LABOR RELATIONS AND THE LAW

LABOR RELATIONS
AND THE LAW

Compiled by a group of
Teachers and Practitioners of Labor Law

ROBERT E. MATHEWS

EDITOR IN CHARGE

LITTLE, BROWN AND COMPANY · BOSTON

1953

PRINTED IN THE UNITED STATES OF AMERICA

Foreword

This book is the product of a series of events dating back to the winter of 1946. The program of the Round Table Council on Labor Law of the Association of American Law Schools for that year was devoted to a discussion of the topic, "A New Prospectus for Labor Law." [1] Under the stimulus of this critical approach to the inadequacies of contemporary teaching materials in this field, the Association authorized the Round Table Council to hold a conference on this subject during the following year. With the aid of a generous grant from the Carnegie Corporation of New York and the hospitality of the University of Michigan Law School, such a conference was held at Ann Arbor during June, 1947. This was known as the Conference on the Training of Law Students in Labor Relations. [2] The Conference, which continued for two weeks, was attended by representatives of thirty-two law schools and was addressed by outstanding figures representing the points of view of labor, management, and the public in the field of labor-management relations. The persistent emphasis throughout this Conference was, first, on the function of lawyers in the labor-management field; second, on the training of law students so that they may perform these functions more effectively and with a fuller realization of both the magnitude of the public interest at stake and their own professional responsibilities in relation to it; third, on the fact that contrary to popular impression the normal and prevalent relationship between labor and management in this country is one of practical cooperation rather than of friction, conflict, and violence; and fourth, on the lawyer's duty to further this cooperative relationship in every possible way.

A majority of the law teachers in attendance at this Conference later expressed a desire to make the fullest possible use of their experience by putting into trial form a collection of materials for

[1] Later published as "On Teaching Labor Law," by W. Willard Wirtz, 42 Ill. L. Rev. 1 (1947).

[2] The complete transcript of the proceedings of this Conference has been distributed to the libraries of all schools holding membership in the Association of American Law Schools.

classroom teaching. At various later dates, others expressed a similar interest. In consequence, an editorial group was set up which, with occasional variations in membership, has now been engaged in the compilation of successive editions for a period of over five years. The names of the joint participants in the preparation of this book appear on page xiii.

It should be noted that while most of these editors — twenty-five, in fact — are presently members of faculties belonging to the Association of American Law Schools, the Association is in no sense sponsoring this work. The initial encouragement for a conference on the teaching of labor law was first voiced at the Round Table of the Association, and was later confirmed on the floor of its assembly, but the subsequent project of compilation has been the exclusive responsibility of the editors.

The first preliminary editions of the present work appeared in 1948. They comprised four of the five major units that are contained here, plus two other units later separately available in mimeographed form. During the years 1948 and 1949 these six units were used in seventeen law schools throughout the country. Use was confined, however, to persons engaged in the joint compilation; the book was not made available for general adoption.

During 1949 the editorial group, prompted by their classroom experience with the book, prepared a full set of comments and criticisms on each portion of it. In June, fourteen members spent a week together in detailed re-examination of the materials in the light of these comments. In consequence, a complete revision was agreed upon, a portion of which first appeared in January, 1950, when the materials now entitled Parts I and II were mimeographed and distributed. Thereafter, certain changes and additions were made in Part I, and a complete revision was accomplished of Parts II, III, and IV. These four units were then published by lithographic process, by Little, Brown and Company, in September of that year.

During the following months the book was again subjected to classroom testing, and the editors' comments and criticisms were again used as a basis of a week-long conference in June, 1951. On this occasion, further revisions were agreed upon, a major one being the inclusion of Part V in the present volume. This concerns problems relating to internal union affairs. The present work therefore embodies the third and final selection and arrangement of these materials.

In the field of Labor Law there are already casebooks written by outstanding members of the teaching profession. Several have appeared since the present project was undertaken. There is, therefore, little justification for a volume that is "just another book." It is, however, the belief of the editors of this work that it makes certain contributions of its own which in their judgment are needed even today for the adequate training of law students in this field. These contributions, we feel, are of four types: (1) a new approach to the process of compiling a casebook; (2) a major shift in emphasis; (3) an expansion in the use of problems as teaching devices; and (4) the introduction of materials from foreign countries as a basis for comparative study.

Without the financial assistance of the Carnegie Corporation of New York, the program adopted for assuring a group approach to the preparation of these materials would have been impossible. Not only did this grant finance the large conference at Ann Arbor in 1947, but it made possible the holding of the two week-long conferences in 1949 and 1951, each attended by fourteen or fifteen persons, coming from widely distributed areas from coast to coast, from Chicago to Texas. It also made possible several small committee conferences at various stages of the work. At the same time, it need hardly be said that the Corporation is not to be understood as in any way approving, by virtue of this grant, any of the statements, views, or materials contained in this work. These, of course, are the sole responsibility of the editors.

As a matter of administration, the otherwise unwieldy editorial staff was broken up into seven sections, six dealing with each of the major Parts, and the seventh concerned with servicing each Part with materials on foreign law. Except for the latter group, the membership, even the chairmanship, of each committee was rotated from time to time as the materials proceeded through their two temporary editions to the present final volume.

Casebooks by several editors are no novelty; indeed they have been highly successful. Nor can any real contribution be claimed for an approach by thirty-one as against a previous maximum of perhaps five editors. The difference in the present product, editorially speaking, is qualitative rather than merely quantitative. It is this: each portion of the book has been worked and reworked by each editor. This has been on both an individual and a group level. The reassignment of small sections to new committees, the total revision by group conference — these methods of organizing editorial participation have produced a book that is by its very nature a joint group product. It reflects the summation of total judgment brought to bear on the creative process itself. Not unnaturally, we hope that the merit of this total effort will be greater than could have been attained by any of the editors alone. In any event, there can be little doubt that it has now been established that it is both possible and practical for a large number of individuals to combine their editorial work so as to produce what is in reality a unit, rather than a mosaic of individual effort.

In terms of emphasis, this volume reflects a conscious and deliberate attempt to shift the weight of discussion from the breakdown in labor relations to the constructive working program that today, happily, is vastly more characteristic of this relationship. That this is the only true emphasis is well substantiated by the 75,000 or more collective agreements currently in operation, renegotiated annually and usually without strife, and periodically interpreted by hundreds of arbitrators whose final awards are seldom questioned. Casebooks and law-teaching too often have been directed to the peripheral area of legal pathology, rather than to the healthy core of practical working cooperation.

It is the aim of this book, then, to rectify that historic unbalance and to develop in the student's mind a realistic sense of his functions as a lawyer in working with and playing his part in this long-established cooperative practice. To this end, the book opens with an introductory section on the significance of the labor movement in our sort of free enterprise democracy, and then proceeds to prepare the groundwork for collective bargaining through the discussion of its meaning and the ways of establishing it, including determination of the bargaining unit, the selection of bargaining representatives, and the issues about which bargaining must take place. Next comes what in a real sense is the heart of the book — a discussion of the actual process of bargaining itself and the administration of the resulting collective agreement, with particular emphasis on the disposition of grievances and the use of voluntary arbitration.

It is not until the student reaches the fourth section, dealing with economic pressures, that he is faced with the tactics that are consequent upon the failure of the bargaining process. Here he sees the lawyer's function in that happily smaller area of labor-management relationship where conflict is rife and where the lawyer's job is more to attack or defend than to construct and work cooperatively.

The final portion of the casebook contains materials that traditionally have been dealt with lightly if at all in general courses in Labor Law. These relate to the internal problems of unions:

intra-union democracy, admission policies, discipline, elections of officers, finances, local-parent relations, and jurisdictional conflicts. With the increasing emphasis on representation, collective bargaining, and administration of agreements, the modern lawyer, whether he is retained by labor or management, needs at least a rudimentary grasp of these practices.

The use of problems in casebooks is no longer novel. An attempt has been made here, however, to expand this use in a substantial degree and to give continuity to a series of extensive problems that run in sequence throughout Parts II and III. By improvising the fictitious Enderby Rubber Company, a Rubber Workers Union, and a cast of characters attached to each, it has been possible to develop graphically a case study of labor-management relations from the early pre-organization days through the choice of representatives, the processes of negotiations, and the administration of a succession of contracts through grievance procedure to final arbitration. Problems are not used in Part IV, but in Part V there is a series of short ones without the continuity of the successive "Enderby cases." This plan affords ample material and incentive for the application of a teaching method that has lately come to have increasing use for third-year students, a method that substitutes discussion of problems for recitation of individual decisions.

The fourth contribution is the inclusion of materials that may be best described as comparative labor law. In addition to a major section at the end of Part I on Basic Features of Foreign Labor Law, there have been inserted from time to time discussions calculated to provide contrast between the solutions of similar problems and conflicts in our own and other countries. The function of these items is in no sense to prepare the student for the practice of labor law in Germany, for instance, but to widen his perception of how other peoples with other traditions have dealt with situations comparable to those that confront us here at home, to enrich his appreciation for the diversity of solutions, and to stimulate that characteristic so essential to all competent lawyers — imagination.

It has not proved practicable for all members of the editorial group to participate to the same degree in this project. However, it is only proper to name specifically those whose contributions have been outstanding, in order that they may have credit for their part of the work, whatever its merits or demerits may be. Thus Part I, Organized Labor in a Free Enterprise Society, was initially prepared by Professor Alexander H. Frey of the University of Pennsylvania and Professor Sylvester Garret, then of Stanford University, and later revised by Professor W. Willard Wirtz of Northwestern University. The comparative law treatment at its conclusion, as well as the many excerpts and notes in that field throughout the book, was prepared by Professor Arthur Lenhoff of the University of Buffalo, with substantial editorial help from Professor William G. Rice of the University of Wisconsin. Part II, Establishment of Collective Bargaining, was originally prepared by Professor Nathan P. Feinsinger, with the cooperation of Professor William G. Rice, both of the University of Wisconsin; was rearranged and revised by Professor M. T. Van Hecke of the University of North Carolina, and Professor William H. Soule of Wake Forest College; and was further revised by Professor Donald H. Wollett of the University of Washington. Part III, Collective Bargaining, was prepared by Professor W. Willard Wirtz of Northwestern University with the cooperation of Benjamin Aaron, Labor Arbitrator and Research Associate, Institute of Industrial Relations, University of California at Los Angeles. Later revisions were under the direction of Professor Charles A. Reynard of Louisiana State University. Part IV, Legal Limitations on Economic Pressure, was prepared by Professor Bertram Willcox of Cornell University. Its final revision was under the direction of Professor Clyde W. Summers of the University of Buffalo. Part V, Unions and Their Members, was prepared by Professor Summers, and subsequently revised by Professor Jerre S. Williams of the University of Texas. In each instance, the person named worked in cooperation with a committee of three to five other members of the editorial group. By means of correspondence and group conferences, each of the editors has made his own contribution to each portion of the book.

According to current plan, this work will be followed shortly by two others. One of these will contain a selection of readings and source materials for use with the present casebook. Preparation is already under way. The other is intended as a casebook for a separate course in Employees' Rights, a field now coming to be known as Social Legislation. It will concern the employee as an individual, irrespective of union membership, and will cover such matters as the nature of the employment relation, both at common law and under statutes, protection against physical risks — safety appliance acts and workmen's compensation — and protection against economic exploitation. This latter will include rights to inventions, wage-and-hour rights, and rights to unemployment benefits. This is already available in temporary form, and is now in process of revision before submission for publication as part of this series.

One further feature of this project is, we believe, unique. No part of the royalties on any edition of any of the volumes will be distributed to the editors personally. On the contrary, they are already being accumulated to finance further group conferences on the teaching of Labor Law, and to make possible periodic group revisions. By this device it will be feasible, through subsequent editions over an indefinite period, to include significant materials from the constant flow that so characterizes this field of law, and to explore new teaching arrangements and methods as they may suggest themselves by the repeated exposure of the product to the trial of classroom use.

The editors wish to express their appreciation to Dr. George W. Taylor of the Wharton School of the University of Pennsylvania, Dr. Edwin E. Witte, Chairman of the Department of Economics at the University of Wisconsin — former Chairman and Public Member of the National War Labor Board respectively — and to Dr. William M. Leiserson, former member of the National Labor Relations Board and former Chairman, National Mediation Board, for their reading of portions of the manuscript and for their most helpful comments and suggestions.

Personal gratitude is also here expressed by the Editor in Charge for the conscientious and intelligent help rendered by Professor Don W. Sears of the University of Colorado Law School who, as a Senior law student at Ohio State University, gave substantial assistance both editorially and administratively to the publication of the original preliminary edition in 1948.

> *For the Editorial Group*
> ROBERT E. MATHEWS
> *Editor in Charge*

Ohio State University
November, 1952

Cooperating Editors

Table of Contents

PART I

ORGANIZED LABOR IN A FREE ENTERPRISE SOCIETY

PART II

ESTABLISHMENT OF COLLECTIVE BARGAINING

PART IV

LEGAL LIMITATIONS ON ECONOMIC PRESSURE

PART V

UNIONS AND THEIR MEMBERS

APPENDIX

Table of Cases

Principal cases are indicated by roman page numbers, while cases cited in the text and footnotes are designated by italic numbers.

Table of Secondary Authorities

When excerpts from the cited works are set forth in the text, the
reference page is printed in roman type.

LABOR RELATIONS AND THE LAW

Throughout this book, where there are footnotes in quoted material — that is, cases, articles, and so forth — the original numbers have been retained. Editor's notes are numbered beginning with 1 at the start of each Part. Whenever these notes are keyed to quoted material they are signed "Ed."

PART I

Organized Labor in a Free Enterprise Society

I. INTRODUCTORY NOTE

The law of labor relations must be distinguished in two respects from that which governs most of the other relationships constituting the democratic social order. A comparatively small proportion of this "law" is embodied in the ordinary kind of legislative enactments and in the decisions of courts; of at least equal importance here are the collective bargaining agreements which constitute the codes or constitutions of particular industrial or commercial communities, and what are called the "grievance" settlements which make up the "common law" of these communities. What formal law there is in this field is still in such a state of flux that none of it can be considered meaningfully unless it is evaluated in terms of its social and economic and political context; most of it was different two decades ago and will probably be changed again within the next short span of years.

There is, nevertheless, a continuity in these changes. The roots of contemporary doctrine are discernible in century-old precedents, and a relatively stable basic pattern has emerged in the period since 1935.

This first part of these materials has been designed to suggest a little of the history of labor law in this country, something of its context, and something, too, of the problem of identifying the role that "government" and "law" may be expected to play in this area. The case of Enterprise, Inc. v. Amalgamated Assn., Local 619, AFL is an apocryphal case, at least as far as the parties and the facts are concerned. The precedents discussed in the opinion are, however, actual cases, and the quotations which are used are from the sources indicated. The case has been set up as the basis for a consideration of those high points in the evolution of labor law in this country which still seem to illuminate contemporary problems, and as an instrument for bringing into "legal" focus the representative points of view illustrated in the materials which follow the case. The "opinion" in the case should by no means be accepted uncritically, for it has been deliberately designed to stimulate independent reactions.

II. ENTERPRISE, INC. v. AMALGAMATED ASSN.
LOCAL 619, AFL
(*Unreported*)

EDITOR, J., delivered the opinion of the Court:

Both parties to these proceedings have appealed from the decision of the court below. That court had before it the suit of Enterprise, Inc. for an injunction prohibiting the officers and members of Amalgamated Assn., Local 619, AFL, from striking, or picketing the Company to enforce their collective bargaining demands. These demands, described below in fuller detail, were for (1) a certain wage increase, and (2) a guarantee against loss of employee earnings resulting from the introduction by the Company of laborsaving devices. The court below issued an injunction prohibiting any concerted action for the purpose of enforcing the second of these demands. The Union has appealed this action. The lower court denied the Company's request for a broader injunction. The Company, in turn, appeals from this denial, insisting that the narrower injunction has proven to be meaningless.

There is no material dispute about the facts. Enterprise, Inc. produces at its plant in New City 73 per cent of the ray-bulbs used in this country by the manufacturers of electronics equipment of various types. The 1250 production workers at Enterprise are virtually all members of Local 619.

On January 3 of this year, an impasse was reached in the efforts of Enterprise and Local 619 to agree upon the terms of a new collective bargaining contract. This impasse developed as a consequence of the Union's insistence upon the two contract changes already referred to and from the Company's refusal to make these changes.

The Union has demanded an increase of 50 cents per hour in all wage rates, justifying this demand on the ground that the net increase in labor costs to the Company (about $1,250,000 per year) is less than half of the average annual earnings realized by the Company (after taxes) during the past five years. The Company has offered an increase of 10 cents per hour, pointing out that this would give the Enterprise employees the highest wage levels paid any manufacturing employees in the New City labor market area.

The Union's second demand is that the Company agree in the contract that if any new laborsaving devices are installed, this will not reduce either the number or earnings of employees affected by the introduction of the new equipment. The Union's proposal is that hours of work (but not take-home earnings) be reduced if the Company installs laborsaving devices which cut down the number of man-hours required. The Company has refused to consider this proposal.

On January 5, the Enterprise employees went out on strike. Pickets were placed at the several entrances to the plant. There has at no time been any violence. There have been sporadic attempts at renewal of negotiations but neither side has been willing to move from its earlier position.

The Company went into the Circuit Court on April 20 and asked for an injunction against continuation of the striking and picketing. A hearing was held on April 25. Evidence was introduced, and was not denied, which shows that this strike has had a very substantial effect upon the entire electronics industry in the country and that production in this industry is now at about 50 per cent of normal. It appears that some 250,000 employees have been laid off by users of Enterprise ray-bulbs. Some types of electronics equipment used in hospitals and by various public utilities are in exceedingly short supply.

On April 27, the Circuit Court issued an injunction prohibiting the union officers and its members from "proceeding, in concert, to strike against or picket the premises of Enterprise, Inc. for the purpose of forcing said Company to yield to demands that the Company not install laborsaving devices except on terms inconsistent with the welfare of the people of this State." The pickets were withdrawn from the plant immediately upon the issuance of this injunction, but no employees returned to work. A statement was issued by the President of Local 619 that "in view of the pending court proceedings Local 619 has temporarily abandoned all of its demands except that for increased wages." When Company representatives suggested that another bargaining session be convened, they were advised by the Union that "we will not negotiate on anything while your injunction is in effect." The appeals to this Court were filed on May 3.

This case has attracted great attention in the community in which the dispute has developed, in this State, and, in fact, in the nation. As will hereinafter appear, the problem involved has become the subject of legislative as well as judicial concern. This Court has been favored by exhaustive and illuminating argument of outstanding counsel. It has become evident that any reliance by the Court upon what might appear to be convenient precedents would constitute only a rationalization of a result actually rooted in more basic considerations. It must be recognized that the issues presented here warrant and require the analysis of economic and political and social forces which have not been finally reconciled in any definitive statutory or common law pronouncements.   To the extent that these issues present questions under the state or federal constitutions, it is clear that these questions have not been finally resolved and that the answers are, indeed, less clear than they seemed to be fifty or even ten years ago.   It is almost, if not quite, true that the circumstances warrant the treatment of this case as one of first impression.   The position which it appears proper and necessary for this Court to take, in its ultimate disposition of this case, would perhaps justify a very brief opinion.   Yet this disposition might appear to be an avoidance of responsibility if the considerations prompting it were not fully detailed.

We have started from an attempt to familiarize ourselves with the full details of the relationship between the parties to this dispute, going back as far as considerations of relevancy seem to permit.   Only the more significant features of the picture disclosed to us are recorded here.

Prior to 1938, Enterprise was a very small company which manufactured miscellaneous electrical devices and equipment. In that year, A. R. Rudow, the Enterprise president, manager, and holder (then and now) of over 80 per cent of its stock interest, took out a patent on a device for making ray-bulbs.   This device permitted the manufacture of such bulbs at one tenth of the cost of manufacture by any other method.   Within two years, Enterprise was making and selling virtually all of the ray-bulbs used by the electronics industry.   There have, since that time, been some other processes developed which have resulted in some competition, but Enterprise still dominates this field.

Between 1938 and 1942, the number of employees in the production department at Enterprise increased from 32 to 476.   The employees were not organized.   There is evidence that Rudow, handling his own employee relations, paid high wages and provided good working conditions, but exercised what was at least considered by some of his employees to be dictatorial control. On two occasions, for example, employees were discharged for asking wage increases.   All complaints by individual employees were handled exclusively by the foremen in the plant, and Rudow always backed up the foremen's decisions.

On one occasion in 1940, an employee who had been discharged at Enterprise (allegedly because he supported a Presidential candidate whom Rudow opposed) joined a labor union after he was discharged, and then, in company with two union organizers, picketed the Enterprise plant. Over half of the employees refused to cross the picket line and the plant was closed for three days. The Company then obtained an injunction against the picketing and, when it was stopped, virtually all the employees returned to work. No appeal was taken from the court order.

In late 1942, Local 619 began its organizational activities in the plant. Rudow opposed this movement with unusual aggressiveness. Several men were discharged when it became known that they had joined the Union. A substantial wage increase was given to most of the employees, but not to those in the Shipping Department, where the union movement had apparently started. Rudow announced that he "would close the plant before he would deal with any union." Charges were filed by Local 619 and a number of employees with the National Labor Relations Board, alleging violations of subsections (1) and (3) of Section 8 of the Wagner Act, 49 Stat. 449, 29 U.S.C. §151. In March, 1943, the Board issued an order directing Enterprise to cease and desist from a continuation of its discriminatory practices and to reinstate with back pay eleven employees found to have been discharged for union activity. Enterprise appealed this order to the Circuit Court of Appeals and there followed a two-year period of litigation. The Board's order was finally upheld.

While this litigation was pending, Local 619 also instituted proceedings under Section 9 of the Wagner Act seeking certification as exclusive bargaining representative of the Enterprise production workers. After appropriate hearings, the National Labor Relations Board held an election (in December, 1943). An overwhelming majority of the employees indicated their desire to be represented by Local 619, and the Union was certified as provided in the Act. The Company still refused to bargain with the Union. Charges were then filed under Section 8(5) of the NLRA, and the Board ordered the Company to bargain.

Although at first the Company indicated that it would adhere to its position of refusal to bargain, on account of which enforcement proceedings were instituted by the Board (under Section 10 (e) of the Act), Rudow finally announced (in August, 1944) that he would negotiate with Local 619. Three months of futile "bargaining" followed. No agreement could be reached on any substantial issue.

When a strike threatened, in early December, 1944, this contract dispute was certified by the Secretary of Labor, acting under the War Labor Disputes Act of 1943 (57 Stat. 163, 50 U.S.C.

§§1501–1511), to the National War Labor Board.   After extended hearings, the Board issued a "directive order" covering all of the disputed issues: wages, seniority, grievance procedure, union security, hours of work, vacations, etc.   The various provisions of this directive order were in the form of collective bargaining contract clauses.   Upon receipt of the order the Company and Union signed an agreement incorporating the provisions of the NWLB order.   This agreement covered the period from May 1, 1945, to April 30, 1946.

Rudow apparently decided, at about this time, to retire from the active management of the Company's affairs, or at least from that part of them relating to employee relations.   An Industrial Relations Manager was added to the Enterprise top staff and was given virtually a free hand in dealing with the employees and with the Union.   Relationships improved very materially. Renewal contracts were worked out each year, and there is virtual agreement that these were substantially satisfactory to both parties. A grievance procedure was included in the contracts and any grievances which were not settled by the parties were referred to arbitration.

The last of these annual renewal contracts expired six months ago.   The Union had, some thirty days before that, filed with the Company demands for the contract changes previously referred to.   The strike followed approximately three months of futile negotiation.

This is the record of labor relations at Enterprise.   It is singularly free of any evidence, at least during the past several years, of untoward or "illegal" action on either side.   The record leaves the present dispute standing almost in isolation.   The question seems to be whether the employees may, acting peacefully but in concert, decide not to work except for the wages and on the terms they have stated.   We are required to review a court order enjoining them from doing so.

Our questioning of counsel reveals that the grounds for the requested exercise of judicial authority here are two: first, that the Union's wage demands and its proposal for covering technological displacement of its members are too expensive to the employer; second, that there is a "public interest" in getting production at the Enterprise plant started up again.   It is virtually conceded that no injunction could reasonably be granted (1) if the wage demands were for a 10-cent instead of a 50-cent hourly increase and the other demand were for "reasonable severance pay" to cover technological displacements, and (2) if there were other substantial sources of ray-bulb supply in the country.   (There has been much argument as to whether the proposition just stated should be in the disjunctive rather than the conjunctive.)

Our predisposition, in view of this clarification of the issue, has been to say that this is not an appropriate area for the functioning of the judiciary.   We have relied, in this country, upon the "decentralized decision-making of the market place" rather than upon the personal predilection of judges to determine what are proper industrial wage rates.   If we would have no authority to protect a small ray-bulb manufacturer's bargaining interests we cannot escape the conclusion that the public's concern about a larger producer's interests must be reflected by legislative action rather than by courts' drawing of lines which are not within any special competence of judges.

We have been pressed, however, with the argument that "ever since the first labor case was decided in this country, the courts have stood as bulwarks against the power of small groups of employees to hold the community and society in ransom."   See Appellant Company's Brief, pp. 86–87.   The citation of extensive authority gives this statement more weight than its flamboyance might suggest.   We have accordingly felt compelled to review the evolution of this area of the law.   We agree with counsel for appellant Company that "the significance of this evolution lies not so much in particular precedents as it does in the courts' identification of the responsibility of the judiciary in situations of this kind."   Id. at p. 87.

Emphasis is properly placed upon the very earliest period of labor litigation in this country.   The doctrine of criminal conspiracy which emerged in the early nineteenth-century labor cases in Pennsylvania and New York and Massachusetts is today anachronistic.   Those early courts were faced, however, with the basic problems of fitting "law" into "labor relations" and even though they may, as it is now generally agreed, have erred in expressing their conclusions in a particular legal form, their analysis of the problem is important as suggesting the roots from which subsequent doctrines have grown and from which these doctrines probably still take some nourishment.

The first recorded "labor relations" case in this country was one in which a group of journeymen shoemakers in Philadelphia were indicted, convicted, and fined eight dollars each when they "did combine, conspire and confederate, and unlawfully agree together . . . that they . . . would not . . . work . . . but at certain large prices and rates."   Philadelphia Cordwainers' Case of 1806

(Commonwealth v. Pullis, 3 Commons and Gilmore, A Documentary History of American Industrial Society 59–248 (1910) Phila. Mayor's Court). The pattern which was developed here, involving the identification of the most common activity of employee groups as a "criminal conspiracy," was followed in eight of the ten similar cases which arose during the next twenty years in Pennsylvania, Maryland, New York, and Massachusetts. See Professor Nelles' illuminating article, Commonwealth v. Hunt, in 32 Col. L. Rev. 1128, 1166 (1932).

If these precedents had prevailed in the evolution of this branch of the law, the case before us would present no problem, for the employees at Enterprise stand in basically the same relationship to their employer as did the Philadelphia shoemakers to their masters, and the effect of their actions upon the broader community may be properly considered even more serious. These precedents did not prevail. It remains for us, however, to identify whatever the record discloses as to what it was that seemed to prompt these earliest state courts to intervene in private disputes of this kind.

The charge which Moses Levy, one of the judges of the Mayor's Court in Philadelphia and its Recorder, made to the jury in the 1806 Cordwainers' case is illuminating, if not particularly helpful. The charge, very different in nature from those which are today considered customary, started from an exposition of economic theory. A brief excerpt will give the flavor. "The usual means by which the prices of work are regulated, are the demand for the article and the excellence of its fabric. . . . To make an artificial regulation, . . . governed by no standard, controlled by no impartial person, but dependent on the will of the few who are interested; this is the unnatural way of raising the price of goods or work." Turning, somewhat later, to "the law," Recorder Levy summed it up as follows: "A combination of workmen to raise their wages may be considered in a two fold point of view: one is to benefit themselves . . . the other is to injure those who do not join their society. The rule of law condemns both. If the rule be clear, we are bound to conform to it even though we do not comprehend the principle upon which it is founded. We are not to reject it because we do not see the reason of it." The Recorder then turned the case over to the jury with these words: "If you can reconcile it to your consciences, to find the defendants not guilty, you will do so; if not, the alternative that remains, is a verdict of guilty." The verdict of guilt which followed was not surprising. [The opinion in this case is given at page 637. — Ed.]

In the subsequent cases, there was increasing emphasis upon the factor of concert of action, rather than the purpose of such action, as the criminal element in what the journeymen groups (usually shoemakers, but sometimes tailors, spinners, weavers, or hatters) did.   See, e.g., the New York Cordwainers' Case of 1809 (People v. Melvin, 2 Wheeler's Crim. Cases 262–282).   A further insight into the economics from which the legal conclusion was drawn is supplied by Judge Roberts' charge to the jury in the Pittsburgh Cordwainers' Case of 1815 (Commonwealth v. Morrow, 4 Commons and Kilmore 15–87), where the facts were very much like those of the Philadelphia case:

> In the investigation of subjects like that now presented . . . the mind is easily misled . . . here we see on the one hand, a number of journeymen, whom we are led to regard as poor men, opposed to their employers, some of whom are represented as wealthy.   The human mind spontaneously revolts at the idea of oppression; and the attention of the jury is invariably drawn to this point; as if the true question were, whether the journeymen were the oppressed, and the masters the oppressors — whether the profits of the one class be not too great, and the remuneration of the other inadequate . . .
>
> With the regulation of wages, or the profit of the one or the other, you have nothing to do. . . .   It is not for demanding high prices that these men are endicted, but for employing unlawful means to extort those prices. . . .   Confederacies of this kind have a most pernicious effect, as respects the community at large.   They restrain trade: they tend to banish many artizans, and to oppress others.   It is the interest of the public, and it is the right of every individual, that those who are skilled in any profession, art, or mystery, should be unrestrained in the exercise of it.

Here was, near the headwaters of American labor law, economic jurisprudence of a kind usually associated with a much later period.   It prompts the inquiry as to whether there are basic similarities, or basic differences, between the economics of bootmaking in Pittsburgh in 1815 and ray-bulb manufacture in New City almost a century and a half later.   Does it make a difference that there are not substantial alternative sources of ray-bulb supply, and that New City is not, like early Pittsburgh as described by Professor Nelles, "an outfitting station for westward-moving pioneers"?   As we make these inquiries we look not only for an answer to the question of whether a court should direct its participation in a controversy such as this toward conviction or acquittal, but also for some suggestion as to whether there is here,

in today's society, justification for *any* exercise of judicial function.
Judge Roberts insisted that questions of wage rates and prices
were not for either the court or the jury. It is at least one view
of it to identify the current controversy at Enterprise as involving,
primarily and basically, only wages and prices.

One other of the early criminal conspiracy conviction cases
warrants notation here, not for the result it reached, but for the
suggestion it contained regarding another factor in the equation in
which labor unions, on the one hand, and government (of which
the courts are part), on the other, appear as factors. The case was
that of People v. Faulkner, or Twenty Journeymen Tailors. It
was tried before the Court of Oyer and Terminer in New York
City in 1836, and is reported in 4 Commons and Gilmore 315
et seq. on the basis of accounts appearing in contemporary issues
of the New York papers. The tailors had struck first for wages and
then (after they had received substantial increases) for a kind of
seniority system. Highhanded tactics were used against employers
of "dungs," tailors who took work when more senior tailors were
without jobs. The trial was on an indictment for conspiring to
injure trade and commerce (based on a New York statute) and
was apparently not based on another indictment for "riot, and
assault and battery." The result in the case was virtually certain
in view of the conviction a year earlier of a group of bootmakers
who had engaged in similar tactics. People v. Fisher, 14 Wend. 9
(N.Y. 1835). The tailors were convicted of conspiracy. In imposing fines totalling $1150, Judge Edwards addressed the tailors
at length, in part as follows:

> Associations of this description are of recent origin in this
> country. Here, where the government is purely paternal,
> where the people are governed by laws of their own creating;
> where the legislature proceeds with a watchful regard to the
> welfare not only of the whole, but of every class of society;
> where the representatives ever lend a listening ear to the com-
> plaints of their constituents, it has not been found necessary
> or proper to subject any portion of the people to the control
> of self-created societies. Judging from what we have wit-
> nessed within the last year, we should be led to the conclusion
> that the trades of the country, which contribute immeasurably
> to its wealth, and upon which the prosperity of a most valu-
> able portion of the community hinges, [are] rapidly passing
> from the control of the supreme power of the state into the
> hands of private societies. . . . Every American knows, or

ought to know, that he has no better friend than the laws, and that he needs no artificial combination for his protection. . . . They [the "private societies" of the journeymen groups] are of foreign origin, and I am led to believe are mainly upheld by foreigners. . . .

Here, in what proved to be virtually the climax of the criminal conspiracy development, Judge Edwards added the "political science" dimension to Recorder Levy's legalism and Judge Roberts' economics. If his premises were sound — that "the government is purely paternal," that legislative representatives in the government show due regard to the interests of "every class of society" — then so were his conclusions that "private societies" are unnecessary and that the employee "has no better friend than the laws." But this is the whole problem of "political pluralism" as against "monism," to use the labels which have subsequently emerged in political theory. At the more practical level, the trouble at Enterprise, Inc., like that in the early nineteenth-century New York tailoring shops, arises from the fact that American labor has never accepted the Edwards premises and has accordingly rejected his conclusions. Labor in this country rejects the concept of Hobbes' Leviathan, and any discussion of labor controversies which ignores the basic problem, even today unresolved, of the relationship of State and "private societies" must be recognized as superficial.

It is relevant to our present inquiry that the courts' application of the criminal conspiracy doctrine to early employee group activities eventually aroused a storm of public protest. The people felt that the courts had overreached their authority. The reaction was typified by the official in Judge Edwards' court who stepped forward, when the fines were imposed on the twenty tailors, and contributed his last three weeks' salary toward a fund to pay them. The public concern was not limited to working groups; it included also those who voted Federalist, wanted high tariffs, and owned mills and factories which would be closed if labor feeling grew too strong. Labor was already recognized as a strong, if not cohesive, economic and political force.

These were undoubtedly among the considerations which prompted the Supreme Judicial Court of Massachusetts, in 1842, to set aside the conviction (for criminal conspiracy) of seven members of the Boston Journeymen Bootmakers' Society who had indicated that they would refuse to work in shops where nonmembers of the Society were employed at less than the scheduled rate (obtained by the Society in a recent strike) of $2 per pair of boots. Commonwealth v. Hunt, 4 Metc. 111 (1842). The court, while not rejecting the doctrine of criminal conspiracy as being inapplicable to organized employee activity, cut the heart from the old approach by insisting that it was the *purpose* of the concerted action rather than the fact of such concert itself which was important. "We cannot perceive," Chief Justice Shaw wrote, "that it is criminal for men to agree together to exercise their own acknowledged rights, in such a manner as best to subserve their own interests." The court found that the "manifest intent of the association" was only "to induce all those engaged in the same occupation to become members of it," and concluded that "such a purpose is not unlawful." Chief Justice Shaw's opinion relied upon legal technicalities to patch thin places in economic and social theory which was itself more a reflection of contemporary politics than an application of clear premises. We find it significant, however, that this "first period" in American labor law started with an announcement of a legal concept which seemed to warrant judicial interference in employment disputes, and ended with a recognition that the "requirements of the community," as well as contemporary politics, prompted judicial withdrawal from this arena. See Nelles, Commonwealth v. Hunt, above; Gregory, Labor and the Law 27–29 (1946); Schlesinger, The Age of Jackson 339–341 (1945).

The most significant developments in the three or four decades following the decision of the Massachusetts court in Commonwealth v. Hunt appeared in a group of cases in which actions were instituted to collect money damages from associations which, it was charged, had by combination placed restraints upon the operation of "free market place" controls over prices, the supply of labor, and the terms and conditions of employment. Professor Gregory has best illuminated this period of development in his Labor and the Law, c. III (1946), and his casebook (edited with H. A. Katz) on Labor Law, c. II (1948).

Two cases decided in 1867, one by the New York Court of Common Pleas and the other by the Massachusetts Supreme Judicial Court, involved actions against combinations of *employers*, but they bore a direct relationship to the matter of *employee* freedom to act in concert. In Master Stevedores' Assn. v. Walsh, 2 Daly 1, the New York court upheld the right of an incorporated association of master stevedores (i.e., the entrepreneurs in this industry) to penalize any member of the association who charged less for any job than the prices fixed in the association's schedule.

The labor cases in the Cordwainers' series were considered in detail but were distinguished on the ground that those cases all involved coercion of nonmembers of the "conspiring" group. As for "voluntary" agreements as to wage or price fixing, with sanctions applied only among the collaborators themselves, the New York court (in an opinion by Daly, J.) declared, "It is better for the law to leave such matters to the action of the parties interested — to leave master workmen or journeymen free to form what associations they please in relation to the rate of compensation, so long as they are voluntary." Satisfied that market forces will soon operate to defeat any agreement whereby "workmen demand too much, or the masters offer too little," Judge Daly concluded that the master stevedores' price-fixing agreement "imposes no restraint upon one party which is not beneficial to the others, and is not . . . prejudicial to the interests of the public."

The Massachusetts case was Bowen v. Matheson, 96 Mass. 499 (1867). It involved the activities of an association made up of most of the Boston "shipping-masters and agents" — men whose business it was to sign crews up for ship captains and who, incident to this business, housed and boarded the seamen between voyages. The association members adopted the policy of refusing to supply any sailors to a captain who dealt with any nonmember shipping-master. Bowen, one such nonmember, sued the association in tort, alleging that his business was being destroyed. The Massachusetts court upheld the association's demurrer to the complaint, finding no illegal acts alleged, but only "a new method of transacting business" and "such a result as in the competition of business often follows" such invention. "Sometimes associations break down the business of individuals," Judge Chapman commented for the court, adding broad-mindedly, "and sometimes an individual is able to destroy the business of associated men."

These precedents must have given substantial encouragement to the Journeymen Freestone Cutters' Association of Boston when, only a few months later, they decided to enforce their bylaw which provided, in effect, that the association members would not allow any employer for whom they worked to subcontract the cutting of ornamental stone out of his yard (and, in normal circumstances, away from association members). When Carew, a large cut-stone supplier in Boston, subcontracted some ornamental stonework to a New York firm, the association fined him $500 and forced him to pay it on threat of withdrawing all of his journeymen cutters (who were members of the association). Carew paid, but then, when he had finished some contracts he was working on, he sued mem-

bers of the association for the $500, charging a tort of conspiracy
to extort, as well as for "money had and received."

The Massachusetts Supreme Judicial Court, with Judge Chapman again writing the opinion, reversed a lower court decision
favorable to the defendants and in effect ruled for Carew, the contractor. Carew v. Rutherford, 106 Mass. 1 (1870). Bowen v.
Matheson was mentioned, but the purported distinguishing of the
two cases became confused in an exegesis on the subject of freedom,
developed by the court as an abstraction which would appear to
cover everything or nothing, depending upon what result was being
rationalized. It is only a fair reading of the opinion, in its factual
context, that Judge Chapman and his colleagues were righteously
offended by the arrogance of the association in "levying a fine."
But the court's analysis offers no basis for telling what its answer
would have been if the journeymen stonecutters, like the shipping-
masters, had resorted to the perhaps more subtle but hardly less
effective or expensive tactic (from the victim's standpoint) of
simply refusing to deal with anyone who gave them only part of his
business. It was obvious that Carew preferred paying $500 to
having his journeymen walk out on him.

The fact of the "fine" in the Carew case apparently distracted
the court's attention from the more basic issue, thrown into unusually sharp relief when this case arose so soon after Bowen v.
Matheson, in the same community and before the same court, of
whether the attitude of "the law" should be different in the
presence of combinations of employers from what it is when the
combination is that of employees. We regret this particularly
because a related point has been much pressed on us in the present
case. Counsel for Local 619 has argued strongly that nothing
which the Union has done here would have been considered at all
exceptionable, in the eyes of the law, if the Company had done the
same thing. We are impressed with the suggestion that no court
would have considered issuing an injunction if Enterprise, Inc. had
said to the Union, "Business is bad and profits are too small, and we
are going to close down unless you accept a reduction of 50 cents
an hour in wages." It would appear to be true that Rudow, as
owner of the factory, could have closed it any day he chose, and
that as owner of the patent on the device for making ray-bulbs
he could have withdrawn it from use if he had wanted to. The
effect on the users of ray-bulbs and upon the public would have
been the same as it is now that the employees have struck, and
yet that effect would appear to have had no legal consequences.

We cannot help commenting, however, upon the danger that we

may fall back too easily in this field upon a "sauce for the goose" kind of thinking. It may or it may not be true that the Boston stonecutters' action, even if they had shown a little more delicacy, amounted to neither more nor less than that of their fellow townsmen who hired sailors. Similarly it cannot be lightly assumed, without analysis that is broad as well as penetrating, that the community — and the offices of its public servants — face the same problem when a group of employees close a factory as when its owner does. It may or may not be true that society feels the same way about the implications of corporate and labor union group activity. The difficulties the commentators have had in squaring the Bowen and Carew results, the conclusions they have drawn that judges are revealed in these two decisions as pro-capital and anti-labor, confirm the concern here expressed.

The decisions which followed the cases just discussed bear ample testimony, however, to the fact that the great majority of common law judges have approached these cases involving labor controversies by borrowing "concepts" from convenient areas of legal doctrine and then squeezing the facts of industrial life into them. Carew v. Rutherford was followed a year later by the case of Walker v. Cronin, 107 Mass. 555 (1871), in which a union program of permitting its members (shoemakers) to work only in shops which provided acceptable terms and conditions of employment was held an actionable tort. In this and other cases of the period, the courts developed the principle that organized labor's pressures constitute a "prima facie tort." If there was "intentional infliction of harm" on employers or on nonunion employees, which there invariably was, this was "in itself wrong." But there might be "justifiable cause" shown, and then this was a defense.

Perhaps these rubrics constituted more reliable indices to predictable results in the hands of their originators than it is today possible to understand. It is true that something of a pattern of results did emerge, at least if that pattern be described in terms of the specific employee goals which were being sought. If the purpose of the "infliction of harm" was the procuring of higher wages, this was an instance of justifiable cause as far as most courts were concerned, and therefore the strike was not tortious but only "competition." Some courts felt the same way about action designed to enlarge union membership; others, notably those in Massachusetts, considered such strikes to be "without justification" and therefore a sufficient basis for recovery of damages. It is difficult, however, to be fully persuaded that the tort doctrines which emerged during this period were very much more than professional sophistications which were used to dignify judicial fiats.

It was toward the end of the nineteenth century that the third phase of judicial participation in the working out of the employment relationship was initiated. Labor activities which had first been considered as the subject of criminal proceedings, and then as torts, were identified, almost suddenly, as matters enjoinable in the equity courts.

The English courts have steadfastly, throughout the centuries, denied the applicability of the injunctive process to labor disputes involving no damage to physical property. Counsel for Enterprise suggests that the English courts' position results from the making of a conceptualistic distinction between injuries to an employer's plant facilities and injuries to the productive output of those facilities. It is insisted that the latter may be much more costly than the former and even more irreparable. Our own reading, which has required the piercing of the legalistic gloss which occasionally obscures the basis of the English rule, suggests that it rests in fact upon the recognition that in the field of business activity, including that of employee groups, most non-corporeal hurts are properly identified as only "competition" and, as such, not enjoinable in the courts. There is also reflected an obvious concern about the procedures which lead to the issuance of injunctions.

Counsel for Local 619 argues that it was only by accident that the courts in this country stumbled into a departure from the English rule against the issuance of injunctions in labor disputes. It is apparently true that the American practice developed as a by-product of the fact that so many railroads were in receivership in the 1880's and 1890's, under the control of agents of the courts of equity. When the railroad employees struck for something or other, the equity court's handiest weapon was turned on them. The technique worked so well and so quickly that it was almost immediately applied to strikes at plants where the equity court had no interest until the strike broke.

Some courts, notably those in New York, refused to lend their powers to the perpetration of wholesale interferences with the operation of the economic forces of the employment market place. E.g., National Protective Association v. Cummings, 170 N.Y. 315 (1902) (injunction against a kind of closed shop practice denied). Probably the substantial majority of courts, almost from the first, declined to issue injunctions against strikes which represented only attempts to secure wage increases or reduced work schedules. We find in this record almost no evidence of any support for the position that the members of Local 619 could be prevented, by judicial order, from refusing, even in concert, to work for less than the prices which, whether with or without justification, they choose to set on their labor.   It may or may not add to whatever theoretical support there is for the development of the labor injunction practice, that the courts issuing them have consulted almost exclusively the interests of the immediate parties to these disputes rather than what might be considered the broader interests of consumers and "the public."

There is no denying the fact, however, that in the late nineteenth century, and after that in the first decades of this one, there accumulated many precedents which would support the enjoining of the Enterprise employees' action in seeking to deter the company's installation of laborsaving devices.   It is difficult for us to see how this is very basically different from a demand for extravagant wage increases, at least different to the point that it presents an occasion for judicial participation where the strike for wages does not.   As far as the purchaser of ray-bulbs is concerned, it will not matter to him whether he pays a higher price as a consequence of the Union's successful demand for a large general wage rate increase or because of the Company's capitulation to a demand that employees be paid existing wages (in terms of take-home earnings) even though a machine has assumed most of the burden of their labors.   It is, nevertheless, true that American courts which have declined to issue injunctions against strikes for higher wages have shown a ready willingness to enjoin concerted labor activities where the immediate objective is something other than wage increases even though the ultimate objective is pretty clearly an improvement in the employees' economic status.   This distinction gave rise, early in the "injunctive period," to the so-called "illegal purpose" doctrine.

It was, again, in the Massachusetts courts that this labor regulation device received its most notable early development.   In Vegelahn v. Guntner, 167 Mass. 92 (1896), the Supreme Judicial Court issued an injunction against any kind of picketing by a union which was seeking only higher wages and shorter hours. These "purposes" were apparently considered legitimate, but the fact that there was here picketing as well as a refusal to work prompted the court to throw its weight on the side of the employer. If there is picketing, the court reasoned, there is bound to be more serious trouble, and it was deemed best to nip it in the bud.   Four years later the same court enjoined the refusal of members of one union of painters to work for contractors who used employees who refused to join this union.   Plant v. Woods, 176 Mass. 492 (1900).

In this case, however, it was the *purpose* of the organized movement which the court found so exceptionable as to warrant prohibition by injunction, and it was this element which came to be emphasized in most of the later injunction cases.

Appellant Company of course relies upon these two landmark cases in Massachusetts as illustrating what it terms the "now traditional willingness of equity courts to enjoin employee action where either the object or the means is such as to result in injury to the public." See Brief, p. 103. The truth of the matter is, however, that these cases are given widest recognition today because of the analysis of the role of the judiciary in labor disputes set forth in the dissenting opinions written by Judge Oliver Wendell Holmes. In Vegelahn v. Guntner, he noted the "numberless instance [in which] the law warrants the intentional infliction of temporal damage," particularly in the area of commerce and business. The reason, he said, "is that the doctrine generally has been accepted that free competition is worth more to society than it costs, and that on this ground the infliction of the damage is privileged." He spoke particularly of the difficulties judges have when they seek to introduce their personal standards of "justification" into determinations as to what activities in this area are proper and what are improper. "The true grounds of decision are considerations of policy and social advantage, and it is vain to suppose that solutions can be attained merely by logic and the general propositions of law which nobody disputes. Propositions as to public policy rarely are unanimously accepted. . . ." It was on another occasion that Judge Holmes expressed most clearly his concept of what the role of law ought to be in situations of this kind:

> As law embodies beliefs that have triumphed in the battle of ideas and then have translated themselves into action, while there is still doubt, while opposite convictions still keep a battle front against each other, the time for law has not come; the notion destined to prevail is not yet entitled to the field. (At a meeting of the Harvard Law School Assn. of New York, 1913. See Speeches 101 (1913).)

Judge Holmes included in his Vegelahn dissent a consideration of the matter of "combinations" which is perhaps even more directly relevant in a case, like the present one, involving basic issues of public welfare, than it was in a case turning only on the issue of whether picketing inevitably breeds violence.

> It is plain from the slightest consideration of practical affairs, or the most superficial reading of industrial history,

that free competition means combination, and that the organization of the world, now going on so fast, means an ever-increasing might and scope of combination.   It seems to me futile to set our faces against this tendency.   Whether beneficial on the whole, as I think it, or detrimental, it is inevitable, unless the fundamental axioms of society, and even the fundamental conditions of life, are to be changed.

One of the eternal conflicts out of which life is made up is that between the effort of every man to get the most he can for his services, and that of society, disguised under the name of capital, to get his services for the least possible return.   Combination on the one side is patent and powerful.   Combination on the other is the necessary and desirable counterpart, if the battle is to be carried on in a fair and equal way. . . .

If it be true that workingmen may combine with a view, among other things, to getting as much as they can for their labor, just as capital may combine with a view to getting the greatest possible return, it must be true that, when combined, they have the same liberty that combined capital has, to support their interests by argument, persuasion, and the bestowal or refusal of those advantages which they otherwise lawfully control.

In Plant v. Woods, Judge Holmes identified the union's action in seeking a closed shop as being "one degree more remote" than one "directly concerned with wages" but as "a preliminary and means to enable [the union] to make a better fight on questions of wages or other matters of clashing interests."   He opposed the enjoining of the strike, and in passing offered a notable comment both upon the economics of organized labor's wage demands (which economics may or may not appear as acceptable today as in 1900) and upon the divorcement of judges' personal credos and their decisional functions (as to which there would appear to have been little occasion for change) :

I think it well to add that I cherish no illusions as to the meaning and effect of strikes.   While I think the strike a lawful instrument in the universal struggle of life, I think it pure phantasy to suppose that there is a body of capital of which labor, as a whole, secures a larger share by that means.

The annual product, subject to an infinitesimal deduction for the luxuries of the few, is directed to consumption by the multitude, and is consumed by the multitude always.   Organization and strikes may get a larger share for the members of an organization, but, if they do, they get it at the expense of the less organized and less powerful portion of the laboring mass.   They do not create something out of nothing.

It is only by divesting our minds of questions of ownership and other machinery of distribution, and by looking solely at the question of consumption, — asking ourselves what is the annual product, who consumes it, and what changes would or could we make, — that we can keep in the world of realities.

But . . . I think it lawful for a body of workmen to try by combination to get more than they are now getting, although they do it at the expense of their fellows . . .

We have set out these passages from the Holmes opinions at length because they embody so fully our own reactions to the case before us.   What Judge Holmes seems to us to have said is that peaceful labor disputes are only part of the field of industrial and commercial competition, that attitudes toward them are inevitably different because people hold conflicting economic views, and that in these circumstances there is no occasion for judges issuing injunctions in a manner suggesting that they consider themselves possessed of some higher understanding.

There could be little point in tracing closely the developments in the period lying between the granting of these early injunctions and the passage of the Norris-LaGuardia Act in 1932.   The practice developed of employers' counsel coming into the equity courts with handfuls of affidavits charging striking unions with all manner of unconscionable designs and tortious tactics, and with deviously and legalistically worded restraining orders all made out and ready for judicial signature.   They usually left, minutes later and without notice having been given or hearing held, with the signature where they wanted it.   Sometimes a hearing would be held — days later, after the strike had been broken — and not infrequently the statements in the affidavits were found to be almost wholly false.   See Judge Amidon's opinion in Great Northern Ry. v. Brosseau, 286 Fed. 414 (D.N.D. 1923).   Sometimes cases eventually went on appeal to higher courts, in pursuit of what could only be hollow vindication.   The results there were less predictable and uniform, but no more can be said than that the appellate judges developed a somewhat refined rationale which they expressed in terms of "justifiable cause" or "illegal purpose," hardly concealing that they were simply expressing their personal predilections in obtuse legal language.

Many of the precedents cited by counsel from this period are, we recognize, against the conclusion we have reached in the present case. But those precedents were all, in effect, rejected by the nation when, in 1932, the Norris-LaGuardia Act (47 Stat. 70, 29 U.S.C. §101) received the endorsement, by overwhelming majorities of both the U.S. Senate and the House of Representatives. That enactment represented perhaps the strongest condemnation the American judiciary has ever received. The federal courts were told, in so many words, to *stop* issuing injunctions in labor disputes where there was no violence involved. Most people had thought that substantially this had been done in 1914, in the Clayton Act (38 Stat. 731, 15 U.S.C. §17; 38 Stat. 738, 29 U.S.C. §52). But the prohibition there was in language which the courts could and did convert to meaninglessness. In the 1932 Act, however, no loopholes were left, no limiting of the prohibition to "legal" strikes, no exceptions permitting judicial evaluations of "purpose," and the like. The courts to which the Act applied, being the only ones subject to Congressional authority, were simply prohibited from further participation in a practice which it was recognized had been badly abused. The legislative history of the Act, as well as its statement of purpose, left no question about the reasons for its enactment.

This 1932 enactment is not, technically, binding upon this Court. Half of the state legislatures enacted "little Norris-La Guardia Acts," applicable to the state courts. The legislature in this state has taken no similar action, although a proposal of like kind is presently before it. We rely, however, upon what we consider the complete justification for these restrictive statutes. We find in them the reflection of a public recognition of what we ourselves sense in our approach to this dispute: namely, that there is here only a competitive struggle between two economic units, that there is nothing in "the law" that confines this struggle so long as neither party injures the corporeal interests of the other, and that until the people speak on this subject through the democratic process of legislation, judges have no authority to dictate results which only their own private consciences might suggest.

It may well be, although our conclusion is not based on this point, that there is in fact an applicable legislative dictate here. Section 7 of the Wagner Act of 1935 (49 Stat. 449, 29 U.S.C. §§151–166), substantially unchanged in the Taft-Hartley Act of 1947 (61 Stat. 136, 29 U.S.C. §§141 et seq.), guarantees to employees, where there is interstate commerce involved, the right to engage in "concerted activities for the purpose of collective bargaining." This phrase and this guarantee would seem to cover all that has happened at the Enterprise plant. It may be, too, as has been alleged, that the employees' picketing finds protection in the "freedom of speech" concept which has been read into the Fourteenth Amendment to the Constitution of the United States. These contentions lie, however, in areas of doubt upon which we do not feel compelled to venture. Whatever they might add to the analysis of this issue could only point more certainly toward the conclusions that the controversy before us does not contain elements which make it actionable in the courts.

This conclusion is confirmed by the fact that the legislature of our own state, being presently in session, is currently giving its attention to this matter. There are three bills before the two houses. Two of them have been introduced, apparently, as a result of the public attention which has been directed at the Enterprise dispute. Senate Bill 517 is in effect a proposal that this state adopt a "little LMRA," its provisions paralleling closely those of the Federal Act of 1947. One proposed change, however, embodied in Section 12 (f) of S.B. 517, would make it an unfair labor practice for a union to "strike or picket or engage in any boycott for the purpose of opposing the installation of any labor saving devices by an employer." Senate Bill 625 takes a different approach. It prohibits strikes in any situation determined by the Governor to involve "substantial threat or danger to the public welfare," and provides that any dispute underlying such a situation shall be submitted to arbitration which shall be final and binding upon the parties. House Bill 119, on the other hand, is a proposal to place upon the courts in this state the same restraints put upon the federal courts by the Norris-LaGuardia Act. Here again it cannot be said that this pending legislation controls, technically, the authority or discretion of this court. But here again there is evidence of a strong disposition to deal legislatively with the problems arising in this area.

We agree with our dissenting colleague that the present situation at Enterprise is, in a sense, the product of the recognition and protection given labor unions generally, Local 619 among them, by the Wagner and Taft-Hartley Acts. The strike at Enterprise is a much more serious matter than was the one in 1940, at least as far as its immediate incidents are concerned. We agree, too, as we have said, that the pendency of state legislation does not necessarily tie our hands. We insist, however, that these legislative developments make perfectly clear, what might in their absence be in doubt, that what is involved here is within the proper control of legislators rather than judges. The basic issue is that of the kind of balance this society wants to achieve between corporate and labor interests, and, beyond this, the issue of whether government is to fix the terms of labor relationships or leave this to be determined by the parties themselves.   The Wagner and Taft-Hartley Acts are clear legislative determinations that the prevailing policy is one of balancing the economic power of organized capital with that of organized labor and then accepting the settlements which are bargained out.   This means, at least in theory, less government rather than more.   See Frey, Democracy, Free Enterprise, and Collective Bargaining.   [Ed. note: See below at pages 29–49.]   The adoption of this choice will inevitably mean occasional impasses of the kind we have here.   But if that is a defect in the system which has been established legislatively, it is the responsibility of the legislature to repair it.

One final word.   We are asked to approve and to enlarge the injunction which has already been issued.   That injunction has been obeyed but it has accomplished nothing.   Nor, we think, would a broader injunction have any fuller effect unless we simply ordered every Enterprise employee to go back to his bench and to stay there — on the employer's terms.   We do not assume that there is a constitutional right to strike.   We do, however, question both the legality and the policy of the kind of order which would be required here to achieve the end the Appellant Company desires.   We should be concerned about how such an order would be enforced.   A democracy does not advisably put itself in a position of having to resort to what would seem to be totalitarian sanctions, nor does it needlessly reveal the impotence which is actually its basic strength.

This case is remanded to the court below with instructions that the injunction be set aside.

WRITER, J., dissenting.   I feel compelled to say that the decision of the majority of the Court in this case seems to me to represent an almost intolerable avoidance of judicial responsibility.   It does not change the fact to disguise this decision as one based upon deference to the will of the legislature.   The fact remains that the welfare of this country is threatened by what is today occurring at the Enterprise plant.   The majority of this Court, in saying that the decision is not for it, has in fact made a decision.   It is a decision in favor of this Union and in favor of permitting one small group of strategically placed men to hold up an important phase of this country's economy.

Perhaps it is true that a situation of this kind warrants legislative attention.   There may be legislation enacted which will cover it. The question for this Court, however, like the question which has faced all courts since time immemorial, is what must be done in the interests of society where the legislature has not acted. Is it the position of the majority of the members of this Court that there shall be no common law in the field of employment relations? Why should this be? But there *is* a common law here. The courts of this state have granted scores of injunctions in labor disputes. The setting aside of the lower court's order in the present case admittedly rests upon a decision to ignore established precedent. What is camouflaged as an aversion for reliance upon personal predilection is in hard fact an expression of exactly such predilection.

The court majority recognizes that the present difficulty at Enterprise is the product of legislation protecting labor unions in their exercise of raw economic power. The 1940 dispute at this same plant created no national crisis in this industry. The timely issuance of an injunction in that situation avoided today's deplorable consequence, wherein an entire industry is forced to suffer for a disagreement between a handful of men. The 1940 injunction kept a local dispute from spreading its effects across a nation. The Wagner Act is referred to by the majority. There is something almost ironic in the fact that that Act, representing in theory an exercise of the Federal Government's commerce power, was based on findings that it was necessary to free the flow of commerce from the obstructions created by strikes in labor disputes. See Section 1. So a state court is to refrain from continuing its traditional practice of restraining unlawful strikes because of the enactment of a federal statute expressly stated as being for the purpose of diminishing the effect of strikes upon interstate commerce! Here, indeed, is blind logic and circuitous sophistry.

The majority opinion in this case pretends at frank analysis and stark jurisprudential realism. This labor problem, it is said, involves so much of social dynamics that judges must hide their heads in the sand. It is fair to ask why the realism of the majority's approach carries only part way through the analysis of this problem. If this situation at the Enterprise plant is to be approached as a problem in social dynamics, affected to some degree by legislation which has been enacted, it is the obligation of this Court to deal with this situation in terms of social consequence. This Court has marched bravely *part way through* the social implications of this problem. It has, however, refused even to face the real issues outlined in such analyses as that of Professor Simons in his article entitled "Some Reflections on Syndicalism." [Ed. note: See below at page 49.]

This strike is pure waste — from everyone's standpoint. It is waste resulting from the avarice of this company or this union or both. Unfortunately, hundreds of thousands of others are being forced to pay a high price for this avarice. This is because these two "groups" — this "union" and this "corporation" — have built up a potential private power which apparently exceeds that of the Government. All of the legislation the majority opinion refers to protects, if it does not create, this private group power. This is not democracy as I know it. I reject a position that a democratic government is either obligated or permitted to let these two little private groups so interfere with the interests of millions upon millions of other citizens of this country.

The majority's eloquent plea for judicial self-restraint overlooks entirely this crucial problem of private group power. It is, of course, true that unlimited and indiscriminate resort to the injunctive process in private labor disputes without observance of rudimentary procedural requirements was responsible for many abuses, which finally led an aroused public opinion to demand legislation curbing the labor injunction. But it is one thing not to interfere with picketing or strikes which bring inconvenience or even hardship to the employer and his workers only; it is quite another to stand idly by and watch important segments of the nation's economy being crippled with disastrous consequences to hundreds of thousands and possibly millions of our people. In such a situation abnegation of judicial authority and responsibility would destroy the foundations of a democratic society, and thus have particularly catastrophic potentialities in view of present international conditions. By now most Americans seem to agree that the holocaust of a Third World War can be avoided only by building military *and economic strength*. Since the dispute involved here affects a vital strategic industry, it would almost certainly undermine the national effort, were it permitted to continue.

The majority apparently feels that these considerations cannot override the clear expression of legislative policy which gives to employees in interstate commerce "the right . . . to engage in concerted activities for the purpose of collective bargaining" (Section 7 of the Wagner Act, substantially unchanged in the Taft-Hartley Act of 1947). Thus the majority ignores the fact that Congress and numerous state legislatures have indicated that they are aware that certain labor disputes affect not only the private interests of the participants but inflict damage on the general public; in such a case, the danger to the public may become so great and continuance of the dispute so intolerable to civilized society as to *require* the intervention of executive or judicial power.

These principles have found their most notable expressions in the provisions of the Taft-Hartley Act concerning "national emergencies" caused by disputes which will "if permitted to occur or to continue, imperil the national health or safety." (Section 206 et seq.), and in the statutes enacted by many states for the settlement of labor disputes between public utilities and their employees, through seizure or compulsory arbitration or both, where an interruption of an essential service would threaten the "public interest, health and welfare." (N.J.S.A. 34: 13B–13. See, generally, Teller, Government Seizure in Labor Disputes, 60 Harv. L. Rev. 1017 (1947); France and Lester, Compulsory Arbitration of Utility Disputes in New Jersey and Pennsylvania (1951).) Although the power of the states to enact such legislation is now uncertain because of possible conflict with federal law (Amalgamated Assn. of Street, Electric Railway and Motor Coach Employees v. Wisconsin Employment Relations Board, 340 U.S. 383 (1951)), the general philosophy of these statutes is eminently pertinent to the case at bar in view of the majority's finding that the Appellant's products are needed by hospitals and various public utilities, where they are now "in exceedingly short supply." Continuation of the strike will thus prevent surgeons from performing operations to save the lives of their patients; the sick and injured may not secure help, houses may not be saved from fire, property may be stolen by burglars because there is no telephone to call a doctor, the fire department, the police. I do not comprehend the equanimity with which the majority must have contemplated these seemingly inevitable consequences of its decision. More important, I do not understand how it can be seriously contended that the inherent powers of a court of equity do not include the power of preventing such irreparable injuries.

It should be added that the inherent powers of a court of equity may be invoked in the case at bar not only on the basis of such general considerations. Indeed, a more specific principle is readily available to justify the exercise of such powers. "Combinations in restraint of trade" were not deemed valid at common law and the Sherman Anti-Trust Act, 26 Stat. 209, 15 U.S.C. §1, has added criminal penalties and government injunctions as additional weapons of enforcement. In many states the common law rules against such combinations were also supplemented by local statutory enactments.

It is true that the Appellant here has not invoked the Sherman Act and it is doubtful whether it could have successfully done so (Allen-Bradley Co. v. Local Union No. 3, 325 U.S. 797 (1945)). However, in many states, statutes outlawing restraints of trade have been interpreted as justifying injunctions against labor activities of infinitely less harmful effect than those presented here (see Carpenters & Joiners Union, Local 213 v. Ritters Cafe, 315 U.S. 722 (1942), and Giboney v. Empire Storage & Ice Co., 336 U.S. 490 (1949)), and these decisions have been sustained by the Supreme Court of the United States as giving proper effect to the public policy of those states (ibid.).   Even in a state like our own, where there is no specific local statute, combinations in restraint of trade were universally condemned at common law as contrary to public policy unless they were merely ancillary to some other transaction (United States v. Addyston Pipe & Steel Co., 85 Fed. 271, 281, 282 (6th Cir. 1898)).   This rule has consistently been invoked by our courts to restrain combinations by employers to restrict output, raise prices, and exclude competitors from the markets.   It is hardly necessary to belabor the point that, according to the statement of facts in the majority opinion, trade in the electronics industry has been substantially and disastrously curtailed to a degree never accomplished by employer combinations, as a result of Defendants' actions.   Hence, it is clear that the Defendants have violated the public policy of this jurisdiction and that this Court has ample authority to restrain such violation.   (Compare Building Service Employees International Union v. Gazzam, 339 U.S. 532, 537 (1950); Outdoor Sports Corp. v. AFL, 6 N.J. 217, 231 (1951)..)

The judgment of the court below should be affirmed.

III. DEMOCRACY, FREE ENTERPRISE, AND COLLECTIVE BARGAINING [1]

By Alexander Hamilton Frey [*]

Democracy and freedom of enterprise are the cornerstones of our political and economic structure, and any conditions that

---

[1] This essay is based in considerable part upon material appearing in the Introductory Chapter of Frey's Cases on Labor Law 1–6 (1941), and in an article by the same author entitled "The Logic of Collective Bargaining and Arbitration," 12 Law & Contemp. Prob. 264–280 (1947).

[*] Professor of Law, University of Pennsylvania. — ED.

threaten the permanence of these basic institutions are matters of the gravest concern to the vast majority of the American people. The primary purpose of this essay is to inquire into the role of labor law and labor relations in the maintenance of democracy and freedom of enterprise in the United States. Essential to this inquiry is a preliminary analysis of the terms "democracy" and "freedom of enterprise."

"Democracy" is one of the most revered words in the American vocabulary. If challenged, the people of the United States would, with very few exceptions, proclaim their passionate devotion to democracy, and their strenuous insistence that any substantial, imminent threat to democracy in the United States, whether from within or without, be promptly suppressed. But it is doubtful whether the average person who subscribes to these views has any adequate conception as to the *details* of his belief.

The term "democracy" is usually employed in a political sense; it is also used in an economic sense (as when Harold Laski suggests that there is more democracy in Russia than in the United States). But when Americans express a devotion to democracy, they are using the term as a synonym for certain ideals or human values which they regard as fundamental. A precise definition of democracy is not practicable. But the term is nevertheless useful, and in this country its most frequent usage is for the purpose of contrasting the basic desires of the American people, and the methods of achieving them, with those of dictator-ridden nations.

Democracy is a concept that arises out of *group* existence. To an individual living completely alone, democracy would have no personal significance. The term applies only to the relations of an individual to others in his group. The very idea of a group connotes a number of individuals associated together for the achievement of some common objective. The people of the United States are a vast continental community and *as a group* they have one dominant desire to which all else is subordinate, namely, that each member of the group shall have the maximum individual freedom that is consistent with like freedom for every other member of the group. "Democracy" is the term by which we Americans summarize this group objective, for when we express our belief in democracy, it is our underlying belief in this great ideal and its eternal rightness that we seek in shorthand fashion to express.

But the attainment of this degree of freedom for each devolves responsibilities upon all. For example, as part of our belief in individual freedom we prescribe freedom of the ballot, but we recognize that universal suffrage could be an insidious thing unless the voters are equipped to vote with at least a modicum of intelligence; to this end, we have embraced the idea of general education, and have entrusted to government the establishment and administration of a public school system.   Freedom of expression and freedom of assembly we also recognize as fundamental to our democratic ideal, so fundamental indeed as to warrant constitutional protection.

We appreciate, however, that this fine democratic ideal of individual freedom cannot stand completely alone.   It can attain reality only within a group or nation from which physical want has been eliminated.   A sick man, a hungry man, a man struggling long and mightily for subsistence, is not in reality free to cultivate for himself the good life which it is our democratic objective to enable him to achieve.   Therefore, collateral to the idea of maximum individual freedom for every American is a secondary objective that each American able and willing to work shall receive at least a minimum of decent subsistence.

In our modern, complex industrial society few men can be self-sufficient.   The Industrial Revolution projected an age of specialists, which seems destined to be with us for all time.   In such a society it is practically impossible for a single, unaided individual to provide himself with even a minimum of decent subsistence. Job specialization must obtain, and the specialists in each field must produce enough of their specialty to supply the needs not only of themselves but also of specialists in other fields.

The achievement by a modern nation of its group objectives necessitates, first, organization and allotment of functions to the individual members of the group, and, second, the furnishing of incentives to the doing of the allotted tasks.   If the group consists of free people, each individual has an equal voice, and delegation of authority is by majority rule.   In such a group every individual is both a master and a servant.   Even those who give orders acquire their power only by the consent of the majority; moreover, in directing they are also serving the group by thus making their allotted contribution to the group objectives.

We Americans *are* a free people, and hence the will of the majority determines the means we utilize to attain our group ends. For ascertaining the special function which each individual shall perform as his contribution to our democratic objectives, we have adopted two procedures: governmental and non-governmental.

Some of the tasks we expressly allot to those whom we call, collectively, the "government."   Now government is merely a group device for attaining a group objective.   Government arises out of the desire of a group of people to achieve certain results which the members of the group regard as important, and which it would be either inconvenient or impossible for the individuals to accomplish separately.   Government then is a means and not an end.   Moreover, it is not a fictitious entity foreign to ourselves, or an ogre seeking to exploit us to our eventual disadvantage.   The term "government" refers to flesh and blood human beings — part of a group — to whom the group has delegated the accomplishment of certain desired results.   For example, each of us might attempt to provide himself with protection against thieves and marauders and fire hazards, but we find it more convenient, and perhaps less expensive, to delegate these functions to policemen and firemen employed by and serving all of us.

But only a very small part of the specialized tasks which our group objectives necessitate do we expressly delegate to "government."   In keeping with our American conviction as to the basic importance of individual liberty, we have for the most part refrained from *prescribing* individual functions.   So, in general, we privilege each to determine for himself what activity he will engage in, what contribution he will make to the welfare of the group.

Among a free people such as ours the rights and privileges of each rest upon the consent of the others.   An individual can be deprived even of the right to life if an appropriate majority of his fellows so determines.   And when the controlling majority refrains from asserting its power to prescribe individual rights and privileges, it is in effect allotting to the specialists, in the fields of their own choosing, the duty of supplying the needs of others to the same extent as if they had had their chosen tasks expressly delegated to them.   This type of representative or "delegated" conduct we do not call "government."   But when we go through certain formalities such as announcing the delegation in a writing called a constitution or a statute, then we are accustomed to refer to the persons performing the delegated functions as "government."

This privilege of each American to determine for himself, free from dictation by government, what contribution he will make to the well-being of the national group, to select the uses to which his labor or his property is to be subjected, is in essence what is denoted by the term "freedom of enterprise."   Obviously, if we are to be free from governmental dictation as to the production and distribution of economic goods, there must be some process whereby a decision is reached as to what each one of us shall contribute to the national economic pool, and as to what each one of us shall receive in return. In the United States these all-important questions have in general always been determined by a process of *bargaining*.

All over the United States, day in and day out, individuals or groups or associations are negotiating, bartering, dickering, contracting, buying and selling, lending and borrowing, renting and leasing, producing and distributing, supplying and demanding, all upon terms and under conditions reciprocally accepted — in short, bargaining. Out of this unending welter of bargaining come food, shelter, clothing, amusements, the cost of living, inflation, deflation, wealth, poverty, success, failure — freedom of enterprise.

The antithesis of freedom of enterprise is dictation by government: economic decisions proclaimed by governmental fiat instead of emerging from an untrammeled bargaining process. Experience demonstrates, however, that even in the United States, enterprise is not entirely free and that government does from time to time intervene. This is especially noticeable when conditions develop which are conceived of as threatening to thwart the attainment of our national objectives, i.e., individual freedom of a high order and physical security at least from indecent living conditions. If widespread want appears, or if men's liberties are drastically curtailed, we Americans have come to regard this as an emergency. And in emergencies we have not been content to rely upon the miracle of enough men voluntarily altering their conduct and selecting for themselves the right tasks by which the crisis might be averted. At such times we have tended to enlarge the functions of government by expressly empowering those comparatively few persons whom we call "government" to correct the evil conditions by any appropriate means, even if this involves curtailing the freedom of choice or action of certain members of the national group.

An emergency, in the form of widespread individual physical insecurity, may result from some dramatic act of nature such as flood or drought or pestilence; in such an event we authorize government to take from those who have and give to those in want, but we call it increased taxation, or possibly an exercise of the power of eminent domain. Such an emergency may also result from human greed, indolence, or stupidity, or from the failure of those to whom we have delegated the effective accomplishment of a specialized task of their own choosing. Again we authorize government to fill in the gap; we call it truth in securities, or insurance of bank deposits, or subsidies to farmers, or social security. The emergency may, however, take the form not only of a lack of physical security, but also of a deprivation of individual freedom. If small businessmen are having their freedom destroyed by unfair tactics of huge combinations, we authorize government to restrain such actions; we call it an antitrust statute. If large numbers of people are being denied the freedom of the ballot, we authorize government to interfere, but we call it the Fifteenth Amendment.

Thus we have come to recognize that it is the proper function of those whom we denominate "government" not only to specialize in certain delegated tasks such as police and fire protection, road building, education, postal service, etc., but also to intervene and exercise a measure of control over the activities of the self-chosen specialists whenever either the security or the liberty of numbers of people is threatened. The threat may come from within or from without the nation, but from whatever source, whenever it occurs, an emergency exists and the vast majority of the members of the national group will favor governmental action or control.

Whenever government intervenes to protect the security or liberty of some, it destroys the liberty, actual or potential, of others. There is always this price which the group must pay whenever it establishes a new rule or delegates a new power.

For the preservation of our system of freedom of enterprise it is essential to minimize conditions that will be regarded by the majority of the people as emergencies justifying governmental intervention. In any given transaction there may be a considerable disparity between the bargaining powers of buyer and seller without any noteworthy effect upon our economy. Some inequality of bargaining power is the rule rather than the exception, and our free-enterprise system does not, and cannot reasonably be expected to, concern itself with minor advantages that may accrue to the stronger party. But if there is an absence of bargaining power, or if a pronounced disparity of bargaining power develops as to a significant *class* of buyers (or sellers), then experience has taught that government will intervene, either by dictating to buyer and seller the terms of the sale (thus removing it from the traditional process of free enterprise), or by attempting to improve the bargaining power of the weaker side, so that the bargaining process, and the free-enterprise system, may continue to function without the injustice inherent in inequality. (Infancy laws, usury statutes, and fiduciary standards are traditional examples; so, too, are temporary controls on rents, commodities, wages, etc., when emergency conditions disrupt the normal balance of bargaining power.)

Whatever the subject matter of the transaction may be, a "bargaining" situation does not obtain between a buyer and a seller unless each is able to force upon the other some concession, some abandonment of a preferred position. The seller can exert very little pressure with respect to the terms of the sale unless there is some degree of scarcity, some limitation upon the supply of that which he seeks to sell. This is the first essential of "bargaining power." If the seller is offering something for which the buyer is willing to pay *a* price, i.e., which it is advantageous to the buyer to purchase at *some* price, the ultimate price which the seller receives, whether he controls all or only a fraction of the supply, depends upon the respective resources with which each of the parties can withstand a deadlock. In other words, if the seller has no capital, if he must sell to live — even in the extreme case where he controls the entire supply — he must accept the best terms offered, however far below what he regards as a "fair" price. Without some resources at the seller's command, there is no element of "give and take" in the situation. This is the second essential of "bargaining power."

Since "bargaining" is the core of freedom of enterprise, those who lack one or both of these essentials of bargaining power are in reality not within the framework of the system, and if such persons constitute a considerable class of buyers or sellers, the deficiency must be eliminated, or governmental intervention to promote their interests may be anticipated, with the attendant danger of a chain reaction resulting in extensive inroads upon the free-enterprise system.

The Industrial Revolution, i.e., the mechanization of the processes of production and the introduction of the factory system, brought about conditions which have terminated the ability of any but the most highly skilled workers to bargain individually with their employers on a basis of equality. In earlier times employer and employee generally belonged to the same community, attended the same church, participated in the same political activities, and were not very far removed in the economic scale. There was no great surplus of labor; if the terms of employment offered to a given employee by his employer were unsatisfactory, more likely than not they would talk face to face and reach an accord. Or if the terms were regarded by the employee as utterly unreasonable, he could do odd jobs for others, farm on his own land, and look forward to the security of at least subsistence for himself and his family for an indefinite period. And eventually either his employer would feel the need of his services sufficiently to modify his former offer, or the employee would find other satisfactory work in the same community.

But with the coming of the Industrial Revolution all this was changed. Great cities developed which were the centers of the factory system. The individual worker and his employer grew farther and farther apart socially and economically. The favorable atmosphere for personal conferences and adjustment of disputes disappeared. Mass production methods resulted in huge concentrations of labor and in a great increase in the percentage of jobs not requiring skilled work. Thus unskilled workers are today the vast majority of those employed or seeking employment, and their labor has little or no element of scarcity. Moreover, whether skilled or unskilled, the individual factory worker normally has no capital with which to withstand a "buyers' strike." He owns no land, has no tools, and hence has few resources with which he and his family can hope to survive an extended deadlock with his employer over terms of employment. Furthermore, labor cannot be preserved and held for a more favorable market: a worker cannot tomorrow sell today's unexpended labor. Nor does the labor of an individual worker have the fluidity that attaches to most commodities or to credit seeking a market: a workman in Philadelphia does not have the resources with which to avail himself of an opportunity for employment that may exist in Chicago or even in Pittsburgh. He and his family are effectively bound to a limited geographical area of job opportunity; and within this area the job opportunities may, as in many a mill town, all be controlled by a single employer.

This unfavorable bargaining position of the individual worker has been greatly accentuated by the phenomenal growth in the use of the corporation as a device for conducting business enterprises, both large and small. In the commercial world the corporation has become much the most important employer of labor. Many persons, however, are still accustomed to think of labor problems in terms of the relations between an individual small businessman and his few employees. One so conditioned is very apt to overlook the most significant factors behind the current labor movement, factors arising out of the present commanding and expanding position of the modern corporation in national affairs.

In any large-scale enterprise, and especially if such enterprise is incorporated, the ultimate product is the result of the contributions of a number of groups among whom the benefits or losses of the joint endeavor are eventually distributed. First, there are those who contribute what is termed "capital," i.e., money or property permanently dedicated to the enterprise; such persons are most frequently designated as the "owners" or, in the case of corporations, the "shareholders." Second, there are those who contribute money or property for a temporary period; such persons are normally designated as "lenders" or "creditors" — they are the ones who are said to have "lent" money or to have "sold goods on credit" or to have "leased" property to the enterprise. Third, there are those who contribute "labor"; such persons may be skilled or unskilled workers, and their labor may be primarily physical or primarily mental or a combination of both. Finally, there are those who "manage," who are at or near the top of the hierarchy of those who direct the activities of others; such persons are in the main the directors and principal executive officers of corporations. These four categories are obviously neither all-inclusive nor mutually exclusive. They may well overlap, as in the case of a financial institution that lends a large sum to a corporation on condition that it be accorded significant representation on the board of directors. Nevertheless, for an adequate understanding of modern labor problems, it is essential that one bear in mind that various divergent interests (whether they be the ones just enumerated or others) contribute to the ultimate product of the enterprise and participate in its eventual distribution.

Obviously there must be some process whereby a decision is reached as to what each of these groups shall contribute to the enterprise and be entitled to receive in return. This is a matter of bargaining — bargaining, in the final analysis, between each of the first three groups (capital, credit, and labor) and the fourth (management). Shall the corporation attempt to obtain more capital? This the management determines. If so, upon what terms? Shall it issue common or preferred shares, par or no par, voting or non-voting, convertible, redeemable, cumulative, participating, etc.? As to these terms the management bargains. But with whom? With the individual prospective shareholders? Rarely, if ever, in the case of a stock issue of any magnitude. The bargaining is with a group having at least as much bargaining power as the corporation itself — with a financial institution which will make a considerable capital contribution if the terms are satisfactory, with bankers or brokers who will underwrite certain types of issues on certain conditions, with the management of another corporation which will merge or consolidate only pursuant to an approved plan.

If the management determines to borrow funds for the corporation, it negotiates as to the terms with virtually the same powerful bargaining groups as in the case of an issue of stock. If the management determines to buy for the corporation raw materials or machinery or other property, today it bargains for the most part with another corporation. Although the law conceives of a corporation, for many purposes, as an entity — a single fictitious person — it is patent that the influential corporations are in fact huge combinations of persons, strongly equipped for bargaining purposes on all fronts.

But when the management seeks to obtain labor for the corporation (not the results of labor in the form of raw materials or processed goods), it does not bargain with another group. In the absence of an effective labor union, it deals with the individual worker, who, as we have observed, has no bargaining power. If four groups each contribute to a joint enterprise and only three of the groups participate in the determination of how the joint product shall be divided, the inevitable result is that the fourth group receives a disproportionately small share. And this is precisely what has happened and is happening in areas where labor unions are not permitted to flourish.

In short, under modern industrial conditions the individual worker is powerless to bargain on an equal basis with his employer with respect to the terms of his employment. Acting alone, he has no practical alternative but to accept the terms offered to him. And this unfavorable bargaining position is reflected in the development of the case law relating to the economic hazards which confront the individual worker. He has no job security, no protection from discharge without "cause." Where any ambiguity exists, or if the term is indefinite, courts tend to construe employment contracts not as contracts for a term but as a hiring at will.

The individual worker is not only unable to insure job security for himself; he is also powerless to influence the amount or frequency of his wage payments. Legislative attempts to improve his situation have frequently been neutralized by the courts. When "overtime" work is required of the individual, the courts will not aid him in recovering compensation therefor. Even where statutes have been enacted declaring the number of hours that shall constitute a day's work, courts have held that employees are not entitled to additional compensation for work required beyond the statutory number.

The individual worker is likewise not in a position effectively to resist if his employer demands of him an excessive number of hours of labor; despite this fact, legislative enactments limiting the hours of labor of adult male workers in a wide variety of occupations, i.e., not in a single specified occupation, have been held to be unconstitutional in a majority of the decided cases.

The individual worker cannot force his employer to install safety devices and other protections against industrial accidents. Yet prior to the enactment of workmen's compensation laws, the courts afforded little relief to those avoidably injured. See, for example, Hayden v. Smithville Mfg. Co., 29 Conn. 548 (1861) (the plaintiff, a boy of ten years, employed in defendant's mill, got his hand caught in a gear, and charged defendant with negligence in not providing the spinning frame with a bonnet; in reversing judgment for the plaintiff, the court said that no recovery could be had for injury due to defective or obsolete machinery "unless the employer knew or ought to have known the fact, and the employee did not know it or had not equal means of knowing it").

If it be conceded that under modern industrial conditions the individual worker, acting alone, has little or no bargaining power, then it must be recognized that he will endeavor to foster his interests by acting in concert with his fellow workers. To labor leaders and other students of labor problems the desirability of organizations through which workers can bargain collectively is axiomatic, for labor unions can do much to offset the lack of bargaining power of the individual member. In the first place, they provide a medium for concerted action by which the supply of labor available to an employer may be restricted, so that even unskilled labor in an era of unemployment will have some scarcity value. Secondly, their treasuries constitute a potential source of that minimum of capital which the individual worker must have if he is to be able to resist at all when deadlocked with his employer over terms and conditions of employment. Thus, through unionization, the individual worker is enabled to secure at least a measure of the two essentials of bargaining power.

If workers fail in their efforts to bring themselves within the framework of our free-enterprise system by achieving collective bargaining power — and they had failed signally prior to the passage of the National Labor Relations Act in 1935 — then governmental intervention to promote the interests of a group of such proportions may be anticipated. Apparently the Congress and various state legislatures ultimately came to regard the unequal bargaining position of the individual worker as an emergency justifying legislative attention. They might have attempted by legislative fiat to force upon employers and employees prescribed wages, hours, prices, and other standards. But in a society such as ours, dedicated to the perpetuation of a system of free enterprise, the function of government is not to displace that system but to protect it, and fortunately government has elected to put its faith in the ability of labor and capital voluntarily to reach agreements that in the long run will be in the best interests of society. Accordingly, the Federal Government has thus far sought to safeguard the individual worker in interstate commerce not by dictating the wages to be paid to him, but by facilitating the development of organization through which he may achieve the only kind of realistic freedom of enterprise available to him, namely, collective bargaining.

For decades the American legislature has sought to minimize the unequal combat over unionization by depriving employers of some of the weapons with which they had been thwarting union development. As early as 1898, Congress passed the Erdman Act. This statute aimed to promote unionization of interstate railroad employees by outlawing "yellow dog" contracts and forbidding railroads to discriminate against union members. But in 1908 the United States Supreme Court, in the noted case of Adair v. United States (208 U.S. 161), held the Act to be unconstitutional under the Fifth Amendment, which declares that no person shall be deprived of liberty or property without due process of law. A companion case, Coppage v. Kansas (236 U.S. 1) arose in 1915 out of a Kansas statute also declaring "yellow dog" contracts to be unlawful. Again the United States Supreme Court thwarted the legislative effort to stimulate unionization by declaring this state statute unconstitutional as in conflict with the "due process" clause of the Fourteenth Amendment. In each of these cases Mr. Justice Holmes was among those dissenting.

Rebuffed in its effort to lessen the severity with which employers treat union workers, Congress addressed itself to another obstacle in the path of the labor movement, namely, the injunction. In 1914, Congress passed Section 20 of the famous Clayton Act. Although the wording of this section leaves room for some construction (this is inevitably true of a statute covering a broad field), it might reasonably have been interpreted as manifesting a Congressional purpose to take away from the federal courts the power to issue injunctions in labor disputes except where necessary to prevent irreparable injury. But in 1921 the United States Supreme Court, in Duplex Printing Press Co. v. Deering (254 U.S. 443), held that the benefits of this statute extended only to "those who are proximately and substantially concerned as parties to an actual dispute respecting the terms or conditions of their own employment, past, present or prospective." This decision reversed both the District Court and the Circuit Court of Appeals and evoked dissents from Justices Brandeis, Holmes, and Clarke. The value to labor of the Clayton Act was largely destroyed by this narrow construction, since it left union officials and other labor leaders as vulnerable to the injunction as formerly.

Not until 1932 could sufficient strength be mustered in the Senate and in the House to enable Congress to attempt to override these judicial vetoes. In that year the Norris-LaGuardia Act was passed, and approved by President Hoover. This statute embraces the subjects dealt with by both the Erdman and the Clayton Acts. Instead of making it a crime for an employer to require an employee to enter into a "yellow dog" contract, the Norris-La Guardia Act provides that such contracts shall not be enforceable by injunction or otherwise in any federal court. The Act also denies to the federal courts the power to enjoin any person "interested" in a labor dispute from doing a number of specified acts, such as "giving publicity to the existence of, or the facts involved in any labor dispute, whether by advertising, speaking, patrolling, or by any other method not involving fraud or violence," and "assembling peaceably to act or to organize to act in promotion of their interests in a labor dispute." One of the features of the Act is that it protects defendants in actions for labor injunctions from many of the grave procedural abuses to which they were theretofore subject. The United States Supreme Court has apparently accepted the constitutionality of this statute, although there is no decision of that court directly in point.

In 1926, Congress enacted the Railway Labor Act, which, although confined to a single industry, was a most important step in the development of national labor policy; and the famous Section 7 (a) of the ill-fated National Industrial Recovery Act of 1933 was in some significant respects a forerunner of the next Congressional enactment on behalf of labor, namely, the National Labor Relations Act of 1935, popularly referred to as the Wagner Act. This statute characterizes a number of acts by employers as "unfair labor practices." These "unfair labor practices" are in general the more common activities of employers in their attempts to defeat the development of labor unions. They include (a) coercing employees not to join labor organizations, (b) dominating the formation of labor organizations (this relates especially to company unions), (c) discriminating, in the hiring or firing of employees, against union members or against employees who have availed themselves of the rights established by the Act, and (d) refusing to bargain collectively with employees' representatives. The Act provides that representatives selected for the purpose of collective bargaining by the majority of the employees in an appropriate unit shall be the exclusive representatives of all the employees for the purpose of collective bargaining as to conditions of employment. A National Labor Relations Board is established by the Act. If a complaint is made to this Board that an employer has committed one of the unfair labor practices designated in the Act, the Board may conduct an inquiry, hear testimony, and, if the Board finds that the employer has been committing the unfair labor practice charged, it may issue a "cease and desist" order and may also direct the employer to reinstate employees with back pay where improper discharge is involved. If the employer ignores the Board's order, the Board must petition one of the federal Circuit Courts of Appeals for enforcement of the order; and if the employer desires, he may petition the Circuit Court of Appeals for a review of the Board's order.

In a series of historically startling opinions delivered April 12, 1937, the United States Supreme Court completely upheld the constitutionality of the Wagner Act. This statute, of course, is applicable only within the domain of the Federal Government, that is, where interstate commerce is concerned, and the Norris-La Guardia Act only affects the jurisdiction of the federal courts. But both statutes have been supplemented by similar state legislation in a number of states.

In 1947, Congress enacted the Labor-Management Relations Act, commonly known as the Taft-Hartley Act. This statute is much more comprehensive than the Wagner Act and also deals with certain union activities as unfair labor practices, but the employer unfair labor practices created by the Wagner Act are incorporated into the Taft-Hartley Act virtually unchanged.

These labor relations acts, state as well as federal, struck down the most important barriers theretofore erected by employers against the development of labor unions. The anti-injunction statutes, state and federal, have drastically limited the power of the judiciary to enjoin activities in furtherance of unionization. By the summer of 1949 there were approximately sixteen million workers in the ranks of organized labor. These statutes, particularly the Wagner Act, may well have as profound effect upon the growth of the labor union movement in this country as did the Trade Disputes Act of 1906 in England, and in that case collective bargaining will become a reality.

There can be little doubt that if the collective bargaining endeavor fails significantly to bring about substantial equality of bargaining power between employers and employees,[2] the government will be forced to attempt to aid whichever is the weaker side by dictating wages to be paid and received. Dictation by government of the terms of any sale (even the establishment of "floors" and "ceilings") tends to set off a chain of governmental actions which increasingly restrict the areas of free enterprise. This is particularly true with respect to the establishment of labor costs by governmental fiat, for in order to effectuate its wage policy the government would find it had also to concern itself with other costs and with prices, which in turn would involve profits, and the investment of capital, and the use of property, and the myriad decisions which are now reached by the traditional process of free bargaining.

If the alternatives are substantial equality of bargaining power for the individual employee in relation to his employer through the device of collective bargaining, or governmental dictation of wages and a congeries of related interests, then collective bargaining emerges as a potential bulwark of the free-enterprise system, and labor unions are seen as organizations having significance to society as well as to their own members. An understanding of the factors without which collective bargaining cannot succeed is of the utmost importance to the preservation of our national economy.

Since individual workers can bring themselves within the framework of our free-enterprise system only by bargaining collectively, the first essential is that employers shall bargain with their employees only on a collective and not on an individual basis. Even though a group of workers form an organization and agree to negotiate only as a unit with a given employer or potential employer, they do not in fact achieve any bargaining power with reference to that employer so long as he is able to obtain an adequate supply of competent employees on his own terms by dealing individually with other, unorganized workers. Hence, if there is a sincere desire to have labor relations determined by a genuine bargaining process, and not by governmental fiat, it is necessary either that employers voluntarily refrain from dealing with individual employees for their labor except on terms that have emerged from collective bargaining negotiations, or that employers be precluded from engaging in such individual transactions by virtue

[2] Collective bargaining might fail either because employers succeed in reducing unions to an impotent state, or because unions become so powerful and arrogant as to make a mockery of bargaining negotiations.

of the organization of substantially all available employees as members of one or more labor unions through which they will bargain collectively only.

The suggested self-restraint is hardly likely to occur: each employer (even corporations employing huge aggregates of workers) will discount the danger of eventual governmental intervention on a national scale because of the absence of genuine bargaining in his plant; each employer will convince himself that the terms and conditions of employment which he will uni-laterally establish if the opportunity presents itself are fair and reasonable. Accordingly, it is difficult to escape the conclusion that bargaining as to labor relations can exist only if employers cannot obtain adequate supplies of labor except by first negotiating terms and conditions of employment with an association of workers organized to bargain collectively.

It must be borne in mind that, just as in an ordinary sale there is always a specific subject matter of the bargain, so in collective bargaining the bargaining is as to the terms and conditions of employment of the employees *in a given bargaining unit*. A bargaining unit is not a union; it is a group of jobs. It may be the jobs connected with a particular machine or operation; it may be the jobs of a particular craft, such as painters; it may be the jobs in a particular department of a plant; it may be clerical jobs or production jobs; it may be all nonsupervisory jobs in a given plant or in all the plants of the employer. Collective bargaining cannot proceed until the bargaining unit has been established, whether by prior practice or custom, decision of an administrative agency, or agreement of the parties. With reference to a given bargaining unit, there may be more than one union to which divergent groups of the available workers belong. If so, the employer will have a choice of organized sources of his labor supply with which to bargain collectively, unless the operation of a labor relations statute controls his choice.

Even if the employer has, however, no choice but to deal with one union representing all of his employees or potential employees in a given bargaining unit, this does not place the employer in the unfair position of a would-be buyer of a commodity which has been monopolized by a single seller. The monopolistic commodity seller has many potential buyers to pit against one another, they being unorganized, while each individual buyer has, by hypothesis, no alternate seller with whom to deal.[3] A labor

[3] Except where labor is involved, individual sellers and individual buyers are in general deemed to have comparable bargaining power. Hence, when

union is a bargaining agency only if the workers comprising it act as one man in selling their labor. The difficulty or impossibility which an employer encounters in finding another group of employees, when all are organized, is thus matched by the difficulty or impossibility which the union members, as a unit, encounter in finding another employer. The first element of bargaining equality is therefore present, i.e., the opportunities for the buyer to buy and the seller to sell elsewhere are equal.

This unitary aspect of organized workers is an essential element of collective bargaining. There can be no bargaining as to the sale of labor without the right to strike and to lock out. Unless those available for work in a given bargaining unit are permitted to act in concert in refusing to work on the job or jobs involved in the bargaining unit, and unless the employer is permitted to withhold job opportunities from the members of the bargaining unit as a group, a bargaining condition as to labor relations cannot exist. There are several interesting corollaries to this conclusion. Where a condition of collective bargaining does exist, and the workers in a given bargaining unit embark upon an economic strike,[4] they ought not to be privileged to exert other economic pressure upon the employer, such as inducing or persuading third persons to cease or refrain from dealing with him, so long as he either does not or cannot obtain labor to replace that of the striking members of the bargaining unit; and a refusal by another employer to employ the strikers while the strike is in progress ought not to be adjudged an unfair labor practice on his part. So-called "secondary" boycotts and sympathetic strikes are defensible, if at all, only in situations where the conditions of collective bargaining do not exist, or where the strike is provoked by a statutory unfair labor practice of the employer. In many states there is no local counterpart of the National Labor Relations Act, so that, if interstate commerce is not affected, efforts to form a union and to achieve union recognition may be unsuccessful because no applicable statute deprives the employer of the devices, such as discrimination, which he is privileged at com-

---

unions of commodity sellers have been formed, government has sought, through antitrust statutes, to restore the bargaining process by breaking up such combinations. With respect to individual sellers of labor, government has attempted, through labor relations statutes, to reestablish the bargaining process by stimulating the development of unions of such sellers.

[4] An "economic" strike is a strike to force wage or other concessions from the employer which he is not required by law to grant. A strike to induce an employer to abide by the requirements of the National Labor Relations Act (or of some other federal or state labor statute) is commonly referred to as an "unfair labor practice" strike.

mon law to use to thwart the establishment of a collective bargaining organization among his employees. If, however, the employer replaces the striking members of the bargaining unit with non-union employees, neither the strikers nor the unorganized replacements have any actual bargaining power, and almost inevitably the strikers will attempt to exert other forms of economic pressure upon the employer than the futile withholding of their own services.

Outside the field of labor relations, the equivalent of a strike or a lockout is a normal element in the bargain process. When buyer A (usually a corporation) is unable to reach an accord with seller X (usually another corporation), buyer A refuses to deal further with seller X, or vice versa, and each seeks a seller or a buyer elsewhere. But, as indicated above, when a bargaining impasse occurs between an employer and a union, resulting in a strike or a lockout, there is normally no other seller (i.e., the entire group of workers involved in the bargaining unit) for the buyer (i.e., the employer) to turn to, and there is no other employer from whom the workers *as a body* can obtain employment. The accuracy of this statement is not affected by the fact that a few employees, as individuals, may be able to get some kind of temporary work elsewhere, or that the employer may be able to obtain a trickle of replacements for individual workers. If a strike develops in any plant in which the organized workers constitute a sizable segment of the community, the possibility of other jobs or other workers being obtained on a substantial scale is illusory. Consequently, so long as the deadlock continues, the parties have no alternatives but to wait each other out, or to resume negotiations with each other.

The vast body of consumers constituting the public has a very real interest in not having the production of coal, steel, transportation, automobiles, housing, food, and goods and services of many other sorts interrupted while employers and employees engaged in such production slug out their differences over labor relations. Consequently, there are recurring proposals for federal or state legislation aimed at precluding strikes and lockouts, at least in those situations in which the public interest is vitally affected. If such an inroad on collective bargaining should ever be ordained, the omnivorous character of the concept of a "vitally affected" public interest can readily be imagined. But very few members of the public fully comprehend that there is no bargaining power available to most workers in modern industry unless those who can perform the jobs in a given bargaining unit are able to act as one man, and unless that "one man" is given the privilege which any individual has of refusing to work upon the terms or under the conditions proffered.   Too many employers are unmindful of the long-range probability that the absence of collective bargaining as to labor relations will lead to the destruction of their freedom of enterprise and the emergence of some form of state socialism or planned economy.

Here, then, is a perplexing dilemma: [5] strikes which materially affect the production or distribution of essential commodities are inimical to the public interest, but legislation which curtails the right to strike, thus in effect eliminating collective bargaining, is not an expedient way to protect the public interest, for the consequences of the cure may too readily be worse than the disease.   The situation is not, however, hopeless.   There are two relatively untried avenues of approach to the solution of this dilemma.   The first lies in an intensive and unremitting search for methods of improving the processes of collective bargaining, thereby bringing about a dramatic decrease in the number of ultimate disagreements, which are the sources of strikes and lockouts.

Despite the gains that may be expected from wise legislation, from intelligent administrative procedures, and from a far better understanding and acceptance by the parties of their grave responsibility so to conduct themselves as not to endanger the institution of collective bargaining, no doubt there will remain an irreducible minimum of disagreements as to which the disputants are unable to negotiate a mutually acceptable solution. Within this area, the protection of the public interest in the avoidance of strikes and lockouts lies in promoting measures which will encourage self-restraint on the part of both employers and organized labor — a not impracticable task, for together these groups constitute a preponderant part of the public.

[5] It is of the utmost importance constantly to bear in mind that the basic purpose of collective bargaining is not the process of negotiating and dickering, but the reaching of an agreement between labor and management.   Toward the achievement of this purpose the strike, or the possibility thereof, fulfills an essential function.   Strikes occur when the parties have failed to reach agreement, i.e., when collective bargaining has not achieved its purpose.   A strike thrusts both ways — it visits financial detriment upon both the employer and his employees.   Hence it ultimately renders each side more amenable to compromise, more willing to recede somewhat from a position that may have contributed to the impasse.   In the realm of labor relations the free-enterprise system can exist only if strikes, actual or potential, are permitted to fulfill this function.   Here then is the real dilemma: the public has admittedly an interest in the production lost through strikes; it also has an interest in the preservation and strengthening of the free-enterprise system of which voluntary agreement is the core.   Which interest is, or should be, paramount?

If a buyer and a seller are fairly evenly matched as to bargaining power, there are several things that may happen: each may make some concessions, may recede somewhat from a preferred position, and thus an agreement may be concluded; or one may ultimately regard the other as so unreasonable as to render further negotiations futile, whereupon they will part company at least for the time being — the equivalent of a strike or a lockout in collective bargaining; or, while unable to agree upon one or more of the terms of their bargain, they may both consent to take a chance within defined limits by submitting the controversy to an impartial third person for final and binding determination. This last procedure is arbitration, and in it lies the major hope of preserving the bargaining process in labor relations, and thus of saving both industry and labor from the evils of domination by officialdom.

There are no more important people in the United States today than those who, on both sides of the table, have been entrusted with doing the bargaining as to terms and conditions of employment in just a few industries, such as coal, oil, steel, and transportation. Their importance lies not in the fact that their decisions can materially affect the people and the interests they respectively represent, but in the extent to which their conduct may forever affect the freedom of millions whom they do not represent. If collective bargaining does not work in these key industries, if the negotiators are unable to agree upon labor relations, or even upon a procedure for resolving disputed issues, if much needed production is seriously and frequently curtailed while the parties sulk in their corners (even if they do not engage in miniature civil war), government will surely intervene, a succession of regulations, controls, and dictates will follow, and freedom of enterprise will become a historic memory.

The responsibility resting upon a handful of negotiators is colossal. Stupid men do not achieve such positions; and no sane man would consciously, through either stubbornness or greed, invoke so great a national disaster. Those who occupy these vital posts in both labor and industry have every reason to desire the perpetuation of a system of freedom of enterprise, of freedom from state dictation. But have they come to realize the terrible concatenation of events that willful or selfish attitudes on their part can project? This they must be brought to understand; and when they do, collective bargaining will on both sides be carried on with a much greater eagerness for agreement. Few unresolved disputes can survive negotiations con-

ducted in this spirit.   As to these occasional deadlocks the negotiators will be fully conscious of their grave responsibility to
society.   One may confidently predict that from such a bargaining
atmosphere voluntary arbitration will emerge as the generally
accepted final step in labor contract negotiations.

IV. SOME REFLECTIONS ON SYNDICALISM [1]

By Henry C. Simons [*]

Students of social science must fear popular approval; evil is
with them when all men speak well of them.   If there is any set
of opinions by the advocacy of which a newspaper can increase its
sales, then the student . . . is bound to dwell on the limitations
and defects and errors, if any, in that set of opinions; and never to
advocate them unconditionally even in an ad hoc discussion.   It
is almost impossible for a student to be a true patriot and to have
the reputation of being one at the same time.

— ALFRED MARSHALL.[2]

Questioning the virtues of the organized labor movements is
like attacking religion, monogamy, motherhood or the home. . . .
One simply cannot argue that organization is injurious to labor;
one is either for labor or against it, and the test is one's attitude
toward unionism.   But let me indicate from the outset that my
central interest, and the criterion in terms of which I wish to
argue, is a maximizing of aggregate labor income and a minimizing
of inequality.   If unionism were good for labor as a whole, that
would be the end of the issue for me, since the community whose
welfare concerns us is composed overwhelmingly of laborers.

Our problem here, at bottom, is one of broad political philosophy. . . .   What we generally fail to see is the identity of interest
between the whole community and enterprises seeking to keep

[1] Author's note: The manuscript of this article was prepared in 1941.   It
was designed, not for publication, but as an exercise in formulating some
persuasions or prejudices which kept creeping into discussions of other subjects
or problems.   Later, several friends looked at the manuscript.   Some of them,
thought not all, questioned the presumption against publication.   So the matter was referred to the editors.   After they decided to publish, one insert and
a few footnotes were added to the original draft.   [This article originally appeared in the March, 1944, issue of the Journal of Political Economy and is
reprinted here with the permission of the copyright owner.   The article has
been reduced to somewhat less than half its original length for the purpose of
this volume.   The deletions have been of paragraphs, of sentences, and, in a
few instances, of phrases.   All deletions are indicated by ellipsis points.
— ED.]

[*] Late Professor of Economics, University of Chicago Law School. — ED.

[2] Quoted in A. C. Pigou, Economics in Practice (London, 1935), pp. 10–11.

down costs. Where enterprise is competitive — and substantial, enduring restraint of competition in product markets is rare — enterprisers represent the community interest effectively; indeed, they are merely intermediaries between consumers of goods and sellers of services. Thus we commonly overlook the conflict of interest between every large organized group of laborers and the community as a whole. What I want to ask is how this conflict can be reconciled, how the power of strongly organized sellers can be limited out of regard for the general welfare. . . .

In an economy of intricate division of labor, every large organized group is in a position at any time to disrupt or to stop the whole flow of social income; and the system must soon break down if groups persist in exercising that power or if they must continuously be bribed to forgo its disastrous exercise. There is no means, save internal competition, to protect the whole community against organized labor minorities and, indeed, no other means to protect the common interests of organized groups themselves. . . . This minority-monopoly problem . . . is the rock on which our present system is most likely to crack up. . . .

All the grosser mistakes in economic policy, if not most manifestations of democratic corruption, arise from focusing upon the interests of people as producers rather than upon their interests as consumers, i.e., from acting on behalf of producer minorities rather than on behalf of the whole community as sellers of services and buyers of products. One gets the right answers usually by regarding simply the interests of consumers, since we are all consumers; and the answers reached by this approach are presumably the correct ones for laborers as a whole. But one doesn't get elected by approaching issues in this way! People seldom vote in terms of their common interests, whether as sellers or as buyers. . . .

I am arguing . . . as an advocate of the elaborate mixed system of traditional economic liberalism. The essence of this practical political philosophy is a distrust of all concentrations of power. No individual may be trusted with much power, no organization, and no institution save the state itself. The state or sovereign must, of course, possess great reserves of power, if only to prevent other organizations from threatening or usurping its monopoly of violence. But the exercise of power inherent in government must be rigidly economized. Decentralization of government is essential. Indeed, the proper purpose of all large-scale organization or federation — as should be obvious to people facing the problem of world order — is that of dispersing power. . . .

A community which fails to preserve the discipline of competition exposes itself to the discipline of absolute authority. . . . An obvious danger in collectivism is that the vast powers of government would be abused in favoritism to particular producer groups, organized to demand favors as the price of maintaining peace, and available to support established authorities against political opposition. Adherence to competitive, productivity norms is, now or under socialism, a means for avoiding arbitrariness and, to my mind, the only feasible means. . . .

Monopoly power must be abused. It has no use save abuse. Some people evidently have believed that labor organizations should have monopoly powers and be trusted not to use them. Collective bargaining, for the Webbs, was evidently a scheme whereby labor monopolies were to raise wages to competitive levels, merely counteracting monopsony [1] among buyers, but eschewing further exercise of organizational powers. A trade-unionism, affecting wages and working rules only within such limits, and doing all the many other good things that unions can do, would be a blessing all around.[5] No one could seriously question its merits in the abstract. But monopsony in the labor market is, I think, very unsubstantial or transitory; and it is romantic and unreasonable to expect organizations to exercise powers only within limits consistent with the common interest. All bargaining power is monopoly power. Such power, once attained, will be used as fully

---

[1] A situation where a single buyer (as distinguished from a producer or seller), or several buyers acting in unison, control substantially the entire demand for a commodity. See Wilcox, Investigation of Concentration of Economic Power (TNEC Monograph No. 21, p. 10 (1940)). — ED.

[This is the first editor's footnote in Part I. Editor's notes are numbered beginning with 1 at the start of each Part. Whenever these notes are keyed to quoted material they are signed Ed. The original numbers have been retained for all notes in quoted material.]

[5] . . . I wish I could honestly and tactfully propose that large unions be protected and fostered in their good functions and deprived of their socially bad ones (monopoly power). Like others, I can wish for this solution, but, also like others, I cannot honestly propose it, for I have no notion how it could be done. Politicians may go on advocating schemes defined merely in terms of everyone's ends, without any reference to means or implementation — and fearlessly opposing sin in general. Professors, after a prodigious spree, should now eschew such rhetorical intoxicants and go back to work. However, it is perhaps not merely wishful to suggest that many of the good features of unionism could be preserved, and monopoly powers perhaps kept within reason, by limiting the size of unions and proscribing collusion among them. Having said this, one must pause for riotous heckling about "company unions" and then try calmly to assert that the case against company unions is strongest when asserted only against bad ones and, like the case against means tests, is not impressive when stated categorically or when supported only by bad (i.e., historical) evidence.

as its conservation permits and also used continuously for its own accretion and consolidation. . . .

I do not assert that our only monopoly problems lie in the labor market. Save for the monopolies which government is promoting in agriculture, however, no others seem comparably important for the future. It is shameful to have permitted the growth of vast corporate empires, the collusive restraint of trade by trade-associations, and the gross abuse of patent privilege for extortion, exclusion, and output restriction. But enterprise monopoly is also a skin disease, easy to correct when and if we will, and usually moderate in its abuses, since its powers are necessarily small, and since the danger of political reckoning is never very remote. Enterprise monopoly, enjoying very limited access to violence and facing heavy penalties for unfair methods against rivals, is always plagued by competition, actual and potential, and must always operate against a deeply hostile, if lethargic, attitude of courts, legislatures, and the public. . . . The proper remedies here are not very difficult technically or politically.

Labor monopolies are, now or potentially, a different kind of animal. If much violence has been used against them as they struggled into existence, this should not obscure the fact that, once established, they enjoy an access to violence which is unparalleled in other monopolies. If governments have tolerated flagrant violations of law by employers, they are nearly impotent to enforce laws against mass minorities even if majority opinion permitted it. Thus, unions may deal with scabs in ways which make even Rockefeller's early methods seem polite and legitimate. They have little to fear from chiselers in their own midst; and they have now little to fear from Congress or the courts. . . .

Frankly, I can see no reason why strongly organized workers, in an industry where huge investment is already sunk in highly durable assets, should ever permit a return on investment sufficient to attract new capital or even to induce full maintenance of existing capital. . . . If I were operating, as labor leader, without the valuable hostages of large sunk investment, I should be obliged to behave more moderately. But I should still seek, controlling prices via labor costs, to restrict production as rapidly as consistent with decline of my membership by death and retirement and, while permitting some return to investors, should try always to induce only as much employment and production as my original constituents could take care of without new members. If investors dislike my high wages, they would like the high prices which I could assure them by excluding lower-wage competitors. . . .

I am here arguing merely the classical case for free trade, free markets, and free occupational migration. The argument is equally sound whether invoked against external or internal barriers, against governmental restrictions on trade, or against those imposed by private monopolies. . . . The public interest demands free exchange and free movement of workers among occupations. Above all, it demands the easiest possible access by workers in low-wage occupations to highly productive and unusually remunerative employment. Unionism implies ability of established workers in high-wage areas and occupations to insulate themselves from competition, excluding inexperienced new workers and qualitatively inferior labor from their markets. . . .[8]

Consider . . . the untoward effects of standard rates on new and venturesome enterprise. The most vital competition commonly arises from firms content to experiment with new locations and relatively untrained labor. Such enterprises must offer workers better terms than they have received in alternative previous employment but cannot offer the wages paid to highly specialized, selected workers in established centers. If compelled to offer such terms, they will not arise. . . . Here again one sees an alarming identity of interest between organized workers and employers and a rising barrier to entry of new firms, as well as to entry of new workers.

Let me now propose some generalizations about wages and ideal wage policy, whether for a democratic capitalism or for a democratic socialism. . . . The proper wage in any area or occupational category is the lowest wage which will bring forth an adequate supply of labor in competition with other employment opportunities. "Adequate supply" . . . may . . . be defined as . . . the wage which will permit the maximum transfer of workers from less attractive, less remunerative, less productive employments. . . . The basic principle here is freedom of entry — freedom of migration, between localities, between industries, between occupational categories. If such freedom is to exist — and it is limited inevitably by costs and by defects of training and experience — wages must fall to accommodate new workers in any area to which

---

[8] . . . Incidentally, I am wholly intolerant of the apology usually made, for labor monopolies and for almost every particular racket, that "everyone is doing it." A prominent educator is alleged recently to have said, also by way of apology: "There is no public interest any more; there are only interests." If such statements are true, moral or realistic, we should all make careers in the army and assert that military dictatorship is the only feasible foreign policy and the only means to internal peace or prosperity! Another implication is that nothing should be done about anything until everything has been done about everything else.

many qualified persons wish to move. . . . Freedom of entry is peculiarly essential in the case of unusually remunerative employments, if one believes in greater equality of opportunity. Only by permitting the freest movement upward through wage categories can we minimize economic inequality and maximize incomes at the bottom of the scale. But it is exactly the high-wage industries which invite and facilitate organizations; and it is the favorably situated who have most to gain by exclusion, restriction, and monopolistic practices. At best, no labor organization is likely to be more unselfish or to make less use of its powers than the American Medical Association; and, considering its loose organization and small power, the comparison is surely alarming.

Organization is a device by which privilege may be entrenched and consolidated. It is a device by which the strong may raise themselves higher by pressing down the weak. Unionism, barring entry into the most attractive employment, makes high wages higher and low wages lower. Universally applied, it gets nowhere save to create disorder. Surely we cannot all get rich by restricting production. Monopoly works when everyone does not try it or when few have effective power. Universally applied, it is like a universal uniform subsidy paid out of universal, uniform taxation, save that the latter is merely ridiculous while the former is also incompatible with economy of resources and even with order. But the dictator will be installed long before monopoly or functional organization becomes universal. Must we leave it to the man on horseback, or to popes of the future, to restore freedom of opportunity and freedom of occupational movement? . . .

Labor demands may be rationalized and popularized as demands for a larger share of earnings — as part of a contest over the shares of labor and capital in particular outputs. But enterprises remain essentially intermediaries between sellers of services and buyers of product. The semblance of struggle between labor and capital conceals the substantial conflict between a labor monopoly and the community; between organized workers and consumers; and especially between established workers in more remunerative occupations and workers elsewhere. The masses of the unorganized and unorganizable lose as consumers; they lose by being denied access to higher-wage areas; and they lose by an artificial abundance of labor in the markets where they must sell, i.e., by being forced to compete with workers who should have been drawn off into the higher-wage occupations. . . .[12]

[12] One may recognize the possibility that, with wide or universal organization of workers, federations of unions might enforce some moderation of wage

If we are to preserve modern industrial production without totalitarian control, we must solve the problem of private investment. . . . I believe that investment opportunities were never so large as now; that our highest thrift would not for generations permit enough investment to lower interest rates substantially, if owners of new capital assets could be assured of free-market access to labor and other complementary factors (mainly indirect labor). But the prospect of such access has diminished everywhere. Every new enterprise and every new investment must now pay heavy tribute to labor (and other monopolies) in acquiring its plant and equipment; and it faces the prospect of increasing extortion in its efforts to utilize facilities after they are constructed. . . .

We face a real problem in economic inequality. This problem can be handled easily and without serious diseconomies, if one is not hysterically in a hurry, by progressive taxation of income and inheritance. Merely by repairing a few structural flaws in our income tax, we could assure steady reduction of inequality in property incomes and continuous correction of wide disparities in non-property incomes. But radicals and powerseekers have little interest in such dull, peaceful, orderly, efficient, gradualist methods. So they have simply ignored critical issues in tax reform and plumped for labor organization. They have promoted the organization of innumerable industrial armies, with implicit sanction to employ force, coercion, and violence to the full extent of their power, at least to prevent competing sales of services at rates below their own offers. We are told that violence is essential only in the organizing phase; that it will disappear afterward as organization is achieved and recognized — which, of course, is true. Organizations which have attained power need use little overt violence to maintain it. However, it is only the middle phase of unionism or syndicalism which is non-violent. There is much violence at the start inevitably; but there is more and worse violence at the end, involving total reconstruction of the political system. Somehow, sometime, the conflict between the special interests of

demands and of exclusive, restrictive practices among the labor aristocracies. Such internal discipline among and between unions is a real contingency in small, homogeneous nations like Sweden (especially if complemented by a strong free-trade traditions). In a vast nation or a culturally heterogeneous population, the possibility may be dismissed as utterly unsubstantial. Moreover the development of such effective "regulation" would involve radical constitutional change in the political system, i.e., reduction of the Congress or national legislature to a status not unlike that of the British crown.

It is interesting to note that Swedish co-operatives have at times discharged functions of our Anti-Trust Division — which is not a decisive reason for abolishing that agency here!

labor monopolies and the common interest must be reconciled. Beyond some point their exactions become insufferable and insupportable; and their power must be broken to protect the general welfare. . . .

Progressive taxation is a workable, democratic method for dealing with inequality. The alternative of unionists is to send workers out in packs to exploit and expropriate by devices which resemble those of bandit armies. The one device is inherently orderly, peaceful, gradualist, and efficient. It is the device of law. The other is inherently violent, disruptive, and wasteful in the extreme. One calls for debate, discussion, and political action; the other, for fighting and promiscuous expropriation. . . .

Few Americans will straightforwardly espouse syndicalism or look with approval on Il Duce's corporative state. Few likewise will face the patent fact that we are rushing pell-mell toward and into the political order in the United States. Our formal political structure, of course, retains its traditional character. Our legislators, state and federal, still represent geographic sections of the nation. But alongside this formal political structure arises now a structure of powerful organizations of labor, immune to prosecution as monopolies and largely immune to the proscriptions or penalties of other laws. An essentially syndicalist order (or disorder) may, of course, evolve or arise without formal participation of industrial or occupational organizations in the legislative process. Indeed, such organizations may exercise greater power as extra-constitutional political agencies than they could if they had direct representation in Congress, in state assemblies, and in county and local government.

The intricate pluralism of modern democracies is, of course, a commonplace among students of sociology and politics. Equally commonplace, however, is the fact that organized minorities are a continuing threat to democratic order and internal peace. The danger may arise dramatically in the case of churches, secret societies, vigilante movements, a Ku Klux Klan, or less dramatically, in the case of political machines, tariff lobbies, silver Senators, veterans' organizations, and farm blocs. In the main, however, we have rarely or briefly endured political usurpation by minorities practicing violence and intimidation; and (save at federal levels!) we manage somehow to stop corruption and vote-buying short of insolvency and short of disintegration in political morality. . . . But . . . we have never faced the kind of minority problem which widespread, aggressive, national and regional unions and their federations present. . . . Peaceful strikes, even in the absence of overt violence or intimidation, are a meaningless conception when they involve disruption of an elaborate production process with intricate division of labor. What is obvious in the case of railways and utilities is similarly true of coal-mining, steel production, and ultimately of every important industry and occupation. . . .

The obvious struggle within particular industries over division of earnings tends largely to obscure the more substantial identity of interest and functional complementarity of labor and employer organizations. Popularly regarded and defended as counterpoises to industrial concentration or enterprise monopoly, unions in fact serve mainly to buttress effective monopoly in product markets where it already obtains, and to call it into existence when it does not. Labor leaders have, indeed, a quite normal appetite for monopoly prices and for monopoly profits which bargaining power permits them to appropriate and to distribute among their members.

While extremely ill-informed, I know of no instance where a powerful union has proposed reduction of a monopolistic product price or given real support, singly or in federations, to anti-trust policy. On the other hand, N.I.R.A., like extreme tariff protection, was strongly supported by organized labor. The formal and enforced cartelization of the coal industry may be credited largely to U.M.W. And, if some proposals of C.I.O. leaders for labor participation in management are not pure cartel schemes, I cannot identify the beast when I see it. If labor remains and becomes increasingly cartelized along industry lines, enterprises must be similarly organized for bargaining purposes — not only to present a united front and to recoup wage-increases from consumers but because labor itself will prefer, demand, and, in any case, compel such employer organization. . . .

We must alter our labor policy or abandon our anti-trust policy — as English businessmen so urgently recommend. If one big union is a fait accompli in, say, the automotive industry, that industry is all through as a competitive sector of our economy — and damned to full cartelization, if not to General Motors. . . . If labor is tightly cartelized or syndicalized, enterprises must adjust themselves to the political realities. . . .

It is easy to argue that the whole problem is so hard and ominous politically that no effort should be made to solve or even see it — that the real choice lies between a certain, gradual death of economic democracy and an operation or treatment which would cure if successful but is almost certain to kill. I . . . maintain that it is immoral to take such absolute dilemmas seriously. . . .

With free trade the world can gradually be welded into a securely peaceful, democratic whole; with it, we may work miracles in monetary and political co-operation, in raising standards everywhere by economic integration and by relatively unrestricted movements both of goods and of investment funds. . . . But there can be no free world trade without free internal trade in the dominant post-war nation. Free access to markets implies, not merely absence of tariffs, exchange-controls, and quota limitations, but opportunity to sell to competitive buyers and to buy from competitive sellers in every national market. Free trade among collectivisms is a meaningless conception. Much the same must be said of free trade between substantially syndicalist nations. There can be no really free access to raw materials produced by monopolists or cartels, or to raw materials produced by workers organized to price their services monopolistically.

Given free internal trade . . . we can prosper far more abundantly as part of a world economy and can lead the whole world into durable prosperity and peace. Thus, I submit that the peace will be won or lost in the field of American domestic economic policy, . . . on issues in the field of labor policy. . . .

The peace will be won or lost on the simple issue of economic disarmament. The extreme nationalism of high protection, quota limitations, exchange controls, and bilateral trading must be swept away, at least among the leading protagonists in the present conflict. But movement in this direction cannot come unless there is wholesale economic disarmament also within these nations. As nations, we must abandon the contest for dominance and subjugation, finding our proper places in a close-knit, integrated world economy whose markets and commodities are freely and equally available to all. As individuals, we must find and make our places in a domestic system of free exchange, instead of organizing into occupational or industrial states to pursue domestically a power contest which is the analogue of war among nations, and perhaps its most important cause.

V. WHY WORKERS JOIN UNIONS
By E. Wight Bakke *

Analysis of our interviews with workers has indicated almost universal recognition that one is living successfully if he is making progress toward the experience and assurance of:

A. The society and respect of other people.

B. The degree of creature comforts and economic security possessed by the most favored of his customary associates.

C. Independence in and control over his own affairs.

D. Understanding of the forces and factors at work in his world.

E. Integrity.

. . . What effect might union membership have on the desire of the worker for *the society and respect of his fellows?* He knows what is expected of one who "stands in well." Socially respected roles are recognized among workers as among all groups. The man who plays these roles is "a right guy."

Some of these roles are closely related to his job. Let us consider them first. Men whose jobs are interchangeable and carry very few prestige differentials are provided by the union with an opportunity to function in roles which do provide variations in prestige. As a shop steward or union officer or member of the grievance committee, a worker can become "a fellow your buddies look to." Such positions give him the opportunity to win the other workers' approval by being "a fellow who stands up to the boss" with impunity. The role of "a fellow who stands up to the boss" is made more significant because the definition of the boss has been enlarged to include not merely the foreman but "the head office in Pittsburgh." He can win prestige as "a guy that gets results" in such matters as the distribution of work, assignment to jobs, seniority policy, and protection from discrimination. In shops where union security has proceeded far enough to permit union-management co-operation, the role of "producer" takes on new meaning. Moreover, since being a "producer" is dependent on holding a job, and since the union promises to provide greater job security, the possibility of playing this role may be enhanced.

Not only in the shop, but in union associations, the worker has

* Professor Bakke, Director of the Labor and Management Center, and Sterling Professor of Economics, Yale University, report in 22 Personnel (American Management Association) No. 1, pp. 2–11 (1945), on the study made by the Yale Institute of Human Relations (Division of Labor Studies) of "what causes workers to join, or not to join, a union." The excerpts from this report suggest the outline of the Institute's conclusions. — ED.

increased opportunities for distinction among his fellows. The "good union man" who is loyal to his "brothers" denotes a new status. It is defined and buttressed by a code of conduct, by symbols such as buttons and the union card, and by responsibilities and opportunities for service which distinguish him from non-union workers. The very contrast with those laggard workers who "don't pull their own oar" and who at worst may be "scabs" or "finks" or "traitors" makes him more aware, by negative implication, of his status and the consequent role he plays as a "good union man." He is sent to conventions and deliberations on policy of the larger organization of which he is a part, and when he returns, his brothers hang on his words.

His role as a "union man" may readily provide an opportunity to appear in a new role before other citizens in the community. As a representative of the union before community groups, before public agencies of various sorts, before organizations of citizens concerned with community improvements (such as getting a new trade school) , he is conscious of a new importance of his group and himself in community affairs. . . .

Whether or not he achieves individual distinction as a union man, the whole process of union organization and activity makes the worker aware of the dignity and importance of the class in society to which he belongs. It allies him with a larger group in all parts of the country and the world, a group which has a history. He is no longer playing an isolated individual role. He is part of a movement. . . .

The second major goal of workers is to achieve that *measure of creature comforts and economic security possessed by the most favored of their customary associates.* We have found little evidence that the average worker's definition of economic security goes much beyond this. Comparisons of the incomes of the "upper 10 per cent" and that of workers play very little part in their appraisal of their own fortunes. "Enough for three square meals a day, and not the same damn thing tomorrow." . . . "Enough to keep me and the family in good health." . . . "Enough to pay my bills and not to worry." . . . "Enough not to be a burden on anyone in my old age." . . . "Enough to have a margin so I can enjoy myself." . . . "A steady job I can count on" — these are the recurring elements in the definition. What is meant by "enough" is measured in terms of the most favored of one's customary associates, although the emphasis upon "an American standard of living" is beginning to make itself felt. Yet the incomes of most workers are so close to the margin of want in terms of those standards that the statement of one worker may represent the judgment of most: "I guess what I really mean by *fair* wages is *more* wages, and *more regular* wages."

We need not labor the point that union promises and efforts in the field of wage and job betterment strike a ready response at this point unless the workers' hopes in this respect are dependent upon the behavior of those who are in a position to make union membership an obstacle. A specific union, of course, may have a record for favoritism in job allocations or for internal corruptness which would give the worker pause before counting on union membership to better his economic position. Memories of lost or long-drawn-out strikes are effective in reducing the enthusiasm of many workers. "Better wages, hours, and working conditions" are promises, however, which do not seem likely to lose their appeal in the near future.

The third goal common to most workers and exceptionally important in the case of a large minority is *to gain an increasing measure of independence in and control over their own affairs*. This goal can be stated negatively, and perhaps more realistically, as the objective of reducing the control exercised by others. To this end the union has a large contribution to make. Almost every item in the union program and in the trade agreement promotes this contribution by placing restrictions on management discretion. The employer's control is governed by a body of industrial jurisprudence, and his action must follow a due process of law before substantial changes are made in the value of the worker's "property in a job."

Not only does the union provide the worker with an instrument for reducing the employer's control, but the arrangements of collective bargaining help him to reach the employer. The union and collective bargaining provide institutional arrangements consistent with the fact that the employer who exercises control is, in many cases, not an individual but an institution. Whatever, then, may be the worker's definition of his employer — be it foreman, general manager, or the "head office in Pittsburgh" — the union helps him locate the employer and provides an instrument of control consistent with the nature of the one who holds power over his job, his wages, and his working conditions.

More than this, the power of the union extends beyond the factory gates to bring pressure to bear upon business, industrial community, and government agencies which are responsible for dealing with those larger impersonal social, political, and economic forces of which the worker is vaguely conscious. As an individual, he is powerless before the sweep of such forces.   As a union member, he becomes increasingly aware that "something can be done" about them.   The action may be more or less effective, but he need not simply bow his head and "take it." . . .

We should neglect a very important factor in explaining some workers' hesitation or refusal to join unions, however, if we did not recognize that they fear that the transfer of control from employers to union officials will only further frustrate their efforts to achieve an increasing measure of control over their own affairs.

Another goal which we have found shared by most workers is a desire *to understand the forces and factors whose impact they experience.*   This desire is not merely indicative of a search for an instrument of control.   Indeed, it is quite possible that the discovery of the realistic nature of these factors and forces might well increase their awareness of the difficulties in or impossibility of controlling them.   That is not the point.   It may not be true that "knowledge is power," but it is equally untrue that "ignorance is bliss."   In a culture which has glorified the thinking man, a lack of understanding of why things happen as they do is intolerably frustrating.   Workers share the general culture in this respect.

The dominant folklore in America, in terms of which explanations are sought, stresses individual opportunity and responsibility for success or failure, freedom of choice and contract, the social benevolence resulting from individual effort in the pursuit of profit, the ultimate justice in an uncontrolled and impersonal operation of the laws of supply and demand, and the certainty of all forms of progress.   This does not give many workers a satisfactory explanation of why things are as they are in their particular part of the world.   Their attempts to apply the dominant folklore as it is usually interpreted have resulted in confusion as frequently as in understanding. . . .

Most difficult of all the worker's goals to define clearly is the one we have called *the experience and assurance of integrity.*   We use the word in the sense of "wholeness."   Perhaps the best way to introduce the matter is to list some of the recurring comments which suggested this as a major objective: "You've got to keep your self-respect." . . . "No use being crooked with yourself." . . . "As Lincoln said, 'You can fool a part of the people all the time,' but why try to fool yourself any of the time?"   This is one aspect of the goal of integrity.   We shall label it "self-respect." It involves an inner conviction that a man should be consistent within himself; his acts and thoughts should jibe with his personal standards.

There is another aspect of integrity which demands that not only shall he "be fair" with himself but that other people shall treat him "right," that is, in harmony with his own conception of himself and his worth. "They ought to treat you like a human being, you know." . . . "I'm as good as they are, any day." . . . "That sort of treatment goes against my sense of justice. Whatever justice is, that ain't it." We may label this aspect "justice." In its simplest form it looks toward a consistency between the worker's own conviction of personal worth and the way he is treated. That sense of justice may be violated by treatment afforded to others to whom an individual ascribes the same worth; and it may be violated, not only by people, but by the more impersonal forces that operate on human beings, such as technology, depressions, and societal institutions. (God, Himself, has on occasion come in for criticism on this score!)

Finally, in the comments of a number of workers we can identify another aspect of integrity which we may term "relationship." The emphasis here is upon the individual's being geared into a larger whole. The comments on such integration range from those relevant to the job, through those referring to social institutions and pertaining to the nature of the universe itself. What is the significance of what one is and does and thinks? How is all of that caught up and made a significant part of the total effort of the plant, the community, the nation, the world?

The worker may view membership in a particular union as an improvement in or a challenge to his opportunities for realization of self-respect. The union may promise a technique of closer approximation to justice, or may in its program and policies violate his sense of justice. Membership in the union may offer just that channel of relationship to the whole process of production and societal activity which he seeks, or it may disturb a satisfactory adjustment which he has already made in this respect. . . .

VI. BASIC FEATURES OF FOREIGN LABOR LAW

A. *The Background of European Labor Law*

The striking distinctions between the labor law of the United States and that of the European continent are due to two historical factors: (1) most significant, the more political background of European labor law, and (2) the diversity between the civil or Roman law system and the common or Anglo-American law system.

From these two influences come four characteristics of European

labor law that set it off from American: preponderance of legislation in the government of the employer-employee relationship,
including social legislation; differentiation between salaried and
wage-earning employees; works councils; and labor courts.

While the discussion of these four differences that follows will
reveal the influence of civil law concepts, the political factor demands some explanation at the outset.   In Germany, the entrance
of labor into politics dates back to Ferdinand Lassalle's formation
of the German Workers Association in 1863.   In 1875 this Association merged with the Social-Democratic Workers Party which
had been founded in 1868 by Karl Marx's pupil Wilhelm Lieb-
knecht and the ex-bourgeois, August Bebel.   The fight of this
party in the German Diet and in the provincial parliaments of the
German states set the pace and the pattern for all other nations.[2]
As late as 1880, the Socialist votes cast for the elections to the German Diet were the only socialist votes on the globe.   Before the
outbreak of the First World War, the Social-Democratic Party
had become the largest political party in the Diet, and, until the
Nazis seized the government, was by far the strongest labor party
in the world.   At first the Socialist representatives in the Diet
advanced revolutionary ideas, but gradually their emphasis shifted
to translating political strength into legislative protection of the
workers.   "Interventionism," as this approach is sometimes called,
thus became the characteristic trait of labor law in Germany.

On the other hand, trade-unions in Great Britain during the
nineteenth century were devoted to "business unionism."   John
Bright, the famous British reformer, expressed throughout his
political career his distrust of governmental interference in labor
contracts.   The gospel for British unionism was "self-organization," a gospel which the English-born Samuel Gompers successfully preached in America.   No wonder the Germans Ferdinand
Lassalle and Karl Marx (therein in full agreement [3]), did not
think very highly of unionism in this sense.   Had not Lassalle as
early as 1862 derided, before a meeting of Berlin workers, the
liberals of his day as the champions of a government whose scope
was restricted to that of a night watchman (*Nachtwächterstaat*)?
In 1872, quite a number of eminent German scholars in economics,
headed by G. Schmoller, Ad. Wagner, and L. Brentano, formed
the Society for Social Policy.   These men, ridiculed by their opponents, the Manchester liberals, as professorial socialists (*Katheder-
socialisten*), propagandized for reform of the existing social order

[2] Sombart, Socialism and Social Movement 142 (5th ed. 1905) (in German).
[3] Id. at 143–144.

by state intervention in favor of the working class.   Outside of
Central Europe, such advocacy of social reform was rare before the
twentieth century.   In 1900, however, the Paris Exposition was
the occasion for the founding of the International Association for
Labor Legislation.

The tremendous growth of the Social-Democratic Party in Germany caused Bismarck to enact the notorious antisocialist law of
1878, after he had at first watched the progress of the labor movement sympathetically, since the Party no longer served his purpose
in the fight against his "liberal" political adversaries.   The introduction of compulsory industrial accident and health insurance
in Germany, used by Bismarck as a political weapon against the
Social-Democratic Party, was in line with prevalent traditional
notions in Germany as to the task of the state.[4]   When the first
German National Assembly met in Frankfort on Main in 1848, a
deputy sponsored a bill to declare that "one of the most important
tasks of the government in new Germany must be the protection
of the proletarians."[5]   The Democratic Congress of October, 1848,
in Berlin, called for state workshops, for a guaranty by the state
for the livelihood of every person who is able to work, and for
governmental care of unemployed workers.[6]   After the repeal, in
1890, of Bismarck's antisocialist law, the objective of attaining
socialism through securing a majority in the legislatures seemed
even nearer.[7]   And the steady growth of the unions strengthened
the expectation that socialism would be established through legislation, in spite of the revolutionary phraseology used now and
then by the political leaders prior to the First World War.

Thus in Germany — and the development was similar in Austria — the unions were the Party's creatures rather than its masters,[8] in diametrical contrast to the situation in Great Britain.
Until the advent of the Third Reich, the leaders of the unions
regarded themselves as party men first, and as union men second.

In the period immediately following the First World War, the
most impressive novelty in German and Austrian labor law was
the establishment by statute of "works councils," and the enforcement of union terms far beyond unionized enterprises by legislative and administrative commands.

The development in other Continental countries followed that

[4] See also Rubinow, Social Insurance, 14 Encyc. Soc. Sc. 134 (1933).
[5] 2 Valentin, History of the German Revolution, 1848–49, 101 (1932) (in
German).
[6] Id. at 257.
[7] Cf. Rosenberg, Socialist Parties, 14 Encyc. Soc. Sc. 212 et seq. (1933).
[8] See 1 Gulick, Austria — From Habsburg to Hitler 299 (1948).

in Germany in both time and direction. In 1871, when the Commune was set up in Paris, no socialistic party existed — and the Commune's failure postponed the emergence of such a party for a considerable time. But after 1900 the French Socialists influenced politics decisively.[9] Already, before the First World War, when most British industrial workers were still voting Conservative or Liberal, the great majority of their brothers in France, Belgium, Netherlands, and Scandinavia were Socialists.

B. *Legislative Assurance of Employment Rights*

In this country, neither common law nor statute gives an employee a right to continued employment for any time. Neither the labor relations statutes nor the Railway Labor Act abrogate the employer's right to hire or discharge employees, except to the extent of preventing discrimination for organizational activities. Unless a collective contract or an individual contract affords them protection, employees may be discharged at the employer's pleasure.[10]

But in Europe every employee, whether a member of a union or not, enjoys by statute many of the rights and privileges which in this country can be acquired only by contract. Not merely protection against abrupt discharge, but also vacations with pay, wages during absence due to illness or other urgent, personal reasons, and during a period of idleness caused by reduction of plant operations, pay upon permanent discharge, and many other benefits, are here obtained only as contracts so provide, that is, practically, only if the labor union has enough bargaining power to make the employer agree to the creation of such rights by collective contract.

European legal systems recognize a multiplicity of categories of contracts, depending on their content. Thus the employer-employee relationship, following the Roman law tradition, arises from a labor contract (*Arbeitsvertrag, contrat de travail, contratto di lavoro*) entered into between the one who promises to work and the other who promises to pay. Within this type of contract there are subtypes each of which is a subject of special legislation. Illustrations are contracts of salaried employees, industrial wage earners, agricultural workers, theatrical personnel, newspaper employees, domestic personnel, and workers in the mining industry

[9] Sombart, Socialism and Social Movement 209 (5th ed. 1905) (in German).
[10] See Judge Allen's opinion in Thomas v. N.Y., Chic. & St.L. R.R., 185 F.2d 614 (6th Cir. 1951).

and in transportation enterprises. In our law also distinctions exist. Some of these categories as, for example, agricultural laborers and domestics, are altogether excluded from basic labor statutes, such as acts relating to bargaining, hours of work, and wage rates; for other categories, such as railway employees and seamen, there are specific enactments; while still others, such as supervisors or persons employed in an executive or professional capacity, are partially excepted from general laws. While our law in this way distinguishes such classification, Continental laws have proceeded much further and more systematically, and probably too far, toward pluralism of employment relationships.

In the second place, while the common law in its pure or classical form has few, if any, rules concerning the content of contracts,[11] the Continental legal system, with differences in degree, distinguishes between contractual terms that are open to the parties to stipulate according to their free desires, called in French *dispositions facultatives,* and those terms which are mandatory, *dispositions impératives* or *obligatoires.*[12] The German terminology expresses this distinction in the words *ius dispositivum* and *ius cogens.* The Continental doctrine has, from an early day, presented contracts in general, and labor contracts in particular, as transactions which are pervaded with terms prescribed by the law.[13] By contrast, the prevalent American concept of freedom of contract (derived from English law) identifies a contract with promises voluntarily made by the parties.[14] That even the leading text has ignored the fact that the law may attach to promises legal obligations that modify the actual promises,[15] shows how strange to our law the concept of compulsory minimum terms has remained. As late as 1915, the U.S. Supreme Court read into the due process clause a guaranty of "freedom of contract" which barred prescription or proscription of terms of labor contracts. (See Coppage v. Kansas, 236 U.S. 1.) Were it not for the many puzzling problems which the Wage and Hour Law of 1938 offered to lawyers trained

[11] For details see Lenhoff, Optional Terms (*Jus Dispositivum*) and Required Terms (*Jus Cogens*) in the Law of Contracts, 45 Mich. L. Rev. 39, 43 (1946).

[12] See e.g., 1 Planiol, Traité élémentaire de droit civil, no. 295 (9th ed. 1922).

[13] 1 von Gierke, German Private Law 111, 116 (1895) (in German).

[14] See, e.g., 1 Restatement of Contracts, Sec. 1 (1932).

[15] See the criticism of Williston's work on Contracts, by W. W. Cook, 33 Ill. L. Rev. 497, 500 (1939), and see the most recent definition of contract in the final draft of the Uniform Commercial Code (1950), Sec. 1–201 (10): "Contract means the *total* obligation in law which results from the parties' agreement as affected by this Act and any other applicable rules of law" (emphasis added).

exclusively in private contractualism, the idea of compulsory terms imposed upon contracting parties would still be little known in this country.   Is the American lawyer puzzled by what might be called the "unwaivability" of the seamen's right to maintenance and cure?   It is because "unwaivability" does not fit into the traditional concept of common law contract, law on admiralty being derived from the Continental law.[16]   Alien as was the notion of terms imposed by law upon contracting parties, the idea of nonwaivability could be explained here only by the fiction that seamen are the "wards of the court."   It would be somewhat difficult, however, to carry this explanation over to the unwaivable right to overtime rates of thirty million American workers!   Knowledge of the labor law of other countries would have eased understanding of such American labor legislation.

Present-day American labor law has become, at last, slightly acquainted with compulsory terms, but in civil law countries terms imposed by law on the employment relation or status have been pervasive.   Very early, indeed, the social character of the employer-employee relationship was recognized on the Continent.   This is well illustrated in the mining industry.   The medieval miners digging silver and ore in the Bohemian, Saxon, or Tyrolese mountains were the first free laborers in the history of industry (as distinguished from craftsmanship).   It was in medieval mining that for the first time large groups of employees served one employer, and that, for this reason, industrialism and, as Gustav Schmoller says,[17] class differentiation between employers and employees, arose for the first time.   The state, therefore, intervened by writing into employment contracts such compulsory statutory terms as weekly payments, maximum hours, minimum wages, and the prohibition of the truck system (the payment of wages in goods instead of in money).   Mining laws containing such provisions as are found in the *Ferdinandea,* the mining code of Austria (1553), or in the Joachimsthaler Code in Bohemia (1548) remained in effect until the Austrian Law of 1854.   Thus, the concept of compulsory terms in labor contracts long preceded the Industrial Revolution of the last century.   Centuries of interventionism [18]

[16] Pappenheim, Historical Development of Maritime Trade and Law, 103 Publications of the Association for Social Policy 173 et seq. (1903) (in German).

[17] 10 Jahrbücher (1891), p. 683.   At about 1526, in one of the Tyrolese mines, 4600 miners were employed.   Wolfskron, Tiroler Erzbergbaue 1301–1665.

[18] Incidentally, the far-reaching social insurance laws in present-day Europe can likewise be traced to early developments in mining law, where as early as 1300, in the mining district of Kuttenberg, the law required employers and

led the way to the present European labor law,[19] under which the parties cannot alter, modify, or exclude what the statute provides for.

Under this system, in case contract terms conflict with compulsory provisions (e.g., provisions concerning statutory Christmas bonuses, vacation periods, holidays, working time, time for notice, and other clauses of this type), the statutory terms are *ipso jure* substituted for the party-made ones to the extent that the former are more favorable to an employee than the latter. An agreement with an employer that an employee waive such statutory rights is ineffectual. The compulsory provisions become a part of the contract just as if stipulated by the parties. But the parties to a contract — either an individual or a collective contract — have power to stipulate terms that are *more favorable* to the employee or employees than those required by statute.

Modern American labor law imposes a few compulsory terms. The Wage and Hour Law, workmen's compensation, and social security are the chief examples.[20] But they are "largely peripheral and hitting only at extremes." [21] No broad theory as to compulsory provisions has developed here, important particularly for the question of substitutionality.[22] As yet,[23] not even draftsmen of legislation seem to visualize the problem.[24]

In American labor law of the last decade, contractualism seems to have been given new life by trade-unionism. The powerful unions are more interested in control over employments by their own contractual terms than in state control which, of course, could be exercised only through legislation. While on the Continent more favorable conditions than those fixed by collective agreements *may* be granted individual workers and are even welcomed,

---

miners to pay periodical contributions to the miners' accident and sickness funds (*Knappschaftskassen, Bruderladen*).

[19] Menzel, Social Ideas in Mining Law, 18 Grünhuts Zeitschrift 494 (1891) (in German).

[20] For a general provision see, e.g., California Civil Code, Sec. 3513.

[21] Cox, Cases on Labor Law vii (1948).

[22] The interpretative approaches turn upon the validity of a departure from the prescribed terms in favor of the party which belongs to the class protected by the statute, or of a variation offering substantially the same as the compulsory terms. A civilian lawyer is startled when learning of the technical-legalistic sticking-to-the-letter American rules on compulsory provisions.

[23] Lenhoff, Optional Terms (*Jus Dispositivum*) and Required Terms (*Jus Cogens*) in the Law of Contracts, 45 Mich. L. Rev. 39 (1946), and Comments, Cases and Materials on Legislation 43–54 (1949). See also Sperbeck v. A. L. Burbank, 190 F.2d 449 (2d Cir. 1951).

[24] See the example taken from the Taft-Hartley Act, Sec. 301, in Lenhoff, Comments, Cases and Materials on Legislation 46 (1949), and that involving the same Act, in Conway's Express, 87 N.L.R.B. 972 (1949) (hot cargo clause).

since the state enacts compulsory terms in order to give an economic counterweight to the weaker,[25] the United States Supreme Court has pointed out the fact that the practice and philosophy of (American) collective bargaining regards such individual advantages with suspicion.[26]

In the civil law countries, legislative control over labor did not stop at the protection of employment terms for the individual employee as such, nor at his protection against impairment or loss of earning power by means of social insurance. This stage had already been reached prior to the First World War. The last thirty years have witnessed an expansion. Thus employees in many civil law countries have a bargain-proof statutory right to elect works councils, a statutory representative with infinitely greater power to protect them than the representative of the members of an appropriate bargaining unit certified by the National Labor Relations Board. Representation in this country requires a collective contract in order to become effective, but representation under the laws referred to does not depend on the existence of a collective contract or even a bargaining agent.

More recently in Austria, in important West German states such as Hesse and Württemberg-Baden, and in the Federal Republic (West Germany), employees in mining, and iron or steel manufacturing have been granted by law the right of *Mitbestimmung* (codetermination). Owing to these new laws, the employer is no longer sole master of hiring and even of business policies. More will be said on this subject later. On the other hand the whole course of labor legislation tends away from contractualism and toward a *régime dirigé* (government-controlled system, *Gemeinwirtschaft*). Not many topics are left for collective bargaining. Even prior to the World Wars, collective contracts in Germany were called *Tarifverträge*. The use of this word is even better founded at present, for settlement of a *Tarif* (wage schedule) remains the only important subject for bargaining.

C. *Differentiation Between Salaried Employees and Wage Earners*

Common law makes no distinction between the contracts made by a department store with the managerial personnel, with salesmen, with saleswomen, or with janitors and cleaning women, and

[25] Rouast and Durand, Précis de législation industrielle 59 (3d ed. 1948).
[26] J. I. Case & Co. v. NLRB, 321 U.S. 332, 339 (1944). See also NLRB v. J. H. Allison & Co., 165 F.2d 766 (6th Cir. 1948).

if the contracts did not make distinctions — differences in wage and other terms — there would not be any. Our public law, such as labor relations statutes, however, sets managerial personnel and supervisors (who have to act in the interest of the employer) apart from all other employees.

The Roman law had sharply separated the type of contract which pertained to the performance of mental work from that of manual services.[27] When, toward the end of the medieval era, Roman law was adopted as the legal system of the Continent, manual work got a legal treatment different from that given to mental work.[28] The first traces of legal distinction between the two groups of employees are to be seen in the Italian cities of the eleventh and twelfth centuries.[29] The differentiation projected itself into the terminology and pervaded all the labor laws outside the Anglo-American legal world. Employees performing "higher," i.e., primarily mental, work are called *Angestellte, employés, impiegati, empleados,* while those employees whose services are chiefly manual are called, in legal parlance, *Arbeiter, ouvriers, operai, obreros.*

The influence of Roman law, however, was not the only historical factor which accounted for the emergence of a privileged class of employees. The civil service has been professionalized since the seventeenth century on the Continent, and especially in Austria and many German states such as Prussia, Bavaria, Saxony, and Hanover. By the end of that century professional personnel with permanent tenure, based on a hierarchic organization, operated not only the entire revenue system — including forests, mines, and customs, as well as taxes — but also the postal administration and public education.[30] About the same time there developed legal protection of salaried personnel of the Hanseatic enterprises which operated branches abroad.[31] In more modern times, this was extended to all salaried workers. Otto von Gierke pointed out the important influence of the public service law on the law of the salaried personnel in private enterprises.[32] In the era prior to the First World War, political motivations accounted for the considerable increase of job protection given by legislation to salaried employees. Though the codes which are of recent origin,

[27] 2 Windscheid, Lehrbuch des Pandektenrechts 771 (9th ed., Kipp, 1906).
[28] Von Gierke, The Origin of the Employment Contract, Festschrift für Heinrich Brunner 37, 55 (1914) (in German).
[29] Goldschmidt, Universal History of Commercial Law 248 et seq. (1891) (in German).
[30] Morstein-Marx, Civil Service Abroad 161–170 (White ed. 1935).
[31] 1 Ehrenberg, Handbuch des gesamten Handelsrechts 217 (1913).
[32] 3 German Private Law 598–599 (1917) (in German).

such as the German and Swiss Civil Codes, declare the employment
contract to be uniform, one still finds many differences in the
status between salaried employees and wage-earning employees,[33]
among others:

1. Differences in the influence exercised by employee representation through works councils for salaried employees.
   Recently, however, there has been a tendency to eliminate the
   differences in this field.[34]

2. In many countries, notice preceding dismissal must be given
   much sooner to salaried employees than to wage earners.

3. By Austrian and Italian law, payment on severance of employment is required only for salaried employees.

4. All the laws which provide for the continuation of wages
   during illness or other justifiable absence, and for vacation
   pay, set longer periods for white-collar workers than for wage-
   workers.

D. *Works Councils*

An outstanding work on Austria, written by an American
scholar, describes the changes in the relations between the special
classes in the period after World War I as follows: [35] "Legal protection of the workers on a scale unheard of before, works councils,
chambers of labor and other institutions considerably restricted
the freedom of entrepreneurs in a great many respects. These
changes, apart from the modest attempts at direct socialization,
were thought of by at least one leading representative of the
Austrian labor movement [36] as new forms of a *partially socialized
economy*." Austria was the first country which, in this way, established a system of "shop democracy" embedded within political
democracy. The Act of May 15, 1919, required that employees
in each shop having from five to nine employees should elect one
representative, and those in a shop having ten to nineteen should

[33] The cleavage in legislative protection between salaried and wage-earning
employees abroad was never so deep as that between unionized and non-
unionized employees in the United States.

[34] The French Act of July 7, 1947, has introduced the principle of proportional representation for the so-called *comités d'entreprises* as well as for
the *délégués du personnel*. Engineers and foremen form an electoral college.
Following the Control Council Law No. 22 (April 10, 1946), many German
acts such as the Hessian Works Council Act of May 26, 1948, and the Bavarian
Act of Oct. 25, 1950, eliminated all distinction, deliberately and clearly. See
Engels, The Hessian Works Council Act 9 (1948) (in German).

[35] 1 Gulick, Austria from Habsburg to Hitler 50 (1948).

[36] Gulick's reference is to Karl Renner (the late President of the Austrian
Republic), Wege der Verwirklichung (1929).

elect two.   If there were more than nineteen employees, a shop council had to be elected.   The right to vote for representatives or a council was granted by statute to all employees who have attained the age of eighteen years, irrespective of sex and nationality.

The German Works Council Act [37] applied to all industrial and commercial establishments in which five or more persons were employed.   Czechoslovakia followed very soon with a similar law.

We must bear in mind the distinction between the Continental works councils on the one hand, and the Whitley [38] joint industrial councils of the between-the-wars period and the joint production committees during World War II in England,[39] as well as American joint labor-management committees sponsored in the same period by the War Production Board, on the other hand.   The latter are voluntary bodies with advisory function, created by an agreement between management and labor.   Such also are the numerous Canadian labor-management production committees.   They have been helpful in promoting the safety and health of the employees, in stimulating the interest of the employees in the quality of the product, and in bringing about a better understanding of all the problems inherent in the operation of a plant.   Productivity had been raised as a result of this kind of labor-management cooperation.

Of the shop councils on the Continent, those established since 1945 in the three Scandinavian countries come closest to our joint committees.   They have, with one exception,[40] no statutory basis. Their foundations are nation-wide collective contracts entered into between the top confederations of employers and unions.   A council may be created provided that the union in whose jurisdiction the shop falls consents to its establishment.   The council's functions are similar to those of our joint committees.

The legal basis, the form, and the objectives of the shop councils in other Continental countries — such as Austria, Germany, France, Italy, Czechoslovakia, Belgium, and the Netherlands — are

[37] Act of Feb. 4, 1920, enacted in compliance with the mandate of the (Weimar) Constitution, 1919, art. 65.

[38] The name is derived from that of the chairman of the committee which was established in October, 1916, as a special subcommittee of Prime Minister Asquith's Cabinet Committee on reconstruction.   The Report of the Whitley Committee (1917) proposed, inter alia, joint councils, district councils, and shop councils in each industry.

[39] Cf. International Labour Office, Studies and Reports, Series A: British Joint Production Machinery (Montreal, 1944).

[40] In Norway, a "provisional" law enacted on July 22, 1920, concerning workers councils in companies employing fifty or more employees, granted them only advisory functions.

substantially different.   After the Second World War particularly, the constitutions — for example, those of Baden, Bavaria, Hesse, or the Rhenish Palatinate — decreed the establishment of works councils.   The French Constitution of 1946 proclaims the right of workers, through their delegates, to participate in the management of business.   The Italian Constitution of 1947 contains an analogous declaration, but its language is more reserved, and the declaration has to wait for legislation to execute it.   The labor-management committees formed in Italy in almost every factory (after the liberation) had no statutory basis; but labor, Communist-controlled as it was (and to a substantial degree still is), exacted the formation of these committees, which have interfered with management mostly in questions concerning the hiring and the discharging of employees.[41]

In the other European countries, where the law requires the setting up of works councils, the conditions and procedures for their formation as well as their jurisdiction, are regulated by law. The advantage of a statute-based system lies in securing effective employee representation independently from the degree of unionization on the one hand, and from undemocratic, overcentralized, or bureaucratic union methods on the other.   However, one must not overlook the drawbacks of such a system.   Experience has demonstrated that statutory provisions prescribing a minimum of functions have been regarded as so adequate that neither management nor council has shown any desire to extend the mutual relations beyond the provisions of the law.   Under our system of voluntary councils, cooperation is stimulated; over there, it is, rather, stifled.

These remarks point to a second distinction from our joint labor-management committees.   The power of the statutory works councils is not merely advisory.   They are the representatives of the employees and the powerful tribune of their interests in the shop.   For this reason, within their jurisdiction, their decisions are binding, even though administrative review is permitted from their decisions to an administrative tribunal.

In the third place, in their pre-war form they were composed of employees only.   This is still true of the post-war Austrian and German works councils.   There is some deviation from this principle in the Belgian and the French post-war legislation.   The French laws of 1945, 1946, and 1947 distinguish between committees (*comités d'enterprises*) and delegates of the employees

[41] Shaw, Management-Labor Committees, 3 Indust. & Lab. Rel. Rev. 229 (1949).

(*délégués du personnel*). The function of a committee headed
by the employer (or his representative) and composed of the
latter and representatives elected by all employees ("higher" and
manual alike) is to secure and control welfare institutions, especially pension plans, housing projects, canteens, and consumer
cooperatives for the employees. The delegates, composed exclusively of employees of the enterprise, have authority to take up
with the employer any grievances, individual and collective, concerning the application and interpretation of wage schedules and
job classifications, and to see that the laws and regulations concerned with the safety, health, and social insurance of employees
are observed in the shop.

The Dutch Act on Works Councils of June 6, 1950, makes the
establishment of works councils mandatory for all plants with
more than twenty-five employees. In the Netherlands, for a long
time, joint committees for collective bargaining and administration of collective contracts have existed on a voluntary basis in
certain industries. The Dutch Act on the Organization of Industry of January 27, 1950, has created a national council, representative of management, labor, and the public, which has
the function of setting up joint supervisory labor-management
committees in each branch of industry. These committees determine the functions of works councils in the different enterprises.

A fourth characteristic of works councils is that they offer not
union-member but shop-employee representation, for they are
elected by all employees, regardless of whether or not a union is in
the shop. The new Austrian Act of March 28, 1947, requires that
candidates for the council be employees or else officers of a trade-
union [42] which has the capacity to bargain collectively — a qualification barring company unions. Employees who are members
of the employer's family or are related to him by blood or marriage
up to the second degree or are his adopted children or wards are
ineligible.

In the Weimar era, the German law had conditioned eligibility
to the council upon employment in the shop. Under Control
Council Law No. 22, which in 1946 restored plant councils after
their suppression during the Nazi regime, unions were given the
right to nominate candidates from the employee roster. The
works council laws subsequently enacted in the *Länder* in the wake
of that law followed the pattern of increasing the union influence.

[42] But three quarters of the council members shall be employees of the
enterprise.

This has been further confirmed in the enactment of July, 1952,[43] superseding the works council laws.

In post-war Germany, and also Austria, though there is now a single national federation of labor, and the pre-war pattern of rival federations distinguished from each other by political leanings has disappeared, yet "Union influence on the works councils election procedure is often subordinated to the influence of political groups . . . Actually most works councils elections are held along strict party lines." [44] The statutes have adopted a system of elections which is based on proportional representation.

The statutes established strong legal safeguards for the purpose of making the councils independent of management. By Austrian law, the employer has no right to attend council meetings. Furthermore, he must grant to the councilmen the full time required for the performance of their official duties. Wages must be paid to the members of the council without any deduction for the time they spend on council business and at meetings. There are ample provisions for the protection of the members from victimization and discrimination by the employer. No member of the council can be given notice of termination of his employment without previous consent of an administrative tribunal.

The functions of the Austrian and German type of works councils can be grouped under six heads:

1. Joint control with management of the hiring and dismissal of employees.
2. Participation in making shop rules and in handling disciplinary matters.
3. Settlement of grievances.
4. Participation in the economic phases of management; co-determination of business policy (*Mitbestimmungsrecht*).
5. Relation to public authorities and to trade-unions.
6. Establishment and administration of shop welfare schemes.

The first five of these functions will be briefly described.

1. HIRING AND FIRING

Considering the jurisdiction of the councils over this field, the new Austrian Act of March 28, 1947 (sec. 14 (5)) and new German

---

[43] Federal Works Basic Law, July, 1952 (Betriebsverfassungsgesetz).

[44] For details, particularly for the influence of the unions on the operation of works councils in the post-war era in Western Germany, see Fisher, Works Councils in Germany (Visiting-Expert Series No. 18, Office of Labor Affairs, Office of the U.S. High Commissioner for Germany) (1951).

acts such as that of Hesse of May 26, 1948 (sec. 37 (2)) place the employer under the obligation of informing the works council about the employment of an applicant before he can start work. The Austrian act does not specify the legal effectiveness of objections raised by the works council against the engagement of a new employee. The Hessian law, on the other hand, empowers an administrative agency, upon such objections, to direct the employer to revoke his action if it considers the employee objectionable. In German acts such as those of Hesse (May 26, 1948) and Bavaria (October 25, 1950) one finds a statement of criteria for decisions on objections to a hiring: "Such objections can be founded only upon the ground that the action would not be in the best interest of the shop or of the personnel." However, the acts contain an express warning against the use of political, religious, or ideological differences as basis for objections; nor could, therefore, nonmembership in the controlling union supply a basis for them.

As for the discharge of employees, the German Works Council Act of February 4, 1920, gave an employee the right to file (with the council) objections to his discharge. Aside from discharge without the mention of a ground and discriminatory discharge, a discharge not warranted by economic or technical conditions affecting the establishment could properly be objected to if the worker was subjected to an inequitable hardship. However, the Austrian Works Council Act of March 28, 1947, goes far beyond that law. It requires the employer to notify the works council (by notice) in advance of the termination of an employment. Otherwise, the discharge is invalid. The works council may communicate its disapproval of the planned discharge within three days to the employer; and it is authorized to contest the discharge (in the event that the employer carries it out despite the disapproval) before an administrative tribunal which has the misleading name of Conciliation Board (*Einigungsamt*). If the works council refuses to act, the employee may contest his dismissal before that tribunal. Similar is the new law of the German state of Hesse. Both likewise restrict general layoffs.[45]

2. RULES FOR WORK PERFORMANCE AND SHOP DISCIPLINE

In the United States, in the absence of collective-contract provisions, an employer lays down the conditions and terms for the

---

[45] Lenhoff, Some Basic Features of American and European Labor Law: A Comparison, 26 Notre Dame Law. 389, 405 (1951).

performance of the work, such as the hour for beginning work, shift schedules, safety measures, lunchtime, requirements for short absences, and penalties for violation of these and similar rules (work discipline).

In most European countries, before the rise of works councils, statutes required a company (with twenty or more employees) to draft shop rules, i.e., rules for work performance and factory discipline (*Arbeitsordnung, règlement d'atelier*), and to submit the document to the competent administrative agency for approval, before which no rules for work performance could operate. Now approval by the works council replaces governmental approval. (Thus a French Act of 1945 ordains that shop rules may be drawn up only after consultation with the delegates of the employees.[46]) And the Works Council Act of Hesse (1948), and laws of other German *Länder,* require that shop rules be established jointly by employer and works council.[47] Though power to make shop agreements is subordinate to the power of the *unions* and employers or, usually, *associations of employers,* to establish shop rules by collective contract, ordinarily shop rules are set by shop agreements only.[48]

Discipline, erstwhile a purely managerial matter, has now become one which lies within the sphere of the works council's codetermination, pursuant to shop rules.[49]

A British student of the German Works Council Act of February 4, 1920, in the pre-Nazi era has remarked:

> Rules for work performance and factory discipline form in a sense the written constitution of the works and are binding not merely on the workers but also on the employer. The power given to the works council to agree to these rules with the employer, in so far as they are not determined by a collective agreement, represents a very real and vital extension of the principles of industrial democracy within the factory.[50]

[46] French Code du Travail, pt. I, art. 22, as amended by Act of Nov. 2, 1945.
[47] Hesse: Works Council Act, May 26, 1948, sec. 35 (1); Austria: Works Council Act, Mar. 28, 1947, sec. 14 (4); Norway: Worker's Protection Act, June 19, 1936, sec. 34 et seq.
[48] Ibid.; also German Act of April 9, 1949, [1949] W.G.B. 11, sec. 4; Fisher, op. cit. supra note 44, at 15; Haemmerle, Employment Contract 166 (1949) (in German).
[49] Cf. Austrian Collective Contract Act, Feb. 26, 1947, sec. 21, and Works Council Act, Mar. 28, 1947, sec. 14 (1), (13).
[50] Guillebaud, The Works Council: A German Experiment in Industrial Democracy 157 (1928).

An American, after making a field study of councils in 1950, wrote:

> A further contribution towards industrial peace may be seen in works council insistence upon industrial discipline and plant morale.   It may appear strange to hear of a works council chairman standing at the door of the shop to berate late comers.[51]

3. SETTLEMENT OF GRIEVANCES

The new German and Austrian statutes (1947 and 1950) grant works councils a right of codetermination, not only respecting employment and discipline but also as to transfer, promotion, and demotion.   In case of disagreement between management and council, decision rests with an administrative agency.[52]

As for wages, the Austrian law provides for an agreement between management and council on the amount of a job rate or piece rate in case neither a collective contract nor an individual agreement between the employee concerned and the management can be reached concerning the rate for particular work.[53]   Various laws provide also for participation by the council in the determination of the vacation roster, for its initiating inquiries concerning the company's performance of its duties with regard to factory and social legislation, payment of wages and salaries, and compliance with collective contracts and shop agreements.   It is therefore not surprising that works councils play a great part in the settlement of individual grievances.

The new laws in the German *Länder* expressly direct the councils to promote industrial peace and to settle grievances through negotiation.   Paul Fisher reports that in the twenty plants visited by him, approximately 98 per cent of all grievances were settled amicably and finally, and that in well-organized plants only test cases were submitted to labor courts.[54]

4. ECONOMIC CODETERMINATION

After the First World War, the basic objective sought by labor through works councils was representation of the employees for

[51] Fisher, op. cit. supra note 44, at 36.
[52] E.g., Austrian Works Council Act, Mar. 28, 1947, sec. 13 (1), (6) and sec. 26 (c) ; Hesse: Works Council Act, May 26, 1948, secs. 37 and 40.
[53] Id. (Austria), sec. 14 (1), (2), and (3) ; analogous, in the Hessian Law, sec. 35 (1).
[54] Fisher, op. cit. supra note 44, at 36.

the promotion of their economic and social interests, with the emphasis upon the protection of an individual's job. Characteristic of the period following the end of the Second World War is the use of works councils as an instrument for the greatest possible preservation of employment for the personnel as a whole by obtaining for employees' representatives a share in the management of the enterprise, said by an Austrian spokesman for labor to be necessary for "a true and effective system of industrial democracy." [55]   (The preceding Austrian law already had given the works council the right to appoint two delegates to the control board in every stock corporation.[56])

In France the statutes require the management of any enterprise having fifty or more employees to consult the enterprise committee previously described, upon all questions concerning its management, and to supply necessary information.   Where the company is a stock corporation, two members of the committee are admitted — in an advisory capacity — to the board of directors.[57]   The committee has a right to the assistance of experts for the examination of the books.

Experience in the pre-war era proved that the employee-delegates who served on the boards had neither the training nor the education to take an active part in the control of business affairs. French workers now have opportunities to learn business theory and operations through courses given periodically in the larger cities.[58]   In Germany likewise training for shop council members is now provided.   The Federation of Trade Unions offers also classes on the responsibilities of economic codetermination.[59]   A new law in Hesse even provides for a paid leave of absence up to four weeks, to enable works councilors to attend training courses.[60]

The Austrian law requires the employer to deliver annually to the works council (one month after the filing of his income tax return) a balance sheet and a profit and loss statement, to explain them, and to give information about the economic situation, the

[55] Hillegeist, The Austrian Works Council Act 7 (1947) (in German).

[56] The control board (*Aufsichtsrat*) has supervisory rather than directive functions; the latter are lodged in the board of directors (*Vorstand*).

[57] For details, see Chambelland, The Enterprise Committees (1949) (in French), and International Labour Office, Labor-Management Cooperation in France (1950).

[58] See Labour-Management Cooperation in the Undertaking, 59 Int. Lab. Rev. 121 (1949).   For a report on the activities of the French works committees and the cavalier fashion in which many employers comply with the obligations mentioned in the text, see 1949 Revue française de travail 287.

[59] See the detailed description by Fisher, op. cit. supra note 44, at 13.

[60] Act of Sept. 10, 1950.

output, the orders on hand, the demand of the market, and the business policy to be followed for the purpose of increasing the economic efficiency of the company.[61]   In addition, the employer must meet with the works council every month for the purpose of joint consultation on the general policy of the management and on improvements of the methods of operation.   One of the functions of the works council is to make suggestions for the promotion of greater working efficiency and profits.   But the real novelty of the Austrian Act of 1947 is the provision which gives the works council in establishments employing more than five hundred persons the right (through the district office of the Confederation of Trade Unions) to object to the conduct and management of the business if the employer has not paid heed to its proposals.   These objections go to the Federal Economic Commission, which is headed by a cabinet member.

Laws of Hesse and Württemberg-Baden, enacted in 1948, include economic codetermination provisions (which were suspended by the U.S. High Commissioner until April, 1950).   The powers given the councils resemble those created by the new Austrian law.   However, the introduction of technological changes, shutdown of plant, substantial change in size of shop operations and in labor methods as well as in product, are also matters which come under "codetermination" by the works council, according to those German laws.

Likewise the Labor Code of April 19, 1950, of the German Democratic Republic — the official name of Russian-occupied Eastern Germany — grants the employees the right to share in the management of a privately owned enterprise.[62]

The latest German development is the codetermination law of May 21, 1951 (of the Federal Republic of Germany, i.e., Western Germany), relating to companies engaged in mining, and iron or steel manufacturing with more than a thousand employees.   It is the first statutory experiment in having employee representatives share in all economic phases of management of a free enterprise. Of the control board (*Aufsichtsrat*) of eleven members, five are representatives of capital (shareholders), five of labor, and one a neutral person.   In the choosing of the labor members one observes again a strengthening of union influence at the expense of

---

[61] Provided that in the undertaking at least thirty employees are permanently employed.

[62] International Labor Office, Industry and Labor, Vol. 4, p. 214 (1950). See, also, Note on that law for Eastern Germany in 1 Rivista giuridica del lavoro 307 (1950) (first part).

works councils. The statutory provision for the selection of the five labor members requires the nomination of three by the labor federation, and of the other two (who must be employees) by the works council "after consultation with the federations and the unions." The control board elects and removes — for cause — by majority vote the three directors who run the enterprise and are its legal representatives. The new law ordains that, of the three directors — one in charge of production, another of sales, and the third of labor relations — the labor director (*Arbeitsdirektor*) cannot be elected or removed without consent of the majority of the labor members of the control board. Like the other members of the control board, the eleventh member is elected by the shareholders; because of the equal representation of capital and labor on the board, he holds a key position. This accounts for the complicated provisions concerning his election.[63]

Whether industrial production and shop cooperation will be greatly stimulated by this new structure of coal, steel, and iron enterprises cannot yet be answered. Meanwhile it is likely that this legislation will be extended to other industries.[64] The German legislation of 1951 has no analogue in other countries.

5. RELATION OF SHOP COUNCILS TO PUBLIC AUTHORITIES AND
TO TRADE-UNIONS

Shortly before statutes established works councils in Austria, Germany, and Czechoslovakia, radicals among the working class in those countries were enraptured by the glamour of the Russian Revolution based on workers' councils or soviets. These radicals mentally associated the name "councils" with a new form of government aimed at the dethronement of capitalism.[65] The Social-Democratic Parties prevented a copying of the Russian system in two important respects. First, they broke up the attempts to incorporate works councils into the political machinery. Second,

[63] See Section 8 of the Act of May 21, 1951, [1951] B.G.B. I No. 24. For details, see Fisher, Labor Codetermination in Germany, 18 Social Research 449, 480 (1951). One can agree with him that the complicated provisions result in a fair amount of freedom in the designation of "the eleventh man," given to the stockholders.

[64] See also McPherson, Codetermination: Germany's Move toward a New Economy, 4 Indust. & Lab. Rel. Rev. 20 (1951).

[65] For a historical picture, especially the first formation of workers' councils (soviets) in a strike in January, 1918, in Austria, see 1 Gulick, Austria from Habsburg to Hitler 71 (1948). For development in Germany, see Guillebaud, The Works Council: A German Experiment in Industrial Democracy 3–7 (1928); Fisher, op. cit. supra note 44, at 6: "The works council of 1918 was not of the union's making."

they blocked legislation designed to hand over to works councils functions which previously were regarded as the exclusive domain of the trade-unions, which was particularly true of collective contracts.   In the struggle with the radical workers, the (socialistic) trade-unions won.[66]   The "trade" organizations maintained their superiority over "shop" organizations.

In the previous discussion of the councils' activities, their role in negotiating shop agreements was described.   In general, these agreements are only supplementary and ancillary, because wage scales and such questions as those relating to apprenticeship, job training, welfare institutions, and shop canteens are not dealt with by works councils.   These matters are controlled by collective contracts which, however, may expressly delegate jurisdiction to works councils.

Nevertheless, the position of councils in shops is strong because of their control over employment as far as their power of personnel codetermination reaches.   In addition, the councils check company compliance with regulations concerning accident prevention, safety appliances, and other fields of protective labor legislation and may report violations to the competent public authorities.

Works councils have taken over also the functions of the union-shop stewards, who still exist, but only as agents of the councils rather than as principals.[67]   However, since the unions derive their influence not only from the legal powers conferred in recent years, but also — and perhaps even more — from the fact that most employees are union members, it is safe to say that at present the councils will not depart from union policies.   Some 85 per cent of all elected works council members in Western Germany are union members.[68]

From a realistic — a sociological rather than a legal — standpoint, our system and the foreign system of labor relations have much in common.   For full functioning of both systems, unionism is an indispensable ingredient.   It is a matter of general knowledge in Germany that if there is no union in a shop, interest is rarely shown in the election of a works council.   However, works councils are elected in many small factories which are not unionized, a characteristic difference between the two systems; for here, without collective contracts, labor relations remain in their com-

[66] By the Austrian law, works councils have no capacity to negotiate and agree upon matters left open in collective contracts unless express reference to such a negotiation for a shop agreement had been made in those contracts.

[67] Fisher, op. cit. supra note 44, at 15.

[68] Id. at 19: "This does not mean that the unions have organized 85 percent of all employees."

mon law state of incidents of the employer's control over his enterprise, but in Europe, employees have representation whether collective contracts exist or not.

E. *Labor Courts*

If an individual employee in this country feels aggrieved in any
of his employment rights, the only practical redress he can obtain
is through the grievance procedure and, finally, through arbitration.   Both steps presuppose a collective contract.   Likewise in
foreign countries most grievances are settled through intra-shop
machinery: the works councils.   Where the latter do not exist or
operate, or cannot reach a settlement, a party may get redress by
an action in the labor courts.   Thus, one finds that in its bearing
upon the determination of individual grievances the significance of
labor courts abroad is analogous to that of labor arbitration here.
The analogy is weakened if one realizes that the invocation of our
grievance procedure by a party presupposes the existence of a collective contract, whereas in the foreign countries *labor courts* take
care of his grievances regardless of the existence of a collective
contract.   The contract may add to his substantive rights, but it
cannot affect the jurisdiction of the labor courts to protect all of
his employment rights.   Needless to say, unorganized workers have
access to them for the redress of their grievances to the same extent
as organized workers.

The first labor courts were created in 1806 in France under the
name council of *probi viri* (*Conseil des prud'hommes*) , the name
indicating their composition of men with expert knowledge in a
trade.   The idea was carried along with the French law by the
Napoleonic armies, and spread during the last century to Germany,
Austria, Italy, many Swiss cantons, and later to the Scandinavian
countries.

The principle of having labor courts settle labor rights has become so deeply ingrained in European, particularly German thinking, that soon after the collapse of Germany the Interallied Control
Council revived the labor courts — with the exception of the
Federal (*Reich*) Supreme Labor Court.[69] The structure and
jurisdiction of the courts vary between countries.   The characteristic feature is the limitation of their jurisdiction to legal
claims.   None of these European courts has anything to do with
the negotiation or fixing of wages, hours, and working conditions;

[69] Control Council Act No. 21 of April 4, 1946, [1946] K.R.A. Bl. 124 on
Labor Courts.

they have no power to decide disputes over terms under which, in the future, work should be performed. European labor courts therefore are quite different from Australian or New Zealand courts of arbitration.

Characteristic of the French labor court is the restriction of jurisdiction to controversies arising out of employment contracts, and their composition of laymen only. They work in divisions consisting of an equal number of employers and employees — ordinarily two on each side with an employer and an employee alternating in the chairmanship year by year.

The German type, re-established in the *Länder,* is now closer to the French than in the pre-Hitler era, for the chairman of a division of the first instance may be a layman. It still differs from its French analogue in many regards; for example, its jurisdiction extends to collective disputes. German labor courts work in divisions of three men: a chairman, one member from an employer panel, and one from a union panel. The panels consist of persons from various trades and occupations, and in the individual case the chairman will call men and women of the trade or occupation of the parties involved.[70]

The Scandinavian courts, jurisdictionally, are of a type dia-metrically opposite to the French. Jurisdiction is restricted to enforcement of collective contracts or of the statutory right to organize, including redress of discriminatory discharges and settle-ment of jurisdictional disputes. The Swedish labor court consists of a chairman and six other members, of whom two are taken from nominees of employers' associations, two from those of unions. The other three, two of whom, including the chairman, must be qualified for and experienced in judicial service, are chosen by the government.

F. *Labor in Nationalized Industries*

After the end of the last war, a process of nationalization of busi-ness enterprises commenced in nearly the whole of Europe. The operation of public utilities, from gas and electric power plants to railroads, telephone, telegraph, and broadcasting, by the state or its subdivisions originated before the First World War. When, after the liberation, statutes nationalizing the key industries, banks, in-surance companies, and basic branches of the food industry in Czechoslovakia were enacted in 1945, this nationalization was set in operation "with full acceptance by the Western Powers under

[70] For the era prior to 1945, see Wunderlich, German Labor Courts (1946).

the early Beneš regime." [71]   In other words, it was the pressure
engendered by economic needs rather than by political decision
which must account for the launching of a nationalization program
in the eastern part of Europe, where simultaneously the expulsion
of a substantial portion of the native population and the confisca-
tion of its property, caused by a chauvinistic surge of emotion and
retaliation, called for state control of industrial property which
had become and was properly called "masterless."

Post-war nationalization in France of coal mines, large banks
and insurance companies, the greatest automobile factory (Renault), aircraft engine company, and airline, and the power and
gas industries, might be explained partly by the immense need for
fast, though planned, recovery and reconstruction — hardly feasible under private ownership — and partly by the understandably
prevalent desire for penalization of Nazi-collaborationists.[72]

Nationalization of important areas of British industry was undertaken in response to the will of the majority of the voters, expressed
in the result of the first post-war national elections, in 1945.

Modern industrialism has taken many forms in democratic
countries, and nationalization of industries, which means their appropriation by the state or transfer to the state acting through
public corporations, with compensation for the former owners, is
only one of them.   Similarly, compulsory norms or consensual
bargaining or a combination of these may exist within the framework of a political democracy.   The degree to which one form
prevails over another may be expressed by terms such as "capital-
istic" or "socialistic."

But a "socialistic" economy does not entail a totalitarian governmental system as present-day Great Britain, France, Germany,
and Austria clearly demonstrate.   And neither nationalization nor
regulation affects substantially the form of labor relations.   All
over the world, the experience with government-run industries
"proved that their management is ordinarily exactly as interested
in the undertaking's making profits as any private business enterprise." [73]   This is true also of that type of nationalized enterprise

[71] Herman, War Damage and Nationalization in Eastern Europe, 16 Law
& Contemp. Prob. 498, 501 (1951).

[72] DeVries and Hoeniger, Post-Liberation in France, 50 Col. Law Rev. 629
(1950); Pinkney, The French Experiment in Nationalization, 1944–1950,
Modern France 354–367 (Earle ed. 1951).

[73] Wiedenfeld, Industrial Policy 180 (1927) (in German). Haemmerle,
op. cit. supra note 48, at 9 (speaking of the effect of nationalization in
Austria): "To the employee it makes no difference who is the owner of the
capital of the enterprise."

which, as in Great Britain, is in the form of a public corporation.[74] In the nationalization of the Bank of England and six commercial industries,[75] each is administered by one board, or, as in the gas industry, by area boards. The boards are appointed by the appropriate minister, e.g., in the case of the coal industry and the gas industry by the Minister of Fuel and Power, in the case of the British and South American Airways by the Minister of Civil Aviation. The boards in these public corporations follow commercial principles in the pursuit of their objectives. Accordingly, appointment to the boards has been guided by nonpolitical considerations; [76] "the complex and technological nature of the undertakings involved, the need for managerial boldness, and most of all, the desire to escape from the political interference resulting from direct responsibility of government departments, determined the choice of the instrument." [77]

Consequently, none of the British nationalization acts contains any provision which would require that delegates of the employees be members of the boards. Thus, any conflict inherent in acting at the same time as trustee for management and as trustee for labor is spared to the members of the board.[78] The boards act in labor matters like management in other industries. Each board is admonished "to enter into consultation with organizations appearing to them to represent substantial proportions of the persons in the employment of the Board . . . as to the Board's concluding with those organizations agreements providing for the establishment and maintenance of joint machinery for (a) the settlement

[74] E.g., Bank of England Act, 1946, 9 & 10 Geo. VI, c. 27, an act to bring the capital stock of the Bank of England into public ownership and bring the bank under public control. Nationalization of British Industries, 16 Law & Contemp. Prob. 555 (1951).

[75] Bank of England Act, 1946, note 74 supra; Coal Industry Nationalization Act, 1946, 9 & 10 Geo. VI, c. 59; Civil Aviation Act, 1946, 9 & 10 Geo. VI, c. 70; Cable and Wireless Act, 1946, 9 & 10 Geo. VI, c. 82; Transport Act, 1947, 10 & 11 Geo. VI, c. 49; Electricity Act, 1947, 10 & 11 Geo. VI, c. 54; Gas Act, 1948, 11 & 12 Geo. VI, c. 67. And for nationalization of steel the act has been passed: Iron and Steel Act, 1949, 12 & 13 Geo. VI, c. 72 (96 companies are affected).

[76] Friedman, The New Public Corporations and the Law, 10 Mod. L. Rev. 233, 237 (1947).

[77] Note, The Role of the Public Corporation in British Nationalized Industry, 97 U. of Pa. L. Rev. 534–535 (1949).

[78] By contrast, according to the French nationalization statutes (except those concerning Air France), the employees are represented on the boards of directors. For details see DeVries and Hoeniger, op. cit. supra note 72, at 636, 637, 639, 642, 645. The French Act of Feb. 11, 1950, on collective contracts, extends its rule to the personnel of a nationalized industry in which the employment conditions are not regulated by statute, e.g., insurance, banks, Renault. Id. at sec. IV, art. 3lo.

by negotiation of terms and conditions of employment, with provision for reference to arbitration in default of such settlement in such cases as may be determined by or under the agreements; and (b) consultation on (1) questions relating to the safety, health, or welfare of such persons; (2) the organization and conduct of the operations in which such persons are employed and other matters of mutual interest to the Board and such persons arising out of the exercise and performance by the Board of their functions." [79]

What is the effect of this legislative policy? First labor law, even in the nationalized industries, remains subject to the control of principles of contractualism. In contrast to Continental law, terms and conditions of employment are not established by legislation or administrative regulations, but are left to the free domain of collective bargaining. Workers' representation remains a matter of agreement. Second, in contrast to American law, there is no difference in organizational rights between employees of state-owned corporations and employees of private corporations.[80] In 1940, under the impact of the war, the Conditions of Employment and National Arbitration Order was enacted — since then repeatedly renewed — which under criminal sanctions forbade strikes and lockouts in a trade dispute until twenty-one days after the dispute had been reported to the Minister of Labour without the latter's having taken any steps toward a settlement.[81] If he had taken such steps — by reference to the machinery set up by a collective contract or by him — without success, he had to refer the dispute to the National Arbitration Tribunal. The award of the Tribunal was compulsory. In 1951, that Order was replaced by the Industrial Disputes Order, 1951.[82] The structure of the Order has been, on the whole, maintained. However, the 21-day cooling-off period has been abolished along with the criminal sanctions. The compulsory-arbitration procedure before what is now renamed the Industrial Disputes Tribunal, after failure of a settlement through other machinery, is embodied also in the new Order. Third, closed-shop clauses also may be agreed upon, for the provision of Section 6 of the Trade Disputes and Trade

[79] Coal Industry Nationalization Act, 1946, 9 & 10 Geo. VI, c. 59, s. 46. The other acts have analogous provisions.

[80] For a comparison see Section 2 (2) of the Taft-Hartley Act, excluding from the scope of the NLRA the United States or any wholly government-owned corporation.

[81] Conditions of Employment and National Arbitration Order, S.R. & O., 1940, N–1305, 33 Halsbury 734 (1940).

[82] S.I., 1951, No. 1376. For details see McKelvey, Compulsory Arbitration in Britain, 37 Cornell L.Q. 403 (1952).

Unions Act, 1927, which made it illegal for public authorities to enter into such clauses, fell with the repeal of that Act in 1946. Moreover, from the provision of the nationalization acts which was previously quoted, it can be seen that the boards are directed to bargain only with the one union which is most representative in the industry concerned.

In conclusion, one must admit that the differences in structure and characteristics between American and Continental labor laws are significant, but it is perhaps proper to warn against exaggerations on this score. It is true that abroad legislation rather than contracts controls the specific content of employment relations. However, it is the power of labor organizations which influences the direction of that legislation. Since the end of the war, the employment of organizational force is in France, Italy, and in all German *Länder* guarantied in the constitutions (see p. 110 and p. 742). Unionism represented in collective contracts and, more or less in control over the works councils in all the larger enterprises, also shows its power through legislation which extends collective contract terms to other than to contracting parties and their members. At the same time, the unions in America, through the National Labor Relations Board and the courts, have greatly widened the subjects on which bargaining can be compelled — subjects which reach from simple wage rates to work loads, technological changes, work standards, and pension systems. This, though contractual in form, is in substance legislation. Thus, in spite of important distinctions, there is more than one bridge between the two powerful streams of foreign and American labor law.

PART II

Establishment of Collective Bargaining

I. INTRODUCTORY NOTE

This section of the casebook deals with the government facilities for the establishment of collective bargaining relations and with the consequences of the statutory duties of employers and unions to bargain collectively. Mainly, the emphasis is upon the effects of the National Labor Relations Act, as amended by the Taft-Hartley Act, with occasional consideration of the Railway Labor Act and the state labor relations acts. Comparisons with the labor law of other countries are made at appropriate points, emphasizing differences and similarities in the approach to common problems.

The policies and procedures developed by the administrative process in the designation of the bargaining agent of the employees in an appropriate bargaining unit are explored in the material on representation proceedings, based principally upon the various reports of the National Labor Relations Board. Incidentally, light is thrown upon the factors taken into account by an administrative agency with a specialized experience, as it interprets and applies the changes in the statute constituting its frame of reference.

The consequences of the statutory duties of employers and unions to bargain collectively are set forth, primarily in terms of court decisions rendered in the course of judicial enforcement or review of Board orders in unfair labor practice cases of refusal to bargain under the NLRA, with incidental references to the enforcement of statutory duties to bargain under the National Industrial Recovery Act and under the Railway Labor Act. These indicate the basic attitudes and methods with which employers and unions approach the bargaining table, the types of unilateral action in the plant which are intolerable because of their destructive impact upon collective bargaining, and the changing scope of the subject matter of collective bargaining. The material raises the problems encountered when the government seeks to compel some employers and some unions to comply with the standards of negotiation voluntarily achieved by the more statesmanlike representatives of labor and management.

II. AGENCIES FOR BARGAINING

A. *The Evolution of the National Labor Relations Act*

The firm development of a labor policy embodying the concept that workers have a right to bargain collectively through representatives of their own choosing can be traced to World War I, when that right was recognized by the Federal Government. With the termination of hostilities and the wartime agencies, e.g., the War Labor Board, general acceptance of the principle disappeared, but it emerged as the core of governmental labor policy on a narrower front — the railroad industry.

The Transportation Act of 1920 (41 Stat. 456, 469), which returned the railroads to the companies, urged interstate carriers and their employees to settle their disputes peacefully by direct conference. The statute also established a Railroad Labor Board to settle disputes which the parties could not resolve either by direct conference or by reference to an adjustment board of their own choosing. Compliance with the statute and the decisions of the Board was entirely voluntary.

In 1926, Congress repealed the 1920 Act and passed the Railway Labor Act, which developed the policy further.[1] This statute recognized the right of both carriers and their employees to choose their collective bargaining representatives, free from the interference, influence, or coercion of the other (Sec. 2, Third), directed them to exert every reasonable effort to make and maintain agreements concerning rates of pay, rules, and working conditions and to settle all disputes by conference between their respective representatives (Sec. 2, First and Second). It then established a Board of Mediation with the duty to facilitate settlement between disputants who had failed to reach agreement, and directed the Board to discharge this duty either by using techniques of mediation or by trying to persuade the parties to accept arbitration (Secs. 4 and 5). This statutory policy was enforced by the decision in Texas and New Orleans Railroad Co. et al. v. Brotherhood of Railway & Steamship Clerks et al., 281 U.S. 548, 50 Sup. Ct. 427, 74 L. Ed. 1034 (1930), in which the court enjoined an employer from interfering through a "company" union with the freedom of his employees to select a collective bargaining agent of their own choice.

In 1934, Congress amended the Railway Labor Act. This was

---

[1] The full text of this statute, as subsequently amended, is set out in the Appendix.

because of a belief that continued interference by carriers with the right of their employees to join or organize unions of their own choice and to designate them as their bargaining representatives, and continued denial by carriers of the authority of the representatives so chosen, were major causes of labor disputes. The amendments specifically prohibited carriers from interfering "in any way" (including the "company" union device) with the right of their employees to organize and bargain collectively through representatives of their own choosing, and recognized that employees have the right to designate as their representatives persons who are not in the employ of the carrier. Further, the amendments stated that the principle of majority rule would determine which bargaining agent, if any, a particular craft or class of employees wanted (Sec. 2, Third and Fourth). They provided that the Mediation Board should investigate representation questions, determine which representative had majority support among the particular group of employees, and certify it (Sec. 2, Ninth). The amendments also directed carriers to "treat with" the certified representative as the representative of the craft or class for the purposes of collective bargaining (Sec. 2, Ninth).

In a landmark decision, the United States Supreme Court held in Virginian Railway Co. v. System Federation No. 40, 300 U.S. 515, 57 Sup. Ct. 592, 81 L. Ed. 789 (1937), that the amended Act, while it did not require agreement, did impose the affirmative and judicially enforceable duty to meet and confer, to listen, and to make reasonable efforts to compose differences and to reach agreement, as well as the negative duty not to "treat with" any other representative for the purpose of collective bargaining. In addition to directing the carrier to recognize and bargain with the petitioning union (which had been certified, after an election, by the National Mediation Board) as the representative of its mechanical department employees, the court restrained the railroad from interfering with, coercing, or influencing the employees in their free choice of a collective bargaining representative.

BROOKS, UNIONS OF THEIR OWN CHOOSING *

37–43 (1939)

The intense suffering of millions of people during the depression [of the early '30's] fixed the attention of the nation on the anomaly of poverty amid plenty. The spectacle of slow starvation in the

* Reprinted by permission of the copyright owner, Yale University Press. — ED.

face of almost unlimited productive resources could be overlooked only by the socially blind.   The belief gained wide currency that this anomaly was caused primarily by the immense and increasing inequality in the distribution of income.   This inequality resulted in the piling up of superabundant means of production in the face of inadequate mass consuming power.   It could be traced to restriction of output and the maintenance of semimonopoly prices by business combinations side by side with the holding down of the wage income of the great mass of consumers.   Wages had a constant tendency to lag behind increasing productivity because workers did not have the organized power to drive them up.   Prices did not fall in consonance with increasing productive power because organized business had the power to keep them from falling.

There were two possible ways out of this situation.   Prices could be driven down by government regulation or persuasion backed by a renewed trust-busting campaign.   Or wages could be driven up by minimum-wage and maximum-hour laws backed by increased governmental protection of the workers' right to organize. Government policy with respect to trust-busting and price regulation during the last six years has consistently reflected the confusion of public thought and the conflict of private interests on the issue.   Whether to break up business combinations and allow competition among smaller units to take care of prices, or whether to allow the persistence of large-scale semimonopolistic enterprises under government price regulation, or neither or both — this was the question.   The past history of neither policy offered much comfort to the advocates of either program.   It cannot be said that a clear-cut decision has as yet emerged.   Meanwhile the proponents of government ownership as the solution of this problem bide their time.

With respect to wage regulation and governmental protection of the workers' right to organize, the policies of the New Deal have been far more clear.   In the closing days of the Hoover administration and in the first special session of Congress under the Roosevelt administration, the Black Bill to regulate the hours of labor in interstate manufacture had an excellent chance of passing both houses of Congress.   To the idea of regulating hours the regulation of wages was necessarily added in order to protect the weekly wages of workers.   From this conception the National Industrial Recovery Act [of 1933], emerged by a process of accretion.   The regulation of hours and wages necessitated the regulation of prices if the actual consuming power of workers was to be improved.   It was then observed that any such complicated regulation of wages, hours, and prices would have to be sufficiently flexible to conform to the variety of conditions in different industries and localities. The idea of legislative regulation was therefore dropped in favor of administrative regulation through semi-self-governing code authorities. Finally, as a result of pressure from labor lobbyists and supporters, the now famous Section 7a [2] was added. Section 7a gave formal governmental sanction to labor's right to collective bargaining through representatives of its own choosing and forbade employers to use their superior economic and social power to prevent the exercise of this right by workers.

The theory back of Section 7a was clear. Government could not police industry. Employers were organized and would unquestionably use their organized power, in spite of governmental warnings to the contrary, to continue traditional practices of undue restriction of production and raising of prices. Consumers, as such, could not be adequately organized or represented to protect their own interests. Labor, acting in a dual capacity as the largest body of consumers and as the receiver of wages, must be organized to protect the consumers from extravagant price increases and provide the workers with wage increases. But labor was not organized. Less than 10 per cent of American workers had had any continued experience in unions. One of the obstacles to the growth of organized labor was the antiunion economic power of employers. If labor was to be organized, this power had to be curbed. Section 7a was designed to call into existence a new deal to redress the balance of the old.

The effects of Section 7a were psychological rather than legal and judicial. As a declaration of governmental policy, its "guarantee" of the right to collective bargaining was a powerful stimulus to trade-union membership. Unionism ceased to be associated in the minds of thousands of workers with Moscow and became associated with the personality of President Roosevelt. The explicit prohibition of interference and coercion by employers in union affairs temporarily removed the fear of employer reprisals from the minds of other thousands of workers. By the same token,

[2] Section 7 (a) (1). That employees shall have the right to organize and bargain collectively through representatives of their own choosing, and shall be free from the interference, restraint, or coercion of employers of labor, or their agents, in the designation of such representatives or in self-organization or in other concerted activities for the purpose of collective bargaining or other mutual aid or protection; (2). That no employee and no one seeking employment shall be required as a condition of employment to join any company union or to refrain from joining, organizing, or assisting a labor organization of his own choosing. — ED.

many employers accepted the spirit of this legislative declaration, altered their antiunion attitudes, and dropped their antiunion policies. The result was that hundreds of thousands of workers poured into unions, old and new, and the government's purpose promised to be achieved.

Very soon, however, the administration began to have the same experience with its efforts to equalize the economic power of workers and employers that legislatures had previously had with their efforts to equalize the legal position of the two groups. As employers' confidence and prosperity returned, those who retained their antiunion attitudes simply refused to comply with the intention of Congress. It was not difficult to abide by the letter of Section 7a, which was vaguely worded, and yet violate its intent. There was an important minority which did not trouble to concern itself with the letter. Verbal and written opposition to unions expressed inside and outside the shop, company-dominated unions, black lists, discharge of union members, and the use of professional strikebreakers, spies, and deputy sheriffs flourished on an unprecedented scale. The administration of Section 7a rapidly disintegrated in the face of this opposition. Organized labor soon felt the effects of this disintegration.

The refusal of many powerful employers to abide by the spirit of Section 7a led to a wave of strikes by unions attempting to enforce their rights by their own strength. These strikes interfered with the recovery program of the N.R.A. Consequently, President Roosevelt, in August, 1933, appointed a National Labor Board to mediate these strikes and settle them if possible. The National Labor Board was composed of three labor members, three employer members, and Senator Wagner as chairman.

The difficulties of this board were immense. Its legal status (creation by an executive order of the President) was doubtful. It had to attempt a mixture of mediatory functions in settling strikes and judicial functions in enforcing Section 7a. Back of it lay a government and a people torn between a recovery and a reform program. Frequently this conflict was reflected in the problems before the board. Most important, however, was the fact that the board had no real powers of enforcement. After exhausting efforts to secure voluntary compliance, the board had no recourse except to turn its cases over to the compliance division of the N.R.A. for removal of Blue Eagles, or to the Department of Justice for court enforcement.

Neither of these agencies was equal to its task. The compliance division of the N.R.A. was powerfully influenced by em-

ployer sentiment and was unwilling to antagonize business interests.   The Department of Justice was hamstrung, first, by the
fact that it could not accept the evidence developed by the Labor
Board.   It had to prepare its own case anew.   It had had no experience with this type of case and its sympathy with the board's
position was not impressive.   Second, there were grave doubts
about the constitutionality of the National Industrial Recovery
Act which gave the Labor Board its presumed authority.   The
administration in general and the Department of Justice in particular were unwilling to test the constitutionality of the act upon
a labor issue.   The result was that powerful employers were able
to flout the orders of the board, destroy its prestige, and pave
the way for disregard by lesser industrial figures.

Because of this situation, sentiment mounted in Congress in
favor of a federal law which would remedy these defects.   The
Wagner Labor Disputes Bill of 1934 was designed to accomplish
this purpose.   Employer opposition and an administration divided
within itself prevented the passage of this bill.   In its place a
compromise measure called Public Resolution No. 44 was adopted
in June, 1934, in the face of a wave of strikes.   In July, the President appointed a National Labor Relations Board of three impartial, expert members empowered to hold elections for workers'
choice of bargaining representatives, investigate labor disputes,
and hold hearings on charges of violations of Section 7a.

This board marked an advance over the National Labor Board
in that it was created independent of the N.R.A., although its legal
status depended upon the powers granted to the President in the
Recovery Act.   It was composed of full-time experts and could
relegate its mediatory and voluntary compliance work to semi-
official panels of citizens connected with the regional offices while
it devoted its full time to judicial work on cases of primary importance.   But it still lacked power to compel compliance.   In
the crucial Houde Engineering Company case,[3] for example, the
employer successfully defied the board.

---

[3] Decisions of the National Labor Relations Board, July 9, 1934 — December
1934, p. 35.   Opinion by Garrison, Chairman, and Millis and Smith, Members.   The company manufactured automobile parts and appliances.   An
AFL union had been certified as the bargaining agent of the employees after
an election.   The company met separately on alternate Saturdays with representatives of the certified union and with representatives of a company union
to which a minority of the employees belonged.   These meetings dealt mainly
with grievances.   The company acted unilaterally on all matters presented
and refused to negotiate an agreement with either union.   Labor relations
were characterized by confusion, friction, and suspicion.   The Board ordered
the company to bargain in good faith with the certified union chosen by the

In spite of this difficulty, the first N.L.R.B. was of considerable importance in protecting workers' rights to bargain collectively. It secured a notable amount of voluntary compliance with the intent of Section 7a. It began the process of building up a body of informed and experienced personnel. And it moved a long way toward clarifying and defining the issues involved in governmental protection of collective bargaining. Without this experience the National Labor Relations Act would not have taken its present definite form, nor could the new board have achieved the remarkable record which will be discussed in later pages.

Nevertheless, from the point of view of protecting unions from the economic attack of a crucially important minority of belligerently antiunion employers, Public Resolution No. 44 must be put down as a failure. The invalidation of the National Industrial Recovery Act, from which the board received its basic authority, put the final quietus on the board's efforts to accomplish its *raison d'être*.

One result of the Supreme Court's decision against the N.R.A. in May, 1935,[4] was the immediate renewal of pressure from organized labor and its friends for the passage of the Wagner Labor Disputes Bill. This bill had already had extended hearings in February, March, and April. The Supreme Court decision precipitated its passage. On June 27, the bill was approved by both houses and on July 5, [1935] was signed by President Roosevelt.

There are several aspects of the National Labor Relations Act which should be made clear. First, it was not an innovation. There lay back of it an extended experience with governmental attempts to protect the rights of workers to organize. This experience had been gained in the railroad industry under the National Mediation Board as well as under the National Labor Board, the first National Labor Relations Board, and the numerous satellite boards created during the N.R.A. period. The issues attending the passage of the N.L.R.A. were perfectly clear to interested parties. They were thoroughly aired during the debates on Section 7a and Public Resolution No. 44.

---

majority of the employees, as the exclusive representative of all of the employees. This idea of majority rule was based upon an interpretation of Section 7a in the light of the policies of the National War Labor Board in 1918, the Transportation Act of 1920, various "employee representation plans," the President's Executive Order of February 1, 1934, creating the National Labor Board, and Public Resolution No. 44, of June 19, 1934. — ED.

[4] Schechter Poultry Corporation v. United States, 295 U.S. 495, 55 Sup. Ct. 837, 79 L. Ed. 1570 (1935). See Notes, 49 Harv. L. Rev. 332 (1935), 11 Wis. L. Rev. 88 (1935). — ED.

Second, the N.L.R.A. is concerned only with making collective bargaining possible in the face of the antiunion economic power of employers . . .

B. *The National Labor Relations Act* [5]

The National Labor Relations Act of 1935 carried forward the substance of the ill-fated Section 7a and Public Resolution No. 44. It guaranteed to employees in industries other than transportation the right to form, join, or assist labor organizations, to bargain collectively through representatives of their own choosing, and to engage in concerted activities for mutual aid or protection. It implemented these guarantees by imposing on employers the administratively and judicially enforceable duty not to commit unfair labor practices by restraining or coercing employees in the exercise of these rights, by promoting or supporting company unions, or by discriminating against employees in order to encourage or discourage union membership.   To put it simply, the statute established the policy that employees are free to form unions, to designate them as their bargaining representatives, and to strike to attain their objectives, and directed employers to remain neutral. (Secs. 7, 8 (a) (1), (2), and (3).)

Further, the NLRA made it an unfair labor practice for employers to refuse to bargain collectively with the designated representatives of their employees.   (Sec. 8 (a) (5).)

In explaining the meaning of this obligation in NLRB v. Jones & Laughlin Steel Corp., 301 U.S. 1, 45, 57 Sup. Ct. 615, 628, 81 L. Ed. 893, 916 (1937), which upheld the constitutionality of the NLRA as applied to manufacturing, the Court commented: "The Act does not compel agreements between employers and employees.   It does not compel any agreement whatever.   It does not prevent the employer 'from refusing to make a collective contract and hiring individuals on whatever terms' the employer 'may by unilateral action determine . . . The theory of the Act is that free opportunity for negotiation with accredited representatives of employees is likely to promote industrial peace and may bring about the adjustments and agreements which the Act in itself does not attempt to compel.' "

---

[5] The original statute, generally known as the Wagner Act, was substantially amended in 1947 by Title I of the Labor Management Relations Act (the Taft-Hartley Law.)   The statute was again amended in 1951.   The full text of the amended statute is set out in the Appendix.   The material is set up in such a way as to indicate which portions of the Act are the result of the Taft-Hartley amendments and which are the result of the 1951 amendments.

As administered, the NLRA did, however, compel employers to sit down with the representatives of their employees and make a good-faith effort to reach an agreement governing the terms and conditions of employment, and it imposed on them the negative duty to treat with no bargaining representative other than the one selected by their employees.

The NLRA established the National Labor Relations Board to administer the statute. The Board was composed of three persons appointed by the President and was authorized to determine appropriate bargaining units and to ascertain, by election and otherwise,[6] the wishes of the employees as to their bargaining agent. (Sec. 9.) Further, the Board was empowered to determine whether or not a particular employer had engaged in an unfair labor practice and to prevent such misconduct by cease and desist and restitutionary orders.[6a] The orders were enforceable by, and subject to the review of, the United States Circuit Courts of Appeals. (Secs. 10 (e) and (f).) The NLRB was centered in Washington, D.C., but it established regional offices throughout the country.

At the time that the NLRA was passed, organized labor consisted almost entirely of unions affiliated with the American Federation of Labor. Many AFL unions traditionally gained status as the bargaining agent in particular plants by putting sufficient economic pressure on the employer to force him into agreement. The wishes of the employees involved were often ignored or at least not regarded as decisive. The emphasis of the NLRA on employee preference and free choice in the selection or rejection of bargaining representatives disturbed this organizational technique. But the requirement of employer neutrality and the absence of any restrictions on unions in influencing employees made the statute appear to be a net gain to the AFL unions.

However, the Congress of Industrial Organizations was formed in 1936 and struggles began to arise between AFL and CIO affiliates over the organization of workers. The NLRA, which concerned itself with employer-employee disputes over organization, was not designed to handle inter-union conflicts. Employers, hemmed off by the policy of neutrality, frequently found themselves in the middle of bitter jurisdictional quarrels. They were hamstrung by the statute from resolving the dispute by throwing

---

[6] See text on page 168 and note 39 infra, for a comment on devices other than elections used to resolve representation questions.

[6a] See pages 566–572 infra for a discussion of the procedures followed in disposing of unfair labor practice cases.

their weight on the side of one of the disputants, and they were frequently subjected to severe economic pressures by one or both of the unions who were seeking collective bargaining status.

This development, and the failure of the statute to meet it, created considerable dissatisfaction on the part of some employers and some AFL unions with the terms and the administration of the NLRA.[7]

After World War II there was a sharp swerve to the right on socio-economic matters generally, and a change in the attitude of a substantial part of the public toward organized labor. With a membership of 15 millions in 1947, as compared with three millions in 1933, unions were thought by many to have attained a degree of power that menaced collective bargaining, individuals, minority groups, and the political status quo. It was believed in some quarters that the War Labor Board, the Labor Relations Board, the Wage and Hour Division of the Department of Labor, and the Conciliation Service, through a strong pro-labor bias, had accelerated these developments. The dynamic unionization of millions of unskilled workers in the mass production industries was especially disturbing. The arrogant abuses of power by some labor leaders had lessened public confidence in union responsibility. Communism was feared to have gained control of a number of unions and to be threatening others. Sentiment was growing for government control of unions to protect the public interest. And a fraction of management had initiated antiunion campaigns.

As a result of these and other factors the Labor Management Relations Act (the Taft-Hartley Law) was passed in 1947. Only Title I of the statute, the part that amended the National Labor Relations Act, is relevant here.[8]

The preamble of the original NLRA was modified to limit the blame for labor disputes obstructing and burdening commerce to *some* employers and to extend the blame to the conduct of *some* unions. (Sec. 1.) The employer unfair labor practices were retained, with some modification due to the regulation of union security agreements, but were made less restrictive by giving employers a greater privilege to speak freely in labor controversies than had been permitted by the original statute. (Secs. 8 (a), (c).) The freedom of unions to exercise economic pressures on em-

---

[7] The point is well developed in Gregory, Labor and the Law 223–228 (2d ed. 1949).

[8] The other titles of the LMRA are treated elsewhere in these materials.

ployers and employees was restricted for the first time, by forbidding certain union unfair labor practices. (Sec. 8 (b) .)

Under the original NLRA, employees had the privilege of rejecting unionization and choosing to remain unorganized. This privilege was expressly spelled out by the amendments as a right and protected against union restraint and coercion except when a certain type of union-shop agreement was in existence. (Secs. 7, 8 (b) (1) .)

Under the original statute employers were privileged to enter into closed-shop, union-shop, maintenance-of-membership, and other types of union security contracts, even though such agreements required employees to be union members and encouraged membership in one union and discouraged membership in others.[9] The amendments limited this privilege to certain types of union-shop and maintenance-of-membership agreements, and unions were prohibited from attempting to cause illegal employer discrimination. (Secs. 8 (a) (3) , 8 (b) (2) .) Probably the most important single effect of these changes was to outlaw the closed-shop agreements which had become common in many of the industries that were characterized by collective bargaining. The obligation to bargain collectively, which had been imposed by the original statute only on employers, was extended to unions. (Sec. 8 (b) (3) .) In both cases, a refusal to bargain was made an unfair labor practice.

In addition, unions were prohibited from engaging in certain types of secondary strikes, from engaging in strikes to force an employer to recognize any union other than the one certified by the Board as the bargaining agent in his plant, and from striking to force an employer to assign jurisdiction over particular work tasks to one union rather than to another. Secs. 8 (b) (4) (A) , (B) , (C) , and (D) .) Moreover, the Board was empowered and directed to resolve such jurisdictional disputes. (Sec. 10 (k) .)

An effort was made to regulate the admission policies of unions by prohibiting, under certain circumstances, the imposition of excessive or discriminatory fees. (Sec. 8 (b) (5) .) Featherbedding practices were restricted to some extent by prohibiting unions from extorting payments from employers for work not performed. (Sec. 8 (b) (6) .)

Administratively, the statute was amended so that the NLRB's functions became almost entirely judicial. The Board was in-

[9] The union had to be one not established, maintained, or assisted by the employer in violation of Section 8 (2) and it had to have support of a majority of the employees in an appropriate unit.

creased from three members to five, and its administrative and prosecuting functions were authoritatively vested in a General Counsel.   (Secs. 3 and 4.)

A careful reading of Title I of the Act, to be found in the Appendix, will bring out more clearly the nature of all these changes.

C. *The Reach of the National Labor Relations Act*

1. JURISDICTIONAL POWER

The authority of the NLRB over labor relations is, of course, coextensive with the power granted by the statute.   This power extends to all industries affecting interstate or foreign commerce. It does not "embrace effects upon interstate commerce so indirect and remote that to embrace them, in view of our complex society, would effectually obliterate the distinction between what is national and what is local and create a completely centralized government."   NLRB v. Jones & Laughlin Steel Corporation, 301 U.S. 1, 37, 57 Sup. Ct. 615, 624, 81 L. Ed. 893, 911–912 (1937).   But it does reach activities which, although they may be intrastate when separately considered, "have such a close and substantial relation to interstate commerce that their control is essential or appropriate to protect that commerce from burdens and obstructions . . ." Ibid.

NOTES

1. What about the power of a state to regulate labor relations in industries affecting commerce?   Does a state labor relations board have jurisdiction over a question of representation raised by a group of employees in a plant when the NLRB has taken jurisdiction over similar questions raised by a different group of employees in the same plant?   See Bethlehem Steel Co. et al. v. New York State Labor Relations Board, 330 U.S. 767, 67 Sup. Ct. 1026, 91 L. Ed. 1234 (1947).   See also Note, 15 U. of Chi. L. Rev. 362 (1948).   Compare with Pittsburgh Railways Company Substation Operators and Maintenance Employees' Case, 357 Pa. 379, 54 A.2d 891, 174 A.L.R. 1045, Anno. 1051 (1947).

2. Does a state labor relations board have jurisdiction over a question of representation raised in a plant which affects interstate commerce and is part of an industry over which the NLRB customarily exercises jurisdiction, when the NLRB has never taken jurisdiction over any aspects of labor relations in the particular

plant?   See La Crosse Telephone Corporation v. Wisconsin Employment Relations Board, 336 U.S. 18, 69 Sup. Ct. 379, 93 L. Ed. 463 (1949).

3. See Salney, Jurisdictional Conflicts Under National and State Labor Relations Acts, 10 U. of Pittsburgh L. Rev. 327 (1949).   See also, Cox and Seidman, Federalism and Labor Relations, 64 Harv. L. Rev. 211, 212–218 (1950).

4. Other aspects of the problem of state versus federal regulation of labor relations — viz., employer labor practices and concerted labor activities — are taken up at pages 835–850 infra.

2. JURISDICTIONAL POLICY

The NLRB does not, despite its power, take jurisdiction over all industries that affect interstate commerce.

In Waitresses and Cafeteria Womens Local No. 305, etc. (Haleston Drug Stores, Inc.), 86 N.L.R.B. 1166, 25 L.R.R.M. 1040 (1949), after the General Counsel, through the Regional Director, had taken jurisdiction of an unfair labor practice issue in Portland, Oregon, and had issued a complaint, a trial examiner for the Board proceeded to dismiss the complaint "on the ground that the assertion of jurisdiction would not effectuate the policies of the Act."   The Board affirmed this action in spite of the vigorous contention of the General Counsel that when he had taken jurisdiction the Board was without power to dismiss the proceedings on purely jurisdictional grounds.   The Board replied that once the complaint had issued, the General Counsel's authority was exhausted, that the Board might then dismiss it "because it believes the legal theory urged in support of the case inapplicable or that the factual allegations of the complaint are unproved, or that the policy of the Act will not be effectuated by entertaining jurisdiction."   This decision was upheld in Haleston Drug Stores, Inc. v. NLRB, 187 F.2d 418 (9th Cir. 1951), cert. denied, 342 U.S. 815 (1951).[10]

The NLRB's practice of "self-abnegation" has created considerable confusion among employers and unions who, although within the Board's statutory power, cannot predict with confidence whether they are within or without the Board's jurisdictional policy.   In order to dispel some of this confusion, the Board, in NLRB Release No. 342 (Oct. 6, 1950), spelled out jurisdictional

[10] On this conflict as to assertion of jurisdiction, see Note, The Taft-Hartley Act, 64 Harv. L. Rev. 781, 781–85 (1951).

"yardsticks" evolved in eight unanimous decisions issued simultaneously. According to the release jurisdiction will be taken over:

1. Instrumentalities and channels of interstate and foreign commerce (examples: banks, radio stations, and taxicab companies serving interstate bus and railway terminals).

2. Public utility and transit systems.

3. Establishments which operate as integral parts of a multi-state enterprise (for example, chain stores, or franchised dealers in new automobiles and trucks).

4. Enterprises which produce or handle goods destined for out-of-state shipment, or performing services outside a state, if the goods or services are valued at $25,000 a year.

5. Enterprises which furnish services or materials necessary to the operation of enterprises falling into categories 1, 2 and 4 above, provided such goods or services are valued at $50,000 a year.

6. Any other enterprise which has:
   (a) a direct inflow of material valued at $500,000 a year; or
   (b) an indirect inflow of material valued at $1,000,000 a year; or
   (c) a combination inflow or outflow of goods which add up to at least a total of "100%" of the amounts required in items 4, 5, 6 (a) and (b) above.

[*Example:* The employer annually buys $65,978.04 worth of goods directly out of state. This is 15 per cent of $500,000.

The employer annually sells $22,596.99 worth of goods directly out of state. This is 90 per cent of $25,000. Fifteen per cent plus 90 per cent equals 105 per cent. Jurisdiction will be taken. Rutledge Paper Products, Inc., 91 N.L.R.B. 625, 26 L.R.R.M. 1544 (1950).]

7. Establishments substantially affecting national defense.

NOTES

1. Does the NLRB uniformly adhere to these jurisdictional rules?

In Hotel Association of St. Louis, 92 N.L.R.B. 1388, 27 L.R.R.M. 1243 (1951), the Board refused to take jurisdiction over an association of hotels in a representation case despite the fact that the members of the association annually received $2,400,000 from out-of-state guests, annually bought over $800,000 in supplies shipped from points outside the state, and that several of the members were units of large multistate hotel chains. Compare with Westport Moving and Storage Company, 91 N.L.R.B. 902, 26 L.R.R.M. 1581 (1950), in which the Board took jurisdiction over an individual proprietorship in Kansas City, Missouri, which had two employees engaged in moving and storage operations and ten employees engaged in making packing boxes for Fifth Army Headquarters to use in shipping the personal effects of military personnel. The employer's gross annual receipts during 1949 amounted to about $21,000.

2. Prior to 1947 the NLRB was reluctant to exercise jurisdiction over the building and construction trades, in part because of the short-term and often sporadic employer-employee relationship which characterizes the industry. See Covington, Jurisdiction of the National Labor Relations Board over the Building and Construction Industry, 28 N.C.L. Rev. 1 (1949).

"Since the enactment of the amended Act in 1947, however, the Board has treated this industry the same as any other industry, asserting jurisdiction when the facts in the case pointed to a substantial effect on commerce, and declining to assert jurisdiction . . . otherwise." Plumbing Contractors Association of Baltimore, 93 N.L.R.B. 1081, 27 L.R.R.M. 1514 (1951).

3. For a general discussion of Board policy see NLRB, 16th Ann. Rep. 15–39 (1951).

3. EXCLUDED GROUPS

The jurisdiction of the NLRB not only excludes industries and other economic activities which are intrastate or purely local in character. It also excludes certain types and classes of wage and salary earners and their employers.

Supervisors are not within the term "employee" as used in the NLRA.[11]

Similarly, independent contractors are outside the coverage of the Act.[12] In Matter of Kansas City Star, 76 N.L.R.B 384, 21 L.R.R.M. 1185 (1948), the Board found home delivery newspaper

---

[11] Section 2 (3). This exclusion of foremen from the rights and responsibilities of the statute is discussed more extensively at pages 153–155 infra.

[12] Section 2 (3). See Matter of Morris Steinberg et al., 78 N.L.R.B. 211, 22 L.R.R.M. 1201 (1948).

carriers to be independent contractors, and said, at page 388: "The amended Act, as already noted, specifically excludes 'independent contractors' from the category of 'employees.' The legislative history, in this connection, shows that Congress intended that the Board recognize as 'employees' those who 'work for wages or salaries under direct supervision,' and as 'independent contractors,' those who 'undertake to do a job for a price, decide how the work will be done, usually hire others to do the work and depend for their income not upon wages, but upon the difference between what they pay for goods, materials, and labor and what they receive for the end result, that is, upon profit.' 80th Congress, 1st Session, House of Representatives Report No. 245, April 11, 1947, page 18."

Relying upon these and other conventional criteria of the law of agency, such as degree of control, the Board has found the individuals concerned to be independent contractors: operator of rural telephone exchange, Matter of Southwestern Associated Telephone Co., 76 N.L.R.B. 1105, 21 L.R.R.M. 1298 (1948) ; net fishermen, Alaska Salmon Industry, Inc., 81 N.L.R.B. 1335, 23 L.R.R.M. 1497 (1949). But in other cases the Board has found the individuals concerned to be employees: insurance salesmen, Phoenix Mutual Life Ins. Co., 73 N.L.R.B. 1463, 20 L.R.R.M. 1116 (1947), enforced, 167 F.2d 983 (7th Cir. 1948), cert. denied, 335 U.S. 845 (1948); muskrat trappers, Morris Steinberg, 78 N.L.R.B. 211, 22 L.R.R.M. 1201 (1948); an accountant, Sam Marcos Telephone Co., 81 N.L.R.B. 314, 23 L.R.R.M. 1341 (1949); and station agents and commissioned drivers, Standard Oil Co., 81 N.L.R.B. 1381, 23 L.R.R.M. 1536 (1949). See also 16th Ann. Rep. 113–115 (1951).

The statute does not cover as "employers" corporations or associations operating a hospital, if no part of the net earnings inures to the benefit of any private shareholder or individual. (Sec. 2(2).)

It does not apply either to employers or employees in the railroad and air transport industries. (Secs. 2 (2) and (3).) These exclusions are explained by the fact that government facilities for settling representation questions and labor disputes in those industries are made available through the Railroad Labor Act. See Note, The Air Carrier's Duty to Bargain Under the Railway Labor Act — The National Airlines Strike, 16 Air L. 113 (1949); McNatt, Labor Relations in the Air Transport Industry Under the Amended Railway Labor Act, 45 U. of Ill. Bull. 64 (1948).

Section 2 (2) of the NLRA excludes from the term "employer" . . . "the United States or any wholly owned Government corporation, or any Federal Reserve Bank, or any State or political subdivision thereof. . . ." As to the first phrase see Schnell, Federally Owned Corporations and Their Legal Problems, 14 N.C.L. Rev. 238, 337 (1936). Perhaps the second phrase is limited to the twelve Federal Reserve Banks, in the light of Bank of America National Trust & Savings Assn. California, 14 N.L.R.B. 207, 4 L.R.R.M. 423 (1939) (national bank discriminatorily discharged ten messengers; Board order to cease and desist and to offer reinstatement; though the national bank was a member of Federal Reserve System, it was held not to be "the United States" under Section 2 (2) of the Wagner Act), enforced, 130 F.2d 624 (9th Cir. 1942), cert. denied, 318 U.S. 792 (1943).

Government contractors have been held to be employers subject to the NLRA in the following cases: carrier of mail by truck, William H. Carroll, 29 N.L.R.B. 343, 7 L.R.R.M. 219 (1941), enforced, 120 F.2d 457 (1st Cir. 1941); lessee of cannery, Alaska Salmon Industry, Inc., 33 N.L.R.B. 727, 8 L.R.R.M. 294 (1941); operator of atomic energy plant at Oak Ridge, Monsanto Chemical Co., 76 N.L.R.B. 767, 21 L.R.R.M. 1239 (1948). On the other hand, a harbor improvement district created under a state statute has been held to be a political subdivision of the state and excluded as an employer from the Board's jurisdiction. Oxnard Harbor District, 34 N.L.R.B. 1285, 9 L.R.R.M. 73 (1941).

In addition to the above, the statute excludes agricultural laborers, domestic servants, and individuals employed by parent or spouse. (Sec. 2 (3).) In respect to agricultural labor, see NLRB 15th Ann. Rep. 55 (1950), and Report of the President's Commission on Migratory Labor 105–118 (1951).

D. *Other Jurisdictions*

1. STATE CONSTITUTIONS

New York, Article 1, Section 17: "Employees shall have the right to organize and to bargain collectively through representatives of their own choosing."

Missouri, Article 1, Section 29: Provision identical to the above.

New Jersey, Article 1, Section 19: "Persons in private employment shall have the right to organize and bargain collectively. Persons in public employment shall have the right to organize, present to and make known to the State or any of its political subdivisions or agencies, their grievances and proposal through representatives of their own choosing."

2. STATE LEGISLATION

A number of states such as New York, Massachusetts, Utah, Wisconsin, and others have enacted labor legislation somewhat similar to the NLRA.   See Note, The State Labor Relations Acts, 51 Harv. L. Rev. 722 (1938) ; Smith and De Lancey, The State Legislatures and Unionism, 38 Mich. L. Rev. 987 (1940) ; Killingsworth, State Labor Relations Acts (Univ. of Chicago Press, 1948).

Many jurisdictions have no extensive statutory scheme for resolving labor-management problems.   How are these problems handled in such jurisdictions, e.g., Illinois, Ohio, and Washington?

By com l princas

3. CANADIAN LEGISLATION

The Canadian Industrial Relations and Disputes Investigation Act, 1948, Statutes of Canada, 1948, 11 & 12 Geo. VI, c. 54, secs. 1–74, imposes the duty to bargain on the union as well as the employer (secs. 12–15).   Although a refusal to bargain is not listed among the unfair labor practices (sec. 4), after such a refusal and the unsuccessful intervention of a conciliation officer (sec. 16), and an ad hoc conciliation board (secs. 17 and 28), the Canada Labour Relations Board may, after notice and hearing, issue an appropriate order (sec. 43).   Compliance therewith is made a statutory obligation; noncompliance is punishable by fine (sec. 40).   Only indirectly does the Act furnish a statutory basis for determining the scope of collective bargaining; pending negotiations, except by consent, changes are forbidden in "rates of wages, or . . . any other term or condition of employment" (secs. 14 and 15).   See 23 L.R.R. 103 (1948).

For the prior law, see Laskin, Labour Law; 1923–1947, 26 Can. B. Rev. 286, at nn. 4, 5, 299–307 (1948).

4. RIGHT OF GOVERNMENT EMPLOYEES TO ORGANIZE AND TO BARGAIN IN EUROPE

At the present time, nearly all European countries — except the Russian satellites — have lifted the ban which was laid upon organizations of civil servants when they began to be formed in European countries in the later eighteen eighties.   The first groups to organize were postal employees, workers in governmental industries, and teachers.   With a few exceptions,[13] no legal obstacle

[13] The Swiss federal law on civil servants of 1927 contains a prohibition against membership of civil servants in those labor organizations which do not forbid the use of strikes.   Norway allows civil servants to be organized in organizations of their own only.

prevents civil servants of any category from joining any labor organizations. The British statute of 1927 prohibiting civil servants from belonging to any organization whose membership was not confined to civil servants was repealed in 1946.

In the same year, the legislature of France expressly repealed the settled rule which had proclaimed the illegality of unions of career employees (*fonctionnaires*).[14] Now, those French unions of civil servants, which are the "most representative," have the right to designate delegates to the appropriate minister's service committees [15] entrusted with the power to work out rules for the organization of the service.[16]

The capacity to enter into collective bargaining contracts is also expressly guaranteed in Germany, Austria, Norway, and Sweden to organizations of civil servants and to labor unions acting for groups of civil servants. For those groups for which the terms of service such as rules of promotion, transfer, discharge, and, above all, salaries are fixed by law, the scope for bargaining is not very broad. Moreover, in all these countries, the schism between public law and private law is marked in their legal systems. As far as a civil service position rests upon an administrative law basis, it lies beyond the range of any collective contract. The latter can reach only "employments," a term indicating a contractual basis, i.e., a concept of private law.

On the other hand, in the works council acts which have most recently been enacted in many West German *Länder*,[17] e.g., Hesse, and in Austria, all civil servants, including career employees (*Beamte*), are given the right to representation by works councils both in governmental departments and in administrative agencies.[18] A Belgian act on civil servants provides — similarly to the French legislation mentioned above — for "committees of the personnel" consisting of an equal number of delegates, on the one hand, of the competent ministries and, on the other, of the competent unions of the civil servants; it is the office of the committees to discuss the demands made by the latter and their views in mat-

[14] France: Act of Oct. 19, 1946, art. 6. Cf. Preamble to the Constitution, 1946, (cl. 5), assuring everybody the right to join a union.

[15] They are called *comités techniques*.

[16] Waline, Traité élémentaire de droit administratif 344–345 (5th ed. 1950). Professor Waline regards this favoritism towards the politically most powerful unions as a symptom of the "politicization" of public functions.

[17] Any idea of reviving works councils behind the "iron curtain" was suppressed by the Soviet-controlled authorities.

[18] Hesse: Constitution, 1946, art. 37, and Act of May 26, 1948, secs. 2(1), 4(1). Austria: Act of March 28, 1947, sec. 1(3). In Austria, the representatives in the public service are not called works councils.

ters of the service and the improvement of the conditions of work.[19]

However, the law of all countries considers a *strike* in public services as an illicit act. In Italy a participation therein is even a crime.[20] This is all the more remarkable because in Italy and in France "the right to strike" is safeguarded by their new constitutions. Those constitutions contain, however, a clause which restricts the right to strike "to the limits to be set by legislation." [21] Until such legislation is enacted, the law as it has been remains in effect.[22] The only legislation of that kind which, at this writing, has been enacted in France, prohibits — for the personnel of the police — the resort to a concerted discontinuance of services, placing serious sanctions on the violation of the prohibition.[23] Also, the recent legal literature,[24] along with decisions of the highest administrative court,[25] condemns strongly a strike of civil servants. The tenor of those opinions rests upon the notion that to be in governmental service means to be under a duty to act for the public.[26] Consequently, a strike of governmental employees is, in the first place, a self-contradiction, and, in the second place, an impediment to the exercise of governmental functions, inflicting a serious blow on the public order. According to those opinions, the idea of government calls for the subordination of an individual's right (to participate in a strike) to public interest in the continuity of governmental functions.[27]

[19] *Arrêté royal* of Dec. 14, 1937, as amended by the *arrêté* of Oct. 12, 1949.

[20] Italy: Penal Code (R.D. of Oct. 19, 1930, n. 398), art. 328. The bill which was introduced by the Italian government in December, 1951, grants — in Article 34 — manual workers in public service the right to strike for proper purposes upon compliance with very strict requirements.

[21] Preamble to French Constitution, 1946, cl. 7. Italian Constitution, 1947, art. 40.

[22] Waline, op. cit. supra note 16, at 344.

[23] Act of Sept. 28, 1948.

[24] Elia, The Strike of Civil Servants, 3 Rivista di diritto del lavoro 89 (1951) (in Italian) ; Waline, op. cit. supra note 16, at 345; Orianne, Recognition, Sanctions and Limitations on the Right to Strike in the Law of Belgium, 27 Revue de droit international et de droit comparé 132, 138 (1950) (in French).

[25] Decisions of the Council of State: Anon. (1950), 13 Droit social 317 (1950) (suspension of clerks of provincial government, who had participated in a strike, sustained) ; Matter of Tarrigion (1947), D. 1947. 3. 37; Matter of Minaire (1937), D. 1938. 3. 49.

[26] Elia, op. cit. supra note 24, at 96: "As the 'duty to act' (*dovere d'agire*) denies a public entity the power to effect a voluntary dissolution, so it prohibits a civil servant from participating in a strike." (Author's translation.)

[27] Waline, op. cit. supra note 16, at 345 (discussion on the several theories which, however, agree on the condemnation of strikes of *fonctionnaires*).

5. AUSTRALASIAN LEGISLATION

Commonwealth Conciliation and Arbitration Act, 1904–1947, sec. 2: "The chief objects of this act are — (a) To establish an expeditious system for preventing and settling industrial disputes by the methods of conciliation and arbitration." [28]

The Act further provides (sec. 70) that any employer or association of employers who employ an average of at least one hundred persons per month for a six-month period or any association of at least "one hundred employees in or in connection with any industry" or "engaged in any industrial pursuit or pursuits whatever" is eligible to be registered. When any of these groups is registered it thereby attains the status of an "organization" with the right of perpetual succession and is empowered to own and deal in property rights (sec. 75) and to appear as a party before governmental tribunals. (See page 149 infra, for a comment on the significance of "registration.")

Once these systems had been established, the obstacles to union recognition, to preliminary negotiation, and to effective presentation of plaints before the tribunals, for the most part, became simply elements in the "disputes" with which the tribunals dealt. The tribunals could then deal with such obstacles by terms in the relevant award settling the disputes. For example, they might provide for the following: permission to union officials to enter industrial premises and address employees, Murdoch Manufactories Ltd. v. Gibb, Arbitration Rep. (N.S.W. 82) (1925); permission to union members to wear union badges when at work, Australian Tramway Employees Association v. Prahran etc. Trust, 17 Commonwealth Law Rep. 680 (1913); preference in employment to members of unions, AWU v. Pastoralists' Fed. Council, 1 Commonwealth Arbitration Rep. 62 (1907). Some obstacles to unionization are dealt with in the Acts, e.g., Commonwealth Conciliation and Arbitration Act 1904–1947, sec. 5, which makes it an offence for an employer to dismiss or adversely affect an

[28] When using Australian statutory material, it is necessary first to make oneself familiar with the method of consolidation or reprinting and amendment used by the relevant legislature. Notice in particular that the Commonwealth Conciliation and Arbitration Act 1947 not only amended many sections of the preceding Acts, but also (in the Second Schedule) renumbered them. Hence it is advisable to obtain the Government Printer's reprint (which does not appear in the annual bound volumes but is sold separately) or the reprint in McWilliam and Boyt, Commonwealth Industrial Arbitration Law — Supplement (Law Book Co. of Australia, 1948). Except where otherwise indicated, the Australian notes cover the situation as it existed until June, 1952.

employee because he is a union officer or member or has appeared in arbitration proceedings. This section correspondingly makes it an offence for employees to cease work because an employer is an officer, witness, etc. of or for an employers' organization.

New Zealand has followed the policy of encouraging unionization to its logical conclusion, by establishing compulsory unionization. Industrial Conciliation and Arbitration Amendment Act, 1936, sec. 18 (1) : . . . "It shall not be lawful for any employer bound [by an award] to employ or to continue to employ in the industry to which the award relates any adult person who is not for the time being a member of an industrial union of workers bound by that award" . . . .

E. *Representation Proceedings* [29]

The following problem is the first of six in this Part of the book that concern the same manufacturing company. While this enterprise, and the people and their experiences, are all fictitious, every fact that is portrayed in these episodes is of the type that has actually happened in some industry somewhere in the country. In fact, several of the incidents are built upon the actual experiences of one of the editors.

Read these episodes carefully and try to figure out what you as a lawyer would consider worth noting, worth calling to the attention of your client, worth warning him about or commending him for. The questions and notes will give you leads, will refer you to citations or to pages of this book where you can learn to detect more clearly the issues involved, and the way the NLRB and the courts have dealt with them.

You will notice that each problem is followed by several pages of case material. It is possible for the instructor to use this for recitation purposes in the conventional classroom approach, referring back to the Enderby problem as each case bears on points contained in it. It is also possible, however, to use what has come to be called the "problem method" as distinguished from the case method of classroom discussion and to devote the class

[29] At this point we are interested in the NLRA only as a mechanism for the establishment and maintenance of collective bargaining relationships. Accordingly, the ensuing materials in this Part concern themselves largely with two matters: (1) the implementation of the policy of freedom of choice through the principle of majority rule and the election device; (2) the process of getting the parties together through legal compulsion — viz., the duty to bargain.

The development and meaning of other unfair labor practices and aspects of the NLRA are discussed in Parts III, IV, and V of this volume.

hour to an analysis of the facts in each problem and to the identification of legal issues by discovering their presence, and their disposition in the notes, references, and opinions which follow.

You will now read the first portion of The Enderby Case — I.

1. PROBLEMS

THE ENDERBY CASE — I

A

The Enderby Rubber Company operates an automobile tire and miscellaneous rubber products plant on the outskirts of Chicago. This Company employs approximately 1000 men and women, the work force being divided roughly as follows:

Production employees — Tire Division	500
Production employees — Miscellaneous Division	350
Foremen	50
Clerical	75
Executive	25

There has been, prior to the time at which this account starts (latter part of 1947), no union organization of the Enderby employees.

Five employees form a committee and send a letter to Mr. Leslie White, the Industrial Relations Manager of the Enderby Company, advising him that a majority of the production workers in the plant have become members of the United Rubber, Cork, Linoleum and Plastic Workers of America, CIO, and that this Union has established Local No. 417 for the employees of this plant. The letter asks that the Company recognize Local No. 417 and start immediately on the negotiation of a collective bargaining agreement.   In response to White's request, the committee, accompanied by George Layton, a representative of the International Office of the URCL & PWA, go to White's office for a conference.

White asks the committee how many members they have.   The only answer is that "we've got over half the men lined up."   White asks for a list of the Union members.   This is refused, and Layton tells White that he considers the request highly improper.   White calls attention to the fact that all except one of the committee are from the Tire Division, and asks whether this indicates that most of the union membership is in that division.   The answer is that there are "some from both divisions, — over 100 from the Miscellaneous Division." After further discussion, White tells the committee he will "talk the matter over with some of our people," and suggests a meeting for the following Monday.

At the Monday meeting, White tells the committee that the Company "has decided not to recognize Local 417 as the bargaining representative for the employees of the plant unless and until the NLRB conducts an election and certifies the United Rubber Workers as the bargaining agent." Oliver Curme, one of the employees, who has been elected President of Local 417, reverses the position taken by Layton at the previous meeting and offers to submit membership cards to White for a cross-check against the Company's employment records. White refuses this offer, stating that he does not trust such evidence, and he reaffirms his position that the Company will not negotiate with the Union until it has been certified. White calls to Curme's attention the fact that, two days after the first meeting at which the Union presented its request for recognition, he was visited by three employees from the Miscellaneous Division who gave him a petition signed by 100 workers in that division stating that they were not members of the United Rubber Workers, and had no intention of becoming members or authorizing it to bargain for them.

Curme tells White he thinks it is a mistake to get this new relationship started off this way. He says he "doesn't know what the boys will do, and there may be trouble." White refuses to discuss the matter further at this time.

The next day, White calls into his office, individually, for conferences four of the five employees who had been in to see him the day before (Curme was not called), and several other employees of the plant who had been active in organizing Local 417. During each of these conferences, White reminds the employees of how generous and liberal the Company has been in its treatment of its employees in the past. He states that the Company is now paying higher wages than the average of the companies engaged in the same line of business. He also points out that all employees of the Company are receiving pensions, life insurance, sickness and accident benefits, vacation with pay, and Christmas bonuses, and that all of these are paid for entirely by the Company. When asked by one of the employees what his attitude is toward the Union, White replies, "I am opposed to the Union — it causes trouble and does no good. All it does is take dues, and it gives nothing in return." He asks each employee to compare conditions in plants where the Union is certified as the bargaining representative of the employees, and suggests if this were done, the

Enderby Company would compare extremely favorably with these other companies. White adds, however, that "under the law the choice is yours — not mine."

1. What considerations besides the antipathy toward unions expressed by White may have motivated the management decision not to recognize Local 417?

2. What is the legal effect under the NLRA of White's statements made in the individual conferences held the day after the Monday meeting with Curme? Is such conduct permissible? Would your answer have been the same prior to the 1947 amendments?

3. If you were legal counsel for the Company, would you have advised it (a) to hold the individual conferences and (b) to refuse to recognize Local 417?

4. Are the employees free, under the NLRA, to strike to force the Company to recognize Local 417? What considerations, aside from the applicability of the statute (if it is applicable), will affect the decision on the question of whether or not to strike?

5. If it appeared that the Union was not going to take the matter to the NLRB, but planned to strike instead, could the Company file a petition with the NLRB? Would your answer have been the same prior to the 1947 amendments? What would be your advice to the Company if it appeared that Curme and Layton had told two of the employees with whom White talked individually, "If you renege now, we will ride you out of the plant?"

6. If the Union decides to take the matter to the NLRB, should it file an unfair labor practice charge, a representation petition, or both? Would your advice be different if Curme had been discharged three days after the Monday meeting "for being a troublemaker?"

7. If the Union files a representation petition, what kind of proof should it submit?

READINGS

For material germane to most of the issues raised by this part of the Enderby Case — I, see pages 123–131.

For references, both to material in the text and to other sources, which bear on each of the six questions, see the following notes. The numbers of these notes correspond to those of the questions.

1. Consult NLRA, Secs. 9 (a) , (b) , and 8 (a) (5) ; NLRB, 16th Ann. Rep. 159–160 (1951). But see NLRB v. Standard Steel Spring Co., 180 F.2d 942 (6th Cir. 1950) .

2. NLRB policy with respect to employer "free speech" prior to the adoption of Section 8 (c) in the 1947 amendments to NLRA, both as to unfair labor practice and representation cases: Daykin, Employer's Right of Free Speech in Industry Under the National Labor Relations Act, 40 Ill. L. Rev. 185 (1945) ; Killingsworth, Employer Freedom of Speech and the N.L.R.B., 1941 Wis. L. Rev. 211. See also Bausch and Lomb Optical Co., 72 N.L.R.B. 132, 19 L.R.R.M. 1145 (1947) ; Armour and Co., 14 N.L.R.B. 682, 4 L.R.R.M. 463 (1939) ; Elias Savada, d.b.a. Model Blouse Co., 15 N.L.R.B. 133, 5 L.R.R.M. 116 (1939) ; NLRB v. Jones Foundry, etc., 123 F.2d 552 (7th Cir. 1941) .

For the effect of Section 8 (c) of the 1947 amendments to the National Labor Relations Act on NLRB policy with respect to employer "free speech," see Note, 58 Yale L.J. 165 (1948) ; NLRB, 13th Ann. Rep. 49–50 (1948) ; Mathews Lumber Co. v. United Brotherhood, etc., 96 N.L.R.B. No. 52, 28 L.R.R.M. 1513 (1951) ; NLRB, 14th Ann. Rep. 54–55 (1949) , 16th Ann. Rep. 151–152 (1951) .

See pages 593–595 infra.

3. Consult pages 123–126 infra; NLRB, 16th Ann. Rep. 190–191 (1951) .

4. Consult NLRB, 15th Ann. Rep. 127, 148–149 (1950). See text, pages 169–172 infra, for rules governing eligibility of strikers to vote. See also pages 725–742, and 688–692 infra, for rules governing the right of strikers to reinstatement and the right of unions to strike for recognition.

5. See pages 126–130 infra; NLRA, Sec. 9 (c) (1) (B) ; NLRB, 13th Ann. Rep. 19, 26 (1948) ; NLRB, Rules and Regulations; Ser. 6 (effective March 1, 1951), Secs. 102.52 and 102.53. See also pages 820–822 infra.

6. NLRA, Secs. 8 (a) (1) , (3) , (5) , 9 (a) , (b) , (c) , 10 (a) , (b) ; Silverberg, How to Take a Case Before the N.L.R.B. (1949) ; NLRB, Rules and Regulations, Ser. 6 (effective March 1, 1951) , Secs. 102.9–102.19, 102.52. See pages 616–620 infra.

7. NLRB, Rules and Regulations, Ser. 6 (effective March 1, 1951) , Sec. 102.53.

B

After two weeks of consideration by the Union members (of whom there are actually only some 250 — over 150 of them in the Tire Division) , Local 417 decides to file a petition with the Regional Office of the NLRB under Section 9 (c) of the Act, requesting that this Union be certified as the representative of "all employees of the Enderby Rubber Company Chicago plant." In this petition the Local alleges that this action is supported by "a substantial number of employees," and submits 250 cards signed by individual employees authorizing the Union to act as their representative.   Shortly after this petition is filed, the Board receives another one from the Enderby Employees Association, requesting that it be certified as the representative of all the employees in the Miscellaneous Division at the Enderby Chicago plant.   A third communication is received from a group of employees from both the Chicago plant and the Gary, Indiana, Enderby plant.   Those employees state that they are members of District No. 50, United Mine Workers, and that they desire its certification as the representative of all the employees in both the Chicago and Gary plants. In this petition, the UMW alleges that the Gary plant (located approximately twenty miles from the Chicago plant) is likewise a rubber plant, manufacturing miscellaneous rubber products, with total employment of 2000 men and women, divided into the following groups:

Production employees	1700
Foremen	100
Clerical	150
Executive	50

In addition, the UMW petition states that there is a great deal of centralized control of the labor policies, wages, and general policies between the two plants.   Likewise, the nature of the work performed in the plants is very similar, resulting in a high degree of transferability of employees between the two plants.   The UMW petition requests, however, that no election be held at the present time because "this Company is actively encouraging membership of its employees in an organization calling itself the Enderby Employees Association."   There is finally a petition by the Teamsters Union (AFL), requesting representation rights in behalf of all employees in the Receiving and Shipping Department at the Chicago plant.   (This department is technically part of the Miscellaneous Division but actually handles materials for and from both divisions.   There are 45 employees in this department.)

1. Does the Regional Director of the Board have any discretion as to whether or not to act upon this matter of representation at the Enderby plants?

2. Assuming that the Regional Director proceeds, what, if any, hearings must be held before there is an election at the plant?

3. If hearings are held, which of the four employee organizations will be entitled to appear?

4. What problem is presented by the UMW request for the right to represent employees of both the Chicago and Gary plants? How will the Board dispose of this request?

5. Suppose the Enderby Company alleges that it has for a number of years been a member of the Mid-West Rubber Association, an organization consisting of nine companies engaged in the manufacture of automobile tires and miscellaneous rubber products in and around Chicago. The Association is a very informal organization, with no bylaws, no constitution, and no regularly scheduled meetings. It does have a president, vice-president, and secretary, elected annually. The primary function of the Association is to meet occasionally (about three times a year) to discuss common personnel problems. However, for the past four years it has, through its three-man executive committee, negotiated agreements with the Chemical Engineers Protective League. The League is an organization consisting of over 80 per cent of all the chemists and engineers employed by the nine plants which are members of the Mid-West Rubber Association. In 1943 the League was certified by the NLRB as the collective bargaining representative for all of the chemists and engineers employed by the nine plants. As a result collective bargaining has been between the Association and the League. The Association has no authority to bind the nine member plants. But in each of the last four years the agreement negotiated by the Association committee has been accepted, and each of the nine plants has executed a uniform contract, signed individually. The United Rubber Workers have thus far not attained collective bargaining status in any of the nine companies. So far as is known, they have no substantial support in any of the plants except those operated by the Enderby Company. The Enderby Company asserts that an association-wide unit is appropriate. How would the NLRB dispose of this contention?

6. What problem is presented by the UMW allegation regarding the Enderby Employees Association? What would the Regional Director do if he determined that these allegations were in fact true?

7. Suppose the Enderby management, acting on the request of a number of its clerical employees, files a petition with the Regional Office of the Board requesting that the clerical employees "not be included as employees eligible to vote in any election which may be held to determine a bargaining representative for the production employees." What consideration would be given to this petition?

8. How would the Board have disposed of a request from the

plant foremen that they be recognized as a separate bargaining unit and that the Enderby Foremen's Club be certified as their representative? (Compare applicable provisions of the 1935 Act and the 1947 Act.)

READINGS

For material germane to most of the issues raised by this part of The Enderby Case — I, see pages 130–168 infra.

For references to sources other than the text which bear on each of the eight questions, see the following notes. The numbers of these notes correspond to those of the questions.

1. Consult NLRB, 13th Ann. Rep. 26–28 (1948); NLRB, Rules and Regulations, Ser. 6 (effective March 1, 1951), Secs. 102.55 and 102.63; NLRB, Statements of Procedure, as amended Nov. 29, 1949, Secs. 101.16–101.17. With respect to filing requirements, consult NLRA, Secs. 9 (f), (g), (h).

2. NLRA, Sec. 9 (c) (1); NLRB, Statements of Procedure, as amended Nov. 29, 1949, Secs. 101.18–101.20, NLRB, Rules and Regulations, Ser. 6 (effective March 1, 1951), Sec. 102.54–102.60.

3. Consult NLRB, 15th Ann. Rep. 32–33 (1950), 16th Ann. Rep. 56–58 (1951).

4. Matter of Libby-Owens-Ford Glass Co., 31 N.L.R.B. 243, 8 L.R.R.M. 135 (1941); Matter of Swift and Co., 4 N.L.R.B. 779, 1A L.R.R.M. 387 (1938); Matter of Standard-Coosa-Thatcher Co., 80 N.L.R.B. 50, 23 L.R.R.M. 1035 (1948); NLRB, 14th Ann. Rep. 35–37 (1949).

5. Matter of Associated Shoe Industries, 81 N.L.R.B. 224, 23 L.R.R.M. 1320 (1949); NLRB, 12th Ann. Rep. 21 (1947), 14th Ann. Rep. 36–37 (1949).

6. NLRA, Sec. 8 (a) (2); NLRB, 3d Ann. Rep. 112 (1939); Matter of Ewing-Thomas Corp., 72 N.L.R.B. 1450, 19 L.R.R.M. 1290 (1947); Matter of Central Truck Lines, Inc., 3 N.L.R.B. 317, 1A L.R.R.M. 130 (1937); H. J. Heinz Co., 10 N.L.R.B. 963, 3 L.R.R.M. 482 (1939); Matter of Cudahy Packing Co., 17 N.L.R.B. 302, 5 L.R.R.M. 314 (1939); Matter of Armour and Co., 8 N.L.R.B. 1100, 3 L.R.R.M. 202 (1938); Matter of Security Warehouse and Cold Storage Co., 35 N.L.R.B. 857, 9 L.R.R.M. 106 (1941); NLRB, 14th Ann. Rep. 56–58 (1949); 16th Ann. Rep. 62 (1951). See also NLRA, Secs. 10 (a), (b), (c) and 9 (c) (2). See pages 595–612 infra.

7. NLRA, Sec. 9 (b); Farwell, Ozmun, Kirk & Co., 61 N.L.R.B. 875, 16 L.R.R.M. 125 (1945); R.C.A. Mfg. Co., 2 N.L.R.B. 159, 1 L.R.R.M. 95 (1936); Western Electric Co., Inc., 62 N.L.R.B. 1505 (1945); NLRB, 15th Ann. Rep. 56–58 (1950), 16th Ann. Rep. 108–109 (1951).

8. Under 1935 Act: Packard Motor Car Co. v. NLRB, 330 U.S. 485, 67 Sup. Ct. 789, 91 L. Ed. 1040 (1947), affirming 157 F.2d 80 (6th Cir.

1946), enforcing 64 N.L.R.B. 1212, 7 L.R.R.M. 163 (1945); Jones & Laughlin Steel Corp., 66 N.L.R.B. 386, 17 L.R.R.M. 304 (1946). Under 1947 Act: Sections 2(3), 2(11), and 14(a). Apparently, "supervisors" cannot now be included in, nor themselves constitute, a bargaining unit under the Act. In accord with this changed status see Merris & Monroe, 77 N.L.R.B. 1375, 22 L.R.R.M. 1142 (1948). See also NLRB, 16th Ann. Rep. 110–113, 186 (1951).

C

A Board hearing is held, and an election date set. The notice of election states that "all production and clerical employees of the Enderby Rubber Company Chicago plant" shall be entitled to vote in the election. (This description is spelled out in greater detail in the full text of the notice.) It also indicates that the employees in the Miscellaneous Division of the Chicago plant will be considered as a separate group for the purposes of the election, and that the ballot for them will include the following choices: Local 417 of URW, the Enderby Employees Association, and "no union." For the rest of the eligible voters, the choices will be Local 417 of URW, and "no union."

On receipt of this notice of election, 35 of the employees in the Shipping Department at the Chicago plant go out on strike. They are joined by 40 other employees at the same plant who are apparently members of the UMW. The Company immediately hires new employees to fill these 75 jobs.

Three days before the election, White calls a meeting of the production employees (both Tire and Miscellaneous Divisions). He reiterates what he had told the key members of Local 417 in individual conferences the day after the Monday meeting with Curme. (See section A of this problem, pages 114–115 supra.)

1. Has Local 417 a valid basis for protesting the recognition of the Miscellaneous Division employees as a separate voting group?

2. Have the members of the Teamsters Union any valid basis for protest?

3. Will the 75 striking employees be permitted to vote in the election? How about the 75 employees who have been hired to fill their jobs? Will S, an active URW worker whom one of the foremen fired the day before the election "to show the rest of these guys what I think of this Union," be allowed to vote?

4. Will ten men who are employed as night watchmen and who are members of Local 417 be eligible to vote at the election?

5. Suppose, changing the above-stated facts, the Enderby Employees Association had been formed a year prior to the time the URW committee called on White, and a contract had been entered into between the Company and the Association (which contract was in effect at the time the URW made their overtures). In what respects would this affect the URW rights and its decision as to how to proceed in its pursuit of representative authority? How would this affect the probable disposition of this case by the Board? What additional facts are necessary to answer these questions definitively?

6. The results of the election are as follows:

Miscellaneous Division

Local 417, URW	126
Enderby Employees Association	44
No union	110
Challenged votes	2
	282

Other Production and Clerical Employees

Local 417, URW	204
No union	190
Challenged votes	10
	404

What is the next step to be taken by the Board (or by the parties)?

7. Suppose the number of votes for each choice listed above had been exactly half what is actually was. Would this have made any difference in the effect of the election?

8. Suppose that in the Miscellaneous Division balloting, the Enderby Employees Association had received 145 votes, with 126 going for Local 417, URW, and 11 for "no union" (with no votes challenged). How would this have affected the disposition of this case? Would the URW have a basis for challenging this election as improper?

9. Suppose that after the election, the AFL Teamsters file a petition in the Circuit Court of Appeals to have the results set aside, requesting that the Board be ordered to recognize the Shipping Department as a separate bargaining unit and to hold another election. What disposition will be made of this petition? Suppose that after the election, the Teamsters, instead of going to court, picket for recognition as the collective bargaining representative of the employees in the Receiving and Shipping Department? What would be your advice to the Company?

READINGS

For material germane to most of the issues raised by this part of The Enderby Case — I, see pages 144–150, 150–152, and 168–202 infra.

For references to sources other than the text which bear on each of the nine questions, see the following notes. The numbers of these notes correspond to those of the questions.

1. With respect to the unit appropriate for purposes of collective bargaining in general, see NLRB, 14th Ann. Rep. 31–35 (1949) (for criteria used by the Board see id. at page 32). See Section 9 (c) (5), NLRA for its possible relation to this factual situation. See also NLRB, 16th Ann. Rep. 85–96 (1951).

2. See Note, 6 U. of Chi. L. Rev. 673 (1939); Underwood Machinery Co., 74 N.L.R.B. 641, 20 L.R.R.M. 1208 (1947); Conference Report on Section 9 (b) (2), N.L.R.A., 93 Cong. Rec. 6465 (June 3, 1947); NLRB, 14th Ann. Rep. 32–33 (1949) (particularly note 26). See some recent determinations made by the Board in various industries: Sunshine Biscuits Inc., 94 N.L.R.B. 770, 28 L.R.R.M. 1094 (1951); Aluminum Foils Inc., 94 N.L.R.B. 806, 28 L.R.R.M. 1109 (1951); Reilly Electrotype Co., 94 N.L.R.B. 810, 28 L.R.R.M. 1110 (1951); Hudson Pulp and Paper Corp., 94 N.L.R.B. 1018, 28 L.R.R.M. 1125 (1951).

3. Section 9 (c) (3), NLRA; Pipe Machinery Co., 79 N.L.R.B. 1322, 22 L.R.R.M. 1510 (1948); NLRB, 13th Ann. Rep. 32–33 (1948), 14th Ann. Rep. 27 (1949); Times Square Stores Corp., 79 N.L.R.B. 361, 22 L.R.R.M. 1373 (1948); NLRB, 15th Ann. Rep. 77–79 (1950). With respect to employee S, see Section 8 (a) (3), NLRA; Consumers Cooperative Refinery Association, 77 N.L.R.B. 528, 22 L.R.R.M. 1055 (1948); Ames Spot Welder Co., 75 N.L.R.B. 352, 21 L.R.R.M. 1040 (1947); Differential Steel Car Co., 75 N.L.R.B. 714, 21 L.R.R.M. 1074 (1948); Container Manufacturing Co., 75 N.L.R.B. 1082, 21 L.R.R.M. 1105 (1948); NLRB, 13th Ann. Rep. 55–56 (1948). With respect to limitations imposed by Section 10 (c) of NLRA on the Board's policies in these cases, see NLRB, 14th Ann. Rep. 59–61 (1949).

4. Section 9 (b) (3), NLRA. For a definition of the term "guard" as used in that section, see C. V. Hill and Co., Inc., 76 N.L.R.B. 158, 21 L.R.R.M. 1172 (1948); Radio Corp. of America, 76 N.L.R.B. 826, 21 L.R.R.M. 1250 (1948); Steelweld Equipment Co., Inc., 76 N.L.R.B. 831, 21 L.R.R.M. 1252 (1948); Brinks, Inc., 77 N.L.R.B. 1182, 22 L.R.R.M. 1133 (1948). With respect to certification of unions as affected by Section 9 (b) (3), see Schenley Distilleries, Inc., 77 N.L.R.B. 468, 22 L.R.R.M. 1040 (1948); E. R. Squibb and Sons, 77 N.L.R.B. 84, 21 L.R.R.M. 1336 (1948). See also NLRB, 16th Ann. Rep. 106–107 (1951).

5. Pressed Steel Car Co., Inc., 36 N.L.R.B. 560, 9 L.R.R.M. 164

(1941) ; Matter of American Tobacco Co., 62 N.L.R.B. 1239 (1945) ; Matter of Eicor, Inc., 46 N.L.R.B. 1035, 11 L.R.R.M. 201 (1943) ; Matter of John Morrell and Co., 69 N.L.R.B. 1446, 18 L.R.R.M. 1316 (1946) ; Matter of Wheland Co., 72 N.L.R.B. 351, 19 L.R.R.M. 1173 (1947) ; Murdock, Some Aspects of Employee Democracy Under the Wagner Act, 32 Cornell L.Q. 73 (1946) ; Note, 51 Yale L.J. 465 (1942) ; NLRB, 13th Ann. Rep. 29–32 (1948) , 14th Ann. Rep. 22–26 (1949) .

6. NLRA, Sec. 9 (c) (3) ; NLRB, Rules and Regulations, Ser. 6 (effective March 1, 1951) , Secs. 102.61–102.62; NLRB, 13th Ann. Rep. 35 (1948) , 14th Ann. Rep. 30–31 (1949) ; United States Rubber Co., 83 N.L.R.B. 378, 24 L.R.R.M. 1087 (1949) ; Bauer-Schweitzer Hop & Malt Co., 79 N.L.R.B. 453, 22 L.R.R.M. 1409 (1948) .

7. See NLRB, 11th Ann. Rep. 23 (1946) , 12th Ann. Rep. 18 (1947) , on the question of the representative number of the eligible employees within the unit casting ballots; NLRB, 14th Ann. Rep. 31 (1949) , with respect to the Board rule that the majority of votes of employees participating in the election rather than the majority of those eligible to vote is the decisive factor.

8. Direct Laboratories, Inc., 94 N.L.R.B. 380, 28 L.R.R.M. 1053 (1951) ; Wilson & Co., 95 N.L.R.B. No. 103, 28 L.R.R.M. 1377 (1951) ; NLRB, 13th Ann. Rep. 34–35 (1948) , 16th Ann. Rep. 128–136 (1951) .

9. See Fitzgerald v. Douds, 167 F.2d 714 (2d Cir. 1948) ; Ohio Power Co. v. NLRB, 164 F.2d 275 (6th Cir. 1947) . See also CCH Labor Law Rep. (4th ed.) ¶2750 (1948) . See pages 200–202 and 688–692 infra; NLRB, 14th Ann. Rep. 98–99 (1949) .

2. THE DUTY TO RECOGNIZE

NOTES

The unfair labor practices spelled out in the National Labor Relations Act are dealt with in detail in Part IV of this volume.[30] However, since some of them bear directly on organizational activities and affect the course and disposition of representation questions, they are either discussed or referred to in this Part.

One such unfair labor practice which has an important bearing on the establishment of a collective bargaining relationship is set out by Section 8 (a) (5) , which makes it unlawful for an employer to refuse to bargain collectively with the representative of his employees. It has been held that this section imposes, among other things, the duty on an employer to recognize as the exclusive

[30] For a brief summary of the substance of the unfair labor practices, see pages 566–570 infra.

bargaining agent the union which a majority of the employees in an appropriate unit have selected as their representative.

1. In Roanoke Public Warehouse, 72 N.L.R.B. 1281, 19 L.R.R.M. 1267 (1947), the Union claimed that it had majority support and asked for recognition. The Company refused recognition on the ground that the Union lacked majority support. The Union offered to prove its status by submitting to the Company membership cards showing that 16 of the 17 employees involved supported it. The Company refused this offer and proposed a Board election, offering to join with the Union in a consent election. The Union rejected this proposal, quit the conference, and threatened to strike — a threat which it carried out. Despite a finding that prior antiunion remarks by two of the Company's supervisors unlawfully restrained the employees in the exercise of their right to self-organization, the NLRB found that the Company's refusal to recognize the Union was not a refusal to bargain collectively.

2. In Jackson Press, Inc., 96 N.L.R.B. No. 132, 28 L.R.R.M. 1615 (1951), two Unions requested that the Company recognize them as the collective bargaining representatives for its "pressroom employees." The Company refused on the ground that the Unions' majority support was questionable. The Company took the position that it would not grant recognition unless and until the Unions were certified. The unit was appropriate, and the Unions did in fact represent a majority at the time of the Company's refusal. The Unions filed a representation petition which, after a strike, they withdrew. In ruling on a complaint subsequently issued against the Company, the NLRB said: ". . . an employer, when faced with a demand for recognition by a union, may in good faith insist on a Board election as proof of the union's majority, but . . . an employer unlawfully refuses to bargain if its insistence on such an election is motivated, not by any bona fide doubt as to the union's majority, but rather by a rejection of the collective bargaining principle or by a desire to gain time within which to undermine the union." The Board, having found that the Company had committed numerous violations of Section 8 (a) (1) both before and during the strike, held that the refusal of the Company to recognize the Unions at the time of their original request violated Section 8 (a) (5).

3. Wood, representing the Hotel and Restaurant Employees Union, Local 146 (AFL), met with Kommelter and Leverton, two officers of the Chamberlain Corporation, stated that the Union represented a majority of the Company's cafeteria employees, and

requested exclusive recognition. Leverton replied that all matters pertaining to labor relations were handled by Kamenow, the Company's labor relations adviser, and stated that the Union would have to talk to him. Wood then referred to certain coercive statements made to the employees by Pikell, the cafeteria manager. Leverton denied knowledge of such statements, stated that he would investigate, and assured Wood that if the charge were true, corrective action would be taken. Subsequently Pikell was warned by Company officials not to repeat the questioned conduct. Wood then met with Kamenow, claimed majority status, and requested recognition. He offered to prove his claim with membership cards. Kamenow refused, stating that the only proof of majority acceptable to the Company would be through a Board-directed election. Kamenow refused to agree to a consent election, as suggested by Wood. The Union then filed a petition with the Board. Subsequently, and in response to a request from Wood, the business agent of a Union which represented another group of employees of the Chamberlain Corporation asked Kamenow to meet with Wood. Kamenow refused. The cafeteria was shut down within two weeks after the Union filed its petition with the Board. Two days after this shutdown the Union sent a letter to Kamenow requesting a conference. This letter was ignored. The union then withdrew its petition and filed an unfair labor practice charge. The Board, despite a finding that the Chamberlain Corporation had, through Pikell, restrained the employees in the exercise of their right to self-organization, held that the Company's insistence on an election was a good-faith request for reasonable proof of the Union's majority status and that the refusal to recognize until the Union's representative status was established in such an election did not constitute an unlawful refusal to bargain. Chamberlain Corporation, 75 N.L.R.B. 1188, 21 L.R.R.M. 1122 (1948).

4. See also: doubt as to majority status, Artcraft Hosiery Co., 78 N.L.R.B. 333, 22 L.R.R.M. 1212 (1948) ; doubt as to appropriate bargaining unit, Matter of W. W. Holmes, 72 N.L.R.B. 39, 19 L.R.R.M. 1143 (1947), Matter of Palm Beach Broadcasting Co., 63 N.L.R.B. 597, 17 L.R.R.M. 9 (1945), enforced, 155 F.2d 805 (5th Cir. 1946) ; request not made to responsible company official, Bausch and Lomb Optical Co., 69 N.L.R.B. 1104, 18 L.R.R.M. 1290 (1946). Generally, see NLRB, 13th Ann. Rep. 59–60 (1948), 14th Ann. Rep. 70–72 (1949), 16th Ann. Rep. 189–191 (1951).

Consult Reliance Mfg. Co., 28 N.L.R.B. 1051, 7 L.R.R.M. 165

(1941), enforced, modified, 125 F.2d 311 (7th Cir. 1941); Biles-Coleman Lumber Co., 4 N.L.R.B. 679, 688–89, 1A L.R.R.M. 368 (1937), enforced, 98 F.2d 18 (9th Cir. 1938); Phillips Transfer Co., 69 N.L.R.B. 493, 18 L.R.R.M. 1231 (1946); NLRB v. Louisville Refining Co., 102 F.2d 678, 680 (6th Cir. 1939).

3. PROCEDURE

FELDESMAN, PRINCIPLES IN REPRESENTATIVE CASES *

When a formal proceeding is instituted before the National Labor Relations Board praying, in effect, that the Board dispose of a question concerning representation, we have a "Representation Case."   Unlike unfair labor practice cases, which are initiated by the filing of a charge under Section 10, Representation Cases are instituted by the filing of a petition under Section 9 (c).   Representation Cases are not always necessary to establish the exclusive representative status of a bargaining agent.   But when substantial issues are raised in good faith, the Representation Case is the legal instrument for determining such status. . . .

Section 9 (c) of the Wagner Act contained language of a very general nature.   Under that language the Board permitted Representation Cases to be brought in but two instances: By a labor organization or other employee-representative seeking certification as bargaining agent.   And by an employer in limited circumstances; these were the necessary circumstances: More than one labor organization or employee-representative must have asserted a claim to representation and the claims must have been conflicting in that the very same unit or overlapping units of employees were being sought.   Thus, the employer-petition was designed to take the employer "off the spot" by permitting him to place before the Board for resolution the question concerning representation raised by two or more labor organizations with conflicting representation claims.

In Board terminology the case brought by the employee-representative was known as an "R" case and that instituted by the employer as an "RE" case.

Section 9 (c) of the amended Act has broadened the field of

* Excerpts from an address delivered at the University of Virginia Law School, July 31, 1948, which is printed in 22 L.R.R.M. 31 (1948).   William Feldesman is Assistant General Counsel, National Labor Relations Board. Other excerpts are reprinted elsewhere in this Part of the casebook. — ED.

Representation Cases to a considerable extent. The old "R" case is still preserved under Section 9 (c) (1) (A) (i) ; in Board parlance it is now called an "RC" case. But the employer is no longer circumscribed as heretofore in bringing a representation case. He may institute a proceeding under Section 9 (c) (1) (B) even when one labor organization claims to represent employees. The employer proceeding is now an "RM" case in Board jargon. . . .
Under Section 9 (c) (1) (A) (ii) an entirely new representation proceeding is permitted — a proceeding wherein employees seek to "decertify" a certified or currently recognized bargaining agent. This type of proceeding is called an "RD" case, the third and last kind of Representative Case under the Amended Act. . . .

In "RC" and "RM" cases a question concerning representation generally arises when a labor organization demands recognition as exclusive bargaining agent in a given unit and the employer refuses to accede to the union's demand. The employer's refusal may stem from a bona fide doubt as to the union's majority status or the appropriateness of the unit sought. His refusal may be occasioned by an existing contract with another union or an outstanding certification of another union. Or it may be that more than one union is seeking recognition as agent for the affected employees and the employer wisely declines to pick and choose. In "RD" cases the question usually arises by the filing of a petition by employees seeking to oust the incumbent union. . . .

As I have already indicated, Representation Cases are commenced by the filing of a petition. The Board has established Regional Offices throughout the United States for case handling and the petition should ordinarily be filed in the Regional Office wherein the alleged appropriate bargaining unit exists. The form of petition is supplied by the Regional Office. This form must be completed by supplying certain information indicated on the face of the form. After the petition is filed the Regional Office conducts a preliminary investigation through a Board agent who is assigned the case by the Regional Director. This investigation is made for the purpose of determining administratively whether the Board has jurisdiction, whether there is a question concerning representation, whether the unit sought is appropriate and other relevant matters. In "RC" and "RD" cases the investigation is also concerned with ascertaining whether or not the petitioner has a sufficient showing of interest to warrant further proceedings. In the "RC" case the petitioner is required to submit authorization cards or other documentary evidence indicating that a substantial number of employees have designated the petitioner as collective bargaining representative.   And in the "RD" case the petitioner is obliged to submit similar documentary evidence to demonstrate that a substantial number of employees desire to decertify the certified or currently recognized bargaining representatives.   This is the "showing of interest." . . .

If at the Regional level the Regional Director is persuaded that the Board has no jurisdiction, or that there is no question concerning representation, or that the unit sought is in fact inappropriate, or that the petitioner's showing of interest in "RC" and "RD" cases does not amount to 30 percent of the employees in the affected unit, or that there are other reasons in line with Board policy and decisions for not proceeding with the case, he will ask the petitioner to withdraw the petition.   If the petition is withdrawn, that ends the case.   On the other hand, if the petition is not withdrawn, the Regional Director will serve notice on the petitioner that he is refusing to issue notice of hearing.   This is tantamount to an administrative dismissal of the petition.   If the petitioner is dissatisfied with the Regional Director's determination, he may appeal to the Board under the Board's Rules and Regulations.   Note that the appeal is to the Board.   In unfair labor practice cases an administrative dismissal of the charge is appealed to the General Counsel as he has final authority, on behalf of the Board, with respect to the investigation and prosecution of unfair labor practice proceedings.

An appeal from a Regional Director's dismissal must be taken within ten days.   The Board in Washington may sustain the dismissal or may reverse the Regional Director's action and direct him to proceed with the case.

When a Representation Case has merit the Regional Director encourages informal adjustment before issuance of notice of hearing.   There are two methods of informally adjusting a case.   Both involve the consent election agreement, wherein all interested parties stipulate generally as follows: That there is a question concerning representation affecting commerce; that there is an appropriate unit and precisely what that unit consists of; that there shall be an election conducted to ascertain the exclusive bargaining status of claiming labor organizations; and that eligibility to vote shall be determined by an agreed pay roll date.   In the consent election agreement all parties waive a formal hearing.

One type of consent election agreement calls for a Regional Director's certification.   All interested parties agree that the Regional Director's determinations with regard to all issues arising shall be made in accordance with Board procedure and principles and shall be final and binding. The Regional Director is the final arbiter; he issues the certificate attesting to representative or lack of representative status. The other type of consent election agreement calls for a Board certification. Under this agreement, issues which are properly raised are determined by the Board.

In the event that there are matters upon which the parties cannot agree [31] and the consent election procedure cannot be followed, the Regional Director issues a Notice of Hearing. Copies of the petition and notice of hearing are served upon all interested parties and the notice of hearing specifies a time and place for the hearing.

The hearing, usually open to the public, is held before a Hearing Officer, who normally is an attorney or field examiner attached to the Regional Office but may be another qualified official of the Board. The hearing, which is non-adversary in character, is actually part of the investigation of the question concerning representation, and the primary interest of the Hearing Officer is to insure that the record contains as full a statement of the pertinent facts as may be necessary for determination of the case by the Board. The parties are afforded full opportunity to present their respective positions and to elicit the significant facts in support of their contentions. In most cases a substantial number of the relevant facts are undisputed and stipulated. The parties are permitted to argue orally on the record before the Hearing Officer. The petitioner's showing of interest, in "RC" and "RD" cases, is not a litigable issue. In days gone by a form prepared by the investigating Board agent reflecting the showing of interest of the various labor organizations involved was introduced into evidence. The showing then, as now, was an administrative matter and could not be attacked directly or indirectly. Evidence of showing of interest

---

[31] During the twelve years under the Wagner Act, 74.1 per cent of the representation cases were adjusted informally, including 5.5 per cent by recognition, 42.4 per cent by consent election and cross-check, 18 per cent withdrawn, and 7.3 per cent dismissed. Only 25.9 per cent went to formal proceedings, and an eighth of these were settled before Board decision. NLRB, 12th Ann. Rep. 84, 87 (1947). During the first year under the Taft–Hartley Act, 82.3 per cent of the representation cases were adjusted informally, including 1.4 per cent by recognition, 30.6 per cent by consent election, 8.7 per cent by stipulated election, 27.6 per cent withdrawn, and 13 per cent dismissed. Only 17.7 per cent went to formal proceedings, and a third of these were settled before Board decision. NLRB, 13th Ann. Rep. 105 (1948). See also NLRB, 14th Ann. Rep. 165 (1949). During the fiscal year 1951, 74.4 per cent of the representation cases were adjusted informally. Only 25.6 per cent required formal action, and 3.9 per cent of these were settled before hearing, 2.9 per cent were settled after hearing, and 18.8 per cent required a Board decision. NLRB, 16th Ann. Rep. 300 (1951). — ED.

is no longer introduced, since introduction evoked much argument and many legal objections — and unnecessarily so.

The Hearing Officer does not decide the case. Nor, under the amendments to the Act, does he make recommendations as to how the issues are to be resolved or the case finally decided. The Hearing Officer does transmit to Washington after the close of the hearing a case analysis memorandum which sets out all the pertinent facts and issues, but the case is thoroughly considered in Washington. After a careful review of the record the Board issues its decision, making findings of fact and resolving all legal issues, and either directs an election or the dismissal of the petition.

The close of the hearing marks the transfer of the case to the Board. At any time before the close of the hearing the Regional Director may permit withdrawal of the petition. After the closing of the hearing, however, the petition may be withdrawn only with the consent of the Board. Whenever the Regional Director or the Board approves withdrawal of the petition the case is closed.[32]

4. INITIAL REPRESENTATION PROCEEDINGS

a. The Question Concerning Representation

GENERAL BOX CO.
National Labor Relations Board, 1949
82 N.L.R.B. 678, 23 L.R.R.M. 1589

HERZOG, Chairman, and HOUSTON and REYNOLDS, Members: . . .

At the hearing, the Employer contended that there is no ques-

---

[32] For the procedure in representation cases, see also NLRB, Rules and Regulations, Ser. 6 (effective March 1, 1951), Secs. 102.52–102.63; NLRB, Statements of Procedure, Secs. 101.16–101.20, as amended November 29, 1949; and Silverberg, How to Take a Case Before the N.L.R.B. (1949). The chart on page 131 illustrates the procedures followed in representation cases.

The Canadian Industrial Relations and Disputes Investigation Act, 1948, makes no provision for employer petitions or for decertification petitions. However, Section 7(5) provides: "Two or more trade unions claiming to have as members in good standing of the said unions a majority of employees in a unit that is appropriate for collective bargaining, may join in an application under this section and the provisions of this Act relating to an application by one union and all matters or things arising therefrom, shall apply in respect of the said application and the said unions as if it were an application by one union."

And Section 11 provides: "Where in the opinion of the Board a bargaining agent no longer represents a majority of employees in the unit for which it was certified, the Board may revoke such certification and thereupon, notwithstanding sections fourteen and fifteen of this Act, the employer shall not be required to bargain collectively with the bargaining agent, but nothing in this section shall prevent the bargaining agent from making an application under section seven of this Act." — ED.

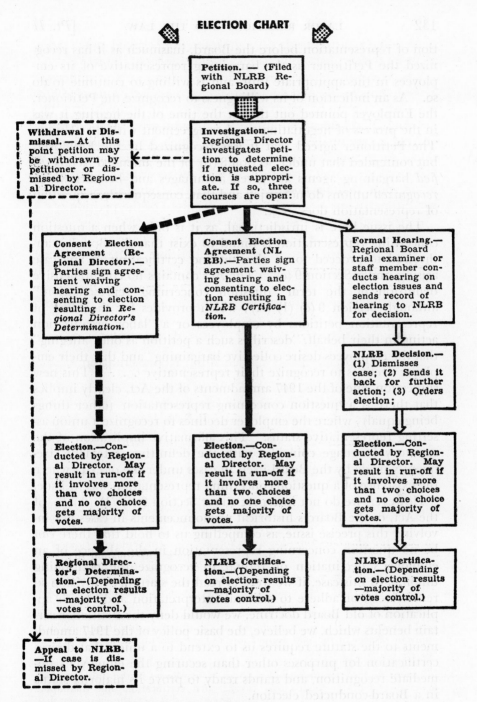

Petition. — (Filed with NLRB Regional Board)

Investigation. — Regional Director investigates petition to determine if requested election is appropriate. If so, three courses are open:

Withdrawal or Dismissal. — At this point petition may be withdrawn by petitioner or dismissed by Regional Director.

Consent Election Agreement (Regional Director). — Parties sign agreement waiving hearing and consenting to election resulting in *Regional Director's Determination.*

Consent Election Agreement (NLRB). — Parties sign agreement waiving hearing and consenting to election resulting in *NLRB Certification.*

Formal Hearing. — Regional Board trial examiner or staff member conducts hearing on election issues and sends record of hearing to NLRB for decision.

NLRB Decision. — (1) Dismisses case; (2) Sends it back for further action; (3) Orders election;

Election. — Conducted by Regional Director. May result in run-off if it involves more than two choices and no one choice gets majority of votes.

Election. — Conducted by Regional Director. May result in run-off if it involves more than two choices and no one choice gets majority of votes.

Election. — Conducted by Regional Director. May result in run-off if it involves more than two choices and no one choice gets majority of votes.

Regional Director's Determination. — (Depending on election results —majority of votes control.)

NLRB Certification. — (Depending on election results —majority of votes control.)

NLRB Certification. — (Depending on election results —majority of votes control.)

Appeal to NLRB. —If case is dismissed by Regional Director.

tion of representation before the Board, inasmuch as it has recognized the Petitioner as the bargaining representative of its employees in the appropriate unit, and is willing to continue to do so. As an indication of its willingness to recognize the Petitioner, the Employer pointed out that at the time of the hearing it was in the process of negotiating another agreement with that Union. The Petitioner agreed that it was recognized by the Employer, but contended that under Section 8 (b) of the amended Act, *certified* bargaining agents are given advantages and benefits which *recognized* unions do not enjoy and that, consequently, a question of representation does exist.

The issue here is jurisdictional, as it is only when a question concerning representation is found to exist that the Board is authorized to proceed to an election and certification in any case arising under Section 9 (c). The Act contains no comprehensive definition of the term "question concerning representation," although Section 9 (c) (1) (A), which provides for the filing of representation petitions by employees or a "labor organization acting in their behalf," describes such a petition as one "alleging" that the employees desire collective bargaining "and that their employer declines to recognize their representative . . ." This new subsection, one of the 1947 amendments of the Act, clearly implies that there *is* a question concerning representation (other things being equal), where the employer declines to recognize a union asserting representative status. This affirmative implication of the statutory language coincides with the definitive statements frequently made by the Board itself in cases under the old Act where the existence of a question concerning representation was in issue.

However, we do not interpret either Section 9 (c) (1) (A) (i) of the Act, or the Board's historical pronouncements in cases not involving this precise issue, as compelling us to hold that there *can* be no question concerning representation in the absence of an employer's declination or refusal to recognize the petitioning union. In this case, if we were to read the statutory provision so restrictively, or adhere to a literal interpretation and slavish application of old Board doctrine, we would deny the Petitioner certain benefits which, we believe, the basic policy of the 1947 amendments to the statute requires us to extend to a union that desires certification for purposes other than securing the employer's immediate recognition, and stands ready to prove its majority status in a Board-conducted election.

Recently in the Advance Pattern case, 80 N.L.R.B. 29, on reconsideration, Members Murdock and Gray dissenting, we decided an issue as to the effect of Section 9 (c) (1) (A) (i) that is closely related to the problem in this case.   In that case, the petition filed by a labor organization which sought an election and certification failed to conform to the specifications set forth in Section 9 (c) (1) (A) (i). It did not allege that the employer had "declined" to recognize the petitioner, and the record showed that there was no declination by the Employer until a date after the petition was filed.   The Board majority nevertheless directed an election, holding that the language of the Act, describing certain types of petitions that may be filed, is not to be construed as restrictively defining the Board's jurisdiction.   In reaching this conclusion, the Board in effect anticipated the situation now presented in this case. We pointed out that to construe Section 9 (c) (1) literally and restrictively would preclude certification of unions which, although they already enjoy recognition, may still desire to be certified in order to secure protection under Section 8 (b) (4) (C) of the Act. By virtue of this provision it is an unfair labor practice for one union to take concerted action directed to accomplish the overthrow of an established certified representative.   As a prohibition against "raiding," its value to the certified union is immediately apparent.

Furthermore, if we were to treat the Employer's recognition of the Petitioner in this case as negating the existence of a question concerning representation, we would be compelled to deny the petitioning union an opportunity to secure still other benefits which the amended statute reserves to *certified* unions.   Under Section 8 (b) (4) (B) , for example, it is only a *certified* union that can lawfully induce the employees of some "other employer" to engage in a strike or other concerted activity for the purpose of compelling the primary employer to recognize it.   The legality of certain concerted activities sponsored by one union in aid of another union's effort to secure recognition, too, depends upon whether or not the latter union is certified.   Moreover, a Board certification is a defense in certain situations where a respondent union is charged with engaging in a strike or other concerted activity in support of a jurisdictional dispute within the ambit of Section 8 (b) (4) (D) of the Act.

These statutory privileges and immunities that accompany certification are not the only significant advantages that accrue to certified unions, as distinguished from those that enjoy recognition without certification.   Under the so-called "one-year rule" enunciated by the Board long before the 1947 amendments were enacted, a certified union's right to recognition as the exclusive bargaining agent is stabilized and fully protected for a "reasonable" period of time, ordinarily one year from the date of certification. This rule operates to limit the freedom of the employees to select and change their bargaining representative at will, once they have selected a union in a secret ballot conducted by the Board; it derives from the statutory policy of encouraging and stabilizing collective bargaining in the interest of industrial peace; it endows a *certified* union's status with a measure of security and permanence not enjoyed by a union whose majority standing and right to recognition is established otherwise than by Board election and certification.

For example, although an uncertified union may prove its majority to the employer's satisfaction, properly secure recognition and negotiate with the employer for many months, the successful completion of this collective bargaining effort may be frustrated. If, at the eleventh hour before a contract is signed, a rival union, or employees seeking to "decertify" the merely recognized union, assert that its majority is dissipated and file a petition with the Board, the employer may not lawfully execute a contract until the Board has disposed of the petition. But if the union has a vital *certification,* neither the employer himself nor a rival union, nor the employees, can effectively raise a question of representation; and if a contract otherwise valid is signed or renewed within the certification year, even in the face of a petition, it will bar an election for its term. In short, under the "one-year rule," a Board certification not only resolves any dispute as to the employer's duty to recognize and bargain with the certified union; it also precludes other possibly interested parties from raising a question of representation, and for a definite period of time.

In enacting the 1947 amendments, Congress left unchanged the Board's practice of according this special value to certifications. Moreover, it greatly expanded and implemented the protection of certified unions in Section 8 (b) (4), and restated the statutory policy of stabilizing collective bargaining relationships in the public interest. It would be a retrogressive step tending to defeat that basic policy to hold that an employer's willingness to recognize and bargain with a union makes it impossible for the union to secure the other manifest advantages which flow from a Board certification. In many instances, indeed, it is the employer — although concededly not this one — who seeks these advantages and particularly those conferred by Section 8 (b) (4) (C).

For these reasons, as well as those more fully stated in the Advance Pattern case, we conclude that, in view of the 1947 amendments, an employer's recognition of a union which asserts representative status does not, in and of itself, negate the existence of a question concerning representation. In this case, we are of the opinion that there is such a question, created by the Petitioner's assertion of majority standing, its expressed desire to secure a certificate, and its formal petition that the Board investigate its status by the statutory method of conducting an election.

. . . . Employers and unions do not require Board certifications as a prerequisite to collective bargaining if recognition of a majority representative suffices for their purposes. But if a certification is deemed desirable because of its special advantages, the use of the ballot box is not too high a price to pay.

[An election was directed. Members Murdock and Gray concurred specially, conceding jurisdiction but suggesting certification without an election. Their opinions and the footnotes to the majority opinion have been omitted.]

NOTES

1. Compare California Consumers Corp., 82 N.L.R.B. 484, 23 L.R.R.M. 1577 (1949). This was a petition for decertification. The Union, certified in 1945, entered into successive contracts with the Employer for three years. The Union won a union-shop election in 1947. The 1948 contract was terminated by the Employer and not renewed. The Union appeared and participated in decertification hearing and filed a post-hearing brief urging dismissal or reopening of proceedings. Held: A question concerning representation exists, election directed.

2. In Ny-Lint Tool and Mfg. Co., 77 N.L.R.B. 642, 22 L.R.R.M. 1061 (1948), the petition was filed by the Employer. The Union had represented the production and maintenance employees for several years, under successive contracts with this Employer, but had never been certified. The Board said: "In August, 1947, the Union, having given timely notice that it would not renew the contract about to expire in September, 1947, submitted to the Employer a proposed contract covering the same unit of production and maintenance employees. The Employer expressed doubt that the Union represented a majority of its production and maintenance employees, refused to negotiate a new contract, and filed this petition.

"At the hearing, the Union disavowed any claim to represent a majority of the Employer's production and maintenance workers. However, it did claim to represent a majority of the Employer's toolroom employees, who, it contended, constitute an appropriate craft unit, and requested an election among them.

"The question of representation, although brought to the Board's attention by the Employer's petition, was raised by the affirmative claim of the Union to represent a majority of the Employer's employees in the production and maintenance unit. The Union has now withdrawn its claim to represent the employees in the production and maintenance unit, which is the unit designated in the Employer's petition as well as the unit designated in the Union's own proposed contract. The Union has thereby abandoned its right to represent these employees, and has waived any obligation the Employer may have had to recognize it as the bargaining representative of such employees. In the absence of a claim by the Union to represent the employees in the aforesaid unit, a question concerning representation does not exist, and the Board is, under these circumstances, without jurisdiction to proceed with its investigation under Section 9 (c) (1) of the Act, as amended. Accordingly, we shall dismiss the petition." [Member Reynolds dissented. See NLRB, 13th Ann. Rep. 26–27 (1948).]

3. In J. P. O'Neil Lumber Co., 94 N.L.R.B. 1299, 28 L.R.R.M. 1190 (1951), the Board declined to dismiss the petition of an employer who, although currently negotiating with an uncertified union which it had recognized for several years, had reason to doubt the union's majority status. The majority opinion, following the reasoning of the General Box Co. case, said that an employer should not be denied "the opportunity to secure the benefits attendant upon dealing with a certified union." See also Matter of Continental Southern Corporation, 83 N.L.R.B. 668, 24 L.R.R.M. 1127 (1949).

(1) *The Petitioner's Interest*

NLRB, 13TH ANNUAL REPORT 27–28 (1948): "For many years it has been the Board's practice to require the petitioning union in a representation case to show, prima facie, that it represented a substantial number of the employees in the bargaining unit for whom it seeks to be certified as representative. Absent that prima facie demonstration that the petitioner's interest was substantial, the Board dismissed the petition in order to avoid the useless expenditure of time and effort involved in conducting an election where there was little likelihood that the petitioner would be designated as majority bargaining representative. The amended act prescribes that employees or their representatives petitioning for certification or decertification under section 9 (c)

(1) (A) shall allege that their petition is supported by 'a substantial number of employees.' The Board views this provision of the statute as codifying its prior practice, and as leaving unimpaired the established rule that a petitioner's prima facie showing of interest is to be investigated only administratively by the regional director, and may not be a subject of litigation at the hearing. However, the statute makes no reference to a showing of interest in proceedings initiated by an employer petition; a majority of the Board (Member Murdock dissenting) has construed this to mean that no showing is required of the labor organization or organizations claiming a majority in cases where the employer is the petitioner." [39]

(2) *Effect of Company Domination*

Evidence of unfair labor practices, such as allegations of domination of one of the unions involved in a representation proceeding by the employer, is not ordinarily admissible in a representation proceeding.

However, in the Baltimore Transit Co. case [33] decided under the

[39] Matter of O. E. Felton d/b/a/ Felton Oil Co., 78 N.L.R.B. 1033 (1948). The majority gave effect by this decision to sec. 202.17 (a) of the Board's Rules and Regulations, Series 5, effective August 22, 1947. It held that, aside from the fact that nothing in the Act or the legislative history of the amendments precludes the Board from adhering to this rule, the rule will best effectuate the intent of Congress in enacting 9 (c) (1) (B), "that employers confronted with a union claim for recognition be afforded an opportunity to ascertain through a Board election the representative status of the union." It added that to "require the petitioning employer to obtain and submit evidence of a union's representative interest in the same manner as other petitioners" would at the very least "require the employer to engage in an unfair labor practice in procuring such data." The dissenting opinion, however, would not require the employer to supply the proof as to the union's representation; it would place the burden on the union to appear and support its prior claim of representative status and, absent such proof, would resolve the employer's petition by a finding that the claimant is not the representative of the employees. And, in disagreement with the majority, it finds authority for insisting on a showing being made in "the plain language of 9 (c) (2) which provides that the same rules of decision shall be applied in determining the existence of a question concerning representation irrespective of the identity of the persons filing the petition or the kind of relief sought."

[See Norris, Inc. v. NLRB, 177 F.2d 26, 24 L.R.R.M. 2084 (D.C. Cir. 1949) (employer sought restraining order against Board election in RC case because petitioning union was not required to prove substantial interest at hearing. Board contended it properly determined whether petitioner's interest is substantial, administratively, and that it is not required to spread upon the record the evidence on the point. Held: Question not reached, trial court's denial of restraining order affirmed, and Board's conduct of representation proceedings not subject to direct judicial intervention in absence of showing of threatened irreparable injury). — ED.]

[33] 59 N.L.R.B. 159, 15 L.R.R.M. 118 (1944).

1935 National Labor Relations Act the Board stated: "The full freedom to choose bargaining representatives which the procedure set forth in Section 9 of the Act is intended to insure would be limited drastically were the Board powerless to determine which unions shall appear on the ballot in elections directed thereunder and thus be available for choice by employees. The absence of such power might well result in the defeat of one of the prime objectives of the Act, the promotion of peaceful relations between employees and employers to the end that interferences with the free flow of commerce may be lessened thereby. Accordingly the Board has found on many occasions that the purposes of the Act would best be effectuated by enlarging the usual scope of its inquiry in a representation proceeding and considering matters pertaining to unfair labor practices. In all instances, the object has been to guarantee that full freedom of choice, which must prevail if the provisions of Section 9 are to have any substantial meaning, by denying places on the ballot to tainted unions. Thus, where the articles or constitution of a labor organization participating in a representation proceeding indicated on their face subservience to the employer, such organization has been denied a place on the ballot. . . . We believe it follows logically that, in a case such as the instant one, where a union seeking a place on the ballot allegedly is a successor to or a continuation of a union previously ordered disestablished, this Board may inquire into the formation of such union to determine whether it is subject to the same taint of employer control and influence and thus not to be foisted upon employees in a Board-conducted election. As previously stated, this has indeed been the Board's practice, and where a finding of successorship has been made, the tainted union has been denied a place on the ballot, and its petition, if any, has been dismissed."

The union which was denied a place on the ballot in the foregoing representation proceeding subsequently sought to obtain an injunction restraining the National Labor Relations Board from conducting an election in accordance with its order, on the ground that the Board did not have power to deny a union a place on the ballot because of successorship to a company-dominated organization unless such successorship had been established in an unfair labor practice proceeding. The lower court granted the injunction but the Fourth Circuit Court of Appeals reversed,[34] emphasizing that the Board may proceed to determine a question of repre-

[34] Madden v. Brotherhood and Union of Transit Employees, 147 F.2d 439 (4th Cir. 1945).

sentation without having the finding of company-domination or successorship determined prior to that time in an unfair labor practice proceeding. See also Matter of Flint Mfg. Co., 62 N.L.R.B. 1003, 16 L.R.R.M. 241 (1945) ; NLRB, 10th Ann. Rep. 26–27 (1945), 12th Ann. Rep. 14 (1947). Where unfair labor practice charges have been filed, or previously determined unfair labor practices have not been remedied, the Board will not usually proceed to an immediate election, unless the union charging such unfair labor practices agrees not to raise such practices as objections to the conduct or results of the election.

The 1947 amendments to the National Labor Relations Act made several changes in the administrative structures of the NLRA. Under the original Act, the General Counsel of the Board was appointed by the Board and subject to its control. Under Section 3 (d) of the present NLRA, the General Counsel is appointed by the President, by and with the advice and consent of the Senate, just as are the Board members themselves. Likewise, under Section 3 (d) the General Counsel is given the final authority on the Board's behalf, in investigation of charges and the issuance of complaints under Section 10 (unfair labor practice cases) and in the prosecution of these complaints before the Board. Thus, there resides in the General Counsel the sole authority to decide whether action will be taken when an unfair labor practice charge is filed.

Taking cognizance of this change, in Matter of Times Square Store Corporation,[35] a representation case in which the Board had to dispose of a large number of challenged ballots cast by striking employees, the Board held that the statutory scheme of separation of functions of the General Counsel and the Board precluded it from deciding in a representation proceeding, solely on the basis of the record made in such proceeding, that a strike had been caused by an unfair labor practice of the employer. Such a determination, the Board concluded, could only be made by it in an unfair labor practice proceeding initiated by the General Counsel through the issuance of a complaint. Accordingly, the striking employees in this case were found to be "economic" strikers,[36] and, as they had been replaced, their challenged ballots were ruled invalid. The Board, in a unanimous opinion, stated at page 365: ". . . [T]he Act, as written, compels this conclusion. To hold otherwise would not be consistent with the Congressional intent to

[35] 79 N.L.R.B. 361, 22 L.R.R.M. 1373 (1948).
[36] Strikes are "economic" unless they are found by the Board to have been caused by unfair labor practices of the employer.

endow the General Counsel with *final authority* over the issuance and prosecution of complaints under Section 10. It would, in addition, create the undesirable situation of the Board's acting in practice as a forum for considering the content of charges which the General Counsel, for reasons satisfactory to himself, has thought it proper to dismiss.

"In the light of the foregoing, we conclude that an initial finding that a strike was caused by unfair labor practices may be made only in unfair labor practice proceedings. No such proceedings are now before us, for those with sole power to initiate them have chosen not to do so. Nor have findings of unfair labor practice on the facts here involved been made in any other proceeding. We therefore have no choice but to find, without further examination of the facts, that the strike was an economic strike, and that the strikers who participated therein are economic strikers." See also Marine Optical Mfg. Co., 92 N.L.R.B. 571, 27 L.R.R.M. 1137 (1950), where the Board held that a charge that an intervening union is employer inspired and dominated may be heard only in a complaint proceeding.

Section 9 (5) of the Canadian Industrial Relations and Disputes Investigation Act, 1948, provides: "Notwithstanding anything in this Act, no trade union, the administration, management or policy of which is, in the opinion of the Board, (a) influenced by an employer so that its fitness to represent employees for the purpose of collective bargaining is impaired; or (b) dominated by an employer; shall be certified as a bargaining agent of employees, nor shall an agreement entered into between such trade-union and such employer be deemed to be a collective agreement for the purposes of this Act."

(3) *Effect of a Jurisdictional Dispute*

MOUNTAIN STATES POWER CO.
National Labor Relations Board, 1944
58 N.L.R.B. 109, 15 L.R.R.M. 29

MILLIS, Chairman, and REILLY and HOUSTON, Members: . . . During December 1943, the I.B.E.W. requested the Company to recognize it as the exclusive collective bargaining representative of the employees involved herein. The Company refused this request on the ground that the Engineers also claimed to represent such employees.

The Engineers contend that the petition should be dismissed because it and the I.B.E.W. are both affiliated with the American Federation of Labor. In the past the Board has, as a matter of policy, refused to permit rival unions affiliated with the same parent organization to resort to the administrative processes of the Act for settlement of their representation disputes where adequate and appropriate machinery was available to them under the procedures of the parent organization. . . . In the instant case the record indicates that the dispute between the I.B.E.W. and the Engineers is of long standing and universal in scope. Thus it is apparent that effective resolution of the existing conflict cannot be had without resort to the administrative processes of the Act.

A statement of the Regional Director, introduced into evidence at the hearing, indicates that the I.B.E.W. and the Engineers each represents a substantial number of employees in the unit hereinafter found to be appropriate.

We find that a question affecting commerce has arisen concerning the representation of employees of the Company, within the meaning of Section 9 (c) and Section 2 (6) and (7) of the Act . . .

[An election was directed to determine whether the employees wished to be represented by the I.B.E.W. or by the Engineers, or by neither. The Board's footnotes have been omitted.]

NOTES

1. Accord, as to cases arising under the Wagner Act, Grinnell Company of the Pacific, 71 N.L.R.B. 1370, 19 L.R.R.M. 1134 (1947) ; Pacific Car and Foundry Co., 76 N.L.R.B. 32, 21 L.R.R.M. 1161 (1948).

2. After a year's operation under the Taft-Hartley Act, the Board reported: "Other familiar prerequisites to the resolution of a question concerning representation still obtain, although not similarly codified. Thus the Board . . . is reluctant to entertain proceedings involving a jurisdictional dispute concerning representation between two or more unions affiliated with the same parent organization, but will proceed where the dispute cannot be resolved by submission to the authority of the parent body, [citing the Pacific Car and Foundry case]." NLRB, 13th Ann. Rep. 28 (1948).

3. Compare Air Conditioning Co. of Southern California, 81 N.L.R.B. 946, 23 L.R.R.M. 1440 (1949) (where petitioning local had seceded from international, was suspended by international

and its jurisdiction transferred to another local.   Held: Controversy over right to administer petitioner's contract is not a "jurisdictional dispute," and in any event is no bar) ; Mathieson Chemical Corp., 81 N.L.R.B. 1355, 23 L.R.R.M. 1533 (1949) (principle that Board will dismiss petition in jurisdictional dispute where issue is which of two unions had right to conduct negotiations on behalf of certain employees, held inapplicable to case where one union no longer regards itself as affiliated with parent body and has been denied some of the privileges of such affiliation) .

4. Compare the Board's handling of jurisdictional disputes in unfair labor practice cases, under Sections 8 (b) (4) (D) and 10 (k) of the Taft-Hartley Act and Sections 102.74–102.78 of the Board's Rules and Regulations.   See pages 1000–1007 infra.

5. Compare the New York State Labor Relations Act, Sec. 705.3 (Representatives and elections) : ". . . provided, however, that the board shall not have authority to investigate any questions or controversy between individuals or groups within the same labor organization or between labor organizations affiliated with the same parent labor organization."   See Rubel Corp. v. Boland, 177 Misc. 638, 31 N.Y.S.2d 572 (1941), and New York Post Corp. v. Kelley, 61 N.Y.S.2d 264 (1946), affirmed, 270 App. Div. 916, 61 N.Y.S.2d 762 (1st Dept. 1946), affirmed, 296 N.Y. 178, 71 N.E.2d 456 (1947) (action for declaratory judgment that Board without power to direct election; motion to dismiss denied) .

6. For further treatment of the problem of jurisdictional disputes, see pages 984–1007 infra.

7. In Australasia, union demarcation disputes are "industrial disputes" with which the tribunals of the various systems can deal. Such disputes, however, are not common.   One factor discouraging them is the existence of statutory provisions giving the registrars of the relevant tribunals power to refuse registration to new organizations if there is an existing registered organization to which the persons who would be included in the new organization might conveniently belong.   (See especially New Zealand Industrial Conciliation and Arbitration Amendment Act, 1936, sec. 4) .

(4) *Effect of Filing Requirements*

The Board is prohibited specifically by Sections 9 (f) , (g) , and (h) of the NLRA from investigating any questions concerning representation which grow out of petitions submitted by labor unions which have not complied with the filing requirements contained in the above-named sections. Petitions for decertification do not fall within these prohibitions, however, as the Board has determined that in this situation it is the petitioning employees, not a labor union, who raise a question concerning representation. The Board stated that this result must follow, since otherwise the union's own dereliction in failing to file the necessary papers and documents would protect it from decertification.[37]

See NLRB, 13th Ann. Rep. 23–25 (1948) and 14th Ann. Rep. 13–16 (1949) for a résumé of how the Board has ruled with respect to what acts constitute compliance specifically with these sections. For the impact of Sections 9 (f), (g), and (h) on the union's right to set up its current contract as a bar to an election, see NLRB, 13th Ann. Rep. 32 (1948); and for the impact of Sections 9 (f), (g), and (h) on the ability of a union to file objections to election procedure, see id. at 34. The NLRB has continued to hold that compliance is a matter for administrative determination by the Board. NLRB, 15th Ann. Rep. 19 (1950). The circuit courts have upheld the Board. NLRB v. Greensboro Coca Cola Bottling Co., 180 F.2d 840 (4th Cir. 1950); NLRB v. Red Rock Co., 187 F.2d 76 (5th Cir. 1951); NLRB v. Wiltse, 188 F.2d 917 (6th Cir. 1951). See pages 934–947 infra, for more exhaustive treatment of the filing requirement. Compare Crown Can Co., 22 L.R.R.M. 1369 (1948) (Wisconsin Employment Relations Board proceeding). But see NLRB v. Highland Park Mfg. Co., 341 U.S. 322, 71 Sup. Ct. 758, 95 L. Ed. 680 (1951).

Under the arbitration systems of Australia and New Zealand, industrial associations have to pay for the encouragement and privileges they receive by a good deal of subjection to statutory regulation of their internal affairs, and to disciplinary control by the relevant tribunals. The extent to which this should be carried is a current topic of political dispute. Examples of existing controls are: Commonwealth Conciliation and Arbitration Act 1904–1947, sec. 72, empowering the Court of Conciliation and Arbitration to conduct secret ballots to ascertain the views of members of an organization at any stage of a dispute; N.S.W. Industrial Arbitration Act 1940, sec. 115, prohibiting unreasonable refusal of admission to membership of organizations and giving the Industrial Commission power to police this requirement; N.Z.

[37] Matter of Harris Foundry and Machine Co., 76 N.L.R.B. 118, 21 L.R.R.M. 1146 (1948); Matter of Magnesium Casting Co., 76 N.L.R.B. 251, 21 L.R.R.M. 1179 (1948); Matter of Bethlehem Steel Co., 79 N.L.R.B. 1271, 22 L.R.R.M. 1499 (1948); Matter of Ives-Cameron Co., 81 N.L.R.B. 287, 23 L.R.R.M. 1360 (1949); Matter of Univis Lens Co., 82 N.L.R.B. 1390, 23 L.R.R.M. 1679 (1949).

Industrial Disputes and Arbitration Act 1925, sec. 17, requiring organizations to file records of the names and number of members and providing for a report to Parliament on such matters.

The Anzac statutes require as conditions of registration compliance with general requirements as to rules governing union affairs. It is not usual to compel the adoption of any particular types of rules, but there are general powers of refusing registration unless the rules are reasonable. For example, the Commonwealth Conciliation and Arbitration Act, Schedule B, Part IV of the Conciliation and Arbitration Regulations 1947, and sec. 70A of the Act (inserted by No. 18 of 1951), require the organization to include in its rules provision for union elections by secret ballot "under a system of voting which makes adequate provision for absent voting," the removal of members of committee and of officers, the control of officers by members and the control of branch officers by branch members, the mode in which property is to be controlled and funds invested, yearly or more frequent audit, the keeping of a register of members, provision for alteration of rules and other such matters. The Regulations, sec. 106 (b), require that the rules should exclude from office any person who has within a year before nomination advocated the overthrow of government by force and violence.

b. Unit Determination

Unit questions may come in three situations: (1) Where no collective bargaining relationship exists in a plant, and the NLRB must make a formal determination as to the appropriate unit or units for the first time; (2) Where a collective bargaining relationship does exist, there has been prior Board action, and the NLRB must determine whether or not the unit (s) defined in its previous action is still appropriate; (3) Where a collective bargaining relationship does exist, there has been no prior Board action, and the NLRB must determine whether or not the unit (s) defined by the employer and the union (s) is appropriate.

Only the first of these situations is discussed in the following material. The other two situations are covered under Subsequent Representation Proceedings, pages 177–188 infra.

(1) *In General — Crafts*

NLRB, 13TH ANNUAL REPORT 35 (1948) : "Under section 9 (a) of the amended act, as before, the collective bargaining representative designated by the majority of the employees *in an appro-*

priate unit is the exclusive representative of all the employees in that unit, 'for the purposes of collective bargaining in respect to rates of pay, wages, hours of employment, or other conditions of employment.' And it is the Board's responsibility under section 9 (b) of the act to 'decide in each case whether, in order to assure to employees the fullest freedom in exercising the rights guaranteed by this act, the unit appropriate for the purposes of collective bargaining shall be the employer unit, craft unit, plant unit, or subdivision thereof . . .' Guided by this general statement of statutory purposes and standards, the opening part of which was slightly rephrased but not substantially changed by the amendments, the Board, over a period of years, has formulated certain criteria which are applicable to the determination of all questions concerning the appropriate bargaining unit."

———

NLRB, 14TH ANNUAL REPORT 31–33 (1949) : "In any case where there is a controversy as to the bargaining unit, one or more of the following questions is usually presented to the Board for decision: What should be the *general type* or character of the unit, for example, whether it should be an industrial unit embracing all the employees in a broad class such as production and maintenance workers, or a craft unit confined to a small, specialized group within the class of production or maintenance employees; what the *scope* of the unit should be, i.e., whether it would embrace all employees in a given class at only one plant or establishment of one employer or at several plants of one employer or at all or several plants of a group of associated employers; and, finally, what the specific *composition* of the unit should be, that is, whether or not it should include occupational groups of employees such as clerks, inspectors, helpers, technical employees, and a host of others who, in a particular case, may be on the 'fringe' of the class constituting the unit as a whole. Related to questions in this last category are problems of determining what personnel, otherwise akin to the employees in the unit, must be excluded because they are specifically exempted from the definition of 'employee' in section 2 (3) of the act — for example, 'supervisors.'

"As noted in the last annual report, the 1947 amendments to the act have, in the main, left unchanged the familiar basic tests of appropriateness formulated by the Board during the years in administering the act prior to the amendments. Thus, in resolving unit issues, the Board is still guided by the fundamental concept that only employees having a substantial mutuality of interest in wages, hours, and working conditions, as revealed by the type of work they perform, should be appropriately grouped in a single unit. Various factors are taken into consideration by the Board in applying this general rule to the particular facts of each case. Chief among these criteria of appropriateness are: (1) The extent and type of union organization and the history of collective bargaining in behalf of the employees involved or other employees of the same employer or of other employers in the same industry; (2) the duties, skill, wages, and working conditions of the employees; (3) the relationship between the proposed unit or units and the employer's organization, management, and operation of his business, including the geographical location of the various plants involved; and (4) the desires of the employees themselves."

NLRB, 13TH ANNUAL REPORT 36 (1948) : "In deciding each case on its own facts, as it must do, the Board is vested with broad discretion, but its discretion in certain instances is now limited by provisions of the amended act. In brief outline, the innovations are as follows: 'professional employees,' 'guards,' and 'supervisors,' respectively, are now defined in the statute; and supervisors, as well as 'independent contractors' are expressly excluded from the definition of 'employees' covered by the act. Two new provisos added to Section 9 (b) dictate conditions affecting the unit placement of professional employees and guards. Another proviso, Section 9 (b) (2) , affects the Board's consideration of certain cases involving the familiar controversy over craft versus industrial units.[38] Finally, Section 9 (c) (5) prescribes that the extent of employee organization shall not be 'controlling' in unit determinations."

NLRB, 14TH ANNUAL REPORT 34–35 (1949) : "The Board, prior to its decision in Matter of Armstrong Cork Company (80 N.L.R.B. 1328 (1948)) , consistently refused, even in the absence of any prior history of industrial bargaining, to recognize the appropriateness of a departmental unit limited to the maintenance employees of a typical manufacturing plant, on the ground that such a unit embraced essentially a multicraft grouping of em-

[38] Section 9 (b) (2) is relevant only to situations where the Board has made a prior unit determination. Hence, it is discussed under Subsequent Representation Proceedings, pages 177–188 infra. — ED.

ployees with varying skills and therefore lacked sufficient homogeneity and cohesiveness to warrant establishment as a separate bargaining unit. The Armstrong Cork case, however, marked a partial abandonment of this policy. In finding that the maintenance department unit sought therein by one of the petitioning unions might constitute an appropriate unit, the Board said:

" 'The unit sought by the IAM is essentially a multicraft unit of maintenance employees. Although such a group may lack the inherent cohesiveness of a unit limited to employees of a single craft, it is clear that, as a group composed primarily of maintenance craftsmen, the members possess interests in common, distinct from those of the production employees, which are sufficient to warrant their original establishment in a separate unit.'

"Under certain circumstances, however, the Board has refused, even since the Armstrong Cork decision, to find appropriate a separate unit of maintenance employees. Thus, maintenance employees, as a departmental group, will not be severed where there has already been a bargaining history at the plant involved on an industrial basis. The Board also disapproved a separate maintenance unit in one case where there was no separate maintenance department, but where there was common supervision of maintenance and production employees and a high degree of integration between maintenance and production, and where the maintenance employees performed tasks of specialists rather than of true craftsmen."

NOTES

1. See Feldesman, Principles in Representative Cases, 22 L.R.R.M. 31, 41 (1948): "Absent a history of collective bargaining at the plant involved, where A union seeks a small unit of employees and B union seeks a more comprehensive unit including the employees sought by A, the Board, if it concludes that the employees desired by A could either be a separate unit or part of the all-inclusive unit requested by B, directs a 'Globe' election. A 'Globe' election derives its name from the old Globe Stamping case [3 N.L.R.B. 294 (1937)], wherein the Board used this type of election device I will now describe. The employees sought by A are set up as a separate voting group — A, B, and neither are placed on the ballot. The remaining employees are established as another voting group with B on the ballot in a yes — no vote. If the employees sought by A vote for A, this is indicative of their desires as to the form of unit they want — the Board will

find them to be a separate appropriate unit and certify A in that unit. If they vote for B, however, they also indicate the type of unit they want — a more comprehensive unit — and if B receives a majority vote in the residual voting group, the Board will certify B in a large single unit composed of the 2 voting groups, finding that unit to be appropriate. This is usually done where A union desires a craft unit and B union desires an industrial unit, absent a history of collective bargaining." See Note, The "Globe Rule" for Units Under the Wagner Act, 6 U. of Chi. L. Rev. 673 (1939).

As to whether such ascertainment of the wishes of the employees is an improper delegation of the Board's responsibility for unit determination, see NLRB v. Underwood Machinery Co., 179 F.2d 118 (1st Cir. 1949).

For a case where a Globe election was denied in a unit of radio, phonograph, and television repairmen as not truly craft and supportable only on basis of extent of organization, see Grinnell Bros., 80 N.L.R.B. 1268, 23 L.R.R.M. 1223 (1948); for a case where a Globe election was granted in a unit consisting of a multicraft group possessing interests in common distinct from those of production workers, see Armstrong Cork Co., 80 N.L.R.B. 1328, 23 L.R.R.M. 1232 (1948).

As to whether the amended NLRA requires as a prerequisite to the Board's ordering of a "self-determination" election among an unrepresented residual group of employees in a plant that a determination be made that such group may constitute a separate appropriate unit and that no election is being sought by a union in the broader unit, see Matter of Great Lakes Pipe Line Co., 92 N.L.R.B. 583, 27 L.R.R.M. 1123 (1950); Matter of Boeing Airplane Co., 92 N.L.R.B. 716, 27 L.R.R.M. 1148 (1950); NLRB, 16th Ann. Rep. 93–97 (1951).

2. See Woll, Glenn, and Thatcher, Craft Unionism and the N.L.R.A., 1 Lab. L.J. 33 (1949); Rathbon, The Taft-Hartley Act and Craft Unit Bargaining, 59 Yale L.J. 1023 (1950).

3. With the effect of Section 9 (c) (5) of the Taft-Hartley Act, compare Note, Recent Trends of the New York State Labor Relations Board in Determining the Appropriate Bargaining Unit, 47 Col. L. Rev. 1220 (1947).

4. The proviso to the unit-determination section of the New York Labor Law (705 (2)) reads: ". . . in any case where the majority of employees of a particular craft shall so decide the board shall designate such craft as a unit appropriate for the purpose of collective bargaining." For a discussion of the effects of this statute, see Arenwald and Landay, Representation Problems Under

the New York State Labor Relations Act, 8 U. of Chi. L. Rev. 471, 483–489 (1941).

5. Compare Section 8 of the Canadian Industrial Relations and Disputes Investigation Act, 1948: "Where a group of employees of an employer belong to a craft or group exercising technical skills, by reason of which they are distinguishable from the employees as a whole and the majority of the group are members of one trade union pertaining to such craft or other skills, the trade union may apply to the Board subject to the provisions of section seven of this Act, and shall be entitled to be certified as the bargaining agent of the employees in the group if the group is otherwise appropriate as a unit for collective bargaining."

6. The Australasian systems of compulsory arbitration grew up against a background of rapid and intensive unionization, encouraged by legislative policy and also by the policy of the industrial arbitration tribunals. Hence the creation of "bargaining units" has long since ceased to be a significant problem in those systems. The corresponding activity is the registration of industrial associations, i.e., employer and employee organizations recognized as capable of representing their members in the raising and settling of industrial disputes.

Whether an organization should be on a craft or an industrial basis has been determined for the most part by custom and historical development. The tribunals have had no bias in either direction. The general policy of the industrial tribunals is to require separate organization of managerial and supervisory employees. (See, e.g., Australian Workers' Union v. Wool Classers' Association of Australia, 32 Commonwealth Arbitration Rep. 733 (1933).)

These systems have fostered the growth of organizations covering complete groups of employers, plants, and employees so that it is very rare for a dispute to concern one employer only. Disputes are usually started by a union which covers the whole of a particular craft or a particular type of industry serving a "log" of demands upon all employers of the craftsmen or in the industry. Owing to constitutional restrictions, the Australian Commonwealth awards can cover only the actual parties to a dispute (but persons and corporations can become "parties" for this purpose by being members of registered associations which are parties, and by being assignees or successors in business of actual parties). The State and New Zealand systems authorize the relevant tribunals to make the terms of an award into a "common rule" — that is, a determination binding all persons in the craft or industry in which the dispute originated, even though not themselves actually parties to the dispute.

(2) *Guards, Professional Employees, and Supervisors*

(a) Guards

NLRB, 13TH ANNUAL REPORT 39 (1948): "The third proviso to section 9 (b) of the amended act, provides: 'The Board shall not . . . (3) decide that any unit is appropriate . . . if it includes, together with other employees, any individual employed as a guard to enforce against employees and other persons rules to protect property of the employer or to protect the safety of persons on the employer's premises; but no labor organization shall be certified as the representative of employees in a bargaining unit of guards if such organization admits to membership, or is affiliated directly or indirectly with an organization which admits to membership, employees other than guards.' It was the Board's practice in the past to insist upon separate units for monitorial guards, plant policemen, and watchmen. But the statute now adds two additional restrictions: (1) In effect, only unaffiliated unions representing guards exclusively may be certified to represent guard units. Accordingly, the Board held, in Matter of Schenley Distilleries, Inc., 77 N.L.R.B. 468, that a local union chartered by the American Federation of Labor was ineligible for certification as the representative of a unit consisting of plant guards because it was affiliated, through the American Federation of Labor, with unions admitting to membership employees other than guards. But in the converse situation, in Matter of E. R. Squibb and Sons, 77 N.L.R.B. 84, the Board rejected a contention that an international union affiliated with the American Federation of Labor could not be certified as the representative of production and maintenance employees, merely because one of its chartered locals happened to be the certified representative of guards at another plant of the same employer. (2) As the amendment contains language defining the term 'guard,' the Board now holds that watchmen, even though they do not function as monitors of fellow employees, must be excluded from bargaining units of production and maintenance employees. This is because watchmen normally have a duty to protect their employer's property against theft, whether by employees or 'other persons' who might gain access to the employer's premises. Matter of C. V. Hill & Co., Inc., 76 N.L.R.B. 158. But in Matter of Radio Corp. of America, 76

N.L.R.B. 826, and Matter of Steelweld Equipment Co., Inc., 76 N.L.R.B. 831, the Board held (Members Reynolds and Murdock dissenting) that an employee who spends less than half of his working time in guard duties is not an individual "employed as a guard" within the meaning of Section 9 (b) (3) and that such employees may therefore be included in units of production and maintenance employees. Similarly, a majority of the Board (Member Murdock dissenting) held in Matter of Brinks, Inc., 77 N.L.R.B. 1182, that the restrictions contained in Section 9 (b) (3) do not apply to armored truck drivers who have no duty to report derelictions or violations of rules by fellow employees and who are engaged to guard property belonging not to their own employer, but to their employer's customers."

NOTES

1. For further application of the "guard" proviso, see Levitt, The Taft-Hartley Act — A Year and a Half of Administrative and Judicial Construction, 24 N.Y.U.L.Q. Rev. 76, 127–129 (1949).

2. Compare: night watchmen at fruit packing plant, who are neither armed nor deputized, have no responsibility for enforcement of rules, and spend most of their time on regularly assigned maintenance duties, are not "guards" within meaning of the Act, California Growers, Inc., 80 N.L.R.B. 578, 23 L.R.R.M. 1194 (1948); firemen and dressing-room custodians and matrons at livestock-slaughtering and meat-packing plant are not "guards" under the Act; their enforcement of no-smoking rules and certain monitorial duties, respectively, are merely incidental to their respective responsibilities for fire prevention and dressing-room maintenance, Wilson & Co., Inc., 81 N.L.R.B. 504, 23 L.R.R.M. 1383 (1949); oil refinery's bathhouse employees are not "guards" within meaning of the Act although, on occasion, they have reported cases of theft and drunkenness and performed duties of gatemen; facts showed they spend more than 50 per cent of their time performing janitorial work and that they are part of unit along with company's watchmen as result of consent election held in 1945, Gulf Oil Corp., 92 N.L.R.B. 700, 27 L.R.R.M. 1140 (1950).

3. Compare NLRB v. E. C. Atkins Co., 331 U.S. 398, 67 Sup. Ct. 1265, 91 L. Ed. 1563 (1947), and NLRB v. Jones & Laughlin Steel Corp., 331 U.S. 416, 67 Sup. Ct. 1274, 91 L. Ed. 1575 (1947), in which, under the Wagner Act, it was held, three justices dissenting, that plant guards, both militarized and nonmilitarized,

although having disciplinary functions with respect to other personnel, were employees entitled to the protection of the Act.

(b) Professional Employees

NLRB, 13TH ANNUAL REPORT 39–40 (1948): "Section 9 (b) (1) [see Appendix] of the amended act provided that the Board 'shall not . . . decide that any unit is appropriate . . . if such unit includes both professional employees and employees who are not professional employees unless a majority of such professional employees vote for inclusion in such unit.' [17] This amendment substantially codifies the Board's prior practice of placing professional employees in separate bargaining units, or excluding them from units of other employees wherever the record in a particular case indicated that the professional personnel desired to be segregated.   But it removes the matter from the Board's discretion and permits no exceptions to the general rule.   Persons employed in a professional capacity [18] are accordingly now excluded from all units consisting of nonprofessional workers; or, in a proper case, the professionals are voted separately to determine whether or not they desire to be included or continue to be included in a unit of nonprofessional employees." [19]

[17] Section 2 (12) of the amended act contains an elaborate definition of the term "professional employees."   The Board has held that the following are professional employees: time-study and standards men, Matter of Worthington Pump and Machinery Corp., 75 N.L.R.B. 678 [but see Florence Stove Co., 94 N.L.R.B. 1434 — Ed.]; attorneys in the claim department of an insurance company, Matter of Lumbermen's Mutual Casualty Co., 75 N.L.R.B. 1132; plant engineers and right-of-way agents employed by a telephone company, Matter of Illinois Bell Telephone Co., 77 N.L.R.B. 1073; estimators employed by a company engaged in the business of designing and constructing office and industrial buildings and structures, Matter of the Austin Co., 77 N.L.R.B. 938.

On the other hand, the Board has held that the following are not professional employees: reporters, special editors, and rewrite men employed by a newspaper, Matter of Jersey Publishing Co., 76 N.L.R.B. 467; wire editor, sports editor, society editor, and clerks on a newspaper staff, Matter of Free Press Co., 76 N.L.R.B. 1047; announcers, singers, and writers employed by a radio station, Matter of West Central Broadcasting Co., 77 N.L.R.B. 366; accounting employees who do cost analysis and other accounting work, Matter of American Window Glass Co., 77 N.L.R.B. 1030.

[18] But not individuals possessing professional qualifications who are not employed in a professional capacity.   See Matter of Charles Eneu Johnson & Co., 77 N.L.R.B. 41; Matter of Starrett Bros. & Eken, Inc., 77 N.L.R.B. 275.

[19] See Matter of Illinois Bell Telephone Co., 77 N.L.R.B. 1073, where a decertification election was directed for a group of professionals who petitioned for severance from a previously established unit consisting predominantly of nonprofessional personnel.   But in Matter of Continental Motors Corp., 77 N.L.R.B. 345, the Board held that the statute did not require a separate election where the unit (in which an election had been held prior

(c) Supervisors

Section 2 (3) of the NLRA as amended by the Taft-Hartley Act, in 1947, provides that the "term 'employee' . . . shall not include . . . any individual employed as a supervisor . . ." Section 14 (a) provides: "Nothing herein contained shall prohibit any individual employed as a supervisor from becoming or remaining a member of a labor organization, but no employer subject to this Act shall be compelled to deem individuals defined herein as supervisors as employees for the purposes of any law, either national or local, relating to collective bargaining." The term "supervisor" is defined in Section 2 (11). Supervisors were not mentioned in the Wagner Act.

This statutory exclusion of supervisors as employees entitled to the protection of the NLRA reversed the power of the Board as sustained, four justices dissenting, in Packard Motor Car Co. v. NLRB, 330 U.S. 485, 67 Sup. Ct. 789, 91 L. Ed. 1040 (1947). In this case, 61 N.L.R.B. 4, 16 L.R.R.M. 43 (1945), and 64 N.L.R.B. 1212, 17 L.R.R.M. 163 (1945), the Board, Member Reilly dissenting, had originally ordered the employer to bargain with the Foremen's Association of America, an independent supervisors' union representing 1100 foremen in an automobile plant employing 32,000 rank and file production workers represented by the United Automobile Workers, CIO.

Supervisors had long been organized, and some 38 unions had been recognized for collective bargaining in their behalf by most of the employers in the building and construction, maritime, metalworking, postal, printing, and railroad industries. Usually, the supervisors were members of the same 29 craft unions that represented the rank and file; sometimes, as in the maritime, postal, and parts of the railroad industries, they were in 9 separate supervisors' unions. Whatever difficulties had arisen within the unions, on the job and at the bargaining table, the unionization of supervisors in these industries had presented no problem for the Board

to the effective date of the amended act) consisted predominantly of professional employees and included only a very small fringe of nonprofessionals.

[For further application of the "professionals" proviso, see Levitt, The Taft-Hartley Act — A Year and a Half of Administrative and Judicial Construction, 24 N.Y.U.L.Q. Rev. 76, 129–130 (1949).

Compare Cutter Laboratories, 80 N.L.R.B. 213, 23 L.R.R.M. 1077 (1948), holding that biological chemists, engineers, bacteriologists, biologists, and physicists are professional employees within the meaning of the Act; F. W. Sickles Co., 81 N.L.R.B. 390, 23 L.R.R.M. 1354 (1949), to the effect that manufacturing-methods engineers of radio parts manufacturing plant are not professional employees within the Act. — ED.]

under the original NLRA. Presumably, these traditional bargaining relations are not necessarily impeded by the amended Act. See Peterson, American Labor Unions 90–97 (1945) ; Note, Union Membership and Collective Bargaining by Foremen, 56 Mo. Lab. Rev. 1049 (1943).

The problem for the Board arose in the early 1940's, in the mass production industries, where the rank and file were organized in CIO industrial unions. Many supervisors claimed that, while representing management in relation to the production workers, their own economic relationships as employees with management required the protection of the Act. See the Foreman's Cases, 26 War Labor Rep. 644 (1945). Employers objected that this would mean the extension of the Act to management personnel, for supervisors acted "in the interest" of the employer under Section 2 (2) of the Wagner Act, and had often perpetrated the unfair labor practices for which employers had been held responsible. Because of changes in economic and labor conditions and in Board membership, the Board in 1942 made the protection of the Act available to supervisors, withdrew it in 1943, granted supervisors protection in 1944 against some discriminatory practices, granted them full protection in 1945 in the Packard case, referred to above, where the union involved was an independent supervisors' union, and in 1946 did likewise where the union involved was closely affiliated with that representing the rank and file.

The various cases and changes in Board policy are discussed in NLRB, 10th Ann. Rep. 30–35 (1945), 11th Ann. Rep. 26–32 (1946), and in Notes, 59 Harv. L. Rev. 606 (1946), 13 U. of Chi. L. Rev. 332 (1946), 55 Yale L.J. 754 (1946). See also Bethlehem Steel Co. v. N.Y. State Lab. Rel. Bd., 330 U.S. 767, 67 Sup. Ct. 1026, 91 L. Ed. 1234 (1947).

Thus, the impact of the 1947 amendments in excluding supervisors from the NLRA has been mainly felt in the mass production industries.

The definition of a "supervisor" in Section 2(11) of the amended Act provides: "The term 'supervisor' means any individual having authority, in the interest of the employer, to hire, transfer, suspend, lay off, recall, promote, discharge, assign, reward, or discipline other employees, or responsibly to direct them, or to adjust their grievances, or effectively to recommend such action, if in connection with the foregoing the exercise of such authority is not of a merely routine or clerical nature, but requires the use of independent judgment."

Applying these tests, the Board has held the following to be supervisors excluded from the protection of the Act: assistant soda department managers in charge of department half of the time, Liggett Drug Co., Inc., 80 N.L.R.B. 1099, 23 L.R.R.M. 1209 (1948); assistant foremen in charge part-time who had effectively recommended hire and fire, Underwood Machinery Co., 80 N.L.R.B. 1264, 23 L.R.R.M. 1222 (1948); electric utility company's working foremen, Carolina Light and Power Co., 80 N.L.R.B. 1321, 23 L.R.R.M. 1226 (1948); newspaper assistant city editors, telegraph editors, chiefs of copy desk, and assistant sports editors, A. S. Abell Co., 81 N.L.R.B. 82, 23 L.R.R.M. 1298 (1949). The following have been held not to be supervisors and so were included in the bargaining unit: managers of men's shoe store, where all decisions as to hiring, firing, promotion, and pay were made by general manager of chain, Florsheim Retail Boot Shop, 80 N.L.R.B. 1312, 23 L.R.R.M. 1234 (1948); electric utility's control operators, Ohio Power Co., 80 N.L.R.B. 1334, 23 L.R.R.M. 1242 (1948); newspaper editorial writers, make-up editors, night librarian, racing editor, dramatic critic, and financial editor, A. S. Abell Co., supra. As to time-study men, see NLRB v. Brown & Sharpe Mfg. Co., 169 F.2d 331 (1st Cir. 1948). However, see Baltimore Transit Co., 92 N.L.R.B. 688, 27 L.R.R.M. 1148 (1950).

The New South Wales Industrial Arbitration Act 1940, sec. 20 (I) (a), provides that "no award shall be made for the payment of wages or remuneration of persons occupying managerial positions" (other than managerial positions in governmental instrumentalities); sec. 5 excludes shop-walkers, gangers, and foremen stevedores from the definition of "managerial positions." Most of the tribunals, however, have no objection to making awards for such employees provided they are separately organized and their disputes are heard separately from those of the general craft and industry unions, and legislative policy in general permits this.

(3) *Multiple Plants*

PITTSBURGH PLATE GLASS CO. v. NLRB
Supreme Court of the United States, 1941
313 U.S. 146, 61 Sup. Ct. 908, 85 L. Ed. 1251

MR. JUSTICE REED delivered the opinion of the Court.
The petitioners in the two cases covered by these certioraris are

the Pittsburgh Plate Glass Company, an employer, and the Crystal City Glass Workers Union, an "independent" or "local" union, that is a union unaffiliated with any other employee organization. Charged with an unfair labor practice in refusing to bargain collectively with duly accredited representatives of its employees, the Company countered the complaint with the assertion that it had and did bargain collectively with the proper representatives of its employees but that it denied the validity of a Board decision including the Crystal City plant of the Company as a part of the appropriate bargaining unit.   The central issue thus is the legality of the Labor Board's decision, under §9 (b) of the National Labor Relations Act, determining that "the production and maintenance employees of the Company" at all six plants of its flat glass division, as a whole, constitute the appropriate unit for collective bargaining for the Crystal City employees rather than the employees of the Crystal City plant only.   The Board's conclusion is challenged on the merits, on procedural and on constitutional grounds. The certioraris were granted because of the importance of the "appropriate unit" problem in the administration of the Act.

The six plants of the flat glass division are located in five different states: Ford City, Pennsylvania; Creighton, Pennsylvania; Mount Vernon, Ohio; Clarksburg, West Virginia; Henryetta, Oklahoma; and Crystal City, Missouri.   The normal number of employees in the whole division is about 6,500.   The Crystal City plant, with 1,600, and the slightly larger plants at Ford City and Creighton account for the bulk of these workers; the remaining three together employ only about 1,000.   The Federation of Flat Glass Workers, an affiliate of the Congress of Industrial Organization, has a majority of all the employees in the flat glass division and also a majority at each plant except Crystal City.   Its position, which the Board sustained, is that the entire division should be a single bargaining unit.   The Crystal City Union, which claims a majority at that plant, and the Company both contend that the circumstances of this case require Crystal City to be separated from the rest of the division for the purpose of fixing the unit.

The present proceedings are the third stage of this labor dispute.   Originally, in June, 1938, the Board filed a complaint against the Company alleging domination of and interference with the Crystal City Union in violation of §§8 (1) and (2), 29 U.S.C.A. §158 (1,2).   The Crystal City Union was not named as a party in that proceeding.   Before any hearing had been held the Company consented to entry of an order that it would cease and desist from dominating or contributing to the Crystal City Union or from recognizing or dealing with it as a labor organization.   The Board issued the stipulated order in September, 1938, and later, also pursuant to the stipulation, obtained an enforcement order from the Circuit Court of Appeals.[5]   The Federation of Flat Glass Workers, which had filed the charges leading to the issuance of the complaint, also had requested an investigation and certification of representatives pursuant to §9 (c) of the Act.   Extensive hearings on this second stage took place in October, 1938, at which the Crystal City Union appeared and participated.   On January 13, 1939, the Board issued its decision fixing the bargaining unit and certification of representatives.   The Board found that the Company's production and maintenance employees throughout the entire flat glass division (with the exception of window glass cutters, clerical employees not directly connected with production, and supervisory employees) constitute an appropriate unit, and it certified the Federation as the exclusive representative of all the employees in the unit.[6]   This order, under our ruling in American Federation of Labor v. National Labor Relations Board,[7] was not subject to direct judicial review under §10 (f) of the Act [29 U.S.C.A. Sec. 160 (f)].   The Company, however, continued to assert that the Crystal City plant should be excluded from the unit, and refused to bargain with the Federation with respect to that group of employees.   Accordingly, about a month after its certification order, the Board issued a complaint in this proceeding, the third and pending stage of the labor dispute, alleging a refusal to bargain collectively in violation of §§8 (1) and (5).   At the hearing on this complaint, at which the Crystal City Union was permitted to intervene, the trial examiner excluded a certain offer of proof by it and the Company.   For various reasons the Board found that the exclusion was in part proper and for the rest non-prejudicial.   On the merits, the Board, with one member dissenting, adhered to its original view that the Crystal City plant should be included in the unit and therefore found that the Company had committed an unfair labor practice.[8]   The Company and the Crystal City Union sought review of the Board's decision in the Circuit Court of Appeals, which affirmed the ruling of the Board,[9] and we brought the case here on certiorari . . .

The petitioners' contention that §9 (a) grants to the majority

[5] 8 Cir., 102 F. (2d) 1004, enforcing 8 N.L.R.B. 1210.
[6] 10 N.L.R.B. 1111.
[7] 308 U.S. 401, 60 Sup. Ct. 300, 84 L. Ed. 347.
[8] 15 N.L.R.B. 515.
[9] 8 Cir., 113 F. (2d) 698.

of employees in a unit appropriate for such purposes the absolute
right to bargain collectively through representatives of their own
choosing is correct only in the sense that the "appropriate unit" is
the one declared by the Board under §9 (b), not one that might
be deemed appropriate under other circumstances.   In its Annual
Reports, the Board has stated the general considerations which
motivate its action:

> In determining whether the employees of one, several, or
> all plants of an employer, or the employees in all or only a
> part of a system of communications, transportation, or public
> utilities, constitute an appropriate unit for the purposes of
> collective bargaining, the Board has taken into consideration
> the following factors: (1) the history, extent, and type of
> organization of the employees; (2) the history of their collec-
> tive bargaining, including any contracts; (3) the history,
> extent, and type of organization, and the collective bargain-
> ing, of employees of other employers in the same industry;
> (4) the relationship between any proposed unit or units and
> the employer's organization, management, and operation of
> his business, including the geographical location of the vari-
> ous plants or parts of the system; and (5) the skill, wages,
> working conditions, and work of the employees.[12]

In its hearings on the appropriate unit the Board received evidence as to the organization of the Company, the variety of its
business, its distribution of this business into divisions and the
location, size and method of operation of its flat glass plants, which
composed the flat glass division.   The history of collective bargaining in the business was developed.   Finally the relation of the
several plants of the flat glass division was examined and the
characteristics of each plant and their respective employees gone
into.   From this evidence the Board determined that the production and maintenance employees of the six scattered flat glass plants
were the appropriate unit and that the Federation, which had
majorities of the employees in all the plants except Crystal City,
was the labor representative for purposes of collective bargaining.
The Company and the local union contend that Crystal City's
inclusion was erroneous because neither in the hearings on the
appropriate unit nor on this unfair labor practice did the Board
permit the introduction of material evidence on the question of

[12] Fourth Annual Report (1939) 89–90. See also First Annual Report
(1936) 112–20; Second Annual Report (1937) 122–40; Third Annual Report
(1938) 156–97; Fifth Annual Report (1940) 63–72.

appropriate units, the exclusion of which was prejudicial to the respondents.

While the ruling of the Board determining the appropriate unit for bargaining is not subject to direct review under the statute, the ruling is subject to challenge when, as here, a complaint of unfair practices is made, predicated upon the ruling.[13] Petitioners press that challenge upon the ground (1) that the procedure denied due process of law, (2) that there was no substantial evidence to justify the ruling, and (3) that the authority granted the Board is an unconstitutional delegation of legislative power. . . .

[After sustaining the refusal of the Board to admit evidence as to (1) the desires of the Crystal City employees for a separate local unit, (2) the freedom of the Crystal City Union from employer domination, (3) the fact that the Crystal City employees had distinct interests from employees at the other plants, (4) the fact that the Crystal City Union had bargained for the employees with the company until disestablished, and (5) the fact that the membership of the Crystal City Union had recently increased, Mr. Justice Reed concluded]:

Petitioners find failure of evidence to establish the appropriateness of the division-wide unit. It is true the record shows a substantial degree of local autonomy. Crystal City is a separate industrial unit, not one mechanically integrated into the division. The local superintendent deals with labor grievances, the plant has its own purchasing agent and there is no exchange of employees. On the other hand, labor policies and wages come from the central office in Pittsburgh; there is great similarity in the class of work done. Wages, hours, working conditions, manufacturing processes differ only slightly among the plants. An independent unit at Crystal City, the Board was justified in finding, would frustrate division-wide effort at labor adjustments. It would enable the employer to use the plant there for continuous operation in case of stoppage of labor at the other plants. We are of the view that there was adequate evidence to support the conclusion that the bargaining unit should be division-wide.

Finally petitioners urge that the standards for Board action as to the appropriate unit are inadequate to give a guide to the administrative action and the result is necessarily capricious, arbitrary and an unconstitutional delegation of legislative power. We find adequate standards to guide the Board's decision. While the

---

[13] A.F. of L. v. Labor Board, 308 U.S. 401, 408–411, 60 Sup. Ct. 300, 303, 304, 84 L. Ed. 347 (1939).

exact limits of the Board's powers or the precise meaning of the terms have not been fully defined, judicially, we know that they lie within the area covered by the words "employer," "plant," and "craft." The division-wide unit here deemed appropriate is well within these limits. As a standard, the Board must comply, also, with the requirement that the unit selected must be one to effectuate the policy of the Act, the policy of efficient collective bargaining. Where the policy of an act is so definitely and elaborately stated, this requirement acts as a permitted measure of delegated authority.

Affirmed.

[Justices Stone and Roberts and Chief Justice Hughes dissented. Their opinion has been omitted.]

NLRB, 6TH ANNUAL REPORT 65 (1941): "In Matter of Libbey-Owens-Ford Glass Company,[40] a labor organization, previously certified by the Board as the exclusive representative of the employees at all seven plants of the company,[41] filed charges alleging that the company had refused to bargain collectively with it concerning one of these plants, at Parkersburg. An opposing organization filed a petition requesting certification as the representative of the employees of the Parkersburg plant. The Board found that the Parkersburg plant constituted an appropriate bargaining unit, dismissing the charges that the company had refused to bargain collectively with the charging organization.[42] The Board stated:

" 'The Parkersburg plant, as we pointed out in our Decision and Certification of Representatives of January 30, 1939, has a history of separate organization and bargaining. Since January 30, 1939, the respondent (the employer), faced with the conflicting claims of the Federation (certified representative) and the National (petitioner) has refused to bargain with either as the representative of the Parkersburg employees. The Federation had no members at the Parkersburg plant when it was certified, and it has apparently gained none in the period of approximately 2 years which has elapsed since the prior proceeding. There is no showing that it now has any representation there. The record shows,

[40] Matter of Libbey-Owens-Ford Glass Co. and Federation of Glass, Ceramic and Silica Sand Workers, etc., 31 N.L.R.B. 243 (1941).
[41] Matter of Libbey-Owens-Ford Glass Co. and Federation of Flat Glass Workers, etc., 10 N.L.R.B. 1470 (1939).
[42] Board Member Edwin S. Smith dissented.

and it is not disputed, that the National is and has been the designated representative of almost all the employees at the Parkersburg plant.' "

The Pittsburgh Plate Glass and Libbey-Owens-Ford cases are discussed in Note, Determination of the "Appropriate Bargaining Unit" in Multi-plant Enterprises, 51 Yale L.J. 155 (1941).

GRAND UNION CO., 81 N.L.R.B. 1016, 23 L.R.R.M. 1444 (1949) : "The Petitioner seeks a unit limited to the employees in the Employer's Pittsfield, Massachusetts, store. The Employer contends that the unit requested is inappropriate and that only a unit embracing all the stores in its Northern Division, which includes the Pittsfield store, is appropriate.

"The Employer operates approximately 130 retail grocery stores, grouped, for administrative purposes, into 3 divisions. The Northern Division consists of 98 stores, which in turn are divided into 8 districts. In District 3 are the Pittsfield store, located in Massachusetts, and 11 others in Vermont and New York.

"The Northern Division is supervised by a division manager; under him, district sales managers supervise the stores within their respective districts. Purchases for all stores within the division are centralized in the division head, and each operates on a budget set by the division manager. All merchandise, except for local produce and dairy products, is requisitioned by each store from the division warehouse. The wage structure within the entire division is set by the division manager, who administers the Employer's general policies, some of which are determined by the president. The district sales manager coordinates all personnel policies within his district, but all promotions and transfers are subject to final approval by the division head. However, local store managers may discharge employees with less than 5 years' seniority without submitting such recommendations for approval. Though infrequent, there is some interchange of employees among the stores within the Northern Division, either to suit the need of the Employer or the desires of the employees themselves.

"Despite the geographic separation of the stores in the Northern Division, we believe that the centralized management control over all the stores, and the uniformity of wage rates and other terms and conditions of employment throughout the division, make a unit limited to the employees of a single store inappropriate.

Relying at least in part on the extent of organization among an employer's employees, the Board did at times establish units similar to that requested by the Petitioner herein.   But we are now precluded, by the amended Act, from giving controlling weight to this factor in any unit determination. . . .

"Herzog, Chairman, dissenting: I would direct an election among the employees at the Pittsfield store, the only one located in the Commonwealth of Massachusetts.   It is 25 miles away from the Employer's nearest store, located in New York State.   The many other stores in District 3 and in the Northern Division, one or the other of which must be believed by my colleagues to be the appropriate unit, are even more remote.   The furthest is on the Canadian border, over 200 miles away.

"Although a broader base for bargaining would certainly be preferable, I believe that the objective facts in the record disclose that there is more to support the Petitioner's position than the present extent of its organization of the employees.   Geographical factors alone provide a logical basis for setting up a unit of employees who are not interchanged with and have no contacts with their fellows in distant communities."

TEXAS ELECTRIC SERVICE CO., 77 N.L.R.B. 1258, 22 L.R.R.M. 1143 (1948): "The Petitioner seeks a single unit composed of all production and maintenance employees in the Employer's Fort Worth and Handley plants, excluding watchmen, engineers, student engineers, clerical employees, and supervisors as defined by the Act.   On the other hand, the Petitioner indicates it is not 'unfriendly' to single-plant units.   The Employer, which has no history of collective bargaining, is in substantial accord with this unit definition, but contends that there should be a separate production and maintenance unit for each plant; . . .

"The Forth Worth and Handley Plants, although located within the city limits of Fort Worth, are approximately 7 miles apart. Except for their geographical proximity, which is not disproportionate in relation to some of the Employer's other plants, there seems to be no reason for grouping these plants together. Of the two involved, the Handley plant is the newer, and uses a type of equipment different from that found in the Fort Worth plant. The record is clear that additional training would be required before employees of the Forth Worth plant would be qualified to work at the Handley plant.   Likewise there is evidence to indicate that employees are not interchanged between the two plants involved, or between any of the seven other plants owned by the employer. In view of the above, and the fact that each of the employer's nine plants is under separate supervision, we believe that the unit problem should be resolved on an individual plant basis.

"Under all the circumstances, we find that separate bargaining units for the employees of the Fort Worth and Handley plants, respectively, are appropriate for the purposes of collective bargaining."

Compare Note, Recent Trends of the New York State Labor Relations Board in Determining the Appropriate Bargaining Unit, 47 Col. L. Rev. 1220 (1947). See NLRB, 16th Ann. Rep. 97–102 (1951).

(4) *Multiple Employers*

NLRB, 12TH ANNUAL REPORT 21 (1947) : "As already noted, the Board sometimes found units appropriate which went beyond the confines of the employees of a single employer. It had established single units of employees of independent and competing employers if it appeared that the employers, either as members of an employer association or otherwise, had in practice handled their labor relations jointly and had demonstrated by customary adherence to uniform labor agreements resulting therefrom that they desired to be bound by group rather than individual action.[83] The Board, however, recognized the right of a member of such a group to withdraw from that type of bargaining. In this connection, it found appropriate a unit confined to the employees of one such employer provided that the employer in question demonstrated an intent to pursue an individual or separate course with reference to his labor relations.[84] However, this was not to say that the Board would always refuse to find a multiple employer

[83] Matter of T. C. King Pipe Company et al., 74 N.L.R.B. 468; cf. Matter of Foreman & Clark, 74 N.L.R.B. 77, and Matter of Martinolich Shipbuilding Company, et al., 73 N.L.R.B. 1304. Cf. also Matter of California Metal Trades Association, 72 N.L.R.B. 624, in which the employer association's power to bind its members to collective bargaining agreements stemmed not from mere membership in the association but from powers of attorney. Under these circumstances the unit was limited to those member firms which had delivered outstanding powers of attorney to the association before the execution of the last master contract, thereby properly indicating their desire to be part of the association-wide unit.

[84] Matter of Canada Dry Ginger Ale, Incorporated, 73 N.L.R.B. 460, and Matter of General Baking Company (Bond Plant), 73 N.L.R.B. 44.

unit appropriate in a situation where the constituent employers who had functioned jointly in the past oppose such a finding. Thus, in two cases generally designated as Matter of Waterfront Employers Association of the Pacific Coast et al., 71 N.L.R.B. 80 and 71 N.L.R.B. 121, the Board held, despite contentions to the contrary by employer associations and by many of their member companies, that they did not wish to bargain on a multiple employer basis, that it was empowered under the act to find multiple employer units appropriate, and that the circumstances justified exercise of that power.   In both cases, the employer associations, by their activities, were found to have brought themselves within the statutory definition of employer.   Further, the state of organization of the associations and the union involved, as well as the character of their activities, showed that adequate machinery for the conduct of multiple employer bargaining existed."

NOTES

1. See Note, The N.L.R.B. and Multi-Employer Units in a Competitive Economy, 43 Ill. L. Rev. 877 (1949) ; Levy, Multi-Employer Bargaining and the Anti-Trust Laws (1949).

2. Compare Section 9 (3) of the Canadian Industrial Relations and Disputes Investigation Act, 1948: "Where an application for certification under this Act is made by a trade union claiming to have as members in good standing a majority in a unit that is appropriate for collective bargaining, which includes employees of two or more employers, the Board shall not certify the trade union as the bargaining agent of the employees in the unit unless (a) all employers of the said employees consent thereto; and (b) the Board is satisfied that the trade union might be certified by it under this section as the bargaining agent of the employees in the unit of each such employer if separate applications for such purpose were made by the trade union."

3. Air Conditioning Co. of Southern California, 79 N.L.R.B. 1396, 23 L.R.R.M. 1014 (1948) : "The Petitioner seeks a multi-employer unit of all refrigeration fitters and apprentices employed by the 50 Employers (consisting of the 31 members of the Association, the 2 former members and the 17 non-member Employers). The Intervenors oppose the 50-employer unit upon the ground that there is no history of bargaining in a multi-employer unit by the 17 non-members of the Association.   The Association takes a neutral position with respect to the requested unit.   The 17 non-

member Employers were not represented at the hearings; therefore, their position with respect to the unit is not indicated.   Neel Refrigeration Company and Thompson Refrigeration Service, who were former members of the Association, but who resigned after the petition was filed in this proceeding, appeared at the hearing and requested that they be excluded from any multi-employer unit that might be found appropriate.

"The petitioner relies solely upon the history of collective bargaining to support its request for a multi-employer unit of 50 Employers.   On January 1, 1947, the Association, for and on behalf of its members, negotiated a master collective bargaining agreement with the Petitioner.   There is no evidence, however, that the 17 non-members of the Association participated in these negotiations.   Without any semblance of bargaining, the 17 non-members signed agreements identical to the master agreement executed by the Association.   This course of conduct cannot be considered as true collective bargaining on a multi-employer basis covering employees of both the members of the Association and the 17 non-members, particularly as the latter were in no way obligated to follow the Association's lead.   We find, therefore, the unit sought by the Petitioner is inappropriate."

Air Conditioning Co. of Southern California, 81 N.L.R.B. 946, 23 L.R.R.M. 1440 (1949) : "[In the original decision in this case] an area-wide multi-employer unit, including the employees of the Members and of the Non-members, as originally requested by the Petitioners, was found inappropriate.   The Petitioner now requests a single unit of refrigeration fitters and apprentices employed by the Members, based upon past bargaining history of the Association, and separate units of similar employees of each of the Non-members.   [The intervenors] contend that the employees of each of the Members, as well as the employees of each of the Non-members, constitute [separate units]. . . .

". . . One of the main functions of the [employer trade association] is the establishment of sound labor relations policies for the Members.   To this end, the negotiating committee of the Association has been authorized by the Members to represent them jointly in collective bargaining negotiations with the union representing their employees. . . .   The Association has negotiated at least one contract on behalf of the Members, and, but for the schism within the membership of Local 508, was ready in 1947 to enter into further negotiations [for another contract].

"The negotiating committee did not, however, have authority

to execute contracts binding upon the Members; instead the draft of the proposed master contract was submitted to the Members individually for their respective signatures. . . .

"The Intervenors contend that, inasmuch as the Members have not delegated to the Association negotiating committee power to bind the Members in its negotiations, no true pattern of bargaining has been established upon an association basis, and hence no ground exists for finding appropriate a unit coextensive with the bargaining conducted by the Association. However, the decided cases do not support the Intervenors' contention.

"The Board has recently had occasion to reexamine the question of the prerequisites for the establishment of multiple-employer units, Matter of Associated Shoe Industries of Southeastern Massachusetts, Inc. et al., 81 N.L.R.B. 224 [23 L.R.R.M. 1320] . . . The Board therein affirmed its prior decisions which held that participation in joint bargaining negotiations and the uniform adoption of the agreement resulting from such negotiations by the participants in the negotiations indicated a desire on the part of said participants to be bound by joint rather than individual action and therefore warranted the establishment of a multiple-employer unit. [See Matter of Rayonier Incorporated, 52 N.L.R.B. 1269, 1274–1275; Matter of Dolese & Shepard, 56 N.L.R.B. 532, 539; Matter of Advance Tanning Company, 60 N.L.R.B. 923, 931. . . .] In the present case, the Members through having authorized the negotiating committee to negotiate on their behalf, and by their uniform acceptance of the agreement negotiated by the committee, have met the prerequisites which warrant the inclusion of their employees in a multiple-employer unit."

[The Board also held that separate individual employer units of refrigeration fitters and apprentices employed by companies which are not members of the employer trade association are appropriate even assuming that three of such employers are technically members of the association, since these three employers have manifested an intent to pursue their own courses of action with respect to labor relations by opposing the inclusion of their employees in the multiple-employer unit, by giving notice that they will not be bound by an extension of the existing contract, and by stating that the negotiating committee of the association is no longer authorized to bargain on their behalf.]

"[Houston and Murdock, Members, concurring in the result]: In Matter of Associated Shoe Industries of Southeastern Mass., Inc., et al., 81 N.L.R.B. 224 [23 L.R.R.M. 1320 (1949)], we have recently expressed disagreement with the Board's policy with respect to multiple-employer units involving association members and non-members, set forth in Matter of Advance Tanning Company, 60 N.L.R.B. 923 (1945).

"Here, no less than in the Associated Shoe case, we disagree with so much of the rationale of our colleagues as makes participation in preliminary negotiations of collective bargaining agreements a prerequisite for a multiple-employer unit. The record before us, however, does not disclose the existence of such *other* facts as impelled us to find appropriate a unit including the non-members in the Associated Shoe case. We are not persuaded, on the basis of the present record, that the non-members have truly manifested a desire to be bound by group action to such an extent that they should be included with the Association members in order to "assure to the employees the fullest freedom in exercising the rights guaranteed" by the Act. Section 9 (b) of the amended Act. In these circumstances, we concur in the result reached by our colleagues."

4. What authority has the NLRB, in light of the language of Section 9 (b) of the NLRA, to establish multiple-employer units?

5. Compare the Board's policy of resolving multiple-employer unit questions by ascertaining whether the employers have manifested a desire to be bound by group rather than individual action with (a) the policy lying behind self-determination elections (see pages 147–148 supra), and (b) the policy reflected by Sections 8 (b) (1) (B) and (4) (A) of the NLRA.

6. In Matter of Marcellus M. Murdock, d.b.a. the Wichita Eagle, 69 N.L.R.B. 1270, 18 L.R.R.M. 1315 (1946), the Board, in finding a separate unit appropriate (as petitioned by the union), said that a history of multiple-employer bargaining for printers does not determine the extent of the unit for editorial employees. In Matter of Epp Furniture Company, 86 N.L.R.B. 120, 24 L.R.R.M. 1618 (1949), the Board, in finding a multiple unit appropriate (as petitioned by the union), said that a history of multiple bargaining for shipping and repairing employees manifested a desire by the employers to be bound in collective bargaining by joint rather than individual action and controlled the type of unit appropriate for salesmen. Can these cases be reconciled?

To what extent is the Board still guided in these unit cases by the extent to which the employees have organized, despite the language of Section 9 (c) (5) of Taft-Hartley? Should the Board find a multiple-employer unit appropriate when the Union does not have majority support of the employees of each employer, in light of Section 9 (b) of Taft-Hartley, which sets up the standard of assurance to employees of the fullest freedom in exercising the rights guaranteed by the Act (which includes, in Section 7, the right to refrain from collective bargaining) ? To what extent did Congress, in Taft-Hartley, intend to adopt the Canadian rule? (See Note 2, page 164 supra.)

c. Conduct of the Election

NLRB, 13TH ANNUAL REPORT 32 (1948) : "Section 9 (c) of the act, as amended, prescribes the election by secret ballot as the sole method of resolving a question concerning representation, and leaves the Board without the discretion it formerly possessed (but rarely exercised) [39] to utilize other 'suitable means' of ascertaining representatives. With certain significant exceptions, discussed below, the Labor Management Relations Act of 1947 has left to the Board's discretion all other matters pertaining to the determination of representatives, including, for example, selection of the time and place when elections are to be conducted, the method whereby a forthcoming election is to be publicized, the mechanics of the balloting, the identification of eligible voters, and appraisal of the election results. And, except for adaptations required by the new statutory provisions, the Board has adhered to its previously enunciated rules and practices governing representation elections, without significant change during this fiscal year."

NLRB, 13TH ANNUAL REPORT 28–29 (1948) : "The Board also continued to invoke the rule that an election will not be delayed merely because of an imminent reduction or expansion in force, unless the change-over will involve material alterations in the character of the bargaining unit, or the adoption of new or materially different operations or processes requiring personnel with different job classifications and skills. Matter of Allied Container Corp., 76 N.L.R.B. 1186; see Twelfth Annual Report, p. 8 ff. However, section 9 (c) (3) has put an end to the prior practice, in situations where less than 50 percent of the anticipated full complement was employed at the time of the election, of providing in the

---

[39] But see A Guide to the N.L.R.A. (U.S. Dept. of Labor, Div. of Labor Statistics, Bull. No. 81, 1946), p. 21, stating that 15 per cent of the petitions filed from 1935 to 1945 were disposed of by consent cross-checks or recognition agreements. — ED.

decision that the Board would entertain a new petition 6 months after any certification which might be issued, upon a showing that the unit had expanded to more than twice the number of employees eligible to vote in the election.

GOODALL CO., 80 N.L.R.B. 562, 23 L.R.R.M. 1138 (1948): ". . . The Employer urges that an election among the employees in its Talladega plant would be premature at this time, as it is engaged in an expansion program and expects to increase the number of its production and maintenance employees from 550 to 1,200 within the next 18 months. It further asserts that the present complement of employees does not constitute a fair cross section of the personnel which will ultimately be in its employ. The Petitioner desires an immediate election. The employees of the Talladega plant currently perform 541 operations essential to the production of wash suits. Although the plant expansion program calls for an increase of approximately 100 per cent in both personnel and machinery, the Employer does not anticipate a material change in these operations or an increase in their number. We are, therefore, of the opinion that the unit herein found appropriate is representative of the work force which the Employer may reasonably anticipate. Accordingly, we find that the employer's plant expansion program does not prevent an election at this time. Matter of Western Electric Company, Incorporated, 76 N.L.R.B. 400. Election directed."

Compare Sparton Teleoptic Co., 81 N.L.R.B. 1228, 23 L.R.R.M. 1515 (1949) (employer had arranged to terminate production).

NLRB, 13TH ANNUAL REPORT 32-33 (1948): "The standards determining eligibility to vote in Board-directed elections are familiar; generally all persons who were employed in the appropriate unit at the time when the direction of [sic] election issued are eligible to vote, unless they quit or were discharged for cause between that date and the date of the election itself. But the old rule that employees engaged in a current strike are eligible to participate in the choice of a collective bargaining representative has been modified by Section 9 (c) (3) of the Act, as amended, which provides in part, 'Employees on strike who are not entitled to reinstatement shall not be eligible to vote.' This statutory provision must be read in the light of the Board's long-standing rule that employees participating in an 'economic strike,' as contrasted with those engaged in a strike caused by unfair labor practices, are not entitled to be reinstated if, when they apply, their jobs have been filled by replacement workers. Despite this rule, under which economic strikers, so called, are not absolutely 'entitled' to reinstatement, it was the Board's consistent view, prior to the 1947 amendments, that such strikers were eligible to vote in representation elections, even though they had been replaced.[39a]   This was partly because their status as employees was expressly preserved by that portion of Section 2 (3) of the Act which defines the term 'employee' as including 'any individual whose work has ceased as a consequence of, or in connection with, any current labor dispute or because of any unfair labor practice.'

"This doctrine is now specifically overruled by the quoted language of Section 9 (c) (3).[39b]   Accordingly, in cases where a strike is current at the time of an election, the Board now denies the franchise to those striking employees who have been 'permanently replaced.'[82]   Frequently as in the leading Pipe Machinery

---

[39a] ". . . [E]ven if strikers have been replaced by other employees, it is impossible during the currency of an economic strike to determine, despite what an employer may predict, whether or not the strikers will return to their jobs. It is common knowledge that strikes frequently have been concluded by settlements pursuant to which the strikers have been reinstated. Were we to hold that, during the height of an economic contest, strikers are ineligible to vote because they have no expectancy of returning to work, our holding would be tantamount to a determination that the struggle had been lost by the strikers . . . Although economic strikers certainly have no absolute right to their jobs, . . . they should be permitted, while the strike is still current, to select representatives to bargain with the employer on the question of their possible reinstatement." Matter of Columbia Pictures Corp., 64 N.L.R.B. 490, 520, 17 L.R.R.M. 103, 105 (1945). — ED.

[39b] "The Intervenor contends that to apply Section 9 (c) (3) so as to deny such strikers the right to vote would be to sanction a readily contrived device for breaking strikes, and that such a result would be contrary to the protection of the right to strike afforded by Section 13 of the amended Act. But Section 9 (c) (3) places no limitation on the right to strike although it may indeed discourage its exercise in some situations by denying the franchise to those strikers who lose their right to reinstatement. The Intervenor asserts that this places such hazards upon the exercise of the right to strike as to make the guarantee of that right in Section 13 of the Act a nullity. This contention . . . should be directed to the Congress. . . . Accordingly, in determining the voting eligibility of the strikers, we confine ourselves to the question of whether or not particular strikers are entitled to reinstatement. The questions are questions of fact." Matter of Pipe Machinery Co., 79 N.L.R.B. 1322, 1324, 22 L.R.R.M. 1510, 1511 (1948). — ED.

[82] The general rule that temporary employees, as distinguished from those who have a substantial expectancy of future employment, are ineligible to vote in Board-directed elections still stands. Consequently a crucial issue commonly presented in the economic strike cases is whether or not replace-

case, 76 N.L.R.B. 247, which was first before the Board in February 1948, it cannot be accurately determined at the time the election is directed which strikers have been validly replaced and which are still entitled to reinstatement. The Board therefore provided in the cited case and others like it that both the strikers and the replacement workers would be deemed presumptively eligible and permitted to cast ballots subject to challenge. In the Pipe Machinery case, a supplemental hearing on challenged ballots was held after the election; the Board then (in the October 1948, decision) disposed of the issues upon the basis of the evidence showing the status of strikers and their replacements as of the time of the election."

Compare Section 8 (d) of the N.L.R.A., as amended, the last sentence: "Any employee who engages in a strike within the sixty-day period specified in this subsection shall lose his status as an employee of the employer engaged in the particular labor dispute, for the purposes of Sections 8, 9 and 10 of this Act, as amended, but such loss of status for such employee shall terminate if and when he is re-employed by such employer." [40]

In Times Square Stores Corp., 79 N.L.R.B. 361, 22 L.R.R.M. 1373 (1948), on an employer's petition, the Board held that it could not, from the facts presented in a representation case, determine whether or not a strike was an unfair labor practice strike in order to rule on challenges to ballots cast by 109 strikers. Stating that "an initial finding that a strike was caused by unfair labor practices may be made only in unfair labor practice proceedings," the Board found that the strike was "economic," that

---

ment workers are "permanent" employees. In Matter of The Pipe Machinery Co., 79 N.L.R.B., 1322 (Supplemental Decision and Direction issued October 13, 1948), the Board found that a group of economic strikers had been permanently replaced and that the strikers were therefore not "entitled" to reinstatement within the meaning of Section 9 (c) (3). The Board stressed the following facts: The replacement workers as well as the strikers themselves had been told by the employer that the newly hired employees were being employed on a permanent basis and would not be "bumped" by strikers seeking to return to work after a certain date; most of the replacement workers had previously engaged in the same or similar work as that for which they were hired by this employer; and the new employees were recruited from the geographical area in which the plant was located. In addition, the Board pointed out that there was no showing that any of the individuals currently on strike had ever made an unconditional application for reinstatement.

[40] See pages 725–742 infra, for rules governing the right of strikers to reinstatement.

the 121 replacements were eligible to vote, and that the strikers were not.

FELDESMAN, Principles in Representative Cases, 22 L.R.R.M. 31, 44 (1948): "If the Board finds that a question concerning representation affecting commerce has arisen in an appropriate unit, it now invariably directs an election to resolve the question and determine which, if any, labor organization is the exclusive bargaining representative. A majority of the valid votes cast determines representative status in all three types of Representation Cases.[41]

"In one union case [involving a single union only], employees are asked to indicate on the ballot 'Yes' or 'No' to the question 'Do you wish to be represented by X union for the purposes of collective bargaining?' In two or more union cases [cases involving two or more unions], the employees are asked to indicate on the ballot if they wish to be represented for collective bargaining purposes by X union or Y union, or neither [by no union].

"The pay-roll period immediately preceding the Direction of Election ordinarily determines eligibility to vote. To be eligible a person must have been employed during the pay-roll period and on the day of the election. Employees transferred into or out of the voting unit between the pay-roll period and date of the election are not eligible. Employees who are ill or on vacation or temporarily laid off are eligible. . . .

"A ballot must be challenged when the voter seeks to cast it at the election — not after it had been cast and commingled. Where an employer failed to challenge a ballot at the election and sought to do so afterward, one vote being determinative of the election, the Board refused to permit him to do so. The Board's position in that case, the Tower case, was upheld by the Supreme Court, in 329 U.S. 324. If, however, a Board agent is aware of the ineligibility of a voter and fails to challenge him, the Board will entertain a post-election challenge and set aside the election if necessary."[42]

---

[41] Provided a representative number of the eligible employees cast ballots. See NLRB, 12th Ann. Rep. 18 (1947), 11th Ann. Rep. 23 (1946). The "representative number" voting requirement was held satisfied when 40 per cent voted, in A. A. Fagan, 73 N.L.R.B. 680, 20 L.R.R.M. 1043 (1947), and when 32 per cent voted in Evans & Son, 75 N.L.R.B. 811, 21 L.R.R.M. 1081 (1948), but not when only 40 out of 218 voted, in Northwest Packing Co., 65 N.L.R.B. 890, 17 L.R.R.M. 249 (1946). — Ed.

[42] For the details of the Board's election and run-off election procedure,

WILLCOX and LEVY, The "Run-off" Election Under the Wagner Act — A Review and a Proposal, 32 Cornell L.Q. 490, 491 (1947): ". . . the problems of the industrial election are matters of considerable public importance.

"One of the knottiest of these problems, and one of the most crucial, is that of the 'run-off' election. If the initial ballot contains spaces in which to vote for one of two unions or more and contains also a space in which the worker may vote against having any union at all, it may happen that none of these choices will receive a majority of all the ballots cast. In such a case the Board usually orders a run-off election. What choices ought to appear upon the second, or run-off ballot?

"Should it present a choice between the highest union and no union at all? The Board so decided in the Coos Bay case [5] in October, 1939. Should it present a choice between the two highest unions? The same Board so decided five months later in the LeBlond case.[6] If more workers vote for 'no-union' than for either of the two unions, should any run-off at all be held? At the end of another three months the same Board said 'no' and dismissed the petitions for investigation in the General Motors case.[7] No two of the three Board members could agree. Should all except the two highest choices be eliminated in every case? This would follow the logic and the analogy of the political run-off election.[8]

"Where 'no-union' has a plurality, as in the General Motors case, should a run-off be held between the higher union and 'no-union'? Where 'no-union' comes in second, or worse than second, should a run-off be held between the two highest unions only? These two solutions, with some exceptions and qualifications, represent the policy of the Board as expressed in a Regulation which it adopted, after public hearings, in the summer of

---

see NLRB, Rules and Regulations, Ser. 6 (effective March 1, 1951), Secs. 102.61 and 102.62. — ED.

[5] In the Matter of Coos Bay Lumber Co., 16 N.L.R.B. 476 (1939), Mr. William M. Leiserson dissenting. . . .

[6] In the Matter of R. K. LeBlond Machine Tool Co., 22 N.L.R.B. 465 (1940), partial dissents by Chairman Madden and Mr. Leiserson.

[7] In the Matter of General Motors Corp., 25 N.L.R.B. 258 (1940). Each of the three Board members took a different view. The results of this trio of decisions are easier to understand if it is noted that the Board takes two votes in each case: the first, on the question whether a run-off election shall be ordered; and the second, if the motion for a run-off has carried, on the question whether a proposed ballot-form shall be adopted.

[8] The Board temporarily adopted this view, as among unions, in In the Matter of Aluminum Co. of America, 12 N.L.R.B. 237 (1939).

1943.[9]　One of the most important of the qualifications is that no union shall find a place upon the run-off ballot unless that union polled at least 20% of the votes cast in the original election. Since the average for each of three choices would be $33\frac{1}{3}\%$, this limitation upon the other rules must operate to eliminate a considerable number of third-choice unions.　The other important qualification is that no more than one run-off will ever be held. In this the Board Rule departs from previous Board policy as expressed in 1939."

NLRB, 13TH ANNUAL REPORT 35 (1948) : "Section 9 (c) (3) of the act as amended provides in part, 'In any election where none of the choices on the ballot receives a majority a run-off shall be conducted, the ballot providing for a selection between the two choices receiving the largest and second largest number of valid votes cast in the election.' . . .　[See N.L.R.B., 14th Ann. Rep. 30–31 (1949).]　It alters certain features of the Board's practice respecting run-off elections in this respect: whereas, under the rules and regulations in effect before the 1947 amendments, the 'neither' or 'none' choice was eliminated from the run-off ballot unless it received a plurality of votes cast in the original election, this choice now must appear on the run-off ballot if it received either the highest or second highest number of votes."

NLRB, 13TH ANNUAL REPORT 34–35 (1948) : "The Board is keenly aware of its responsibility to the parties in representation cases and to the public for the maintenance of high standards governing the conduct of elections under its auspices.　Its objective in each case is to insure that the secret ballot is held under conditions enabling employees to register a free and untrammeled choice for or against a bargaining representative.　When a party in a representation case files timely objections, the Board will set the election aside if its investigation reveals that there was any substantial defect or irregularity in the conduct of the balloting or that the employees' freedom to express their true desires in the election was inhibited by 'antecedent conduct or episodes which were both (1) coercive in character, and (2) so related to the election in time or otherwise as to have had a probable effect upon

---

[9] . . . National Labor Relations Board, Rules and Regulations, Series 4, issued August 28, 1946.　The change had become effective on August 23, 1943, Sec. 203.56

the employees' action at the polls.' On the other hand, the Board eschews the role of censor and declines to vacate elections because of activities in the nature of 'campaign propaganda.'

"Unremedied unfair labor practices constituting coercion of employees are generally regarded by the Board as grounds for vacating an election,[42a] but the converse is not always true. The Board has the power to set aside an election, in the exercise of its discretion, because of any conduct or circumstances militating against the employees' freedom of choice, even though the objectionable conduct in a particular case may not quite be an unfair labor practice subject to prevention in complaint proceedings. In such a case, the Board will occasionally set aside the election if it is convinced that there was serious interference with the employees' free exercise of their franchise; but, as the majority remarked in Matter of General Shoe Corp., 77 N.L.R.B. 124, it will exercise its power in this area only 'sparingly.' If the alleged interference consists solely of an employer's antiunion propaganda falling within the 'free speech' privilege defined in Section 8 (c) of the amended Act, the Board is disinclined to vacate the election. There are, of course, many representation cases in which the validity of an election is called into question by an objecting party, but there is no companion unfair labor practice case presenting the issue whether the alleged interference with the election is also a violation of the Act. In those cases, the Board determines only the question whether there has been substantial interference with the election, and does not consider the possible applicability of the unfair labor practice provisions of the statute." [43]

Elections were set aside in Marshalltown Trowell Co., 81 N.L.R.B. 1050, 23 L.R.R.M. 1481 (1949) (employer announced first vacation and holiday plan, "if the union doesn't come in," between filing of petition and date of election) ; Craddock-Terry Shoe Corp. (Farmville plant), 82 N.L.R.B. 161, 23 L.R.R.M. 1529 (1949) (in former years, on last pay day before plant closed for vacation, paymaster had distributed single checks including

---

[42a] If unfair labor practice charges affecting the bargaining unit are pending, the Board will not ordinarily hold an election immediately — unless the charging party files a waiver to the effect that the alleged unfair practice will not later be used for the purpose of objecting to the election. NLRB, 16th Ann. Rep. 127–128 (1951) . — ED.

[43] Compare this with pages 588–595 infra, dealing with the privilege of free speech in unfair labor practice cases. — ED.

pay for week worked and vacation pay; this year, the day after the election was the last payday before the plant closed for vacation; but on the day before the election, the foreman distributed checks for vacation pay only) ; G. H. Hess, Inc., 82 N.L.R.B. 463, 23 L.R.R.M. 1581 (1949) (the union organizer, three days before the election, told a woman employee: (1) "If you don't vote for the union, the girls will refuse to work with you"; (2) "When four o'clock comes [quitting time on election day, just before polls to open], to keep from causing hard feelings, will you put your hat and coat on and walk out of the factory"; and (3) "There has been a lot of rough stuff at these union elections."   Members Reynolds and Gray voted to set aside the election because of all three statements.   Chairman Herzog concurred solely because of the last two statements, and Members Houston and Murdock dissented).

The Board refused to set aside the election in Fairbanks Co., 81 N.L.R.B. 864, 23 L.R.R.M. 1420 (1948) (union official, coming out of manager's office several hours before election, told several employees, including chairman of shop committee, he had seen manager's papers arranging for a wage cut if the union lost the election; manager issued statement 40 minutes before election began, specifically denying report.   Member Gray dissented) ; L. H. Butcher Co., 81 N.L.R.B. 1184, 23 L.R.R.M. 1479 (1949) (on day of election, president of employer read prepared address to employees, in which he listed certain benefits given the employees in the past, including personal loans, overtime and rest-period arrangements, and a pension and insurance plan, saying that if the union won, the employees would have a "stranger" in their midst and from that time forward would have to go to the "stranger for everything").

The existence of an economic strike is not sufficient, per se, to prevent the holding of an election; absent violence or other gross misconduct the presence of the usual activity accompanying strikes away from the restricted polling area, e.g., picketing, does not, per se, invalidate an election.   West-Gate Sun Harbor Co., 93 N.L.R.B. 830, 27 L.R.R.M. 1474 (1951).

5. SUBSEQUENT REPRESENTATION PROCEEDINGS

The problems that now follow arise, if at all, after a collective bargaining relationship has been established between the employer and the representative of the employees.   Frequently the collective bargaining relationship bears the stamp of an NLRB certification. But it may have come into existence without any prior Board action.

An employer, when confronted with evidence that the union seeking recognition as the representative of the employees has majority support among the employees in the plant or in the area of the plant which has been organized, may voluntarily recognize the union and sign a contract with it. Many impelling considerations and circumstances may persuade an employer to take this action rather than to instigate NLRB proceedings himself, or to await the union's action in filing a petition.

a. Unit Redeterminations

In the Matter of

NATIONAL TUBE COMPANY
National Labor Relations Board, 1948
76 N.L.R.B. 1199, 21 L.R.R.M. 1292

The issue before us is whether the amended Act requires or should induce the Board to conduct an election among certain bricklayers in order to afford them an opportunity to sever themselves from a long-established industrial unit, in the basic steel industry.

The Petitioner [Bricklayers' Union, AFL] seeks a craft unit of bricklayers and apprentices, employed at the Employer's Lorain, Ohio plant. They are engaged primarily in the construction and repair of blast furnaces and related equipment used in the production of basic steel. In support of its position, the Petitioner contends that, regardless of prior decisions of the Board with respect to craft severance in this industry, the Board is now required under Section 9 (b) (2) [2] of the amended Act, to grant an election to a group of craft employees seeking separate representation for the purposes of collective bargaining. The Petitioner also contends that, in any event, the Board should, upon the facts in the present record, find appropriate the unit it requests.

The Intervenor [USA–CIO] and the Employer both oppose as inappropriate the unit sought by the Petitioner herein . . . In addition, both the Intervenor and the Employer contend that, if

---

[2] Section 9 (b) (2) provides, in part, that the Board shall not "decide that any craft unit is inappropriate for such purposes on the ground that a different unit has been established by a prior Board determination unless a majority of the employees in the proposed craft unit vote against separate representation."

the Board may consider the application of the new Section 9 (b) (2) in the present instance, the Board is not required by this provision to grant craft severance to these bricklayers, because of the degree of integration in the basic steel manufacturing process and the history of collective bargaining by this Employer and by employers generally in the basic steel industry.

On July 30, 1942, the Intervenor was certified, in accordance with a stipulation for a consent election, as exclusive bargaining representative for a multiple-plant unit of the Employer's production and maintenance employees. Thereafter the Intervenor bargained for all such employees, including bricklayers, under a series of collective bargaining agreements, the most recent of which was executed as of April 22, 1947. The record indicates that the collective bargaining history of the Employer has followed the pattern of collective bargaining generally in the steel industry, which has been predominately on an industrial basis. No unit confined to bricklayers has ever been established among the employees in any operation controlled by the United States Steel Corporation, the parent of the Employer. The record further shows that the same situation exists at the plants of 65 other companies engaged in the production of basic steel. . . .

We come, therefore, to the Petitioner's contention that under Section 9 (b) (2) the Board is required to establish a separate bargaining unit for a group of craft employees, unless there is a vote against separate representation by a majority of such employees. This contention is, in effect, that Section 9 (b) (2), which precludes the Board from finding a craft unit inappropriate on the ground that a different unit had been established "by a prior Board determination," removes from the Board's discretion not only the power to rely upon a prior decision as the basis for finding a proposed craft unit inappropriate, but also the power to find a craft unit inappropriate by reason either of any collective bargaining history or of other circumstances upon which we have customarily based a determination as to the appropriateness or inappropriateness of a proposed craft unit.

This argument asserts that no discretion exists, and is not directed to the Board's exercise of discretion. Recent decisions should make it apparent that the Board has been inclined recently to exercise discretion in the direction of easing the path of a union desiring severance of a craft unit. That is not the primary problem before us here, nor is this decision to be taken to mean that that trend is about to be reversed.

. . . the statute clearly states that the Board's action in finding

a craft unit inappropriate shall not be based upon the fact that a
different unit has been established by a prior Board determination.
. . . We find . . . that Section 9 (b) (2) does not itself limit the
Board's discretion to find a craft unit inappropriate in certain
situations, so long as there is no reliance upon the fact that a
different unit has already been established by a prior Board determination.[11]

Had Congress desired to deprive the Board of all discretion in
matters of this sort, it had only to adopt language similar to the
mandatory craft proviso contained in the New York State Labor
Relations Act.[12] Although this was urged at the hearings on the
bill, Congress saw fit not to enact it into law. . . .

Even on the assumption, however, that the legislative history
might be construed as indicating an intent on the part of Congress
to eliminate altogether the American Can doctrine, 13 N.L.R.B.
1252, 4 L.R.R.M. 392 (1939), so that neither a prior Board determination nor the bargaining history of a particular employer
could be relied upon as the controlling factor in a decision finding
a craft unit inappropriate, it is clear that the only restriction imposed by Section 9 (b) (2) is that such prior determination or bargaining history may not be the sole ground upon which the Board
may decide that a craft unit is inappropriate without an election.
In other words, there is no basis for finding a Congressional intent
to prohibit the use of a prior Board determination or any bargaining history based thereon as a factor to be considered in determining the issue of craft severance, so long as neither is made the sole
ground upon which the Board predicates its decision . . . We
conclude that bargaining history in an industry may be considered
as a weighty factor in any Board decision affecting the issue of the
appropriateness of separate craft representation.

. . . there is nothing in either statute or legislative history to
preclude the Board from considering or giving such weight as it
deems necessary to the factors of bargaining history in an industry,

[11] This construction is meaningful in limiting the Board's discretion, because, at the very least, the Board may no longer support administrative or
other dismissal of craft petitions upon the sole ground of a prior Board
determination that a plantwide unit was appropriate. The question of the
appropriateness of the proposed craft grouping must be independently considered on its merits. In this case, therefore, we have explored the entire
situation *de novo*, without particular stress upon the certification issued in
1942 at 42 N.L.R.B. 1121.

[12] The craft proviso of the New York Act (Section 705 (2)) reads as follows: . . . provided, however, that in any case where the majority of employees of a particular craft shall so decide the Board shall designate such
craft as a unit appropriate for the purpose of collective bargaining.

the basic nature of the duties performed by the craft employees in relation to those of the production employees, the integration of craft functions with the over-all production processes of the employer, and many other circumstances upon which the Board has customarily based its determination as to the appropriateness or inappropriateness of a proposed unit.

We find, therefore, that the appropriateness of the unit requested by the Petitioner is a matter that lies within the discretion of the Board, to be determined upon all the factors in the case, including those just mentioned. We turn now to those factors.

The Petitioner's contention that bricklayers and apprentices employed at the particular plant of this Employer constitute an appropriate unit, is based primarily upon craft considerations and the alleged inadequacy of their past representation as part of the present plant-wide bargaining unit. The record discloses that, unlike the usual craft maintenance employees whose work on any particular piece of production equipment occurs for the most part at irregular intervals, the bricklayers and apprentices for whom the Petitioner seeks separate representation are engaged in a definite program of replacing and repairing on regularly succeeding occasions, the instrumentalities used in the continuous production of basic steel. Their functions are therefore intimately connected with the steelmaking process itself. The bricklayers and the steel production employees enjoy similar working conditions and, as already indicated, have been represented under a series of exclusive bargaining agreements between the Employer and the Intervenor, extending from 1942 through 1947, when the current collective bargaining agreement between the Employer and the Intervenor was executed.

The resultant integration of the bricklayers with the steel production employees has been further advanced by a job evaluation program recently completed pursuant to agreements between the Employer and the Intervenor. It covers all employees including bricklayers. The wage rates of production employees, including those of bricklayers and apprentices, have been integrated into a single coordinated wage structure. The experience of the Employer, as disclosed by its long history of collective bargaining with the Intervenor, is parallel to that of other employers in the steel industry, who generally have bargained upon the basis of an over-all unit in which craft employees, including bricklayers, have been included.

The Board is greatly impressed by the argument of the Employer that, due to the integrated nature of operations in the steel industry, any change in the unit governing the bargaining relations between the Employer and its employees would be detrimental to the basic wage rate structure underlying the Employer's present operations, and would necessarily have an adverse effect upon its productive capacity in an industry of vital national concern.

Upon consideration of all the foregoing circumstances, we are of the opinion that the factors relied upon by the Board in Matter of Geneva Steel Company, [57 N.L.R.B. 50], particularly those of integration and bargaining history in the industry, are equally present here. They continue to present a compelling argument in favor of an over-all bargaining unit, and against separate units of these particular craft employees in the basic steel industry. We find, accordingly, that the unit sought by this Petitioner is inappropriate for the purposes of collective bargaining. We shall therefore order that the petition in the instant proceedings be dismissed.

———

NLRB, 14TH ANNUAL REPORT 34 (1949): "During the past fiscal year, the Board continued to apply the National Tube doctrine of denying severance to craft groups in the basic steel industry, because of the complete integration of all employee functions in the steel-making process and the prevailing pattern of industrial units in the industry. For substantially the same reasons, the Board has refused to establish separate units for certain skilled groups in other industries where the work performed by these employees is a regular and indispensable segment of and is inextricably integrated with the production process."

The advent of Section 9 (b) (2) of the amended NLRA has increased the importance of the petition to "carve out," whereby a craft union requests the right to represent a segment of workers who formed a part of the initial bargaining unit. This fact is demonstrated by numerous cases decided recently by the Board.[44] See NLRB, 14th Ann. Rep. 33 (1949), 16th Ann. Rep. 91–92 (1951).

[44] Matter of W. S. Tyler Co., 93 N.L.R.B. 70, 27 L.R.R.M. 1426 (1951); Matter of Gulf Oil Corp., 92 N.L.R.B. 700, 27 L.R.R.M. 1140 (1950); Matter of New England Container Co., 92 N.L.R.B. 1430, 27 L.R.R.M. 1258 (1951).

TIN PROCESSING CORP.
National Labor Relations Board, 1948
80 N.L.R.B. 1369, 23 L.R.R.M. 1253

[The Oil Workers International Union (CIO) filed a petition raising a question concerning representation. At the hearing the employer and the intervening Tin Smelter Workers Union, Local 23198 (AFL) moved to dismiss the petition and to strike the intervention of Lodge 1446, International Association of Machinists.]

REYNOLDS, MURDOCK and GRAY, Members: . . . The Employer and the intervening Tin Smelters are in substantial agreement with the Petitioner that the unit should consist of all production and maintenance employees including laboratory employees and leadmen, but excluding all office and clerical, administrative, executive, and professional employees, plant protection employees, all supervisors and employees of the Electrical Department and the Pipe Department. The intervening Machinists seeks the severance from the production and maintenance unit of four groups which it claims are appropriate craft units. The units requested consist of: (1) All inside and outside machinists classified on the pay-roll as machinists, their helpers, apprentices, and oilers working under the supervision of the machine shop foreman, and including all employees engaged in the erection, assembling, dismantling, maintaining, and/or repairing of machinery by the Employer but excluding supervisors and all other employees; (2) All auto mechanics, truck mechanics, heavy-duty mechanics employed in the auxiliary repair shop, including tool crib attendants, repairmen classified on the pay-roll as machinists but excluding supervisors and all other employees; (3) All truck drivers excluding supervisors and all other employees; (4) All boiler firemen and their helpers, excluding supervisors and all other employees.

The Employer opposes the units sought by the Machinists, urging that the tin smelting industry in the United States is comparable to the basic steel industry and as such should fall under the principles announced in the National Tube Company case. It is urged that the Board erred in ordering an election in Cases Nos. 16–R–2418 and 16–R–2425, Matter of Tin Processing Corporation, 78 N.L.R.B. 96, allowing craft severance elections for separate groups of electricians and pipefitters employed by the Employer.

The Employer's production operations under the supervision

of the Plant Superintendent are carried on in several buildings consisting of three departments, i.e., Ore Storage and Ore Dressing, Roasting and Leaching, and Smelting and Refining. The maintenance departments under the supervision of the Maintenance Engineer service the production operation and consist of the following departments, each under the supervision of a foreman: Auxiliary, Pipefitters, Machinists, Riggers, Welders, Electricians, Carpenters, and Painters. A few employees from each maintenance department are assigned directly to each of the three production departments at all times. The other employees from each department are assigned in gangs to handle specific jobs.

The Board has determined that separate craft maintenance units in the basic steel industry may not be established because, unlike the usual craft maintenance employees whose work on production equipment occurs for the most part at irregular intervals, the craft maintenance employees in the basic steel industry are engaged in a definite program of replacing and repairing on regular succeeding occasions the instrumentalities used in the continuous production of basic steel, and that their functions are therefore intimately connected with the steelmaking process itself. However, the principle announced in the National Tube Company case, supra, is an exception to the general Board policy and is based on the high degree of integration of maintenance craftsmen with the production employees in the basic steel manufacturing process. It does not appear that a similar situation exists in the tin processing industry. On the contrary, it appears here that substantially all employees in each craft group generally remain in the maintenance divisions from which they are sent out in crews to work wherever the occasion may arise, in much the same manner as general maintenance crews in most industries. We therefore conclude that the facts in the instant case do not warrant a finding that any craft maintenance employees herein are an inseparable part of the over-all production unit.

The Tin Smelters oppose the units sought by the Machinists upon the ground that such units are not true crafts but merely heterogeneous groups of maintenance employees, and that such units are based solely on the "extent of organization," a factor to which the Board may no longer give controlling weight by reason of Section 9 (b) (2) of the Act. More specifically, the Tin Smelters contend that a true craft unit of machinists in this plant would be one identical to the unit of machinists set forth in the agreement for a consent election held on August 5, 1947 in a unit consisting of "all machinists and machinist maintenance mechanics, including heavy duty mechanics, automobile mechanics, instrument repairmen, leadmen, helpers and apprentices." It is further contended that oilers are not a part of the machinists craft.

The journeymen machinists, their helpers and apprentices, under the supervision of the machine shop foreman, perform the usual duties required of such employees. Another group classified as machinists, their helpers and apprentices, who do machine repair work in the auxiliary repair shop under the supervision of the auxiliary foreman, also perform highly skilled machine work. Likewise, the group of instrument repairmen, although under the supervision of the foreman of the Electrical Department, are classified as machinists, and do machinist maintenance repair work on electrical panels and equipment. Although the machinists in the three groups mentioned above are under separate immediate supervision, they are under the common ultimate supervision of the Maintenance Engineer. Furthermore they perform similar duties requiring the same high degree of skill and are all a part of the same traditional craft to whom the Board has customarily granted the opportunity of separate representation. Because the proposed machinists and mechanics units sought by the Machinists, respectively, comprise only a segment of a craft group possessing similar skills and performing comparable work, we find that such units are not appropriate for the purposes of collective bargaining under the meaning of Section 9 (b) of the Act. We find, however, that three groups consisting of machinists under the supervision of the machine shop foreman, machinists under the supervision of the auxiliary repair shop foreman, and machinists known as instrument repairmen, their leadmen, helpers and apprentices, may constitute an appropriate unit.

The oilers, on the other hand, follow a regular schedule of lubricating all moving parts in the plant. In this plant they are not machinists but unskilled men who have been trained by the Employer in all phases of proper oiling. Although they are under the same supervision as the shop machinists, the oilers are not a part of the machinists craft nor do they possess mechanical skills comparable to those of the machinists. Accordingly, we shall exclude the oilers from the machinists group.

The Employer opposes the separate unit of truck drivers requested by the Machinists upon the ground that their function is actually a part of the production department. These employees are engaged in loading, hauling, and unloading materials for and between the several operational departments on plant property exclusively. In this process they operate gasoline and electric battery driven lift trucks of a type which are not used on highways. Labor crew employees without previous experience are trained in from 6 hours to 2 weeks to perform this type of work for which chauffeur's licenses are not required. While we have on occasions permitted separate representation for truck drivers who constitute a traditional homogeneous group of skilled employees, the truck drivers herein concerned have duties too closely associated with those of production employees to warrant their being separately represented apart from the production employees. Accordingly, we find that the proposed unit of truck drivers is inappropriate for purposes of collective bargaining.

As previously noted, the machinists also seek a unit of boiler firemen and their helpers. The boiler firemen and their helpers tend the pumps, gauges, and various controls of two isolated waste heat boilers and perform other related duties. The boiler firemen and helpers are a well defined homogeneous group to which the Board has customarily accorded the right of separate representation. Accordingly, we believe that the boiler firemen and helpers may in the present instance constitute an appropriate unit. The Board will, however, make no unit determination until it has further ascertained by separate elections the desires of these and other employees in the voting groups described below. If, in these elections, a majority of the employees in any voting group select the Machinists, they will have been taken to have indicated their desire to constitute a separate bargaining unit. If, on the other hand, the majority of those employees in any voting group select either the Petitioner or the Tin Smelters, they will be taken to have indicated their desire to remain a part of the existing production and maintenance unit.

We shall direct that the questions concerning representation which exist be resolved by separate elections by secret ballot among employees within the following voting groups:

(a) All machinists, including machinists under the supervision of the machine shop foreman, machinists under the supervision of the auxiliary repair shop foreman and machinists known as instrument repairmen, their leadmen, helpers, apprentices, and tool crib attendants, but excluding oilers, supervisors and all other employees of the Employer;

(b) All boiler firemen and their helpers, excluding supervisors and all other employees of the Employer; and

(c) All remaining production and maintenance employees of the Employer including laboratory employees and leadmen, but excluding all office and clerical, administrative, executive, professional, and plant-protection employees, the electricians and pipe-fitters, and all supervisors.

NOTES

1. In Permanente Metals Corp., 89 N.L.R.B. 804, 26 L.R.R.M. 1039 (1950), the Board overruled Reynolds Metals Co., 85 N.L.R.B. 110, 24 L.R.R.M. 1363 (1949), and held that craft severance is not consistent with the policies of the Act in the reduction and rolling mill phases of the aluminum industry, and that the National Tube case applies.

2. In Mueller Brass Co. v. NLRB, 180 F.2d 402 (D.C. Cir. 1950), the Board was upheld in constituting 149 diesinkers among 370 employees in a toolroom a craft unit, severed from a previous service unit of toolmakers, repair and maintenance men, distinct from the production unit.

3. An employer is engaged in the retail department store business and operates, under one management, a store in New York City, with 3200 employees, and a warehouse two miles away in Long Island City, with 250 employees. For more than ten years the collective bargaining agreements have covered all the non-supervisory personnel of the employer in both the store and the warehouse.

The warehouse serves as a reserve stockroom for 30 per cent of the sales departments in the store. It handles the receiving, marking, checking, and stocking of merchandise ultimately destined for retail customers. There is a constant interchange of employees between the store and the warehouse.

The engineering department consists of the following non-supervisory employees: six licensed engineers (two at the warehouse and four at the store), six firemen (two at the warehouse and four at the store), and three mechanics. The engineers and firemen operate the heating, refrigeration, plumbing, and air-conditioning systems. The mechanics repair and maintain this equipment. All of these employees are separately supervised by a single supervisor.

The electrical department consists of 12 maintenance electrical journeymen, two electrical elevator maintenance mechanics, one electrical escalator maintenance mechanic, and three electrical apprentices. All of these workers have served or are serving an apprenticeship of five years or its equivalent.

The cash-register mechanics are two employees who do nothing but repair National Cash Registers. Each has had about six months' training.

Intervenors Retail, Wholesale and Department Store Employees Union, Local 75 (CIO), and International Brotherhood of Teamsters, Local 804 (AFL), ask for a unit consisting of warehouse employees only. International Union of Operating Engineers, Local 30, petitions for a unit consisting of all employees in the engineering department. The International Brotherhood of Electrical Workers, Local 3 (AFL), requests a unit of electrical maintenance mechanics and their assistants. The International Brotherhood of Operating Engineers, Local 94, requests a unit of cash register mechanics. Retail Clerks International Association (AFL) intervenes for a unit similar to that asked for by Local 3 (Independent), but agrees with the contentions of Local 30, Local 94, and the IBEW. Bloomingdale Department Store Employees Union, Local 3 (Independent) contends that the present contract unit is appropriate.

How would the NLRB dispose of these requests and contentions? See Bloomingdale Bros., Inc., 81 N.L.R.B. 1252, 23 L.R.R.M. 1495 (1949).

4. Refer to Notes, page 147–148 supra, in respect to "Globe" elections.

5. NLRB, 15th Annual Report 47–48 (1950): "While the Board takes into consideration the bargaining history, it is primarily guided by the desires of the parties in determining the appropriateness of multiemployer units. For example, where, after the Board's finding of such a unit, the employers involved abandoned all group bargaining and elected to pursue individual courses of action, the Board, upon a motion for reconsideration, set aside its prior finding and held individual employer units appropriate. In another case, the Board excluded from an association-wide unit the employees of those association members who affirmatively indicated a desire to bargain individually. And, where originally a single unit had been found for the employees of seven employers, a separate unit for the employees of one of these employers was established after he indicated his desire to pursue an independent course of action. However, in the Johnson Optical Case, 85 N.L.R.B. 895, the Board found a multiemployer unit appropriate despite the fact that the employers had concurred in the petitioning union's request for separate units. The Board, while relying mainly on the successful 13-year bargaining history of the group during which a labor relations consultant had bargained on behalf of the several employers, took into consideration

the additional fact that the employers' agreement with the union's request for separate units was not accompanied by any indication that they intended to abandon their concerted course of action on labor relations."

In order to make a single unit appropriate, withdrawal from a multiple unit must take place at a proper time.   The resignation of an employer from an association after the contract negotiated by the association on a group basis has become effective does not serve as a basis for finding a single employer unit appropriate. Purity Stores, Ltd., 93 N.L.R.B. 199, 27 L.R.R.M. 1359 (1951). This is so because the employer has, by entering into the contract, manifested an intent to be bound in collective bargaining by group rather than by individual action for the life of the agreement.   Engineering Metal Products Corp., 92 N.L.R.B. 823, 27 L.R.R.M. 1162 (1950).   For an appropriate and effective withdrawal from a multiple unit, see Economy Shade Co., 91 N.L.R.B. 1552, 27 L.R.R.M. 1046 (1950).

b. The Election Bar

TIN PROCESSING CORP.[45]
National Labor Relations Board, 1948
80 N.L.R.B. 1369, 23 L.R.R.M. 1253

REYNOLDS, MURDOCK and GRAY, Members: . . .

The Employer and Tin Smelters, [Intervenor] urge, in view of the provisions of Section 9 (c) (3) of the Act, as amended, that no elections should be conducted at this time.   Thus, it is contended that the elections held on July 28, 1948, among the electricians and pipefitters, pursuant to Board Direction issued July 2, 1948, in which the Petitioner [Oil Workers] participated, were conducted in subdivisions of the unit petitioned for herein; that pending the lapse of a 12-month period from the date of the earlier elections, the Act specifically precludes the Board from directing an election at this time in the production and maintenance unit petitioned for herein or in any other subdivision thereof.   The Machinists, [Intervenor] on the other hand, take the position that because the earlier elections were in craft units, they do not affect employees in the plant other than those employees in the craft units involved

[45] The facts of this case are set out at pages 182–183 supra.

in such elections, and relies on Section 9 (b) as support for this position.

Inasmuch as the earlier elections were conducted for groups other than those for whom elections are sought in this proceeding, we find that such elections were not held in the same bargaining unit or subdivision thereof within the meaning of Section 9 (c) (3) of the Act, as amended. Accordingly, we find that the elections do not preclude a present election in any unit or units which may be found appropriate in this proceeding.

Elections directed.

NOTES

1. NLRB, 13th Annual Report 31 (1948) : "Section 9 (c) (3) of the amended statute, which proscribes the holding of more than one valid election in a bargaining unit or any subdivision thereof in a 12-month period, amounts in part to a codification of the Board's 1-year certification rule. [The Board relied upon this statutory provision in Matter of Lehrolite, Inc., 75 N.L.R.B. 607, in dismissing a petition filed 5 months after a consent election in the same unit won by a rival union, because only 11 months had elapsed at the time of its decision.] In addition, however, it creates a prohibition against holding a second election within the same year after a valid election lost by a union, where the election does not result in a certification. The significant term, 'valid election,' has been interpreted by the Board in several cases. The Board has held that this term does not embrace an informal card check; [Matter of Arrow, Hart and Hegeman Electric Co., 77 N.L.R.B. 258.] or an election in which the balloting was inconclusive; [Matter of N.A.P.A. New York Warehouse, Inc., 76 N.L.R.B. 840.] or an election which resulted in a dismissal of the petition, without disposing of objections, because of the petitioning union's non-compliance with section 9 (f) and (h) of the act. [Matter of Nashville Corp., 77 N.L.R.B. 145.]"

2. The Great Atlantic and Pacific Tea Co., 81 N.L.R.B. 880, 23 L.R.R.M. 1421 (1949) . This was a petition for craft representation filed on April 12, 1948. Decertification of the industrial representative was sought in a petition filed on June 3, 1948. A consent decertification election was held on June 30; the industrial representative won; the craft petitioner was not a party through Board error. Held: The decertification election was not a "valid" election within Section 9 (c) (3) ; craft election directed.

3. Gilchrist Timber Co., 76 N.L.R.B. 1233, 21 L.R.R.M. 1302

(1948). Sections 9 (c) (3) and 9 (e) (3) do not preclude a union-shop election within 12 months after a representation election.

c. The Contract and Certification Bars

REED ROLLER BIT CO.
National Labor Relations Board, 1947
72 N.L.R.B. 927, 19 L.R.R.M. 1227

HERZOG, Chairman, and HOUSTON and REYNOLDS, Members: . . .

We must decide whether a contract of 2 years' duration is a bar to an election when it has been in effect for more than 1 year, although the customary term of agreements in the industry in which the Employer is engaged is only 1 year.

On August 30, 1945, the Employer and the Intervenor made a contract which provided that it was to remain in operation for 2 years. On June 28, 1946, the Petitioner filed the petition in this proceeding. Both the Employer and the Intervenor contend that their agreement, which will not expire until August 30, 1947, precludes a current determination of representatives.

The problem of the contract bar was presented to the Board early in its history. In its first decisions, the Board held that a contract for a term of 1 year, whose expiration date was not imminent, would bar a determination of representatives, but that no contract which had been in effect for more than 1 year could foreclose an election. On the basis of these decisions, the Board frequently found that a 2-year contract was no bar after it had been in operation more than 1 year. It was also held, however, that a 2-year contract which was customary in the industry served to preclude a determination of representatives, although it had already run for more than 1 year.

Beginning in 1945, the Board modified previous decisions and ruled that a contract for a term of 2 years was presumed to be of reasonable duration, and that the burden was on the petitioning union to prove the contrary by showing that 2-year agreements were not customary in the industry. Failure to sustain the burden of proof resulted in the dismissal of the petition.

We thus progressed from the rule that no contract which had been in effect for more than 1 year could operate as a bar to a determination of representatives to the principle that a 2-year agreement is presumed to be of reasonable duration and therefore operates as a bar to an election unless the presumption is over-come.   In the present case the Petitioner rebutted the presump-tion by proving that 1-year agreements are customary in the in-dustry in which the Employer is engaged.   Consequently, the question before us now is whether we should complete the cycle by holding that a 2-year contract operates as a bar to an election until the approach of its terminal date, even in the face of contrary custom in the industry.

Whenever a contract is urged as a bar, the Board is faced with the problem of balancing two separate interests of employees and society which the Act was designed to protect: the interest in such stability as is essential to encourage effective collective bargaining, and the sometimes conflicting interest in the freedom of employees to select and change their representatives.   In furtherance of the purposes of the Act, we have repeatedly held that employees are entitled to change their representatives, if they so desire, at reason-able intervals; or conversely, that a collective bargaining contract may preclude a determination of representatives for a reasonable period.

In the light of our experience in administering the Act, we be-lieve that a contract for a term of 2 years cannot be said to be of unreasonable duration.   We have already held that 2-year con-tracts are presumptively of reasonable duration.   In applying this rule, we have not discovered any compelling conditions which indicate that such agreements unduly limit the right of employees to change their representatives.   Moreover, in entertaining rival petitions several months before the expiration of the numerous 1-year contracts which are made, we have found in many instances the contracting parties, having composed their differences and ex-ecuted collective bargaining contracts after the expenditure of much time, effort and money, can feel truly secure in their re-spective positions only for the brief period of approximately 8 or 9 months.

For large masses of employees collective bargaining has but recently emerged from a stage of trial and error, during which its techniques and full potentialities were being slowly developed under the encouragement and protection of the Act.   To have in-sisted in the past upon prolonged adherence to a bargaining agent, once chosen, would have been wholly incompatible with this ex-perimental and transitional period.   It was especially necessary, therefore, to lay emphasis upon the right of workers to select and change their representatives.   Now, however, the emphasis can better be placed elsewhere.   We think that the time has come when stability of industrial relations can be better served, without unreasonably restricting employees in their right to change representatives, by refusing to interfere with bargaining relations secured by collective agreements of 2 years' duration. Such contracts, even in the presence of a contrary custom in the industry, should ordinarily preclude a determination of representatives until shortly before their terminal dates.

As the agreement between the Employer and the Intervenor will not terminate until August 30, 1947, we shall dismiss the petition, without prejudice to the right to file a new petition a reasonable time before this terminal date.

NOTES

1. In California Walnut Growers Association, 77 N.L.R.B. 756, 22 L.R.R.M. 1082 (1948), the Board said: "The Petitioner takes the position that the 3-year contract entered into by the Employer and the Intervenor on September 18, 1945, is not a bar to the instant proceedings, because the contract was opened for negotiations during the contract period, and because the contract is of unreasonable duration.

"We do not agree with the Petitioner's contentions. We have frequently indicated in previous cases that negotiations pursuant to the terms of reopening provisions, will not remove the contract as a bar.[45a]

"We have taken the position in the past that a contract for 2 years is a contract for a reasonable term, and, therefore, a bar, but that a contract for more than 2 years, in the absence of showing of custom in the industry, is presumed to be unreasonable and, therefore, no bar. The Employer in the instant petition controls the output of more than 9,000 walnut growers in Southern California. While the record does not indicate that the Employer's operations dominate the walnut industry, it does clearly indicate that the Employer's operations represent a not inconsiderable portion of all walnut growers in the industry and that the instant 3-year contract is not an innovation.

"Under these circumstances, we find that the 3-year contract is not of unreasonable duration and is a bar. Therefore, at this time, no question exists concerning the representation of the employees covered by this petition. We shall dismiss the petition, without

---

[45a] The Board now follows the same rule even though the reopening is not specifically provided for in the contract. NLRB, 16th Ann. Rep. 73–75 (1951). — ED.

prejudice, however, to the filing of a new petition prior to thirty (30) days before the terminal date of the contract."

2. In Puritan Ice Co., 74 N.L.R.B. 1311, 20 L.R.R.M. 1268 (1947), a 4-year contract was found to be unreasonable but a bar to petitions during its initial 2-year period.   What will be the effect of the UAW-General Motors 5-year contract signed in the spring of 1950?

3. Feldesman, Principles in Representative Cases, 22 L.R.R.M. 31, 40 (1948) : "After the Act was amended there was considerable speculation as to whether the Board would continue its contract bar rule.   It has.   And there was conjecture as to whether it would apply contract bar principles to RD cases.   In the Snow & Nealley case, 76 N.L.R.B. 390 (1948), the Board flatly stated that it would. In fact, it pointed to the language of Section 9 (c) (2), which reads: 'In determining whether or not a question of representation affecting commerce exists, the same regulations and rules of decision shall apply irrespective of the identity of the persons filing the petition or the kind of relief sought,' and commented, in substance: '. . . indeed it would appear that we must apply contract bar rules to RD cases.' "

4. Compare the Canadian Industrial Relations and Disputes Investigation Act, 1948:

"Section 7 (4).   Where a collective agreement is in force, the application [for certification] may be made at any time after the expiry of ten months of the term of the collective agreement, but not before, except with the consent of the Board.

"Section 10 (c).   Where a trade union is certified under this Act as the bargaining agent of the employees in a unit, if, at the time of certification, a collective agreement binding on or entered into on behalf of employees in the unit is in force, the trade union shall be substituted as a party to the agreement in place of the bargaining agent that is a party to the agreement on behalf of employees in the unit, and may, notwithstanding anything contained in the agreement, upon two months' notice to the employer terminate the agreement in so far as it applies to those employees."

5. A contract containing a clause contrary to the basic policies of the NLRA does not bar an election.   Prior to the 1951 amendments abolishing the union-shop authorization poll, the Board said that a contract containing a clause which conforms to the union-security provisions of the Act but was not authorized by a referendum of employees is not a bar.   See General Electric Co., 80 N.L.R.B. 169, 23 L.R.R.M. 1057 (1948) (maintenance-of-membership clause); Hager & Sons Hinge Manufacturing Co., 80

N.L.R.B. 163, 23 L.R.R.M. 1044 (1948) (union-shop provision).
A contract containing a clause that goes beyond the limited union
security permitted by the Act is similarly not a bar. American Export Lines, Inc., 81 N.L.R.B. 1370, 23 L.R.R.M. 1499
(1949) (contract between employer and intervenor required
preferential treatment in the hire, retention, and promotion of
employees to those who are union members; held, these provisions
go beyond the limited union shop permitted by Section 8 (a) (3)
of the amended NLRA and are thus illegal without regard to
whether their execution was authorized by an election under Section 9 (e) of the Act). But compare Wyckoff Steel Co., 86
N.L.R.B. 1318, 25 L.R.R.M. 1062 (1949), where an unauthorized
maintenance-of-membership clause was preceded by this statement
in the contract: "These provisions shall take effect . . . only if
and when they may take effect in accordance and consistent with
provisions of Federal Laws." And see In re Port Pub. Co., 231
N.C. 395, 57 S.E.2d 366 (1950), (void closed-shop provision
separable; printers and pressmen granted lien against insolvent
employer for vacation pay due under collective agreement).

GENERAL ELECTRIC X–RAY CORP.
National Labor Relations Board, 1946
67 N.L.R.B. 997, 18 L.R.R.M. 1047

Herzog, Chairman, and Reilly and Houston, Members: . . .

The Company has, in effect, refused to recognize the CIO
United Electrical, Radio & Machine Workers of America as the
representative of certain of its employees because of its contractual
obligations to the IAM.

On May 18, 1943, the IAM was designated, after a consent election, as the representative of the Company's hourly paid production and maintenance workers. A collective bargaining agreement
executed by the Company and the IAM terminated on September
20, 1945. At that time the parties began negotiations for a new
contract. During the course of these negotiations they reached
an impasse, which was followed by a strike lasting until October
22, 1945. Negotiations were thereafter resumed, and, by October
29, 1945, the parties agreed upon, but did not reduce to writing,
all of the terms of a new contract.

On November 2, 1945, the CIO addressed a letter to the Company, advising it that "a majority of [its] production and maintenance workers have indicated their desire to be represented by
[the CIO]," and requesting the Company not to enter into any

agreement with any other labor organization claiming to represent these employees.   It filed no petition at that time.

On November 22, 1945, the Company and the IAM signed a collective bargaining agreement covering the production and maintenance employees.   This agreement is to continue in operation until October 21, 1946, and is automatically renewable for yearly periods thereafter in the absence of notice of a desire to modify or terminate given by either party to the other at least 30 days before any anniversary date.   Five days later the Company addressed a letter to the CIO wherein it stated:

> Since the Board has not certified to us that the [CIO] has displaced the [IAM] as the bargaining representative and has not, even though twenty days have passed since the receipt of your letter [of November 2, 1945], notified us that the matter of representation is in dispute, we had no alternative . . . but to enter into an agreement with [the IAM] in respect of which the parties had been in substantial agreement since October 22, 1945.

The CIO did not file its petition herein until November 30, 1945.

It is the position of the CIO that the agreement of November 22, 1945, cannot bar an immediate determination of representatives, because it was executed after the Company had been notified of the CIO's claim of majority representation.   The Company and the IAM contend that their agreement does bar a present election, because the CIO did not promptly follow up its timely but informal claim by filing a petition with the Board.   At the oral argument the IAM argued that only a formal petition should be permitted to prevent a subsequent collective agreement from becoming a bar.

Our precedents support the CIO's position.   We have not applied the contract bar rule in situations in which a rival claim antedates the execution or automatic renewal of the agreement. Until now, moreover, our decisions have made no distinction between informal claims and formally filed petitions.   But the record and oral argument in this and a companion case persuade the Board that it is no longer desirable to accord a mere naked assertion of majority equal dignity with that accorded a petition.

By filing a formal representation petition with a Regional Office of the Board, a claimant submits its claim to the Board's administrative process, including a prompt investigation of the substantiality of the petitioner's prima facie showing of interest. The issuance of a notice of hearing constitutes a preliminary but official recognition that the claim has color. Conversely, where substance is found wanting, the Regional Director refuses to proceed. By subjecting the petition to this preliminary scrutiny, and risk of rejection, the Board's processes serve to discourage baseless claims. The Board may reasonably require restraint on the part of an employer and a labor organization, engaged in negotiations, during the relatively short period necessary to conclude these preliminary investigations, and hold that they act at their peril in consummating an agreement with knowledge of the pendency of the proceeding before the Board.

But the presentation of a mere naked claim of representation, such as was here advanced, places no onus on the claimant to substantiate its claim and thus gives rise to no inference of substantial interest. To permit such a claim to defeat, without limitation as to time, a subsequent but otherwise valid collective agreement appears to us to place too great burden and impairment upon the bargaining process. The now great and growing familiarity on the part of labor organizations and their advisers with the Board's policies and practices enables abuse, inviting claimants without representation strength to play the role of dog-in-the-manger, and indefinitely to frustrate collective bargaining.

For the foregoing reasons we have concluded that where a petition is filed more than 10 days after the assertion of a bare claim of representation, and no extenuating circumstances appear, an agreement otherwise valid, which is executed in the interval should be held to constitute a bar.

[The CIO petition was dismissed.]

NOTES

1. Accord, American Container Corp., 77 N.L.R.B. 732, 22 L.R.R.M. 1075 (1948) (claim, Sept. 18, 1947; contract with Intervenor, Oct. 2, 1947; petition, Oct. 17, 1947). But when a rival union presents an employer with a claim for recognition which has a substantial and recognizable basis, the subsequent execution or renewal of a contract with another union does not bar an election. For example, the Board has held that a claim for recognition accompanied by notice of schism within the incumbent union and followed by unfair labor practice charges was substantial and had demonstrated foundation and that a

contract between the employer and the incumbent union made after this claim did not bar a petition filed two months later. Swift & Co., 94 N.L.R.B. 917, 28 L.R.R.M. 1138 (1951).

2. Feldesman, Principles in Representative Cases, 22 L.R.R.M. 31, 37 (1948): "What happens when the employer and B union are already under contract and the contract contains an automatic renewal clause — a clause saying that unless notice of termination or desire to amend is given by either party a certain number of days before the contract's anniversary date, the contract should be automatically renewed for another year?   Under the rule which obtained before General Electric X-Ray and under the Mill B doctrine, 40 N.L.R.B. 346, if A union gave notice of its rival claim a reasonable time before the operative date of the automatic renewal clause — the Mill B date, as it is now known — the contract was held not to be a bar.   The Mill B date was equated with the execution date of a new contract.   But the considerations which led to the formulation of the General Electric X-Ray doctrine were also present in this type of situation.   And so in the Henry & Allen case, 68 N.L.R.B. 724 (1946), the Board extended the General Electric X-Ray doctrine to contracts with automatic renewal clauses.   Now if A union apprises the employer of its claim to representation, and then the Mill B date arrives and passes, A union must file a petition within 10 days of its claim to prevent the contract from operating as a bar to an election."

3. Compare Triboro Coach Co. v. N.Y. State Lab. Rel. Bd., 286 N.Y. 314, 36 N.E.2d 315 (1941), discussed in Notes, 41 Col. L. Rev. 524 (1941) and 26 Minn. L. Rev. 640 (1942), and by Willcox, in The Triboro Case — Mountain or Molehill, 56 Harv. L. Rev. 576 (1943).

4. What is known as the "premature extension" doctrine has been applied by the Board in two situations: (1) where there is an automatic renewal provision contained in a contract already in operation and the new contract is entered into before the operative date for automatic renewal stipulated in the contract, and (2) where a new contract is entered into before the termination date of the contract already in existence and operation.   The question arises in each of these two situations where a union files a petition raising a question of representation after the new contract has been entered into either before the operative date of the original automatic renewal provision or before the termination date of the original contract.   In these instances the Board has refused to bar the petition.   Matter of Mill B., Inc. 40 N.L.R.B. 346. 10 L.R.R.M. 62 (1942); Wichita Union Stock-

yards Co., 40 N.L.R.B. 369, 10 L.R.R.M. 65 (1942); Matter of Little Rock Furniture Mfg. Co., 80 N.L.R.B. 65, 23 L.R.R.M. 1033 (1948); Matter of General Electric X-Ray Corp., 67 N.L.R.B. 997, 18 L.R.R.M. 1047 (1946). But see Matter of Republic Steel Corp., 84 N.L.R.B. 483, 24 L.R.R.M. 1286 (1949).

5. The contract between A Union and the employer contains a clause stating that the contract will run until January 29, 1951, and be automatically renewed in the absence of a modification or termination notice given 30 days prior to that date. On December 4, 1950, the parties, after a 60-day notice as required by Section 8 (d) of the Taft-Hartley Act, execute a new contract which is to be effective from December 28, 1950, to December 29, 1952, and automatically renewable for yearly periods thereafter in the absence of a 60-day modification or termination notice. On December 6, 1950, B Union files a petition. Does the "premature extension" doctrine apply to this situation? See De Soto Creamery & Produce Co., 94 N.L.R.B. 1627, 28 L.R.R.M. 1234 (1951).

6. In Con P. Curran Printing Co., 67 N.L.R.B. 1419, 18 L.R.R.M. 1086 (1946), X Union was certified on November 24, 1944. Prior to that time, it and several other unions had submitted a disputed wage demand to the War Labor Board for increases in one of the three departments in the unit. This was granted, and, similarly, increases were granted in the other two departments. However, many other issues which would comprise the final contract between the company and X Union were still in dispute and negotiations were still under way. The C Union requested bargaining rights claiming a majority in the unit; the company refused, claiming X Union was the certified representative. C Union filed a representation petition. Afterwards, the Company and X Union completed a contract to last for one year. Held: The contract bars election at this time, even though it was executed ten months after date of certification, and this bar remains for the duration of the contract term of one year. Representative status is not subject to challenge for a "reasonable period" after certification, usually one year, except in unusual circumstances.

7. For further applications of the certification bar, see NLRB, 11th Ann. Rep. 17–19 (1946), 13th Ann. Rep. 31 (1948).

8. Compare the Canadian Industrial Relations and Disputes Investigation Act, 1948:

"Section 7 (3). Where no collective agreement is in force but a bargaining agent has been certified under this Act for the unit, the application may be made after the expiry of twelve months from the date of certification of the bargaining agent, but not before, except with the consent of the Board.

"Section 10 (b). Where a trade union is certified under this Act as the bargaining agent of the employees in a unit, if another trade union had previously been certified as bargaining agent in respect of employees in the unit, the certification of the last mentioned trade union shall be deemed to be revoked in respect of such employees; . . ."

9. In the Quaker Maid case, 71 N.L.R.B. 915, 19 L.R.R.M. 1069 (1946), the B Union was certified on July 3, 1945. It executed a 1-year contract on July 30, 1945, with reopening and 30-day automatic renewal clauses. On May 13, 1946, B Union and the employer executed a supplemental agreement, changing wages and extending the original contract to July 30, 1947. The A Union petitioned on June 20, 1946. Held: The extended contract was a bar for its duration. The "premature extension" doctrine does not apply for a period of one year after certification. See NLRB, 12th Ann. Rep. 12–14 (1947).

10. What happens when a local union which has entered a contract with the employer secedes from the parent organization? What happens to the contract? Suppose the parent body organizes another local union to replace the seceding one? Which local is entitled to the contract? See Secession of Locals, pages 976–984 infra. See also NLRB, 16th Ann. Rep. 70–72 (1951).

d. Decertification

A new type of election introduced by the amended NLRA was the decertification election. Any employee, group of employees, or labor union may petition for an election to test the majority status of the union which is now acting as the bargaining representative of the employees in the particular unit, as a result of either a previous certification by the Board or of the employer's voluntary recognition. NLRA, Sec. 9 (c) (1) (A) (ii). If, as the result of this election, the union is shown to have lost its majority status among the employees within the unit, it will lose its bargaining rights. As stated in the section on Filing Requirements, page 142 infra, the Board has not applied the restrictions of Sections 9 (f), (g), and (h) of the NLRA to decertification petitions because of the difference in the nature of the proceedings, on the theory that any other result would allow a union to use its own dereliction in failing to file the necessary documents to protect itself from decertification. Thus, the Board has held that the union which is the employees' current representative, and which the employees seek to have decertified, must be allowed to participate in the hearing, be granted a place on the ballot, and be given the right of objecting to the conduct of the election, even though it has not complied with the filing requirements of Sections 9 (f) , (g) , and (h) of the Act. See NLRB, 15th Ann. Rep. 59–60 (1950) .

6. COURT REVIEW OF REPRESENTATION PROCEEDINGS

Neither the Wagner Act nor the NLRA as amended in 1947 by the Taft-Hartley Act provided for direct or immediate judicial review of Board actions in representation proceedings. On the contrary, Sections 9 (d) and 10 (c) , (e) , and (f) , unchanged in this respect, provide for such review only indirectly, i.e., when enforcement or review by the U.S. Court of Appeals is sought of an order of the Board in an unfair labor practice case (usually refusal to bargain) involving the representation proceeding in question.

On the whole, the courts have adhered to this procedure and have declined by injunction, declaratory judgment, or otherwise to review directly the propriety of hearings, elections, certifications or unit determinations. In part, this has been based upon the view that the statutory method of review was exclusive and that resort to administrative procedures should be completed before court action is invoked.[46] Mainly, however, the courts have shared with Congress and the Board a fear, based upon experience under Public Resolution 44 in 1934 and during the first two years of the Wagner Act, that judicial interference in representation proceedings would tend to delay and disrupt facilities for collective bargaining. See Madden v. Brotherhood of Transit Employees, 147 F.2d 439 (4th Cir. 1945) .

There has not been much distress over this procedure when it

---

[46] This same principle has been applied to the review of complaint cases. Thus where the Board had taken jurisdiction and issued a complaint charging an employer with domination of and interference with a labor organization, the District Court has been held to be without jurisdiction to enjoin the Board from holding a hearing, at the request of either the employer or an employee. This was so even though it was claimed in the injunction proceeding that interstate commerce was not involved and that the holding of a hearing would cause irreparable damage to complainants. Mr. Justice Brandeis, speaking for a unanimous Court, stated (p. 50) that the complainant's "contention is at war with the long settled rule of judicial administration that no one is entitled to judicial relief for a supposed or threatened injury until the prescribed administrative remedy has been exhausted." Myers v. Bethlehem Shipbuilding Corp., 303 U.S. 41, 58 Sup. Ct. 459, 82 L. Ed. 638 (1938) .

was the employer who wanted to contest a Board action in a representation proceeding: he could refuse to bargain with the designated union and not be hurt until a Board order compelled him to act. Then he could raise the allegedly defective hearing, election, certification, or unit as an issue in the enforcement or review case in the Court of Appeals. See Pittsburgh Plate Glass Co. v. NLRB, 313 U.S. 146, 61 Sup. Ct. 908, 85 L. Ed. 1251 (1941), printed at page 155 supra; NLRB v. National Plastic Products Co., 175 F.2d 755 (4th Cir. 1949); Norris, Inc. v. NLRB, 177 F.2d 26 (D.C. Cir. 1949); Note, Judicial Review of Representation Cases Under the National Labor Relations Act, 28 Geo. L.J. 666, (1940).

However, a union adversely affected by Board action in representation proceedings may suffer immediate harm and may sometimes need a direct court test of the administrative decision. Moreover, under the Wagner Act the union was not in a position later to precipitate a statutory judicial review by a refusal to bargain. For these reasons, the courts have indicated that, while no relief is available to the union under the NLRA, a district court, in the exercise of its equity jurisdiction, may enjoin Board action in order to prevent irreparable injury. Although a number of such injunctions have been granted by the district courts, they have seldom survived the scrutiny of the appellate courts. See AFL v. NLRB, 308 U.S. 401, 60 Sup. Ct. 300, 84 L. Ed. 347 (1940); Inland Empire v. Millis, 325 U.S. 697, 65 Sup. Ct. 1316, 89 L. Ed. 1877 (1948); Madden v. Brotherhood and Union of Transit Employees, 147 F.2d 439 (4th Cir. 1945); Fitzgerald v. Douds, 167 F.2d 714 (2d Cir. 1948); International Union, Local 148 v. Same, Local 2, and NLRB, 173 F.2d 557 (8th Cir. 1949); Norris, Inc. v. NLRB, 177 F.2d 26 (D.C. Cir. 1949) (employer denied injunction, injury not irreparable). See Note, 55 Harv. L. Rev. 875 (1942).

The Administrative Procedure Act of 1946 has worked no change. Ohio Power Co. v. NLRB, 164 F.2d 275 (6th Cir. 1947); International Union, Local 148 v. Same, Local 2, and NLRB, supra.

For the Board's appraisal of the availability of injunctive or declaratory relief against representation proceedings, see NLRB, 10th Ann. Rep. 74–75 (1945), 11th Ann. Rep. 65–67 (1946), 12th Ann. Rep. 62–63 (1947), 13th Ann. Rep. 72, 80 (1948), 14th Ann. Rep. 149–151 (1949), 15th Ann. Rep. 212–214 (1950).

As to judicial review under the state labor relations acts, compare Jordan Marsh v. Mass. Lab. Rel. Comm., 312 Mass. 597, 45

N.E.2d 925 (1942) (employer denied certiorari to test certification and unit); Wisconsin Statutes (1947), Sec. 111.05 (3): "The board's certification of the results of any election shall be conclusive as to the findings included therein unless reviewed in the same manner as provided . . . for review of orders of the board"; New York Post Corporation v. Kelley, 296 N.Y. 178, 71 N.E.2d 456 (1947), criticized in Benjamin, Judicial Review of Administrative Adjudication, 48 Col. L. Rev. 1, 4–10 (1948) (employer sought declaratory judgment to test board's certification, board's motion for judgment on the pleadings denied, two judges dissenting with opinion).

III. The Duty to Bargain

References: NLRA, Secs. 8 (a) (5), 8 (b) (3), 9 (a), 8 (d) set out in the Appendix; Excerpt from NLRB v. Jones and Laughlin Steel Corp., page 98 supra.

A. *Status of the Bargaining Agent*

THE ENDERBY CASE — II

Refer to the facts of The Enderby Case — I, page 113 supra. Suppose that Curme, instead of filing a petition with the NLRB raising a question of representation, had filed a charge alleging certain unfair labor practices, and that, after investigation, the Regional Office of the NLRB had issued a complaint charging the Enderby Company with violating Sections 8 (a) (1) and (5) of the NLRA.

Assume the following additional facts:

By the time the matter came up for a hearing before a trial examiner four months later, White felt that his position was quite secure. At his request a second petition had been submitted from the workers in the Miscellaneous Division, listing 230 employees. Moreover, there had been a turnover of 125 workers in the Tire Division, and he had been advised by the personnel manager that only a "dozen or so" of the replacements were supporters of the United Rubber Workers.

The trial examiner, after hearing the evidence, made the following findings of fact:

1. The production employees, both the Tire and Miscellaneous Divisions, have an identity of interest.

2. While there is no history of collective bargaining in this

particular plant, collective bargaining in other plants in the industry is done on the basis of a production unit including employees of the Tire and Miscellaneous Divisions.

3. At the time that the Enderby Company refused to negotiate with the United Rubber Workers, the Union was supported by a majority of the production employees in the plant.

4. At the present time the United Rubber Workers is supported by a minority of the production workers.

5. The Company was not instrumental in the submission of the first petition from the workers in the Miscellaneous Division.

6. The high turnover in the Tire Division was primarily the result of economic factors beyond the control of the company.

7. Most of the employees quit voluntarily.

8. In hiring replacements the Company was guided by the following considerations: experience, age, and physical well-being. In a rather large number of cases, the decisive factor in hiring was the fact that the applicant was personally known to some other employee at the supervisory level or above.

With these findings of fact, what conclusions of law will the trial examiner reach? What kind of an order will he issue?

JOY SILK MILLS, INC. v. NLRB
United States Court of Appeals, District of Columbia, 1950
185 F.2d 732, certiorari denied, 341 U.S. 914 (1951)

[After a brief strike, the employees of the Joy Silk Mills at Hartsville, South Carolina, returned to work September 20, 1948.   Four days later Jacobs, the Regional Director of the United Textile Workers of America (AFL), telephoned Gilbert, the President of the Company, and requested recognition for the Union as the bargaining agent of the Company's employees.   Thirty-eight of the fifty-two employees had signed union cards at this time.   The request was made again by Jacobs in a meeting with Gilbert six days later.   Jacobs offered to let Gilbert check the Union's membership cards.   Gilbert declined, and a consent election to be held on October 19 was agreed upon.   Gilbert advised his supervisory employees that they should not interfere with the union activities of the employees and posted a notice advising the employees of their right to vote freely in the forthcoming election.   However, Gilbert and some of his supervisors subsequently engaged in conduct which the NLRB found to be a violation of Section 8 (a) (1) of the NLRA.   The Union lost the election and immediately filed a protest against the conduct of the election.   This protest was sustained by the Board's Regional Director, who ordered the election set aside and directed another one. The Union then withdrew its representation petition and filed charges of unfair labor practices. A complaint was issued charging the Company with, inter alia, a violation of Section 8 (a) (5). On September 13, 1949, the NLRB found the Company guilty of certain unfair labor practices, and ordered the Company to cease and desist from refusing to bargain collectively with the United Textile Workers as the exclusive representative of all its production and maintenance employees and, upon request, to "bargain collectively with the United Textile Workers of America." The Company filed a petition with the Court of Appeals for the District of Columbia to review and set aside this order. Relevant portions of the court's opinion by Washington, Circuit Judge, are set out below.]

. . . Was there a refusal to bargain collectively in violation of Section 8 (a) (5) of the Act? Before there can be a wrongful refusal to bargain, there must have been a request to bargain by the union. N.L.R.B. v. Columbian Enameling & Stamping Co., 306 U.S. 292, 59 S. Ct. 501, 83 L. Ed. 660. The Board concluded that such a request was made by Jacobs in the telephone conversation with Gilbert on September 24. Jacobs testified that he had requested recognition of the union as collective bargaining agent, stating that the union had been authorized to represent the employees; and that he had suggested a cross-check of membership cards with the payroll, by an impartial person, to prove the authorization. He further testified that Gilbert declined both requests, stating he wished to consult his attorney; that he thought the matter had been settled by an election held two years previously, which the union had lost; and that in any event he preferred to have the Board handle the matter. Gilbert testified that no request to bargain was made and that Jacobs merely said he had enough employees to petition the Board for an election if Gilbert wouldn't agree to a consent election. Jacobs also testified that at the meeting of September 30, he suggested negotiating a contract to obviate the necessity of an election. Again there was contradictory testimony. The trial examiner chose to believe Jacobs' version of the conversations, finding Gilbert mistaken in his recollection, and concluded that there had been a request to bargain; these findings were affirmed by the Board. The circumstances of the conversations corroborate this conclusion to some extent. But apart from that, credibility of witnesses is a matter for Board determination, and not for this court. Nor must the request to bargain be in *haec verba,* so long as there was one by clear implication.   The Labor-Management Relations Act "is not a statute of frauds or an act prescribing the formalities of conveyancing.   No seal or writing is required by its terms.   Nor is any special formula or form of words."

The question presented is then whether Gilbert's refusal to bargain was permissible under the Act.   It has been held that an employer may refuse recognition to a union when motivated by a good faith doubt as to that union's majority status.   North Electric Mfg. Co. v. N.L.R.B., 6 Cir., 123 F.2d 887; N.L.R.B. v. Chicago Apparatus Co., 7 Cir., 116 F.2d 753.   When, however, such refusal is due to a desire to gain time and to take action to dissipate the union's majority, the refusal is no longer justifiable and constitutes a violation of the duty to bargain set forth in section 8 (a) (5) of the Act.   N.L.R.B. v. Federbush Co., 2 Cir., 121 F.2d 954, 956; N.L.R.B. v. Remington Rand, Inc., 2 Cir., 94 F.2d 862, 868–869.   The Act provides for election proceedings in order to provide a mechanism whereby an employer acting in good faith may secure a determination of whether or not the union does in fact have a majority and is therefore the appropriate agent with which to bargain.   Another purpose is to insure that the employees may freely register their individual choices concerning representation.   Certainly it is not one of the purposes of the election provisions to supply an employer with a procedural device by which he may secure the time necessary to defeat efforts toward organization being made by a union.   Thus, the problem now before us narrows down to whether or not the evidence warrants the Board's inference that the refusal of recognition was in fact motivated by bad faith.

We think that there was "substantial" evidence, viewing the entire record, from which the Board could conclude that the original refusal of recognition was in bad faith.   Cf. N.L.R.B. v. Consolidated Machine Tool Corp., 2 Cir., 163 F.2d 376, certiorari denied 332 U.S. 824, 68 S. Ct. 164, 92 L. Ed. 399.   The employer engaged in coercive activities immediately preceding the election.   Interference commenced only five days after the consent election had been agreed upon.   The time lapse between the first request to bargain and the election was only 26 days.   In view of the totality of the evidence, it is a reasonable conclusion that the employer did not suddenly suffer a change of heart.   "We are in a field where subtleties of conduct may play no small part . . ." N.L.R.B. v. Express Publishing Co., 312 U.S. 426, 437, 61 S. Ct. 693, 700, 85 L. Ed. 930.   Neither the Board nor the courts can read the minds of men.   As the Board has stated: "In cases of this type the question of whether an employer is acting in good or bad faith at the time of the refusal is, of course, one which of necessity must be determined in the light of all relevant facts in the case, including any unlawful conduct of the employer, the sequence of events, and the time lapse between the refusal and the unlawful conduct." Petitioner has transgressed the bounds of permissible conduct to a sufficient extent to permit the Board to conclude that its refusal to bargain was as ill-intentioned as its other actions. . . .

There remains for consideration whether the Board's order should be enforced in full or should be modified in some respects.

First, as to that portion of the order relating to the refusal to bargain: If the Board is correct in its finding that the employer refused to bargain in violation of Section 8 (a) (5) , its order that the employer bargain collectively with the union is within its authority, and is amply sustained by precedent. This is true despite the fact that the union lost the consent election. The Board has concluded that the union's loss of strength was due to petitioner's coercive activities. It has also concluded that prior to the engagement in that coercion the union had a large majority. The Board is specifically empowered "to take such affirmative action . . . as will effectuate the policies of this chapter." 29 U.S.C.A. §160 (c) . It has been consistently held by the Supreme Court that where an employer refuses to bargain collectively with a majority union, and the union loses its majority status because of the employer's coercive activities, suffering the loss of an election, it is appropriate for the Board to order the employer to bargain with the union. Franks Bros. Co. v. N.L.R.B., 321 U.S. 702, 64 S. Ct. 817, 88 L. Ed. 1020; N.L.R.B. v. P. Lorillard Co., 314 U.S. 512, 62 S. Ct. 397, 86 L. Ed. 380; N.L.R.B. v. Bradford Dyeing Ass'n, 310 U.S. 318, 339–340, 60 S. Ct. 918, 84 L. Ed. 1226. . . .

The decision in Franks Bros. Co. v. N.L.R.B., supra, appears controlling, and the order of the Board is entitled to be enforced in the respect just discussed.

As to that portion of the order requiring the petitioner to cease and desist from refusing to bargain, what has been said above is equally applicable, and the order must likewise be enforced. . . .

[Miller, J., dissented. The Court's footnotes are omitted.]

NOTES

1. Compare NLRB v. Vulcan Forging Co., 188 F.2d 927 (6th Cir. 1951). In an election held at the plant in March, 1947, the

employees voted 12 to 10 to be represented by the International Union, United Automobile, Aircraft and Agricultural Implement Workers of America (CIO). Eight days after the election the employees drew up a statement signed by 19 of the 20 men then employed stating in substance that they wished to sever their relations with the Union. The employees also stated that they were making this decision without any intimidation or influence. Three days later international representatives of the Union met with representatives of management and two employees who constituted the bargaining committee of the local group to consider the request of the Union for a contract. The Company did not receive the aforementioned statement from the employees until a week or so after this meeting. The management then suggested to the Union that it would be wise to defer consideration of the proposed contract until such time as it appeared that the employees desired to have the Union represent them. The NLRB found that the Company had refused to bargain collectively with a duly elected bargaining agent of its employees and petitioned for judicial enforcement of its order. The court held that the loss of majority support by the Union within a short period of time after the certification by an unsolicited shift in employee sentiment relieved the Company of its duty to bargain. In denying the petition for enforcement of the Board order, the court stated at page 931: "To force them [the employees] to bargain through a representative which they had repudiated would be depriving them of their right to bargain through a representative of their choice."

2. Also compare the Joy Silk Mills and Vulcan cases with NLRB v. Inter-City Advertising Co., 154 F.2d 244 (4th Cir. 1946), where it was held that the employer need not bargain with a Union which lost its majority after certification, due to employee turnover not caused by any unlawful acts of the employer. But see NLRB v. Appalachian Electric Power Co., 140 F.2d 217 (4th Cir. 1944), which held that an employer cannot treat the revocation by a majority of his employees of union authority shortly after certification as justification for a refusal to bargain. See also NLRB v. Century Oxford Manufacturing Co., 140 F.2d 541 (2d Cir. 1944), and Celanese Corp. of America, 95 N.L.R.B. 664, 28 L.R.R.M. 1362 (1951).

B. *Good Faith*

THE ENDERBY CASE — III

1. During negotiations in April and May of 1948, Curme asks for the following: a wage increase of 25 cents an hour, double time on Sundays, 10 cents an hour for a night-shift premium, and a pension plan whereby the Company puts an amount equal to 5 per cent of each employee's average annual salary into a trust fund for retirement payment at age sixty. White says, "Impossible. Your demands are out of the question." Curme asks, "Why?" White responds, "We don't have to give our reasons." Is this an unfair labor practice?

2. White offers a 5-cent wage increase, says "no" on the other demands, and refuses to give his reasons. Is this an unfair labor practice?

3. White offers a 5-cent wage increase, says "no" on the other demands. Curme refuses the proffered increase but says he will take 20 cents if White will grant double time on Sunday. White says, "No!" Curme then asks for a counteroffer. White says, "We have made our offer. We won't budge an inch." Is this an unfair labor practice?

4. Agreement is finally reached on all issues but wages. The Union offers to arbitrate. White refuses. Is this an unfair labor practice?

5. White and Curme reach agreement on all issues. Curme says he can't sign a written contract until the local membership ratifies the agreement. At the meeting Curme says, "Don't ratify. We've got the Company on the run. If we reject this contract, I think I can get 5 cents more an hour and an agreement to hire only union men." The membership unanimously rejects the agreement. Curme returns and confronts White with the two new proposals. Is this an unfair labor practice?

NLRB v. BOSS MFG. CO.
United States Circuit Court of Appeals, Seventh Circuit, 1941
118 F.2d 187

KERNER, J. This is a petition by the National Labor Relations Board that the Boss Manufacturing Company and its officers and agents be adjudged in contempt of this court for their failure to comply with the decree of this court, entered on December 19, 1939, wherein enforcement of an order of the Board made with respect to the Boss Manufacturing Company was directed pursuant to an opinion rendered November 7, 1939, 7 Cir., 107 F.(2d.) 574.

The decree ordered the Boss Manufacturing Company (hereafter referred to as "respondent") to cease and desist (1) from interfering with, restraining or coercing its employees in the exercise of their rights guaranteed in Sec. 7 of the National Labor Relations Act, 29 U.S.C.A. Sec. 157, and (2) from refusing to bargain collectively with International Glove Workers' Union of America, Local 85, as the exclusive representative of all its production employees, excepting supervisory and clerical employees. The decree also ordered respondent, (4c), upon request, to bargain collectively with Local 85 as the exclusive representative of all its production employees, in respect to rates of pay, wages, hours and other conditions of employment.

In its petition the Board alleged that respondent has failed to comply with, and had disobeyed and resisted compliance with, the paragraphs of the decree above set forth, and prayed that respondent and Thomas R. Stokes, Thomas H. Blair and C. W. White, its president, vice-president and superintendent, respectively, be adjudged in contempt.

In support of its petition the Board presented affidavits from officials of the union and from members of its collective bargaining committee to the effect that there has been no compliance with the above paragraphs of the decree.

In opposition to the Board's petition the respondents filed a joint and several answer denying that they have disobeyed and failed to comply with the decree, and averred that they did bargain in good faith in respect to all matters under consideration and have reached an agreement in all matters in which respondent could reach an agreement with the union.

An analysis of all the affidavits, after excluding all immaterial matters, leads us to the conclusion that the facts are that on January 20, 1940, a collective bargaining committee, representing Local 85, and Blair and White, representing respondent, held a conference at which Youngfelt, a member of the committee, inquired what respondent intended to do about complying with the decree, to which Blair replied: "We will meet with the committee of Local 85, but according to law it was (we are) required to meet with any employee or group of employees for the purpose of hearing any complaints they might have to make." Youngfelt thereupon stated that the union could not accept this limited recognition; that exclusive bargaining meant that respondent would deal with the committee of Local 85 and no other; that collective bargaining meant a program of meeting and getting the views of the employees which would lead to friendly relations and that all matters relating to working conditions and changes in rates of pay would have to be taken up with the committee; and that Blair replied: "We could never do anything like that . . . that would interfere with management."

The parties held a second conference on February 3, at which the union presented a proposed agreement. Blair voiced opposition to several of its provisions, but upon request of the committee agreed to give the proposal further consideration. They met again on February 17 to consider the agreement consisting of 12 paragraphs. It provided (1) that Local 85 represents all of the employees working in respondent's factory; (2) that the divisions of work would be left to the discretion of the employer and the shop committee; (3) that new kinds of work shall be submitted to the shop committee; (4) that overtime work shall be paid for at the rate of time and one-half, but no work to be performed on Sundays or holidays; (5) that Saturday shall be a holiday throughout the year; (6) that no discrimination shall be made against any member of the union; (7) that no solicitation nor union business shall be transacted upon the premises of the employer during working hours; (8) that no strikes or lockouts should take place during the life of the agreement and that all questions not settled by the agreement shall be referred to arbitration; (9) that the employer shall recognize and deal with shop stewards for discussion and adjustment of grievances; (10) that shop stewards shall be allowed to collect dues; (11) that present wages shall remain in force during the life of the agreement; and (12) that the agreement shall be in force for a definite period subject to cancellation by either party giving a 30-day written notice.

It will not be necessary to discuss all of the paragraphs. Blair objected to (4) and (6) on the ground that the payment of overtime and the question of discrimination were covered by the Fair Labor Standards Act, 29 U.S.C.A. Sec. 201 et seq., and the National Labor Relations Act, 29 U.S.C.A. Sec. 151 et seq. — consequently, there was no need to bargain about these points. He objected to (5) because, although it was respondent's policy not to work on Saturdays, there were times when it was necessary to do a limited amount of work. He objected to (8) on the ground that there was no law prohibiting men going out on a strike nor compelling respondent to operate its plant, and that he could not agree to arbitration on the ground that if the employees and the company could not work out their problems and have confidence in each other, operations could not be successful for either side.

With respect to (9) he stated that shop stewards would interfere with the duties of the foremen and were unnecessary, and as to (10) that he could not permit the collection of dues. Regarding (11) Blair would not embody wages in any agreement nor discuss the length of time that wages would remain in effect on the theory that wages were open for discussion at any time by either side. Finally, respecting (12) Blair in substance stated that respondent had accepted a number of provisions of the proposed agreement, requested changes in others and refused several of the provisions because they were contrary to respondent's policies; that the provisions accepted would be carried out to the letter but respondent would not sign any agreement. Thereupon Blair was informed that respondent had not made any counter-proposals and that the union would not consider that respondent had engaged in collective bargaining unless a written agreement was signed.

One further conference was held on March 9 and the proposed agreement was again the subject of discussion. Respondent insisted that matters covered by law could not be the subject of bargaining. As to matters covering wages, rates of pay and working conditions, respondent stated it would not agree to them as these would interfere with management. It declined to make counter-proposals because such a procedure would be against the company's principles.

On the record before us the question is whether the respondents have in fact refused to bargain collectively with Local 85.

Collective bargaining, as contemplated by the Act, is a procedure looking toward the making of a collective agreement between the employer and the accredited representative of his employees concerning wages, hours and other conditions of employment. Collective bargaining requires that the parties involved deal with each other with an open and fair mind and sincerely endeavor to overcome obstacles of difficulties existing between the employer and the employees to the end that employment relations may be stabilized and obstruction to the free flow of commerce prevented. [Citing cases.] Mere pretended bargaining will not suffice. National Labor Relations Board v. Whittier Mills Co., 5 Cir., 111 F. (2d) 474, 478, neither must the mind be hermetically sealed against the thought of entering into an agreement. Somerset Shoe Case, 111 F. (2d) 688. To do less than is required by the decisions above cited is a refusal to bargain collectively and violates the spirit and tenor of the Act. National Labor Relations Board v. Griswold Mfg. Co., 3 Cir., 106 F. (2d) 713, 720.

Respondent insisted that it would not discuss the scheduling of new rates except after they were put into effect; that it refused to discuss and to make any agreements as to overtime, Sunday or holiday work, because they were covered by laws; that it would not consider contractually binding itself against lockouts or agreeing to arbitrate any differences that might arise; and, finally and boldly, that it would not sign any written agreement even though satisfactory to both parties.

This attitude of the respondent upon these most essential principles convinces us that respondent participated in the discussions with Local 85 with a fixed intention not to agree with any proposal, irrespective of whether the proposed terms were otherwise acceptable. Such an attitude shows a total want of good faith and makes genuine collective bargaining impossible.

An order will be entered adjudicating the Boss Manufacturing Company, Thomas R. Stokes, Thomas H. Blair and C. W. White in contempt of the decree of this court entered on December 19, 1939. We await the suggestions of the parties as to the penalty to be imposed.

SPARKS, J., dissented.

NOTES

1. The following conduct has been held to be bad faith: refusal to sign a written contract which embodies the terms of a collective agreement, H. J. Heinz Co. v. NLRB, 311 U.S. 514, 61 Sup. Ct. 320, 85 L. Ed. 309 (1941); refusing to execute an agreement with the Union until it complies with a condition which is outside the area of compulsory bargaining, NLRB v. Dalton Telephone Co., 187 F.2d 811 (5th Cir. 1951) (insisting that Union register under a state statute so as to make it suable as an entity in the state courts); refusing to provide financial data, upon request, to support a claim of inability to pay, Southern Saddlery Co., 90 N.L.R.B. 1205, 26 L.R.R.M. 1322 (1950). See also NLRB v. Yawman & Erbe Manufacturing Co., 187 F.2d 947 (2d Cir. 1951), and Electric Auto-Lite Co., 89 N.L.R.B. 1192, 26 L.R.R.M. 1092 (1950).

2. Refusal to make a counterproposal when requested is evidence of bad faith. Landis Tool Co., 89 N.L.R.B. 503, 26 L.R.R.M. 1001 (1950). Compare Adler Metal Products Co., 79 N.L.R.B. 219, 22 L.R.R.M. 1359 (1948). See also NLRB v. Montgomery Ward, 133 F.2d 676 (9th Cir. 1943).

Section 8 (d) of the NLRA states: ". . . but such obligation does not compel either party to agree to a proposal or require the making of a concession."

3. During negotiations the company insisted upon including in any collective bargaining agreement a strong management prerogative clause. This clause provided that the company should have the right to exercise the customary functions of management, the right to hire, suspend, discharge, or otherwise discipline an employee for violation of rules or for other proper and just cause, the right to maintain the discipline and efficiency of employees, and the right to determine the schedules of work. The clause stated that an employee who felt himself aggrieved by the company's exercise of any of these rights had the right to have the decision reviewed by top management officials under the grievance machinery in the agreement, but that the final decision of the company should be made by these officials and "shall not be further reviewable by arbitration." The company in effect insisted upon this prerogative clause as a condition of agreement.

A union spokesman commented that "we never could agree to the prerogative clause even if he [the employer] gave us five hundred dollars a month increase . . ." The union in effect insisted upon the elimination or modification of this clause as a condition of agreement.

The NLRB ordered the employer, among other things, to cease and desist from "refusing to bargain with the union by in effect insisting on the prerogative clause." *he insisting on cl' = not bargaining in good faith — S Ct*

Is this a proper order? See NLRB v. American National Insurance Co., 343 U.S. 395, 72 Sup. Ct. 824, 96 L. Ed. 721 (1952). *held improper order he mgmt's insistence was legit.*

4. A refusal to bargain is usually based on a pattern of conduct rather than on a single act. Reed and Prince Manufacturing Co., 96 N.L.R.B. No. 129, 28 L.R.R.M. 1608 (1951); I.B.S. Manufacturing Co., 96 N.L.R.B. No. 200, 29 L.R.R.M. 1027 (1951).

5. For discussions of the characteristics of negotiations which have been regarded as indicative of a willingness or a refusal to bargain in good faith, see Note, Good Faith Bargaining in Labor Negotiations, 61 Harv. L. Rev. 1224 (1948); NLRB, 13th Ann. Rep. 61–62 (1948), 14th Ann. Rep. 75–77 (1949); Tower Hosiery Mills, 81 N.L.R.B. 658, 23 L.R.R.M. 1397 (1949), order enforced, 180 F.2d 701 (4th Cir. 1950), Soper, J., dissenting. In this case the Board said at page 662 of its report: "The respondent, it is true, went through many of the motions of collective bargaining. It met on numerous occasions with the union, conferred at great length regarding contract proposals, made concessions on minor issues, and discussed and adjusted several grievances. These sur-

face indicia of bargaining, however, were nullified by the respondent's manifest determination to deprive the union of any voice in determining such major issues as wage rates, and working conditions. Such conduct on the part of the respondent demonstrates that its participation in discussions with the union was not intended to lead to the consummation of an agreement with the union, but merely to preserve the appearance of bargaining."

Compare NLRB v. Corsicana Cotton Mills, 178 F.2d 344, 347, 179 F.2d 234 (5th Cir. 1949, 1950), where contempt proceedings were dismissed on the ground that company insistence that non-union employees be allowed to vote on an agreement negotiated by the bargaining agent was a mistake of judgment.

NOTES

1. NLRB v. Columbian Enameling & Stamping Co., 306 U.S. 292, 59 Sup. Ct. 501, 83 L. Ed. 660 (1939). The Supreme Court sustained a judgment refusing to enforce a Board order that the Company bargain with the representative of its employees. The Board order resulted from a refusal by the Company to meet with the Union at the request of conciliators. In so holding, the Court said at page 297: "While the Act . . . makes it the employer's duty to bargain with his employees, and failure to perform that duty entails serious consequences to him, it imposes no like duty on his employees. Since there must be at least two parties to a bargain and to any negotiations for a bargain, it follows that there can be no breach of the statutory duty by the employer — when he has not refused to receive communications from his employees — without some indication given to him by them or their representatives of their desire or willingness to bargain . . .

"However desirable may be the exhibition by the employer of a tolerant and conciliatory spirit in the settlement of labor disputes, we think it plain that the statute does not compel him to seek out his employees or request their participation in negotiations for purposes of collective bargaining, and that he may ignore or reject proposals for such bargaining which come from third persons not purporting to act with authority of his employees, without violation of law and without suffering the drastic consequences which violation may entail. To put the employer in default here the employees must at least have signified to respondent their desire to negotiate. Measured by this test the Board's conclusion that respondent refused to bargain with the Union is without support, for the reason that there is no evidence that the

Union gave to the employer, through the conciliators or otherwise, any indication of its willingness to bargain or that respondent knew that they represented the Union. The employer cannot, under the statute, be charged with refusal of that which is not proffered."

2. After a period of negotiations over a new contract which proves fruitless because the international union will not permit the local union to accept an agreement unless it contains a provision that the laws of the international will govern working conditions, the local union, shortly before August 1, 1945, presents the employer with a document, stating that the union "establishes the wages, hours and working conditions" as set forth. The local union's president states that this document is not a contract, need not be executed by the employer, but admits that it is practically a "take-it-or-leave-it" proposition. With a choice of accepting these conditions or taking a strike, the employer accepts the union's conditions, posts them, and operates in accordance with them.

In September, pursuant to a provision in the conditions, the union reopens the question of wages. During the ensuing bargaining sessions, the employer twice offers to increase wage rates and also offers to increase daily working hours from seven and one half to eight in order to increase take-home pay. The union refuses these proposals, fails to modify its original wage proposals, does not accept the employer's suggestion of arbitration, and finally, on November 2, 1945, without notification to the employer, goes on strike. The union does not communicate with the employer until December 15, 1945, when it informs him of an increase in the wage demands.

On December 17, 1945, the company advises the union that it is forming a new corporation to continue operations. On January 10, 1946, the union begins picketing. The company representative tells the union that the new corporation is to begin hiring employees and requests a meeting with the union membership. At the meeting the company representative reads the conditions of employment pursuant to which the new corporation is about to hire employees, states that the union members have the first opportunity to be hired, points out that under the laws of the union 51 per cent of the voting members can decide to end the strike, warns that if these conditions are rejected, the corporation will have to bring in a few key journeymen to train apprentices who will be recruited from returning war veterans and others, promises that no outside employees will be hired before January 21, and asks for a response. A union member at the meeting asks the company representative if the corporation is willing to negotiate with the union on conditions of employment. He replies that the corporation has no employees but that when it gets them it will be willing to negotiate conditions with their majority representative. He adds that the corporation will not negotiate with strikers who are not employees.

The union makes no response to the company's proposals. After the company representative leaves, a representative of the international union insists that the union membership vote to reject the company's proposals. He states, before the vote, that if the members vote to accept the proposals, he will have them deprived of their membership cards and will have the local union's charter permanently revoked. The members vote to reject.

A couple of days later a federal conciliator asks the company representative if he will meet with the union. He says that he is willing. He hears nothing further from the conciliator. On March 21, 1946, a representative of the international union calls on the company representative. The latter states that settlement is now difficult because replacements have been hired, but he proposes settlement with the understanding that the company will refuse to aid other struck companies, that the union will remove his company from its unfair list, and that the strikers will be hired to fill vacancies as they occur. On March 23 they meet again, and the union representative submits proposals for a contract. He states, however, that he has no authority to present them as a firm and final offer from the union, and that the proposals are only a basis for negotiations. At the union's request company representatives meet with the union strike committee on March 26. The union makes no specific proposals, and one union representative refers to the meeting as merely "exploratory."

On April 11 the representative of the international union who had met with the company representative on March 23 submits another proposed contract. The company asks the union by letter whether he is its official representative and if it has ratified the proposal. The union replies by stating that the questions are academic, but answers them affirmatively. On April 30 the company rejects the proposed contract on the grounds that it provides for blanket recognition of the rules of the international union, that it sets out an inadequate arbitration clause, and that the wage demands are even higher than those previously rejected. The company asks if the union will accept the arbitration procedure set out in the company's conditions of employment. On May 27 the union asks that the strikers be reinstated, with all rights provided by the union's conditions of employment as of August 1, 1945, and asks that the wage issue be arbitrated. On June 12 the company sends a letter to the union summarizing the negotiations, arguing that a joint arbitration committee is necessary, and asking a number of questions seeking clarification of the union's position. The company also asks to continue negotiations. The union makes no reply. The company is charged with a refusal to bargain, and a complaint is issued.

How will the NLRB dispose of this issue? See Times Publishing Co. et al., 72 N.L.R.B. 676, 19 L.R.R.M. 1199 (1947).

3. Section 8 (b) (3) of the amended NLRA makes it an unfair labor practice for a labor organization or its agents to refuse to bargain collectively. The NLRB has held that this section imposes upon labor unions a duty to bargain coextensive with the duty long since imposed upon employers.

(a) Would the conduct of the union described in Note 2, supra, constitute a violation of Section 8 (b) (3)?

(b) On or about August 21, 1947, the International Typographical Union and its subordinate locals met in convention and voted to follow a uniform bargaining policy, avowedly designed to circumvent those provisions of the amended NLRA which make the closed shop unlawful (see pages 475–483). Pursuant to this objective the Union adopted a "Conditions of Employment" form which set forth the only conditions under which ITU members would work — one such condition being that they would not work with nonunion men — and which contained the threat that any employer who did not provide these conditions would be struck. (In ITU terms, the Union would declare a "lockout.") Under this policy no contract would be entered into.

In October, 1947, the Union modified the policy so that local unions would submit to employers an alternative proposal, known as a "P–6A" contract, which embodied the Union's offer to enter into a bilateral agreement cancelable at any time upon 60 days' notice. See International Typographical Union et al., and American Newspaper Publishers Association, 86 N.L.R.B. 951, 25 L.R.R.M. 1001 (1949).

(1) Chicago Typographical Union No. 16, pursuant to the policy, refuses, during negotiations with the Chicago Newspaper Publishers Association from August 23 to October 21, 1947, to make any bilateral agreement, written or oral, with respect to terms and conditions of employment. The Union does, however, make it clear that it is prepared to negotiate wages and other economic conditions. Is this a refusal to bargain?

(2) On October 21, 1947, the Union offers the "P–6A" contract as an alternative, thus in effect offering to enter into a written bilateral agreement of 60 days' guaranteed duration. Does this constitute good-faith bargaining?

(3) The Union makes it clear, after proposing the "P–6A" contract, that if any of its conditions are violated (if, for example, non-union men are hired), the Union will cancel the contract pursuant to the 60-day cancellation clause, and strike. Does this additional fact affect your answer to Question (2) supra?

(4) Throughout negotiations the employer adamantly refuses to discuss wages or to submit a complete counterproposal. Does this constitute good-faith bargaining? Does this additional fact affect your answers to Questions (2) and (3) supra? See the following cases: Chicago Typographical Union No. 16 and International Typographical Union and Chicago Newspaper Publishers Assn., 86 N.L.R.B. 1041, 25 L.R.R.M. 1010 (1949) ; International Typographical Union and Baltimore Typographical Union No. 12 and Graphic Arts League et al., 87 N.L.R.B. 1215, 25 L.R.R.M. 1218 (1949) ; International Typographical Union and Its Subordinate Unions and Union Employers' Section of Printing Industry of America, Inc., 87 N.L.R.B. 1418, 25 L.R.R.M. 1243 (1949) .[46a]

(5) On July 17, 1947, prior to the effective date of the Taft-Hartley amendments to the NLRA, an employer and a local union orally reach agreement on the terms of a one-year contract to be effective on July 2, the expiration date of the prior contract. The contract contains the customary closed-shop provision and a clause providing that if any part of the contract is declared illegal or inoperative by any agency or court, the entire agreement shall become null and void. The Company fails to execute the July 17th agreement in writing. The Union indicates that it is primarily interested in obtaining written employer agreement to the July 17th contract, and the International Union gives its approval of this objective. Pursuant to this end, on August 8 the Union posts in the plant the conditions of employment under which its

[46a] The American Newspaper Publishers Association petitioned for review and modification of, and the NLRB petitioned for enforcement of, its order against the International Typographical Union. The NLRB also petitioned for enforcement of its order against the ITU and Chicago Typographical Union No. 16. The Printing Industry of America petitioned for review and modification of the Board order entered against the ITU in its case. The petitions for enforcement were granted, and the petitions to review and modify were denied except in one respect. American Newspaper Publishers Assn. v. NLRB, 193 F.2d 782 (7th Cir. 1951) .

members shall work.   These conditions are the same as those embodied in the oral agreement of July 17.

On August 9 the Company advises the employees that it rejects these conditions and purports to reinstate the 1945–1947 agreement, which the oral agreement of July 17 had presumably superseded.   On August 13 the Union serves a notice of termination. At a subsequent bargaining conference the Union, apparently following the policy of the International Union, proposes no contract and suggests that ITU-approved conditions of employment be followed.   No agreement is reached.   About the middle of October the Union submits the "P–6A" contract as the only contract which it will be willing to sign.   Again no agreement is reached.   The employer does not at any time offer to sign a written agreement embodying the terms of the oral contract of July 17.

Does the Union's conduct constitute a refusal to bargain?   See Nassau County Typographical Union No. 915 and International Typographical Union and the Daily Review Corporation, 87 N.L.R.B. 1263, 25 L.R.R.M. 1189 (1949).

(c) The 1947 agreement between a maritime union and the employer provides that the "Union agrees to furnish satisfactory men and the Company agrees that . . . all replacements shall be hired through the offices of the Union, as vacancies occur."   If the company validly rejects a man sent to it, the union must supply a replacement.   If it cannot, the company has the "right to obtain replacements wherever possible."

In practice the union operates under this hiring-hall clause as follows: Jobs are assigned in rotation to applicants who have registered.   Only union members are permitted to register. Nonunion members can come into the hiring hall and may be given job vacancies if no union member is available and willing to take the job.   A nonunion member who is assigned a job from the hiring hall is given a "trip card," which entitles him to keep his job for one round trip or for 30 days, whichever is sooner.   At the end of that period, he can be "bumped" by any union member who wants the job, unless during the trip he has joined the union.

(1) On November 19, 1947, the union requests by letter certain changes in the existing contract to be effective January 20, 1948. These changes include elimination of the no-strike clause.   It asks, however, that the hiring-hall provision be continued in effect without change.   On November 26 the company replies by letter and requests certain changes.   One of these changes is a modification of the hiring-hall provision.

On December 19 the parties meet. The union's proposals are discussed. A union spokesman says that "the demands were but a starting point" and that he would "willingly negotiate with respect to them." No agreement is reached on these proposals. The company's proposals are also discussed. Among other things, the company states that the hiring hall has to be modified to conform with the amended NLRA. The union insists that the provision is legal as it stands. No agreement, other than to extend the existing contract to February 19, 1948, is reached.

At subsequent negotiations the company proposes that the hiring-hall provision be modified so as to permit the company to reject a replacement sent by the hiring-hall if, in order to accept him, the company will have to discriminate against some other applicant on account of membership or non-membership. The company insists that some such modification is necessary in order to comply with the statute. The union insists that since the provision does not on its face require discrimination on the basis of union membership or the lack of it, the present hiring-hall clause is legal as it stands, and insists upon its retention. The parties negotiate for many months over this and other issues. They are able to reach tentative agreement on some issues. But they reach a complete impasse on this issue.

Does the union's conduct constitute a refusal to bargain?

(2) The union finally states that all substitute proposals for the hiring-hall provision are rejected and that it cannot settle for less than the standard hiring-hall clause. A union spokesman says: "We have got to have a hiring hall or your ships stay tied up."

Does the taking of this position constitute a refusal to bargain? See National Maritime Union of America et al. and the Texas Company, 78 N.L.R.B. 971, 22 L.R.R.M. 1289 (1948).

(d) An employer and a union in the shipping business have an oral agreement. The union goes on strike, alleging breach of agreement. A conference is called to settle the strike. The union says that it will end the strike only if the employer posts a $5000 performance bond. The employer cannot comply, and the strike is not settled.

Does the union's demand for a performance bond as a condition to settlement of the strike constitute a refusal to bargain? At the time of the strike the employer owed other carriers between $9000 and $10,000, and in times past he had paid wages with worthless checks, once being $3000 arrears in wage payments. See International Brotherhood of Teamsters, Chauffeurs, Warehousemen and Helpers of America, Local 294, and Henry V.

Union here acting reasonably, but its insistence was delaying coll. barg. & ... not in good faith

Rabouin, d.b.a. Conway's Express, 87 N.L.R.B. 972, 25 L.R.R.M. 1202 (1949).

Under Australian systems (excluding Wages Board procedure) there is no "compulsion to bargain."   Normal steps are
  (a) Calling of compulsory conferences by Court of Commissioner (e.g., Commonwealth Act sec. 15).
  (b) If conciliation can produce agreement, registration of this agreement so that it has the effect of an award (Commonwealth Act sec. 37).
  (c) If it appears that no agreement is possible, reference to a court or (if legislation allows) immediate making of an award (e.g., Commonwealth Act sec. 38).
The compulsion to attend conferences, court proceedings, etc., is in lieu of the compulsion to bargain.

Since 1947 the jurisdiction of the Court of Conciliation and Arbitration and the Conciliation Commissioners have been mutually exclusive.   However, by legislation passed in 1952 the Court has been given appellate and supervisory powers over the Commissioners.   The latter may continue to make binding awards (they are not restricted to "conciliation" in the strict sense), but appeals from their action may be taken to the Court.

The 1952 amendment represents the policy of non-labor parties in the Federal Parliament.   It was strongly opposed by the Labour Party.   Probably this is one of the features of the system which is likely to be changed from time to time in accordance with the politics of the government in power.

C. *The Individual Employee and Collective Bargaining*

J. I. CASE CO. v. NLRB
Supreme Court of the United States, 1944
321 U.S. 332, 64 Sup. Ct. 576, 88 L. Ed. 762

MR. JUSTICE JACKSON delivered the opinion of the Court.

This case was heard by the National Labor Relations Board on stipulated facts which so far as concern present issues are as follows:

The petitioner, J. I. Case Company, at its Rock Island, Illinois, plant, from 1937 offered each employee an individual contract of employment.   The contracts were uniform and for a term of one year.   The Company agreed to furnish employment as steadily as conditions permitted, to pay a specified rate, which the Company might redetermine if the job changed, and to maintain certain hospital facilities. The employee agreed to accept the provisions, to serve faithfully and honestly for the term, to comply with factory rules, and that defective work should not be paid for. About 75% of the employees accepted and worked under these agreements.

According to the Board's stipulation and finding, the execution of these contracts was not a condition of employment, nor was the status of individual employees affected by reason of signing or failing to sign the contracts. It is not found or contended that the agreements were coerced, obtained by any unfair labor practice, or that they were not valid under the circumstances in which they were made.

While the individual contracts executed August 1, 1941 were in effect, a C.I.O. union petitioned the Board for certification as the exclusive bargaining representative of the production and maintenance employees. On December 17, 1941 a hearing was held, at which the Company urged the individual contracts as a bar to representation proceedings. The Board, however, directed an election which was won by the union. The union was thereupon certified as the exclusive bargaining representative of the employees in question in respect to wages, hours, and other conditions of employment.

The union then asked the Company to bargain. It refused, declaring that it could not deal with the union in any manner affecting rights and obligations under the individual contracts while they remained in effect. It offered to negotiate on matters which did not affect rights under the individual contracts, and said that upon the expiration of the contracts it would bargain as to all matters. Twice the Company sent circulars to its employees asserting the validity of the individual contracts and stating the position that it took before the Board in reference to them.

The Board held that the Company had refused to bargain collectively, in violation of Sec. 8 (5) of the National Labor Relations Act, and that the contracts had been utilized, by means of the circulars, to impede employees in the exercise of rights guaranteed by Sec. 7 of the Act, with the result that the Company had engaged in unfair labor practices within the meaning of Sec. 8 (1) of the Act. It ordered the Company to cease and desist from giving effect to the contracts, from extending them or entering into new ones, from refusing to bargain and from interfering with the employees; and it required the Company to give notice accordingly and to bargain upon request.

The Circuit Court of Appeals, with modification not in issue here, granted an order of enforcement.   The issues are unsettled ones important in the Administration of the Act, and we granted certiorari.   In doing so we asked counsel, in view of the expiration of the individual contracts and the negotiation of a collective contract, to discuss whether the case was moot.   In view of the continuing character of the order we think it is not, and will examine the merits.

Contracts in labor law is a term the implications of which must be determined from the connection in which it appears.   Collective bargaining between employer and the representatives of a unit, usually a union, results in an accord as to terms which will govern hiring and work and pay in that unit.   The result is not, however, a contract of employment except in rare cases; no one has a job by reason of it and no obligation to any individual ordinarily comes into existence from it alone.   The negotiations between union and management result in what has often been called a trade agreement, rather than in a contract of employment.   Without pushing the analogy too far, the agreement may be likened to the tariffs established by a carrier, to standard provisions prescribed by supervising authorities for insurance policies, or to utility schedules of rates and rules for service, which do not of themselves establish any relationships but which do govern the terms of the shipper or insurer or customer relationship whenever and with whomever it may be established.   Indeed, in some European countries, contrary to American practice, the terms of a collectively negotiated trade agreement are submitted to a government department and if approved become a governmental regulation ruling employment in the unit.

After the collective trade agreement is made, the individuals who shall benefit by it are identified by individual hirings.   The employer, except as restricted by the collective agreement itself and except that he must engage in no unfair labor practice or discrimination, is free to select those he will employ or discharge. But the terms of the employment already have been traded out. There is little left to individual agreement except the act of hiring. This hiring may be by writing or by word of mouth or may be implied from conduct.   In the sense of contracts of hiring, individual contracts between the employer and employees are not forbidden, but indeed are necessitated by the collective bargaining procedure.

But, however engaged, an employee becomes entitled by virtue of the Labor Relations Act somewhat as a third party beneficiary to all benefits of the collective trade agreement, even if on his own he would yield to less favorable terms.   The individual hiring contract is subsidiary to the terms of the trade agreement and may not waive any of its benefits, any more than a shipper can contract away the benefit of filed tariffs, the insurer the benefit of standard provisions, or the utility customer the benefit of legally established rates.

Concurrent existence of these two types of agreement raises problems as to which the National Labor Relations Act makes no express provision. We have, however, held that individual contracts obtained as the result of an unfair labor practice may not be the basis of advantage to the violator of the Act nor of disadvantage to employees. National Licorice Co. v. Labor Board, 309 U.S. 350. But it is urged that where, as here, the contracts were not unfairly or unlawfully obtained, the court indicated a contrary rule in Labor Board v. Jones & Laughlin Steel Corp., 301 U.S. 1, 44–45, and Virginian Ry. Co. v. System Federation, 300 U.S. 515. Without reviewing those cases in detail it may be said that their decisions called for nothing and their opinions contain nothing which may be properly read to rule the case before us. The court in those cases recognized the existence of some scope for individual contracts, but it did not undertake to define it or to consider the relations between lawful individual and collective agreements, which is the problem now before us.

Care has been taken in the opinions of the Court to reserve a field for the individual contract, even in industries covered by the National Labor Relations Act, not merely as an act or evidence of hiring, but also in the sense of a completely individually bargained contract setting out terms of employment because there are circumstances in which it may legally be used, in fact, in which there is no alternative. Without limiting the possibilities, instances such as the following will occur: Men may continue to work after a collective agreement expires and, despite negotiation in good faith, the negotiation may be deadlocked or delayed; in the interim express or implied individual agreements may be held to govern. The conditions for collective bargaining may not exist; thus a majority of the employees may refuse to join a union or agree upon or designate bargaining representatives, or the majority may not be demonstrable by the means prescribed by the statute, or a previously existent majority may have been lost without unlawful interference by the employer and no new majority have been formed. As the employer in these circumstances may be under no legal obligation to bargain collectively, he may be free to enter into individual contracts.

Individual contracts, no matter what the circumstances that justify their execution or what their terms, may not be availed of to defeat or delay the procedures prescribed by the National Labor Relations Act looking to collective bargaining, nor to exclude the contracting employee from a duly ascertained bargaining unit; nor may they be used to forestall bargaining or to limit or condition the terms of the collective agreement. "The Board asserts a public right vested in it as a public body, charged in the public interest with the duty of preventing unfair labor practices." National Licorice Co. v. Labor Board, 309 U.S. 350, 364. Wherever private contracts conflict with its functions, they obviously must yield or the Act would be reduced to a futility.

It is equally clear since the collective trade agreement is to serve the purpose contemplated by the Act, the individual contract cannot be effective as a waiver of any benefit to which the employee otherwise would be entitled under the trade agreement. The very purpose of providing by statute for the collective agreement is to supersede the terms of separate agreements of employees with terms which reflect the strength and bargaining power and serve the welfare of the group. Its benefits and advantages are open to every employee of the represented unit, whatever the type or terms of his pre-existing contract of employment.

But it is urged that some employees may lose by the collective agreement, that an individual workman may sometimes have, or be capable of getting, better terms than those obtainable by the group and that his freedom of contract must be respected on that account. We are not called upon to say that under no circumstances can an individual enforce an agreement more advantageous than a collective agreement, but we find the mere possibility that such agreements might be made no ground for holding generally that individual contracts may survive or surmount collective ones. The practice and philosophy of collective bargaining looks with suspicion on such individual advantages. Of course, where there is great variation in circumstances of employment or capacity of employees, it is possible for the collective bargain to prescribe only minimum rates or maximum hours or expressly to leave certain areas open to individual bargaining. But except as so provided, advantages to individuals may prove as disruptive to industrial peace as disadvantages. They are a fruitful way of interfering with organization and choice of representatives; increased compensation, if individually deserved, is often earned at the cost of breaking down some other standard thought to be for the welfare of the group, and always creates the suspicion of being paid at the long-range expense of the group as a whole. Such discriminations not infrequently amount to unfair labor practices. The workman is free, if he values his own bargaining position more than that of the group, to vote against representation; but the majority rules, and if it collectivizes the employment bargain, individual advantages or favors will generally in practice go in as a contribution to the collective result. We cannot except individual contracts generally from the operation of collective ones because some may be more individually advantageous. Individual contracts cannot subtract from collective ones, and whether under some circumstances they may add to them in matters covered by the collective bargain we leave to be determined by appropriate forums under the laws of contracts applicable, and to the Labor Board if they constitute unfair labor practices.

It is also urged that such individual contracts may embody matters that are not necessarily included within the statutory scope of collective bargaining, such as stock purchase, group insurance, hospitalization, or medical attention. We know of nothing to prevent the employee's, because he is an employee, making any contract provided it is not inconsistent with a collective agreement or does not amount to or result from or is not part of an unfair labor practice. But in so doing the employer may not incidentally exact or obtain any diminution of his own obligation or any increase of those of employees in the matters covered by collective agreement.

Hence we find that the contentions of the Company that the individual contracts precluded a choice of representatives and warranted refusal to bargain during their duration were properly overruled. It follows that representation to the employees by circular letter that they had such legal effect was improper and could properly be prohibited by the Board.

One minor matter remains for consideration. The literal terms of the Board's order require the Company to "cease and desist from (a) giving effect to the individual contracts of employment or any modification, continuation, extension, or renewal thereof, or entering into any similar form of contract with its employees for any period subsequent to the date of this decision," and to give written notice to each to that effect and that "such contract will not in any manner be enforced or attempted to be enforced" and that "such discontinuance of the contract is without prejudice to the assertion of any legal rights the employee may have acquired under such contract."

These provisions, it has been argued, go beyond the Board's power, leave employees free to bring but the Company powerless to defend actions on the contract, and prohibit making future contracts even when not obnoxious to the law or to any collective agreement.

The Board, of course, has no power to adjudicate the validity or effect of such contracts except as to their effect on matters within their jurisdiction. National Licorice Co. v. Labor Board, supra. The Board, however, would construe the order more narrowly than its terms suggest. It says, "The provision in question, as we have seen, is based upon the finding that the contracts were utilized as a means of interference with rights guaranteed by the Act and constituted an obstacle to collective bargaining. Read in the context of this finding, the requirements of the cease and desist provisions enjoins petitioner only from continuing to derive benefits from the contracts heretofore utilized to forestall collective bargaining and deter self-organization, and from entering into new contracts either for the purpose of again thus utilizing them or under circumstances in which similar infringement of the collective bargaining process would be a probable consequence. The paragraph does not prevent petitioner from contracting with individual employees under circumstances which negative any intent to interfere with the employees' rights under the Act . . . Thus construed, the challenged requirement is but a reasonable safeguard . . ."

We agree, but the literal language of the order may well be read in quite different meaning, especially when separated from findings and standing alone in the Court's enforcement order. It then becomes the language of the Court, and the Court would not be bound to look upon the Board's construction as its own. Questions of construction had better be ironed out before enforcement orders issue than upon contempt proceedings. A party is entitled to a definition as exact as the circumstances permit of the acts which he can perform only on pain of contempt of court. Nor should he be ordered to desist from more on the theory that he may violate the literal language and then defend by resort to the Board's construction of it. Court's orders are not to be trifled with, nor should they invite litigation as to their meaning. It will occur often enough when every reasonable effort is made to avoid it. Where, as here, the literal language of the order goes beyond what the Board admits was intended, correction should be made. Paragraphs 1 (a) and 2 (a) of the decree of the court below are hereby modified, by adding the words in italics to read as follows:

1. Cease and desist from:
   (a) Giving effect to the individual contracts of employment or any modification, continuation, extension,
   or renewal thereof *to forestall collective bargaining
   or deter self-organization,* or entering into any similar form of contract with its employees for any
   period subsequent to the date of this Decree *for such
   purpose or with such effect.*

2. Take the following affirmative action which the Board
finds will effectuate the policies of the Act:
   (a) Give separate written notice to each of its employees
   who signed an individual contract of employment
   or any modification, continuation, extension, or renewal thereof, or any similar form of contract for any
   period subsequent to the date of this Decree, that
   such contract will not in any manner be enforced or
   attempted to be enforced *to forestall collective bargaining or deter self-organization,* that the employee
   is not required or expected by virtue of such contract to deal with respondent individually *in respect
   to rates of pay, wages, hours of employment, or other
   conditions of employment,* and that such discontinuance of the contract is without prejudice to the assertion of any legal rights the employee may have
   acquired under such contract *or to any defenses
   thereto by the employer.*

As so modified the decree is

Affirmed.[47]

MR. JUSTICE ROBERTS is of the opinion that the judgment should
be reversed.

NOTES

1. May a company and a union enter into an agreement which
provides that individual employees who are within the appropriate
bargaining unit but are not members of the union have the right
to deal individually with the employer? See United Automobile,
Aircraft & Agricultural Implement Workers, Local 180 (CIO) v.
J. I. Case Co., 250 Wis. 63, 26 N.W.2d 305, 170 A.L.R. 933 (1947).

[47] Cf. Note, Employee's Rights Under Conflicting Terms in Collective
Agreement and Individual Contract, 50 Yale L.J. 695 (1941); Weyand,
Majority Rule in Collective Bargaining, 45 Col. L. Rev. 556 (1945). —ED.

2. May a company and a union properly enter into a collective bargaining agreement which prescribes minimum rates for each job classification and expressly permits the company to negotiate and conclude individual contracts with employees providing for rates of pay higher than the minimum?

May the employer properly refuse, during negotiations with the union over the terms of a new collective bargaining agreement, to agree to any proposals which deprive individual employees of any rights they have acquired under the individual contracts?

3. In Order of Railroad Telegraphers v. Railway Express Agency, Inc., 321 U.S. 342, 64 Sup. Ct. 582, 88 L. Ed. 788 (1944), the Company had entered into contracts with some individual employees changing their wages, without giving notice to the Union as required by the collective agreement. The Union brought an action to enforce an award of the Railway Adjustment Board made under the wage provisions of the collective agreement and Section 2, Sixth and Seventh, of the Railway Labor Act, awarding the employees the difference between the amounts they actually were paid under the individual contracts and the amounts they would have been paid under the collective agreement. The Supreme Court sustained the Board and held that the employees were entitled to the compensation provided by the collective agreement.

Suppose the individual contract between the employer and the employee long antedates the collective bargaining agreement and gives the employee certain seniority rights. The collective agreement purports to abrogate these seniority rights. Does the individual contract which is more favorable to the particular employee prevail over the collective contract? See Lewellyn v. Fleming, 154 F.2d 211 (10th Cir. 1946).

4. Medo Photo Supply Corp. v. NLRB, 321 U.S. 678, 64 Sup. Ct. 830, 88 L. Ed. 1007 (1944), involved a petition by a union to have the National Labor Relations Board find the Company guilty of an unfair labor practice. The Company had recognized the Union as the representative of a unit of 26 employees (18 of whom supported the Union) and had agreed to meet for the purposes of collective bargaining. Two days prior to the date set for the meeting, at the request of 12 of the 18 Union members, the employer met with them and agreed to grant them wage increases when they stated that if he would do so they would deal directly with the Company rather than through a union. The Supreme Court affirmed the Board, holding that the Company had engaged in an unfair labor practice by granting individual wage increases in response to an offer to leave the Union.

5. A local union was certified in January, 1945, after an NLRB election. On May 29, 1945, the union and the company entered into a contract to run from January 26, 1945, to January 26, 1946. The parties could not agree on several issues, including wages and hours, and referred them to the War Labor Board. After June, 1945, the members showed a lack of interest in the union. A quorum failed to attend meetings, and only two members paid up their dues in July. In November, 1945, the president of the local union asked the War Labor Board to withdraw the case. An international representative of the union objected, however, and the matter went to hearing.

On December 19 the War Labor Board issued its recommendations. At a conference called by the company to consider these recommendations, the members of the bargaining committee of the local union indicated that they wanted to get out. In response to a question, the company president suggested that the employees prepare a written resignation form for signatures. A company stenographer was called in, and the two employees dictated a resignation form. The company president then suggested that a form be dictated for the signature of those desiring to stay in the union. This form was also dictated. On December 28 one of the employees who had dictated the forms used a company truck, with the approval of a company superintendent, to get the signatures of absent employees and out-of-town employees. He presented both forms to each employee and told him to sign the one he preferred. All the members (23 employees out of 42 in the unit — none in good standing), except one who could not be located, signed the withdrawal form. Subsequently, the employee who had obtained the signatures asked the company superintendent: "Are you going to adjust the wages, or are you going to let us go back in the union and let them get it for us?" A meeting was held on January 18 between company representatives and 21 employees. The employees indicated that all they were interested in was a little more money. On January 30 or 31 the company granted a wage increase.

Was the employer's conduct proper? See West Ohio Gas Co., 76 N.L.R.B. 179, 21 L.R.R.M. 1156 (1948), enforcement denied, 172 F.2d 685 (6th Cir. 1949).

NLRB v. CROMPTON–HIGHLAND MILLS, INC.
Supreme Court of the United States, 1949
337 U.S. 217, 69 Sup. Ct. 960, 93 L. Ed. 1320

Mr. Justice Burton delivered the opinion of the Court.

In this case a collective bargaining representative was certified, under the National Labor Relations Act, to represent all employees working in a certain appropriate bargaining unit. Their employer engaged in extended negotiations with this representative as to many matters, including rates of pay. December 19, 1945, the negotiations reached an impasse. The question here presented is whether this employer engaged in an unfair labor practice when, on January 1, 1946, it put into effect as of December 31, 1945, without prior consultation with the bargaining representative, a general increase in the rates of pay applicable to most of the employees who had been represented in the negotiations. This increase was a substantially greater one than any which the employer had offered during the negotiations. For the reasons to be stated, we hold that, under the circumstances, this action constituted an unfair labor practice and that a decree should be entered enforcing an order prohibiting such conduct. The case also raises questions as to the nature of the impasse which was reached and as to the proper scope and terms of the enforcement decree. . . .

I. The employer engaged in an unfair labor practice when, without consulting the employees' collective bargaining representative, it put into effect, for most of its employees who had been represented in the bargaining negotiations, a general increase in rates of pay which was substantially greater than any that the employer had offered.

The specific findings of the Board, coupled with the findings adopted by it from the trial examiner's report, leave no room for doubt as to the adequacy of the facts upon which its cease and desist order was based. The facts so found distinguish this case from any in which no collective bargaining representative has been certified or otherwise authorized to represent the employees in an appropriate unit. In the instant case, the wish of the employees to be consulted and to bargain collectively as to the terms of any general wage increase is established by the findings and the negotiations. Cf. Labor Board v. Columbian Enameling & Stamping Co., 306 U.S. 292, 297. We do not have here a case where the bargaining had come to a complete termination cutting off the outstanding invitation of the certified collective bargaining representative to bargain as to any new issue on such a matter as rates of pay. Cf. Labor Board v. Sands Mfg. Co., 306 U.S. 332. The opening which a raise in pay makes for the correction of existing inequities among employees and for the possible substitution of shorter hours, vacations or sick leaves, in lieu of some part of the proposed increase in pay, suggests the infinite opportunities for bargaining that are inherent in an announced readiness of an employer to increase generally the pay of its employees. The occasion is so appropriate for collective bargaining that it is difficult to infer an intent to cut off the opportunity for bargaining and yet be consistent with the purposes of the National Labor Relations Act.

We do not here have a unilateral grant of an increase in pay made by an employer after the same proposal has been made by the employer in the course of collective bargaining but has been left unaccepted or even rejected in those negotiations. Such a grant might well carry no disparagement of the collective bargaining proceedings. Instead of being regarded as an unfair labor practice, it might be welcomed by the bargaining representative, without prejudice to the rest of the negotiations. See In the Matter of W. W. Cross & Co., 77 N.L.R.B. 1162; In the Matter of Exposition Cotton Mills Co., 76 N.L.R.B. 1289; In the Matter of Southern Prison Co., 46 N.L.R.B. 1268.

We hold that the Board's order to cease and desist is justified, under the circumstances of this case, to the extent that the order requires the employer to cease and desist from refusing to bargain collectively by taking action, without prior consultation, with the authorized collective bargaining representative of the employees, with respect to general rates of pay which are substantially different from, or greater than, any which the employer has proposed during its negotiations with such representative. The need for this order depends in part upon the Board's finding that the action by the employer, on January 1, 1946, taken so soon after the meeting on December 19, 1945, showed that "the respondent (employer) was not acting in good faith during the negotiations, and is manifestly inconsistent with the principle of collective bargaining." 70 N.L.R.B. at p. 207. See May Dept. Stores Co. v. Labor Board, 326 U.S. 376; Medo Photo Supply Corp. v. Labor Board, 321 U.S. 678; Labor Board v. Newark Morning Ledger Co., 120 F. (2d) 262; Jeffery-Dewitt Insulator Co. v. Labor Board, 91 F. (2d) 134.[7]

[7] Even though the employer, since January 1, 1946, may have carried on collective bargaining in good faith as to rates of pay and other matters, a

MR. JUSTICE DOUGLAS, MR. JUSTICE MURPHY and MR. JUSTICE RUTLEDGE join in Part I of this opinion, but think the Board's order should be enforced without modification.

NOTES

1. In Central Metallic Casket Co., 91 N.L.R.B. 572, 26 L.R.R.M. 1520 (1950), a contract was executed on May 20, 1948, between an employer association and the union, to run until February 1, 1949. On November 28, 1948, the union notified all association members of certain changes in the contract which it desired, and requested a conference. From December 2, 1948, to May 19, 1949, the union and the association met six times but reached no agreement. In December and January the union also met six times with a representative of Central Metallic Casket Co. to discuss company proposals for new rates of pay and a production schedule with a bonus plan which involved the substitution of pay for day-work based on hourly rates rather than piece rates.

After the meeting of January 24, at which no agreement was reached, the company made no further attempts to negotiate with the union. However, the company general manager held individual conferences with the three members of the bargaining committee whom he thought were the principal obstacles to acceptance of his proposal. He refused their request to let an outside union agent sit in the conferences. His objective was to obtain from each of the three employees individual agreement to the bonus plan and hourly rates. Each refused, on the ground that such action would be inconsistent with his union obligations and therefore he would have to consult with the union. On

decree enforcing the original order against making a general increase without consulting the collective bargaining representatives is justifiable. ". . . an order of the character made by the Board, lawful when made, does not become moot because it is obeyed or because changing circumstances indicate that the need for it may be less than when made." Labor Board v. Pennsylvania Greyhound Lines, 303 U.S. 261, 271. See also, Federal Trade Comm'n. v. Goodyear Tire & Rubber Co., 304 U.S. 257.

[This case is discussed in Note, 35 Cornell L.Q. 192 (1949). See also NLRB v. Union Mfg. Co., 179 F.2d 511 (5th Cir. 1950) (unilateral wage, bonus, and vacation benefits).

Compare NLRB, 13th Ann. Rep. 61 (1948); Penokee Veneer Co., 74 N.L.R.B. 1683, 20 L.R.R.M. 1273 (1947), enforcement denied, 168 F.2d 868 (7th Cir. 1948) (employer, after having bargained to impasse with union, submitted final proposal directly to strikers individually by mail, requesting vote on enclosed ballot whether they would return to work on terms proposed by employer but rejected by union). The case is discussed in Note, Employer By-passing Designated Bargaining Agent, 27 N.C.L. Rev. 266 (1949).
— ED.]

February 14 the company posted notices that piecework was abolished and that the new rates were in effect. The general manager met with the three employees again. Once more they refused to agree individually to the bonus plan. They were discharged.

Did the company's conduct constitute a refusal to bargain?

2. In May Dept. Stores v. NLRB, 326 U.S. 376, 66 Sup. Ct. 203, 90 L. Ed. 145 (1945), the Board was held justified in finding that the employer, in seeking War Labor Board approval of employee wage increases without bargaining collectively with the certified representative on the matter of wages, was guilty of violating Section 8 (1) of the NLRA.

Compare United Welding Co., 72 N.L.R.B. 954, 19 L.R.R.M. 1241 (1947); Hudson Hosiery Co., 72 N.L.R.B. 1434, 19 L.R.R.M. 1288 (1947).

3. Suppose Company A has an agreement with Union X. Thirty days before the agreement expires, the Company joins Association B established for the purpose of collective bargaining. At the expiration of the agreement, a representative of the Union approaches the Company and makes certain bargaining demands. The Company says, "We are now bargaining through the Association. Take your demands there." The business agent of the Union says, "No. Seven years ago we were certified by the NLRB as the bargaining agent for your store. We will bargain with you, and you only. We will not meet with the Association under any circumstances. If you persist in your attitude, we will strike and picket your store and file charges with the NLRB." The Association hires you as counsel. What will be your advice?

In Morand Bros. Beverage, 91 N.L.R.B. 409, 26 L.R.R.M. 1501 (1950), the union reached an impasse in joint negotiations with an employer association. It then called a strike of the employees of one employer-member of the association, proposed that he enter separate negotiations, and sent a copy of its proposed contract to the other employer-members. The struck employer discharged all the union employees for going on strike. The other employer-members of the association refused employment to their union employees. The NLRB held that the union's conduct did not constitute a refusal to bargain within Section 8 (b) (3), nor did it constitute restraint or coercion in the selection of the employers' bargaining representative in violation of Section 8 (b) (1) (B). The Board said that to prohibit the union's conduct after the collapse of joint negotiations would be inconsistent with the basic policy of the NLRA to encourage collective bargaining, since the parties would be prevented from exhausting the possibilities of settling the dispute by that method rather than by economic attrition. However, the Board held that the employers' conduct violated Sections 8 (a) (1) and (3).

On a petition to review and set aside the Board order, it was held that the order would be enforced against the employer who had discharged the strikers but that, in respect to the other employers, it would be remanded to the Board for a finding as to whether those employers had discharged their employees for the purpose of interfering with the rights guaranteed to employees by Section 7 of the NLRA or had locked them out as a counter-measure to the strike. Morand Bros. Beverage Co. v. NLRB, 190 F.2d 576 (7th Cir. 1951).

THE ENDERBY CASE — IV

The Enderby Company and the United Rubber Workers finally reached agreement on May, 20, 1948. The contract provided, inter alia, that "all veterans of World War II hired on or before December 9, 1947, shall be given a seniority credit of one fourth of one year for each year of active military service, up to a maximum of one full year's credit, even though the particular employee was not employed by the Enderby Company prior to his entrance into military service." On September 23, 1948, the Enderby Company found it necessary, because of a shrinking market, to curtail its work force. The contract provided that "seniority shall be the decisive factor in determining who is laid off when economic conditions necessitate a reduction in work force." Seven non-veteran employees who had been hired on September 23, 1945, were laid off. Seven employees, with four years army service from 1941 to 1945, who had been hired on June 1, 1946, were retained.

1. The seven nonveterans brought action in the federal district court to restrain the Enderby Company from enforcing the clause of the agreement giving veterans preferential treatment. What result?

2. On April 19, 1949, one month before the contract expired, the seven nonveteran employees petitioned the NLRB to "decertify" the United Rubber Workers on the ground that they were guilty of "hostile discrimination" against nonveterans. What result?

STEELE v. LOUISVILLE & NASHVILLE
RAILROAD CO. et al.

Supreme Court of the United States, 1944
323 U.S. 192, 65 Sup. Ct. 226, 89 L. Ed. 173

STONE, C.J.   The question is whether the Railway Labor Act, 48 Stat. 1185, 45 U.S.C. secs. 151 et seq., imposes on a labor organization, acting by authority of the statute as the exclusive bargaining representative of a craft or class of railway employees, the duty to represent all the employees in the craft without discrimination because of their race, and, if so, whether the courts have jurisdiction to protect the minority of the craft or class from the violation of such obligation.

The issue is raised by demurrer to the substituted amended bill or complaint filed by petitioner, a locomotive fireman, in a suit brought in the Alabama Circuit Court against his employer, the Louisville & Nashville Railroad Company, the Brotherhood of Locomotive Firemen and Enginemen, an unincorporated labor organization, and certain individuals representing the Brotherhood.   The Circuit Court sustained the demurrer, and the Supreme Court of Alabama affirmed.   245 Ala. 113, 16 So. (2d) 416.   We granted certiorari, 322 U.S. 722, the question presented being one of importance in the administration of the Railway Labor Act.

The allegations of the bill of complaint, so far as now material, are as follows: Petitioner, a Negro, is a locomotive fireman in the employ of respondent Railroad, suing on his own behalf and that of his fellow employees who, like petitioner, are Negro firemen employed by the Railroad.   Respondent Brotherhood, a labor organization, is, as provided under sec. 2, Fourth of the Railway Labor Act, the exclusive bargaining representative of the craft of firemen employed by the Railroad and is recognized as such by it and the members of the craft.   The majority of the firemen employed by the Railroad are white and are members of the Brotherhood, but a substantial minority are Negros who, by the constitution and ritual of the Brotherhood, are excluded from its membership.   As the membership of the Brotherhood constitutes a majority of all firemen employed on respondent Railroad, and as under sec. 2, Fourth, the members, because they are the majority, have the right to choose and have chosen the Brotherhood to represent the craft, petitioner and other Negro firemen on the road have been required to accept the Brotherhood as their representative for the purposes of the Act.

On March 28, 1940, the Brotherhood, purporting to act as representative of the entire craft of firemen, without informing the Negro firemen or giving them opportunity to be heard, served a notice on respondent Railroad and on twenty other railroads operating principally in the southeastern part of the United States. The notice announced the Brotherhood's desire to amend the existing collective bargaining agreement in such manner as ultimately to exclude all Negro firemen from the service. By established practice on the several railroads so notified only white firemen can be promoted to serve as engineers, and the notice proposed that only "promotable," i.e., white, men should be employed as firemen or assigned to new runs or jobs or permanent vacancies in established runs or jobs.

On February 18, 1941, the railroads and the Brotherhood, as representative of the craft, entered into a new agreement which provided that not more than 50% of the firemen in each class of service in each seniority district of a carrier should be Negros; that until such percentage should be reached all new runs and all vacancies should be filled by white men; and that the agreement did not sanction the employment of Negros in any seniority district in which they were not working. The agreement reserved the right of the Brotherhood to negotiate for further restrictions on the employment of Negro firemen on the individual railroads. On May 12, 1941, the Brotherhood entered into a supplemental agreement with respondent Railroad further controlling the seniority rights of Negro firemen and restricting their employment. The Negro firemen were not given notice or opportunity to be heard with respect to either of these agreements, which were put into effect before their existence was disclosed to the Negro firemen. . . .

Protests and appeals of petitioner and his fellow Negro firemen, addressed to the Railroad and the Brotherhood, in an affort to secure relief and redress, have been ignored. Respondents have expressed their intention to enforce the agreement of February 18, 1941 and its subsequent modifications. The Brotherhood has acted and asserts the right to act as exclusive bargaining representative of the firemen's craft. It is alleged that in that capacity it is under a duty and obligation imposed by the Act to represent the Negro firemen impartially and in good faith; but instead, in its notice to and contracts with the railroads, it has been hostile and disloyal to the Negro firemen, has deliberately discriminated against them, and has sought to deprive them of their seniority rights and to drive them out of employment in their craft, all in order to create a monopoly of employment for Brotherhood members. . . .

The Supreme Court of Alabama took jurisdiction of the cause but held on the merits that petitioner's complaint stated no cause of action. It pointed out that the Act places a mandatory duty on the Railroad to treat with the Brotherhood as the exclusive representative of the employees in a craft, imposes heavy criminal penalties for willful failure to comply with its command, and provides that the majority of any craft shall have the right to determine who shall be the representative of the class for collective bargaining with the employer. See Virginia R. Co. v. System Federation, 300 U.S. 515, 545. It thought that the Brotherhood was empowered by the statute to enter into the agreement of February 18, 1941, and that by virtue of the statute the Brotherhood has power by agreement with the Railroad both to create the seniority rights of petitioner and his fellow Negro employees and to destroy them. It construed the statute, not as creating the relationship of principal and agent between the members of the craft and the Brotherhood, but as conferring on the Brotherhood plenary authority to treat with the Railroad and enter into contracts fixing rates of pay and working conditions for the craft as a whole without any legal obligation or duty to protect the rights of minorities from discrimination or unfair treatment, however gross. Consequently it held that neither the Brotherhood nor the Railroad violated any rights of petitioner or his fellow Negro employees by negotiating the contracts discriminating against them. . . .

But we think that Congress, in enacting the Railway Labor Act and authorizing a labor union, chosen by a majority of a craft, to represent the craft, did not intend to confer plenary power upon the union to sacrifice, for the benefit of its members, rights of the minority of the craft, without imposing on it any duty to protect the minority. Since petitioner and the other Negro members of the craft are not members of the Brotherhood or eligible for membership, the authority to act for them is derived not from their action or consent but wholly from the command of the Act. Section 2, Fourth provides: "Employees shall have the right to organize and bargain collectively through representatives of their own choosing. The majority of any craft or class of employees shall have the right to determine who shall be the representative of the craft or class for the purposes of this Act . . ." Under secs. 2, Sixth and Seventh, when the representative bargains for a change of working conditions, the latter section specifies that they are the working conditions of employees "as a class." Section 1,

Sixth of the Act defines "representative" as meaning "Any person or . . . labor union . . . designated either by a carrier or group of carriers or by its or their employees, to act for it or them." The use of the word "representative," as thus defined and in all the contexts in which it is found, plainly implies that the representative is to act on behalf of all the employees which, by virtue of the statute, it undertakes to represent.

By the terms of the Act, sec. 2, Fourth, the employees are permitted to act "through" their representative, and it represents them "for the purposes of" the Act. Sections 2, Third, Fourth, Ninth. The purposes of the Act declared by sec. 2 are the avoidance of "any interruption to commerce or to the operation of any carrier engaged therein," and this aim is sought to be achieved by encouraging "the prompt and orderly settlement of all disputes concerning rates of pay, rules, or working conditions." Compare Texas & New Orleans R. Co. v. Brotherhood of Clerks, 281 U.S. 548, 569. These purposes would hardly be attained if a substantial minority of the craft were denied the right to have their interests considered at the conference table and if the final result of the bargaining process were to be the sacrifice of the interests of the minority by the action of a representative chosen by the majority. The only recourse of the minority would be to strike, with the attendant interruption of commerce, which the Act seeks to avoid.

Section 2, Second, requiring carriers to bargain with the representative so chosen, operates to exclude any other from representing a craft. Virginian R. Co. v. System Federation, supra, 545. The minority members of a craft are thus deprived by the statute of the right, which they would otherwise possess, to choose a representative of their own, and its members cannot bargain individually on behalf of themselves as to matters which are properly the subject of collective bargaining. Order of Railroad Telegraphers v. Railway Express Agency, 321 U.S. 342, and see under the like provisions of the National Labor Relations Act J. I. Case Co. v. Labor Board, 321 U.S. 332, and Medo Photo Supply Corp. v. Labor Board, 321 U.S. 678. . . .

Unless the labor union representing a craft owes some duty to represent non-union members of the craft, at least to the extent of not discriminating against them as such in the contracts which it makes as their representative, the minority would be left with no means of protecting their interests or, indeed, their right to earn a livelihood by pursuing the occupation in which they are employed. While the majority of the craft chooses the bargaining representative, when chosen it represents, as the Act by its terms makes plain, the craft or class, and not the majority. The fair interpretation of the statutory language is that the organization chosen to represent the craft is to represent all its members, the majority as well as the minority, and it is to act for and not against those whom it represents. It is a principle of general application that the exercise of a granted power to act in behalf of others involves the assumption toward them of a duty to exercise the power in their interest and behalf, and that such a grant of power will not be deemed to dispense with all duty toward those for whom it is exercised unless so expressed.

We think that the Railway Labor Act imposes upon the statutory representative of a craft at least as exacting a duty to protect equally the interests of the members of the craft as the Constitution imposes upon a legislature to give equal protection to the interests of those for whom it legislates. Congress has seen fit to clothe the bargaining representative with powers comparable to those possessed by a legislative body both to create and restrict the rights of those whom it represents, cf. J. I. Case Co. v. Labor Board, supra, 335, but it has also imposed on the representative a corresponding duty. We hold that the language of the Act to which we have referred, read in the light of the purposes of the Act, expresses the aim of Congress to impose on the bargaining representative of a craft or class of employees the duty to exercise fairly the power conferred upon it in behalf of all those for whom it acts, without hostile discrimination against them.

This does not mean that the statutory representative of a craft is barred from making contracts which may have unfavorable effects on some of the members of the craft represented. Variations in the terms of the contract based on differences relevant to the authorized purposes of the contract in conditions to which they are to be applied, such as differences in seniority, the type of work performed, the competence and skill with which it is performed, are within the scope of the bargaining representation of a craft, all of whose members are not identical in their interest or merit. Cf. Carmichael v. Southern Coal Co., 301 U.S. 495, 509–510, 512 and cases cited; Washington v. Superior Court, 289 U.S. 361, 366; Metropolitan Casualty Co. v. Brownell, 294 U.S. 580, 583. Without attempting to mark the allowable limits of differences in the terms of contracts based on differences of conditions to which they apply, it is enough for present purposes to say that the statutory power to represent a craft and to make contracts as to wages, hours and working conditions does not include the authority to make among members of the craft discriminations not based on such relevant differences. Here the discriminations based on race alone are obviously irrelevant and invidious. Congress plainly did not undertake to authorize the bargaining representative to make such discriminations. Cf. Yick Wo v. Hopkins, 118 U.S. 356; Yu Cong Eng v. Trinidad, 271 U.S. 500; Missouri ex rel. Gaines v. Canada, 305 U.S. 337; Hill v. Texas, 316 U.S. 400.

The representative which thus discriminates may be enjoined from so doing, and its members may be enjoined from taking the benefit of such discriminatory action. No more is the Railroad bound by or entitled to take the benefit of a contract which the bargaining representative is prohibited by statute from making. In both cases the right asserted, which is derived from the duty imposed by the statute on the bargaining representative, is a federal right implied from the statute and the policy which it has adopted. It is the federal statute which condemns as unlawful the Brotherhood's conduct. "The extent and nature of the legal consequences of this condemnation, though left by the statute to judicial determination, are nevertheless to be derived from it and the federal policy which it has adopted." Deitrick v. Greaney, 309 U.S. 190, 200–201; Board of County Commissioners v. United States, 308 U.S. 343; Sola Electric Co. v. Jefferson Co., 317 U.S. 173, 176–7; cf. Clearfield Trust Co. v. United States, 318 U.S. 363.

So long as a labor union assumes to act as the statutory representative of a craft, it cannot rightly refuse to perform the duty, which is inseparable from the power of representation conferred upon it, to represent the entire membership of the craft. While the statute does not deny to such a bargaining labor organization the right to determine eligibility to its membership, it does require the union, in collective bargaining and in making contracts with the carrier, to represent non-union or minority union members of the craft without hostile discrimination, fairly, impartially, and in good faith. Wherever necessary to that end, the union is required to consider requests of non-union members of the craft and expressions of their views with respect to collective bargaining with the employer and to give to them notice of and opportunity for hearing upon its proposed action. . . .

We conclude that the duty which the statute imposes on a union representative of a craft to represent the interests of all its members stands on no different footing and that the statute contemplates resort to the usual judicial remedies of injunction and award of damages when appropriate for breach of that duty.

The judgment is accordingly reversed and remanded for further proceedings not inconsistent with this opinion.

Reversed.[48]

NOTES

1. Compare Betts v. Easley, 161 Kan. 459, 169 P.2d 831 (1946). Defendant union was certified under the Railway Labor Act as the collective bargaining agent for a unit of railroad shop employees. The plaintiffs were Negro members of the unit who had been segregated into a "Jim Crow" lodge. The Union's constitution provided that any such separate lodge "shall be under the jurisdiction of and represented by the delegate of the nearest white local in any meeting of the Joint Protective Board Federation or Convention where delegates may be seated." The Negro members were not permitted to participate in any determination of policy, or to vote in the selection of those who were to represent them. The plaintiffs sought an injunction to restrain the defendants from excluding eligible Negro workmen from full participation in privileges incident to the Railway Labor Act and to restrain them from requiring segregation into separate lodges. Held: The acts complained of constituted a violation of individual rights guaranteed by the Fifth Amendment; judgment of the lower court sustaining defendant's demurrer reversed, with directions to overrule the demurrer and grant equitable relief by injunction.

Apparently, this decision goes beyond the cases holding the "closed union" (discriminatory admissions practices) illegal because the labor union enjoyed the benefit of a closed-shop contract[49] and applies wherever a union serves as exclusive bargaining agent under a federal statute, thus denying such union the right to restrict membership on the basis of race.

2. In Haynes v. United Chemical Workers, 190 Tenn. 165, 228

[48] In Brotherhood of Locomotive Firemen and Enginemen v. Tunstall, 163 F.2d (4th Cir. 1947), cert. denied, 332 U.S. 841 (1947), Tunstall, a Negro fireman on the Norfolk Southern Railway, was awarded declaratory judgment, injunction and damages against the Brotherhood and the Railway, because of discriminations (parallel to those alleged in the Steele case) found to constitute a cause of action in Tunstall v. Brotherhood, etc., 323 U.S. 210, 65 Sup. Ct. 235, 89 L. Ed. 187 (1944). See Note, 3 Nat. B.J. 148 (1945).

See also, The Elimination of Negro Firemen on American Railways, 4 Law. Guild Rev. 32 (March–April, No. 2, 1944). For more recent cases see Brotherhood of Railroad Trainmen v. Howard, 343 U.S. 768, 72 Sup. Ct. 1022, 96 L. Ed. 917 (1952), and Rolax v. Atlantic Coast Line R. Co., 186 F.2d 473 (4th Cir. 1951). — Ed.

[49] James v. Marinship Corp., 25 Cal. 2d 721, 155 P.2d 329 (1944); Williams v. Int. Brotherhood of Boilermakers, 27 Cal. 2d 586, 165 P.2d 903 (1946).

S.W.2d 101 (1950), the provision of a contract between a union and an employer entitling war veterans who entered the service of the employer prior to a specified date to seniority credit was held not to be contrary to public policy.   However, in Huffman v. Ford Motor Co., 195 F.2d 170 (6th Cir. 1952), the provision of a contract giving seniority credit to veterans for military service subsequent to a specified date, even though they were not employed by the Company prior to entrance into service, was held to violate the doctrine of the Steele case.   In Hartley v. Brotherhood of Railway and S.S. Clerks, Freight Handlers and Station Employees, 283 Mich. 201, 277 N.W. 885 (1938), the provision in a collective agreement providing that all married women would be laid off irrespective of seniority acquired under the prior agreement was enforced against a married woman who, despite acquired seniority under prior agreement, was laid off.

3. See also Legal Protection Against Exclusion, pages 855–873 infra.

4. In Australia, discrimination of an undesirable type is systematically discouraged under the general power of the tribunals to have regard for the public interest, and prohibitions of various types of discrimination sometimes occur in the legislation.   See, e.g., Commonwealth Conciliation and Arbitration Act sec. 43: "In determining an industrial dispute under this Act, the Court or a Conciliation Commissioner shall provide, so far as possible, and so far as the Court or Conciliation Commissioner thinks proper, for uniformity throughout an industry carried on by employers in relation to hours of work, holidays and general conditions in that industry."

NLRB, 10TH ANNUAL REPORT 17–18 (1945) : "Lacking any specific authority to regulate directly the structure and practices of labor organizations except as an incident to the enforcement of Section 8 (2) of the Act, the Board has uniformly declined to treat a union's status as statutory bargaining agent as affected by alleged violation on its part of general civil or criminal law or moral and democratic precepts.   However, in Matter of Larus & Brother Company, Inc., 62 N.L.R.B. 1075 (1945), the Board held that a union which, in its collective bargaining contracts and representative practices, discriminates against employees in the bargaining unit in regard to tenure of employment, rates of pay, or other substantive conditions of employment on the basis of race, color, or creed, will not be permitted to secure or retain the Board's certificate as a statutory representative.   This holding, in which the Board applied doctrines foreshadowed in earlier decisions and recently approved by the Supreme Court, interprets the term 'representative' employed in Sections 7, 8, and 9 of the Act in the light of the express policies of the statute as well as the national policy against racial discrimination.   A statutory representative, the Board held, has a duty 'to represent all members of the unit equally and without discrimination on the basis of race, color, or creed.'

"The Larus decision affords an answer to a question mooted in a number of other cases decided earlier in the fiscal year; namely, whether a union seeking certification as exclusive bargaining agent is bound to offer membership to all employees in the bargaining unit.   The Board indicated that, in general, a labor organization's right to prescribe the qualifications of its members will be respected, but that a union acting as an exclusive representative under the statute must not exclude employees upon a discriminatory basis if it holds a contract with the employer containing closed-shop features.   Earlier, in Matter of Atlanta Oak Flooring Company, 62 N.L.R.B. 973, the Board had held that a statutory bargaining agent may segregate racial groups within its membership into separate but equally privileged locals or branches of its organization.   Thus, the rule has evolved: Neither exclusion from membership nor segregated membership per se represents evasion on the part of a labor organization of its statutory duty to afford 'equal representation.'   But in each case where the issue is presented the Board will scrutinize the contract and conduct of a representative organization and withhold or withdraw its certification if it finds that the organization has discriminated against employees in the bargaining unit through its membership restrictions or otherwise."

See also NLRB, 15th Ann. Rep. 36–37 (1950).

In Wallace Corp. v. NLRB, 323 U.S. 248, 65 Sup. Ct. 238, 89 L. Ed. 216 (1944), the Court enforced a Board order which reinstated with back pay forty-three members of a CIO union who had been discharged by the employer on demand of a company union under a closed-shop contract executed by the employer with knowledge that the local union would not admit to membership the CIO people who had lost the election and would insist on ousting them from their jobs.   Four Justices dissented.   The majority said, at page 255 of the official report: "The duties of a bargaining agent selected under the terms of the Act extend beyond the mere representation of the interests of its own group members. By its selection as bargaining representative, it has become the agent of all the employees, charged with the responsibility of representing their interests fairly and impartially. Otherwise, employees who are not members of a selected union at the time it is chosen by the majority would be left without adequate representation. No employee can be deprived of his employment because of his prior affiliation with any particular union. The Labor Relations Act was designed to wipe out such discrimination in industrial relations."

The case is discussed in Note, 40 Ill. L. Rev. 149 (1945).

D. *Subject Matter of Bargaining*

THE ENDERBY CASE — V

For many years prior to the establishment of a bargaining relationship with the United Rubber Workers, the Enderby Company had subcontracted certain types of work. During negotiations in April, 1950, the Union demanded a wage increase of 10 cents per hour, an extension of eligibility for vacations with pay, a night-shift premium of 12 cents per hour, a pension plan with voluntary retirement at sixty, and a clause whereby the Company agreed not to subcontract any work except in accordance with past practice. The Company offered, by way of a counterproposal, a wage increase of 3 cents an hour, a vacation plan substantially in accord with the one proposed by the Union, and a night-shift premium of 5 cents an hour. The Union countered by proposing a wage increase of 7 cents an hour, a night-shift premium of 10 cents an hour, and a pension plan with voluntary retirement at sixty-two. Agreement was finally reached on a wage increase of 6 cents an hour and a night-shift premium of 8 cents an hour. The Union dropped the demands for pensions and a clause on subcontracting. On November 1, 1950, the Company subcontracted a large amount of work normally done in Department X. The Company had not subcontracted this type of work since July, 1945. The Union objected vigorously and asked for negotiations on the point. The letter from the Union stated: "We propose that the Company agree not to subcontract any work unless it is of a type which cannot be performed by the Company without substantial capital investment." The Company refused to meet with the Union to discuss the proposal. The Company's letter of reply cited the "management prerogative" clause in the 1950 agreement (see page 326), as well as Sections 9 (a) and 8 (d) of the NLRA. The Union filed a complaint with the Regional Office of the NLRB. What result?

INLAND STEEL CO. v. NLRB
United States Court of Appeals, Seventh Circuit, 1948
170 F.2d 247, certiorari denied, 336 U.S. 960 (1949)

MAJOR, J. . . . In the beginning, it seems appropriate to set forth that portion of the Board's order which gives rise to the questions here in controversy. The order requires the Company to "Cease and desist from:

" (a) Refusing to bargain collectively with Local Unions Nos. 1010 and 64, United Steel-workers of America (CIO), with respect to its pension and retirement policies . . ."

The Company, in case No. 9612, attacks that portion of the order which requires it to bargain with respect to its retirement and pension policies . . .

The Company relates in lengthy detail the complicated nature of its retirement and pension plan, for the purpose, as we understand, of showing that it is impossible, or at any rate highly impractical, for it to bargain relative thereto with the multiplicity of bargaining units which the Board has established in its plant. . . .

The Company concedes that "Congress could have established a requirement of compulsory collective bargaining upon any subject which a representative of the employees chose to present for that purpose," and we understand from some parts of its argument that it tacitly concedes that some retirement and pension plans may be within the scope of the bargaining requirement. . . . We . . . are of the view that the bargaining requirements of the Act include all retirement and pension plans or none. Otherwise, as the Board points out, "some employers would have to bargain about pensions and some would not, depending entirely upon the unit structure in the plant and the nature of the pension plan the employer has established or desires to establish." Such a holding as to the Act's requirements would supply the incentive for an employer to devise a plan or system which would be sufficiently comprehensive and difficult to remove it from the ambit of the statute, and success of such an effort would depend upon the ingenuity of the formulator of the plan. We are satisfied no such construction of the Act can reasonably be made.

It is, therefore, our view that the Company's retirement and pension plan, complicated as it is asserted to be, must be treated and considered the same as any other such plan. It follows that the issue for decision is, as the Board asserts, whether pension and retirement plans are part of the subject matter of compulsory collective bargaining within the meaning of the Act . . .

Briefly, the plan as originally initiated on January 1, 1936, provided for the establishment of a contributory plan for the payment of retirement annuities pursuant to a contract between the Company and the Equitable Life Assurance Society. Only employees with earnings of $250.00 or more per month were eligible to participate. Effective December 31, 1943, the plan was extended to cover all employees regardless of the amount of their earnings, provided they had attained the age of 30 and had five years of service. The plan from the beginning was optional with the employees, who could drop out at any time, with rights upon retirement fixed as of that date. . . .

An integral and it is asserted an essential part of the plan from the beginning was that employees be compulsorily retired at the age of 65. (There are some exceptions to this requirement which are not material here.)

The Company's plan had been in effect for five and one-half years when, because of the increased demands for production and with a shortage of manpower occasioned by the war, it was compelled to suspend the retirement of its employees as provided by its established program. In consequence there were no retirements for age at either of the plants involved in the instant proceeding from August 26, 1941 to April 1, 1946. This temporary suspension of the compulsory retirement rule was abrogated, and it was determined by the Company that no retirements should be deferred beyond June 30, 1946. By April 1, 1946, all of the Company's employees, some 224 in number, who had reached the age of 65, had been retired. Thereupon, the Union filed with the Company a grievance protesting its action in the automatic retirement of employees at the age of 65. The Company refused to discuss this grievance with the Union, taking the position that it was not required under the Act to do so or to bargain concerning its retirement and pension plan, and particularly concerning the compulsory retirement feature thereof. Whereupon, the instant proceeding was instituted before the Board, with the result already noted.

This brings us to the particular language in controversy. Sec. 8 (5) of the Act requires an employer "to bargain collectively with the representative of his employees, subject to the provisions of Sec. 9 (a)," and the latter section provides that the duly selected representative of the employees in an appropriate unit shall be their exclusive representative "for the purposes of collective bargaining *in respect to rates of pay, wages, hours of employment, or other conditions of employment . . .*" (Italics supplied.) The instant controversy has to do with the construction to be given or the meaning to be attached to the italicized words; in fact, the controversy is narrowed to the meaning to be attached to the term "wages" or "other conditions of employment."

The Board found and concluded that the benefits accruing to an employee by reason of a retirement or pension plan are encompassed in both categories. As to the former it stated in its decision:

> With due regard for the aims and purposes of the Act and the evils which it sought to correct, we are convinced and find that the term "wages" as used in Section 9 (a) must be construed to include emoluments of value, like pension and insurance benefits, which may accrue to employees out of their employment relationship. . . . Realistically viewed, this type of wage enhancement or increase, no less than any other, becomes an integral part of the entire wage structure, and the character of the employee representative's interest in it, and the terms of its grant, is no different than in any other case where a change in the wage structure is effected.

The Board also found and concluded that in any event a retirement and pension plan is included in "conditions of employment" and is a matter for collective bargaining. After a careful study of the well written briefs with which we have been favored, we find ourselves in agreement with the Board's conclusion. In fact, we are convinced that the language employed by Congress, considered in connection with the purpose of the Act, so clearly includes a retirement and pension plan as to leave little, if any, room for construction. . . .

The opening sentence in the Company's argument is as follows: "Sections 8 (5) and 9 (a) of the Act do not refer to industrial retirement and pension plans, such as that of the petitioner, *in haec verba.*" Of course not, and this is equally true as to the myriad matters arising from the employer-employee relationship which are recognized as included in the bargaining requirements of the Act but which are not specifically referred to. Illustrative are the numerous matters concerning which the Company and the Union have bargained and agreed, as embodied in their contract of April 30, 1945. A few of such matters are: a provision agreeing to bargain concerning nondiscriminatory discharges; a provision concerning seniority rights, with its far reaching effect upon promotions and demotions; a provision for the benefit of employees inducted into the military service; a provision determining vacation periods with pay; a provision concerning the safety and health of employees, including clinic facilities; a provision for in-plant feeding, and a provision binding the Company and the Union to bargain, in conformity with a Directive Order of the National War Labor Board concerning dismissal or severance pay for employees displaced as the result of the closing of plants or the reduction in the working force following the termination of the war. . . .

The Company in its brief states the reasons for the establishment of a uniform fixed compulsory retirement age for all of its employees in connection with its retirement annuity program, among which are (1) "The fixed retirement age gives the employee advance notice as to the length of his possible service with the Company and enables him to plan accordingly," (2) "The fixed retirement age prevents grievances that otherwise would multiply as the question of each employee's employability arose," (3) "A fixed retirement age gives an incentive to younger men," and (4) "It is unfair and destructive of employee morale to discriminate between types of jobs or types of employees in retiring such employees from service." These reasons thus stated for a compulsory retirement age demonstrate, so we think, contrary to the Company's contention, that the plan is included in "conditions of employment."

The Supreme Court in National Licorice Co. v. N.L.R.B., 309 U.S. 350, 360, 60 S. Ct. 569, 84 L. Ed. 799, held that collective bargaining extends to matters involving discharge actions and, as already noted, the Company in its contract with the Union has so recognized. We are unable to differentiate between the conceded right of a Union to bargain concerning a discharge, and particularly a nondiscriminatory discharge, of an employee and its right to bargain concerning the age at which he is compelled to retire. In either case, the employee loses his job at the command of the employer; in either case, the effect upon the "conditions" of the person's employment is that the employment is terminated, and we think, in either case, the affected employee is entitled under the Act to bargain collectively through his duly selected representatives concerning such termination. . . . The Company's position that the age of retirement is not a matter for bargaining leads to the incongruous result that a proper bargaining matter is presented if an employee is suddenly discharged on the day before he reaches the age of 65, but that the next day, when he is subject to compulsory retirement, his Union is without right to bargain concerning such retirement.

The Company, however, attempts to escape the force of this reasoning by arguing that the retirement provision affects tenure of employment as distinguished from a condition of employment. The argument, as we understand, rests on the premise that the Act makes a distinction between "tenure of employment" and "conditions of employment," and attention is called to the use of those terms in Secs. 8 (3) and 2 (9) of the Act. Having thus asserted this distinction, the argument proceeds that tenure of employment is not embraced within the term "conditions of employment." Assuming that the Act recognizes such distinction for some purposes, it does not follow that such a distinction may properly be made for the purpose of collective bargaining, as defined in Sec. 9 (a). "Tenure" as presently used undoubtedly means duration or length of employment. The tenure of employment is terminated just as effectively by a discharge for cause as by a dismissal occasioned by a retirement provision. . . .

The Company also concedes that seniority is a proper matter for collective bargaining and, as already noted, has so recognized by its contract with the Union. It states in its brief that seniority is "the very heart of conditions of employment." Among the purposes which seniority serves is the protection of employees against arbitrary management conduct in connection with hire, promotion, demotion, transfer and discharge, and the creation of job security for older workers. A unilateral retirement and pension plan has as its main objective not job security for older workers but their retirement at an age predetermined by the Company, and we think the latter is as much included in "conditions of employment" as the former. What would be the purpose of protecting senior employees against lay-off when an employer could arbitrarily and unilaterally place the compulsory retirement age at any level which might suit its purpose? . . .

The Company in its brief as to seniority rights states that it "affects the employee's status every day." In contrast, the plain implication to be drawn from its argument is that an employee is a stranger to a retirement and pension plan during all the days of his employment and that it affects him in no manner until he arrives at the retirement age. We think such reasoning is without logic. . . . It surely cannot be seriously disputed but that such a pledge on the part of the Company forms a part of the consideration for work performed, and we see no reason why an employee entitled to the benefit of the plan could not upon the refusal of the Company to pay, sue and recover such benefits. In this view, the pension thus promised would appear to be as much a part of his "wages" as the money paid him at the time of the rendition of his services. But again we say that in any event such a plan is one of the "conditions of employment." . . .

The Board cites a number of authorities wherein the term "wages" in other fields of law has been broadly construed in support of its conclusion in the instant case that the term includes retirement and pension benefits for the purpose of collective bargaining. . . . For instance, the Board has been sustained in a number of cases where it has treated for the purpose of remedying the effects of discriminatory discharges, in violation of Sec. 8 (3) of the Act, pension and other "beneficial insurance rights of employees as part of the employees' real wages and, in accordance with its authority under Sec. 10 (c) , to order reinstatement of employees with . . . back pay," and has required the employer to restore such benefits to employees discriminated against. See Butler Bros., et al. v. N.L.R.B., 7 Cir., 134 F. (2d) 981, 985; General Motors Corp. v. N.L.R.B., 3 Cir., 150 F. (2d) 201, and N.L.R.B. v. Stackpole Carbon Co., 3 Cir., 128 F. (2d) 188. In the latter case, the court stated (128 F. (2d) at page 191) that the Board's conclusion "seems to us to be in line with the purposes of the Act for the insurance rights in substance were part of the employee's wages."

In the Social Security Act, 49 Stat. 642, Sec. 907, 42 U.S.C.A. sec. 1107, the same Congress which enacted the National Labor Relations Act defined taxable "wages" as embracing "all remuneration . . . [for services performed by an employee for his employer], including the cash value of all remuneration paid in any medium other than cash . . ." This definition has been construed, as the Supreme Court noted, in Social Security Board v. Nierotko, 327 U.S. 358, 365, 66 S. Ct. 637, 90 L. Ed. 718, 162 A.L.R. 1445 (note 17) , as including "vacation allowances," "sick pay," and "dismissal pay."

In the field of taxation, pension and retirement allowances have been deemed to be income of the recipients within the Internal Revenue Act definition of wages as "compensation for personal services." 26 U.S.C.A. Int. Rev. Code sec. 22 (a) . Thus, in Hooker v. Hoey, D.C., 27 F. Supp. 489, 490, affirmed, 2 Cir., 107 F. (2d) 1016, the court said: "It cannot be doubted that pensions or retiring allowances paid because of past services are one form of compensation for personal service and constitute taxable income . . ."

The Company places great stress upon the bargaining language used in the Railway Labor Act of 1926, 45 U.S.C.A. sec. 151 et seq., on the theory that the instant Act is *in pari materia*. It points out that numerous retirement and pension plans were put into effect by the railroads and that they were never subjected to the process of collective bargaining. This showing is made for the purpose of demonstrating that Congress in the enactment of the legislation now before us did not intend to include such matters. In this connection, we think it is pertinent to note that in the Railway Labor Act the bargaining language was quite different from that of the instant legislation. There, it read, "rates of pay, rules, or working conditions." Here, it reads, "rates of pay, wages, hours of employment, or other conditions of employment." A comparison of the language of the two Acts shows that Congress in the instant legislation must have intended a bargaining provision of broader scope than that contemplated in the Railway Labor Act. Certainly the term "wages" was intended to include something more than "rates of pay." Otherwise, its use would have served no purpose. Congress in the instant legislation used the phrase, "other conditions of employment," instead of the phrase, "working conditions," which it had previously used in the Railway Act. We think it is obvious that the phrase which it later used is more inclusive than that which it had formerly used. . . .

It is our view, therefore, and we so hold that the order of the Board, insofar as it requires the Company to bargain with respect to retirement and pension matters, is valid, and the petition to review, filed by the Company in No. 9612, is denied. . . .

NOTES

1. See Note, Pension and Retirement Matters — A Subject of Compulsory Collective Bargaining, 43 Ill. L. Rev. 713 (1948); Note, Proper Subjects for Collective Bargaining: Ad Hoc v. Predictive Definition, 58 Yale L.J. 803 (1949); Cox and Dunlop, Regulation of Collective Bargaining by the National Labor Relations Board, 63 Harv. L. Rev. 389 (1950); Taylor, Government Regulation of Industrial Relations 280–282 (1948); Note, The Scope of Required Collective Bargaining Under the L.M.R.A., 50 Col. L. Rev. 351 (1948).

2. In W. W. Cross & Co. v. NLRB, 174 F.2d 875 (1st Cir. 1949),

in reliance on the Inland Steel case, the Court enforced an order of the Board that the employer bargain with the Union as to a group health and accident insurance program which the employer had unilaterally initiated.

3. In Weyerhauser Timber Co., 87 N.L.R.B. 672, 25 L.R.R.M. 1163 (1949), the NLRB held that the price of meals served at the place of employment is a subject of compulsory bargaining. The Board took a similar position with respect to leases on company homes in Elgin Standard Brick Manufacturing Co., 90 N.L.R.B. 1467, 26 L.R.R.M. 1343 (1950).

4. The NLRA, as amended, and other provisions of the Taft-Hartley Act have placed certain matters beyond the scope of permissible bargaining.

Thus, closed-shop agreements are made unfair labor practices of employers and unions. So are union-shop and maintenance-of-membership agreements, unless authorized in secret ballot by a majority of the employees eligible to vote.[50] (Secs. 8 (a) (3), 8 (b) (2), and 9 (e).) State laws absolutely prohibiting or more severely regulating closed-shop, union-shop, or maintenance-of-membership agreements prevail over the federal law. (Sec. 14 (b).) The check-off of union dues, when authorized only by the collective agreement, is made a crime. (Secs. 302 (a), (c) (4).)

Certain types of featherbedding agreements are made unfair labor practices. (Sec. 8 (b) (6).)

And the terms of agreements for employer contributions to union welfare funds are regulated in detail, subject to criminal penalties. (Secs. 302 (a), (c) (5).)

What is the significance of such statutory restraints upon the negotiation of agreements: (1) as to cause and effect, and (2) as to long-run tendencies of government?

5. In the Australian arbitration systems the subject matters of awards are defined in the relevant legislation in very wide terms, the trend being to extend the range of "industrial disputes," as the original definitions are treated by the tribunals, so as to include matters on which disputes have in fact occurred. For example, Commonwealth Act, sec. 4, defines "industrial matters" as "all matters pertaining to the relations of employers and employees . . . and includes all questions of what is right and fair in relation to an industrial matter having regard to the interests of the persons

---

[50] On October 29, 1951, the President signed a bill which amends the Taft–Hartley Act by eliminating the requirement that a special election must be conducted by the NLRB before a union-shop provision can be embodied in a collective bargaining agreement. 28 L.R.R. 360 (1951).

immediately concerned and of society as a whole," and without prejudice to the generality of this, a list of seventeen specific matters is set out covering wages, hours, apprenticeships, preference, seniority, discipline, sex of workers, demarcation of functions, rest rooms, canteens, leave, and indeed "all matters or things affecting or relating to work done or to be done." The definitions are so wide as apparently to exclude the possibility of a matter being held not "industrial," but see the King v. Kelly, (1951) A.L.R. 287, where the Commonwealth award was held invalid insofar as it fixed hours of trading of butchers' shops.

The industrial tribunals frequently use their discretionary powers in relation to organizations and awards in order to discourage strikes, refusal to work overtime, "job control," and other undesirable labour practices.

NLRB v. J. H. ALLISON & CO.
United States Court of Appeals, Sixth Circuit, 1948
165 F.2d 766, certiorari denied, 335 U.S. 814 (1948)

MARTIN, Circuit Judge.   The National Labor Relations Board ordered the respondent, J. H. Allison & Company, a Tennessee corporation doing business in Chattanooga, Tennessee, to cease and desist from refusing to bargain collectively concerning so-called "merit wage increases" with a labor union (affiliated with the American Federation of Labor), as exclusive representative and bargaining agent of its production workers; and to grant no merit wage increases to such employees "without prior consultation with the Union."

Respondent was affirmatively ordered to bargain collectively with the union regarding merit wage increases; and, upon request, to furnish the union "full information with respect to merit wage increases, including the number of such increases, the amount of such increases, and the standards employed in arriving at such increases." The customary directions as to notice-posting and notification of the Regional Director were given. This court is petitioned to enter a decree enforcing the Board's order in entirety. Respondent vigorously opposes the petition. . . .

The material facts are not in dispute. The respondent company for approximately five years had dealt with the union and had executed exclusive bargaining contracts with it as representative of the employees. At the time of the occurrences during 1945 upon which the complaint is based, one of these annual agreements, dated January 7, 1945, was in effect. This contract provided for a minimum wage scale; but no provision was made therein for merit increases. Indeed, the subject was not mentioned in the signed agreement. A few months after the execution of this contract, the company, in conformity with its past practice, gave some thirty-one out of a total number of from one hundred and five to one hundred and fifteen, of its employees wage increases. Upon learning this, an official representative of the union requested respondent on May 2, 1945, to furnish the union with a list of the names of the employees who had received increased pay, together with the amount of the raise granted each. He stated that such information was necessary as a basis for further collective bargaining negotiations on wage rates. Respondent refused to divulge the desired information, and was likewise adamant to similar later requests from the union. The reasons given by the company for rejection were that merit wage increases are not proper subject matter for collective bargaining, but fall within exclusively managerial function; and that the union could obtain from its own membership the information which it sought. . . .

Upon the substantial evidence, the Labor Board found that during negotiations for 1946, the ensuing year, the union requested respondent to include in the contract a clause concerning the union's rights with respect to merit increases and other changes in wages, but that respondent "presumably adhering to its previously announced position that merit increases are not a bargainable issue," refused the request of the union, which "then dropped its request stating that the matter would probably be settled in the proceedings which it had instituted before the Board."

In its decision, the Board expressed concurrence in the Trial Examiner's conclusion that the respondent had not fulfilled its obligation to bargain collectively with the union. No merit was found in the company's contention that merit increases are a prerogative of management; but they were deemed by the Board "an integral part of the wage structure" and, as such, a proper subject for collective bargaining. The refusal of respondent, during the formulation of the 1946 contract, to negotiate with the union concerning merit wage increases and to furnish information upon the subject so that the union could adequately represent the employees, was declared to be the basis of the Board's finding that respondent had refused to bargain within the meaning of section 8 (5) of the Act. . . .

. . . the constant position of respondent has been and now is that merit increases are not, under the National Labor Relations

Act, a proper subject for collective bargaining; and that the company will not negotiate or bargain with the union upon the subject until "ordered so to do by final authority." This pat position of the employer necessitates the course pursued by the union to enforce the rights of its membership claimed under the Act. Nor do we see logical justification in the view that in entering into a collective bargaining agreement for a new year, even though the contract was silent upon a controverted matter, the union should be held to have waived any rights secured under the Act, including its right to have a say-so as to so-called merit increases. Such interpretation would seem to be disruptive rather than fostering in its effect upon collective bargaining, the national desideratum disclosed in the broad terms of the first section of the National Labor Relations Act, 29 U.S.C.A. sec. 151.

In its brief, respondent states its insistence that "the ex parte giving of merit increases does not come within the scope of collective bargaining in the absence of a provision in its contract to the contrary, and that under the existing contract and usage obtaining between the Company and the Union, the merit increases were not the subject of collective bargaining." . . . Respondent argues that it is common practice for employers to grant merit increases; and that, unless there is an express stipulation in the bargaining agreement to the contrary, the employer may at any time during the term of the contract give an individual employee a merit increase within "the network" of the wage scale negotiated between the employer and the union representing its employees as bargaining agent. . . .

In our judgment, the argument of the respondent will not stand. We think the logical deduction to be drawn from the opinions of the Supreme Court is that by virtue of the National Labor Relations Act the obligation of the employer to bargain collectively with representatives of its employees with respect to wages, hours, and working conditions, includes the duty to bargain with such representatives concerning individual merit wage increases. The labeling of a wage increase as a gratuity does not obviate the fact that a gratuitous increase on the basis of merit does, in actuality, effectuate changes in rates of pay and wages, which are by the Act made the subject of collective bargaining.

In J. I. Case Co. v. National Labor Relations Board, 321 U.S. 332, 337–339, 64 S. Ct. 576, 580, 88 L. Ed. 762, the Supreme Court discusses generally the relation of individual contracts to collective bargaining, and declares that regardless of the circumstances justifying the execution of individual contracts the procedures prescribed by the National Labor Relations Act, looking to collective bargaining, may not by individual employment contracts be defeated or used to forestall collective bargaining or "to limit or condition the terms of the collective agreement." . . .

On the same day that the opinion in the case just discussed was announced, the Supreme Court held, in Order of Railroad Telegraphers v. Railway Express Agency, Inc., 321 U.S. 342, 346, 347, 64 S. Ct. 582, 585, 88 L. Ed. 788, that the failure of a carrier to give notice to the bargaining representative of its employees of an intended change affecting rates of pay of certain individual employees constituted a violation of section 6 of the Railway Labor Act of 1926 (the 1934 Railway Act containing a similar provision), 48 Stat. 1197, 45 U.S.C.A. sec. 156. Mr. Justice Jackson, who also wrote the opinion in J. I. Case Co. v. National Labor Relations Board, supra, said: "From the first the position of labor with reference to the wage structure of an industry has been much like that of the carriers about rate structures. It is insisted that exceptional situations often have an importance to the whole because they introduce competitions and discriminations that are upsetting to the entire structure. Hence effective collective bargaining has been generally conceded to include the right of the representatives of the unit to be consulted and to bargain about the exceptional as well as the routine rates, rules, and working conditions. . . ."

Even though the foregoing decisions of the Supreme Court do not hold directly that so-called merit increases are so closely identified with "rates of pay" as to be properly considered within the coverage of that phrase as used in the Act, we think that the discussion and reasoning in the cases leads to the conclusion that the union, as collective bargaining agent, may not be ignored by refusal of the employer to furnish information as to the basis of such increases, or the names of those receiving betterments in the wage scale and the amounts of the increased wages received by them.

Aluminum Ore Co. v. National Labor Relations Board, 7 Cir., 131 F. (2d) 485, 486, 487, 147 A.L.R. 1, is closely in point. There, the complaint was that the employer had taken unilateral action as to certain wage increases, and had withheld from the union "information as to pay rates which was necessary and basic to collective bargaining." . . .

The company declared . . . that it would determine for itself what the wages and rates of pay should be, as it had done for many years; that it was making presently certain increases of which it had advised the union [as was not done by respondent in the instant case]; and that such increases would stand unless and until there should be objections by any individual member of the union, in which event the company would permit any aggrieved person to present his complaint, either personally or through the union.

The Court of Appeals held justifiable the finding of the Labor Board that the employment of unilateral procedure by the company was not within the spirit and contemplation of the Act. In enforcing the order of the Board, with immaterial modifications insofar as the opinion is authoritative here, the court said: "In determining what employees should receive increases and in what amounts, it could have been only helpful to have before the bargainers the wage history of the various employees, including full information as to the work done by the respective employees and as to their respective wages in the past, their respective increases from time to time and all other facts bearing upon what constituted fair wages and fair increases. . . . Petitioner announced the increases it would be willing to make but it refused to supply the wage history. From this refusal, we think the Board was justified in concluding that petitioner had failed to cooperate wholeheartedly in collective bargaining."

The Aluminum Ore Co. case is not distinguished by the fact, that, there, the employer insisted upon making all wage changes unilaterally, while the employer in the case at bar asserts the right to grant wage increases only to certain individuals of its own choice. In both cases, the insistence is upon impermissible unilateral company action as to wage increases.

For the reasons which have been indicated, a decree of enforcement of the order of the National Labor Relations Board will be entered as prayed in its petition to this court. [Simons, J., dissented. The dissenting opinion and the Court's footnotes are omitted.]

NOTES

1. In General Controls Co., 88 N.L.R.B. 1341, 25 L.R.R.M. 1475 (1950), the Board found the employer guilty of a refusal to bargain by refusing to furnish the union "the name, classification, rate of pay, and merit rating score of each employee . . . and full information with respect to individual periodic merit wage increases or decreases, including the names of employees who received such increases or decreases, the amount of such in-

creases or decreases, and the dates on which such increases or decreases were put into effect."   Member Reynolds dissented.

The majority said at page 1343: "All the information requested by the Union was necessary in order for the Union effectively to police the existing contract, and in order for it intelligently to bargain with respect to future contracts.   Without such information, the Union would be seriously hampered.   Under these circumstances, we have consistently held that withholding this type of information, when requested, constitutes a violation of the Act. The courts have approved this doctrine.   And the result has been the same whether the demand and refusal occurred at the time of contract negotiations, or in the middle of the term."

Under the contract, the employer had complete power to make merit ratings and increases without consulting the union.   The merit ratings were also used by the employer in determining layoffs, discharges, and promotions.   The company was willing to disclose information in respect to the complaints and grievances of specific employees, but it steadfastly refused to give such information on an over-all basis.

2. In Allied Mills, Inc., 82 N.L.R.B. 854, 23 L.R.R.M. 1632 (1949), the Board held that an employer must bargain on a subject (pensions) which is part of rates of pay, wages, hours, or other conditions of employment within the meaning of Section 9 (a) and is not written into the contract, unless the agreement contains a clear and specific waiver.   In Tide Water Associated Oil Co., 85 N.L.R.B. 1096, 24 L.R.R.M. 1518 (1949), the Board held that a management prerogative clause stating that "This Agreement shall in no way affect the operation of, or the status of any Employee with respect to any welfare or benefit plan of the Company . . . that may be in effect during the term hereof" was not a waiver of the union's right to bargain on a Retirement Allowance Plan, even though the plan had been in existence for some time and had been administered unilaterally by the employer.

3. See NLRB, 14th Ann. Rep. 78 (1949).   Compare Cox and Dunlop, The Duty to Bargain Collectively During the Term of an Existing Agreement, 63 Harv. L. Rev. 1097, 1125 et seq. (1950).

JACOBS MANUFACTURING CO.
National Labor Relations Board, 1951
94 N.L.R.B. 1214, 28 L.R.R.M. 1162
enforced, 196 F.2d 680 (2d Cir. 1952)

[In July, 1948, the Company and the UAW (CIO) executed a two-year contract which by its terms could be reopened one year after its execution date for a discussion of "wage rates." In July, 1949, the Union invoked this reopening clause and gave written notice of wage demands. These included a request for a wage increase, a request that the Company take over the full cost of an existing group insurance program, and a request for the establishment of a pension plan. The Company refused to discuss the insurance and pension requests on the ground that they were not appropriate items of discussion under the reopening clause. At the time of negotiations in 1948 the Company and the Union had discussed changes in the insurance program and had agreed to increase certain of the benefits as well as the costs. However, neither the changes nor the insurance program was mentioned in the agreement. No pension plan was in effect in the plant, and the subject was not discussed during the 1948 negotiations, nor was it mentioned in the contract. For refusing to discuss the insurance and pension requests (and other conduct not pertinent here) the Company was charged with a refusal to bargain. The opinion of Board Members Houston and Styles is set forth in part below.]

. . . We are satisfied, too, that the 1948 contract did not in itself impose on the Respondent any obligation to discuss pensions or insurance. The reopening clause of that contract refers to *wage rates,* and thus its intention appears to have been narrowly limited to matters directly related to the amount and manner of compensation for work. For that reason, a requirement to discuss pensions or insurance cannot be predicated on the language of the contract.

On the other hand, a majority of the Board believes that regardless of the character of the reopening clause, the Act itself imposed upon the Respondent the duty to discuss *pensions* with the Union during the period in question.

It is now established as a principle of law that the matter of pensions is a subject which falls within the area where the statute requires bargaining. And, as noted above, the 1948 contract between the Respondent and the Union was silent with respect to the subject of pensions; indeed, the matter had never been raised or discussed by the parties.   The issue raised, therefore, is whether the Respondent was absolved of the obligation to discuss pensions because of the limitation contained in Section 8 (d) of the amended Act dealing with the duty to discuss or agree to the modification of an existing bargaining contract.   The pertinent portion of Section 8 (d) of the Act provides:

> . . . the duties so imposed shall not be construed as requiring either party to discuss or agree to any modification of the terms and conditions contained in a contract for a fixed period, if such modification is to become effective before such terms and conditions can be reopened under the provisions of the contract.

So far as the matter of pensions is concerned, the issue presented is not novel.   On the contrary, it is one which has twice before, in the Allied Mills and Tide Water cases, been before the Board, and which, in the Tide Water case was fully considered and squarely passed upon in the unanimous opinion of the full Board.   The crucial point at issue here, as in the earlier cases, is the construction to be given the phrase "terms and conditions *contained in* a contract."   (Emphasis supplied.)   The Board, in the Tide Water case, concluded that the pertinent portion of Section 8 (d) : *refers to terms and conditions which have been integrated and embodied into a writing.*   Conversely it does not have reference to matters relating to "wages, hours and other terms and conditions of employment," which have not been reduced to writing.   As to the written terms of the contract either party may refuse to bargain further about them, under the limitations set forth in the paragraph, without committing an unfair labor practice.   With respect to unwritten terms dealing with "wages, hours and other terms and conditions of employment," the obligation remains on both parties to bargain continuously.

Thus, as already construed by this Board in the Tide Water case, Section 8 (d) does not itself license a party to a bargaining contract to refuse, during the life of the contract, to discuss a bargaining subject unless it has been made a part of the agreement itself.   Applied here, therefore, the Tide Water construction of Section 8 (d) means that the Respondent was obligated to discuss the Union's pension demand.

Members Houston and Styles have carefully reexamined the Board's construction of Section 8 (d) in the Tide Water case. and are persuaded that the view the Board adopted in the Tide Water case best effectuates the declared policy of the Act.   Chairman Herzog, while joining in the result with respect to the obligation to bargain here concerning pensions — never previously discussed by the parties — joins in the rationale herein only to the extent that it is consistent with his views separately recited below, concerning the insurance program.

By making mandatory the discussion of bargainable subjects not already covered by a contract, the parties to the contract are encouraged to arrive at joint decisions with respect to bargainable matters, that, at least to the party requesting discussion, appear at the time to be of some importance. The Act's policy of "encouraging the practice and procedure of collective bargaining" is consequently furthered. A different construction of Section 8 (d) in the circumstances — one that would permit a party to a bargaining contract to avoid discussion when it was sought on subject matters not contained in the contract — would serve, at its best, only to dissipate whatever the good will that had been engendered by the previous bargaining negotiations that led to the execution of a bargaining contract; at its worst, it could bring about the industrial strife and the production interruptions that the policy of the Act also seeks to avert.

The significance of this point cannot be overemphasized. It goes to the heart of our disagreement with our dissenting colleague, Member Reynolds. His dissent stresses the need for "contract stability," and asserts that the furtherance of sound collective bargaining requires that the collective bargaining agreement be viewed as fixing, for the term of the contract, all aspects of the employer-employee relationship, and as absolving either party of the obligation to discuss, during that term, even those matters which had never been raised, or discussed in the past. We could hardly take issue with the virtue of "contract stability," at least in the abstract, and we would certainly agree that everyone is better off when, in negotiating an agreement, the parties have been able to foresee what all the future problems may be, to discuss those problems, and either to embody a resolution of them in the contract, or to provide that they may not be raised again during the contract. But we are here concerned with the kind of case in which, for one reason or another, this has *not* been done, and the question is what *best* effectuates the policies of the Act in *such* a case.

In this connection we cannot ignore the fact that to say that a party to an agreement is absolved by Section 8 (d) of an obligation to discuss a subject not contained in a contract does not mean that the other party is prohibited from taking economic action to compel bargaining on that subject.   The portion of Section 8 (d) we are here considering does no more than provide a *defense* to a charge of a refusal to bargain under Section 8 (a) (5) or 8 (b) (3) of the Act.   It does not render unlawful economic action aimed at securing lawful objectives.   That being so, the view urged by Member Reynolds achieves "contract stability" but only at the price of industrial strife, and that is a result which now more than ever, we must avoid.   The basic policy of this Act to further collective bargaining is founded on the proposition — amply demonstrated by experience — that collective bargaining provides an escape valve for the pressures which otherwise result in industrial strife.   With this policy in mind, we are loath to narrow the area of mandatory bargaining, except where the amended statute, in the clearest terms, requires that we do so.

The construction of Section 8 (d) adopted by the Board in the Tide Water case serves also to simplify, and thus to speed, the bargaining process.   It eliminates the pressure upon the parties at the time when a contract is being negotiated to raise those subjects that may not then be of controlling importance, but which might in the future assume a more significant status.   It also assures to both unions and employers that, if future conditions require some agreement as to matters about which the parties have not sought, or have not been able to obtain agreement, then some discussion of those matters will be forthcoming when necessary.

We cannot believe that Congress was unaware of the foregoing considerations when it amended the Act by inserting Section 8 (d) , or that it sought, by the provision in question, to freeze the bargaining relationship by eliminating any mandatory discussion that might lead to the addition of new subject matter to an existing contract.   What Section 8 (d) does do is to reject the pronouncements contained in some pre-1947 Board and court decisions, — sometimes *dicta,* sometimes necessary to the holding — to the effect that the duty to bargain continues even as to those matters upon which the parties have reached agreement and which are set forth in the terms of a written contract.   But we believe it does no more.   Those bargainable issues which have never been discussed by the parties, and which are in no way treated in the contract, remain matters which both the union and the employer are obliged to discuss at any time.

In so holding, we emphasize that under this rule, no less than in any other circumstance, the duty to bargain implies only

an obligation to *discuss* the matter in question in good faith with
a sincere purpose of reaching some agreement. It does not require that either side agree, or make concessions. And if the
parties originally desire to avoid later discussion with respect to
matters not specifically covered in the terms of an executed contract, they need only so specify in the terms of the contract itself.
Nothing in our construction of Section 8 (d) precludes such an
agreement, entered into in good faith, from foreclosing future
discussion of matters not contained in the agreement.

Chairman Herzog, for reasons set forth in his separate opinion,
believes that — unlike the pensions issue — the Respondent was
under no obligation to bargain concerning the *group insurance
program.*

However, Members Houston and Styles — a minority of the
Board on this issue — are of the further opinion that the considerations discussed above leading to the conclusion that the Respondent was obligated to discuss the matter of pensions, also,
impel the conclusion that the Respondent was obligated to discuss
the Union's group insurance demand. Like pensions, the matter
of group insurance benefits is a subject which has been held to be
within the area of compulsory bargaining; and like pensions, the
Respondent's group insurance program was not mentioned in the
terms of the 1948 contract. Members Houston and Styles therefore believe that so far as the controlling facts are concerned, the
ultimate issues presented by the Union's pension and group insurance demands are identical; and that the views already expressed hereinabove with respect to the matter of pensions are
equally applicable, and equally controlling, with respect to the
matter of the Respondent's group insurance program.

Members Houston and Styles believe, moreover, that the view
adopted by Chairman Herzog on the insurance issue is subject to
the same basic criticism as is the view of Member Reynolds — it
exalts "contract stability" over industrial peace; it eliminates
mandatory collective bargaining on subjects about which one of
the parties now wants discussion, and concerning which it may
well be willing to take economic action if discussion is denied,
solely because the matter has once been discussed in a manner
which may warrant an inference that the failure to mention that
subject in the contract was part of the bargain. Members Houston
and Styles are constrained to reject the view of Chairman Herzog
for the further reason that it would establish a rule which is administratively unworkable, and would inject dangerous uncertainty into the process of collective bargaining. Apart from the

extremely difficult problems of proof — illustrated in this very case — which would constantly confront the Board in cases of this type, the parties to collective bargaining negotiations would always be faced with this question after a subject has been discussed — "Have we really negotiated, or are we under an obligation to discuss the subject further if asked to?"   To this query the rule of the Tide Water case gives a clear and concise answer: "You are obligated to discuss any bargainable subject upon request unless you have reduced your agreement on that subject to writing or unless you have agreed in writing not to bargain about it during the term of the contract."   Members Houston and Styles would apply that rule without deviation.

CHAIRMAN HERZOG, concurring in part:

I believe that this Respondent was *not* under a duty to discuss the Union's *group insurance* demand.   The individual views which lead me, by a different road, to the result reached on this issue by Members Reynolds and Murdock, are as follows:

Unlike the issue of pensions, concerning which the contract is silent and the parties did not negotiate at all in 1948, the subject of group insurance was fully discussed while the Respondent and the Union were negotiating the agreement.   True, that agreement is silent on the subject, so it cannot literally be said that there is a term "contained in" the 1948 contract relating to the group insurance program.   The fact remains that during the negotiations which preceded its execution, the issue was consciously explored. The record reveals that the Union expressly requested that the preexisting program be changed so that the Respondent would assume its entire cost, the very proposal that was again made as part of the 1949 mid-term demand which gave rise to this case. The Respondent rejected the basic proposal on this first occasion, but agreement was then reached — although outside the written contract — to increase certain benefits under the group insurance program.

In my opinion, it is only reasonable to assume that rejection of the Union's basic proposal, coupled in this particular instance with enhancement of the substantive benefits, constituted a part of the contemporaneous "bargain" which the parties made when they negotiated the entire 1948 contract.   In the face of this record as to what the parties discussed and did, I believe that it would be an abuse of this Board's mandate to throw the weight of Government sanction behind the Union's attempt to disturb, in mid-term, a bargain sealed when the original agreement was reached.

[Member Reynolds dissented from the holding that the Company had violated Section 8 (a) (5) of the Act by refusing to bargain on the subjects of pensions and insurance.   He stated, inter alia, at page 1233: ". . . I would find that a contract would be modified within the meaning of Section 8 (d) by an addition to, deletion from, or change in the written agreement, or by any change in the basic terms and conditions of employment existing at the time the collective bargaining agreement was executed but which were not incorporated into the written instrument.   Eliminating the duty to bargain in midterm concerning items not mentioned in the contract does not mean that the collective bargaining process ends with the negotiation of the contract.   Day-to-day grievances and other disputes arising out of the employer-employee relationship are ever present.   The settlement of these matters is part and parcel of the bargaining process, and it is in this regard that there remains upon the parties the continuing duty to bargain collectively . . . negotiating or legislating the basic terms of the agreement need be undertaken only periodically, usually at annual or biennial conferences mutually agreed upon by the parties.   Collective bargaining during the term of the contract therefore would be mandatory only with respect to administering or interpreting the terms of the contract in accordance with the procedure outlined in the contract."

Member Murdock also dissented from the holding that the refusal to discuss pensions and insurance violated Section 8 (a) (5).   His position was based on the argument that the Union had never requested bargaining on pensions and insurance independent and divorced from a discussion of wage rates under the reopening clause and that, therefore, the Company's willingness to bargain on those issues independently was never put to test.]

NOTES

1. The union asks the employer for a wage increase or a decrease in the price of the employer's product.   Proper?

2. The union asks the employer to install more modern equipment so the employees can earn more on incentive.   Proper?

3. The union asks the employer to manufacture additional products so as to relieve seasonal unemployment.   Proper?

4. The union demands an immediate increase in wages.   Wages are covered in the existing contract.   The union also demands a pension.   Pensions are not covered in the agreement.   What kind of a bargaining position is the employer in if the union makes it clear that it will drop the pension demand if, but only if, the employer agrees to the wage demand?   (See Note,

The Taft-Hartley Act, 64 Harv. L. Rev. 781, 839–841 (1951).)

5. The employer proposes a clause in the agreement giving him unilateral control over a subject within the ambit of Section 9 (a). Proper?

6. The employer, party to a lawful union-shop agreement, asks the union to reduce its initiation fees and monthly dues.   Proper?

See Cox and Dunlop, Regulation of Collective Bargaining by the National Labor Relations Board, 63 Harv. L. Rev. 389 (1950) ; Findling and Colby, Regulation of Collective Bargaining by the National Labor Relations Board — Another View, 51 Col. L. Rev. 170 (1951) ; Note, The Impact of Collective Bargaining on Management Prerogatives, 16 U. of Chi. L. Rev. 568 (1949).

E. *Value of Statutory Duty to Bargain*

NLRB, 11TH ANNUAL REPORT 1–2 (1946) : ". . . The fact is that the only kind of strikes which the Board was created to discourage, those involving recognition and the commission of unfair labor practices, have declined sharply, both absolutely and relatively, since 1937. [Organizational strikes in 1938, the first year of relatively unhampered operation of the Act, accounted for only 44 per cent of the strike idleness in that year, as compared with 76 per cent in 1937.   Except for 1939, the figure for 1938 has never been exceeded.   In the years 1942 through 1945, for instance, the percentage has never been greater than 35 per cent.   In 1945, . . . such idleness accounted for only 29 per cent of the total, as compared with 76 per cent for 1937.   Likewise, the number of workers involved in organizational strikes has declined since 1937, when 60 per cent of the workers on strike were involved in organizational disputes.   In 1938 the percentage dropped to 32 per cent and it has never exceeded 33 per cent in the years 1940 through 1945. In 1945, only 22 per cent of the strikers were involved in organizational strikes . . .]"   (In 1946 this figure was 12 per cent. NLRB, 12th Ann. Rep. 1 (1947).)

MILLIS and BROWN, FROM THE WAGNER ACT TO TAFT–HARTLEY *
91–92 (1950)

Strikes for recognition were not eliminated by the work of the N.L.R.B., in spite of its provision of a peaceable means of settling

* Reprinted by permission of the University of Chicago Press. — Ed.

issues over claims to recognition. The United States Department of Labor reports almost 10,000 strikes involving the issue of recognition from 1935 through 1946, 2,200 of which occurred during the great organization drive of 1937.   Included, however, are intrastate disputes not under the Act.   Moreover, strikes over this issue, which were 30 per cent or more of all strikes in 1934 and the first years of the Act, greatly decreased during the war to less than 500 annually, under 10 per cent of all strikes, and even in 1946 were back only to 16 per cent.   Meantime the 37,000 elections conducted by the Board during the twelve years prevented many potential strikes and developed habits of peaceable procedures. The increase in recognition strikes in the two postwar years can probably be attributed in large measure to the fact that inadequate appropriations for the Board made it impossible for the staff to handle cases promptly and led many unions to resort to use of their economic power in order to avoid delays.

F. *Suspension of the Duty to Bargain*

THE ENDERBY CASE — VI

The 1950 agreement between the Enderby Company and the United Rubber Workers contains a reopening clause which permits either party, upon written notice, to open up for negotiations the question of "general wage rates."   (See contract, page 329 infra.)   On May 21, 1951, the Union filed such a notice with the Company, demanding a wage increase of 10 cents an hour and an agreement on subcontracting.

On July 1, 1951, agreement had still not been reached.   At that point 127 production workers struck, disgruntled because the Company had recently subcontracted a large volume of work. The Company broke off negotiations at once, advising Curme that "the Company refuses to negotiate further until such time as the Union lives up to the contract [see Art. III, page 321 infra] and the men return to work."   Curme insisted that the strike did not have the sanction of the union.   Indeed, he stated that "the Union is flatly opposed to strike action at this time."

Curme called an emergency meeting of the Union.   He urged the strikers to return to work, and, at his suggestion, a resolution was passed stating that the strikers should go back to work at once. Thirty-seven men did return as a result of this action.

White, speaking for the Company, still refused to resume negotiations.   He stated: "We are not satisfied that the Union is in good faith in this matter. The contract calls for the Union 'to exert every effort' to terminate a strike during the life of the agreement. Until the Union directs these unlawful strikers to return to work under a specific threat of discipline for failure to do so, the Company will refuse to negotiate concerning either the proposed wage increase or subcontracting."

At the regular weekly meeting of the Union three days later, Curme proposed a motion to the effect that "effective immediately, each striker shall be fined $5 for each day he remains away from the job." The motion was defeated by a vote of 312 to 289.

When advised by Curme that "the Union has done everything it can," White reiterated his former position. Three days later the Company repudiated the contract and began hiring replacements. Fifty-seven more men returned to work, but seven of them were refused employment on the ground that they had been ringleaders of the strike.

The Union filed a grievance (see contract, pages 318–321 infra), alleging a violation of Section 2 of Article I (see contract, page 318 infra). The Company agreed to meet with the Grievance Committee. The Company refused in the meeting to discuss any issue other than reinstatement of the strikers, stating that *any* discussion was a mere gratuity since the contract had been vitiated by the illegal strike. The Union agreed to the Company's position, with the understanding that when the reinstatement issue had been settled, other negotiations would be resumed. The Company agreed. After four days of discussion without agreement, the Union proposed that other negotiations be resumed. The Company refused. The Union, at an emergency meeting, voted overwhelmingly to strike. The Company refused to discuss the issue of reinstatement, wages, or subcontracting until the strike had been terminated. It also instituted a wage increase of 5 cents an hour effective immediately and began hiring replacements on a large scale. The Union filed a complaint with the Regional Office of the NLRB. What result?

NOTES

1. The contract between the United Steelworkers and the Timken Roller Bearing Company contained a no-strike clause stating in part: "There shall be no lock-outs on the part of the Company and no strikes on the part of the Union during the term of this agreement." The parties also agreed to cooperate in disciplining employees who caused a work stoppage.

The contract contained a grievance procedure which provided that any grievance or dispute involving the interpretation or application of the contract not adjusted through the grievance machinery should be submitted to arbitration. The grievance procedure also contained a statement that in the case of differences as to the meaning and application of the agreement or "local trouble of any kind," there should be no suspension of work but an earnest effort to settle the differences through the grievance machinery.

The contract also contained a management clause which stated: "The management of the works and the direction of the working forces, including the right to hire, suspend or discharge for proper cause, or transfer, and the right to relieve employees from duty because of lack of work, or for other legitimate reasons, is vested exclusively in the Company, provided that this will not be used for purposes of discrimination against any member of the Union."

In 1945 the Company took disciplinary action against certain employees who had left their jobs because of a shortage in the work-crew, and it also placed certain work schedules in effect for maintenance employees. The Union thereupon instituted a general strike. The Company stopped bargaining on two grievances then in process and refused to participate in any grievance proceedings relating to the causes of the strike until the men returned to work. It did indicate, however, that it would meet with the Union when the men had returned and grievances had been filed. The strike was called off after a month.

The Union had also made a demand for consultation on the matter of subcontracting work. The Company had refused on the ground that subcontracting was a management function.

The NLRB, in Matter of The Timken Roller Bearing Company and United Steelworkers of America (CIO), 70 N.L.R.B. 500, 18 L.R.R.M. (1946), held that the Company had refused to bargain during the pendency of the strike concerning (1) grievances then in process, (2) the causes of the strike, and (3) subcontracting. It found the Company in violation of Section 8 (5) on the theory that there is a continuous statutory obligation to bargain which exists independently of all contractual obligations, and that a breach of contract on the part of the Union does not relieve the employer from this obligation.

In granting the petition to set aside the Board's order and denying the Board's petition for enforcement in Timken Roller Bearing Co. v. NLRB, 161 F.2d 949 (6th Cir. 1947), the court said at page 955: "Though the duty to bargain is absolute, it may be channeled and directed by contractual agreement . . . The law invites, though it may not compel, a collective bargaining agreement. If adjudication bases no sanctions on commitments made therein by the bargaining agent, it imparts futility to a bargaining process hopefully developing in the interest of industrial peace. If the law penalizes one party to the contract for standing on a bargain not itself violative of law, there may still be compulsion to bargain, but the virtue of agreement vanishes. It may well be that industry will concede much for a no-strike covenant and orderly grievance procedures. It may also result that it will concede little for promises, the performance of which may be insisted upon only at the risk of condemnation for unfair labor practices. The law, we think, does not compel such a result."

2. In Boeing Airplane Co. v. NLRB, 174 F.2d 988 (D.C. Cir. 1949), the court held that a union which strikes in violation of the 60-day notice requirement of Section 8 (d) of the NLRA and in breach of a promise not to strike loses its standing as the collective bargaining agent, thereby freeing the company from its obligation to bargain. Further, the court held that the "Company was at liberty to treat the employees as having severed their relations with the Company . . . and to consummate their separation from the Company's employ by hiring others to take their places."

3. In United Packinghouse Workers, 89 N.L.R.B. 310, 25 L.R.R.M. 1556 (1950), the NLRB held that a strike pursuant to demands made under a reopening clause is not violative of Section 8 (d) of the NLRA and hence a refusal to bargain if it is not effected for 60 days after notice, even though the contract is still in effect.

4. United Elastic Corp., 84 N.L.R.B. 768, 24 L.R.R.M. 1294 (1949). The employees of respondent corporation, in violation of a no-strike clause in their collective agreement, went on strike in protest of an alleged accumulation of unsettled grievances. The union officially sanctioned the strike and respondent thereupon offered unilateral wage increases, solicited individual strikers to return to work, and refused to deal with the union until the employees returned to work. The trial examiner found this a refusal to bargain. The Board found that the union had breached its obligations under the contract but rejected the finding of a refusal to bargain by respondent. Pointing out that the detailed grievance procedure was intended to be a substitute for strike action, the majority held that "Respondent's statutory obligation to bargain . . . was suspended as long as such wrongful strike action continued. In our opinion, the stability of labor relations that the statute seeks to accomplish by the encouragement of the

collective bargaining process ultimately depends upon the chan-nelization of the collective bargaining relationship within the framework of a collective bargaining agreement *and the adherence thereto* by the contracting parties. We feel, therefore, that the broad purpose of the statute and the interest of the parties will *best* be served by requiring *such adherence.*" Member Houston dissented on the ground that the union, in his opinion, had not breached the agreement; the strike had been by the union mem-bers without union authority, and the union had made every reasonable effort to persuade them to return.

5. In Ohio Oil Co., 91 N.L.R.B. 759, 26 L.R.R.M. 1579 (1950), the Board held that the 60-day period required by Section 8 (d) of the NLRA does not begin to run until the employer actually receives the written notice of a desire to modify the agreement. The Board also held that the day of receipt is one of the 60 days.

6. See U.S. Cold Storage Corp., 96 N.L.R.B. No. 176, 29 L.R.R.M. 1011 (1951), where refusal to meet with the union during a strike was held to violate Section 8 (a) (5) even though an impasse in bargaining had been reached before the strike. Compare with the cases discussed and cited supra, page 232, note 7, and pages 231–235.

7. See also NLRB, 14th Ann. Rep. 65–67, 73–79 (1949).

G. *Methods for Establishing Peaceful Labor Relations in Foreign Countries*

The "appropriate unit" and its representative, chosen by the majority of its members, are characteristic of our labor relations laws and those of Canada. But neither the law of Great Britain nor that of any Continental country has adopted them. Bargain-ing abroad is carried out, as a rule, for a whole branch of industry in a national or regional area. At present, competing unionism does not exist in the Scandinavian countries, or Germany, or Austria, and even where it does exist, as in France [51] and Italy, [52]

[51] The several French federations are usually distinguished in French and other foreign publications and speeches by combinations of alphabetic sym-bols which are abbreviations of their names, such as C.G.T., C.F.T.C., C.G.C., and C.G.T.–F.O. They stand for Confédération Générale du Travail; Con-fédération Française des Travailleurs Chrétiens; Confédération Générale des Cadres, and Confédération Générale du Travail-Force Ouvrière, respectively. The first mentioned one, the C.G.T., is the strongest among them; it is con-trolled by the Communists and often seeks, therefore, to attain political objectives under the cloak of labor demands. On the whole, unionism is weak in France. The statistical figures don't give a true picture, because the number of members paying dues actually falls far behind the number of mem-

the law — upon certain requisites to be discussed later — tends to make terms fixed in contracts of the most important unions control all employment relations in the enterprise. There is no need for the certification of a representative. In addition, governmental extension of terms worked out between an association of employers and a union plays an important role in several countries.

Naturally the objective is the same in all countries: to determine jointly wages and other terms of employment without interruption of production. In Europe there are three general types of procedure, the Scandinavian, the British, and the Continental — each of them reflecting a particular normative structure of labor relations.

1. STATUTORY DUTY TO BARGAIN

The structure of Sweden's labor law has this important feature in common with ours: it keeps governmental control of employment terms to a minimum.[53] Moreover, Section 4 of the Swedish Law on the Right of Association and the Right of Collective Bargaining of September 11, 1936, declares that a party — which means an association of employers, or an employer, or the appropriate union — has the right to require the other party to bargain. Prior to this Act, an employer was free to resist bargaining and the union was free to resort to a test of economic power. The only prohibition against concerted activities on the part of employers and unions had been the statute of 1928, which placed both parties under a "peace obligation" during the existence of a collective contract. The matter is discussed at page 421 infra.

In addition, discrimination against an employee because of his organizational activities is a violation of the statutory "right of association." But, unlike the American pattern as presented in the 1947 amendment to Section 7 of the National Labor Relations

bers on union rolls. See Park, The Government of France, in Foreign Governments and Their Backgrounds 303–306 (Adams, ed. 1950); Sturmthal, Collective Bargaining in France, 4 Indust. and Lab. Rel. Rev. 236, 246 (1951).

[52] Immediately after the collapse of Fascism and the revival of a free labor movement, the coalition of political parties set up the C.G.I.L. (Confederazione Generale Italiana del Lavoro), in which soon the Communist influence became predominant. This, together with the breakdown of the coalition government, gave rise to the formation of other federations such as the L.C.G.I.L. (Libera Confederazione Generale Italiana dei Lavoratori), controlled by the Christian Democratic Party, and the F.I.L. (Federazione Italiana del Lavoro), controlled by the Republican Party and the Socialist Workers' Party.

[53] Schmidt and Heineman, Enforcement of Collective Bargaining Agreements in Swedish Law, 14 U. of Chi. L. Rev. 184 (1947).

Act, the Swedish right of association since 1940 has not included the right to remain unorganized. Moreover, Sweden has not followed our principle that the majority union shall be the exclusive representative of all employees in the unit; more than one union may have a statutory right to bargain for a collective contract with the same employer.[54]

In most respects, the Mexican Federal Labor Act of 1931 (Section 43) may be grouped with the Swedish law, but it provides an even greater degree of union recognition, for it charges every employer with a duty to bargain collectively with a union if any of his employees are members. Where more than one union operates in one undertaking, the employer must bargain with the union which represents the greatest number.[55] Venezuela, in its Labor Code of 1945, has followed the Mexican pattern.

The sanctions of cease and desist orders provided for by our law for the violation of the duty to bargain are unknown to the Swedish law. The administration of the law on collective contracts (June 22, 1928) and of that on the right of association (September 11, 1936) is entrusted to the labor court,[56] which applies only civil sanctions, primarily that of damages. The only other sanction provided in the Act of 1936 is the negative one — that failure of an employer or a trade-union to comply with the duty to bargain bars the party from access to the mediation machinery provided by the State. Conversely, where the parties have bargained but were unable to agree, an independent conciliator, appointed by the State Department of Social Affairs, will take up the negotiations.

2. COMBINATION OF BARGAINING AND REGULATION

The British law presents three types of governmental intervention. There is, first, the one represented by the Wages Councils Act, 1945. This Act provides for the establishment of boards through an order of the appropriate minister (Minister of Labour; Secretary of State for Scotland), the purpose of which is to establish appropriate wages and terms of employment. The minister will create a board whenever it becomes evident that some class of workers lacks adequate machinery for the effective regulation of

[54] See Adlercreutz, Some Features of Swedish Collective Labor Law, 10 Mod. L. Rev. 137, 149 (1947).

[55] The contract made with that union excludes any contract with another union.

[56] For the Swedish labor court, see page 85 supra.

their remuneration, or when, although such machinery has been set up in a collective contract for the settlement of remuneration and conditions of employment, that machinery is likely to cease to exist or to become inadequate for that purpose. The principal consideration for the establishment of such boards is whether the remuneration actually paid to the workers involved is in accordance with the prevailing terms of collective agreements and awards for that type of work.

The parties to a collective contract, to prevent undercutting of wage rates, can therefore take the initiative in the establishment of a board under the Wages Councils Act.[57]

It must be borne in mind that, in the first place, it is the councils (boards) and not the bureaucracy (i.e., the minister) which work out the proposals relating to the terms of the employment contracts; and that, in the second place, the minister will set up a board only upon a recommendation of a "commission of inquiry" consisting of representatives of management and of labor and three independents, persons not connected with the industry.[58] The wages councils (boards) are constituted in a similar manner, so that the representatives of labor and management have a majority.[59] Before boards or councils submit a recommendation to the appropriate minister, they must give the public notice of a hearing, stating the questions under consideration and fixing a time for the presentation of statements or protests.

On the receipt of wage regulation proposals, the minister is bound to give all persons who might be affected by the regulation an opportunity — by public notice of the contemplated order — to be fully heard. The merits of the objections may influence the minister's decision. Once an order is issued, its provisions become the statutory minimum terms which are read into any employment contract and thus supplant any individual stipulation contrary to them.[60] They have, in this respect, the same effect as minimum wages statutes, of which we have plenty in this country.

An order of the minister is a kind of provisional statute; the

---

[57] The statements in the text are far from being comprehensive. For details on the complicated matter, see Kahn-Freund, Minimum Wage Legislation in Great Britain, 97 U. of Pa. L. Rev. 778 (1949).

[58] The Agricultural Wages Act, 1948, 11 & 12 Geo. VI, c. 47, itself established a board authorized to regulate wages; aside from that Act, only the Catering Wages Act, 1943, 6 & 7 Geo. VI, c. 24, has provided for a permanent (Catering Wages) commission.

[59] Cooper, Outlines of Industrial Law, 201 (1947).

[60] Id. at 202; Kahn-Freund, op. cit. supra note 57, at 807.

order must be laid before the two Houses of Parliament, either of which may annul it by a resolution. In this country, collective contracts similarly control the terms of employment of all workers in a unit. They have this statutory quality by force of Section 9 (a) of the National Labor Relations Act and similar legislation.[61]

Without a statutory basis, neither the terms of the American collective contracts nor the British "orders" could have such an effect. The idea of enforceability of collective contracts is alien to British common law.[62] But what the new boards do is actually to negotiate among the board members representing industry and labor, assisted by the independent members.[63] The consensus reached in the negotiations constitutes the boards' proposals to the minister. In contradistinction to the American-Canadian and Swedish method, the Government's intervention in Great Britain is much more than a mere command to bargain, for the administrative order represents a governmental decision on the contents of the bargain.[64]

Second, a few statutes give the minister power to extend the terms of a collective contract to enterprises of employers who are not parties to the contract. The Cotton (temporary) Act, 1934, was the first to authorize the minister "to bring into force by order the wage rates contained in a collective contract." If he proceeds in this manner, those rates apply to all persons employed in the industry of the class and description to which the agreement relates. The minister can issue such an order only upon a joint application by organizations of employers and employees, which must be representative of a majority of the operators and of the employees in question, respectively.

In the third British type, found in the nationalization laws, 1945–1948, a duty to bargain is imposed upon the (managerial) boards of the nationalized industries.[65] This type has been discussed at page 87 supra.

The Belgian labor law displays a similar aspect in its bipartite

[61] See Lenhoff, Comments, Cases and Other Materials on Legislation 7 (1948), and The Present Status of Collective Contracts in the American Legal System, 39 Mich. L. Rev. 1109, 1137 (1941).

[62] See Final Report of the Balfour Committee on Industry and Trade to Parliament (1929) Cmd. 3282 p. 125.

[63] Kahn-Freund, op. cit. supra note 57, at 785.

[64] Such an order does not — as the former Trade Boards Act orders did — embrace a "trade"; its scope is defined by a certain type of employee as well as by a certain locality and type of work.

[65] Robson, Nationalized Industries and Industrial Law, 2 Indust. L. Rev. 192 (1948).

commissions *(commissions paritaires)*. The Act of June 9, 1945, provides that they shall be established by a royal ordinance in each branch of industry; to the present time, forty-four commissions have been set up. Their composition is based on the principle of equal representation of management and labor. The members are appointed by the King (that is, the Cabinet) from panels presented by the appropriate employers' associations and trade-unions. The commissions are headed by a president and a vice-president, also appointed by the King, who have, however, no right to vote. As the law points out, the president and the vice-president must be experts in the field of economics and labor relations, but they must not be in any manner interested in any cause or matter within the jurisdiction of the commission.

What the commissions have to do is nothing less than collective bargaining for wage schedules in the industry concerned. The bargaining process there differs from ours only insofar as the bargaining in Belgium is industry-wide — on a national or regional level. It is a real bargaining; unanimity is requisite for a decision, which amounts to an agreement among the employer members and labor members. At the request of such a commission, an executive decree gives the decision of the commission compulsory effect, so that then any private stipulation which is contrary to the decision is null and void.

In case a labor dispute arises in an industry controlled by a bipartite commission, the latter may — after an investigation and report made by one or more members delegated as conciliators — render a decision which presents the solution of the dispute. Naturally, the requisite of unanimity extends also to such a solution.

3. COMPULSORY ARBITRATION: A MATTER OF THE PAST

As for Continental types represented by French and German law, a duty to bargain is not imposed upon either party. But, prior to World War II, the German as well as the French labor law included compulsory arbitration in their concepts. While the Swedish and British labor laws generally require bargaining (at present, British law still includes a vestige of compulsory arbitration, noted in Part I of this book [66]), the French and German laws of the recent past would, in the last resort, force employment terms upon management and labor through compulsory arbitration.

By German law (Decree of October 30, 1923), the administra-

[66] See the text preceding the reference to footnote 82, on page 88 supra.

tive decision declaring an award binding upon the parties was subject to judicial review, but review restricted to procedural legality of the award and its conformity with the terms of reference. Legal errors of substance did not justify reversal on such review.[67] In the famous Ruhr-Eisen conflict, the award, rejected by the parties, contained reversible error because of its inroad upon a collective contract.   What was fixed in the contract, said the court, could not be varied by compulsory arbitration.[68]   Differences as to the collective contract had to be decided by the labor courts; only negotiation disputes were within the authority of administrative boards.

The French call such disputes on "interests," *conflits de règlementation* or *conflits économiques,* in contrast to disputes on legal rights, *conflits juridiques.*

The French Act of March 4, 1938, provided for compulsory arbitration of conflicts on interests in cases for which no arbitration agreement was made by the parties, with wide appeal to the Superior Court of Arbitration (Cour supérieure d'arbitrage).[69] In contrast to German law the appeal could be based not only on jurisdictional grounds, or excess of power, but also on violation of law.[70]   An interesting novelty was the right of appeal given the Minister of Labor in cases where he believed that considerations of public interest called for it whenever an award, although not contrary to law, seemed to be bad from an economic or social standpoint.

4. THE PRESENT STATUS OF A PEACEFUL SETTLEMENT OF LABOR
QUESTIONS IN GERMANY, FRANCE, AND SWITZERLAND

(a) The German system of compulsory arbitration died with the Weimar Republic.   When, after the collapse of the Hitler regime, the Allied Control Council restored essential features of pre-Hitler conciliation and arbitration proceedings, it did not revive compulsory arbitration.   The Control Council Law No. 35 of August 20, 1946, expressly declares that an arbitration award shall be binding upon the parties only if they accept it, or have previously agreed to be bound by it.   (Where the dispute "affects

[67] R.A.G., 3 Bensheimer (Reports of Labor Courts Decisions) 147 (1928).
[68] R.A.G., 5 Bensh. 167, 176 (1929).
[69] That so-called court was composed of seven members none of whom was a representative of capital or labor; the Vice-President of the Supreme Administrative Court (Council of State) presided over it.   See Colton, Compulsory Arbitration in France, 1936–1939 (1951).
[70] See the decision of Jan. 25, 1939 (1939) Droit social 107.

the interests of the Allied Occupation," the Allied Commander may direct the German authorities to require the parties to submit the dispute to an arbitration board.)   In general the principle requiring a cooling-off period before the opening of hostilities has not won acceptance.

(b) France suspended her compulsory arbitration laws by a decree of September 1, 1939, at the outbreak of the war.   During the post-war period of controlled economy (*dirigisme*) there was no need for a resort to arbitration.   But the Act of February 11, 1950, restored the parties' autonomy in the field of labor relations and without a compulsory arbitration provision.   Examination of the Act's legislative history reveals why the idea of restoration of compulsory arbitration, included in the governmental bill,[71] was rejected.   In the first place, as a speaker in the French National Assembly put it:

> To impose the principle of compulsory arbitration against a unanimous expression of opposition of all the employers' as well as workers' associations — such an arbitration being a field over which the only efficient dominion can be exerted by public opinion — at a moment when public opinion is not willing to accept that principle, means to make compulsory arbitration absolutely inefficient, and even dangerous.[72]

In the second place, the principle of compulsory arbitration could not be reconciled with the Constitution of 1946, because the latter proclaims a *right* to strike, which seems inconsistent with a duty to submit labor disputes to a peaceful solution.   In the third place, the employers' resistance to compulsory arbitration was a reflection of their aversion towards "statism." [73]

However, to prevent work stoppages by strikes and lockouts a new approach was made, namely compulsory conciliation for "collective disputes" (*conflits collectifs de travail*) .   The Act of February 11, 1950, omitted a definition of this term, but in general one can identify "collective disputes" with disputes about "interests." [74] The Act goes into detail with respect to the formation of official "Commissions for Conciliation" on the national and regional

---

[71] In France, as in other European countries, most bills are introduced by the government.

[72] This quotation from M. Gazier's speech is taken from Rivero, Conciliation and Arbitration in the Law of Feb. 11, 1950, 13 Droit social 145 (1950) (in French) .

[73] Rivero, id. at 146.

[74] Malézieux, Les Conventions collectives de travail 12 n.48 (1950) .   For the explanation of disputes on interests, see page 278 supra.

levels. These commissions are presided over by the Minister of Labor and regional commissioners of labor respectively, each commission being composed of representatives, in equal number, of industry and labor, on the one hand, and three or fewer representatives of government on the other. Where a collective contract provides for a negotiation procedure, the latter replaces the governmental machinery.

The difficulty with the French compulsory conciliation system is its lack of sanctions for noncompliance, even for a refusal to participate in the conciliation procedure.[75] Where a conciliation attempt is made, its results are put on record and signed by the parties. In case of success, the record has the effect of a collective contract; in the opposite case it is a "record of nonconciliation," and, if the collective contract contains an arbitration provision, it has to state the topics to be submitted to arbitration.[76]

The statute emphasizes that an arbitral decision in a dispute on "rights" must be based on "law," while "equity" (équité) should guide labor arbitration in disputes on "interests." "Equity" in civil law means something different from "equity" in our legal system.[77] As used in the Act of 1950 it points to a fair compromise between conflicting proposals.[78]

Though the new law has restored the Superior Court of Arbitration, with reviewing functions not essentially changed,[79] there can be no question that the important, if ever so short-lived role which the Court played in the process of developing French labor law during the era of compulsory arbitration, cannot be expected of the Court any longer.

(c) Following the adoption of a constitutional amendment federalizing labor regulation, the Swiss Law of February 12, 1949, was passed to supplement the earlier law on peaceful settlement of economic disputes. As early as 1914, the Swiss Factory Act (June 18) directed the cantons to provide for conciliation and arbitration services, labor law being cantonal law. Parties to a dispute were bound, under the various cantonal laws, to participate in

[75] For a sharp criticism, see Rivero, op. cit. supra note 72, at 148.

[76] Rivero, op. cit. supra note 72, at 148–151. For the statute, see the Act of Feb. 11, 1950, (1950) J.O. 1688, tit. II, c. II, arts. 5–18, and Decree No. 50–241 of Feb. 27, 1950, concerning the Commissions for Conciliation.

[77] Buckland, Roman Law and Common Law, c. XV (1936); Jolowicz, Historical Introduction to the Study of Roman Law 516 (1932).

[78] Rouast and Durand, Précis de législation industrielle 282, no. 232 (3d ed. 1948): "The arbiter acts [in disputes on interests] as a law maker . . . as a friendly peace-maker."

[79] The right of appeal, which was given under the Act of March 4, 1938, to the Minister of Labor, has not been restored.

hearings held before such cantonal authorities and to furnish information. The new act provides for the establishment of a tripartite Federal Conciliation Board having jurisdiction in those labor cases which affect more than one canton. Its jurisdiction is conditioned upon a failure of the parties to come to terms through their own bargaining and upon the absence of conciliation and arbitration provisions in their collective contract. Unless the parties agree to abide by the decision of the Board, its decision is enforceable only by the force of public opinion. But the parties are bound under the sanction of fines to take part in negotiation proceedings, during which strikes and lockouts are forbidden for a period of forty-five days, or longer by order of the Board.

5. EXTENSION OF COLLECTIVE CONTRACT EMPLOYMENT TERMS
TO OUTSIDERS

a. The German Type

Another feature of Continental labor law is the power to extend the coverage of collective contracts, a power given by legislation to particular administrative agencies. The idea originated in the New Zealand Industrial Conciliation and Arbitration Act of 1894. Germany adopted the idea at the outbreak of the First World War.[80] Immediately following the war, on December 23, 1918, came the decree on collective contracts, which provided for an extension of collective contracts by the Minister of Labor.[81] The present law of April 9, 1949, the collective contracts statute, prescribes these conditions for extension: first, that application be made by a bipartite committee appointed by the federations of employers' and employees' organizations, respectively; second, that the contract already applies to at least 50 per cent of the employees to be covered by the contract after the proposed extension; and third, that public interest calls for such an extension.

The new Austrian law (1947) on collective contracts, following the first law (of 1919) on this subject, requires only that the contract, to be extended, have pre-eminent significance.[82] The

[80] Umbreit, Der Krieg und die Arbeitsverhältnisse 117 (Economic and Social History of the World War, 1914–1918, German Ser. 1928).

[81] The German title of the decree is *Tarifvertragsordnung.*

[82] Act of Feb. 26, 1947, B.G.B. No. 76, sec. 14. The Austrian law has, from the beginning, vested power to pronounce such an extension in a particular administrative agency, the Conciliation Board (*Einigungsamt*), composed of an impartial chairman, who is a judge, and two associates chosen respectively from panels of representatives of employer associations and trade-unions.

Swiss executive decree sets up as requisites for extension that the collective contract already encompasses the majority of the employees and of the employers who will be covered by the contract after the proposed extension, that there is need for such an extension, and that it is not contrary to the national interest.[83]   Besides Switzerland, other countries have adopted the extension feature of the German model — for example, Brazil, Czechoslovakia, Quebec, and Mexico.   The British power to issue wage orders for an entire branch of industry based on employers' and labor's cooperation, is similar.

b. The New French Approach

Collective contracts were first recognized by French statute in 1919.   The extensible contract, however, did not exist prior to the Act of June 24, 1936, and differs from the ordinary collective contract in its foundation.   To qualify for the extensible category, a collective contract had to be framed by a "mixed commission" convened by the Minister of Labor, and composed of delegates of "the most representative organizations" of employers and employees in the branch of industry concerned.   Such agreements may be "national," "regional," or "local."

Upon the outbreak of the war, a system of administrative regulation of wages and working conditions was created which, as *dirigisme,* survived the downfall of Pétain, under whom all labor organizations had been dissolved.   Even when, after the war, the Law of December 23, 1946, revived collective bargaining, a collective contract could come into effect only upon its approval by the Minister of Labor, and then had binding effect on the whole branch of the industry concerned within a specified region, so that the terms of the contract affected all persons and companies whether or not members of the contracting parties.   There was, for this reason, no need for extension.[84]

With the abandonment of a policy of governmental wage regulation and the return to a "free economy," the Law of February

[83] Fed. Order 1941 (10.1), Recueil Officiel (1941) 1141 (repeatedly renewed since 1941).   For the legal significance of this piece of delegated legislation, see Tschudi, 43 Schweizerische Juristenzeitung 56 (1947).   The authority to extend the control of the collective contract schedules beyond the parties to the contract is granted to a cantonal government where the extension does not reach beyond the cantonal boundaries, otherwise to the Federal Council.

[84] For the statute see Brethe de la Gressaye, Le Nouveau statut des conventions collectives de travail, 1947 Droit social 103.   Incidentally, the approach of the Irish Act on Industrial Relations of Aug. 27, 1946, sec. 27, is very similar to that of the French statute, enacted four months later.

11, 1950, was passed. This repealed the Law of December 23, 1946, and readopted basic features of the Law of June 24, 1936.

Thus the decision on the question of which factors make an association "most representative" is extremely important.[85] This phrase was used in the Treaty of Versailles, 1919, Part XII, Art. 389, as the criterion of the organizations to be consulted by governments in selecting delegates representing employers and employees at the Conferences of the International Labor Organization (ILO). When called on to interpret this criterion with respect to the selection of a worker delegate by the Netherlands, the Permanent Court of International Justice in 1922 pointed to the number of employees embraced in the federation as the most important factor.[86] The French government considered also other factors,[87] and the Act of 1950 mentions, in addition to the number of members, the amount of dues regularly paid, the degree of independence of the organization — company unions are very much distrusted — and the patriotic attitude during the German occupation. The decision on this question of representation, being an administrative decision, is, on the national level, in the hands of the Minister; while, on the regional or local level, it is left to the courts to pass judgment on representativeness.[88]

The recognition of the principle of bargaining through the most representative organization of employers and employees was under the legislation of 1936 considered as compatible with the principle that more than one organization might be "most representative." [89] Obviously, the formation of the "mixed commission" presupposes an understanding among the leaders of the rival organizations on their share in the representation in the Commission. As the practical failure of the Act of 1936 shows — only one contract on national level was made — the difficulty lies with the arriving at such an understanding. This innate weakness of the structure proved

[85] The principle is also applied to other fields of labor representation, such as the composition of the "committees of the enterprise," discussed at page 72 supra.

[86] Publications, Permanent Court of International Justice, Ser. B, No. 1 (1922). Part XII of the Treaty of Versailles was the original constitution of the ILO. The "most representative" phrase remains in Article 3 of the revised ILO Constitution.

[87] For details of the historical development from 1936 on, see Sturmthal, Collective Bargaining in France, 4 Indust. & Lab. Rel. Rev. 236 (1950).

[88] From the decision of the Minister, appeal may be taken to the Conseil d'Etat (Council of State, i.e., Supreme Administrative Court). As for "regional" or "local" representation, see Malézieux, op. cit. supra note 74, at 6 n.14.

[89] Circular of Aug. 17, 1936 (J.O. 1936, Sept. 3) ; Malézieux, op. cit. supra note 74, at 6 n.12.

to be fatal when the Law of December 23, 1946, previously mentioned, had established a hierarchy of collective contracts so that no regional or local contract could be entered into before a national contract had come into existence.   The new Law of February 11, 1950, permits the making of regional or local contracts independent of the existence of a "national" contract.   However, if a national contract exists, its terms cannot be varied by the regional and local contracts.   Naturally, the latter may, in such a case, regulate those matters which are not treated in the former. Understanding between rival organizations on a regional or local level meets with far fewer difficulties than an understanding on the national level.   Hence the law accords the most representative organizations the power to enter into regional or local contracts on their own initiative.   It is to be observed that also the new law of 1950 cleaves to the principle that the extensibility of a contract requires that the organizations on either side represent one of the twenty-three branches into which the industry of France is for organizational purposes divided.   Among these branches, the chemical, textile, metal, and construction industries along with transportation, stevedoring, and public works, each of them forming one branch, may be mentioned.   Only within the terms of an extensible contract for a branch, can agreements be "appended" — *conventions annexes* — for the chief professional groups: manual workers, salaried employees, engineers, and employees engaged in executive or technical work.   It will have been noted that by eliminating from the extensible class contracts made *only* for a certain "category" (group) — defined by terms of professional education or skill, craft, or other characteristics — or contracts applicable only to a single shop, the Law of 1950 sought to confront the employer with a unified front on the employees' side.

It is clear that the new law presents a philosophy which is nearer to the laws of 1919 and 1936 than to that of 1946.   This interpretation points to the tendency of the new law to strengthen union power as well as to limit governmental control over the contracts. The characterization of the new law is not contradicted by its return to the idea that the scope of national, regional, or local contracts *may* be expanded by an administrative decree so as to bring outsiders within their control.   Such an approach based on a merely technical similarity overlooks the fact that in 1946 no wage schedule could be freely bargained for.   Compared with this difference, the fact that by the Act of 1946 the law itself widened the domain controlled by the contract, while the Act of

1950 provides for an administrative decree (issued by the Minister of Labor) to effect an extension, loses its significance.

In extending the scope of extensible contracts, the Minister of Labor may proceed on his own initiative or upon the request of one or more of the "most representative" organizations of employers or employees. The decree of extension has to be preceded by preliminaries similar to those under the recent British law on wage orders. He publishes[90] a notice of his plan to extend a certain national, regional, or local collective contract[91] to all other employers and employees embraced in the branch and professional groups or group stated in the contract; the notice requires all persons interested in the matter to make known their views on the plan within fifteen days. Before extending a contract (or terminating extension of a contract) the Minister must consult (but is not required to follow the advice of) the High Commission for Collective Contracts, headed by the Minister of Labor and composed of two of the highest public officers,[92] of fifteen representatives of labor and fifteen of management, and — a very interesting feature — of three persons representing the interests of families.[93] Before extending a contract, the Minister must purge it of any terms forbidden by statute[94] and within defined limits may exscind others.

"Ordinary"[95] collective contracts are of two types, one made by a single employer with the "most representative" unions, the other by one or more employers with one or more unions representing the particular groups concerned. Like individual contracts, both types of ordinary collective agreements are subordinate to extensible contracts; the terms of the latter prevail over nonconforming terms of the former. However, individual contracts or ordinary collective agreements may effectively provide for terms

[90] The "notice" is to be published in the official publication of French legislation (*Journal officiel*).

[91] The labor court or the justice of the peace, with the secretary of which collective contracts have to be filed — Labor Code, bk. I, tit. II, c. IV bis, art. 31d — must also be mentioned in the notice.

[92] The President of the Council of State and the Minister in charge of the National Economy.

[93] They are designated by the National Federation of Associations for Domestic Relations.

[94] Those compulsory provisions (*lois impératives*) limit, of course, the freedom of the parties in negotiating collective contracts. French Labor Code, bk. I, tit. II, c. IV bis, art. 31a (2). Since it is not always self-evident whether a term is in the teeth of such a provision, the Minister must ask the High Commission for its "reasoned view," which, however, he need not follow.

[95] The term, distinguishing other collective contracts from extensible collective contracts, is used in recent French legal literature. Cf. Malézieux, op. cit. supra note 74, at 4 n.4.

which are more favorable to the employee or employees than the terms of an extensible contract.   This is the so-called "more favorable terms" exception.   Analogous subordination, along with this exception, exists in the relation between individual contracts and ordinary collective agreements.

Another limitation is expressed in a rule likewise established in the Act of 1950.   This rule prohibits the making of a collective agreement on any other matter than wages, in absence of an extensible collective contract.[96]

Whatever the type of a collective contract, its terms, if valid, have an immediate effect upon individual employment relationships.   The terms enter by themselves, without any further private, administrative, or judicial act into the individual employment relationships and replace any nonconforming provisions which the individual parties have stipulated.   This effect is called *l'effet automatique.*

One important expression of a policy favoring collective bargaining over individual bargaining is the permission of noncontracting groups' "joining in the operation of the ordinary contract" (*adhésion*).[97]   In contrast to extension, adhesion is an entirely private act.   An association of employers or employees in the same branch of industry[98] may notify the office in charge of registration of collective contracts — this requisite, characteristic of European collective contract law, is discussed at page 340 infra — of its adhesion.

The decree of extension by German and French law terminates upon the expiration or termination of the contract.

c. The Italian Type

The Italian Constitution of 1947 provides for an all-embracing scope of collective contracts.[99] Like the French labor movement, Italy's trade-unionism is not unified.   The idea embodied in the Constitution presupposes the formation of unified agencies to bargain on organized labor's behalf with management.   Recently the Italian Government introduced a bill in the Italian parliament to carry out that idea.[100]   Characteristic features of the bill

[96] French Labor Code, bk. I, tit. II, c. IV bis, art. 31n (and Act of Feb. 11, 1950, tit. III, art. 21).

[97] French Labor Code, bk. I, tit. II, c. IV bis, art. 31c (6), (7).

[98] See the decision of the Supreme Court of Arbitration of June 15, 1938, Gaz. Pal. 1938. 2. 229.

[99] Article 39 (4).

[100] Official draft (of an Act to regulate labor relations) of Dec. 4, 1951; for the present status of the law, see Pergolesi, Diritto del lavoro 54 (1949).

are, first, that only registered organizations can share in the formation of the agency.   Second, registration requires a membership
which covers at least 10 per cent of all employees in the branch
of industry related to the organization concerned.   In the third
place, the agency (*rappresentanza unitaria*) shall be propor-
tionate to the number of enrolled members in each of the organizations.   The Minister of Labor shall decide controversies
concerning the composition, the Council of State having appellate
jurisdiction over his decision.

6. PROLONGATION BY LAW OF THE EFFECT OF COLLECTIVE AGREEMENTS AFTER THEIR EXPIRATION

Between the two World Wars the German labor courts evolved
a theory which excellently served as a shock absorber against the
impact of brusque expiration of collective contracts on wage rates
and other terms in a period of declining prosperity.   In this
country, contractualism demands its price.   Once the collective
contract has come to its normal end without being renewed or
replaced by a new one, employers may cut down the wage rates
and lessen or drop the benefits which were provided for by the
contract, although often — except in coal mining — work goes
on according to the terms of the expired contract until a new
collective contract has been arrived at, without pecuniary gains
of the workers made retroactive to the date of expiration of the
old contract.

The German theory is that terms of employment agreed upon
in a collective contract become automatically contractual terms
of all individual employment relationships controlled by that contract.   As a consequence, after the expiration of the collective
contract the individual employment relationships continue to be
controlled by these terms until they are replaced by those stipulated in a new collective contract, or, in the absence of the latter,
by those laid down in individual contracts (*Nachwirkung*).
Accordingly, the terms of the expired contract remain effective
until the parties expressly reach a new agreement.[101]

The German law of 1949 adopted this theory: "After the expiration of a collective contract, its provisions continue to be in
effect until they are replaced by another agreement." [102]   The
Austrian and Italian laws contain a similar provision.[103]   The

[101] Kaskel, Labor Law 99, 128 (4th ed. 1932) (in German).

[102] Germany: Act on Collective Contracts, April 9, 1949, sec. 4 (5).

[103] Austria: Act on Collective Contracts, Feb. 26, 1947, secs. 9 (1) and 15.
Italy: Civil Code (1942), art. 2074.

pending Italian law on labor relations provides even for a pro-
longation of the operation of a collective contract by a decree of
the Minister of labor.[104]

The French Act of February 11, 1950, on collective contracts
goes farther, providing that upon its expiration a collective contract, although made for a specified time, shall remain in effect
as if it were entered into for an indeterminate period,[105] till it is
terminated by notice, provision for which shall be included in
every collective contract.[106]

The Norwegian law, which does not provide for an extension
of the terms of a collective contract beyond the parties — the high
degree of organization in Norway must not be overlooked —
contains features similar in effect, though not in form, to those
discussed previously.   As in Sweden, provisions were made in pre-
war Norway for state-mediation proceedings which had to terminate [107] before work-stoppages were allowed.   Post-war legislation
added various provisions.   One of them provides for compulsory
arbitration by the Wage Board so that an agreement proposed
by the State Mediator but rejected by the employer or by the
employees, and then submitted by the Mediator to that Board,
becomes a collective contract upon its approval by a decree of the
Board.[108]   But whether the legal force of a contract originates in
such a decree or in purely voluntary acts of the parties, it cannot
be terminated without governmental approval, and where the
parties are affiliated with the top organizations of management
and of labor, not without their approval.[109]

7. GENERAL NATURE OF COLLECTIVE BARGAINING IN AUSTRALIA AND NEW ZEALAND

The compulsory disputes settlement systems of Australia and
New Zealand rest on legal compulsion to accept terms and conditions of employment arrived at in the last resort by authorities

[104] See Article 21 (2) of the bill cited at note 100 supra.
[105] Cf. Labor Code, bk. I, tit. II, c. IV bis, art. 31c (3).
[106] Id. arts. 31c (5) and 31g (7).
[107] Labor Disputes Act of August 6, 1915.   Only a party who cooperates
with the state mediator has — after ten days of mediation — a right to request
such a termination of the ban laid upon concerted action.   Galenson, Labor
in Norway 101 (1949).
[108] The Wage Board consists of seven members appointed by the Minister
of Labor, two of which are nominated by employers' associations, two are
nominated by trade-unions, and the remaining three are independent.
[109] For details on the Act of 1948, see Galenson, op. cit. supra note 107
at 285.

having compulsive quasi-legislative authority. There are three main procedures, which merge into each other and can exist in various combinations. First, there is the "Wages Board," which in principle is a straight-out legislative process by which a Board consisting of workers' and employers' representatives, with an independent chairman, lays down from time to time wages, hours, and other conditions for the whole of a trade or group of trades. In principle, this system does not depend upon the existence of disputes, though in practice the Boards tend not to act until some degree of dissatisfaction has become known to them. Trade-unions are in principle in no way necessary to this system, but in practice, the Boards take notice of them, and the workers' representatives are usually trade-union officials. There is no formal provision for recognition of collective agreements; any such agreement would have to be adopted as an award of the relevent Board. Tasmania and Victoria employ this system exclusively, and South Australia employs it for certain industries.

Secondly, there is the Arbitration Court system, in which a tribunal having judicial status and many of the forms of a court makes awards in settlement of specific industrial disputes, interprets those awards, and polices the system. The necessity for representation of workers and employers as "parties" in this system gives a maximum encouragement to the formation of employers' organizations and trade-unions, and there is a tendency to the elaboration of an "industrial jurisprudence," with some corresponding loss of flexibility. The dominant constitutional position of the Commonwealth (federal) Court of Conciliation and Arbitration in the Australian system, and the readiness with which "disputes" are manufactured so as to invite its jurisdiction, have produced a situation in which this tribunal is in substance an economic planning organization, though its judges frequently repudiate such a function. This system is also employed by the states of New South Wales, Queensland, Western Australia, and (with the qualification mentioned above) by South Australia.

Thirdly, there is the Conciliation Commissioner system, in which disputes are settled by awards made by officers who are usually not lawyers, and who have a lower status than that of judges and work with more speed, informality, and flexibility than the Courts. They are now used in association with the Court system by the Commonwealth and New South Wales; the Commissioners attend in principle to disputes on questions of detail, and the Courts to major basic issues such as standard hours, the basic wage, and paid holidays. The Commissioner system tends to produce greater fragmentation of industrial law and occasional anomalies because different Commissioners follow different policies in related trades.   Under the Commonwealth system, Commissioners are permanently allocated to specified groups of occupations and keep constantly in touch with their problems.

The long-term trend of the Australian systems is to employ trained lawyers as judges of Arbitration Courts, and to exclude them from the other types of industrial tribunal.   The trend is also to discourage the employment of lawyers to argue cases, subject to the following exceptions:

(a) In enforcement cases (prosecutions for illegal strikes, breaches of awards, etc.) the function is recognized as "judicial" in the traditional sense, and lawyers have right of audience.

(b) It is usual to provide that counsel may appear if both parties (and sometimes the presiding Judge or Commissioner) consent.   The parties usually do consent at the hearing of basic policy cases such as variation of standard hours and basic wage.

Lawyers hardly ever play any part in the activities of Wages Boards.

The Court and Commissioner systems make provision for the registration of collective agreements between registered organizations, e.g., Commonwealth Act, sec. 37.

(1) If an agreement between all or any of the parties as to the whole or any part of the dispute is arrived at, a memorandum of its terms shall be made in writing and certified by the Court or by the Conciliation Commissioner, and the memorandum shall when so certified, be filed in the office of the Registrar, and, unless otherwise ordered, and subject to any direction of the Court or Conciliation Commissioner, shall, as between the parties to the agreement or any successor, or any assignee or transmittee of the business of a party bound by the agreement, including any corporation which has acquired or taken over the business of such a party, have the same effect as, and be deemed to be, an award for all the purposes of this Act.

(2) The Court or a Conciliation Commissioner may refuse to certify any such memorandum if it or he is of opinion that —

    (a) the agreement is not in settlement of an industrial dispute;

    (b) the agreement contains clauses which the Court

or a Conciliation Commissioner has no power to insert in awards; or

(c) it is not in the public interest that the agreement should be certified.

[The last proviso was originally intended to prevent the overreaching of weak unions by powerful employer interest. In recent years it has been used to refuse consent to "inflationary" wage agreements in a period of labor shortage.]

PART III

Collective Bargaining

I. THE GENERAL NATURE OF THE COLLECTIVE BARGAINING PROCESS

A. *Introduction*

1. WHAT IS THIS THING . . . ?

The relationships between employers and employees in about 75,000 plants in this country are today controlled, in part, by the terms of "collective bargaining contracts."

The general purpose and coverage of these contracts has been suggested in Parts I and II. It is appropriate now to explore the collective bargaining process in further detail. Before turning, however, to a treatment of the various typical and basic contract issues, attention may be profitably directed to some additional aspects of the general nature of this process. Experience has proved that lawyers' minds are likely to be conditioned to a type of thinking about "contracts" which not infrequently prejudices their approach to the collective bargaining problem. It is important to get the clearest possible picture of what these labor agreements are in terms of their purpose and use rather than from what may well have been the accident of nomenclature which has resulted in their being called "contracts." [1]

Mr. Justice Jackson, writing for the Supreme Court majority in J. I. Case Co. v. NLRB, 321 U.S. 332, 64 Sup. Ct. 613, 88 L. Ed. 762 (1944), dealt with this problem of how these labor-management agreements are to be categorized in minds which are, perhaps to a fault, indexed and cross-indexed:

> The negotiations between union and management result
> in what often has been called a trade agreement rather than
> a contract of employment. Without pushing the analogy

[1] Except for the fact that they are negotiated bilaterally, labor-management agreements are quite unlike commercial contracts. They place few obligations on unions and resemble statements of company policy. Many unorganized companies have issued statements of policy and rules dealing

too far, the agreement may be likened to the tariffs established by a carrier, to standard provisions prescribed by supervising authorities for insurance policies, or to utility
schedules of rates and rules for service, which do not of
themselves establish any relationships but which do govern
the terms of the shipper or insurer or customer relationship
wherever and with whomever it may be established.

Others have suggested that lawyers' thinking about these
employer-employee "understandings" is best oriented if they are
analogized to statutes or ordinances, or perhaps to constitutions.
"Industrial codes" is a suggestive phrase which is finding increasing usage in the developing literature on the subject.   The particular phrase is, of course, not in itself important.   It is only
important that "collective bargaining contracts" be recognized as
a phrase describing a particular economic and political and social
phenomenon rather than as a key phrase to a body of doctrinal
concept.

Mr. Justice Jackson makes passing note of the fact that these
contracts "do not themselves establish any relationships."   The
employment relationship existed at the Enderby plant before the
first collective bargaining contract was signed there.   It will continue indefinitely in the future.   It may be temporarily interrupted while the parties exert pressure upon one another to secure
certain new concessions in the renewal contract.   "No contract,"
the United Mine Workers' battle cry goes, "no work."   Yet the
important fact remains that the employment relationship in a
plant *must*, save in the very rare case, go on.   This basic fact,
if its implications are understood, translates into innumerable
common-sense principles for handling the "legal" aspects of any
collective bargaining relationship.   They perhaps emerge more
clearly if a contrast is drawn between this situation and another
in which the question is that of handling the drawing of a contract
between two "legal fictions" each of which will deal elsewhere
if this particular bargain is too harshly, or too loosely, driven.

Mention of the strike or lockout aspect of collective bargaining
warrants a note of caution regarding another danger here of dis-
torted perspective.   It is a commonly accepted axiom that "the
power to strike and to lock out is the motive force of collective

with most of the matters covered in labor-management agreements.   Such
statements of policy were very common before unions ever came into the
picture.   The present-day labor-management agreements differ from these
in that they are negotiated between representatives of labor and management
and are not promulgated unilaterally.

bargaining." A corollary is that "there is no bargaining power if there is no freedom and opportunity to refuse to continue the relationship."[2] It is as easy to accept this axiom and its corollary too uncritically as it is to ignore what is at least the percentile truth they incorporate. Collective bargaining is a catch-as-catch-can kind of business in which disdain for such uncouthness as is labeled "duress" in more polite contract circles has no place. Yet it is essential that it be realized that regardless of the significance of the strike or lockout potential in any collective bargaining negotiation, over 95 per cent of the agreements of this type are concluded without any interruption of production. In probably 75 per cent of all the cases each year there is never any real thought by either side about a strike, with only a few irresponsible union members, and perhaps a newspaper reporter or two, engaging in any loose talk of this kind. Furthermore, to the extent that what is one-sidedly labeled the "strike" problem is important, it is worth considering whether there may not be alternative motive forces which would serve as activators of this particular law-making process, and whether society will continue indefinitely to accept the risk of having to pay so much for labor's and management's occasional legislating by muscle.[3]

To the extent that the use of economic force may constitute a factor in this collective bargaining process, the problems which result where that economic force is exerted are developed in Part IV infra. The present Part is organized in no naïve disregard of the fact that the terms of grievance, seniority, disciplinary, union-security, and wage clauses will vary from contract to contract depending upon the relative power of the respective companies and unions and their willingness to use that power. This treatment does proceed, however, on the assumption that the evolving "law of collective bargaining" already reveals principles and common denominators which are never negatived, but only affected in degree, by the comparative power and militancy of the participants.

A further basis for understanding the basic nature of this collective bargaining process lies in an appreciation of the significant parallels between labor law and international law. These are the two areas in which we are today still experimenting with the substitution of law for force. Wars and strikes (or lockouts) are related phenomena. Both represent utterly wasteful attempts to

[2] See Taylor, The Voluntary Arbitration of Labor Disputes, 49 Mich. L. Rev. 787, 789–790 (1951).
[3] Id. at 790.

settle by force disagreements which seemingly defy rational adjustment. In both areas we are relying today primarily on law-by-agreement or "contract" between powerful groups. In both areas, although in different and in changing degrees, the terms of what "laws" we have (treaties and collective bargaining agreements) are in part dictated by the use of force, or the threat to use force. It is a characteristic feature of our experimentation in both areas that we have so far accepted the group sovereignty concept. There are beginnings, in the United Nations Organization and in the "emergency dispute" provision of the LMRA, of a recognition of a higher authority. But the individuals in unions and in corporate organizations retain, as do the citizens of individual nations, primary allegiance to their respective groups. As a practical matter, the groups set up governmental systems to control their affairs without establishing governmental institutions possessing power greater than that retained by each of the groups. This is, in effect, law without government; or perhaps, more accurately, it is government directly by the governed themselves, dependent largely, in the final analysis, upon the self-restraint of the groups. Compare here, Mr. Justice Frankfurter's concurring opinion in the American Sash & Door Co. case, page 489 infra.

2. LEGISLATORS IN OVERALLS

The law-making process by which these industrial plant codes are arrived at is a rudimentary one.[4] It usually starts with a request, from the union, either oral or in writing, that company representatives meet with the union negotiating committee for the purpose of negotiating an agreement. Today, when there are many more renewal contracts each year than there are "first contracts," this initiatory step typically takes the form of a service of notice (usually by the union), in accordance with terms contained in the expiring contract, of a desire to make certain changes in the old agreement.

Assuming that there are no issues of recognition of the union pending (see page 123 supra), the company complies with the union request, and a series of negotiating meetings follows. Where only a single plant is to be covered by the agreement, these meetings are usually conducted in a room in the plant which has been set aside as neutral territory. The proceedings are, under these circumstances, extremely informal. Where there

[4] See Kelley, Collective Bargaining, 30 Mich. St. B.J. 14 (1951).

is company-wide or industry-wide bargaining the proceedings may take on a much more formal, and formidable, quality.

These negotiations usually proceed from the submission of an inflated list of union demands. The company representative, commonly the Industrial Relations Manager, says "No" with varying degrees of emphasis. Then he agrees to consider points 3, 7, 8, and 15. The union spokesman goes over the list again, not mentioning four or five of the points originally included. Both groups have a pretty good idea right from the start about where they will come out. It will depend on the strength and cohesion of the union, the competitive position of the company, the local manpower situation, the personalities involved, and the experience of the negotiators in covering various problems of industrial administration by written rules. There are factors present, however, which make it almost part of the folklore of the process that these bargains are arrived at slowly and arduously.

The "code" which emerges from this tug-of-war legislative process is, as has been indicated, called a contract and put in what approximates contract form. Characteristically, however, the language used is not typical contract language, and by lawyers' standards the document is often loosely drawn. Look, for example, at Section 7 of Article II of the Enderby contract, page 321 infra, and at Article IX, page 326 infra. The sentences are usually short and so are most of the words, although there is likely to be extensive use of plant idiom which makes it difficult for a stranger to understand many of the provisions. A careful reading of the contract will usually suggest numerous situations which the negotiators must have anticipated, but which are not actually covered by the language adopted.

3. LEARNING WHAT IS IN THE CONTRACT

The contract, when it is completed, is usually printed up, not on legal-size paper, but in little booklets about 6″ by 4″, and distributed among the union's members. Experience has indicated, however, that this is frequently a wholly inadequate means of communicating a full and complete understanding of the contract and its implications to the rank and file of the employees. In its 1950 Report, the Committee on Improving the Administration of Union-Employer Contracts of the American Bar Association, composed of lawyers active in labor relations and representatives of labor, management, and the public, emphasizes this breakdown in communication and sets forth several proposals which have been suggested for its elimination. The Report reads in part:

> One management lawyer has discoursed at length and with effectiveness on the need for his clients to explain to the union and the employees the reasons for company action. As he puts it "understanding on the part of both sides of their respective places in the industrial scene generally and at the plant involved is the key." He advocates better acquaintance and relegation of "class consciousness," and suggests the need of competent industrial relations people who appreciate these needs. Another points out how little of the information that the negotiators have at their finger tips ever gets passed on to the union members, the stewards or the foremen. A labor representative who advocates complete information warns, however, that untrained employees with more information than understanding often cause serious difficulties and that the only answer is a "well considered course of training of shop stewards by the union and of foremen by the employer."

Union training programs of the type just mentioned have been adopted by many of the leading trade-unions of the country in recent years [5] to cope with this and allied problems.

4. COLLECTIVE BARGAINING AND THE LAWYER

Where does the lawyer fit into this legislative and administrative process?

The profession's "bankruptcy" function in labor relations is obvious enough. When the collective bargaining process breaks down, with a resultant strike or a lockout, either the company or the union may want to go to court. We come to that in Part IV infra.

But how about the prophylactic phase of collective bargaining? The "court" aspects of this phase are negligible. There is no point in spending more time studying the applicability of judicial and state or federal legislative rules to the bargaining process. There are only a very few of these rules. The employer and employee representatives *must*, as a matter of public statutory law bargain together. This rule has been discussed at page 202

[5] Kotrotsios, IAM Training for Active Participation in Local Lodges, 74 Mo. Lab. Rev. 653 (1952); Brooks and Allen, Union Training Program of the AFL Unions, id. at 395; Smith, CIO Training for Active and Effective Local Leadership, id. at 140; Smith, ILGWU Approach to Leadership Training, 73 Mo. Lab. Rev. 529 (1951); Brooks and Gamm, A Union's Steward-training Program, 4 Indust. & Lab. Rel. Rev. 249 (1951).

supra. There are also a handful of substantive matters with respect to which these parties' freedom to contract is expressly limited by statutory or court-made law. They cannot, if the employer's operations are covered by the Fair Labor Standards Act, agree upon wage rates of less than 75 cents per hour, or upon less than time-and-one-half rates for all work over 40 hours per week. They cannot, if the LMRA is applicable, agree upon a closed shop; and in some states local legislation places still more severe strictures upon their agreement as to union security. If they decided on a check-off or on a plan for employer payments to a union trust fund, they must make their agreement conform to the provisions of Section 302 of the LMRA. There is some question about the extent to which they can agree, at least effectively, not to take one another into court in cases of alleged contract violation.

To note these few statutory provisions specifically is only to emphasize, however, the fact that collective bargaining is in predominant measure a "private law" process, very largely uncontrolled by public statute or by common law as to either the procedures to be followed or the results to be reached. That there is substantial similarity between thousands of collective bargaining agreements is only a reflection of the emergence of certain generally recognized principles of industrial relations. Thus, most of these contracts contain the provision that an employee can be discharged only "for just cause." Yet there is today nothing whatsoever in "the law of the land" which prevents an employer from discharging an employee on the basis of the color of his hair or on the ground that he dreamed about him the night before. Virtually all contracts contain seniority provisions, and they bear a remarkable similarity. Yet no federal or state laws (except those giving war veterans certain preferential rights) touch on this seniority matter.

Our principal interest here is not in studying the few instances of public-law control over the employer-employee private lawmaking process. It is rather in studying the private law-making process itself, the process by which two private groups, a corporation (in most cases) and a union, make their own "private law" and then proceed to administer it.

Whether this is lawyers' business may be debated, futilely, as a matter of defining terms. The question ought to be whether there is something here for which legal training and experience represents a qualification superior to that which others, with different training, are likely to have. Here are documents to be drawn up and "cases" to be argued. The test of the effectiveness of the document will be whether it says what the parties to it will, on hindsight, wish they had said. The arts of anticipation of problems, effectiveness of written incorporation of ideas and principles for future guidance, and persuasive argumentation are all involved. If lawyers have nothing to offer here, some soul-searching is in order. The only explanation would be that the practice of law has become so rigidified that it is confined to trafficking in particular forms of technicality and is unable to accommodate itself to new demands upon the effectuation of its purposes.

Many collective bargaining agreements are today drawn, and many arbitration cases argued, by lawyers. The number is increasing. Yet it is advisable to face, as one of the preliminaries to our further consideration of this subject, the fact that substantial question has arisen as to the usefulness of lawyers in connection with this particular law-making process. Some unions, especially, have taken the position that lawyers do more harm than good in the working out of collective bargaining agreements, and this view is also taken, or at least espoused, by a good many management industrial relations people. The AFL Electrical Workers make it a firm policy to insist that no lawyers be permitted to participate in collective bargaining negotiations and to include in their contracts the following provision: "No legal adviser of either party is to serve on any grievance committee."

Leaders of the bar are alert to this attitude and have frankly recognized that too many lawyers approach the negotiation, drafting, and administration of a collective agreement as though it were just another commercial contract. It has been pointed out by the American Bar Association Committee on Improving Administration of Union-Employer Contracts (1950 Report) that for the lawyer's effective participation in these processes:

> . . . one basic assumption must unquestionably be accepted; that is, that the lawyer understands the interplay of forces we describe as labor relations, and that he realizes that his client's position is ordinarily best served by the maintenance of working relationship in the spirit of mutual cooperation. A lawyer who thinks in terms of abstractions, of legal rights and duties, and who conducts himself as if he were representing a litigant in an adverse proceeding before a court, is little fitted for the responsibilities in the field here under discussion.

The Report also reflects a generally accepted opinion that with such an attitude there is a real place for lawyers at the initial stage of informal consultation as to the meaning and application of the contract and at the final stage of arbitration of disputes as to these same matters. On the contrary there is little support for the lawyer's participation in personnel practices or in the early pre-arbitration steps for processing such a dispute.

Insofar as the handling of collective bargaining cases themselves are concerned, some appreciation of the difficulties of working out the lawyer's role, may be suggested by looking at what happened in an actual case (unreported) involving a relatively small Chicago manufacturer and a newly organized local of one of the large CIO unions.

After three weeks of prolonged negotiations (between Union and Management committees on which no lawyers were included) tentative agreement was reached on a contract which included, among other things, the following seniority clause:

> Seniority will be followed in all cases of layoff and rehire, but only to the extent the employee is qualified to do the work available.

The Company insisted on showing this tentative agreement to its lawyer before signing. After much shaking of his head, he took the tentative agreement back to his office and proceeded to make certain "changes deemed absolutely essential." Two days later, and at a point where the Union negotiating committee tempers had reached a temperature of approximately 211° F., the lawyer submitted his revision. The seniority clause had been reworked to read as follows:

ARTICLE V. SENIORITY

Seniority means length of service with the Company; provided that said service shall not have been interrupted for any period of more than ninety (90) days. An employee's seniority shall be recognized as continuing to accumulate during any period during which he serves in a supervisory capacity, either in his own or any other department.

In the case of layoffs in any department of the Company's plant, employees shall be laid off in the reverse order of their seniority in that department and shall be rehired on the basis of their seniority; provided, however, that no employee shall, in the case of a layoff, be retained or returned to work unless there is work in his department which, in the judg-

ment of the Company, he is qualified to perform; and provided, further, that the term "layoff," as used herein, shall
be interpreted to mean, exclusively, a reduction in work force
resulting from a curtailment of production schedules by decision of the Company and necessitating the dismissal of one
or more employees in the department for periods equal to
or greater than one full work shift.

Seniority shall not be considered by the Company, as a
matter of contractual obligation, in the case of transfers from
one job to another or in the case of promotions to higher
paying jobs, the right to make such transfers and promotions
being recognized as a prerogative of the Company.

The Executive Vice-President of the Company involved in this
case refused to authorize the Industrial Relations Manager to
sign the contract until he had taken up with the Union some of
the matters, including the seniority clause, covered in the lawyer's
memorandum. This was done. The contract was finally signed
ten days later. The seniority clause, in the final form, was as
follows:

Employees will be laid off and rehired on the basis of their
seniority in their department, provided that there is work
available in that department which they are qualified to do.
This provision will not apply to cases of dismissal for less
than a full shift or to layoffs resulting from any strike or
work stoppage.

Several months later an issue arose in this plant when the installation of a new machine necessitated laying off three operators
in the press room. One of these three operators, who may be
identified here as Emanuel Ferreira, had been transferred only
three months before the layoff from the paint room to the press
room. He had worked in the paint room for eleven years and
was one of the oldest employees there. But he was the lowest
seniority employee in the press room, which is in a separate
department.

The Industrial Relations Manager wanted to move Ferreira
back into the paint room. The paint room foreman objected,
however, apparently in large measure because of his personal dislike for Ferreira. The Company lawyer also advised against the
transfer on the ground that it was not required under the contract
and that it would "set a bad precedent." Ferreira was accordingly discharged.

The Union filed a grievance in this case, setting out in some detail the record of Ferreira's eleven years of service, and concluding with the statement that "if Emanuel Ferreira's service to this Company doesn't mean any more than this his fellow workers will feel that the Company is willing to take eleven years of a man's life and then forget about him when it wouldn't cost anything to give him another job he can do." On advice of counsel, the Company filled in the space on the grievance form for the Management answer with the statement: "No contract violation alleged or proven."

The case went to arbitration, the Company lawyer handling it for the Company. The Union's presentation to the arbitrator was largely in terms of Ferreira's ability to do the paint-room work and in terms of the inequity of his being laid off. The Company lawyer objected repeatedly to the Union representative's argument, insisting that it was "irrelevant and immaterial." At the end of the Union representative's statement the lawyer asked the arbitrator to "enter a summary judgment here and now in favor of the Management, for no evidence has been submitted, only argument by some friend of the allegedly aggrieved employee."

Upon the arbitrator's refusal to rule as requested, the Company lawyer developed, through examination of Company witnesses (principally the paint-room foreman) the following points: 1. That Ferreira had once (three years before) been laid off for three days for having someone else punch in his time card for him. 2. That Ferreira had protested bitterly in 1943 when the Company refused to seek a draft deferment for him. (When the Union representative tried to explain the 1943 incident to the arbitrator, Company counsel protested that he should not be permitted to proceed because "his argument can amount at best to no more than hearsay testimony.") In his closing argument, the Company lawyer of course stressed the provision in the contract for departmental seniority. "Expressio unius," he reminded the arbitrator, "exclusio alterius." He submitted an exhibit summarizing the holdings of seven different arbitrators in similar cases at other plants, and adjured the arbitrator to "recognize here the clear and unequivocal application of the principal of stare decisis."

The arbitrator's decision was in favor of the Company.

Despite the doubts and objections which have been raised, more and more the collective bargaining job is being done by legally trained men and women, a good many of them lawyers in general practice, some of them in the legal divisions of large corporations and unions, and not a few of them in positions where they do only this kind of work and may have abandoned their identity (sometimes considered a disadvantage) as "lawyers." This increase in lawyer-participation is in part the consequence of lawyers' increasing acceptance of the fact that practice in this field requires the playing of a different role from that which they play in some of their other professional pursuits, the use of a different vocabulary, and the acceptance of some harder standards of performance than the writing of air-tight documents and the winning of cases. It is in part, too, the consequence of an increasing realization by both labor and management that the adoption of a set of formal rules as the basis for their relationship, or as part of it, creates a whole new set of demands and difficulties which require a substantial degree of expertness in their handling. Carelessly drawn collective bargaining contracts have created worse relationships than those which existed before. Misguided and awkward amateur advocacy has proved expensive economy when the arbitration awards have come in. Just as the adoption of incentive systems has produced, of necessity, corps of industrial and time-study engineers, the adoption of collective bargaining contracts is requiring the services of men expert and experienced in establishing and administering written codes of working relationships. These are not all lawyers, and fortunately there has been no inclination to expand here the "illegal practice of law" concept, but it is obvious that the legislative, administrative, and adjudicative functions which actually constitute the collective bargaining process are the kind of things which good lawyers do particularly well. The record is that where lawyers have learned that a collective bargaining contract is *only part* of a *necessarily continuing* relationship, one party to which is a very different thing from a corporation, they have made substantial contributions in this field.[6]

5. THE ENFORCEABILITY OF COLLECTIVE BARGAINING AGREEMENTS

a. Introductory Note

Discussion of the enforceability of collective agreements prior to an analysis of their substance is in a sense anomalous. Yet

[6] An interesting enumeration of management's errors in the bargaining process is presented in an article by Cyrus Ching, Director of the Federal Mediation and Conciliation service. Good Bargaining Is Good Business, The Nation's Business, 37:41, December, 1949.

general misunderstanding about it has contributed to prevailing attitudes regarding the nature and efficacy of the entire process. It is accordingly important to clear up this matter at the outset.

There are "legal" issues regarding the enforceability of these agreements by the courts. But they loom much larger in the minds of lawyers and legislators than in the minds of union officers and personnel managers. For not one in a hundred of these agreements will ever be taken to the courts, even though one or both parties to them may commit innumerable breaches of their terms.

There are two reasons for this. One is that most management and union officials feel that the price which has to be paid for judicial redress of a contract breach is too high. The adversary process as practiced in the courtroom is often characterized by acrimonious exchange and by exaggerated charges and counter-charges which injure a relationship which has to continue throughout the proceedings and after they are over. Judgment is as likely to be based on anachronistic precedent or ill-fitting doctrines of the law of contracts as on what the parties consider the merits of the case. The decision will, in any event, probably not come down until after the parties have completed another series of negotiations in which the mooted issue has been cleared up as far as the new contract is concerned. Opportunities for revision come so frequently that adjudication is minimized.

The other reason why in America so few of these cases go to the courts is that the parties usually set up in these agreements their own private adjudicative system designed to meet their specific needs. This is the grievance and arbitration procedure, which the parties substitute for judicial settlement.

b. The Rise and Legal Recognition of Collective Agreements

The modern collective bargaining agreement is a natural outgrowth of the Industrial Revolution of the nineteenth century which drew masses of workers into gigantic productive enterprises in all of the industrially advanced countries of the world. In an entirely different sense from that intended by Karl Marx, it may be said that the spread of machine technology into such societies has revolutionized the contractual relationship between employer and employee.[7] During medieval times, working conditions in

---

[7] 1 Marx, Das Kapital 360, 361 (5th ed., Engels, 1903) (in German). Marx, of course, contended that industrialism, if not regulated by the state, leaves the industrial worker no freedom of bargaining.

most European countries were controlled by the guilds.   This system later gave way to governmental regulation which denied
workers the right to seek improved employment conditions
through combination, usually under threat of criminal prosecution.   This type of governmental regulation, in turn, collapsed
during the nineteenth century when France in 1864, Germany in
1869, and England by a series of acts in 1825, 1859, and 1871,
enacted legislation which established the immunity of workers'
combinations from criminal prosecution.   In America the common law theory of criminal conspiracy flourished as a restraint
upon collective bargaining until approximately the middle of the
nineteenth century, when it fell into disuse without legislative
repudiation.[8]

When workers were thus released to pursue their economic destiny through combination, the stage was set for the rise of collective
contracts.   Most foreign countries encountered problems similar
to our own in seeking to fit this novel instrumentality into the
framework of their existing legal systems.   As late as 1910 a leading German text announced that a collective bargaining agreement
had no legal effect at all, its principal force being its "social"
(moral) significance,[9] and in the same year the highest court of
France held that those agreements had no effect on nonconforming
individual contracts of employment.[10]   This has likewise been the
English view.   The Trade Union Act, 1871, gave trade-unions
legal status, but provided that collective agreements should neither
be enforceable nor, if breached, give rise to a cause of action for
damages.[11]   Elsewhere in Europe the problem of recognition was
ultimately resolved by legislation providing in substance that
where collective agreements have been negotiated, individual contracts of employment which undercut the terms so created are invalid.   The first of such acts were adopted by the Netherlands and
Switzerland in 1907 [12] and provided that collective agreements
could be specifically enforced and that they override nonconform-

---

[8] Its place was taken, in a sense, by a great expansion of the civil remedy of
injunction, until the use of the injunction in labor disputes was severely
restricted in 1932 by the Norris–LaGuardia Act, relating to federal courts,
and about the same time by similar legislation in many states.

[9] Oertmann, The Law on Obligations 669 (3d and 4th eds. 1910) (in
German).

[10] Cour de Cassation (Civ.) 1 D.P. 201 (1911).

[11] Trade Union Act, 1871, 34 & 35 Vict., c. 31, s. 4 (4).   But note the
Conditions of Employment and National Arbitration Order, S.R. & O., 1940,
N-1305, 33 Halsbury 734 (1940).   See also Kahn-Freund, Minimum Wage
Legislation in Great Britain, 97 U. of Pa. L. Rev. 778, 779 (1949).

[12] Dutch Law on Labor Contracts and Swiss Law on Obligations (effective
1912).

ing terms of individual contracts of employment. Similar laws
were enacted in France in 1919,[13] Finland in 1924,[14] Norway in
1927,[15] and Sweden in 1928.[16] Germany in 1918 and Austria in
1919 adopted acts of like effect and also provided for administrative extension of the contract schedules, which is now authorized
in many countries.[17]

In the absence of legislation, courts both here and abroad dis-
agreed.[18] In the United States, J. I. Case Co. v. NLRB [19] interpreted the National Labor Relations Act to mean that the collective agreement overrides conflicting individual contracts of employment; and Section 301 of the Labor Management Relations Act
confirmed the enforceability of the collective agreement.

c. Legal Effects of Collective Contracts in the Absence of Legislation

Many people confuse collective agreements with employment
contracts. But the collective agreement does not create employment relationships, for, in the language of Mr. Justice Jackson
in the Case case, "no one has a job by reason of it and no obligation to any individual ordinarily comes into existence from it
alone." [20] The confusion has been due in part to the fact that
many of the early cases were suits between individual employers
and employees; the immediate issue presented was the effect, if
any, which the collective agreement had upon the individual employment relationship.

1. *The Usage Theory.* The oldest theory concerning the nature
of collective agreements in the United States and England is the
"usage theory," which developed in cases between individual employees and their employers involving collective agreements. The

---

[13] However, withdrawal from membership in one of the parties to the contract restored full freedom of contract to individuals, and there were other
"exits" left to them.

[14] Act of March 22, 1924.

[15] Act of May 15, 1927.

[16] Act of June 22, 1928.

[17] See pages 281 et seq.

[18] See Fuchs, Collective Labor Agreements in American Law, 10 St.L. L.
Rev. 1 (1924); Rice, Collective Labor Agreements in American Law, 44 Harv.
L. Rev. 572 (1931); Witmer, Collective Labor Agreements in the Courts,
48 Yale L.J. 195 (1938); Lenhoff, The Present Status of Collective Contracts
in the American Legal System, 39 Mich. L. Rev. 1109 (1941); Witmer, Trade
Union Liability, 51 Yale L.J. 40 (1941).

[19] 321 U.S. 332, 64 Sup. Ct. 576, 88 L. Ed. 762 (1944). The opinion in this
case appears at page 221 supra.

[20] Id. at 335. On the other hand the exclusion of "contracts of employment
of seamen, railroad employees, or any other class of workers engaged in foreign

courts refused to look upon the collective agreement as a contract, but did regard it as a "usage" that the individual parties to the employment relationship incorporated into their employment agreement.[21] The collective agreement had legal significance only to the extent that it was so adopted.

2. *The Agency Theory.* A few courts, holding that the collective agreement was not enforceable because negotiated by or between unincorporated associations, which lacked juristic personality, nevertheless gave it effect in actions between individual employees and employers on the theory that the negotiators were agents of the individual members of the unions (or employers' group) so that the collective agreement was the members' contract.[22]

3. *The Third Party Beneficiary Theory.* A third theory, invoked in actions between individuals involving collective agreements, was the "third party beneficiary theory." Unlike the two theories thus far considered, this holds that the collective agreement itself is valid and enforceable; and that an individual could obtain relief pursuant to the terms of the collective agreement because the contracting parties so intended.[23] Germany's highest court invoked this principle as early as 1910 to sustain the rights of individual members of a contracting employers' association against the other contractor, the union.[24] But in 1925, in a reciprocal situation the same court refused to grant relief when a union

---

or interstate commerce" from the U.S. Arbitration Act, 9 U.S.C. Sec. 1, embraces collective contracts. Amálgamated Assn. v. Pa. Greyhound Lines, 192 F.2d 310 (3d Cir. 1951), noted in 65 Harv. L. Rev. 1239 (1952).

[21] The leading case is Hudson v. Cincinnati, etc. R. Co. 152 Ky. 711, 154 S.W. 47 (1913). This and other cases are discussed in Fuchs, op. cit. supra note 18, at 3–7. See also Rice, op. cit. supra note 18, at 581–593.

[22] The leading case is Barnes & Co. v. Berry, 169 Fed. 225 (6th Cir. 1909).

[23] The doctrine is discussed in Rice, op. cit. supra note 18, at 595–597. The cases and their language are: Hall v. St. Louis-San Francisco Ry., 224 Mo. App. 431, 28 S.W.2d 687 (1930) ("We hold that the agreement referred to was binding, and the plaintiff was entitled to the benefit of its provisions."); Blum & Co. v. Landau, 23 Ohio App. 426, 155 N.E. 154 (1926) ("It clearly appears that [it] . . . was a contract for the benefit of third parties . . . That such a contract is valid and enforceable is supported by unquestioned authority."); Gulla v. Barton, 164 App. Div. 293, 149 N.Y. Supp. 952 (1924) ("The agreement referred to was a valid contract, which may be enforced in any proper manner . . . It was a contract made by [plaintiff's] representative for his benefit, and its validity is not affected by the independent agreement, express or implied, between him and the defendant."). The principle was recently invoked in the case of In Re Norwalk Tire & Rubber Co., 100 F. Supp. 706 (D. Conn. 1951).

[24] Arbeitgeber-Schutzverband der Holzindustrie (Wood Manufacturers' Assn.) v. Deutscher Holzarbeiter Verband (Union of Woodworkers), 73 R.G.Z. 92, 105 (1910).

sought to enforce the *duties* imposed upon an individual employer-member of a contracting group, asserting that the concept of third-party-obligor is unknown to the German law.[25]

4. *The Moral Obligation Theory.*   In a few cases the collective agreement is held to be a "moral obligation," not enforceable but influential in determining whether equitable relief shall be given.[26]

5. *The Contract Theory.*   A substantial body of case law, both in this country and abroad, has dealt with collective agreements according to the traditional pattern of contract litigation.   In many instances American courts held agreements unenforceable because negotiated by unincorporated associations which, lacking legal personality, had no standing to sue or be sued.[27]   In others they examined the agreements, found numerous promises on the part of employers but no express undertakings on the part of the unions, and declared them to be invalid for lack of consideration.[28] Still other courts denied specific enforcement in terms of the rule against compelling the performance of personal services,[29] or in converse situations, because of the lack of mutuality of remedy.[30] But courts in many American states and many foreign countries, proceeding along traditional lines of contract law, held them to be enforceable.   The courts of France, Denmark, and Sweden had reached this conclusion, at least with respect to some aspects of liability, prior to the enactment of legislation which established enforceability beyond all question.[31]   Both Czechoslovakia [32] and Yugoslavia [33] held to the contrary, as did Germany.[34]

In a number of comparatively early American cases, employers obtained injunctions against strikes, the courts basing their action

[25] Verband der Bergarbeiter (United Mineworkers) v. Arbeitgeberverband für Braunkohlenbau (Assn. of Operators of Brown-Coal Mines), 111 R.G.Z. 166, 178 (1925).

[26] Both the principle and the cases are discussed by Fuchs, op. cit. supra note 18, at 7–12.

[27] See generally Witmer, Trade Union Liability, 51 Yale L.J. 40 (1941); and for a comparatively recent case, see Hallman v. Wood, Wire and Metal Lathers' International Union, 219 N.C. 798, 15 S.E.2d 361 (1941).

[28] See generally Witmer, Collective Labor Agreements in the Courts, 48 Yale L.J. 195, 203 (1938).

[29] *Ibid.*

[30] *Ibid.*

[31] See Rice, op. cit. supra note 18, at 575–581.

[32] Cf. Czechoslovakian Supreme Court (in banc), (1925) Važny No. 5479, pronouncing the superiority of individually contracted terms over collective contract schedules.

[33] Bilimovic, Arbeitsrecht des Königreichs der Serben, Kroaten und Slowenen, 5 Zeitschrift für Ostrecht 369, 379 (1929).

[34] See discussion under Third Party Beneficiary Theory, supra.

on the ground that the contracts contained no-strike clauses.[35]
More numerous, however, are suits instituted by unions. The
New York case of Schlesinger v. Quinto [36] is generally regarded as
the fountainhead of this line of cases. The court enjoined the
employers from reducing the wages and increasing the hours contrary to the collective agreement. The allegation that this constituted an order of specific performance of a contract for personal
services was rejected, the court taking the position that this was
not a contract for personal services but an agreement between two
responsible organizations. There have been innumerable subsequent holdings of the same kind in New York, and the same
position has been taken in many other states. The opinion of
the Texas Court of Civil Appeals in Harper v. Local Union No.
520, IBEW,[37] contains an illuminating discussion of the issue and
of the developing precedent. The Mississippi court in 1931 noted
this trend and commented:

> The time has at last arrived when, under patriotic and intel-
> ligent leadership [the labor unions'] place has become secure
> in the confidence of the country, and their contracts are no
> longer construed with hesitancy or strictures, but are accorded
> the same liberality, and receive the same benefits of the appli-
> cation of the principles of modern law, bestowed upon other
> agreements which pertain to the important affairs of life.[38]

A minority of state courts still maintains the contrary position.

d. Effect and Enforceability of Collective Contracts Under Statutes

As previously indicated, the enforceability of collective labor
agreements is established in many European countries by legislation. In their interpretation of such legislation the courts of some
countries, notably Germany and France, have recognized the dual
character of the collective agreement. It contains some terms
which are contractual or promissory; and others which are normative or regulatory. It is contractual insofar as it imposes conditions and obligations to be performed by the contracting parties

---

[35] E.g., Burgess v. Georgia F. & A. Ry., 148 Ga. 417, 96 S.E. 865 (1918);
Gilchrist Co. v. Metal Polishers Union, 113 Atl. 320 (N.J. Eq. 1919); Neder-
landsch Amerikaansche Stoomvaart Maatschappij v. Stevedores' & Longshoremen's Benev. Soc., 265 Fed. 397 (E.D. La. 1920).

[36] 201 App. Div. 487, 194 N.Y. Supp. 401 (1st Dept. 1922).

[37] 48 S.W.2d 1033 (Tex. Civ. App. 1932).

[38] Yazoo & M.V.R. Co. v. Sideboard, 161 Miss. 4, 13, 133 So. 669, 671 (1931).

themselves. It is regulatory insofar as it establishes work schedules, wages, etc., which control employment relationships within
its scope.[39]

The regulatory or normative provisions are enforced between
individuals not because of custom, usage, agency, third-party-bene-
ficiary, or any other contractual considerations, but because the
law directs that the terms of the collective agreement shall control.
It cannot be objected that this is private law-making, despite the
fact that it is the terms of a private agreement that are being imposed upon the parties. We have here merely a variant of referen-
tial legislation, a technique well known in all countries. Its application here is found in the legislative declaration that the terms
for work fixed by collective bargaining shall be the terms for *all*
employments within the bargaining unit or occupational field.
It is not the collective agreement alone that imposes its conditions
upon nonmembers of unions, but the combination of the agreement and the statute that brings about this result.[40] This is essentially the American view of the matter as a result of the Supreme
Court's decision in the Case case,[41] where it was held that individual contracts of employment were no bar to the union's efforts to
negotiate a collective agreement for all the employees in the appropriate unit.

The contractual aspects of the collective agreement are enforceable in actions between the parties and are not the concern of individuals. This principle was recently applied by the United
States Court of Appeals for the Ninth Circuit, which affirmed the
dismissal of an action brought by a group of individual employees
to enforce a closed-shop clause in the collective agreement between
their union and employer.[42] Litigation for the enforcement of
these types of provisions, when brought by proper parties, calls for
the application of traditional legal concepts of contract law.
Where, as in many foreign countries and in some states in this

[39] The first scholar to approach the problem from this point of view was
H. Sinzheimer in the first volume of his work, The Corporate Contract on
Employment Norms 68, 107 (1907) (in German). See also Durand, Dualism
in Collective Bargaining Contracts, 1939 Revue trimestrielle de droit civil 353
(in French); Hueck and Nipperdey, Textbook on Labor Law 117 (1929)
(in German).

[40] See Lenhoff, Werden und Wesen der Kollektivverträge, Festschrift für
Maurovic 625, 650, 665 (1935), and The Present Status of Collective Contracts in the American Legal System, 39 Mich. L. Rev. 1109, 1137 (1941).

[41] J. I. Case Co. v. NLRB, 321 U.S. 332 64 Sup. Ct. 576 88 L. Ed. 762 (1944).
See also Burstein, The Status of the Collective Bargaining Agreement, 2 Lab.
L.J. 902 (1951).

[42] Mackay v. Loew's, Inc., 182 F.2d 170, 18 A.L.R. 2d 348 (1950), cert.
denied, 340 U.S. 828 (1950). See the annotation in 18 A.L.R. 2d 352.

country, it is concluded that these concepts prevent enforcement, legislation could alter the law. The chief industrial countries of Europe except Great Britain have adopted such measures. So has the United States by enacting (to govern the federal courts) Section 301 (a) of the Labor Management Relations Act of 1947, 29 U.S.C.A. Sec. 185 (a) , which was sustained against constitutional attack in the case of Wilson & Co. v. United Packinghouse Workers of America, reprinted infra.

A few State Labor Relations Acts, such as those of Wisconsin and Colorado, have included a breach of a collective contract among the cases of unfair practices, thus providing for an administrative enforcement of a collective contract.[43]

There are other problems of judicial enforceability of collective bargaining agreements which might be explored if time did not require a more selective emphasis. The important point, however, is that the collective bargaining process has almost completely substituted private arbitration as the method of settlement in the United States.

WILSON & CO., INC. v. UNITED PACKINGHOUSE WORKERS OF AMERICA
United States District Court, Southern District, New York, 1949
83 F. Supp. 162, 23 L.R.R.M. 2391

KAUFMAN, District Judge.

The defendants move pursuant to Rule 12 (b) of the Federal Rules of Civil Procedure, 28 U.S.C.A., to dismiss this action upon the grounds that (1) the court lacks jurisdiction over the subject matter of the action, and (2) the court lacks jurisdiction over the person of the defendant, United Packinghouse Workers of America.

Plaintiff, an employer, has brought this suit to recover the sum of $50,000 as damages for an alleged breach of a written collective bargaining agreement made by it with the defendants in October of 1947. Plaintiff alleges that it is engaged in a business affecting commerce and that the defendants are labor organizations and voluntary unincorporated associations representing employees in an industry affecting commerce and have officers and agents engaged in such representation in this district. The defendants are alleged to have breached the terms of the agreement by causing

[43] See Rice, A Paradox of Our National Labor Law, 34 Marq. L. Rev. 233, 237, 238 (1951) .

strikes and work stoppages in March of 1948 in certain of the plaintiff's plants located in New York.

Jurisdiction is invoked under Section 301 (a) of the Labor Management Relations Act, 1947, 29 U.S.C.A. Sec. 185 (a) (hereinafter referred to as the "Act"), which provides that "suits for violation of contracts between an employer and a labor organization representing employees in an industry affecting commerce as defined in this Act, or between any such labor organizations, may be brought in any district court of the United States having jurisdiction of the parties, without respect to the amount in controversy or without regard to the citizenship of the parties"; and under 28 U.S.C.A. Sec. 1337, which provides that "the district courts shall have original jurisdiction of any civil action or proceeding arising under any Act of Congress regulating commerce. . . ."

The constitutionality of Section 301, 29 U.S.C.A. Sec. 185, has been drawn in question by the defendants' motion and the United States has intervened.   28 U.S.C.A. Sec. 2403.

First.   It is contended by defendants that Section 301 (a) is unconstitutional as applied to this case, in that it extends the jurisdiction of this court beyond the limitations prescribed by Article III, Section 2, of the Constitution of the United States, which, insofar as here material, provides that "the judicial power shall extend to all Cases, in Law and Equity, arising under this Constitution, the Laws of the United States . . . to Controversies . . . between Citizens of different States. . . ."

Defendants argue that the action is one for breach of contract, to enforce a right existing under the common law of the State of New York; that there is no diversity of citizenship, and the case is not one arising under the Constitution or laws of the United States or upon any other ground set forth in Article III, Section 2 of the Constitution.   Consequently, runs the argument, Congress was without power to confer jurisdiction over the case on the District Court.   [Citing cases.]

The argument must fail.

The spirit as well as the letter of the Act makes it clear that in setting up the machinery for the negotiation of collective bargaining agreements, their execution, effect and enforcement, Congress recognized and regarded the observance and enforcement of such contracts as a matter of federal concern incident to the regulation of commerce, and intended to create a right in each of the parties to such contracts to the observance and the performance thereof by the other.   Section 301 (a) of the Act, authorizing suits for violation of such agreements, would be meaningless on any other hypothesis and would attribute to Congress the anomalous action of providing for remedy and a forum in which to enforce it, without creating a right to remedy or to enforce. The very inclusion of Section 301 shows, on its face, and the legislative history of the Act confirms the Congressional intention, that other provisions of the Act, for redressing unfair labor practices, were not an exclusive statement of the rights created by the Act, and did not eliminate or militate against the right to seek relief in the federal courts for violations of collective bargaining agreements between employers and labor organizations.

There can be no doubt that Congress, under its power to regulate commerce, could constitutionally create such substantive rights (see Section 22 (a), Securities Act, 1933, as amended, 15 U.S.C.A. Sec. 77v (a) ; Section 16 (b), Fair Labor Standards Act, 1938, as amended, 29 U.S.C.A. Sec. 216 (b) ; and the legislative history of the Act fully supports the conclusion that Congress not only intended to do so, but that it regarded the language it used as sufficient and effective to do so. S. Rept. No. 105, 80th Cong., 1st Sess., pp. 3, 15–17; H. Rept. No. 245, 80th Cong. 1st Sess., pp. 6, 45, 46; House Conference Rept. No. 510, 80th Cong., 1st Sess., p. 52; 93 Cong. Rec. 6443, 7537.

To adopt the defendants' contention would violate the cardinal principles that a court should adopt that construction of a statute which will sustain its constitutionality, [citing cases]; worse than that, it would give to the Act a construction at variance with the one put upon it by the Congress which enacted it.

The question now under discussion was raised and decided in Colonial Hardwood Floor Co. v. International Union, D.C. Md., 76 F. Supp. 493, affirmed 4 Cir., 168 F.2d 33. In overruling the contention on which defendants rely here, Judge Chesnut said, 76 F. Supp. 493, at page 496:

> The defendants also raise various constitutional questions. First, it is said that the court is without jurisdiction of the case in the absence of diversity of citizenship. The point made is that under Article III of the Constitution judicial power is limited to cases of diverse citizenship or to cases arising under the Constitution, Treaties or laws of the United States; and that the controversy in this case does not arise under a law of the United States. See Barnhart v. Western Maryland Ry. Co., D.C. Md. 41 F. Supp. 898, affirmed 4 Cir., 128 F.2d 709. But I think this contention untenable here. Osborn v. Bank of United States, 9 Wheat. 738, 6 L. Ed. 204;

Markham v. Allen, 326 U.S. 490, 66 S. Ct. 296, 90 L. Ed. 256. The Labor Management Act creates important substantive rights between employers and employees engaged in interstate commerce, and section 301 expressly authorizes suits of this character in district courts of the United States. It is clearly, therefore, a suit arising under a law of the United States.

See also Note, 57 Yale L. J. 630.

Second. It is contended by defendants that Section 301 infringes upon the rights reserved to the States under the Tenth Amendment in that it sets forth the circumstances when and the manner in which a Union may be sued in a case which does not involve the enforcement of a federal right. In view of the fact that the enforcement of a federal right is involved in the instant case, the argument falls. It is clear that Congress, having created a substantive right in the exercise of its power under the commerce clause, art. 1, Sec. 8, Cl. 3, may also provide the procedure for enforcing that right by making voluntary labor organizations legal entities for the purpose of suit. United Mine Workers of America v. Coronado Coal Co., 259 U.S. 344, 383–392, 42 S. Ct. 570, 66 L. Ed. 975, 27 A.L.R. 762; cf. Rule 17 (b) of the Federal Rules of Civil Procedure. In so far as state laws may conflict, they must yield to the paramount congressional legislation when a federal right is asserted as the basis of suit.

Third. It is contended by defendants that Section 301 subjects voluntary unincorporated labor organizations to suits in foreign forums and to service of process by procedures which are inapplicable to other unincorporated organizations; and that in so doing Congress has made an unreasonable and arbitrary discrimination against unincorporated labor organizations which deprives the defendant, United Packinghouse Workers of America, of the equal protection of the laws as guaranteed by the due process clause of the Fifth Amendment.

Unlike the Fourteenth Amendment, the Fifth Amendment has no equal protection clause and it restrains only such discriminatory legislation as amounts to a denial of due process. [Citing cases.]

Section 301 is not invalid by that test. Its purpose was to do away with the difficulties which arose in attempting to enforce the provisions of collective bargaining agreements by reason of the fact that in many states labor unions were not suable as entities and in others only under certain circumstances, and that relief against the members individually was generally impracticable, if not unattainable. By holding the parties to such agreements to a higher degree of responsibility, Congress endeavored to carry out the purpose and policy of the Act. It was not necessary for Congress to make that statute applicable to all unincorporated associations for there is no requirement of uniformity in connection with the commerce clause. Currin v. Wallace, 306 U.S. 1, 14, 59 S. Ct. 379, 83 L. Ed. 441; Sunshine Anthracite Coal Co. v. Adkins, 310 U.S. 381, 401, 60 S. Ct. 907, 84 L. Ed. 1263. Connolly v. Union Sewer Pipe Co. 184 U.S. 540, 22 S. Ct. 431, 46 L. Ed. 679, upon which defendants rely, "has been worn away by the erosion of time, and we are of opinion that it is no longer controlling." Tigner v. State of Texas, 310 U.S. 141, 147, 60 S. Ct. 879, 882, 84 L. Ed. 1124, 130 A.L.R. 1321.

Fourth. It is contended by defendants that Section 301 as applied in this case deprives the defendant, United Packinghouse Workers of America, of due process of law in violation of the Fifth Amendment, in that it provides that service of process upon an agent shall constitute service on a labor organization. The argument is made that since the principal offices of defendant are located in Illinois, it is to be regarded as having a residence in that forum; and that service of process upon its agent in New York is not such as will subject it, a non-resident, to the jurisdiction of this court. Service in the instant case was effected on the defendant's District Director for this area, who is also a member of its Executive Board. The defendant does not contend that it is not engaged in representing employees in this district through its agents, nor does it contend that service was not effected upon its agent within the meaning of Section 301 (d) of the Act. Neither is it urged that the service was not such as was reasonably calculated to give the defendant notice and an opportunity to appear and defend. In these circumstances the defendant was not deprived of due process of law. [Citing cases.]

Fifth. It is contended that this court has no jurisdiction over the defendant, United Packinghouse Workers of America, by reason of the fact that service was not effected in accordance with Section 13 of the New York General Associations Law, McK. Consol. Laws, c. 29. Inasmuch as service was effected in the manner provided by Rule 4 (d) (7) of the Federal Rules of Civil Procedure and Section 301 (d) of the Labor Management Relations Act, the argument is without merit.

Motions denied. Settle order on notice.

NOTES

1. Observe that the relief sought in Wilson & Co. was money damages. Subsection 301 (b) of the LMRA provides that "Any money judgment against a labor organization in a district court of the United States shall be enforceable only against the organization as an entity and against its assets."

2. Suppose, however, that the employer, apprised in advance of a union's intention to breach its contract, asks for an injunction to restrain the breach. See Mercury Oil Refining Co. v. Oil Workers etc. Union, 187 F.2d 980 (10th Cir. 1951) ; AFL v. Western Union Tel. Co., 179 F.2d 535 (6th Cir. 1950) ; Textile Workers of America v. Aleo Mfg. Co., 94 F. Supp. 626 (M.D.N.C. 1950) ; Mountain States Div. No. 17, etc. v. Mountain States Tel. & Tel. Co., 81 F. Supp. 397 (D. Colo. 1948) ; Lewittes & Sons v. United Furniture Workers, 95 F. Supp. 851 (S.D.N.Y. 1951) ; Rice, A Paradox of Our National Labor Law, 34 Marq. L. Rev. 233 (1951).

3. Would it make any difference whether the breach of contract is also an unfair labor practice prescribed by Section 8 (a) or (b) of the Act? See Amazon Cotton Mill Co. v. Textile Workers Union, 167 F.2d 183 (4th Cir. 1948) ; International Longshoremen's Union v. Sunset Line & Twine Co., 77 F. Supp. 119 (N.D. Cal. 1948).

4. Suppose an employer breaches a contract in two particulars, one of which is an unfair labor practice and the other not. See Reed v. Fawick Airflex Co., 86 F. Supp. 822 (N.D. Ohio 1949).

5. May a union be held liable for damages attributable to a "wildcat" strike? Consult the language of Section 301 (e) and see Shirley-Herman Co. v. Int. Hod Carriers, etc., 182 F.2d 806 (2d Cir. 1950).

6. Is a union responsible for the damages resulting from a prolonged strike called in violation of a "no-strike" clause in its contract with the employer, if the employer has in the interim exercised its election to terminate the contract because of the union's breach? See Boeing Airplane Co. v. Int. Assn. of Machinists, 188 F.2d 356 (9th Cir. 1951).

B. *A Typical Collective Bargaining Agreement*
(The Enderby Contract)

Agreement Between
The Enderby Rubber Company
and
United Rubber, Cork, Linoleum
and Plastic Workers of America,
CIO, Local Union No. 417

This Agreement is made this twenty-first day of May, 1950, by and between the Enderby Rubber Company, its successors or assigns (hereinafter referred to as the "Company"), and Local Union No. 417 of the United Rubber, Cork, Linoleum and Plastic Workers of America, affiliated with the Congress of Industrial Organizations, its successors or assigns, and on behalf of the employees covered by this contract (hereinafter referred to as the "Union").

WITNESSETH:

That it is the intent and purpose of the parties hereto that this agreement will promote and improve industrial and economic relationship between the Union and the Company, and to set forth herein the basic agreement covering rates of pay, hours of work, and all other conditions of employment to be observed between the parties hereto.

Now therefore, in consideration of the premises and the mutual agreements hereinafter stated, it is agreed as follows:

ARTICLE I. UNION-MANAGEMENT RELATIONSHIP

SECTION 1. The Company recognizes the Union as the sole and exclusive collective bargaining agency for all production and maintenance employees of the Company with respect to wages, rates of pay, hours of work, and all other conditions of employment, excluding watchmen, draftsmen, technical employees, engineers, nurses, clerical and supervisory employees. "Supervisory employees" as used in this section, shall include employees who do not perform productive labor (work of employees covered by this contract), except when necessary in the following instances namely:

1. To assist or instruct in making set-ups.

2. To straighten out production and maintenance difficulties.

3. To instruct or train employees.

SECTION 2.   The Company will not interfere with the right of its employees to become members of the Union and will not interfere with, restrain, coerce, or discriminate against any employee because of membership in the Union, or activities in its behalf. The Union agrees not to intimidate or coerce any employee into membership in the Union, and also not to solicit membership on Company time.

SECTION 3.   The Company or the Union shall not discriminate against any employee because of race, sex, political or religious affiliation or nationality.

SECTION 4.   All employees who, on June 5, 1950, are members of the Union in good standing in accordance with its constitution and bylaws and all employees who become members after that date, shall, as a condition of employment, maintain their membership in the Union in good standing for the duration of this agreement.   If any dispute arises as to whether an employee is a member of the Union in good standing, or has been such a member on or after June 5, 1950, this dispute shall be disposed of as a grievance and in the manner provided for in Article II.

The Company will deduct from the first pay check each month, for each employee authorizing such deduction by writing to the Company, Union dues, initiation fees (not to exceed $3.00) and assessments (not to exceed $4.00).   The sums so deducted shall be paid promptly to the Secretary-Treasurer of the Union.

ARTICLE II.   REPRESENTATION AND GRIEVANCES

SECTION 1.   The Company agrees to recognize Department Stewards for each shift in each department for the purpose of handling and settling of grievances.   The Steward shall work in the department he represents.   The Steward shall be granted time off from work in order to present grievances to the Foreman.   The Stewards will also be excused from work to attend meetings between the Grievance Committee and the management upon written request of the Chairman of the Grievance Committee where the grievance involves a matter arising in the Steward's department. The Steward shall obtain permission from the Foreman before leaving the department.

SECTION 2.   The Company agrees to recognize a Plant Grievance Committee for the purpose of handling and settling grievances in all appeal steps in the grievance procedure.   This Plant Grievance

Committee shall consist of five (5) members of the Union who are employees of the Company.

Members of the Plant Grievance Committee shall be afforded such time off as may be required: (1) To attend regular scheduled meetings with Company representatives, without loss of pay; (2) To attend special meetings arranged by the Chairman of the Grievance Committee and the Industrial Relations Manager pertaining to discharges and other matters which cannot be reasonably delayed until the time of the next regular meeting without loss of pay; (3) To visit departments wherein they have legitimate business as labor representatives.

Before leaving their place of employment representatives shall give notice and receive permission from the Department Foreman.

SECTION 3. A total of five hours per week will be paid for stewards attending meetings under items 1 and 2 of Section 2 above. Committeemen and stewards attending meetings pursuant to Sections 1, 2, and 3 of this Article will be paid their guaranteed hourly rate for all such meeting time within the limitations herein stipulated.

SECTION 4. The Union agrees to submit the names of the Plant Grievance Committee, and the Department Stewards to the Company and to notify the Company of any changes.

SECTION 5. A grievance is a difference of opinion as to the meaning and application of the provisions of the agreement, or as to the compliance of either party hereto with any of its obligations under this agreement. This does not limit the Union from bringing up for discussion and possible agreement any other differences which might arise between the parties hereto. Should grievances arise between the Company and the Union, an earnest effort shall be made to settle such grievance immediately.

Step 1. Employees shall take up their grievance with their Foreman or with the Department or Group Steward who shall take up the matter with the Foreman. The aggrieved employee or employees may be present at the time the grievance is submitted to the Foreman.

Step 2. If no satisfactory settlement is reached, the grievance may be reduced to writing in triplicate on forms which will be provided by the Company. Two copies of the grievance shall be filed with the foreman and one copy shall be filed with the Chairman of the Grievance Committee by the Steward of the department. If the Grievance Committee decides to take up the grievance, it shall present the grievance within eight (8) days after it has been filed or at the next weekly meeting between the Grievance

Committee and the Divisional Superintendent.   The superintendent shall answer the grievance taken up in this manner as promptly as possible, but in no event later than eight (8) days following such meeting.   A specific time each week shall be agreed upon for the presentation of grievances referred by the Plant Grievance Committee to the Superintendent.

Step 3.   If the answer of the Superintendent is not satisfactory, the grievance may be appealed to the Industrial Relations Manager or his designated representative.   Such appeal shall be in writing and shall be filed within twenty-four (24) hours.   Upon receipt of the appeal a meeting shall be scheduled between the Grievance Committee and the Industrial Relations Manager or his designated representative, within five (5) working days of receipt of the appeal.   The Grievance Committee shall have the right to call in International Representatives of the United Rubber Workers at this meeting.   The Industrial Relations Manager's answer on any grievance appealed in this manner will be presented to the Grievance Committee in writing within two (2) days following the meeting.

Step 4.   In the event the answer of the Industrial Relations Manager or his designated representative on a particular grievance is not satisfactory, the Union may request that this grievance be submitted to arbitration.   If such a request is made, it shall be made by letter addressed to the Industrial Relations Manager within ten (10) days from the date of the answer of the Industrial Relations Manager.   An arbitrator shall be selected in the following manner: The Union shall submit the names of seven (7) recognized arbitrators.   The Company may select an arbitrator from the list but if no arbitrator is selected within ten (10) days, a request shall be made of the Federal Mediation and Conciliation Service for the names of five (5) arbitrators.   The Union shall first have the right to strike from this list two (2) names and the Company shall then strike from the list two (2) names and the remaining shall be the name of the arbitrator.

The arbitrator shall have the authority to settle only a grievance which concerns the interpretation and application of this contract.   Any grievance appealed to an arbitrator over which he shall have no power to rule shall be referred back to the parties without decision.   The arbitrator shall have no power to add to, subtract from, or modify this agreement.

Any decision or award by the arbitrator shall be final and binding on both parties for the life of this agreement.   No decision shall be made retroactive prior to the date that the grievance was filed under Step 2 of the grievance procedure. The expense of such arbitration shall be divided equally by the parties to this agreement.

SECTION 6.   Grievances (except cases involving claim of wrongful suspension or discharge), to be considered under the procedures provided for in this Article, must be filed within thirty (30) working days after the event occurs which is alleged to give rise to the grievance. Grievances must be filed and appealed within the time limit established in each step of the above procedure or they shall be considered settled on the basis of the last answer given. If the Company fails to answer a grievance within the time limit specified, the Union may appeal the grievance to the next step.

SECTION 7.   In the event an employee shall be suspended or discharged from employment and believes he has been unjustly dealt with, such suspension or discharge shall constitute a case to be handled in accordance with the method of adjustment of differences herein provided. Should it be decided under the provisions of this contract that an injustice has been done with regard to the employee's suspension or discharge, the Company agrees to reinstate him and pay full compensation at his prevailing rate for the time lost. No grievance may be filed claiming wrongful suspension or discharge unless it is filed within five (5) working days after same occurs. The Department Steward will be advised of all discharges promptly and in no event later than twenty-four (24) hours after such discharge. The Personnel Department or the Night Superintendent will make arrangements for a discharged or disciplined employee to call in a Union Steward before leaving the plant, if such employee so desires. The grievance shall be taken up promptly and diligent efforts made to dispose of it within five (5) working days.

ARTICLE III. NO STRIKE OR LOCKOUT

SECTION 1.   During the life of this agreement the Union agrees not to call any strike or to instigate any slowdowns or interruptions of production. If there are any violations, the Union agrees to exert every effort to terminate such violations immediately. Any participation by an individual in any strike, slowdown, or other interruptions with production during the life of this agreement, shall be a breach of this agreement by the employee. Any obligation on the part of the Company to check off dues shall cease if there is any violation of this Section by the Union.

SECTION 2. During the life of this agreement the Company agrees that there shall be no lockouts.

ARTICLE IV. SENIORITY

SECTION 1. New employees of the Company shall be considered probationary employees until they have had sixty (60) days' continuous service with the Company, after which their seniority shall date from sixty (60) days prior to the close of such probationary period. Grievances shall not be presented in connection with the discharge or layoff of probationary employees.

SECTION 2. Whenever there is a reduction in the working forces of an occupation, the probationary employees in the occupation shall be laid off first. If there is a further reduction, the order in which employees with seniority in that occupation shall be laid off from that occupation shall be determined by the following factors as listed below.' However, only where factors (b) and (c) are relatively equal shall factor (a) govern:

(a) Departmental seniority (length of continuous service in the department involved) ;

(b) Ability to perform the work available satisfactorily;

(c) Physical qualifications to perform the work available.

SECTION 3. An employee who is laid off from his occupation in accordance with the provisions of Section 2 above shall have the following opportunities for a job in the order set forth below:

(a) He may use his departmental length of service to return to former job or jobs that he held in another occupation or occupations in the same department in the reverse order that he worked on such jobs.

(b) He may replace the employee in his department with the least amount of departmental length of service in the department.

(c) If the employee has nine (9) months or more of service he may return to a job that he held for a period of at least sixty (60) days in any department in the plant, provided that he has more plant-wide length of service than the employee who is then working on the job.

(d) He may use his plant-wide length of service for an available laboring job in any department of the plant.

SECTION 4. Employees shall be recalled to the occupation from which they were laid off or transferred at the time of a reduction in the working forces in the reverse order of their layoff.

SECTION 5. In determining an employee's length of service for seniority purposes, computation will begin on the day the employee began work and no deduction will be made for lost time due to any reason, except that continuity of service shall be broken for the following reasons:

　(a)　If the employee quits.

　(b)　If the employee is discharged for cause, and the decision is not reversed under provisions of Article II herein.

　(c)　If the employee overstays an agreed leave of absence, and does not give the Company a satisfactory reason.

　(d)　If the employee who has been laid off because of lack of work fails to report when properly recalled within a period of five (5) working days.

　(e)　If an employee is laid off for twenty-four (24) consecutive months.

SECTION 6.　The Company agrees to furnish the Union with a new seniority list once every six months.

SECTION 7.　Employees who desire to be transferred to a different class of work may file an application for a transfer to the particular class of work they desire on a standard form which will be available upon request from the Foreman.　As a vacancy occurs on any job, or when a new job is created, the Company will first examine the list of applicants for that type of work, and select a qualified applicant for the job, based on seniority, before a new employee is hired for the job.　Any employee requesting and receiving a transfer in this manner shall be limited to one transfer a year.　Employees so transferred shall be given a reasonable break-in period on such jobs, to be determined by the Foreman, and in the event they fail to qualify, they shall be returned to their original jobs without prejudice.

SECTION 8.　When a permanent vacancy occurs in a department on any shift, preference for such vacancy shall be given to qualified employees in line with their departmental seniority.

SECTION 9.　Employees transferred on account of layoffs to other departments will, upon request, be retransferred to their original job and department where they were regular employees when production warrants.

SECTION 10.　When a job or operation is moved from one department to another within the plant, and is not otherwise altered, the employee holding such job shall have the privilege of transferring with the job, subject to the seniority provisions of this agreement.

SECTION 11.　At each layoff, or recall following layoff, the Company may designate certain individual employees whose services are required under the special circumstances then existing.

Such employees may be retained in or recalled to service, regardless of their seniority. No such designation shall become effective until after consultation with the Union and approval by the Works Manager.

SECTION 12. Local officers and plant Grievance Committee men not to exceed thirteen (13) shall have plant-wide preferential seniority at times of layoff during their respective terms of office.

ARTICLE V. HOURS OF WORK AND OVERTIME

SECTION 1. This Article is intended only to provide a basis for calculating overtime and shall not be interpreted as a guarantee of hours of work per day or per week.

SECTION 2. A day shall consist of twenty-four (24) consecutive hours from the time an employee begins the shift in which the work is performed. The normal workday shall be eight (8) hours of work.

SECTION 3. The normal work week shall consist of five (5) consecutive days, Monday to Friday, inclusive, except for continuous operations. A week shall consist of any seven (7) consecutive days.

SECTION 4. Should it be necessary, in the interest of efficiency or emergency operations, to establish schedules departing from the normal work week, the Company shall confer with the Grievance Committee in the establishment of such schedules, but the final right to arrange such working schedules rests with the Management in order to avoid adversely affecting operations of the plant.

SECTION 5. Time and one-half wage compensation shall be paid for work in excess of eight (8) hours in any day or forty (40) hours in any work week or for work performed on the sixth day worked in any regularly scheduled work week.

SECTION 6. Double time compensation shall be paid for all time worked over twelve (12) hours in any one day, or on Sunday (except to employees on continuous operations), or on the seventh day of any regularly scheduled work week.

SECTION 7. Double time compensation shall be paid for work performed on any of the following holidays: New Year's Day, Memorial Day, Fourth of July, Labor Day, Thanksgiving Day, Christmas Day.

SECTION 8. Overtime payments shall not be duplicated for the same hours worked under any of the above provisions. An employee shall be paid daily or weekly overtime, whichever is greater, but not both.

SECTION 9. The Company agrees that an employee shall not

be required to take time off for overtime worked, or to be worked. Overtime shall be allocated as evenly as possible among the employees in each department working on the job where overtime is required.

SECTION 10.   An employee reporting for work shall be provided with at least four hours of work, or at the Company's option, two hours' pay if he performs no work, unless he has been notified not to report for work before his scheduled starting time.   An employee refusing to do the work assigned to him shall not receive any pay.   In the event of fires, storms, floods, strikes, work stoppages, or any other causes beyond the control of the Company, which interfere with the work being provided, the provisions of this Section shall not apply.*

ARTICLE VI.   BULLETIN BOARDS

For the sole use of the Union, the Company will erect and maintain a suitable number of bulletin boards throughout the plant.   Such boards shall be the only place in the plant for the purpose of disseminating information concerning Union meetings, Union elections, social events, and notices of other Union affairs of general interest.   No matter shall be posted until it has been submitted and approved by the Works Manager or someone designated by him for that purpose.

ARTICLE VII.   LEAVE OF ABSENCE

SECTION 1.   A leave of absence, without pay, shall be understood to mean an absence from work requested by an employee and consented to by the Company, covering an agreed period of time and for such reasons as: settlement of an estate, serious illness or death of a member of the family, an extended trip, Union activity, or school under the G.I. Bill of Rights, etc.   The Company agrees to grant leaves of absence for such reasons, if it is practical to do so. Any employee elected or designated as a delegate to a Union convention shall be granted a temporary leave of absence without pay for a stated period of time not to exceed thirty (30) days.

SECTION 2.   Any employee on leave of absence who engages in other gainful employment shall lose his status as an employee of the Company.   Employees who fail to return on the expiration date of their leave shall be considered to have quit their employment unless the leave is extended in writing by the Company prior to the expiration of the leave.

* Section 10 was not included in the agreement until renegotiation in 1951. — ED.

ARTICLE VIII. SAFETY AND SANITATION

SECTION 1.   The Company agrees to provide healthful working conditions and adequate devices with regard to safety and sanitation in accordance with all state and federal laws.

SECTION 2.   The Company and the Union agree that in order to promote and encourage more healthful and safer working conditions, there shall be a Labor-Management Safety Committee as follows: three members of the Union selected by the Union, and three representatives of the Company, designated by the Company, whose duty it will be to refer recommendations to the Company for appropriate action.   The Committee shall, from among its number, elect its own chairman, vice-chairman, and secretary. The elective positions of said committee shall not all be held simultaneously by representatives of the Company or Union.   The Committee shall meet at least once each month on Company time.

SECTION 3.   Any female employee who becomes pregnant shall be allowed a leave of absence not to exceed twelve (12) months.

ARTICLE IX. PLANT MANAGEMENT

The Company shall exercise the normal and usual functions, duties, and responsibilities such as scheduling production, making work assignments, hiring, promoting, demoting, transferring, discharging, classifying, reclassifying, and disciplining for just cause, and maintaining discipline and the efficiency of employees, provided, however, in the exercise thereof the Company shall not take any action which violates any of the terms and provisions of this Agreement.

ARTICLE X. VACATIONS

SECTION 1.   Each employee who has been continuously in the employ of the Company for one or more years and who also has a regular record of attendance during the preceding year, shall upon this completion of one or more years' service, receive one week's vacation with pay, and each employee who has been continuously in the employ of the Company for five years or more and who also has a regular record of attendance during the preceding year shall, upon completion of five or more years receive two weeks' vacation with pay.   In determining eligibility, a regular record of attendance shall mean employment of at least sixty per cent (60%) of the time within the prior period which entitles him to vacation privilege.

SECTION 2.   Vacation pay for one week shall consist of the number of hours in the scheduled work week of the plant but not less than forty (40) hours nor more than forty-eight (48) hours at the employee's average straight time hourly earnings for the first three months in the calendar year in which the vacation occurs.

SECTION 3.   No employee shall be eligible to receive any benefits under this Article if he resigns from the employment of the Company, or if he is discharged, prior to the beginning of his vacation, provided, that such discharge for cause is not reversed under the provisions of Section 7, Article II.   Vacation will, so far as possible, be granted at times most desired by employees, but the final right to allot vacation periods is reserved to the Company in order to insure orderly operation of the Plant.   Any temporary shutdown in any department, for any reason, may be designated as vacation period.

ARTICLE XI.   WAGES

SECTION 1.   The hourly wage rates to be paid by the Company effective 12:01 A.M., June 9, 1950, for the life of the contract are set forth in Exhibit 3 attached hereto and made a part of this agreement.   [Ed. note: Exhibit omitted.]

SECTION 2.   The hiring rate for each classification shall be as set forth in Exhibit 3.   The employee will be increased to the minimum rate for the job classification as set forth in Exhibit 3. Employees on incentive work will follow the Schedule.   Employees on day work may be advanced farther than the automatic progression set forth in Exhibit 3.

SECTION 3.   The rates for apprentices shall be established as set forth in Exhibit 3, Part II.   The general provision of the apprentice program will be negotiated separately and made a part of this Agreement.

SECTION 4.   A day work employee's classification within the rate range for his occupation shall be determined by the Company on the basis of the ability and employment record of the employee as demonstrated in the performance of his assigned duties, except for such automatic progressions to the mid-point of rate ranges as shown in Exhibit 3.   A grievance may be presented regarding a merit increase.

SECTION 5.   Employees receiving an hourly rate as of the date of this contract, over the maximum of the rate range set forth in Exhibit 3, shall not have their wage reduced as long as they remain in their current job classification.

SECTION 6.   The Company will pay a shift premium of six (6) cents per hour to all employees who are scheduled to work on the afternoon shift and a premium of eight (8) cents per hour to all employees who are scheduled to work on the night shift.   Employees paid on an incentive basis will receive the premium as an additional amount per hour over their incentive earnings.   The premium shall be part of the regular pay for the purpose of computing overtime.   However, no such premium shall be paid by reason of overtime work which extends beyond the employee's regular shift other than the premium specified for his regular shift.

SECTION 7.   All base or occupational and hourly rates on newly created jobs and on jobs where there has been a change in job content shall be arrived at by the use of job evaluation practices in line with established comparable operations in the plant. When the job evaluation has been completed, the Union shall be advised as to what the rate will be as far in advance of the effective date as possible.   Any dispute that may arise respecting the rate shall be subject to immediate review as provided for in the grievance procedure.   Any increase made in the rate shall be retroactive to the effective date of the rate.

SECTION 8.   When it is necessary to establish new or changed piecework rates or standards, the Company will make necessary studies of the factors which determine what the new or changed rate or standard should be.   When the necessary studies have been completed, the Union shall be advised as to what the rate or standard will be as far in advance as possible, but not less than two (2) working days, prior to the effective date.   The parties shall agree upon a local basis as to the length of a trial period. During this trial period the employees involved shall give the rate or standard a fair trial.   At the end of the trial period if a dispute exists concerning the rates or standards, such dispute shall be subject to immediate review under the grievance procedure. Any increase made in the rates or standards shall be retroactive to the effective date of the rates or standards.

SECTION 9.   It is agreed that no change in established piecework rates or standards will be made unless changes are made in job content, such as method, construction, compound, group arrangement, breakdown, layout, equipment, material, or material specifications, which either increase or decrease the time necessary to produce a unit of production or where an obvious inaccuracy has been made.   Any change in established piecework rates or standards will be made commensurate with the degree of change in job content unless otherwise mutually agreed upon.

SECTION 10.   It is agreed that the Company shall base its piecework rates or standards on the full use of an employee's time, which consists of full productive time on the job, less necessary allowances, such as rest periods, fatigue, personal allowance, etc., for the work day at normal operating speeds attainable by any average operator.

SECTION 11.   Incentive workers shall be entitled to payment at base rates if their earnings opportunities are affected adversely by defective conditions of material or equipment.

ARTICLE XII.   DURATION OF AGREEMENT

SECTION 1.   This Agreement supersedes the contract dated May 21, 1949, between the parties and constitutes the entire Agreement between the parties.   This contract may be amended from time to time in writing by mutual Agreement.

SECTION 2.   This Agreement shall become effective on May 21, 1950, and shall continue for two years, and shall renew itself from year to year unless either party serves upon the other written notice of termination thirty (30) days prior to the expiration date.

SECTION 3.   Once during the life of this Agreement either party upon ten (10) days' written notice to the other party may open up for negotiation the question of general wage rates.   Both parties agree that this right shall not be exercised at least for a period of one year after the effective date of this Agreement.

THE ENDERBY RUBBER COMPANY

By J. L. WELLER, *Executive Vice President*
C. S. CHRISTIAN, *Plant Manager*
LESLIE WHITE, *Industrial Relations Manager*

UNITED RUBBER, CORK, LINOLEUM AND PLASTIC WORKERS OF AMERICA, CIO, LOCAL NO. 417

By OLIVER CURME
STANLEY LEVIN
NEWTON KLEINES
DAN SAGER
HOWARD O'BRIEN
Negotiating Committee

C. *Some Further Aspects of Collective Contracts in Foreign Countries*

1. EXTENT OF COLLECTIVE BARGAINING IN EUROPE

In the Federal Republic of Germany (i.e., Western Germany, with a population of about 45 million), five and a half million industrial workers — this is more than 50 per cent of the working population — are organized in the DGB, the (unified) German Labor Federation. However, owing to the administrative-extension feature of German collective contract law (see page 281 supra), a substantial number of unorganized workers are also controlled by collective contracts. The coverage, therefore, reaches at times 100 per cent in Germany! The collective contracts themselves at the Mine Workers' Union, one of the largest unions in Germany, cover all workers within its jurisdiction because all of them are organized. The existence of the German Salaried Employees Union (embracing about 300,000 members) — side by side with the DGB — does not change the result in substance, because in most cases affecting salaried employees (banks, insurance companies, business enterprises) that union has joined the DGB as a party in collective contracts made with those enterprises.

As for the Republic of Austria (with a population of a little less than 7 million), the number of industrial employees, salaried included, amounts to approximately 1 million; the number of all persons active in any occupation whatsoever, to about 2 million. A little more than 1000 collective contracts have been in operation since 1947. The contracts affect all employees in the enterprises. The number of members of the Austrian Labor Federation — likewise a unified federation — was 1,290,581 at the end of 1950 (the percentage of industrial employees among the members was not available).

The number of collective contracts in France made after the enactment of the new collective contract law of February 11, 1950 (see page 282 supra) amounted, as of May 1, 1950, to 75 wage agreements, 11 of which were nation-wide. (Between the Second World War and 1950, all wages were regulated by the government.) Unions have never been really strong in France. Out of 12 million French employees, not even 4 million were organized and a great many of the latter were nominal members only, paying no dues.

Scandinavian countries show, in contrast to France, a very high percentage of organized workers, strong unions, and therefore an impressive status of collective contracts.   Thus in Denmark, with a population of 3,500,000, two-year labor contracts covering 500,000 industrial workers were concluded in 1950.   One collective contract, in addition, covers about 50,000 agricultural workers.[44]

2. THE SCOPE OF COLLECTIVE CONTRACTS

The coverage of a particular collective contract has been considered, in Continental jurisprudence, in terms of the coverage of (a) occupations, (b) categories of employees, (c) territory, and (d) persons.

a. Occupational Coverage

The French law is based on the concept of occupationally differentiated unions and associations (together called *organisations syndicales*).   Economics rather than law has created twenty-eight groups, organized along occupational lines [45] in such *organisations syndicales*.[46]   Voluntary membership in an organization determines which collective contract governs an employment.   But an administrative decree may extend the terms of a contract made by an organization of a certain occupational group to people in the group not members of the organization.[47]

Concerning German law, the principle of industrial organization is generally recognized.   There can be no more than *one* contract for *one* shop.[48]   This is an example: A collective contract made with an association of construction firms controls each and every activity in a construction job, therefore also the work of the woodworkers and glassworkers, whereas in turn, construction work done in the glass industry places a construction worker under the control of the glass industry contract.   Even if the purposes of

[44] The sources of the statistical data are as follows: for Germany, Dr. Bodo Boerner, Assistant in the Law School Seminar, University of Hamburg, and the German Labor Federation (District Nordmark); for Austria, Professor Hermann Haemmerle, Innsbruck, Tyrol; for France, see Sturmthal, Collective Bargaining in France, 4 Indust. & Lab. Rel. Rev. 236 (1950), and Malézieux, Les Conventions de travail (1950); for Denmark, Notes in Labor Abroad (U.S. Dept. of Labor Bull. No. 15, 1950).   See also Kerr, Collective Bargaining in Postwar Germany, 5 Indust. & Lab. Rel. Rev. 323, 328 (1952).

[45] The French expression is *les branches d'activité*.

[46] Rouast and Durand, *Précis de législation industrielle* 249 (3d ed. 1948).

[47] For the problem of "extension" see the discussion at page 284 supra.

[48] So-called principle of singleness of the collective contract (*Tarifeinheit*).

one plant are diversified, the principle of the control of one sole contract over all the employment relationships applies. Thus, where the business includes, for example, chemical and iron production (i.e., its activity extends to more than one trade), the courts have been guided by the preponderant-business-activity test. This means that depending upon whether the chemical branch outweighs the iron manufacturing branch in economic significance or vice versa, the chemical industry or the iron industry contract is deemed to be applicable.[49]

b. Coverage of Categories of Employees[50]

By French law, the four categories of employees within the same occupational group, an identity which is conclusively established by the appropriate trade-union, are covered by the same contract, but supplementary provisions may be agreed on for each category.[51] German decisional law reaches the same result provided the contract itself does not restrict its domain to a certain category only, e.g., commercial personnel in contrast to technical employees.[52] Where an employee performs diversified services which fall within more than one category, the principle of the preponderant nature of his whole activity applies. In other words, where, for instance, only a part of the work comes within the jurisdiction of another union, the courts have been guided by the determination of the category to which the principal part of the job belongs.[53]

c. Territorial Scope

Elsewhere [54] reference was made to the principle in the French law that, within the same occupational range, a contract made for the entire national territory prevails over a contract covering a region, and the latter over a local contract.[55]

The dominant opinion in Germany does not accord one contract the quality of superiority over another because the former has been made for a larger territory. The parties have to define

---

[49] For a collection of cases see Hueck and Nipperdey, Collective Contract Law 94, 95 (1950) (in German).

[50] The Germans call the occupational scope *betrieblich* and the scope as to employee categories *fachlich*.

[51] French Labor Code, bk. I, tit. II, c. IV bis, art. 31f. These supplementary contracts for the several categories have been discussed at page 284, supra.

[52] For decisions see Hueck and Nipperdey, op. cit. supra note 49, at 95.

[53] Id. at 96.

[54] See page 284 supra.

[55] French Labor Code, bk. I, tit. II, c. IV bis, art. 31i.

the area which is to be ruled by their contract.[56]   Most litigated
cases concern the question as to which among several local contracts shall be applied to work performed outside the locality
of the store or plant or office.   As a matter of principle, German
labor courts have resorted to the concept of the localization of the
employment for the question of extraterritorial application in
about the same way as New York courts do in questions of conflicting workmen's compensation laws.   In other words, it is the
German view that a shop is ruled by the contract which controls
the area in which the shop is situated.   This contract is also applicable to services performed outside the area if the employment
relationship is localized, i.e., has its basis in the shop.[57]

d. Persons Subject to the Contract

See the discussion on union security at page 494 infra.

e. How Problems of Scope Are Solved

Problems of all the four types come up in foreign countries
usually in connection with an individual's complaint.   Here, an
individual's grievance procedure presupposes a settlement of the
question of a union's jurisdiction.   Abroad, labor courts are
readily available to solve such problems as the determination of
the applicable contract.

3. THE CONTENTS OF FOREIGN COLLECTIVE CONTRACTS

It is important to distinguish rights and obligations that relate
to the employer-employee relationship from rights and obligations
that relate to the groups that are the contracting parties.

As for the former, the normative provisions, the contract may
contain schedules of wage rates and salaries and provisions relating to working time, overtime, vacations with pay, absences with
pay because of sickness or performance of civic duties or other important reasons, service inventions, profit sharing, promotion, demotion, transfer to other branches of the enterprise, insurance,
pension, and retirement.   Many of these items are regulated by
statutes.[58]   If so, the collective contract clauses are subordinate to
them.   Likewise by statute or by contract the terms of individual

[56] Hueck and Nipperdey, op. cit. supra note 49, at 93.
[57] Compare German cases collated in Hueck and Nipperdey, id. at 93, with
Cameron v. Ellis Construction Co., 252 N.Y. 394, 169 N.E. 622 (1930).
[58] See the discussion at page 66 supra.

employment are subordinated to the collective contract with some exceptions.

Concerning the question how far the parties to an individual employment contract, although bound by a collective contract, are entitled to vary the terms of the latter, four classes of cases reflecting the variations among the acts of different countries may be considered.

A collective contract statute may tolerate individual departures, whether or not more favorable to an employee, from the terms of the collective contract, provided the latter contains an express provision to this effect. The Germans call such a provision in the collective contract a *Zulassungsklausel* (right of variation). The German law of December 23, 1918, was and the German law of April 9, 1949, still is, of this type. So is the Swedish Collective Contract Act of June 22, 1928 (sec. 3). The Irish Industrial Relations Act, August 27, 1946 (sec. 28), lays down as requisite for such departures not only the inclusion of a right of variation in the contract, but, in addition, the approval of any variation by the labor court. A collective contract act of this pattern allows the parties to a collective contract to change its employment terms from compulsory terms into terms modifiable by agreement of employer and employee.[59] Collective contracts in the United States may, of course, contain such provisions, but actually they are extremely rare.

A collective contract statute may allow "more favorable" individual agreements, i.e., such agreements as are more favorable to an employee than the terms of a collective contract. Under such statutes the provisions of the contract are minimum standards. Such are the present French Act (1950), the Italian Civil Code (1942), art. 2077, and the Irish Industrial Relations Act, 1946, sec. 30 (3). Also the German Act of 1949 allows, in the absence of the clause mentioned in the preceding paragraph, individual agreements on more favorable terms.

Many other collective-contract statutes allow more favorable conditions by individual contract only if the collective contract does not foreclose them. The Austrian law is of this type.[60] Under these acts, the parties to the collective contract may change the collective contract schedules from minimum standards to absolute standards.

---

[59] For the significance of the distinction, see Lenhoff, Optional Terms (*Jus Dispositivum*) and Required Terms (*Jus Cogens*) in the Law of Contracts, 45 Mich. L. Rev. 39 (1946).

[60] For the Austrian law, see Act of Feb. 26, 1947 (B.G.B., no. 76), sec. 1 (3).

Finally, there are statutes which bar any kind of individual agreement, whether or not in favor of an employee. This theory can be seen in the Dutch Act of December 24, 1927.[61] By such statutes the terms of a collective contract are absolutely compulsory for both employer and employee.

The question whether a provision is more favorable to an employee may face some difficulties. Thus the German and Austrian courts have refused to embark upon an isolated comparison of a single item, e.g., wages. So when an employee accepted a rate of pay lower than that of the collective contract, but his employer undertook to meet all taxes and all costs of social insurance and health insurance and disability insurance, thus relieving the employee from payments which otherwise would fall upon him, the courts refused to let the employee take both the higher collective-contract wage rates and the individually stipulated relief from payment of taxes and premiums. On the other hand, the courts were reluctant to take a bird's-eye view of the whole employment picture, i.e., to set off the plus of one item against the minus of another. They deemed it to be improper, for instance, to weigh a smaller salary together with a longer vacation against a larger salary and a shorter vacation fixed in the collective contract. The dominant practice has chosen to balance only items closely related to each other, e.g., wages and contributions made to a pension fund.[62]

With respect to less favorable individual agreements, most laws have not departed from the general principle that agreements prohibited by law are invalid. In other words, the provisions of individual employment contracts, as far as they undercut collective contract terms, are simply replaced by the latter. Characteristic is the new Irish Act of 1946. Its section 30 (2) reads:

> If a contract between a worker of a class, type or group to which a registered employment agreement [i.e., collective contract] applies and his employer provides for the payment of remuneration at a rate . . . less than the rate . . . provided by such agreement and applicable to such worker, the contract shall, in respect of any period during which the agreement is registered, have effect as if the agreement rate were substituted for the contract rate.

[61] For this point, see Nipperdey, Der Niederländische Entwurf eines Tarifvertragsgesetzes, 1 Zeitschrift für Ausländisches und Internationales Privatrecht 74, 84 (1927).

[62] For cases, see Kaskel, Labor Law 102 (4th ed. 1932) (in German).

The same is true of the Dutch Act of December 24, 1927, article 12 (1), the Finnish Act of March 22, 1924, section 6, the German Law of April 9, 1949, section 4 (3), and the Austrian Law of February 26, 1947, section 9 (1).

It is obvious that if an act does not allow for individual terms, an employee cannot, in advance, renounce his rights which derive from the collective contract. However, jurisdictions differ on the question of whether or not, subsequent to the performance of his service, an employee may waive such rights, e.g., by accepting sub-collective-contract-standard wages. The French, Swiss, and Austrian courts have held that as long as the employment relationship lasts, an employee cannot be deemed, by accepting such sub-standard wages, to have waived his right to claim the balance.[63] The Austrian Supreme Court has, in a leading decision,[64] denied the validity of such a waiver upon the ground of the economic disparity in bargaining position between the employer and the employee. Waiver by an ex-employee is, of course, an entirely different matter.

In contrast, under the law of December 23, 1918, the highest German labor court recognized the validity of a person's waiver as to past wages, although, when such a waiver occurred, the person was still employed and therefore subject to the economic risk of discharge for refusal to waive. The only qualification made by that court was with regard to waivers inherent in the acceptance of wages undercutting collective contract rates. In the latter case, the burden was on the employer to show that an employee, when he unreservedly accepted payment, acted under no economic pressure and did not even feel that he acted under pressure.[63] Lest an employer be later overwhelmed even by bona fide claims for wage balances, collective contracts frequently contain a provision limiting the time for raising claims based upon the schedules fixed therein. Courts have regarded such limitations as valid, but the present German statute allows them only if based on a collective contract.[66]

This new statute greatly differs from the previous German view

[63] Compare for the French law, Lorch, Trends in European Social Legislation Between the Two World Wars 68 (1943); for the Swiss law, see 1 Guhl, Das Schweizerische Obligationenrecht 189 (2d ed. 1936).

[64] Austrian Supreme Court in 1929, *Judikat* (in banc) no. 26, Slg. Labor Courts, no. 3725.

[65] E.g., decisions of R.A.G. in 1929, 7 Bensh. 219 (1930) and 8 Bensh. 468 (1930). But see for criticism, 2 Hueck and Nipperdey, Labor Law 299 (1929–1930) (in German); Kaskel, op. cit. supra note 62, at 97; Jacobi, Fundamentals of Labor Law 223 (1927) (in German).

[66] Act of April 9, 1949, on Collective Contracts, sec. 4 (4) (3).

of waiver and estoppel. A waiver now requires approval of the organizations which are parties to the collective contract.[67]   In addition, the new law denies estoppel which would cut off rights arising out of collective contracts in favor of individuals.[68]   The former German decisional law had come to the result that an employee's failure to make a demand, e.g., for wages within a reasonable time, estopped him from bringing an action for recovery later, e.g., after termination of his job.[69]   Whereas the new law bars the defense of estoppel, it does not exclude the defense of fraud.[70] Where, for instance, an employer had paid a substandard wage rate in good faith because his employee had concealed his membership in a union which was the party to a collective contract setting up a wage standard, that defense would prevail even under the new law.[71]

The foreign law most like the American as to the subjects to which the duty to bargain extends, is presented in the French Collective Contract Act of February 11, 1950. It provides for national, regional, and local collective contracts to be entered into by the "most representative" labor organization on the one hand, and the "most representative" employers' association for the trade or profession concerned, on the other.[72]   If the appropriate minister so decrees, these contracts become binding for each member of the trade, employer and employee alike, within their spatial scope even if neither of them belongs to the contracting organizations.[73]   Unless and until such collective contracts come into existence and effect, employers and unions can freely enter into collective contracts on wage schedules (including vacation pay), and so can associations of employers with respect to their members.[74]

In contrast, the previously mentioned national, regional, and

---

[67] Id. sec. 4 (4) (1).

[68] Id. sec. 4 (4) (2). See the comments on this provision in Hueck and Nipperdey, op. cit supra note 49, at 114.

[69] The basis for the doctrine was deemed to be the German Civil Code, sec. 242: An obligor has to perform his obligation in good faith with due regard to customs of the trade.

[70] The civil law theory calls this *exceptio doli.*

[71] Cf. Hueck and Nipperdey, op. cit. supra note 49, at 118. For the former law see R.A.G. (Supreme Labor Court), 9 Bensh. 496 (1930).

[72] It is the Minister of Labor and the Minister of Agriculture, respectively, who at the demand of one of those organizations and associations convenes their representatives for the purpose of making contracts. The representatives for the execution of a nation-wide contract are called a "mixed commission." French Labor Code, bk. I, tit. II, c. IV bis, art. 31f.

[73] Id. art. 31j. For "extension" see the discussion at page 284 supra.

[74] Id. art. 31n, and Act of Feb. 11, 1950, tit. III, art. 21.

local contracts not only can but must embrace many other subjects besides wage schedules.[75]　Among them:

(a) Guaranty to an individual employee of his freedom to join a labor organization and to express his opinion.[76]

(b) Hiring and discharging of employees. (Such provisions are valid only if they are not at variance with the foregoing guaranty.)

(c) Procedure for election of employee delegates and of employee members of the joint councils.[77]

(d) Procedure for revision or rescission of the contract.

(e) Conciliation machinery covering all kinds of collective disputes (in contrast to individual conflicts), not only those on jural matters but also those on interests.　The difference between collective and individual disputes lies in the collective or individual interest in the subject of the dispute rather than in the person (whether a group or an individual) who raises the issue.[78]　Thus a discharge of an employee for the expression of his political opinions might result in a collective dispute, whereas the deduction of a loan from the wage of an employee would not.　It must be borne in mind that it is conciliation, not arbitration, to which this regulation relates.

As far as subjects are dealt with by statute, the contractual regulation is subordinate to legislative: for example, provisions on delegates or on conciliation, on wages, as far as minimum wages are fixed by administrative decree,[79] and on vacations with pay, for these subjects are regulated by legislation.

The dominant theory is that provisions governing individual employment constitute the essence of the collective contract,[80] for which the statute requires written form.　So an oral agreement between an employers' association and a trade-union, e.g., concerning the establishment of a labor exchange, is valid if no provisions affecting individual employment relationships are included.

As for those obligations which bind the contracting groups themselves, and not individuals — that is, the obligations which

[75] French Labor Code, bk. I, tit II, c. IV bis, art. 31g (1) (no. 1–10).

[76] The subject is discussed at page 498 infra, in connection with closed-shop clauses.

[77] For this subject see the foreign law material at page 74 supra.

[78] Rouast and Durand, op. cit. supra note 46, at 277, no. 226.

[79] After consulting a Superior Commission for Collective Contracts upon whose reports the appropriate ministers may issue an administrative order fixing such wages.　French Labor Code, bk. I, tit. II, c. IV bis, art. 31x.　Such orders have been issued ever since August, 1950.

[80] For details see Hueck and Nipperdey, op. cit. supra note 49, at 17.

constitute the so-called contractual part of a collective contract — the principle of freedom of contract controls; the parties are free with regard to both subjects and contents. The law, however, imposes very important obligations upon associations as parties to such a contract, namely the peace obligation [81] and the obligation to use authority over members to keep them in compliance with the contract.[82] Whether the parties can bargain away these obligations by an express stipulation is disputed.[83]

A characteristic feature of this part of German collective contracts is a clause providing for the establishment of so-called collective contract commissions. Such commissions may be established for a variety of objectives, e.g., for job classification and "slotting" (placing individual employees in the diverse wage and job classes) and supervision of compliance with wage and work schedules. Frequently there is an arbitration clause. If its scope is dubious, — whether, for instance, it covers disputes between the parties to the collective contract only or also controversies that arise out of individual employment relationships — its interpretation is for the labor courts.[84]

4. VALIDITY AND DURATION OF COLLECTIVE CONTRACTS

a. Validity

1. *Form.* In the vast majority of foreign laws, written form is requisite for a collective contract.[85] Also most laws require its deposit in some public office before it becomes effective.[86] In Germany, however, such recording is not requisite.[87] When the

---

[81] The peace obligation is treated at page 420 infra.

[82] In German, *Einwirkungspflicht.* Similar is the Swedish Right of Association Act of September 11, 1936, art. 22.

[83] For the authorities pro and con, see Hueck and Nipperdey, op. cit. supra note 49, at 42.

[84] See, e.g., Supreme Labor Court (R.A.G.), 2 Bensh. 188 (1928), and 3 Bensh. 53 (1928).

[85] E.g., Swiss Law on Obligations, art. 322 (2); Dutch Law on Collective Contracts, art. 3 (a public officer's certificate of such a contract being the alternative); French Labor Code, bk. I, tit. II, c. IV bis, art. 31c; German Collective Contract Act of April 9, 1949, sec. 1 (2); Austrian Collective Contract Act of Feb. 26, 1947, sec. 2 (1).

[86] See, e.g., Ireland: Industrial Relations Act, Aug. 27, 1946, sec. 27; Italy: Civil Code (1942), art. 2072; Austria: Collective Contract Act of Feb. 26, 1947, sec. 7 (conciliation board); France: Labor Code, bk. I, tit. II, c. IV bis, art. 31d (labor court).

[87] Germany: Collective Contract Act of April 9, 1949, sec. 6 (Federal Minister of Labor; Register of Collective Contracts).

German Statute of April 9, 1949 was a subject of legislative deliberation, those German zonal governments which operated under British and American control offered a substitute bill which would have made recording requisite for validity. Unions along with employers' associations vigorously objected to such a plan, for it violated the principle of self-control by the parties of the contract.

Most of the foreign laws require the recording office to send the contract to the ministry of labor for registration. But only in Ireland, Italy, Mexico, and Venezuela is the effectiveness of a collective contract conditioned upon its registration. In those countries registration is granted only if the contract conforms with the statute.[88] In other countries, e.g., Austria, in providing for registration, the registrar has only to check for compliance with the statutory formalities for registration.[89] Publication in an official journal is prescribed in several countries.[90]

2. *Capacity for Making Collective Contracts.* With very few exceptions, the trade-union is the only group of workers authorized by foreign laws to make collective contracts.[91] On the employers' side, however, the laws permit both employers' associations and single employers to enter into collective contracts. Both German law and French law distinguish between a contract made by an employer and one made by an employers' association even though it be for one member's enterprise only (group contract for one firm). For example, only the association can terminate the latter contract by notice; the firm is bound by it as long as it is kept in effect by the association.[92]

In contrast to our law on labor relations and collective bargaining, foreign collective contract laws apply to agricultural labor. Also by French and German law the state and other corporations *publici juris* such as municipal corporations or social insurance carriers have capacity to make collective contracts. It is particularly the new French law of February 11, 1950, which extends its

[88] Ireland: Industrial Relations Act, Aug. 27, 1946, sec. 27; Italy: Civil Code (1942), art. 2072; Mexico: Labor Code (1931), sec. 45; Venezuela: Labor Code (1945), sec. 44.

[89] The Austrian Administrative Court expressly held that the fact that a collective contract contains invalid provisions does not justify administrative refusal of its filing and recording. Decision 1930 Sammlung No. 16466A.

[90] Austria: Collective Contract Act of Feb. 26, 1947, sec. 7. The failure to publish the contract does not affect its validity. Austrian Supreme Court S.Z. (Reporter) XIII/220 (1931).

[91] The Germans call the capacity *Kollektivvertragsfähigkeit*.

[92] Rouast and Durand, Précis de législation industrielle 246 (3d ed. (1948)); Hueck and Nipperdey, op. cit. supra note 49, at 63.

scope to all public offices and ministries.[93] As for public enterprises, such as nationalized banks, the law on collective contracts
applies, unless a particular legislative enactment governs their
personnel.[94] Also professional people, e.g., lawyers and doctors,
may be covered by collective contracts.

In further contrast to our law, French law and German law
deny the capacity to make collective contracts to organizations
that restrict membership to employees of one firm. In other
words, company unions lack that capacity.[95]

In addition, labor unions and employers' associations must meet
three requirements to qualify as parties to a collective contract.
First, membership must be restricted to persons of the same class,
i.e., employer or employee. This is called the principle of purity.[96]
So-called mixed organizations, those including persons of both
classes, lack contractual capacity.[97] Second, an association must
be, in its formation and operation, independent of and opposed to
the other party, its "social antagonist." With regard to these
two requisites for the contractual capacity of a labor organization,
foreign law hardly differs from our own. However, the German
theory has added a third requisite for which there is no counterpart
on this side of the Atlantic. It is considered essential that resort
to concerted actions, such as strikes, must not, as a matter of principle, be excluded from the policy to be followed by a labor organization;[98] were it excluded, such an organization could not be
regarded as having capacity to be a party to a collective contract.
Though the principle is held in theory to apply also to employer
groups, no well-established test exists as to them.

The Netherlands, Austria, and Finland require incorporation
for capacity to contract.[99] Licensing of labor unions and employer
associations is required by the pending Italian Labor Relations
Act, described at page 286 supra.

An association's capacity to contract is dependent upon the

[93] See Professor Paul Durand's article on the new law of 1950 in 13 Droit
social 93, 100 (1950).

[94] Id. at 101; French Labor Code, bk. I, tit. II, c. IV bis, art. 31o. A list of
such enterprises is to be published in an administrative regulation.

[95] French Labor Code, bk. I, tit. II, c. IV bis, art. 31a; German Collective
Contract Act of April 9, 1949, sec. 2 (1) ; Hueck and Nipperdey, op. cit. supra
note 49, at 71.

[96] In the German phraseology, the association must be *gegnerfrei*.

[97] Rouast and Durand, op. cit. supra note 92, at 183; Hueck and Nipperdey,
op. cit. supra note 49, at 68.

[98] Hueck and Nipperdey, Collective Contract Law 75 (1950) (in German).

[99] By Dutch law the corporate quality of an association not for profit can
be obtained only by royal grant, according to a law of 1855, while the Austrian
and Finnish laws authorize incorporation freely.

existence in its constitution or bylaws of a provision which shows that the making of collective contracts falls within the range of its activities. An express provision to this effect is not required by French or German law, but according to the former, the absence of such a provision must be replaced either by a special resolution of the board or express authorization of each and every member,[100] whereas it has been generally accepted in Germany that such a capacity might be recognized upon an association's contractual record alone.[101]

Some countries have accorded confederations of associations the capacity for making collective contracts.[102]

b. Duration of Collective Contracts

1. *Initial date.* The parties may fix the date for the contract to become operative.[103] They may stipulate that some or all provisions have retroactive effect.[104]

2. *Terminal date.* (a) *Contract for a specified time.* Contracts may be made for a specified time or without fixed duration.[105] Since the American idea of majority rule is not adopted, a subsequent change in union allegiance of the employees covered has no significance from a contractual point of view. Nevertheless, the French law establishes a five-year period as the maximum term for a contract.[106] It has been noted elsewhere in this book [107] that some foreign laws, e.g., the French law, treat such a contract upon the completion of its term as if it were a contract of indeterminate duration, as far as its effects on individual employment relationships are concerned. The German law contains no provision to that effect. However, the automatic continuation of the wage and working conditions schedules after the expiration of a con-

[100] French Labor Code, bk. I, tit. II, c. IV bis, art. 31b.

[101] Decisions refer to an "implied" purpose for which the association is formed. Cf. R.A.G., 12 Bensh. 136 (1930).

[102] Sweden: Collective Contract Act of June 12, 1928, sec. 1; Ireland: Industrial Relations Act, Aug. 27, 1946, secs. 25, 59 (Joint Industrial Council); Germany: Collective Contract Act of April 9, 1949, sec. 2 (3).

[103] The French law declares that in the absence of provision for effective date the contract shall come into effect on the day following its filing at the appropriate public office; the Austrian law, on the day following its official publication. French law, Labor code, bk. I, tit. II, c. IV bis, art. 31d(1); Austrian Collective Contract Act of Feb. 26, 1947, sec. 9(2).

[104] For the German law, see Hueck and Nipperdey, op. cit. supra note 98, at 23.

[105] See French Labor Code, bk. I, tit. II, c. IV bis, art. 31c(2).

[106] Id. art. 31c(2). The possibility of a change of economic conditions weighs against the legality of a too long term.

[107] At page 288 supra.

tract has been held there to be highly desirable in order to avoid an interval fraught with all the socioeconomic perils inherent in the absence of a contract.[108]

(b) *Contract for an indeterminate time.* The French law requires that a provision concerning notice of termination be included in a contract. The Germans take it for granted that either party has a right to terminate such a contract at will by a notice having immediate effect unless a time of notice was stipulated in the contract. There is no form requirement for the notice.

The Dutch and the Norwegian law, however, prescribe advance notice of a certain number of days. In those countries and in Sweden the notice must be in writing.

(c) *Premature termination.* Collective contracts which, through administrative decree,[109] have been extended to others than the persons subject thereto by their membership in one of the contracting associations, may be deprived of that "extended" effect by an administrative decree although their contractual term has not yet expired.[110] By the French and the German law, the decree must be based on a substantial change in the situation,[111] and may be issued by the minister only after consultation with the advisory commission,[112] and after public notice and hearing. Termination of the extension decree has no effect on the contract itself.

All collective contracts, like other contracts, may for cause be ended prematurely by notice, according to dominant German opinion. Unilateral termination by a party is unknown to the French law by which rescission of any contract may be pronounced only by a court for cause recognized by law.[113] Likewise the Swedish Act on collective contracts recognizes judicial rescission only. The labor court may, at the request of a party, cancel for a material violation of the Act or of the contract, committed by the other party.[114]

[108] See the Labor Minister's suggestion to insert a continuation clause in (1929) Reich Labor Register I, p. 3.

[109] The subject is discussed at page 281 supra.

[110] French Labor Code, bk. I, tit. II, c. IV bis, art. 31m; German Collective Contract Act of April 9, 1949, sec. 5 (5).

[111] The German Collective Contract Act of April 9, 1949, sec. 5 (5), speaks of "public interest."

[112] This is a statutory commission called Superior Commission for Collective Contracts. Cf. French Labor Code, bk. I, tit. II, c. IV bis, art. 31v; German Collective Contract Act of April 9, 1949, sec. 5 (1).

[113] 2 Planiol, Traité élémentaire de droit civil, no. 1166 (9th ed. 1923).

[114] Swedish Act of June 22, 1928, sec. 7. For judicial rescission see also Finnish Act of March 22, 1924, sec. 11 (1), and Dutch Civil Code, art. 1302.

Termination or modification of a contract by agreement of the original parties, as well as termination by its own terms or for cause, terminates the effect of the extension decree.[115]

II. The Drafting and Administration of Collective Bargaining Agreements

A. *Procedures for Settling Grievances Arising During the Contract Term*

1. IN GENERAL

As is apparent from the Enderby contract above, the typical collective bargaining agreement covers a variety of "substantive" matters, establishing rules governing union security, seniority, disciplinary standards, and the like. The significance of these rules, and of the practices which have become general in connection with their establishment and administration, cannot be grasped or evaluated, however, without an understanding of the general administrative procedures whereby the employment relationship is carried out under a collective bargaining agreement. It has therefore been deemed advisable to take up first, in this section, the problem of the "grievance clause."

It is in the grievance clause that the parties establish the procedures for their day-to-day working relationship. Before there was a collective bargaining agreement in the plant, John Sappolio, if he was told to get out of the plant and stay out, got and stayed. That was all there was to it. Today, however, there is probably a provision in the collective bargaining agreement to the effect that "there shall be no disciplinary action or discharge without just cause." What happens now if Sappolio is told that he is fired? He leaves, just as he did before. But he doesn't feel that there was "just cause" for his discharge. So he wants to exert his contract right. How does he do it? Who sees whom, and where is the decision made as to whether there was or was not "just cause" for the particular discharge? How is the seniority clause administered, so that Employee A can challenge, if he wants to, the decision by the Company that he, rather than Employee B, should be laid off temporarily because of reduction in production schedules?

Reference to Article II of the Enderby contract (page 318 supra) will illustrate the type of procedure which has today become the

---

[115] Hueck and Nipperdey, op. cit. supra note 98, at 149.

answer of most large employers and their employees to these questions.   That article, particularly the fifth section of it, should be
studied here in some detail.   It represents one of the most significant developments in the jurisprudence of the twentieth century.
If this statement seems carelessly broad, consideration should be
given to the fact that there are perhaps today more private disputes being resolved daily under provisions such as this one than
are being handled in all the state and federal courts in the country.

The materials which follow are designed to develop some of
the problems which arise in connection with the development and
use of this private administrative and adjudicative machinery.
Much of this development is built around the Enderby Case, a
case made up by combining for the purposes of this volume, the
facts of a number of actual cases.

2. HOW BROAD SHOULD THE COVERAGE OF THE GRIEVANCE CLAUSE BE?

a. Introductory Note

A contract provision that "all grievances" shall be taken up
through the prescribed procedure is obviously ambiguous.   What
is a "grievance"?   The dictionary definitions suggest that it is "a
sense of wrong or of oppression" or "a cause of annoyance."
Does this contract clause mean then that a union which is disgruntled because it could get only a 4-cent wage increase in its
annual bargaining with the company can turn around as soon as
the contract is signed and file a grievance requesting an additional
6 cents?   Is this a proper question to put to arbitration as the
fifth step of the grievance procedure?   Does such a contract provision warrant an employee's filing a grievance if he is "annoyed"
by the way one of the members of his crew blows his nose?

An extraordinary degree of trouble has developed as a consequence of the failure, in many collective bargaining agreements,
to define what is meant by the term "grievance."   Such failure
usually results in the union's filing claims covering matters which
the company maintains were either settled conclusively in other
provisions of the agreement or were meant to be left within management's discretion.   The union insists then on taking the case
to arbitration.   The company either refuses to participate in the
arbitration or limits its presentation to a challenge of the arbitrator's jurisdiction.   A small point is expanded into an issue which

may result in serious misunderstanding and trouble in the plant.

This is obviously a good deal more than a question of contract forms. The issue involves judgments as to the extent to which matters, once considered as within the scope of managerial prerogative, are to be identified now as warranting bilateral consideration by the company and the union. The problem also involves questions of the desirable degree of rigidity or flexibility which should be given to the substantive provisions of the collective bargaining agreement. Present here too, where the grievance procedure includes arbitration as its last step (as it usually does), is the consideration of the degree to which it may be desirable to turn certain matters over for settlement to a third person who is an independent stranger so far as the particular employment relationship is concerned. The fact that not all disputes which arise in a plant during the contract term are to be considered grievances (in the sense that they are covered by the grievance procedure), of course, leaves the question of how these other disputes are to be settled. Is the company entitled to ignore them, on the ground that issues arising during the year should be held over until the next contract-negotiating period? Is the union free to strike in order to win its point on one of these non-grievance disputes, or is it obligated to wait the year out?

These questions arise in different forms, at three stages of the collective bargaining process. There is, first, the question of the form in which the grievance procedure clause of the contract is to be drafted. The illustrative forms which are set out below offer a basis for analyzing the differences in the approach which may be taken at this initial stage. There is, secondly, the question of how this problem is to be handled by the parties themselves in the private handling of their affairs. The two excerpts from statements by lawyers who have participated in this private administrative process suggest the considerations which affect the handling of this stage of the problem. (See pages 354 and 357 infra.) There is, finally, the matter of how this issue of grievance definition will be handled when a case goes before an arbitrator. It usually takes the form, at that stage, of a question of the arbitrator's jurisdiction. Sometimes the same issue is presented when the company or the union takes to a court the question of the arbitrability of a particular dispute. It is of course obvious that the underlying issue is substantially the same regardless of whether the matter arises at one of these three stages or another. The division is in some degree academic. It should also be obvious that this issue is not a narrow one of word meaning but a basic issue of administrative law in the plant community.

b. THE ENDERBY CASE — VII

[Editorial note: The general situation at the Enderby Rubber Company's Chicago plant has been described in The Enderby Case — I, at page 113 supra.   There are approximately 1000 employees, 500 of them production workers in the Tire Division, 350 production workers in the Miscellaneous Division, 50 foremen, 75 clerical workers, and 25 executive officers.   There was no union organization in the plant prior to 1947.   During the latter part of 1947, two organizational movements developed.   A group in the Miscellaneous Division organized the Enderby Employees Association.   Its membership, at no time large, has been made up of employees strongly opposed in principle to large-scale unionization.   A substantial majority of the production workers in both the Tire and Miscellaneous divisions joined, in 1947, a new Local (No. 417) of the United Rubber, Cork, Linoleum and Plastic Workers of America, CIO.   This Union requested recognition by the Company but such recognition was denied, the Company insisting upon the holding of a representation election.   An election was held in March, 1948, and on March 30, 1948, the NLRB certified Local 417 as the exclusive bargaining representative of all production workers in the two divisions of the plant.]

On April 6, 1948, Oliver Curme, the President of Local 417, addressed a letter to the President of the Enderby Company asking that a conference be arranged for some early date to discuss the matter of a collective bargaining agreement.   This letter was answered on April 8 by Leslie White, the Industrial Relations Manager of the Company.   He suggested that the parties meet in the plant conference room at 9:00 A.M. the following Saturday morning to consider whatever proposals the Union might have.

Curme called at White's office to discuss the arrangement for this first meeting.   He told White that the Union negotiating committee wanted to hold this meeting during working hours instead of "on their own time," and that they would prefer to have the meeting at some place outside the plant.   It was finally agreed that the negotiating meetings would be held in the plant conference room, that they would be held during working hours, but that the Union committee members would not be paid by the Company for the time spent in the bargaining meetings.   White agreed to have the members of the Union committee released from their jobs during such time as might be necessary for the bargaining. He insisted, however, that the Committee be limited to five members and indicated that the management would refuse to release more than that number from their jobs. He also told Curme that the Company was going to insist on dealing only with members of Local 417 and that it would not bargain with "anybody from the International." Curme told White that he could not accept his position on either of these matters, but suggested that they cross these bridges when they came to them.

The first meeting was held on April 12. The Union delegation included Curme, a Negotiating Committee made up of seven members of Local 417, and Arthur Sawyer, a business agent assigned to this case by the Rubber Workers' International Office. Present for the Company were White, Paul Fisher (the Plant Manager), Grant Burr (Manager of Industrial Engineering), Ralph Locke (White's assistant), and Harold Blair, a local practicing attorney. White immediately raised questions as to the size of the Union Committee and as to the presence of Sawyer. Curme replied that the Union had elected the seven-man committee, that the Local had asked the International to send Sawyer in, that Sawyer was going to take a very active part in the negotiations, and that "the Union is standing on its rights under the Act." Curme went on to say that the Union was very much disturbed by Blair's presence at this session and that he doubted whether it would be worth while proceeding "if we're going to have a lawyer sticking in his two cents' worth every time we start getting anywhere."

After a good deal of discussion and a series of caucuses by both sides, it was finally agreed: (a) that the entire group present would remain for the rest of this opening day's session, but that thereafter (b) the Company would be represented by White, Locke, Burr, and Blair, and (c) the Union by Curme, Sawyer, and a subcommittee of three from the seven-man Negotiating Committee. The Union representatives held out quite a while regarding Blair, but they had obviously been impressed by the fact that White admitted at one point that Blair had told him the Company's objection to Sawyer's participation "wouldn't stand up as a matter of law and was probably inconsistent, as a matter of fairness, with the Company's retaining a lawyer."

After these preliminaries had been cleared up, Curme handed over to White a copy of a proposed contract. It was read through, section by section, by Curme, with White asking a few questions here and there but with little discussion. White asked, when Curme was through, whether this proposed contract "had been approved by the membership of Local 417." Curme told him that it had been, but declined to add any details as to the formalities of approval. The meeting was adjourned upon White's request that the Company be given an opportunity to go over the contract in detail. Another meeting was set for April 15, White indicating that the Company would probably be in a position at that time to submit to the Union its own proposal for a contract.

This first session was followed by a series of meetings at which the various points were discussed at length and in detail. Both sides evidenced a willingness to cooperate in getting a contract worked out, although there was basic disagreement on a number of points. On May 15, the two committees finally concluded their negotiations and reached agreement as to all the provisions to be included in the contract. The terms of this contract were approved by the Enderby Board of Directors and were ratified by the Union membership, by majority vote, at one of the regular Union meetings.

This first contract was signed on May 20, 1948, and was made effective for a period of twelve months. The termination clause provided that the contract should "be automatically renewed for another year, or until May 19, 1950, unless one party or both parties shall give notice in writing on or before April 19, 1949 of a desire to change or modify the terms of this Agreement or to cancel it in its entirety."

A number of problems affecting the interpretation of this contract arose during the first year it was in effect. On April 15, 1949, the Union notified the Company that it desired to make a number of changes in the agreement for the 1949–1950 term. These were described in general terms, in the Union's letter. Several negotiation meetings were again held and a new contract was finally worked out. It was signed on May 20, 1949. This contract included the same termination provision that had been in the 1948 agreement except that the dates were all moved one year ahead.

Additional problems arose during this second contract term and again, in April, 1950, the Union served notice of a desire to make some further changes. A third contract was signed, after another period of prolonged negotiations, on May 20, 1950. This 1950 contract is the one set out at page 317 supra.

Among the problems which caused the parties greatest difficulty was that of working out a satisfactory grievance procedure. This story included the following developments:

A

The original Union contract proposal (submitted to the Company committee on April 12, 1948) contained this provision:

All disagreements which arise between the Company and the Union will be settled by representatives of the Company and the Union and by arbitration if no agreement can be reached by the parties.

The Company's counterproposal on this point was in the following form:

Any employee may, if he so desires, submit any grievance to his Foreman. Any question which arises concerning the interpretation of the terms and conditions of this agreement may be presented by the Union as representative of any individual employee. The following procedure shall be followed:

Step 1. The Steward in the department in which the aggrieved employee is employed shall take the matter up with the Foreman of said department.

Step 2. If a mutually satisfactory agreement is not reached at Step 1, the Union Grievance Committee Chairman shall submit the grievance complaint in writing to the Industrial Relations Manager.

Step 3. If a mutually satisfactory agreement is not reached at Step 2, the grievance shall be considered by the Union Grievance Committee and a committee representing the management of the Company.

No questions regarding matters other than those involving the interpretation of the terms and conditions of this Agreement shall be raised by the Union with the Management during the term of this contract.

No employee of the Company may receive payment from the Company for time spent in the handling of his or any other employee's grievance.

The agreement finally signed on May 20, 1948, contained the following provisions:

ARTICLE II.   GRIEVANCE PROCEDURE

All grievances involving the terms and conditions of this contract shall be handled through the following procedure, provided, however, that any individual employee or group of employees shall have the right at any time to present grievances directly to the Management:

Step 1.   Employee and/or department or group steward to Supervisor or Foreman.

Step 2.   Union Grievance Committee and Divisional Superintendent.

Step 3.   Union Grievance Committee and Industrial Relations Manager.

In case any grievance is not settled at one of the three steps set out above, the grievance shall be referred to arbitration, provided, however, that there must be mutual agreement that the issue in dispute involves the meaning of the terms and conditions of this agreement.

Time spent by employees in the handling of grievances will not be paid for by the Company.

B

In September, 1948, there was a change in the scheduling of shifts in the Molding Department, Tire Division. The entire plant had been on a two-shift basis, one shift running from 7:00 A.M. to 3:30 P.M. (with a half hour off for lunch) and the other from 3:30 P.M. to 12 midnight (also with a half hour off). The half-hour lunch periods were not paid for. On September 10, 1948, however, the Molding Department was put on a three-shift basis, these shifts starting at 7:00 A.M., 3:00 P.M., and 11:00 P.M. The employees on these shifts were given 30 minutes off for lunch in the middle of each shift and were not paid for it.

On September 20, 1948, the employees in the Molding Department, after the steward had spoken to the foreman and had his request turned down, filed a written grievance in the following form:

Union demands 8 hours' pay for everyone who works any full shift. We should not be made to lose earnings resulting from cutting down the length of some shifts to suit the convenience of Management.

The Superintendent of the Tire Division replied to this demand in a letter to the Grievance Committee chairman, stating the reasons for making the change in shift schedules and adding the following:

Article IX of the Agreement dated May 20, 1948, provides that the Management shall exercise the function of "scheduling production." No other section of the Agreement is relevant to the issue which you raise, and Article II (Grievances) covers only "grievances involving the terms and conditions of this contract." Inasmuch as the grievance filed by you on September 20, last, does not allege any contract violation on the part of the Company, and in view of the fact that no right of the Union can here be said to have been infringed, we must decline to consider this matter further with the Union at this time.

This grievance was taken by the Union to the third step of the grievance procedure, but the Company's position remained unchanged. The Union then insisted that the case go to arbitration. The Company refused to agree to arbitration, relying upon the terms of Article II. On October 15, the employees in the Molding Department left their jobs in protest against the Company position. The strike lasted three days, ending after an agreement had been reached that the Company and the Union would "give special consideration to the matter of payment for 7½ hour shifts at the time the present contract is open for modification or amendment."

C

Article II was amended, in the May 20, 1949, agreement, so that the first paragraph read as follows:

All grievances involving the interpretation or application of the terms and conditions of this agreement, and all disputes which may arise regarding the terms and conditions of employment in the plant (not including wages) shall be handled through the following procedure, provided, however, that any individual employee or group of employees shall have the right at any time to present grievances directly to the Management: . . .

The rest of Article II remained as it had been in the 1948 Agreement.

D

In December, 1949, the following grievance was filed:

Joe Garrity and Tom Silvers were sent home early on December 7 and December 8 because Foreman Thomas said there was not enough work for them to do.   They are experienced Tool and Die Makers.   There would have been plenty for them to do if Management had let them work on the Die now being made for the Company over at The Acme Tool Mfg. Co.   Demand pay for time lost by J. Garrity and T. Silvers on December 7 and 8.

How should this grievance be handled by the Industrial Relations Manager?   (There was nothing in the 1949 contract about either a guaranteed workday or the matter of subcontracting work.)

E

The grievance clause of the contract was completely remodeled in the 1950 contract.   See Article II, page 318 supra, noting particularly Section 5.   What effect would the change in contract language have upon the handling, if they arise again, of problems like those involved in the 1948 lunch-period case and the Garrity-Silvers case?

c. Illustrative Contract Definitions of the Scope of the Grievance Procedure [116]

(i) "Should any differences arise between the Company and the Union or its members employed by the Company, an earnest effort shall be made to settle such differences immediately in the following manner . . ."   Compare: "any complaints, grievances, difficulties, disagreements or disputes . . ."; "a dispute as to any question or grievance . . ."; "should any trouble of any kind arise in the plant . . ."

(ii) "A grievance is defined to be any question or controversy . . . concerning any matter relating to wages, hours of employment, tenure, or other conditions of employment which are not covered by this Agreement."

(iii) "Neither the justice nor propriety of any specific provision of this agreement, nor any matter reserved solely to the discretion of the Company by the terms of this agreement, shall be made the subject of a grievance, except as otherwise specifically provided in this agreement."

[116] These illustrations are taken from actual contracts as reported in Collective Bargaining Negotiations and Contracts, Contract Clause Finder (Bureau of National Affairs), pp. 51:11 et seq.

(iv) "All disputes arising out of the application or interpretation of any provision of the agreement of the parties shall be deemed grievances."

KATZ,* MINIMIZING DISPUTES THROUGH THE ADJUSTMENT OF GRIEVANCES

The grievance channel must be deeply dug to receive all complaints.

Grievances are complex reactions by workers to the interplay of psychological, social, and economic forces. A proper grievance procedure will be so designed that it will carry all grievances. Yet, in the early stages of the collective relation, management's bargainers tend to be concerned with preventing the adjustment of all but a restricted class of grievances. The grievances they would consider are only those which involve the interpretation and application of the terms of the agreement. This limitation misses the entire point of the grievance procedure and its office in the collective relation. The error derives from failure to appreciate the multi-faceted nature of the collectively bargained agreement.

The collective bargaining agreement is at once a business compact, a code of relations and a treaty of peace. As an economic accord it sets forth the terms which will govern hiring, work and pay. Normally it is not a contract of employment. As a peace pact it assures against strikes and lockouts. As a code of relations it seeks to create a *system of government* through the processes of which grievances are resolved, understanding achieved, a line of communication opened between management and employees, and a self-disciplining labor force secured.

The collective agreement is thus a different kind of document from the commercial agreement. The ordinary contract does not partake of the nature of governmental systems; the adjustment clause sometimes incorporated in it serves merely to provide a substitute for a court to resolve disputes over interpretations of the other contract terms which define with care the boundaries of a limited relation between the parties. Thus it is merely ancillary to the other terms of the contract. In the collective agreement, on the other hand, the grievance procedure is a "sys-

* The full text of this statement by Isadore Katz, General Counsel to Textile Workers Union of America, CIO, may be found in 12 Law & Contemp. Prob. 249–263 (1947), from which the above selections have been taken with the permission of the editors of that publication. — Ed.

tem of government" which exists independently of the other clauses of the agreement.[117]

The narrow view that a complaint need not be considered unless it involves the interpretation or application of the provisions of the agreement is the least desirable approach to the objective of adjusting grievances. It is not only at odds with the ultimate goal of developing a harmonious and amicable relation in which each worker feels that he is a vital and worthy part, but it proceeds on the erroneous assumption that the relation is capable of precise definition in the contract. It predicates a static relationship in which every point of contact between the contracting parties can be fully reflected in words. Though this may be true of commercial relationships in which the only interest one party has in the other is the article bought or sold, the premises leased or sold, or the money earned or lent, it is not true of the dynamic relation between management and labor. Here the relationship is a multifarious web made up of economic, social and psychological strands inextricably interwoven yet continuously changing in pattern. This community is affected by changes in population, outside competitive forces, outside community activities, changes in production techniques, scientific discoveries, market conditions, internal group relations, and a host of other unpredictable events necessitating quick accommodations — in short, it is a dynamic field of adversary and co-operative group relations. The contingencies in such a relationship can no more be set forth in a contract than can the contingencies of the marital relation. Both defy definition.

Any effort thus to limit the scope of the grievance procedure to the interpretation and application of the provisions of the agreement presupposes that the agreement's provisions can be made so clear and precise as to rule future developments not contemplated by the parties. Such a collective agreement has never been drawn. If it were drawn it would be a particularized code of such length as to destroy its utility. The drafting of it would keep the parties at the bargaining table engaged in interminable exercises in semantics. Such an agreement, if it were ever com-

---

[117] Syme, Arbitrability of Labor Disputes, 5 Rutgers L. Rev. 455, 472 (1951), emphasizes the contrast as follows: "A parallel has been drawn between commercial and labor arbitration. The two are entirely dissimilar. Their origin is different, their purposes are disparate and their functioning is antithetic. *Commercial arbitration evolved as a substitute for litigation.* The parties either litigated or arbitrated. They invoked the use of either one type of tribunal or the other. *Labor arbitration is not a substitute for litigation. Labor arbitration is a substitute for the strike.*" — ED.

pleted, would serve merely as a vehicle for endless disputes over the meanings to be attached to each phrase. Instead of settling grievances by ameliorating the conditions which nourish them, the parties would be engaged in conflicts over words. The dynamics of the relation preclude such an agreement. Even legislative bodies of political government, when confronted with the necessities of enacting law to govern a kinetic field of action, turn to the administrative process to deal with unanticipated developments. . . .

The unwise demand that the complaints of the workers must come within particular categories described in the various contract headings recalls the procedural intricacies of the early common law, when a cause of action had to fit the rigid requirements of the available writs. If the cause of action could not be made to meet the technical requirements of the writ, the doors to the courts of justice were not opened. How this denial of process affected social and economic relations in those days is not fully recorded, but we do know that even the common law had to be augmented by equity jurisprudence because of the need to afford means for the adjustment of disputes. In the industrial community we know at the very outset of bargaining that grievances will arise because of occurrences not envisaged by the negotiators and that they cannot be exercised by pronouncing them out of contract bounds. All grievances, whether real or fancied, reflect discontent and affect production and should be settled. Grievances which are banned find expression in reduced morale, or have the curious trait of assuming the guise of admissible grievances. This is well known to all production men. The excluded and therefore unsettled grievance has the annoying characteristic of making itself known through a drop in efficiency, absenteeism, slowdown, controlled production, quit or turnover. These have always been symptoms of protest. Obviously, the grievance procedure is installed in a plant not to seal up avenues of expression and protest but to open up paths to adjustment. . . .

The grievance procedure furnishes a means of orderly life in the mill. . . . It serves as an outlet for the aggrieved worker and at the same time keeps management in close touch with the tone and temper of the relationships in the plant. It reveals to management the reactions of the individuals and the code of behavior of the group of which they are a part. The knowledge thus gained is of utmost importance to the policy makers on both sides. To block up this index of plant morale is not the way to minimize labor disputes but rather the way to remain ignorant of their physiology. . . .

FAIRWEATHER AND SHAW,* MINIMIZING DISPUTES IN LABOR CONTRACT NEGOTIATONS

A labor contract is a statement of policy which is established through negotiations and which is to remain in effect for a fixed period of time.

If it is a policy to control the relationship between the parties, it must clearly set forth the rights and obligations of the parties so that they can properly perform their respective functions. . . .

Management's prime function is to manage — that is, to plan the work and to direct the working forces. Management is a group of individuals trained, at great expense, in industrial "know-how." If management does not do its job properly, the plant will not be as efficient as it would otherwise be. Management must have the right under the contract to manage the plant efficiently if the efficiency principle considered above is to be followed.

Management is charged with carrying out many policies. One of these policies is contained in the contract with the union. Therefore, it becomes management's job to manage the plant under this contractual policy. The management is always the "acting" party; there is no basis for the idea that, because a labor contract exists, the union shares jointly the obligation to manage the plant efficiently. That is solely management's obligation. . . .

Since efficient operation is necessarily a management function, the provisions of a labor contract should make it clear that management has the rights which are necessary to the performance of this function. It is interesting to note how this functional concept of management's rights has been reflected in the War Labor Board's decisions and in arbitration awards, which together are the only source of "common law" on rights of unions and managements under labor contracts. . . .

During the life of the contract the union's concern is to see that management, in its everyday operation of the plant, does not violate the contractual policy. The union's function can properly be considered to be that of "watch dog," in contrast to

---

* Partners, Seyfarth, Shaw and Fairweather, Chicago. The full text of this statement by Owen Fairweather and Lee C. Shaw may be found in 12 Law & Contemp. Prob. 297–329 (1947), from which the above selections have been taken with the permission of the editors of that publication. — Ed.

the management's function, which is to carry the responsibility as the "acting" party for efficient operations.

If being the watch dog is the union's function, then the union must have the right under the contract to perform this function. The grievance procedure established by the contract provides the method by which the union challenges management on the ground that it has not followed the contract. . . .

The purpose of the grievance procedure is simply to provide a method whereby the union can obtain compliance with the contract itself. It should not be a method by which the union questions all of management's decisions, nor should it be written so that the union can force management to place questions of managerial judgment before outside arbitrators who bear none of the responsibility for mistakes of judgment. A "grievance" should be considered simply as an allegation that management has not properly followed a given provision of the agreed policy. . . .

NOTE

What are the consequences of the refusal by one of the parties at the request of the other to process a grievance in accordance with the procedure established by the collective agreement? [118] It has already been indicated in the materials in Part II supra that it is an unfair labor practice under the provisions of the Labor Management Relations Act for an employer (Sec. 8 (a) (5)) or a labor organization (Sec. 8 (b) (3)) to refuse to bargain collectively with the other in appropriate circumstances. This duty to bargain is defined in Section 8 (d) to include "the obligation . . . to meet at reasonable times and confer in good faith with respect to . . . the negotiation of an agreement, or any question arising thereunder."

Even prior to the adoption of the provisions of Sections 8 (b) (3) and 8 (d) employers' failures to discuss grievances and matters of contract interpretation were held to constitute refusals to bargain collectively within the meaning of the language presently found in Section 8 (a) (5). This conclusion was predicated upon the principle that the obligation to bargain was a continuing one which was not extinguished by the execution of the agreement; and it persisted despite the fact that the agreement made no provision for grievance procedure. Rapid Roller Co. v. NLRB, 126

[118] As to prematurity in resort to arbitration, see Decca Records, Inc. v. Van Clief et al., 107 N.Y.S. 2d 64, 17 L.A. 223 (Sup. Ct., N.Y. County, 1951).

F.2d 452 (7th Cir. 1942); NLRB v. Bachelder, 120 F.2d 574 (7th Cir. 1941); NLRB v. Highland Shoe Co., 119 F.2d 218 (1st Cir. 1941). During the same period, it was held that an employer was relieved of its duty in this respect where a union, in violation of a no-strike clause and in complete disregard of a detailed grievance procedure contained in its agreement, went on strike in protest of an alleged accumulation of unsettled grievances. The fact that the union's conduct was neither denominated nor forbidden as an unfair labor practice was regarded as immaterial. United Elastic Corp., 84 N.L.R.B. 768, 24 L.R.R.M. 1294 (1949), foreshadowed, perhaps, by Timken Roller Bearing Co. v. NLRB, 161 F.2d 949 (6th Cir. 1947).

With the enactment of Section 8 (b) (3), the action of labor organizations of the kind involved in the United Elastic and Timken cases is itself an unfair labor practice and may be directly redressed rather than serving as a defense in an unfair labor proceeding against the employer. Consequently the principle has emerged that if either of the parties to a collective agreement requests the other to participate in the processing of a grievance in accordance with the procedure established therein, the refusal of the other will constitute a violation of Section 8 (a) (5) or 8 (b) (3). For a detailed discussion of this and related problems, see Cox and Dunlop, The Duty to Bargain Collectively During the Term of an Existing Agreement, 63 Harv. L. Rev. 1097 (1950), and Jacobs Mfg. Co., 94 N.L.R.B. 1214, 28 L.R.R.M. 1162 (1951).

The Federal Declaratory Judgments Act, 28 U.S.C. Sec. 2201 et seq., may also provide a remedy for the aggrieved party in this type of situation. Northland Greyhound Lines v. Amal. Assn. of Street, Electric Ry. & Motor Coach Employees, Division 1150, 66 F. Supp. 431 (D. Minn. 1946). In this case the Union insisted that the Company was obligated, under the terms of an existing collective bargaining agreement, to submit to arbitration the Union's demands for certain changes to be made in the contract (incident to its extension or renewal). The Company sought a declaratory judgment that the contract arbitration clause did not cover the matter of proposed changes in the present agreement. The court decided this issue in favor of the Union, stating that "the type of contract involved is a proper subject for the invocation of the Declaratory Judgment statute." Id. at 432. See also Texoma Natural Gas Co. v. Oil Workers Int. Union, 58 F. Supp. 132, affirmed, 146 F.2d 62 (5th Cir. 1944), cert. denied, 324 U.S. 872 (1944). Would the court similarly accept jurisdiction of a case, for example, where the Union is claiming that the seniority provision of the collective bargaining agreement requires that layoffs be on the basis of company-wide seniority, whereas the Company's position is that seniority in the *department* should control?   How about a case in which the issue is whether, under the incentive-rate provisions of the contract, the piece rate for Job 1346L should be $1.24 per 100 pieces (as it will be if Section IV–B of the parties' contract is determined to be controlling) or $1.38 per 100 pieces (which is the answer apparently dictated by Section IV–G)?   Do these cases present a different issue, insofar as the applicability of the Declaratory Judgments Act is concerned, from that presented in the Northland Greyhound case?

3.   THE ARBITRATION STEP IN THE GRIEVANCE PROCEDURE

a.   Introductory Note

The abitration step is the capstone of the grievance procedure. Just as the negotiation steps, considered in the previous section, evolved as an appropriate method for resolving the innumerable and unforeseeable disputes which arise over the meaning and application of particular contract terms, arbitration has become quite generally accepted as the means for achieving final settlement in the event of disagreement between company and union representatives.   In 1950 the United States Department of Labor reported that a comprehensive study of representative collective bargaining agreements showed that some type of arbitration was provided for in more than 80 per cent of them.[119]

Although grievance arbitration has been common in some industries for many years, its widespread utilization has developed since World War II, and was unquestionably prompted by the practice of the National War Labor Board to direct the parties in disputes before it to include such provisions in their agreements.   Prior to that time American employers were in general

---

[119] Arbitration Provisions in Union Agreements, 70 Mo. Lab. Rev. 160 n.2 (1950), states that "Agreements included in this study were in effect in all or some part of 1949.   Of the 1,482 in the sample, 1,036 were in manufacturing industries and 446 in nonmanufacturing.   Employment data were available for 3,020,000 workers covered by 977 of the agreements.   About 47 percent of the agreements were concluded with unions affiliated with the American Federation of Labor, 39 percent by affiliates of the Congress of Industrial Organizations and 14 percent by independent unions."

opposed to arbitration as the terminal point of the grievance machinery.   President Truman's Labor-Management Conference of November, 1945, reached unanimous accord in recommending that "Collective bargaining agreements should . . . provide for the adjustment of . . . grievances and disputes (involving the interpretation or application of the terms of the agreement) by an effective grievance procedure with arbitration as its final step."

The extent to which arbitration has become accepted by the representatives in the ranks of both labor and management, as well as their views of the process itself, are well summarized in a comprehensive survey by Warren and Bernstein, entitled "A Profile of Labor Arbitration," 4 Indust. & Lab. Rel. Rev. 200 (1951), and see also, Taylor, The Voluntary Arbitration of Labor Disputes, 49 Mich. L. Rev. 787 (1951).

It should be kept clearly in mind that the arbitration procedure involved here is a very different matter from the arbitration of new contract terms.   The question for the arbitrator, or arbitration board, in "grievance arbitration" is not what the terms of the parties' relationship *should be,* but what they *are* under the contract already in effect.   In contrast, the parties may at the end of a contract term find themselves unable to agree upon proposed revisions in the contract (covering wages or any other matter), and they may decide to submit that issue to arbitration. They may even have provided in their previous contract for this method of resolving future "contract revision" disputes.   This has been the practice in the local transit industry for many years. But this is not a general practice, and there is still, except in the East, comparatively little resort to arbitration in the settlement of "new contract" disputes.   What we are talking about in this section is "grievance arbitration" — the kind of arbitration which is now generally provided as the last step in the settlement of grievances arising during the contract term.[120]

In the materials which follow, a basis is offered for consideration of some of these particular matters: (a) the establishment of the arbitration procedure in the contract; (b) the scope of arbi-

---

[120] For one of the best descriptions of the various steps that constitute what is called the "grievance procedure," see Settling Plant Grievances (U.S. Dept. of Labor, Div. of Standards, Bull. No. 60, 1943). This contains diagrams illustrative of the types customarily used in both large and small enterprises. While there are no known tabulations of the proportion of disputes disposed of satisfactorily at each pre-arbitration step, it is a frequently expressed opinion that where labor-management relations are healthy, only about 5 per cent of all grievances filed ever reach the point of arbitration; all others are amicably settled at earlier stages.

tration under a particular contract; (c) illustrative problems of evidence and procedure in arbitration proceedings; (d) the enforceability of agreements to arbitrate and of arbitration awards.

b. THE ENDERBY CASE — VIII

Employees D. Lewis and B. Walton were advised, when they reported for work at the beginning of the 8:00 A.M. shift on February 6, 1951, that the rolling mill on which they normally worked would not be run that day or the next day and that they were dismissed until 8:00 A.M., February 8. When they asked what the trouble was the foreman told them there had been a breakdown on the rolling mill. Lewis and Walton protested mildly but went on home without raising any formal objection. They returned to work on the eighth. When they picked up their checks the following Monday they found that they had not been paid for these two days.

A grievance was filed [121] in the following form on February 14:

GRIEVANCE NO. 1113

Demand two days' pay for D. Lewis and B. Walton, laid off on February 6 in violation of seniority.

This grievance was discussed at the second step grievance meeting (see Article II, Section 5 of the agreement, page 319 supra) on Monday afternoon, February 19. The divisional superintendent said he would look into it. On Friday, February 23, he wrote to the Chairman of the Plant Grievance Committee as follows:

RE GRIEVANCE NO. 1113

I find that Employees D. Lewis and B. Walton were sent home for two days because the C Rolling Mill was down for repairs. It has never been the practice to consider seniority in cases of this kind and the claim made in this grievance must accordingly be denied.

[121] "Filing" implies, of course, a written form. Many companies have these printed up, with copies available at the Industrial Relations Office and from shop stewards. These provide for a brief summary signed statement of the employee's grievance, often a place for an entry by the foreman of his ruling, and occasionally places for entries of the disposition at each subsequent step. A set of sample forms will be found in Settling Plant Grievances (U.S. Dept. of Labor, Div. of Labor Standards, Bull. 60, 1943).

An appeal to Leslie White, the Industrial Relations Manager, was filed on Monday, February 26. It stated merely, "The superintendent's decision in Grievance No. 1113 is hereby appealed."

This grievance was discussed by the Grievance Committee and White at a meeting held on Friday, March 2. White charged that the Union was "just trying to read into the contract the call-in pay provision you tried to get us to agree to during negotiations last May." The Union representatives' answer was (a) that this was a seniority case under the contract, and (b) that "common fairness" required paying Lewis and Walton "at least for the day they had come into the plant." Emphasis was placed on the facts that both men had to drive over ten miles to reach the plant, and that Lewis had to come back at 4:30 to pick up the other men in his car pool. No agreement was reached at this meeting. When the Union representatives indicated that they would take this case to arbitration, White replied that the Company did not consider the issue arbitrable and that it would probably refuse to go to arbitration with it.

White's formal denial of the grievance claim was sent to the Grievance Committee on March 3. It read simply, "Claim in Grievance No. 1113 denied because no showing of contract violation." On March 6, the Union President, Oliver Curme, wrote to White that "the Union requests that Grievance No. 1113 be submitted to arbitration." This letter included a list of seven names of proposed arbitrators.

White, upon receiving this letter of March 3, discussed with Harold Blair, the Enderby attorney, the matter of taking the case to arbitration. Blair's advice was that the Company should go through with it. He felt that W. M. McKinney, one of the arbitrators listed by the Union, with whom Blair had worked before, would, when he heard the case, "throw it out for lack of jurisdiction." White was reluctant. He asked Blair whether the Company could be forced "by law" to arbitrate the case. Blair's answer was that it probably could not be but that he would be concerned about the effect upon relationships in the plant of a refusal to arbitrate. White finally decided to take Blair's advice.

Blair insisted that there should be a written stipulation by the Company and the Union of the issue to be arbitrated. This caused quite a wrangle. Blair's original proposal was for a stipulation in the following form:

> The issue to be decided is whether the arbitrator has jurisdiction under Section 5 of Article II of the Agreement of

May 21, 1950, to award call-in pay to D. Lewis and B. Walton for work not performed on February 6 and 7, 1951.

The Union lawyer (Dan Cooper) to whom this case had been referred rejected Blair's proposed stipulation as a "flagrant manifestation of bad faith." Cooper held out for quite a while against having any stipulation at all, insisting that the contract did not call for one. Blair indicated that the Company would not go ahead with the case until a stipulation of the issue was worked out and signed. Agreement was finally reached on the following form:

AGREED STATEMENT OF ISSUE

The arbitrator shall decide whether D. Lewis and B. Walton are entitled to payment for all or any part of the 16 hours they would have worked on February 6 and 7, 1951, if they had not been dismissed by their foreman. It is agreed that this issue must be decided under the terms of the agreement of May 21, 1950, and that the arbitrator will have to pass upon any question which is raised as to his jurisdiction.

OLIVER CURME
LESLIE WHITE

McKinney accepted the parties' appointment as arbitrator and a hearing was held on March 30. A number of questions arose at the hearing:

1. Blair asked the arbitrator, at the outset, to "dismiss this proceeding for lack of jurisdiction in the arbitrator, and to refer it back to the parties as provided in Article II, Section 5 of the Agreement." Blair insisted that this was required because the contract contained no provision for call-in pay and there was therefore "no possible issue of 'interpretation and application' of the contract." McKinney said that he would rule on this point in his written award but that he would "hear full argument first."

2. Blair, in the course of his preliminary argument on the jurisdictional point introduced, as Company Exhibit 4, a typewritten copy of what he said had been a Union proposal made in the May, 1950, contract negotiations. It read as follows:

To be added as Section 11 to Article V:
"A minimum of four hours' pay will be provided for any employee who is called to work and who is then dismissed without being given at least four hours' of work."

Cooper, the Union attorney, objected to this exhibit being admitted on the ground that it was irrelevant and was, in any event, "only a copy of something or other typed up for this hearing by one of the Company stenographers."

3. Objections were made by Blair to the Union's introduction of the following:

(a) Testimony by an employee from another department of the plant that the foremen there always provided at least four hours' pay to any employee called in even though there was nothing for him to do.

(b) An arbitration award in a case involving a similar dispute at the U.S. Rubber Co. plant in Eau Claire, Wisconsin.

(c) A statement by Cooper that "a survey of 117 Chicago plants, all organized, shows that there are call-in pay guarantees in 107 of the collective bargaining agreements." Cooper had the survey with him. It had been made by the research office of one of the other CIO unions.

(d) Testimony by an employee in the division where Lewis and Walton worked, to the effect that only about 30 minutes' repair work was done on the C Mill on the two days in question, and that the "real reason" for Lewis' and Walton's layoff was that there was not enough work for them to do. Cooper stated that this, in view of the fact that two other men in this same division with less seniority than Lewis and Walton worked on February 6 and 7, established a violation of Article IV, Section 2 of the contract. Blair objected to this testimony on the ground that the Union had made no claim at any step of the grievance procedure that the dismissal was for any reason other than machinery repairs.

4. In his summary statement Blair made the point that there had not been any "real proof" of any of the facts in issue, not even of the allegation that Lewis and Walton reported for work on the morning of February 6. Cooper called this, in his reply, "the silliest d—— nonsense ever heard outside a court room."

McKinney's award was received by the parties on April 17. He rejected the Company's claim on the jurisdictional point, describing it as "in keeping only with the overemphasis upon legalistic technicality which has unfortunately characterized the handling of this case throughout its history, particularly at the arbitration hearing." The opinion emphasized, on the jurisdictional point, the language in the first paragraph of Section 5 of Article II. McKinney held that there was "clearly a seniority issue here as well as one of claimed call-in pay." He decided, however, that "the Union's claim is really only for partial payment for the time which was lost," and he accordingly awarded Lewis and Walton four hours' pay apiece.

Neither the Union nor the Company received this award with any satisfaction. Curme and White, talking it over, agreed that they wanted "no more compromising arbitrators who try so hard to satisfy everybody that they only foul things up."

Both parties consulted their lawyers as to the possibilities of court review of McKinney's award. Lewis and Walton wanted to go after their other twelve hours' pay. Cooper told them that they "wouldn't have a chance." White pressed Blair a good deal harder about the possibility of either getting a court to set the award aside or of just not making payments to Lewis and Walton and letting the Union take the case up if they wanted to. Blair told White that he was relatively sure no court would enforce the award. Blair's stock had gone down, however, in the course of his handling of this case, and White finally decided to pay the two men as directed in the award and let it go at that. This was done.

Several weeks later another situation of the same kind developed in another department, there being no work for five men who had reported in the Shipping Department. They were sent home, and, on White's advice, were not paid. The Union officers objected strenuously to the Company's "refusal to accept the arbitrator's decision," and filed another grievance. This case also went to arbitration, before a different arbitrator. He referred the case back to the parties without decision, making no mention of the McKinney award and ruling that he had no authority to decide what he termed "a demand for call-in pay not provided for in the contract." The Union sought Cooper's advice as to whether this decision could be effectively appealed to the courts.

c. Some Illustrative Arbitration Clauses

It has not been unusual for companies and unions to include in one of their first contracts, a clause such as the following:

> If a grievance is not settled [at the first steps of the grievance procedure] it will be submitted to an arbitrator for final and binding decision.

The report of the Enderby Case, set out above, illustrates some of the problems which can develop as a consequence of the use of this kind of loose language. The principle of arbitration is accepted by both parties, but they create for themselves a situation in which the effectuation of that principle may prove so difficult that relationships will actually be worsened rather than improved.

The two problems which are most likely to arise under clauses of the type illustrated have to do with (a) the selection of an arbitrator, and (b) the matter of submission to arbitration of a particular dispute which one party feels is not the appropriate subject of arbitration. It is perhaps true that neither of these problems presents issues which are actually basic in the administration of a collective bargaining relationship. They are, on the other hand, typical of the administrative considerations which parties unfamiliar with the demands of any "legal" system are likely to overlook and they are accordingly illustrative of the kind of thing with respect to which the counsel and advice of lawyers may prove most helpful. It is very much the essence of this counseling job that attention be called to the impracticability of relying too far upon "settlements in principle" which will not hold water when occasions arise for the application of those principles to specific cases.

The circumstances of particular cases (e.g., the size of the plant, the past history of the relationship, etc.) will of course affect very substantially the question of what will be satisfactory arbitration clauses in particular contracts. See Comment, The Arbitrator's Approach to Labor Contract Interpretation, 64 Harv. L. Rev. 1338 (1951). The following clauses offer some basis, however, for an understanding of the kinds of measures which may be taken to avoid the most obvious problems which are likely to arise under the looser form of contract provision.

(i) In the event that the Company and the Union are unable to adjust a grievance, such grievance or dispute shall, on the written demand of either party, be submitted to arbitration.

(ii) Grievances not satisfactorily settled in Step 4 shall, in the absence of mutual agreement in writing to the contrary, be appealed to an impartial umpire, to be appointed by mutual agreement of the parties hereto. [Note, however, the inadequacy of such a clause (without other provision in the contract) with respect to the naming of the umpire in case the parties do not agree.]

(iii) Within five working days after receipt of written notice of a demand for arbitration sent by either party to the other, the parties shall mutually agree upon a single arbitrator who shall hear and decide the dispute. If the parties shall fail to agree upon a single arbitrator within the aforesaid five-day period, then and in that event the arbitrator shall be appointed by the American Arbitration Association in accordance with its rules.   [In other clauses of similar type, provision is made for the appointment of the arbitrator, in case the parties cannot agree, by the Federal Mediation and Conciliation Service, the City Club of Chicago, the Labor Council of Toledo, the dean of a law school, the judges of a circuit court of appeals or of a state court, the mayor of a city, or by other similar offices.]

(iv) The Board of Arbitration shall consist of one representative to be selected by the Company and one representative to be selected by the Union; the Federal Mediation and Conciliation Service, Washington, D.C., shall be called upon to select a third member, who will also act as Chairman. The third member shall be selected in the following manner: The Conciliation Service will submit the names of five persons, and the representatives of the Union and the representatives of the Company shall each have the choice of rejecting the names of two of these five persons, and the remaining, or fifth, shall be the said third member.

[One of the problems which is most likely to arise under these tripartite arbitration provisions is covered specifically in the North Carolina statute (1949 Supp., Sec. 95–36.5; providing for arbitration, where desired, under the terms of the statute) : "If any panel is unable to reach a unanimous decision on the merits of any issue, the finding and decision of a majority of the members of the panel shall constitute the award of the panel on that issue; if a majority vote cannot be obtained on any issue, the finding and decision of the chairman shall constitute the award of the panel on that issue."]

(v) Disputes arising as to the application and meaning of the terms of the agreement concerning wages that cannot be settled satisfactorily through the grievance procedure shall be submitted to the Massachusetts Board of Conciliation and Arbitration for arbitration and the decision of such board shall be final and binding on both parties. [Note the rather basic difference between the type of arbitration provided for here as compared with that in the other clauses set out above.]

(vi) For the purpose of settling any unsettled disputes and grievances, the parties agree to use as arbitrator .... of Portsmouth, Ohio. At any time after three months from the date, either party may by written notice to the other, object to the continuance of said arbitrator and thereupon they shall forthwith agree to his successor . . . [This particular contract provided that the successor arbitrator should be appointed by the National War Labor Board if occasion for such an appointment developed. The more usual practice is, however, where permanent arbitrators or umpires are provided for, that the parties will always do this appointing themselves.]

The contracts almost invariably provide that the expenses of the arbitration proceedings, insofar as the arbitrator's charges are concerned, will be divided equally between the company and the union. See Warren and Bernstein, A Profile of Labor Arbitration, 4 Indust. & Lab. Rel. Rev. 200, 217 (1951).

d. The "Jurisdiction" of the Arbitrator

In re LOEW'S, INC., METRO–GOLDWYN–MAYER STUDIOS and OFFICE EMPLOYEES' INT. UNION (AFL), LOCAL NO. 174
10 L.A. 227 (1948)

[Betty Schwartz, who had been working for M–G–M for eleven years in a position not included within the bargaining unit, was moved by the Company to a job within the unit. She was then, shortly afterward, promoted to another job on the basis that she was entitled to it by virtue of her eleven years' seniority. The Union protested that moving Miss Schwartz into the unit without the Union's approval, was a violation of Article 3 (g) of the contract: "The Producer shall notify the Union when the producer desires to hire new employees, and agrees to accept applicants furnished by the Union provided the Producer finds such applicants competent and capable of performing the duties of the position." The Union also contended that Miss Schwartz' service outside the bargaining unit did not give her seniority credit under Clause 68 of the contract and that her promotion was therefore a violation of the seniority rights of another employee. When the Company rejected these protests the Union took the case to arbitration. The Company challenged, before the umpire, his authority to rule on the issue, or at least to rule on it favorably to the Union. The arbitration clause in the contract was as follows: "The . . . Impartial Chairman shall have power to interpret and apply the provisions of this Agreement, but shall not have power to amend or modify any of its provisions, nor shall . . . he have power to effect a change in any of its provisions." That part of Umpire Benjamin Aaron's Decision dealing with the jurisdictional issue is as follows:]

Obviously, the first point which must be disposed of is the Company's contention that the arbitrator cannot decide the principal issue in the Union's favor without amending the collective agreement and thus exceeding his authority under the submission. As previously noted, the Company buttresses this argument by pointing out that the collective agreement contains no provision which specifically covers the issue here involved. Stated in other terms, the Company's contention is that the arbitrator has no power (1) to interpret the words "new employees" in Article 3 (g) as meaning "new employees in the bargaining unit," and (2) to interpret Clause 68 as applying only to employees within the bargaining unit.

It is hardly an exaggeration to state that the great majority of those experienced in collective bargaining recognize the collective bargaining agreement as a comprehensive, but necessarily flexible, instrument which governs the relations between the parties. The very fact that almost all of such agreements (including the one here involved) provide for the arbitration of grievances concerning the interpretation of various provisions suggests that the parties recognize the impossibility of foreseeing and providing for all questions which may arise during the life of the agreement.[9] In some instances the parties deliberately use general rather than specific language, in order to avoid the hazards of the rule of construction, "*expressio unius est exclusio alterius.*" Thus, collective agreements frequently provide that an employer shall be permitted to discharge an employee "for just cause";

[9] One eminent authority in this field has stated that the collective agreement is merely a skeleton of intent, the bare bones of which are covered by the flesh of interpretation supplied by the parties; and whether the end product turns out to be a Hedy Lamar or a Boris Karloff depends upon the modeling skill of the creators. To this may be added the further observation that the attractiveness or repulsiveness of the complete agreement will probably depend upon the attitude of the party construing it; after all, beauty lies in the eye of the beholder.

and what shall constitute "just cause" in each case is determined by collective bargaining, and sometimes by arbitration. This type of case is illustrative of the many others in which an arbitrator may be called upon to apply the terms of a collective agreement to situations not specifically covered therein.

In some instances, it is true, the issue involved is clearly outside the scope of the agreement, in which case one of the parties usually objects to the submission of the matter to arbitration; and the arbitrator may have to make a preliminary finding as to his jurisdiction in the premises. In so doing, however, he is obligated to avoid a destructively literal construction which clearly does violence to the intent of the parties. It is not irrelevant to note that courts of law have been criticized for their "scrupulousness to the written word" in statutory construction and their consequent frustration of the legislative intent.[10] Holmes' observation that "it is not an adequate discharge of duty for courts to say: We see what you are driving at, but you have not said it, and therefore we shall go on as before," [11] applies equally to arbitrators.

In the instant case the arbitrator is satisfied that the principal issue may be determined on the merits within the confines of the collective agreement. This process does not require an "amendment" of the collective agreement; what is involved is simply the interpretation of certain provisions on the basis of its complete context and background. [The umpire held, in his award, that the Company had violated the contract by placing Miss Schwartz in a bargaining unit job.]

NOTES

1. In re John Deere Tractor Company, Dubuque Works and United Farm Equipment Workers (CIO), Local No. 241, 9 L.A. 73 (1947); Arbitrator — George N. Gorder. The Union sought in this grievance to require the Company to reinstate an employee who had been discharged (for alleged incompetence) while he was still a probationary employee. The contract provided that "nothing contained (herein) shall be construed so as to limit in any manner the right of the Company to discipline or to terminate finally and without recourse to the Grievance Procedure the employment of any probationary employee for failure satis-

[10] Learned Hand, The Speech of Justice, 29 Harv. L. Rev. 617, 620 (1916), cited in Frank, Words and Music: Some Remarks on Statutory Interpretation, 47 Col. L. Rev. 1259, 1263 (1947).

[11] Johnson v. United States, 163 Fed. 30, 32 (1st Cir. 1908).

factorily to meet job performance requirements." The arbitrator denied the grievance claim on the ground that under the quoted contract clause "this grievance is not arbitrable. The arbitrator is without jurisdiction to consider the question presented." Was this properly considered a jurisdictional question? In Twentieth Century-Fox Film Corporation v. Screen Publicists' Guild, Local No. 114, 78 N.Y.S.2d 178, 21 L.R.R.M. 2401 (Sup. Ct., Spec. Term, N.Y. County, Part I (1948)), the Company refused to arbitrate a question similar to that involved in the John Deere Tractor Company case, and sought a court order staying arbitration. The order was granted, the court stating that where the agreement makes the company's decision final, the matter is not arbitrable.

2. Compare In re International Harvester Company, McCormick Works and United Farm Equipment Workers (CIO), Local No. 108, 9 L.A. 1021 (1948); Arbitrator — Herbert Blumer. The Union request here was that employees be paid for time spent in visits to the doctor requested by the Company. The defense relied on by the Company was that an affirmative award by the arbitrator would be beyond his jurisdiction. The contract provided that the arbitrator "shall not have power to add to, to ignore or to modify any of the terms and conditions of this agreement." The arbitrator rejected this defense on the ground that the contract was clear that "hours worked" were to be paid for, and the question raised was whether the time spent on visits to the doctor came within this description. Inasmuch as only the jurisdictional joint had been argued at the hearings before the arbitrator the merits of the case were left for further proceedings. Compare In re International Harvester Company, Farmall Works and United Farm Equipment Workers (CIO), Local 109, 9 L.A. 965 (1948); Arbitrator — Joseph D. Lohman.

Consideration should be given to the effect of cases of this kind on the general plant relationship. Jurisdiction is a technical point, at least in the minds of most laymen, and they may be expected to react unfavorably to decisions revolving on technicalities, particularly when the consequence is that a second hearing must be held. On the other hand it is important that the arbitrator not usurp the "legislative" functions of the parties. Could cases of the type illustrated above be handled on other than "jurisdictional" grounds?

In Mosaic Tile Co., 14 L.A. 953 (1950), Arbitrator R. E. Mathews found that the Union's complaint over the operation of a particular incentive plan was a grievance under the collective bargaining agreement.　But he ruled the issue was not arbitrable because it fell within a provision of the contract expressly stating the arbitrator had "no authority over wage rates established by this agreement."　His opinion stated in part:

> Let it be said in closing that this arbitrator views with extreme reluctance an award of non-arbitrability.　The function of a collective agreement is essentially that of industrial self-government, and the grievance procedure with its culminating step of arbitration is the administrative mechanism which the parties have themselves set up to resolve all their differences as to the meaning or application of that agreement. Their contract should, wherever consistent with its language, be viewed as a flexible body of principles capable of governing all relations between the company and the members of the bargaining unit for which it was negotiated.　By no amount of human foresight can all the possible frictions between these many persons be anticipated and the agreement should therefore be given liberal coverage with a view to encompassing as many of these as its language permits. Where, however, the parties have expressly excluded from arbitration certain enumerated issues, an award of arbitrability of such issues would expose the arbitrator to the just criticism that he was in fact writing into the contract a term the parties had agreed to exclude.

In re NEW JERSEY WORSTED MILLS, GERA MILLS and TEXTILE WORKERS UNION (CIO)
10 L.A. 310 (1948)

DAVID L. COLE, Arbitrator: The Company questions the arbitrability of certain issues presented by the Union.　They are all disputes which arose during the 1947 agreement.　The 1947 agreement has been replaced by an agreement signed on February 27, 1948, effective as of February 1, 1948.　It is the Company's view that when the 1947 contract terminated on February 1, 1948, the powers granted to the permanent arbitrator "likewise ceased to exist," and that the use of practically identical language on arbitration in the 1948 contract, in which the same permanent arbitrator was named, had no bearing on the question presented.

Artificial or technical rules or conditions which serve no good purpose should not be read into an agreement regulating labor relations.　The Company has said: "To hold that the arbitrator named in the 1947 contract has power to arbitrate issues, after the contract has expired, when one of the parties thereto did not take such issues to arbitration during the contract period, would be a very dangerous precedent to establish. To hold that the arbitrator named in the 1948 agreement has power to hear and determine issues which arose before the contract was negotiated would be contrary to the language and intention of the parties as expressed in the 1948 contract."

It would be a much more dangerous precedent to hold that wrongs should be left uncorrected in a relationship of this kind because of the failure to give technical notice of a fact of which the other side is quite aware and which the agreement does not require.

Labor arbitration is a proceeding which is basically equitable, not legal. Its very flexibility is what commends it. It moulds itself procedurally and in the forms of remedies, which it adopts to the objectives of the contracting parties. Thus, nonadherence to formal rules of evidence or to courtroom procedures is taken for granted. An award is not bad simply because, on the evidence or form of evidence offered, a court would have come to a different conclusion. The purpose of labor arbitration, both express and implied, under broad contract provisions is to provide a definite, non-technical means of clearing up disagreements between the employer and employees; to search for reasons to exclude disputes from adjustment in this manner is quite inconsistent with this purpose. When a question over arbitrability is raised, subject only to clear limitations stated in the agreement, the ruling suggested is that of the maximum that equity will not suffer a wrong to be without a remedy.

Having agreed to forgo all forms of self-help, the employees who believe they have not received what the contract assures them should be given the opportunity to seek redress through arbitration, under the circumstances of this case. Whether there has been undue delay which may reflect on the merits of their contentions is a totally different consideration and does not affect their right to have the arbitrator pass on their grievances. . . .

NOTES

1. In re The Shook Bronze Company and United Electrical, Radio and Machine Workers of America, Local 763 (CIO), 9 L.A. 656 (1948); Arbitrator — Paul N. Lehoczky. "The contract involved in this case provided that 'All differences, disputes, and grievances between the parties that are not satisfactorily settled fol-

lowing the [first steps of the grievance procedure] shall, at the request of either party, promptly be submitted to arbitration.' The Union filed a grievance requesting pay for certain holidays not worked. The Company refused to grant this request, and the Union thereupon insisted that the issue be submitted to arbitration. The Company acquiesced in submitting the case to arbitration, but insisted, before the arbitrator, that this was not an appropriate subject for arbitration because it involved no question of 'applying the general terms of the contract to specific factual situations.' The contract did not provide for paid holidays but did include a provision stating that 'The parties have discussed the matter of paid holidays, . . . [but] have agreed to pass this matter at this time, . . . [and] that they will again enter into negotiations concerning this matter [later].' " The Union's position was that this was a dispute between the parties and that they had agreed to arbitrate all disputes.

The arbitrator denied the Union request, holding that this issue was not properly arbitrable. He recognized the literal wording of the agreement as supporting the Union position, but concluded that "the parties meant arbitration to apply only to matters involving the interpretation of the Agreement." The opinion includes the following statement: "Legally, the language of the Agreement permits the arbitration of any and all issues either party may wish to raise, whether related to the provisions of the Agreement or not. This, we hold, is neither in accordance with the spirit or the intent of Labor-Management agreements as they now exist in the United States. Accordingly, we rule that the Agreement permits the arbitration only of differences which arise between the parties regarding the meaning or application of the terms of the Agreement."

The arbitrator, in this same case, granted a Union request for average earnings payments to all incentive operators for "down time" resulting from "short runs, machine breakdowns, experimental runs and work done for the Company's convenience." This request was considered to present an arbitrable issue inasmuch as the parties' contract included the following provision: "The Employer expects to revise its incentive pay system. A supplement will be entered into concerning the incentive pay system and the system will be agreed upon after negotiations between the parties and embodied in said supplement."

2. In re Air Reduction Sales Company and Int. Assn. of Machinists (Ind.), Jersey City Lodge No. 304, 10 L.A. 528 (1948); Arbitrator — Frederick R. Livingston. The contract involved

here included a wage-reopening clause. This clause provided that upon reopening notice "negotiations shall proceed between the parties, with a view toward making such changes as may be mutually satisfactory." The contract was reopened by the Union and the negotiations proceeded as specified. No agreement being reached, the Union sought to have the issue arbitrated. The arbitrator held the matter not arbitrable, relying in part on the fact that the contract limited the grievance procedure to "the meaning and application of this agreement." He pointed out more broadly, however, that the "very process of collective bargaining might be impaired where the parties know in advance that failure to reach an agreement would result in a determination by a third party in arbitration." Is this less true, and important, in cases which *are* covered by the grievance procedure in a contract?

In other cases involving issues similar to that in the Air Reduction Sales case, the Company has refused to go to arbitration and the union has sought court orders directing that arbitration be compelled. Such orders were denied in Matter of Int. Assn. of Machinists v. Cutler-Hammer, Inc., 271 App. Div. 917, 67 N.Y. S.2d 317 (1st Dept. 1946), affirmed, 297 N.Y. 519, 74 N.E.2d 464 (1947); In re Berger, 21 L.R.R.M. 2595, 79 N.Y.S.2d 490 (Sup. Ct., Special Term, N.Y. County Part I (1948)); In re Vasek v. Matthews & Co., 21 L.R.R.M. 2588 (1947) N.Y.L.J., Nov. 5, 1947, p. 1175.

In United Electrical, Radio and Machine Workers of America, Local 411, CIO v. National Pneumatic Co., 134 N.J.L. 349, 48 A.2d 295 (1946), however, the Court granted the Union's request for an order requiring the Company to submit to arbitration a wage issue which had been reopened during the contract period in accordance with the contract terms. The contract provided for the arbitration of "all differences, disputes, complaints and grievances between the parties." Bodine, J.: "The purpose desired in labor contracts is that disputes, as the contract in question expressly provides, shall be promptly settled in the interest of a continuance of sound relations between the Union and the Company. If the contract so provides, as it does in this case, it is not the function of the court to so construe it so [sic] as to defeat the intention of the parties." Cf. Northland Greyhound Lines, Inc. v. Amalgamated Assn. of Street, Electric Ry. and Motor Coach Employees of America, Division 1150, 66 F. Supp. 431 (D. Minn. 1946) (declaratory judgment granted).

e. Arbitration Practice and Procedure

Very few collective bargaining agreements contain provisions governing the procedures to be followed in arbitration hearings or the rules to be observed by the arbitrator in reaching his conclusions (except, of course, as he is usually directed to limit himself to an application of the contract terms). The following clauses are, however, illustrative of the type of contract provision which is sometimes included:

(i) The party desiring arbitration shall give notice in writing to the other party, defining the issue to be arbitrated and it is understood and agreed that only one issue at a time may be arbitrated. [The last part of this provision is not typical, the very general practice being for an arbitrator to handle several grievances upon the occasion of his visit to the plant.]

(ii) The decisions of the Board of Arbitration shall not be governed by strict legal rule, but may be based on any logical evidence which to the Board may seem to have probative value . . .

(iii) The Arbitration Board shall organize and promulgate such rules as are proper for conducting the arbitration . . .

(iv) It is agreed that . . . International officers . . . are entitled to be present [at the arbitration hearings] as counsel and advisers, and that the employer may be similarly represented by persons engaged in the industry; provided that not more than three such representatives may be present on behalf of each party. Such representatives may if they desire call and question witnesses called before such Board.

Some contracts entered into by the AFL Electrical Workers provide that neither party shall be represented in arbitration proceedings by "legal advisers."

This matter of arbitration practice and procedure has been covered in detail in Updegraff and McCoy, Arbitration of Labor Disputes, cc. 3 and 4 (1946).[122] Some aspects of it were also covered in the 1948 Report of the American Bar Association's Committee on Improving the Administration of Union-Employer Contracts. The following paragraphs are excerpts from that report:

[122] See also Wirtz, Collective Bargaining: Lawyers' Role in Negotiations and Arbitrations, 34 A.B.A.J. 547 (1948); Singer, Labor Arbitration: Should It Be Formal or Informal? 2 Lab. L.J. 89 (1951), and Labor Arbitration: Use of Legal Rules of Evidence, id. at 185.

Written stipulations of the issue to be arbitrated. The
Committee calls attention to the importance, from the standpoint of good administration, of the clearest and most precise
possible formulation of the issue which is to be submitted to
the arbitrator.   Such a formulation offers two advantages.
The most obvious one is that the subsequent award will bear
directly on the point at issue, and will be no broader than is
necessary.   Stipulations would appear to have particular justification when the arbitrator who has been selected is relatively unknown to the parties.   The second advantage is that
the process of clarifying the precise issue involved in any dispute leads not infrequently to a settlement of the dispute itself.
It may reveal a previous misunderstanding the removal of
which will disclose substantial agreement as to the point
actually in issue.

The Committee notes at the same time, however, the danger
of needless misunderstanding which may result from adaman-
tine insistence upon the drawing up of written stipulations in
all cases.   There is no point in ignoring the fact that many
Unions object strenuously to the introduction into these proceedings of what they consider "legalistic" technicalities.
The "stipulation" has become identified as perhaps the most
characteristic of such technicalities.   Because the question
of whether there is to be a stipulation arises at the very outset
of the arbitration proceeding, the handling of this matter
may affect everything that follows.   The type of attitude referred to does not warrant the abandonment of precautionary
measures which appear to be essential in any particular case.
It does suggest, however, the desirability of not insisting upon
such measures' being taken on a rule-of-thumb basis and regardless of whether there is any purpose actually to be served.
Where, for example, a grievance form has been used in the
handling of the case at the lower steps of the procedure, there
would seem to be little reason for a special stipulation covering the arbitration. . . .

Rules of evidence. The principles underlying most of the
evidentiary rules are no less applicable to arbitration than to
other fact finding and adjudicative proceedings.   The Committee recommends consideration, however, of two adaptations of these rules for purposes of their use in arbitration
proceedings.

There would seem to be every reason, in the first place, for
a recognition of these established principles in arbitration pro-

ceedings as rules for the weighing of evidence rather than for its admissibility.   The circumstances attending an arbitration hearing do not warrant restrictions upon employee or employer representatives telling the arbitrator anything which they honestly feel, regardless of the error of their judgment, is relevant to the case.   Arbitration awards and the arbitration process depend, for their acceptability, upon the confidence which both parties retain in the arbitrator, and rulings excluding testimony sincerely offered will reduce or destroy that confidence.   Arbitrators who cannot be relied on to weigh properly what they hear, aided of course by counsels' argument regarding its relevance and probity, are not qualified for this particular function.

The second consideration here is only the obvious one that these "rules" should be stripped, for purposes of arbitration, proceedings of their legalistic and Latin trappings. It is exceedingly difficult for the lawyer to realize how much "shorthand" has become a part of his natural conversation regarding these tools of the trade. His failure in this connection is at least in part responsible for the misunderstanding which has developed regarding his participation in problems of industrial relations.

The use of witnesses and the interrogatory form of testimony. It has already become apparent that the departure from courtroom procedural formalities is resulting in a substantial diminution in the use of witness testimony in arbitration proceedings. The tendency is toward reliance upon general statements of both fact and argument by the representatives of the respective parties, with foremen and stewards (or the allegedly aggrieved employee) being called upon only to fill in corroborative or technical details.

The Committee calls attention to the importance of these representative "advocates" being men who are qualified on some basis other than their familiarity with the facts of the case involved.   It is just as important that the arbitrator understand the case as that the advocate does.   If he does not get his story over the advocate has failed, regardless of his mastery of his subject matter.   The typical steward and the typical industrial engineer share the common weakness of being so close to their subject that they assume far too much with respect to its understanding by the arbitrator. . . .

Methods of advocacy.   The Committee . . . calls attention to one feature of the arbitration process which gives particular significance to the type of advocacy which may be used in these proceedings. That feature . . . is that the relationship involved in any arbitration case is more important than the case itself and is one which will continue after the case is over. The corollary of this general proposition is that the "winning of the case" cannot, in an arbitration proceeding, be an exclusive consideration. Cases won on technicalities may mean only that the settlement of an issue will be postponed while trouble develops. Exaggerations which are sometimes recognized as inherent in advocacy may cause unnecessary animosity when they get back to the shop. Clever obfuscation may produce the desired award from the befuddled arbitrator, but it may mean too, some language in his opinion which will create new confusion in the plant. The adversary system, as it has been developed in the courtroom, requires some adaptation before it will become well suited to all the purposes of the arbitration proceeding.

In re TEXTRON, INC., ESMOND MILLS and TEXTILE WORKERS UNION OF AMERICA (CIO)
12 L.A. 475 (1949)

WALLEN, Arbitrator. The issue in this case is whether or not under the agreement between the parties the employees of the Esmond Mills, Incorporated are entitled to severance pay.

On January 1, 1948 the Esmond Mills and the Textile Workers Union of America, CIO, entered into a collective agreement which is effective until March 15, 1950. In May, 1948, Textron, Incorporated, purchased the Esmond Mills, closed the plant, and proceeded to liquidate the machinery and equipment. The employees of the Company were terminated. It was acknowledged that Textron assumed the obligations resident in Esmond's agreement with the Union.

The Union requested severance pay for the employees. Forty-six percent of the 1100 employees involved have had ten or more years of service, some as much as thirty years; 28 percent from five to ten years of service; 12.6 percent from three to five years of service; and 12.8 percent less than three years of service.

The closing of the mill came as a surprise to the employees and to the Union. The laid-off employees found an employment market in which textile mill jobs were scarce. After long training in the textile industry the employees found it difficult to transfer their skills to other industries. They felt that they had built up an equity in their jobs, the abrupt termination of which caused them to be entitled to severance pay.

The Union presented a long and detailed justification for its demand for severance pay. Considered solely in the light of the human problem involved, there is ample justification for some measure of compensation to these employees for the loss of their power to market their labor resulting from the abrupt closing of the plant in which many of them have spent such a large portion of their lives. The closing of the plant apparently was decided upon with little or no regard for the human beings involved. The new owner appears to have regarded the plant solely as a physical asset to be disposed of as he pleased without limitation or inhibition. Likewise, the prior owners callously disposed of their property without making provision for the men and women who helped to make its growth and development a living fact.

In short, if the arbitrator had the power he would award the terminated employees severance compensation in some amount to assist them in their readjustment until they find employment. But the central question is whether a third party has the power under the existing contract to make such an award.

The Union argues that such power exists. It bases this argument on Article VI of the contract which is entitled, "No Strikes or Lockouts — Arbitration" and which contains in part the following language:

"Any dispute, difference, disagreement or controversy of any nature or character, whether or not a grievance between the Union and the Employer which has not been satisfactorily adjusted within fifteen (15) working days after the initiation of conferences may be referred by either party to arbitration . . ."

It also cites the preamble to the contract which reads as follows:

"WHEREAS, it is the intent and purpose of the parties hereto to promote and improve the industrial and economic relations between the Employer, its employees and the Union, to establish a basic understanding relative to rates of pay, hours of work and other conditions of employment, and to provide means for the amicable adjustment of any and all disputes and grievances."

In addition, it points to the absence of a so-called "Management Prerogative Clause" from this Agreement.

The Union contends that the phrase "any dispute, difference, disagreement or controversy" is language without limit and clearly conveys the parties' intention that not only matters concerning specified provisions of the agreement as written can be arbitrated, but also any other matters encompassed by the parties' relationship

which might be brought up by them during the contract's life.
There are no words, expressed or implied, denoting exception,
inclusion or limitation as to what constitutes any "dispute, difference, disagreement or controversy." This broad clause, while
unusual in labor contracts, the Union reasoned, was nonetheless
drawn in this instance by parties well versed in the contents of
such agreements. By virtue of their previous experience they
realized the impossibility of foreseeing all the problems which
might arise under a contract and they purposely used the phrase,
"any dispute, difference, disagreement or controversy of any nature
or character, whether or not a grievance . . ." to allow for the
arbitration of disputes the nature of which they did not anticipate
when the agreement was signed. There is nothing in this language
that reflects an intention to limit the arbitrator's jurisdiction in any
way, the Union argues. If the parties had intended such a limitation, they had ample opportunity to express it in specific language. They would have written language to limit the arbitration
provision to matters arising out of the application or interpretation
of the agreement such as most contracts contain.

In short, the Union argues that the parties signed a blank check
in the sense that they left open to the possibility of arbitration any
matter coming within the scope of the relationship of the parties.
The Union denies the applicability to this case of the decision by
Professor Douglass V. Brown in a case involving the same Union
and the Naushon Mill in New Bedford. It points out that while
the contract involved in that case made any dispute, difference, disagreement or controversy arbitrable, it also contained a sentence
which read, "It is understood and agreed that questions involving
changes in the terms and provisions of this agreement shall not be
subject to the foregoing grievance procedure or to arbitration
thereunder." The contract at hand does not contain such language.

The Company maintains that the agreement between the
parties dated January 1, 1948 covers in detail wage adjustments,
piecework adjustments, hours of work, overtime, holiday pay,
vacations, leaves of absence, layoffs, seniority, insurance benefits
and all matters normally covered in a collective bargaining agreement. The contract was the outgrowth of negotiations of demands
made by both sides. Severance pay was not included among these
demands, and in any event no reference to it was included in the
agreement. When the contract was entered into the Union's demand for a general wage increase was not settled by agreement
but was submitted to arbitration. The written submission to

arbitration stated that "all the requests of the Union have been negotiated and agreed upon, and it is understood all of the provisions in the new contract except the matter of a general wage increase have been settled." The Company argues that the Union's request for severance pay for the employees is therefore outside the scope of the contract and not an arbitrable issue. While admitting that the language of the arbitration clause is broad, the Company maintains that it is the intent and purpose of the clause to permit arbitration only of matters arising under the contract and not to permit either party to raise and arbitrate issues not under the contract. To hold otherwise, it is argued, would destroy the validity of collective bargaining agreements and lead to chaos and strife.

Despite my conviction that on equitable grounds there is much merit to the Union's request for severance pay, I am compelled as an arbitrator to give careful consideration to the parties' rights under their collective agreements. Granted the broad nature of the arbitration clause in this agreement, one must nevertheless consider whether the parties intended to permit a third party, through the medium of the arbitration clause, to drastically alter the basic nature of their contractual commitments. I cannot believe this to be the case. The substantive contract issues are contained in the parties' agreement which was drawn for a specific period. It could hardly be deemed an agreement if there could be constant additions to its basic terms by virtue of new demands carried to arbitration during its life. One of the basic purposes of a collective agreement is to furnish stability to the parties' relationship by defining the limits of their rights and obligations. This end is hardly served by a holding that additions to the structure of their relationship of an unknown and unforeseen character can constantly be carried to arbitration during the agreement's existence.

The parties in this case bargained over a contract, reached an agreement on its salient features, and determined that it was to govern their relationship for a fixed period. All of the important elements involved in their relationship were discussed, considered, and negotiated. On certain ones the parties reached common understandings and reduced them to writing. With respect to others, demands were made by one side and rejected by the other. Provisions covering such subjects were omitted from the contract. The agreement as finally written was an embodiment of all of the major elements in the parties' commitments. It defined the limits of their respective obligations. By reasonable implication, major categories of obligations not included in the agreement were not intended to be covered by it.

In this case, the above conclusion is reinforced by the fact that when the parties submitted the wage question to arbitration they acknowledged that "all the requests of the Union have been negotiated and agreed upon, and it is understood all of the provisions in the new contract except the matter of a general wage increase have been settled." In the light of this fact, the arbitrator cannot add to the parties' agreement an obligation to pay severance pay without fundamentally altering the understanding they had themselves reached. If he did so, he would not be effectuating the terms of the parties' agreement; he would be extending those terms to a field usually written into a contract by direct collective bargaining. It is not a reasonable conclusion from the instrument as drawn that such an extension of the agreement by arbitration to an area usually the subject of direct negotiations was contemplated by the parties.

The arbitrator is without power to grant the Union's request for severance pay under the parties' agreement.

In re GORTON–PEW FISHERIES et al. and INTER–
NATIONAL LONGSHOREMEN'S ASSN. et al.
16 L.A. 365 (1951)

[This case involved the question of the amount of overtime compensation due to employees pursuant to the terms of a collective bargaining contract. During the week in question the employees had worked eight hours per day for five days and four hours on Saturday morning. One of the eight-hour days was a holiday.

The contract provided that "All hours worked in excess of eight (8) per day or in excess of forty (40) hours per week shall be paid at the rate of time and one-half. Employees shall not be paid overtime both daily and weekly for the same overtime hours worked. . . . All work performed on . . . holidays shall be paid for at the rate of double time."

The Company paid these employees 52 straight time hours (eight each for the four eight-hour non-holiday days, 16 for the holiday and four for the Saturday work) construing the holiday premium pay as being creditable against the Saturday overtime (in excess of forty) hours. The Union contended that the holiday compensation was premium pay, not overtime, and hence not so creditable.

It was shown that the same issue had previously arisen under the identical language contained in a prior contract and had been interpreted favorably to the Company's contention in an arbitration proceeding before a State Board of Arbitration. It also appeared that upon the termination of the prior contract and following a long strike, negotiations had proceeded to a point where the parties had tentatively agreed upon a new and different overtime clause which would have set aside the interpretation of the State Board. However, in the course of bargaining, this clause had been "traded off" in return for other concessions offered by the Company, and the same overtime clause was carried forward from the old agreement. Based upon these facts, the question was put to the arbitrator: Were the employees entitled to overtime pay for the Saturday morning work?]

WALLEN, Arbitrator [after stating the facts]. From these facts the Companies argued that inasmuch as the State Board award favored their interpretation, and the parties chose not to change the clause, they in fact adopted the State Board's ruling as the accepted meaning of the clause. Failure to follow this principle, it was averred, would result in rearbitration of all prior cases that either party had lost. In addition, the Companies argued that the agreement by the Union to drop its demand for a revision of Article IV, Section 1, was made with the full knowledge that the prior State Board decision would continue to be applied. The employers got this minor concession in return for their major concession in the matter of production schedules.

The Union argued that the principle of res judicata does not apply in arbitration and that on its merits, the outcome is clear. It urged this arbitrator to look at the question de nouveau, stressing that no opinion was written by the State Board, that the point was at that time a minor one among several others simultaneously arbitrated, and that the Companies at that time offered to settle this point on terms favorable to the Union in return for Union concessions on other matters. The Union denied the validity of the argument that the parties' action in abandoning the tentatively agreed-upon Article IV, Section 1, in return for another concession gave status to the prior State Board award. The purpose of the tentatively agreed-upon Article IV, Section 1, was not to set aside the effect of the State Board award, which was never discussed. Its purpose was to get premium pay for Saturday as such and a basic 40-hour week. Because the Companies wished to avoid having Saturday as an extra premium in a week in which an unworked paid holiday fell, the phrase "except during weeks in which a paid holiday occurs" was included.

The arbitrator has given much thought to this case because it poses so squarely the problem of the relation of prior awards to current controversies, and their status under a succeeding contract and before a different arbitrator. These problems are difficult and delicate because they involve a balancing of concepts of justice, the sanctity of agreements freely bargained, and the need for stability and order in contract administration.

At the outset, it must be stated that if this arbitrator were to consider this case as an isolated matter apart from the agreement's history, the question at issue would be given an affirmative answer. It is clear that Section 11 and the parties' admitted practice under it provides for the payment of holiday pay in the amount of eight hours to eligible employees, who if they work on the holiday, also get paid for working at their regular rate. The holiday pay was not originally intended to be an offset against overtime pay earned under other provisions of the agreement. If this arbitrator had been presented with the question at the time it was presented to the State Board, he would have so ruled. He is at a loss to understand the State Board's decision, especially since it was not accompanied by an opinion or explanation of any kind.

The Union argued that the State Board's decision is not binding on this arbitrator and he is free to rule on his own understanding of the merits. With this thesis the arbitrator is in general agreement. He would be loath, when passing on the same question under the identical contract language, to arrive at a different conclusion when there is any ground at all for arriving at the same conclusion, because of the unstabilizing effect of different interpretations on the parties' day-to-day administration of their agreement. However, if he could find no justification for the prior decision in logic or equity, he would not abdicate to his predecessor that function of judgment for which he was engaged. Hence the existence of the State Board decision *alone* does not serve to deter this arbitrator from answering the question at issue in the affirmative.

What does deter him in this particular case is the conduct of the parties in their negotiations since the date of the State Board award. When the parties negotiated their current agreement they were fully aware of the interpretation that had become attached to Article IV, Sections 1 and 11 by virtue of the prior award. For a while they contemplated, and actually tentatively agreed to, a substitute clause which would set aside the interpretation contained in the State Board award. But in the give and take of bargaining, and in exchange for other benefits, the Union withdrew its demand for a revised Article IV, Section 1 and agreed to the very clause that had previously been interpreted by the State Board to the disadvantage of the Union. The Union and the Companies knew that the interpretation advanced by the State Board remained attached to the prior Article IV, Sections 1 and 11. Nevertheless, it agreed to continue to live with that interpretation because in exchange it secured an important concession in the matter of production schedules. It clearly agreed to live with this disadvantage in return for an advantage in another respect. This is the bargain it made. This arbitrator would under the circumstances be making a basic change in the nature of the parties' bargain were he now to give the disputed provisions an interpretation the parties both knew was not attached to them at the time they concluded their bargaining.

The arbitrator is aware that the disputed clauses were agreed to only after a long and exhausting strike and that they may have been the product of a less than perfect justice. But in the imperfect state of things, labor agreements are compounded not only of sweet reason but also relative strength and staying power. The outcome of the struggle was the agreement in controversy in this case. The Union, whether out of conviction or not, yielded on its demand to change Article IV, Section 1 in return for another benefit. The arbitrator may not alter the fundamental character of the parties' bargaining, a result that would follow, under all of the circumstances of this case, if he answered the question at issue in the affirmative.

NOTES

1. Arbitrator Wallen's clearly expressed intimation that in the absence of the extraordinary circumstances presented in the Gorton-Pew case he would feel free to disregard prior awards was demonstrated in his decision in In re General Electric Company and United Electrical, Radio and Machine Workers of America, CIO, 9 L.A. 757 (1948), by the following language: ". . . the doctrine of stare decisis has a limited application in the field of labor arbitration. Decisions of other arbitrators have value as indications of the thinking of others on the same subject. The following of precedent in arbitration rests upon the assumption that the precedent has a sound and continuing validity. But where a conflict in decisions results from a clear and supported conviction that the earlier decision does not reasonably resolve the issue, a given arbitrator need not abdicate to his predecessor that function of

judgment for which he was engaged." This language was quoted with approval and followed in In re North American Aviation, Inc., 15 L.A. 626 (1950), where it was stated that "it is well established that the doctrine of stare decisis in labor arbitrations has only a limited application. It is true that it is desirable and conducive to good labor relations for decisions to have precedent value. This avoids an unnecessary multiplicity of disputes. But there are circumstances where precedent should not be followed." See also Roberts Numbering Machine Company and United Electrical Workers (CIO), Local 1217, 9 L.A. 861 (1948); McPherson, Should Labor Arbitrators Play Follow the Leader? 4 Arb. J. (N.S.) 163 (1949); a symposium, Precedents in Labor Arbitration, 1949, Wash. U.L.Q. 71 (1949); Gray, Some Thoughts on the Use of Precedents in Labor Arbitration, 6 Arb. J. (N.S.) 135 (1951).

2. In the case of Pan American Refining Corporation and Oil Workers International Union (CIO), Local No. 449, 9 L.A. 731 (1948), Arbitrator McCoy, after expressing himself as being in fact sympathetic to a Union claim for reclassification of certain employees from "helpers" to "painters," denied the claim on the following ground:

> However, the matter is not one of first impression: the precise question was presented by this Company and Union, under identical contract provisions and job descriptions, to another arbitrator and was decided adversely to the Union's contention. Matter of Pan American Refining Corporation and Oil Workers International Union, Local 449, 4 L.A. 773, decided September 2, 1946. That decision, based upon a finding that the parties had agreed upon a consolidation of the duties of helper and 3rd class painter, held that when a helper applies a priming coat he is not performing painter's work within the meaning of the contract clause in question, but is performing helper's work. It thus construed that contract clause as not covering facts in all respects identical with the facts before me. This raises the question as to how far one arbitrator's decision should be binding upon another.
>
> Of course it should not be binding at all when another company and union are involved, but should be at most merely persuasive, entitled to as much weight as, but no more than, its inherent logic, common sense, and reasonableness dictate. Where the prior decision involves the same company and union but is essentially a decision on facts rather than on the interpretation of a contract clause, it is entitled to no

weight whatever under a different set of facts, though general statements of principle may or may not be persuasive. But where, as here, the prior decision involves the interpretation of the identical contract provision, between the same company and union, every principle of common sense, policy, and labor relations demands that it stand until the parties annul it by a newly worded contract provision.

Otherwise, in what position would the parties find themselves? If I should decide to the contrary of the prior decision, which decision would be binding for future cases? Obviously neither, for if Dr. Abernethy's decision is not binding neither is mine. When similar facts arose next week, the Company would refuse to pay, the case would go to arbitration, and a third arbitrator would be called upon to decide the same question because both Abernethy and I would have to refuse to serve if appointed, having already expressed an opinion. So every week or two the parties would find themselves arbitrating the same question, each time with a new arbitrator. Such a situation would be intolerable.

I find that the precise issue before me, having been already decided between these parties adversely to the Union's contention, is not open to a new determination in arbitration, but must be settled, if at all, by agreement of the parties. The questions submitted will therefore be answered in the negative.

3. An agreement between the Merchants' Ladies' Garment Assn. and the Int. Garment Workers, AFL, contains the following clause: "Each case shall be considered on its merits and the collective agreement shall constitute the basis upon which decisions shall be rendered. No decision shall be used as a precedent for any subsequent case."

4. The arbitrator "is not required except by specific agreement of the parties to follow precedent. He should not, however, prevent the parties from presenting the decisions of other arbitrators in support of their positions. When the parties have selected a continuing arbitrator, it is generally recognized that he may establish or follow precedents for the same parties." Quoted from Code of Ethics and Procedural Standards for Labor-Management Arbitration, prepared by the American Arbitration Association and the National Academy of Arbitrators, Part II, Sec. 4 (f), 15 L.A. 961, 964 (1950). See discussion in 6 Arb. J. (N.S.) 6 (1951).

LOCAL 474, NATIONAL FOOD CHAIN STORE EMPLOYEES, CIO v. SAFEWAY STORES, INC.
New York Supreme Court, New York County, 1948
79 N.Y.S.2d 493

[The Company changed the working hours of certain of its employees so that they were required to start at 11:00 A.M. and work until 9:00 P.M. on Fridays, whereas before they worked every day from 8:30 A.M. to 6:30 P.M. The employees filed a grievance asking for overtime pay for the hours between 6:30 P.M. and 9:00 P.M. When this request was denied, the Union sought to take the dispute to arbitration. The Company insisted that it was not arbitrable under the contract terms. The Union then applied to the court for an order to compel arbitration. The contract provided for the arbitration of "any dispute . . . concerning interpretation or application of the terms of this Agreement." The contract contained several references to "normal working hours," but, as the court noted, "the agreement is silent on what the parties intended by . . . [the] use [of this phrase]." The court granted the order, stating, in part, as follows:]

Obviously, if the dispute is not one which, under the agreement properly construed, is arbitrable, the court may not direct the parties to proceed to arbitration (Matter of International Association of Machinists v. Cutler-Hammer, Inc., 271 App. Div. 917 [19 L.R.R.M. 2233], aff'd. 297 N.Y. 519 [20 L.R.R.M. 2445]; Matter of Belding-Hemingway Co., 295 N.Y. 541).

In ascertaining whether a given dispute is one under the contract, it must be borne in mind that from the very nature of things, specific provision cannot be made in a collective agreement for every detail which may arise in the day to day operations under it. If it covers broadly a given field, the mere failure to foresee every possible contingency should not be treated as a purposeful exclusion of the unforeseen contingency from the operation of the agreement and its arbitration machinery.

The underlying purpose to establish peaceful relations is to be balanced against the inherent right of management to regulate its business. Though the respondent employer may have the right to fix the hours during which its stores shall be open for business, it does not follow that under a collective agreement the hours so established necessarily constitute normal working hours for the employees. While the question is not free from doubt, the court inclines to the view that, bearing in mind the purpose and general scope of the collective agreement, it cannot be said that a dispute as to what hours constitute normal working hours must be treated as one not "concerning interpretation or application of the terms of this agreement."

Accordingly, the motion to direct arbitration is granted. Settle order.

NOTE

See also North American Philips Company v. Assn. of Machinists, 103 N.Y. Supp. 520 (Sup. Ct., N.Y. County, 1951), in which the court dismissed an employer's petition to stay arbitration of a dispute concerning the employer's right to assign work normally performed by employees in the bargaining unit to persons outside that unit. The contract in that case provided that "All differences, disputes and grievances that may arise between the Union and the Employer" should be submitted to arbitration if they remained unsettled by negotiation. The court concluded that arbitrability thus broadly stated was not qualified by other provisions of the contract, including a so-called management prerogatives clause as well as a provision that arbitrators "shall have no power to modify or supplement the provisions of this Agreement or to impose any obligations on the parties which are not specifically provided."

The proceedings in the Safeway Stores and North American Philips Company cases both arose under the terms of Article 84 of the New York Civil Practice Act (Secs. 1448–1469) providing for the specific enforcement of agreements to arbitrate controversies, including labor disputes. The scope and application of provisions are discussed in Nordlinger, The Law and Practice of Arbitration in New York, 13 Mo. Lab. Rev. 196 (1948), where the author points out that "A person aggrieved by the failure of the other party to proceed with arbitration as agreed has a choice of two remedies. He may proceed under Sec. 1450 of the Civil Practice Act with a proceeding to compel arbitration. . . . Or the party aggrieved may simply serve a notice of his intention to proceed with the arbitration as agreed (Sec. 1458). In that case, the adverse party must prove (move) within ten days to stay the arbitration, or he is bound by a conclusive presumption that he has agreed to arbitrate. . . . The arbitration must be adjourned pending the determination of the motion for a stay." See also Report of Committee on Arbitration of National Academy of Arbitrators, 16 L.A. 994 (1951).

In re INTERNATIONAL HARVESTER CO., EAST MOLINE WORKS and UNITED FARM EQUIP-MENT WORKERS (CIO), LOCAL NO. 104
9 L.A. 894 (1947)

[The Union request in this case was for payment at the average rate for incentive workers who had been assigned to new jobs without being informed in advance of the assignment, as to the rate for the new job. The contract provided, in Section 10, that "When an employee is assigned to a new and different job he will be informed in advance of the piece-work price, day-work rate, or allowance to be paid for such job." One of the defenses relied on by the Company was that Section 10 established only a "good faith" guide to Company action and that it created no contractual obligation. It was argued, in this same connection, that since the contract included no specific "damages" provision, no damages could be awarded here by the arbitrator. The Company contended that the arbitrator could not grant the request of the Union because to do so would be to "add to the contract" in violation of the clause restricting the arbitrator's jurisdiction. The following excerpt from the opinion of the arbitrator (W. Willard Wirtz) relates to the issues of the obligatory nature of the notice clause and the measure of damages.]

There is similarly no substantial basis for the contention made by the Company that Section 10 establishes only a "good faith" guide to Company action and creates no real contractual obligation. This contention is unsupportable either in terms of general contract construction, as applied to collective bargaining agreements, or in terms of the parties' previous construction of this particular clause. The Company contention is that no "money award" is permissible in these cases because the contract "did not provide a penalty for a violation of (this) section." (C. B. p. 54.) This is similarly true of any number of other provisions in the Agreement, including those in which the Union assumes certain obligations. (See Art. II and Art. X.)

The conclusion that no money arbitration award is proper in the case of violations of contract provisions which do not specifically provide for damages would have two effects. The first would be the substitution of some other method of settlement in the place of arbitration. The second would be the cluttering up of the contract with a lot of "liquidated damage" provisions which would invite more trouble than they could ever be expected to prevent. It will be unfortunate if collective bargaining agreements develop along the lines of the revenue laws, with provision necessarily being made for every little hairline question which may arise between adverse parties pressing conflicting interests.   They will lose their effectiveness when they become so involved that laymen cannot follow or understand them.   It would contribute dangerously to that tendency if it were required that every contract clause had to include a damages provision.   This is the kind of thing which it must be assumed the parties intended would be handled in the light of the applicability of a particular clause to the particular problems that might arise under it.

As far as the application of Section 10 itself is concerned, the Company's contention regarding its unenforceability is weakened by two specific considerations.   The first of these is that the parties have themselves, in their past practice, taken a very different view of the matter from that which is advanced here.   Section 10 was taken over in the 1946 Agreement, without change, from the previous contract.   The Union introduced several other grievance records which showed a disposition of Section 10 issues by payment of what Company counsel identifies here as "money damages."   Some of these cases arose under the 1942 contract. Two of them arose and were settled under the 1946 Agreement here in question and *after the four grievances presented here had been processed.*   Counsel for the Company explained these other grievances as being atypical and as representing nothing more than instances of Management's willingness to make payments over and beyond those required of it.   No evidence whatsoever is presented, however, of a single instance wherein any different settlement was made.   There is greater support for the Union contention that the cases presented here are the ones which represent possible departures from the norm.

The other point of significance here is that the Company position as to non-enforceability was presented for the first time at the arbitration hearing and is, furthermore, inconsistent with the position which is implicit in the Company's answer at the earlier steps in the handling of some of these particular grievances.

Thus in the second step answer in Grievance No. 588 A, the Company denial of the grievance request is expressed solely in terms of the fact that notice was given before the end of the shift. The statement is made that "we understand that *it is our obligation* to notify the operator within the working hours of the shift." The phrase which has here been italicized suggests that the Company did not, prior to the arbitration hearing, deny *any* obligation but that it has, in these grievances, contested only the time as of which its obligation is created. The possibility of construing this language as referring to some merely moral obligation is removed by additional language which appears in the Company's answer in Grievance No. 633 A. Here it is stated that the fact of notification before the end of the shift is what supports the contention that "no *penalty payment* is to be made."

It is clear in the light of the practice of the parties in other similar cases and in their handling of these particular cases, as well as against the background of broader principles of contract construction, that Section 10 creates a contractual obligation and is not simply a testimonial of good faith and intentions.

These cases present two further questions, both involving what lawyers refer to as the "measure of damages." There is first the question of whether the employees involved in these cases are entitled to reparation on the basis of a showing that Section 10 was violated, or whether it must also be shown that this violation was actually the cause of an impairment in their earnings. The Union's proof in these cases is limited to a description of the general types of injury which *may* result from a lack of the required notice. The theory upon which recovery is sought is that Section 10 requires no showing of specific injury and that the interests involved are such that they will be prejudiced unless it is *uniformly* adhered to.

It is not shown in any of the four cases that the failure to supply the requisite information actually caused an impairment of the particular operator's earnings. The related question is as to whether the average piecework earning rate is the proper basis for computing the reparation payment which is due if the requisite degree of damage is shown.

These questions would present real difficulty if they were presented as novel issues. They are not so presented. They have arisen before and have been dealt with by the parties themselves under both this 1946 Agreement and the 1942 contract. The record of those other settlements shows affirmatively in each case (a) that the fact of undue delay in supplying the price information was itself considered by both parties to be the controlling factor, and (b) that where there was this delay, the operator involved received average earnings payments for the time covered by the delay. The Company implied at the hearing that there may have been other facts in those cases. If so, they should have been pointed out, for a careful scrutiny of the record does not reveal them.

There is a strong insistence by the Company in this group of cases, that an award upholding the "damages" claims presented would constitute an assumption by the Arbitrator of an authority not given him by the contract. It would much more accurately be said that a decision by the Arbitrator to substitute his own rule of "damages" for that adopted by the parties would, in the absence of any contract basis, constitute a violation of his carefully prescribed duties. Counsel for the Company himself expressed the view that the question presented here should be considered in the light of "the construction of [the contract provisions] by the parties over the period of years." If a new rule regarding this point was to have been established it should have been done at the time the parties had before them the question of whether or not to include Section 10 in the new contract in its old form.

NOTE

What was the arbitrator's ultimate disposition of the point involving the Company's failure to raise the defense of nonenforceability during the prearbitration steps of the controversy? Did he conclude that the contract created an obligation, thereby overruling the defense on its merits? Did he conclude that custom or usage under the contractual provision implied an obligation? Did he conclude that the Company's failure to raise the defense at a prior stage constituted a waiver? What should be the rule in such cases?

WESTERN UNION TEL. CO. v. AMERICAN COMMUNICATIONS ASSN., CIO
Court of Appeals, New York, 1949
299 N.Y. 177, 86 N.E.2d 162

[The Company suspended certain employees because of their refusal to handle telegraph traffic transmitted to Western Union by nonstriking employees of four international telegraph companies whose other employees were on strike. The Union demanded the reinstatement of the suspended employees, and the case eventually went to arbitration. The arbitrator ordered the employees reinstated, with back pay. The basis of his award was stated as being that there is a tradition in the telegraph industry of refusing to handle "hot traffic" and that the no-strike clause in the contract (upon which the Company had relied) had to be interpreted in the light of that practice. The Company refused to comply with the award. The Union then sought a court order confirming this award.   This order was granted by Justice Pecora at Special Term, with the statement that "it is to be expected that the impartial chairman named in the contract will render decisions in conformity with the practices of the industry and not act in total disregard of them by making literal interpretations of the text."   The Appellate Division reversed this decision, setting aside the order.   274 App. Div. 754, 79 N.Y.S.2d 545.   The case was then appealed to the Court of Appeals.]

LEWIS, J. . . . In view of the clearly expressed agreement by the parties that in the event of their disagreement with respect to the interpretation of their contract an arbitrator shall have no authority to modify its express provisions, and in view of the express provision in section 31 of the contract that "there shall be no strikes or other stoppages of work during the life of this contract," the award before us, as we view it, amply demonstrates that the arbitrator exceeded the power granted to him.   Civil Practice Act, Section 1462, subd. 4.

Where, as in the contract which the arbitrator was here called upon to interpret, "the language is unambiguous, the words plain and clear, conveying a distinct idea, there is no occasion to resort to other means of interpretation.   Effect must be given to the intent as indicated by the language employed."   Settle v. Van Evrea, 49 N.Y. 280, 281.   Upon that subject this court has said that "Evidence of custom is permitted for the purpose of qualifying the meaning of a contract *where otherwise ambiguous* and of providing for incidents not in contradiction of the fundamental provisions of the contract and of supplying omissions under certain circumstances which have occurred in agreement of the parties.   Evidence of it is not permitted for the purpose of contradicting the agreements which the parties have made or for the purpose of accomplishing an unfair or immoral construction of their contract."   Emphasis supplied.   [Citing cases.]   That no provision in section 31 of the contract impressed the arbitrator as ambiguous is indicated by his statement — "If we were to construe that language in vacuo we might well find that the Union's direction to the employees not to handle 'hot traffic' violated the letter if not the spirit of the clause."   Although the record is clear that "stoppages of work" did result from refusal by employees of Western Union's landlines division to handle "hot traffic," the arbitrator found that such refusal conformed to a practice generally prevalent in the telegraph industry.   Thereupon, despite his own disclaimer of ambiguity in the contract, he concluded that "the language of Section 31 must be read in the light of this practice and that so read it does not prohibit the Union from directing employees not to handle 'hot traffic' or the employees from following such directions."

By that conclusion, as we view it, the arbitrator — entering a field of decision from which the parties had expressly excluded him — modified an express provision of the contract by which the union had agreed that "there shall be no . . . stoppages of work during the life of this contract." As the language employed to express the Union's agreement leaves no doubt as to its meaning "there is no occasion to resort to other means of interpretation." [Citing cases.]

We know of no case where a court, in construing a contractual obligation expressed in language as clear as is the clause here in controversy, has found it necessary to employ extrinsic means to ascertain a party's obligation thereunder. The lack of such authority may well be due to the early rule in Collender v. Dinsmore, 55 N.Y. 200, 208–209, 14 Am. Rep. 224: "Custom and usage is resorted to only to ascertain and explain the meaning and intention of the parties to a contract when the same could not be ascertained without extrinsic evidence, but never to contravene the express stipulations; and if there is no uncertainty as to the terms of the contract, usage cannot be proved to contradict or qualify its provisions. . . . Usage is sometimes admissible to add to or explain, but never to vary or contradict, either expressly or by implication, the terms of a written instrument, or the fair and legal import of a contract."

The modification of the contract here accomplished, being, as we believe, in excess of the arbitrator's authority as limited by the parties, serves to vitiate the award. Civil Practice Act, Section 1462, subd. 4. . . .

[The Court went on to hold that the suspended employees' refusal to handle the messages was in violation of certain provisions of the Penal Law, particularly Sections 552 and 1423, Consol. Laws, c. 40.]

The order should be affirmed, with costs.

DESMOND, Judge (dissenting). These parties agreed (Section 6, subd. [a]) to send to the named arbitrator for determination, all disputes "with respect to the application or interpretation of this contract." A dispute arose between them as to the application or meaning of so much of Section 31 of the agreement as provided that "there shall be no strikes or other stoppages of work during the life of this contract." The union, in connection with a strike called by another union, had refused to handle "struck traffic." The arbitrator, after hearings, held that, in view of the tradition and customs of the industry, which he felt he could not ignore and in the light of which the language "stoppages of work" had to be construed, the phrase did not prohibit employees refusing to handle "hot" or "struck" messages. That was a pure question of interpretation and application, and the very kind of question which the parties themselves had agreed should be decided by the arbitrator alone. Accordingly, his decision must stand. Matter of Wenger & Co. v. Propper Silk Hosiery Mills, 239 N.Y. 199, 202, 146 N.E. 203. Whether we consider the decisions to be "right" or "wrong" is beside the point. "The courts in this State have adhered with great steadiness in the general rule that awards will not be opened for errors of law or fact on the part of the arbitrator." Fudickar v. Guardian Mut. Life Ins. Co., 62 N.Y. 392, 400. "The conclusiveness of awards is based upon the principle that, the parties having chosen judges of their own and agreed to abide by their decision, they are bound by their agreement and compelled to perform the award." [Citing cases.] "It is the duty of the court to enforce their agreement rather than to undertake itself to settle the dispute or to narrow the field of arbitral disputes." Matter of Wenger & Co. v. Propper Silk Hosiery Mills, supra, 239 N.Y. at page 202, 146 N.E. at page 204. . . .

The order of the Appellate Division should be reversed and the order of Special Term affirmed, with costs in this court and in the Appellate Division.

CONWAY, DYE and BROMLEY, JJ., concur with LEWIS, J.

DESMOND, J., dissents in opinion in which LOUGHRAN, C.J., and FULD, J., concur.

Order affirmed.

NOTES

1. Compare with the Western Union case, Motor Haulage Co. v. International Brotherhood of Teamsters, Local 807, 272 App. Div. 382, 71 N.Y.S.2d 352 (1st Dept. 1947). In that case the arbitrator awarded damages to the Company for losses resulting from a strike. The strike was apparently not authorized by the Union. The no-strike clause in the contract provided that "No strikes, lockouts or walkouts shall be ordered or enforced by either party. . . ." The arbitrator apparently suspected, however, that there had been at least tacit approval of the strike by the Union. He concluded that the Union officials at least shared some respon-

sibility for its continuance, and noted that denying the Company's claim would mean that it "would be without remedy of any kind because he could not prove that the Union, as such, had 'ordered or sanctioned' the walkout." The Company filed a motion before the court at Special Term to have the award in its favor confirmed. Justice Eder denied this motion, finding that the arbitrator's statements were "inconsistent . . . and contrary to the facts as reported by the arbitrator." 189 Misc. 152, 69 N.Y.S.2d 656 (Sup. Ct., Special Term, N.Y. County, Part I, 1947) (reversed and remitted for further proceedings on the ground that judgments may not be entered against an unincorporated association in its proper name in New York, 298 N.Y. 208, 81 N.E.2d 91 (1948)). The Appellate Division reversed this ruling and granted the motion to confirm the award, stating, per curiam:

> The award of an arbitrator cannot be set aside for mere errors of judgment either as to the law or as to the facts. If he keeps within his jurisdiction, and is not guilty of fraud corruption, or other misconduct affecting his award, it is unassailable, operates as a final and conclusive judgment, and, however disappointing it may be, the parties must abide by it. Matter of Wilkins, 169 N.Y. 494, 496, 62 N.E. 575; see also Matter of Delma Eng. Corp. (Johnson Contr. Corp.), 267 App. Div. 410, 45 N.Y.S. (2d) 913, affirmed 293 N.Y. 653, 56 N.E. (2d) 253.
>
> By their contract the parties here agreed to submit to arbitration any dispute arising between them "concerning the application or interpretation of any provision of this agreement or concerning any term or condition of employment, or otherwise." It was further stipulated that the decision of the arbitrator "shall be final and binding upon the parties hereto."
>
> Notwithstanding this agreement and the aforementioned well settled principle of law, the court at Special Term not only inquired into the facts, but has reviewed the law and denied the motion to confirm the award of the arbitrator on its independent determination of the facts and the law. The court, in the circumstances, was not warranted in interfering with the arbitrator's award.

Compare with this result in the Motor Haulage Co. case, the holding in the United Elastic Co. case, discussed at page 271 supra.

2. In Stein v. Local 680, Milk Drivers and Dairy Employees of New Jersey, 141 N.J. Eq. 226, 56 A.2d 715 (1948), it was held that

where an arbitrator proceeds with hearings in the face of an injunction restraining such proceedings, the award which he renders will not be enforced.

UTILITY WORKERS UNION OF AMERICA (CIO), LOCAL NO. 116 v. OHIO POWER CO.
Court of Common Pleas, Ohio, Tuscarawas County, 1947
49 Ohio Abs. 619, 77 N.E.2d 629, 36 Ohio Op. 324

LAMNECK, J.: The plaintiff union in this case asks the court to decree specific performance of the arbitration provisions in a labor agreement between the plaintiff union and the defendant corporation by mandatory injunction.

According to Article III, Section b of the agreement attached to the petition, it is provided in substance that any grievance, difference or dispute that may arise between the parties under the agreement which is not satisfactorily adjusted and settled according to other provisions of the agreement shall be submitted to three arbitrators, one appointed by the union, a second by the employer, and a third by the director of conciliation of the United States Department of Labor. It is also provided in the agreement attached to the petition that a decision of a majority of the arbitrators shall be binding upon both parties to the agreement.

The plaintiff union contends that a wage dispute exists between the parties and that the defendant corporation, after demand therefor, refuses to take steps to arbitrate said dispute.

The matter is now before the court on the defendant corporation's demurrer in which it contends that the petition does not state a cause of action. It is the contention of the defendant corporation that an agreement to arbitrate a labor dispute can not be specifically enforced under the statutes of this state.

In the absence of a statute requiring the specific performance of a contract to arbitrate, it is generally held throughout the various jurisdictions in this country that an agreement to arbitrate either an existing or a possible future dispute, while not illegal, will not be specifically enforced, prior to the making of an award. [Citations omitted.]

Among the reasons given by the courts for refusing to specifically enforce arbitration agreements under the common law were the following:

(1) That the arbitrators at common law had no authority to administer oaths or to compel the attendance of witnesses or the production of books, documents or papers.

(2) That under the common law contracts to arbitrate could always be revoked by a party prior to the making of an award. [Citing case.]

(3) That the court could not compel the arbitrators to make an award.   [Citing case.]

In Ohio, prior to the enactment of the present arbitration statutes, and in cases exempted from the provision of the present act since the enactment thereof, the courts have consistently held that agreements to arbitrate will not be specifically enforced before the making of an award, nor will the arbitrators be compelled to act. . . .

Because the courts would or could not decree specific enforcement of arbitration agreements before the making of an award, many states in the Union have enacted arbitration statutes authorizing the specific enforcement of arbitration agreements.

Some of the states have passed in substance the "Draft State Arbitration Act" sponsored by the American Arbitration Association which provides three stringent methods of enforcing both submissions and clauses:

(1) Direct enforcement of arbitration agreements by an order compelling arbitration.

(2) Indirect enforcement by an order staying any action brought in violation of an arbitration agreement.

(3) Collateral enforcement by an order appointing arbitrators empowered to proceed with the arbitration.

Under such statutes, in the absence of exceptions, labor disputes arising under a labor agreement providing for the submission of disputes to arbitration are within their terms, and specific performance will be decreed.   (Williston on Contracts, Section 1930.)

Following the lead of a number of other states, Ohio repealed its former arbitration laws originally enacted in 1831, Sections 12148 to 12160 inclusive of the General Code, and enacted most of the provisions of the "Draft State Arbitration Act." The present arbitration act, Sections 12148–1 to 12148–17 General Code of Ohio, became effective July 28, 1931, and is known as "The Ohio Arbitration Act." Under this act, for agreements coming within its provisions, the court can decree specific performance of an arbitration agreement by mandatory injunction because it is specifically provided under Section 12148–3 General Code of Ohio that if "there is a default in proceeding thereunder, the court shall make an order summarily directing the parties to proceed with the arbitration in accordance with the terms thereof."

(American Laundry Machinery Co. v. Prosperity Co., Inc., 27 O.O. 393; Gilbert v. Burnside, 255 N.Y. 348.)

If there were no exceptions of certain arbitration agreements in the Ohio Act, the court would overrule the defendant's demurrer, because the court is of the opinion that the petition would then state a cause of action.   [Citing case.]

However, Section 12148–1 of the General Code of Ohio specifically provides:

"The provisions of this act shall not apply to (a) collective or individual contracts between employers and employees in respect to terms or conditions of employment."

Consequently, the Ohio Arbitration Act excludes labor arbitration agreements from its provisions.

Under Sections 871–12, 871–22, and Sections 1063 to 1074, inclusive, of the General Code, either a group of employees or an employer, or both, may voluntarily submit an existing controversy or difference between them which may not involve an action or proceeding in court to the Industrial Commission of Ohio which is authorized to hold a hearing and make a finding.   However, the finding of the Commission is unenforceable unless the parties make a joint application to the Commission which contains a stipulation that the decision of the Industrial Commission under it shall be binding upon the parties.   Then and in that event, the decision of the Industrial Commission may be enforced in the Common Pleas Court.   (Section 1066, General Code.)

These statutes, however, have no application to an agreement between a labor union and an employer providing for the submission of a future dispute to a Board of three arbitrators.

The plaintiffs contend that they have no adequate remedy at law, and in a sense this contention may be partially correct, because only nominal damages could be awarded in an action at law under the facts alleged in the petition.   In 47 L.R.A. (N.S.) 410, the rule is stated thus:

"Damages recoverable in such action are merely nominal where nothing has been done to carry out the agreement beyond a request by one party and a refusal by the other to submit a controversy, afterward made the ground of an action at law."

If an employer arbitrarily refuses to proceed to take any action in a dispute with its employees arising under a labor agreement to arbitrate under the provisions of the agreement, it may be that the employees would be entitled to revoke the entire agreement.   In Insurance Co. v. Appel, 76 Ohio St. 1, 80 N.E. 952, the court held that when one of the parties to an arbitration acts in bad faith, or, which is tantamount thereto, unreasonably refuses to carry out the agreement, the other party is absolved from compliance therewith.

The court is not adverse to accepting the view that all valid contracts made by mature men should be specifically enforced; that pretexts should not be resorted to, to evade them; and that where no argument exists based on reason and justice or common morality for avoiding a valid agreement, compulsory performance of such agreements should be decreed. Yet no court can contravene positive legislative enactments, or ignore the pronouncements of its superior courts. No court is free to disregard the law because the Judge may think that the law should be otherwise. If the situation in Ohio relative to the specific enforcement of arbitration provisions in labor agreements is not what it should be, the remedy lies with the legislature and not in the court.

The court is of the opinion that under the present Ohio law a contract between a [company and a] labor union which provides that disputes as to wages and conditions of labor shall be submitted to arbitration is not invalid in this state, but since there is no statute in Ohio authorizing a court to decree specific performance of a labor arbitration agreement, and as an arbitration agreement is not specifically enforceable prior to the making of an award under the common law, the court is without authority to entertain the plaintiff's petition.

For the reasons given herein, it follows that the court must and does sustain the defendant's demurrer. Exception will be noted.[123]

NOTES

1. The Ohio Power case reflects the generally prevailing rule of the common law that agreements to arbitrate are not enforceable. The principle has been modified by legislation in many states, but the lack of uniformity is astonishing. Most statutes provide only for the enforcement of an agreement to arbitrate an existing, specific dispute, rather than agreements for the arbitration of all future disputes between the parties. Some are restricted to commercial arbitration, one applies solely to labor agreements, and the others make no distinction between the types of contracts involved. Local statutory provisions should be consulted and studied carefully. See Gregory and Orlikoff, The Enforcement of Labor Arbitration Agreements, 17 U. of Chi. L. Rev. 233 (1950);

[123] This case is commented on in 9 Ohio St. L.J. 329 (1948). See also, Local 1111, United Electrical Workers v. Allen-Bradley Co., 259 Wis. 609, 49 N.W.2d 720, 17 L.A. 429 (1951), turning on a local statute. — ED.

Updegraff and McCoy, Arbitration of Labor Disputes, c. VII (1946) ; Comment, 43 Ill. L. Rev. 678 (1948) .

The Federal Arbitration Act [124] provides that arbitration provisions of contracts involving "commerce . . . shall be valid, irrevocable and enforceable." [125]   The term "commerce" is defined to include "commerce among the several states" to which is appended the proviso that "nothing herein contained shall apply to contracts of employment." [126]   Section 3 provides for the stay of proceedings in any suits brought in federal courts which involve issues referable to arbitration, pending their submission to the arbitration process; and Section 4 authorizes the specific enforcement of agreements to arbitrate.   The Supreme Court has never passed upon the question whether the provisions of this Act apply to collective bargaining agreements, and the decisions of the circuit courts of appeals have not been consistent.   The Fourth [127] and Sixth [128] Circuits have held that such agreements are "contracts of employment" and thus exempted from the Act's coverage.   The Third Circuit, which was the first to pass upon the point, held in 1943 that the Act did apply to collective contracts, and directed the stay of litigation pending arbitration of the issue involved under the terms of the contract.[129]   This decision was approved and followed by the same court in 1945.[130]   Both of these cases were suits by employees to recover unpaid overtime compensation alleged to be due to them under the provisions of the Fair Labor Standards Act, which applies to employees engaged in the production of goods for interstate commerce.   In both cases the plaintiffs were coal miners employed by firms which had signed agreements with the United Mineworkers, containing provisions for the arbitration of all claims arising under them.   In 1951, however, it reversed these earlier cases in a suit brought by a union to compel the submission of a dispute to arbitration pursuant to a collective agreement, thereby aligning itself with the rule established in the Fourth and Sixth Circuits.[131]   The reason which the court assigned for the change was the 1947 Act of Congress, which, without

[124] 9 U.S.C.A. Sec. 1 et seq.
[125] Section 2.
[126] Section 1.
[127] Int. Union United Furniture Workers v. Colonial Hardwood Flooring Co., 168 F.2d 33 (4th Cir. 1948) ; cf. Agostini Bros. Bldg. Co. v. United States, 142 F.2d 854 (4th Cir. 1944) .
[128] Gatliff Coal Co. v. Cox, 142 F.2d 876 (6th Cir. 1944) .
[129] Donahue v. Susquehanna Collieries Co., 138 F.2d 3 (3d Cir. 1943) .
[130] Watkins v. Hudson Coal Co., 151 F.2d 311 (3d Cir. 1945) .
[131] Motor Coach Employees v. Greyhound Lines, 192 F.2d 310, 17 L.A. 372 (3d Cir. 1951) .

changing the prior wording of the 1925 law, was designed to enact it as positive law into the United States Code.   In the course of this re-enactment the compilers of the Code had taken the former catchline which followed the enacting clause of the old Act and set it out as Section 1 of the present Act.   There was no mention of the case of Evans v. Hudson Coal Co.,[132] decided in 1948, after the adoption of the 1947 legislation, in which the court continued to follow its earlier view of the matter.   The Second Circuit has not passed on the point, but the District Court for the Southern District of New York has held the Act applicable to collective bargaining agreements.[133]   See also Gregory and Orlikoff, supra at 259 et seq.; Kaye and Allen, The U.S. Arbitration Act and Collective Bargaining Agreements, 4 Arb. J. (N.S.) 41 (1949) ; Note, 28 N.C.L. Rev. 225 (1950).

2. Could the Union in the Ohio Power case avoid the common law principle applied there by involving the jurisdiction of the federal courts under the provisions of Section 301 (a) of the Labor Management Relations Act of 1947?   See AFL v. Western Union Tel. Co., 179 F.2d 535 (6th Cir. 1950), and Textile Workers Union, etc. v. Aleo Mfg. Co., 94 F. Supp. 626, 27 L.R.R.M. 2164 (M.D.N.C., 1950).

3. Would the Ohio Power Company be guilty of a refusal to bargain under Section 8 (a) (5)?   See Timken Roller Bearing Co. v. NLRB, 161 F.2d 949 (6th Cir. 1947), and United Elastic Corp., 85 N.L.R.B. 768, 24 L.R.R.M. 1294 (1949).   (See page 271 supra, Note 4.)

4. Even though, according to the principal case, no judicial remedy is available for a refusal to arbitrate, will the courts deny other judicial remedies on the ground that the claim should have been processed through the grievance procedure?   Thus, an employee sues for wrongful discharge in violation of the collective agreement.   Should his complaint be dismissed and he be told to file a grievance?   Ott v. Metropolitan Jockey Club, 107 N.Y.S.2d 854, 17 L.A. 276 (Sup. Ct., Special Term, Queen's County, Part I, 1951).[134]

[132] Evans v. Hudson Coal Co., 165 F.2d 970 (3d Cir. 1948).

[133] Lewittes & Sons v. United Furniture Workers of America, 95 F. Supp. 851, 27 L.R.R.M. 2490 (S.D.N.Y. 1951); cf. Shirley-Herman Co. v. Int. Hod Carriers, etc., 182 F.2d 806 (2d Cir. 1951).

[134] Although not referred to in the case, the New York Arbitration Statute provides for the staying of any action "brought upon any issue otherwise referable to arbitration under any contract . . . until such arbitration has been had . . ." (C.P.A., Sec. 1451).   See also Mencher v. B. & S. Abeles & Kahn, 274 App. Div. 585, 84 N.Y.S.2d 718, 11 L.A. 954 (1st Dept. 1948); Ilgenfritz v. Westinghouse Elec. Corp., — Pa —, 16 L.A. 486 (C.P. Pa. 1951);

In non-labor cases, the courts have prevailingly favored the granting of a declaratory judgment despite existing alternative remedies. Borchard, Declaratory Judgments 331 (2d ed. 1941); 172 A.L.R. Anno. 847 (1948). But in the case of application for a declaration of rights under a collective agreement having an appropriate grievance procedure not as yet resorted to, there are certain policy factors that may well lead to a different result: (1) the parties have expressly agreed to settlement through the grievance procedure and (2) the arbitration proceeding there provided for has become generally recognized by both labor and management as a more suitable forum for dealing with this type of dispute than courts of law. There are but few decisions, but a declaratory judgment on the merits has been denied in Northland Greyhound Lines, Inc. v. Amalgamated, etc. Employees of America, 66 F. Supp. 431, 18 L.R.R.M. 2205 (D. Minn. 1946), and the requirement of prior exhaustion of administrative remedies has been upheld where an order of a Regional War Labor Board to use the existing grievance procedure had not yet been carried out. Worthington Pump & Mach. Corp. v. Local 259, U.E., 63 F. Supp. 411, 17 L.R.R.M. 608 (D. Mass. 1945).

The issue of arbitrability, not ordinarily expressly covered in a collective agreement, does not raise policy considerations of the same order. Possibly a court will issue a judgment declaring the issue arbitrable,[135] in which case it should direct recourse to the grievance procedure,[136] or nonarbitrable, in which case it might proceed to dismiss the proceeding if petitioner had by his own laches lost his right to arbitration, or to dispose of the issue on the merits in case it were the type to which the arbitration provisions of the contract did not apply.

f. The Enforceability of Arbitration Awards

If arbitration is to bring about orderly and peaceable settlement of disputes without resort to the economic weapons of the strike and the lockout, it is obviously essential that the parties accept

---

In re Atlantic Basin Iron Works, 16 L.A. 51 (N.Y. Sup. Ct. 1951); In re Julius Wile Sons & Co., 102 N.Y.S.2d 862, 16 L.A. 88 (Sup. Ct., Special Term, N.Y. County, Part I, 1951).

[135] The court in Local 1111, UE v. Allen-Bradley, 259 Wis. 609, 49 N.W.2d 720 (1951), declared plaintiff's grievance subject to arbitration, but because of a local statute, refused to require it to be arbitrated.

[136] United Office, etc. Workers of America, CIO v. Monumental Life Ins. Co., 88 F. Supp. 602 (E.D. Pa. 1950). But see Key v. Breece Lumber Co., 45 N.M. 397, 115 P.2d 622 (1941).

and comply with the awards which are made in the proceedings. The record of voluntary compliance with these awards is almost phenomenal. "For example, during the ten years ending in 1945, over 1,500 cases were heard by the impartial chairman in the full-fashioned hosiery industry, without one case of non-acceptance. In the men's clothing industry in New York, out of 898 cases referred to arbitrators between 1924 and 1936, in only seven was there wilful non-compliance with an arbitrator's decision, and only two went to the courts. Not one of the first 1,616 cases heard by the National Railway Mediation Board went to the courts. Only six of the first 5,000 cases heard by the Railroad Adjustment Board were litigated." Dowell, Judicial Enforcement of Arbitration Awards in Labor Disputes, 3 Rutgers L. Rev. 65 (1949). A later study, more general in character, has disclosed that "In only 51 of the 16,819 arbitrations — 0.3 per cent — in which the respondents participated in the prior two year period did either party refuse to accept the award." Warren and Bernstein, A Profile of Labor Arbitration, 4 Indust. & Lab. Rel. Rev. 200, 217 (1951).

A valid award may be enforced by an action at law or a suit in equity for specific performance where the remedy at law is inadequate, even in those jurisdictions which refuse to compel performance of the executory agreement to arbitrate. The obligation to comply with the award in such cases is regarded as a contractual one, growing out of the submission agreement. See Updegraff and McCoy, Arbitration of Labor Disputes, c. V (1946) and Dowell, supra. In either type of proceeding the defendant may question the validity of the award, or he may bring an action of his own to have the award declared invalid. Validity is usually attacked upon either of two grounds (1) that the arbitrator exceeded his jurisdiction or failed to answer the question submitted (see Lusher v. Jewish Welfare Organizations, 16 L.A. 340 (Cal. Super., Los Angeles County, 1951), and Scoles, Review of Labor Arbitration Awards on Jurisdictional Grounds, 17 U. of Chi. L. Rev. 616 (1950)), or (2) that there was a lack of due process in the proceedings. See Note, Court Review of Arbitration Cases, 19 L.R.R.M. 110, 114–116 (1947).

In many jurisdictions the common law principles just enunciated have been modified or varied by statutory enactments. Local provisions should be consulted.

4. NO-STRIKE-NO-LOCKOUT CLAUSES

a. THE ENDERBY CASE — IX

A

The 1948 contract between the Enderby Rubber Company and Local 417, URCL & PWA (CIO) did not contain a "no-strike-no-lockout" provision. There were no substantial work-stoppages in the plant during that contract year. There were, however, brief "wildcat strikes" in four different departments, three of them lasting only part of a day, the other one for three days. The Union officers cooperated with the Company officials in getting the men back to work on these occasions. There was more question about the Union's position when, during a four-week period, the operators on one of the tennis-shoe lines cut their production rate to about 60 per cent of normal in protest against a change in piecework standards.

The Company insisted, when the contract was reopened in 1949, that the new agreement include a no-strike clause. The Union's first reaction was strongly negative, Curme, the President of the Local, insisting that there was no point in "looking for trouble we haven't had." Curme eventually asked, however, what kind of clause the Company had in mind. White, the Industrial Relations Manager, took a piece of paper and wrote out the following:

> In case there is a strike or work-stoppage or slowdown by any employee or a lockout of any employee by the Company this Agreement shall be null and void.

The vigor of Curme's objection to this proposal was matched only by the eloquence of the frown with which the proposal was greeted by Blair, the Enderby attorney. Quite a lot of talk followed. Curme insisted that "if there is to be any such clause at all, you can't expect the Union to take the rap for what a few hotheads may do if some foreman starts throwing his weight around." Blair finally came up with this proposal:

> The Union agrees that it will not cause, instigate, sanction, authorize or permit any strike, slowdown, stoppage or other interruption of production during the period of this contract; and the Company agrees that, during this same period, there shall be no lockout of any employees.

Curme objected to the word "permit" in this proposed clause, and also said he thought that some of the other phrases were repetition.   After quite a lot more talk, agreement was finally reached on the following clause:

ARTICLE III. NO STRIKE OR LOCKOUT

During the life of this agreement the Union agrees not to call any strike or to instigate any slowdowns or interruptions of production, and the Company agrees that there shall be no lockouts.

B

In December, 1948, there was another slowdown on the tennis-shoe line, again in protest against an allegedly "tight" piecework standard.   One of the operators involved in the slowdown was Gene McDonald, the steward in the department.   White, the Industrial Relations Manager, asked Curme to do what he could as President of Local 417, to get the operators to put their production back up and to persuade them to use the grievance procedure if they had any complaint.   Curme said that there was nothing he could do, mentioning the fact that McDonald had opposed Curme at the last Union election.

McDonald was discharged by the Company "for instigating a slowdown in violation of Article III of the Agreement."   Three days later, the scheduled production on the shoes carrying the disputed piecework standard having been completed, production on the tennis-shoe line went back up to normal.   The Union then filed two grievances, one alleging that McDonald had been discharged without just cause in violation of Section 7 of Article II, the other demanding a readjustment of the disputed piecework rate "in accordance with the provisions of Article XI."

In the discharge case, the Union argued that in Article III in the 1949 contract the Union had agreed not to instigate any slowdown, but that this agreement did not cover the acts of individual employees.   It was finally agreed, at the third step of the grievance procedure, that McDonald would be reinstated (without back pay) but that the matter of "individual breach" would be considered at the time the contract would be again reopened.

The piecework standard grievance went to arbitration.   There was a sharp disagreement at the hearing as to whether the Company should be permitted to introduce testimony regarding the slowdown.   The arbitrator did admit it.   The Company argued that by disregarding the contract no-strike clause and by choosing "self-help" instead of recourse to the grievance procedure the tennis-shoe line operators had sacrificed any rights they might have to a change in the disputed rate. The arbitrator did not expressly rule on this issue, basing his finding instead on an interpretation of Article XI (denying the relief requested).

C

The Company and Union agreed, in the 1950 contract negotiations, to the revised form of Article III which appears at page 321 supra.

D

Two problems arose in the application of Article III in the 1950–1952 agreement.

1. In March, 1951, there was a threatened strike in the toolroom when it developed that the Company was subcontracting to another company some tool-making which the tool-and-die makers in the toolroom felt they could do. Two of the Enderby tool-and-die makers had been laid off for lack of work.

White told Curme that a strike by the other men in the toolroom would be considered a breach of the Article III commitment and that any strikers would be summarily discharged. Dan Cooper, the Local 417 attorney, was called in. He argued that the no-strike agreement was intended only as an adjunct of the grievance procedure, being a commitment not to use "self-help" when a more orderly procedure was available. He asked whether the Company would agree to submit the subcontracting issue to arbitration, without holding the arbitrator to a "contract interpretation" decision. White said, "Certainly not." "Then," Cooper insisted, "you have no right to deny these men their only other method of seeking redress. We're willing to go either route, but you can't deny us both."

White insisted that Cooper's view did not square with the language of Article III. Cooper's reply was that the matter was "not one of contract interpretation alone but of equity and of interpretation of Sections 7 and 8 of the Labor Relations Act."

2. In June, 1951, the Union reopened the contract on the general wage rate issue. The Union demanded a 25-cent general wage increase. (The details of this negotiation are set out in The Enderby Case — XIV, at page 545 infra.) On June 17 the Union advised the Company in writing that the plant would be struck on July 17 if no agreement had been reached by that date. The

negotiators could not get together and on July 17 the plant went down.   It was closed for two weeks.

Shortly after the strike started White asked Blair, the Enderby attorney:

(a) Whether it would be "safe" to notify all employees that they would be discharged if they did not return to work within two days;

(b) Whether the Union officers could be discharged;

(c) Whether arbitration or court proceedings could be instituted to collect damages from the Union "for violating Article III of the contract."

(Editorial note: These three questions can be more fully answered in the light of the materials presented in Part IV infra. They should be considered here only as they present issues of contract application and administration.)

 NOTE

A concomitant of the development of the bilateral settlement of contract grievance disputes has been the very general inclusion in the collective bargaining contracts of agreements by both parties that they will not resort to the alternative of settling these disputes by force.   The prescribed grievance procedure is conceived of as the exclusive method of settlement.   The coverage of the no-strike-no-lockout clause is sometimes broader than that of the grievance procedure in that the agreement is not to strike or lock out for any reason whatsoever, but in general the two types of clauses have a parallel and related purpose and effect.

The two problems which are of primary importance in connection with the drafting of these "no-force" provisions are (a) the degree of responsibility which is to be imposed upon the union for wildcat strikes, and (b) the sanctions which are to be imposed for a breach by either party of its agreement not to use force as a weapon in these cases.   The matter of the applicability of these clauses to strikes over issues other than grievances has also caused difficulty.

This subject of no-force provisions in the collective bargaining agreement is treated at greater length in Part IV of these materials.   As is indicated there, the provisions of Section 8 (d) of the LMRA (see Appendix) take this matter to some extent out of the hands of the parties themselves and make it, at least to some degree, more than a collective bargaining question.   It is accordingly appropriate at this point only to note the contract-drafting problem which is presented in connection with these no-force clauses and to indicate their relationship to the contract provisions for the settlement of certain disputes (grievances) by prescribed, and peaceful, methods. See Daykin, The No-Strike Clause, 11 U. of Pitt. L. Rev. 13 (1949).

The form in which the drafting problem is presented may be briefly illustrated by the development of the no-strike clause in the 1945, 1946 and 1947 contracts between the Chrysler Corporation and the United Automobile Workers (CIO). The 1945 agreement contained the following clause:

> The Union will not cause or permit its members to cause, nor will any member of the Union take part in, any sit-down, stay-in or slow-down in any plant of the Corporation, or any curtailment of work or restriction of production or interference with production of the corporation. The Union will not cause or permit its members to cause nor will any member of the Union take part in any strike or stoppage of any of the Corporation's plants or premises until all the bargaining procedure as outlined in this agreement has been exhausted, and in no case until after the negotiations have continued for at least five days and not even then unless sanctioned by the International Union, United Automobile, Aircraft and Agricultural Implement Workers of America. In case a strike shall occur, either before or after all bargaining procedures have been exhausted, this agreement shall terminate at once. The Corporation reserves the right to discipline any employee taking part in any violation of this section of this agreement. The management will not cause or sanction a lock-out until all the bargaining procedure as outlined in this agreement has been exhausted, and in no case until after the negotiations have continued for at least five days.

The Company had proposed in the 1945 negotiations, but did not succeed in obtaining, the inclusion of the following language as the fourth sentence in the above clause:

> The Corporation reserves the right to discharge or otherwise discipline any employee causing or taking part in any unauthorized strike, and the Union agrees it will not take any step to oppose such discharge or discipline.

In the 1946 agreement, the following provision was added following the fourth sentence:

The Union agrees that it will not oppose the discharge or discipline of anyone who instigates, leads or induces another employee to take part in an unauthorized strike.

In the course of negotiations incident to the renewal of this contract in 1947, the Company proposed the following amendment:

The Corporation reserves the right to discipline any employee taking part in any violation of this section of this agreement. The Union agrees that it will not oppose the discharge or discipline of anyone violating this Section of the Agreement.

This proposal was not accepted and the 1946 clause was left unchanged in the new agreement.

For a case involving the application of this clause, see In re Chrysler Corporation, Chrysler-Kercheval Plant and United Automobile Workers (CIO), Local No. 7, 9 L.A. 789 (1947), and Note, 49 Mich. L. Rev. 142 (1950). See also the check list for such clauses in P–H Lab. Rel. Ser., ¶¶52,641 and 53,391.

A variety of interesting and significant problems develops from the fact that the no-strike clause represents (unlike virtually all of the other provisions in the typical collective bargaining agreement) an affirmative commitment on the part of the union. Virtually all grievance cases have traditionally been instituted by the unions, the allegation being that the company has violated one of the contract provisions. The question arises now as to whether a breach by a union of a no-strike clause is to be taken up by the company as a grievance. There is, similarly, the question of whether a breach of such a clause gives the company a "dependent conditions" defense against a grievance, instituted by the union, which alleges a breach by the company of some other contract provision.

APPLICATION OF METROPOLITAN LIFE INSURANCE COMPANY
Supreme Court, New York, Special Term, New York County, 1949
86 N.Y.S.2d 718, 12 L.A. 107

Proceeding in the matter of the motion of Metropolitan Life Insurance Company for a stay of arbitration demanded by United Office and Professional Workers of America, CIO.

HOFSTADTER, Justice. This application to stay arbitration under a collective bargaining agreement presents a somewhat unusual phase. The proposed arbitration concerns the termination by the petitioner of the employment of one of its agents. The union asserts that the termination was not justified. The agreement provides for arbitration of such a dispute but limits the scope of the arbitration. The applicable clause is:

"In arbitrating such grievance, the arbitrator shall determine only whether or not the facts alleged by the Company, or any other facts presented, justified such action. Should the arbitrator decide that such termination was not justified, the Company shall offer the agent reinstatement. The arbitrator shall have the power to award the payment of back pay in full or in part. If the Agent shall promptly accept such reinstatement, the Company agrees to pay such Agent for the period specified in the Arbitrator's award at a weekly rate equivalent to his average weekly earnings from the Company for the year prior to the termination of his Agreement, or for such period as he may have been employed, if less than a year, less any compensation paid by the Company or any other employer to such Agent while he was not employed by the Company."

The collective agreement also contains a prohibition against strike, demonstration, work stoppage or "any other action the effect of which may be to impede or interfere with the operations of the Company . . . or to incite sympathy or protests concerning the relations between the parties."

In protest against the dismissal of the agent he and others with the sanction of the union picketed, distributed handbills and otherwise demonstrated against the petitioner. The petitioner contends that the foregoing conduct was a breach of the agreement and as a result a waiver by the union of its right to arbitration.

I assume that the picketing and demonstration violated the agreement. If so, it may perhaps seem anomalous that the union which has broken the agreement in protesting against the dismissal should be permitted to invoke the arbitration procedure of the agreement for settlement of the dispute growing out of that very dismissal. The rule, however, is that as long as the agreement has not been terminated arbitration thereunder may be ordered, even though it is claimed that the applicant for arbitration has committed a breach justifying rescission. Matter of Lipman v. Haeuser Shellac Co., 289 N.Y. 76, 43 N.E.2d 817, 142 A.L.R. 1088; Matter of Kahn's Application , (National City Bank) 284 N.Y. 515, 32 N.E.2d 534.

The petitioner insists that because of the restricted nature of the arbitration prescribed in the agreement the foregoing rule is inapplicable to the present situation. It argues that the arbitrator is without power to determine the question of waiver and that the court alone is competent to decide it. Even so, it does not follow that there has been a waiver. The petitioner has not attempted to abrogate the agreement because of the union's breach. Admittedly the parties still are operating under the collective bargaining agreement. I am of the opinion that the union's breach, if such it was, did not forfeit the right to arbitration. There is no claim that the union has persisted in its course. Indeed, by the notice of arbitration the respondent seems to indicate a purpose to retrace its steps and to return to the more orderly method of adjusting grievances established by the agreement. In the circumstances, I do not think that the respondent's conduct was so destructive of the essence of the agreement as irretrievably to take away the right to seek its protection. Lane v. Endicott Johnson Corporation, Sup., 75 N.Y.S.2d 171, 175, 176.

The motion to stay the arbitration is accordingly denied.[137]

NOTES

1. In Colonial Hardwood Flooring Co. v. International Union, United Furniture Workers of America, 76 F. Supp. 493 (D. Md 1948), affirmed, 168 F.2d 33 (4th Cir. 1948), the Company instituted proceedings in the federal court under Sections 301 and 303 of the LMRA to recover damages from the Union (both the Local and International) resulting from a strike. Article 4 (K) of the parties' agreement provided that: "During the life of this agreement, the Company agrees that there shall be no lockouts and the Union agrees that it will not cause or permit its members to cause nor will any member of the Union take part in any strike or stoppage of work. It is understood and agreed that the grievance procedure provided in this Article shall be the only method for settling disputes which are the subject of this agreement." The Union moved to dismiss the complaint on the ground, among others, that the Company should have resorted, under the contract, to arbitration instead of to suit. What would seem to you the proper action upon this motion?

Compare Textile Workers Union of America v. Aleo Mfg. Co., 94 F. Supp. 626, 27 L.R.R.M. 2164 (M.D.N.C. 1950); Lewittes &

[137] Cf. Rice & Holman v. United Electrical, Radio & Machine Workers, etc., 3 N.J. Super. 258, 65 A.2d 638 (1949). — ED.

Sons v. United Furniture Workers, 95 F. Supp. 851, 27 L.R.R.M. 2490 (S.D.N.Y. 1951).

2. Arthur C. Miller, permanent umpire under the contract between the Waterfront Employers Assn. of the Pacific Coast and the International Longshoremen's and Warehousemen's Union, CIO, was asked by both parties on October 7, 1947, to issue rulings regarding the legality, under the contract, of an alleged lockout and an alleged strike which were at that time in progress. He issued rulings on October 7 and October 10, finding that there was a strike and a lockout and that these were both in violation of the contract; he ordered the parties to discontinue them. His opinion, filed subsequently (see 9 L.A. 5 (1947)), contains the following statement:

> The document embodying the contract between the parties does not itself contain an express provision forbidding strikes, lockouts, or other work stoppages. However, contractual obligations to that effect exist by necessary implication from the arbitration provisions. The opening paragraph of the contract incorporates by reference the interpretations of arbitrators in awards rendered under the basic Award of the National Longshoremen's Board of 1934, and the agreements which have been in effect since that time. It is firmly established by a whole series of these Awards that in accepting the arbitration provisions the parties, by necessary implication, have agreed to forego economic action as a means for settling disputes arising during the term of the contract and in lieu thereof have agreed to refer all such disputes for settlement under the grievance procedure before resorting to such action. With exceptions not pertinent to the immediate questions raised by the Union's motion, the contract thus imposes upon the members of both organizations an obligation to refrain from attempts to enforce the contentions of either party in a dispute between them by resort to a work stoppage.

See also Matter of Dorsey Trailers, Inc. 80 N.L.R.B. 478, 23 L.R.R.M. 1112 (1948).

3. Frequently the question may arise whether a particular strike (or lockout) may properly be imputed to the union (or employer) so as to impose liability under the agreement. This is an issue which will be resolved in part by the language of the clause itself. Thus, obviously, a union assumes a far greater risk when it "agrees that during the term of this agreement there shall be no strikes, etc.," than is the case when "the Union agrees that

during the term of this agreement it will not cause or permit or take part in any strike." Upon the basis of the language employed, the issue will then be finally resolved in terms of applicable principles of the law of agency. A comparable problem is encountered by the National Labor Relations Board when it is asked to find that the acts of a particular person are imputable to an employer or a labor organization thereby making it guilty of an unfair labor practice proscribed by Section 8 of the Labor Management Relations Act of 1947. Section 2 (13) of the Act reads: "In determining whether any person is acting as an agent of another person so as to make such other person responsible for his acts, the question of whether the specific acts were actually authorized or subsequently ratified shall not be controlling."

The Board first construed this section in International Longshoremen's Union and Sunset Line and Twine Co., 79 N.L.R.B. 1487, 23 L.R.R.M. 1001 (1948). The following quotations are taken from the decision in that case:

> We have found that, on various occasions described in the foregoing sections of this opinion, certain acts of restraint and coercion, within the purview of Section 8 (b) (1) (A) of the Act, were committed. The actors were Vail and Lynch, officers of Local 6, assisted on some occasions by striking employees of the Company, other members of the Respondent Unions (the Local and the International), regularly detailed pickets and unidentified persons. None of these individuals is named in the complaint as a respondent. . . .
>
> Therefore, the only question before us is whether or not the conduct of these individuals can properly be imputed to one or both of the Respondent Unions, for, unless the record justifies that imputation, there was no violation of the Act in this case. . . .
>
> The Act, as amended, envisages that the Board shall now hold labor organizations responsible for conduct of their agents which is proscribed by Section 8 (b) of the statute, just as it has always held employers responsible for the acts of their agents which were violative of Section 8 (a). For this purpose we are to treat labor organizations as legal entities, like corporations, which act, and can only act, through their duly appointed agents, as distinguished from their individual members. . . .
>
> Because this is a case of first impression in that sense, we shall set forth, in abstract, those fundamental rules of the law

of agency which we believe must control our decision of the
issue of the responsibility in this and similar cases:

1. The burden of proof is on the party asserting an agency
relationship, both as to the existence of the relationship
and as to the nature and extent of the agent's authority.
(Mechem, Outlines of Agency (3d ed.) Secs. 106, 223.)   In
this case, for example, it was incumbent upon the General
Counsel to prove, not only that the acts of restraint and coercion alleged in the complaint were committed, but also that
those acts were committed by agents of the Respondent
Unions, acting in their representative capacity.   The Respondent's failure to introduce evidence *negating* the imputation in the complaint did not relieve the General Counsel
of that burden.

2. Agency is a *contractual relationship* deriving from the
mutual consent of the principal and agent that the agent shall
act for the principal.   But the principal's consent, technically called authorization or ratification, may be manifested
by conduct, sometimes even passive acquiescence as well as
by words. . . .

3. A principal may be responsible for the acts of his agent
within the scope of the agent's general authority, or the
"scope of his employment" if the agent is a servant, even
though the principal has not specifically authorized or indeed
may have specifically forbidden the act in question.   It is
enough if the principal actually empowered the agent to
represent him in the general area within which the agent
acted. . . .

Vail, mentioned above, was the business agent of the Local
and had authority for the lawful carrying out of the strike.   While
doing that, he wrongfully assaulted strikebreakers and instigated
picketers to chase them.   The Union was responsible.   The General Counsel also urged (see id. at 1511 n.49) that the individual
picketers themselves were agents, picketing for the Union and on
its behalf.   The Board did not have to pass upon "the manifold
implications of this argument" because the complaint did not
charge that the individuals had engaged as agents in any unfair
labor practice, nor did it ask any order running against them as
individuals.   Whether they were the Union's agents, therefore,
or mere instrumentalities of Vail, made no difference.

After holding that the Local was liable for the acts of Vail, the
Board turned to a consideration of the International's responsi-

bility. The International's answer did not deny that it, itself, had a direct and immediate interest in the strike. It joined with the Local in pleading certain affirmative defenses (which the Board dismissed) and it nowhere either pleaded, or proved, that the strike was anything other than a joint enterprise of the Local and the International together. A majority of the Board concluded that "this record establishes, . . . that the International was a co-sponsor of the strike in the course of which the lawless acts were committed."

Chairman Herzog and Board Member Houston dissented, on this point alone, on the ground that admissions in the International's answer, plus "surmises as to the probabilities" were all there was to support a finding that the International was responsible for the acts of restraint and coercion committed during the strike by individuals. A party has a privilege of pleading all defenses. Admissions in pleadings cannot serve as substitutes for proof.

In answer to this, the majority had said:

> Of course, if the International had offered evidence to show that it was not a co-sponsor of this strike, the members of the Board majority would not disregard that evidence merely because it conflicted with the allegations of the answer. Like their dissenting colleagues, they think pleadings are relatively unimportant as compared with evidence. The majority's objective is to get at the real facts rather than to serve as referee in a competition of skill between pleaders. Nevertheless, where, as here, there is not a single word in the entire record to contradict a party's clear admissions as to a material fact, made by its counsel in a formal pleading before the Board, the majority believes that it is entirely just to take the pleader at his word. Id. at 1514 n.59.

4. In United States v. Brotherhood of Railroad Trainmen, 96 F. Supp. 428 (N.D. Ill. 1951), the defendant Union was found guilty of civil and criminal contempt of court for violating the terms of an injunction ordering the cessation of strike action. The Union had disclaimed responsibility for the continuation of the work stoppage following the issuance of the injunction and it was shown that abnormally large numbers of employees had reported themselves as being sick. At one point in its opinion the court stated "that as long as a Union is functioning as a Union it must be held responsible for the mass actions of its members. That means this, that when the members go out and

act in a concerted fashion and do an illegal act the Union is responsible."

b. The "Peace Obligation" — A Characteristic Feature of Foreign Collective Contract Law

Characteristic of European labor law is the sharp line drawn between a work stoppage by the workers or lockout by the employer during the term of a collective contract, on the one hand, and economic warfare in the absence of contractual relationships, on the other.

The law of collective contracts in the civil law countries reads into every collective contract an obligation by each party to abstain from economic warfare during the term of the contract (*Friedenspflicht*). The German doctrine has evolved the distinction between a "relative" and an "absolute" obligation. The second exists only if the *Friedenspflicht* is expressly stated in the collective contract; while the "relative" obligation inheres in the nature of the contract, or as one would say in this country, it is an implied term thereof.[138]

In the case of the absolute obligation, it is immaterial whether the objective of the hostile action lies within or without the range of the contract; it is, in any case, deemed to be wrongful. But the implied (relative) obligation is held to be breached only if the hostile action affects a matter covered in the contract. Consequently, if a collective contract, made for a year's duration, leaves the wage question open (for new negotiation) after the expiration of the first four months, a strike after the breakdown of such negotiation would violate an absolute (in case the contract contains an express no-strike clause) but not a relative obligation to maintain peace.[139] One must also bear in mind that, just as in this country, organizations, both companies and unions, are the only parties to the most important contracts over there. Although it is a contract provision,[140] the peace obligation is not itself a term of individual employment. Nevertheless it inures to the benefit of individual members of organizations which are parties to the contract. Thus, Germany's highest court has held that a member

---

[138] Cf. S.P. and K. v. Zentralverein Lederarbeiter, 111 R.G.Z. 105 (1925); R.A.G., 2 Bensh. 194 (1928); R.A.G., 10 id. at 252; Reiner's study in 5 Zeitschrift für Soziales Recht 17, 19 (1933).

[139] 118 R.G.Z. 200 (1927).

[140] See the discussion on the theories of enforceability in foreign law at page 309 supra.

of the employers' organization is entitled to damages against the union as a third party beneficiary.[141]

Breach of the obligation leads to all the consequences of a breach of contract, including liability for damages.[142]   Parties act at the risk of guessing wrong, e.g., as to what is covered by the contract.   Thus the fact that the union believed that the dispute arose upon an issue not covered by the contract (a belief confirmed by a lower court), has been held to be no defense where the highest labor court has found the issue to be the interpretation of the contract.[143]

The French law of 1950 (Labor Code, bk. I, tit. II, c. IV bis, art. 31q) states: "The groups of employees and of employers are during the term of a collective contract under an obligation to abstain from doing anything that might affect the due performance of the contract.   The groups are not guarantors for its performance except as far as the contract determines otherwise."

The Canadian Industrial Relations and Disputes Investigation Act, 1948, sec. 19, imposes upon the parties to a collective contract the duty to include therein a provision securing settlement — without stoppage of work — of disputes concerning its meaning or violation; in the absence of such a provision, the Board is required upon application of either party to the contract, to prescribe such a provision which is then deemed to be a term of the contract.

In countries where the law provides for the extension of the "normative" part of collective contracts to nonmembers, the peace obligation, belonging to the "contractual" part, does not bind them.   However, the Swiss law on extension constitutes an exception; for it also burdens with this obligation persons whose employments are controlled by the contract on the sole basis of the extension decree.[144]

But where the contract is imposed upon the parties by means of a compulsory arbitration award (*Zwangstarif*), foreign courts have held that a relative peace obligation must be deemed to be included by operation of law.[145]

The Swedish Collective Contract Act of June 22, 1928, Sec. 4, contains these provisions:

[141] 113 R.G.Z. 198 (1926).

[142] Cf. S.K. & Co. v. Verband der Bergarbeiter Deutschlands, 119 R.G.Z. 291 (1927).

[143] X. v. Verband Süddeutscher Textilarbeiter, R.A.G., 5 Bensh. 224 (1929).

[144] Swiss executive decree of June 23, 1943, arts. 15 and 23.

[145] R.A.G., 10 Bensh. 252 (1931).

Employers or employees who are bound by a collective contract shall not, during the term of the contract, engage in stoppages of work (lockout or strike), blockade, boycott, or other hostile action of similar nature:

1. On account of a dispute respecting the validity, existence or correct interpretation of the contract, or on account of a dispute as to whether a particular act constitutes an infringement of the contract or of the provisions of this Act;
2. In order to bring about an alteration in the contract;
3. In order to enforce a provision which is to come into operation on the expiration of the contract;
4. In order to assist others in cases in which the latter cannot themselves commit hostile actions.[146]

If an association or a member of an association is bound by a collective contract, the association shall not induce or otherwise bring about the commission of hostile actions which under the first paragraph are unlawful, nor take part in unlawful hostile actions committed by a member, either by giving assistance or in any other way. An association which is bound by a collective contract must endeavor to prevent its members from committing unlawful hostile actions, or, if such actions have already been committed, must endeavor to cause such members to discontinue them.

The provisions of this section shall apply even to contracts which contain clauses contrary thereto. If a collective contract contains provisions imposing further obligations, the latter shall apply.

Thus, the relative peace obligation is a compulsory contractual term (*jus cogens*). The Act unnecessarily adds that the parties may bind themselves to more stringent peace obligations than the compulsory one, e.g., provide for a notice of warning before any economic weapons can lawfully be used, or even, although rarely, provide that no sanction at all is to be used against the other party.[147]

---

[146] This clause has been added in order to dispel any doubts about the scope of the peace obligation. Where a local union is the party to the contract, the national union is deemed to be equally bound by the peace obligation and so is an organization to which members of that local transfer their allegiance. Cf. Schmidt and Heineman, Enforcement of Collective Bargaining Agreements in Swedish Law, 14 U. of Chi. L. Rev. 184, 190 (1947).

[147] Robbins, The Government of Labor Relations in Sweden 254 (1942).

5. THE RIGHTS OF INDIVIDUAL EMPLOYEES AND MINORITY UNIONS IN THE PRESENTATION OF GRIEVANCE CLAIMS

a. THE ENDERBY CASE — X

Local 417 of the Rubber Workers (CIO) has been the "exclusive representative" of the production workers at the Enderby Rubber Company's Chicago plant for bargaining purposes ever since its certification by the NLRB, following a representation election, in 1948. There has also existed at the plant, however, an independent minority union, the Enderby Employees Association. The Association has had as members some 50 or 60 employees in the Miscellaneous Division. They are mainly older employees, most of them in higher skilled jobs, and all of them allergic to the CIO. There have at most times been another 75 or 100 employees who have not been members of either union.

There was disagreement, when the 1948 contract between the Company and Local 417 was being negotiated, about the handling of the grievances of employees who were not members of Local 417. The proposals and counterproposals on this point are set forth in The Enderby Case — VII, at page 347 supra. Article II in the agreement finally reached in May, 1948, provided that "all grievances involving the terms and conditions" of the contract would be handled through the three-step grievance procedure, but that *"any individual employee or group of employees shall have the right at any time to present grievances directly to the Management."* This provision for the presentation of grievances other than through Local 417 was carried over into the 1949 contract, the only change in Article II being a broadening of the clause describing "grievances" so that it included not only matters of contract interpretation and application but also "all disputes which may arise regarding the terms and conditions of employment in the plant (not including wages)."

This matter of grievance handling became a hotly disputed issue during the 1949 contract term. Three cases came up:

A

Mike Angelo, a pattern-maker, was denied a merit increase to which he thought he was entitled. He insisted that Local 417, of which he was a member, file a grievance for him. This was done, although somewhat reluctantly, for the Chairman of the Grievance Committee did not think that Angelo had a very strong case under Section 4 of Article XI of the agreement. (This section was the same in the 1949 as in the 1950 agreement; see page 327 supra.) The grievance was taken to the third step. At that point the Union Grievance Committee and the Industrial Relations Manager, after an honest discussion of the claim, agreed that it was without merit and should be dropped. The minutes of the meeting recorded: "Grievance No. 423 — Mike Angelo — Badge #14–23B. Agreed denial."

Angelo then called on White, the Industrial Relations Manager, and demanded further consideration of his case. White, referring to the Step 3 settlement, told Angelo he would not reopen the case. Angelo's reply was that he had consulted a lawyer and had been advised that he was entitled, under the Labor Management Relations Act and the decisions of the Supreme Court, to handle his own grievance and to take it to court if he was denied satisfaction. Angelo claimed, to White, that the Union had "sold him down the river because they know I don't like Curme, the Union President." Angelo also told White that the Chairman of the Grievance Committee had asked him, the day before the Step 3 meeting, to agree to a withdrawal of the merit increase grievance and that he (Angelo) had told the Chairman, "You have no right to give my grievance away."

White, as soon as Angelo left, called in Curme (the Local 417 President) and Harold Blair (the Enderby attorney) to discuss this case.

B

The second case involved a claim for vacation payments. The 1949 contract included in Article X (Vacations) only what appears as Section 1 in the 1950 contract, set out at page 326 supra. This meant that although vacations "with pay" were provided for, nothing was said about the *rate* of pay.

Employee Floyd Dean, who was a member of the Enderby Employees Association, took his two-week vacation right at the start of the 1949 vacation period. His vacation pay check was for $80, this being equal to 80 times his basic hourly rate of $1. Shortly after Dean received his check, the president of the Employees Association (R. M. Endicott) wrote to White, the Industrial Relations Manager, claiming that Dean was entitled to receive $108.30 instead of $80. The larger figure was arrived at by taking account of the fact that Dean, who had been doing piecework, had been working 45 hours a week (5 hours overtime at time and a half) and had been averaging earnings of $1.14 an hour. The Association claim was that vacation pay should, under the contract, be computed on an average-earnings rather than basic-hourly-rate basis. White called Endicott in and discussed this matter with him.

Several days later White wrote to Endicott, stating that the practice in the plant had always been to figure vacation pay on a basic-hourly-rate basis, that there had been no intention to change this practice when Article X was added to the contract, and that "the Floyd Dean claim must therefore be, and hereby is, denied."

White received, within the next several days, two letters. One was from Curme, the President of Local 417 of the Rubber Workers. It charged the Company with having violated "both our contract and the Labor Relations Act" by "handling a grievance involving the interpretation of this agreement with an alleged representative of a group of employees who have no standing either in the plant or in the eyes of the law." Curme threatened to "have an unfair labor practice charge filed immediately with the NLRB unless your letter to the alleged Association is withdrawn" and to "strike the plant if any more grievances are handled with anybody except the legally certified exclusive bargaining agency."

The second letter was from Endicott. It stated that the Employees Association was referring this "grievance claim" to arbitration under Article II of the Agreement of May 21, 1949, and that a meeting was desired for the purpose of selecting an arbitrator. "I am authorized by the membership of the Association to tell you," Endicott's letter stated, "that should this request be denied, the members of the Association will have no alternative but to leave their jobs." Endicott concluded by saying, "We are advised by counsel that such arbitration constitutes the only method of giving substance to the rights assured Mr. Dean under Section 9 (a) of the Labor Relations Act, and that our strike, if we are forced to that unfortunate extreme, will be legal under the decisions of the courts."

White, realizing that both Curme and Endicott had relied upon legal counsel, called Blair, the Enderby attorney, for advice.

C

The Company and Local 417 had agreed, as part of the wage negotiations in May, 1949, to "eliminate present inequities between the rates for comparable jobs in the Miscellaneous Division." The agreement provided that this would be done through continuing negotiations by a joint committee of union and management representatives, that this committee should have authority to agree upon both increases and decreases in individual job rates, and that the adjustments "shall not have a net effect of increasing the average of hourly rates in the Division by more than 1½ cents."

This joint committee met during the months of June, July, and August. Agreement was finally reached upon a whole new schedule of rates for jobs in the Miscellaneous Division. Some old hourly rates were left unchanged, some were raised by from ½ cent to 7 cents, others were reduced by from ½ cent to 4 cents. The net effect of the changes was to increase the average of the hourly rates by 1.4932 cents. The Company immediately put the new rates into effect.

It developed that a somewhat disproportionately high percentage of the jobs on which the rates were either reduced or left the same were held by employees who were either members of the Enderby Employees Association or of no union. There had, however, been some cuts in the rates of jobs held by members of Local 417.

A petition was prepared by one of the adversely affected employees. Addressed to the Enderby Plant Manager, this petition protested "the discriminatory treatment given the undersigned in the recent re-scheduling of job rates" and concluded with a demand "for full hearing of our grievances." Thirty-seven employees signed this petition, 21 of them members of the Employees Association, 9 of them members of Local 417, and 7 of them members of no union. All of the signers except three held jobs on which the rates had been reduced; the three were on jobs for which the rates had not been changed.

Each of the 37 received, in reply, a polite letter advising him that these adjustments had been "worked out in collective bargaining participated in by your duly certified exclusive representative" and that the rate changes had been considered "exclusively in terms of the content of the jobs involved so as to eliminate inequities between comparable jobs."

The 37 employees decided to take up with an attorney the matter of whether they could do anything about their claim.

The experience with the problem of grievance handling during the 1949 contract term made it a big issue in the 1950 contract renewal negotiations. Both the Company and the Union submitted proposals for clarifying the old Article II references to the processing of grievances other than through the union channel. Negotiation seemed to widen rather than narrow this gap. Reference to this article as it finally appeared in the 1950–1952 agreement will reveal how the difficulty was finally resolved — or postponed. (See page 318 supra.)

NOTES

Virtually all grievance procedure clauses contemplate some degree of representation of individual employees by the union insofar as the presentation and settlement of grievances are concerned. In most plants, this causes no difficulty. The employee usually wants to have the shop steward with him when he presents his protest to the foreman. He is normally glad to have the union committee take his case on up with the higher management officials if the talk with the foreman fails to produce results. If the case has to go to arbitration, the employee invariably wants it handled by someone who knows the ropes. The company's interest in union representation of the individual employees is frequently just as strong as the employees', at least in a large plant. Many companies prefer, assuming that the union in the plant is a responsible organization, to deal with the named grievance representatives instead of with hundreds of different claimants. A responsible union will screen out a lot of the unsubstantial claims. The grievance representatives know the contract much better than do the individual employees, and much less time need be wasted with them in repeated explanation of its terms. Where the relationship is a really effective one, the company will realize benefit from the union's having agreed that a particular grievance claim is not well founded.

The picture is not, however, in actual practice, always so idyllic or so simple. Some of the employees may not belong to the union which has bargaining rights in the plant, and may not trust or want it to handle their claims. Others may be willing to have the union handle their cases so long as things go well, but may decide to press them themselves if the union brings back an unfavorable answer. The company may feel that it can settle its problems better with the men themselves than with the union officials. The union may have proved to be something less than a responsible organization.

Where these problems have arisen, they have caused difficulty. The status of a union in relationship to its members, and particularly to employees who are in the unit which it represents but are not members, has not as yet become clear. This subject has, as a result, had the attention of the Congress, the NLRB, and the federal courts.

Section 9 (a) of the National Labor Relations Act provided as follows: "Representatives designated or selected for the purpose of collective bargaining by the majority of the employees in a unit appropriate for such purposes, shall be the exclusive representatives of all the employees in such unit for the purposes of collective bargaining in respect to rates of pay, wages, hours of employment or other conditions of employment; *Provided,* That any individual employee or a group of employees shall have the right at any time to present grievances to their employer."

The proviso to this section received its best-known judicial interpretation in the following case.

HUGHES TOOL CO. v. NLRB
United States Court of Appeals, Fifth Circuit, 1945
147 F.2d 69

[The United Steelworkers, CIO, had been certified as agent for collective bargaining in the plant and had charged in unfair labor practice proceedings that the Company had committed an unfair labor practice by taking up with a minority union in the plant, at the latter's insistence, grievances involving employees who were members of the minority union. The Board issued a cease and desist order against the Company, and this was an appeal by the Company for a review of the order.]

SIBLEY, C.J. [After stating the facts and quoting Section 9 (a) of the National Labor Relations Act.] Taking the quoted provisions together, it is plain that collective bargaining in respect to rates of pay, wages, hours of employment and other conditions of employment which will fix for the future the rules of the employment for everyone in the unit, is distinguished from "grievances," which are usually the claims of individuals or small groups that their rights under the collective bargain have not been respected. These claims may involve no question of the meaning and scope of the bargain, but only some question of fact or conduct peculiar to the employee, not affecting the unit. They may, however, raise a question of the meaning of the contract, or present a situation not covered by the contract touching which an agreement ought to be made. In the latter cases it is plain that the representative ought to participate, for bargaining, rather than the mere decision of a case according to the contract, is involved. Attention to grievances is therefore mentioned in Section 2 (5) as part of the business of the representative, but Section 9 (a) does not give him the *exclusive* right to handle them unless they really involve a bargaining for the unit, or an interpretation of the bargain.   On the contrary, it expressly gives each employee or group of employees the right to present their own grievances to the employer. The purpose is to preserve in each employee as a right this direct approach to the employer to secure full consideration of his case. . . .

But the Board thought that this right did not include a presentation of the grievance through a union not the bargaining representative, and did not exclude the latter, who ought on its request to be admitted to the hearing to see if any grievance was in fact an individual one, or involved in the sufficiency or interpretation of the collective contract. . . .   [W]e agree with the Board in principle. . . .   We think an inexperienced or ignorant griever can ask a more experienced friend to assist him, but he cannot present his grievance through any union except the representative.   On the other hand, the representative, when not asked to present the grievance, but is attending to safeguard the collective bargaining, cannot exclude the griever, and withdraw his grievance or destroy it by not permitting its consideration.

We take it to be a proper matter for collective bargaining to establish an orderly and just method of presenting and adjusting grievances.   This was done in the collective contract made with the Steelworkers.   According to it, an employee, feeling aggrieved, may take the matter up directly with his foreman, with or without the presence of a member of the Steelworker's grievance committee as he may elect. . . .   The procedure provision concludes: "Whenever the Union so desires, it may have present any of its representatives during any of the proceedings above set out in this article."   This recognizes and emphasizes the privilege of the bargaining representative to be present at the settlement of grievances. . . .

We find no evidence that there has been any refusal by the Company to comply with any particular bargaining request of the Steelworkers made since the collective bargaining in connection with the old plant, or in connection with the new plant for which no bargain had been made.   Permitting the rival union to present grievances of its members we have held to be not intended by the Act, but it can hardly be called a refusal to bargain, unless the representative, in a grievance which really called for bargaining rather than mere decision, had offered to bargain but was refused.

. . . The order ought to be merely that the Company cease and desist from adjusting grievances through the Independent, and from adjusting grievances not presented through the representative without notifying the representative, except the informal adjustments with the foreman provided for in the contract.

The evidence offered and rejected if true, would show that the representative in this case is discriminating between its members and the members of the rival union by refusing to present the grievances of the latter, and making use of the discrimination to force employees to join it in order to get their grievances adjusted. When the Steelworkers union accepted certification as the bargaining representative for the group, it accepted a trust. It became bound to represent equally and in good faith the interests of the whole group. Steele v. Louisville and Nashville R.R. Co., 65 S. Ct. 226. It ought not to discriminate in the execution of its duties between its own members and employees who belong to another union or to no union. . . . If the griever is a member of another union and cannot be represented by his own union, it is the more necessary that he have the aid of the representative. It may be true that the Board has no power to order the representative specifically to do anything, but the rule making authority granted in Section 6 (a) might be used to curb conduct which is unfair and not according to law. If no remedy exists under the Act, a judicial remedy might be found, as in the Steele case, supra. But because we shall modify the order as to bargaining so as to require only notification of the intention to adjust grievances not presented by the Steelworkers, and to require cessation of presentation of them through other unions, and because this case is not a proceeding to compel the representative to present grievances for others than its members, we shall not direct the evidence to be taken. We will assume that conduct so plainly at war the bargaining agent's duty will not be repeated, if it has occurred in the past. . . .

NOTES

1. The subject case is annotated in 158 A.L.R. 1174 (1945), where it is indicated that other circuit courts of appeals have taken a broader view than that expressed by the Fifth in the Hughes Tool Co. case, e.g., NLRB v. North American Aviation, Inc., 136 F.2d 898 (9th Cir. 1944) ; NLRB v. Union Pacific Stages, 99 F.2d 153 (9th Cir. 1938) ; Humble Oil & Refining Co. v. NLRB, 113 F.2d 85 (5th Cir. 1940).

2. In Steele v. Louisville & Nashville Railroad Co. et al. (see page 236 supra), it was held that the provisions of the Railway Labor Act conferring the exclusive power to bargain upon the representative of the majority of those employed in a craft in an appropriate unit also imposed the duty to exercise fairly the power conferred, without hostile discrimination against minority members of the craft. Query, whether the collective bargaining agent in such a case would be guilty of discrimination if it refused to process a minority member's grievance? Could the minority member compel final submission of an unsettled grievance to arbitration? See Kordewick et al. v. Brotherhood of Railroad Trainmen et al., 181 F.2d 963 (7th Cir. 1950). See also In re Julius Wile Sons & Co., 102 N.Y.S.2d 862, 16 L.A. 88 (Sup. Ct., Special Term, N.Y. County, Part I, 1951).

3. A related question concerns the right of individual union members who may be dissatisfied with the grievance settlement which is concluded between union representatives and management, to challenge the settlement or to seek an independent adjudication of the grievance at the hands of the courts in suits against the employer.[148]

Shortly after the Hughes Tool Co. case was decided, the Supreme Court of the United States handed down its opinion in Elgin, Joliet & Eastern Ry. v. Burley, 325 U.S. 711, 65 Sup. Ct. 1282, 89 L. Ed. 1886 (1945). Burley and nine other employees were seeking back pay over a period of years to which they maintained they were entitled under the starting-time provisions of the collective bargaining agreement between the Company and the Brotherhood of Railway Trainmen. This claim had been handled by the Grievance Committee of the Brotherhood and a compromise settlement had been worked out and agreed to between the Committee and the Company. The ten employees were not satisfied with the settlement and they protested that they had not authorized the Committee to compromise their claim. The case was then taken to the Railroad Adjustment Board under the provisions of Section 3 of the Railway Labor Act (see Appendix), but that Board accepted the agreed settlement as conclusive and issued an award denying the claim. The ten employees then filed suit in the federal district court based on their original claim of contract violation. The district court rendered summary judgment for the Company. The Circuit Court of Appeals reversed this judgment (140 F.2d 488), holding that the district court had

[148] A recent case in point is In re Norwalk Tire & Rubber Co., 100 F. Supp. 706 (D. Conn. 1951).

erred in not deciding the factual issue of whether the employees had authorized the Union to compromise the contract claim.

The Supreme Court granted certiorari and subsequently affirmed, by a five-to-four vote, the decision of the Court of Appeals. The Court majority held that the ten employees could not be said "as a matter of law," to have assented to the final settlement of their claim, at least on a compromise basis; and that the district court was obligated to determine whether the basis for such assent could be found in the collective bargaining agreement, the Brotherhood's regulation (which authorized the Grievance Committee to settle claims), or in the ten employees' action in originally submitting their claim through the Brotherhood offices. The holding was based in substantial part upon the Court's interpretation of various provisions of the Railway Labor Act.

Part of the basis for the Court majority's opinion (by Rutledge, J.) is indicated in the following paragraph at page 738:

> . . . For an award to affect the employee's rights, therefore, more must be shown than that the collective agent appeared and purported to act for him. It must be that in some legally sufficient way he authorized it to act in his behalf. Authority might be conferred in whatever ways would be sufficient according to generally accepted or "common law" rules for the creation of an agency, as conceivably by specific authorization given orally or in writing to settle each grievance, by general authority given to settle such grievances as might arise, or by assenting to such authority by becoming a member of a union and thereby accepting a provision in its constitution or rules authorizing it to make such settlements.

The holding in the Burley case seems also to have rested, however, upon a broader ground. Mr. Justice Rutledge devoted much of his opinion to a discussion of the differences between "disputes concerning the making of collective agreements" and "disputes over grievances." The following excerpts suggest the Court's approach, and raise interesting questions about the scope of the union's exclusive bargaining authority and about the relationship between the union and its members:

> . . . disputes over the formation of collective agreements or efforts to secure them. . . . look to the acquisition of rights for the future, not to assertion of rights claimed to have vested in the past.
>
> [Grievance disputes], however, contemplate the existence

of a collective agreement already concluded, or at any rate, a situation in which no effort is made to bring about a formal change in terms or to create a new one. The dispute relates either to the meaning or proper application of a particular provision with reference to a specific situation or to an omitted case. In the latter event the claim is founded upon some incident of the employment relation, or asserted one, independent of those covered by the collective agreement, e.g., claims on account of personal injuries. In either case the claim is to rights accrued, not merely to have new ones created for the future. [Id. at 723.]

Whether or not the agent's exclusive power [recognized in the case of contract formation disputes] extends also to the settlement of grievances, in conference or in proceedings before the Board, presents . . . difficult questions. . . .

It would be difficult to believe that Congress intended . . . to submerge wholly the individual and minority interest, with all power to act concerning them, in the collective interest and agency, not only in forming the contracts which govern their employment relation, but also in giving effect to them and to all other incidents of that relation. Acceptance of such a view would require the clearest expression of purpose. For this would mean that Congress had nullified all pre-existing rights of workers to act in relation to their employment, including perhaps even the fundamental right to consult with one's employer, except as the collective agent might permit. [Id. at 729.]

To settle for the future alone, without reference to or effect upon the past, is in fact to bargain collectively, that is, to make a collective agreement. That authority is conferred independently of the power to deal with grievances, as part of the power to contract "concerning rates of pay, rules, or working conditions." It includes the power to make a new agreement settling for the future a dispute concerning the coverage or meaning of a pre-existing collective agreement. For the collective bargaining power is not exhausted by being once exercised; it covers changing the terms of an existing agreement as well as making one in the first place.

But it does not cover changing them with retroactive effects upon accrued rights or claims. [Id. at 739.]

Mr. Justice Frankfurter wrote a dissenting opinion, concurred in by Chief Justice Stone and Justices Roberts and Jackson. Here

a different view was taken of the scope of the union's authority
and the relationship of unions to their members (or at least of
the proper scope of judicial scrutiny of this relationship) :

This is not a simple little case about an agent's authority.
Demands of the employees' representative imply not only
authority from those for whom he speaks, but the duty of respect from those to whom he speaks. . . . We do not have the
ordinary case where a third person dealing with an ostensible
agent must at his peril ascertain the agent's authority. In
such a situation a person may protect himself by refusing to
deal. Here petitioner has a duty to deal. If petitioner refuses to deal with the officials of the employees' union by
challenging their authority, it does so under pain of penalty.
If it deals with them on the reasonable belief that the grievance officials of the Brotherhood are acting in accordance with
customary union procedure, settlements thus made ought not
to be at the hazard of being jettisoned by future litigation.
To allow such settlements to be thus set aside is to obstruct
the smooth working of the Act. It undermines the confidence
so indispensable to adjustment by negotiation, which is the
vital object of the Act. [*Id.* at 755.]
. . . Union membership generates complicated relations.
Policy counsels against judicial intrusion upon these relations. If resort to courts is at all available, it certainly should
not disregard and displace the arrangements which the members of the organization voluntarily establish for their reciprocal interests and by which they bound themselves to be governed. The rights and duties of membership are governed
by the rules of the Brotherhood. Rule 10 concerns objections to official action: "Whatever action may be taken by the
general grievance committee . . . shall be law to the lodges
on that road until the next meeting of the board of appeals,
and if any member refuses to vote or abide by the action of
such general grievance committee or board of adjustment he
shall be expelled from the Brotherhood for violation of obligation." To ask courts to adjudicate the meaning of the
Brotherhood rules and customs without preliminary resort
to remedial proceedings within the Brotherhood is to encourage influences of disruption within the union instead of
fostering these unions as stabilizing forces. Rules of fraternal
organizations, with all the customs and assumptions that give

them life, cannot be treated as though they were ordinary legal documents of settled meaning. [Id. at 757.]

The Supreme Court's decision was greeted by a storm of protest. A rehearing was set, and briefs amicus curiae (in opposition to the holding) were filed by the Solicitor General of the United States and by a number of labor organizations. The Court reaffirmed its previous decision, Mr. Justice Rutledge writing another opinion (327 U.S. 661, 66 Sup. Ct. 721, 90 L. Ed. 928). This second opinion insisted that "no all-inclusive rule can be formulated" regarding the fact of employee authorization of union settlement of grievance claims, and that the only holding in this case was that a factual question of authorization did exist and that the district court should have determined that question. "Custom and usage," Mr. Justice Rutledge wrote, at page 663, "may be as adequate a basis of authority as a more formal authorization for the union, which receives a grievance from an employee for handling, to represent him in settling it . . ." Mr. Justice Frankfurter, in another dissenting opinion, charged that by this language (and some other) the Court majority, although in form adhering to its original decision, did so "by extracting from it almost all of its vitality."

For the Attorney General's opinion as to the effect of this decision on the right to be represented by a minority union under the Railway Labor Act, see 40 Op. Atty. Gen. 494, 18 L.R.R.M. 48 (1946).

4. In Moore v. Illinois Central Railroad Co., 312 U.S. 630, 61 Sup. Ct. 754, 85 L. Ed. 1089 (1941), the Supreme Court sustained the right of an employee to maintain an action in the courts for his wrongful discharge from employment without first having resorted to administrative remedies available under the provisions of the Railway Labor Act. In the recent case of Broady v. Illinois Central Railroad Co., 191 F.2d 73 (7th Cir. 1951), cert. denied, 342 U.S. 897, 72 Sup. Ct. 231, 96 L. Ed. 140 (1951), the Circuit Court of Appeals for the Seventh Circuit directed the dismissal of a suit brought by a dining-car waiter seeking restoration to his job and damages for his discharge in alleged breach of the collective agreement. The court distinguished the Moore case on the ground that that case had involved diversity of citizenship while the Broady case did not. Query, whether the cases weren't further distinguishable on the ground that relief by way of restoration to a position involves questions of future relations between the

railroad and its other employees?   See Slocum v. Delaware L. & W.R. Co., 339 U.S. 239, 70 Sup. Ct. 586, 94 L. Ed. 15 (1950), and Order of Railway Conductors v. Pitney, 326 U.S. 561, 66 Sup. Ct. 322, 90 L. Ed. 318 (1946), and cf. Newman v. Baltimore & Ohio R. Co., 191 F.2d 560 (3d Cir. 1951).

5. Both the Hughes Tool and the Burley cases, and the language in those opinions, were considered extensively by the House and Senate Labor Committees in connection with the drafting of the 1947 amendments to the NLRA.   The Senate Committee stated its position in the Report which accompanied its submission of Senate Bill 1126 (S. Rep. No. 105, 80th Cong., 1st Sess. 25 (1947)): "The revised language would make it clear that the employee's right to present grievances exists independently of the rights of the bargaining representative, if the bargaining representative has been given an opportunity to be present at the adjustment, unless the adjustment is contrary to the terms of the collective bargaining agreement then in effect."

The resultant amendment of the Section 9 (a) proviso should be carefully considered.   See Appendix.   The following case illustrates the interpretation which this revised language has been given.

DOUDS v. LOCAL 1250, RETAIL WHOLESALE DEPARTMENT STORE UNION OF AMERICA, CIO
United States Court of Appeals, Second Circuit, 1949
173 F.2d 764, 9 A.L.R. 2d 685

[On September 1, 1948, the NLRB certified the Retail Clerks Int. Assn., AFL, as the representative of the employees of Oppenheim Collins & Co., Inc.   Some of the Company's employees then went on strike in an attempt to force the Company to recognize and bargain with Local 1250 of the CIO union.   The Regional Director of the NLRB (Douds) issued a complaint against Local 1250, charging a violation of Section 8 (b) (4) (C) of the 1947 Act, and on September 14 sought and obtained an injunction in the federal district court under Section 10 (1) of that Act.   The strikers then demanded reinstatement.   The Company offered to take them back only as vacancies might develop, refusing to discharge replacement employees who had been hired during the strike.   The employees who were not taken back, along with other members of Local 1250 (who had never worked for Oppenheim Collins), then picketed the Company's stores.   The picket signs demanded reinstatement, referred to the employees of the Company as "scabs," and urged that no one patronize the stores.   On October 8, the NLRB Regional Director instituted contempt proceedings against Local 1250 and certain of its agents.   The District Court held the Union and its agents in contempt of the injunction, finding the picketing an attempt to force the Company "to recognize and bargain with the respondent, Local 1250, concerning reinstatement of striking former employees."   The Union was fined $20,000, with provision for another $1,000 for each day of future continuing contempt.   The Union appealed this order to the Circuit Court of Appeals.

By unanimous decision the Court of Appeals reversed the order of the court below and dismissed the petition.   Judge Hand, who wrote the opinion, first considered the scope of the injunction issued by the trial judge.   He concluded that the latter must have thought the action taken by the Local had violated the 1947 Act, even though the injunction was not, in all details, modeled after Section 8 (b) (4) (C) ; otherwise, for the judge to levy such "large fines" would have been a "plain abuse of discretion."

To discover what the Act itself meant to allow and to prohibit, Judge Hand then turned to Section 9 (a) of the Wagner Act providing that "any individual employee or a group of employees shall have the right at any time to present grievances to their employer."   Noting that there was some confusion as to what this meant, he briefly reviewed the North American and Hughes Tool cases.

Taking up next the significance of the Taft-Hartley amendment to the old Section 9 (a) , Judge Hand quoted from the Senate Report of the Act, which declared that the amendment made it "clear that the employee's right to present grievances exists independently of the rights of the bargaining representative" so long as the adjustment is not inconsistent with the terms of an existing collective bargaining agreement.   Judge Hand then continued:]

This amendment put an end to the distinction between "grievances" and other disputes.   It may well be that it was proper to assume the existence of such a distinction, while the certified agent's powers and the powers of a "group" were mutually independent; but any such necessity disappeared as soon as the authority of the certified agent was made expressly paramount.   It then became the natural understanding that those "grievances" which could be "adjusted" comprised all disputes which could be covered in a collective agreement; and that meant every kind of dispute, for all disputes can be covered by a collective agreement.

[Judge Hand thus interpreted the Act as investing the certified representative with no more than the authority to contract for all the employees in the unit, for "until he chooses to contract, and in so far as his contract leaves open any points in dispute, present or future, the employees retain their common-law right to bargain for themselves, singly or collectively." But he continued, "any bargain they may make is subject to his power to cancel it, for in so doing he acts for them as their agent, as much as though they had expressly authorized him to do so."

May a rival union act for "a group" in the "adjustment" of a "grievance"? Two reasons have been advanced, according to Judge Hand, for "implying" that such a rival union may not enter the picture: (1) that to allow a rival union to take such action would result in friction between it and the certified agent; and (2) that while the original National Labor Relations Act was in Congress, there were deleted from the proviso in Section 9 (a) the words, "through representatives of their own choosing."

The "friction" question did not worry Judge Hand. He noted that "[u]nder the present act . . . the certified agent has it always in his hands to take over the 'adjustment' of any 'grievance,' whether it has been already 'adjusted,' or is in the process of 'adjustment,' and by including it in a collective agreement with the employer, finally to dispose of it. Whatever friction remains, therefore, will arise from the possible presence of the certified agent at the negotiations which lead up to an 'adjustment' which a rival union is conducting for a 'group.' " And Judge Hand continued, "[S]ome measure of friction appears to us inevitable, once the right granted by the proviso is conceded. . . . [W]e cannot take seriously the difference in resulting friction between letting the union, or its lawyers, conduct the actual negotiation, and requiring the employees to keep going back and forth for advice and counsel between the employer and the union as the negotiation proceeds . . . [T]he question would be constantly arising just what degree of intervention in the adjustment brings the union out of the wings and upon the stage."

With respect to the effect of the deletion, by Congress, of the words, "through representatives of their own choosing," from the original Section 9 (a) proviso, Judge Hand argued that]

Congress having expressly provided that a "group" need not "adjust" their "grievances" through the certified agent, meant either that they should have no representative except one of their number, or that they might choose one. Inexperienced persons are not adepts in labor controversies; there has grown up an elaborate system of law, complicated and technical, which demands special proficiency and training . . . It seems to us incredible that Congress should have meant that an unassisted group of employees must shift for themselves in negotiating with their employer, who was free to protect himself by whatever armor the market afforded.

[On the basis of the foregoing analysis of Section 9 (a), Judge Hand concluded that "it would not have been an 'unfair labor practice' for the employer to 'adjust' the 'grievance' of the 51 employees: *i.e.,* their claim to reinstatement, through the Local's attorneys acting as negotiators; and . . . [that] it was not an 'unfair labor practice' under Section 8 (b) (4) for the Local to try to induce other employees to strike, as a sanction upon the employer to compel him to reinstate those employees." As Judge Hand interpreted Section 8 (b) (4) (C), its purpose was to protect both the certified agent and the employer from interference by an outside union in the discharge of the certified agent's bargaining authority; but "in so far as he has not exercised it, the relative rights of the employer and employed remain what they were, including the right of the employed to choose whom they will to represent them."

What Section 8 (b) (4) (C) did forbid in this case, according to Judge Hand, was the following:]

Striking or inducing others to strike, (1) in order to force the employer to recognize the Local as the bargaining agent for the "unit"; or (2) in order to force the employer to "adjust" any "grievance" which the certified agent had already "adjusted" by a collective agreement.

[In this latter connection, the opinion pointed out that "no collective agreement of any kind had ever been made," or at least, "if there was one, it had not 'adjusted' the question of the reinstatement of those of the 51 employees who had not been taken back."

Judge Hand recognized that perhaps the Local aimed at much more than merely securing the reinstatement of those employees who had not been reinstated, and that "perhaps out of the turmoil, agitation and ill feeling which the picketing would inevitably engender," the Local thought it might "displace the certified union." He noted, however, that "the judge did not find that the Local harbored such a purpose, and there would have been little, if any, basis for it, if he had."

In reversing the lower court and dismissing the petition, the court observed that possibly its interpretation of the meaning of the Act shows the Congressional plan to be defective; but "we think that Congress knew what it meant and expressed it in what seems to us inescapable terms."

Following the court's decision, both the employer and the NLRB filed briefs asking the court to reverse its interpretation of the proviso to Section 9 (a). They argued that in application the ruling would "cause confusion in administration and introduce that strife between rival unions which it was one of the chief purposes of the Act to prevent."

In denying the petition for a rehearing (p. 770), the court stated that it was not unmindful of these possibilities: "We were aware of the possibility, and mentioned it before; and it is indeed a circumstance not to be lightly dismissed in interpreting the statute." "But," the court continued (again speaking through Judge Hand), "the argument comes to not more than that, in granting to minorities the measure of individual representation which it did, Congress clogged, and perhaps even frustrated, the venture as a whole." Referring once again to the legislative history of the 1947 Act, Judge Hand concluded that "Congress for the sake of the limited minority representation which it granted, was willing to accept the chance that the Board might be right. That choice it is not for us to review."

Judge Hand's opinion concluded:]

Specifically the Board's argument is that the distinction between 'grievances" and the stipulations appropriate to a collective bargain was well fixed in the law of this subject; and that it was carried over into the amendment Act, which, as both parties appear to think, was written with the decision in mind of the Supreme Court in Elgin, Joliet & Eastern Railway Co. v. Burley. Curiously enough, so far as concerns the actual holding in that case, it rather confirms our view than otherwise, for it denied power to the certified agent to settle the claims of individual members for violations of a collective agreement. It is true that in his opinion Rutledge, J., did distinguish "grievances" from those matters with which collective agreements deal. However, although he mentioned among "grievances" complaints founded upon an employer's failure to observe the terms of an existing collective agreement, he also included disputes for which the agreement did not provide — "an omitted case." Indeed, had he not so enlarged the term, although the interpretation would of course have been authoritative as to the Railway Labor Act of 1934, it could not have been so as to the provisos of Section 9 (a), because these plainly presuppose that a "grievance" may not have been covered by the collective agreement, and indeed, that there may not be any such agreement in existence.   Once it be conceded that "grievances" do cover disputes which no collective agreement has attempted to settle, it becomes to the last degree difficult to draw the line, if there be a line, between "grievances" proper, and those other disputes which are not "grievances."   It was on this account that we said before that the provisos include any disputes, which no existing collective agreement has settled.   If that be not true, there will merge in every case a question perplexing, and pregnant with controversy, which will be as troublesome as any of the evils of which the Board complains.   However, since it is never desirable for a court to go beyond what the decision demands; and, since all that the case at bar does demand is to decide whether the reinstatement of the employees at bar was a "grievance," we will confine our decision to that issue; and will let it be understood that we do not finally commit ourselves upon the proposition which we announced before and have just restated.

We cannot see how it can fail to be, unless the term is to be confined to such complaints as the oppression of foremen, the unfair distribution of the work, or other details of factory management. That it cannot be so confined follows from the fact that under the first proviso a "grievance" may be a dispute which conflicts with the collective agreement.   The Board protests that the reinstatement of aggrieved employees cannot be considered as though it stood *in vacuo,* for it may disturb the relations of the employer with other employees, or the relations of those employees with the aggrieved employees themselves.   That is true; any industrial establishment is, as it were, an elastic medium, which transmits everywhere a disturbance originating in any part.   That may be a good objection to the procedure set up; but it is a reason which applies to the adjustment of any "grievance" whatever.   No doubt, it was the recognition of this which caused the addition of the second proviso giving the certified agent the right to intervene whenever the proposed adjustment would be inconsistent with an existing collective agreement.   If, as the Board argues, that gave an employer an opportunity to "play off" one faction against another, it also gave the certified agent an opportunity by exercising his paramount authority, backed by the formidable sanctions at his command, to insure the unimpeded performance of any collective agreement.   We hold that, whatever the overall scope of the term may be, the reinstatement of these employees was a "grievance" within the first proviso.

There only remains the question whether an individual employee or a minority — a "group" — must negotiate the adjust-

ment of their "grievance" without the help of a union which it has
been their custom to use as their representative.   We have little to
add to what we said before.   Behind the whole Act, indeed its
main presupposition, is the assumption that in industrial negotiations an individual, or a minority, does not bargain on equal terms
with an employer.   It is not reasonable to suppose that Congress,
after giving a minority this privilege, should wish to deprive it of
that means of exercising it, which for this reason is the putative
condition of its effective use.   But that is not all.   The present
Act provides for the intervention of the certified agent, and he will
seldom, if ever, intervene if he is in sympathy with the minority's
"grievance"; for if he is, they are likely to ask him to do the "adjusting."   Hence they will ordinarily be called upon to face two
opponents, each better qualified in such negotiations than they.   It
appears to us extremely unreasonable to impute that purpose to
Congress.   To match these considerations the Board invokes the
fact that, while the original Act was before Congress, it struck out
from the proviso, as it then was, the clause: "of their own
choosing."   That was done, so far as one can now tell, because it
was feared that a "group" might use a "company union" as its
representative.   The deletion is not a safe guide in the interpretation of the amendment unless we recall the content of the original
proviso.   It had even been debated whether that gave employees
any further privileges than to "present" their "grievances"; but if
it did — and the better opinion would appear to be that it did —
it was left uncertain whether the adjustment had to be consonant
with any existing collective agreement.   Perhaps that too was to
be implied, but it was not plain.   At any rate the original proviso
gave the certified agent no right to appear, not only to protect the
agreement if one existed, but — what is far more important — to
protest that the whole issue was a covert attempt to infiltrate the
influence of a "company union."   No such possibility any longer
exists; and we cannot believe that the deletion of the clause from
the original proviso is valid evidence of the purposes which dictated
the amendment.   Finally, we note that, after the Elgin case, supra,
the Attorney General reached the conclusion under the Railway
Labor Act of 1934, that the minority might make use of a union
as its representative.

Petition denied.[149]

---

[149] See Dunau, Employee Participation in the Grievance Aspect of Collective
Bargaining, 50 Col. L. Rev. 731 (1950), which discusses the subject case at
page 755.   The subject case is also discussed in a Comment, 17 U. of Chi. L.
Rev. 533 (1950), and in Notes, 34 Cornell L.Q. 655 (1950), 63 Harv. L. Rev.
361 (1949). — ED.

b. Foreign Law Regarding Group Participation in Complaints and Grievance Procedure

In European countries, other than Ireland and the United Kingdom, collective agreements do not contain what we here call grievance procedure provisions. On the contrary, these functions, so far as they exist, are vested in works councils and labor courts provided by statute. The statutory works councils have a strong position, independent of the existence of collective contracts and appropriate provisions therein, as to the treatment of grievances. This subject has been discussed at page 79 supra.

For breach of a normative provision of a collective contract the law of all countries grants a remedy at the suit of the aggrieved individual. In many of them there are labor courts or special proceedings for controversies relating to employment, through which an employer or an employee (particularly after he has left the job) readily asserts his claim. Such is the case, for instance, in Germany, Austria, Italy, France, most cantons of Switzerland, the Netherlands, and Belgium.[150] In France, but not in Germany, statutory provisions enable an association also to protect an individual's rights based on a collective contract. This has various advantages. First, it provides a more effective sanction for the observance of collective contract terms than merely the vigilance of individuals. An association is usually not economically or socially under as much pressure to refrain from action against the violator. Second, a right to vindicate individuals' claims before the court makes it possible for an association to obtain a judicial declaration or interpretation. Finally, time and costs may be saved by substituting a single case for many individual actions which otherwise would have to be brought against the adverse party.

French law provides that the union may sue for a violation affecting an individual only after it has given him notice of its intention to do so and provided he does not object.[151] The Swedish law confers the primary right to sue upon the union in such instance, but permits the individual to bring the action upon a showing that

---

[150] For details, see Herzog, The Representation of the Parties before the Labor Courts in Germany and Other European Countries (1934) (in German). The competence of the labor courts in the Scandinavian countries is restricted to controversies arising between the parties to the collective contract.

[151] Labor Code, bk. I, tit. II, c. IV bis, art. 31t; Rouast and Durand, Précis de législation industrielle 259 (3d ed. 1948). The individual may intervene in the suit.

the union has refused to do so.[152]   The Dutch law forbids a suit
by the group only when the individual has already brought his
action.[153]   However, the group may intervene in the individual's
action.   The French law and the Italian law also allow such
intervention.[154]

Under the systems of Australia and New Zealand such grievances
could be dealt with as if they were initial disputes.   In practice,
however, such matters tend to be dealt with by subordinate authorities such as the Commonwealth conciliation commissioners,
or by boards of reference appointed when an original award is
made.   Since the awards create legal rights enforceable by summary procedure, grievances such as disputes over the computation
of a wage claim are frequently determined in courts of summary
jurisdiction on appropriate civil action, or on statutory prosecution for breach of award.

This gives rise to the possibility of individual employees prosecuting claims in summary fashion in respect of legal rights created
by awards.   A peculiar situation arises from the constitutional
limitations on the federal arbitration power in Australia.   A
registered organization may validly raise a dispute with employers
as to the conditions of employment of nonunionists who refused
to participate in the dispute, and the Commonwealth Court of
Arbitration may then make an award which settles the dispute by
specifying the conditions of employment of the nonunionists.   An
employer failing to comply with the award can then be prosecuted,
but the nonunionists concerned derive no rights from the award
and cannot themselves either prosecute or bring a civil action
(Metal Trades Case, 54 C.L.R. 387).   There is no such constitutional restriction on the states, and it is common for awards of the
state courts and wage boards to be made a "common rule," giving
full protection and rights to all individual employees in the trades
specified.   For further discussion, see page 289 supra.

Both the German law and the French law give rights likewise to
the individual employer.   Such a right exists, for example, when
an employer whose individual economic interest is affected by a
union's complacent attitude towards its members' working at
lower wages for his competitor.   If the association of which they
both are members has made a collective contract which is being

[152] Swedish Labor Court Act, June 22, 1928, sec. 13; Robbins, The Government of Labor Relations in Sweden 214 (1942).

[153] Dutch Collective Contract Act of Dec. 24, 1927, art. 15.

[154] France: see note 151 supra.   Italy: Italian Royal Order (1934), No.
1073, art. 7.   For an analogous enactment, see Mexico Labor Act (1931),
sec. 54.

violated, the employer may sue the union to compel it to perform its obligation to take all measures available to it, disciplinary ones included, against its members to compel the competing employer to comply with the contract.[155]   Failure to carry out the judgment entered in such a case may lead to a proceeding analogous to the Anglo-American contempt sanction,[156] and to a damage action.

While in Germany a union may not sue merely because employees are not paid rates fixed in the collective contract schedules, yet such violation of individuals' rights may simultaneously affect the interests of the group.   In that event, the German labor courts have recognized that the union may recover; a case of what is called "mockery" [157] of the collective contract may be made out by proving frequent or willful violation of collective contract schedules.[158] The kind of relief for this will depend on whether the violator is himself a party to the collective contract or only a member of a party thereto.   In the former case, a judgment may be entered enjoining him from further violations and ordering him to pay the wage-balance [159] to those employees who are affected.   In the latter case, the action will be against the association and the judgment will direct the association to use its full authority against its violator-member in order to make him comply with the contract.   By French law too the group which is a party to the contract may bring an action for damages in its own behalf for violation of the contract.[160]

c. Union Participation in Grievance Settlements in the United States

In the United States, to date, no general or definitive policy has been adopted respecting a union's standing to maintain an action for the enforcement of individual employees' claims.   Section

---

[155] That obligation (*Einwirkungspflicht*) is discussed at page 339 supra.

[156] Germany: Civil Code, sec. 315 (3) ; Civil Practice Act. sec. 888; Labor Court Act, sec. 61 (4) .   France: Labor Code, bk. I, tit. II, c. IV bis, art. 31s. For the French concept of enforcement of a judgment of the described type (the so-called *astreinte*), see 2 Planiol, Traité élémentaire de droit civil (9th ed. 1923) , and the discussion at page 834 infra.

[157] This is offered as a translation of the German legal term *Tarifuntreue*.

[158] For German judicial authorities see Hueck and Nipperdey, Collective Contract Law 48, no. 88 (1950) (in German) .

[159] The payment of substandard wages is only one example.   Another is systematic violation of a collective contract obligation to employ union members.   Cf. Nikisch, The Peace Obligation, Its Performance and Execution 77 (1932) (in German).

[160] Labor Code, bk. I, tit. II, c. IV bis, art. 31t; Rouast and Durand, op. cit. supra note 151, at 259.

9 (a) of the Labor Management Relations Act authorizes the certified union to represent him in the private handling of grievances, subject, however, to the significant proviso involved in the Douds case, page 436 supra, that he may elect to proceed on his own or retain the services of a minority union.   Even here, however, there is a legislative recognition of the interest of the certified union, as the collective representative of all the employees, in the requirement that any private adjustment reached be consistent with the agreement and that the certified union be accorded the right to attend the adjustment proceedings.

Recent developments in cases arising under the Railway Labor Act also reflect a judicial recognition of the union's interest in the settlement of individual employee claims arising under the collective agreement, at least insofar as the adjustment reached may bear upon or control the future relations of the contracting parties. The Burley case indicates that the union, on the basis of "custom and usage" *may be* regarded as the agent for individual employees for the purpose of making irrevocable settlements of claims growing out of alleged contract violations.   And the cases cited in the Notes following the discussion of the Burley case at page 431 supra have demonstrated a growing reluctance on the part of the courts to entertain suits by individual employees until there has been an exhaustion of administrative remedies available to them under the Railway Labor Act.   Finally, the Circuit Court of Appeals for the Ninth Circuit has recently held that individual union members may not maintain an action for damages growing out of their wrongful discharge by an employer in violation of his closed-shop contract with the union, saying that "For such injury, the union alone could seek redress." [161]

B. *Union Security*

1. INTRODUCTORY NOTE

A union is a social institution, and like all other institutions it is subject to growth and decline.   Since its vitality and continued existence depend, in large part, upon its ability to meet the specific needs of its members, the union itself needs to be strong.   It therefore seeks to achieve sovereignty and to obtain rights for itself as an organization.   In this way it is better able to protect and to implement rights gained for the workers.

Threats to the welfare of organized workers come from three

---

[161] MacKay v. Loew's, Inc., 182 F.2d 170, 172 (9th Cir. 1950).

principal sources: employers, other unions, and the workers themselves.   The history of employer opposition to the growth of labor organization is still vivid in the minds of union leaders and their members; and the basic feeling of insecurity of most unions has yet to be completely dispelled.   Rival unionism and jurisdictional disputes are outstanding characteristics of the American labor movement; and many unions have successfully met the challenge of employers, only to succumb to attacks by their more powerful competitors within the "house of labor."   Finally, union standards have constantly been undermined by the tendency of individual workers to compete against each other; this has been true particularly in periods of economic depression.

The most important means by which unions attempt to establish their own strength with respect to employers, other unions, and workers are the so-called "union security provisions" frequently included in collective bargaining agreements.   These provisions generally fall into the following categories:

a. Closed Shop

Under closed-shop agreements, the employer contracts not to hire anyone except members of the appropriate union, and to discharge any employee who does not remain a union member in good standing throughout the life of the agreement.   Most of the closed-shop agreements require employers to hire through the union unless the latter is unable to furnish suitable persons within a given period; in such cases the persons hired elsewhere must join the union before starting to work.

Example.   The Company hereby agrees to employ only members of Local No. 114 . . . and only those in good standing in the above-named Local; all positions to be supplied through the employment office of said Local.

b. Union Shop

Under union-shop agreements, employers are permitted to hire workers on the open market, but all new employees must join the union within a specified period and must continue their membership in good standing throughout the life of the agreement. Failure to do so results automatically in discharge by the employer.

Example.   All present employees shall be required to join the union within 30 days of the date of this agreement and shall remain members in good standing in the union as a condition of employment. All new employees shall be required to join the union within 30 days from the date of their employment and shall remain members in good standing as a condition of employment.

c. Preferential Shop

Some agreements provide that preference in employment shall be given to union members. Under such agreements the employer is free to hire workers on the open market only if no suitable union members are supplied within a specified period of time. A preferential hiring provision is frequently incorporated as a supplement to a union-shop agreement. In that event, the union-security provision as a whole has practically the same effect as a closed shop.

> *Example.* It is agreed that in hiring new employees the employer shall give preference to union members but in the event union members are not available, new members may be hired from any source.

d. Maintenance of Membership

In order to avoid the compulsory aspects of the closed and the union shop, some employers and unions have agreed upon maintenance of membership as a compromise. Under this arrangement, membership in the union is not required of new employees; they may join or not, as they prefer. Once they do join, however, they are obligated to maintain their union membership in good standing for the life of the collective agreement as a condition of employment. Some maintenance-of-membership provisions specify an "escape period," usually at the end of the contract term, during which time members may withdraw from the union with impunity. For an example of a typical maintenance-of-membership clause, see the Enderby Agreement, Article I, Section 4, at page 318 supra.[162]

It is significant that the issue of union security is confined almost exclusively to the United States. American workers have

[162] Note the modified union-security provision in the Pittsburgh Steel Company contract with the United Steel Workers, CIO: maintenance of membership for all present members plus those who join the union voluntarily; required application for membership by all new employees, revocable in writing within between twenty and thirty days of date of employment. 3 L.R.R. (BNA) 175 (1952).

been more difficult to organize and to keep organized than European workers.   In European industrial relations the union shop has been accepted more or less tacitly by employers and its tradition with workers dates back to the period of the guilds.[163]   There are a number of reasons why this is so.   In Europe, the higher degree of unionization, the homogeneity of the working classes, and the relative lack of opportunities for the wage earner to progress up the economic scale have made for a stronger feeling of solidarity among the workers.   In the United States, however, the presence of great numbers of immigrants, the relatively frequent opportunities for wage earners to rise out of the ranks of labor, as well as other economic and social factors, have retarded the development of a spirit of class solidarity.   The American worker has traditionally been individualistic rather than class-conscious; the knowledge that he might some day be a "boss" has tended to spur his ambition and to make him less amenable to discipline and control.

This tradition has been largely responsible for the emphasis which American labor unions have placed upon union security. Threatened on the one hand by those workers who were willing to accept low wages and long hours, in the belief that their position as wage earners was only temporary, and on the other hand by immigrant workers with lower standards of living, most American unions have come to regard the closed or union shop as their only real protection.   Thus, in the early 1800's American craftsmen refused to work with nonunionists, and by the time of the Civil War virtually all unions favored excluding nonunionists from employment.   The principle of the closed shop was officially adopted by the American Federation of Labor, and the beginning of the twentieth century saw the closed shop firmly established as a keystone of union bargaining policy.

The principle of union security, and indeed of unionism itself, was strongly attacked by organized American industry, which favored the open (i.e., nonunion) shop.   The industry program was launched on a broad scale in the first decade of the 1900's by the National Association of Manufacturers.   This antiunion cam-

---

[163] Sweden is something of an exception.   The famous "Section 23 clause" of the powerful Swedish Employers' Federation statutes provides that every collective agreement entered into by a member association or firm of the Federation must include a stipulation to the effect that the employer shall have "full freedom to take on and to employ workers regardless of whether they belong to organizations or not."   So far as hiring is concerned, however, this clause is of minor significance today, since more than 90 per cent of all workers in mining, manufacturing, and construction are organized.

paign was partially effective but union membership and strength increased tremendously during World War I. Industry's second organized attempt to retard the growth of unionism, begun in 1919, met with considerably more success. By 1920, militant unionism in the United States had been largely suppressed, and the open shop, or "American Plan" as it was then called, prevailed generally. The moral which American unions drew from this defeat was that real collective bargaining was possible only if they could secure the closed or union shop.

During the years which have elapsed since the passage of the Wagner Act in 1935, the principle of collective bargaining has become firmly established in American industry. A union which is the certified representative of a majority of employees within an appropriate bargaining unit is authorized to bargain exclusively for all employees in that unit, regardless of their union affiliation. The issue of the degree of union security to which the employer should agree, however, is still unresolved in a major part of American industry.

Certain more or less stereotyped arguments have been developed both in support of and in opposition to union security, which is usually discussed in terms of either the closed or the union shop. Employers frequently argue that one of the fundamental freedoms is the freedom to work, and that union security constitutes an abridgement of that basic right. Unions attack this contention principally on the ground that the individual has only the right to seek work, and that the exercise of this right is conditioned upon the willingness of some employer to hire him. Therefore, it is argued, compulsory union membership does not deny workers their "inalienable right to work" because no such right exists. In addition, unions are openly skeptical of the employers' interest in the welfare of individual workers; they assert that it was the continuing failure of employers to respect the dignity or to meet the minimum needs of individual workers which led to the rise of unionism as an institution.

Another argument advanced by employers is that since they are forbidden by law to prevent workers from joining unions, it is equally wrong for them to compel workers to join unions. To this unions reply that the collective agreements which they negotiate benefit all employees in the bargaining units covered, and that all who participate in these advantages should bear their fair share of the corresponding obligations. Employers contend, however, that it is undemocratic to force employees to join any organization of which they do not approve. Unions answer that this principle has its counterpart in political democracy: the tax-payer who votes against the victorious party must still abide by the laws passed by that party. This example is labeled a fake analogy by employers, however, who point out that any government by its very nature has the right to tax for its support, whereas no private organization has such a right.

One point stressed heavily by unions is that in an industrial democracy minority groups are not entitled to pursue their own objectives with the same freedom accorded their counterparts in a political democracy. Under existing law minority unions or groups of individuals have no right to bargain with the employer; indeed, his affirmative duty to bargain with the majority representative implies a negative duty to treat with no other. Unions argue, therefore, that compulsory union membership is the only means by which individual workers can be assured of a voice in the determination of their wages, hours, and working conditions. Employers reply that the law still permits individual workers to present grievances, and that, in any case, they should be permitted to decide for themselves whether or not they wish to participate in the governance of their own affairs.

With respect to the effects of union security upon the freedom and efficiency of business enterprise, businessmen are of divided opinion. Opponents of the closed or union shop charge that it tends to create a labor monopoly; that it destroys discipline and efficiency in the plant by vesting greater authority in union officials than in foremen; that it places the union, which has no financial interest or responsibility for the welfare of the enterprise, in a position effectively to check management's operating policies; that it tempts union officials to become increasingly dictatorial and arbitrary; and that as a consequence of all these factors, it tends to increase costs of production and to raise prices.

Some employers take the position, however, that the closed or union shop has certain attendant advantages. They argue that it eliminates factional strife within the working force by giving the exclusive bargaining representative an assured status; that it improves discipline by making the union answerable to management for violations of the collective agreement or of plant rules by individual employees; that it ends the frequent demands by the union for concessions from the employer solely for the purpose of holding the membership, and permits the union to devote its full energies to promoting maximum production; that it tends to standardize wages, hours, and working conditions within the industry; and that it brings about a greater feeling of responsibility and interest in their jobs on the part of employees, because they have a voice in determining the conditions under which they work.

The passage of the Labor Management Relations Act, 1947, which contains certain restrictions upon union security provisions discussed later in this section, has made the task of determining the number of workers covered by such provisions more difficult. For the year 1946, however, the United States Department of Labor, Bureau of Labor Statistics, reported that of approximately 15 million workers governed by collective agreements, 33 per cent were covered by the closed shop, 17 per cent by the union shop, and 25 per cent by maintenance of membership. An additional 3 per cent were covered by preferential hiring, and the remaining 22 per cent had no explicit form of union security. In 1951 the Bureau made a further study based upon a sample of 2651 agreements, covering 5,581,000 workers. Fifty-eight per cent of these workers were covered by union-shop clauses and 16 per cent by maintenance-of-membership provisions. Contracts covering the remaining 26 per cent of the workers provided only for sole recognition.

2.   THE ENDERBY CASE — XI

A

The Enderby Rubber Company and Local 417, URCL & PWA (CIO), agreed in their 1949 contract upon a "maintenance-of-membership clause" with a "voluntary check-off." (Cf. Art. I, sec. 4 of the 1950 contract, page 318 supra).

At the time of the 1950 contract renewal the Union included in its written demands one for a union shop. When this point was reached in the negotiations, the Company representatives indicated that they would refuse to consider any union-security provision which would force the "old-timers," most of whom belonged to the Enderby Employees Association, to join the CIO union. When it became clear that the Company was not going to yield on this point, the Union negotiators changed their demand to one for "a check-off of Union dues *or their equivalent* for all employees in the bargaining unit regardless of whether they are members of Local 417 or not." It was argued that such an arrangement would be "completely equitable" in that it would put an end to the "hitch-hiking" of the nonunion employees who had been sharing the gains the Union had won but had not been paying their share of the costs.

The initial Company reaction to this proposal was strongly negative. Blair, the Enderby attorney, pooh-poohed the proposal as being "ridiculously out of line with the limitations in the Taft-Hartley Act." Cooper, the Union lawyer, who was participating in the negotiations, had evidently anticipated this objection. "Would you accept," he asked Blair, "the opinion on that of the Hon. Senator Robert A. Taft himself?" Blair asked Cooper what he was talking about. "I am quoting," Cooper answered, taking a sheet from his brief case, "from Taft's statement in the 1947 debates. The citation is 93 Cong. Record 5088, and you'll find most of this in the NLRB opinion in the Union Starch and Refining Co. case, 87 N.L.R.B. 137 (1949):

> 'The rule adopted is substantially the rule now in effect in Canada . . . that . . . the union does not have to admit an employee . . . but the employee must nevertheless pay dues, even though he does not join the union. If he pays the dues without joining the union, he has the right to be employed. . . . Under the Canadian rule and under the rule of the committee, we pretty well take care of [the "free ride"] argument. There is not much argument left.' "

This quotation obviously shook the Company's negotiators a little bit. Blair insisted, however, that he could not fit the proposal in with the language of Section 8 (a) (3) of the LMRA, "at least unless the Company is willing to pay the 'dues' of non-CIO employees out of its own pocket." Cooper said he saw no difficulty at all, but he was obviously not quite clear about the matter. The Company negotiators finally rejected the proposal.

The Company committee then indicated that there was one change they were going to insist be made in this Section 4 of Article I. This was to write into it a provision that the Company would not be obligated to discharge any employee who had lost his "good standing" in the Union except where the reason for his being dropped by the Union was nonpayment of Union dues. Blair had apparently advised the Company officials that the old Section 4 was itself inconsistent with the provisions of the LMRA.

The Union negotiators opposed the Company proposal. "Would that mean," Curme (the Union President) asked, "that we could not enforce this clause against a fellow who stole union funds?" Blair admitted that this would be the effect of the proposed change but he insisted that this conclusion would be required by the language of Section 8 (a) (3) of the LMRA regardless of what the contract provided. "Suppose," Curme continued, "we had a fellow who kept on paying his dues to us but joined another union — which is a violation of our constitution and bylaws." "Same law," Blair replied, "same answer." Curme then asked about the case of a union member who might refuse to pay a special assessment "for political purposes," pointing out that nothing is said about such assessments in Section 8 (a) (3) of the Act. Blair's answer was that he had a little doubt about this case but assumed that discharge would not be permitted under the Act.

At this point Curme stated flatly that the Union would strike before they would agree to the proposed changes in Article I, Section 4. Blair advised the Company negotiators privately that there was probably no point in pressing this matter further, but that the Company would have to be careful not to apply this section of the agreement except in a manner consistent with the federal statute.

There was one other proposal made with respect to a change in the union security provisions of the contract. The Union negotiators made the offer to "drop everything out of Section 4 of Article I except the check-off if you will agree to leave up to the Union the determination of seniority for the purpose of applying Article IV of the Agreement." This suggestion never got very far, but it was not clear whether the objections to it were on the basis of legal or of practical difficulties.

Section 4 of Article I was finally, after all this discussion, carried over into the 1950–1952 agreement in the same form that had been used in the 1949 contract.

B

Three problems arose, during the 1950–1952 contract term, with respect to the application of Section 4 of Article I of the May 21, 1950, agreement.

1. Employee R. Loftin, a member of Local 417 on June 5, 1950, was subsequently expelled by the Union for "nonpayment of his dues." He was immediately, at the Union's request, discharged by the Company. He filed with the NLRB an unfair labor practice charge against both the Union and the Company, claiming violations of Sections 8 (a) and (b). His attorney offered to prove (a) that Loftin's "nonpayment of dues" was only

...

a matter of being two days late in making his tender of payment; (b) that other Union members were given at least a 30-day grace period on dues payment; (c) that the real reason for the hasty action by Union and Company was that Loftin was an admitted member of several "allegedly Communist" organizations.

The General Counsel of the NLRB faced the question of whether to prosecute Loftin's complaint before the Board.

2. Local 417, facing a problem of nonattendance at regular union meetings, increased its regular monthly dues (by a change in its bylaws duly made on October 10, 1950) from $2 to $2.50 with a provision that those who attended the monthly meetings would not have to pay the additional 50 cents.

Sherman Staunchly, a member of Local 417, did not attend the October, November, or December union meetings. The only dues he paid were those of $2 per month which were checked off by the Company pursuant to his earlier written authorization. He refused the demands of the Local 417 Secretary-Treasurer for the additional 50-cent items. He was thereupon expelled by the Union, and the Union advised the Company that Staunchly must be discharged.

White, the Enderby Industrial Relations Manager, concerned about the point raised by attorney Blair during the contract negotiations, sought Blair's advice about what could and should be done.

3. In May, 1951, Gordon Glibly, previously a leading member of the Enderby Employees Association, joined Local 417 of the Rubber Workers. He made no bones about his purpose, announcing it as being to work inside Local 417 to oust the incumbent president and officers. The Local 417 officers had been reluctant to admit Glibly but felt that a refusal to do so might crystallize a feeling they knew existed among some of their members and particularly because of their realization that they had no choice in view of the provision in the first part of Article 23 of the Local 417 bylaws. This Article, in full, was as follows:

> Membership shall be open to all non-supervisory employees of the Enderby Rubber Company regardless of race, creed, color or political belief; provided that any applicant for membership who has ever engaged in rival union activity against this organization shall serve a probationary period of one year during which time his monthly dues shall be one dollar ($1.00) more than those paid by regular members of this organization.

Glibly paid his initiation fee and for three months he paid his monthly dues, including the extra dollar. The fourth month he tendered only the regular dues, refusing to pay the dollar. After a stormy session at the Local 417 monthly meeting, a bare majority of the membership present voted to expel Glibly. The Company was advised that this necessitated Glibly's discharge. Acting on Blair's advice, White notified the Union that the Company was refusing to discharge Glibly because to do so would be in violation of the Labor Management Relations Act.

A grievance was then filed by the Union and, settlement proving impossible at the preliminary steps of the grievance procedure, the case was referred to arbitration. The argument t the arbitration hearing covered a wide range of contract, statutory, and "practical" considerations. The arbitrator, whether rightly or wrongly, ruled that the contract (Section 4 of Article I) required the Company to discharge Glibly, and that any "legal or statutory considerations are not within the province of the arbitrator." This left the Company at best in an uncertain position, and again attorney Blair's advice was sought.

3. DECISIONS OF COURTS AND ARBITRATORS

BERRY v. DONOVAN
Supreme Judicial Court, Massachusetts, 1905
188 Mass. 353, 74 N.E. 603

[Action in tort for damages for malicious interference with plaintiff's contract of employment. Plaintiff had been employed for four years as a shoemaker by Goodrich & Co. under a contract terminable at will. The employer entered into a contract with a national union of shoe workers of which the defendant was a representative and member. The contract provided, inter alia, that ". . . the employer agrees to hire, as shoe workers, only members of the Boot and Shoe Workers' Union in good standing, and further agrees not to retain any shoe worker in his employment after receiving notice from the union that such shoe worker is objectionable to the union, either on account of being in arrears for dues, or disobedience of union rules or laws, or from any other cause." Shortly after the contract was signed, the defendant, as a representative of the union, demanded that plaintiff be discharged. The record disclosed that the sole ground for the demand was that plaintiff, though repeatedly requested to do so, had refused to join the union.　Plaintiff had verdict and judgment for $1500.　Defendant appeals.]

KNOWLTON, C.J.　The primary right of the plaintiff to have the benefit of his contract and to remain undisturbed in the performance of it is universally recognized.　The right to dispose of one's labor as he will, and to have the benefit of one's lawful contract, is incident to the freedom of the individual, which lies at the foundation of the government in all countries that maintain the principles of civil liberty.　Such a right can lawfully be interfered with only by one who is acting in the exercise of an equal or superior right which comes in conflict with the other.　An intentional interference with such a right without lawful justification is malicious in law, even if it is from good motives and without express malice.

The only argument that we have heard in support of interference by labor unions in cases of this kind is that it is justifiable as a kind of competition.

[The court then acknowledged that rival businessmen were customarily justified in the name of competition for visiting harm on their competitors so long as their action was in the furtherance of their own self-advancement.　(See Bowen v. Matheson, 96 Mass. 499, 1867).　Similar considerations, said the court, would justify individual workmen competing with each other for job opportunities, but not "interference by a combination of persons. . . . In such a case the action taken by the combination is not in the regular course of their business as employees, either in the service in which they are engaged or in effort to obtain employment in other service."]

We understand that the attempted justification rests entirely upon another kind of so-called competition, namely, competition between employers and the employed, in an attempt of each class to obtain as large a share as possible of the income for their combined efforts in the industrial field.　In a strict sense this is hardly competition.　It is a struggle or contention of interests of different kinds, which are in opposition, so far as the division of profits is concerned.　In a broad sense, perhaps, the contending forces may be called competitors.　At all events, we may assume that, as between themselves, the principle which warrants competition permits also reasonable efforts, of a proper kind, which have a direct tendency to benefit one party in his business at the expense of the other.　It is no legal objection to action whose direct effect is helpful to one of the parties in the struggle that it is also directly

detrimental to the other.   But when action is directed against
the other, primarily for the purpose of doing him harm, and thus
compelling him to yield to the demand of the actor, and this
action does not directly affect the property or business or status
of the actor, the case is different, even if the actor expects to derive
a remote or indirect benefit from the act.   The gain which a labor
union may expect to derive from inducing others to join it is not
an improvement to be obtained directly in the conditions under
which the men are working, but only added strength for such
contests with employees as may arise in the future.   An object of
this kind is too remote to be considered a benefit in business, such
as to justify the infliction of intentional injury upon a third person
for the purpose of obtaining it.   If such an object were treated as
legitimate, and allowed to be pursued to its complete accomplishment, every employee would be forced into membership in a
union, and the unions, by a combination of those in different
trades and occupations, would have complete and absolute control
of all the industries of the country.   Employers would be forced
to yield to all their demands or give up business.   The attainment
of such an object in the struggle with employers would not be
competition, but monopoly.   A monopoly, controlling anything
which the world must have, is fatal to prosperity and progress.
In matters of this kind the law does not tolerate monopolies.
The attempt to force all laborers to combine in unions is against
the policy of the law, because it aims at monopoly.   It therefore
does not justify causing the discharge, by his employer, of an
individual laborer working under a contract.   It is easy to see
that for different reasons an act which might be done in legitimate
competition by one or two or three persons, each proceeding independently, might take on an entire difference of character, both
in its nature and its purpose, if done by hundreds in combination.

We have no desire to put obstacles in the way of employees who
are seeking by combination to obtain better conditions for themselves and their families.   We have no doubt that laboring men
have derived and may hereafter derive advantages from organization.   We only say that under correct rules of law, and with a
proper regard for the rights of individuals, labor unions cannot be
permitted to drive men out of employment because they choose
to work independently.   If disagreements between those who
furnish the capital and those who perform the labor employed in
industrial enterprises are to be settled only by industrial wars, it
would give a great advantage to combinations of employees, if

they would be permitted by force to obtain a monopoly of the labor market. But we are hopeful that this kind of warfare will soon give way to industrial peace, and that rational methods of settling such controversies will be adopted universally.

We hold that the defendant was not justified by the contract with Goodrich & Company, or by his relations to the plantiff, in interfering with the plantiff's employment under his contract. How far the principles which we adopt would apply under different conceivable forms of contract, to an interference with a workman not engaged, but seeking employment, or to different methods of boycotting, we have no occasion in this case to decide. . . .

Exceptions overruled.

NOTES

1. This case represents the attitude expressed by many of the early common law decisions. However, most of these decisions have been overruled and the majority of courts now hold that such provisions are enforceable. The language of the Massachusetts court in Hamer v. Nashawena Mills Inc., 315 Mass. 160, 52 N.E.2d 22 (1943), is typical: "The validity of a closed shop agreement, if freely and voluntarily made primarily for the mutual advantage of the parties, has always been upheld and enforced even if the opportunity for securing employment by other workmen, not members of the contracting union may thereby be greatly restricted or practically destroyed. Such an agreement has been recognized as a legitimate means which a labor union may employ to secure for its members all the work of their employers that they are competent to perform."

2. Although a union-security provision may be held valid and enforced, many courts still hold that concerted activity to obtain such a provision is illegal and can be enjoined. In Fashioncraft, Inc. v. Halpern, 313 Mass. 385, 48 N.E.2d 1 (1943), the Massachusetts court enjoined peaceful picketing for a closed shop. It held that such picketing was illegal and therefore not within the "free speech doctrine" or the state anti-injunction act. The court relied upon the same reasoning in enjoining peaceful picketing for the purpose of retaining a maintenance-of-membership provision originally adopted at the direction of the National War Labor Board. Colonial Press, Inc. v. Ellis, 321 Mass. 495, 74 N.E.2d 1 (1947), noted in 48 Col. L. Rev. 156 (1948).

3. The Supreme Judicial Court of Massachusetts has long

struggled with the problem of reconciling its conception of "legality of purpose" with an intelligible theory of competition. See, for example, Plant v. Woods, 176 Mass. 492, 57 N.E. 1011 (1900), and Pickett v. Walsh, 192 Mass. 572, 78 N.E. 753 (1906), discussed in Gregory, Labor and the Law 60–76 (2d ed. 1949). Compare with the Massachusetts decisions the results reached by the California Supreme Court in Smith Metropolitan Market Co. v. Lyons, 16 Cal. 2d 389, 106 P.2d 414 (1940), and Park and Tilford Import Corp. v. Int. Brotherhood of Teamsters, 27 Cal. 2d 599, 165 P.2d 891 (1946).

EXCHANGE BAKERY & RESTAURANT, INC. v. RIFKIN
Court of Appeals, New York, 1927
245 N.Y. 260, 157 N.E. 130

[Plaintiff operated its restaurant as a nonunion shop, hiring waitresses on a basis of employment at will, exacting from each of them the written commitment that they were not union members when hired and would not make any efforts to unionize the establishment. At the instigation of the defendants, members of a union, four of the plaintiff's employees were induced to join the union and to participate in a strike of the restaurant, accompanied by peaceful picketing for the purpose of forcing the employer to recognize and bargain with the union. Plaintiff seeks an injunction to restrain the defendants from continuing the picketing. Relief was denied in the trial court, but the decision was reversed by the Appellate Division, and this is an appeal.]

ANDREWS, J. A workman may leave his work for any cause whatever. He need make no defense, give no explanations. Whether in good or bad faith, whether with malice or without, no one can question his action. What one man may do, two may do or a dozen, so long as they act independently. If, however, any action taken is concerted; if it is planned to produce some result, it is subject to control. As always, what is done, if legal, must be to effect some lawful result by lawful means, but both a result and a means lawful in the case of an individual may be unlawful if the joint action of a number.

A combination to strike or to picket an employer's factory to the end of coercing him to commit a crime, or to pay a stale or disputed claim would be unlawful in itself although for an individual, his intent in leaving work does not make wrongful the act otherwise lawful. His wrong, if wrong there be, would consist of some threat, of something beyond the mere termination of his contract with his employer. Likewise a combination to effect many other results would be wrongful. Among them would be one to strike or picket a factory where the intent to injure rests solely on malice or ill will. Another's business may not be so injured or ruined. It may be attacked only to attain some purpose in the eye of the law thought sufficient to justify the harm that may be done to others.

The purpose of a labor union to improve the conditions under which its members do their work; to increase their wages; to assist them in other ways may justify what would otherwise be a wrong. So would an effort to increase its numbers and to unionize an entire trade or business. It may be as interested in the wages of those not members, or in the conditions under which they work as in its own members because of the influence of one upon the other. All engaged in a trade are affected by the prevailing rate of wages. All, by the principle of collective bargaining. Economic organization to-day is not based on the single shop. Unions believe that wages may be increased, collective bargaining maintained only if union conditions prevail, not in some single factory but generally. That they may prevail it may call a strike and picket the premises of an employer with the intent of inducing him to employ only union labor. And it may adopt either method separately. Picketing without a strike is no more unlawful than a strike without picketing. Both are based upon a lawful purpose. Resulting injury is incidental and must be endured.

Even if the end sought is lawful, the means used must be also. "Picketing" connotes no evil. It may not be accompanied, however, by violence, trespass, threats or intimidation express or implied. No crowds may be collected on or near the employer's property. The free entrance of strangers, customers or employees may not be impeded. There may be no threats — no statements oral or written, false in fact, yet tending to injure the employer's business. We here make no attempt to enumerate all the acts that might make picketing illegal. Doubtless there are others. When the situation in a particular case comes to be reviewed by the courts there will be no difficulty in drawing the line between acts permissible and acts forbidden.

We have been speaking in terms of the workman. We might equally have spoken in terms of the employer. The rule that applies to the one also applies to the other. The latter may hire and discharge men when and where he chooses and for any reason. But again any combination must be for lawful ends secured by lawful means. If believed to be for their interests employers may agree to employ non-union men only. By proper persuasion they may induce union men to resign from their unions. They may not, however, because of mere malice or ill will, combine to limit the opportunities of any one to obtain employment. The means adopted must be lawful. No violence or intimidation, no threats, no trespass, no harmful false statements, no means that would be improper were the workman the actor. . . .

In the case before us findings of fact were made by the Special Term resulting in a judgment for the defendants. Most of such findings were reversed by the Appellate Division. As a substitute new findings were made by that court and a sweeping injunction was granted to the plaintiff. It, therefore, becomes our duty to review these findings and to determine for ourselves whether they are sustained by the weight of the evidence.

In 1918 the plaintiff corporation was formed. From the first its intention was to employ only non-union waitresses in its restaurant. Always, with one exception, an applicant for employment was questioned as to her membership in any union and only those who denied such a connection were engaged. No contract as to this matter was then made but the applicant was hired at the rate of $8 per week for full time or $5 for half time. This hiring was at will and might be ended at any time by either party. (Cuppy v. Stollwerck Brothers, 216 N.Y. 591.) Thereafter the waitresses were asked repeatedly if they had joined a union. They always denied it. If it had been discovered that their denials were untrue they would have been at once discharged. Also after beginning work each waitress signed a paper stating that it was the understanding that she was not a member of any union, pledging herself not to join one or if she did to withdraw from her employment. She further promised to make no efforts to unionize the restaurant, and says that she will attempt to adjust by individual bargaining any dispute that may arise. This paper was not a contract. It was merely a promise based upon no consideration on the part of the plaintiff. . . .

The Appellate Division has based its decision in part upon the theory that the defendants wrongfully attempted to persuade the plaintiff's employees to break this alleged contract. Even had it been a valid subsisting contract, however, it should be noticed that whatever rule we may finally adopt, there is as yet no precedent in this court for the conclusion that a union may not persuade its members or others to end contracts of employment where the final intent lying behind the attempt is to extend its influence. . . .

The judgment of the Appellate Division should be reversed

and that of the Special Term affirmed, with costs in this court and in the Appellate Division.

[The dissenting opinion of Crane, J., with whom Kellogg and O'Brien, JJ., concurred, is omitted.]

NOTES

1. In Polk v. Cleveland Ry. Co., 20 Ohio App. 317, 151 N.E. 808 (1925), a union of streetcar employees in Cleveland sought an injunction against threatened violation of their closed-shop agreement. The court refused injunctive relief with the following statement: "Contracts by which an employer agrees to employ only union labor are contrary to public policy when they take in an entire industry . . . in a community so that they operate generally in that community to prevent or seriously deter craftsmen from working at their craft or workmen from obtaining employment under favorable conditions without joining a union . . ."

However, a majority of the more recent decisions hold that a closed-shop agreement is valid even though the union has a monopoly of the available jobs in the community. F. F. East Co. v. United Oystermen's Union, 130 N.J. Eq. 292, 21 A.2d 799 (1941); Corpus v. Hotel and Restaurant Employees, 61 Ariz. 483, 151 P.2d 705 (1944); Williams v. Quill, 277 N.Y. 1, 12 N.E.2d 547 (1938).

2. Where the union's membership is restricted so that the employee is prevented from working although he is willing to join the union, the courts have enjoined enforcement of union security provisions. This matter is more fully discussed at pages 857 et seq. infra.

In re PHOENIXVILLE PUBLISHING CO. and AMERICAN NEWSPAPER GUILD, NEWSPAPER GUILD OF PHILADELPHIA AND CAMDEN (CIO)
2 L.A. 10 (1946)

FREY, Arbitrator: — In Phoenixville, Pa., the company produces and distributes The Daily Republican, a six-day evening newspaper and conducts a commercial job shop. The union is a local of the American Newspaper Guild, and, since December 1944, the editorial, advertising, business, and circulation employees of the company have been a unit of the Philadelphia-Camden local . . . [This proceeding was to resolve certain issues upon which the parties were unable to reach a negotiated agreement. The one here discussed is union security.]

The Guild proposes the inclusion in the contract of the following article:

> The Publisher agrees that it will not, without the written consent of the guild, employ or retain as an employee any person to whom this agreement is made applicable under Art. 1 unless he is a member of the Guild in good standing or becomes a member within thirty (30) days of the date of his employment and thereafter remains a member in good standing.   The Guild agrees that it will admit to membership and retain in good standing any such employee who complies with the constitution and by-laws of the Guild provided he shall not have previously been expelled or suspended from any unit of the American Newspaper Guild.

The guild points out that it is not requesting a closed shop but a union shop, i.e., the employer, in hiring new employees, is not confined to those who are already members of the guild but may hire non-members of the guild provided they thereafter become members within the stipulated period.

The guild maintains that the guild (or union) shop for which it is contending would insure more harmony among the members of the staff as it would remove the natural resentment of the overwhelming majority of the employees against the occasional "free riders."   The guild refers to the fact that the great preponderance of guild contracts contains guild-shop provisions.   The guild asserts that the guild shop is of especial importance to it in the present situation because of alleged efforts on the part of representatives of management to discourage membership in the guild.

The publisher is alleged by the guild to have previously adhered to the principle of the union shop: In January 1938, the company entered into a collective bargaining agreement with an unaffiliated union of its employees and, in February, 1938, the company and that union agreed to a supplement to the contract which provided that the employees must become members of the union within two weeks, and this supplementary agreement was in fact enforced among the employees.

Finally, the guild points out that, while 11 of the 12 employees in the bargaining unit at the time of the hearing were members of the guild, the remoteness of Phoenixville from the center of activity of the guild local makes it difficult to combat any apathy which might develop among the employees with respect to union membership.

The publisher contends that the guild-shop provision "would

contravene the essential freedom of action guaranteed to all Americans in the Constitution and the Bill of Rights."

The publisher points out that the newspaper is published and circulated in a small community where the residents are particularly jealous of their rights and prerogatives of "belonging or not belonging," "joining or not joining"; that employees are recruited from this community and that any kind of requirement of union membership as a condition of employment (union security) would jeopardize the publisher's ability to hire suitable employees.

The publisher emphasizes that the guild has no rival union, that the War Labor Board did not direct a "guild shop" but only maintenance of union membership, and that the guild, itself, has accepted "open-shop" provisions in some initial contracts.

There are about 190 contracts between locals of the American Newspaper Guild and various publishers throughout the United States. Of these contracts, 92 contain provisions for the "guild" (or union) shops, and 42 contain the maintenance-of-membership provision evolved by the War Labor Board. It would thus appear that a contract provision for union security is the rule rather than the exception where the guild is by contract the collective bargaining agent of the employees in the bargaining unit.

I do not believe that the present management of the Phoenixville Publishing Company is antagonistic to the existence of the guild as the collective bargaining representative of its employees or that it has a policy or practice of discouraging its employees from becoming or remaining members of the guild. I do believe, however, that a provision in the contract requiring permanent employees to be members of the guild would, so long as the guild remains worthy of their membership, make for greater harmony among the employees, and to this extent would be to the mutual advantage of the publisher and the guild. In my opinion, such a provision would not seriously interfere with the publisher's selection of competent new employees despite the local conditions emphasized by the company, especially if the trial or probationary period is as long as 90 days, which is the period stipulated in Art. 15 or the partial agreement the parties have already executed.

The major reason offered by those who oppose provision for a closed shop or a union shop or for maintenance of membership is that it is un-American, and undemocratic to require an employee to belong to a union or any other organization as a condition of getting or holding a job. In general this argument has great merit. But one may question its validity when applied to organizations existing for the purpose of enabling the individual em-

ployee to achieve through collective action, a degree of equality of
bargaining power when dealing with his employer.   The process
of bargaining is the traditional and revered American way of arriving at the terms and conditions of all manner of commercial and
industrial situations — and this is the significant distinction between our economy and that of a totalitarian state, like Russia,
where such terms and conditions are established by governmental
fiat.   Even in the United States we have experienced the fact that,
where drastic inequality of bargaining power does exist, as for
example, between adult and child or lender and borrower, the
Government will move in and impose regulations upon the parties.

There can be no doubt that the average individual worker,
acting alone, has no capacity to bargain with his employer, and this
situation presents a constant threat of Government intervention
for the protection of those otherwise unable to protect themselves.
To the extent that there are labor organizations through which, by
collective action, workers can exert an influence for themselves
upon the development of the terms and conditions of their employment, this threat is removed or at least minimized.   From this
standpoint, therefore, labor unions, far from being un-American,
are a bulwark against an ever-expanding encroachment by Government upon the American processes of free enterprise.

Organizations having such a vital role in the perpetuation of our
American way of life, perform an important public function and
accordingly are not to be indiscriminately lumped with social clubs
and private societies of all sorts.   To require an employee, as a
condition of employment, to be a member of such an organization
is to require him not merely to participate in benefiting himself
and his fellow-workers but also to promote a long-range public
interest.

For the foregoing reasons, I cannot with sincerity oppose a contract provision requiring permanent employees to belong to the
collective bargaining agency provided the union is worthy of that
status.   The Philadelphia-Camden local has not been attacked
by the publisher.   To my knowledge there are few unions that
rival the guild with respect to the complete internal democracy
which it practices; and the Phoenixville unit appears to live up
to the best traditions of its parent organizations. . . .

Provision for neither maintenance of membership nor a union
shop should be included in the contract if the union in question
is not worthy of this trust.   There remains, however, a very important problem; how to deal with the situation which arises when
a union which has been accorded either maintenance of member-

ship or a union shop so conducts itself during the life of the contract as to furnish members with just cause for a desire to disaffiliate. This is a dilemma for which neither the maintenance-of-membership nor the union-shop provisions supplies an answer . . .

[In making his award on this issue, the arbitrator directed the parties to include a union security provision, and prescribed the form which it should take.]

NOTE

Newspapers and news-gathering agencies have frequently contended that the First Amendment to the Constitution guarantees them freedom from any legislative constraint or compulsion relating to their dealings with their employees. The argument that the NLRA was unconstitutional insofar as it applied to the employment practices of a news-gathering agency was rejected by the Supreme Court in Associated Press v. NLRB, 301 U.S. 103, 57 Sup. Ct. 650, 81 L. Ed. 953 (1937). Similarly, the contention of a newspaper that the National War Labor Board lacked the authority to direct the inclusion of a maintenance-of-membership provision in its contract with the American Newspaper Guild was held to be without merit in Matter of Patriot Co. and American Newspaper Guild, 14 War Lab. Rep. 355 (1944).

In re FORD MOTOR COMPANY OF CANADA (WINDSOR, ONT.) and UNITED AUTOMOBILE, AIRCRAFT AND AGRICULTURAL IMPLEMENT WORKERS OF AMERICA (CIO)
1 L.A. 439 (1946)

ARBITRATOR: . . . Justice I. C. Rand of Supreme Court of Canada. Basing my judgment on principles which I think the large majority of Canadians accept, I am unable, in the circumstances, to award a union shop. It would subject the company's interest in individual employees and their tenure of service to strife within the union and between them and the union which, with extraordinary consequences in one instance, has proved a serious matter for the company concerned; and it would deny the individual Canadian the right to seek work and to work independently of personal association with any organized group. It would also expose him, even in a generally disciplined organization to the danger of arbitrary action of individuals and place his economic life at the mercy of the threat as well as the action of power in an un-

controlled and, here, an unmatured group. It may be said that
that is the danger to the individual in society, but, while we must
run the risk of the latter, certainly, in some situations, it is desirable to withhold the same power from smaller units.   This points
to a field within labor organization affecting the interest of the individual, the employer, and the public which perhaps must be left
for legislation.   At least a code of these relations cannot be made
a conditional annex to the determination of a limited point of
dispute as I have it here.

I should point out that the employer can, by his consent, subject
his employees to the full force of the organized power of unionism,
and, in many groups in trades and employment in Canada, that
has taken place; e.g., printing trades, including that work in many
newspapers, longshoremen, theatrical and moving picture operators, hotel and restaurant employees, building workers, pulp and
paper mill workers, miners, milk and dairy employees, seamen, and
others.   Some of these trades are organized as exclusive crafts, but
their power is recognized and strengthened whenever, in a plant,
permanent or temporary employees are taken from their ranks.
In these cases, the employer's interest in his personnel, except as to
competency, is surrendered, and the individual's right against the
organization, except as a member of it, is destroyed.   It may be of
some interest that the Ford Motor Company in the United States,
with over 100,000 employees affected, has accepted the union shop
and check-off in all of its production and assembly plants and units
in that country.

On the other hand, the employees as a whole become the beneficiaries of union action, and I doubt if any circumstance provokes
more resentment in a plant than this sharing of the fruits of
unionist work and courage by the nonmember.   It is irrelevant
to try to measure benefits in a particular case; the protection of
organized labor is premised as a necessary security to the body of
employees.   But the company, in this case, admits that substantial
benefits for the employees have been obtained by the union, some
in negotiation and some over the opposition of the company.   It
would not then, as a general proposition, be inequitable to require
of all employees a contribution towards the expense of maintaining the administration of employee interests, of administering the
law of their employment.

What I am dealing with is employment in a mass production
industry.   The employees are coordinated with mechanical functions which in large measure require only semi-skilled operators.
No long apprenticeship is necessary to acquire those skills; some

operations can be taken on at once, and there is a general rise in complexity. But it is essentially the utilization of concentrated manpower in a framework of machines in which the initiative and artistry of the individual is either nonexistent or becomes stereotyped. The large body of employees, from their stature and their average skills, are inescapably of a class that must be governed more or less in the mass and by mass techniques, and one chief object of the plant law is to diffuse authority among the labor representatives to make administration as flexible as possible. But, in such a body, we cannot look for that generalized individuality in understanding and appreciation of the necessity for employee organization which craftsmen have tended to evolve. Their objectives and their conception of union function are much too simplified for that. With the aggravation of an annual layoff, the result is that the union is subject to a periodic disorganizing tendency. Then, too, the union has little to offer the men except their plant law: There is less individual appeal of or opportunity for social activities or union benefit provisions than in other classes of labor. In these conditions, it is, in my opinion, essential to the larger concern of the industry that there be mass treatment in the relation of employees to that organization that is necessary to the primary protection of their interests.

I consider it entirely equitable then that all employees should be required to shoulder their portion of the burden of expense for administering the law of their employment, the union contract; that they must take the burden along with the benefit.

The obligation to pay dues should tend to induce membership and this, in turn, to promote that wider interest and control within the union which is the condition of progressive responsibility. If that should prove to be the case, the device employed will have justified itself. The union, on its part, will always have the spur to justify itself to the majority of the employees in the power of the latter to change their bargaining representatives.

It may be argued that it is unjust to compel nonmembers of a union to contribute to funds over the expenditure of which they have no direct voice and even that it is dangerous to place such money power in the control of an unregulated union. But the dues are only those which members are satisfied to pay for substantially the same benefits, and, as any employee can join the union and still retain his independence in employment, I see no serious objection in this circumstance. The argument is really one for a weak union. Much more important to the employee will be the right which is being secured to him in the conditions to be attached to the check-off, to have a voice in that of which he is now a victim, the decision to strike.   Whether the constitution of the union is sufficiently democratic in securing the powers of the members or such money power is dangerous are matters which concern the members and the public.   The remedy lies essentially in the greater effectiveness of control in the members; but outside interference with that internal management is obviously a matter of policy for the legislature.   Apart from the strengthening of the union on which I have made observations in these reasons, I see no special interest of the employer as such in these possible dangers, and, in the present state of things, those who control capital are scarcely in a position to complain of the power of money in the hands of labor.   The company's suggestion was that, in relation to the union shop, the union should be left to its own resources until such time as legislation was passed placing controls and requirements on the constitution of unions, their accountability to members and the public, and other features of their internal organization.   But this assumes the exhaustion of the resources of private negotiation which I think unwarranted, and, in the actual circumstances and for the reasons I have given, it would perpetuate a ruinous hostility in labor relations; and Mr. Aylesworth conceded that the scheme I am about to make effective went "quite" a way to meet his objections to a union shop.

My award is a check-off compulsory upon all employees who come within the unit to which the agreement applies.   It shall continue during the period of the contract.   The amount to be deducted shall be such sum as may from time to time be assessed by the union on its members, according to its constitution, for general union purposes; it shall not extend to a special assessment or to an increment in an assessment which relates to special union benefits such as, for instance, union insurance, in which the nonmember employee, as such, would not participate or the benefit of which he would not enjoy.   The deduction shall be made only in the conditions and circumstances laid down by the constitution and bylaws of the union, but it shall not include any entrance fee. At the end of each calendar month, and prior to the 10th of the following month, the company shall remit by check the total of the deductions to the local union.

This mechanism, from the orthodox standpoint, preserves the basic liberties of company and employee which I have mentioned. The assessment affects only the employees; the employer is concerned only in the expense of the check-off and the strength which it may give to the union.   But the expense can properly be taken as the employer's contribution toward making the union, through its greater independence, more effective in its disciplinary pressure even upon employees who are not members, an end which the company admits to be desirable. I should perhaps add that I do not for a moment suggest that this is a device of general applicability. Its object is primarily to enable the union to function properly. In other cases, it might defeat that object by lessening the necessity for self-development. In dealing with each labor situation, we must pay regard to its special features and circumstances.

Note that Judge Rand suggests that the "field . . . must be left for legislation." Two years later the Canadian Parliament adopted the Industrial Relations and Disputes Investigation Act, 1948. (11 & 12 Geo. VI, c. 54.) It makes provisions for union security which are substantially similar to those which were contained in our own National Labor Relations Act of 1935. Section 4 (3) of the Act provides that "No employer . . . shall seek . . . to compel an employee to refrain from becoming or to cease to be a member . . . of a trade union and no other person shall seek by intimidation or coercion to compel an employee to become or refrain from becoming or to cease to be a member of a trade union." Section 6 authorizes permissive closed-shop as well as preferential-hiring clauses, with the proviso that "No provisions in a collective bargaining agreement requiring an employer to discharge an employee because such employee is or continues to be a member of, or engages in activities on behalf of a union other than a specified trade union, shall be valid." Does this meet the problem the judge had in mind?

The Dominion Act encourages the adoption of comparable legislation by the provinces and makes provision for integrated enforcement. Section 62. In 1950, Ontario substantially revised its labor legislation to conform with the Dominion Act and adopted provisions similar to those cited above. Revised Statutes of Ontaro, 1950 (c. 194, secs. 33 and 47 (c)).

NOTES

1. What arguments would you present at the bargaining table on behalf of management and on behalf of the union in the following situation?

A plant employing 600 men was established for the purpose of producing certain auto parts. Most of its labor was semiskilled or unskilled, and because of the kind of work it had a high labor turnover. During the first six months after it began operations the United Auto Workers and the Machinists engaged in a vigorous organizing drive. Management posted bulletins urging the employees to "preserve their freedom," and both unions accused management of discharging union members but no charges were ever filed and the accusations were never proved. In a Board election the vote was UAW, 280; Machinists, 190; No Union, 80. The UAW, upon certification, demanded a union shop with a check-off of dues. Management offered a maintenance-of-membership provision without a check-off.

2. May there be situations where the union will prefer not to have a union shop? For years the UAW struggled to obtain a foothold in the Ford Motor Company but was able to develop only a relatively small nucleus of members in an underground organization. Many employees, although favoring the Union, were afraid to join, but others were either extremely anti-Union or planted spies. In 1941 the Union staged a walkout and a bitter strike ensued. The Company, which was reported to have said that it would never sign a contract, suddenly offered not only to recognize the Union but also to grant a union shop. What dangers are involved in the Union accepting this offer? Is it practical for the Union to refuse the union shop?

THE FORD MOTOR COMPANY and UAW–CIO,
LOCAL NO. 906
14 L.R.R.M. 2625 (1944)

[Smith and Elvin were test drivers of army trucks. They were expelled from the Union and the Company was asked to discharge them under the union-shop agreement. The Company refused on the grounds that the men were expelled solely because they were testing their trucks in half the time taken by the other drivers. The umpire, after thorough consideration of the evidence, found that the expulsion was because Smith and Elvin were causing discord among Union members, but he also found that the discord arose from their high production rate. The Union contended that even though an employee was expelled because he failed to slow down, the Company must discharge him.]

PERMANENT UMPIRE — Harry Shulman. Protection of union members against unjust expulsion in general is not the function, privilege, or duty of the employer. His interest in the general justice of an expulsion is no different from or greater than that of an outsider. His special interest is in the maintenance of proper personnel for his business. So long as that special interest is satisfied, it is of no importance to him that a particular employee must be discharged, because of his loss of membership in the union and replaced by one who is a member in good standing . . . even when the expulsion interferes with the operation of his business, he enters the arena not as gladiator to champion the cause of the expelled member, but as a party fighting for his own interests and against interference with his own right.

Now the provision for a union shop at Ford is not the whole agreement of the parties. Their agreement sets down many other rights, obligations and procedures. It sets down, for example, the Union's "adherence to the principle of a fair day's work for a fair day's pay" and its agreement to "use its best efforts in behalf of the company both as to work and as to conduct in its performance." It states the agreement of the union and of its members not to cause or take part in "any slowdown, curtailment of work, restriction of production, interference with work," or the like; and it recognizes the right of the Company to discipline any employee taking part in any violation of this provision . . . These are provisions which must be read along with that for a union shop.

The provision for a union shop is an integral part of the whole agreement. It is not inconsistent with these provisions. On the contrary it is meant to aid in the achievement of these same objectives . . . It follows that a use of the union shop provision to slow-down or interfere with production is a perversion of its agreed upon function and is a betrayal of its promised objectives . . . There can be no threat to union security in recognizing the defense advanced by the Company in this case. The defense is narrow. It does not touch the Union's freedom to require from its members loyalty and conduct becoming a union member. The defense is limited to cases in which the expulsion infringes rights assured to the Company.

Recognition of the defense here asserted is not an undue interference with the internal affairs of the Union. As stated above, we are not concerned with any attempt of an expelled member to get back into good standing in the union. We are not here required to determine the rights of a union member, to affect his relationship to the Union or to alter the decision of the Union with respect to the good standing of a member. Insofar as this case is concerned those are matters which can properly be left to the Union, for here the issue is, what is the employer required to do.

But even if the issue were different, the view that a decision of the Union respecting the standing of a member cannot under any circumstances be the concern of the employer or arbitrable under the contract is unrealistic, reactionary and without support . . . If a member is expelled because he refused to slow down his production and if the employer is required to honor the expulsion, then the decision surely must concern him since it directly affects him. To say that he is not concerned is to say that he is not to be concerned about his own production.

To require termination of employment under these circumstances would be to impair the rights and obligations which the union shop was designed to implement rather than impede. I hold, therefore, that the Company need not discharge Smith and Elvin.

NOTES

1. Six members of the UAW–CIO were expelled for dual unionism in supporting the Mechanic Educational Society of America. The Union asked the Electric Auto-Lite to discharge them under a maintenance-of-membership clause, and the Company refused. Arbitrator Ralph Seward held: "The employer is required, upon the union's demand under maintenance of membership clause, to discharge employees suspended from membership in the union without inquiry into the fairness of the union's trial proceedings or into the merits of the dispute between the union and the employees involved." Electric Auto-Lite and UAW–CIO, 14 L.R.R.M. 2631 (1944).

2. Other arbitrators have not so narrowly limited the power of the company to inquire into the propriety of expulsion under a union-security agreement. In Re John Wood Manuf. Co. and UAW — AFL, 1 L.A. 43 (1945), seven employees were summarily suspended for criticizing the local officers and negotiating committee. The Company refused to discharge them under a maintenance-of-membership agreement. The Arbitration Board (Jacob B. Courshon, Chairman) held that the Company's refusal to discharge was proper, and stated: "The union's contention that it is not for the company to inquire into the reason of the suspension of the employees in question nor how the suspension was effected as those are matters of internal functions of the union is usually and ordinarily true. However, when the internal functioning of the union results in adversely affecting the rights of a party outside the union, then it becomes the privilege of the party

so affected to determine on such action as is lawfully open to it to prevent the adverse effect . . . Since summary discharge from the company was demanded, then the Company, in exercise of its rights to maintain its organization had the right to inquire into the reasons for the suspension and the propriety thereof."

3. Not only the employer's right to question the propriety of union disciplinary action, but also that of the arbitrator, was challenged by the union in In re American Tel. and Tel. Co. and Nat. Fed. of Telephone Workers, 6 L.A. 31 (1947). The case involved the expulsion from the Union of some Company employees, following their refusal to pay fines imposed as a consequence of their crossing a picket line during a strike against the Company. The arbitrator held that the men must either pay the fines or be discharged. He ruled that the Union's disciplinary action was "subject to scrutiny" by an arbitrator only on limited, specific grounds, namely, if the disciplinary action was the result of the member's refusal to violate some law or public policy, or to violate the collective agreement between a union and an employer; or if the disciplinary action contravened the Union's constitution or bylaws.

4. Suppose the union improperly refuses readmission of the inactive member holding a valid withdrawal card and insists that he be discharged under a union-shop agreement. May the company or an arbitrator question or set aside the union's decision? See In re RKO Radio Pictures, Inc. and Office Employees Int. Union, 11 L.A. 268 (1948).

4. LEGISLATION — FEDERAL

It was not until 1951 that the Railway Labor Act of 1926 was amended to permit the inclusion of union-shop and check-off provisions in agreements within the coverage of that statute. Act of January 10, 1951, Pub. L. No. 914, 81st Cong., 1st Sess. (45 U.S.C.A. Sec. 152). Such clauses had been expressly forbidden by the 1934 amendments at the request of the unions themselves because of their fears that company-dominated organizations would threaten the existence of bona fide unions.

As early as 1935, however, Congress had approved union security in principle through the enactment of the National Labor Relations Act:

Section 8. . . . It shall be an unfair labor practice for an employer (3) by discrimination in regard to hire or tenure

of employment or any term or condition of employment to
encourage or discourage membership in any labor organization: *Provided,* That nothing in this Act . . . shall preclude
an employer from making an agreement with a labor organization (not established, maintained, or assisted by any action
defined in this Act as an unfair labor practice) to require as
a condition of employment membership therein, if such labor
organization is the representative of the employees as provided in section 9 (a) , in the appropriate collective bargaining
unit covered by such agreement when made.

One of the most interesting questions faced by the Board in the
administration of Section 8 (3) arose in connection with the treatment of maintenance-of-membership clauses. In May, 1941, the
Kearny, N.J., shipyard of the Federal Shipbuilding & Dry Dock
Co. was seized by the Federal Government, following its refusal to
accept a recommendation of the National Defense Mediation
Board that a maintenance-of-membership provision be incorporated in the Company's contract with the Industrial Union of
Marine & Shipbuilding Workers, CIO.[164] Company officials
charged publicly that they were being forced to accept the closed
shop. This the Board denied. The point was then raised that if
maintenance of membership was not synonymous with the closed
shop, it was not covered by the proviso in Section 8 (3) of the
Wagner Act and was therefore illegal.[165] This matter was referred by President Roosevelt to Board Chairman William H.
Davis with the suggestion that "you and your associates consider
this question — if necessary, with the members of the National
Labor Relations Board — in order that the Government may avoid
any conflict in its position." Chairman Davis thereupon obtained
the memorandum from Robert B. Watts, General Counsel of the
NLRB, which is summarized below.

> The proviso to Section 8 (3) of the Act provides that noth-
> ing in the Act or in any other statute of the United States
> shall preclude an employer from making certain agreements.
> Consequently, if a maintenance-of-membership clause comes
> within the terms of the proviso to Section 8 (3) it is not un-
> lawful under Section 8 of the Act. . . .

[164] A complete history of the case may be found in Report on the Work of
the National Defense Mediation Board (U.S. Dept. of Labor, Bureau of
Labor Statistics, Bull. No. 714, 1942) .
[165] See Opinion on Legality of Union Maintenance Clauses, 10 L.R.R.M.
1294.

The agreements protected by the terms of the proviso to Section 8 (3) are those which "require as a condition of employment membership" in the contracting labor organization. Clearly the maintenance-of-membership clause does no more than "require as a condition of employment membership" in the contracting union. By virtue of this type of clause an employee who becomes a member of the union must upon pain of discharge remain a member for a limited period. The closed shop provision and the maintenance-of-membership clause differ only in that the former makes union membership a condition of employment with respect to all employees, whereas the maintenance-of-membership clause is more limited, making membership a condition of employment only with respect to employees who have already joined the union, either before or during the life of the contract. While one provision is more severe than the other, both fall within the terms of the proviso, since they "require as a condition of employment membership" in the contracting union.

. . . the legislative history of the Act does not warrant any conclusion that Congress intended to confine the protection of the proviso to closed shop contracts. . . . In sum, although the legislative history of the Act shows specific discussion of the relation between the proviso and closed shop contracts, there is no reason to believe that Congress intended the proviso to Section 8 (3) to protect only one species of agreement requiring as a condition of employment membership in a contracting labor organization.

The National Labor Relations Board has frequently held, of course, that the closed shop contract may be lawful because of the proviso to Section 8 (3) . . . . The Board, however, has not confined the protection of the proviso to closed shop contracts. . . .

Upon the basis of the above discussion I conclude: (1) that the proviso to Section 8 (3) makes it lawful under the National Labor Relations Act and under any other statute of the United States for an employer to make an agreement with an unassisted union, which is the exclusive representative of the employees in an appropriate unit, requiring as a condition of employment that such employees be members of the contracting union; (2) that the proviso is not confined to the closed shop variety of contract; and (3) that an employer does not engage in unfair labor practices within Section 8 of the National Labor Relations Act by including in a contract with a proper labor organization, a maintenance-of-membership clause.

Much of the public debate which preceded the enactment of the LMRA in 1947 was focused on the union-security issue. Many people were "for" or "against" the Taft-Hartley amendments depending upon how they (or their ancestors) felt about the "closed shop," a phrase used loosely in the common parlance to cover not only what is technically a closed shop, but also the union shop, maintenance-of-membership provisions, and the "closed union." From this welter of emotional confusion emerged four amendments to the old Wagner Act, which became Sections 8 (a) (3), 8 (b) (1) (proviso), 8 (b) (2), and 9 (e) of the 1947 Act. The provisions of Sections 8 (a) (3) and 9 (e) were further amended by Act of October 22, 1951, Pub. L. No. 189, 82d Cong., 1st Sess. These provisions of the Act (which is set forth in the Appendix) should be studied carefully.

In very brief summary it may be said that the amendments brought about the following changes:

(a) The union shop, rather than the closed shop, is the most severe form of union-security provision which may now be included in collective bargaining agreements. Under the former, the employer is free to hire new employees without regard for their membership or nonmembership in the union, with the proviso that such new employees must join the union within thirty days after becoming employed. Under the latter, authorized by the Wagner Act, union membership is a condition of hire. (Section 8 (a) (3) first proviso.)

(b) Prior to the adoption of the 1951 amendments the Act required as a condition precedent to the inclusion of a union-shop clause in collective bargaining agreements that "a majority of the employees eligible to vote in [an election called for that purpose] have voted to authorize such labor organization to make such an agreement." [166] This is no longer necessary. The inclusion of union-security provisions is now solely a matter of bargaining, subject only to the proviso contained in Section 8 (a) (3) (ii) which forbids the making of such an agreement between an employer and

[166] Sections 8 (a) (3) (ii) and 9 (e) (1) of the Labor Management Relations Act of 1947. Hogan, The Meaning of the Union Shop Elections, 2 Indust. & Lab. Rel. Rev. 319 (1949), presents a forceful portrayal of the significance of these elections, and gives some indication of the reasons which led to the repeal of these provisions. Among the statistical data presented, for example, is a table showing that during the first year following the enactment of the 1947 legislation, a total of 23,584 such elections were held, resulting in the authorization of the union shop in 23,055 or more than 97 per cent of the cases.

a union whose authority to do so otherwise has been rescinded within one year prior thereto by an election conducted in the manner prescribed in Section 9 (e).

(c) The employer will not be justified in discharging an employee for nonmembership in the union, even under a union-shop clause, if membership was denied the employee on discriminatory grounds or for any reason other than his refusal to pay initiation fees and dues.   (Section 8 (a) (3) second proviso.)

(d) Unions, while free to adopt and enforce rules governing membership (Sec. 8 (b) (1) proviso), may not force an employer to discharge an employee under the circumstances enumerated in the preceding paragraph.   (Section 8 (b) (2).)

Neither the Wagner Act nor the amendments give protection to an employer who discharges an employee under a union-security agreement made with a union which he has in any manner assisted or dominated.   The Board and the courts have not hesitated to invalidate such provisions even though the employer has given only slight assistance to a bona fide affiliated union.   See NLRB v. Electric Vacuum Cleaner Co., 315 U.S. 685, 62 Sup. Ct. 846, 86 L. Ed. 1120 (1942).

In Wallace Corp. v. NLRB, 323 U.S. 248, 65 Sup. Ct. 238, 89 L. Ed. 216 (1944), an employer entered into a consent election agreement with two contending unions, stipulating that he would grant a closed shop to the winner.   This agreement, which was approved by the NLRB Regional Director, also provided that one union, affiliated with the CIO, would drop its charges that the rival Independent union was company dominated and assisted. The Independent won the election and demanded the closed shop, indicating at the same time that it intended to refuse admission to certain members of the losing CIO union, and thereby procure their discharge.   The employer protested but, nevertheless, carried out the agreement.   The Independent thereupon made good its threat; as a consequence, 43 of the CIO members were discharged.   The Board subsequently found that the employer's discharge of the CIO members constituted a violation of Section 8 (a) (3) of the Act.   In upholding this finding in a five-to-four decision the Supreme Court stated at page 256:

No employee can be deprived of his employment because of his prior affiliation with any particular union.   The Labor Relations Act was designed to wipe out such discrimination in industrial relations.   Numerous decisions of this Court dealing with the Act have established beyond doubt that workers shall not be discriminatorily discharged because of their affiliation with a union. We do not construe the provision authorizing a closed shop contract as indicating an intention on the part of Congress to authorize a majority of workers and a company, as in the instant case, to penalize minority groups of workers by depriving them of that full freedom of association and self-organization which it was the prime purpose of the Act to protect for all workers. It was as much a deprivation of the rights of these minority employees for the company discriminatorily to discharge them in collaboration with Independent as it would have been had the company done it alone. To permit it to do so by indirection, through the medium of a "union" of its own creation, would be to sanction a readily contrived mechanism for evasion of the Act.

The Court then affirmed the Board's conclusion that such conduct was sufficient to revive the pre-election charges filed by the CIO against the employer and the Independent. Accordingly, it ordered reinstatement of the discharged CIO members and disestablishment of the employer's contract with the Independent.

The essence of any closed- or union-shop or maintenance-of-membership provision is that employees who fail to maintain their membership in good standing must be discharged by the employer. The Board's position under the Wagner Act, reflected in the Wallace case, was first established in Matter of Rutland Court Owners, Inc., 44 N.L.R.B. 587, 11 L.R.R.M. 42 (1942), clarified, 46 N.L.R.B. 1040, 11 L.R.R.M. 200 (1943). In that case, unlike the facts in the Wallace case, the contracting union was not company dominated nor did the employer know, when he entered into the closed-shop agreement, that it contemplated using it to eliminate the rival union members from the shop. The Board there held that the employer had committed an unfair labor practice in knowingly making discharges for engaging in conduct protected by Section 7 of the Act at a time when such conduct was proper. Further extensions of the Rutland Court doctrine were made in Matter of Cliffs Dow Chemical Co., 64 N.L.R.B. 1419, 17 L.R.R.M. 185 (1945), and in Matter of Portland Lumber Mills, 64 N.L.R.B. 159, 17 L.R.R.M. 88 (1945). Ultimately, however, the doctrine was rejected by the Supreme Court in Colgate-Palmolive Peet Co. v. NLRB, 338 U.S. 355, 70 Sup. Ct. 166, 94 L. Ed. 161 (1949), where the Court said: "Shorn of embellishment, the Board's policy makes interference and discrimination by fellow employees an unfair labor practice of the employer. Yet the legislative history [of the Wagner Act] conclusively shows that Congress . . . refused to word Section 7 so as to hamper coercion of employees by fellow employees."

The amendments in the Taft-Hartley Act in effect revive the Rutland Court doctrine, but they go further. It is now an unfair labor practice (1) for an employer to discharge an employee for nonmembership if he has reason to believe that such status is attributable to discrimination or reasons other than nonpayment of dues and initiation fees (Section 8 (a) (3)) and (2) for a union to seek such a discharge or to take discriminatory action of its own (Section 8 (b) (2)). These provisions have frequently been invoked in proceedings before the Board and it is most probable that increasing resort will be made to them in the future. Principal developments thus far may be summarized as follows:

(a) The union-security provision, to be valid in any case, must be inserted in the contract as the result of "an agreement" between the parties; hence, such clauses cannot be forced upon the parties in awards made under compulsory arbitration proceedings held pursuant to state legislation. New Jersey Bell Tel. Co. v. Communication Workers of America, etc., 5 N.J. 354, 75 A.2d 721 (1950), and Amalgamated Assn., etc. v. Wisconsin Employment Relations Board, 340 U.S. 383, 71 Sup. Ct. 359, 95 L. Ed. 364 (1951). (The issue of precedence of federal over state law, involved in the latter case, is treated in detail at pages 842 et seq.)

(b) The Board has accorded literal interpretation to the language contained in the second proviso of Section 8 (a) (3) which forbids discharge for nonmembership pursuant to a union-security clause if the employer has reasonable grounds for believing that membership was (A) not available on the same terms applicable to others, or (B) denied or terminated for reasons other than failure to tender dues or initiation fees. In the leading case of Union Starch & Refining Company [167] an employer was found to have violated the (B) portion of this proviso when it was shown that the employees in question had in fact tendered dues and initiation fees but failed to file applications for membership, take an oath of loyalty to the union and attend a union meeting for the purpose of being voted upon. Other cases have established that employees may not be excluded from the union (and discharged as a consequence) for failure to pay dues and initiation fees which accrued prior to the current contract,[168] although they

---

[167] 87 N.L.R.B. 779, 25 L.R.R.M. 1176 (1949), enforced, 186 F.2d 1008 (7th Cir. 1951), cert. denied, 342 U.S. 815 (1951).
[168] New York Shipbuilding Corp., 89 N.L.R.B. 1446, 26 L.R.R.M. 1124

may be required to pay dues for the month in which they join the union in addition to the initiation fee.[169] Neither general assessments [170] nor fines [171] levied by the union are "dues" within the meaning of the proviso, and attempts to disguise "fines" as "dues" have proved ineffectual.[172] The Board has recently held in one case [173] and intimated in another [174] that the employer violates the (A) portion of the proviso by discharging an employee who was excluded from the union for failure to pay back dues (accrued prior to current contract) because membership in such cases is not available on the same terms and conditions generally applicable to others.   Some of these cases as well as their implications, including an analysis of the employer's duty to inquire into the internal affairs of the union, are appraised in Macaluso, The NLRB "Opens the Union," Taft-Hartley Style, 36 Cornell L.Q. 443 (1951).

(c) The closed shop is now prohibited and appropriate relief may be sought in proceedings before the Board.   Hence, equitable relief for the victims of discrimination in closed-shop-union situations, to the extent formerly granted by the courts,[175] will now be withheld (in cases where interstate commerce is affected) since they fall within the Board's exclusive jurisdiction over unfair labor practice proceedings.[176]

(d) The Board has been alert in the detection of superficially harmless and nondiscriminatory contractual provisions which, upon close examination, have the effect of compelling the employer to maintain a noncontractual closed shop.   Thus in the

---

(1950) ; General American Aerocoach, etc., 90 N.L.R.B. 239, 26 L.R.R.M. 1188 (1950).

[169] Chisholm-Ryder Co., 94 N.L.R.B. 508, 28 L.R.R.M. 1062 (1951).

[170] International Harvester Co., 95 N.L.R.B. 730, 28 L.R.R.M. 1337 (1951).

[171] Pen and Pencil Workers Union, 91 N.L.R.B. 883, 26 L.R.R.M. 1583 (1950); Eclipse Lumber Co., 95 N.L.R.B. 464, 28 L.R.R.M. 1329 (1951).

[172] Electric Auto-Lite Co., 92 N.L.R.B. 1073, 27 L.R.R.M. 1205 (1950), noted in 12 Ohio S.L.J. 297 (1951).   See also New York Shipbuilding Co., 89 N.L.R.B. 1446, 26 L.R.R.M. 1124 (1950).

[173] Eclipse Lumber Co., 95 N.L.R.B. 464, 28 L.R.R.M. 1329 (1951).

[174] Foley's Mill & Cabinet Works, 95 N.L.R.B. 743, 28 L.R.R.M. 1378 (1951).

[175] Clark v. Curtis, 76 N.Y.S.2d 3, 21 L.R.R.M. 2139 (1947), affirmed without opinion, 297 N.Y. 1014, 80 N.E.2d 536 (1948); Wilson v. Newspaper and Mail Deliverers' Union, 123 N.J. Eq. 347, 197 Atl. 720 (1938); Dotson v. Int. Alliance, 34 Cal. 2d 362, 210 P.2d 5 (1949); Williams v. Int. Brotherhood of Boilermakers, 27 Cal. 2d 586, 165 P.2d 903 (1946); James v. Marinship Corp., 25 Cal. 2d 721, 155 P.2d 329 (1944).

[176] Ryan v. Simons, 100 N.Y.S.2d 18 27 L.R.R.M. 2003 (1950); cf. Amalgamated Assn, etc. v. Wisconsin Employment Relations Board, 340 U.S. 383, 71 Sup. Ct. 359, 95 L. Ed. 364 (1951).

maritime industry the Board has found that a provision requiring the employer to recruit men through a union hiring hall, while nondiscriminatory on its face, nevertheless resulted in practice *in that case* in the maintenance of closed-shop conditions.[177]   A similar result was reached in the so-called ITU cases involving the printing industry.[178]   At the same time, it is clear that the Board to date has not held that hiring through the offices of the union is per se an unfair labor practice.   In a recent dictum it said, "assuming, *arguendo* that the Respondent Company and the Respondent Unions entered into such an agreement, we have not found a provision that personnel be secured through the offices of a union violative of the Act, absent evidence that the union unlawfully discriminated in supplying the company with personnel.   [Citing cases.]" [179]

(e)   What effect, if any, will the inclusion of an invalid union-security provision have upon the remainder of the contract?   Is the contract severable or entire?   Re Port Publishing Company, 231 N.C. 395, 57 S.E.2d 366 (1950) ; Polk v. Cleveland Ry. Co., 20 Ohio App. 317, 151 N.E. 808 (1925) ; International Union v. J. I. Case, 250 Wis. 63, 26 N.W.2d 305 (1947).   If the contract would otherwise be construed as an entirety, will a general severability clause be effective to preserve the valid portions?   Slater & Son, 96 N.L.R.B. 1026, 29 L.R.R.M. 1001 (1951).   Suppose a maintenance-of-membership provision, unauthorized by an election, is to take effect only "in accordance and consistent with provisions of Federal Laws"?   Wyckoff Steel Co., 86 N.L.R.B. 1318, 25 L.R.R.M. 1062 (1949).

5.   LEGISLATION — STATE

Section 14 (b) of the amended NLRA provides: "Nothing in this Act shall be construed as authorizing the execution or application of agreements requiring membership in a labor organization as a

---

[177] National Maritime Union of America, 78 N.L.R.B. 971, 22 L.R.R.M. 1289 (1948), enforced, NLRB v. National Maritime Union of America, 175 F.2d 686 (2d Cir. 1949), cert. denied, 338 U.S. 954 (1950).

[178] International Typographical Union (ANPA), 86 N.L.R.B. 951, 25 L.R.R.M. 1001 (1949); Chicago Typographical Union No. 16 (CNPA), 86 N.L.R.B. 1041, 25 L.R.R.M. 1010 (1949); International Typographical Union (Graphic Arts League), 87 N.L.R.B. 1215, 25 L.R.R.M. 1218 (1949); International Typographical Union et al (Printing Industry of America), 87 N.L.R.B. 1418, 25 L.R.R.M. 1243 (1949).   For further developments in connection with the first two cases cited, see American Newspaper Publishers Assn. v. NLRB, 190 F.2d 45 (7th Cir. 1951).

[179] Hunkin-Conkey Construction Co., 95 N.L.R.B. 433, 28 L.R.R.M. 1327 (1951).

condition of employment in any State or Territory in which such execution or application is prohibited by State or Territorial law."

The Conference Report explained this provision as follows:

> Under the House bill there was included a new section 13 of the National Labor Relations Act to assure that nothing in the act was to be construed as authorizing any closed shop, union shop, maintenance of membership, or other form of compulsory unionism agreement in any State where the execution of such agreement would be contrary to State law. Many States have enacted laws or adopted constitutional provisions to make all forms of compulsory unionism in those States illegal. It was never the intention of the National Labor Relations Act, as is disclosed by the legislative history of that act, to preempt the field in this regard so as to deprive the States of their powers to prevent compulsory unionism. Neither the so-called 'closed shop' proviso in section 8 (3) of the existing [original] act nor the union shop and maintenance of membership proviso in section 8 (a) (3) of the conference agreement could be said to authorize arrangements of this sort in States where such arrangements were contrary to the State policy. To make certain that there should be no question about this, section 13 was included in the House bill. The conference agreement, in section 14 (b), contains a provision having the same effect. [H.R. Rep. No. 510, 80th Cong., 1st Sess. 60 (1947).]

By 1950, seventeen states [180] and the Territory of Hawaii had approved some measure relating to the control or regulation of union-security agreements and of union activities directed toward their execution. Twelve states [181] appear to have outlawed all forms of union security. Three states [182] and the Territory of Hawaii require certain voting procedures as a condition precedent to the execution of a valid union-security agreement, and four states [183] and the Territory of Hawaii specifically outlaw certain kinds of discrimination in the enforcement of union-security agreements.

[180] Arizona, Arkansas, Colorado, Florida, Georgia, Iowa, Kansas, Massachusetts, Nebraska, North Carolina, North Dakota, Pennsylvania, South Dakota, Tennessee, Texas, Virginia, Wisconsin.

[181] Arizona, Arkansas, Florida, Georgia, Iowa, Nebraska, North Carolina, North Dakota, South Dakota, Tennessee, Texas, Virginia.

[182] Colorado, Kansas, Wisconsin.

[183] Colorado, Massachusetts, Pennsylvania, Wisconsin.

Massachusetts has directed particular attention to the rights of union members employed under union-security agreements. Its State Labor Relations Law provides that any employee who is required as a condition of employment to become or remain a union member may appeal to the Labor Relations Commission from any alleged unfair denial of admission to, or suspension or expulsion from, the union. A hearing before the Commission is provided for, and if the Commission finds that the employee was unfairly denied admission to membership in the union, or that the discipline complained of:

(1) Was imposed by the labor organization in violation of its constitution and bylaws; or

(2) Was imposed without a fair trial, including an adequate hearing and opportunity to defend; or

(3) Was not warranted by the offense, if any, committed by the employee against the labor organization; or

(4) Is not consistent with the established public policy of the Commonwealth;

then the Commission can order the labor union to admit or restore the employee to membership, or to refrain from seeking to procure his discharge.

This section of the law became effective in September, 1947. As of April 27, 1949, nine formal charges of unfair denial of, or suspension from, membership had been filed against unions. Four were settled by amicable adjustment, without the issuance of a formal complaint, and the remaining five were under investigation. In addition, there were about twenty instances in which the Commission settled informal complaints against unions, thus obviating the need for the filing of formal charges.

The Colorado, Pennsylvania, Wisconsin, and Hawaii statutes approach this particular regulatory problem indirectly, by making it an unfair labor practice for an employer to enter into a union-security agreement which does not meet specified conditions. The Pennsylvania Labor Relations Act, while permitting union-security agreements under conditions similar to those prescribed in Section 8 (3) of the Wagner Act, adds the following proviso:

> . . . if such labor organization does not deny membership in its organization to a person or persons who are employees of the employer at the time of the making of such agreement, provided, such employee was not employed in violation of any previously existing agreement with said labor organization.

The Wisconsin Employment Peace Act permits "all-union" agreements under certain circumstances, but adds the following requirement:

> The [Employment Relations] Board shall declare any such all-union agreement terminated whenever it finds that the labor organization involved has unreasonably refused to receive as a member any employee of such employer, and each such all-union agreement shall be made subject to this duty of the Board.

Identical language is used in the Colorado Labor Peace Act and in the Hawaii Employment Relations Act.

LINCOLN FEDERAL LABOR UNION v. NORTHWESTERN IRON & METAL CO.

WHITAKER v. STATE OF NORTH CAROLINA
Supreme Court of the United States 1949
335 U.S. 525, 69 Sup. Ct. 251, 93 L. Ed. 212

MR. JUSTICE BLACK delivered the opinion of the Court.

A North Carolina statute and a Nebraska constitutional amendment provide that no person in those states shall be denied an opportunity to obtain or retain employment because he is or is not a member of a labor organization. To enforce this policy North Carolina and Nebraska employers are also forbidden to enter into contracts or agreements obligating themselves to exclude persons from employment because they are not labor union members.

[The validity of these provisions was appropriately challenged in legal proceedings in state courts by union officials who contended that the laws in question violated rights secured by the First Amendment, the contract clause and the equal protection and due process clauses of the Fourteenth Amendment of the Constitution of the United States.

The Court rejected the claim grounded on the First Amendment's guarantees of freedom of speech, assembly, and petition, observing that "Nothing in the language of the laws indicates a purpose to prohibit speech, assembly or petition. . . . And appellants do not contend that the laws expressly forbid the full exercise of those rights by unions or union members . . . There cannot be drawn from a constitutional right of workers to assemble and discuss improvement of their own working standards, a further right to drive from remunerative employment all other persons who will not or cannot, participate in union assemblies."

The objection based upon the contract clause was dismissed summarily, and the Court then proceeded to treat the objections based upon the equal protection and due process clauses, as follows:]

Third.   It is contended that the North Carolina and Nebraska laws deny unions and their members equal protection of the laws and thus offend the equal protection clause of the Fourteenth Amendment.   Because the outlawed contracts are a useful incentive to the growth of union membership, it is said that these laws weaken the bargaining power of unions and correspondingly strengthen the power of employers.   This may be true.   But there are other matters to be considered.   The state laws also make it impossible for an employer to make contracts with company unions which obligate the employer to refuse jobs to union members.   In this respect, these state laws protect the employment opportunities of members of independent unions.   See Wallace Corporation v. National Labor Relations Board, [323 U.S. 248]. This circumstance alone, without regard to others that need not be mentioned, is sufficient to support the state laws against a charge that they deny equal protection to unions as against employers and non-union workers. . . .

Fourth.   It is contended that these state laws deprive appellants of their liberty without due process of law in violation of the Fourteenth Amendment.   Appellants argue that the laws are specifically designed to deprive all persons within the two states of "liberty" (1) to refuse to hire or retain any person in employment because he is or is not a union member, and (2) to make a contract or agreement to engage in such employment discrimination against union or non-union members. . . .

There was a period in which labor union members who wanted to get and hold jobs were the victims of widespread employer discrimination practices.   Contracts between employers and their employees were used by employers to accomplish this anti-union employment discrimination.   Before hiring workers, employers required them to sign agreements stating that the workers were not and would not become labor union members.   Such anti-union practices were so obnoxious to workers that they gave these required agreements the name of "yellow dog contracts."   This hostility of workers also prompted passage of state and federal laws to ban employer discrimination against union members and to outlaw yellow dog contracts.

[The Court then discussed the cases of Allgeyer v. Louisiana, 165 U.S. 578; Lochner v. New York, 198 U.S. 45; Adair v. United States, 208 U.S. 161; and Coppage v. Kansas, 236 U.S. 1.]

The Allgeyer-Lochner-Adair-Coppage constitutional doctrine was for some years followed by this Court. It was used to strike down laws fixing minimum wages and maximum hours in employment, laws fixing prices, and laws regulating business activities.

This Court beginning at least as early as 1934, when the Nebbia case (291 U.S. 502) was decided has steadily rejected the due process philosophy enunciated in the Adair-Coppage line of cases. In doing so it has consciously returned closer and closer to the earlier constitutional principle that states have power to legislate against what are found to be injurious practices in their internal commercial and business affairs, so long as their laws do not run afoul of some specific federal constitutional prohibition, or of some valid federal law. . . . Under this constitutional doctrine the due process clause is no longer to be so broadly construed that the Congress and state legislatures are put in a strait jacket when they attempt to suppress business and industrial conditions which they regard as offensive to the public welfare.

Appellants now ask us to return, at least in part, to the due process philosophy that has been deliberately discarded. Claiming that the Federal Constitution itself affords protection for union members against discrimination, they nevertheless assert that the same Constitution forbids a state from providing the same protection for non-union members. Just as we have held that the due process clause erects no obstacle to block legislative protection of union members, we now hold that legislative protection can be afforded non-union workers.

Affirmed.

[Mr. Justice Frankfurter and Mr. Justice Rutledge filed separate concurring opinions.]

NOTES

1. The Supreme Court decided, as a companion case to the principal cases, the case of American Federation of Labor v. American Sash & Door Co., 335 U.S. 538, 69 Sup. Ct. 258, 93 L. Ed. 222 (1949). This involved the validity under the United States Constitution of the following amendment to the Arizona Constitution, adopted at the 1946 general election: "No person shall be denied the opportunity to obtain or retain employment because of non-membership in a labor organization, nor shall the

State or any subdivision thereof, or any corporation, individual or association of any kind enter into any agreement, written or oral, which excludes any person from employment or continuation of employment because of non-membership in a labor organization."

What important difference, if any, is there between the Arizona amendment and the North Carolina and Nebraska enactments? What difference in analysis is required?

2. Mr. Justice Frankfurter filed a separate concurring opinion in these cases. The following are excerpts from that opinion:

> Unions are powers within the State. Like the power of industrial and financial aggregations, the power of organized labor springs from a group which is only a fraction of the whole that Mr. Justice Holmes referred to as "the one club to which we all belong." The power of the former is subject to control, though, of course, the particular incidence of control may be brought to test at the bar of this Court . . . Neither can the latter claim constitutional exemption. Even the Government — the organ of the whole people — is restricted by the system of checks and balances established by our Constitution. The designers of that system distributed authority among the three branches "not to promote efficiency but to preclude the exercise of arbitrary power." Mr. Justice Brandeis, dissenting in Myers v. United States, 272 U.S. 52, 293, 47 Sup. Ct. 21, 85, 71 L. Ed. 160. Their concern for individual members of society, for whose well-being government is instituted, gave urgency to the fear that concentrated power would become arbitrary . . .
>
> If concern for the individual justifies incorporating in the Constitution itself devices to curb public authority, a legislative judgment that his protection requires the regulation of the private power of unions cannot be dismissed as insupportable. A union is no more than a medium through which individuals are able to act together; union power was begotten of individual helplessness. But that power can come into being only when, and continue to exist only so long as, individual aims are seen to be shared in common with the other members of the group. There is a natural emphasis, however, on what is shared and a resulting tendency to subordinate the inconsistent interests and impulses of individuals. From this, it is an easy transition to thinking of the union as an entity having rights and purposes of its own. An ardent

supporter of trade unions who is also no less a disinterested student of society has pointed out that "As soon as we personify the idea, whether it is a country or a church, a trade union or an employers' association, we obscure individual responsibility by transferring emotional loyalties to a fictitious creation which then acts upon us psychologically as an obstruction, especially in times of crisis, to the critical exercise of a reasoned judgment."   Laski, Morris Cohen's Approach to Legal Philosophy, 15 U. of Chi. L. Rev. 575, 581 (1948).

The right of association, like any other right carried to its extreme, encounters limiting principles.   See Hudson County Water Co. v. McCarter, 209 U.S. 349, 355, 28 Sup. Ct. 529, 531, 52 L. Ed. 828, 14 Ann. Cas. 560.   At the point where the mutual advantage of association demands too much individual disadvantage, a compromise must be struck.   See Dicey, Law and Public Opinion in England 465–66 (1905).   When the point has been reached — where the intersection should fall — is plainly a question within the special province of the legislature . . .

3. In January, 1947, a Wisconsin employer (in interstate commerce) discharged an employee for failure to pay his union dues. This was required by the terms of the maintenance-of-membership clause in the collective bargaining agreement between this employer and the union representing the employees in his plant. The employee then filed a complaint with the Wisconsin Employment Relations Board alleging that his discharge constituted a violation of the Wisconsin statute (Section 111.06 (1) (c) (1)) which, in effect, forbids enforcement of a maintenance-of-membership clause unless the contract containing it has been approved by two thirds of the covered employees in a referendum conducted by the state Board. There had been no such referendum here. The Board issued a cease and desist order against the employer and ordered him to reinstate the employee with back pay. Was this order supportable against a claim, made to the courts, that it was in conflict with the NLRA and the LMRA? Algoma Plywood & Veneer Co. v. Wisconsin Employment Relations Board, 336 U.S. 301, 69 Sup. Ct. 584, 93 L. Ed. 691 (1949).

4. In Giant Food Shopping Center, Inc., 77 N.L.R.B. 791, 22 L.R.R.M. 1070 (1948), the National Labor Relations Board ruled that it would not hold union-shop elections if union-shop provisions were barred by state law, or until all requirements of state law had been met; if bargaining units extend into two or more

states which have different laws, the units will be split along state lines for purposes of union-shop elections.

6. THE CHECK-OFF

The check-off is a form of union security. It is a device whereby employers aid unions by insuring the collection of dues and initiation fees (and sometimes fines and assessments) with a minimum of trouble to the unions. In practice, the employer makes a deduction from the pay check of those employees who have dues obligations and transmits the amounts so deducted to the union. The deduction may be automatic and compulsory, or it may be made only upon the consent of the individual employee. Such consent may be written or oral, revocable or irrevocable.

The chief argument advanced in support of the check-off is that it benefits the employer as well as the union. No time is wasted by union representatives during working hours in the effort to collect dues, and the union is never forced to establish a "dues picket line" as a means of handling delinquent members. The efforts of union representatives can thus be directed into more constructive channels.

The principal objection to the check-off, particularly the compulsory form, is that it is undemocratic and tends to make the union leadership less responsive to the wishes of the rank and file. Many employers, and some unions as well, believe that the union which does its job well will have no difficulty in collecting dues; conversely, it is argued that the union which is assured membership dues by means of the automatic check-off tends to shirk its responsibilities to the membership. Another point which is frequently stressed is that an employer who checks off union dues thereby assumes an active role in the administration of internal union affairs.

NOTES

1. A rather unusual situation came before the War Labor Board in In re Hamilton Watch Co. and American Watch Makers' Union, 27 War Lab. Rep. 9, 17 L.R.R.M. 1537 (1945). The Union asked for maintenance of membership. The employer urged simply that if the Union's request were granted, it be accompanied by compulsory check-off. The reasons given by the employer were its desire to avoid implication in questions of good standing of Union members and to minimize interference with production

resulting from the collection of dues by shop stewards. The Union vigorously opposed the compulsory check-off, partly on the ground that it lessened personal contracts of shop stewards with members. Held: Voluntary, irrevocable check-off directed.

2. The theory of the War Labor Board with respect to the value of the check-off is set forth by Public Member Frank D. Graham in the "Little Steel" Companies case, 1 War Lab. Rep. 325, 341, 10 L.R.R.M. 969, 979 (1942):

> The check-off eliminates the picket lines for collecting dues and their attendant abuses. With a maintenance-of-membership clause, the check-off prevents the necessity for the discharge of a would-be delinquent. As pointed out in the panel report, the check-off will save the time of the union leaders for the settlement of grievances and the improvement of production. This sharing by the company and the union of their common problems and their responsibilities for shop discipline and efficient production through the maintenance of a stable membership and the prompt collection of union dues, makes for a better and more cooperative company, and a more responsible and more cooperative union. The time, thought, and energy given in tense struggles for the organization, maintenance of membership, and collection of dues, necessary and educationally valuable as they are, should as fairly and wisely as possible now be concentrated on winning the war. The intense struggle to maintain the labor unions should, by a stabilization of the union, give way to the more intense and larger struggle to maintain the American Union as the hope of freedom and peace in the world.

3. Section 302 of the Taft-Hartley Act, which prohibits the automatic check-off, provides, in part, as follows:

> (a) It shall be unlawful for any employer to pay or deliver, or to agree to pay or deliver, any money or other thing of value to any representative of any of his employees who are employed in an industry affecting commerce.
>
> (b) It shall be unlawful for any representative of any employees who are employed in an industry affecting commerce to receive or accept, or to agree to receive or accept, from the employer of such employees any money or other thing of value.
>
> (c) The provisions of this section shall not be applicable . . . (4) with respect to money deducted from the wages of

employees in payment of membership dues in a labor organization: *Provided,* That the employer has received from each employee, on whose account such deductions are made, a written assignment which shall not be irrevocable for a period of more than one year, or beyond the termination date of the applicable collective agreement, whichever occurs sooner.

The Attorney General has ruled that under Section 302 (c) (4) of the Act an authorization card which provides for the checking off of both regular dues and assessments is proper, and that the card may provide that it shall be irrevocable for one year with automatic renewals for successive periods of one year unless written notice is given to both the employer and the union not more than twenty and not less than ten days prior to expiration. Op. Atty. Gen., May 13, 1948, P–H Lab. Eq. ¶37,024, 22 L.R.R.M. 46 (1948).

In an arbitration case (unreported) involving the Furniture Employers' Council of Southern California and Local 576, United Furniture Workers of America, CIO, the issue involved the legality under the Taft-Hartley Act of an existing check-off provision requiring the employer to deduct "the union initiation fees of new employees, the regular monthly union dues of all employees, and any fines and assessments authorized by the Union in accordance with its By-Laws." The Union's constitution provided that "membership dues" should include initiation or reinstatement fees, monthly fees ("herein referred to as dues or monthly dues") and special fees ("herein referred to as assessments, penalty assessments and fines") which are levied by the union . . .

Relying upon the above-quoted opinion of the Attorney General, the arbitrator stated: "This reasoning is applicable here. The . . . Attorney General concluded that 'initiation fees' and 'assessments' fell within the classification of 'membership dues' because they were 'incidents of membership.' Likewise, in the present case, the penalty assessments or fines are . . . equally incidents of membership."

In State of Utah v. Montgomery Ward & Co., 233 P.2d 685 (Utah, 1951), it was held that Congress, by enacting Section 302, had pre-empted the field of legislation on the subject of the check-off (in employments affecting interstate commerce), thereby invalidating state legislation affecting the matter. Hence it was held that an employer was not subject to prosecution for violation of a state act which made it a misdemeanor to fail to comply with the terms of a written check-off authorization executed by one of its employees. Two justices dissented. Certiorari denied, 342 U.S. 869 (1951).

4. Section 95–82 of North Carolina General Statutes, which prohibits involuntary check-off in all cases, provides as follows: "Payment of dues as condition of employment prohibited. — No employer shall require any person, as a condition of employment or continuation of employment, to pay any dues, fees, or other charges of any kind to any labor union or labor organization."

5. The purpose of wage assignment laws is to protect workers against the temptation to anticipate their wage payment and to assume improvident obligations. International Textbook Co. v. Weissinger, 160 Ind. 349, 65 N.E. 521 (1902); Braddom v. Three Point Coal Corp., 288 Ky. 734, 157 S.W.2d 349 (1941). The purpose of full payment and anti-kickback statutes is to protect not merely the legal form of employment contracts but also the substantive rights of workers actually to receive the benefit of the stipulated wage schedules. See United States v. Laudani, 320 U.S. 543, 64 Sup. Ct. 315, 88 L. Ed. 300 (1944). Generally, the check-off of union dues has not been held to violate federal or state laws of these types. This view was adopted by the National War Labor Board in a number of cases during World War II. "Little Steel" Companies case, 1 War Lab. Rep. 325, 356, 10 L.R.R.M. 969 (1942); In re J. Greenbaum Tanning Co. and Int. Fur & Leather Workers Union, 10 War Lab. Rep. 527, 545, 13 L.R.R.M. 1501 (1943). Compare United States v. Carbone, 327 U.S. 633, 66 Sup. Ct. 734, 90 L. Ed. 904 (1946); United States v. Baker 155 F.2d 16 (3d Cir. 1946).

6. In Sanford v. Boston Edison Co., 316 Mass. 631, 56 N.E.2d 1 (1944), the court granted specific performance of a check-off provision in a collective bargaining agreement.

7. UNION SECURITY UNDER FOREIGN LAW

For the purpose of classifying legislation concerning union security, foreign countries may be divided into three groups.

a. Jurisdictions Barring Security Clauses

The laws of some countries absolutely forbid the making of collective agreements which impose membership in a union as a condition of employment. This is the attitude, for instance, of the Danish law. It regards, in general, such an agreement as an unreasonable restriction of an individual's right to work.[184] Since,

[184] Danish Act of March 27, 1929, sec. 1.

however, there is hardly an unorganized employee in Danish industries,[185] the rule is not of practical significance.

The Belgian law treats a security clause as void,[186] imposing a criminal sanction upon the execution of an agreement conditioning employment upon the affiliation or nonaffiliation with a union. A strike for the closed shop has, therefore, been held a crime.[187] Under the Irish law "the agreement must not be intended to restrict unduly employment generally or the employment of workers of a particular class, type, or group . . ." [188] Similarly the Nicaraguan Labor Code requires the "maintenance of an open shop." [189] The Venezuelan Labor Law states: "It shall not be lawful to require or compel any person directly or indirectly to become a member of an industrial association or to refrain from doing so." [190]

b. Jurisdictions Permitting Security Clauses

In its Declaration of Human Rights (1948) the United Nations has likewise dealt with the subject. Article 20 (2) reads: "No one may be compelled to belong to an association." [191] This, however, does not exclude making union membership a condition of employment. The Right to Organize and Collective Bargaining Convention (1949), adopted by the U.N.'s "specialized agency," the International Labor Organization, forbids "the employment of a worker subject to the condition that he shall not join a union or shall relinquish trade union membership." (Art. 1, Sec. 2 (a).) This leaves each country free to allow or forbid the union shop.

Prior to the Act of May 17, 1940 the Swedish labor court invalidated clauses which conditioned employment upon membership in *the* contracting labor union. That Act has validated such clauses. Agreements requiring membership in *a* labor organization — Swedish law permits the coexistence of two or more unions for the same branch of industry — have always been regarded as valid.[192] However, ever since 1906 the leading employer organiza-

---

[185] Cf. Galenson, Some Aspects of Industrial Relations in Denmark, Proceedings of the Industrial Relations Research Association 230, 231 (1949).

[186] Act of May 24, 1926, arts. 3 and 4. See Orianne, 27 Revue de droit international et droit comparé 132, 134 (1950).

[187] Belgian Penal Code, sec. 310.

[188] Irish Industrial Relations Act, 1946, sec. 27 (3) (d).

[189] 52 International Lab. Rev. 231 (1945).

[190] Section 165.

[191] U.S. Dept. of State Pub. No. 3381 (Int. Org. and Conf. Series III, 20). UN Doc. A/811, Dec. 16, 1948.

[192] Robbins, The Government of Labor Relations in Sweden 282–317 (1942).

tion (S.A.F.) has forbidden its members to include any union-security clause whatsoever in a collective contract.[193]

The law of Norway shows analogous features, and the attitude of organized Norwegian employers toward security clauses has corresponded ever since 1907 to that of their Swedish brothers.[194] In both countries, the clause is legal but in fact is not a part of any contract of any significance. In many industries unorganized employees cannot be found.[195] In the Netherlands, the closed shop is allowed. The closed-shop clause prevails in certain types of industry, notably the printing industry.[196]

Union-security clauses in Great Britain are not invalid. They, like all other terms of a collective contract, lack enforceability, but it is by no means unlawful to bring pressure upon employers to give their consent to them. In Reynolds v. Shipping Federation, Ltd.,[197] the court had this to say:

> For many years past no one has questioned the right of a trade union to insist, if they are strong enough to do so, under penalty of a strike, that an employer or a group of employers shall employ none but members of the trade union. And the result of any such effective combination of workmen has, of course, been to impose on the other workmen in the trade the necessity of joining the union as a condition of obtaining employment. Here, the employers, instead of being forced against their wills into employing union men only, have recognized that advantages may arise from adopting such a course voluntarily, and have accordingly made an agreement with the trade union to that effect. The incidental result to the other workmen in the trade is the same as if the employers had yielded against their wills instead of agreeing voluntarily. But I fail to see that workmen who are unwilling to join the union have any greater reason to complain of a violation of their legal rights in the second case than in the first.

Moreover, the legality of a closed-shop clause at common law is to be inferred from the fact that a legislative act was thought necessary in 1927, as an aftermath of the unsuccessful general strike of 1926, to make it unlawful for any local or other public authority to make membership or nonmembership in a union a

[193] Id. at 70, 285.
[194] Galenson, Labor in Norway 205–207 (1949).
[195] Ibid.
[196] Information from Jacqueline C. Rutgers, Board of Conciliators, Netherlands Ministry of Labor.
[197] [1924] 1 Ch. 28, 39.

condition of employment or of continuance in employment of any person.[198]   No sooner had the Labour Party taken office after the war than the act was repealed.[199]

Similarly, the federal law of Canada allows closed-shop contracts.   However, a clause requiring an employer to discharge an employee because of his affiliation with a union other than a specified one, is not valid.[200]   In Switzerland, likewise, the law has recognized the validity of union-security clauses.[201]   Note the information at page 112 supra concerning compulsory unionism in New Zealand.

c. Intermediate Solutions

All the Australian statutes of the Court and Commissioner types (see page 111 supra) authorize the granting of preference to union members as part of the terms of an award.   The general policy is to grant preference as between prospective employees of equal efficiency.

In pre-Nazi Germany the problem of union-security clauses had played a large part in the organization of labor, owing to rivalry among unions holding different political views.   After the collapse of the Nazi regime and the revival of free labor relations, the crazy quilt of politically diversified labor organizations was replaced by nonpartisan unionism, unified in one single confederation, the German Labor Federation (DGB).[202]   Closed-shop and similar clauses have, therefore, lost their significance in Germany.   There is hardly any mention made of them in textbooks or articles; no decision of the courts dealing with them can be found after World War II.   Unified unionism has shown its strength in the codetermination question (see page 81 supra).   This alone may have served as an adequate inducement for union membership.

The legal situation in present-day Austria with respect to union-security questions is analogous to that in Germany.   Since the war

[198] Trade Disputes and Trade Unions Act, 1927, 17 & 18 Geo. V, c. 22 s. 6.
[199] Trade Disputes and Trade Unions Act, 1946, 9 & 10 Geo. VI, c. 52.
[200] Canadian Industrial Relations and Disputes Investigation Act, 1948, 11 & 12 Geo. VI, c. 54, s. 6.
[201] Egger, 1 Kommentar zum Schweizerischen Zivilgesetzbuch 430 (2d ed. 1930).
[202] To be exact, one has to note that the German Salaried Employees Union (DAG) and the Civil Servants Federation (DBB) stand outside of the DGB.   However, those organizations, as their names indicate, are confined to classes of employees, relatively small in number (if compared with 5 million workers organized in the DGB), having a legal and social status different from that of wage earners.   See page 70 supra.

there has been one unified union in each branch of business and industry, and all unions are affiliated with the Austrian Labor Federation (OeGB). Incidentally, the Act of 1930, outlawing union-security clauses, is regarded by labor law experts as repealed.[203]

The situation in France is not clear. The courts have not yet generally determined the validity of union-security clauses. A French employer may discharge an employee from an employment at will, at any time, after a period of notice if this is customary.[204] But if the discharge is not based on a just ground, he is liable to damages for "abusive exercise of a right" (*abus de droit*).[205] In 1938 the Cour de Cassation held that an employer had committed such an abuse by discharging an old and deserving employee, for refusal to join a union with which the employer had entered into a union-shop clause.[206] In 1916 the same court had recognized the validity of such a clause.[207] In contrast to Germany, France still suffers, and more than ever, from a multiplicity of more or less weak federations warring against one another.[208] French employers are very hostile to union-shop clauses of any kind and the discussion seems to center also around the question of the constitutionally guaranteed freedom of association. For some, that freedom means only the freedom to form and operate an association, for others, it includes also the freedom to abstain from any association.

Concerning Latin America, the Mexican Labor Act of 1931 (Sec. 49) permits inclusion in a collective contract of a clause by which the employer agrees to refuse employment to any person who is not a member of a labor organization. Also, where there is such a clause, any labor organization may request and obtain from the employer the dismissal of any member who resigns or is expelled from the organization.[209] It should be noted, however, that the statute makes these clauses prospective only, in that it provides that they cannot be made applicable to those employees who were

[203] Order D.R.G. Bl. 1938 I 851 and Order G. Bl. Oe. 1938, 366, no. 11 (lit. b).

[204] Labor Code, bk. I, tit. II, c. II, art. 23.

[205] Rouast and Durand, Précis de législation industrielle, no. 350 (3d ed. 1948). The words *abus de droit* designate the use of a right in a manner which perverts the socially desirable purpose for which it was created. For a discussion of this concept, see page 746 infra.

[206] Decision March 9, 1938, D.H. 1938, 305; see the note of Professor Pierre Henri Teidgen in 1938 Droit social, 185.

[207] Raquet v. Syndicat d'Halluin, D.P. 1916. 1.246. The action brought by nonmembers who had been discharged was dismissed.

[208] See the discussion at page 272 supra.

[209] Mexican Labor Act (1931) sec. 236.

not members of the union at the effective date of the collective agreement.

C. *Seniority*

1. INTRODUCTORY NOTE

The seniority principle, in its simplest terms, implies employment preference based upon length of service: employees with the longest service are given the greatest job security and the best opportunities for job promotion. An employer not bound by the seniority principle is free to base promotions, layoffs, and rehirings on such factors as ability, age, sex, race, or personal favoritism. Substitution of the principle of strict seniority results in the establishment of a specific and exclusive basis for employee selection in place of a wide variety of random, unrestricted bases.

The seniority principle is not generally accepted as inherent in the employment relationship as such. The average employer assumes, in the absence of a collective agreement, that layoffs or promotions will be determined primarily, if not exclusively, on the basis of his unilateral determination of relative skill and efficiency. While the notion of making length of service the controlling criterion may have a strong ethical appeal, it frequently encounters strong resistance predicated upon considerations of productive efficiency. In most collective bargaining contracts, therefore, seniority is not the sole consideration, but is taken into account along with such factors as skill, physical capacity, and the like.

Seniority appears to have been accepted first in the railroad industry, the earliest formal recognition of that principle being embodied in an agreement between the Brotherhood of Locomotive Engineers and the New York and Hudson River Railroad in 1875. It became a major issue on the railroads because employment tenure was broken by frequent transfers and layoffs due to consolidation and technological improvements. Printing trades unions were also among the first to establish a seniority program, the object of which was to protect the established workers against itinerant craftsmen.

With these major exceptions union seniority rules have, until recently been rather exceptional in the United States. As a result of the frequent layoffs during the depression of the 1930's, however, the desire for recognition of seniority became stronger. Moreover, the organizational struggles of the New Deal period brought seniority rights to the fore as a method of protecting union men

from discrimination.   Today most collective agreements contain
seniority clauses.

Seniority usually figures in layoffs, rehirings, transfers, and promotions.   It may be computed on an industry-wide, company-
wide, or plant-wide basis; or on the length of service within
a particular department or occupational group, or on some combination of these methods.   There are often specific exceptions
to the general rule for skilled workers or for union officials.

However applied, seniority is one of the most difficult problems
confronting unions and employers; and also, under normal circumstances, there is no matter more important to the rank-and-file
membership.   When employment slacks off, the younger employees prefer share-the-work programs, under which the work of all
employees is reduced to a minimum number of hours per week
before any layoffs are made.   Older workers, on the other hand,
tend to favor strict seniority provisions.   This situation is further
complicated by the fact that, particularly in newly organized industries, younger employees frequently are the most militant union
members.   Problems of seniority are especially important in industries characterized by seasonal fluctuations, in those where the
great majority of jobs are not skilled, and where the emphasis is on
youth and speed.

The seniority principle is most generally accepted in industries
characterized by relatively continuous employment with a single
employer, such as the railroad and various mass production industries.   This is not always the case, however; there are some
notable instances (e.g., in some of the motion-picture craft agreements) of industry-wide seniority agreements covering workers
who are sporadically employed by a large number of employers in
the industry for short-term periods.   With the passage of the Labor
Management Relations Act of 1947 many unions and employers
have sought to circumvent the prohibition against the closed shop
by entering into such industry-wide seniority agreements.   The
effect of these arrangements is to provide for the continued exclusive employment of union members, much as it would have
been under the closed-shop conditions previously in operation.
Assuming the legality of these provisions, their effectiveness would
appear to be complete, except in the case of future expansion of
the industries involved which would create job opportunities in
excess of the number of union members with seniority.

Viewed objectively, the principle of seniority has both its
strengths and its weaknesses.   It protects the worker against uncertainty and discrimination in the tenure of his employment; but

it also inhibits the employer in his efforts to improve the efficiency of his employees.   Seniority tends to provide a given employer with a stable, loyal, experienced group of workers; to a corresponding degree it discourages labor mobility and the infusion of younger men into the work force.   Within the plant, a system of strict seniority results in the transference to the union of much of management's normal responsibility; and even modified seniority rules give great power to union leaders over their members. The relative security of various groups within the union, for example, will be vitally affected by the decision to predicate seniority on a plant-wide, as opposed to departmental, basis.   In some plants, the seniority provision has been changed each time a new group has assumed control of union affairs.

The administration of seniority provisions in collective bargaining contracts has proved to be one of the major trouble spots in the labor-management relationship.   The Committee on Improving the Administration of Union-Employer Contracts of the American Bar Association's Section of Labor Relations Law submitted a report in 1950, wherein, in reporting upon specific issues which it found to occasion friction in the administration of collective agreements, it was said:

> The second point of emphasis in terms of specific issues is the seniority provisions of the agreement.   By and large the management attorneys [on the committee] feel this to be one of the lesser causes of friction, but one observes that while changes in production "cause more big troubles, seniority causes tens of thousands of little ones which are a constant source of annoyance and do much harm to production."   As for most of them though, the major specific cause of friction has related to rate adjustments that have been consequent upon changes or modifications of production processes and practices.   Other members [of the committee, representing labor unions and the public] have not apparently found this sort of issue troublesome, for both groups place seniority issues as the top ground of discord.   A labor lawyer deprecates the "loose language sometimes used to qualify seniority provisions" and believes that the contract should not contain any such qualifications; but that "the good judgment of both management and union leadership should be relied upon to take care of those cases in which strict application of seniority would interfere with efficiency."

It is interesting to note that the public members are unanimous in their view that seniority is the most frequent specific cause of friction.   One such lawyer states "there is a woeful ignorance, among management people particularly, as to the political implications within unions of the seniority provision. In many ways it is the most important source of power available to special interest groups within the union."   His illustration is a large aircraft plant where each year "the basic issue was, should there be plant-wide or departmental seniority?   This in turn could be translated into a power fight between the skilled craftsmen and the semi-skilled and unskilled workers within the union."   Another makes a point of the definition of terms; does "plant-wide seniority" mean (a) plant-wide bumping by choice of the employee or (b) that the company lays off the youngest man and then makes its own shift of senior employees to available jobs?

For a detailed analysis of the many problems involved, see Mitchem, Seniority Clauses in Collective Bargaining Agreements, 21 Rocky Mt. L. Rev. 156, 293 (1949).

In the materials which follow here, some of the more typical seniority problems are illustrated, first by reference to another set of developments in the Enderby Case, and then by the inclusion of excerpts from various arbitration awards, collective bargaining contracts, and court decisions.

2. THE ENDERBY CASE — XII

A

The Union's original proposal for a seniority clause, submitted on April 12, 1948, at the first bargaining session between representatives of Local 417, URCL & PWA (CIO) and the Enderby Rubber Company was as follows:

> Length of service shall control all layoffs, rehires, promotions and transfers, the employee with the greatest seniority being given preference in any case involving questions regarding these matters. Union officers shall be given top seniority.

The Company offered, at a subsequent negotiating session, the following counterproposal with respect to the form and substance of a seniority clause:

> In case of a reduction of work force, employees will be laid off in accordance with their ability and their length of service

in the department; provided, that the Company shall be the judge as to ability.

Article IV (Seniority) in the contract finally signed on May 20, 1948, was in this form:

> In cases of layoffs, rehires, and so forth, the Company will give primary consideration to length of service with the Company, but skill and ability will also be taken into account.

B

Article IV, as it was included in the 1948 agreement, proved highly unsatisfactory.

The Union tried to use the clause to gain preferred treatment of older employees in cases involving bids on vacant jobs, transfers from one shift to another, and the granting of merit increases under Section 4 of Article XI. The Company took the position that Article IV had no bearing on any of these matters.

There was another disagreement when an employee who had formerly been a drill press operator and had subsequently been made a foreman was moved back to his old job, being put on a press in place of an employee who had more years on the press than the ex-foreman had.

When a wildcat work stoppage in Department 11 (a "feeder" department) meant that some men in the Assembly Department had to be sent home early one afternoon because they had no parts (from Department 11) to work on, the Union objected when some of the older men were dismissed and some of the younger ones kept on. The Company's answer was that what was involved here was not a "layoff" within the contract language, and that in any event the Union was responsible for the interruption of production.

None of these questions was taken to arbitration, the Union attorney advising Curme, the Union president, that the contract clause would not hold water. Some of the individual cases were worked out to the satisfaction of everyone involved but some of the others created extremely hard feelings in the plant.

C

The seniority clause did not receive much attention in the 1949 negotiations. Everyone agreed that it needed cleaning up, but the main pressure was on the wage issue and no time was spent on seniority until the last day of the negotiations.   Article IV was finally revised as follows:

> The following factors will be taken into account whenever a question arises as to layoffs, rehires or promotions (to jobs within the bargaining unit) : (a) length of service in the department and in the plant; (b) skill and ability.   Where skill and ability are equal, length of service shall govern.
>
> Employees with three or more years' seniority who are subject to layoff will replace younger employees in the plant on work of a similar nature, if capable of performing operation available.
>
> Union officials shall be given top seniority.

D

There was a substantial layoff at the Enderby plant in September, 1949, and it soon became evident that the revised seniority clause was not much more helpful than the old one.

1. Frank Klaus, who had five years' seniority, was laid off.   A grievance was filed, the Union claiming that Klaus should have been given a job held by a female employee, with less seniority, in the same department.   The Company's answer was (a) that it would take Klaus "at least a week" to learn the female employee's job, and (b) that "it has been traditional practice in the plant to consider male and female jobs as entirely separate and there has never been any transfer of employees from one set of jobs to the other."   This grievance went to the third step.

2. Clem Barker, who had twelve years' seniority in Department 39, was advised that his job would have to be closed down.   The foreman in Department 39 told Barker that he would be given a job held by R. E. Mabie, who had been working in the plant (in Department 39) for only nine months.   This job paid 57 cents an hour less than Barker's job.   Barker refused to accept this transfer insisting that he be moved, instead, to a job very much like his own but in Department 72.   This job was held by Fred Wilson, who had eleven years' seniority.   The foreman finally told Barker that he would either have to take the Mabie job or be laid off.

Barker stuck to his position, claiming that Article IV of the contract entitled him to the job in Department 72.   A grievance was immediately filed, and was finally taken to arbitration.

3. The job held in Department 319 by R. E. Krotz, vice-presi-

dent of the Union, had to be shut down completely.   It was agreed by Company and Union representatives that Krotz should be given a job held by Sam Butler.   There was nothing else to give Butler, so he was laid off.   Butler had eight years' seniority and Krotz only six.   When the Union refused to process a grievance for Butler (who was not a member of Local 417), Butler retained a lawyer who instituted legal proceedings against the Company seeking to collect damages for his layoff.

E

The seniority clause was completely overhauled in the 1950 contract renewal negotiations.   See Article IV, page 322 supra.   It is interesting to note the extent to which this much expanded set of provisions covers, or fails to cover, the issues which had arisen under the 1948 and 1949 contracts.

3.   SELECTED CONTRACT CLAUSES AND ILLUSTRATIVE CASES

1. In Tioga Mills, Inc. and Federal Labor Union, American Federation of Grain Processors, Local 22682 (AFL), 10 L.A. 371 (1948), the contract clause subject to interpretation provided (in Sec. 8) that "In the event of a layoff, preference shall be given to qualified workers on a seniority basis.   This rule to apply also to reinstatements."   The Union was protesting certain layoffs on the grounds (a) that they had not been acquiesced in by the Union, and (b) that they had been made in disregard of the seniority clause.   The opinion of Arbitrator Bertram F. Willcox includes the following statement:

> If the Company was exercising a discretionary function of management, the arbitrator must not set himself up as a better judge than the Company of how it should exercise its discretion.   Deciding how many men to employ, and what jobs given men can do, is normally a function of management.   If a contract takes away the discretion of management in such matters, the contract, of course, controls.   Since the present contract, as the parties interpret it in practice, does not transfer these functions from Company to Union, the Company has not violated the contract unless its action was arbitrary and unreasonable, a mere sham or subterfuge for the purpose of avoiding the seniority clause.   Whether it was or not, that is what the arbitrator has to decide. . . .   To have efficient ad-

ministration one must make the first decision on who are qualified under Section 8. Since the contract does not provide otherwise . . . the first decision remains — as it was before the contract — one to be made initially by the Company. It is subject to challenge, of course, in the grievance proceedings. . . . [The Union's claim was denied.]

2. The question in In re Keuffel and Esser Co., and United Electrical, Radio and Machine Workers of America, Local 427 (CIO), 10 L.A. 216 (1948), was whether the layoff provision of a seniority clause applied to suspensions of work not in excess of one day each, occasioned by a temporary shortage of work consequent to a change in production. The clause read that "All layoffs and all rehiring following layoffs shall be made according to seniority." The arbitration board decided that the clause applied to the short-term work suspensions in the case of the five employees involved in the grievance. Part of the Company's argument in this case was that "in practice it would involve a greater amount of time to make the adjustments required under the Union's interpretation of this clause than the total time lost by the employees in the short period involved."

3. A question which has arisen in a substantial number of cases involves the matter of the relation of a contract seniority provision to a compulsory pension and retirement plan established unilaterally by the Company. Employee X is advised by the management shortly before he reaches his sixty-fifth birthday, that he is to be retired on a pension of $60 a month. He protests to the Union (not wanting to lose his current earnings of $45 a week) that his layoff is in violation of the seniority clause of the contract, he being in fact the top seniority man in the plant. The Union files a grievance, taking the matter to arbitration, or, in the alternative, institutes court proceedings. The problem presented in this situation is discussed, and several arbitrator's decisions on the point are reviewed, in Bakery and Confectionery Workers' Int. Union, Local 492 v. Nat. Biscuit Co., 78 F. Supp. 517, 22 L.R.R.M. 2304 (E.D. Pa. 1948). See Comment, Compulsory Retirement of Superannuated Workers Under Collective Bargaining Agreement, 45 Ill. L. Rev. 88 (1950).

BELANGER et al. v. LOCAL DIVISION NO. 1128, AMAL–
GAMATED ASSN. OF STREET, ELECTRIC RAILWAY &
MOTOR COACH EMPLOYEES OF AMERICA et al.
Supreme Court, Wisconsin, 1949
254 Wis. 344, 36 N.W.2d 414

[Plaintiffs in this case were bus drivers employed by the Duluth-
Superior Bus Company; they had been originally employed as *bus
drivers* prior to 1935 by a predecessor company.   All of the other
employees of the company were streetcar operators employed by
a different predecessor company prior to 1935 when streetcar
operations were discontinued, and they were retained in the
Duluth-Superior Bus Company's employ as bus drivers.

For many years there was a dispute between the plaintiffs and
the former streetcar operators regarding seniority, the contention
of the plaintiffs being that seniority should date from the time that
an employee began driving a bus, which would place the plaintiffs
at the head of the list.   The former streetcar operators claim that
the seniority should date from the time the employee was employed by the company, which would have the effect of placing the
bus drivers lower on the seniority list.

In 1937, the plaintiffs and the former streetcar operators and
the Company entered into an agreement which incorporated an
agreed upon seniority list, referred to as the "compromise seniority
list."

Thereafter the employees of the Company, including the plaintiffs, organized the defendant Union.   The issue of seniority continued to provide a bone of contention among the employees and
became a subject of controversy within the Union.   In 1946 the
Union and the Company negotiated changes in their collective
agreement, including changes in the matter of seniority which
materially altered the scheme set forth in the 1937 "compromise
seniority list."   The plaintiffs exhausted all remedies available
to them within the Union in an effort to prevent the change, but
to no avail.   They then instituted this suit against the Union and
the Company, seeking relief by way of declaratory judgment and
injunction.

The trial court declared the 1937 agreement a valid contract and
adjudged the 1946 seniority list void and of no effect.   This is an
appeal by the Union.]

MARTIN, Justice.   The question involved in this case is whether
the agreement entered into by the original bus drivers, the former
streetcar operators, and the Duluth-Superior Bus Company on

April 6, 1937, which agreed on a seniority list, known as the "compromise seniority list," is a valid and enforceable contract.

Seniority rights are things of value to the employees which are capable of determination. The main consideration in determining these rights is length of service. It was stated in Dooley et al, v. Lehigh Valley R. Co. of Pennsylvania et al. 1941, 130 N.J. Eq. 75, 21 A.2d 334, 335, syllabus 4: " 'Seniority' rights result from desire of railway labor organizations to protect men of extended service in right to their jobs and to select their jobs in preference to men who have had shorter periods of service."

Seniority rights here do not flow from any union bargaining but exist because of a written agreement or contract involving the "compromise seniority list" which existed before the union was formed or before its present members joined, and was in effect for some years. See Annotations in 142 A.L.R. 1055 and 153 A.L.R. 60, and cases cited therein. The individual rights of seniority in this case were determined and remained fixed.

Bargaining for seniority rights is quite different than bargaining for wages, hours, working conditions, etc. The latter conditions affect the union as a whole and are ever changing. A collective bargaining agreement may be necessary and its results are final and binding under the union's by-laws when the union bargains for benefits for all its members.

In its letter of July 12, 1946 to the employer, the union set out sixteen different matters which it desired to bargain with the employer. All points except No. 2 (Seniority of Superior Division Bus Operators *to be determined by the Union* (Italics ours)) were proper matters for collective bargaining. The agreement of 1937 in no way affected the union's rights to bargain on any of the other points set out.

Our decision in this case in no way conflicts with Section 9 (a) of the Taft-Hartley Act, 29 U.S.C.A. Sec. 159 (a). We hold here that seniority was determined by the 1937 agreement. This also applies to sec. 111.05 (1) of the Wisconsin Statutes which provides: "Representatives chosen for the purposes of collective bargaining by a majority of the employees voting in a collective bargaining unit shall be the exclusive representatives of all of the employees in such unit for the purposes of collective bargaining, provided that any individual employee or any minority group of employees in any collective bargaining unit shall have the right at any time to present grievances to their employer in person or through representatives of their own choosing, and the employer shall confer with them in relation thereto." J. I. Case Co. v.

National Labor Relations Board, 321 U.S.332, 64 S. Ct. 576, 580, 88 L. Ed. 762, relied on by appellants, is not in conflict with this position. In that case there was a dispute between the company and the union relating to contracts which the company had entered into with individual employees fixing wages and hours of employment. In the present case we have no dispute between the company and the union. It is wholly within the union. The contract entered into by the original bus drivers, former streetcar operators, and the Duluth-Superior Bus Company previous to the formation of the union, does not in any way "forestall bargaining or . . . limit or condition the terms of the collective agreement." The court continued at page 332 of 321 U.S., at page 580 of 64 S. Ct., at page 767 of 88 L. Ed.: " 'The Board asserts a public right vested in it as a public body, charged in the public interest with the duty of preventing unfair labor practices.' National Licorice Co. v. National Labor Relations Board, 309 U.S. 350, 364, 60 S. Ct. 569, 577, 84 L. Ed. 799 [810]. Wherever private contracts conflict with its functions, they obviously must yield or the Act would be reduced to a futility."

Here the private contract does not conflict with the functions of the bargaining agent nor the company. It does not bar the union from bargaining for any advantages regarding wages, working conditions, etc.

Appellants also relied on International Union v. J. I. Case Co., 1947, 250 Wis. 63, 73, 26 N.W.2d 305, 310, 170 A.L.R. 933, and quoted: "Collective bargaining is a continuing and developing process by which, under present law, the relationship between employer and employee is to be molded, and the terms and conditions of employment progressively modified along lines mutually satisfactory to all concerned. Changing conditions require continuing collective bargaining and changed contracts of employment. The written contract of yesterday does not become a final and permanent result. National Labor Relations Board v. Newark Morning Ledger Co., 3 Cir., 120 F.2d 262, 137 A.L.R. 849."

There are no cases cited involving seniority rights which had once been established by contract as here. The matters in dispute were matters between the union and the employer, and not wholly matters between the members of the union as in the present case. Also, the authorities hold that there must be some changes in economic conditions to enable the contract to be changed.

It was stated in Yazoo & M.V.R. Co. v. Sideboard, 1931, 161 Miss. 4, 133 So. 669, at page 671: "So that, although only a few years ago the courts were holding that an individual member of a labor union could not maintain an action for the breach of an agreement between an employer and the union of which the plaintiff was a member in respect to wages and other rights fixed in the contract (cases cited), these rulings have been left in the rear in the advancement of the law on this general subject, and the holdings now are that these agreements are primarily for the individual benefit of the members of the organization, and that the rights secured by these contracts are the individual rights of the individual members of the union, and may be enforced directly by the individual.   [Citing cases.]

The case of Piercy v. Louisville & N. Ry. Co. et al., 198 Ky. 477, 248 S.W. 1042, 33 A.L.R. 322, involved the seniority rights of a conductor on the railroad.   The conductor had a good run; the railroad acceded to the request of the union, of which Piercy was a member, to change his seniority, to his detriment.   He sought to be reinstated to his rights by a suit against the railroad and the union.   The action of the union was not indorsed or brought about by Piercy; it had volunteered in the matter for purposes of its own.   There was no necessity because of business conditions for any change in the seniority of Piercy.   The lower court held that Piercy was entitled to be reinstated to his rights, and the railroad did not appeal.   The union appealed, and the court sustained the decree of the lower court, and also held that such agreement between organizations of employees and their employers were not designed to place it within the power of the organization to change or modify the contract at pleasure, so as to affect injuriously the individual rights of its members theretofore secured by the agreement; that the officers of labor unions were not the agents of the members to affect their individual rights, and that a labor organization could not, by arbitrary act, deprive one of its individual members of rights secured to him by the agreement which it had made with the employer.   It was stated at pages 1045 and 1046 of 248 S.W.:

"The primary purpose in the organization of labor unions and kindred organizations is to protect their individual members and to secure for them a fair and just remuneration for their labor and favorable conditions under which to perform it.   Their agreements with employers look always to the securing of some right or privilege for their individual members, and the right or privilege so secured by agreement is the individual right of the individual member, and such organization can no more by its arbitrary act deprive that individual member of his right so secured than can any other person." . . .

There is no evidence here showing any such change which would justify an amendment of the contract of 1937.   The change in this case was merely to give the former streetcar operators better seniority than they had under the compromise agreement.   They were in the majority in the union and arbitrarily, unfairly, and capriciously changed the contract to suit themselves.   Under such facts, the courts have held the change unlawful.   In Hartley v. Brotherhood of Ry. and S. S. Clerks, etc., 1938, 283 Mich. 201, 277 N.W. 885, the court in that case agreed that a union and the employer can bargain as to seniority even though an individual member might lose some of his rights, but stated, 277 N.W. at page 887: "A different situation might be presented had the agreement of 1932 been accomplished as a result of bad faith, arbitrary action, or fraud directed at plaintiff on the part of those responsible for its execution."

We hold that the union acted arbitrarily and without authority.

Judgment affirmed.[210]

NOTE

In 1921 a union and an employer entered into an agreement relating to working conditions, including inter alia, a provision controlling seniority.   During the depression years of 1930–1931 the employer was compelled to reduce its working force, and in doing so adhered to the seniority schedule created in the 1921 contract.   The employer received many complaints because this adherence to the contract resulted in married women being retained while others, who had no other source of income, were discharged.   At the employer's request, the seniority provision was renegotiated to permit the layoff of married women in the absence of extenuating circumstances.   H, a married woman employee who had been in the company's employ since 1919 was discharged under the new provision in 1932.   Held: Contract alteration and discharge pursuant to it proper, suit against the union for damages dismissed.   Hartley v. Brotherhood of Railway and Steamship Clerks, etc., 283 Mich. 201, 277 N.W. 885 (1938).   See also Leeder v. Cities Service Co., 199 Okla. 618, 189 P.2d 189 (1948); Edelstein v. Duluth Ry. Co., 225 Minn. 508, 31 N.W.2d 465 (1948); Langhurst v. Pittsburgh & L.E.R.R. Co., 97 Pa. L.J.R. 516, 24 L.R.R.M. 2432 (1949); Donovan v. Travers, 285 Mass. 167, 188 N.E. 705 (1934).

[210] For further developments in the case see 256 Wis. 274, 40 N.W.2d 504 (1949). — ED.

D. *Disciplinary Action*

THE ENDERBY CASE — XIII

A

The Enderby Company representatives insisted, in the 1948 collective bargaining negotiations with Local 417, URCL & PWA (CIO), upon including the following clause in the contract as Article XI:

> It is recognized that Management retains the right to discharge or demote any employee for any action deemed by it to constitute a threat to productive efficiency.

During the 1948–1949 contract term, the Union filed grievance protests in several cases involving disciplinary action. One of these, in which Robert Horak, an employee with nine years' seniority, was discharged for being absent for three days without notifying the foreman, went to arbitration. The arbitrator dismissed the grievance, his opinion including the following statement as to the basis for his award:

> Company representatives stated in their answer to this grievance request, and again at the hearing, that they considered Horak's dismissal a necessary step in the attempt which was being made to eliminate the absenteeism problem which was threatening productive efficiency in the plant. These were apparently honest representations as to the sole and exclusive reason for Horak's discharge. That settles this case under the terms of Article XI of the agreement, for the language of that clause makes the Company's judgment controlling.

> The arbitrator went on to say that he considered the action taken to have been extremely severe in view of the fact that Horak's record was no worse than that of many other employees and inasmuch as he had been given no warning. He therefore added to his formal ruling (dismissing the claim for reinstatement as a matter of contract right) a recommendation that Horak be re-employed by the Company. This recommendation was in fact carried out, but White (the Industrial Relations Manager) wrote the arbitrator a letter protesting his having gone beyond his authority in adding the recommendation to his ruling.

Article XI was revised in the 1949 contract to read as follows:

It is agreed that Management is entitled to discharge or discipline any employee, but only for just cause. In case the Union desires to protest any disciplinary action taken under this section the case will be processed through the regular grievance and arbitration procedure.

Two serious disciplinary cases arose during the 1949–1950 contract term:

1. Allen Seward, an employee in Department 94, was discharged for alleged incompetence. He was given a separation notice which stated, in the blank provided for Cause of Discipline: "Spoilage of 320 yards of stock on August 20, 1949, and previous showing of incompetent workmanship."

A grievance was filed and this case eventually went to arbitration. The arbitration hearing got off to a bad start when Cooper, the Union lawyer, insisted that, contrary to usual arbitration practice in other types of cases, the Company should state its case and develop its evidence first. Cooper's claim was that the "burden of proof and of going ahead" was here on the Company. Blair, the Enderby attorney, protested this and insisted that the Union, "as plaintiff or at least claimant," had to go ahead.

Later in the hearing there was a heated argument when Blair made the point that although the contract in effect prohibited any disciplinary action except for "just cause," by its failure to specify any damages for any disciplinary action the contract clause could only be interpreted as "hortatory," and that for the arbitrator to award damages by way of back payment for time lost would be to "add to the contract rather than simply to interpret it." The arbitrator rejected this argument, asking Blair in passing whether he (the arbitrator) was not going to be required "to add something or other of my own when I try to give content to what the parties meant by 'just cause.'"

There was still another argument about whether the arbitrator was to decide, under the contract, whether there was just cause for *some* disciplinary action or whether there was just cause for the discharge. Blair contended that the only issue for the arbitrator was whether there was or was not employee fault warranting disciplinary action by management and that if there was such fault the measure of disciplinary penalty was up to the Company.

Finally, there was disagreement about the Company's introduction (a) of evidence that Seward had on three previous occasions been orally reprimanded for incompetent work and had once been given a one-week layoff for poor work; (b) of evidence that Seward

had, according to the Company's records, been absent without
prior notice on two occasions during his five years with Enderby;
and (c) of evidence that Seward had falsified his Application for
Employment in 1944 by stating that he had been honorably discharged from the Navy when, as a matter of recently (since the discharge) discovered fact, he had been in the merchant marine and
had been discharged for repeated drunkenness. The Union position was that Seward would not have been discharged except for
what happened on August 20, 1949, and that nothing else was
relevant in this arbitration proceeding.

2. Employee Allan Simkin, a punch-press operator, had been
told by his foreman at the end of his shift on November 2, 1949,
to truck the pieces he had produced that day to the warehouse.
The trucker who was supposed to do this had gone home during
the shift because of illness. Simkin asked the foreman whether
he would be paid for this trucking at his guaranteed classification
rate ($1.64 per hour). The foreman told him he would receive
only the trucker's hourly rate ($1.26 per hour). Simkin insisted
that he was entitled under the contract to payment at the higher
rate, and finally said he would not do the trucking unless the foreman agreed to put this work on the time sheet at this rate. The
foreman told him that if he refused to do the work he would be
fired. Simkin finished his punch-press work and left the plant.
He received a discharge notice by telegram that night. The Company refused, at the first three steps of the grievance procedure,
to modify this discharge action. Union attorney Dan Cooper was
asked by the Union officers whether it would be advisable to take
this case to arbitration.

C

In the 1950 contract renewal negotiations the Company insisted
upon an enlarged "management rights" clause. Article IX as it
appears above at page 326 supra was eventually agreed upon.
Note the further coverage given the "disciplinary" issue in Article
II, Section 7, at page 321 supra.

NOTES

1. The difficult question of the standard to be applied in determining the meaning of "just cause" in a disciplinary provision was
given special consideration in Arbitrator Lewis Tyree's opinion
in In re Campbell Soup Co. and Food, Tobacco, Agricultural and

Allied Workers Union of America (CIO), Local 80, 10 L.A. 207 (1948). The case was one in which an employee had been discharged for alleged excessive absenteeism and alcoholism. The arbitrator's opinion includes the following statements:

> About all that an impartial arbitrator can do, therefore, is to decide the justice or the injustice of the discharge here in question, in the light of (a) common sense, (b) common knowledge of generally prevailing industry standards for employee deportment and (c) common understanding of when — *absent specific criteria mutually agreed on* — an employer may fairly and justly discharge an employee with seniority rights. Common sense would seem to indicate the right of an employer to discharge any employee when his absences are so frequent as to impair substantially output or efficient production. . . . It is also a matter of common knowledge that alcoholism — on or off the premises — is harmful to plant efficiency and discipline, and is not commonly tolerated in competitive industry. . . .
>
> In the instant case is any man on the street likely to say — in the light of all the facts that appear in N's record — that he got a raw deal or that the Company action was arbitrary, or capricious, or without just cause? On the contrary, it would seem that the standards of any ordinary man-on-the-street are adequately satisfied in this case. . . . [Grievance claim dismissed.]

In some contracts, although this is the exception, an attempt is made to spell out what is meant by "just cause." There is sometimes a very lengthy enumeration of matters which purports to be all inclusive. A contract between the Allis-Chalmers Manufacturing Company and the United Automobile Workers (CIO) lists twenty-three reasons for which an employee may be disciplined. A more general approach is taken in the following provision of the contract between the Fall River Manufacturers Assn. and the Textile Workers Union (CIO):

> The right to discharge employees shall remain in the sole discretion of the Employer, except that no discharge shall be made without just cause — just cause to mean, among other things, inefficiency, insubordination or persistent or serious infraction of rules reasonably promulgated by the management relating to the actual operation of the plant, or engaging in a strike or group stoppage of work of any kind, slow-down strike,

sabotage, picketing or failure to abide by the terms of this agreement or by the award of the arbitrator.

2. "Any member who does not perform his duties to the satisfaction of his employer is subject to his immediate discharge."

3. "It is mutually agreed that any employee, supervisory or otherwise, who violates or advocates the violation of this agreement may be discharged by the company and barred from membership by the Union."

4. In a contract between Air Associates, Inc., and the United Automobile Workers (CIO) it is provided that "just cause" for discharge shall include, among other things, "A deliberate attempt to destroy harmonious relations between the Company and the Union."

5. Some contracts provide that the reasons for discharge shall include "Advocating, or being a member of or affiliated with any organization which advocates the overthrow of the American social order and the American form of government."

6. "The Union shall have the right to recommend to the employer the discharge of any employee for whom the union is the bargaining agent under this contract. In the exercise of this right, the union shall be guided by the same considerations and bound by the same restrictions by which, under this contract, the employer is bound in the discharge of an employee, and in no event shall such request be predicated on the fact that the employee is or is not a member of the union. Upon the employer's refusal to follow any such recommendation, the matter shall be submitted to arbitration in accordance with this contract, and in the event that the arbitrator orders that the union's recommendation be followed by the employer, the employer shall forthwith discharge the employee."

7. A contract between the Gaylord Container Corporation and Retail, Wholesale and Department Store Union, Wholesale and Warehouse Workers Union, Local 65 (CIO) contained the following discharge clause:

> The Employer shall have the right to discharge employees for just cause, such as, but not limited to: slow-down in production, dishonesty, intoxication, falsifying time cards, insubordination, inefficiency, lateness or tardiness without reasonable excuse in excess of three times in any one month; having his salary garnished or his wages assigned more than three times; or for any violation of the Employer's reasonable working rules. If the Union shall dispute such discharge,

the same shall be handled as provided for in the grievance procedure hereof. . . .

In interpreting this clause, an arbitrator (F. W. Naggi) made the following statement (see 10 L.A. 439, 440 (1948)):

> The arbiter agrees that by the terms of the contract it is management's prerogative to determine what constitutes inefficiency, but in determining inefficiency it must have facts upon which to base its conclusions. When management does have facts from which it can conclude, its judgment cannot be questioned, but in the absence of such facts its position is untenable. The Union's claim for reinstatement with back pay for an employee discharged for inefficiency was granted in this case on the ground that the employer has merely pleaded inefficiency and has failed to produce the witnesses and production records to establish the facts warranting its conclusions.

8. Clauses of the following type are frequently included in contract disciplinary provisions:

> The employer shall have the right to discharge or suspend for just cause, but shall first notify the Union representatives of the reasons for such discharge. . . . It is the intent of the parties that the employer shall give at least one warning to any employee before taking disciplinary action except in cases involving a serious breach of discipline. Said warning shall be made known to a Union Representative.

Compare the following provision in the agreement between Shell Oil Company and Oil Workers Int. Union:

> Shell may discharge any Employee for any reason whatsoever, without assignment of cause, if agreed to by the Union.

Would an employee have any standing before an arbitrator or a court to challenge a discharge under this clause? Suppose the employee was not a member of the Union.

9. In Retail Drug Union v. Sun Ray Drug Co., 12 L.A. 418 (Pa. C.P. No. 5, Pa. County, 1949), the Union petitioned for an order that the Company show cause why it was refusing to arbitrate a "discharge" case, as provided in the parties' agreement. The Company alleged that the employee involved had not actually been discharged but had been persuaded to take employment in another store. The Union alleged that the employee had thought this other store (which had a similar name) was part of the defendant

company's system. It was, in fact, independently owned. The court dismissed the petition. It held, first, that the question of fact as to whether the employee resigned voluntarily "should . . . be determined by a court and jury, or by a court alone." Smith, J., went on to say that even if this case had gone to arbitration and the arbitrator had ordered reinstatement the court could not thereafter have upheld such an order in view of the rule against ordering specific performance of contracts for personal service. "The collective bargaining agreement itself is a contract for personal services between a union representing its members and the employer of members of the union." Does this holding raise an issue of the consistency of all reinstatement arbitration orders with the specific performance rule referred to by Judge Smith? Is his analysis of the nature of a collective bargaining agreement sound?

In re SAGER LOCK WORKS [NORTH CHICAGO, ILL.]
and UNITED STEELWORKERS OF AMERICA,
LOCAL 1647 (CIO)
12 L.A. 495 (1949)

Board of Arbitration: Otto J. Baab (chairman, appointed by parties); D. W. McClay (employer-appointed arbitrator); and Ernest Sirvidas (union-appointed arbitrator), dissenting.

BAAB, Arbitrator: . . .

The grievance filed by Carl O. Benson reads as follows:

"Having been unjustly discharged from my employment at the Sager Lock Works, North Chicago, Illinois, on December 17, 1948, I request that I be replaced on my job as Stock Chaser and be reimbursed for any monies lost during the period of unemployment caused by the discharge."

On the basis of this grievance, the Union requests the arbitrators to reinstate Carl Benson in the job he held at the time of his discharge and award him compensation for loss of earnings since that time.

The employee involved in this grievance — Carl Benson — was hired by the Company on August 20, 1946, with a full knowledge of his physical disability, caused by infantile paralysis in his youth. This worker had served his probationary period of thirty days, during which the Company had its contractual opportunity to determine whether or not it desired to retain Benson. Following this probationary period all of the terms of the contract became effective in this employee's case, including those relative to discharge. The Union maintains that the purpose of the probationary clause is to give the employer a chance to study the work of new employees and to eliminate those who proved to be incapable of performing their jobs. Benson survived this test, as is evidenced by the fact that he remained in the Company's employ until the date of his discharge — December 17, 1948.

The discharge was not due to an actual reduction of the working force in the employee's department — Stock Room Dept. On the contrary, one week before Benson's discharge another worker was hired in this department, with the obvious intention of replacing Benson. In the meantime, one employee assigned to the Stock Room Department had worked part time in the Shipping Department and continued to do so after Benson's discharge. This is submitted to refute the Company's argument that he was discharged because he was not physically able to do the work of both departments. The only employee in the Stock Room who works part time in the Shipping Department had previously worked in both departments and the worker who replaced Benson did work in the Stock Room only. Thus the replacement was given a job, upon which he was retained, although only a probationary employee, while Benson, with over two years of service with the Company, was discharged.

The Company has not demonstrated the alleged inability of Benson to do his job as Stock Handler. At the hearing it admitted it had no exact proof of the amount of work done by Benson in relation to other workers on the same job. This employee climbed the ladders provided for placing the stock and wrote figures upon the records clearly and legibly, as seen by the exhibits submitted by the Company. The fact that he was continued as an employee by the Company for more than two years is in itself evidence that he was viewed as performing the duties of his job acceptably. This fact and the failure of management to prove that the discharge was based upon the Contract fully support the Union position.

The Company contends that its discharge of Carl Benson should be sustained upon the basis of Article 2 of the Contract, which provides that it may discharge an employee "for proper cause" and transfer or relieve him from duty "because of lack of work or for other legitimate reasons." When the personnel needs and production requirements of a plant demand it, management has the right to hire and fire, provided only that such action is not used to discriminate against any member or members of the Union. It is clear and beyond dispute that no charge of discrimination is involved in this grievance case. Solely on the basis of production requirements and of the proven inability of Benson to meet these, does the Company argue that its discharge of this employee is entirely justified. If the Union's position is accepted, the Company could then discharge no employee for cause, as is permitted by the Contract. The officials of the Company have patiently given Benson every opportunity to prove his competence and ability to do the work, and discharged him only after retaining him for more than two years. There is no evidence of bad faith or an attempt at discrimination. The sole cause of the discharge is the inability of the worker to do his job. The Union must demonstrate the presence of unfairness or bad faith if it expects to carry conviction in its argument. This it has been unable to do. . . .

The facts in this case are clear and undeniable. After an employment period of more than two years, the aggrieved employee was discharged. During this period, Benson had held two jobs — first that of records clerk and then that of stock handler. As records clerk he had been warned — how often has not been determined — by management as to the unsatisfactory nature of his work. At least some effort was made to help his [sic] improve. During his service on this job he worked for a short time each day in handling stock, with the apparent reason of improving his efficiency as records clerk. When reduction in the working force in the Shipping Department took place, he was discharged on the ground of inability to do the work in both departments — Stock Handling and Shipping. A further fact of record includes the Company's knowledge that Benson was handicapped by infantile paralysis when he was hired, and that he was hired at a time when it was difficult to secure able-bodied men.

Even though the normal production expectation of this job [stock handler] has never been measured by the Company and only rough estimates were made that Benson did about one-fourth of the work done by other individuals handling stock, the conclusion can surely be reached that the handling and moving of stock by this unfortunately handicapped employee would take place at a considerably slower pace than that of other employee doing similar work. Casual observation, such as was possible before and after the hearing, of the movements of this employee compels one to come to this conclusion. The work may have been done dependably and well, from the standpoint of care and accuracy in placing the cartons, yet in such an amount as to fall far behind the production requirements and rate of the rest of the plant. Incompetence produced by this man's physical handicap can be blamed on neither the workmen nor the Company, but neither can existence be denied.

It now becomes appropriate to consider the Union's contention as to the Company's failure to exercise its right to discharge Benson before the expiration of the probationary period.

[This contention was rejected with the statement, inter alia, that "the probation clause with regard to discharge simply means that after the probationary period the company shall be *responsible* for any discharge; that is to say, it may occasion a grievance such as the present one, and must defend its acts on the basis of other parts of the Contract." The opinion then continues as follows:]

This interpretation of the agreement, therefore, at no time obligates the Company to give a guarantee of permanent tenure in a job to any employee who may have survived the probationary period. On the contrary, it permits management to exercise control of its working force, its size and its assignment to jobs, at all times, in the light of production needs and economic conditions. Since management directs an economic organization whose primary function is to produce efficiently and profitably, as well as to provide jobs, the retention of an employee for humanitarian reasons cannot be its primary motive. At this point the appropriateness of Article 2, defining the so-called prerogatives of management, is made clear. Direction of the working force, its expansion or reduction, and direction of the individual worker, as well as the control of production methods, are well recognized powers of management, and of it alone.

This means that management's decision to discharge an employee on the basis of its own judgment as to his competence cannot be disputed, even though it can make no statistical showing or scientific demonstration of the precise character or degree of incompetence. In the absence of a bilaterally negotiated merit system, the judgment of management on this point must be final, providing there is no showing of discrimination or prejudice. Consequently proof of Benson's incompetence in the job of records clerk or of his lack of speed in the job of stock handler is not a crucial matter. It may be presumed that management, in discharging this employee, acted in its own interests for the sake of production efficiency, as the Contract clearly permits it to do. Mere delay in bringing about the discharge, no matter what the reason for the delay, does not bar this employer from using his contract rights as set forth in Art. 2. Since there has been no showing of arbitrary or unfair discrimination, the Company's position must be upheld.

The majority of the panel of arbitrators awards as follows:

The request of the Union that Carl Benson be reinstated in his former job and be reimbursed for lost earnings is denied.

NOTES

1. A general hiring without reference to time is prima facie at will according to common law decisions: Martin v. New York Life Ins. Co., 148 N.Y. 117, 42 N.E. 416 (1895). See annotations 11 A.L.R. 469 (1921), 100 A.L.R. 839 (1936), and 161 A.L.R. 706 (1946), Restatement of Agency, Sec. 442.

2. In view of Arbitrator Baab's finding that "The Company has not demonstrated the alleged inability of Benson to do his job as Stock Handler," and his assertion that "The Union must demonstrate the presence of unfairness or bad faith if it expects to carry conviction in its argument," where do you believe that the so-called burden of proof should rest in these cases of discharges for incompetence or misbehavior?

In most grievance arbitration cases it is generally accepted that the aggrieved party has the responsibility of establishing his position. In strict courtroom language this would be referred to as the burden of proof, but in arbitration proceedings it is rarely given any formal designation. In discipline cases, however, arbitrators have demonstrated a marked tendency to force the employer to justify the action which he has taken, as demonstrated by the following excerpts from reported cases.

In the frequently cited case of In re Campbell, Wyant & Cannon Foundry Company, 1 L.A. 254 (1945), Arbitrator Harry H. Platt concluded that, "In a case of discharge, the burden of proof rests upon the company to show, by a fair preponderance of the evidence, that the discharge was for good and sufficient cause."

In American Smelting and Refining Company, 7 L.A. 147 (1947), Arbitrator Robert J. Wagner referred to the passage quoted above and said, "While I cannot always hold with that position, particularly where a history of amicable union-management relations is evident, I do not believe it to be sound where the 'management rights clause' qualifies discharge for cause by the word 'just' or 'proper' (as in the instant case); and where the discharged employee has established a substantial equity in his job."

Elsewhere in his opinion Arbitrator Wagner observed: "Neither party offered a substantial amount of undisputed testimony at the hearing in this case. Aside from that of Foreman Murphy and Grievance Committee Chairman — and fellow-employee — Jackson, little of the testimony stems from actual observation. The arbitrator cannot presume to substitute his judgment for that of a management with whom the union had admittedly good relations in the past. But, in the discharge of two employees with over 13 and 12 years' service respectively, it would seem to be the responsibility of management to show, beyond a reasonable doubt, that the employees are unable to perform a fair day's work."

In the case of Walter Butler Shipbuilders, Inc., 2 L.A. 633 (1944), Arbitrator George A. Gorder drew a distinction between disciplinary discharges and temporary layoffs, using the following language: "It may be conceded the evidence is insufficient to sustain a discharge where the burden would be upon the company to justify it, but, on a three-day suspension, where the burden is upon the union to establish the incorrectness of the order, the action must be upheld where there appears any reasonable ground to show that the officer acted fairly, without caprice or discrimination, upon facts evidencing an infraction of rules. The acts constituting infractions are admitted. The sole question is whether or not the evidence seeking to justify them is sufficient to prove that the suspensions were improperly imposed upon a misconception or misinterpretation of them. The arbitrator feels that, where an officer acts in good faith without caprice or discrimination, upon appearances which prima facie constitute an infraction of known rules, the burden should be placed upon the employee and his union to show that the officer's inferences and actions are mistaken or improper. The evidence in this case does not meet that requirement, when weighed against a three-day suspension."

A further factor was injected into the burden of proof issue by Arbitrator James J. Healy in In re Swift & Company, 12 L.A. 108 (1948), when, accepting the view that the burden is on the employer to show that the discharge was for *proper cause,* he added that "once an employee is proved guilty of certain offenses, his guilt and the penalty invoked by the Company therefor shall stand unless it is shown by the Union that the *penalty* was improper for the proved offense." (Italics added.)

Compare with the statement just quoted, the following language from the award of Arbitrator Russell A. Smith in the case of In re Armen Berry Casing Co., 17 L.A. 179, 181 (1950): "In a discharge case, when the collective agreement between the parties protects employees against discharge where there is not 'proper cause,' it is well accepted that the burden of justifying the discharge or other discipline is upon the employer. This involves the necessity on the employer of showing *both the infraction of some established rule of employee conduct and the propriety of the disciplinary action taken,* in this case, of discharge."   (Italics added.)

3. Do these cases suggest an analysis of the burden of proof issue as follows: The Union must prove the discharge (its case as plaintiff) and the Company the justification?   In a word, and reducing or converting it to the courtroom vernacular, can it be said that justification in discharge cases is an "affirmative defense" as that term is used in pleading?

4. It will be recalled that the Union in the Enderby Case — XIII objected to the Company's introduction of evidence in Seward's case of prior oral reprimands for incompetent work.   Suppose the Company's practice had been to give warnings before taking disciplinary action, and none had been given in this case?   What is the relevance of the following excerpt from Arbitrator Stein's opinion in In re Pyrene Manufacturing Company, 9 L.A. 787 (1948) :

> A warnings system has several purposes.   On the one hand, it puts the employee on notice that the Company takes a serious view of his behavior and that repetition thereof will lead to discharge.   On the other, it focuses attention clearly on the particular behavior of which the Company complains; if the employee feels the warning unjustified, he may resort to the grievance procedure in order to clear himself.   At the very least, such recourse permits a finding of the facts when these are still fresh in people's minds.   Miller conceded that he had on various occasions received verbal "spankings" from supervisors, but these are not the same as written warnings.   We are not impressed by Company testimony that the reluctance of supervisors to issue written warnings should be taken into account in evaluating the record.   The Company must either use its warnings system or abandon it, and supervisors' laxness cannot condone not using the system on appropriate occasions, if it is to remain.   Where a warnings system is in effect, the workers have a right to be warned, and they may well feel that the misbehavior which is known to management but which is not followed by a warning is not regarded seriously by management.   To discharge a man without a previous warning may amount to a denial of procedural "due process."   We believe, therefore, that the Company's failure to follow its own disciplinary procedures makes its action in discharging Miller improper.

In re BURNDY ENGINEERING CO., INC. [NEW YORK, N.Y.] and UNITED ELECTRICAL, RADIO & MACHINE WORKERS OF AMERICA, LOCAL 475 (CIO)
12 L.A. 1012 (1949)

ARBITRATOR: Sidney Cahn, arbitrator under contract. . . .

Prior to reporting for work on a certain day a dispute arose between Denahy and Rowel. It was later settled between them by means of a fist fight which occurred during their lunch hour and off company property.

Their supervisor, Elliot D. Braush, learned of the proposed fight and left the plant in an attempt to prevent it. He arrived at the scene after the fight was over and after the participants had "forgotten" and "forgiven." The entire incident took place during the participants' lunch hour.

Denahy, as a result of the fight, sustained an injury to his eye and was sent to a physician for treatment. At Braush's request Rowel accompanied him. Denahy, after visiting the physician, did not return to work that day.

Upon Rowel's return to the plant at about 1:20 P.M., he was met by Braush, who first directed him to "get to work." Three or four minutes later Braush, after a conference with the shop steward, told Rowel that as Denahy had lost his afternoon's work because of the fight, it was no more than fair that Rowel should suffer the same penalty. Rowel was laid off without pay for the balance of the day.

In answer to one of my questions Braush testified that he laid Rowel off for the half day because he felt that a fist fight was no way to settle a dispute and further, to set an example for all other employees. Braush also testified that the suspension was imposed on Rowel so as to avoid disruption in the department, for he feared that upon Rowel's return to work, other employees would leave their jobs for the purpose of questioning Rowel concerning the result of the fight.

Rowel and Denahy returned to work the next day but each of them suffered a loss of one-half day's pay. The Union claimed that such action was unjustified, in view of the fact that the fight took place "off company time and off company property." The Employer, on the other hand, contended that its action was justified as a means of preventing disruption in the department and as an example to other employees.

Insofar as Denahy is concerned, I am of the opinion that the

Employer's action, in refusing to pay him for the half day lost, was justified. In fact, Denahy was not laid off or suspended for the period in question. He actually did not report for work, due to an injury which he sustained "off company time and property" and in no way related to his employment. Under such circumstances there is no reason to require the Employer to compensate Denahy for the time so lost.

The facts, insofar as they concern Rowel, however, require a different conclusion. For the time which Rowel lost, beginning with the end of his lunch hour and up to the time he reported for work at 1:20 P.M., the Employer was not justified in refusing to pay him, for this time was taken by Rowel at the supervisor's request that he accompany Denahy to the physician. But for this request Rowel would have reported for work at the end of his regular lunch period.

The Employer's action in laying off Rowel for the balance of the day was likewise unwarranted for the following reasons:

The Employer's interest in its employees, under the particular facts as here exist, must be deemed to apply only to prohibited acts committed on the Employer's property or time and to such acts as directly affect the Employer in the operation of its business. To treat the act complained of, i.e., improper conduct committed while off duty and not on the Employer's property or business, as sufficient to control or to discipline an employee, would be tantamount to an unjust and improper intrusion upon an employee's personal rights and life. No more so would an employer be justified in disciplining an employee who had abused his wife while at home. Such disciplinary action is not within an employer's province. It follows, therefore, that the Employer's action, in making an example of Rowel, was unwarranted under the facts as here disclosed.

Concerning the second reason advanced by the Employer seeking to justify Rowel's lay-off, i.e., that Braush was afraid Rowel's presence would disrupt departmental operations, I am of the opinion that discipline based on such assumption was likewise unjustified.

During the three or four minutes that Rowel actually worked that afternoon, no other employee sought to question him concerning the fight. Despite this, Rowel was laid off for the balance of the afternoon because Braush was "afraid" Rowel's presence "might" disrupt operations. Braush admitted that no facts existed upon which he based this fear. It was speculative and conjectural and I am of the belief that the assertion of such fear was seized upon merely as a pretext for an attempt to equalize penalties with Denahy. Braush did not have the right to suspend Rowel for a half day merely on a supposition, but if after Rowel had returned to work his actions did tend to disrupt the department, then Braush would have been completely within his rights. To discipline an employee under these circumstances, however, is in effect penalizing him for something he has not done.

The Employer will be directed to reimburse Rowel for the one-half day in question. For the reasons hereinabove stated, Denahy is not entitled to any reimbursement for the time he lost.

The undersigned, constituting the duly authorized Arbitrator, and to whom was voluntarily submitted the matters in controversy, awards as follows:

Burndy Engineering Co., Inc. was justified in laying off David Denahy on April 7, 1949.

Burndy Engineering Co., Inc. was not justified in laying off Clayton Rowel on April 7, 1949. Burndy Engineering Co., Inc. is directed to reimburse Clayton Rowel for one-half day of April 7, 1949 at his regular straight time rate.

TELLER, MANAGEMENT FUNCTIONS UNDER COLLECTIVE BARGAINING *

75–80 (1947)

The question whether "just cause" or simply "cause" exists to sanction the discharge of an employee under a contractual provision authorizing management to take disciplinary action, depends upon the facts of the particular case. . . .

In one case the collective agreement provided that the arbitrator should not substitute his judgment for that of management unless he finds that it acted arbitrarily or in violation of the terms of the agreement. The agreement also provided that discharge of employees should be for cause only. The arbitrator held, overruling the opposite contention of management, that the discharge clause takes precedence over the provisions of the management clause, and authorized the arbitrator to make his own decision as to whether cause exists in the given case.[72]

This is not to say, however, that the employer's judgment is completely irrelevant to the inquiry. His judgment as to the

---

* Reprinted by permission of the publisher, Baker Voorhis & Co.—ED.

[72] See Matter of Bakelite Corporation (Chemical & Crafts Union, Inc. (Ind.)). Arbitrators: Arthur R. Lewis, Edward C. Moffett, William C. Treanor (dissenting), 1 Lab. Arb. Rep. 227 (1945).

effect of the employee's conduct upon plant efficiency and plant morale should undoubtedly be considered as a factor to be weighed with other factors in the case.

Insubordination is the kind of specific cause which most arbitrators will accept as sufficient to justify the employer in discharging the insubordinate employee. But this rule, like most of the rules established in the field of labor relations, may prove unrealistic as applied to special facts in a specific case. It was held in one case, for example, that insubordination cannot be charged where the refusal to obey directions is not defiant, but is a precautionary action reasonably taken to avoid the risk of injury due to defective plant machinery.[73]

Borderline cases involving alleged insubordination frequently occur in cases of disputes over contract interpretation. In such cases the question arises whether the employer's right to discharge will be sustained simply because the arbitrator upholds the employer's view in regard to the disputed question of interpretation. In Matter of Modernage Furniture Corporation,[74] the union was in dispute with the employer over the question whether certain employees had supervisory powers in the light of the contract provisions. The union instructed the employees not to accept the directions of the supervisor in question. The employer discharged some of the employees for so doing. The arbitrator refused to uphold the employer's right to discharge them, notwithstanding that the employer's contention was upheld as to the right of the supervisor to give the directions in question. While the decision would seem to be logically incorrect, it might possibly be justified as an effort to dispose of a dispute between an employer and a union without penalizing certain employees who acted in innocent compliance with union instructions.

An impression commonly found in some management circles, as well as among union spokesmen, is that "cause," under a contractual provision limiting the employer's right to discharge employees, must be specific. To the extent that this impression implies that there must be tangible evidence to support the employer's contention, it is probably correct, but the decisions do not support it insofar as it denies that cause may be proved by general conduct evidencing an unsatisfactory worker. As stated in Matter of Bakelite

[73] Matter of The Key Company (International Molders & Foundry Workers, A.F.L.), Arbitrator: John E. Dwyer, 1 Lab. Arb. Rep. 192 (1945).

[74] Matter of Modernage Furniture Corporation (Retail Furniture and Floor Covering Employees, C.I.O.), Arbitrator: I. Robert Feinberg, 3 Lab. Arb. Rep. 680 (1946).

Corporation: [75] "It should be reasonably clear that discharge for cause may be justified even without the incidence of a single effective occurrence such as dishonesty or intoxication. The right of management to determine the desirability of continued employment of a worker may not be fairly curtailed by any such rigid requirement. It is entirely consistent with the determination of proper cause that an employee may be found by trial of substantial duration to be unsuited for particular employment or unreliable or in some other way an unsatisfactory worker. The fact that the conclusion is reached only after extended trial and on the basis of numerous details independently insufficient is not enough to preclude the exercise of fair judgment."

May "cause" be proved by incidents occurring outside the plant? A negative answer to this question was made in Matter of Pioneer Gen-E-Motors Corporation.[76] It appeared in this case that an employee assaulted her supervisor off the company premises and after working hours. The arbitrator held that this did not constitute cause to justify her discharge, stating: "to hold otherwise would, in effect, be to extend company or employer supervision over the private lives of their employees." While the arbitrator's opinion in support of his decision does not indicate the background against which the case arose, there seems to be at least plausible ground for questioning the correctness of the decision, since the antagonism between the parties might very well be expected to overflow into the plant and impair its efficiency. Cases of immoral conduct, for example, may easily disrupt plant morale though engaged in by employees outside the plant.

The arbitrator laid stress upon the fact that the employee engaged in the assault was not convicted for so doing. But it would seem that he was obliged to inquire as to the facts just as he would have been obliged to do had the assault taken place inside the plant, if it could be proven in the light of the specific facts that the assaulting employee was at fault and that the assault precluded cooperation between the supervisor and the employee in the plant.

It seems clear, under a contract reserving to management the right to discharge for cause, that management is not obliged to discharge employees where just cause exists; it may impose a lesser

[75] Matter of Bakelite Corporation (Chemical & Crafts Union, Inc. (Ind.)), Arbitrators: Arthur R. Lewis, Edward C. Moffett, William C. Treanor (dissenting), 1 Lab. Arb. Rep. 227 (1945).

[76] Matter of Pioneer Gen-E-Motors Corporation (United Electrical, Radio and Machine Workers), Arbitrator: Jacob J. Blair, 3 Lab. Arb. Rep. 486 (1946).

measure of discipline.[77]   But the question arises whether the arbitrator may properly assume jurisdiction to cut down the disciplinary action taken by the employer or whether the measure of discipline is in the employer's discretion absent any provision in the contract.

It would seem logically that the measure of discipline is in the employer's discretion.   As stated in Matter of Perkins Oil Company: [78] "Where, as in this case, no schedule of offenses and punishment has been put into effect, either by agreement, by company rules, or by practice, the penalty to be imposed for an offense rests in the sound discretion of management.   Arbitrators have no right to substitute their judgment for that of management except where there has been an abuse of such discretion.   While the (arbitrator), if he had had (the employer's) decision to make in the first place, might have imposed a ten-day layoff instead of discharge, it does not follow that discharge was unreasonable or an abuse of discretion, especially in view of the admitted warning. The remedy of the union lies in negotiating with the company for a schedule of offenses, with provisions for warnings and specification of penalties."

Cases exist, however, where arbitrators have assumed such jurisdiction.[79]   In Matter of Campbell, Wyant & Cannon Foundry Company,[80] the employee's discharge was based on a proper ground, but on the mistaken assumption that the employee had been disciplined on a prior occasion.   The arbitrator cut down the measure of discipline for this reason.   It has also been held that an employer may not apply different measures of discipline to several employees each of whom was guilty of the same offense.[81]

[77] Matter of Auto-Lite Battery Corporation (United Auto Workers, C.I.O.), Arbitrator: Maxwell Copelof, 3 Lab. Arb. Rep. 122 (1946).

[78] Matter of Perkins Oil Company (Food, Tobacco, Agricultural and Allied Workers, C.I.O.), Arbitrators: Whitley P. McCoy, L. P. Brown III, W. A. Copeland (union-appointed arbitrator, dissenting), 1 Lab. Arb. Rep. 446 (1946).   See also Matter of Diemolding Corporation (Interstate Copper and Brass Workers Union, C.U.A.), Arbitrators: Ralph E. Kharas, James Di Bella, Henry Fraser, 2 Lab. Arb. Rep. 274 (1945).

[79] See Matter of Campbell, Wyant, & Cannon Foundry Company (United Auto Workers, C.I.O.), Arbitrator: Harry H. Platt, 1 Lab. Arb. Rep. 254 (1945).

[80] Matter of Campbell, Wyant & Cannon Foundry Company (United Auto Workers, C.I.O.), Arbitrator: Harry H. Platt, 1 Lab. Arb. Rep. 254 (1945).

[81] See Matter of Ford Motor Company (United Auto Workers, C.I.O.), Arbitrator: Harry Shulman, 3 Lab. Arb. Rep. 779 (1946).   Compare Matter of General Motors Corporation (United Auto Workers, C.I.O.), Arbitrator: George W. Taylor, 10 Lab. Rel. Ref. Man. 1183 (1942).

The student should also consult Copelof, Management-Union Arbitration 110–150 (1948) ; Elkouri, How Arbitration Works 162, 253 (1952) ; Comment, Discharge and Discipline Cases in Labor Arbitration, 43 Ill. L. Rev. 847 (1949).

FEDDERS–QUIGAN CORP.
15 L.A. 209 (1951)

Arbitrator: Morrison Handsaker

The question presented to the arbitrator for determination in the case of the grievance of Mr. Lonnie Brown is set forth in the submission as follows:

"Is Lonnie Brown entitled to pay for the period between his discharge on June 6, 1950 and his reinstatement by the Company on July 10, 1950."

While there is some slight disagreement concerning facts in the history of the case, the differences in this regard are minor, and, in the view of the arbitrator, not significant.   It appears that the following events took place in the order listed.   (Since the timing of events is of more than usual significance in this case they are listed chronologically.)

On June 6, 1950, Mr. Lonnie Brown was discharged by the Fedders-Quigan Corporation.

On June 14, the Union protested the discharge and requested arbitration.   The Company waived the provision in the contract which required protests of discharges within five days, and the case is properly before the arbitrator even though more than the five days elapsed between the discharge and the protest.

On either June 16 (this is the Union view) or June 20 (this is the Company view) a conference was held in the office of Mr. Joseph K. Reichbart, attorney for the Union, dealing with the discharge of Mr. Brown and also with the interpretation of the vacation clause which is the subject matter of the second grievance, dealt with below.   Present at this conference were Mr. Reichbart, Mr. Joseph Gullotta, international representative of the Union, and Mr. U. V. Musico, representing the Company.   After considerable discussion of the second grievance in this case, briefer attention was turned to the grievance arising from the discharge of Lonnie Brown.   It appears that a suggestion (according to the Union) or a proposal (according to the Company) was made by Mr. Gullotta to Mr. Muscio.   This suggestion or proposal appears to have been as follows: "The Company would be well advised to make the following proposal to the Union: the Company will rehire Mr. Brown on condition that the Union waive any questions of retro-active pay for the time lost due to the discharge." It appears that Mr. Gullotta backed up his suggestion or proposal by the con-tention that if the case came to arbitration the Union had such a strong case that they would win reinstatement without any ques-tion. The worst that could happen, in Mr. Gullotta's view, was that the arbitrator might deny back pay for the time lost, thus in effect imposing a disciplinary layoff, rather than a discharge for the offense committed by Mr. Brown.

Before the proposal or suggestion was made the parties in the conference had agreed that Mr. Gullotta would take up the in-terpretation of the vacation clause directly with Mr. Giordano, president of the Company. When the proposal or suggestion con-cerning Mr. Brown was made Mr. Muscio indicated that this mat-ter also might well be taken up with Mr. Giordano, and Mr. Gullotta indicated that he would do so.

Since the Company has several plants and the President travels from one to another, it was not until June 26 that Mr. Gullotta and Mr. Giordano were able to get together to discuss these mat-ters. On that date, a conference was held in the Stacy-Trent Hotel in Trenton. Again the matter of the interpretation of the vacation clause was the main point under discussion but near the end of the conference the subject of Mr. Brown's discharge again came up. Mr. Gullotta again proposed reinstatement. It appears that there was no discussion at all concerning retroactive pay at this conference. Mr. Giordano stated that he would take the matter up with Mr. Muscio to get the background of the case before deciding what position the Company would take. Later that same day Mr. Gullotta advised Mr. Muscio that he had dis-cussed the matter with Mr. Giordano and that the matter would be considered by Mr. Giordano.

On June 28 Mr. Giordano discussed over the telephone a num-ber of matters with Mr. Muscio, and among other things told Mr. Muscio that Mr. Brown should be rehired.

On July 5 or 6 Mr. Malloy, shop chairman for the Union, asked Mr. Muscio about the status of the case of Mr. Brown and Mr. Muscio advised Mr. Malloy that the Company was going to rehire Mr. Brown. At that time it was arranged that Mr. Malloy would have Mr. Brown report to Mr. Muscio on Friday, July 7.

On July 7, as planned, Mr. Malloy and Mr. Brown came to Mr. Muscio's office and it was explained to Mr. Brown that because of the intervention of the Union on his behalf, Mr. Brown was to be rehired. He reported back to work on Monday, July 10.

On July 17 or thereabouts, Mr. Gullotta asked Mr. Malloy what was being done about the Brown case, since he had heard nothing concerning it. He was advised by Mr. Malloy that Mr. Brown had been rehired. Mr. Gullotta then asked concerning retroactive pay and Mr. Malloy said he knew nothing about any retroactive pay.

Subsequent to this the Union pressed its claim for retroactive pay and carried the case to arbitration. A hearing on this matter was held before the undersigned on August 3, 1950 in the offices of the New Jersey State Board of Mediation in Newark.

The Company contends that a proposal was made to them, namely that if they would rehire Mr. Brown, the Union would waive back pay for time lost due to the discharge. The Company contends further that they accepted this proposal, rehired Mr. Brown and that, therefore, there is no basis for the Union claim for retroactive pay. The Company is willing to rest their case against retroactive pay on the basis of this proposal, made and accepted.

The Union contends that they did not make a proposal; Mr. Gullotta merely gave some good advice to the Company namely that the Company should make a proposal to the Union. The Union indicates that they might have accepted such a proposal (for reinstatement without back pay) at the time it was suggested, namely (according to the Union time-table) June 16, 10 days after the discharge. They would not, however, waive their claim for retroactive pay, they contend, when the case ran on as long as it did, for a period of 5 weeks.

It is the award of the arbitrator that Lonnie Brown is entitled to pay for the time lost due to the discharge, except that he shall not be paid for the first two weeks of the time lost due to the discharge. It is the further award of the arbitrator that in computing the pay due Mr. Brown, a deduction shall be made for money, if any, earned elsewhere by Mr. Brown during the period after the first two weeks of the discharge and a further deduction shall be made for money, if any, received by Mr. Brown as unemployment compensation during the period following the first two weeks of the discharge period.

The above award has been rendered by the arbitrator for the following reasons:

It appears to the arbitrator that this case must be determined on the basis of the broad equities of the situation. The collective

bargaining agreement between the parties gives no guidance to
the arbitrator.   It provides permissive but not mandatory awarding of back pay by an arbitrator when discharge has not been for
cause.

Looking at the broad equities of the matter the arbitrator has
concluded that a decision entirely in favor of the Union or a decision entirely in favor of the Company would be unjust.   The
Company, the arbitrator is persuaded, acted in good faith in accepting, as they thought, what they regarded as an offer from the
Union.   A suggestion such as that made by Mr. Gullotta comes
close to being a proposal if in fact it is not a proposal.   It is true
that Mr. Gullotta would have had to take back to his committee
and to the aggrieved employee, the proposal which he urged the
Company to make.   But it is also true that if he felt, as apparently
he did, that this would have been a good solution of the difficulty,
he would have urged acceptance of this by the Committee and the
employee affected and in all probability it would have been accepted.   When no discussion of retroactivity took place in the
conference with Mr. Giordano on July 26, it was not unreasonable
for Mr. Muscio to conclude that the earlier offer for the waiving
of back pay still stood.   In the light of the foregoing, it would,
in the view of the arbitrator, be unfair to award back pay for all
time lost.

This view is further strengthened by the following point: In
this case the Union, apparently, took the frequently held view
that while some disciplinary action may have been justified, nothing stronger than a disciplinary lay-off was in order, and they
believed, apparently that they could defend this position, is [sic]
necessary, before an arbitrator.   It appears, however, that the
Union did not believe that they could defend Mr. Brown's actions
completely, else they would not have indicated that they might
accept a settlement that waived back pay.   Thus it appears that
both Company and Union believed that Mr. Brown's actions
(whatever they were; this matter was not developed at the hearing)
warranted some penalty.   On the other hand, the arbitrator believes that there would be an injustice done if no back pay were
granted.   In the first place, his reinstatement was ordered by Mr.
Giordano on June 28, but it was not until July 10 that he was
actually put back to work.   Clearly, in the view of the arbitrator,
he is at the very least entitled to back pay for that period of time.
Further, the Union makes a valid argument when it contends that
while they might, in the interests of getting a settlement of a dispute, agree to waive back pay for a period of some days, they

would not waive it for as long as five weeks.   The Union also, it appears to the arbitrator, acted in good faith when they believed that some back pay would be forthcoming after Mr. Brown had been off the job so long.

It appears to the arbitrator that there was a genuine misunderstanding at the time of the conference in Trenton: the Company believed that the Union suggestion of reinstatement without back pay was still in force and the Union believing that the Company understood its view that so much time had elapsed that the previously made suggestion was not in force.   When no mention was made of back pay by either party, each party thought that the other accepted his view of the back pay issue.

If, then, the facts indicate that some penalty, short of discharge should lie against Mr. Brown as a disciplinary measure, and if, for reasons cited above, he should not be denied all back pay, for what period of time should back pay be awarded?   The Union made their suggestion or proposal (according to their version) on June 16.   At that time, apparently, they believed that their suggestion was equitable.   We may reasonably use that date as one limiting factor.   On the other hand, the President of the Company instructed that he should be reinstated on June 28 (though he was not actually reinstated until July 10).   The date of June 28 accordingly appears to establish a date when, without question, retroactive wage adjustment should begin.   We have then narrowed the limits down to a period of 12 days.   Any decision within that period is, probably, more or less arbitrary.

Within these limits the arbitrator has ruled as he has since it appears that a two week disciplinary layoff is about as severe a penalty as the evidence (such as it is) would justify.

NOTE

The arbitrator allowed for deduction "for money, if any, earned elsewhere" and for unemployment compensation.   How will these amounts be determined?   Suppose Brown had never tried to get a job, but just took it easy, confident that since his discharge was not for just cause, he would get back pay anyway?

JUSTIN, ARBITRATION UNDER THE LABOR CONTRACT — ITS NATURE, FUNCTION AND USE *

THE ARBITRATOR'S FUNCTION IN DISCIPLINARY CASES

Now, there are two schools of thought as to how the arbitrator should function in disciplinary cases. One school holds that in the absence of any qualifying contract provision or facts showing a contrary intent, the arbitrator must be satisfied on three points:

(1) That the employee was guilty of the charge — that he committed the offense complained of;

(2) That punishment was warranted under the circumstances; and

(3) That the degree of punishment imposed — say discharge — was just and proper, i.e., that the "penalty fitted the crime."

The last consideration, says this school, is just as much a part of "just cause" under the contract as are the first two. A punishment that fits the crime is equally a part of "just cause" and must be proved to the arbitrator's satisfaction.

Thus, in a number of discharge cases, arbitrators have reinstated an employee, without back pay, or modified in some other form the penalty of discharge. In other disciplinary cases, arbitrators have, in various ways, reduced the penalty imposed by management.

It doesn't follow, however, that in these cases, the arbitrator has "compromised" the case or his judgment. Neither can it be correctly said that he has tried to act as an "industrial statesman," making both parties happy with an award that he thinks will be "mutually acceptable" to them. Rather, he has acted under the above-stated three criteria. He has, in effect, judged that the disciplinary action taken, including the degree of penalty imposed, was not for "just cause." The offense, the facts and circumstances under which the offense was committed, and the degree of penalty imposed — all these did not add up to or prove "just cause" on management's part.

In such a case, the arbitrator has unquestionably substituted his judgment for that of management. He has determined the degree of penalty that, in his judgment, the offense warranted. But if, in the absence of other agreed upon criteria, or by acquiescence, the

* The full text of this article may be found in 27 Personnel 286 (1951), from which the above selections have been taken with the permission of the editor of that publication, the American Management Association, Inc. The article has been reprinted in 6 Arbitration Journal (N.S.) 139 (1951). — ED.

parties permit him to act under these three criteria, he is acting within his authority. Under these circumstances, he has not, as such, "compromised" the case or "split" his decision. Of course, if the parties do not want the arbitrator to act under these three criteria, they have the power to so instruct him. Theirs is the responsibility to exercise this power, and not leave it to guess-work or the individual arbitrator's choice.

The other "school" maintains that the arbitrator does not have the authority to substitute his judgment, as to the degree of penalty imposed, for that of management. They say that under the typical discharge clause cited above, only the first two criteria — whether the wrong was committed and whether punishment was warranted — are the only relevant subjects of inquiry. They are the only subjects over which the arbitrator has been given authority to act.

The nature of the punishment, or the degree of the penalty, they say, is not part of "just cause" under the contract. Thus, it is contended, if the arbitrator finds that the employee committed the wrong complained of, and he was disciplined for that wrong, the action of management must be sustained, whatever the penalty was. Neither the union nor the employee can then be heard to complain. The arbitrator's action in changing the penalty constitutes, under this position, an abuse or usurpation of authority, not given by the contract.

In these opposite positions, we find revealed the source of misunderstanding of the arbitrator's function in disciplinary and discharge cases. Each position has points of merit, and a good case can be made out to support each one.

STUDY OF AWARDS IN DISCIPLINE CASES

A recent study of arbitrators' actions in disciplinary and discharge cases, was made by Professor J. M. Porter, Jr.[9]

Professor Porter's study covered nearly 200 reported awards. He found that in

> . . . 74 cases, which represents 38 per cent of the total number studied, the arbitrator's award sustained the disciplinary action taken by management. In the remainder of the cases studied, 121, which was 62 per cent of the total, the effect of the arbitrator's award was to either revoke or modify the

[9] Professor of Psychology, Rensselaer Polytechnic Institute, Paper presented at the Proceedings of the Second Annual Meeting of Industrial Relations Research Association, 1949.

discipline imposed by management. In this latter group of cases, the effect of the award was to completely revoke management's action in 49 per cent of the instances and to modify (i.e. reduce in severity) the discipline in 51 per cent of the instances.

The report further stated:

Where the original discipline had taken the form of a suspension (24 cases) the arbitrator's decision sustained the action taken in two-thirds of the instances. Where the original discipline imposed had been the discharge of the employee (170 cases) the arbitrator's award sustained the action in 34 per cent of the cases.

SOME IMPLICATIONS OF THE STUDY

Though the study showed "that discharge is the form of discipline most frequently resorted to by management," Professor Porter was careful to point out that the "data were gathered from disputes which had been taken to arbitration and such findings may merely mean that unions are more apt to press discharge cases to arbitration than lesser forms of discipline."

Where management imposes a disciplinary punishment short of discharge, unions are less prone to test out the propriety of the company's action. As Professor Porter points out: "When suspension rather than discharge is involved, the awards sustain management's action two to one."

In re INTERNATIONAL HARVESTER CO. and UNITED AUTOMOBILE, AIRCRAFT & AGRICULTURAL IMPLE-MENT WORKERS OF AMERICA, LOCAL 98 (CIO)
16 L.A. 307 (1951)

McCoy, Arbitrator. . . . The facts are entirely without dispute, and in stating them I shall rely, as to some of the most vital matters, upon the testimony of the Company's General Foreman, Kenneth Brown. Virgil Cain, a Union steward, works in a seven man pool, so when he desires to check out for his Union duties it is necessary that a relief be supplied. When he reported to work on February 8, he requested his foreman, Mr. Lawrence, to get him a relief, as he desired to consult with his Zone Committeeman about Grievance No. 19–6, which was a protest against alleged undue curtailment by the Company of Cain's performance of Union duties.

A half-hour later the relief had not been supplied, so Cain repeated his request of Mr. Lawrence. Mr. Lawrence replied that the Committeeman, Neal, had not requested consultation with Cain. Cain then acquainted Mr. Lawrence with the provisions of Article VI, Section 8 (j), under which it is plainly supervision's duty to "call such Grievance Committeeman promptly" upon request of a steward and identification of the grievance and grievant. About 8:30 A.M. relief was supplied. Cain then filled in the form required by Article VI, Section 8, to be used, containing such information as his name, date, grievance number, and time of leaving (see form in Exhibit C to Contract), and gave it to Mr. Lawrence. The latter did not sign it, but the General Foreman, Mr. Brown, came up and said, "I thought I told you the other day that we would make out those passes." After some argument Mr. Brown signed it.

Just why Mr. Brown took the position that supervision should fill in the blanks I do not know, as Mr. Brown did not explain it when he took the stand. But clearly there is no Contract requirement to that effect, but rather to the contrary. The Contract provides that "Stewards and Grievance Committeemen will be required to use the authorizations required on the forms which will be provided by the Company. . . ." It would appear from this that the Company provides the forms and the Steward must "use" them, which I should think means fill in the required information.

This incident is trivial, but coming as it did on top of Mr. Lawrence's failure to provide a relief with reasonable promptness, or to explain the delay, and his mistaken argument with Cain as to Cain's right to have his Committeeman sent for, it assumes some importance as showing a general attitude that morning on the part of supervision that could not have a tendency toward harmony or mutual respect for the rights of Company and Union.

Neal, the Committeeman, then came to the Department, and he and Cain went into consultation. While they were conferring, a probationary employee, one Draga, went up to them and told them he had been discharged for not wearing his safety glasses.

Since a discharge takes precedence over other grievances, Cain immediately went to Mr. Brown, inquired whether it was true, and then asked why the Union representative had not been informed. Mr. Brown stated, "Mr. Draga has no bargaining rights whatsoever." In that Mr. Brown was quite mistaken. Article XI, Section 4, covering all employees, both seniority and probationary, provides, "The employee's Steward, and the Chairman of the Grievance Committee will be notified promptly of such disciplinary action."

Mr. Brown then denied Cain's request that he be allowed to represent Draga in the Industrial Relations Office, to which Draga was to be taken. Neal then intervened and asked permission to go to Industrial Relations to represent Draga. Brown told him he could go but he would not be paid for it. Again Mr. Brown was mistaken. Under the same Section 4 of Article XI Draga and Neal both had the right which Brown denied absolutely to Cain and granted only conditionally to Neal.

The Company subsequently admitted the error, and paid Neal for his time spent in Industrial Relations, but not until after a representative of the Industrial Relations Department had repeated Brown's error and refused payment.

Cain then checked out on another grievance, on an authorization signed by Assistant General Foreman Vance. When he failed to settle that grievance, he was signed back in by Vance at 10:35. Cain immediately made out an authorization to investigate the Draga discharge, and submitted it to Foreman Lawrence for signature. He refused to sign it. This was a clear violation of Article VI, Section 8 (a) , reading: [quoting the section].

In refusing to sign the pass, Mr. Lawrence referred Cain to the Assistant General Foreman, Mr. Vance. The latter was not to be found, and Cain so advised Lawrence and told him he was going ahead with his investigation and would ask Mr. Brown to sign the pass when he returned. Mr. Lawrence made no reply. Cain then went to the desk that has been assigned to Stewards, consulted his Contract, and was making notes when Mr. Brown came in. He asked Brown to sign the pass, and Brown refused, saying, "Draga is gone now, and I don't see where you would have a grievance on him. It would be best if you would go back to work."

Cain then consulted Neal, who advised him that he should continue to investigate the grievance, and that the most that could happen to him would be failure to receive pay for his time. Cain was writing a grievance when Brown came back and asked him what he was doing. Cain replied that he was writing a grievance on Draga, and Brown told him that he had no connection with that, that Draga had no rights, and that Cain should go back to work. Cain replied that he had two jobs, one on production and one to represent employees, that he was on the latter job and was going to continue on it. Brown told him that if he did not go back to his job in the paint booth he would discharge him. Cain said, "I am not going back."   Brown thereupon discharged him.

Cain was clearly within his rights in investigating the grievance, under Article VI, Section 8 (a) , and the Company expressly admits it in the post-hearing brief.   The "comedy of errors" committed by Supervision throughout the morning culminated in an unlawful order to Cain to go back to work, that order being based upon Mr. Brown's decision as to whether the Union could work up a valid grievance concerning the discharge of a probationer.   Of course Mr. Brown had stepped entirely outside his province when he started making decisions for the Union.   The Company's protection, under the Contract, lies in refusing pay.

One further fact needs to be noted.   Before Cain was taken to Labor Relations for formal discharge, he went back to Mr. Brown and said, "Wait a minute.   Let's compromise on this a little bit." Evidently Mr. Brown interpreted this, as I would, to be an offer to discuss the matter, and to go back to work if Brown insisted on it because he replied, "Virgil, you have had all the chance in the world, come on, let's go," and proceeded to take him to Labor Relations.   At the hearing there he was not offered a chance to go back to work, but was simply asked whether he had refused, and on his replying in the affirmative the discharge was completed.

In view of the facts stated in the last paragraph, a discharge could not be sustained regardless of all other facts.   A studied, persistent refusal to obey orders is ground for discharge.   But in the very first case I arbitrated between these parties, Case No. 1, 11 L.A. 1007, in sustaining the discharge of Union Briody, I said, ". . . I would have seized upon any reasonable ground for lessening the penalty, for discharge is the ultimate penalty.   If Briody had been discharged . . . without warning or opportunity to change his mind, such reasonable ground would have existed. But despite argument and advice extending over the period of an hour, despite his having the advice of his Steward . . . he persisted in his refusal."   The principle that an employee should have a *locus penetentiae,* room or time for repenting, was referred to in the Willis Blow case at this Works, Case No. 7, 12 L.A. 653, and was applied in the Max Plant case, Case No. 15, 13 L.A. 582.   Cain sought an opportunity to "compromise," which I take to mean to go back to work, and met with refusal from his General Foreman.

So the only real question in this case is whether some lesser penalty should be imposed.   I have applied a very strict rule in other cases concerning refusal of orders, and am cited to those cases by the Company's post-hearing brief.   In applying that strict rule, that it is the employee's duty to obey an order, and contest it afterward by the orderly processes of the grievance procedure, I have been in good company. The Company quotes from decisions by Arbitrators Harry Platt, David Wolff, and Harry Shulman, as well as from my own decision in Dwight Mfg. Co., 12 L.A. 990.

If production is to be had, the plant cannot be turned into a debating society. And a special duty in this respect lies upon Union Stewards, committeemen, and officers. They, above all, should set an example for obedience to orders and strict adherence to the contract for redress rather than resort to self-help. I recognized this principle in Stockham Pipe Fittings Co., 4 L.A. 744, bottom p. 745.

I have recently had my attention called to the fact that in these and similar cases I (and other arbitrators) have applied to industrial plants a stricter rule than is applied in the United States Army. I am informed by eminent authority [1] that under military law, a man declines to obey an order at his peril; if it turns out later that the order was lawful, he is guilty of insubordination; but if it turns out later that the order was unlawful, he is not guilty.[2] An example given me is this: a soldier appears at inspection with a button unbuttoned. His commanding officer says, "For that you do guard duty tonight." The soldier says, "I decline that duty," and he is court-martialed. He will be acquitted, because the order was unlawful in that it violates the rules of military law that duty shall not be imposed as punishment lest it demean duty.

I know of no organization where the strictest rule as to insubordination would be so justified and necessary as in the Army. Had I applied that Army rule in the Dwight case, 12 L.A. 990 (Hathcock's grievance), his layoff for one shift would have been set aside. I presume that principle of military law is based upon the premise that the responsibility for discipline rests not alone upon the lower ranks, to obey their superiors, but also upon the higher ranks, not to issue orders that can lawfully be declined. Of course the same principle applies to an industrial plant, and I recognized it in that same Dwight case, when I said: "The maintaining of discipline is not the responsibility entirely of the employees. Supervision has an equal responsibility."

Much as knowledge of the principle applied in military law has shaken me, I am not prepared to confess error in the decision where I have applied a stricter rule. I have been in too distinguished company in applying that rule to lightly overturn it. Military

---

[1] Brigadier General James E. Morrisette, ret., formerly Asst. Judge Advocate General.

[2] See Manual for Courts Martial, 1948 Ed., Par. 134, p. 149.

organization contains no adequate grievance machinery, such as is afforded by modern labor contracts. And the recognized exceptions to the strict rule (endangering life or health, suffering humiliation, etc.) afford adequate protection to the employee.

But while adhering to the rule, I do not feel inclined to extend it to unlawful orders issued by the Company to the Union. There is a clear distinction between the case of a supervisor telling an employee to go back to his job, and a supervisor telling the Union to stop investigating a grievance. The Company and the Union have met on equal terms and adopted a Contract recognizing each other's rights. Each has its dignity to uphold. Organization and corporations can act only through agents and representatives. When the duly authorized representative of the Company (Brown) told the duly authorized representative of the Union (Cain) to stop investigating a grievance, it was the Company issuing orders to the Union. If Brown had been right, it would have been Cain's duty as an employee to go back to his job. But Brown was wrong, by the Company's express admission, and it was Cain's duty, speaking as the representative of the Union, to insist firmly but respectfully upon the Union's rights.

The Company argues that with such a principle supervisors will never dare issue orders to Union representatives, and discipline will be gone. That is a slightly exaggerated view. The rule of military law referred to above has produced no such result in the Army. But it has had the effect of causing officers to learn the rules so as to avoid the giving of orders that can be declined with impunity. If this decision has that effect upon supervisors, causes them to study the Contract and be sure before they act, and causes them to refrain from arrogating to themselves the power to decide from stewards whether grounds for a grievance exist, no unfortunate results need be anticipated. The Company has express protection in the Contract against abuse of the privileges of Union representatives, in that it can refuse pay to them.

It was doubtless considerations such as these which led Permanent Umpire Alexander to set aside a 2½ day layoff imposed by General Motors on a Union representative under similar circumstances (G.M. Case No. E-319, decided May 2, 1949), cited by the Union. This decision was only one of a long line of similar decisions at General Motors under Umpire George Taylor, Allen Dash, and Ralph Seward.

If Cain had been rough, rowdy, belligerent, or insolent in his attitude, I might have sustained a brief layoff. But so far as the record shows, his attitude was calm, dignified, and respectful. If he could rightly be penalized it would put the entire grievance machinery, set up by agreement of the parties at the highest levels, at the mercy of supervisors, with the possibility of great harm to the relations of the parties, even to a complete breakdown of the grievance machinery. The Company is in the anomalous position here of asking that a rule be laid down that a steward must rely upon a grievance machinery that is even then under attack and being violated. Cain was insisting upon the inviolability of the grievance machinery, and for that he was discharged. The Company is virtuously insisting on adherence to the grievance machinery, but asks me to do that which amounts in effect to sustaining a foreman in denying the Union access to it. I cannot in common sense, in the light of principle, or in the light of the distinguished authorities cited, do so. For these reasons the grievance will be sustained.

E. *Wages*

Two distinct types of wage problems must be recognized in connection with any general discussion of the collective bargaining process. The first of these has to do with the matter of wage rates themselves. The second relates to the administration of the incentive system which is a feature of the payment plan established in a large number of manufacturing plants in this country.

The wage rate question frequently dominates the annual negotiations between company and union. The union request for a general wage increase, to be added, either in flat cents per hour or in percentages, to the wages of all employees in the unit, has become a hardy perennial. This is the issue which becomes the principal subject of public notice and interest if the negotiation is of a type which attracts the attention of the newspapers. It is probably true, however, that there is less occasion for lawyer participation in the handling of this issue than of any other which may come up. The wage adjustment, if there is one, is finally agreed upon by the company and the union and the increase is incorporated in the employees' next pay checks. Very frequently the terms of this settlement are not even included in the collective bargaining agreement itself, but are the subject of a separate and comparatively informal memorandum. The drafting problem is negligible. The labor relations lawyer must know, in general, how the wage question is handled, but it will be only if there are questions of the applicability of statutes relating to wage minimums (Fair Labor Standards Act) or maximums (e.g., Defense

Production Act of 1950) that he will play much of a part in annual wage negotiations.

The other wage problem, that of incentive plan administration, is a good deal more likely to be encountered by the lawyer who participates in the collective bargaining process. The provisions in the agreement covering this matter are among the most difficult to draft, presenting both basic policy issues and the necessity of covering countless little points. A high percentage of the grievances arising during the year may be expected to involve the interpretation and application of contract provisions of this type.

Neither of these wage problems can be covered in detail here. It is important, however, to get at least a feel of how they develop and what they involve, and to test what may be general predilections by applying them to a concrete situation. There is accordingly set forth here another chapter in The Enderby Case, part of it having to do with the 1951 wage reopening negotiations (contemplated in Article XII, Section 3 of the 1950 contract — see page 329 supra), the other part relating to the handling of a group of wage system administration issues arising under Article XI (page 327 supra).

THE ENDERBY CASE — XIV

A

On June 3, 1951, Oliver Curme, President of Local 417, URCL & PWA (CIO) wrote to C. S. Christian, Plant Manager of the Enderby Rubber Company, Chicago Plant, advising Christian that "Local 417 desires to open the question of general wage rates as provided for in Section 3 of Article XII of the agreement of May 21, 1950." Christian replied, on June 5, that "in view of the failure of the Union to make any specific demand for adjustment in present wage rates, your letter cannot be considered proper notice under Article XII of the Agreement." There was another letter from Curme to Christian on June 9. Its tone was not friendly, Curme protesting that Christian's "legalistic attempt to avoid bargaining or at least to delay it so as to save a few pennies has caused much bad feeling in the plant." Curme's letter went on to say that "although it had been hoped to seek a common grounds for negotiations, and to avoid 'demands,' your letter leaves no alternative. We hereby demand a general wage increase of 25 cents per hour, effective as of June 3, 1951; an additional 10 cents per hour per employee to be paid into a health and welfare fund; an increase in the shift premiums to bring them all up from 5 cents to 10 cents per hour; and a revision of the piecework rates and standards, on the following jobs: [listing 36 jobs the piecework rates for which had been the subject of dispute during the preceding twelve months]."

Arrangements were made for a negotiating conference to be held on June 14. A long series of conferences followed. It became clear in the course of these meetings that the Union's real demand was for a general increase in the neighborhood of 12 or 15 cents an hour. It also developed that the Company was willing to grant some increase, that it was insistent upon an increase in terms of percentages rather than so many cents across the board, and that it would probably go along on an adjustment of from 3 to 4 per cent in all hourly and base rates. (The weighted average of the hourly and base rates of all of the employees in the plant was determined to be $1.564; the common labor rate was 96 cents per hour and the highest base rates paid for skilled labor (on incentive work) was $2.11 per hour; the hourly earnings of some incentive workers were up around $2.75 per hour.)

It became apparent, too, as the negotiations developed, that the Union would not press its health and welfare demand but that it was going to be insistent upon either an adjustment in the shift premiums or a substantial change in a number of the 36 disputed piece rates. The Company's position was that none of these points could be considered in any way until the end of the contract term (May 21, 1952). At one session, however, the Industrial Relations Manager said something about realizing that "some of those 36 rates are on the low side, but we'll never do anything about them until you agree to changes in some others we all know are too high."

The arguments relied upon by the Union in defending its general wage increase (in terms of cents across the board) included the following:

1. That the cost of living in Chicago had increased 12 per cent between May, 1950, and June, 1951; that it would take a 19-cent general increase in hourly rates to neutralize this change in living costs; that the cost of living could be expected to rise at least another 5 per cent before May, 1952 (the contract termination date), and that the wage increase should therefore be 26 cents or 27 cents an hour.

2. That general wage increases of 11 cents, 12 cents, 16 cents and 19 cents had been granted the employees of the "Big Four" rubber

companies (U.S. Rubber, Goodyear, Goodrich, and Firestone) in the period between May, 1950 and June, 1951.

3. That an 11-cent increase had been granted by the big meat-packing companies (three of which have plants within five miles of the Enderby plant) in February, 1951; and that this represented "a higher percentage increase in the average rate in the meat-packing plants (formerly $1.30 per hour) than Local 417 is seeking here."

4. That employees at the Enderby plant in Tulsa, Oklahoma, had received a wage increase averaging 16 cents per hour in January, 1951; that the Chicago plant rates had been 20 cents an hour above the Tulsa plant rates in 1949, but were, after the 1951 increase at the Tulsa plant, only 8 cents above those rates (there having been some other adjustments in 1950).

5. That the net profits of the Enderby Company for 1950 had been, after taxes, $9,300,000; that the Company's statement showed that at least 33 per cent of these earnings were allocable to the Chicago plant's operations; that the comparable earnings figure for the first quarter of 1950 was roughly $3,000,000; that the 25 cents per hour general increase would cost the Company only $500,000 a year and that the employees were more entitled to this than the shareholders.

6. That there was no justification for a percentage increase because this would mean the largest increases to those who needed it least.

7. That any increase agreed upon should go into the base rates of all incentive workers.

8. That "general wage rates" in the contract reopener clause covered all "money items"; that it clearly covered any items which go directly into wage rates affecting a group of employees; that the 36 disputed piecework rates "ought to be cleaned up for everybody's good regardless of any argument about the words in the contract."

9. That there "will be a strike on July 17 unless this thing is cleared up."

The Company's position was based on the following arguments:

1. That any increases in the cost of living since May, 1950, had been substantially matched by increases in the take-home pay of Enderby employees, many of whom had been upgraded and almost all of whom had been working considerable amounts of overtime during recent months; that the average rate at the Enderby plant (in Chicago) had risen, since 1939, from 67 cents per hour to

$1.564, compared with an increase in the cost of living of only 80 per cent; and that the rate increase since 1945 had also been larger than the cost-of-living increase.

2. That the increases in the Big Four plants had no bearing on the Enderby wage negotiations; that Enderby wage rates had historically been lower and that "they must be if Enderby is to remain competitive, in view of the economies which the bigger companies' larger-scale operations permit"; that the Big Four plants are (with one or two little exceptions) not located in the Chicago labor market area.

3. That the percentage increase in the meat-packing plants was irrelevant; that the relevant point was that the Enderby present average rate of $1.564 was 15 cents higher than the meat-packing rate even after the February, 1951, increase; that, furthermore, the Enderby rates "are, on the average, 4 cents higher than those paid by comparable companies for comparable jobs in the Chicago area, a fact reflected in the unusually low turnover rate at the Enderby plant."

4. That the rates paid at the Enderby plant in Tulsa have nothing to do with the Chicago rates; that the 16-cent increase in January, 1951, was the result of a union's (AFL) just being recognized there; that the Tulsa rates were still 8 cents below the Chicago rates and that a 33-cent differential would be ridiculous.

5. That profits have no place in the discussion of wage rates; that the Union is in no position to evaluate the significance of the "earnings" figure; that dividend payments to stockholders had increased less than wage payments to employees, whether the comparison was made with 1939, 1941, 1945, or 1950; that most of the corporate earnings had been earmarked for an expansion of the Chicago plant and that this would mean creating 600 new jobs by 1955; that the Union "cannot argue ability to pay unless it is willing to agree to take wage cuts when profits go down."

6. That a percentage increase is the only fair way of recognizing skill differences, and that the spread between the common labor rate and the highest skilled rates had already been compressed unduly (the 1947, 1948, and 1950 increases having been in cents per hour across the board).

7. That increases to incentive workers, if any, should be added to their earnings figures and could not be put in their base rates without discriminating against hourly workers.

8. That the contract reopener provision "obviously does not apply to anything except wage adjustments affecting all employees

the same way," and that the shift differentials and individual job rates could therefore not be considered.

9. That a strike would be a violation of Article III of the May 21, 1950, contract and would be considered by the Company as so serious a breach that the whole contract would fall; that such a strike would be an "unfair labor practice" and that the Company would "have no choice but to seek court assistance."

On July 12, the Union negotiators told the Company conferees that they had been authorized by the membership of Local 417 to agree to either of the following settlements: (a) a 12-cent general increase, a 2-cent increase in all shift premiums, and arbitration of the 36 disputed piecework rates; or (b) a 15-cent general increase in all hourly and base rates.

On July 13, the Company negotiators told the Union group that the Company directors had turned down the July 12 proposition but had authorized the negotiating committee to agree to a "five per cent increase, effective August 1, 1951." This was, the committee reported, "the Company's last offer." The Union committee rejected the Company proposition.

Another meeting was held on July 14. Both committees reported that there had been no change in their principals' positions, and that there would be none. The chairman of the Union group then asked the Company representatives whether they would agree to submit the dispute to arbitration, indicating that the Union would be willing to follow this course. This offer was immediately rejected.

On July 17 the plant was struck.

QUESTIONS

1. What factors, other than those enumerated in the above statement, probably entered into the consideration of this problem by the respective parties?

2. What would you, as a representative of the Federal Mediation and Conciliation Service assigned to this dispute, have said to each of the parties (privately) with respect to the various points enumerated above?

3. How would you, as an arbitrator, have resolved this issue if it had been submitted to you? What disposition would you have made of the enumerated points? What account would you have taken of any factors not enumerated?

4. How would you, as counsel for Local 417, have advised the Union regarding its rights to strike?

B

Sections 5 to 11 of Article XI in the 1950 contract between the Enderby Rubber Company and Local 417 (see page 327 supra) cover the matter of administration of the incentive wage system. That these provisions did not remove all areas of doubt and disagreement is illustrated by the following cases which arose under these sections:

1. In September, 1950, Employee A. M. Sampson demanded of his foreman that the packing job on which he was working be taken off the incentive basis and put on a flat hourly basis. He claimed that he was killing himself on the job but that he was still averaging only three or four cents an hour over his base rate ($1.17). Sampson also made the point that one reason for the low earnings was that he had to spend a lot of his time keeping a tally of work performed and that the only purpose of the tally was to give the timekeeper a basis for figuring the incentive earnings. The foreman, recognizing some merit in Sampson's objection and admitting that the present incentive rate was "pretty tight compared with some others in the department," said he would be willing to recommend putting this job on an hourly basis with an hourly rate of $1.17. Sampson insisted that the hourly rate should be at least $1.21 and that any lower rate would mean a reduction in his wages "in violation of the contract." When the foreman then refused to do anything further about the matter, the Union filed a grievance in Sampson's behalf demanding that "the base rate on the packing job being performed by A. M. Sampson be adjusted to permit earnings at 110 per cent of base rate as is possible in other incentive jobs in the Packing Department, or that this job be placed on an hourly basis at a rate of $1.21 per hour."

What, if anything, does Article XI of the 1950 contract give the Union as a basis for pressing this demand? Would you, as counsel for Local 417, advise its being carried beyond the second step of the grievance procedure if no settlement is reached there?

2. A dispute developed, in November, 1950, about the incentive rate for a job in the Tire Department which involves the inspection of large rolls of fabric. This fabric is wound, by machine, off one roller and on to another, passing in front of the inspector who stands between the two rollers. As originally set up, in March, 1949, the job called for the inspector's stopping the machine when he spotted a flaw in the fabric so that he could clip a piece of colored cloth to the fabric next to the flaw. Different colors were used for different kinds of flaws.

In April, 1950, the employee who had been performing this job quit and R. S. Bosun transferred to it. After about a month on the job Bosun asked the foreman whether he could mark the flaws with colored chalk instead of clipping on the pieces of cloth. The foreman said he had no objection. This change in practice meant that Bosun could mark the flaws without stopping the machine which unwound and wound the two rollers. This resulted in almost doubling the amount of fabric which could be inspected in a given period of time. Since the piece rate for the job was figured in terms of yards of fabric inspected per minute, Bosun's earnings jumped from $1.65 per hour to $3.15 per hour.

When the Company's Industrial Engineering Department learned about this change (which was in October) they had the inspection job restudied. On November 3, 1950, the Company advised Bosun and the Union that a new piece rate would be established on this job, to take effect on November 7. The new rate was set in such a manner that the inspector's earnings, using the chalk method of marking, and working at the pace Bosun had been working, would be about $1.85 an hour. The "job description" covering this inspection operation was changed to provide for chalk marking of flaws instead of cloth marking.

A grievance was filed by the Union on November 4. On November 7, the day the new rate became effective, Bosun instituted the practice of stopping the machine every time he made a chalk mark on the fabric. The result was to cut the inspection rate back to just about what it was under the old marking method. Bosun's earnings rate dropped to $1.05 per hour. He demanded, however, that he receive the base rate ($1.45) for the job. When this demand was denied another written grievance was filed.

Neither grievance could be settled at the first three steps of the grievance procedure and both were submitted to arbitration. What factors or considerations should the arbitrator deem to be controlling?

3. Operators on a stamping job in the Miscellaneous Division filed a grievance on January 19, 1951, demanding that they "be compensated for time lost on sticky stock." There were no other details set forth. The following facts emerged at the second step grievance hearings: the operators on this job are paid on an incentive basis; their base rate is $1.27 per hour; their earnings for the entire year of 1950 averaged $1.52 per hour (or about 120 per cent of their base rate); between January 2 and January 19, 1951, their earnings averaged only $1.37 per hour; this drop resulted

from the fact that a new processing method had been instituted for the making of the rubber stock which comes to these operators for stamping and some of the new stock was exceedingly sticky; the stamping operators would occasionally get batches of stock so sticky that their normal production rate would be cut in half; these abnormal situations would continue for from 15 to 30 minutes, after which the stock would again be all right. The Union insisted that these operators were entitled to base rate pay for all periods during which they handled defective stock, no matter how short these periods were.

The Company representatives denied this grievance claim at Steps 1, 2, and 3 on the grounds (a) that no specific compensation was asked for in the grievance; (b) that there was no ground for any claim because the stamping operators' earnings never dropped below base rates on either a daily or a weekly basis; and (c) that the Union's claim presented an impossible administrative problem.

The Union insisted that this case be referred to arbitration.

How would you, as counsel for Enderby, advise the Company in this matter?

F. *Pensions*

The subject of pensions has come to occupy a position of major importance in collective bargaining negotiations. See Wilson, Employee Pension Plans, 1 Lab. L.J. 1035 (1950), and Unterberger, Function of the Arbitrator in the Administration of Pension Plans, 1 Lab. L.J. 348 (1950). A substantial number of the contracts concluded in 1949 and 1950 between the larger companies and unions, particularly in the heavy manufacturing industries, included pension plans. It is impossible, within the limited scope of these materials and this course, to explore this subject in many of its ramifications. Some idea of the problems it raises is offered, however, by the following checklist prepared by the Bureau of National Affairs, Inc., in 1949 and issued as part of its Collective Bargaining Service. Some deletions have been made from the full text.

CHECKLIST FOR PENSION BARGAINING *

This checklist, prepared by CBNC editors, lists some of the questions which management and union negotiators should expect

* Reprinted by permission of the copyright owner, Bureau of National Affairs, Inc. — ED.

to face in collective bargaining over pension plans. A brief comment follows each question, outlining some of the details of the problem which must be considered. Where possible, reference is made to existing pension plans, and to union pension demands as they were being presented in 1949.

The subject of pensions for wage earners is due to appear on bargaining tables with increasing frequency in coming months. Hitherto, pensions plans were adopted unilaterally by management, in most instances, only after careful examination of the problem and consultation with experts and advisors in the field. Now that unions are getting into the pension field, the union negotiators, too, will have to study carefully the ramifications of the pension problem.

Most companies have recognized the desirability of pensions. The chief deterrent has been the cost commitment involved. Pension experts estimate that even a modest plan will cost somewhere in the neighborhood of eight per cent of payroll, while elaborate systems with additional benefits will run considerably higher. Nevertheless, this cost may be offset, in part at least by improved employee morale, and better production which can be secured by removing older, inefficient employees from the active rolls. In addition, considerable tax advantage can be secured if the plan meets the qualifications laid down in Internal Revenue laws and regulations, as most plans now in existence do. The cost situation changes also if employees will forego a wage increase and agree that the money be applied on a pension plan instead.

This checklist assumes that employer and union negotiators agree on the need for a plan and want to study the problem of getting one started or amending an existing plan. It lists the various possibilities which should be considered in tailoring a plan to suit the individual situation. It does not preclude the need for getting expert advice from an insurance company, or an independent pension consultant, but should lay the groundwork for intelligent discussions of the various points with the consultant and at the bargaining table.

Who Should be Eligible?

Treasury regulations — which must be met if tax advantages are to be gained — allow pension plans to be set up with eligibility and coverage requirements to suit the individual company, provided there is no discrimination in favor of officers, stockholders, supervisory or highly-paid employees.

Which Employees Should Be Covered?

Most unions will insist that all employees in the bargaining unit be covered, although they will not object if the company wants to blanket others under the same plan.

Should There Be a Salary Limitation?

Although Treasury regulations allow a plan to be set up which excludes those earning less than $3,000 a year, there could hardly be a collective bargaining situation where a union would agree to such a limitation.

Should There Be a Waiting Period?

Most company officials think of a pension plan as applying to long-service employees, consequently they seek to limit participation to employees who have passed through the employment period when turnover is largest. They do this in two ways: (1) by excluding those employees under a certain age, such as thirty, and (2) by requiring that employees work a certain length of time, such as two years, before becoming eligible.

When Is Eligibility Lost?

Pension plans should specify carefully the circumstances under which employees lose their pension rights, such as discharge, resignation, etc. Special provision should be made for short-term layoffs, leave of absence, military service, and other temporary breaks in service.

Should There Be a Maximum Age Limit?

Because of the high cost of retiring those close to retirement age when a plan is installed, some plans specifically exclude them from coverage. Provision could be made, however, for paying these employees a pension outside the established plan, or establishing a later retirement age for them.

What About Non-participating Employees?

Under a contributory pension plan, where the employee pays part of the cost, each employee is usually allowed to elect whether to come under the plan or not.

When Should Employees Retire?

Almost all existing retirement plans put the retirement age at 65 for both men and women, although a very few lower the age for women to 60.   It is estimated that to lower the age from 65 to 60 for all participants would increase pension costs about 50 per cent.   Nevertheless, C.I.O.'s United Auto Workers have pitched their pension demands on retirement at age 60, and the United Mine Workers now have a 60-year retirement age in effect for coal miners.   Many of the existing plans with a 65-year age are integrated with Social Security benefits which begin at that age; if Social Security laws are liberalized to provide earlier retirement, many of these plans will also shift to the lower age.

Should Retirement Be Compulsory When Retirement Age Is Reached?

There is some advantage to a company in letting a skilled worker stay on the job after retirement age, but pension experts point out that an exception in one case will make it more difficult to pension unnecessary oldsters, whose automatic removal is one prime reason why a pension plan is introduced in the first place.   C.I.O.'s Newspaper Guild maintains that if workers have the right to retire at age 65, they will not elect to do so, on the average, for several years. On the other hand, the Guild points out that if large enough pensions are provided, older workers who have passed peak usefulness will voluntarily retire.

If Employees Work Past Retirement Age, Should Pension Be Paid?

Here there are three alternatives: (1) Begin regular retirement payments at retirement age regardless of whether annuitant goes off the payroll, (2) defer his pension until he actually retires, and pay him a larger annuity based on his larger accumulation in the fund and his shorter life expectancy, or (3) defer his pension but pay him when he retires the same monthly pension he would have received if he had retired at the stipulated age.

How Much Pension Should Be Paid?

Most pension plans now in existence compute annuities as a percentage of annual compensation during each year of service. For example, if the plan provides benefits of 1 per cent for each year's compensation, and a worker had worked 30 years, receiving an average of $2,000 a year for his first 15 years of service and $3,000 a year for the next 15 years of service, his total compensation would be $75,000.00 and his annual pension would be $750.00 (probably payable in monthly installments of $62.50 each) .

In most cases credit for past service (years worked before the pension plan was installed) is given at a lower rate in the benefit formula; for example the plan might provide benefits of 1 per cent for future service (as above) and one-half of one per cent for past service. In addition, a top limit is sometimes placed on the formula, so that no employee can get more than a fixed amount as a pension.

Some plans average salary paid during the last 5 or 10 years before retirement, multiply this by years of service, and pay benefits of a fixed percentage of this amount. This gives larger credit for early years when salaries are usually lower.

Other plans pay a flat percentage of present salary, for example, 25 or 30 per cent, regardless of years of service, or after a minimum number of years of service.

A pension plan may provide a fixed sum as annual retirement income after completion of a minimum number of years of service. The United Mine Workers plan currently provides $100 a month to all miners aged 60 or over who have worked at least 20 years in the mines. The UAW demand is for pensions of $100 a month at age 60 for employees with 25 years of service with the company (and graduated downwards for employees with less than 25 years of service). The Newspaper Guild asks a minimum pension of $175 a month.

Should Social Security Benefits Be Included?

In planning a pension program, some companies have started out with an estimate of pension needs as a flat percentage of salary, then deducted Social Security benefits to determine how much supplemental retirement income would have to be provided to reach the fixed amount. For example, it may be agreed that a pension equal to 40 per cent of salary, including Social Security, should be provided. It is then possible to arrange a formula which, after Social Security benefits are included, will total that amount. Sometimes the wife's benefits under Social Security are added in, by computing the husband's benefit at 150 per cent of the primary amount. It is important that such a plan take into consideration possible changes in Social Security benefits.

How Should "Compensation" Be Defined?

If the retirement benefits formula is based on a percentage of compensation, it is important to define this term carefully. It may include all annual earnings, or it may be restricted to the basic wage for a 40-hour week and a 52-week year, excluding certain bonuses, overtime, and other special payments.

Should There Be a Minimum Pension?

Special arrangements are sometimes made for employees who are so close to retirement when the plan is begun that the benefit formula would provide practically no pension. For these persons a nominal amount, such as $20 a month, is set as a minimum pension.

Should There Be a Maximum Pension?

Where high-salaried officers are covered by a plan, a top limit may be placed on the total amount of pension which any individual can receive. However, this is not likely to be a bargaining problem, since negotiated plans will be primarily concerned with wage-earner coverage.

Should the Plan Provide Disability Benefits?

Most pension plans now in existence permit early retirement, after certain age and service requirements are met, with company approval. These early retirements are designed to take care, in most cases, of employees who become so disabled that they are unable to work. They are permitted, however, only at substantially reduced pension benefits, which are actuarially computed so as to place no additional liability on the employer. That is, the amount the employee would have been paid if he had reached retirement age is recomputed to take into account his younger age, longer life expectancy, fewer years of service, and smaller accrued fund. This results in a substantial reduction in monthly pension amounts.

Although some unions want pensions for diasbled workers as an *integral* part of the pension plan, most union plans call for *separate* disability allowances, not tied to the pension system. The UAW, for example, is asking for a separate health fund outside the pension program, from which disability benefits would be provided.

What About Workers Who Leave Before Retirement Age?

A large proportion of existing pension plans allow some form of "vesting" — that is, they give some benefits to workers who quit or leave the company for one reason or another before reaching retirement age. Sometimes this is an immediate cash refund, but more often the amount which has been credited to the employee is held in the retirement fund and a pension, based on this amount, is paid him when he later reaches the specified retirement age. In almost all cases there are age and service requirements on vesting. For example, vesting is frequently limited to those employees who have reached 50 or 55 years of age and who have 15 or 20 years of service with the company.

Why Is Vesting Desirable?

Although a liberal vesting provision raises the cost of a pension plan to the employer, it has certain advantages. For one thing, unless there is a vesting provision, it is practically impossible, without bad feeling, to lay off or discharge employees who are nearing retirement age. Also, workers will regard employer contributions on their behalf as money in the bank if they know it will revert to them when they leave (and therefore may be more willing to forego a wage increase as an exchange for a pension plan). On the other hand, it should be remembered that one purpose of a pension plan is to prevent large turnover. A liberal vesting provision removes the incentive to stay on with a company, and there is even a danger that employee quits will be encouraged, if employees know they can immediately get their hands on a large sum of money in the fund.

Should Employee Contributions Be Vested?

In plans where employees contribute a share of the costs out of their wages, this share is returned to them almost without exception when they leave. Usually the interest which these contributions have earned is also given the employee.

How About Discharge for Cause?

The only exception to some liberal vesting provisions is a clause which denies vesting to those discharged for "just cause." Experience has proved this difficult to enforce, however, without bad effects on employee morale. Even without any actual enforcement, existence of such a qualification reduces the value of the pension benefit in the eyes of employees.

What About Workers Who Die Before Retirement?

Although older pension plans were limited in scope to provide only retirement income for those who lived to retirement age and beyond, newer plans have adopted the philosophy that employees need protection against three hazards: death, disability, and old age. In these newer plans it is customary to pay the beneficiary of an employee who dies before reaching retirement age a lump sum which equals the amount accumulated in his name in the retirement fund. Others pay the beneficiary only the amount in the fund which the employee himself has contributed. Pension experts point out that if the pension plan includes death benefits, it is much more likely to get and hold the interest of younger workers, whose primary interest is in immediate protection of family rather than future old age.

Should Employees Contribute?

Existing pension plans are split almost equally between the contributory and non-contributory variety. (However, the employer always bears the cost of past service benefits — those based on service before the adoption of the plan.) Union demands are pitched strongly in favor of having the employer bear the entire share of the cost. Some unions, for example, point out that under contributory plans, employees have the choice of joining the plan or not. Many will elect not to contribute and others will do so at the expense of current living standards. Moreover, they add, the employer's contribution is tax free, while the employee's contribution is not.

Some pension experts see definite advantages in employee contributions. It may be shown that employees will receive larger benefits only if they share in the cost of the pension and, if given a choice, they will elect to "purchase" these larger benefits. These experts are convinced that in nearly every case the employee will elect to participate even though it means a reduction in current income, and that there is no less interest and appreciation of a plan by employees if they bear a share of the cost. They point out further that once a plan is started on a non-contributory basis, it is almost impossible to shift it to a contributory basis.

How Much Should Employees Contribute?

If it is decided that employees should contribute, what should the contribution be? Only very rarely do employees assume more than half of the cost. The most popular type of contribution is a percentage of salary — 2%, 2½% or 3% depending on the benefits provided by the plan. In some other plans the employee contribution is fixed at a certain sum, and the company adds an equal amount or a greater amount to make up the employee's credit in the retirement fund.

How Should the Plan Be Administered?

Pension funds are usually handled by a trustee, who is responsible for keeping and investing the money contributed to the trust, and for paying out the money to eligible claimants. He operates under powers given him by the trust agreement. Often a bank or trust company is named trustee to insure continuity over the long period of years during which the plan is expected to be in effect. In some cases the trustee also *administers* the plan, deciding who is eligible for pensions, and making other administrative decisions as they arise. More often, however, these administrative duties are separated from the financial duties of handling the money. In this case, a pension committee is set up to make the administrative decisions (sometimes this is called a Pension Advisory Committee or a Board of Trustees).

Should the Union Participate in Administration?

Present union thinking is to demand the right to participate, on an equal basis with management, in the administration of the pension plan covering the bargaining unit. Because the decisions which the pension committee has to make are often "bread-and-butter" matters to union members, unions feel that they must have a voice in them. The Taft-Hartley Act allows union participation in welfare fund administration, provided some provision is made for a neutral member or for impartial settlement of deadlocks if they occur on the bipartisan board. The United Mine Workers' fund is administered by a board made up of one representative of each side and a third elected by these two. The UAW demands equal voice with management in administering social security funds. The Newspaper Guild also wants either a tripartite board or a bi-partisan board with provision for neutral breaking of deadlocks.

What Are the Duties of a Pension Committee?

The pension committee does the record-keeping, applies for the insurance policies (if the plan is insured), reviews employee records to arrange for participation by eligible employees, keeps track of changes in beneficiaries, etc., and advises the trustee on all terminations and retirements under the plan. The functions of the advisory committee may be broadened or limited by the trust agreement. The Newspaper Guild lists these questions which an administrative body may have to consider and decide: (1) determination of disability or recovery from disability, (2) how to make payments to protect the interests of elderly or disabled persons whose mentality may be clouded, (3) reviewing experience under the plan, (4) seeing to it that adequate contribution rates are maintained, (5) making decisions with respect to investments or selection of outside agencies for that purpose, (6) recommending changes in plan terms, (7) taking whatever steps are necessary to see that the plan functions effectively.

How Should the Plan Be Financed?

There are two basic methods by which pension plans are financed: (1) through a pension trust, where money is held in a trust fund and administered by a trustee, and (2) through an insurance company, where money is invested in group annuity or individual annuity policies. Each of these types has its own partisan advocates — arguments pro and con are outside the scope of this checklist. However, management and union negotiators, once a plan has been agreed on, would be well served to call in representatives of both types of financing to secure cost estimates on the plan best suited to the individual company.

It should be noted that some unions have become interested in financing of pensions through purchase of Government bonds. Essentially this is no different than any other type of trust fund, except that investments are limited to Government bonds, which are purchased in the name of the individual employee who participates in the plan.

What Provisions Should Be Made for Amendment or Termination?

Under N.L.R.B. rules, any change in pension plan which affects employees in the bargaining unit must be discussed with the union before the change is put into effect, unless the union has specifically waived the right to bargain over the plan. If the pension plan is incorporated in the collective bargaining agreement, no change may be made in the plan during the life of the contract without the union's consent.

In negotiations over a pension plan, it may be wise to specify in advance the conditions under which the plan may be amended or terminated. The Newspaper Guild, for example, suggests that it might concede that a plan should be modified if the employer could show, by an accounting system approved by the Guild, that the company had failed to make a profit for three consecutive years.

As to termination, special problems arise on the distribution of assets of the retirement fund. The money credited to the employee may be returned to him as a lump sum or it may be held for later payment of an annuity (reduced in size) when the employee reaches retirement age.

It should also be noted that certain Treasury Department regulations exist concerning termination of a pension plan. Unless the Department is convinced that the termination is in good faith, it may disallow certain tax deductions which the company has taken *in the past* on account of contributions to the fund.

PART IV

Legal Limitations on Economic Pressure

I. INTRODUCTION

Collective bargaining is customarily a peaceful process through which unions and management agree upon the terms and conditions of employment under which the plant or job shall operate. Strikes are news, peaceful settlements are commonplace. The publicity given to shutdowns beclouds the fact that they are the exceptional cases. Even in the turbulent postwar year of 1946, nine out of ten contracts were rewritten without any interruption of production.

If the parties are unable to find terms mutually acceptable to the workers who supply the labor and to the employer who supplies the jobs, then production ceases. Each withholds from the other its economic contribution until a bargain can be made. Like a buyer and a seller who are unable to agree upon a price, they refuse to make a contract. The strike is the labor equivalent of "no sale."

The strike is itself a part of the bargaining process. It tests the economic bargaining power of each side and forces each to face squarely the need it has for the other's contribution. As the strike progresses, the worker's savings disappear, the union treasury dwindles, and management faces mounting losses. Demands are tempered, offers are extended, and compromises previously unthinkable become acceptable. The very economic pressure of the strike is the catalyst which makes agreement possible. Even when no strike occurs, it plays its part in the bargaining process, for the very prospect of the hardship which the strike will bring provides a prod to compromise. Collective bargaining is a process of reaching agreement, and strikes are an integral and frequently necessary part of that process.

Unfortunately, unions and management are not always content with this simple and direct test of economic strength. Both parties may feel that their very existence is at stake, and resort to any means available to save themselves. Emotions run high as each proclaims the justness of its cause and denounces the evil

of its enemy's.   All too often, the orderly strike which should
serve as the final step in collective bargaining degenerates into
virtual warfare with every possible weapon capable of inflicting
economic injury brought into action.   Each side seeks allies in
the struggle.   The employer may seek to resume operations by
the use of strikebreakers or a back-to-work movement and to
protect the entry of these workers with court injunctions and
special police.   He may attempt to move his operations to another
plant or to enlist the aid of other employers by subcontracting
his work to them during the strike.   The union also may seek
allies by urging customers not to patronize, by threatening other
employers who deal with the employer on strike with economic
sanctions of picket lines and boycotts, and by ordering other union
members not to perform any work on "unfair" goods.

Devices for exerting economic pressure, however, are not used
solely to resolve deadlocks in bargaining.   In fact, the most bitter
battles may come in the prelude to bargaining, for the union's
effort to organize the employees for collective action is frequently
countered by the employer's effort to prevent unionization.   In
this struggle each resorts to its whole arsenal of economic weapons.
Employers may discharge union leaders and black-list them with
other employers, threaten to close the plant if a union is organized,
or require all employees to sign "yellow dog" contracts not to
join a union while employed.   They may bribe union officials,
infiltrate the union with spies and *agent provocateurs* or sponsor
a company union to confuse and divide the workers.   Unions, on
the other hand, may use a picket line to keep employees or customers out until the plant is organized.   It may enlist the aid of
other unions in shutting off necessary deliveries or other services,
black-list the employer's goods as nonunion, and threaten other
employers with strikes or picket lines if they continue to handle
those goods.   Either party may in desperation or in the heat
of passion resort to even the most extreme forms of terrorization
and physical violence.

The use of economic pressure is an inherent part of any free
collective bargaining system.   However, the law has not left it
wholly unrestrained.   This Part is devoted primarily to a study
of some of the legal limitations placed upon economic pressures
which may be used by the parties in labor disputes.   When either
party goes beyond the permissible limits, various types of legal
action may be available.   Criminal prosecution may be used not
only to punish physical violence but also to curtail peaceful picketing and in some instances prohibit strikes.   Suits for damages

may be brought for breach of contract or for injuries coming within the common law theory of torts. Courts of equity may be sought for injunctive relief, and administrative agencies such as the National Labor Relations Board may be sought for cease and desist orders. The arsenal of legal weapons available in these disputes is as varied as the economic weapons used by the parties.

In the study of these legal limitations on economic weapons two important factors must be kept in mind. First, the law cannot stand as an impartial arbiter between the parties, for it cannot judge the merits of the economic demands without destroying collective bargaining itself. On the contrary, each party seeks the aid of the law in disarming its enemy. The very placing of limits on the economic weapons of one party makes the law to that degree an ally of the other. Second, resort to legal action may be a desperate expedient. After the dispute is over, the employer and his employees must live and work together. Divorce, in most cases, is out of the question. For the employer to enlist the aid of the courts by obtaining injunctions, bringing damage suits against the union, or pressing for criminal prosecution will leave a deep scar on labor relations in the plant which even time cannot fully heal. The lawyer dare not forget that far more important than the question whether legal relief is available is the question what action is advisable.

II. Legal Limitations on Employers

A. *Introductory Note*

The common law placed no effective legal limitations on the employer's use of his economic strength to combat unions. He was free to use that strength not only to obtain concessions at the bargaining table, but also to prevent bargaining itself. He was free to exact "yellow dog" contracts, discharge union sympathizers, place spies within union ranks, and organize his own subservient company union. Even violence committed by professional thugs hired to terrorize employees went unpunished for lack of prosecution. Most employers did not wait until the union had organized and bargaining had reached a deadlock, but made vigorous use of their economic strength to prevent unions from organizing and thus forestall any effective collective action.

Legal limitations on employers spring almost wholly from statutes such as the National Labor Relations Act, the Railway Labor Act, and similar state labor relations acts which are designed to give affirmative protection to free collective bargaining.[1] These statutes curtail the employer only in those activities which interfere with union organization and hinder collective bargaining.

B. *Outline of Unfair Labor Practices and Procedures*

Section 7 of the Wagner Act provided: "Employees shall have the right to self-organization, to join, or assist labor organizations, to bargain collectively through representatives of their own choosing, and to engage in concerted activities for the purpose of collective bargaining."

This section constituted the very heart of the law limiting employers' activities. The specific unfair labor practices in which employers were forbidden to engage were set forth in more detail in Section 8, but they must always be viewed in the light of the basic rights enunciated in Section 7.

Section 8 listed five unfair labor practices: (1) interference with any rights enumerated in Section 7; (2) domination or interference with the formation or administration of any labor organization; (3) discrimination in terms of employment to encourage or discourage membership in any labor organization (followed by the closed-shop proviso) ; (4) discrimination because of filing charges or giving testimony under the Act; and (5) refusal to bargain collectively.

These unfair labor practices were purposely stated in general terms, for precise definition would have been impossible and would have tempted employers to devise new methods not reached by the law. Congress delegated to the National Labor Relations Board the power to give these provisions substantive content by applying them to each case in the light of the underlying policies of the Act. The scope of each of these, as applied by the Board, will be indicated in the sections which follow.

The Taft-Hartley Act did not repeal these provisions. The employer is still prohibited from using his economic strength to obstruct unionization and collective bargaining.[2] The principal

---

[1] For an analysis of various state labor relations acts, see Killingsworth, State Labor Relations Acts (1948) ; Millis and Katz, A Decade of State Labor Legislation, 15 U. of Chi. L. Rev. 282 (1948) .

[2] The proviso of Section 8 (3) of the Wagner Act which permitted union-security agreements was amended by Taft-Hartley to prohibit the closed-shop form of union security, but to permit all other variations provided they were approved by a majority of the employees in a special election. Section 8 (c), by providing that the expressing of views should not be evidence of an unfair labor practice if it contained no threat of reprisal or promise of benefit, was intended to guarantee employers greater freedom of speech than the Board

change made by the Taft-Hartley Act was to add a new set of unfair labor practices that apply only to unions, and place further legal limitations on their use of economic pressure.[3]

The impact of the Wagner Act on industrial relations was due not only to the forthright pronouncement that certain employer practices were illegal, but also to the fact that Congress placed its enforcement in the hands of a special agency charged with effectuating the purposes of the Act. The National Labor Relations Board entered upon its task with a crusading zeal seldom equaled by an administrative agency. The provisions were broadly construed and violations vigorously prosecuted. Only continual criticism in Congress and finally the Taft-Hartley amendments were able to temper its enthusiasm.

Before dealing in detail with the substantive content of employer unfair labor practices, it will be helpful to understand the procedure by which these cases are handled.[4] This procedure must be sharply distinguished from representation cases wherein the practices and procedures are radically different.[5]

Proceedings in unfair labor practice cases are initiated by the filing of a sworn charge with the regional office of the Board in the area where the alleged violation took place.[6] Although the Board, through its General Counsel, acts as a public prosecutor, it cannot act on its own motion, but only upon the filing of a charge by some individual or labor organization. If the charge is filed by a union, it must show that it has complied with Sections 9 (f), (g), and (h) which require the filing of organization and financial reports with the Secretary of Labor, the furnishing of members with financial reports, and the signing of non-Communist affidavits by the officers.[7] Any individual can file a charge so long

had once permitted. Other provisions restricting union activity indirectly changed the legal obligations of employers.

[3] To Section 7 was added the clause, "and shall also have the right to refrain from any or all of such activities except to the extent that such right may be affected by an agreement requiring membership in a labor organization as a condition of employment as authorized in Section 8 (a) (3) ." This reflects the shift in policy from one of governmental encouragement of organization to one of government neutrality. Individuals were protected in organizing or in refusing to do so.

[4] For a full description of NLRB procedure, see Attorney General's Committee on Administrative Procedure, Monograph No. 18 (1940); Silverberg, How to Take a Case Before the National Labor Relations Board (1949).

[5] See pages 126 et seq. supra.

[6] The discussion that now follows in the text will be more readily understood if the student follows it on the Prentice-Hall NLRB Complaint Procedure Chart at page 571 infra.

[7] Not only the officers of the parent, or international, union must sign, but the officers of the AFL or CIO to which it is affiliated must also sign. NLRB v.

as it is shown that he is not "fronting" for a noncomplying union.[8] The charge must be filed and a copy served on the party against whom the charge is made within six months after the unfair labor practice occurred.[9]

When a charge is filed, the case is assigned to a field examiner who interviews the parties, obtains signed statements from witnesses, and arranges an informal joint conference with the parties. If, after full investigation, he believes there is insufficient evidence to support the charge, he may ask the charging party to withdraw its charge. If the charge is not withdrawn, the Regional Director will dismiss it. The charging party then has ten days in which to appeal to the General Counsel. His decision is final.[10] If the investigation reveals merit in the charge, the field examiner will attempt to obtain voluntary compliance through a settlement agreement made with the party accused of the violation. Again, the charging party, if dissatisfied with this adjustment, may appeal to the General Counsel.

These informal procedures dispose of the great bulk of unfair labor practice charges. During the fiscal year of 1951, 4168 cases of employer unfair labor practices were closed by the Board; 89.8 per cent were disposed of during the preliminary stages before formal action; 47 per cent of these were withdrawn, the remainder dismissed or settled. Only 10.2 per cent of the cases required formal action.[11]

If the charge has merit and efforts to settle the case are unsuccessful, the Regional Director issues a formal complaint stating the violations charged and serves it upon all of the interested

---

Highland Park Mfg. Co., 341 U.S. 322, 71 Sup. Ct. 758, 95 L. Ed. 969 (1951). The local unions which are active among the employees must also comply with the filing requirements. In Matter of Sunbeam Corp., 98 N.L.R.B. No. 98, 29 L.R.R.M. 1366 (1952).

[8] NLRB v. Augusta Chemical Co., 187 F.2d 63 (5th Cir. 1951); NLRB v. Clausen, 188 F.2d 439 (3d Cir. 1951). For a case in which it was determined that a union officer in filing a complaint of discrimination was in fact fronting for the union, see NLRB v. Alside Inc., 192 F.2d 678 (6th Cir. 1951).

[9] Section 10(b).

[10] The refusal to issue a complaint is not considered a "final order," and therefore is not reviewable in the courts. General Drivers v. NLRB, 179 F.2d 492 (10th Cir. 1950). This places a broad power of discretion in the General Counsel to grant dispensations from strict compliance with the statute. Even though the General Counsel issues a complaint, the Board may exercise its discretion in refusing to accept jurisdiction. Haleston Drug Stores v. NLRB, 187 F.2d 418 (9th Cir. 1951).

[11] NLRB, 16th Ann. Rep. 299 (1951). In the same year 1198 cases of union unfair labor practices were closed; 88.3 per cent were disposed of during the preliminary stages, over half of which were withdrawn; the remainder were dismissed or settled. Only 10.2 per cent required formal action, the same fraction as in the case of employer unfair practices.

parties. After issuance of the complaint, the Board, under Section 10 (j), may apply for a temporary injunction against the unfair labor practice pending final disposition of the case.[12] However, such application is rarely made.

The hearing is held before a trial examiner appointed by the Board, but under Section 11 of the Administrative Procedure Act he is independent of the Board in tenure and compensation. Furthermore, he is barred by Section 5 (c) of that Act from participating in any investigatory or prosecuting functions of the Board.[13] Since the Board is the charging party, its legal staff prosecutes the complaint, although the attorney for the charging party frequently participates and gives substantial aid to the Board attorneys. Other interested parties are allowed to intervene.

The hearing is essentially judicial in nature. Witnesses are subpoenaed, placed on the stand to testify, and subjected to cross-examination by the opposing party. Documentary evidence is introduced, and a complete record made. However, the strict rules of evidence are often relaxed and the hearing is marked by the informality characteristic of such administrative proceedings.[14] At the conclusion of the hearing, the trial examiner issues an intermediate report which contains a summary of the evidence, findings of fact, and a recommended order. If he finds that the unfair labor practice is not proved by "the preponderance of the testimony taken," he will recommend dismissal of the complaint. If the practice is found to be so proved, the order will typically require that (a) the party cease and desist from the practice, (b) take specified affirmative action to remedy the evil effects of the practice, (c) post a conspicuous notice of the contents of the order, and (d) report the details of its compliance to the Regional Director.[15]

[12] Under Section 10 (1) the Board is directed to seek such temporary injunction in every case in which the union is found on preliminary investigation to be violating Sections 8 (b) (4) (A), (B), or (C) (secondary boycotts).

[13] The trial examiner's function in complaint cases is to be contrasted with that of the hearing officer in representation cases. The latter is not independent, but is an employee of the Board, and he is authorized to make only findings of fact with no power to make recommendations or to suggest an appropriate order.

[14] Although Section 10 (b) of the Taft-Hartley Act provides, "Any such proceedings shall, so far as practicable, be conducted in accordance with the rules of evidence applicable in the district courts of the United States . . . ," the rules of evidence have not been changed substantially. Eastern Coal Corp. v. NLRB, 176 F.2d 131 (4th Cir. 1949).

[15] The Board's order to cease and desist cannot be made so broad as to cover all violations of the Act when only a single type of unfair labor practice, such as a refusal to bargain, has been proved. Although a violation of Section 8 (a) (5) may also be a violation of the catchall provision of Section 8 (a) (1),

Copies of the intermediate report are served on the parties, and if no exceptions to it are filed within twenty days, it automatically becomes the decision and order of the Board. If exceptions are filed, the parties are given an opportunity to submit briefs and may be granted oral argument before the Board. The Board then makes its decision and order on the basis of the whole record in the case.

The Board's order carries in itself no legal compulsion, no power to punish for contempt in event of violation. If the party against whom the order runs refuses to comply, the Board must obtain an enforcement order from the appropriate Circuit Court of Appeals. Further disobedience then is punishable as contempt of court.

Any person aggrieved by the final order of the Board may obtain judicial review of the order by petitioning the appropriate Circuit Court of Appeals to modify or set aside the order. Review may also be obtained by contesting the Board's petition for an enforcement order. The Wagner Act provided that the Board's findings on all questions of fact are conclusive on the court, "if supported by evidence." The Taft-Hartley Act changed this to read, "if supported by substantial evidence on the record considered as a whole." [16] The Supreme Court, in Universal Camera Corp. v. NLRB, [17] construed this change as making clear that the "substantial evidence rule" as applied to other administrative tribunals and codified in Section 10 (e) of the Administrative Procedure Act applied equally to the National Labor Relations Board. Without attempting to define "substantial evidence," the Court said, "that courts must now assume more responsibility for the reasonableness and fairness of Labor Board decisions than some courts have shown in the past." In discussing the weight to be given the findings of the trial examiner, and the effect of the Board's reversing an examiner, the Court said that the Board could reject his findings even though they were not "clearly erroneous." However, reviewing courts should give the examiner's report "such probative force as it intrinsically commands."

The fact that judicial review is available does not mean that it is regularly used. Out of nearly 5000 cases formally decided by the Board between 1935 and 1950 only 873 were appealed. Out of those appealed, the Board's order was upheld in 525 cases,

the cease and desist order cannot include such a blanket clause unless there has been a showing of systematic antiunion activities. NLRB v. Express Publishing Company, 312 U.S. 426, 61 Sup. Ct. 693, 85 L. Ed. 930 (1941).

[16] Section 10 (e).

[17] 340 U.S. 474, 490, 71 Sup. Ct. 456, 95 L. Ed. 456 (1951).

NLRB COMPLAINT PROCEDURE CHART

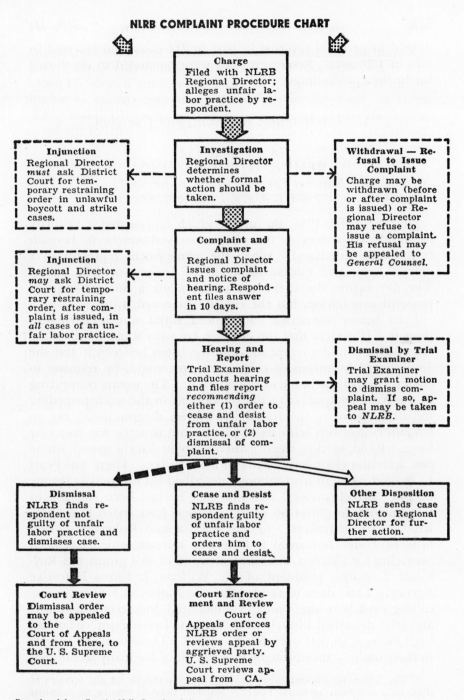

Charge
Filed with NLRB Regional Director; alleges unfair labor practice by respondent.

Investigation
Regional Director determines whether formal action should be taken.

Injunction
Regional Director *must* ask District Court for temporary restraining order in unlawful boycott and strike cases.

Withdrawal — Refusal to Issue Complaint
Charge may be withdrawn (before or after complaint is issued) or Regional Director may refuse to issue a complaint. His refusal may be appealed to *General Counsel.*

Complaint and Answer
Regional Director issues complaint and notice of hearing. Respondent files answer in 10 days.

Injunction
Regional Director *may* ask District Court for temporary restraining order, after complaint is issued, in *all* cases of an unfair labor practice.

Hearing and Report
Trial Examiner conducts hearing and files report *recommending* either (1) order to cease and desist from unfair labor practice, or (2) dismissal of complaint.

Dismissal by Trial Examiner
Trial Examiner may grant motion to dismiss complaint. If so, appeal may be taken to *NLRB.*

Dismissal
NLRB finds respondent not guilty of unfair labor practice and dismisses case.

Cease and Desist
NLRB finds respondent guilty of unfair labor practice and orders him to cease and desist.

Other Disposition
NLRB sends case back to Regional Director for further action.

Court Review
Dismissal order may be appealed to the Court of Appeals and from there, to the U. S. Supreme Court.

Court Enforcement and Review
Court of Appeals enforces NLRB order or reviews appeal by aggrieved party. U. S. Supreme Court reviews appeal from CA.

upheld in part and reversed in part in 211 cases, and reversed in toto in 120 cases.   Seventeen cases were remanded to the Board for further proceedings.

C. *Interference, Restraint, and Coercion*

In the Matter of
REMINGTON RAND, INC.
National Labor Relations Board, 1937
2 N.L.R.B. 626, 1 L.R.R.M. 88

[During April, 1936, the union which represented a majority of Rand's employees at the plants involved sought to bargain collectively with Rand.   When the management representatives delayed and gave evasive answers, the union voted to strike. The day before the strike the union made a final attempt at peaceful negotiation, but the company ignored it.]

Even before the strike commenced Rand was preparing to meet it.   It is clear that the decision lay with Rand whether the respondent would attempt to settle the issues between it and the Joint Board by means of conferences, or would, by refusing to confer, compel the latter to call a strike.   The events transpiring in the New York offices of the respondent in the week preceding the strike point to the respondent's grim determination not to bargain collectively with its employees but to settle the issues by force.   Rand in that week gathered about him a group whose past activities eloquently testify to that resolve.   There was Pearl L. Bergoff, who, in his testimony described his business as simply that of "strikebreaking" and who said he had been engaged in that business for "over 30 years."   Others have styled him "The King of Strikebreakers."   There was Captain Robert J. Foster, head of Foster Industrial & Detective Bureau, which has been operating for 25 years.   A third member of this group was Raymond J. Burns, president of the William J. Burns Detective Agency.   Later there was added Captain Nathaniel S. Shaw, whose calling card bore the words "Confidential Industrial Missions," and who described himself as a "Radical Investigator" who had been engaged in that work for 27 years.[40]   These men are experts in their trade — they brought to Rand all of the many techniques

[40] The following amounts were paid by the respondent for the services of these men and their agencies: Foster — $30,000; Bergoff, who in all supplied 200 men — $25,850; Burns — $25,000, "a good substantial job," according to his testimony. Shaw was promised $50 a day and expenses but aside from $300 in expenses did not receive any more due to a dispute with Rand.

they had developed through years of experience. They know how to operate "propaganda factories" designed to spread demoralizing rumors among striking employees, how to use "missionaries" to visit the homes of these employees and, posing as members of the company's personnel department, persuade them to return to work, how to organize "back to work movements" that would cause an ever widening breach in the ranks of strikers. They appreciate how the devices of the law can be used to advantage and so they know the technique of securing a labor injunction by framed "acts of violence." They understand the aid which state and local police protection can offer in opening a plant so they know how "to get to the Sheriff or the Chief of Police, maybe to the Mayor," or how to bring about "violence" that can be used to support a demand for such protection. When small towns are involved, they are aware of the opportunity offered to divide the community by bringing pressure on the business groups through threats to move the plant elsewhere. Finally, they have at their command the forces necessary for all these purposes — "guards," whose police records are not without significance, undercover men, missionaries, ordinary strikebreakers. All these resources were placed at Rand's disposal. To them he added the invaluable device of a skillful publicity campaign to mould public opinion as yet unacquainted with the issues involved or the forces at play, against the striking employees. With these men and the techniques and resources they offered, Rand, supported by his publicity expert, Earl Haring, and his attorney, J. A. W. Simson, proceeded to evolve the strategy of the respondent in fighting the strike. . . .

There remained only the final touch — Rand's christening this technique the "Mohawk Valley Formula" and proudly offering it . . . as an example of modern strikebreaking. . . . We repeat this technique of strikebreaking, interpolating our interpretations:

First: When a strike is threatened, label the union leaders as "agitators" to discredit them with the public and their own followers. In the plant, conduct a forced balloting under the direction of foremen in an attempt to ascertain the strength of the union and to make possible misrepresentation of the strikers as a small minority imposing their will upon the majority. At the same time, disseminate propaganda, by means of press releases, advertisements, and the activities of "missionaries," such propaganda falsely stating the issues involved in the strike so that the strikers appear to be making arbitrary demands, and the real issues, such as the employer's refusal to bargain collectively, are obscured. Concurrently with these moves, by exerting economic pressure through threats to move the plant, align the influential members of the community into a cohesive group opposed to the strike. Include in this group, usually designated a "Citizens Committee," representatives of the bankers, real estate owners, and businessmen, i.e., those most sensitive to any threat of removal of the plant because of its effect upon property values and purchasing power flowing from payrolls.

Second: When the strike is called raise high the banner of "law and order," thereby causing the community to mass legal and police weapons against a wholly imagined violence and to forget that those of its members who are employees have equal rights with the other members of the community.

Third: Call a "mass meeting" of the citizens to coordinate public sentiment against the strike and to strengthen the power of the Citizens Committee, which organization, thus supported, will both aid the employer in exerting pressure upon the local authorities and itself sponsor vigilante activities.

Fourth: Bring about the formation of a large armed police force to intimidate the strikers and to exert a psychological effect upon the citizens. This force is built up by utilizing local police, State Police if the Governor cooperates, vigilantes, and special deputies, the deputies being chosen if possible from other neighborhoods, so that there will be no personal relationships to induce sympathy for the strikers. Coach the deputies and vigilantes on the law of unlawful assembly, inciting to riot, disorderly conduct, etc., so that, unhampered by any thought that the strikers may also possess some rights, they will be ready and anxious to use their newly acquired authority to the limit.

Fifth: And perhaps most important, heighten the demoralizing effect of the above measures — all designed to convince the strikers that their cause is hopeless — by a "back to work" movement, operated by a puppet association of so-called "loyal employees" secretly organized by the employer. Have this association wage a publicity campaign in its own name and coordinate such campaign with the work of the "Missionaries" circulating among the strikers and visiting their homes. This "back to work" movement has these results: It causes the public to believe that the strikers are in the minority and that most of the employees desire to return to work, thereby winning sympathy for the employer and an endorsement of his activities to such an extent that the public is willing to pay the huge costs, direct and indirect, resulting from the heavy forces of police. This "back to work" movement also enables the employer, when the plant is later opened, to operate it with strikebreakers if necessary and to continue to refuse to bargain collectively with the strikers. In addition, the "back to work" movement permits the employer to keep a constant check on the strength of the union through the number of applications received from employees ready to break ranks and return to work, such number being kept secret from the public and the other employees, so that the doubts and fears created by such secrecy will in turn induce still others to make applications.

Sixth: When a sufficient number of applications are on hand, fix a date for an opening of the plant through the device of having such opening requested by the "back to work" association. Together with the Citizens Committee, prepare for such opening by making provision for a peak army of police by roping off the areas surrounding the plant, by securing arms and ammunition, etc. The purpose of the "opening" of the plant is threefold: To see if enough employees are ready to return to work; to induce still others to return as a result of the demoralizing effect produced by the opening of the plant and the return of some of their number; and lastly, even if the manoeuvre fails to induce a sufficient number of persons to return, to persuade the public through pictures and news releases that the opening was nevertheless successful.

Seventh: Stage the "opening," theatrically throwing open the gates at the propitious moment and having the employees march into the plant grounds in a massed group protected by squads of armed police, so as to give to the opening a dramatic and exaggerated quality and thus heighten its demoralizing effect. Along with the "opening" provide a spectacle — speeches, flag raising, and praises for the employees, citizens, and local authorities, so that, their vanity touched, they will feel responsible for the continued success of the scheme and will increase their efforts to induce additional employees to return to work.

Eighth: Capitalize on the demoralization of the strikers by continuing the show of police force and the pressure of the Citizens Committee, both to insure that those employees who have returned will continue at work and to force the remaining strikers to capitulate. If necessary, turn the locality into a warlike camp through the declaration of a state of emergency tantamount to martial law and barricade it from the outside world so that nothing may interfere with the successful conclusion of the "Formula," thereby driving home to the union leaders the futility of further efforts to hold their ranks intact.

Ninth: Close the publicity barrage, which day by day during the entire period has increased the demoralization worked by all of these measures, on the theme that the plant is in full operation and that the strikers were merely a minority attempting to interfere with the "right to work," thus inducing the public to place a moral stamp of approval upon the above measures. With this, the campaign is over — the employer has broken the strike.

NOTES

1. The whole gamut of interferences and restraint and coercian has been vigorously exploited in combating the efforts to unionize the South. See Hearings on Labor Management Relations in the Southern Textile Industry, 82d Cong., 1st Sess. (1951). The Report of the Subcommittee of the Committee on Labor and Public Welfare, at pages 17–21, gives a graphic narrative of the events at one plant:

> During and after World War II, attempts were made by both the United Textile Workers Union of American, A.F. of L., and Textile Workers Union of America, CIO, to organize the American Thread Co. mill at Tallapoosa, Ga.
>
> The first attempt came in March of 1945. Mr. C. C. Collins, a representative of the United Textile Workers of America, A. F. of L., went to Tallapoosa in response to an invitation from employees at the mill. On this first visit he talked to about 12 employees; all but one signed union cards. About 2 weeks later he returned to continue his work and was informed that two of the union adherents had been discharged. Collins had made an appointment to meet an employee in a cafe a short distance outside of Tallapoosa. While he was waiting there a group of persons, two of whom were armed with revolvers, entered the cafe. Collins was interrogated by their leader, Mr. Don Howe, as to whether he was an A. F. of L. organizer. Collins admitted that he was. Howe, speaking for the group which he identified as representing the citizens of Tallapoosa, ordered him to leave town and ". . . don't come back." Collins had no choice other than to comply. He got into his car and was followed by the group until he had crossed the Alabama line, some 2 miles distant. Howe has been identified as the local attorney for the American Thread Co. Five of the group were identified as employees of the mill, one of them being a minor supervisor. The remainder were Tallapoosa businessmen

. and city officials. The UTWA–A. F. of L. did not file charges and made no further attempt to organize the Tallapoosa mill.

1. *TWUA organizer kidnaped*

In 1947, several Tallapoosa employees wrote to TWUA–CIO requesting help in organizing a union. TWUA sent two organizers to Tallapoosa in October. One of them, Mrs. Edna Martin, stayed in a neighboring town, Bremen, Ga., for the first several weeks. On November 17, she decided that the situation had progressed sufficiently to justify her in moving to Tallapoosa and devoting her full time to organizing the employees. She made arrangements to live at a rooming house and then made calls on a number of employees. During her activities she was kept under constant surveillance by the company policeman, Mr. Wyatt Davis, and Mr. H. O. McGill, the company superintendent. That night her room was invaded by a mob of armed men and women. She was bound, forcibly loaded into a truck, driven out of town, and finally ejected on a lonely country road with the instruction, "Don't come back to Tallapoosa or you will be shot on sight."

Subsequently, Mrs. Martin identified several of her abductors as employees of the American Thread Co. The leader of the group, according to Mrs. Martin, was Mr. Elzie Teal, a nonsupervisory employee, who will be referred to again in connection with other incidents in the campaign against union organization.

2. *Labor espionage*

Union charges of espionage involved Wyatt Davis, company policeman and special police officer of Tallapoosa; the American Thread Co. mill superintendent; and the chief of police.

The labor espionage activities of Wyatt Davis command attention. He was deputized as a special police officer of the city of Tallapoosa, but was employed by and received his pay from the company. As company policeman he divided his time about equally between duties at the mill and around the town. However, about October 15, 1947, with the beginning of the union organization campaign, he devoted his full time to outside duties, which according to the NLRB field examiner, "appeared to have consisted principally of watching union organizers, watching mill employees interested in the union, and watching field examiners." Few persons, it appears, escaped his surveillance if they came to . Tallapoosa.

Davis was interrogated by NLRB field examiner Willis Hay, and stated that part of his duties were to "report the presence in town of strangers or unknown persons if they are doing anything questionable." Hay himself was kept under surveillance by Davis and McGill. On November 13, 1947, Davis followed union organizers from a meeting, trailed them around town, and followed them along the highway as they left Tallapoosa. On November 17, 1947, Mrs. Martin was followed about town by Davis. She was also kept under surveillance by plant superintendent McGill. Thus, while Mrs. Martin was arranging for her room he drove by the house; a few hours later when she drove out of town with union adherents, McGill followed. On November 24, after the kidnaping, Mrs. Martin met with union members at Bremen. Davis was there, watching them. He managed to precede them as they drove to Tallapoosa, and kept them under observation. Others reported similar activities by Davis.

The extent to which the police department participated in this espionage is unknown. However, the employment of Davis as a police officer argues that the department at least knew about it and approved it. (McGill is no longer connected with the American Thread Co. and could not be found in Tallapoosa. No member of the police department was subpoenaed by the subcommittee because of the shortness of time available for the hearings.)

3. *Employer interference*

The abduction of Mrs. Martin occurred in the midst of a series of other events connected with the union's organizing campaign. Shortly after the opening of the organizing drive an intensive interrogation of employees suspected of union sympathies was carried on by the American Thread Co. supervisors. The campaign was led by the mill superintendent H. O. McGill, and overseer Monroe Brooks. The following are some of the incidents reported: J. P. Abercrombie, one of the prominent union adherents, wore a CIO pin in the plant, and was told by Brooks, "You better get that damn thing off of there." Other employees were interrogated as to their union membership by overseers Gordon and George. Overseer Brooks attempted to secure the cooperation of Earline Rochester, another employee, to "frame"

Rufus Mulkey, a very active advocate of the union. **Mrs.**
Rochester testified that Brooks attempted to get her to sign
a union card and say that Mulkey had induced her to sign it
while she was working at her job. Mrs. Rochester refused.

Allen Abercrombie, one of the employees who had invited
TWUA organizers to Tallapoosa, testified before the NLRB
trial examiner that Plant Superintendent McGill had warned
him to "just go ahead and forget about this union business."
Allen apparently complied. . . .

Mrs. Dicie Little, a union adherent, was questioned by
another employee, Mrs. Leonora Morris, about her union
sympathies. When Mrs. Little expressed a favorable attitude toward the union and asked Mrs. Morris if the company
had hired her to get the names of the union sympathizers,
Mrs. Morris became very angry. Mrs. Little believed that
Mrs. Morris was acting as a spy for the company, because the
following day Mrs. Little was approached by Overseer Brooks
who asked if she were satisfied with her job. She told Brooks
that, in spite of her statement the day before, she knew very
little about unions and that her chief concern was in keeping
her job so she could support her three children. Mrs. Little
was thereafter subjected to constant harassment by being
transferred from job to job and from shift to shift. In spite
of the fact that she had to care for three children, she was
assigned to night work, 11 P.M. to 7 A.M.

4. *The company union*

The campaign against the union was also prosecuted
through a company-supported employees' organization known
as the TATCO Council. This council, which was formed
in 1945, had neither constitution, bylaws nor rules. Membership in the council was automatic and carried no obligation to pay initiation fees or dues. There were no meetings
of the membership. Apparently it performed none of the
functions of a legitimate union. It did, however, provide
the management with a convenient corral for "captive audiences." For example, Mrs. Little was invited to attend
one of the meetings of the council. Plant Superintendent
McGill, according to Mrs. Little's testimony before the subcommittee, addressed the group as follows:

"We have a nice mill here, but someone or something is
fixing to come in and tear up your playhouse. This outside
influence is just a bunch of pot-bellied Yankees with big

cigars in their mouths, and the dues they collect will just go up North, and you should want to keep your money in Tallapoosa. If they come in you will share the same rest rooms with Negroes and work side by side with them. It comes right out of Russia and is pure communism and nothing else. In one place the people who went out on strike had to eat raw cabbage."

5. Discriminatory discharges

While these actions undoubtedly had an adverse effect on the progress of union organization their impact was mild as compared to that of lay-offs and discharges of leading union sympathizers. Although the reasons for the discharges given by the company superficially appeared to be valid, other employees regarded it as more than coincidence that the persons discharged were also active in the union organizing campaign.

Thus, J. P. Abercrombie, one of the most active employees in behalf of the union, was discharged on December 31, 1947, for allegedly leaving his machine and using abusive language to a supervisor. On this same night Eunice Arnold and Gladys Moore were discharged for "not making production." Mrs. Little doubted the reason assigned and expressed the opinion that she would probably be fired next. Superintendent McGill heard of her remark and interrogated Mrs. Little about it. When she questioned the stated reason for the discharge of Arnold and Moore, McGill replied: "We don't have to have a reason. We can get up anything on them and there is nothing that they can do about it. . . . The ones that are sticking to us, we are going to take care of them; but the ones that are joining these organizations, we don't care anything about."

Rufus Mulkey was discharged in May 1948 for allegedly talking in favor of the union on the job. However, antiunion employees who had left their jobs and warned him to cease his union activities were not even reprimanded. An antiunion petition was circulated in the plant during working hours with the direct knowledge of the company's supervisors, and without any disciplinary action on the part of the company. It appears that the company rules were strictly applied to union sympathizers, but relaxed for the benefit of those who opposed or were indifferent to the union.

2. It is no defense to a charge of violating Section 8 (a) (1) that almost all employees testifying denied any actual intimida-

tion. Matter of Chicopee Mfg. Co., 85 N.L.R.B. 1439, 24 L.R.R.M. 1572 (1949). Nor is it a defense to a charge of surveillance that the employees did not know they were being spied upon. NLRB v. Grower-Shipper Vegetable Assn., 122 F.2d 368 (9th Cir. 1941). "In answer to these contentions it will be enough to say that this court has recognized that the test of interference, restraint and coercion under §8 (1) of the Act does not turn on the employer's motive or on whether the coercion succeeded or failed. The test is whether the employer engaged in conduct which, it may reasonably be said, tends to interfere with the free exercise of employee rights under the Act." NLRB v. Illinois Tool Works, 153 F.2d 811, 814 (7th Cir. 1946). It is likewise an unfair labor practice to give the employees the impression that they are being spied upon when no spying is in fact being done. Matter of Roxboro Cotton Mills, 97 N.L.R.B. No. 201, 29 L.R.R.M. 1249 (1952).

3. It should be noted in passing that the all-inclusive wording of Section 8 (a) (1) is broad enough to comprise within its prohibition every other employer unfair labor practice, even though it may also fall within one of the later subdivisions of Section 8 (a). The occurrence of violations of Section 8 (a) (1) only, called "independent 8 (a) (1) violations," is relatively rare. See NLRB, 16th Ann. Rep. 141 (1951).

REPUBLIC AVIATION CORP. v. NLRB
NLRB v. LE TOURNEAU CO.
Supreme Court of the United States, 1945
324 U.S. 793, 65 Sup. Ct. 982, 89 L. Ed. 1372

MR. JUSTICE REED delivered the opinion of the Court:

In the Republic Aviation Corporation case, the employer, a large and rapidly growing military aircraft manufacturer, adopted, well before any union activity at the plant, a general rule against soliciting which read as follows: "Soliciting of any type cannot be permitted in the factory or offices." The Republic plant was located in a built-up section of Suffolk County, New York. An employee persisted after being warned of the rule in soliciting union membership in the plant by passing out application cards to employees on his own time during lunch periods. The employee was discharged for infraction of the rule and, as the National Labor Relations Board found, without discrimination on the part of the employer toward union activity.

Three other employees were discharged for wearing UAW–CIO

union steward buttons in the plant after being requested to remove the insignia. The union was at that time active in seeking to organize the plant. The reason which the employer gave for the request was that, as the union was not then the duly designated representative of the employees, the wearing of the steward buttons in the plant indicated an acknowledgment by the management of the authority of the stewards to represent the employees in dealing with the management and might impinge upon the employer's policy of strict neutrality in union matters and might interfere with the existing grievance system of the corporation.

The Board was of the view that wearing union steward buttons by employees did not carry any implication of recognition of that union by the employer where, as here, there was no competing labor organization in the plant. The discharges of the stewards, however, were found not to be motivated by opposition to the particular union, or, we deduce, to unionism.

The Board determined that the promulgation and enforcement of the "no solicitation" rule violated §8 (1) of the National Labor Relations Act as it interfered with, restrained and coerced employees in their rights under §7 and discriminated against the discharged employee under §8 (3). It determined also that the discharge of the stewards violated §8 (1) and 8 (3). As a consequence of its conclusions as to the solicitation and the wearing of the insignia, the Board entered the usual cease and desist order and directed the reinstatement of the discharged employees with back pay and also the rescission of "the rule against solicitation in so far as it prohibits union activity and solicitation on company property during the employees' own time." 51 N.L.R.B. 1186, 1189. The Circuit Court of Appeals for the Second Circuit affirmed, 142 F.2d 193, and we granted certiorari, 323 U.S. 688, because of conflict with the decisions of other circuits.

In the case of Le Tourneau Company of Georgia, two employees were suspended two days each for distributing union literature or circulars on the employees' own time on company owned and policed parking lots, adjacent to the company's fenced-in plant, in violation of a long standing and strictly enforced rule, adopted prior to union organization activity about the premises, which read as follows: "In the future, no Merchants, Concern, Company, or Individual or Individuals will be permitted to distribute, post, or otherwise circulate handbills or posters, or any literature of any description, on Company property without first securing permission from the Personnel Department."

The rule was adopted to control littering and petty pilfering from parked autos by distributors. The Board determined that there was no union bias or discrimination by the company in enforcing the rule.

The company's plant for the manufacture of earthmoving machinery and other products for the war is in the country on a six thousand acre tract. The plant is bisected by one public road and built along another. There is one hundred feet of company-owned land for parking or other use between the highways and the employee entrances to the fenced enclosures where the work is done, so that contact on public ways or on non-company property with employees at or about the establishment is limited to those employees, less than 800 out of 2100, who are likely to walk across the public highway near the plant on their way to work, or to those employees who will stop their private automobiles, buses or other conveyances on the public roads for communications. The employees' dwellings are widely scattered.

The Board found that the application of the rule to the distribution of union literature by the employees on company property which results in the lay-offs was an unfair labor practice under §8 (1) and 8 (3). Cease and desist, and rule rescission orders, with directions to pay the employees for their lost time, followed. 54 N.L.R.B. 1253. The Circuit Court of Appeals for the Fifth Circuit reversed the Board, 143 F.2d 67, and we granted certiorari because of conflict with the Republic case. 323 U.S. 698.

These cases bring here for review the action of the National Labor Relations Board in working out an adjustment between the undisputed right of self-organization assured to employees under the Wagner Act and the equally undisputed right of employers to maintain discipline in their establishments. Like so many others, these rights are not unlimited in the sense that they can be exercised without regard to any duty which the existence of rights in others may place upon employer or employee. Opportunity to organize and proper discipline are both essential elements in a balanced society.

The Wagner Act did not undertake the impossible task of specifying in precise and unmistakable language each incident which would constitute an unfair labor practice. On the contrary, that Act left to the Board the work of applying the Act's general prohibitory language in the light of the infinite combinations of events which might be charged as violative of its terms. Thus a "rigid scheme of remedies" is avoided and administrative flexibility within appropriate statutory limitations obtained to accomplish the dominant purpose of the legislation. Phelps Dodge Corp. v. Labor Board. 313 U.S. 177, 194. So far as we are here concerned, that purpose is the right of employees to organize for mutual aid without employer interference. This is the principle of labor relations which the Board is to foster.

The gravamen of the objection of both Republic and Le Tourneau to the Board's orders is that they rest on a policy formulated without due administrative procedure. To be more specific it is that the Board cannot substitute its knowledge of industrial relations for substantive evidence. The contention is that there must be evidence before the Board to show that the rules and orders of the employers interfered with and discouraged union organization in the circumstances and situation of each company. Neither in the Republic nor the Le Tourneau cases can it properly be said that there was evidence or a finding that the plant's physical location made solicitation away from company property ineffective to reach prospective union members. Neither of these is like a mining or lumber camp where the employees pass their rest as well as their work time on the employer's premises, so that union organization must proceed upon the employer's premises or be seriously handicapped. . . .

In the Republic Aviation Corporation case the evidence showed that the petitioner was in early 1943 a non-urban manufacturing establishment for military production which employed thousands. It was growing rapidly. Trains and automobiles gathered daily many employees for the plant from an area on Long Island, certainly larger than walking distance. The rule against solicitation was introduced in evidence and the circumstances of its violation by the dismissed employee after warning was detailed.

As to the employees who were discharged for wearing the buttons of a union steward, the evidence showed in addition the discussion in regard to their right to wear the insignia when the union had not been recognized by the petitioner as the representative of the employees. Petitioner looked upon a steward as a union representative for the adjustment of grievances with the management after employer recognition of the stewards' union. Until such recognition petitioner felt that it would violate its neutrality in labor organization if it permitted the display of a steward button by an employee. From its point of view, such display represented to other employees that the union already was recognized.

No evidence was offered that any unusual conditions existed in labor relations, the plant location or otherwise to support any contention that conditions at this plant differed from those occurring normally at any other large establishment.

The Le Tourneau Company of Georgia case also is barren of special circumstances. The evidence which was introduced tends to prove the simple facts heretofore set out as to the circumstances surrounding the discharge of the two employees for distributing union circulars. . . .

The Board has fairly, we think, explicated in these cases the theory which moved it to its conclusions in these cases. The excerpts from its opinions just quoted show this. The reasons why it has decided as it has are sufficiently set forth. We cannot agree, as Republic urges, that in these present cases reviewing courts are left to "sheer acceptance" of the Board's conclusions or that its formulation of policy is "cryptic." See Eastern-Central Assn. v. United States, 321 U.S. 194, 209.

Not only has the Board in these cases sufficiently expressed the theory upon which it concludes that rules against solicitation or prohibitions against the wearing of insignia must fall as interferences with union organization, but, in so far as rules against solicitation are concerned, it had theretofore succinctly expressed the requirements of proof which it considered appropriate to outweigh or overcome the presumption as to rules against solicitation. In the Peyton Packing Company case, 49 N.L.R.B. 828, at 843 . . . the presumption adopted by the Board is set forth.

In the Republic Aviation case, petitioner urges that irrespective of the validity of the rule against solicitation, its application in this instance did not violate §8 (3), because the rule was not discriminatorily applied against union solicitation but was impartially enforced against all solicitors. It seems clear, however, that if a rule against solicitation is invalid as to union solicitation on the employer's premises during the employee's own time, a discharge because of violation of that rule discriminates within the meaning of §8 (3), in that it discourages membership in a labor organization.

Republic Aviation Corporation v. National Labor Relations Board is affirmed.

National Labor Relations Board v. Le Tourneau Company of Georgia is reversed.

MR. JUSTICE ROBERTS dissents in each case.

NOTES

1. Claims by an employer that "special circumstances" justify him in prohibiting union solicitation during nonworking hours will be closely scrutinized by the Board. For example, a depart-

ment store can prohibit all solicitation on the selling floors, in elevators, and on stairways because this might create traffic and safety hazards, or seriously disrupt business. It can keep non-employee organizers out of stock rooms, and can regulate their activities in public restaurants and waiting rooms. However, it cannot curtail solicitation in employee restaurants, nor prohibit employees from soliciting in non-public areas of the store during their free time. Matter of Marshall Field, 98 N.L.R.B. No. 11, 29 L.R.R.M. 1305 (1952). See also NLRB v. May Department Stores, 154 F.2d 533 (8th Cir. 1946); Daykin, Employee's Right to Organize on Company Time and Company Property, 42 Ill. L. Rev. 301 (1947).

2. In the Peyton Packing Company case (cited in the Republic Aviation case supra), the Board stated that a nonsolicitation rule would be presumed invalid. This presumption could be rebutted only by a showing that such union activity would impair production or discipline. See Matter of Scullin Steel Co., 49 N.L.R.B. 405, 12 L.R.R.M. 163 (1943). However, more recent cases suggest that distribution of union literature does not enjoy the same protection as other forms of solicitation. The employer may prohibit leaflet passing during nonworking hours because of his interest in keeping the plant clean and orderly. Matter of Monolith Portland Cement Co., 94 N.L.R.B. 1358, 28 L.R.R.M. 1204 (1951). The burden is then on the union to show that the restrictive rule constitutes a "serious impediment to the freedom of communication." Matter of Newport News Children's Dress Co., 91 N.L.R.B. 1521, 27 L.R.R.M. 1029 (1950). Under these rules could the union insist on the right to distribute handbills in the parking lots if the employees can be conveniently reached elsewhere? See Matter of Caldwell Furniture Co., 97 N.L.R.B. No. 240, 29 L.R.R.M. 1274 (1952).

3. In NLRB v. Stowe Spinning Co., 336 U.S. 226, 69 Sup. Ct. 541, 93 L. Ed. 638 (1941), it was held to be an unfair labor practice for an employer, in a company-owned town, to deny the Union use of the only suitable meeting hall in the town while making it generally available to other groups. Would it be an unfair labor practice for the employer to close the hall to all groups, including the union? Compare Marsh v. Alabama, 326 U.S. 501, 66 Sup. Ct. 276, 90 L. Ed. 265 (1946), holding unconstitutional an employer's rule against pamphlet distribution on the streets of the company-owned town.

4. In Maryland Drydock Co. v. NLRB, 183 F.2d 538 (4th Cir. 1950), the employer had permitted the Union to distribute its

newspaper on the premises for four years. Without notice it barred two issues. The first, continuing the prior tenor of the paper contained "articles further lampooning French (the Company's president) and holding him up to ridicule in doggerel verse as a goose and vulture." The second offered a reward to anyone who would submit suitable music for the verse, which would then "become the union's official theme song." The NLRB found the Company guilty of an unfair labor practice because there was no other feasible method of distribution and no affirmative evidence of injury to production or discipline in the plant. The Circuit Court of Appeals set aside the Board's order, stating:

. . . The company must maintain order and discipline in its plant; and we see no reason why it may not forbid the circulation on its premises of defamatory and insulting statements which reasonably tend to destroy such discipline, for it is well settled that the employer is not to be held guilty of an unfair labor practice because of action reasonably taken to protect his property or preserve discipline against the unlawful conduct of employees. . . .

. . . The right of the company to prohibit the distribution of insulting and defamatory literature must necessarily depend upon the character of the literature itself and the effect which it might normally be expected to produce, not upon ex post facto proof of the results which actually flowed from its distribution. . . .

Counsel for the Board argue that the action of the company was an abridgement of the freedom of speech guaranteed by the act; but we regard this contention as so utterly lacking in merit as hardly to warrant consideration. Freedom of speech nowhere means freedom to publish libelous and defamatory matter and nowhere does it mean freedom to wantonly lampoon or insult anyone. . . . Counsel for the Board argue that the employer should not be permitted a censorship over the literature of the union; but no censorship is involved in holding that the employer may forbid the distribution on his premises of statements which are defamatory and insulting and which tend to disrupt discipline. . . .

. . . The trouble here is that the Board has proceeded upon an erroneous theory of law in holding that, because no actual disruption of discipline is shown, the company may not forbid the distribution of literature the reasonable tendency of which is to cause its disruption. . . .

Does this holding permit private censorship and prior restraint by the employer? Compare Near v. Minnesota, 283 U.S. 697, 51 Sup. Ct. 625, 75 L. Ed. 1357 (1931). Has the court erred in failing to apply the clear and present danger test to a situation involving freedom of the press?

Compare Montgomery Ward & Co. v. United Department Store Employees, 400 Ill. 38, 79 N.E.2d 46 (1948), in which the court refused to enjoin publication in a Union newspaper of highly defamatory statements about the Company and its officers but indicated that a libel action might lie.

NLRB v. VIRGINIA ELECTRIC & POWER COMPANY
Supreme Court of the United States, 1941
314 U.S. 469, 62 Sup. Ct. 344, 86 L. Ed. 348

MR. JUSTICE MURPHY delivered the opinion of the court:

The Board specifically found that the bulletin of April 26 and the speeches of May 24 "interfered with, restrained and coerced" the Company's employees in the exercise of their rights guaranteed by §7 of the Act. The Company strongly urges that such a finding is repugnant to the First Amendment. Neither the Act nor the Board's order here enjoins the employer from expressing its view on labor policies or problems, nor is a penalty imposed upon it because of any utterances which it has made. The sanctions of the Act are imposed not in punishment of the employer but for the protection of the employees. The employer in this case is as free now as ever to take any side it may choose on this controversial issue. But, certainly, conduct, though evidenced in part by speech, may amount, in connection with other circumstances, to coercion within the meaning of the Act. If the total activities of an employer restrain or coerce his employees in their free choice, then those employees are entitled to the protection of the Act. And in determining whether a course of conduct amounts to restraint or coercion, pressure exerted, vocally by the employer may no more be disregarded than pressure exerted in other ways. For "Slight suggestions as to the employer's choice between unions may have telling effect among men who know the consequences of incurring that employer's strong displeasure." International Association of Machinists v. National Labor Relations Board, 311 U.S. 72, 78.

If the Board's order here may fairly be said to be based on the totality of the Company's activities during the period in question, we may not consider the findings of the Board as to the coercive effect of the bulletin and the speeches in isolation from the findings as respects the other conduct of the Company. If the Board's ultimate conclusion is based upon a complex of activities, such as the anti-union background of the Company, the activities of Bishop, Edwards' warning to the employees that they would be discharged for "messing with the C.I.O.," the discharge of Mann, the quick formation of the Independent, and the part which the management may have played in that formation, that conclusion would not be vitiated by the fact that the Board considered what the Company said in conjunction with what it did. The mere fact that language merges into a course of conduct does not put that whole course without the range of otherwise applicable administrative power. In determining whether the Company actually interfered with, restrained, and coerced its employees, the Board has a right to look at what the Company has said, as well as what it has done.

But, from the Board's decision, we are far from clear that the Board here considered the whole complex of activities, of which the bulletin and the speeches are but parts, in reaching its ultimate conclusion with regard to the Independent. The Board regarded the bulletin, on its face, as showing a marked bias against national unions by implying that strikes and unrest are caused by the organizational campaigns of such bodies, by stressing the "happy relationship of mutual confidence and understanding" prevailing in the absence of organization since the defeat of the Amalgamated in 1922, and by emphasizing the negative "right" of the employees to refrain from exercising their rights guaranteed under the Act, after paying "lip service" to those rights. Summing up its conclusions, the Board said: "We interpret the bulletin as an appeal to the employees to bargain with the respondent directly, without the intervention of any 'outside' union. We find that by posting the bulletin the respondent interfered with, restrained, and coerced its employees in the exercise of the rights guaranteed in Section 7 of the Act."

The Board was of the view that the speeches delivered in the meetings of May 24 provided the impetus for the formation of a system-wide organization, that they reemphasized the Company's distaste for "outside" organizations by referring to the bulletin, and that, after quoting the provision of the Act forbidding employer domination of labor organizations, they suggested that the employees select their "own" officers, and adopt their "own" by-laws and rules. The Board's finding was: "We find that at the May 24 meetings the respondent urged its employees to organize and to do so independently of 'outside' assistance, and that it thereby interfered with, restrained, and coerced its employees in the exercise of the rights guaranteed in Section 7 of the Act."

It is clear that the Board specifically found that those utterances were unfair labor practices, and it does not appear that the Board raised them to the stature of coercion by reliance on the surrounding circumstances.   If the utterances are thus to be separated from their background we find it difficult to sustain a finding of coercion with respect to them alone.   The bulletin and the speeches set forth the right of the employees to do as they please without fear of retaliation by the Company.   Perhaps the purport of these utterances may be altered by imponderable subtleties at work, which it is not our function to appraise.   Whether there are sufficient findings and evidence of interference, restraint, coercion, and domination, without reference to the bulletin and the speeches, or whether the whole course of conduct, evidenced in part by the utterances, was aimed at achieving objectives forbidden by the Act, are questions for the Board to decide upon the evidence.

Here, we are not sufficiently certain from the findings that the Board based its conclusion with regard to the Independent upon the whole course of conduct revealed by this record.   Rather, it appears that the Board rested heavily upon findings with regard to the bulletin and the speeches, the adequacy of which we regard as doubtful.   We therefore remand the cause to the Circuit Court of Appeals with directions to remand it to the Board for a re-determination of the issues in the light of this opinion. . . .

Reversed and remanded.

Mr. Justice Roberts and Mr. Justice Jackson took no part in the consideration of decision of this case.

[Upon remand, the Board found that in view of the totality of conduct of the company, the bulletin and speeches amounted to unfair labor practices.   Upon appeal the Supreme Court affirmed, 319 U.S. 533, 63 Sup. Ct. 1214, 87 L. Ed. 1568 (1943).]

NOTES

1. Compare the following:

The respondent's right to freedom of speech and of press does not sanction its use of speech or press as a means of employing its economic superiority to interfere with, restrain, or coerce its employees in the exercise of the rights guaranteed by the Act.   By its distribution of the "Viewpoint on Labor" to the plant employees, the respondent was not addressing or attempting to influence the public at large; nor was the respondent addressing an argument to the intellect of its employees which they were free to accept or reject without compulsion.   The respondent was not attempting to engage in the "free trade in ideas . . . in the competition of the market."   On the contrary it was issuing a stern warning that it was bitterly opposed to the Union and that it would throw the weight of its economic power against the efforts of its employees to form or carry on such an organization.   The respondent's right so to interfere with, restrain, and coerce its employees is not sanctioned by the First Amendment. . . . [Matter of Ford Motor Co., 23 N.L.R.B. 342, 353, 6 L.R.R.M. 310 (1940).]

Free speech on both sides and for every faction on any side of the labor relation is to me a constitutional and useful right. Labor is free . . . to turn its publicity on any labor oppression, substandard wages, employer unfairness, or objectionable working conditions.   The employer too, should be free to answer and to turn publicity on the records of the leaders of the unions which seek the confidence of his men.   And if the employees or organizers associate violence or other offenses against the laws with labor's free speech, or if the employer's speech is associated with discriminatory discharges or intimidation, the constitutional remedy would be to stop the evil, but permit the speech, if the two are separable; and only rarely and when they are inseparable to stop or punish speech or publication.   [Concurring opinion of Justice Jackson in Thomas v. Collins, 323 U.S. 516, 547, 65 Sup. Ct. 315, 89 L. Ed. 430 (1945).]

2.   The Virginia Electric & Power Company case gave employers a fairly wide range of freedom to express their views.   As another example of such freedom, the following statements were held to be immune from unfair labor practice charges in NLRB v. J. L. Brandeis & Sons, 145 F.2d 556, 560 (8th Cir. 1944):

"Who pays the salaries and expenses of those zealous, hardworking gentlemen, the union organizers, who have been in Omaha for months campaigning unceasingly for the proposal to make the A.F. of L. the bargaining agents in our store? Who is paying the costs of those circulars they are distributing each week, setting forth over and over again their appeals to our employees to accept their proposal? There is an old saying that we 'shouldn't look a gift horse in the mouth.' It is just possible that the 'giver' in this case will profit more by the 'gift' than we will.

"The union organizers almost never refer to the fact that their little gift will cost us all an initiation fee of $2.00 and $1.50 a month dues. But, if we look into the meaning of this $1.50 a month it isn't so difficult to understand why the union is going to so much trouble to make its great 'gift' to us. There are approximately a thousand of us 'eligible' to union membership according to the organizers. That means $1,500 a month. And $1,500 a month means $18,000 a year. And this $18,000 a year is only the smaller part of what the union organizers expect to receive from the 'favors' they want to do for us.

"If employees of our store become unionized, it will be only a short time, no doubt, until all employees of retail stores in Omaha will be unionized. The total is around 3,500. The little $1.50 a month from 3,500 people adds up to the tidy sum of $5,250 a month. And that much money per month means $63,000 a year. Of course, there will be some expense in collecting dues, sending out bills, keeping a few people on the union payroll and other expenses; but the net from the $63,000 per year should be very substantial. When we examine the 'favors' which the union wants to do for us and look into the financial side of it from the union's point of view, we really shouldn't be surprised and annoyed that the union boys and girls work so hard to get us in. Who wouldn't work hard and diligently for $63,000, a year?

"Of course, any employee of this store has a perfect right to join any union. Our employees have always had that right. But like every other question we ever heard of, this one also has two sides. . . .

". . . Do you want to be represented in your dealings with the store, by the people who, in trying to organize you, resorted to the kind of statements that you have heard and read for many months, and which, as illustrated above, are plainly untrue? Do you think that their efforts to organize you are for your interests or for theirs?" [Id. at 562.]

See also NLRB v. American Tube Bending Co., 134 F.2d 993 (2d Cir. 1943) ; NLRB v. West Kentucky Coal Co., 152 F.2d 198 (6th Cir. 1945) . However, if the language becomes defamatory the employer may be sued in libel. Kirkman v. Westchester Newspapers, 287 N.Y. 373, 39 N.E.2d 919 (1942).

3. How does Section 8 (c) of the Taft-Hartley Act affect the totality of conduct test as applied in Virginia Electric & Power Company? The Board took the position, in NLRB, 13th Ann. Rep. 45, 49 (1948), that

> This section appears to enlarge somewhat the protection previously accorded by the original statute and to grant immunity beyond that contemplated by the free speech guarantees of the Constitution. . . .
>
> Not only does section 8 (c) declare that noncoercive statements shall not constitute unfair labor practices; it also provides that such statements shall not "be *evidence* of an unfair labor practice under any of the provisions of this act." Previously, noncoercive anti-union remarks of an employer, although themselves privileged, were admissible to show an employer's motive where that fact was in issue. In view of the language of section 8 (c), however, the Board found in several cases that privileged expressions of opinion were not admissible to show motive.

The Circuit Courts of Appeals, however, have interpreted the section more narrowly. Thus in NLRB v. Kropp Forge Co., 178 F.2d 822 (7th Cir. 1949), the court stated at page 828:

> As this court said in N.L.R.B. v. LaSalle Steel Company, 178 F.2d 829 [7th Cir. 1949], the language of Section 8 (c) "seems to us no more than a restatement of the principles embodied in the First Amendment. . . ."
>
> It also seems clear to us that in considering whether such statements or expressions are protected by Section 8 (c) of the Act, they cannot be considered as isolated words cut off from the relevant circumstances and background in which they are spoken. A statement considered only as to the words it contains might seem a perfectly innocent statement, including neither a threat nor a promise. But, when the same statement is made by an employer to his employees, and we consider the relation of the parties, the surrounding circumstances, related statements and events and the background of the employer's actions, we may find that the statement is a part of a general pattern so coercive as to entirely destroy his employees' freedom of choice and action. To permit statements or expressions to be so used on the theory that they are

protected either by the First Amendment or by Section 8 (c) of the Act, would be in violation of Section 7 and contrary to the expressed purpose of the Act.

See also NLRB v. Bailey Co., 180 F.2d 278 (6th Cir. 1950) ; NLRB v. O'Keefe & Merritt Mfg. Co., 178 F.2d 445 (9th Cir. 1949). The Supreme Court has still reserved decision on the point. NLRB v. Pittsburgh Steamship Co., 340 U.S. 498, 71 Sup. Ct. 453, 95 L. Ed. 479 (1951).

4. Prior to the Taft-Hartley Act, the Board held it to be an unfair labor practice under the Wagner Act for an employer to call his employees together during working hours to compel them to listen to his point of view. The Circuit Courts of Appeals were doubtful. The rule was wholly disapproved in NLRB v. Montgomery Ward & Co., 157 F.2d 486 (8th Cir. 1946) ; but it was approved, where no "similar opportunity to address" the employees was "accorded representatives of the union," in NLRB v. Clark Bros. Co., 163 F.2d 373 (2d Cir. 1947).

This doctrine was grudgingly abandoned by the Board in 1948 out of deference to "Section 8 (c) of the amended Act, and its legislative history." Matter of Babcock & Wilcox Co., 77 N.L.R.B. 577, 22 L.R.R.M. 1057 (1948). However, it has had a remarkable return to life. In a series of cases, the Board re-established the doctrine to the extent that it was approved in the Clark Bros. case. If the employer addresses his employees on company time, he must provide the same opportunity to the union to present its case. Matter of Bonwit Teller, Inc., 96 N.L.R.B. 608, 28 L.R.R.M. 1547 (1951) ; Matter of Bernadin Bottle Cap Co., 97 N.L.R.B. No. 241, 29 L.R.R.M. 1255 (1952) ; Matter of Belknap Hardware & Mfg. Co., 98 N.L.R.B. No. 88, 29 L.R.R.M. 1360 (1952).

This revival of the doctrine may have been influenced by the fact that the Senate Subcommittee of the Committee on Labor and Public Welfare, after a study of the Southern textile industry, recommended repeal of Section 8 (c) , stating, "one effect of this provision has been the stimulation and encouragement of 'captive audiences,' a device used by employers to discourage self-organization and collective bargaining."

5. The Board has refused to extend the protection of Section 8 (c) to interrogation of employees about their union activities, but has held it to be coercive and therefore per se an unfair labor practice. Standard-Coosa-Thatcher Co., 85 N.L.R.B. 1358, 23 L.R.R.M. 1035 (1949) ; Matter of General Shoe Co., 97 N.L.R.B.

No. 71, 29 L.R.R.M. 1113 (1951). There is some doubt whether this view is shared by the courts. Sax v. NLRB, 171 F.2d 769 (7th Cir. 1948); NLRB v. Minnesota Mining & Manufacturing Co., 179 F.2d 323 (8th Cir. 1950); NLRB v. Montgomery Ward & Co., 192 F.2d 160 (2d Cir. 1951); Atlas Life Ins. Co. v. NLRB, 195 F.2d 136 (10th Cir. 1952).

6. The employer may question an employee about his union membership where the employee is entrusted with confidential information, Matter of American Book–Stratford Press, Inc., 80 NLRB 914, 23 L.R.R.M. 1171 (1948); or where it is necessary for his to prepare his defense to a complaint, so long as he does not go beyond the necessities of the situation. Joy Silk Mills v. NLRB, 185 F.2d 732 (D.C. Cir. 1950).

D. *Company Unionism — Domination and Support of Labor Organizations*

NATIONAL LABOR RELATIONS BOARD v. NEWPORT NEWS SHIPBUILDING & DRYDOCK CO.
Supreme Court of the United States, 1939
308 U.S. 241, 60 Sup. Ct. 203, 84 L. Ed. 219

MR. JUSTICE ROBERTS delivered the opinion of the court:

In a case duly instituted and heard, the National Labor Relations Board issued an order, pursuant to the provisions of §10 (c) of the National Labor Relations Act, requiring the respondent, Newport News Shipbuilding & Dry Dock Company; (1) to cease and desist from (a) dominating or otherwise interfering with the administration of the Employees' Representative Committee, a labor organization, or the formation or administration of any other labor organization of its employees; (b) from interfering with, restraining, or coercing its employees in the exercise of the right guaranteed them by §7 of the Act. The order further required the company (2) to take affirmative action, namely: (a) to withdraw all recognition from the Committee as the representative of any of its employees for the purpose of dealing with the company concerning labor conditions and wages, and completely to disestablish the Committee as such representative; (b) to post copies of the order throughout the plant; (c) to maintain said notices for thirty days; and (d) to notify the Board's Regional Director of the steps taken to comply with the order.

The order was based upon findings that the respondent had dominated and interfered with the formation and administration of the Committee, had contributed to it financial and other support, and was still dominating and interfering with the Committee, contrary to §8 (1) and (2) of the Act.

The Company petitioned the Circuit Court of Appeals for review. The Board answered praying that the court dismiss the company's petition and decree enforcement. The court held that the Board had jurisdiction of the cause, but that its holding that the company had dominated and interfered with the formation and administration of the Committee was without support in the evidence. The court decreed that §1 (a) and (b) and §2 (b), (c) and (d) of the Board's order should be enforced but that §2 (a), which required the withdrawal of recognition of the Committee and its disestablishment as a representative of the employees, should be stricken from the order. We granted certiorari because of asserted conflict with decisions of this court.

The respondent does not press the claim advanced in the court below that the Board lacked jurisdiction. The sole issue here joined is as to the propriety of that portion of the Board's order which constrained the respondent to withdraw recognition of the Committee and to disestablish it as the bargaining representative of the employees. Resolution of the issue requires that we determine whether the Board's ultimate finding of domination and interference by the employer has substantial support in the evidence.

The Board's subsidiary findings of fact are not the subject of serious controversy. The respondent attacks the ultimate conclusion of fact as unjustified by the subsidiary findings and further contends that the conclusion could not have been reached had not the Board ignored and refused to find other relevant facts which were either stipulated or proved without contradiction.

The Board's findings were to the following effect: In 1927, in cooperation with its employees, the respondent put into effect a plan of employee representation known as "Representation of Employees." The preamble of the plan stated that its purpose was to give employees a voice in respect of the conditions of their labor and to provide a procedure for the prevention and adjustment of future differences. Under the plan the employees were to elect representatives each of whom was paid $100 per year for services as such. No one holding a supervisory position was eligible to serve as a representative or to vote for a representative Administration of the plan was vested in certain joint committees each of which consisted of five elected representatives and not more than five representatives chosen from amongst the employees by the management. There was provision for a Management's Representative whose function was "to keep the management in touch with the representatives and represent the management in negotiations with their officers and committees." A provision calling for the arbitration of differences was to become operative only upon concurrence of the respondent's president.

Amendment of the plan could be made only by the affirmative vote of two-thirds of the full membership of the Joint Committee on Rules or of a majority of all the employees' representatives and all the representatives of the management, at an annual conference. The plan set forth that independence of action of elected representatives was guaranteed by permitting them to take questions of discrimination to any of the superior officers, to the Joint Committee, and to the president of the company. There was no provision for the payment of dues.

The original plan was revised in 1929, 1931, 1934, 1936, and 1937.

By the 1931 revision, which was not materially altered until 1937, a General Joint Committee was set up in lieu of several joint committees theretofore constituted, and two representatives were to be elected by the employees in each department while the respondent was to appoint an equal number of management representatives, a majority of each class of representatives constituting a quorum. The annual remuneration to be paid elected representatives by the company was reduced to $60.00. The secretary of the General Joint Committee was paid $5.00 monthly by the company. An Executive Committee was also established constituted of five elected employee representatives and five representatives of management.

Elections were arranged for by the management representatives but, in so far as possible, were conducted by the employees themselves.

A procedure was established for the adjustment of individual employee grievances, whereby, in event of failure of settlement, notice was to be given to the president of the Company. Under the revised plan the General Joint Committee met monthly to take action upon matters presented by the Management Representative or by employee representatives or subcommittees; but finality of the action of the General Joint Committee was dependent upon approval by the respondent's president. Amendment of the plan, which could be accomplished by a two-thirds vote of the entire General Joint Committee, became effective when approved by the president of the company.

The last revision made in May 1937, after the validity of the National Labor Relations Act had been sustained by this court, originated in the General Joint Committee, one-half of whose members represented the interests of the respondent. The amended plan was referred to the Executive Committee, similarly constituted, and to the elected employee representatives, respectively. After announcement by the Management Representative that the revision was acceptable to the respondent it was adopted by the General Joint Committee. The personnel manager, and the general manager of the respondent, took part in the revision of the plan. The secretary of the Committee testified that this revision was undertaken in order to bring the plan within the letter, as well as within the spirit, of the Act.

The two principal changes made were the elimination of payment of compensation by the respondent to elected representatives of the employees and the substitution of an Employees' Representative Committee, composed solely of employee representatives elected by employees, for the former General Joint Committee and the Joint Executive Committee. The revised plan provides that action of the Employees' Representative Committee "shall be final and become effective upon agreement by the company"; and, further, that any article of the plan may be amended by a vote of two-thirds of the entire membership of the committee; and "amendments shall be in effect at the time specified by the Employees' Representative Committee, unless disapproved by the company within fifteen days after their passage."

The grievance procedure permits the presentation of a grievance to the respondent's personnel manager, or its general manager, in the event no settlement has theretofore been effected.

Upon the basis of these findings the Board concluded that, from the inception of the plan in 1927 until its final revision in 1937, the respondent dominated, assisted, and interfered with the administration of the labor organization; and that the method followed for amendment of the plan in 1937, and the provisions of the final revision, left the company still in the position of dominating and interfering in the formulation and administration of the plan, contrary to the provisions of §7 of the Act. The Board held that the Committee is, in the circumstances, incapable of serving the employees as their genuine representative for the purpose of collective bargaining.

The respondent criticises several of the findings as without support or contrary to uncontradicted evidence. We do not stop to consider these contentions, since, without such findings, there would still be a basis in the record for the Board's conclusions.

The principal contention of the respondent is that the Board ignored uncontradicted facts and refused to make findings respecting them. The Board replies that it did not ignore these facts, but omitted to find them because they were immaterial to the pivotal issues in the case. It is uncontradicted that labor disputes have repeatedly been settled under the plan; that since 1927 no labor dispute has caused cessation of activities at the respondent's plant; that overwhelming majorities of the employees have participated in the election of representatives; that the company has never objected to its employees joining labor unions; that no discrimination has been practiced against them because of their membership in outside unions; and that neither officials nor superior employees not eligible to vote in the election of employees' representatives, have interfered, or attempted to interfere, or use any influence, in connection with the election of representatives.

Before the Board's decision and order had been promulgated a referendum was held at which a sweeping majority of the company's employees signified, by secret ballot, their satisfaction with the plan as revised in 1937 and their desire for its continuance. Counsel for the Committee requested the Board to certify these facts to the Circuit Court of Appeals as part of the record before the court. The Board, though not bound so to do, embodied these facts in a supplementary certificate. It now takes the position that the only proper way to bring these additional facts to the attention of the reviewing court would have been by application to the court to remand the cause for further findings, and as this was not done, the certificate was irregular and should not have been considered. We are unable to agree with this contention. We think the Circuit Court of Appeals cannot be convicted of error in accepting the Board's supplemental certificate.

The Board urges that, notwithstanding the facts on which the respondent relies, the structure of the Committee, under the 1937 plan, renders the organization incompetent to meet the requirements of the National Labor Relations Act; and further that, if its fundamental law were free from defect, the history of its organization and administration would require that it be disestablished as the bargaining agency of the employees.

Prior to the adoption of the Wagner Act the plan did not run counter to any federal law, either in conception or administration. The respondent, however, concedes that sundry features of the plan, as then formulated, conflict with the provisions of the statute. Both employer and employees so recognized when they undertook the revision of 1937 for the purpose of bringing the plan within the spirit and the letter of the Act.

The Board has concluded that the provisions embodied in the final revision, whereby action of the Committee requires, for its effectiveness, the agreement of the company, and whereby amendment of the plan can become effective only if the company fails to signify its disapproval within fifteen days of adoption, still give the respondent such power of control that the plan is in the teeth of the expressed policy and the specific prohibitions of the Act. The respondent argues that these provisions affect only the company and not the employees; that, in collective bargaining, there is always reserved to the employer the right to qualify or to reject the propositions advanced by the employees. Whatever may be said of the first mentioned provision, this explanation will not hold for the second. The plan may not be amended if the company disapproves the amendment. Such control of the form and structure of an employee organization deprives the employees of the complete freedom of action guaranteed to them by the Act, and justifies an order such as was here entered. The court below in its opinion, states it was advised in a brief after the hearing in that court, that the plan had been amended by striking out the provisions in question. It concludes, therefore, that their previous existence is immaterial. The statute expressly deprives the reviewing court of power to consider facts thus brought to its attention. The case must be heard on the record as certified by the Board. The appropriate procedure to add facts to the record as certified is prescribed in §10 (e) of the Act.

But we think that if the record disclosed such an alteration of the plan, the order of the Board could not be held erroneous. The Board held that, where an organization has existed for ten years and has functioned in the way that the Committee has functioned, with a joint control vested in management and men, the effects of the long practice cannot be eliminated and the employees rendered entirely free to act upon their own initiative without the complete disestablishment of the plan. On the record as made we cannot say this was error.

While the men are free to adopt any form of organization and representation whether purely local or connected with a national body, their purpose so to do may be obstructed by the existence and recognition by the management of an old plan or organization the original structure or operation of which was not in accordance with the provisions of the law. Sec. 10 (c) was not intended to give the Board power of punishment or retribution for past wrongs or errors.   Action under that section must be limited to the effectuation of the policies of the Act.   One of these is that the employees shall be free to choose such form of organization as they wish.

As pointed out in National Labor Relations Board v. Pennsylvania Greyhound Lines, 303 U.S. 261, disestablishment of a bargaining unit previously dominated by the employer may be the only effective way of wiping the slate clean and affording the employees an opportunity to start afresh in organizing for the adjustment of their relations with the employer.   Compare National Labor Relations Board v. Fansteel Metallurgical Corp., 306 U.S. 240, 262.

The court below agreed with the respondent that, as the Committee had operated to the apparent satisfaction of the employees; as serious labor disputes had not occurred during its existence; and as the men at an election held under the auspices of the Committee had signified their desire for its continuance, it would be a proper medium and one which the employer might continue to recognize for the adjustment of labor disputes.   The difficulty with the position is that the provisions of the statute preclude such a disposition of the case.   The law provides that an employee organization shall be free from interference or dominance by the employer.   We cannot say that, upon the uncontradicted facts, the Board erred in its conclusion that the purpose of the law could not be attained without complete disestablishment of the existing organization which had been dominated and controlled to a greater or less extent by the respondent.   In applying the statutory test of independence it is immaterial that the plan had in fact not engendered, or indeed had obviated, serious labor disputes in the past, or that any company interference in the administration of the plan had been incidental rather than fundamental and with good motives.   It was for Congress to determine whether, as a matter of policy, such a plan should be permitted to continue in force.   We think the statute plainly evinces a contrary purpose, and that the Board's conclusions are in accord with that purpose.

The decree must be reversed and the cause remanded for further proceedings in conformity to this opinion.

Reversed.

NOTES

1. NLRB, 3d Annual Report 112 (1938). "Commonly, labor organizations which the Board has found to be within the ban of section 8 (2) are employer-controlled from their inception. Thus, it may be the employer who has suggested to his employees the desirability of establishing an employee organization and has suggested or dictated the form which the particular organization is to assume. The extent and character of employer participation in labor organizations varies from case to case, but factors which the Board has considered in determining whether an employer's activities constitute an unfair labor practice under section 8 (2) include active solicitation on behalf of a labor organization by officials and other supervisory employees, lack of opportunity for the employees to accept or reject a particular organization proposed to them, the disparagement by supervisory employees of any rival labor organization which may be attempting to organize the employees, the linking of benefits arising from group insurance plans and other such activities with membership in the favored organization, and the advance of money by foremen to employees unable to pay their membership fees. The Board has also considered the effects of employers' activities in permitting the conduct of organizational activities on the employer's premises during working hours with the consent of the employer, and in furnishing financial aid and various facilities to employee organizations, such as the use of bulletin boards, mimeograph machines, the company automobile, stenographic services and office space, and mailing lists. As indicated hereinafter, in many cases, the elements of employer interference and support of a labor organization here described are accompanied by the employer's denial of similar advantages to a competing labor organization. . . .

"Supervisors have dominated and interfered with the formation and administration of labor organizations, in numerous other ways. They have attended meetings of such labor organizations, participated in discussions at the meetings, become members, served as officers and committeemen, signed petitions, circulated on behalf of such organizations, and themselves circulated such petitions and other literature, and aided in drafting of constitutions and bylaws. In its decisions, the Board has also considered instances of less direct participation of supervisors in the affairs of employee organizations, such as solicitation of members by employees during working hours on the employer's premises with the knowledge of and in the presence of supervisors while competing organizations are denied the same privileges."

2. NLRB, 16th Annual Report 155 (1951). "Since the 1947 amendments to the act, the Board has distinguished in the remedy it applies between (a) cases of domination and (b) cases involving no more than unlawful assistance or support of a labor organization by an employer. In cases where employer interference in a labor organization amounts to domination, the Board orders it completely disestablished as the bargaining representative of employees. In cases where the interference and support does not reach the point of domination, the Board orders only that the employer withhold recognition of the organization until it has been certified by the Board as a bona fide bargaining representative of a majority of employees. The Board continued this policy during the past fiscal year."

NLRB, 15th Annual Report 101 (1950). ". . . [I]n determining whether employer conduct constituted unlawful domination or support, or both, the Board again has been guided by the extent and nature of the conduct. Thus, domination as well as support was found where the employer not only granted financial assistance or use of plant facilities, or a checkoff of dues but, in addition, one or more of the following factors were present: The labor organization was formed at the employer's suggestion; supervisory personnel participated in the formation and administration of the organization, or the union bylaws enabled management to exercise effective control over the organization.

"On the other hand, support, but not domination, was found where the employer recognized one labor organization while another union's petition for certification was pending before the Board. Illegal support was found also where the employer agreed to union-security clauses which had not been ratified by a union-shop election and, in another case, where the employer granted a union-security clause which exceeded that permitted by section 8 (a) (3)."

3. One recurring question is the status of a new organization which rises from the ashes of the old dominated organization. The Board has consistently ruled that regardless of the new union's actual freedom from domination, it is tainted with the illegality of its predecessor unless the employer, prior to its formation, establishes a clear line of fracture between the two organizations by publicly and unequivocally disestablishing the old organization and by assuring the employees of their freedom from further interference.

This Board rule was upheld in Westinghouse Electric & Manufacturing Co. v. NLRB, 112 F.2d 657 (2d Cir. 1940), affirmed per curiam, 312 U.S. 660, 61 Sup. Ct. 736, 85 L. Ed. 1108 (1941). An old employee representation plan was reorganized without any company interference or domination.   Judge Learned Hand, in upholding the Board order of disestablishment stated at page 660: "The theory is that in cases such as this, where an unaffiliated union seems to the employees at large to have evolved out of an earlier joint organization of employer and employees, the Board may take it as datum, in the absence of satisfactory evidence to the contrary, that the employees will suppose that the company approved the new, as it did the old, and that their choice is for that reason not as free as the statute demands.   How substantial such a fear really is, it is not for us to say; upon how much evidence the Board may insist to make public the change, the court did not declare; nor need we here; for the company did not make any effort to make it plain to the employees generally that the 'Independent' was not a revision, or amendment, of the 'Plan.' On the surface it seemed to be such, for it emanated from the old elected representatives, and that alone established an appearance of continuity between the two."   See also Matter of Sun Oil Company, 89 N.L.R.B. 833, 26 L.R.R.M. 1057 (1950); Matter of Pacific Telephone & Telegraph Co., 76 N.L.R.B. 889, 21 L.R.R.M. 1255 (1948).

4. The prohibition against domination and control extends only to "labor organizations."   In some instances, organizations allegedly organized for social or recreational purposes but in fact used to combat unionization of a union have been held to be labor organizations.   Matter of Donnelly Garment Co., 50 N.L.R.B. 241, 12 L. R. R. M. 216 (1943); Matter of Essex Rubber Co., 50 N.L.R.B. 283, 12 L.R.R.M. 205 (1943).   If the organization discusses grievances or working conditions with the employer, it will clearly be found to be a labor organization even though it makes no binding settlements or agreements.   Matter of Florida Telephone Co., 88 N.L.R.B. 1429, 25 L.R.R.M. 1499 (1950); Matter of Wrought Iron Range Co., 77 N.L.R.B. 487, 22 L.R.R.M. 1050 (1948).   Compare Matter of Hudson Dispatch, 68 N.L.R.B. 115, 18 L.R.R.M. 1095 (1946).

INTERNATIONAL ASSOCIATION OF MACHINISTS
v. NLRB
Supreme Court of the United States, 1940
311 U.S. 72, 61 Sup. Ct. 83, 85 L. Ed. 50

MR. JUSTICE DOUGLAS delivered the opinion of the Court:

. . . The Board found that the closed-shop contract between petitioner and the employer was invalid under §8 (3) of the Act because it had been "assisted" by unfair labor practices of the employer, because petitioner did not represent an uncoerced majority of the toolroom employees at the time the contract was executed, and because for this and other reasons it was not an appropriate bargaining unit. We think there was substantial evidence that petitioner had been assisted by unfair labor practices of the employer and that therefore the Board was justified in refusing to give effect to its closed-shop contract.

Since the court below has confirmed the findings of the Board there is no need to review the evidence in detail. National Licorice Co. v. National Labor Relations Board, 309 U.S. 350, 357. It is clear that the employer had an open and avowed hostility to U.A.W. It is plain that the employer exerted great effort, though unsuccessfully, to sustain its old company union, the Acme Welfare Association, as a bulwark against U.A.W. And it is evident that the employer, while evincing great hostility to U.A.W. in a contest to enlist its production force, acquiesced without protest in the organization by petitioner of the toolroom employees. The main contested issue here is narrowly confined. It is whether or not the employer "assisted" the petitioner in enrolling its majority.

Fouts, Shock, Dininger, Bolander, Byroad and Baker were all employees of the toolroom. Four of these — Fouts, Shock, Byroad and Bolander — were old and trusted employees. Fouts was "more or less an assistant Foreman," having certain employees under him. Shock was in charge of the toolroom during the absence of the foreman. Dininger and Bolander were in charge of the second and third shifts respectively, working at night. Prior to mid-July, 1937, they had been actively engaged on behalf of the company union. When it became apparent at that time that the efforts to build up that union were not successful, Fouts, Shock, Byroad and Bolander suddenly shifted their support from the company union to petitioner and moved into the forefront in enlisting the support of the employees for petitioner. The general manager told Shock that he would close the plant rather than deal with U.A.W. The superintendent and Shock reported to toolroom employees that the employer would not recognize the C.I.O. The superintendent let it be known that the employer would deal with an A.F. of L. union. At the same time the superintendent also stated to one of the employees that some of the "foremen don't like the C.I.O." and added, with prophetic vision, that there was "going to be quite a layoff around here and these fellows that don't like the C.I.O. are going to lay those fellows off first." During working hours, Byroad conducted a straw vote among the employees and under the direction of Fouts and Shock left the plant to seek out an organizer for petitioner. Fouts solicited among workmen in the toolroom stating that his purpose was to "beat" the U.A.W. For a week preceding August 13, Shock spent much time, as did Byroad, going "from one bench to another soliciting" for petitioner. Baker likewise solicited. Dininger offered an employee a "good rating" if he would join petitioner. Not less than a week before August 13, the personnel director advised two employees to "join the A.F. of L." Byroad spent considerable time during working hours soliciting employees, threatening loss of employment to those who did not sign up with petitioner and representing that he was acting in line with the desire of the toolroom foreman, McCoy. This active solicitation for petitioner was on company time and was made openly in the shop. Much of it was made in the presence of the toolroom foreman, McCoy, who clearly knew what was being done. Yet the freedom allowed solicitors for petitioner was apparently denied solicitors for U.A.W. The plant manager warned some of the latter to check out their time for a conference with him on U.A.W. and questioned their right to discuss U.A.W. matters on company property. The inference is justified that U.A.W. solicitors were closely watched, while those acting for petitioner were allowed more leeway.

Five U.A.W. officials had been discharged in June, 1937, because of their union activities. The known antagonism of the employer to U.A.W. before petitioner's drive for membership started made it patent that the employees were not free to choose U.A.W. as their bargaining representative. Petitioner started its drive for membership late in July, 1937, and its closed-shop contract was signed August 11, 1937. On August 10, 1937, the U.A.W., having a clear majority of all the employees, presented to the employer a proposed written contract for collective bargaining. This was refused. On August 13, 1937, all toolroom employees who refused membership in petitioner, some 20 in number, were discharged.   On August 15, 1937, the management circulated among the employees a statement which as found by the Board, was a thinly veiled attack on the U.A.W. and a firm declaration that the employer would not enter into any agreement with it.

Petitioner insists that the employer's hostility to U.A.W. cannot be translated into assistance to the petitioner and that none of the acts of the employees above mentioned, who were soliciting for petitioner, can be attributed to the employer.

We disagree with that view.   We agree with the court below that the toolroom episode was but an integral part of a long plant controversy.   What happened during the relatively brief period from late July to August 11, 1937, cannot properly be divorced from the events immediately preceding and following.   The active opposition of the employer to U.A.W. throughout the whole controversy has a direct bearing on the events during that intermediate period.   Known hostility to one union and clear discrimination against it may indeed make seemingly trivial intimations of a preference for another union powerful assistance for it. Slight suggestions as to the employer's choice between unions may have telling effect among men who know the consequences of incurring that employer's strong displeasure.   The freedom of activity permitted one group and the close surveillance given another may be more powerful support for the former than campaign utterances.

To be sure, it does not appear that the employer instigated the introduction of petitioner into the plant.   But the Board was wholly justified in finding that the employer "assisted" it in its organizational drive.   Silent approval of or acquiescence in that drive for membership and close surveillance of the competitor; the intimations of the employer's choice made by superiors; the fact that the employee-solicitors had been closely identified with the company union until their quick shift to petitioner; the rank and position of those employee-solicitors; the ready acceptance of petitioner's contract and the contemporaneous rejection of the contract tendered by U.A.W.; the employer's known prejudice against the U.A.W. were all proper elements for it to take into consideration in weighing the evidence and drawing its inference. To say that the Board must disregard what preceded and what followed the membership drive would be to require it to shut its eyes to potent imponderables permeating this entire record. The detection and appraisal of such imponderables are indeed one of the essential functions of an expert administrative agency.

Petitioner asserts that it had obtained its majority of toolroom employees by July 28, 1938, and that there was no finding by the Board that that majority was maintained between then and the date of execution of the closed-shop contract by unfair labor practices. In this case, however, that is an irrelevant refinement. The existence of unfair labor practices throughout this whole period permits the inference that the employees did not have that freedom of choice which is the essence of collective bargaining. And the finding of the Board that petitioner did not represent an uncoerced majority of toolroom employees when the closed-shop contract was executed is adequate to support the conclusion that the maintenance as well as the acquisition of the alleged majority was contaminated by the employer's aid.

Petitioner attacks the Board's conclusion that its membership drive was headed by "supervisory" employees — Fouts, Shock, Dininger, and Bolander. According to petitioner these men were not foremen, let alone supervisors entrusted with executive or directorial functions, but merely "lead men" who by reason of long experience were skilled in handling new jobs and hence directed the set-up of the work. Petitioner's argument is that since these men were not supervisory their acts of solicitation were not coercive and not attributable to the employer.

The employer, however, may be held to have assisted the formation of a union even though the acts of the so-called agents were not expressly authorized or might not be attributable to him on strict application of the rules of respondeat superior. We are dealing here not with private rights nor with technical concepts pertinent to an employer's legal responsibility to third persons for acts of his servants, but with a clear legislative policy to free the collective bargaining process from all taint of an employer's compulsion, domination, or influence. The existence of that interference must be determined by careful scrutiny of all the factors, often subtle, which restrain the employees' choice and for which the employer may fairly be said to be responsible. Thus, where the employees would have just cause to believe that solicitors professedly for a labor organization were acting for and on behalf of the management, the Board would be justified in concluding that they did not have the complete and unhampered freedom of choice which the Act contemplates. Here there was ample evidence to support that inference. As we have said, Fouts, Shock, Dininger and Bolander all had men working under them. To be sure, they were not high in the factory hierarchy and apparently did not have the power to hire or to fire. But they did exercise general authority over the employees and were in a strategic position to translate to their subordinates the policies and desires of the management. It is clear that they did exactly that. Moreover, three of them — Fouts, Shock and Bolander — had been actively engaged during the preceding weeks in promoting the company union. During the membership drive for petitioner they stressed the fact that the employer would prefer those who joined petitioner to those who joined U.A.W. They spread the idea that the purpose in establishing petitioner was "to beat the C.I.O." and that the employees might withdraw from the petitioner once this objective was reached. And in doing these things they were emulating the example set by the management. The conclusion is then justified that this is not a case where solicitors for one union merely engaged in a zealous membership drive which just happened to coincide with the management's desires. Hence the fact that they were bona fide members of petitioner did not require the Board to disregard the other circumstances we have noted.

By §8 (3) of the Act discrimination upon the basis of union membership constitutes an unfair labor practice unless made because of a valid closed-shop contract. But that section authorizes an order under §10 abrogating such a contract with a labor organization which has been assisted by unfair labor practices. The presence of such practices in this case justified the Board's conclusion that petitioner did not represent an uncoerced majority of the toolroom employees. §§7, 8 (1). This conclusion makes it unnecessary to pass upon the scope of the Board's power to determine the appropriate bargaining unit under §9 (b).

. . . Petitioner challenges the order directing the employer to bargain exclusively with U.A.W., on the ground that prior to the issuance of the order petitioner had obtained an overwhelming majority of the production employees and had so notified the Board. Petitioner made no showing at the hearing that a majority of the employees had shifted to it after the employer refused to bargain with U.A.W. Nor did it seek leave from the court below to adduce such additional evidence pursuant to §10 (e). Nevertheless it contends that the Board on receipt of the notification should have ordered an election or at least have made an investigation.

We agree with the court below that the Board in failing to act on this request did not commit error. This was not a certification proceeding under §9 (c) ; it was an unfair labor practice proceeding under §10. Where as a result of unfair labor practices a union cannot be said to represent an uncoerced majority, the Board has the power to take appropriate steps to the end that the effect of those practices will be dissipated. That necessarily involves an exercise of discretion on the part of the Board — discretion involving an expert judgment as to ways and means of protecting the freedom of choice guaranteed to the employees by the Act. It is for the Board, not the courts, to determine how the effect of prior unfair labor practices may be expunged. National Labor Relations Board v. Pennsylvania Greyhound Lines, 303 U.S. 261, 271; National Labor Relations Board v. Falk Corp., 308 U.S. 453, 461. It cannot be assumed that an unremedied refusal of an employer to bargain collectively with an appropriate labor organization has no effect on the development of collective bargaining. See National Labor Relations Board v. Pacific Greyhound Lines, 303 U.S. 272, 275. Nor is the conclusion unjustified that unless the effect of the unfair labor practices is completely dissipated, the employees might still be subject to improper restraints and not have the complete freedom of choice which the Act contemplates. Hence the failure of the Board to recognize petitioner's notice of change was wholly proper. National Labor Relations Board v. Bradford Dyeing Assn., 310 U.S. 318, 339–340.

Sec. 9 of the Act provides adequate machinery for determining in certification proceedings questions of representation after unfair labor practices have been removed as obstacles to the employees' full freedom of choice.

Affirmed.

NOTES

1. Does the fact that one of the competing unions has failed to comply with the filing requirements and is reputed to be Communist-dominated justify the employer in campaigning for the complying union? Can he bargain with the complying union if the noncomplying union has a majority? Can he permit the complying union the right to circulate petitions on company property and deny the Communist-controlled union the right to do so? Compare Stewart-Warner Corp. v. NLRB, 194 F.2d 207 (4th Cir. 1952), with Matter of Monolith Portland Cement Co., 94 N.L.R.B. 1358, 28 L.R.R.M. 1204 (1951).

2. Under the Wagner Act, when the Board found that an unaffiliated union was dominated, it invariably issued a disestablishment order which perpetually barred it from recognition. Affiliated unions, however, were not disestablished. The Board merely

ordered cessation of interference and withdrawal of recognition until the effects had been dissipated. Section 10 (c) of the Taft-Hartley Act eliminated this distinction between affiliated and un-affiliated unions.

In Matter of Carpenter Steel Company, 76 N.L.R.B. 670, 21 L.R.R.M. 1232 (1948), the Board recognized that it may no longer concern itself with the affiliation of a union in framing its remedial order. However, it set forth a new distinction at page 673: "Where we find that an employer's unfair labor practices have been so extensive as to constitute *domination* of the organization we shall order its disestablishment, whether or not it is affiliated. . . . But when the Board finds that an employer's unfair labor practices were limited to interference and support and never reached the point of domination, we shall only order that recognition be withheld until certification, again without regard to whether or not the union happens to be affiliated."

For a case in which the Board found an affiliated union (Teamsters) to be dominated, and ordered it disestablished, see Matter of Jack Smith Beverages, Inc., 94 N.L.R.B. 1401, 28 L.R.R.M. 1199 (1951).

3. The check-off of union dues by an employer is not such support as to constitute a violation of Section 8 (a) (2) per se, but if the union is company-dominated, then it does constitute unlawful support. Utah Copper Co. v. NLRB, 139 F.2d 788 (10th Cir. 1943). In such cases the Board may order the company to refund all of the dues deducted, particularly where membership in the dominated union is compulsory. The Supreme Court has held that such an order is not penal but is similar to a back-pay order and can be found by the Board to be "such affirmative action . . . as will effectuate the purposes of the Act under Section 10 (c)." Virginia Electric & Power Co. v. NLRB, 319 U.S. 533, 63 Sup. Ct. 1214, 87 L. Ed. 1568 (1943).

Section 302 of the Taft-Hartley Act requires a written authorization of check-off signed by the employee. The fact that the deduction is without such authorization does not, however, make it an unfair labor practice where the union is free of domination. Matter of Salant & Salant, Inc., 88 N.L.R.B. 816, 25 L.R.R.M. 1391 (1950).

4. An interesting parallel in foreign law is found in a German case of 1938. The German law contained no reference to a company-dominated union, but did contain references to "economic associations of employees" (Lab. Court's Act, Sec. 11, par. 2) as eligible to appear, through attorneys, as parties to court pro-

ceedings. In a proceeding that ultimately reached the Supreme Labor Court, it became relevant to determine whether a certain union was an "economic association," capable of being so represented. It was claimed that this organization was what we would call "company dominated." The Court found the facts to be otherwise, and that the union was actually independent; but the Court expressed the following opinion, as a dictum:

"A further requirement for the capacity to make collective agreements is, however . . . actual independence of the other bargaining party. A purely formal and superficial independence is not enough; there must be internal independence and freedom from the other party. For it is only through such complete independence that the organization can effectively fulfill its object of safeguarding the interests of its members by making collective agreements." Dersch-Flatow, Decisions of the Reichsarbeitsgericht, IV, p. 239 (Oct. 10, 1938).

Thus it would seem clear that the German Court, without any express statute, would have set aside the contract had it found facts which in our country would have constituted a Section 8 (2) violation.

NOTE ON EMPLOYER RESPONSIBILITY FOR CONDUCT OF EMPLOYEES AND OTHERS

To what extent will the employer be held responsible where the antiunion practices are committed by (a) foremen, (b) other rank-and-file employees, and (c) outsiders? Under the Wagner Act the rule was as stated in International Association of Machinists v. NLRB, page 605 supra. Section 2 (2) of the Wagner Act defined "employer" so as to include those "acting in the interest of the employer." Taft-Hartley amended this to read, "any person acting as an agent of an employer." This must be read with Section 2 (13), which states: "In determining whether any person is acting as an agent of another person so as to make such other responsible for his acts, the question of whether the specific acts performed were actually authorized or subsequently ratified shall not be controlling."

The purpose in enacting this amended section was to establish that "both employers and labor organizations will be responsible for the acts of their agents in accordance with the ordinary common law rules of agency." House Conference Report No. 510 [Legis. Hist. of the LMRA (1947) 540]. Whether these sections make any substantial changes in the employer's responsibility is open to question. Compare Cox, *Some Aspects of the Labor Management Relations Act of 1947*, 61 Harv. L. Rev. 8–15 (1947); and Van Arkel, *An Analysis of the Labor Management Relations Act* 20–22 (1947). However, the test stated by the Board since 1947 is almost identical to that previously applied. See Matter of J. S. Abercrombie Co., 83 N.L.R.B. 524, 24 L.R.R.M. 1115 (1949).

An employer will be held responsible for antiunion statements or threats made by a supervisory employee, who has no power to hire or fire, so long as the employees have reasonable basis for believing his conduct reflects the employer's views. However, the employer can purge himself by a disavowal. Matter of Arkansas-Missouri Power Company, 68 N.L.R.B. 805, 18 L.R.R.M. 1165 (1946). It is not enough for him to prohibit the conduct; he must bring home to the employees generally that the conduct has been prohibited and does not reflect the employer's views. NLRB v. Bird Machinery Co., 161 F.2d 589 (1st Cir. 1947); Matter of Otis L. Broyhill Furniture Co., 94 N.L.R.B. 1452, 28 L.R.R.M. 1211 (1951). The employer may escape responsibility also by showing a background free of antiunion attitudes and practices which makes it clear that antiunion statements of supervisory employees do not reflect the views of the employer. NLRB v. Tennessee Coach Co., 191 F.2d 546 (6th Cir. 1951).

The employer has been held responsible for unauthorized conduct of nonsupervisory employees in some instances. In NLRB v. Dorsey Trailers, 179 F.2d 589 (5th Cir. 1950), the employer was held responsible for an attack on the union representative by a rank-and-file employee. The court said, "We agree with the trial examiner and Board that the company, while not directly responsible for the attack, was certainly cognizant of it and could have prevented, but did nothing to prevent it, and that such conduct certainly constituted an unfair labor practice." For extreme examples of countenancing violence against union members, see NLRB v. Ford Motor Company, 114 F.2d 905 (6th Cir. 1940); Matter of American Thread Company, 94 N.L.R.B. 1699, 28 L.R.R.M. 1249 (1951).

An employer may also be responsible for the conduct of outsiders. Thus, an employer has been held responsible for coercive speeches made by the mayor and a local banker where he organized the meeting and urged employees to attend, Matter of Southland Mfg. Co., 94 N.L.R.B. 813, 28 L.R.R.M. 1104 (1951); and for editorials appearing in an antiunion newspaper where he ordered issues mailed direct to employees, NLRB v. Bibb Mfg. Co., 188

F.2d 825 (5th Cir. 1951). He may also be held liable, at least under Section 2 (2) of the Wagner Act, for union-busting activities engaged in by organizations which he has knowingly joined or to which he has subscribed. NLRB v. Sun Tent-Luebbert Co., 151 F.2d 483 (9th Cir. 1945). However, the courts have been extremely reluctant to extend this principle to well-established organizations such as chambers of commerce or legitimate trade associations. NLRB v. American Pearl Button Co., 149 F.2d 311 (8th Cir. 1945); Matter of Fred P. Weissman Co., 69 N.L.R.B. 1002 (1946), 18 L.R.R.M. 1282; NLRB v. Mylan-Sparta Co., 166 F.2d 485 (6th Cir. 1948).

In a number of cases the Board has found employers guilty of unfair labor practices because of activities of local police; but the courts have refused to enforce the Board's orders. In a recent case, Matter of Bibb Mfg. Co., 82 N.L.R.B. 338, 23 L.R.R.M. 1557 (1949), the Board found that

> . . . [U]pon the advent of union organization in early July 1946, at the Respondent's Porterdale mills, the police force was augmented by the employment of two additional policemen. This 40% augmentation of the police force was utilized primarily in openly trailing the organizers of the Union in their every move within Porterdale, and in a few instances in following the Respondent's employees returning from union meetings. . . .
>
> The town of Porterdale was incorporated under the laws of Georgia a number of years ago. However, despite this act of incorporation, Porterdale remains in effect a "company town." All its property, excepting a railroad right-of-way and churches which the Respondent donated to the various religious congregations, is owned by the Respondent. All of Porterdale's utilities and public services, excepting police protection and education, are controlled directly by the Respondent. The municipal officers of Porterdale, including the mayor, are, like most other Porterdale inhabitants, employees of the Respondent. By virtue of this dominant landlord-employer position, the Respondent effectively controls the civic life of Porterdale . . .
>
> The background evidence in this case shows a flagrant intervention by the Respondent in the affairs of the Porterdale police force in 1934, during the last attempt at intense organizational activity among the Respondent's Porterdale employees and during the occasion of a strike among such

employees. Board witness Reynolds credibly testified without contradiction that at that time, at the request of Respondent's officials, he left his job at one of the Respondent's Porterdale mills, reported to the mayor of Porterdale who swore him in as an armed member of the Porterdale police force, and reported back to the Respondent's general overseer from whom for a period of 2 months he received instructions as to the performance of his police functions aimed at breaking up the existing strike. It should be noted that the policemen who were added to the police force in 1946 also worked for the Respondent immediately before joining the police department; it should be also noted that in 1934, as well as in 1946, the time of the alleged unfair labor practices herein, Will Ivey was mayor of Porterdale.

The record also shows that the Respondent habitually used the facilities of the Porterdale police department to serve eviction notices on employees, obviously a non-police service beneficial to the Respondent. As detailed in the Intermediate Report, a principal actor in this respect was the Respondent's house agent, Will Ivey, the same man who served as mayor of Porterdale and who, in the latter capacity, had complete authority over the police department. So far as the record shows, no person other than the Respondent was in a position to or did use the police department in such a manner.

Finally, there is evidence of a close nexus between the Respondent and the police department with respect to the surveillance here in question. As set forth in the Intermediate Report, Snow, the Respondent's Porterdale plant superintendent, was publicly observed on several occasions in an official Porterdale police car in the company of police officers who were cruising the public streets for the purpose of observing union activities. We are not persuaded by Snow's denial that he personally was not engaging in surveillance or that he was unaware that the police officers were engaging in such activity at that time, in view of his frank admission that it was common knowledge among the residents of Porterdale that the police were trailing union organizers. We are convinced that the Respondent, by this activity of Snow, utilized an instrumentality of the police arm of the municipality of Porterdale to engage in the surveillance of union activity in violation of Section 8 (1) of the Act. We further find, as did the Trial Examiner, that by Snow's association with the police officers on a mission of surveillance, the Respondent made it reasonably clear to the employees that this illegal police activity was for and on its behalf. . . . [Id. at 342–345.]

In spite of these facts, the Circuit Court of Appeals concluded that "the Board's findings in this regard are unwarranted, and without substantial support or foundation in the record." NLRB v. Bibb Mfg. Co., 188 F.2d 825 (5th Cir. 1951). See also NLRB v. Russell Mfg. Co., 187 F.2d 296 (5th Cir. 1951).

If the individual or organization is "acting as an agent of the employer," then the cease and desist order may be directed against it. NLRB v. Sun Tent-Luebbert Co., 151 F.2d 483 (9th Cir. 1945). However, if the person is not shown to be an agent of the employer, the processes of the Board cannot run against him regardless of the viciousness of his acts. NLRB v. Russell Mfg. Co., supra. If the organization is found to be an agent it still may escape where it has limited itself to antiunion propaganda by claiming protection under the free speech clause of Section 8(c). NLRB v. Salant & Salant Inc., 183 F.2d 462 (6th Cir. 1950).

E. Discrimination in Employment

EDWARD G. BUDD MANUFACTURING CO. v. NLRB
United States Court of Appeals, Third Circuit, 1943
138 F.2d 86

BIGGS, C.J.: . . . The complaint, as subsequently amended, alleges that the petitioner, in September, 1933, created and foisted a labor organization, known as the Budd Employee Representation Association, upon its employees and thereafter contributed financial support to the Association, and dominated its activities. The amended complaint also alleges that in July, 1941, the petitioner discharged an employee, Walter Weigand, because of his activities on behalf of the union . . .

The case of Walter Weigand is extraordinary. If ever a workman deserved summary discharge it was he. He was under the influence of liquor while on duty. He came to work when he chose and he left the plant and his shift as he pleased. In fact, a foreman on one occasion was agreeably surprised to find Weigand at work and commented upon it. Weigand amiably stated that he was enjoying it. He brought a woman (apparently generally known as the "Duchess") to the rear of the plant yard and introduced some of the employees to her. He took another employee to visit her and when this man got too drunk to be able to go home, punched his time-card for him and put him on the table in the representatives' meeting room in the plant in order to sleep off his intoxication. Weigand's immediate superiors demanded again and again that he be discharged, but each time higher officials intervened on Weigand's behalf because as was naively stated he was "a representative" (of the Association, found to be a dominated union). In return for not working at the job for which he was hired, the petitioner gave him full pay and on five separate occasions raised his wages. One of these raises was general; that is to say, Weigand profited by a general wage increase throughout the plant, but the other four raises were given Weigand at times when other employees in the plant did not receive wage increases.

The petitioner contends that Weigand was discharged because of cumulative grievances against him. But about the time of the discharge it was suspected by some of the representatives that Weigand had joined the complaining CIO union. One of the representatives taxed him with this fact and Weigand offered to bet a hundred dollars that it could not be proved. On July 22, 1941, Weigand did disclose his union membership to the vice-chairman (Rattigan) of the Association and to another representative (Mullen) and apparently tried to persuade them to support the union. Weigand asserts that the next day he, with Rattigan and Mullen, were seen talking to CIO organizer Reichwein on a street corner. The following day, according to Weigand's testimony, Mullen came to Weigand at the plant and stated that he, Mullen, had just had an interview with Personnel Director McIlvain and Plant Manager Mahan. According to Weigand, Mullen said to him, "Maybe you didn't get me in a jam." And, "We were seen down there." The following day Weigand was discharged.

As this court stated in National Labor Relations Board v. Condenser Corp., supra, 3 Cir. 128 F.2d at page 75, an employer may discharge an employee for a good reason, a poor reason or no reason at all so long as the provisions of the National Labor Relations Act are not violated. It is, of course, a violation to discharge an employee because he has engaged in activities on behalf of a union. Conversely an employer may retain an employee for a good reason, a bad reason or no reason at all and the reason is not a concern of the Board. But it is certainly too great a strain on our credulity to assert, as does the petitioner, that Weigand

was discharged for an accumulation of offenses.   We think that
he was discharged because his work on behalf of the CIO had
become known to the plant manager.   That ended his sinecure
at the Budd plant.   The Board found that he was discharged
because of his activities on behalf of the union.   The record
shows that the Board's finding was based on sufficient evidence. . . .

NOTES

1. NLRB v. Ford Bros., 170 F.2d 735 (6th Cir. 1948).   "The
Respondents strenuously urge upon us that the finding that the
discharge of Pancake was discriminatory and motivated by his
union activity is not supported by the evidence.   They rely upon
a company rule forbidding employees to drain gasoline from the
trailers, the undenied fact that Pancake violated this rule, testimony of Wilbur Ford that he discharged Pancake for violating
the rule and because of Pancake's testimony that he was fired solely
because of taking gasoline.   The evidence is not convincing that
even conceding that such a rule had been at one time promulgated
by the Respondents, it had been brought to the attention of Pancake individually or the drivers generally.   In any event, the great
preponderance of the evidence shows that such a rule, even if in
existence, was not enforced, but was openly and continuously
violated by the drivers with the knowledge and implied consent
of the Respondents . . .   It appears well established by the evidence before the Board that Pancake's discharge, for the reason
given, was not justified.   Wilbur Ford's testimony that that was
the sole reason for his discharge is not conclusive on the issue.
The probative value of such testimony was for the Board.   If it
is substantially contradicted by the other evidence and the accompanying circumstances, the Board is not required to accept it.
Nor does the fact that Pancake, called as a witness for the Petitioner, testified that he knew of no reason for his discharge other
than his taking gasoline, preclude the Petitioner from showing
that another reason existed.   The Board, in view of all the
evidence, was justified in rejecting Respondents' claim that the
discharge was solely because of the gasoline incident.   Whether
Pancake's discharge was for his union activity is another question.   Considering his long experience and satisfactory work as a
driver, it is clear that it was not for inefficiency.   Nor do Respondents so claim.   In view of the Respondents' general antiunion attitude over the preceding few years, the imminence of

compulsory collective bargaining with the Union with the probable resulting increase in its influence among the employees, and Pancake's activity in that respect, the inference drawn by the Board that Pancake's discharge was motivated by such union activities is not an unreasonable one. Such inferences are for the Board, not for the Court, to make, and, if supported by the evidence, are not to be set aside even if a contrary inference is possible, or would have been drawn by the Court."

2. It was said in Fairchild Cafeteria, 92 N.L.R.B. 809, 27 L.R.R.M. 1165 (1950): "The employer is at all times free to discharge an employee, for any reason or for no reason, provided only that the discharge is not for the purpose of encouraging or discouraging union membership, or does not have the effect of otherwise interfering with, restraining, or coercing employees in the exercise of the rights guaranteed in Section 7 of the Act." See NLRB, 16th Ann. Rep. 162 (1951).

3. In Matter of Majestic Metal Specialties, 92 N.L.R.B. 1854, 27 L.R.R.M. 1332 (1951), the employer ordered a local union employee transferred to a different department because the non-union employees in his department refused to work with him. He refused to accept the transfer and left the plant. The Board held that the employer in yielding to the antiunion sentiments of the employees discriminated against the union member because of his union activities. The illegal transfer amounted to a constructive discharge. But see NLRB v. Edinburg Citrus Assn., 147 F.2d 353 (5th Cir. 1945). Will the employer be held responsible if he knowingly permits the ouster of employees by a union or antiunion group? See Matter of Randolph Corp., 89 N.L.R.B. 1490, 26 L.R.R.M. 1127 (1950); NLRB v. Weissman Co., 170 F.2d 952 (6th Cir. 1948).

4. Union-security provisions obviously discriminate on the basis of union membership and would violate Section 8 (a) (3) were it not for the proviso permitting a union shop. If the union-security agreement is not in strict compliance with the proviso, its very presence in the contract is an interference with the right of free organization, and every discharge under it is discriminatory. The scope of the proviso has been discussed in detail in conjunction with the other material on union security at page 475 supra. Even the urging of such a contract on a company is an unfair labor practice under Section 8 (b) (2). Matter of Mackay Radio & Telegraph Co., 96 N.L.R.B. 740, 28 L.R.R.M. 1579 (1951).

5. Is it an unfair labor practice for an employer to discharge a supervisor because he refused to report union activities of rank-

and-file employees; refused to discharge an employee for union activity; or refused in other ways to cooperate with the employer's program of unlawful interference? See Matter of Inter-City Advertising Co., 89 N.L.R.B. 1103, 26 L.R.R.M. 1065 (1950); Matter of Irving Weissman, 27 L.R.R.M. 1539 (1951); Matter of Salant & Salant, Inc., 92 N.L.R.B. 343, 27 L.R.R.M. 1092 (1950). Can a supervisor be discharged for membership or activity on behalf of a rank-and-file union? See NLRB v. Inter-City Advertising Co., 190 F.2d 420 (4th Cir. 1951).

NOTE ON WHAT CONSTITUTES "CONCERTED ACTIVITIES"

Section 7 of the Labor Act declares the right of employees "to engage in other concerted activities for the purpose of collective bargaining or other mutual aid or protection." Section 8 (a) (1) makes it an unfair practice for an employer "to interfere with . . . the exercise of the rights guaranteed in Section 7." Thus the definition of "concerted activities" becomes material. Joining a union, attending meetings, seeking to discuss terms of employment, and participating in a strike are clearly "concerted activities." Other conduct, however, may create problems.

To constitute concerted action, it is not necessary to act through a union as long as it is for "mutual aid and protection." In NLRB v. Phoenix Mutual Life Insurance Co., 167 F.2d 983 (7th Cir. 1948), ten insurance salesmen signed a letter objecting to the employer's policy of hiring an untrained person as cashier because of the confusion and loss of time they suffered during the training period. The employer discharged them for making this protest. The court upheld the Board's finding that this constituted discrimination in employment because of concerted action for mutual aid and protection. In Matter of Ohio Oil Co., 92 N.L.R.B. 1597, 27 L.R.R.M. 1283 (1951), two employees informally protested the elimination of overtime work. Although they had no authorization from the other employees, the Board found them acting on a matter of common concern and within the protection of the Act. See also Matter of Modern Motors Inc., 96 N.L.R.B. 964, 28 L.R.R.M. 1618 (1951). In NLRB v. Nu-Car Carriers, 189 F.2d 756 (3rd Cir. 1951), it was held that a meeting of dissident union members which had as its purpose to obtain a change in the union's policy in collective bargaining constituted concerted action.

The employee's conduct, to be protected, "must be directed toward the collective bargaining process." Thus in Joanna Cotton Mills v. NLRB, 176 F.2d 749 (4th Cir. 1949), the court held that an employee who circulated a petition asking for removal of a foreman was not protected because it was merely a part of a personal vendetta between the employee and the foreman. It was not "for purposes of collective bargaining or other mutual aid and protection."   This principle was radically extended in NLRB v. Jamestown Veneer & Plywood Corp., 194 F.2d 192 (2d Cir. 1952). Two and a half hours before quitting time the employer notified four employees they would be laid off the next day for lack of work.   They thereupon quit without finishing the shift.   After the layoff period was over the employer refused to reinstate them because they had walked off the job.   They claimed they quit as a protest against the short notice of layoff and were, therefore, engaged in "concerted activity."   The court held the discharge did not violate Section 8 (a) (3).   They did not seek revocation of the notice and there was no pending dispute as to the length of notice.   Their leaving was only a protest and "had nothing to do with collective bargaining or other mutual aid or protection either past or future."

There is still uncertainty as to the right of a union member to refuse to cross a picket line.   If the union which represents him pickets the plant in which he works, the refusal to cross is protected activity.   Matter of West Coast Casket Co., 97 N.L.R.B. No. 108, 29 L.R.R.M. 1147 (1951).   In Matter of Cyril de Cordova & Bros., 91 N.L.R.B. 1121, 26 L.R.R.M. 1628 (1950) an employee of a brokerage firm was discharged for refusing to enter the Stock Exchange building on an errand because it would require crossing a picket line placed there by the union of which he was a member.   The Board found this was a discharge for "assistance to a labor organization."   However, in NLRB v. Illinois Bell Telephone Co., 189 F.2d 124 (7th Cir. 1951), eight employees who refused to cross a picket line placed around the telephone exchanges were demoted.   The court held that since they were not represented by this union, but worked in a separate bargaining unit represented by another union this was not for "mutual aid and protection." [17a]

Section 7 was amended by adding a provision guaranteeing employees the right to refrain from engaging in concerted activities.   In Matter of Printz Leather Co., 94 N.L.R.B. 1312, 28 L.R.R.M. 1198 (1951), the Union threatened to strike unless the employer discharged one employee who had refused to cooperate

---

[17a] In NLRB v. Rockaway News Supply Co., Inc., — U.S. — , 73 Sup. Ct. 519, — L. Ed. — (1953), discharge for refusing to cross a picket line was held not to be an unfair labor practice where the collective agreement required the employees to cross such picket lines as were involved in the case.

in a slowdown. When the employer complied, the Board held both him and the Union guilty of an unfair labor practice under Sections 8 (a) (3) and 8 (b) (2). The Union was engaged in concerted activity and the employee was discharged for exercising his right to refrain from engaging therein.

Suppose the employer dismisses a man whom he believes to be engaged in "concerted activities" but who in fact is not? Is the discharge any the less an unfair practice? New York Telephone Co., 89 N.L.R.B. 383, 25 L.R.R.M. 1570 (1950). What evil does the Act seek to prevent: employer's action or bad motives? Elimination of union leaders? Intimidation? Would it matter that none of the employees knew the discharge was for supposed concerted activities?

But it should be noted that not all concerted activity receives the protection of the Act, for in certain instances more insistent policies may prevail. Thus, strikers who engage in strikes for illegal purposes, or who engage in violence on the picket line may be subject to discharge. These problems will be dealt with in detail in later sections.

PHELPS DODGE CORP. *v.* NLRB
Supreme Court of the United States, 1941
313 U.S. 177, 61 Sup. Ct. 845, 85 L. Ed. 1271

MR. JUSTICE FRANKFURTER delivered the opinion of the Court:
The dominating question which this litigation brings here for the first time is whether an employer subject to the National Labor Relations Act may refuse to hire employees solely because of their affiliations with a labor union. Subsidiary questions grow out of this central issue relating to the means open to the Board to "effectuate the policies of this Act," if it finds such discrimination in hiring an "unfair labor practice." Other questions touching the remedial powers of the Board are also involved. . . .

. . . The basis of the Board's conclusion that the Corporation had committed unfair labor practices in violation of §8 (3) of the Act was a finding, not challenged here, that a number of men had been refused employment because of their affiliations with the Union. Of these men, two, Curtis and Daugherty, had ceased to be in the Corporation's employ before the strike but sought employment after its close. The others, thirty-eight in number, were strikers. To "effectuate the policies" of the Act, §10 (c), the Board ordered the Corporation to offer Curtis and Daugherty jobs and to make them whole for the loss of pay resulting from the refusal to hire them, and it ordered thirty-seven of the strikers reinstated with back pay, and the other striker made whole for loss in wages up to the time he became unemployable. . . .

First. The denial of jobs to men because of union affiliations is an old and familiar aspect of American industrial relations. Therefore, in determining whether such discrimination legally survives the National Labor Relations Act, the history which led to the Act and the aims which infuse it give direction to our inquiry. . . .

It is no longer disputed that workers cannot be discharged from employment because of their union affiliations. Is the national interest in industrial peace less affected by discrimination against union activity when men are hired? The contrary is overwhelmingly attested by the long history of industrial conflicts, the diagnosis of their causes by official investigations, the conviction of public men, industrialists and scholars. . . .

. . . Discrimination against union labor in the hiring of men is a dam to self-organization at the source of supply. The effect of such discrimination is not confined to the actual denial of employment; it inevitably operates against the whole idea of the legitimacy of organization. In a word, it undermines the principle which, as we have seen, is recognized as basic to the attainment of industrial peace. . . .

. . . Section 8 (3) is the foundation of the Board's determination that in refusing employment to the two men because of their union affiliations Phelps Dodge violated the Act. And so we turn to its provisions that "It shall be an unfair labor practice for an employer . . . By discrimination in regard to hire or tenure of employment or any term or condition of employment to encourage or discourage membership in any labor organization."

Unlike mathematical symbols, the phrasing of such social legislation as this seldom attains more than approximate precision of definition. That is why all relevant aids are summoned to determine meaning. Of compelling consideration is the fact that words acquire scope and function from the history of events which they summarize. We have seen the close link between a bar to employment because of union affiliation and the opportunities of labor organizations to exist and to prosper. Such an embargo against employment of union labor was notoriously one of the chief obstructions to collective bargaining through self-organization. Indisputably the removal of such obstructions was the driving force behind the enactment of the National Labor Relations Act. The prohibition against "discrimination in regard to hire" must be applied as a means toward the accomplishment of the main object of the legislation. We are asked to read "hire" as meaning the wages paid to an employee so as to make the statute merely forbid discrimination in one of the terms of men who have secured employment. So to read the statute would do violence to a spontaneous textual reading of §8 (3) in that "hire" would serve no function because, in the sense which is urged upon us, it is included in the prohibition against "discrimination in regard to . . . any term or condition of employment." Contemporaneous legislative history, and, above all, the background of industrial experience, forbid such textual mutilation.

Second. Since the refusal to hire Curtis and Daugherty solely because of their affiliation with the Union was an unfair labor practice under §8 (3), the remedial authority of the Board under §10 (c) became operative. Of course it could issue, as it did, an order "to cease and desist from such unfair labor practice" in the future. Did Congress also empower the Board to order the employer to undo the wrong by offering the men discriminated against the opportunity for employment which should not have been denied them?

Reinstatement is the conventional correction for discriminatory discharges. Experience having demonstrated that discrimination in hiring is twin to discrimination in firing, it would indeed be surprising if Congress gave a remedy for the one which it denied for the other. The powers of the Board as well as the restrictions upon it must be drawn from §10 (c), which directs the Board "to take such affirmative action, including reinstatement of employees with or without back pay, as will effectuate the policies of this Act." It could not be seriously denied that to require discrimination in hiring or firing to be "neutralized," Labor Board v. Mackay Co., 304 U.S. 333, 348, by requiring the discrimination to cease not abstractly but in the concrete victimizing instances, is an "affirmative action" which "will effectuate the policies of this Act." Therefore, if §10 (c) had empowered the Board to "take such affirmative action as will effectuate the policies of this Act," the right to restore to a man employment which was wrongfully denied him could hardly be doubted. . . . To differentiate between discrimination in denying employment and in terminating it, would be a differentiation not only without substance but in defiance of that against which the prohibition of discrimination is directed. . . .

But, we are told, this is precisely the differentiation Congress has made. It has done so, the argument runs, by not directing the Board "to take such affirmative action as will effectuate the policies of this Act," simpliciter, but, instead, by empowering the

Board "to take such affirmative action, including reinstatement of employees with or without back pay, as will effectuate the policies of this Act." To attribute such a function, to the participial phrase introduced by "including" is to shrivel a versatile principle to an illustrative application. [Third: Since strangers might be ordered rehired, a fortiori strikers might be too.]

Fourth. There remain for consideration the limitations upon the Board's power to undo the effects of discrimination. Specifically, we have the question of the Board's power to order employment in cases where the men discriminated against had obtained "substantially equivalent employment." . . .

The specific provisions of the Act out of which the proper conclusion is to be drawn, should be before us. Section 10 (c), as we already know, authorizes the Board "to take such affirmative action, including reinstatement of employees with or without back pay, as will effectuate the policies of this Act." The relevant portions of §2 (3) follow: "The term 'employee' shall include any employee, and shall not be limited to the employees of a particular employer, unless the Act explicitly states otherwise, and shall include any individual whose work has ceased as a consequence of, or in connection with, any current labor dispute or because of any unfair labor practice, and who has not obtained any other regular and substantially equivalent employment." . . .

Denial of the Board's power to order opportunities of employment in this situation derives wholly from an infiltration of a portion of §2 (3) into §10 (c). The argument runs thus: §10 (c) specifically refers to "reinstatement of employees"; the latter portion of §2 (3) refers to an "employee" as a person "who has not obtained any other regular and substantially equivalent employment"; therefore, there can be no reinstatement of an employee who has obtained such employment. The syllogism is perfect. But this is a bit of verbal logic from which the meaning of things has evaporated. In the first place, we have seen that the Board's power to order an opportunity for employment does not derive from the phrase "including reinstatement of employees with or without back pay," and is not limited by it. Secondly, insofar as any argument is to be drawn from the reference to "employees" in §10 (c), it must be noted that the reference is to "employees," unqualified and undifferentiated. To circumscribe the general class, "employees," we must find authority either in the policy of the Act or in some specific delimiting provision of it.

The reference in §2 (3) to workers who have "obtained regular and substantially equivalent employment" has a role consonant with some purposes of the Act but not one destructive of the broad definition of "employee" with which §2 (3) begins. In determining whether an employer has refused to bargain collectively with the representatives of "his employees" in violation of §8 (5) and §9 (a) it is of course essential to determine who constitute "his employees." One aspect of this is covered by §9 (b) which provides for determination of the appropriate bargaining unit. And once the unit is selected, the reference in §2 (3) to workers who have obtained equivalent employment comes into operation in determining who shall be treated as employees within the unit.

To deny the Board power to neutralize discrimination merely because workers have obtained compensatory employment would confine the "policies of this Act" to the correction of private injuries. The Board was not devised for such a limited function. It is the agency of Congress for translating into concreteness the purpose of safeguarding and encouraging the right of self-organization. The Board, we have held very recently, does not exist for the "adjudication of private rights"; it "acts in a public capacity to give effect to the declared public policy of the Act to eliminate and prevent obstructions to interstate commerce by encouraging collective bargaining." National Licorice Co. v. Labor Board, 309 U.S. 350, 362; and see Amalgamated Utility Workers v. Edison Co., 309 U.S. 261. To be sure, reinstatement is not needed to repair the economic loss of a worker who, after discrimination, has obtained an equally profitable job. But to limit the significance of discrimination merely to questions of monetary loss to workers would thwart the central purpose of the Act, directed as that is toward the achievement and maintenance of workers' self-organization. That there are factors other than loss of wages to a particular worker to be considered is suggested even by a meager knowledge of industrial affairs. Thus, to give only one illustration, if men were discharged who were leading efforts at organization in a plant having a low wage scale, they would not unnaturally be compelled by their economic circumstances to seek and obtain employment elsewhere at equivalent wages. In such a situation, to deny the Board power to wipe out the prior discrimination by ordering the employment of such workers would sanction a most effective way of defeating the right of self-organization.

[The Board has the power to order employment if it finds that this will "effectuate the purpose of the Act." This adaptation of the remedy to the end is left to the discretion of the Board. However, the Board here made no finding that this order would effectuate the purposes of the Act. It determined only the dry legal question of its power, not the propriety of its exercise. The Board must disclose the basis of its order and give clear indication that it has exercised the discretion with which Congress has empowered it.]

Fifth. As part of its remedial action against the unfair labor practices, the Board ordered that workers who had been denied employment be made whole for their loss of pay. In specific terms, the Board ordered payment to the men of a sum equal to what they normally would have earned from the date of the discrimination to the time of employment less their earnings during this period. The court below added a further deduction of amounts which the workers "failed without excuse to earn," and the Board here challenges this modification.

Making the workers whole for losses suffered on account of an unfair labor practice is part of the vindication of the public policy which the Board enforces. Since only actual losses should be made good, it seems fair that deductions should be made not only for actual earnings by the worker but also for losses which he willfully incurred. To this the Board counters that to apply this abstractly just doctrine of mitigation of damages to the situations before it, often involving substantial numbers of workmen, would put on the Board details too burdensome for effective administration. Simplicity of administration is thus the justification for deducting only actual earnings and for avoiding the domain of controversy as to wages that might have been earned.

But the advantages of a simple rule must be balanced against the importance of taking fair account, in a civilized legal system, of every socially desirable factor in the final judgment. The Board, we believe, overestimates the administrative difficulties and underestimates its administrative resourcefulness. Here again we must avoid the rigidities of an either-or-rule. The remedy of back pay, it must be remembered, is entrusted to the Board's discretion; it is not mechanically compelled by the Act. And in applying its authority over back pay orders, the Board has not used stereotyped formulas but has availed itself of the freedom given it by Congress to attain just results in diverse complicate situations. See (1939) 48 Yale L.J. 1265. The Board has a wide discretion to keep the present matter within reasonable bounds through flexible procedural devices. The Board will thus have it within its power to avoid delays and difficulties incident to passing on remote and speculative claims by employers, while at the same time it may give appropriate weight to a clearly unjustifiable refusal to take desirable new employment. By leaving such an adjustment to the administrative process we have in

mind not so much the minimization of damages as the healthy
policy of promoting production and employment. . . .

[Justice Murphy and Justice Stone wrote separate dissenting
opinions. Chief Justice Hughes concurred in Justice Stone's
dissent.]

NOTES

1. The purpose of a back-pay order is not to penalize the employer but to make the employee whole for the discrimination
practiced against him. Therefore, he cannot recover for the
period during which he would have been laid off because of
a seasonal slack, NLRB v. Carolina Mills Inc., 190 F.2d 675 (4th
Cir. 1951); because of an economic strike, Matter of the Perfect
Circle Co., 70 N.L.R.B. 526, 18 L.R.R.M. 1385 (1946); Matter
of Federal Engineering Company, 60 N.L.R.B. 592, 15 L.R.R.M.
250 (1945); or because of illness, Matter of Ames-Harris Neville
Co., 67 N.L.R.B. 422, 17 L.R.R.M. 454 (1946).

The Board originally held that the entire earnings from other
employment should be deducted. However, in Matter of F. W.
Woolworth, 90 N.L.R.B. 289, 26 L.R.R.M. 1185 (1950), the
Board stated at page 291:

> . . . The cumulative experience of many years discloses
> that this form of remedial provision falls short of effectuating
> the basic purposes and policies of the Act. We have noted in
> numerous cases that employees, after having been unemployed
> for a lengthy period following their discriminatory discharges,
> have succeeded in obtaining employment at higher wages
> than they would have earned in their original employments.
> This, under the Board's previous form of back-pay order, re-
> sulted in the progressive reduction or complete liquidation of
> back pay due.
>
> The deleterious effect upon the companion remedy of
> reinstatement has been twofold. Some employers, on the
> one hand, have deliberately refrained from offering reinstate-
> ment, knowing that the greater the delay, the greater would
> be the reduction in back pay liability. Thus, a recalcitrant
> employer may continue to profit by excluding union adher-
> ence from his enterprise. Employees, on the other hand,
> faced with the prospect of steadily diminishing back pay,
> have frequently countered by waiving their right to rein-
> statement in order to toll the running of back pay and pre-
> serve the amount then owing. . . .
>
> The public interest in discouraging obstacles to industrial
> peace requires that we seek to bring about, in unfair labor

practice cases, "a restoration of the situation, as nearly as possible, to that which would have obtained but for the illegal discrimination." In order that this end may be effectively accomplished through the medium of reinstatement coupled with back pay, we shall order, in the case before us and in future cases, that the loss of pay be computed on a basis of each separate calendar quarter or portion thereof during the period from the Respondent's discriminatory action to the date of a proper offer of reinstatement. . . . Earnings in one particular quarter shall have no effect upon the back pay liability for any other quarter. . . .[17b]

Although the employee may be obligated to mitigate the damages by seeking other employment, Matter of Harvest Queen Mill & Elevator Co., 90 N.L.R.B. 320, 26 L.R.R.M. 1189 (1950), he need not accept a discriminating transfer, Matter of Kopman-Woracek Shoe Mfg., 66 N.L.R.B. 789, 17 L.R.R.M. 357 (1945).

2. In Republic Steel Corp. v. NLRB, 311 U.S. 7, 61 Sup. Ct. 77, 85 L. Ed. 6 (1940), the Board had ordered the employer to deduct amounts the employees had received from "work relief projects" and pay those amounts over to the appropriate governmental agencies. The Supreme Court held this order invalid as imposing a penalty on the employer in order to remedy an injury to the public. The Act is meant to remedy private injuries caused by conduct declared to be against public policy. It was not intended to vindicate public rights in other ways. Penalties cannot be imposed merely because they may deter violations.

In NLRB v. Gullett Gin Co., 340 U.S. 361, 71 Sup. Ct. 337, 95 L. Ed. 337 (1951), the Court held that the Board need not allow the employer to deduct unemployment compensation received by discharged employees, on the theory that this does not make the employees more than whole, for such compensation is a collateral benefit paid by the state. The fact that the order increases the employer's tax under the state statute because of a merit rating system, was not considered to constitute penalty inflicted by the Board. The Court, in a footnote, indicated that a state might require an employee to pay back to the state the unemployment compensation benefits received during the period for which back pay is awarded.

3. Has the Taft-Hartley Act in any way changed the Board's power to order reinstatement back pay? If an employer dis-

---

[17b] This policy was approved and its application to a discharge in a seasonal industry upheld in NLRB v. Seven-Up Bottling Co., 73 Sup. Ct. 287 (1953). — ED.

charges a supervisor who refuses to cooperate in unlawful anti-union activities, can the Board order the supervisor reinstated with back pay? Note that under Section 2 (3) a supervisor is not an "employee" and Section 10 (c) provides for reinstatement of "employees."

Section 10 (c) was amended to provide that the Board should not order reinstatement for back pay "if such individual was suspended or discharged for cause." If there is clear proof of just cause for discharge but the Board finds that this was used as a pretext for discharge and that the underlying motivation was union activity, can the Board order reinstatement with back pay? See NLRB v. Dixie Shirt Co., 176 F.2d 969 (4th Cir. 1949).

4. In a number of cases the employer has been placed in the dilemma of having to placate two rival unions. One union may strike to compel the employer to recognize it instead of the rival union, discharge all members of the rival union, or require all employees to join the striking union. If the employer resists, he cannot operate. If he succumbs, he will be guilty of an unfair labor practice and liable for back pay. NLRB v. Star Publishing Co., 97 F.2d 465 (9th Cir. 1938); NLRB v. Glueck Brewing Co., 144 F.2d 847 (8th Cir. 1944); Matter of Greer Steel Company, 38 N.L.R.B. 65, 9 L.R.R.M. 268 (1942). In only one case, where the employer succumbed to the irresistible pressure of a sit-down strike, did the Board give relief against the back pay liability. Matter of New York & Puerto Rico S.S. Co., 34 N.L.R.B. 1028, 9 L.R.R.M. 56 (1941).

In NLRB v. National Broadcasting Co., 150 F.2d 895 (2d Cir. 1945), the Musicians threatened to strike if the networks bargained with the union certified by NLRB for "platter turners." The Circuit Court, in enforcing the Board's order to the network to bargain with the certified union, suggested that if the Musicians persisted they could be held for contempt of court. The Musicians did not strike and this dictum was never tested.

Under the 1947 amendments, the action of the union in these cases would be a union unfair labor practice under Sections 8 (b) (2) and 8 (b) (4). Will this, however, free the employer from responsibility if he complies with the union's unlawful demands? Note the changes in Section 10 (c) empowering the Board to order the union to pay back pay. May the Board in these cases make the employer and union jointly liable? Compare Union Starch & Refining Co., 186 F.2d 1008 (7th Cir. 1951); Matter of Printz Leather Co., 94 N.L.R.B. 1312, 28 L.R.R.M. 1198 (1951).

F.   *The Right in Foreign Countries to Form and Join Combinations*

On the Continent, laws directed against combinations of artisans and workers have existed through the centuries.   The formation of and the participation in such combinations constituted a crime, which was punishable with imprisonment,[18] and even with death.[19] Political regimes of the authoritarian type — the Bourbon type as well as the twentieth-century Fascist, National-Socialist, and Communist types — have always disliked combinations of workers, because the latter obviously threaten their power.   Even the decrees of the French Revolution, known as Le Chapelier laws, like their British contemporaries, the Combination Acts of 1799 and 1800, struck at combinations of workers.   But, unlike the doctrine of preceding ages, they expressed a political philosophy of freedom of the individual, a freedom which was regarded as impaired by combinations with their implicit pressure.[20]   However, strangely enough, the "liberal period" — as the French called the period between 1789 and 1848 — exhibited on both sides of the English Channel much less zeal for the suppression of combinations of employers than of employees.[21]

In the wake of the Revolution of 1848, a right of association was recognized in the constitutions of several countries but this "natural right" did not clearly include freedom to combine. There were several reasons for this.

In the first place, the concept of "combination" comprises association of workers or employers for the promotion or defense of economic interests, while the idea implicit in "association" is cooperation for any purpose not criminal.   No wonder therefore that it took longer to repeal prohibitions against combinations than to recognize freedom of association.

Secondly, even after penal statutes against combinations had finally been repealed, for more than half a century "freedom" to combine was distinguished from a "right" to combine.[22]   In sev-

---

[18] In the Holy Roman Empire the National Police Order (*Reichspolizeiordnung*) of 1530 and subsequent national statutes were followed finally by the National Guild Order (*Reichszunftordnung*), 1731; in France various *ordonnances,* followed in the eighteenth century by those of 1749 and 1781, contained also the criminal sanctions.

[19] No association of twenty or more persons could exist — pursuant to Article 291 of the French Penal Code of 1810 — without a license.

[20] Rouast and Durand, Précis de législation industrielle, no. 12 (3d ed. 1948).

[21] Id. no. 20.

[22] Gaetcke, Vereinigungsfreiheit 18, 19 (1922).

eral countries, between 1860 and 1870, the stigma of criminality was removed,[23] but simultaneously with the repeal of the penal sanctions against strikes in 1864, France introduced a new crime into its Penal Code, called "attack on freedom to work." [24] This made unlawful any resort to threats or violence, assault and battery, fraud or plots, for the purpose of starting or continuing a work stoppage or for the purpose of restraining an individual's freedom to work. Other countries, such as Germany and Austria, likewise enacted this type of criminal legislation along with the repeal of criminal sanctions against the strike as such.[25] Germany repealed this legislation immediately after the Armistice in 1918,[26] whereas France and many of the Austrian succession states kept it on their statute books. The dominant opinion in Germany is that a general criminal law against assault, extortion, and slander supplies sufficient sanctions against the use of illegal means during a work stoppage caused by a strike or lockout.

Moreover, the freedom from prosecution for joining a combination was not identical with the right to participate in a combination, i.e., legal protection against private impairment of the right. After combinations became lawful, discharge by an employer of his employee because of the latter's organizational activities still remained lawful, and a stipulation by which an employee was prohibited from joining an organization — what here we call a "yellow dog" contract — was still valid.

All this changed in Germany after the First World War. The new (Weimar) constitution proclaimed a right to combine,[27] with the result that "yellow dog" agreements were outlawed, and discharge — with or without a period of notice — because of the employee's organizational activities became illegal.[28]

Likewise the Swedish Act of 1936, "on the right to associate and to bargain" declares "that the right to combine shall be inviolate." [29] An amendment to the Act, enacted in 1940, defines the

[23] In England, following the Combination Act of 1825 (6 Geo. IV, c. 129), combinations were, practically speaking, allowed, and the Trade Union Act of 1871 (34 & 35 Vict. c. 31) added legal protection against any attempt to suppress them; even so, agreements incidental to them lack enforceability. Criminal immunity has been granted, particularly by the Conspiracy and Protection Act of 1875.

[24] *Atteinte à la liberté du travail.* Penal Code, arts. 414, 415.

[25] Germany: Industrial Code (1869), sec. 153; Austria: Combination Act (1870), sec. 3.

[26] Order of Council of Nov. 12, 1918.

[27] Constitution (Weimar) 1919, art. 153, now Basic Law (Bonn) 1949, art. 9 (3).

[28] Supreme Labor Court, 6 Bensh. Slg. no. 27 (1929).

[29] Act of Sept. 11, 1936, (1936) Fslg. no. 506.

right to combine as "the right of every employer and every employee to join an association for the defense of his interests in the employment relationship, to enjoy the associative benefits and to work on behalf of such an association." [30]

The Swedish Labor Court not only reached the same results as the German in the instances mentioned, but found many other situations to constitute violations of the right of association. Thus, an agreement automatically reducing an employee's pay upon his becoming a member of a union has been held violative of the right of association, and the union may claim, in its own right, damages for any violation; also it may sue on behalf of the employee — its member — whose right of association has been violated.[31]

After the Second World War, the French Constitution of 1946 and the Italian Constitution of 1947 created guarantees for an "individual's right to defend his interests by trade-union action." [32] By French law an organization can bring a damage action in its own behalf and in the name of its member concerned where the breach of the right to combine occurred during the term of a collective contract.[33]

The object of both our Labor Relations Acts and those foreign constitutions and statutes, is to protect the right to engage in concerted actions for the promotion and defense of economic interests. The main difference lies in the remedy. In the United States and in Canada [34] a violation of the right constitutes a public wrong, an unfair labor practice, while in the civil law countries it is an actionable tort triable before the labor courts.

German courts, for example, will repress any violation of the right to combine by granting the plaintiff back pay as pecuniary damages and reinstatement. But for an economic strike no such relief is obtainable, as in American law. The cease and desist order has also its analogue in German law, for the latter provides for an action for restraint (*Unterlassungsklage*). The union as plaintiff in such an action can ask for a judgment enjoining the defendant from continuing conduct which violates the right of

---

[30] Act of May 17, 1940, (1940) Fslg. no. 332.

[31] Robbins, The Government of Labor Relations in Sweden 307, 313 (1942).

[32] France: Constitution, 1946, Preamble, cl. 5; Italy: Constitution, 1947, art. 39 (1).

[33] Labor Code, bk. I, tit. II, c. IV bis, art. 31r–31t.

[34] Canadian Industrial Relations and Disputes Investigation Act (1948), 11 & 12 Geo. VI, c. 54, ss. 3–5, 40, 46 (1).

combination, such as black-listing persons who are active in organizational work or persistently refusing to employ plaintiff's
members.[35]   Incidentally, the request for such relief may be
asserted also in the form of an ex parte petition for an injunction.[36]

Do these observations on the similarity between North American and European legal approaches also hold good for the law
of Soviet Russia?   The latter does not reveal any similarity.   In
that country union and management are considered as a team,
each having as its *raison d'être* the achievement of production
quotas set up for the effectuation of a centralized plan decreed by
highest authority.   Costs, scales of wages, and working conditions
for each plant are dictated by the Council of Ministers.   The
unions are required to assist the programs of the government and
cannot, therefore, change the wage scales and other conditions.
The promotion of economic interests of the employees does not
lie within the allowable area of "union" activities.[37]   The use of
the word "unions" cannot hide the fact that such concerted actions are out of the question.

Quasi-authoritarian regimes such as we see in Latin American
countries do not completely forbid strikes but regulate them by
administrative decree.   Strikers are protected pending the decision on the legality of the strike.   Thus, statutes in Ecuador
(1936) and Salvador (1946) require the civil and police authorities to ensure that the right to strike is respected.   If the administrative agency holds that the strike is "illegal," the strikers
must return to work.   Similar provisions are contained in the
Act of the Dominican Republic (1934).[38]   When the decision is
in favor of a strike, then the law throws its full support on the
side of the strikers.   Thus the Labor Code of Panama enjoins an
employer during the strike from entering into new employment

[35] 2 Hueck and Nipperdey, On Labor Law 434, 435, and 592 (1930) (in
German).

[36] See E. J. Cohn in Manual of German Law, vol. I, p. 107 (London,
Foreign Office, 1950).

[37] Note, Collective Bargaining in the Soviet Union, 62 Harv. L. Rev. 1191
(1949). Schlesinger, Justice in Russia: A Dissent, 60 Yale L.J. 976, 985 n.30.
(1951).

[38] In Bolivia, only an "exclusively peaceful suspension of work" can constitute a lawful strike; nor may a strike be validly declared until conciliation and
arbitration have failed and the government conciliation bureau has rendered
a decision, three quarters of the "total number of workers actually employed"
have voted to approve the strike, and a copy of the vote plus the names of
all who favor it has been transmitted to the political authorities and the labor
inspectors.   Infractions may be punished by heavy penalties.   (Busch Labor
Code (1942), secs. 114, 117, and 119).

relationships.[39]   The provisions in the laws of Salvador, Guatemala, and Colombia are similar.   They contain, in addition, a
direction to the administrative authorities to issue decrees ordering the shutdown of plants affected by "legal" strikes.[40]   Several
not only forbid the hiring of strike replacements and the carrying out of plant operations but also burden the employer whose
conduct (unfair practice) has caused the outbreak of the dispute
with the obligation to pay wages to the strikers.[41]

III. Legal Limitations on Unions

A. *Introductory Note*

The common law, while leaving employers unrestrained in
their use of economic force, placed severe limitations on unions.
Originally the courts considered unions illegal combinations obstructing the free play of economic forces in the labor market.
Any concerted action by workers to better their conditions was
unlawful.   This doctrine was repudiated in the famous case of
Commonwealth v. Hunt, 4 Metc. 111 (Mass. 1842), and was
eventually abandoned by the courts.

Although unions came to be recognized as legal combinations,
they were not permitted the same freedom as employers to use
their economic strength.   The courts rigidly circumscribed their
activities, practically frustrating any effective action.   Only gradually was the area of freedom extended, as the judicial attitude
toward unions changed.   The legal limitations on unions, therefore, consist primarily of judge-made rules.   Legislation has
sought to alleviate the harshness of those limitations.   This is
in direct contrast to the limitations on employers which are almost
solely legislative in origin.

The courts, in defining the boundaries of union action, have
attempted to rationalize their decisions by adapting certain basic
theories of legal liability.   The earliest theory was based on the
common law concept of criminal conspiracy — that aggressive conduct which was lawful when done by an individual might be un-

[39] Labor Code (1947), Act of 1947 (Gaceta official, Nov. 26, No. 10459),
sec. 318.   There are some exceptions, e.g., for public utilities or indispensable
operations in the plant.

[40] Salvador: Act 1946 (Dec. 2, 1946), sec. 12; Guatemala: Labor Code
(1947) (Feb. 8, Decree No. 330), sec. 255; Colombia: Act No. 6 of 1945,
sec. 54.

[41] Cf. Guatemala: Labor Code (1947) (Feb. 8, Decree No. 330), sec. 242;
Panama: Labor Code (1947), Act of 1947 (Gaceta oficial, Nov. 26, No. 10459),
sec. 325 (limiting the imputability).

lawful when engaged in by two or more persons joined together. Applied in its extreme form, this theory made all concerted action illegal and collective bargaining impossible. The second, and perhaps most important theory was the doctrine of prima facie tort — that injury intentionally inflicted was actionable unless justified. Under this theory any union action was illegal which the courts found unjustified. Joined with these two major theories were two subsidiary ones which made illegal those combinations that were in restraint of trade, and conduct inducing breach of contract. These theories now receive relatively little explicit attention by the courts, because the substantial body of precedents built upon them makes resort to underlying principles unnecessary. However, these theories are still important, for the central core of each remains. The legality of conduct may still depend on whether it can be characterized as concerted or individual action, on what may be considered its justification, and on the extent to which it induces breach of contract or tends to restrain trade. In this connection, compare the opinion of Editor, J., in the Enterprise case, page 4 supra.

These theories, however, do not decide concrete cases, for they provide no clear lines to separate legality from illegality. Ultimately the problem is one of degree; one of weighing the facts in each case. This does not mean that the matter is left completely at large, for the result depends on subjective weighing of four basic factual elements: First, what objective is sought by the union? Does it seek higher wages, a closed shop, correction of unfair labor practices, or elimination of laborsaving devices? Second, what means does it use to achieve that objective? Does it call a strike, set up a picket line, engage in mass picketing, or boycott the employer's product? Third, against whom does it direct its economic pressure? Does it strike the employer himself, strike his suppliers of material, refuse to handle his goods in the hands of his customers, picket the retail outlets of his products, or refuse to buy the employer's product? Fourth, is the public interest so paramount that resort to economic force by the parties will not be tolerated?

Every exercise by the union of its economic strength inevitably involves these four factors, and the legality of union action depends upon a composite "weighing" of all of them. For the purposes of study and analysis, however, it is helpful to focus attention on one at a time. Therefore, the section on Strikes and Their Objectives will give primary attention to the lawfulness of particular objectives sought by unions. The section on Picketing and Free Speech will emphasize the importance of the means used in determining the legality of union action. The section on Secondary Boycotts will be devoted to the special problems created when the union's pressure is directed against someone other than the employer himself. The problems of the public interest will be considered throughout. The separate treatment of these factors should not be allowed to becloud the fact that defining the legal limitations on union action requires a careful interlacing of all of them.

B. *Unions and the Courts: Theories and Methods of Legal Control*

PHILADELPHIA CORDWAINERS' CASE
(COMMONWEALTH v. PULLIS)
Mayor's Court, 1806
3 Commons and Gilmore, A Documentary History of American Industrial Society 59–248 (1910)

[Indictment for conspiracy of several journeymen cordwainers. The indictment charged them with combining together in a society to refuse to work except at certain rates, to threaten and menace other cordwainers who worked at rates lower than those set, and to refuse to work for any employer who hired any cordwainer who did not abide by the rules of the society. The case, which was prosecuted in the Mayor's Court of Philadelphia, arose out of recurring strife between workmen and employers in the shoe industry and is commonly described as the "First American Labor Case." Recorder Levy, in his charge to the jury said, in part:]

An attempt has been made to show that the spirit of the revolution and the principle of the common law, are opposite in this case. That the common law, if applied in this case, would operate an attack upon the rights of men. The enquiry on that point, was unnecessary and improper. Nothing more was required than to ascertain what the law is. The law is the permanent rule, it is the will of the whole community. After that is discovered, whatever may be its spirit or tendency, it must be executed, and the most imperious duty demands our submission to it. . . .

It is proper to consider, is such a combination consistent with the principles of our law, or injurious to the public welfare? The usual means by which the prices of work are regulated, are the demand for the article and the excellence of its fabric. Where the work is well done, and the demand is considerable, the prices will necessarily be high. Where the work is ill done, and the demand is inconsiderable, they will unquestionably be low . . . To make an artificial regulation, is not to regard the excellence of the work or quality of the material, but to fix a positive and arbitrary price, governed by no standard, controlled by no impartial person, but dependent on the will of the few who are interested; this is the unnatural way of raising the price of goods or work. This is independent of the number of customers, or of the quality of the material, or of the number who are to do the work. It is an unnatural, artificial means of raising the price of work beyond its standard, and taking an undue advantage of the public. Is the rule of law bottomed upon such principles, as to permit or protect such conduct? Consider it on the footing of the general commerce of the city. Is there any man who can calculate (if this is tolerated) at what price he may safely contract to deliver articles, for which he may receive orders, if he is to be regulated by the journeymen in an arbitrary jump from one price to another? . . . Can he fix the price of his commodity for a future day? It is impossible that any man can carry on commerce in this way. There cannot be a large contract entered into, but what the contractor will make at his peril. He may be ruined by the difference of prices made by the journeymen in the intermediate time. What then is the operation of this kind of conduct upon the commerce of the city? It exposes it to inconveniences, if not to ruin; therefore, it is against the public welfare . . .

Consider these circumstances as they affect trade generally. Does this measure tend to make good workmen? No: it puts the botch incapable of doing justice to his work, on the level with the best tradesman. The master must give the same wages to each. Such a practice would take away all the excitement to excell in workmanship or industry. Consider the effect it would have upon the whole community. If the masters say they will not sell under certain prices, as the journeymen declare they will not work at certain wages, they, if persisted in, would put the whole body of the people into their power. Shoes and boots are articles of the first necessity. If they could stand out three of four weeks in winter, they might raise the price of boots to thirty, forty, or fifty dollars a pair, at least for some time, and until a competent supply could be got from other places. In every point of view, this measure is pregnant with public mischief and private injury . . . tends to demoralize the workmen . . . destroy the trade of the city, and leaves the pockets of the whole community to the discretion of the concerned. If these evils were unprovided for by the law now existing, it would be necessary that laws should be made to restrain them . . .

It is in the volumes of the common law we are to seek for information in the far greater number, as well as the most important causes that come before our tribunals . . . Those who know it, know that it regulates with a sound discretion most of our concerns in civil and social life. Its rules are the result of the wisdom of ages. It says there may be cases in which what one man may do with [out] offence, many combined may not do with impunity. It distinguishes between the object so aimed at in different transactions. If the purpose to be obtained, be an object of individual interest, it may be fairly attempted by an individual . . . Many are prohibited from combining for the attainment of it.

What is the case now before us? . . . A combination of workmen to raise their wages may be considered in a two fold point of view: one is to benefit themselves . . . The other is to injure those who do not join their society. The rule of law condemns both. If the rule be clear, we are bound to conform to it even though we do not comprehend the principle upon which it is founded. We are not to reject it because we do not see the reason of it. It is enough, that it is the will of the majority. It is law because it is their will — if it is law, there may be good reasons for it though we cannot find them out. But the rule in this case is pregnant with sound sense and all the authorities are clear upon the subject. Hawkins, the greatest authority on the criminal law, has laid it down, that a combination to maintaining one another, carrying a particular object, whether true or false, is criminal . . .

Verdict: We find the defendants guilty of a combination to raise their wages . . .

NOTES

1. Criminal conspiracy is commonly defined as a combination to achieve an unlawful end or to achieve a lawful end by unlawful means. In the Philadelphia Cordwainers' Case is the objective of raising wages unlawful? Is the means of refusing to work unlawful? Consider the statement by Justice Gibson in Commonwealth v. Carlisle, Brightley's Rep. 36 (Philadelphia, 1821): ". . . a combination is criminal whenever the act to be done has a necessary tendency to prejudice the public or to oppress individuals by unjustly subjecting them to the power of the confederates . . ."

2. The Philadelphia Cordwainers' Case was followed by a number of criminal prosecutions brought against workers who sought to organize and compel higher wages. See People v. Melvin, 2 Wheeler Cr. Cas. 262 (1810); Pittsburgh Cordwainers' Case (1815), 4 Commons and Gilmore, A Documentary History of American Industrial Society 15 (1910); People v. Fisher, 14 Wend. 10 (N.Y. 1835). See also Nelles, The First American Labor Case, 41 Yale L.J. 165 (1931); White, Early American Labor Cases, 35 Yale L.J. 825 (1926).

In Commonwealth v. Hunt, 4 Metc. 111 (Mass. 1842), officers of the Boston Journeymen Bootmakers were indicted for causing the discharge of a member who accepted less than the established rate. Chief Justice Shaw, in declaring the indictment insufficient, said:

> The manifest intent of the association is, to induce all those engaged in the same occupation to become members of it. Such a purpose is not unlawful. It would give them a power which might be exerted for useful and honorable purposes, or for dangerous and pernicious ones. If the latter were the real and actual object, and susceptible of proof, it should have been specially charged . . .
>
> Nor can we perceive that the objects of this association, whatever they may have been, were to be attained by criminal means. The means which they proposed to employ, as averred in this count, and which, as we are now to presume, were established by the proof, were, that they would not work for a person, who, after due notice, should employ a journeyman not a member of their society. Supposing the object of the association to be laudable and lawful, or at least not unlawful, are these means criminal? The case supposes that these persons are not bound by contract, but free to work for whom they please, or not to work, if they so prefer. In this state of things we cannot perceive, that it is criminal for men to agree together to exercise their own acknowledged rights, in such a manner as best to subserve their own interests. . . .
> [See Nelles, Commonwealth v. Hunt, 32 Col. L. Rev. 1128 (1932).]

This decision, though frequently cited as establishing the legality of unions, did not mark the end of the criminal conspiracy doctrine. Even as late as 1867 the New Jersey court held that a combination of workers which sought to compel a discharge of nonunion workers constituted a criminal conspiracy. State v. Donaldson, 32 N.J.L. 151 (1867).

3. The conspiracy theory was scarcely laid to rest as creating a criminal offense when it was reborn as creating a civil liability in tort. In Quinn v. Leatham, [1901] A.C. 495, the Union insisted that Leatham, a meat slaughterer, hire only union members. When he refused they induced his customers, by threats of a strike, to cease buying Leatham's meat. Leatham sued and recovered damages. The House of Lords affirmed, saying at page 510:

> The only other question is this: Does a conspiracy to injure, resulting in damage, give rise to civil liability? It seems to me that there is authority for that proposition, and that it is founded in good sense. . . . That a conspiracy to injure — an oppressive combination, differs widely from an invasion of civil rights by a single individual cannot be doubted. I agree in substance with the remarks of Bowen, L.J., and Lords Bramwell and Hannen in the Mogul Case. A man may resist without much difficulty the wrongful act of an individual. He would probably have at least the moral support of his friends and neighbours; but it is a very different thing . . . when one man has to defend himself against many combined to do him wrong. . . .
>
> I also think that the provision in the Conspiracy and Protection of Property Act, 1875, which says that in certain cases an agreement or combination is not to be "indictable as a conspiracy," has nothing to do with civil remedies.

In the Mogul Case referred to in the opinion, the House of Lords had said:

> . . . [A] combination may make oppressive or dangerous that which if it proceeded only from a single person would be otherwise, and the very fact of the combination may show that the object is simply to do harm, and not to exercise one's own just rights. In the application of this undoubted principle it is necessary to be very careful not to press the doctrine of illegal conspiracy beyond that which is necessary for the protection of individuals or of the public: and it may be observed in passing that as a rule it is the damage wrongfully done, and not the conspiracy, that is the gist of actions on the case for conspiracy: [citing cases]. But what is the definition of an illegal combination? It is an agreement by one or more

to do an unlawful act, or to do a lawful act by unlawful means . . . [Bowen, L.J., in Mogul Steamship Co. v. McGregor, Gow & Co., L.R. 23 Q.B. 598, 616 (1889).]

Compare the more illuminating statement of the doctrine by Justice Holmes:

> I agree, whatever may be the law in the case of a single defendant, Rice v. Albee, 164 Mass. 88, 41 N.E. 122 [1895], that when a plaintiff proves that several persons have combined and conspired to injure his business, and have done acts producing that effect, he shows temporal damage and a cause of action, unless the facts disclose, or the defendants prove, some ground of excuse or justification. And I take it to be settled, and rightly settled, that doing that damage by combined persuasion is actionable, as well as doing it by falsehood or by force. . . . [Holmes, J., dissenting in Vegelahn v. Guntner, 167 Mass. 92, 105, 44 N.E. 1077 (1896).]

See also Central Metal Products Corp. v. O'Brien, noted at page 651 infra.

In the light of these statements, what is the test of whether union action amounts to a civil conspiracy? Does Lord Bowen's classic definition of an illegal combination provide any workable guide? Upon what does lawfulness depend?

ALCO–ZANDER CO. v. AMALGAMATED CLOTHING WORKERS

United States District Court, Eastern District, Pennsylvania, 1929
35 F.2d 203

KIRKPATRICK, District Judge. On September 4, 1929, the complainants, manufacturers of men's clothing engaged in business in Philadelphia, filed two bills in equity against the defendants, an unincorporated labor organization of national extent with headquarters in New York, and against certain of its officers and agents, all citizens and residents of the state of New York, praying for injunctions to restrain certain acts of interference with complainants' business, including combining to bring about strikes in the factories of the complainants. In the first bill, No. 5383, June term, 1929, jurisdiction was based upon alleged restraint of interstate competition in violation of the Sherman Act (15 U.S.C.A. §1 et seq.). In the second bill, No. 5385, June term, 1929, in which only four of the plaintiffs, all Pennsylvania corporations, joined, and in which the national labor organization was omitted as a defendant, jurisdiction was based upon the diverse citizenship of the parties, and the cause of action arises under the common law. The court directed notice to be given to the defendants so far as possible, and fixed September 6, 1929, for a hearing, at which time testimony was taken and affidavits filed. Certain of the defendants, including the Amalgamated Clothing Workers of America, the national organization, appeared at the hearing by counsel, but offered no evidence. On September 9, 1929, the court issued temporary restraining orders substantially as prayed for in the bills; and on September 16, 1929, the orders were modified in order to avoid certain misunderstandings as to their scope which appeared to have arisen. Thereafter, on September 20, 1929, the parties stipulated in writing that the temporary restraining orders should without further proceeding be taken and deemed to be a preliminary injunction.

Appeals have been taken from these temporary injunctions, and, in view of the importance of the issues involved, this opinion is filed in order that the record may show the reasons which prompted the issuance of the restraining orders. Although the two proceedings are entirely different in theory, it will be convenient to deal with the entire controversy in a single opinion. The facts as developed at the hearing are as follows:

In the garment industry, Philadelphia is a nonunion field. None of the complainants' shops are unionized, and if any of the complainants' employees were members of the Amalgamated Clothing Workers of America prior to June, 1929 (which does not appear), their number was negligible. In the year 1927 the production of the Philadelphia market amounted to approximately $80,000,000 in value, 80% of which was shipped in interstate commerce. The wages paid in Philadelphia in the same period amounted to over $14,000,000. On the other hand, the garment industry in New York City has been for some time unionized and New York has been recognized as a union market. In 1927, the production in New York amounted to about $360,-000,000 and the wages paid were over $50,000,000.

The existence of a large nonunion market so close to the unionized New York market had been for some time a source of anxiety to the Amalgamated and its officers. They believe that, by reason of the more favorable wages and conditions of work which labor in New York had been able to obtain, the New York manufacturers were unable to compete effectively with the Philadelphia market, and they were apprehensive that as a result the industry in New York in time either would be injured and curtailed with consequent unemployment of union workers there, or would be compelled to go back to a nonunion basis with reduced wages to its employees.   In point of fact, the production of the New York market had decreased $16,000,000 from 1925 to 1927, while in the same period that of the Philadelphia market had increased $3,000,000, while as early as 1921 strikes had been called in New York to stop New York houses from sending work to Philadelphia to be made up by nonunion labor there.   As the official organ published by the Amalgamated stated: "The open shop basis of operation of the clothing industry in Philadelphia is a menace to the standards of clothing labor everywhere, to the industrial three-fourths of the unionized market." "Philadelphia undersells New York because of its over-worked and under-paid labor.   The Amalgamated does not want Philadelphia employers to compete with New York or other employers on an unfair basis because in the final count that kind of manufacturers' competition means competition between the clothing workers of Philadelphia and of New York and of other cities."   "It was inconsistent with the Amalgamated policy to permit the Philadelphia clothing market to compete with the other markets with the aid of underpaid labor and artificially maintained divisions in the ranks of labor rather than on the basis of industrial ability."   "The open shop in Philadelphia must cease, for the Amalgamated is not safe industrially as long as the open shop continues."   One of the defendants, head of the Eastern Organization Department of the Amalgamated and in charge of the Philadelphia campaign, declared, "The work in Philadelphia is important because Philadelphia can make a graveyard of New York."   A member of the general executive board of the Amalgamated stated: "Just as the coal miners' union died, not because of Pennsylvania, but because of West Virginia, so is New York dependent on what will happen not in New York but in Philadelphia.   It is in Philadelphia that we must first stop reductions.   Fifteen thousand tailors there can break New York."

These considerations moved the Amalgamated Clothing Workers of America to undertake a campaign for the unionizing of the Philadelphia market, the avowed purpose of which was to destroy the advantage which Philadelphia manufacturers had over New York and other parts of the country by reason of nonunion hours and wages.   In 1922 at the convention of the national body a resolution authorizing such a campaign was adopted. This resolution recited that, "The fact that Philadelphia is not fully organized places it in severe competition with the organized centers, especially in New York."   The campaign then under-

taken failed to yield satisfactory results, and at the national convention of the Amalgamated at Cincinnati in 1928, the present
campaign was authorized by a resolution which recited that "conditions in the city of New York are going from bad to worse
daily," and that "our conditions in New York have been undermined and the industry paralyzed."

The above declarations are a few of many. They leave no
doubt whatever that the primary purpose of the campaign for the
unionization of the Philadelphia market was the protection of the
unionized markets in other states, particularly New York, and
that, while the improvement of the condition of the workers in
Philadelphia may have been present as a motive, it was at best a
secondary and remote one. Using the language of industrial
warfare, the move was a piece of major strategy — an offensive
undertaking for the purpose of relieving the pressure upon other
fronts.

The method which the Amalgamated adopted to carry out its
purpose was the calling of strikes in the factories of the complainants and others, totally without notice or warning and
apparently without previously presenting demands of any kind
to the employers. At any rate, it is a fact that in none of the
complainants' plants was there any existing dispute between employers and employees as to wages or conditions of work. Contemporaneous with the calling of the strikes, the employees of the
factories were invited to join the union. In case of some employees, the invitation preceded the calling of the strikes. In general, quitting work meant joining the union, and vice versa.
After a sufficient number of employees had quit to cripple the
business and stop production, they would be organized and
negotiations would be undertaken with the employer for the
recognition of the union. It is not clear whether the agreements
to be made with the employers contemplated an immediate readjustment of wages and working conditions, but that such readjustment was the ultimate purpose and was intended to follow
soon is beyond question. It is quite likely that, in proceeding in
this manner, the union adopted the most effective method to
accomplish its purpose. The mere advocacy of union membership among the plaintiff's employees would have been at best a
slow process and might in the long run have proved futile. This,
however, has no bearing upon the lawfulness of the acts. If the
primary intent were not so clearly apparent, it might be argued
that the calling of strikes was merely an effective means of increasing union membership by a practical demonstration of what

could be accomplished; but, in view of the evidence, it is plain that the object of the strikes was to put an end to all production in Philadelphia under nonunion conditions and only to permit it to be resumed if and when the manufacturers were willing to operate upon an union basis and under union wage scales. Except as a means to the end of compelling the manufacturers to change their methods of operation, the defendants were not seeking to enlarge the union membership. Hitchman Coal Co. v. Mitchell, 245 U.S. at page 256, 38 S. Ct. 65, 62 L. Ed. 260, L.R.A. 1918C 497, Ann. Cas. 1918B, 461.

Some of the complainants, no doubt sensing the impending attack, presented contracts to their employees, and in most cases these contracts were signed by the great majority of the employees. These contracts provided that substantially if at any time while the employee was in the employ of the plantiff such employee desired to become a member of the Amalgamated Clothing Workers of America he would, before becoming so connected, withdraw from the plaintiff's employment. In most cases these contracts were made after the Amalgamated had called a strike in the plant of the particular employer in question. In at least one case they were made before. This, however, seems immaterial, since in all cases they were made with employees who were at the time of making them bona fide employed by the complainants.

There is some testimony going to establish threats, intimidation, and acts of violence on the part of organizers of the union directed against employees who refused to strike. In the view taken of this case, however, this evidence is not important, except so far as it is the basis for certain provisions of the restraining order, which provisions are not specifically complained of or resisted by the defendants.

Each of the restraining orders contains a provision restraining the defendant from combining to bring about a strike or strikes in the factories of the complainants. These are the important provisions of the orders and the only ones that require discussion. If they are proper, the other provisions naturally follow and should be sustained. It will be noted that the orders are broad enough to restrain the defendants from combining to bring about strikes by peaceful persuasion only, and they were so intended to be.

The facts as stated above, together with the provisions of the orders referred to, raise squarely the fundamental issue, namely, the right of a national labor organization, acting through agents who are not employees of the complainants, to bring about strikes in nonunion plants, the primary purpose and object of which is to prevent the shipment of goods produced by nonunion labor to markets of other states where it will by competition tend to reduce the price of the commodity and affect injuriously the maintenance of wages for union labor in competing fields. The question has two aspects, here presented by the two separate proceedings: First, the rights of the parties without reference to the effect of the federal statutes; and, second, their rights as affected by those statutes.

At common law, to induce third persons to leave an employment is actionable if done maliciously and without justifiable cause, although such persons are free to leave at their own will. Hitchman Coal Co. v. Mitchell, 245 U.S. 229, 38 S. Ct. 65, 62 L. Ed. 260, L.R.A. 1918C, 297, Ann. Cas. 1918B, 461; Truax v. Raich, 239 U.S. 33, 36 S. Ct. 7, 60 L. Ed. 131, L.R.A. 1916D, 545, Ann. Cas. 1917B, 283. The question here is whether the self-interest of the national organization in its purpose to protect the unionized markets in New York and elsewhere is a sufficient justification for its interference with the plaintiff's business which, without justifiable cause, concededly would be a legal wrong. The decisions of the Supreme Court compel the conclusion that the question is no longer an open one. The answer of the court to it is to be found in Hitchman Coal Co. v. Mitchell, supra, as modified in American Foundries v. Tri-City Council, 257 U.S. 184, 42 S. Ct. 72, 79, 66 L. Ed. 189, 27 A.L.R. 360. While the decision in the Hitchman Case condemned the method adopted as unlawful, the decision was placed equally upon the unlawfulness of the purpose, and upon that question the entire issue was justification by self-interest for interference with the business of another. The dissenting opinions of Mr. Justice Brandeis in the Hitchman Case and in Duplex Co. v. Deering, 254 U.S. 443, 41 S. Ct. 172, 184, 65 L. Ed. 349, 16 A.L.R. 196, state the case for the defendants here. The conclusion which Justice Brandeis reached in the latter case, and which the majority of the Court did not adopt, was that neither the common law nor the statutes of the United States deny "the right of industrial combatants to push their struggles to the limits of the justification of self-interest." Those limits were subsequently somewhat expanded by the court in American Foundries v. Tri-City Council, supra, but beyond that decision no step has been taken. In that case, it appeared that a local labor body, composed of representatives of a number of trade unions in three adjoining towns in Illinois, assisted in procuring and bringing about strikes in a local foundry which had just begun work after a shutdown and was attempting to run on a nonunion basis at lower than union wages. It appeared (257 U.S. 208, 42 S. Ct. 78) that many members of the local unions represented by the labor body were looking forward to employment when the complainant should resume full operations, and the court held that, even though not employees or ex-employees, they were directly interested in the wages which were to be paid. The decision was that the central body and the members of the local unions which it represented had sufficient interest in the wages paid by the complainant to its employees to justify their use of lawful and peaceable persuasion to induce those employees not to accept such reduced wages and to quit their employment. It will be seen how far short this is of holding that the protection of union laborers in distant markets who have no prospect of employment or direct interest in the wages paid is a sufficient justification.

In the American Foundries Case, the Hitchman Case was distinguished, and, in reviewing it, the court said: "There the action was by a coal mining company of West Virginia against the officers of an International Labor Union and others to enjoin them from carrying out a plan to bring the employees of the complainant company and all the West Virginia mining companies into the International Union, so that the Union could control, through the union employees, the production and sale of coal in West Virginia, in competition with the mines of Ohio and other states. . . . This court held that the purpose was not lawful, and that the means were not lawful and that the defendants were thus engaged in an unlawful conspiracy which should be enjoined. . . . The statement of the purpose of the plan is sufficient to show the remoteness of the benefit ultimately to be derived by the members of the International Union from its success and the formidable, country-wide and dangerous character of the control of interstate commerce sought."   Lest there should be any misunderstanding as to the limited scope of the decision in the American Foundries Case, the court was careful to say: "The principle of the unlawfulness of maliciously enticing laborers still remains and action may be maintained therefore in proper cases. . . ."   True, the court said that the unlawful and deceitful means adopted by the defendants in the Hitchman Case to accomplish their purpose were quite enough to sustain the decision of the court without more, but there was in that case a positive decision that the purpose was also unlawful.   "Where there are two grounds upon either of which an appellate court may rest its decision, and it adopts both, the ruling on neither is obiter dictum, but each is the judgment of the court, and of equal validity." U.S. v. Title Insurance Co., 265 U.S. 472, 44 S. Ct. 621, 623, 68 L. Ed. 1110. If the principle of the unlawfulness of maliciously enticing laborers, which was one of the bases upon which the Hitchman Case was decided, still remains, it must be applied to a case like the instant one, where the self-interest of the defendants is totally unconnected with the employment interfered with. The only alternative would be to hold that any motive, other than personal spite or malignity against the employer, is justifiable cause — a result which would totally nullify the principle itself.

Hitchman Coal Co. v. Mitchell and American Foundries v. Tri-City Council were common-law cases, and a study of them leaves no doubt that, upon the question of justification, the present case is far outside of the limits of the American Foundries Case declaring what is lawful, and well within the limits of the Hitchman Case declaring what is not. When we turn to the common law of Pennsylvania, we find what appears to be a total denial of self-interest as a justification for procuring the employees of another to strike. In Purvis v. United Brotherhood, 214 Pa. 348, 63 A. 585, 589, 12 L.R.A. (N.S.) 642, 112 Am. St. Rep. 757, 6 Ann. Cas. 1275, the court said: "True, the defendants contend and testify that their purpose was to benefit their own members. This doubtless, in a sense, is true, but the benefits sought were the remote purpose which was to be secured through the more immediate purpose of coercing the plaintiffs into complying with their demands, or otherwise injuring them in their business, and the court cannot, in this proceeding, look beyond the immediate injury to the remote results. Such is the doctrine laid down in Eddy on Combinations and quoted with approval in the case of Erdman v. Mitchell, . . . (207 Pa. 79, 56 A. 327, 63 L.R.A. 534, 99 Am. St. Rep. 783), as follows: 'The benefit to the members of the combination is so remote, as compared to the direct and immediate injury inflicted upon the nonunion workmen' (in this case the nonunion millowners) 'that the law does not look beyond the immediate loss and damage to the innocent parties to the remote benefits that might result to the union." The conclusion is that at common law, both in Pennsylvania and under the federal decisions, irrespective of any question of procurement of breach of contract, the efforts of the defendants even by peaceful persuasion to bring about strikes in the plants of the plaintiffs are without justification and therefore actionable.

The element of obtaining breaches of contract is not made a

basis for these injunctions. Similar contracts were in existence in the Hitchman Case. In that case the method of the defendants was slightly different from that adopted by these defendants here. What was done there was to secretly sign up as many employees as possible as members of the union, inducing them to remain in the employ of the complainant in violation of their contracts, and then when a sufficient number had been obtained call a strike which would cripple the operation of the mine. In the present cases, as has been pointed out, there were plenty of instances where the employees were invited to join the union before leaving the plaintiff's employ — also in violation of their contracts. In others the strikes were called first. However, in view of the conclusion reached as to the unlawfulness at common law of the defendant's program, it is unnecessary to decide whether their total disregard of the contracts is within the rule of the Hitchman Case upon that point.

There remains to be considered the proceeding in which the basis of the plaintiff's action is the alleged violation of the anti-trust laws. . . .

NOTES

1. Can you determine whether it is the defendant's objective or the means which they adopted (or both) which illegalized their conduct? What is the "objective" as distinguished from the "means"? Why is the self-interest of the defendants here "totally unconnected" with the employment conditions in the Philadelphia area? If justification depends on the degree of self-interest, how deeply (if at all) should the Court explore the economics of the particular industry? Suppose, for example, that the cost of labor forms a large part of total production cost — what follows? First, that (a) strikes to organize Philadelphia in order to protect wage position in New York are justified? (b) a strike in New York to compel New York producers to maintain their sales prices is justified? Or, second, that neither strike is justified since, (a) it is a direct interference with production schedules, pricing and distribution policies which are all prerogatives of management? and/or (b) it is activity tending to unreasonably enhance prices, restrain trade or promote monopoly? Compare Commonwealth v. McHugh, 326 Mass. 249, 93 N.E.2d 751 (1950), cert. denied, 340 U.S. 911 (1951).

2. In Hitchman Coal & Coke Co. v. Mitchell, 245 U.S. 229, 38 Sup. Ct. 65, 62 L. Ed. 260 (1917), the Court sustained decrees

which thwarted efforts to organize the Hitchman mines for the protection of already organized and competitive mines areas. The Company's nonunion policy (adopted after three years of labor difficulty) was carried out by the so-called "yellow dog" contract device under which employment was conditioned on non-membership in the United Mine Workers. The defendants' tactics centered on inducing the employees to agree to join the Union. As indicated in the Alco-Zander decision supra, the opinion of the Court (Justice Pitney) cumulates as reasons for the result: (a) a constitutional right to exclude union men from employment; (b) combination for illegal purpose; (c) use of illegal means (fraud, deceit, conspiracy, threats, violence, etc.) ; and (d) tortious interference with contract. With respect to the last, consider the Court's statement at page 257:

> Another fundamental error in defendants' position consists in the assumption that all measures that may be resorted to are lawful if they are "peaceable" — that is, if they stop short of physical violence, or coercion through fear of it. In our opinion, any violation of plaintiff's legal rights contrived by defendants for the purpose of inflicting damage, or having that as its necessary effect, is as plainly inhibited by the law as if it involved a breach of the peace. *A combination to procure concerted breaches of contract by plaintiff's employees constitutes such a violation.* Flaccus v. Smith, 199 Pa. 128, 48 A. 894, 54 L.R.A. 640, 85 Am. St. Rep. 779, South Wales Miners' Federation v. Glamorgan Coal Co., [1905] A.C. 239, 244, 250, 253; Jonas Glass Co. v. Glass Bottle Blowers Association, 77 N.J. Eq. 219, 223 [79 A.262, 41 L.R.A. (N.S.) 445]. [Italics supplied.]

3. An interesting and typical application of the interference with contract theory appears in Central Metal Products Corp. v. O'Brien, 278 Fed. 827 (N.D. Ohio, 1922), where the metal workers and carpenters were engaged in a "work" jurisdictional dispute. The plaintiff, which had contracted with the city of Cleveland to install metal doors in the City Hospital, employed members of the Carpenters Union. The defendant metal workers, who claimed that type of installation work pursuant to an award made by the National Board for Jurisdictional Awards (set up by the more important groups in the industry with the approval of the Secretary of Labor), withdrew the union members from work on the hospital as well as from a city auditorium then under construction. City officials acceded to the defendants'

demands by preventing the plaintiff from continuing its work. On the plaintiff's application for a preliminary injunction, what decree?

C. S. SMITH METROPOLITAN MARKET CO., LTD.
v. LYONS
Supreme Court, California, 1940
16 Cal. 2d 389, 106 P.2d 414

EDMONDS, J.   Injunctive relief granted an employer in a controversy with union labor over picketing occasioned this appeal. The market company had no union men employed and the purpose of the picketing was to bring about the establishment of a closed shop in its meat departments.

At the time the dispute arose, C. S. Smith Metropolitan Market Co., Ltd., was a California corporation, engaged in selling groceries, meats, and other commodities at retail.   It owned and operated seven retail markets located in several cities in southern California.   When these markets were picketed, the company sued Amalgamated Meat Cutters and Butcher Workmen Local Union 284, its officers and members, and also Central Labor Council of Long Beach and its secretary.   After trial upon issues framed by the complaint and an answer alleging affirmative defenses, the court made findings and conclusions of law generally favorable to the market company and rendered judgment permanently restraining the appellants from picketing.   The court also found that the market company had been damaged by the appellants' acts, but that the evidence was insufficient to establish the amount which should be awarded therefore.   The appeal is from this judgement . . .

At the time the controversy arose, there was no strike or dispute concerning the terms and conditions of employment between the market company and its employees; the employees were entirely satisfied with their employment and had made no request upon their employer for a discussion concerning any matter involving terms of employment.   The market company discharged several employees, but not because they were members of the butchers' union, and the market company did not discriminate against the organization.   In fact, the president of the company instructed his manager to employ union men at one market and offered to pay the union initiation fee for any employees who desired to join the union, but none accepted the offer.

The business agent of the butchers' union made a request for a discussion concerning the terms and conditions of employment of its employees, but had no authority to represent the employees. So far as the market company was informed none of its employees were members of any labor union and none had any desire to become members, but preferred to work under terms and conditions of their own choosing without interference by labor unions. The market company had not engaged in a course of intimidation against the employees to prevent them from joining labor unions; it had never been a party to any agreement with a labor union and had never requested the appellants to act as collective bargaining agent for its employees.

The sole purpose of the appellants' picketing was to compel the market company's employees to become members of the butchers' union and to compel the market company to discharge those who refused to join the union. For the accomplishment of their purpose, the appellants combined and conspired together to boycott and peaceably picket the market company's places of business. Pickets were stationed for the purpose of interfering with its patronage and inducing other merchants and their employees to cut off business relations. A further purpose of picketing, the court found, was "to obtain employment for union members . . . under good working conditions, fair wages and fair hours of labor," to obtain an agreement with the market company for the employment of union members only, and to persuade "meat cutters employed by . . . [the market company] to become members of the" butchers' union. This union had contracts with a number of markets and butcher shops in Long Beach whereby such markets and butcher shops agreed to employ only members of the union; to pay them union wages for a maximum of 55 hours per week and to close on Sunday.

The respondent paid its butchers more than the union scale, with hours of employment less than the union schedule existing in Long Beach. All of the markets with which the defendant union had contracts did not adhere to union standards. The respondent did not increase its employees' wages and reduce their hours of employment because of the efforts of the butchers' union or for the specific purpose of making it appear to the public that it was paying fair wages or to persuade many of the employees not to join the union. It is not true that if the union's activities were abandoned, the market company would change working conditions in its markets to the detriment of its employees.

The presence of pickets at the market company's places of business led many prospective customers to believe that a labor dispute existed between it and its employees, with a consequent loss of patronage. The picketing also caused other business firms and their employees to refrain from selling or delivering merchandise to the market company. There follow findings of damage to the market company and of the inadequacy of the remedy at law. The conclusions of law stated that the appellants' activities were unlawful, entitling the respondent to injunctive relief. . . .

The findings and evidence in the present case present a further question. They show that the market company's employees, none of whom were members of the union, were satisfied with the terms and conditions of their employment, were not on strike, and were not engaged in a labor dispute with their employer. In its briefs, the market company attaches considerable importance to these findings and argues that peaceful picketing of a closed, nonunion shop by a labor organization is unlawful where there is no strike or dispute between the employer and his employees.

But there is no magic in the words "strike" or "labor dispute" and it is begging the question to make the justification for concerted action depend upon the existence of a strike, which is itself a weapon in the struggle. Justification, or the lack of it, depends upon the purpose for which the means of concerted action are used rather than upon the type of means used. "Picketing without a strike is no more unlawful than a strike without picketing." Exchange Bakery & Restaurant v. Rifkin, 1927, 245 N.Y. 260, 157 N.E. 130, 132. See also, 40 Harv. L.R. 596; 27 Col. L.R. 190 . . .

The gravamen of the charge against the appellants under the findings in the present case is a conspiracy to damage the market company by intentionally interfering with its business. However, here, as in McKay v. Retail Automobile Salesmen's Local Union, . . . (16 Cal. 2d 311, 106 P.2d 373), the damage to the employer was not absolute. The market company was presented with the choice of yielding to the union's demands or continuing to endure the interference with its business relations which the appellants' activities caused. The right of an individual to carry on his business as he pleases is by no means an absolute one. Numerous valid restrictions upon such a right have been enacted by the legislature, as, for example, the Cartwright Act (Stats. 1907, p. 984), the Fair Trade Act (Stats. 1931, p. 583), and many other provisions regulating compensation, hours of labor, and working conditions generally. See Labor Code, passim. And it is now recognized that an employer had no constitutional right to conduct his business as a closed nonunion shop. American Steel Foundries v. Tri-City, etc., Council, 257 U.S. 184, 42 S. Ct. 72,

66 L. Ed. 189, 27 A.L.R. 360; Magruder, A Half Century of Legal Influence Upon the Development of Collective Bargaining, 50 Harv. L. Rev. 1071, 1086. The interference with the employer's business must, therefore, be considered in its relation to the purposes of the appellants.

The law does not invariably give relief against acts causing loss and the field of business competition furnishes numerous examples of intentional infliction of damage without legal remedy. . . . The damage is nonetheless justified when inflicted by a combination of business men than by one (Union Labor Hospital v. Vance Lumber Co., . . . 158 Cal. 551, 112 P. 886, 33 L.R.A., N.S. 1034) ; Mogul Steamship Co. v. McGregor, . . . (61 L.J.Q.B. 295) or by large aggregations of capital in corporate form.

The damage may hit the competitor directly, as when a chain bank or chain grocery enters a community too small to support more than the local establishment already there, or may affect merchants generally, as when a wholesaler opens a retail store solely for the purpose of competing with certain retailers until they withdraw their patronage from a competing wholesaler. Katz v. Kapper, . . . (7 Cal. App. 2d 1, 44 P.2d 1060). In the absence of legislation laying down rules for the contest . . . or where the acts complained of are outside the scope of such legislation, business men are apparently free to inflict damage in the struggle of competition so long as they abstain from violence, fraud or other unlawful conduct.

. . . The justification for such conduct is said to be that free competition is generally considered worth more to society than it costs. Holmes, J., dissenting in Vegelahn v. Guntner, 1896, 167 Mass. 96, 106, 44 N.E. 1077, 35 L.R.A. 722, 57 Am. St. Rep. 443.

The foregoing principles are relevant and have been applied to competition in the field of labor. The use of any of the lawful methods of concerted action in this field — stopping work, persuading others not to work, interfering with advantageous trade relations — all necessarily cause economic loss not only to the parties directly affected but to customers and often to the public generally. Nevertheless, in the struggle for existence the fact of damage to others, intentionally inflicted, does not warrant injunctive relief against workmen any more than it does against business men, if it is inflicted in pursuit of a legally justifiable object. . . .

The underlying reason beneath these rules is a widespread belief in competition, free enterprise, and equality of oppor-

tunity. Statutes such as the Cartwright Act and the Fair Trade
Act . . . represent interference with the free play of competition
in specific situations where the legislature has concluded that the
competitive struggle has become unequal or unfair. And the
inequality of bargaining power between employer and employee
has long been fully recognized by legislation curtailing the employer's freedom to bargain with his employees as he chooses.
For example, California has statutes dealing with compensation
(Labor Code, secs. 200–452), working hours (secs. 510–856, Id.),
women and minors (secs. 1171–1398, Id.), immigrants (sec. 1460–
1486, Id.), employment agencies (secs. 1550–1681, Id.), unemployment relief (secs. 2010–2183, Id.), health (secs. 2260–2606,
Id.), employment relations (secs. 2700–3091, Id.), workmen's
compensation and insurance (secs. 3201–6002, Id.) and safety in
employment (secs. 6300–7601, Id.).

Even more significant is section 923 of the Labor Code which
declares the legislative policy of this state in favor of collective
action by workmen . . . This is not an effort by the legislature
to destroy free competition; it is rather an attempt to insure an
equality of bargaining power upon which the benefits of competition and free enterprise rest, and thus to secure to the individual
workman a larger measure of freedom in his dealings with employers of labor. In other words combination and organization
are permissible on both sides, and the determination of terms and
conditions of employment is to be left to bargaining and competition by these organizations in a free and unrestricted market.

It may very well be that combination and organization on one
side or the other places in the hands of a few persons an immense
power which, in the general welfare, ought to be limited and
controlled. But these are considerations for the law-making
power, not for courts. And considering sections 921 and 923 of
the Labor Code, a court is not more justified in fettering by injunction the bargaining power of workmen merely because they
are organized in a union than it would be in fettering the bargaining power of employers because they are organized in partnerships,
joint ventures or corporations. Accordingly, in cases such as the
present one, the determinative issue is whether the workmen are
demanding something which is reasonably related to employment
and to the purposes of collective bargaining. More specifically,
the propriety of lawful concerted action depends upon whether
the workmen have such an interest in the employment relationship that the attainment of their object will benefit them directly
or will enhance their bargaining power.

The members of a labor organization may have a substantial interest in the employment relations of an employer although none of them is or ever has been employed by him. The reason for this is that the employment relations of every employer affect the working conditions and bargaining power of employees throughout the industry in which he competes. Hence, where union and nonunion employees are engaged in a similar occupation and their respective employers are engaged in trade competition one with another, the efforts of the union to extend its membership to the employments in which it has no foothold is not an unreasonable aim.

Modern industry is not organized on a single shop basis, and it is a logical corollary of the collective bargaining principle that independent labor organizations should be permited to grow and extend their bargaining power beyond the single shop. The market for a product may be so competitive that one producer cannot maintain higher labor standards resulting in higher costs than those maintained by his nonunion competitors.

Nor is the interest of the union in extending its organization any less substantial where the labor standards of the nonunion shop are on an equality with those of its union competitors. Under these circumstances, it may reasonably be believed vital to union interests to organize such a shop, for there can be no doubt that the receipt by other workmen of equivalent benefits without suffering correlative union responsibility serves to create intraunion unrest and disaffections.

Tested by these principles, it is apparent in the present case that the members of the butcher's union have a substantial interest in the employment relations of the market company . . . The appellants were, therefore, privileged to direct against the market company any peaceful form of concerted action within their control. . . .

The judgment is reversed and the trial court is directed to dismiss the action. . . .

CURTIS and SHENK, JJ., and MARKS, Justice pro tem (dissenting).

We dissent for the reasons stated in the dissenting opinions in the case of McKay v. Retail Automobile Salesmen's Local Union No. 1067, Cal. Sup., 106 P.2d 373.

NOTES

1. Does the legality of the picketing in the Smith Metropolitan Market case reasonably follow from the legislature's endorsement of free organizational rights and collective bargaining? Compare Simon v. Schwachman, 301 Mass. 573, 18 N.E.2d 1 (1938), where the opposite result was reached on the basis of the same legislative policy.

2. In Barile v. Fisher, 197 Misc. 493, 94 N.Y.S.2d 346 (1949), the plaintiff, an employee of Watson Manufacturing Company in Jamestown, New York, refused to pay his union dues because the union failed to file non-Communist affidavits pursuant to Section 9 (h) of the Taft-Hartley Act. He was expelled from the Union and the Union obtained his discharge under a maintenance-of-membership contract. The plaintiff alleged that the Union then obtained the cooperation of all CIO and AFL unions in the city to prevent his employment. Regardless of whether they had a union shop or whether he was willing to join, the other unions refused to allow their members to work with him. The plaintiff sued for damages due to the discharge and the black-listing. Judge Halpern held that since under New York law a closed shop was legal, the union was justified in causing his discharge from Watson's. In passing on the added element of union black-listing, he said:

> The question to be ultimately decided in this case is whether there was social or economic justification for this action on the part of the union . . .
>
> The conduct of the defendant union as described in the complaint smacks of revenge rather than of the legitimate protection of the union's economic interests. While it is not explicitly alleged in the complaint, it is reasonably inferable therefrom that the plaintiff claims that the defendant acted out of spite or a desire for revenge rather than any expectation of economic advantage. If this is found to be the case upon the trial, and it is found that the defendant acted out of "disinterested malevolence," the defendant would be clearly liable for the damage caused to the plaintiff.
>
> The singling out of the plaintiff for punishment in the manner alleged seems to me to go beyond the bounds of economic justification. The economic interests of the defendant union were not directly served by the exclusion of the plaintiff from other employment. It is true that this exclusion may

have been of indirect value in that the punishment of the plaintiff in this manner may have served to deter other members from withdrawing from the defendant union, but the defendant's interests in this regard were adequately protected without the adoption of such punitive measures. The plaintiff's discharge by the Watson Manufacturing Company adequately served to deter other members from leaving the union.

The method alleged to have been used by the defendant was far too drastic and cannot be recognized as a lawful means of protecting its economic interests . . .

Is there any legislative policy on which the court can rely in such a case as this? If not, then what is the source of the policy enforced by the court?

Assuming that the business involved in Smith Metropolitan Market v. Lyons or Barile v. Fisher was within the jurisdiction of the National Labor Relations Board, would the specific federal policy expressed in Sections 9 (a) (3) and 8 (b) (2) provide the policy basis for an injunction or damage action in the state court? Compare Park & Tilford Import Co. v. Local 848, 27 Cal. 2d 599, 165 P.2d 891 (1946).

3. The intentional infliction of temporal damage, or the doing of an act manifestly likely to inflict such damage and inflicting it, is actionable if done without just cause. When the defendant escapes, the court is of opinion that he has acted with just cause. There are various justifications. In these instances, the justification is that the defendant is privileged knowingly to inflict the damage complained of. Consider the following statement made nearly sixty years ago:

> But whether, and how far, a privilege shall be allowed is a question of policy. Questions of policy are legislative questions, and judges are shy of reasoning from such grounds. Therefore, decisions for or against the privilege, which really can stand only upon such grounds, often are presented as hollow deductions from empty general propositions . . .
>
> Perhaps one of the reasons why judges do not like to discuss questions of policy, or to put a decision in terms upon their views as lawmakers, is that the moment you leave the path of merely logical deduction you lose the illusion of certainty which makes legal reasoning seem like mathematics. But the certainty is only an illusion, nevertheless. Views of policy are taught by experience of the interests of life. Those

interests are fields of battle. Whatever decisions are made must be against the wishes and opinion of one party, and the distinctions on which they go will be distinctions of degree. . . . The ground of decision really comes down to a proposition of policy of rather a delicate nature concerning the merit of the particular benefit to themselves intended by the defendants, and suggests a doubt whether judges with different economic sympathies might not decide such a case differently when brought face to face with the issue. . . .

I make these suggestions, not as criticisms of the decisions, but to call attention to the very serious legislative considerations which have to be weighed. The danger is that such considerations should have their weight in an inarticulate form as unconscious prejudice or half conscious inclination. To measure them justly needs not only the highest powers of a judge and a training which the practice of the law does not insure, but also a freedom from prepossessions which is very hard to attain. It seems to me desirable that the work should be done with express recognition of its nature. The time has gone by when law is only an unconscious embodiment of the common will. It has become a conscious reaction upon itself or organized society knowingly seeking to determine its own destinies. [Holmes, Privilege, Malice, and Intent, 8 Harv. L. Rev. 1, 3 (1894).]

In Stillwell Theatre, Inc. v. Kaplan, 259 N.Y. 405, 182 N.E. 63 (1932), the plaintiff theatre proprietors had entered into union-shop contracts with an unaffiliated union representing motion picture operators. The defendant rival union (AFL) representatives peaceably picketed with signs which stated that the theatres refused to employ its members. The lower court's injunction was based on the ground that the picketing was illegal because its purpose was to induce breach of contract. The Court of Appeals reversed the judgment, Pound, C.J., saying for the majority at page 412:

. . . [T]o state fairly and truly to the public that the conduct of the employer is socially objectionable to a labor union is no persuasion to break a contract . . . We would be departing from established precedents [New York] if we upheld this injunction. We would thereby give to one labor union an advantage over another by prohibiting the use of peaceful and honest persuasion in matters of economic and social rivalry. This might strike a death blow to legitimate labor activities. *It is not within the province of the courts to restrain conduct which is within the allowable area of economic conflict.* [Italics supplied.]

Does this refusal to intervene avoid — or merely illustrate — the elements of personal predilection which Justice Holmes suggests to be particularly inherent in cases of this character?

DUPLEX PRINTING COMPANY v. DEERING

Supreme Court of the United States, 1921
254 U.S. 443, 41 Sup. Ct. 172, 65 L. Ed. 349

[The complainant manufactured printing presses in Michigan and installed them at the purchasers' places of business. At least 80 per cent of the company's output was sold outside Michigan. After a strike failed to unionize the complainant's factory (the only nonunion establishment of its kind in the country) the International Association of Machinists decided to boycott the complainant's product. In furtherance of this plan, and with the assistance of affiliated unions, trucking companies, repair shops and customers of the complainant were threatened with sympathetic strikes. A majority of the Court ruled that this conduct constituted an enjoinable violation of the Antitrust Acts, Justice Pitney pointing out at page 460:]

. . . The defendants who were brought into court and answered the bill are Emil J. Deering and William Bramley, sued individually and as business agents and representatives of District No. 15 of the International Association of Machinists, and Michael T. Neyland, sued individually and as business agent and representative of Local Lodge No. 328 of the same association. The District Council and the Lodge are unincorporated associations having headquarters in New York City, with numerous members resident in that city and vicinity. There were averments and proof to show that it was impracticable to bring all the members before the court and that the named defendants properly represented them; . . .

The jurisdiction of the federal court was invoked both by reason of diverse citizenship and on the ground that defendants were engaged in a conspiracy to restrain complainant's interstate trade and commerce in printing presses, contrary to the Sherman Anti-Trust Act of July 2, 1890, c. 647, 26 Stat. 209, 15 U.S.C.A. secs. 1–7, 15 note. The suit was begun before but brought to hearing after the passage of the Clayton Act of October 15, 1914, c. 323, 38 Stat. 730. Both parties invoked the provisions of the

Clayton Act, and both courts treated them as applicable. Complainant relied upon also the common law; but we shall deal first with the effect of the acts of Congress . . .

[After discussing the Danbury Hatters' Case (page 666 infra), he continued at page 467:] It is settled by these decisions that such a restraint produced by peaceable persuasion is as much within the prohibition [of the Sherman Act] as one accomplished by force or threats of force; and it is not to be justified by the fact that the participants in the combination or conspiracy may have some object beneficial to themselves or their associates which possibly they might have been at liberty to pursue in the absence of the statute.

Upon the question whether the provisions of the Clayton Act forbade the grant of an injunction under the circumstances of the present case, the Circuit Court of Appeals was divided; the majority holding that under §20 . . . perhaps in conjunction with section 6 . . . there could be no injunction . . . As to section 6 . . . there is nothing in the section to exempt such an organization or its members from accountability where it or they depart from its *normal* and *legitimate* objects and engage in an actual combination or conspiracy in restraint of trade. [Italics supplied.]

The principal reliance is upon section 20 . . .

The first paragraph merely puts into statutory form familiar restrictions upon the granting of injunctions already established and of general application in the equity practice of the courts of the United States. It is but declaratory of the law as it stood before. The second paragraph declares that "no such restraining order or injunction" shall prohibit certain conduct specified — manifestly still referring to a "case between an employer and employees, . . . involving, or growing out of, a dispute concerning terms or conditions of employment," as designated in the first paragraph . . . If the qualifying words are to have any effect, they must operate to confine the restriction upon the granting of injunctions, and also the relaxation of the provisions of the anti-trust and other laws of the United States, to *parties standing in proximate relation to a controversy* such as is particularly described. [Italics supplied.]

. . . The extensive construction adopted by the majority of the court below virtually ignores the effect of the qualifying words. Congress had in mind particular industrial controversies, not a general class war . . .

. . . The emphasis placed on the words "lawful" and "lawfully," "peaceful" and "peacefully," and the references to the dispute and the parties to it, strongly rebut a legislative intent to confer a general immunity for conduct violative of the anti-trust laws, or otherwise unlawful . . .

Reaching the conclusion, as we do, that complainant has a clear right to an injunction under the Sherman Act as amended by the Clayton Act, it becomes unnecessary to consider whether a like result would follow under the common law or local statutes; there being no suggestion that relief thereunder could be broader than that to which complainant is entitled under the acts of Congress."

MR. JUSTICE BRANDEIS, dissenting, with whom MR. JUSTICE HOLMES and MR. JUSTICE CLARKE concur.

First. As to the rights at common law: Defendants' justification is that of self-interest. They have supported the strike at the employer's factory by a strike elsewhere against its product. They have injured the plaintiff, not maliciously, but in self-defense. They contend that the Duplex Company's refusal to deal with the machinists' union and to observe its standards threatened the interest not only of such union members as were its factory em-ployees, but even more of all members of the several affiliated unions employed by plaintiff's competitors and by others whose more advanced standards the plaintiff was, in reality, attacking; and that none of the defendants and no person whom they are endeavoring to induce to refrain from working in connection with the setting up of presses made by plaintiff is an outsider, an interloper. In other words, that the contest between the com-pany and the machinists' union involves vitally the interest of every person whose cooperation is sought. May not all with a common interest join in refusing to expend their labor upon arti-cles whose very production constitutes an attack upon their stand-ard of living and the institution which they are convinced supports it? Applying common-law principles the answer should, in my opinion, be: Yes, if as matter of fact those who so cooperate have a common interest. . . .

Second. As to the anti-trust laws of the United States: Sec-tion 20, of the Clayton Act, declares, — [see Appendix] . . .

This statute was the fruit of unceasing agitation, which ex-tended over more than twenty years and was designed to equalize before the law the position of workingmen and employer as in-dustrial combatants. Aside from the use of the injunction, the chief source of dissatisfaction with the existing law lay in the doctrine of malicious combinations, and, in many parts of the country, in the judicial declarations of the illegality at common law of picketing and persuading others to leave work. The grounds for objection to the latter are obvious. The objection to the doctrine of malicious combinations requires some explanation. By virtue of that doctrine, damage resulting from conduct such as striking or withholding patronage or persuading others to do either, which without more might be damnum absque injuria because the result of trade competition, became actionable when done for a purpose which a judge considered socially or economically harmful and therefore branded as malicious and unlawful. It was objected that, due largely to environment, the social and economic ideas of judges, which thus became translated into law, were prejudicial to a position of equality between workingman and employer; that due to this dependence upon the individual opinion of judges great confusion existed as to what purposes were lawful and what unlawful; and that in any event Congress, not the judges, was the body which should declare what public policy in regard to the industrial struggle demands.

By 1914 the ideas of the advocates of legislation had fairly crystallized upon the manner in which the inequality and uncertainty of the law should be removed. It was to be done by expressly legalizing certain acts regardless of the effects produced by them upon other persons. As to them Congress was to extract the element of injuria from the damages thereby inflicted, instead of leaving judges to determine according to their own economic and social views whether the damage inflicted on an employer in an industrial struggle was damnum absque injuria, because an incident of trade competition, or a legal injury, because in their opinion, economically and socially objectionable. This idea was presented to the committees which reported the Clayton Act. The resulting law set out certain acts which had previously been held unlawful, whenever courts had disapproved of the ends for which they were performed; it then declared that, when these acts were committed in the course of an industrial dispute, they should not be held to violate any law of the United States. In other words the Clayton Act substituted the opinion of Congress as to the propriety of the purpose for that of differing judges; and thereby it declared that the relations between employers of labor and workingmen were competitive relations, that organized competition was not harmful and that it justified injuries necessarily inflicted in its course. Both the majority and the minority report of the House Committee indicate that such was its purpose. If, therefore, the act applies to the case at bar, the acts here complained of cannot "be considered or held to be violations of any law of the United States," and, hence, do not violate the Sherman Act.

The Duplex Company contends that §20 of the Clayton Act does not apply to the case at bar, because it is restricted to cases "between an employer and employees, or between employers and employees, or between employees, or between persons employed and persons seeking employment, involving, or growing out of, a dispute concerning terms or conditions of employment"; whereas the case at bar arises between an employer in Michigan and workingmen in New York not in its employ, and does not involve their conditions of employment. But Congress did not restrict the provision to employers and workingmen in their employ. By including "employers and employees" and "persons employed and persons seeking employment" it showed that it was not aiming merely at a legal relationship between a specific employer and his employees. Furthermore, the plaintiff's contention proves too much. If the words are to receive a strict technical construction, the statute will have no application to disputes between employers of labor and workingmen, since the very acts to which it applies sever the continuity of the legal relationship. Iron Moulders' Union v. Allis-Chalmers Co., 166 F. 45, 52–53, 20 L.R.A., N.S. 315 (C.C.A. 7th) ; Louisville, Evansville & St. Louis R. R. Co. v. Wilson, 138 U.S. 501, 505, 11 S. Ct. 405, 34 L. Ed. 1023; cf. Rex. v. Neilson, 44 N.S. 488, 491. The further contention that this case is not one arising out of a dispute concerning the conditions of work of one of the parties, is, in my opinion, founded upon a misconception of the facts.

Because I have come to the conclusion that both the common law of a State and a statute of the United States declare the right of industrial combatants to push their struggle to the limits of the justification of self-interest, I do not wish to be understood as attaching any constitutional or moral sanction to that right. All rights are derived from the purposes of the society in which they exist; above all rights rises duty to the community. The conditions developed in industry may be such that those engaged in it cannot continue their struggle without danger to the community. But it is not for judges to determine whether such conditions exist, nor is it their function to set the limits of permissible contest and to declare the duties which the new situation demands. This is the function of the legislature which, while limiting individual and group rights of aggression and defense, may substitute processes of justice for the more primitive method of trial by combat.

NOTES

1. Does Justice Brandeis' opinion in this case written in 1927 (with Justice Holmes concurring) differ from Holmes' statement (Note 3, page 642) written in 1894? Does the presence of a statute change the function of the judge in these cases? If these problems of policy are to be left to the legislature, what should the judge do when there is no legislation or the statute is ambiguous?

2. The whole arsenal of legal remedies was used to enforce the Sherman Act against unions. Criminal prosecution, injunctions, and damage actions were freely used. The potency of treble damage suits authorized by Section 7 of the Sherman Anti-Trust Act (see now 15 U.S.C.A., Sec. 15) is cogently illustrated by the Danbury Hatters' Cases (Loewe v. Lawlor, 208 U.S. 274, 28 Sup. Ct. 301, 52 L. Ed. 488 (1908); Lawlor v. Loewe, 235 U.S. 522, 35 Sup. Ct. 170, 59 L. Ed. 341 (1915)); and the Coronado Coal cases (United Mine Workers of America v. Coronado Coal Company, 259 U.S. 344, 42 Sup. Ct. 570, 66 L. Ed. 975 (1922); Coronado Coal Co. v. United Mine Workers of America, 268 U.S. 295, 45 Sup. Ct. 551, 69 L. Ed. 963 (1925)).

In the Danbury Hatters' Cases, the United Hatters of North America (AFL) sought to unionize the shop of a Connecticut hat manufacturer by inducing strikes at his factory and boycotting his products, dealers, and customers throughout the country, all causing an alleged $80,000 damage. The interstate character of the business and boycott were clear, and the Court agreed that the interdiction of the Sherman Act included combinations of labor as well as capital. Questions of motive or justification — as perhaps bearing on the reasonableness of the restraint — received no consideration. Damages in the amount of $240,000 were assessed against the Union and the members were held individually liable.

In the Coronado cases the United Mine Workers attempted to close a nonunion mine (in a generally unionized area) by a strike patterned with criminal violence and substantial destruction of property. Assessed damages of $200,000 were trebled by the court, to which was added a $25,000 counsel fee.

3. The common law incapacity of unincorporated unions to sue or be sued as such, has, at least prior to the Taft-Hartley Act (see Appendix, particularly Secs. 301 and 303), seriously limited use of the damage suit as a usual method of legal control. The Court in the first Coronado case (supra) held that UMW, its

District 21, and certain locals were suable in their own names —
adverting to the entity-like nature of the associations the existence
of statutes which generally treated unions on bases distinct from
other groups, and the softening effects of class suit procedure.   It
should be borne in mind that this realistic approach was somewhat
buttressed by the fact that the word "person" as defined in Section 8 of the Sherman Act (15 U.S.C.A., Sec. 7) includes associations existing under the laws of any state.   The broader procedural implications of the Coronado case, are, however, codified
in substance by Rule 17 (b) , Fed. R. Cir. P. (28 U.S.C.A. following
Sec. 723C), which provides that any unincorporated association
"may sue or be sued in its common name for the purpose of enforcing for or against it a substantive right existing under the constitution or laws of the United States."   If no federal right is
involved — where diversity of citizenship constitutes the basis of
jurisdiction — the law of the state in which the District Court
sits apparently is controlling.   See, for example, Pullman Standard Car Manufacturing Co. v. United Steel Workers, 152 F.2d 493
(7th Cir. 1945), where the Company's action for libel was held
not maintainable although the defendant union had been certified
by NLRB as bargaining representative; compare Worthington
Pump & Machine Corp. v. Local 259, 63 F. Supp. 411 (D. Mass.
1945), a declaratory judgment case.   Modifications which various
states have effected in the common law rule are far from uniform
and the resultant widely variable and uncertain body of local
rules and exceptions forms an important part of the background
of Sections 301 and 303 of the Taft-Hartley amendments.   See,
generally, Sen. Rep. No. 105, 80th Cong., 1st Sess. 15–18 (1947);
Lach v. Hoisting & Portable Power & Eng. Local (AFL), 86 F.
Supp. 463 (D. Mass. 1949).   Cf. Banner Manufacturing Co. v.
United Furniture Workers 90 F. Supp. 723 (S.D.N.Y. 1950).

4. In the first Coronado Coal Case, Note 2 supra, the Court
held that a violation of the Sherman Act was not proved by a
mere showing that union activity had the effect of reducing interstate commerce even by unlawful means.   There must be proof
that the union "intended to restrain commerce" or that its action
"has necessarily such a direct material and substantial effect to
restrain it that the intent must reasonably be inferred."   Upon
retrial of the case additional evidence was introduced to satisfy
the court that at least as to the local union, "the purpose of the
destruction was to stop the production of non-union coal and
prevent its shipment to markets of other states . . . where it
would, by competition, tend to reduce the prices of the com-

modity and injuriously affect the maintenance of wages for union labor in competing mines." Compare United Leather Workers v. Herkert & Meisel Trunk Co., 265 U.S. 457, 44 Sup. Ct. 623, 68 L. Ed. 1104 (1924).

In United States v. Brims, 272 U.S. 549, 47 Sup. Ct. 169, 71 L. Ed. 403 (1926), manufacturers of millwork in Chicago agreed to hire only union carpenters in return for the union's agreement not to install nonunion millwork. This combination of employers with the union was held to be in restraint of trade.

For other famous antitrust cases prior to the New Deal era, see Alco-Zander v. Amalgamated Clothing Workers, page 642 supra; Bedford Cut Stone v. Journeymen Stone Cutters Assn., 274 U.S. 37; 47 Sup. Ct. 522, 71 L. Ed. 916 (1927). See generally, Berman, Labor and the Sherman Act (1930).

5. The strictures of the antitrust laws on unions were substantially loosened in 1940 by the decision in Apex Hosiery Co. v. Leader, 310 U.S. 469, 60 Sup. Ct. 982, 84 L. Ed. 1311 (1940). Apex Hosiery Company annually produced $5,000,000 worth of hosiery at its Philadelphia factory from raw materials shipped to it from outside the state. More than 80 per cent of its product was regularly shipped in interstate commerce, such shipments constituting less than 3 per cent of the total national product. When the Company refused to accede to a closed-shop demand, the Union ordered a strike. Although only eight Apex employees were then members of the Union, assistance was rendered by the Union employees of other local factories. Under the direction of Leader, the Union president, the plant was forcibly seized and a so-called sit-down strike maintained. Machinery was destroyed and during the period of unlawful occupation the strikers repeatedly refused to permit the shipment of $800,000 worth of finished hosiery, 80 per cent of which was on interstate order. Business was thus suspended for more than three months. The Court held that a treble damage suit under the antitrust laws was not available to the complainant. The following points are important highlights of its opinion (Justice Stone):

    (a) Defendants' activities substantially restrained and were intended to restrain inter-state transportation, but

    (b) the issue is whether this is the kind of restraint at which the Sherman Act is directed.

    (c) Common law background, legislative history and prior distinguishable decisions of the Court show that a violation requires a restraint on commercial competition in the marketing of goods and services. Complainant must therefore, show a restraint which has, or is intended to have an effect on market prices or otherwise deprive purchasers or consumers of the advantages which they derive from competition.

Justice Stone had earlier questioned the practical value of speculating on the general inferences to be drawn from a particular antitrust decision (Maple Flooring Manufacturers case, 268 U.S. 563, 579, 45 Sup. Ct. 578, 69 L. Ed. 1043 (1925)). Later treatment of the Apex case has emphasized the importance of the warning. See, for example, United States v. Womens Sportswear Manufacturers Assn., 75 F. Supp. 112 (D. Mass. 1947), where the court relied principally on the Apex decision but was unanimously reversed in United States v. Womens Sportswear, 336 U.S. 460, 69 Sup. Ct. 714 93 L. Ed. 805 (1949); and compare Justice Stone (concurring, at page 237, on the ground that the Apex case was applicable) with Justice Roberts (dissenting at page 243) in United States v. Hutcheson 312 U.S. 219, 61 Sup. Ct. 463, 85 L. Ed. 788 (noted infra). A "labor lawyer" might, nevertheless, inquire concerning the Apex decision whether:

(a) The result would have been different if the volume of complainant's business approximated 10 per cent of the national total?

(b) The Duplex case (page 660 supra) is satisfactorily distinguishable?

(c) The activities in the Alco-Zander case (page 642 supra) are now permissible, or

(d) A local strike to eliminate the use of certain types of labor-saving machinery is permissible?

For a comment on the Apex case, see Landis, The Apex Case, 26 Cornell L.Q. 191 (1941); Gregory, The Sherman Act v. Labor, 8 U. of Chi. L. Rev. 222 (1941).

The final step in freeing unions from the antitrust laws was taken in United States v. Hutcheson, 312 U.S. 219, 61 Sup. Ct. 463, 85 L. Ed. 788 (1940). In this case the Carpenters, who were engaged in a jurisdictional work dispute with the Machinists, attempted to further their position by local strikes called against Anheuser-Busch, Inc. (brewers) and several contractors who were then engaged in the erection of additional facilities for Anheuser and its adjoining tenant. The strike was supplemented by picketing the construction projects and by the nation-wide circularization of a request that union members and their friends refrain from buying Anheuser-Busch beer. The Court held that a Sherman Act *indictment* was demurrable. As noted above, Justice

Stone thought that the Apex case was applicable — at least if aided by some free-speech concepts. Justice Frankfurter, however, in delivering the opinion of the Court chose much broader grounds. He viewed the Norris-LaGuardia Act as a Congressional interpretation of the Clayton Act. "Therefore, whether trade union conduct constitutes a violation of the Sherman Law *is to be determined only by reading the Sherman Law and section 20 of the Clayton Act and the Norris-LaGuardia Act as a harmonizing text of outlawry of labor conduct.*" [Italics supplied.]

For comment on the Hutcheson decision see Nathanson and Wirtz, The Hutcheson Case: Another View, 36 Ill. L. Rev. 41 (1941) ; Cavers, And What of the Apex Case Now? 8 U. of Chi. L. Rev. 516 (1941). In connection with the later evolution of the Apex and Hutcheson decisions, compare Allen Bradley Co. v. Local Union No. 3, IBEW et al., 325 U.S. 797, 65 Sup. Ct. 1533, 89 L. Ed. 1939 (1945), with Hunt v. Crumboch, 325 U.S. 821, 65 Sup. Ct. 1545, 89 L. Ed. 1954 (1945).

6. If unions are to be treated differently from other economic combinations under the antitrust laws and to be freed from its strictures, then it becomes essential to determine what organizations are entitled to this freedom of action.

In Columbia River Packers v. Hinton, 315 U.S. 143, 62 Sup. Ct. 520, 86 L. Ed. 750 (1942), fishermen who leased boats and sold the fish caught to processors formed a union which bargained collectively with the processors to fix the price. Members sold only to processors who had union contracts, and processors under contract bought only from union members. One processor who refused to contract with the union was boycotted. He sought an injunction under the Sherman Act. The Court held that this was not a labor dispute within the Norris-LaGuardia Act but was a dispute between businessmen over the sale of a commodity. There was no employer-employee relationship, but a combination in restraint of trade.

If the purpose of collective bargaining is to equalize bargaining power, why should such an organization be illegal? Does the mere fact that a person's earnings are stated in terms of prices for products, deprive him of the right to concerted action? Can milk drivers or laundry drivers who own their own trucks and are paid on a commission basis organize to obtain higher commission rates? See Gottesman, Restraint of Trade–Employees or Enterprisers, 15 U. of Chi. L. Rev. 638 (1948).

The underlying problem is not met by analysis in terms of employer-employee relationship. In Commonwealth v. McHugh,

326 Mass. 249, 93 N.E.2d 751 (1951), the fishermen were employed by boat owners and were paid according to the price received for the catch. The Union established selling markets for the fish and compelled all employers to sell through these Union markets. If the price bid on a catch was less than the minimum set by the Union, the members refused to unload. The Union thus protected the members' wages by obtaining a minimum price for the catch. The Massachusetts court issued an injunction on the ground that this was an unreasonable restraint of trade.

Would such an arrangement as this be enjoinable in the federal courts? When the Massachusetts court terms this an "unreasonable" restraint of trade, is it applying a test any different from that applied to labor disputes under the prima facie tort doctrine? When John L. Lewis determines that there is too much coal available and orders the miners to refuse to work more than three days a week, is he violating the antitrust laws? If the mine owners agreed among themselves to limit operations to three days a week, would they be violating the antitrust laws?

In the light of these problems reread the excerpt from Simons, Some Reflections on Syndicalism at page 49 supra.

NOTE ON INJUNCTIONS IN LABOR DISPUTES

a. Use, Abuse, and Effectiveness

Justice Brandeis, dissenting in Truax v. Corrigan, 257 U.S. 312, 42 Sup. Ct. 124, 66 L. Ed. 254 (1921), stated at page 366:

> In England, observance of the rules of the contest has been enforced by the courts almost wholly through the criminal law or through actions at law for compensation. An injunction was granted in a labor dispute as early as 1868. But in England resort to the injunction had not been frequent and it has played no appreciable part there in the conflict between capital and labor.[42] In America the injunction did not secure recognition as a possible remedy until 1888. When

[42] Justice Brandeis refers to the infrequency of recourse to the injunction in England. The reasons for this are not clear, but one possibility is that the English courts have followed a much more restricted interpretation than have American courts in determining the nature of the property rights they would protect. In labor cases the property involved is the business, an intangible interest. English courts have been reluctant to extend their jurisdiction to the protection of this sort of interest. Justice Brandeis intimates, too, that since the history of labor legislation in England reveals a more complete definition of the rights and duties of unions than in this country, the courts have been less inclined to engraft their own innovations. — Ed.

a few years later its use became extensive and conspicuous, the controversy over the remedy over-shadowed in bitterness the question of the relative substantive rights of the parties. In the storms of protest against this use many thoughtful lawyers joined. The equitable remedy, although applied in accordance with established practice, involved incidents which, it was asserted, endangered the personal liberty of wage-earners. The acts enjoined were frequently, perhaps usually, acts which were already crimes at common law or had been made so by statutes. The issues in litigation arising out of trade disputes related largely to questions of fact. But in equity issues of fact as well as of law were tried by a single judge, sitting without a jury. Charges of violating an injunction were often heard on affidavits merely, without the opportunity of confronting or cross-examining witnesses. Men found guilty of contempt were committed in the judge's discretion, without either a statutory limit upon the length of the imprisonment, or the opportunity of effective review on appeal, or the right to release on bail pending possible revisory proceedings. The effect of the proceeding upon the individual was substantially the same as if he had been successfully prosecuted for a crime; but he was denied, in the course of the equity proceedings, those rights which by the constitution are commonly secured to persons charged with a crime.

It was asserted that in these proceedings an alleged danger to property, always incidental and at times insignificant, was often laid hold of to enable the penalties of the criminal law to be enforced expeditiously without that protection to the liberty of the individual which the Bill of Rights was designed to afford; that through such proceedings a single judge often usurped the functions not only of the jury but of the police department; that, in prescribing the conditions under which strikes were permissible and how they might be carried out, he usurped also the powers of the legislature; and that incidentally he abridged the constitutional rights of individuals to free speech, to a free press and to peaceful assembly.

It was urged that the real motive in seeking the injunction was not ordinarily to prevent property from being injured nor to protect the owner in its use, but to endow property with active, militant power which would make it dominant over men. In other words, that, under the guise of protecting property rights, the employer was seeking sovereign power, and many disinterested men, solicitous only for the public welfare, believed that the law of property was not appropriate for dealing with the forces beneath social unrest; that in this vast struggle it was unwise to throw the power of the State on one side or the other according to principles deduced from that law; that the problem of the control and conduct of industry demanded a solution of its own; and that, pending the ascertainment of new principles to govern industry, it was wiser for the State not to interfere in industrial struggles by the issuance of an injunction.

Section 20 of the Clayton Act purported to restrict the power of federal courts to issue injunctions in labor disputes. It was hailed by Samuel Gompers as "labor's charter of freedom." Its fate has already been indicated in the Duplex case. The impact of that decision was graphically described by Judge Amidon in Great Northern Ry. v. Brosseau, 268 Fed. 414 (D.N.D. 1923) :

> Notwithstanding the legislative history of the statute, and its highly remedial character, as indicated by its history and the reports of the committees having it in charge, many lower federal courts have studiously striven to disregard its plain language, as well as the actual intent of Congress, as disclosed by the history of the statute. Some have held that all strikes cause irreparable injury, and therefore the employer is entitled to an injunction to prevent such injury. Other courts have gone so far as to hold that the entire statute was a trick by Congress to so frame the measure that one part of it would nullify the other. Other courts have said there was no such thing as peaceful picketing, and hence no such thing as peaceful persuasion, and therefore the plain language of the statute must be disregarded by the court, and all picketing and all attempts by strikers to exercise their rights of peaceful persuasion were to be restrained, and injunctions have been accordingly issued. Other courts, notwithstanding the specific language of the last clause of section 20 that the doing of the acts which it permits should not be held to be in conflict with any federal law, have restrained strikes upon the ground that they violated the Sherman Anti-Trust Law and statutes forbidding the obstruction of the United States mails.

For a full discussion of the evils of injunction, see Frankfurter and Greene, The Labor Injunction (1930). See also a study of trial court practice in issuing labor injunctions over a five-year period: Berwit et al., Survey of Ohio Practice in Issuance of Labor Injunctions, 5 Ohio St. L.J. 289 (1939).

It should be recalled that in addition to the stringency of injunction procedures themselves, the class or representative suit was available to facilitate greatly judicial control of union activities and objectives. (See Duplex Printing Co. v. Deering, page 660 supra.)

Although there was some public reaction against the indiscriminate use of this potent judicial weapon, few courts were willing to abandon its use. Instead they used their judge-made concepts of due process, equal protection, and separation of powers to declare unconstitutional legislation which curbed the injunctive process. See Truax v. Corrigan, 257 U.S. 312, 42 Sup. Ct. 124, 66 L. Ed. 254 (1921); Opinion of the Justices, 275 Mass. 580 (1931).

b. The Norris-LaGuardia Act and State Anti-injunction Acts

"No court of the United States, as herein defined, shall have jurisdiction to issue any restraining order or temporary or permanent injunction in a case involving or growing out of a labor dispute except in strict conformity with the provisions of such sections; . . ."

With these words, Congress in 1932 declared its determination to eliminate the evils of labor injunctions in the federal courts. The Norris-LaGuardia Act is not based on the power of Congress to regulate interstate commerce, but on the power granted to Congress by Article III of the Constitution to regulate the jurisdiction of inferior federal courts. The application of the statute does not depend on the kind of business involved but on the court in which the suit is brought.

A careful reading of its fifteen sections discloses in specific detail the design to prohibit the issuance of injunctions in most labor disputes and to prevent procedural abuses in those situations where an injunction might be issued. Perhaps more important, however, is the Act's firm endorsement of a policy favorable to collective organization and bargaining and the requirement of a general attitude of nonintervention by the courts. The basic framework of the legislative restriction is found in Sections 13, 7, and 4, taken in that order.

    (a) Would these sections prevent the issuance of *any* injunction on the facts of the Alco-Zander case (supra page 642), i.e., is there a case within Section 13?   Can all findings required by Section 7 be made?   What of Section 4?   (See also Section 5.)

(b) What of the applicability of the Act to the situation in the Hitchman case (supra page 650)?   See particularly Sections 3 and 10.

(c) What effect should the statute have on the issuance of an injunction on the facts of Central Metal Products v. O'Brien (supra page 651)?

Following the passage of the Norris-LaGuardia Act, a number of states enacted similar laws.   The pattern of these state anti-injunction laws is far from uniform.   A few states, notably New York (N.Y. Cir. Prac. Act, Sec. 876-a), Pennsylvania (Pa. Stat., tit. 43, §206a et seq. (Purdon, 1941)); New Jersey (N.J. Stat. Ann., Secs. 2:29–77 et seq. (1939)), Wisconsin (Wis. Stat., Sec. 103.51 et seq. (1945)), and Oregon (Ore. Comp. Laws Ann., Sec. 102–902 et seq. (1940)), have enacted legislation substantially modeled on the Norris-LaGuardia Act.   In other states the restrictions are comparatively mild.   For example, the Massachusetts law (Mass. Acts 1935, c. 407) was primarily modeled on Section 7 of the federal law but failed to include the more restrictive provisions of Section 4.   An interesting modification which emphasizes the developing tendency to coordinate judicial intervention with the collective bargaining process is found in the 1950 amendments to the Massachusetts statute (Cox-Phillips Act, Mass. Acts 1950, c. 452, 26 L.R.R.M. 3029).   The technique of this law is to define "lawful" and "unlawful" labor disputes, including within the former type, disputes concerning contract "provisions of a kind commonly found in collective bargaining agreements" and within the latter, non-bargainable demands as well as failure to abide by an arbitration agreement or to circumvent the requirements of the local and national labor relations acts.   State anti-injunction acts (particularly the latter detailed type) may raise interesting problems of federal-state relationships.   (Compare Federal–State Jurisdiction, page 835 infra.)

Where no state legislation has been enacted the old abuses remain.   The most complete study yet published on the prevalence of injunctions in state courts today, despite these statutes, is found in Document No. 7, "State Court Injunctions," Report of the Sub-Committee on Labor Management Relations of the U.S. Senate Committee on Labor and Public Welfare, 82d Cong., 1st Sess. (1951), summarized in 73 Mo. Lab. Rev. 59 (1951).

LAUF v. E. G. SHINNER & CO., INC.
Supreme Court of the United States, 1938
303 U.S. 323, 58 Sup. Ct. 578, 82 L. Ed. 872

MR. JUSTICE ROBERTS delivered the opinion of the Court: . . .

The District Court found the following facts: The respondent is a Delaware corporation maintaining five meat markets in Milwaukee, Wis. The petitioners are, respectively, an unincorporated labor union and its business manager, citizens and residents of Wisconsin. The respondent's employees number about thirty-five; none of them are members of the petitioning union. The petitioners made demand upon the respondent to require its employees as a condition of their continued employment, to become members of the union. The respondent notified the employees that they were free to do this and that it was willing to permit them to join, but they declined and refused to join. The union had not been chosen by the employees to represent them in any matter connected with the respondent. For the purpose of coercing the respondent to require its employees to join the union, and to accept it as their bargaining agent and representative, as a condition of continued employment, and for the purpose of injuring and destroying the business if the respondent refused to yield to such coercion, the petitioners conspired to do the following things and did them: They caused false and misleading signs to be placed before the respondent's markets; caused persons who were not respondent's employees to parade and picket before the markets; falsely accused respondent of being unfair to organized labor in its dealings with employees, and, by molestation, annoyance, threats, and intimidation, prevented patrons and prospective patrons of respondent from patronizing its markets; respondent suffered and will suffer irreparable injury from the continuance of the practice, and customers will be intimidated and restrained from patronizing the stores as a consequence of petitioners' acts. There is more than $3,000 involved in the controversy.

The District Court held that no labor dispute, as defined by federal or state law, exists between the respondent and the petitioners or either of them; that the respondent is bound to permit its employees free agency in the matter of choice of union organization or representation; and that the respondent had no adequate remedy at law. It entered a final decree enjoining the petitioners from seeking to coerce the respondent to discharge any of its employees for refusal to join the union or to coerce the respondent to compel employees to become members of the organization, from advertising that the respondent is unfair to organized labor, and from annoying or molesting patrons or persuading or soliciting customers, present or prospective, not to patronize the respondent's markets.

The Circuit Court of Appeals affirmed the decree.   By reason of alleged conflict with a decision of the Supreme Court of Wisconsin, Senn v. Tile Layers Protective Union, 222 Wis. 383, 268 N.W. 270, 872, and with our decision in Senn v. Tile Layers Protective Union, 301 U.S. 468, 57 S. Ct. 857, 81 L. Ed. 1229, we granted the writ of certiorari.   302 U.S. 669, 58 S. Ct. 35, 82 L. Ed. 516 . . .

Third.   The District Court erred in granting an injunction in the absence of findings which the Norris-LaGuardia Act makes prerequisites to the exercise of jurisdiction.

Section 13 (c) of the Act is: "The term 'labor dispute' includes any controversy concerning terms or conditions of employment, or concerning the association or representation of the persons in negotiating, fixing, maintaining, changing, or seeking to arrange terms or conditions of employment, regardless of whether or not the disputants stand in the proximate relation of employer and employee."

This definition does not differ materially from that . . . [of] the Wisconsin labor Code, and the facts of the instant case bring it within both. . . .   There can be no question of the power of Congress thus to define and limit the jurisdiction of the inferior courts of the United States.   The District Court made none of the required findings save as to irreparable injury and lack of remedy at law.   It follows that in issuing the injunction it exceeded its jurisdiction.

Fourth.   The Court of Appeals erred in holding that the declarations of policy in the Norris-LaGuardia Act and the Wisconsin Labor Code, to the effect that employees are to have full freedom of association, self-organization, and designation of representative of their own choosing, free from interference, restraint, or coercion of their employers, puts this case outside the scope of both acts, since respondent cannot accede to the petitioners' demands upon it without disregarding the policy declared by the statutes.   This view was expressed in the court's first opinion on the appeal from the issue of an interlocutory injunction, and the opinion on the appeal from the final order adopts what was said on the earlier appeal as the law of the case.   We find nothing in the declarations of policy which narrows the definition of a labor dispute as found in the statutes.   The rights of the parties and the jurisdiction of the federal courts are to be determined according to the express provisions applicable to labor disputes as so defined. . . .

The judgment is reversed and the cause remanded to the District Court for further proceedings in conformity with this opinion.

Reversed.

Mr. Justice Cardozo and Mr. Justice Reed took no part in the consideration or decision of this case.

Mr. Justice Butler (dissenting) . . . .

. . . 1. Respondent's business constitutes a property right; and the free opportunity of respondent and its customers to deal with one another in that business is an incident inseparable therefrom. It is hard to imagine a case which more clearly calls for equitable relief; and the court below rightly granted an injunction. Truax v. Corrigan, 257 U.S. 312, 42 S. Ct. 124, 127, 66 L. Ed. 254, 27 A.L.R. 375, and cases cited.

But here it is held that the decree conflicts with the Norris-LaGuardia Act. That the action demanded by petitioners of respondent with respect to its employees, if taken, would have been morally indefensible is plain; that it would have been against the declared policy of the act is equally plain. That act, 29 U.S.C.A. sec. 102, declares that, under prevailing conditions, the individual unorganized worker, "though he should be free to decline to associate with his fellows" should "have full freedom of association, self-organization, and designation of representatives of his own choosing," and should "be free from the interference, restraint, or coercion of employers of labor, or their agents, in the designation of such representatives," etc. This declaration of policy, as the introductory clause plainly recites, was intended as an aid "in the interpretation" of the Act and "in determining the jurisdiction and authority of the courts" under the Act . . .

The opinion of the Court asserts, however, that this definite declaration of policy in no way narrows the definition of the phrase "labor dispute" found in substantive provisions of the Act. . . .

The decision just announced ignores the declared policy of Congress that the worker should be free to decline association with his fellows, that he should have full freedom in that respect and be free from interference, restraint, or coercion of employers. To say that a "labor dispute" is created by the mere refusal of respondent to comply with the demand that it compel its employees to designate the union as their representative unmistakably subverts this policy and consequently puts a construction upon the words contrary to the manifest congressional intent. . . .

2. But putting aside the congressional declaration of policy as an indication of meaning, and considering the phrase entirely apart, the facts of this case plainly do not constitute a "labor dispute" as defined by the act. Undoubtedly "dispute" is used in its primary sense as meaning a verbal controversy involving an expression of opposing views or claims. The act itself, 29 U.S.C.A. sec. 113 (c), so regards it: "The term 'labor dispute' includes any controversy concerning terms or conditions of employment," etc. In this case, there was no interchange or consideration of conflicting views in respect of the settlement of a controversial problem. There was simply an overbearing demand by the union that respondent should do an unlawful thing and a natural refusal on its part to comply. If a demand by a labor union that an employer compel its employees to submit to the will of the union, and the employer's refusal, constitute a labor controversy, the highwayman's demand for the money of his victim and the latter's refusal to stand and deliver constitute a financial controversy. . . .

So far as concerns the question here involved, the phrase "labor dispute" is the basic element of the Act. For unless there was such a dispute — that is to say, a "controversy" — the Act does not even purport to limit the District Court's jurisdiction in equity. The phrase must receive a sensible construction in harmony with the congressional intent and policy. There can be no dispute without disputants. Between whom was there a dispute here? There was none between the union and respondent's employees; for the latter were considered by the union mere pawns to be moved according to the arbitrary will of the union. There was none between respondent and its employees; for they were in full accord. And finally there was none between the union and respondent; for it would be utterly unreasonable to suppose Congress intended that the refusal of a conscientious employer to transgress the express policy of the law should constitute a "labor dispute" having the effect of bringing to naught not only the policy of the law, but the obligation of a court of equity to respect it and to restrain a continuing and destructive assault upon the property rights of the employer, as to which no adequate remedy at law existed. . . .

MR. JUSTICE McREYNOLDS concurs in this opinion.

NOTES

1. The problem of "stranger picketing" for purposes of organizing nonunion shops has been a recurring one. Compare the provisions in Section 20 of the Clayton Act with Sections 13 (a) and (c) of the Norris-LaGuardia Act in this regard. Compare also the definition of an "employee" in Section 2 (3) of the Labor Management Relations Act.

2. Contrast the dissenting opinion of Justice Butler in Lauf v. E. G. Shinner with the majority opinion in Nevada v. Eighth District Court, 66 Nev. 202, 210 P.2d 454 (1949).

3. The requirements of Section 8 of the Norris-LaGuardia Act emphasize the statute's general policy. In Brotherhood of Railroad Trainmen et al. v. Toledo, Peoria & Western Railroad, 321 U.S. 50, 64 Sup. Ct. 413, 88 L. Ed. 534, 150 A.L.R. 810 (1944), the Union (which was engaged in a labor dispute over wages and working conditions) conducted a strike wherein violence had been substantial and the protection of the carrier by public officials had been inadequate. The Company, however, steadfastly refused to submit the dispute to voluntary arbitration as proposed by the National Mediation Board pursuant to the Railway Labor Act (see Appendix). The employees had agreed to such arbitration. The question whether Section 8 barred injunctive relief thus became a principal issue. The Company contended that this section did not apply where violence was involved and that in any event "if 'voluntary arbitration' as the term is used in Section 8 encompasses arbitration under the Railway Labor Act, by that fact the arbitration ceases to be 'voluntary' and the latter Act's requirement that it be so is violated . . . the effect is to force respondent to submit to compulsory arbitration." What decision? Compare Davis Bros. Fisheries Co. Inc. v. Pimentel, 322 Mass. 499, 508, 78 N.E.2d 93 (1948).

4. What is a "labor dispute" within the meaning of the anti-injunction acts? Consider the four following cases:

(a) The complainant operated retail food stores in Washington, D.C., where it employed both white and colored clerks. Petitioners, a philanthropic association of colored persons, requested that the Company adopt a policy of employing Negro clerks in the course of personnel changes. When the request was ignored the petitioners peaceably picketed the stores with placards: "Do Your Part! Buy Where You Can Work! No Negroes Employed Here!" New Negro Alliance v. Sanitary Grocery Co., 303 U.S. 552, 58 Sup. Ct. 703, 82 L. Ed. 1012 (1938). See also Fur

Workers Local No. 72 v. Fur Workers Union 21238, page 688 infra.

(b) The American Medical Association and the Medical Society of the District of Columbia were charged with conspiracy: (1) to restrain member physicians from accepting employment under Group Health (a nonprofit employee organization providing medical care on a risk-sharing prepayment basis and employing full-time physicians on a salary basis); (2) to restrain members from consulting with Group Health doctors, and hospitals from affording facilities to patients of Group Health physicians. American Medical Association v. United States, 317 U.S. 519, 533, 63 Sup. Ct. 326, 87 L. Ed. 434 (1943). Compare Columbia River Packers v. Hinton, page 670 supra (union of fishermen); Outdoor Sports v. AFL, 6 N.J. 217, 78 A.2d 69 (1951) (union of stock car drivers); Rubin v. American Sportsmen Televison Equity Society, 105 Cal. App. 2d 742, 234 P.2d 188 (1951) (organization of professional wrestlers). See also Bakery Sales Drivers Local Union No. 33 v. Wagshal, 333 U.S. 437, 68 Sup. Ct. 630, 92 L. Ed. 792 (1948), page 708 infra.

(c) The Brotherhood of Locomotive Firemen negotiated a collective bargaining agreement with certain carriers, the effect of which was to deprive certain employees in the unit represented by the Union, of promotion and job assignments on a racial basis. A group of these employees sued to enjoin the Union and carriers from complying with the discriminatory clauses of the contract. Graham v. Brotherhood of Locomotive Firemen & Enginemen, 338 U.S. 232, 70 Sup. Ct. 14, 94 L. Ed. 22 (1949).

(d) The United States sued for a declaratory judgment that John L. Lewis and the United Mine Workers could not terminate by unilateral action a contract existing between them and the Secretary of the Interior made after the 1946 seizure of the coal mines under the War Labor Disputes Act of 1943 (50 U.S.C.A. App., Secs. 1501–1511). Ancillary to this declaration, the United States sought a restraining order and preliminary injunction requiring the defendants to cancel the notice of termination of the contract. This had been circulated three days before the complaint was filed and as a result of it the miners had ceased work. When a restraining order was issued it was disregarded by the defendants, who thereupon were cited for contempt. The defendants argued that the Norris-LaGuardia Act barred injunctive relief, and, therefore, that impositions of both civil and criminal contempt penalties by the trial court were improper. United States v. United Mine Workers of America, 330 U.S. 258, 67 Sup. Ct. 677,

91 L. Ed. 884 (1947). Compare International Brotherhood of Teamsters, etc. v. Quick Charge, Inc., 168 F.2d 513 (10th Cir. 1948). See also Cox, The Void Order and Duty to Obey, 16 U. of Chi. L. Rev. 86 (1948).

C. *Strikes and Their Objectives*

A strike symbolizes the failure of unions and management to agree as to terms and conditions of employment. It is the result of the parties' inability to make a bargain. Because the employer controls the plant and issues the pay checks, he is in a position to enforce his will unilaterally so long as the plant continues to operate. The union is then faced with the issue of whether to close the plant by refusing to work. It is the union's basic method of exerting economic pressure.

Two aspects of a strike must be kept clearly in mind. First, it is normally concerted, not individual action. Its effectiveness depends largely upon the element of combined conduct. Second, it is not merely a quitting of a job; rather, it is a temporary refusal to work with an intent to return to work when a bargain is made. Strikers consider themselves as still employees.

The legality of the strike is commonly traced back to the famous case of Commonwealth v. Hunt, 4 Metc. 111 (Mass. 1842), which supposedly repudiated the doctrine of criminal conspiracy. To-day, the right to strike is often termed a "fundamental right" and is given explicit statutory recognition. Section 4 of the Norris-LaGuardia Act barred injunctions which ". . . prohibit any person or persons . . . from doing, whether singly or in concert, any of the following acts: (a) Ceasing or refusing to perform any work or remain in any relation of employment." Compare also Section 13 of the Labor Management Relations Act.

1. LEGALITY OF STRIKE METHODS

INTERNATIONAL UNION, UAW (AFL) v. WERB
Supreme Court of the United States, 1949
336 U.S. 245, 69 Sup. Ct. 516, 93 L. Ed. 651

Mr. Justice Jackson delivered the opinion of the Court:
. . . Briggs & Stratton Corporation operates two manufacturing plants in the State of Wisconsin engaging approximately 2,000 employees. These are represented by the International Union, Automobile Workers of America, A.F. of L., Local No. 232, as collective bargaining agent, it having been duly certified as such

by the National Labor Relations Board in proceedings under the National Labor Relations Act. Under such certification, the Union had negotiated collective bargaining agreements, the last of which expired on July 1, 1944. Negotiations of a new one reached a deadlock and bargaining sessions continued for some time without success.

On November 3, 1945, its leaders submitted to the Union membership a plan for a new method of putting pressure upon the employer. The stratagem consisted of calling repeated special meetings of the Union during working hours at any time the Union saw fit, which the employees would leave work to attend. It was an essential part of the plan that this should be without warning to the employer or notice as to when or whether the employees would return. The device was adopted and the first surprise cessation was called on November 6, 1945; thereafter, and until March 22, 1946, such action was repeated on twenty-six occasions. The employer was not informed during this period of any specific demands which these tactics were designed to enforce nor what concessions it could make to avoid them.

This procedure was publicly described by the Union leaders as a new technique for bringing pressure upon the employer. It was, and is, candidly admitted that these tactics were intended to and did interfere with production and put strong economic pressure on the employer, who was disabled thereby from making any dependable production plans or delivery commitments. And it was said that "this can't be said for the strike. After the initial surprise of the walkout, the company knows what it has to do and plans accordingly." It was commended as a procedure which would avoid hardships that a strike imposes on employees and was considered "a better weapon than a strike."

The employer did not resort to any private disciplinary measures such as discharge of the employees; instead, it sought a much less drastic remedy by plea to the appropriate public authority under Wisconsin law, to investigate and adjudge the Union's conduct under the law of the State. After the prescribed procedures, the Board ordered the Union to cease and desist from " (a) engaging in any concerted efforts to interfere with production by arbitrarily calling union meetings and inducing work stoppages during regularly scheduled working hours; or engaging in any other concerted effort to interfere with production of the complainant except by leaving the premises in an orderly manner for the purpose of going on strike." . . .

The Union contends that the statute as thus applied violates the Thirteenth Amendment in that it imposes a form of compulsory service or involuntary servitude. However, nothing in the statute or the order makes it a crime to abandon work individually (compare Pollock v. Williams, 322 U.S. 4) or collectively. Nor does either undertake to prohibit or restrict any employee from leaving the service of the employer, either for reason or without reason, either with or without notice . . . The facts afford no foundation for the contention that any action of the State has the purpose or effect of imposing any form of involuntary servitude.

It is further contended that the statute as applied invades rights of free speech and public assemblage guaranteed by the Fourteenth Amendment. We recently considered a similar contention in connection with other state action concerning labor relations. Lincoln Federal Labor Union v. Northwestern Iron & Metal Co., and Whitaker v. North Carolina, 335 U.S. 525, and American Federation of Labor v. American Sash & Door Co., 335 U.S. 538. For reasons there stated, these contentions are without merit. . . .

The substantial issue is whether Congress has protected the union conduct which the State has forbidden, and hence the state legislation must yield . . .

The argument is that two provisions, found in §§7 and 13 of the National Labor Relations Act, not relevantly changed by the Labor Management Relations Act of 1947, grant to the Union and its members the right to put pressure upon the employer by the recurrent and unannounced stoppage of work. Both Acts provide that "Employees shall have the right to self-organization, to form, join, or assist labor organizations, to bargain collectively through representatives of their own choosing, and to engage in concerted activities, for the purpose of collective bargaining or other mutual aid or protection." Because the acts forbidden by the Wisconsin judgment are concerted activities and had a purpose to assist labor organizations in collective bargaining, it is said to follow that they are federally authorized and thereby immunized from the state control.

It is urged here that we are bound to hold these activities protected by §7 because that has become the settled interpretation of the Act by the Board charged with its administration. This contention is based on decisions by the Board in American Mfg. Concern, 7 N.L.R.B. 753; Harnischfeger Corp., 9 N.L.R.B. 676; The Good Coal Co., 12 N.L.R.B. 136; Armour & Co., 25 N.L.R.B. 989; Cudahy Packing Co., 29 N.L.R.B. 837; and Mt. Clemens Pottery Company, 46 N.L.R.B. 714. We do not think it can fairly be said that even the cumulative effect of those cases amounts

to a fixed Board interpretation that all work stoppages are federally protected concerted activities . . .

However, in no event could the Board adopt such a binding
practice as to the scope of §7 in the light of the construction,
with which we agree, given to §7 by the Courts of Appeals, authorized to review Board orders.   In similar cases they have
denied comparable work stoppages the protection of that section.
C. G. Conn, Ltd. v. Labor Board, 108 F.2d 390; Labor Board v.
Condenser Corp., 128 F.2d 67; Home Beneficial Life Ins. Co. v.
Labor Board, 159 F.2d 280; and see Labor Board v. Draper Corp.,
145 F.2d 199; Labor Board v. Indiana Desk Co., 149 F.2d 987.
To hold that the alleged fixed Board interpretation has irrevocably
labeled all concerted activities "protected" would be in the teeth
of the Board's own language and would deny any effect to the
Courts of Appeals' decisions. . . .

Reliance also is placed upon §13 of the National Labor Relations Act, which provided, "Nothing in this Act shall be construed
so as to interfere with or impede or diminish in any way the right
to strike."   49 Stat. 449, 457.   The 1947 Amendment carries the
same provision but that Act includes a definition.   Section 501 (2)
says that when used in the Act "The term 'strike' includes any
strike or other concerted stoppage of work by employees (including a stoppage by reason of the expiration of a collective-bargaining agreement) and any concerted slow-down or other concerted
interruption of operations by employees."   61 Stat. 161.

This provision, as carried over into the Labor Management
Relations Act, does not purport to create, establish or define the
right to strike.   On its face it is narrower in scope than §7 — the
latter would be of little significance if "strike" is a broader term
than "concerted activity."   Unless we read into §13 words which
Congress omitted and a sense which Congress showed no intention
of including, all that this provision does is to declare a rule of
interpretation for the Act itself which would prevent any use of
what originally was a novel piece of legislation to qualify or
impede whatever right to strike exists under other laws.   It did
not purport to modify the body of law as to the legality of strikes
as it then existed.   This Court less than a decade earlier had
stated that law to be that the state constitutionally could prohibit
strikes and make a violation criminal.   It had unanimously
adopted the language of Mr. Justice Brandeis that "Neither the
common law, nor the Fourteenth Amendment, confers the absolute right to strike."   Dorchy v. Kansas, 272 U.S. 306, 311.   Dissenting views most favorable to labor in other cases had conceded

the right of the state legislature to mark the limits of tolerable industrial conflict in the public interest.   Duplex Co. v. Deering, 254 U.S. 443, 488.   This Court has adhered to that view.   Thornhill v. Alabama, 310 U.S. 88, 103.   The right to strike, because of its more serious impact upon the public interest, is more vulnerable to regulation than the right to organize and select representatives for lawful purposes of collective bargaining which this Court has characterized as a "fundamental right" and which, as the Court has pointed out, was recognized as such in its decisions long before it was given protection by the National Labor Relations Act. . . .

MR. JUSTICE MURPHY, with whom MR. JUSTICE RUTLEDGE concurs, dissenting. . . .

But the Court, by its reasoning and its quotation from a Congressional report, now makes intermittent work stoppages the equivalent of mutiny, contract-breaking, and the sit-down strike. It stretches the "objectives and means" test to include a form of pressure which is peaceful and direct.   In effect, it adopts the employer's plea that it cannot plan production schedules, cannot notify its customers and suppliers, cannot determine its output with any degree of certainty and that these inconveniences withdraw this activity from §7, of the national statutes.   The majority and the Wisconsin court call the weapon objectionable, then, only because it is effective.   To impute this rationale to the Congress which enacted the Wagner Act is, in my opinion, judicial legislation of an extreme form. . . .

NOTES

1. In C. G. Conn, Ltd. v. NLRB, 108 F.2d 390 (7th Cir. 1939), the court held that the discharge of employees who refused to work overtime was not discriminatory, because they were not "strikers."

> . . . We are unable to accept respondent's argument to the effect that an employee can be on a strike and at work simultaneously.   We think he must be on the job subject to the authority and control of the employer, or off the job as a striker, in support of some grievance. . . .
> . . . We have observed numerous variations of the recognized legitimate strike, such as the "sit-down" and "slowdown" strikes.   It seems this might be properly designated as a strike on the installment plan.
> We are aware of no law or logic that gives the employee

the right to work upon terms prescribed solely by him.   That is plainly what was sought to be done in this instance.   It is not a situation in which employees ceased work in protest against conditions imposed by the employer, but one in which the employees sought and intended to continue work upon their own notion of the terms which should prevail.   If they had a right to fix the hours of their employment it would follow that a similar right existed by which they could prescribe all conditions and regulations affecting their employment. . . .

Similarly, in NLRB v. Condenser Corp., 128 F.2d 67 (3d Cir. 1942), it was held that workers who simply stood at their benches and refused to work were not strikers and could be discharged. Accord, Matter of Elk Lumber Co., 91 N.L.R.B. 333, 26 L.R.R.M. 1493 (1950).   Compare NLRB v. Montgomery Ward & Co., 157 F.2d 486 (8th Cir. 1946), where the employees refused to process orders believed destined for an employer on strike.[42a]

2. In Matter of International Shoe Company, 93 N.L.R.B. 331, 27 L.R.R.M. 1504 (1951), the Union called intermittent stoppages in various departments.   The exasperated employer finally closed the plant and refused to reopen it until the Union signed a no-strike agreement.   Does this constitute a lockout?   Is the employer guilty of an unfair labor practice?   Assuming there is no existing contract, is the Union guilty of an unfair labor practice under Section 8 (b) (1)?

3. In International Union, UAW (AFL) v. WERB, 258 Wisc. 481, 46 N.W.2d 185 (1951), the Union voted to limit production on incentive-paid jobs to 100 per cent of standard.   Before the vote average production on these jobs was 125 per cent to 130 per cent of standard.   The Wisconsin Supreme Court held that this was a "slow-down" and in violation of the state law which made it an unfair labor practice "to interfere with production except by leaving the premises in an orderly manner for purpose of going on strike."

2. LEGALITY OF OBJECTIVES

". . . On the whole, the tests of propriety largely parallel the reasons for permitting concert of action by workers.   A chief purpose of organization of workers is to increase their economic power in bargaining with employers, so that, by concerted action,

---

[42a] Compare also NLRB v. Rockaway News Supply Co., page 621 supra, where the employees refused to make deliveries at establishments that were being picketed.

they may secure a greater share of the fruits of the enterprise in which they are engaged jointly with employers. . . .

"Accordingly, the propriety of the object of workers' concerted activity does not depend upon a judicial determination of its fairness as between workers and employers. The issue is, rather, whether the workers are demanding something which is reasonably related to employment and to the purposes of collective bargaining. Is the object one the attainment of which the workers believe will strengthen their bargaining power in the labor market, or will constitute an immediate benefit to themselves in their present jobs?" 4 Restatement, Torts 118 (1939).

This statement suggests a simple and fairly precise test to determine the legality of objectives. Is this the same test implied in Alco-Zander v. Amalgamated Clothing Workers, page 642 supra? Assuming this test is accepted, may it be that some legal objectives are "more legal" than others? May a certain form of union pressure be used to achieve some legal objectives and not others? May statutes be construed to protect some objectives more than others? These questions should be kept in mind while studying the cases which follow.

FUR WORKERS UNION, LOCAL 72 (CIO) v. FUR WORKERS UNION (AFL)

Court of Appeals, District of Columbia Circuit, 1939
105 F.2d 1, affirmed per curiam, 308 U.S. 522, 60 Sup. Ct. 292,
84 L. Ed. 443 (1939)

[In 1937 the CIO union attempted to organize Zirkin's eleven fur workers, but only two joined. When Zirkin refused to recognize the CIO union, it called a strike and picketed the premises. The other nine fur workers, without any interference or coercion by Zirkin, joined the AFL union, which was thereupon recognized as the bargaining representative. After an agreement was signed, the CIO engaged in mass picketing, accompanied by threats and assaults to compel Zirkin to rescind his recognition and void the contract. The AFL union obtained an injunction in the Federal District Court, which found there was no "labor dispute" within the meaning of the Norris-LaGuardia Act. The CIO appealed.]

STEPHENS, Associate Justice. . . . As will be noted from the provisions of the Norris-LaGuardia Act . . . Section 7 deprives the United States courts of jurisdiction to issue injunctions in any case involving or growing out of a labor dispute except after findings of fact by the court that unlawful acts have been committed and will be continued unless restrained, that substantial and irreparable injury to the complainant's property will follow, that as to each item of relief granted greater injury will be inflicted upon the complainant by the denial of relief than upon the defendants by the granting thereof, that the complainant has no adequate remedy at law, and that the public officers charged with the duty to protect the complainant's property are unable or unwilling to furnish adequate protection. As appears from the foregoing statement of the case, the only one of these findings made by the trial court, was that unlawful acts had been committed. Therefore, if within the meaning of the Act the case is one involving or growing out of a labor dispute the trial court was without jurisdiction to issue the injunction.

When the facts found in the instant case are viewed in terms of the definitions of Section 13, subsections (a), (b) and (c), of the Act, 29 U.S.C.A. §113 (a–c), it is clear, we think, that the case is one involving or growing out of a labor dispute. . . .

But if there is any doubt, looking at the language alone of the Norris-LaGuardia Act, that the controversy in the instant case, comes within it, that doubt is, we think, removed by Lauf v. E. G. Shinner & Co., 1938, 303 U.S. 323, 58 S. Ct. 578, 82 L. Ed. 872. . . . The instant case would parallel Lauf v. E. G. Shinner & Co. if only the appellant union and the appellee Zirkin's were involved. But if in Lauf v. E. G. Shinner & Co., a labor dispute existed within the meaning of the Act, a fortiori a labor dispute exists in the instant case, because the addition to the controversy of a second union, the appellee union, comprising a majority of the employees, makes the controversy not less, but more, a "labor dispute" within the meaning of that phrase. . . .

But the appellees urge further, in support of the trial court's issuance of the injunction, that if it is to be said that a labor dispute existed at some stage of the instant controversy, that dispute terminated once the appellee union was chosen by a majority of Zirkin's employees as their collective bargaining agency. Or, putting it somewhat differently, the appellees say that if what is involved in the instant case is a labor dispute, it is not the kind of labor dispute in which an injunction is forbidden, but is on the contrary one in which despite the Norris-LaGuardia Act an injunction may and should issue. The appellees call attention to Section 7 of the National Labor Relations Act, 29 U.S.C.A. §157, giving employees the right of self-organization, and of collective bargaining through representatives of their own choosing, and urge thereunder that the employees of Zirkin's who have by majority vote chosen the appellee union as their bargaining agency, have a vindicable right of self-organization and collective bargaining. The appellees rely also upon subsection (5) of Section 8 of the same Act, 20 U.S.C.A. §158 (5), making it an unfair labor practice for an employer to refuse to bargain collectively with the representatives of his employees, and further upon subsection (a) of Section 9 of the Act, 29 U.S.C.A. §159 (a), providing that representatives selected for collective bargaining by a majority of the employees in a unit appropriate for such purpose, shall be the exclusive representatives of all of the employees in such unit. Therefore, say the appellees, the picketing by the appellant union after a majority of Zirkin's employees had chosen the appellee union as their bargaining agency, is unlawful, both as an interference with the vindicable right of the employees to self-organization and collective bargaining and as an attempt to compel the employer to commit an unfair labor practice; and therefore, the appellees urge, the picketing is subject to injunction. . . .

We have given attentive consideration to the position taken by the appellees, but we nevertheless reach the conclusion that it is not a supportable one. The essential predicate of the argument is that once a majority of the employees of a particular employer, have, without coercion on his part, made their choice of a bargaining unit, any labor dispute which may be said to have been involved theretofore has ended; therefore the restrictions of the Norris-LaGuardia Act upon the issuance of injunctions are inoperative. . . . But this argument rests upon the assumption that the Federal courts have power to determine the lawful selection of a bargaining agency by employees. . . .

Neither the National Labor Relations Act nor the Norris-LaGuardia Act expressly confers upon the Federal courts power to determine what is the appropriate and lawfully selected collective bargaining unit for employees. And we think no such power is implied in the statutes mentioned. On the contrary, it seems clear that by the National Labor Relations Act Congress intended to confer exclusive initial jurisdiction upon the Board to determine the appropriate and lawfully selected bargaining unit for employees, and intended to give to the Board alone appropriate machinery, to wit, elections machinery for making such determination. . . . The National Labor Relations Act was the culmination of long continued efforts on the part of labor to establish by statute in employees substantive rights of self-organization and selection of collective bargaining representatives; and to define, for the protection of such rights, unfair labor practices by employers; and to constitute, separate from the courts, except in respect of enforcement proceedings, a new agency with both power and machinery appropriate to the enforcement of the rights recognized and to the prevention of the practices denounced. Certainly Congress in the Act did confer upon the Board the power to determine what is the appropriate and lawfully selected collective bargaining unit for employees. And we should not, unless, upon consideration of the Act and its language and purpose, we find it mandatory to do so, put such a construction thereon as would result in the anomalous existence of concurrent initial jurisdiction in both the courts and the Board. In the absence of a principle that as between administrative tribunals and courts, the jurisdiction first attaching shall prevail — and we know of no such principle — the consequence of such double jurisdiction would be most serious. . . .

NOTES

1. Would it make any difference if the AFL union had been certified as bargaining agent after a Board election? Would it be any less of a "labor dispute" within the statutory definition? What weight should be given to the statement of policy in Section 2 of the Norris-LaGuardia Act?

In Stillwell Theatres, Inc. v. Kaplan, 259 N.Y. 405, 182 N.E.63 (1932), the court held that an outside union could not be enjoined from picketing to compel the employer to rescind his recognition of the rival union and breach his contract with it. This was before New York passed statutes modeled on the Wagner Act and Norris-LaGuardia Act. After it passed such statutes the court upheld injunctions against the same type of picketing both where it was against a certified union, Florsheim Shoe Store Co. v. Retail Shoe Salesmen, 288 N.Y. 188, 42 N.E.2d 480 (1942), and where it was against an uncertified union, Dinny & Robbins v. Davis, 290 N.Y. 101, 48 N.E.2d 280 (1943). Does this mean that a union has lost some of its freedom of action by the passage of legislation meant to protect it?

2. What is the effect of the Taft-Hartley Act on the Fur Workers type of situation? Can the employer now compel a resolution of the representation dispute by obtaining an election? If an election is held, will the union's picketing be enjoinable under Section 8 (b) (4)? See Matter of Union Chevrolet Co., 96 N.L.R.B. 957, 28 L.R.R.M. 1620 (1951). Under the decision of Judge Learned Hand in Douds v. Local 1250, 173 F.2d 764 (2d Cir. 1949), page 436 supra, will it make a difference whether

the minority seeks to obtain only a settlement of grievances or attempts to compel exclusive recognition? See also Goodwins v. Hagedorn, 303 N.Y. 300, 101 N.E.2d 697 (1951).

3. Suppose a majority union calls a strike for higher wages and establishes a picket line. The employer then hires new employees who sign statements that they do not want the union to represent them. Can the picketing be enjoined? See Broadway Avenue Realty Co. v. Local 181, Hotel & Restaurant Employees, — Ky. —, 244 S.W.2d 746 (1952); Pomonis v. Hotel, Restaurant & Bartenders Union, 239 P.2d 1003, 29 L.R.R.M. 2355 (N.M. 1952); Sheehy's West Side Restaurant v. Townsend, — Misc. —, 112 N.Y. S.2d 200 (1952). How would the Taft-Hartley Act resolve the issue if the new employees sought an election?

4. Where the union represents a majority of the employees, there is no question about the right to strike to compel recognition. For the employer to refuse recognition is an unfair labor practice and the strikers receive special protection under the National Labor Relations Act. The extent of this protection will be more fully discussed in the section on Rights of Strikers to Return to Work, page 725 infra.

OPERA ON TOUR v. WEBER
Court of Appeals, New York, 1941
285 N.Y. 348, 34 N.E.2d 349

FINCH, Judge. The question presented for decision is far reaching and of vital importance to the best interests of unions of employees, of employers and of the general public. The only issue is whether the leaders of the defendant unions were engaged in promoting a lawful labor objective when the Musicians' Union induced the Stagehands' Union to join in a combination to destroy an enterprise solely because of the use of machinery in the production of music in place of the employment of live musicians.

There is no issue involved in this case of a possible compromise. The defendant Musicians' Union refused all offers of compromise made by the plaintiff. The position of the Musicians' Union cannot be better stated than it is in a letter from that union to the Stagehands' Union: "Our Federation is not in a position to compromise this matter . . . nothing short of ceasing to use canned music can be considered as safeguarding the interests of our organization."

This position was adopted and resolutely held even though such adherence destroyed plaintiff's business. The result was the loss of employment of over fifty stagehands, actors and singers even though this business, which was being destroyed, had created new opportunities of employment where none had existed before.

At the outset we note that there is in the decision of the case at bar no denial of the right to strike. On that issue our decisions are not in doubt. May's Furs and Ready to Wear, Inc. v. Bauer, 282 N.Y. 331, 26 N.E.2d 279; Goldfinger v. Feintuch, 276 N.Y. 281, 11 N.E.2d 910, 116 A.L.R. 477. Individually and collectively, the members of any union may at any time refuse to work, because machinery is employed or for any other reason, and may strike in so doing. The members of these unions are free to refuse to work if they object to working in the presence of a machine. But what is here enjoined is the inducement by the Musicians' Union of the Stagehands' Union to enter into a combination to destroy the business of the plaintiff solely because machinery instead of live musicians is used. Here the members of the Stagehands' Union were ordered and coerced to leave the employ of the plaintiff, causing the ruin of plaintiff's business and the destruction of the opportunity of employment of a larger group of stagehands, actors and singers, and the denial to the public of an opportunity to enjoy the benefits of the classic operas. This, even though the members of the Stagehands' Union were not dissatisfied with respect to wages, hours or terms and conditions of their employment, and no controversy existed or exists between them and plaintiff.

After a trial at Special Term, it was found upon sufficient evidence that plaintiff was engaged in the business of rendering performances of grand opera with an orchestral accompaniment of music mechanically reproduced from records instead of by an orchestra of live musicians. The purpose was to make grand opera available in those cities and towns of the United States which could not afford otherwise this form of entertainment because of the prohibitive cost of transporting a grand opera orchestra. Each of the two defendants is a labor union.

It was found that the members of the defendant unions had no other grievance of any kind, nor did there exist any controversy except this demand to discard machinery, between plaintiff and the defendant unions. The defendant Musicians' Union threatened to and did put plaintiff out of business solely because of the use of recorded music. The defendant Musicians' Union induced the defendant Stagehands' Union to order its members to cease rendering any service to plaintiff, which order had to be obeyed by the members of the defendant Stagehands' Union since over ninety-five per cent of the theatres and auditoria in the United States are closed shop, and without membership in the defendant Stagehands' Union the latter find it practically impossible to obtain employment. In addition, the defendant Musicians' Union ordered that no member of that union render services to plaintiff, and caused the American Guild of Musical Artists to order its members not to render services to plaintiff, and members of the Stagehands' Union not to accept employment from plaintiff. If they had not been so ordered, the members of the defendant Stagehand's Union would have continued to render services to plaintiff. As a result of this conspiracy between the two defendant unions, plaintiff was unable to fulfill its bookings and its contracts which had already been made and was prevented from entering into further engagements for the presentation of opera, and in consequence thereof this entire enterprise was forced to come to a complete stop. . . .

Does this demand of these defendant unions, that plaintiff discard machinery in the interest of the immediate employment of a few individuals, constitute a lawful labor objective? . . .

". . . Prima facie, the intentional infliction of temporal damage is a cause of action, which, as a matter of substantive law . . . requires a justification if the defendant is to escape. . . ." Mr. Justice Holmes in Aikens v. Wisconsin, 195 U.S. 194, 204, 25 S. Ct. 3, 5, 49 L. Ed. 154.

The self-interest of labor, like the self-interest of any other body, receives immunity only for those objectives which have a legitimate and reasonable relation to lawful benefits, which the union is seeking. When the labor objectives are illegal, the courts must control, otherwise there are bodies within our midst which are free from the provisions of the Penal Law. When doubt arises whether the contemplated objective is within the legal sphere, or without and so illegal, it is for the courts to determine. In Exchange Bakery & Restaurant, Inc. v. Rifkin, 245 N.Y. 260, 262, 157 N.E. 130, 132, we said: "If, however, any action taken is concerted; if it is planned to produce some result, it is subject to control. As always, what is done, if legal, must be to effect some lawful result by lawful means. . . ." By way of illustration, the courts condemn the combined effort of employees to coerce an employer to pay a stale or disputed claim, even though it might be to the self-interest of the striking employees. Dorchy v. Kansas, 272 U.S. 306, 47 S. Ct. 86, 71 L. Ed. 248. So a conspiracy is illegal involving extortion or to force the employer to commit a crime;

or one where the intent to injure rests solely on malice or ill will. Or if those engaged in police duty or in the armed forces should conspire in the face of an emergency or otherwise to coerce others to cease maintaining law and order or defense. A secondary boycott has always been held to be an illegal labor objective. Auburn Draying Co. v. Wardell, 227 N.Y. 1, 11, 124 N.E. 97, 6 A.L.R. 901. Harm done to another or to the public may be countenanced only if the purpose, in the eye of the law, is sufficient to justify such harm.

So in Scavenger Service Corporation v. Courtney, 7 Cir., 85 F.2d 825, a labor union joined an employers' association to prevent plaintiff from price cutting in performing scavenger service in the city of Chicago. This labor objective was held unlawful.

To make impossible the continuance of a business and thus to prevent the employment of a full complement of actors, singers, and stagehands merely because a machine is not discarded and in place thereof live musicians employed, is not a lawful labor objective. In Hopkins v. Oxley Stave Co., 8 Cir., 83 F. 912, the labor objective sought was to abandon certain machines for hooping barrels which materially lessened the cost of making the same. The introduction of the machine actually resulted in the dismissal of certain employees, and the court held the labor objective unlawful.

In Haverhill Strand Theatre v. Gillen, 229 Mass. 413, 118 N.E. 671, L.R.A. 1918C, 813, Ann. Cas. 1918D, 650, the owner of a motion picture theatre used an organ played by hand during the presentation of its pictures. A union sought to compel the use of an orchestra of five pieces. The Supreme Court of Massachusetts held that defendants were guilty of an unlawful labor objective.

For a union to insist that machinery be discarded in order that manual labor may take its place and thus secure additional opportunity of employment is not a lawful labor objective. In essence the case at bar is the same as if a labor union should demand of a printing plant that all machinery for typesetting be discarded because it would furnish more employment if the typesetting were done by hand. We have held that the attempt of a union to coerce the owner of a small business, who was running the same without an employee, to make employment for an employee, was an unlawful objective and that this did not involve a labor dispute. Thompson v. Boekhout, 273 N.Y. 390, 7 N.E.2d 674. So, too, in a case just unanimously decided, we held that it was an unlawful labor objective to attempt to coerce a peddler employing no employees in his business and making approximately thirty-two dollars a week, to hire an employee at nine dollars a day for one day a week. Wohl v. Bakery and Pastry Drivers and Helpers Local 802 of International Brotherhood of Teamsters, 284 N.Y. 788, 31 N.E.2d 765.

Since the endeavor to prevent the use of a mechanical device bears no reasonable relation to wages, hours of employment, health, safety, the right of collective bargaining, or any other condition of employment or for the protection of labor from abuses, there is no labor dispute within either the letter or the spirit of the Civil Practice Act. Civil Practice Act, §876-a, subd. 10; Thompson v. Boekhout, 273 N.Y. 390, 7 N.E.2d 674; Luft v. Flove, 270 N.Y. 640, 1 N.E.2d 369. In other words, there is involved in the case at bar solely the demand that a new enterprise shall not make use of machinery in order to create places for live musicians. Neither in the previous judicial decisions of this court has it been held, nor in any statute enacted, that a dispute is a labor dispute which has no connection with or relation to terms or conditions of employment, collective bargaining, protection from abuses, or respective interests of employer and employee. In the case at bar there is no actual employment at all. There is the use of a machine in place of a human relationship between one individual and another. Section 876-a, subd. 10, par. c. defines a labor dispute as any controversy concerning terms or conditions of employment, or concerning representation in arranging terms and conditions of employment, or any controversy arising out of the respective interests of employer and employee whether they stand in such relationship or not. All these words assume the existence of a human relationship. The words of this statute eo nomine relate to terms or conditions of employment, the right of representation for purposes of collective bargaining concerning such terms and conditions of employment, and the respective interests of employer and employee. Such respective interests of employer and employee must be interests that grow out of or have some relationship to employment. Advantage not connected with employment is not the interest referred to in the statute. . . . [Lehman, Chief Judge, dissented.]

NOTES

1. Not all courts have been so positive that preventing the use of laborsaving machinery is an illegal objective. In Harper v. Hoecherl, 153 Fla. 29, 14 So.2d 179 (1943), the employer sought

to enjoin the Painters Union from enforcing its rule prohibiting the use of spray guns. Although the employer was building Army barracks during time of war and had been asked by the Army to rush the work, the court refused to issue an injunction. In Bayer v. Brotherhood of Painters, 108 N.J. Eq. 257, 154 Atl. 759 (1931), a contractor who owned stock in a corporation loaned it money to buy a paint-spraying machine. The Painters Union ordered its members to refuse to work for the contractor on any of its projects and the court refused to issue an injunction.

In United States v. Carrozzo, 37 F. Supp. 191 (N.D. Ill. 1941), the Hod Carriers struck to prevent the use of cement mixers unless the contractor would guarantee no reduction in employment. This was found to be no violation of the antitrust laws. Affirmed, United States v. International Hod Carriers, 313 U.S. 539, 61 S. Ct. 839, 85 L. Ed. 1508 (1941). See also United States v. AFM, 47 F. Supp. 304 (N.D. Ill. 1942), where the Musicians' bar on recordings was held not to be a violation of the antitrust laws.

For the economic aspects of this problem see Lorwin et al., Technology in Our Economy, TNEC Monograph No. 22 (1941); Slichter, Union Policies and Industrial Management, cc. 7, 8, and 9 (1941).

2. The insecurity of employment may induce unions to engage also in "featherbedding" practices. This making of work by requiring employers to hire unnecessary employees has been held by some courts to be an unlawful objective. In Haverhill Strand Theater, Inc. v. Gillen, 229 Mass. 413, 118 N.E. 671 (1918), the court enjoined the Union from demanding that an employer hire a five-piece orchestra instead of a single organist. In La-Fayette Dramatic Productions Inc. v. Ferentz, 305 Mich. 193, 9 N.W.2d 57 (1943), the court voided a contract to employ six musicians for a theatrical production. The Musicians Union two hours before curtain time threatened to call a strike of the stagehands if the musicians were not hired. See also Folsom Engraving Co. v. McNeil, 235 Mass. 269, 126 N.E. 479 (1920); Moreland Theatres v. Portland MPMO, 140 Ore. 35, 12 P.2d 333 (1932). But for decisions finding this to be a lawful objective, see Scott-Stafford Opera House Co. v. Minneapolis Musicians Assn., 118 Minn. 410, 136 N.W. 1092 (1912); Empire Theatre Co. v. Cloke, 53 Mont. 183, 163 Pac. 107 (197).

The legislatures have been as undecided as the courts in determining the legality of this objective. Many states, at the prodding of the railroad brotherhoods, have passed "full crew" laws which have been ostensibly for safety purposes but strongly motivated by the desire to preserve jobs. On the other hand, some state legislatures have made illegal union efforts to require the hiring of stand-ins, to restrict production, or to prevent changes in business methods. See Note, Legislative Shackles on Feather-bedding Practices, 34 Cornell L. Q. 255 (1948).

In 1946, Congress sought to outlaw the Musicians' practices of requiring stand-ins when "canned music" was used in broadcasting. The Lea Act made it a crime to compel an employer to employ "any person or persons in excess of the number of employees needed." 47 U.S.C.A., Sec. 506 (a) (1). Petrillo, the President of the Musicians, was indicted for threatening to strike a station unless it hired three extra musicians. The court allowed an expert to testify that these three were "needed" to satisfy the public demand for "live" music, and to fulfill the station's duty to promote the public interest by providing employment for musicians. The court found there was nothing but evidence of a good faith attempt to obtain honest employment for additional musicians and dismissed the indictment. United States v. Petrillo, 75 F. Supp. 176 (N.D. Ill. 1948).

The Taft-Hartley Act has also attempted to reach featherbedding. Section 8 (b) (6) makes it an unfair labor practice for a union "to cause or attempt to cause an employer to pay or deliver or agree to pay or deliver any money or other thing of value in the nature of an exaction, for services which are not performed or not to be performed."

During the Congressional debates, Senator Pepper argued that this would outlaw paid rest-periods, call-in pay, and other such provisions. Senator Taft denied this, saying, "It seems to me it is perfectly clear what is intended . . . an exaction from the employer for services which he does not want, does not need, and is not even willing to accept." 2 Legis. Hist. of LMRA 1545 (1947).

Which of the following would be an unfair labor practice under Section 8 (b) (6):

   (a) a demand by the union in contract negotiation that the contract include a provision for severance pay?

   (b) a grievance filed by the union requesting back pay for an employee who was laid off out of line of seniority? See Conway's Express v. NLRB, 195 F.2d 906, 29 L.R.R.M. 2617 (2d Cir. 1952).

   (c) a demand by a printer's union that the employer continue a long-established practice of paying employees to set "bogus type" rather than lay them off during slack periods?

See American Newspaper Publishers Assn. v. NLRB, 21 U.S.L. Week 4204, 31 L.R.R.M. 2422 (U.S. Sup. Ct., Mar. 9, 1953).

In NLRB v. Gamble Enterprises, — U.S. — , 73 Sup. Ct. 560, — L. Ed. — (1953), a motion picture theatre had from time to time scheduled performances by "name bands." The local musicians' union insisted that for every performance by a traveling band, the employer must engage a local orchestra to give a separate performance at a later time. The theatre owner refused, claiming he had no need for these services and could not use them. The Board held that this was not an unfair labor practice. "In our opinion, Section 8 (b) (6) was not intended to reach cases where a labor union seeks actual employment for its members, even in situations where the employer does not want, does not need, and is not willing to accept those services." This holding was approved by the Supreme Court.

Under this decision, just what kind of featherbedding does the section prohibit? To what extent does the legality of the union's conduct depend on the verbal phrasing of its demand?

AMERICAN GUILD OF MUSICAL ARTISTS v. PETRILLO
Court of Appeals, New York, 1941
286 N.Y. 226, 36 N.E.2d 123

LOUGHRAN, Judge. The material allegations of the complaint may be divided into four parts which in sum and substance are these:

(1) The members of the plaintiff-guild are musical artists in the field of opera and concert. They are a professional class whose interests and problems are unique. With rare exceptions, each of them employs a manager through whom he makes professional engagements. These managers are paid standard commissions negotiated by the plaintiff-guild. Each engagement is made the subject of a separate contract which fits the repertoire of the artist to the localized requirements of the particular occasion.

(2) The members of the defendant-union are musicians who render service in bands and orchestras for wages pursuant to terms and conditions of employment established by collective bargaining agreements. The defendant-union cannot represent the members of the plaintiff-guild for the purposes of collective bargaining or in any other way act for their mutual business or professional aid or benefit.

(3) In August, 1940, the defendant-union sent to the plaintiff-guild a communication which said in part: "At this time, the

American Federation of Musicians desires to make a request that all instrumentalists belonging to your organization, such as Heifetz, Elman, Hoffman, Horowitz and all symphony orchestra conductors resign from your organization and become members of the American Federation of Musicians where they rightfully belong. As you know, the charter of the American Federation of Musicians granted by the American Federation of Labor calls for all instrumentalists to belong to the American Federation of Musicians. From the inception of the American Federation of Musicians, we have not interfered with such artists, and rightfully so, feeling that they were in a position to take care of themselves and were not in competition with members of the American Federation of Musicians. The request that we are making at this time has been brought about by the reason that these instrumentalists saw fit to join a labor union (the plaintiff-guild), and so long as they desire to belong to a labor union, then they rightfully belong to the American Federation of Musicians. . . . This office is notifying all the radio interests, picture studios, symphony orchestra managements, grand opera companies, recording companies, booking agencies, etc., that these people will not be recognized by the American Federation of Musicians and members of the American Federation of Musicians will not be permitted to render any services at any functions in which they may participate unless they become members of the American Federation of Musicians on or before Labor Day, 1940. . . ."

(4) The parties that were so notified by the defendant-union thereupon informed the plaintiff-guild that instrumental artists and symphony orchestra conductors who did not resign from its membership and join the defendant-union on or before September 2, 1940, would not thereafter be permitted to fulfill any professional engagement. These parties include practically all the business organizations operating in the opera and concert field and were the main source of the existing professional engagements of the instrumental artists and symphony orchestra conductors who are members of the plaintiff-guild. No controversy exists herein as to the standards of wages or conditions of employment of members of the defendant-union.

Upon the foregoing allegations, the complaint demands judgment that an injunction issue against the conduct of the defendant-union so complained of, and, that the plaintiffs recover damages alleged to have been caused to them thereby. The answer of the defendant-union consists of denials of the material allegations of

the complaint.   No defense consisting of new matter is set forth
therein.

Special Term held that the complaint stated a cause of action.
The Appellate Division reversed for reasons stated in its opinion
as follows: "If we strip the complaint of the allegations which are
clearly conclusions of law, we find no facts set forth to indicate
that the plaintiff union is entitled to the relief which it seeks.   It
has not shown that the defendant maliciously or illegally interfered with the contracts of the members of plaintiff's union.
What the defendant is seeking to do, undoubtedly, is to protect
itself and to increase its membership.   Defendant union is well
within its rights in protecting its organization and in not permitting its members to play their instruments wth nonmembers
of their organization. . . .   We have reached the conclusion,
therefore, that the complaint must be dismissed for two reasons:
First, that the controversy between the parties involves a 'labor
dispute' within the meaning of section 876-a, subdivision 10, of
the Civil Practice Act; and secondly, that it fails to state a cause
of action viewed in the light of the law as it stood prior to the enactment of section 876-a."   261 App. Div. 272, 277, 24 N.Y.S.2d,
854, 859.   We think this result cannot be sustained.

In Opera on Tour, Inc. v. Weber, 285 N.Y. 348, 34 N.E.2d 349,
this court applied against a labor union the broad doctrine that
harm intentionally done is actionable if not justified.   Cf. Pollock on Torts, 14th Ed., pp. 43–45.   This complaint, therefore, is
sufficient as such, unless the purpose of the defendant-union must
be presumed to be a lawful labor objective, — an activity having
some reasonable connection with wages, hours, health, safety, the
right of collective bargaining, or some other condition of employment.   Opera on Tour, Inc. v. Weber, supra.   But no sign of
such a justification reveals itself on the face of the complaint; and
even if we should take it upon ourselves to notice all that the briefs
for the defendant-union assert as common knowledge, we would
not yet be competent to contradict the allegation that no part of
the membership of the plaintiff-guild can be represented by the
defendant-union in respect of any labor policy . . .

Unless the objective of the defendant-union is a lawful one, this
controversy is not a "labor dispute" in the sense of section 876-a of
the Civil Practice Act.   Opera on Tour, Inc. v. Weber, supra.
Hence section 876-a is without application to the case stated in the
complaint.

Our conclusion is that the complaint is sufficient on its face.

LEHMAN, Chief Judge (dissenting) : The decision made in this case, throws into bold relief the narrowly restrictive interpretation of section 876-a of the Civil Practice Act, which the court adopted in Opera on Tour, Inc. v. Weber, supra, and emphasizes the grounds for the contrary view put forth in my dissenting opinion in that case, in which Judge Loughran concurs. I still do not understand how a statute which expressly provides that in a case "involving or growing out of a labor dispute," acts specified therein, may not be enjoined "on the ground that the persons engaged therein constitute an unlawful combination or conspiracy or on any other grounds whatsoever" can be construed in manner which would exclude from the statutory definition of a "labor dispute" any dispute with a labor union unless "the objective of the (labor) union is a lawful one."

NOTES

1. Compare this decision with Alco-Zander v. Amalgamated Clothing Workers, page 642 supra. Are the objectives of the union the same in both cases? Compare the objectives here with those in the Fur Workers case, page 688 supra. Must the union be able to show an ability to provide benefits before it can use its economic power to extend its membership? See Dinoffria v. Teamsters Union, 331 Ill. App. 129, 72 N.E.2d 635 (1947).

2. Is a strike to compel all employees in the shop to join the recognized union for a justifiable purpose, or is it merely a strike for union power as in American Guild of Musical Artists v. Petrillo? Compare C. S. Smith, Metropolitan Market Co. v. Lyons, page 652 supra; Barile v. Fisher, page 658 supra.

The legality of various union-security provisions has been discussed in Part III along with the provisions of the Taft-Hartley Act limiting the permissible kinds of union security. A strike to compel an employer to agree to a hiring-hall agreement violates Section 8(a) (2). Matter of Maritime Union of America, 78 N.L.R.B. 971, 22 L.R.R.M. 1289 (1948). Although a strike to obtain an illegal union-security contract is unlawful, it does not follow that a strike to obtain a legal union-security contract is lawful. For example, in Massachusetts a closed-shop contract voluntarily entered into is valid and binding, Hamer v. Nashawena Mills, 315 Mass. 160, 52 N.E.2d 22 (1943) ; but a strike to compel a closed shop is illegal, Fashioncraft v. Halpern, 313 Mass. 385, 48 N.E.2d 1 (1943), Colonial Press v. Ellis, 321 Mass. 495, 74 N.E.2d 1 (1947). Compare, however, Mass. Acts 1950, 452.

3. Is a strike to obtain all available work for union members one for a lawful objective? The problem may arise in two different ways. First, it may be a pure jurisdictional dispute such as one between the Carpenters and Machinists over who should erect and dismantle machinery. Each insists that its members should have exclusive right to do the work. Second, the union may insist on a closed shop, refuse to admit certain workers, and then demand their replacement by union members. In both situations, the union is trying to gain for its members the limited numbered jobs available. This will be discussed in detail in Part V.

4. In many cases employers have sought to escape certain legal obligations by converting their employees into independent contractors. This has been particularly prevalent in the delivering of milk, baked goods, laundry, ice, and so forth. Drivers are turned by their erstwhile employers into "independent peddlers." This destruction of the employment relationship is motivated at least in part by a desire to escape liability for workmen's compensation, unemployment insurance, and social security taxes. It may also seriously handicap the union because its protection under the anti-injunction acts and its immunity from the anti-trust laws as well as its freedom of action at common law, depend on the existence of an employer-employee relation. See pages 670 and 680 supra. Determining the legality of union action to combat this device has caused the courts great difficulty. Compart Wohl v. Bakery & Pastry Drivers Union, 284 N.Y. 788, 31 N.E.2d 765 (1940), reversed, 315 U.S. 769, 62 Sup. Ct. 816, 86 L. Ed. 1178 (1942), with People v. Gassman, 295 N.Y. 254, 66 N.E.2d 705 (1945). In Angelos v. Mesevich, 289 N.Y. 498, 46 N.E.2d 903 (1943), one week after the Union began picketing, the employer had his six employees sign articles of partnership. The court held that since all were proprietors no employment relationship existed, no "labor dispute" existed, and an injunction would issue regardless of the state anti-injunction act. (Reversed on other grounds sub nom. Cafeteria Employees Union, Local 302 et al. v. Angelos et al., 320 U.S. 293, 64 Sup. Ct. 126, 88 L. Ed. 58 (1943).) In Bautista v. Jones, 25 Cal. 2d 746, 155 P.2d 343 (1949), it was held that a union could not strike to enforce a closed-shop agreement against independent peddlers who were denied admission to the union. "The elimination of such persons from our economic life is no more a legitimate object of union activity than would be the elimination of Negroes; and any union which exerts economic pressure to obtain the discharge of the

businessman worker as such, and at the same time excludes him
from union membership on that ground alone, transcends the
bounds of legitimate union activity." Id. at 751. But compare
Emde v. San Joaquin Council, 23 Cal. 2d 146, 143 P. 2d 20
(1943).

In the light of these last two cases, does the union have any
recourse when the employer deliberately eliminates the employer-
employee relationship? Does the illegality of the union's action
arise from the fact that it is interfering with managements rights
to determine how the business should be run, that the "independent peddler" system is to be protected as a matter of public
policy, or that all concerted action by peddlers is in restraint
of trade?

BUILDING TRADES COUNCIL OF RENO v. THOMPSON
Supreme Court, Nevada, 1951
234 P.2d 581

[Thompson, a contractor, employed Ross to help build a residence in Reno. Ross had been assessed a fine of $50 by the
Carpenters because he had done work as a plasterer on a previous
job. The Building Trades Council decided that either Thompson must pay the fine or compel Ross to do so. When Thompson
refused, the Carpenters struck, a picket line was established cutting off deliveries, and Thompson was listed on the Council's "We
Do Not Patronize" list. Later the Council demanded that as
penalty, Thompson contribute $1,000 to the Children's Home
of Carson, Nevada. Thompson sued for damages because of the
Council's action, including injury to the uncompleted house,
and received a verdict for $6750.]

BADT, Chief Justice. . . . (1) Is the compelling of an employer by a union to see that an individual employee pays a $50
fine assessed against him by the union, under the circumstances
herein appearing, a lawful objective of a strike, picketing and
boycott?

(2) Is the compelling of an employer by a union to make $1,000
contribution to a named charity as a penalty for the employer's
employment of an employee not in good standing with his union,
a lawful objective of a strike, picketing and boycott? . . .

We address ourselves first to the second cause of action. Respondent was placed on the "We Do Not Patronize" list, in other
words, boycotted, until such time as he might relieve himself from
that situation by donating $1,000 to the Children's Home in Car-

son City.   Our conclusion is that the learned district judge was correct in holding that this count of the complaint stated a cause of action and in his consistent rulings thereafter denying the motion for nonsuit, the motion for a directed verdict, and the motion for new trial.

The issue is clear-cut.   Plaintiff concedes the right of members of the defendant unions to refuse to work with nonunion men and the right of the defendants to picket the premises and to place the plaintiff on the "We Do Not Patronize" list where the objective of such concerted action is lawful.   The defendants concede that an unlawful objective renders the concerted action unlawful. They insist however that there is nothing unlawful in requiring the plaintiff to pay $1,000 to a worthy charity . . .

The objective of this action, namely, compelling respondent to pay the $1,000 penalty, was clearly unlawful.   Burke v. Fay, 128 Mo. App. 690, 107 S.W. 408.   The rule has been stated in various ways.   In 31 Am. Jur. 942, Labor, §221, it is said that a strike to compel payment of a so-called fine imposed upon an employer by a union is unlawful.   It is said in the Restatement of the Law of Torts, §792: "The payment by an employer of a fine or penalty which he has not agreed to pay is not a proper cause of concerted action against him by workers."   The annotation to Dorchy v. Kansas, 272 U.S. 306, 47 S. Ct. 86, 71 L. Ed. 248, commencing at the last citation, is devoted to "Purposes for which strike may lawfully be called."   Citing Burke v. Fay, supra, and other authorities, it rejects, as a lawful purpose, the compelling of an employer to pay a fine or penalty imposed by the union.   See also annotation, at 116 A.L.R. 486, and prior annotations therein referred to.   No cases have been cited by appellants, and an independent search has failed to disclose any contrary to the rule above stated.

Plaintiff's first cause of action presents a conflict in the evidence. If the contention of the appellants is correct and their concerted action against the plaintiff, was simply for the purpose and objective of compelling the reinstatement of Ross as a member in good standing of the Carpenters Union by his payment of the $50 fine previously assessed against him, we should be inclined to find a close analogy between such situation and the one approved by a majority of this Court in Culinary Workers Union v. Distr. Court, 66 Nev. 166, 207 P.2d 990, 66 Nev. 202, 210 P.2d 454, followed in Jensen v. Reno Central Trades & Labor Council, Nev., — Nev. — , 229 P.2d 908.   There is little, if any, difference in principle between the compulsory payment of union initiation fees and dues there approved as an objective for concerted action and the reinstatement of the employee by the payment of a fine for violation of the rules of the union. . . .

. . . If the jury accepted respondent's testimony, as it manifestly did, it apparently concluded that respondent had agreed to comply with all of the union demands as outlined by Mr. Paley of the Carpenters Union, which demands were coupled with the agreement that Ross might be retained as superintendent without joining or reinstating himself in the Carpenters Union; and that, when all of these matters had been agreed upon, he was then told: "But you still have to make Mr. Ross pay the $50 fine." The jury's acceptance of respondent's testimony is a complete answer to the attack on the $250 judgment on the first cause of action, as Ross' membership or reinstatement in the Carpenters Union then became entirely disconnected with the objective of the concerted action of the appellants. It was no more the province of the District Court on motion for new trial than it is the province of this Court, on appeal, to say that the jury should have disbelieved the detailed testimony of respondent and accepted the more general statement of appellant, Paley, that he told respondent: "Mr. Ross could stay on the job, but he could not use the tools of the trade. That Mr. Thompson, would not agree to. . . ."

Neither appellants nor respondent have cited any authority that may be said to be directly in point. It is true that the rule is stated in 31 Am. Jur. 949, Labor, §231, "Picketing to force an employer to discharge an employee because of delinquency in the payment of his dues is unlawful. . . ." However, the only authorities cited in support of this rule are Harvey v. Chapman, 235 Mass. 1941, 151 N.E. 304, L.R.A. 1917E 389, and St. Germain v. Bakery & Confectionary W. Union, 97 Wash. 282, 166 P. 665, L.R.A. 1917 F. 824. Contrary to the rule in Nevada, to compel unionization of the employees is not a lawful objective of picketing in either Massachusetts or Washington. (See cases cited in the Massachusetts and Washington cases referred to; also Building Service Employees International Union v. Gazzam, 339 U.S. 532, 70 S. Ct. 784, 94 L. Ed. 1045, supporting the right of each state to determine its own policy in such matters, and recently considered at length by this Court in Jensen v. Reno Central Trades & Labor Council, Nev., — Nev., —, 229 P.2d 908 (1951).

Perhaps most clearly approaching the present question, though not quite reaching it, is Dorchy v. Kansas, 272 U.S. 306, 47 S. Ct. 86, 71 L. Ed. 248, decided by the U.S. Supreme Court in 1926. In that case the employer mining company paid wages of $3.55 a day for employees under nineteen years of age and $5.00 a day for those over nineteen.   One Mishmash had been paid, without protest, for a number of months at the lower rate, but subsequently demanded additional compensation under the claim that he was entitled to the higher rate.   The question of fact had arisen over contradictory entries in the family bible as to the date of his birth. The court said:

> The right to carry on business — be it called liberty or property has value.   To interfere with this right without just cause is unlawful.   The fact that the injury was inflicted by a strike is sometimes a justification.   But a strike may be illegal because of its purpose however orderly the manner in which it is conducted.   To collect a stale claim due to a fellow member of the union who was formerly employed in the business is not a permissible purpose.   In the absence of a valid agreement to the contrary, each party to a disputed claim may insist that it be determined only by a court.

Appellants distinguish this case by pointing out that the present case involves no question of a stale claim and that the claim was not even disputed . . .   In the Dorchy case the reference to the claim as a stale claim arose from the fact that it had been pending for two years.   There was no contention that it was barred by limitations nor does any distinction in principle grow out of the fact that Mishmash's claim was against the employer while in the present case it is the union's claim against the employee.   In either event both parties had the right to insist that the claim be subject at least to ultimate determination by a court of competent jurisdiction.   The purpose of courts is to resolve disputes whether the parties be individuals, corporations, union or other persons capable of suing and being sued. . . .

The dissenting opinion of Mr. Justice Jackson in Trailmobile Co. v. Whirls, 331 U.S. 40, 67 S. Ct. 982, 91 L. Ed. 1328, refers to Dorchy v. Kansas in support of the statement: "Neither may a union use its own power over its members to by-pass the courts." This undoubtedly had reference to the unanimous opinion of the court that for the union "to enforce payment by a strike [of a two-year-old claim by a former employee against the employer] is clearly coercion."

Thus we see no logical escape from the extension of the principle of the Dorchy case as quoted supra to any case in which a party not otherwise bound by contract, would be prevented from trying the issues of the disputed money claim in the courts. . . .

NOTES

1. Under the rationale of this case, could a union strike to compel the payment of back wages or to recover for loss to employees due to wrongful layoff? Is there a special danger of abuse of union power when it compels the payment of money for past conduct rather than agreement to future employment rules? In Carew v. Rutherford, 106 Mass. 1 (1870), it was held unlawful for a union to fine an employer $500 for sending work out of town to be done. Would it make any difference if the union demanded that the employer pay the money to the union member who should have been given the work?

2. Mrs. Wagshal owned a delicatessen which sold food and served meals. She bought bread from Hinkle, whose driver delivered at noon. When she insisted he come at some other hour because it interfered with serving lunch, the driver refused and Hinkle stopped deliveries. The Union then claimed she owed the driver $150 for bread previously delivered and demanded that she pay. Instead, she sent a check to Hinkle as she always had in the past. The check was returned by the Union business agent, who insisted that it was $12.22 short and must be paid to the driver. When she refused, the Union prohibited any members from making deliveries to the store. Held: The concerted action of the Union could be enjoined in spite of the Norris-LaGuardia Act, as there was no "labor dispute." The dispute over the hour of delivery was with Hinkle, not with the Union. "To hold that under such circumstances a failure of two businessmen to come to terms created a labor dispute merely because what one of them sought might have affected the work of a particular employee of another, would be to turn almost every controversy between sellers and buyers over price, quantity, quality, delivery, payment, credit, or any other business transactions into a labor dispute." The controversy over the payment of the bill had nothing to do with the driver's employment. He was paid his wages by Hinkle regardless of whether the bill was paid. He was merely the conduit for payment. "The mere fact that it is a labor union representative rather than a bill collector who, with or without the creditor's consent, seeks to obtain payment of an obligation, does not transmute a business controversy into a Norris-LaGuardia labor dispute." Bakery Sales Drivers Local Union No. 33 v. Wagshal, 333 U.S. 437, 68 Sup. Ct. 630, 92 L. Ed. 792 (1948).

If this was purely a dispute between Wagshal and Hinkle, why was the Union so concerned about it? Does this case suggest that intrusion into management functions is an unlawful objective? How does this case escape the definition of "labor dispute" in Sections 13 (a) and (c) of the Norris-LaGuardia Act?

3. Political strikes called to bring pressure on the government have not been common in this country, but it is generally accepted that such strikes are illegal. The non-Communist affidavit provision in Section 9 (h) was presumably based in part on the belief that Communists sought to control unions in order to call strikes for political purposes. In upholding that provision the Supreme Court relied heavily on this objective, saying: "There can be no doubt that Congress may, under its constitutional power to regulate commerce among the several states, attempt to prevent political strikes and other kinds of direct action designed to burden and interrupt the free flow of commerce." American Communications Assn., CIO v. Douds, 339 U.S. 382, 70 Sup. Ct. 674, 94 L. Ed. 925 (1950).

SOCIETY OF NEW YORK HOSPITAL v. HANSON
Supreme Court, New York, Special Term, New York County, 1945
185 Misc. 937, 59 N.Y.S.2d 91, affirmed, 272 App. Div. 998,
73 N.Y.S.2d 835 (1st Dept. 1947)

PECORA, Justice: The plaintiff, the Society of the New York Hospital, has brought this action for a permanent injunction, enjoining and restraining the defendants, a labor union organization called New York Building and Construction Trades Council's Maintenance Organization, its officers, agents, members, representatives, and those acting in concert with them, from interfering with the operation of plaintiff's hospital by causing, instigating, or continuing any strike, work stoppage or action of a similar nature, from picketing in front of or in the vicinity of plaintiff's hospital and from otherwise interfering with the orderly operation of the hospital.

The hospital is wholly dependent upon its power plant operated by its employees, for the electricity required not only to light and heat its premises, but to operate equipment such as oxygen tents, respirators, incubators, sterilizers, and many other modern instruments and machines now recognized as essential to the proper operation of a hospital.

On November 19, 1945, about 116 non-professional employees, including power plant workers, elevator operators and maintenance men, failed to report for work following a statement made two days earlier by an officer of defendant union to plaintiff's officers, that some workers would not report on that day because conferences between plaintiff and defendants had apparently reached an impasse. These workers have not yet returned to their jobs, and their absence has to a certain extent handicapped plaintiff in the performance of its functions. On that day members of the defendant's union and employees of the plaintiff picketed in front of plaintiff's hospital. The picketing was discontinued late that day, as a result of the issuance and service of a temporary restraining order of this Court, and it has not been resumed to this date.

The so-called Little Wagner Act, Chap. 443, Laws of 1937, as amended, Labor Law, Art. 20, §§700–716, is of major significance in the consideration of this case. This article of the Labor Law purports to define certain of the rights of labor. It is prefaced (in Sec. 700) by a full and broad statement of legislative fact finding and policy, outlining the economic necessity for employees to possess full freedom of association, actual liberty of contract and a collective bargaining power equal to that of their employers. It states that "the denial by some employers of the right of employees freely to organize and the resultant refusal to accept the procedure of collective bargaining, substantially and adversely affect the interest of employees, other employers, and the public in general." The act is designed to enforce "the public policy of the state to encourage the practice and procedure of collective bargaining, and to protect employees in the exercise of full freedom of association, self-organization and designation of representatives of their own choosing for the purposes of collective bargaining, or other mutual aid and protection, free from the interference, restraint or coercion of their employers." . . .

The issues in this case have been limited and clarified by concessions of the parties. The defendants have conceded, for the purpose of this case, that Section 715 of the Labor Law does exempt the plaintiff hospital, as a charitable institution, from the operation of the provisions of Article 20. It is also conceded that this case does not involve a "labor dispute" within the meaning of that term as employed in Section 876-a of the Civil Practice Act, and that, therefore, that section is not applicable here. It was so held in Jewish Hospital of Brooklyn v. Doe et al, 2nd Dept. 1937, 252 App. Div. 581, 300 N.Y.S. 1111. Reasoning that Section 876-a of the Civil Practice Act is in pari materia with Article 20 of the Labor Law, the court there held Section 876-a to be inapplicable in the case of a charitable institution, even though Section 876-a contains no explicit exception and Article 20 of the

Labor Law does not directly relate to labor injunctions or to employers' remedies against strikers or pickets.

The plaintiff concedes that its employees have the right to organize for the purpose of collective bargaining, to attempt to bargain collectively with the plaintiff, and to assert and advertise their alleged grievances in any proper manner, not including, however, the picketing of the plaintiff's hospital.

It is also conceded that both the strike and the picketing were entirely peaceful, unaccompanied by violence, misrepresentation, fraud or excesses of any kind. In this connection the record is completely devoid of any evidence of any such practices. The plaintiff asserts that picketing would have the inevitable effect of causing crowds to gather in the immediate vicinity of its hospital, of causing members of wholly unaffected unions, such as truck drivers, to refuse to serve the hospital with the supplies it needs daily in large quantities, and of otherwise interfering with the hospital's orderly operations.

This court, therefore, is called upon to decide whether or not any strike for whatever purpose, involving a stoppage of the essential functions of a hospital which is a charitable institution, should be enjoined; and if so, whether or not picketing, no matter how peaceful, should be permitted . . .

At common law, well established in this state before the passage of Article 20 of the Labor Law, the right to strike was fully recognized as one of the most valuable possessions of labor. Our courts have properly refused to enjoin workers from striking or organizing for the purpose of striking, despite such damage as might incidentally ensue to the property of those affected. In exercising this equitable function, however, the courts have been careful to protect both property and lives from strikes called to achieve improper results or which were violently conducted. Opera On Tour, Inc. v. Weber, 170 Misc. 272, 10 N.Y.S.2d 83, affirmed 285 N.Y. 248, 34 N.E.2d 349, 136 A.L.R. 267; Exchange Bakery & Restaurant v. Rifkin, 1927, 245 N.Y. 260, 157 N.E. 130.

It is the court's duty in each case to determine the purposes and objectives which workers embraced in the categories enumerated in Sec. 715 may lawfully attempt to achieve by striking. In so doing the court must weigh the public interest against that to be served by allowing such workers to obtain fair treatment through the utilization of those economic weapons which are available to them. The right to strike has proven to be of such proper potency to labor in our industrial history that this court would not curtail it in any respect except for the most compelling of reasons. But there are some contravening considerations which can be of even greater importance to the public interests as a whole. It is difficult to conceive of a public service of greater value than the maintenance of hospitals for the care of the sick and the injured. It is almost impossible to conceive of such hospitals functioning properly if they are subject to interference with their activities by strikes or otherwise. Obviously ministration to the sick cannot be delayed. Surgical operations, as well as the routine care of those requiring medical attention, must be permitted to proceed at all times. The effective strength of medicines and serums must be preserved continuously under scientific conditions. The frantic immediacy which is required for the treatment of emergency cases, cannot be suspended while awaiting the outcome of parleys between the hospital management and its employees over terms of labor. These elements imperatively command that the generally broad right to strike be enjoined or otherwise limited in such cases.

A strike by its employees which injuriously affects the essential functions of a hospital, must therefore be held to be improper and inimical to public interest. The public cannot brook any interference with the activities of an institution on which it relies for the treatment of the sick and hurt. A stoppage of electric current, a delay in deliveries of vital supplies or any number of readily conceivable difficulties created by a strike might result in loss of life. The necessity of avoiding such tragic consequences to the public clearly outweighs the sound general policy favoring the protection of labor's right to strike. Hence this court explicitly rules that no strike productive of such results can be permitted against a hospital which is supported by the public through voluntary contributions as well as through contributions made by the local government, and which is maintained for the benefit of the entire public, including those who cannot pay either in whole or in part the cost of their care and medical attention. This is consistent with the holding in Jewish Hospital of Brooklyn v. Doe, supra, in which the Appellate Division enjoined striking and picketing against a charitable hospital. In that case the strike was accompanied by violence and other improper acts, and while it therefore differs somewhat from the case before this court, much of the reasoning there expressed is appropriate here.

An injunction will, therefore, issue permanently restraining the defendants from striking and from organizing for the purpose of striking or inducing others to strike against the plaintiff or the hospital operated by the plaintiff. Such an injunction will not, and cannot, trespass upon the right of the individual to quit his work, — for to give it such effect would be tantamount to giving abhorrent sanction to peonage.   It is aimed only at concerted activities to bring about and support a strike . . .

The many thousands of employees of charitable, educational and religious associations and corporations should not be left entirely without legal protection in their efforts to better their economic status by collective bargaining with their employers. The right to bargain collectively alone is of little value to workers unless they have some means of redress in the event that the employer refuses to meet reasonable demands.   Article 20 of the Labor Law greatly strengthens the bargaining position of workers and recognizes the need for their protection.

In excluding the employees of charitable, educational and religious associations and corporations from the benefits of that law, the legislature recognized the essential difference between such employment and employment in private industries operated for monetary gain and profits.   It may fairly be said that any employee choosing to work for such an institution must realize that the nature of his employment presupposes certain obligations on his part, and the loss of certain rights which would be his if he worked for a private employer.   Nonetheless, it cannot be said that laboring people at all times actually exercise a completely free choice in the selection of employment.   For the most part they are forced to take such jobs as are available in order to support themselves and their families.   Employees of the State, or of any of its political or civil subdivisions or agencies, have certain advantages such as tenure of employment and pensions, which are not usually possessed by the employees of charitable, religious or educational institutions.   Under these circumstances the legislature might well be willing to consider the desirability of legislation designed specifically to cover the cases of the last-named groups of workers.   Whether or not any particular institution is inclined to be niggardly is not important.   The vital factor is that the public interest, which the legislature must have deemed to be served by denying employees of such institutions the fundamental rights which labor, in the face of bitter opposition, has through the years fairly won in its dealings with private employers, may be better served by the enactment of legislation insuring these employees of fair treatment in their relations with their employers, — such legislation, for instance, as may provide for minimum wage scales, hours of labor and arbitration boards to determine disputes.

The defendants in this case would do well to devote a portion of their energies to presenting these matters to the legislature's attention. This court is hopeful that our legislature, which has made the eloquent proclamation of the rights of labor embodied in Art. 20 of the Labor Law, will give adequate heed to the plight in which the employees of charitable, educational and religious organizations presently find themselves because of their exclusion, under the provisions of Section 715, from the benefits of that Article.

NOTES

1. If hospital employees are enjoined from striking, what recourse do they have to protect themselves from depressed wage scales? How satisfactory is the solution of governmental fixing of wages either by legislation or administrative determination? If the choice is between strikes and government wage-fixing, how serious a danger must a strike be before the second alternative is preferable? If we assume that union leaders wish to avoid strike prohibitions and government control, will not self-restraint motivated by self-preservation prevent them from actually prosecuting a strike to the point of public disaster? For discussion of such issues, see Frey, The Logic of Collective Bargaining and Arbitration, 12 Law & Contemp. Prob. 264 (1947); Kennedy, The Handling of Emergency Disputes, 2 Proc. of I.R.R.A. 14 (1949); Smith, The Effect of Public Interest on the Right to Strike, 27 N.C.L. Rev. 204 (1949); Williams, Compulsory Settlement of Contract Negotiation Labor Disputes, 27 Tex. L. Rev. 587 (1949).

2. A number of state statutes have attempted to provide compulsory arbitration for disputes in public utilities. However, such statutes have met numerous obstacles in the courts. The Wisconsin act was held unconstitutional as conflicting with the federal policy of protecting the right to strike in industries affecting interstate commerce. Amalgamated Assn. of Street Railway Employees v. WERB, 340 U.S. 383, 71 Sup. Ct. 359, 95 L. Ed. 364 (1950). The New Jersey statute was held unconstitutional because no standards were provided to guide the arbitration in reaching its decision. State v. Traffic Telephone Workers Federation, 2 N.J. 335, 66 A.2d 616 (1949). The Michigan act was invalidated because the delegation of power to the circuit judges to act as arbitrators violated the principle of separation of powers. Local 170, TWVA v. Gadola, 322 Mich. 332, 34 N.W.2d 71 (1948). Earlier, the United States Supreme Court had declared

that a Kansas arbitration law took property without due process of law when applied to meat packing, but hinted that it might be valid as applied to public utilities. Wolff Packing Co. v. Kansas Court of Industrial Relations, 262 U.S. 522, 43 Sup. Ct. 630, 67 L. Ed. 1103 (1923). This constitutional obstacle probably no longer remains, in view of the Court's present application of the due process clause. See Williams, Note 1 supra. For a discussion of some of the problems faced under the recent state arbitration statutes, see Cushman, Compulsory Arbitration in Action — The New Jersey Telephone Case, 2 Syracuse L. Rev. 251 (1951); Updegraff, Compulsory Settlement of Public Utility Disputes, 36 Iowa L. Rew. 61 (1950).

In the atomic energy industry the nature of the processes and the critical need for sustained production makes strikes intolerable. A strenuous effort has been made to preserve genuine collective bargaining while at the same time prohibiting strikes. For an excellent discussion of this problem and the devices used in attempting to solve it, see Newman, The Atomic Energy Industry: An Experiment in Hybridization, 60 Yale L.J., 1263, 1364 (1951).

3. Government intervention may take less direct forms. During World War II government seizure was used to end strikes in critical industries. In most cases the Army or Navy took possession, operating the plant through the regular management but with the terms of employment fixed by the government. This device was almost exclusively a wartime expedient for enforcing decisions of the National War Labor Board. See Willcox and Landis, Government Seizures in Labor Disputes, 34 Cornell L.Q. 155 (1948); Teller, Government Seizures in Labor Disputes, 60 Harv. L. Rev. 1017 (1947).

The Taft-Hartley Act of 1947 provided a special procedure for national emergency strikes which the President finds "imperil the national health or safety." Sections 206 to 210 provide for appointment of a fact-finding board; an injunction during a cooling-off period of 60 days, and a vote by the union on the employer's last offer. After a total of 80 days the injunction is dissolved and the union is free to strike. Although this procedure has been invoked in disputes in atomic energy, coal-mining, meat-packing, telephone, maritime, and longshore industries, it has not met with marked success. For a critical summary of the experience of the Federal Mediation and Conciliation Service with this procedure, see the First Annual Report (1948) of that agency, pages 55–59.

Some of the problems raised by these procedures are well illustrated by the cases arising out of the coal mine disputes.

In the spring of 1946 the United Mine Workers and the coal operators were unable to come to an agreement in contract negotiations. When the miners struck, President Truman ordered the mines seized under the procedures of the War Labor Disputes Act of 1943 (50 U.S.C.A. App. Secs. 1501–1511). Secretary of Interior Krug then negotiated a contract with John L. Lewis which was to continue in effect only for the period of Government possession. This contract granted most of the Union's demands and made basic departures from earlier contracts. It provided for a new mine safety code, a substantial wage increase, paid vacations, a Welfare and Retirement Fund, and a Medical and Hospital Fund.

In October, 1946, Lewis requested a negotiating conference as authorized by the contract. Krug requested that Lewis negotiate with the mine owners, but Lewis refused and gave notice of termination of the contract on November 20. Although Krug insisted there was no provision giving Lewis the power to terminate the contract, Lewis sent the notice of termination to all local unions as "official information." This was, in effect, a strike call under the miner's rule of "no contract, no work." Two days before the strike date the Government obtained an order in the Federal District Court enjoining Lewis and the United Mine Workers from calling the strike. Lewis refused to withdraw his notice of termination and the miners walked out.

Lewis and the United Mine Workers were cited for contempt and found guilty of both civil and criminal contempt. Judge Goldsborough fined Lewis $10,000, and the union $3,500,000. On December 7, Lewis issued a "back to work" order. On special appeal the Supreme Court affirmed the contempt convictions but reduced the fine against the Union to $700,000.

Two principal issues relating to labor law were involved: (1) Did the Norris-LaGuardia Act prohibit an injunction in this case? (2) If the Norris-LaGuardia Act did apply, were the contempt convictions valid? On the first issue, a five-to-four majority held that the Norris-LaGuardia Act was not applicable. Government seizure made the miners employees of the Government. This was, then, a dispute between the Government and its employees. Since the statute divested pre-existing rights, it would not be applied to the sovereign without express words to that effect. Furthermore, the policies of the Act as stated in Section 2 do not apply to the relations between the Government and its employees. On the second issue five justices held that even though the Norris-LaGuardia Act did apply, the District Court still had power to punish for criminal attempt. The Federal District Courts were not completely stripped of power to issue injunctions in labor disputes. Since they still have the power to adjudicate the subject matter, there is sufficient jurisdiction for the injunction to stand until set aside upon appeal. United States v. United Mine Workers, 330 U.S. 258, 67 Sup. Ct. 677, 91 L. Ed. 884 (1947).

After this Supreme Court decision on March 6, 1947, Lewis wrote Secretary Krug that he "unconditionally" withdrew his notice of termination which had precipitated the strike. However, on March 29 he ordered the miners to stop work during the period of April 1 to 6 as a memorial to 111 miners killed in a mine explosion in Centralia, Illinois, the week before. The "memorial" lasted two weeks and ended only when Lewis ordered the men to return to work.

In June, 1947, the mines were returned to the operators. Lewis obtained a new agreement from them which incorporated all of the concessions refused by them in 1946 but obtained from the Government during the seizure.

The Welfare and Retirement Fund, financed by a 10-cent per ton royalty on coal, created problems because of its doubtful legality under the provisions of Section 302 of the Taft-Hartley Act. In March, 1948, Lewis accused the operators of violating the contract. On March 12 he sent a letter to all local unions stating, among other things, "The winter is now gone. This office now proposes to go forward in requiring the coal operators to honor their agreement." Two days later 450,000 miners quit work. On March 24, President Truman invoked the National Emergency Strike provisions of the Taft-Hartley Act, and appointed a fact-finding board. On April 3, the Government obtained an injunction from Judge Goldsborough ordering Lewis to end the strike. When he failed to act, he and the Union were charged with contempt. On April 12, after he had obtained the desired concessions on the pension system, he "officially advised" the miners to return to work. Judge Goldsborough refused to accept this as a purging of the contempt, ordered Lewis and the Union to stand trial, convicted them of civil and criminal contempt, and fined Lewis $20,000 and the Union $1,400,000. In finding the contempt, Judge Goldsborough held that Lewis's letter, although not an explicit strike call was in reality a code to cause a walkout, and he could have as easily ended it by ordering them to return to work.

In so holding, he stated: "And then this court believes that there is a principle of law, which as far as I know, no court has ever been called upon to announce, because this use of a code in order for a union to avoid responsibility is a new thing. It is a new method of endeavoring to avoid responsibility. . . . The Court thinks the principle is this: that as long as a union is functioning as a union, it must be held responsible for the mass action of its members." United States v. United Mine Workers, 77 F. Supp. 563 (D.D.C. 1948), affirmed, 177 F.2d 29 (D.C. Cir. 1949). Compare United States v. Brotherhood of Railroad Trainmen, 95 F. Supp. 1019 (D.D.C. 1951).

In the summer of 1949 the parties attempted to negotiate a new agreement. Lewis insisted on a union-shop contract although he had not complied with the Taft-Hartley Act, insisted that the Welfare and Retirement Fund should be for members only, and demanded inclusion of the famous "able and willing" clause and a "memorial period" provision designed to enable the miners to suspend operations at any time. When the operators resisted these demands, Lewis ordered a one-week stoppage and then a three-day week. In September another strike was called which lasted seven weeks. Full operation was then restored for three weeks after which the three-day week was again ordered. In January the NLRB invoked Section 10 (j) of the Taft-Hartley Act and obtained a decree in the Federal District Court ordering Lewis to bargain in good faith. The court issued the injunction on the grounds that the above demands were all in violation of the Act. Penello v. United Mine Workers, 88 F. Supp. 935 (D.D.C. 1950). Negotiations resumed on a somewhat doubtful basis, but the miners began leaving the pits. Within a week 370,000 were out, but Lewis declared it was entirely "wildcat."

On February 6, 1950, President Truman appointed a Board of Inquiry under the Taft-Hartley Act. Upon the filing of the board's report on February 11, the Government obtained an injunction restraining the Union and its officers from "in any manner engaging in, permitting or encouraging the strike or its continuation, in whole or in part," and ordered them to "instruct and take all appropriate action necessary to insure that such instructions are carried out, all members . . . to cease the strike and return to their employment forthwith." United States v. United Mine Workers, 89 F. Supp. 187 (D.D.C. 1950).

Lewis sent telegrams to all locals informing them of the restraining order and requesting compliance, and he met with the operators for negotiations. Further letters and circulars were sent to the locals instructing them to cease stoppages, but the men did not return to work. The Government filed charges of contempt against both Lewis and the Union but after a trial held on February 27, Judge Keech acquitted the defendants, holding there was not sufficient evidence of the contempt. He stated that the Union officers had sent instructions to the local unions, had used effort to end the stoppage, and had provided no strike benefits. The only other means available was to revoke local charters, but there was no showing this would be "appropriate" action and therefore was not required under the decree. In the absence of any evidence of bad faith or chicanery, there was no proof of the contempt beyond a reasonable doubt. United States v. United Mine Workers, 89 F. Supp. 179 (D.D.C. 1950).

The dispute was settled by an agreement reached on March 3, which eliminated the "willing and able" clause, limited "memorial periods" to five days per year, and provided for a union shop "to the extent permitted by law." The miners, however, gained a wage increase of 70 cents per day, and an increase to 30 cents per ton for the royalty contribution to the pension fund.

These bouts with the United Mine Workers cost the Government more than exasperation and administrative energy. The Government was still liable to the mine owners for seizing the mines. The Supreme Court held that this was a "taking" within the Fifth Amendment and the Government was liable for just compensation. The Court defined just compensation as being the reasonable value of the property's use. However, in the particular case the mine had been operated at a loss. The Court held that the Government must bear this loss even though the losses to the owners might have been greater if the Government had not seized the mines. United States v. Pewee Coal Co., 341 U.S. 114, 71 Sup. Ct. 670, 95 L. Ed. 809 (1951). Compare Anderson v. Chesapeake Ferry Co., 186 Va. 481, 43 S.E.2d 10 (1947).

4. In the fall of 1949 the Steelworkers included in their demands a request for employer-paid health and welfare plans. The steel companies resisted and a strike was called. The President did not invoke the Taft-Hartley Act, but convened a special board of inquiry to hold hearings and make recommendations. The report of this board, in the main, supported the Union's demands as fair and not unduly inflationary. Shortly after the report was issued the strike was settled on terms substantially equivalent to the board's recommendations. This contract was to expire December 31, 1951.

In January, 1951, the Government inaugurated a wage-and-price stabilization program designed to curb inflationary pressures. Restrictions were placed on both wage and price increases. In the fall of 1951 the Steelworkers notified the steel companies of an intent to demand substantial wage increases in the new contract. The steel companies argued that any such wage increases would violate the letter and spirit of the wage stabilization program. Numerous conferences failed to make any progress toward settlement, and on December 18 the Union served notice of an intent to strike on December 31.

On December 22, the President referred the dispute to the Federal Wage Stabilization Board to investigate and make recommendations for fair and equitable terms of settlement. The parties agreed to maintain production pending these proceedings. Elaborate hearings were held by the Board and efforts were made to induce the parties to reach a settlement. The Board finally made its report on March 20, 1952, recommending wage increases and changes in such fringe items as overtime, holiday and vacation pay totaling more than 25 cents an hour. The Board also recommended that the Union be given a union shop. The steel companies rejected this, stating, that to compensate for such increases they would have to be allowed a price increase of $12 a ton. The Office of Price Stabilization stated that only a $3 price increase could be granted under existing law.

Further meetings between the Union and the companies brought no results and the Union called a strike for April 9. A few hours before the strike deadline the President issued an executive order directing the Secretary of Commerce to take possession of the steel mills and operate them. The President did not claim any statutory authority for the seizure but claimed he had "inherent power" as chief executive and as Commander in Chief of the Armed Forces. He justified his refusal to invoke the emergency provisions of the Taft-Hartley Act on the grounds that in December the Union had agreed that it would voluntarily postpone its strike pending consideration by the Wage Stabilization Board. The Union had delayed 99 days and thereby more than complied with the 80-day cooling-off period required by the Taft-Hartley Act.

In issuing the seizure order the President stated that "a work stoppage would immediately jeopardize and imperil our national defense." The morning after the seizure he sent a special message to Congress informing it of his action and inviting it to take whatever steps it deemed appropriate. In this message he said, "One alternative would have been to permit a shut-down of the steel industry. The effects of such a shut-down would have been so immediate and damaging with respect to our efforts to support our armed forces and to protect our national security that it made this alternative unthinkable." Secretary of Defense Lovett stated that "a work stoppage in the steel industry will result immediately in serious curtailment of production of essential weapons and munitions of all kinds."

Congress debated the seizure with great heat but took no action. In the meantime the battle had moved to the courts. The steel companies brought proceedings in the Federal District Court to enjoin the seizure as unconstitutional. On April 30 the District Court enjoined the seizure and the Union immediately called a strike. This strike call was canceled the same day when the Circuit Court of Appeals stayed the District Court's injunction pending appeal. The Supreme Court granted certiorari and ordered immediate argument of the case. From the time of the seizure until the Supreme Court's decision on June 2, no serious collective bargaining took place.

In a decision entitled Youngstown Sheet & Tube v. Sawyer, 343 U.S. 579, 72 Sup. Ct. 863, 96 L. Ed. 817, the Supreme Court held the seizure unconstitutional. Justice Black, in delivering the opinion of the Court, held that in the absence of any statute granting him the power, the President had no constitutional power to order the seizure of the industry. He did not have the power as Commander in Chief "to take possession of private property in order to keep labor disputes from stopping production. This is a job for the Nation's lawmakers, not for its military authorities." Nor was this power inherent in his position as chief executive. "In the framework of our constitution, the President's power to see that the laws are faithfully executed refutes the idea that he is to be a lawmaker. The Constitution limits his function in the law-making process to the recommending of laws he thinks wise and the vetoing of laws he thinks bad. The Constitution is neither silent nor equivocal about who shall make the laws which the President shall execute." Justice Black reasoned further that there was not only an absence of Congressional authority for seizure but an implied denial of that power. In passing the Taft-Hartley Act, Congress had rejected provisions for seizure and had adopted instead the device of temporary injunctions to permit cooling-off periods.

Justices Jackson, Burton, Clark, Douglas, and Frankfurter each wrote concurring opinions spelling out in more detail the various aspects briefly mentioned by Justice Black.   Justice Clark argued that although the President had power to act to meet an emergency for which Congress had not provided, Congress had provided procedures for meeting this particular kind of emergency.   The Taft-Hartley Act provided for an 80-day delay, and the Selective Service Act provided for seizure of plants which fail to produce goods required by the armed forces.   The President had not exhausted either of these procedures and therefore could not act on any independent power.   Justice Frankfurter, as an appendix to his opinion, set forth in chart form all legislation authorizing seizure of industrial property and all instances of seizure of industrial property by the President.

Chief Justice Vinson, in a dissenting opinion joined in by Justices Reed and Minton, argued that the President did not act in defiance of Congress but in aid of Congress by preserving the status quo until Congress had time to take steps to meet the crisis. This was within the President's power as chief executive in seeing that the laws were enforced.   The Chief Justice further argued that the Defense Production Act, by giving to the Wage Stabilization Board power to deal with labor disputes, provided a procedure which was alternative to the Taft-Hartley Act.   Referral to the Board was an exercise of this alternative and excluded the use of Taft-Hartley emergency strike procedures.

When the Supreme Court enjoined the seizure and returned the mills to the steel companies, the Union called a strike.   Management, in its public appeal, placed great weight on its refusal to submit to the "un-American closed shop."   The Union emphasized the size of the industry's profit.   The President still refused to invoke the Taft-Hartley Act, and some members of Congress talked of impeachment.   Congress, however, refused to take any action to end the strike.

After seven weeks of strike the parties reached a settlement which granted the Union substantially the same economic terms recommended by the Board, and a form of maintenance-of-membership contract.   Simultaneously the industry was granted a price increase of more than $5 a ton.   Although the last weeks of the strike were marked by curtailment of some branches of civilian production, particularly in automobiles, and some layoffs occurred, there was no acute shortage of civilian goods on the market.   No conclusive evidence was ever assembled as to the effect of this stoppage upon our military efforts in Korea or upon our production of military material.

5. Section 305 of the Labor Management Relations Act provides: "It shall be unlawful for any individual employed by the United States or any agency thereof including wholly owned Government corporations to participate in any strike. Any individual employed by the United States or by any agency who strikes shall be discharged immediately from his employment, and shall forfeit his civil service status, if any, and shall not be eligible for reemployment for three years by the United States or any such agency."

This section enacts into statutory form the rule uniformly insisted upon by all branches of government. The judiciary has not lagged behind in enjoining strikes and picketing by government employees. The reasons for this rigid rule have varied, but includes the following: (a) The terms and conditions of employment are fixed by law. Civil service laws regulate hiring, tenure, and job classification practices; appropriations bills fix wages and salaries; and administrative regulations determine the other terms of employment. This leaves no room for collective bargaining and a strike could only compel officials to violate the law. (b) A strike by government employees is a strike against government itself. It is rebellion against constituted authority. (c) Government employees have the obligation to serve the whole people and this obligation is paramount. To strike means to put their welfare ahead of that of the people and violate their obligations. (d) Governmental services are essential for maintaining peace and orderliness in society. Strikes endanger the whole of society.

Consider the merit in these arguments and their applicability to the following situations: (a) A strike by construction workers on city projects for a closed shop. See Los Angeles v. Los Angeles Building and Construction Trades Council, 94 Cal. App. 2d 36, 210 P.2d 305 (1949). (b) A strike by streetcar conductors on a municipally owned transit system against "one-man streetcars." See City of Cleveland v. Division 268, 84 Ohio App. 43, 81 N.E.2d 310 (1948). (c) A strike by school janitors for a three-cent wage increase. See Board of Education v. Public School Employees Union, Local No. 63, 233 Minn. 144, 45 N.W.2d 797 (1951). (d) Strikes by policemen and firemen for tenure rules. See also Norwalk Teachers Assn. v. Board of Education, 138 Conn. 269, 83 A.2d 482 (1951), where a strike of teachers was enjoined; Detroit v. Amalgamated Assn. of Street Railway Employees, 332 Mich. 237, 51 N.W.2d 228 (1952), where a statute prohibiting strikes by public employees was held constitutional as applied to streetcar conductors; Ziskind, One Thousand Strikes of Government Employees (1941) ; Rhyne, Labor Unions and Municipal Employee Law (1946).

Most unions which recognize government employees have express provisions disavowing use of the strike weapon. Others have well-established policies against strikes. Where the strike is eliminated the union must rely almost entirely on political action to obtain benefits through legislative or administrative action. It may also be effective in presenting grievances and in preventing supervisory officials from encroaching on civil service rules and other rules designed to protect the employees. The number and size of these unions suggest that they fill a real need on the part of the government worker.

Note on Conditions Precedent to a Lawful Work Stoppage in Foreign Countries

Under French law compliance with conciliation procedure is a condition precedent to a lawful work stoppage,[43] but no sanction is provided for noncompliance. Neither German nor Austrian law includes any provision relating to the matters discussed in this note. Doubtless this is due to the fact that the terms of the collective agreement, even after its expiration, are there viewed as continuing as terms of the individual employment relation,[44] thus removing the necessity for compulsory conciliation or a cooling-off period.

The Swedish Collective Contract Act prohibits concerted action during the term of a collective contract. Where there is no contract, the Act of September 11, 1936, compels the parties to negotiate. If negotiations fail, the state machinery for mediation comes into action. In addition, a seven-day notice is required prior to the commencement of strikes or lockouts.

The statutes of Norway, 1915 and 1927, make the lawfulness of a strike or lockout dependent upon the expiration of a cooling-off period, starting when a stop order is issued by a public official, the Conciliator. This order issues upon notice of a forthcoming work stoppage which must be given him by the union or employer, planning the action. If, his mediation having failed, a stoppage occurs, the conciliation proceedings must be resumed after the

[43] See Act of Feb. 11, 1950, No. 50–205, tit. II. For further discussion see Methods for Establishing Peaceful Labor Relations in Foreign Countries. page 279 supra.

[44] Discussed at page 287 supra.

expiration of one month, a statutory limitation which makes long-lasting labor disputes almost impossible.

The Mexican Federal Labor Act, 1931, sec. 56, directs either party to a collective contract to transmit a demand for revision not less than sixty days before the expiration of the old contract. If the parties do not reach an agreement within this time and either party fails to express his consent to an extension of time, the matter is referred to a conciliation and arbitration board for decision. During the proceedings before the board the parties are required to observe the terms of the old contract. Under the Labor Code of Venezuela (1945)[45] the lawfulness of a work stoppage depends upon a prior conciliation proceeding and the expiration of at least five days after the demands are handed to a public officer, the Labor Inspector.[46]

The new English Industrial Disputes Order, 1951, prohibits strikes and lockouts without prior notification to the Minister of Labour with a view to possible settlement either through machinery provided for in the collective contract or by him on an ad hoc basis. Violation by the union deprives it of ultimate recourse to the compulsory jurisdiction of the Industrial Disputes Tribunal.[47]

3. RIGHTS OF STRIKERS TO RETURN TO WORK

NLRB v. MACKAY RADIO & TELEGRAPH CO.
Supreme Court of the United States, 1938
304 U.S. 333, 58 Sup. Ct. 904, 82 L. Ed. 1381

[Certiorari to the Ninth Circuit. In this case the Supreme Court reversed a refusal to enforce a Board order. The Mackay Company's headquarters in New York City was bargaining there with American Radio Telegraphists Association; its San Francisco office was bargaining with Local 3 of the same national. The negotiations bogged down. The national officers decided on a general strike. Local 3's representative in New York so informed his Local; and the Local's officers called the San Francisco employees out at midnight on Friday, October 4, 1935. The Com-

---

[45] Secs. 206, 208, 211, and 216.

[46] For similar provisions see Labor Statutes, Salvador, No. 322, secs. 25 and 26 (1946), requiring a thirty-day period after presentation to the Inspector. Cf. Ecuador (Act of July 11, 1926), Dominican Republic (Sec. 1, Act of Jan. 18, 1946), and Bolivia, Busch Labor Code (1942), pt. X, art. 104 et seq., ILO Leg. Ser. 1939 and 1942.

[47] S. Insts., 1951, No. 1376. See McKelvey, Legal Aspects of Compulsory Arbitration in Great Britain, 37 Cornell L.Q. 403, 416 (1952).

pany, to maintain service, brought in replacements from Los Angeles, Chicago, and New York. The strike was unsuccessful throughout the country. The San Francisco strikers, by Monday, had become fearful of losing their jobs forever. One telephoned the Company's local supervisor, who said the Company would take the men back. He then consulted his superior, who agreed the men might come back — except, he said, that the Company had had to promise permanent San Francisco jobs to eleven of the replacements it had brought in, and these must not be ousted against their will. The supervisor then called a meeting of the strikers. But in doing so he omitted eleven men who he said would have to apply for reinstatement, subject to the approval of the Company's New York office. Thirty-six attended the meeting, including a few of the eleven, who had happened to hear about it. The superintendent reiterated his statements about return to work, and also about the eleven. A resolution to return at once was carried, and most did return. Then, or shortly thereafter, six of the eleven in question took their places and resumed their work without challenge as only five of the replacements wanted to stay in San Francisco. The five strikers not reinstated, all of whom were prominent in the union and in the strike, reported for work at various times during the next three days, but were told there were no openings. They were asked to file applications which would be considered for any future vacancies. After three weeks of waiting, the secretary of Local 3 filed a charge of violations of Sections 8 (1) and (3). The Board issued its complaint alleging that the Company's discharge of the five violated Section 8 (1) and also, because discriminatory, violated Section 8 (3). Later, it found that the refusals to reinstate the five men were equivalent to discharges, and issued its usual order including full reinstatement of the five with back pay, posting of notices, and so forth.

In the Circuit Court of Appeals for the Ninth Circuit, the court set the Board's order aside.]

MR. JUSTICE ROBERTS delivered the opinion of the Court: . . .

Second. Under the findings the strike was a consequence of, or in connection with, a current labor dispute as defined in Sec. 2 (9) of the Act. That there were pending negotiations for the execution of a contract touching wages and terms and conditions of employment of point-to-point operators cannot be denied. But it is said the record fails to disclose what caused these negotiations to fail or to show that the respondent was in any wise in fault in failing to comply with the union's demands; and, therefore, for all that appears, the strike was not called by reason of fault of the respondent.   The argument confuses a current labor dispute with an unfair labor practice defined in Sec. 8 of the Act. True there is no evidence that respondent had been guilty of any unfair labor practice prior to the strike, but within the intent of the act there was an existing labor dispute in connection with which the strike was called.   The finding is that the strike was deemed "advisable in view of the unsatisfactory state of negotiations" in New York.   It was unnecessary for the Board to find what was in fact the state of the negotiations in New York when the strike was called, or in so many words that a labor dispute as defined by the Act existed.   The wisdom or unwisdom of the men, their justification or lack of it, in attributing to respondent an unreasonable or arbitrary attitude in connection with the negotiations, cannot determine whether, when they struck, they did so as a consequence of or in connection with a current labor dispute.

Third.   The strikers remained employees under Sec. 2 (3) of the Act which provides: "The Term 'employee' shall include . . . any individual whose work has ceased as a consequence of, or in connection with, any current labor dispute or because of any unfair labor practice, and who has not obtained any other regular and substantially equivalent employment, . . ."   Within this definition the strikers remained employees for the purpose of the Act and were protected against the unfair labor practices denounced by it.

Fourth.   It is contended that the Board lacked jurisdiction because respondent was at no time guilty of any unfair labor practice.   Section 8 of the Act denominates as such practice action by an employer to interfere with, restrain, or coerce employees in the exercise of their rights to organize, to form, join or assist labor organizations, and to engage in concerted activities for the purpose of collective bargaining or other mutual aid or protection, or "by discrimination in regard to . . . tenure of employment or any term or condition of employment to encourage or discourage membership in any labor organization: . . ."   There is no evidence and no finding that the respondent was guilty of any unfair labor practice in connection with the negotiations in New York.   On the contrary, it affirmatively appears that the respondent was negotiating with the authorized representatives of the union.   Nor was it an unfair labor practice to replace the striking employees with others in an effort to carry on the business. Although Section 13 provides, "Nothing in this Act shall be construed so as to interfere with or impede or diminish in any way the right to strike," it does not follow that an employer, guilty of no act denounced by the statute, has lost the right to protect and continue his business by supplying places left vacant by strikers. And he is not bound to discharge those hired to fill the places of strikers, upon the election of the latter to resume their employment, in order to create places for them. The assurance by respondent to those who accepted employment during the strike that if they so desired their places might be permanent was not an unfair labor practice nor was it such to reinstate only so many of the strikers as there were vacant places to be filled. But the claim put forward is that the unfair labor practice indulged by the respondent was discrimination in reinstating striking employees by keeping out certain of them for the sole reason that they had been active in the union. As we have said, the strikers retained, under the Act, the status of employees. Any such discrimination in putting them back to work is, therefore, prohibited by Sec. 8.

. . . The Board found, and we cannot say that its finding is unsupported, that, in taking back six of the eleven men and excluding five who were active union men, the respondent's officials discriminated against the latter on account of their union activities and that the excuse given that they did not apply until after the quota was full was an afterthought and not the true reason for the discrimination against them.

As we have said, the respondent was not bound to displace men hired to take the strikers' places in order to provide positions for them. It might have refused reinstatement on the ground of skill or ability, but the Board found that it did not do so. It might have resorted to any one of a number of methods of determining which of its striking employees would have to wait because five men had taken permanent positions during the strike, but it is found that the preparation and use of the list, and the action taken by respondent, were with the purpose to discriminate against those most active in the union. There is evidence to support these findings.

Sixth. The Board's order does not violate the Fifth Amendment. The respondent insists that the relation of employer and employee ceased at the inception of the strike. The plain meaning of the Act is that if men strike in connection with a current labor dispute their action is not to be construed as a renunciation of the employment relation and they remain employees for the remedial purposes specified in the Act. We have held that, in the exercise of the commerce power, Congress may impose upon contractual relationships reasonable regulations calculated to protect commerce against threatened industrial strife. . . .

Seventh. The affirmative relief ordered by the Board was within its powers and its order was not arbitrary or capricious. . . . .

. . . On the basis of the findings, five men who took part in the strike were discriminated against in connection with a blanket offer to reinstate striking employees. The Board enjoined further discrimination against employees by reason of union affiliation, but it could not grant complete relief in respect of the five men short of ordering that the discrimination be neutralized by their being given their former positions and reimbursed for the loss due to their lack of employment consequent upon the respondent's discrimination. . . .

The judgment of the Circuit Court of Appeals is reversed and the cause is remanded to that court for further proceedings in conformity with this opinion.

Reversed.

MR. JUSTICE CARDOZO and MR. JUSTICE REED took no part in the consideration or decision of this case.

NOTES

1. If the strike is purely economic and the employer has obtained permanent replacements for some of the strikers, are those replaced still employees? Do they have a prior claim to jobs as vacancies occur, or are they merely job applicants protected only against discrimination because they were strikers? See Matter of Union Bus Terminal, 98 N.L.R.B. No. 68, 29 L.R.R.M. 1356 (1952) ; Sax v. NLRB, 171 F.2d 769 (7th Cir. 1948). In NLRB v. Potlatch Forests Inc., 189 F.2d 82 (9th Cir. 1951), the employer, after breaking the strike, rehired the strikers who had not been replaced, but placed them at the bottom of the seniority list, thus giving the strikebreakers superseniority. The court held that this was not a violation of Section 8 (a) (3). "There has been no discrimination between union and non-union employees. The group of replacements includes union members, some of whom had been out on strike but had returned to their jobs before the strike was settled." Id. at 85. "The discrimination between replacements and strikers is not an unfair labor practice despite a tendency to discourage union activities, because the benefit conferred upon the replacements is a benefit reasonably appropriate for an employer to confer in attempting to protect and continue

his business by supplying places left vacant by strikers." Id. at 86.

Does the rule in the Mackay case promote or endanger the peaceful prosecution of a strike? What is the effect of this rule when combined with Section 9 (c) (3) of the Taft-Hartley Act, which deprives employees not entitled to reinstatement of their right to vote? What is its relevance to mass picketing and violence on the picket line? If the employer hires replacements or encourages individual employees to return to work on his terms, is he engaging in individual or collective bargaining? See Boudin, Representatives of Their Own Choosing, 37 Ill. L. Rev. 385 (1943).

2. If a strike in its inception is economic, but during the strike the employer commits an unfair labor practice — such as refusing to bargain, organizing a company union, or discharging strike leaders — and the unfair labor practice has the effect of prolonging the strike, the strike is then converted into an unfair labor practice strike. All strikers replaced after the employer's wrongful act are entitled to reinstatement. NLRB v. Remington Rand, 130 F.2d 919 (2d Cir. 1942); Matter of Crowley's Milk Co., 88 N.L.R.B. 1049, 25 L.R.R.M. 1432 (1950); Matter of De Soto Hardwood Flooring Co., 96 N.L.R.B. 382, 28 L.R.R.M. 1527 (1951); Matter of Pecheur Lozenge Co., Inc., 98 N.L.R.B. No. 84, 29 L.R.R.M. 1367 (1952).

3. Strikers who are entitled to reinstatement are not entitled to back pay during the period of the strike, even though it is caused by an unfair labor practice. However, if they offer to return to work, the refusal to re-employ is a violation of Section 8 (a) (3) and the employer is liable for back pay from the date of the offer. Matter of Andrews Co., 87 N.L.R.B. 379, 25 L.R.R.M. 1117 (1949); Matter of Patterson Steel & Forge Co., 96 N.L.R.B. 129, 28 L.R.R.M. 1492 (1951). The offer to return to work must be unconditional and on the employers' terms. If the strikers demand concessions as the price of their return, it amounts to a continuation of the strike. NLRB v. Crosby Chemicals, Inc., 188 F.2d 91 (5th Cir. 1951); Matter of Pacific Powder Co., 84 N.L.R.B. 280, 24 L.R.R.M. 1243 (1949).

If the strikers offer to return to work only on the condition that the employer cease certain unfair labor practices, is this such an unconditional offer as to make the employer liable for back pay, or is it merely an unfair labor practice strike? The Board has seemingly been unable to resolve this issue. In Matter of Draper Corp., 52 N.L.R.B. 1477, 13 L.R.R.M. 88 (1943), the employer agreed to reinstate some of the strikers who offered to return, but insisted on discharging the others. Those offered jobs refused to return unless all entitled to reinstatement were taken back. The Board held, Member Reilly dissenting, that the employer was liable to these employees for back pay from the date of their offer to return and their replacements were accordingly displaced, their status being regarded as "vulnerable." This rule was approved by the courts. NLRB v. Poultrymen's Service Corp., 138 F.2d 204 (3d Cir. 1943). In two later cases in which strikers refused to return unless they were reinstated as a group, the Board held that their offer to return was not unconditional. From that moment on they were only unfair labor practice strikers and were not entitled to back pay. Matter of Volney Felt Mills, 70 N.L.R.B. 908, 18 L.R.R.M. 1422 (1946); Matter of Pacific Moulded Products Co., 76 N.L.R.B. 1140, 21 L.R.R.M. 1328 (1948). However, in a still later case, the Board apparently reverted to the rule of the Draper Corp. case. Matter of W. T. Rawleigh Co., 90 N.L.R.B. 1924, 26 L.R.R.M. 1421 (1950).

In two other cases involving somewhat different facts, the Board has apparently followed the analysis used in the Draper Corp. case. In Matter of E.A. Laboratories, 80 N.L.R.B. 625, 23 L.R.R.M. 1162 (1948), the employer refused to reinstate the strikers unless they would abandon their union membership and activity; and in Matter of Consolidated Frame Co., 91 N.L.R.B. 1295, 27 L.R.R.M. 1008 (1950), the employer demanded that they withdraw charges filed with the Board. In both cases, the Board held that strikers who offered to return but refused to accept these conditions were entitled to back pay from the date of their offer.

4. Still another problem relating to reinstatement arises out of the use of the term "substantially equivalent employment" found in Section 2 of the Act. The Supreme Court gave this question its first and most extensive consideration in Phelps Dodge Corp. v. NLRB, 313 U.S. 177, 61 Sup. Ct. 845, 85 L. Ed. 1271 (1941), page 622 supra. In that case certain employees had secured other employment which the Company, resisting their reinstatement, contended was "substantially equivalent." The Board found that no such employment had been obtained, but concluded in the alternative that it had the power to order the men reinstated in any event.

Justice Frankfurter, in the opinion for the majority, stated the issue as follows:

> The specific provisions of the Act out of which the proper conclusion is to be drawn should be before us. Section

10 (c), as we already know, authorizes the Board "to take such affirmative action, including reinstatement of employees with or without back pay, as will effectuate the policies of this Act." The relevant portions of Section 2 (3) follow: "The term 'employee' shall include any employee, and shall not be limited to the employees of a particular employer, unless the Act explicitly states otherwise, and shall include any individual whose work has ceased as a consequence of, or in connection with, any current labor dispute or because of any unfair labor practice, and who has not obtained any other regular and substantially equivalent employment."

Merely as a matter of textual reading these provisions in combination permit three possible constructions: (1) a curtailment of the powers of the Board to take affirmative action by reading into §10 (c) the restrictive phrase of §2 (3) regarding a worker "who has not obtained any other regular and substantially equivalent employment"; (2) a completely distributive reading of §10 (c) and §2 (3), whereby the factor of "regular and substantially equivalent employment" in no way limits the Board's usual power to require employment to be offered a worker who has lost employment because of discrimination; (3) an avoidance of this either-or reading of the statute by pursuing the central clue to the Board's powers — effectuation of the policies of the Act — and in that light appraising the relevance of a worker's having obtained "substantially equivalent employment."

Three of the Justices (Frankfurter, Roberts, and Reed) chose the third interpretation, concluding that "the mere fact that the victim of discrimination has obtained equivalent employment does not itself preclude the Board from undoing the discrimination and requiring employment. But neither does this remedy automatically flow from the Act itself when discrimination has been found. . . . In the exercise of its informed discretion the Board may find that effectuation of the Act's policies may or may not require reinstatement. . . . [But] the Board determined only the dry legal question of its power, which we sustain; it did not consider whether in employing that power the policies of the Act would be enforced." Accordingly the case was sent back to the Board for the policy-effectuating determination described.

Two members of the Court (Chief Justice Hughes and Justice Stone) were of the opinion that Section 2 (3) modified and restricted the Board's reinstatement powers conferred by Section 10 (c).

Three of the Justices (Murphy, Black, and Douglas) dissented on the ground that "There is nothing in Section 10 (c) or in the Act as a whole which expressly or impliedly obligates the Board to consider substantial equivalency of other employment or to make findings concerning it before it may order reinstatement."

Suppose a discriminatorily discharged employee seeks a job with another employer in a community where there is a settled policy among employers not to hire men away from other companies in the area? What should be his answer to the prospective employer's query "Have you quit your former job?" Suppose he says, "Yes," is hired, and then discovers that he would prefer to have his old job back. Must his former employer rehire him? See Matter of National Grinding Wheel Company, 75 N.L.R.B. 905, 21 L.R.R.M. 1095 (1948).

NLRB v. FANSTEEL METALLURGICAL CORP.
Supreme Court of the United States, 1939
306 U.S. 240, 59 Sup. Ct. 490, 83 L. Ed. 627

MR. CHIEF JUSTICE HUGHES delivered the opinion of the Court.

The Circuit Court of Appeals set aside an order of the National Labor Relations Board requiring respondent to desist from labor practices found to be in violation of the National Labor Relations Act and to offer reinstatement to certain discharged employees with back pay. While the other portions of the Board's order are under review, the principal question presented relates to the authority of the Board to require respondent to reinstate employees who were discharged because of their unlawful conduct in seizing respondent's property in what is called a "sit-down strike." . . .

First. The unfair labor practices. — The Board concluded that by "the anti-union statements and actions" of the superintendent on September 10, 1936, and September 21, 1936, by "the campaign to introduce into the plant a company union," by "the isolation of the Union president from contact with his fellow employees," and by the employment and use of a "labor spy," respondent had interfered with its employees, and restrained and coerced them, in the exercise of their right to self-organization guaranteed in §7 of the Act, and thus had engaged in an unfair labor practice under §8 (1) of the Act.

Owing to the fact that in September, 1936, the Union did not have a majority of the employees in the appropriate unit, the Board held that it was precluded from finding unfair labor practices in refusing to bargain collectively at that time, but the Board found that there was such a refusal on February 17, 1937, when the Union did have a majority of the employees in the appropriate unit, and that this constituted a violation of §8 (5).

These conclusions are supported by the findings of the Board and the latter in this relation have substantial support in the evidence.

Second. The discharge of the employees for illegal conduct in seizing and holding respondent's buildings. — The Board does not now contend that there was not a real discharge on February 17th when the men refused to surrender possession. The discharge was clearly proved.

Nor is there any basis for dispute as to the cause of the discharge. Representatives of respondent demanded that the men leave, and on their refusal announced that they were discharged "for the seizure and retention of the buildings." The fact that it was a general announcement applicable to all the men in the plant who thus refused to leave does not detract from the effect of the discharge either in fact or in law.

Nor is it questioned that the seizure and retention of respondent's property were unlawful. It was a high-handed proceeding without shadow of legal right. It became the subject of denunciation by the state court under the state law, resulting in fines and jail sentences for defiance of the court's order to vacate and in a final decree for respondent as the complainant in the injunction suit.

This conduct on the part of the employees manifestly gave good cause for their discharge unless the National Labor Relations Act abrogates the right of the employer to refuse to retain in his employ those who illegally take and hold possession of his property.

Third. The authority of the Board to require the reinstatement of the employees thus discharged. — The contentions of the Board in substance are these: (1) That the unfair labor practices of respondent led to the strike and thus furnished ground for requiring the reinstatement of the strikers; (2) That under the terms of the Act employees who go on strike because of an unfair labor practice retain their status as employees and are to be considered as such despite discharge for illegal conduct; (3) That the Board was entitled to order reinstatement or reemployment in order to "effectuate the policies" of the Act.

(1) For the unfair labor practices of respondent the Act provides a remedy. Interference in the summer and fall of 1936

with the right of self-organization could at once have been the subject of complaint to the Board.   The same remedy was available to the employees when collective bargaining was refused on February 17, 1937.   But reprehensible as was that conduct of the respondent, there is no ground for saying that it made respondent an outlaw or deprived it of its legal rights to the possession and protection of its property.   The employees had the right to strike but they had no license to commit acts of violence or to seize their employer's plant.   We may put on one side the contested questions as to the circumstances and extent of injury to the plant and its contents in the efforts of the men to resist eviction.   The seizure and holding of the buildings was itself a wrong apart from any acts of sabotage.   But in its legal aspect the ousting of the owner from lawful possession is not essentially different from an assault upon the officers of an employing company, or the seizure and conversion of its goods, or the despoiling of its property or other unlawful acts in order to force compliance with demands. To justify such conduct because of the existence of a labor dispute or of an unfair labor practice would be to put a premium on resort to force instead of legal remedies and to subvert the principles of law and order which lie at the foundations of society.

As respondent's unfair labor practices afforded no excuse for the seizure and holding of its buildings, respondent had its normal rights of redress.   Those rights, in their most obvious scope, included the right to discharge the wrongdoers from its employ. To say that respondent could resort to the state court to recover damages or to procure punishment, but was powerless to discharge those responsible for the unlawful seizure would be to create an anomalous distinction for which there is no warrant unless it can be found in the terms of the National Labor Relations Act.   We turn to the provisions which the Board invokes. . . .

But the Board, in exercising its authority under §10 (c) to reinstate "employees," insists that here the status of the employees was continued, despite discharge for unlawful conduct, by virtue of the definition of the term "employee" in §2 (3).   By that definition the term includes: "any individual whose work has ceased as a consequence of, or in connection with, any current labor dispute or because of any unfair labor practice, and who has not obtained any other regular and substantially equivalent employment, . . ."

We think that the argument misconstrues the statute.   We are unable to conclude that Congress intended to compel employers to retain persons in their employ regardless of their unlawful conduct, — to invest those who go on strike with an immunity from discharge for acts of trespass or violence against the employer's property, which they would not have enjoyed had they remained at work. Apart from the question of the constitutional validity of an enactment of that sort, it is enough to say that such a legislative intention should be found in some definite and unmistakable expression. We find no such expression in the cited provision. . . .

Here the strike was illegal in its inception and prosecution. As the Board found, it was initiated by the decision of the Union committee, "to take over and hold two of the respondent's 'key' buildings." It was pursuant to that decision that the men occupied the buildings and the work stopped. This was not the exercise of "the right to strike" to which the Act referred. It was not a mere quitting of work and statement of grievances in the exercise of pressure recognized as lawful. It was an illegal seizure of the buildings in order to prevent their use by the employer in a lawful manner and thus by acts of force and violence to compel the employer to submit. When the employees resorted to that sort of compulsion they took a position outside the protection of the statute and accepted the risk of the termination of their employment upon grounds aside from the exercise of the legal rights which the statute was designed to conserve. . . .

. . . We are of the opinion that to provide for the reinstatement or reemployment of employees guilty of the acts which the Board finds to have been committed in this instance would not only not effectuate any policy of the Act but would directly tend to make abortive its plan for peaceable procedure. . . .

The Board stresses the fact that, when respondent was able to obtain possession of its buildings and to resume operations, it offered reemployment to many of the men who had participated in the strike. The contention confuses what an employer may voluntarily and legally do in the exercise of his right of selection and what the Board is entitled to compel. . . .

. . . The important point is that respondent stood absolved by the conduct of those engaged in the "sit-down" from any duty to reemploy them, but respondent was nevertheless free to consider the exigencies of its business and to offer reemployment if it chose. In so doing it was simply exercising its normal right to select its employees.

Fourth. The requirement of reinstatement of employees who aided and abetted those who seized and held the buildings. — There is a group of fourteen persons in this class who were not within the buildings and hence do not appear to have been within the announcement of discharge, but who went on strike and fall within the order for reinstatement. . . .

It cannot be said that independently of the Act respondent was bound to reinstate those who had thus aided and abetted the "sit-down" strikers in defying the court's order.   If it be assumed that by virtue of §2 (3) they still had the status of "employees," that provision did not automatically provide reinstatement. Whether the Board could order it must turn on the application of the provision empowering the Board to require "such affirmative action, including reinstatement of employees" as will "effectuate the policies" of the Act.   We are thus returned to the question already discussed and we think that in that respect these aiders and abettors, likewise guilty of unlawful conduct, are in no better case than the "sit-down" strikers themselves.   We find no ground for concluding that there is any policy of the Act, which justifies the Board in ordering reinstatement in such circumstances. . . .

[Justice Stone concurred except as to the aiders and abettors, who he thought were still employees because they had not been discharged. Justice Reed, joined by Justice Black, dissented.]

NOTES

1. For a fascinating study of the case and a dramatic exposition of how different a case may be in real life from what appears in its pallid reflection glimpsed through an appellate court's opinions, see Hart and Prichard, The Fansteel Case, 52 Harv. L. Rev. 1275 (1939).   This article makes clear that the eviction of the sit-downers did not end the strike.   The Company resumed operations and took back all who would go through the picket line, paying them back wages for the period production was stopped. Included in this group were thirty sit-downers then under citation for contempt and a number who were later convicted of acts of violence.   None of these was dismissed even after conviction. The only ones who were denied reinstatement were those who continued the strike after operations were resumed.   In the light of this the Board found that willingness to abandon the strike, not guilt for seizure or acts of violence was the criterion for reinstatement.   Since the strike was for recognition, reinstatement was granted only to those who would surrender this claim which was supposed to be protected by the statute.

2. The doctrine of the Fansteel case has been extended to other forms of violence.   Mass picketing which blocks entrances to the

plant has been treated as equivalent to physical seizure justifying discharge of any or all who participate. NLRB v. Indiana Desk Co., 149 F.2d 987 (7th Cir. 1945). It is not necessary that physical violence be used if the picketing is intended to and does prevent entry into the plant. W. T. Rawleigh Co. v. NLRB, 190 F.2d 832 (7th Cir. 1951); NLRB v. Perfect Circle Co., 162 F.2d 566 (7th Cir. 1947).

In some instances the doctrine has been limited to gross misconduct. In Republic Steel Corp. v. NLRB, 107 F.2d 472 (3d Cir. 1939), the court stated: "We think it must be conceded that some disorder is unfortunately quite usual in any extensive or long drawn out strike. A strike is essentially a battle waged with economic weapons. Engaged in it are human beings whose feelings are stirred to the depths. Rising passions call forth hot words. Hot words lead to blows on the picket line. The transformation from economic to physical combat by those engaged in the contest is difficult to prevent even when cool heads direct the fight. Violence of this nature, however much it is to be regretted, must have been in the contemplation of the Congress when it provided in §13 of the Act, 29 U.S.C.A. §163, that nothing therein should be construed so as to interfere with or impede or diminish in any way the right to strike. If this were not so the rights afforded to employees by the Act would indeed be illusory. We accordingly recently held that it was not intended by the Act that minor disorders of this nature should deprive a striker of the possibility of reinstatement." The same court had previously held that fist fights between strikers and nonstrikers were such minor disorders as to permit reinstatement. NLRB v. Stackpole Carbon Co., 105 F.2d 167 (3d Cir. 1939). However, they held here that offenses such as discharging firearms, carrying concealed weapons, possession of explosives and malicious destruction of property were so serious as to bar reinstatement. In NLRB v. Elkland Leather Co., 114 F.2d 221 (3d Cir. 1940), the same court held that throwing stones at cars of strikebreakers entering the plant would not bar reinstatement.

What if an employer refuses to reinstate a woman striker when other women in the department refuse to work with her because of her obnoxious language on the picket line? NLRB v. Wytheville Knitting Mills, 175 F.2d 238 (3d Cir. 1949).

3. The burden of proving the misconduct is on the employer who seeks to block the reinstatement order. For an interesting case showing the measure of proof required, see Matter of Standard Oil of California, 91 N.L.R.B. 783, 26 L.R.R.M. 1587 (1950).

4. The growth of the Fansteel doctrine has gone far beyond acts of physical misconduct during a strike. Strikers may lose their right to reinstatement if:

(a) The strike is for an illegal objective —

In American News Co., 55 N.L.R.B. 1302, 14 L.R.R.M. 64 (1944), the workers struck to compel the employer to grant wage increases not yet approved by the War Labor Board. When they were discharged the NLRB denied reinstatement saying: ". . . [W]e think it most improbable that the Congress meant to invest this Board, or the courts in reviewing our action, with any broad discretion to determine what we or the courts might choose to consider the proper objectives of concerted activity. By the same token, we think it most unlikely that Congress intended to exclude from the concerted activities protected by Sec. 7 all conduct deemed tortious, under state rules of decision or statutes, or city ordinances, merely because of the objective sought to be accomplished. It is quite another matter, however, to suggest that Congress, either in 1935 or 1942, intended us to ignore the character of a strike knowingly prosecuted to compel an acknowledged violation of an act of the Congress itself. . . ." Chairman Millis dissented, holding that the Fansteel doctrine should only be applied where the strikers used unlawful means to obtain their objectives, that the legality of the objectives themselves was not in issue.

In a recent case the General Counsel upheld a Regional Director's refusal to issue a complaint alleging discriminatory refusal to hire a group of strikers because the sole purpose of the strike was to compel the employer to discharge all Negro employees. Rulings on Appeals from Interim Decisions of Regional Directors, Case No. 56, 27 L.R.R.M. 1442 (1951). Is the General Counsel, by this action, doing what the Board in the American News Case said it would not do? If this precedent is followed, what would be the status of strikers against laborsaving devices?

(b) The strike is wholly prohibited —

In Southern Steamship Company v. NLRB, 316 U.S. 31, 62 Sup. Ct. 886, 86 L. Ed. 1246 (1942), the Company refused to bargain with the National Maritime Union, which was certified to represent the seamen. While a ship was docked at Houston the men simply sat down and refused to turn on the steam needed for unloading or to tend the fires. No violence occurred and the strike ended when the Company agreed to meet with the Union's attorney. Later some of the strikers were discharged. The Court held that the Board could not order reinstatement. This

strike by sailors while the ship was away from home port constituted mutiny in violation of federal laws. The Board may not
pursue "the policies of the Labor Relations Act so single-mindedly
that it may wholly ignore other and equally important Congressional objectives."

In Matter of Mackay Radio and Telegraph Co., 96 N.L.R.B.
740, 28 L.R.R.M 1579 (1951), the Board held that employees who struck for an unlawful union-security contract for-
feited their rights to reinstatement. However, in NLRB v. E.A.
Laboratories, 188 F.2d 885 (2d Cir. 1951), it was held that failure
on the part of the union to comply with the War Labor Disputes
Act in not giving a 30-day strike notice did not bar the strikers'
right to reinstatement. See also Matter of Thompson Products
Inc., 70 N.L.R.B. 13, 18 L.R.R.M. 1331 (1946).

(c) The strike is in breach of contract —

Under the Wagner Act the Board and the courts evolved the
rule that employees who struck in breach of contract lost their
statutory protection. See NLRB v. Sands Manufacturing Co.,
306 U.S. 332, 59 Sup. Ct. 508, 83 L. Ed. 862 (1939) ; Matter of
Scullin Steel Company, 65 N.L.R.B. 1294, 17 L.R.R.M. 286
(1946) ; Matter of Fafnir Bearing, 73 N.L.R.B. 1008, 20 L.R.R.M.
1063 (1947).

Section 8(d) of the Taft-Hartley Act provides: "Any employee
who engaged in a strike within the sixty day period specified in
this subsection shall lose his status as an employee of the employer
engaged in the particular labor dispute, for purposes of sections
8, 9, and 10 of this Act."

Would this provision apply if the strike was six months before
the termination date of the contract and no notice of a desire
to terminate or modify the contract is given? Compare the following cases: In Matter of Dorsey Trailers, 80 N.L.R.B. 478, 23
L.R.R.M. 1112 (1948), the Board held that such a strike was not
an unfair labor practice under Section 8(d) where the contract
provided for a grievance procedure but no express no-strike clause.
In Matter of Granite City Steel Company, 87 N.L.R.B. 894, 25
L.R.R.M. 1199 (1949), the Board held that the discharge of
strikers was not discriminatory where the contract expressly provided that no strikes should be called until the grievance procedure was exhausted, and the Union had not attempted to use
the grievance procedure. No mention was made of the Dorsey
case. In Matter of United Packinghouse Workers, 89 N.L.R.B.
310, 25 L.R.R.M. 1556 (1950), the Union gave a 60-day notice
while the contract had 17 months to run. The contract did not

contain a no-strike clause. At the end of the 60 days it struck. The Board held that this was not a violation of Section 8 (d). In so holding it argued that although Section 8 (d) (4) provides that the contract continues "for a period of sixty days after such notice is given or until the expiration date of such contract, whichever occurs later," this should not be read literally. If read literally, it "would lead to a situation in which all strikes for modification would be forbidden during the term of a collective bargaining agreement, but only those employees who strike within sixty days after notice is given would be subject to the penalty of loss of employee status."

5. Although the employer is free to deny reinstatement to strikers who are guilty of misconduct, he may lose that freedom if he acts so as to condone it. In NLRB v. E.A. Laboratories, 188 F.2d 885 (2d Cir. 1951), the employer had discharged two Union leaders for extorting money as a price of labor peace, and obtained their indictment. This resulted in a strike in breach of the contract which had a no-strike clause. The employer agreed to take back all of the strikers except the extortionists and certain other leaders. At the trial for extortion the judge asked the employer if he would take back all of the strikers and the employer said he would. The court held that this justified the Board in finding that he had condoned the wrongful strike, wiped the slate clean, and therefore should be compelled to reinstate the strikers. See also Stewart Die Casting Corp. v. NLRB, 114 F.2d 849 (7th Cir. 1940); Matter of Thompson Products, Inc., 70 N.L.R.B. 13, 18 L.R.R.M. 1331 (1946); Matter of Hoover Manuf. Co., 90 N.L.R.B. 1614 (1950).

In the light of the doctrine of condonation, what is the status of the employers' right to rehire any employees he sees fit regardless of their conduct? How can the employer use any criterion in reinstatement other than degree of guilt without condoning the misconduct?

In Matter of Mackay Radio & Telegraph Corp., 96 N.L.R.B. 740, 28 L.R.R.M. 1579 (1951), the Board restricted the application of the condonation doctrine. The strike was for an illegal union-security provision. The Board held that this was not merely unprotected activity but was activity which "constituted from its inception a violation of the very Federal law under which relief was being sought . . . It is the task of the Board to enforce this public policy (expressed in 8 (b) (2)); and even though the Respondent in this case may have condoned conduct violative of such policy, the Board itself has no license to overlook such conduct . . . We are unable to perceive how it will effectuate the Act's policies to give relief to employees who have engaged in conduct violative of those policies." See discussion in Note, 52 Col. L. Rev. 290 (1952).

Note on Tests for the Legality of Concerted Action Under Foreign Law, Particularly of Strikes

1. The new French and Italian Constitutions have proclaimed a new freedom: "the exercise of the right to strike — within the limits set by legislation." [48] A similar provision is included in the constitutions of three states of West Germany, viz., Baden, Rheinland-Pfalz, and Württemberg-Baden.[49] It is noteworthy, however, that those three constitutions recognize the right to strike subject to legislative regulations, as a right of trade-unions only; unauthorized strikes are not lawful. The majority view regards any agreement restricting the exercise of the constitutional privilege as void.[50] German constitutional law subordinates — as does our law — state law (law of the *Länder*) to federal law. Since the Basic Law for the Federal Republic of Germany of 1949 does not include any reference to a right to strike, the German Diet can restrict concerted actions at its pleasure; as can the legislatures of all the other states mentioned, by reason of the constitutional reservations for legislation.[51] All this is practically no different from our law.[52] In Germany, France, Italy, and other European countries, simple legislation may therefore prohibit a concerted stoppage of services, the continuous operation of which is essential to the community. Equally, a statute may condition the legality of concerted action upon giving advance notice to the

[48] France: Constitution, 1946, Preamble, cl. 6; Italy: Constitution, 1947, art. 40.

[49] Baden: Constitution, 1947, art. 38 (II) ; Rheinland-Pfalz: Constitution, 1947, art. 66 (II) ; Württemberg-Baden: Constitution, 1946, art. 23 (III) .

[50] This is expressly laid down in the two constitutions for Baden and Württemberg-Baden respectively. On the question whether the constitutional guaranties warrant a "right" to the individual employee or are mere safeguards against administrative and legislative prohibitions against striking (as they existed during the Nazi regime) , see, for the latter view, Nikisch, The So-called Right to Strike and Its Private-Law Effects, Der Arbeitgeber, no. 18, p. 24 (1951), and, for the former view, Hessel, The Right to Strike and Employment Relationship, 5 Labor L.J. 48 (1952) (in German) .

[51] Of the Western German *Länder* only the Constitutions of Hesse, 1946 (art. 29 (II)) and Bremen, 1947 (art. 51 (III)) proclaim an unqualified right of the unions to strike. Ergo, in those *Länder*, only federal legislation can restrict that right.

[52] In this country there is no constitutional privilege to strike. Dorchy v. Kansas, 272 U.S. 306 (1926) .

other party or upon the exhaustion of conciliation proceedings.[53]

Constitutional or statutory proclamations of a "right to strike" have more significance in Europe than in the United States. Here nearly all employment relationships are terminable at will; an employee need not invoke a right to strike.[54]   By contrast, the lawful quitting of a job in European countries requires that advance notice be given the employer; employment relationships are terminable not at the will of either party but only subject to the statutory provisions requiring notice.   To quit or to dismiss there, without notice, constitutes a breach like quitting or dismissing here before the expiration of the specified term if the contract is for a term.   Consequently, before 1949, the German Supreme Labor Court held that an employee who quit in compliance with a strike order of his union, committed a breach of his obligation toward his employer.   It was further held that a notice announcing the walkout would not prevent the breach because a strike notice is not a notice to terminate employment, since the strikers intend to return to work.[55]   To say that a striker violates his obligation does not, of course, mean that such a breach automatically terminates his employment.   Unless the employer treats the breach as termination, the job is merely suspended but not terminated.[56]

The French law, as expounded by the highest court of France, was the same until the enactment of the law of February 11, 1950.[57]   This law, however, declares: "A strike does not involve a breach of the employment contract except in the case of flagrant wrong." [58]

If a strike is unlawful, the result reached is analogous to that in this country.   The National Labor Relations Board does not hold that participation in an unlawful strike automatically terminates the striker's employment relationship; but it does hold that an employer may discharge such a striker without committing an unfair labor practice, as he would if he discharged participants

---

[53] For Italy see Pergolesi, Diritto del lavoro 44, 215 (1949) ; for France see Trib. Civ. Riom 1948 (Dec. 16) J.C.P. 1949 II, 4655.

[54] In Section 13 of the Labor Management Relations Act, 1947, the phrase "right to strike," by virtue of its antecedents and subsequents, means little.

[55] See, e.g., Supreme Labor Court, 6 Bensh. Slg. 342 (1928) ; 7 Bensh. Slg. 493 (1929).

[56] See, for Belgian decisions, Orianne, 27 Revue de droit international et de droit comparé 132, 143 (1950).

[57] See, e.g., Cour de Cassation, 1924, D.P. 1924, 1. 209. For details see Rouast and Durand, Précis de législation industrielle, no. 345 (3d ed. 1948).

[58] Act of Feb. 11, 1950, tit. II, art. 4.

in a lawful strike.[59] However, the French law does not reinstate an employee who is illegally discharged. In contrast to German and Austrian law, the French law does not give the complainant an alternative choice of remedy. The French law provides solely a claim for pay for a usual period of notice plus an indemnity.[60]

2. Except for concerted action in violation of a contractual obligation or of the peace obligation, organizational pressure is not wrongful in European countries. Naturally, where illegal means are resorted to, such as extortion or fraud or seizure of a plant (sit-down) or force and violence, concerted action, like that of an individual, becomes illegal.

No discussion of the tests for the legality of concerted action should overlook the question of its goal. To be lawful, concerted action must have an objective definable in terms of a goal aimed at by the actors. A boycott for a few hours or a day, only to show readiness or sympathy (*Demonstrationsstreik*), is not lawful.[61]

The dominant doctrine also denies legality to concerted action undertaken for other than "professional" ends. Political strikes are therefore not within the constitutional and statutory privileges mentioned previously.[62] There are some German writers who espouse the doctrine that strikes for political ends are not unlawful per se,[63] but this view is opposed by other German authorities, and is unanimously rejected in France and other European countries.

While the attitude of the American law and the foreign law toward sympathetic strikes or political strikes is similar, there is a difference in the reasoning in support of the legality of the objective of labor disputes. Here, intentional infliction of harm — and, therefore, organized economic pressure — is regarded prima facie as wrongful; in order to escape condemnation as a tort, such an act calls for "justification." It may be noted that views of what constitutes justification in labor disputes — where

[59] See, e.g., Mackay Radio & Tel. Co., 96 N.L.R.B. 740, 28 L.R.R.M. 1579 (1951).

[60] As for France and those countries whose civil laws are modeled upon the Civil Code, see Pekelis, Legal Techniques and Political Ideologies, 41 Mich. L. Rev. 665 (1943). For the "indemnity" in such a case see Lenhoff, Some Basic Features of American and European Labor Law: A Comparison, 26 Notre Dame Law. 389, 401 (1951).

[61] Nipperdey, The Right to Strike, German Reports to the Third International Congress of Comparative Law 744, 746 (1950) (in German).

[62] Malézieux, Les Conventions collectives de travail, no. 47 (1950).

[63] Nipperdey, op. cit. supra note 61, at 745.

the goal of the latter is not wages or hours — have widely differed in this country.

In other countries, however, coercive economic activities of unions such as strikes and boycotts have been held to be allowable because of freedom of employees to bring pressure, in pursuit of their economic interests, upon the employer, and vice versa. The French theory is based upon the liberty to combine forces (*liberté de coalition*) ; similarly the German theory refers to the liberty to engage in economic disputes (*Kampffreiheit*).[64]

The German law of torts does not recognize any general duty to refrain from inflicting harm on others.[65]   It enumerates, on the one hand, absolute rights, interference with which constitutes a· tort; such absolute rights are life, body, freedom, health, safety, property.   On the other hand, the German law also considers it a tort to commit an injurious act which is forbidden by a statutory provision enacted for the protection of others (*Schutz-gesetz*).   However, it has generally been recognized that one's right to carry on his business for profit is neither an absolute right nor a right protected by such a *Schutzgesetz*.[66]   The French law, though, recognizes a general duty to refrain from doing harm [67] but, as is always true under civil laws, it also emphasizes that the infliction of damage in exercise of one's right cannot be regarded as unlawful.[68]

If the foregoing reference to German and French law — and those of all other countries of the Roman law tradition have similar patterns — told the whole story, practically every labor pressure would be lawful.

But there is another general principle that must be taken into account.   It is presented in two propositions.   The one, characteristic of German, Austrian, and Swiss law, declares that the intentional infliction of damage upon another in a manner violating moral standards (*gute Sitten, boni mores*) constitutes a tort.[69] The other, chiefly expressed in French and Italian judicial decisions and legal literature, is well-known as the theory of abuse

---

[64] Rouast and Durand, Précis de législation industrielle, no. 221, p. 270 (3d ed. 1948) ; 2 Hueck and Nipperdey, Lehrbuch des Arbeitsrechts 575 (1930) (in German).

[65] Gutteridge, Abuse of Rights, 5 Camb. L.J. 22, 37 (1933).

[66] Nipperdey, op. cit. supra note 61, at 763.

[67] Gutteridge, op. cit. supra note 65, at 35.

[68] 2 Planiol, Traité élémentaire de droit civil, no. 870 (9th ed. 1923), quoting from Gaius in D. 1. 17. 55: "*Nullus videtur dolo facere qui suo jure utitur.*"

[69] Germany: Civil Code (1896), sec. 826; Switzerland: Civil Code (1907), art. 2; Austria: Civil Code (1811) (as amended, 1916), sec. 1295.

of rights (*abus de droit*).   An act causing damage by the use of one's right takes on a tortious aspect and becomes an "abuse of the right" when the right is exercised contrary to the economic or social purpose for which it was created.[70]

Let us illustrate the principle.   A boycott by a union of an employer is by itself lawful because it rests upon the exercise of the right to bring economic pressure upon the antagonist; but if that right is used for ends alien to the economic interests of the actors or for the sole purpose of inflicting damage, its exercise becomes unlawful under the principle, whether formulated as a violation of moral standards or as an abuse of rights.   Thus, although a strike which does not involve a breach of a collective contract is not prohibited, the French courts have always regarded a strike for obtaining the discharge of a fellow employee who refused to join the labor organization as an *abus de droit* and have, therefore, imposed liability upon the union in favor of the plaintiff.[71] Such a liability has even been placed upon an employer who yielded to the request of the combination and gave notice to the plaintiff.[72]   Likewise, a boycott by employers (black-listing) of union men, if done for the single purpose of damaging the union was held to be an abuse of employers' right to hire and to fire at their pleasure even prior to the present constitutional guaranty of the right to join a union.[73]   A union's continuance of a boycott against an employer from a purely vindictive motive — for example by continuation of the boycott after the termination of the strike — would not be condoned.[74]   (Compare contrary views as to the Sherman Act, but not the common law, expressed by the majority of the Supreme Court in Hunt v. Crumboch, 325 U.S. 821 (1945), page 797 supra.)   Recently a noted French court held that strikers committed an abuse of the right to strike by stopping work abruptly without having previously presented claims, without any previous discussion with the employer, and without the slightest attempt to mediate or arbitrate.[75]

Turning again to German law, we find that in order to determine whether or not a concerted action violates moral standards, the German courts have applied an honest person's sense of fair-

[70] 2 Planiol, op. cit. supra note 68, at no. 872; Saleilles, Etude sur la théorie générale de l'obligation 371 (3d ed. 1914).   See Josserand, De l'Abus des droits (2d ed. 1905).

[71] Trib. Civ. Bordeaux, 1929, Gaz. Pal. 1929. 1. 776. For earlier discussion of this principle of French law, see page 498 supra.

[72] Trib. Civ. de la Seine, 1933, Gaz. des Trib. 1934. 1. 294.

[73] Trib. Civ. Lille, 1906, D.P. 1908, 2. 73.

[74] Cour de Cassation, 1901, S. 1901, 2. 427.

[75] Trib. Civ. de la Seine, 1948, Gaz. Pal. 1948. 2. 20.

ness and decency as the criterion.[76]   Sometimes German labor
courts have qualified that criterion by a reference to the views held
by employers and employees (*Kreise des Arbeitslebens*) rather
than to those held by persons belonging to other classes.[77]   So
tested, the concerted insistence of workers upon a fellow-worker's
discharge because he had been a strikebreaker is, as the German
Supreme Labor Court has held, not violative of good morals.[78]

The Swiss federal court — under a similar theory — has taken
the same view in an analogous case.   But it has taken another view
where the concerted pressure against the nonunionist would interfere with his political freedom because, for example, the union
has pursued political objectives which are repugnant to the political convictions held by the individual employee.   One must not
forget that in France, Italy, Netherlands, and Switzerland there
are several labor organizations for every trade, which are separated from one another along political or religious lines.[79]

If a concerted request for discharge of an employee or a boycott
of an employer is motivated only by desire for reprisal or vengeance
or by political antagonism or is aimed at the economic ruin of the
other man, the German courts have branded it as a violation of
moral standards within the meaning of the Civil Code of that
country.[80]

Where, by means of an agreement with his employer, the discharged employee had violated the terms of a collective contract,
the German Supreme Labor Court has considered the conduct of
the defendant union in causing his discharge — by threatening the
employer with a strike — unobjectionable.   The Court thought
that this conduct was in accord with the ethical views held by the
working class.[81]

When concerted action — for example a boycott against a certain group of employers — is carried out in order to counter
that group's economic pressure on union members, it has been held
to be a proper exercise of the right to combine economic forces.
Likewise a union member who in such a case took a job with

[76] See, e.g., decision of Oberlandesgericht Celle of Dec. 5, 1947, in 2 Monat-
schrift für Deutsches Recht 174 (report to Gestapo by D of a statement made
by P).

[77] Nipperdey, op. cit. supra note 61, at 764.

[78] Supreme Labor Court decision: 10 Bensh. 100 (1930).

[79] Swiss Federal Court decisions (1928) B.G.E. 54 II 146; id. (1925) 51
II 530; 1 Egger, Commentary on Swiss Civil Code 260–261 (2d ed. 1930)
(in German).

[80] Supreme Labor Court decisions: 11 Bensh. 111 (1930); 7 Bensh. 404
(1929); 6 Bensh. 427 (1928).

[81] Id. 7 Bensh. 92 (1929).

one of the boycotted employers — in violation of the proclaimed boycott — has been held liable to pay penalties provided for by the bylaws of his organization.[82]

To sum up the law of the free European countries, the use of coercive pressure such as strikes and lockouts is allowed unless expressly or impliedly proscribed, and prohibition of strikes and lockouts is the exception, not the rule.[83] This attitude is reflected in the Swedish Act (of June 26, 1936) which, during the first three months of the work stoppage, protects workers involved in a strike or subject to a lockout from eviction from homes which had been allotted to them by their employers because of their employment.

3. Much as the two legal systems differ, our labor law and the law of most of the free countries of Europe agree that independent courts have to say the last word on the legality of the objective of a labor dispute. But the law in several Latin-American countries is entirely different. By Mexican law — the laws of the Dominican Republic (of 1934), Ecuador (of 1936), and Salvador (of 1946) are very similar — the objectives for which a strike or lockout can be carried out are stated in the Labor Code. An administrative agency, the Labor Board, has to decide whether the purpose of a strike or lockout falls within the statutory range. No strike or lockout may be proclaimed without previous administrative approval. However, since the statutory definition of grounds for a strike or lockout is shaped in a general fashion, the administrative discretion is very wide. In addition, the consent of the majority of the employees to a strike is a condition of its legality. If the condition is met, and the strike is declared lawful, the members of the minority which voted against the strike are forbidden to continue working in the struck enterprise.[84]

4. The discussion in this section calls for a few supplementary remarks concerning absolutely forbidden actions. Though in the free countries of Europe resort to concerted action is, in principle, at the discretion of the actors, no constitutional obstacle exists to a legislative ban. Thus, as discussed at page 110 supra, strikes of civil servants may be, and are, forbidden. Likewise, concerted actions which threaten to or would in fact cut off public services are forbidden either by general laws or by legislation ad hoc.[85]

It is, of course, generally accepted in France where — in contrast

[82] German Supreme Court decisions: 111 R.G.Z. 199 (1925); 93 R.G.Z. 302 (1918).

[83] Robbins, The Government of Labor Relations in Sweden 234, 239 (1942).

[84] Cf. Cormack and Barker, Mexican Labor Law, 7 So. Calif. L. Rev. 251 (1934).

[85] See, e.g., Robbins, op. cit. supra note 83, at 236.

to Germany — sit-down strikes have now and then occurred, that the taking of possession of the plant by the strikers is absolutely unlawful.[86]

During the Nazi regime (1933–1945) concerted actions in Germany were out of the question. However, even after the right to combine was restored, strikes have been very rare and no lockout has happened from 1945 to this writing.[87] It is otherwise in France, particularly in the case of strikes.

D. *Picketing and Free Speech — The Nature of Picketing Both as Coercion and as Persuasion*

As has been seen, the legality of union action depends not only on the objective sought by the union but also on the means used to attain those ends. The preceding section has focused primary attention on objectives and on the shadowy area separating legal from illegal objectives. This section, by contrast, will emphasize the importance of the means used by the union in determining the ultimate legality of union action.

The picket line is labor's second most important means of exerting economic pressure on the employer. Picketing is commonly used in conjunction with a strike but its usefulness is not limited to strike situations. The union may picket an employer where it has no members either to induce the employees to join the union, to compel the employer to recognize the union, or to compel the employer to cease using nonunion goods.

The picket line exerts pressure on the employer by effecting an economic quarantine, but the quarantine may take one or more of three principal forms. Picketing an industrial plant may be aimed primarily at employees of the employer seeking to keep them from working during the strike — a labor market quarantine. Picketing a retail store may be aimed primarily at customers, seeking to keep them from patronizing the employer — a sales market quarantine. Picketing a warehouse may be aimed primarily at truckers who are employees of other employers and seeks to cut off all deliveries — a goods quarantine. Frequently, of course, the picketing is aimed simultaneously at all three classes of persons.

The picket line may achieve its strength in three distinctly different ways. First, it may provide a notice to all concerned that

[86] E.g., Trib. Civ. Lyon, 1947, Gaz. Pal. 1948. 1. 42.

[87] See the Report on German Labor Law by Professor Erich Molitor (Mainz) to the First International Congress of Labor Law (May, 1951, in Trieste) 9.

the union has a dispute with the employer. Those who believe in the union's particular cause and those who support the union regardless of its cause refuse to cross the line. They act voluntarily on the knowledge which the picket line provides. Second, the picket line may be effective because union rules may make crossing it "conduct unbecoming a union member." A union member who fails to heed the pickets' placards may forfeit his union membership and also his job. Third, a picket line may be effective because persons cannot or dare not enter. Pickets may stand in mass formation or march in lock step so that crossing is impossible, or they may use physical violence to forcibly bar all who try to enter.

Picketing, therefore, cannot be considered as a single method or device used by unions. It describes a class of methods that have in common the physical act of patrolling the employer's premises. Types of picketing vary widely. The persons appealed to may be employees of the employer, customers of the employer, or employees of other employers. It may be effective because the ones to whom the appeal is addressed act voluntarily on the information given, because they are subject to penalties for failing to obey, or because they fear physical injury. Is it little wonder then that it has received such erratic treatment in the courts?

1. COMMON LAW BACKGROUND

a. Judicial Attitudes Toward Picketing

Until about 1921, peaceful picketing was frequently considered to be illegal per se. (Cf. 1 Teller, Labor Disputes and Collective Bargaining, §§38, 112, 117–126 (1940).) With the decision in American Steel Foundries v. Tri-City Central Trades Council, 257 U.S. 184, 42 Sup. Ct. 72, 66 L. Ed. 189 (1921), the tenor of judicial opinion began to change somewhat. But there was no unanimity, either against picketing before 1921 or in its favor after that date.

Compare these judicial statements concerning picketing:

Mere picketing, therefore, if it is peaceful, if there is no threat or intimidation, if it is confined to simple persuasion, I do not regard in any sense as unlawful, whatever may be the motive of the picketers. [Andrews J., in Foster v. Retail Clerks' Protective Assn., 39 Misc. 48, 57, 78 N.Y. Supp. 860, 867 (1902).]

. . . There is and can be no such thing as peaceful picketing, any more than there can be chaste vulgarity, or peaceful mobbing, or lawful lynching. [McPherson, J., in Atchison T. & S.F. Ry. Co. v. Gee, 139 Fed. 582, 584 (S.D. Iowa, 1905).]

The case at bar presents only the right of picketing the employer's premises without trespass thereon. The law recognizes the right of peaceful picketing. Although that term is sometimes criticized as a contradictory one, since the word "picketing is taken from the nomenclature of warfare and is strongly suggestive of a hostile attitude, it has acquired a significance and meaning commonly understood. It connotes peaceable methods of presenting a cause to the public in the vicinity of the employer's premises. Labor has the recognized legal right to acquaint the public with the facts which it regards as unfair, to give notoriety to its cause, and to use persuasive inducements to bring its own policies to triumph. Such picketing or publicity is not per se unlawful. It is only when the evil, tortious factors to which we have alluded are brought into play that it becomes illegal. Nor will peaceable picketing be permitted to become a nuisance. The bounds of legitimacy may be crossed in many and diverse ways. Whatever those ways are, they are wrong and under condemnation. Their commission will be enjoined as irreparable interference and in order to avoid a multiplicity of suits. [Stanley, Commr., in Music Hall Theater v. Moving Picture Machine Operators Local No. 165, 249 Ky. 639, 642, 61 S.W.2d 283, 285 et al. (1933).]

Peaceable picketing, so called, is conceived in battle; its real purpose is to conquer. It would compel acquiescence, not induce it by mere persuasion. Unquestionably its tendency is always militant . . .

. . . [W]e see a distinction between peaceable persuasion by speech and peaceable picketing. True, the latter is said not to have in it force or violence, threats, intimidation or coercion, yet in all picketing, there is an element not appearing in fair argument and a reasonable appeal for justice. [Hudson, J., in Keith Theatre v. Vachon, 134 Me. 392, 413, 187 Atl. 692, 702 (1936).]

Do these judicial statements indicate any distinction between various types of picketing? Does the object sought by the union affect the legality of the picketing?

b. Picketing as Disorderly Conduct

The picket line is an explosive front, charged with the emotions and fierce loyalties of the union-management dispute. It may be marked by colorful name-calling, intimidating threats or sporadic fights between the pickets and those who pass the line. It may degenerate into complete lawlessness and systematic violence. The blame for these acts is often hard to assess. The union may order or condone violent methods such as physically blocking the plant gates, overturning cars, or beating those who cross the line. An antiunion employer, on the other hand, may use strikebreakers or company police to provoke violence and intimidate union members.

When acts of violence occur, for whatever reason, those who participate may be arrested on charges of assault, malicious mischief, mayhem, or manslaughter. Whether conduct on the picket line constitutes a crime is essentially a matter for criminal law. However, one criminal charge, that of disorderly conduct, has caused special difficulty. Its vague limits at common law and as defined by various statutes include conduct less than physical violence, and may be elastic enough to reach conduct that is entirely peaceful. The following examples may be sufficient to suggest the potential use of this criminal charge in regulating picketing.

In People v. Nixon, 248 N.Y. 182, 161 N.E. 463 (1928), twenty pickets were arrested under a statute which made punishable "Any person who with intent to provoke a breach of the peace . . . acts in such a manner as to annoy, interfere with, obstruct, or be offensive to others; congregates with others on a public street and refuses to move on when ordered by the police." The pickets were parading four abreast on a sidewalk 12 feet wide. They occupied about one half of the sidewalk, forcing some pedestrians to step out into the street. There was no evidence of threats, abusive language, or intimidation. A policeman watched them for about ten minutes, and then without any warning arrested them for disorderly conduct. The court dismissed the charges, saying that the pickets were guilty of nothing more than extremely bad manners. However, the same case included some other pickets who had apparently engaged in the same kind of parading but who persisted after they had been ordered by the police to "move on." The court held that in their case the policeman's order converted the lawful picketing into disorderly conduct.

People v. Jenkins, 138 Misc. 498, 246 N.Y. Supp. 444 (1930), was a criminal prosecution based on the same statute. The picketeers carried signs reading "Milgrims on Strike" when in fact there was no strike as none of the employees belonged to the union. The court upheld the conviction on the grounds that the "moral coercion" from such false statements would ultimately lead to some form of disturbance and disorder. This decision was affirmed without opinion in 255 N.Y. 637. See also People v. Levensart, 144 Misc. 671, 259 N.Y. Supp. 309 (1932); People v. Kaye, 165 Misc. 663, 1 N.Y.S.2d 354 (1937). Compare injunction cases involving claims of false bannering or misleading statements. Parkinson Co. v. Building Trades Council, 154 Cal. 581, 98 Pac. 1027 (1908); Hotel and Railroad News Co. v. Clark, 243 Mass. 317, 137 N.E. 534 (1922); Nann v. Raimist, 255 N.Y. 307, 174 N.E. 690, 73 A.L.R. 669 (1931).

In People v. Bellows, 281 N.Y. 67, 22 N.E.2d 238 (1939), the pickets were convicted under the same statute as was involved in People v. Nixon, although the picketing was in small numbers, was entirely peaceful, and the placards were precisely accurate in stating the dispute. The conviction was upheld because it was to enforce a "secondary boycott." Query — does the untruthfulness of the statement or indirectness of the action substantially increase the likelihood of public disturbance? If not, then what makes this conduct "disorderly" and in violation of the statute?

In State v. Zanker, 179 Minn. 355, 229 N.W. 311 (1930), the Union members were arrested under an ordinance prohibiting "disturbance or improper diversion," for picketing in front of the home of a nonunion worker who continued to work during their strike. They carried a sign stating "Norma Christensen, strike breaker, lives here who, is lowering wages and lengthening hours for employees in the City of Minneapolis." The court upheld the conviction, saying, "They disregarded her right to be undisturbed. They resorted to offensive means. . . . It was an annoyance; it tended to disturb the immediate community; . . . Indeed, conduct is disorderly when it is of such a nature as to affect the peace and quiet of persons who witness the same and who may be disturbed or provoked to resentment thereby."

If a man discharges his chauffeur and houseman for joining a union, can the union picket the residence at which the member worked? Under the test stated above does it make any difference whether the place of employment happens to be a home? See State v. Cooper, 205 Minn. 333, 285 N.W. 903 (1939). Compare Petrucci v. Hogan, 27 N.Y.S.2d 718 (1941), enjoining picketing of homes of municipal workers to compel payment of union dues and a closed shop not consistent with the Civil Service Law; People v. Levner, 30 N.Y.S.2d 487 (1941), political picketing of the residence of the Mayor of New York City. Where the legislature expressly makes it a crime to picket the residence of a judge, juror, or witness in any legal proceedings, does that indicate that the picketing of other residences is not a crime or is not enjoinable?

In Leeman v. Amalgamated Retail & Dept. Store Employees Union, 25 L.R.R.M. 2343 (Cal. Super. Ct., 1950), the Union picketed the home of the employer. The court, in refusing to issue an injunction, held that the picketing did not constitute an invasion of the right of privacy, but was merely a publicizing of the existence of the dispute to a portion of the public. It was no more illegal than placing an advertisement in the newspapers bought by a majority of the employer's neighbors. The court further held that there was no conduct likely to lead to a breach of the peace so long as there was no violence or disorderliness.

c. Stranger Picketing

A strike is almost always accompanied by picketing, but picketing may be used where the union is unable to call a strike because none of the employees belongs to the union. This is frequently termed "stranger picketing" because the pickets are not employees but are "strangers" to the employer.

Stranger picketing is used almost exclusively for two purposes — to organize the picketed establishments, or to induce the picketed employer to cease dealing with someone else with whom the union has a dispute. If its purpose is to organize the unorganized, the courts are faced with considerations that pull in opposite directions. Public policy favors the organization of workmen. Therefore, stranger picketing has even a greater claim to legality than the ordinary type of picketing used to support economic demands of workers already organized. On the other hand such picketing has an appearance of wanton interference by a union with a situation in which it has no legitimate interest. The conflicting considerations, weighed differently by every judge according to his economic predilections, has led inevitably to conflicting results and confusion. Contrast the following judicial declarations:

> In this case the picketers not only had no grievances of their own against the plaintiff (theatre) but were not picketing by permission of the employees, or any one else, whether belong-

ing to a union or not, who had any relationship with the theatre company. They were simply attempting to advance the cause of trade unions generally by forcing unionization. That effected [sic] might result not only in the incurrence of indebtedness that the business would not warrant, but in giving to strangers at least substantial partial control and management of the plaintiff's business. These picketers, instead of attempting by their conduct to reconcile a difference that had already arisen between the plaintiff and its employees (for there was none), sought to create trouble between them to the end that the union might indirectly derive a benefit from such newly created trouble. [Hudson, J., in Keith Theatre v. Vachon, 134 Me. 392, 404, 187 Atl. 692, 697 (1936).]

The purposes of a labor union to improve the conditions under which its members do their work; to increase their wages; to assist them in other ways may justify what would otherwise be a wrong. So would an effort to increase its numbers and to unionize an entire trade or business. It may be as interested in the wages of those not members, or in the conditions under which they work as in its own members because of the influence of one upon the other. All engaged in a trade are affected by the prevailing rate of wages. All, by the principle of collective bargaining. Economic organization today is not based on the single shop. Unions believe that wages may be increased, collective bargaining maintained only if union conditions prevail, not in some single factory but generally. That they may prevail, it may call a strike and picket the premises of an employer with the intent of inducing him to employ only union labor. And it may adopt either method separately. Picketing without a strike is no more unlawful than a strike without picketing. [Andrews, J., in Exchange Bakery v. Rifkin, 245 N.Y. 260, 263, 157 N.E. 130, 132 (1927).]

Compare also C. S. Smith Metropolitan Market, Ltd. v. Lyons, page 652 supra, noted in 40 Harv. L. Rev. 896 (1927), 27 Col. L. Rev. 190 (1927).

Out of the welter of decisions grew a substantial body of cases holding stranger picketing illegal even though its objective was to organize nonunion employees in order to protect union standards. Where the purpose of the picketing was to enforce a secondary boycott, the illegality was even more clear-cut.

2. PICKETING AND FREE SPEECH

a. Seeds of the Free Speech Doctrine

In Vegelahn v. Guntner, 167 Mass. 92, 44 N.E. 1077 (1896), a union on strike for higher wages was enjoined from peacefully picketing the employer's premises. Justice Holmes, dissenting, contended at page 96:

. . . [T]he patrol (picketing), so far as it confined itself to persuasion and giving notice of the strike, was not unlawful . . .

. . . [The Majority's injunction] includes refusal of social intercourse, and even organized persuasion or argument, . . . It appears to me that the judgment of the majority turns in part on the assumption that the patrol necessarily carries with it a threat of bodily harm. That assumption I think unwarranted. . . . Furthermore, it cannot be said . . . that two men walking together up and down a sidewalk and speaking to those who enter a certain shop do necessarily and always thereby convey a threat of force. [Id. at 104.]

In 1921 a New York court, referring to the language of Judge Andrews in Foster v. Retail Clerks' Protective Assn., page 750 supra, upholding the right of peaceful picketing, said: "This is sound. It is just. It is the law. It must forever remain the law until liberty of speech ceases to be a human right." Wood Mowing and Reaping Co. v. Toohey, 114 Misc. 185, 186 N.Y. Supp. 95 (1921).

Section 4 of the Norris-LaGuardia Act, passed in 1932, prohibited federal courts from enjoining any act:

(e) Giving publicity to the existence of, or the facts involved in, any labor dispute, whether by advertising, speaking, patrolling, or by any other method not involving fraud or violence;

(f) Assembling peaceably to act or to organize to act in promotion of their interests in a labor dispute;

(g) Advising or notifying any person of an intention to do any of the acts heretofore specified; . . .

In Senn v. Tile Layers Protective Union, 301 U.S. 468, 57 Sup. Ct. 857, 81 L. Ed. 1229 (1937), the Supreme Court upheld the constitutionality of the Wisconsin anti-injunction statute. The Wisconsin court, relying on the statute, refused to enjoin the union from picketing Senn, a tile-laying contractor who hired a few nonunion employees. The Union's purpose was to make Senn hire only union workers and to stop him from doing any tile-laying himself. Although the only issue was whether due process requires a state to give protection against peaceful picketing in this situation, Justice Brandeis made the following fateful suggestion at page 478: "Clearly the means which the statute authorizes — picketing and publicity — are not prohibited by the Fourteenth Amendment. Members of a union might, without special statutory authorization by a state, make known the facts of a labor dispute, for freedom of speech is guaranteed by the Federal Constitution."

Did Justice Brandeis mean that picketing is free speech and therefore constitutionally guaranteed? Or did he mean only that "publicity" and "making known the facts" is free speech constitutionally guaranteed? Compare the interpretation given by the courts in the subsequent cases. See also Gregory, Labor and the Law, 337–341 (2d ed. 1949) ; Teller, Picketing and Free Speech, 56 Harv. L. Rev. 180 (1942) ; Dodd, Picketing and Free Speech, 56 Harv. L. Rev. 513 (1943).

b. The Flowering of the Free Speech Doctrine

THORNHILL v. ALABAMA
Supreme Court of the United States, 1940
310 U.S. 88, 60 Sup. Ct. 736, 84 L. Ed. 1093

[Byron Thornhill had been convicted under an Alabama statute making it a misdemeanor to loiter about a place of business, or to picket it, for the purpose of keeping customers or workers away, without a just cause or legal excuse therefor. The complaint against him had been couched substantially in the words of the statute, simply alleging the offenses described in the statute to have been committed against the Brown Wood Preserving Company. Mr. Thornhill objected that the statute was repugnant to the United States Constitution. The proofs were that Mr. Thornhill was in a picket line and that he dissuaded another man, without threats or even anger, from going to work. There was no evidence of the nature of the labor dispute. The picketing was on land owned by the Company, but the Company had never told the men to stay off that land. Conviction by the Circuit Court for Tuscaloosa County was affirmed by the Alabama Court of Appeals. The Supreme Court granted certiorari.]

MR. JUSTICE MURPHY delivered the opinion of the Court. . . .

First.   The freedom of speech and of the press, which are secured by the First Amendment against abridgment by the United States, are among the fundamental personal rights and liberties which are secured to all persons by the Fourteenth Amendment against abridgment by a State.

The safeguarding of these rights to the ends that men may speak as they think on matters vital to them and that falsehoods may be exposed through the processes of education and discussion is essential to free government.   Those who won our independence had confidence in the power of free and fearless reasoning and communication of ideas to discover and spread political and economic truth.   Noxious doctrines in those fields may be refuted and their evil averted by the courageous exercise of the right of free discussion.   Abridgment of freedom of speech and of the press, however, impairs those opportunities for public education that are essential to effective exercise of the power of correcting error through the processes of popular government.   Compare United States v. Carolene Products Co., 304 U.S. 144, 152–153n. Mere legislative preference for one rather than another means for combating substantive evils, therefore, may well prove an inadequate foundation on which to rest regulations which are aimed at or in their operation diminish the effective exercise of rights so necessary to the maintenance of democratic institutions.   It is imperative that, when the effective exercise of these rights is claimed to be abridged, the courts should "weigh the circumstances" and "appraise the substantiality of the reasons advanced" in support of the challenged regulations.   Schneider v. State, 308 U.S. 147, 161, 162.

Second.   The section in question must be judged upon its face. . . .

Proof of an abuse of power in the particular case has never been deemed a requisite for attack on the constitutionality of a statute purporting to license the dissemination of ideas.   Schneider v. State, 308 U.S. 147, 162–165; Hague v. C.I.O., 307 U.S. 496, 516; Lovell v. Griffin, 303 U.S. 444, 451. . . .   The power of the licensor against which John Milton directed his assault by his "Appeal for the Liberty of Unlicensed Printing" is pernicious not merely by reason of the censure of particular comments but by reason of the threat to censure comments on matters of public concern.   It is not merely the sporadic abuse of power by the censor but the pervasive threat inherent in its very existence that constitutes the danger to freedom of discussion.   See Near v. Minnesota, 283 U.S. 697, 713. . . .

The existence of such a statute, which readily lends itself to harsh and discriminatory enforcement by local prosecuting officials, against particular groups deemed to merit their displeasure, results in a continuous and pervasive restraint on all freedom of discussion that might reasonably be regarded as within its purview.   It is not any less effective or, if the restraint is not permissible, less pernicious than the restraint on freedom of discussion imposed by the threat of censorship. . . .

Third.   Section 3448 has been applied by the state courts so as to prohibit a single individual from walking slowly and peacefully back and forth on the public sidewalk in front of the premises of an employer, without speaking to anyone, carrying a sign or placard on a staff above his head stating only the fact that the employer did not employ union men affiliated with the American Federation of Labor; the purpose of the described activity was concededly to advise customers and prospective customers of the relationship existing between the employer and its employees and thereby to induce such customers not to patronize the employer. . . .   The statute as thus authoritatively construed and applied leaves room for no exceptions based upon either the number of persons engaged in the proscribed activity, the peaceful character of their demeanor, the nature of their dispute with an employer, or the restrained character and the accurateness of the terminology used in notifying the public of the facts of the dispute.

The numerous forms of conduct proscribed by Sec. 3448 are subsumed under two offenses: the first embraces the activities of all who "without just cause or legal excuse" "go near to or loiter about the premises" of any person engaged in a lawful business for the purpose of influencing or inducing others to adopt any of certain enumerated courses of action; the second, all who "picket" the place of business of any such person "for the purpose of hindering, delaying or interfering with or injuring any lawful business or enterprise of another."   It is apparent that one or the other of the offenses comprehends every practicable method whereby the facts of a labor dispute may be publicized in the vicinity of the place of business of an employer.   The phrase "without just cause or legal excuse" does not in any effective manner restrict the breadth of the regulation; the words themselves have no ascertainable meaning either inherent or historical. . . .   An intention to hinder, delay or interfere with a lawful business, which is an element of the second offense, likewise can be proved merely by showing that others reacted in a way normally expectable of some upon learning the facts of a dispute.

The vague contours of the term "picket" are nowhere delineated. . . . In sum, whatever the means used to publicize the facts of a labor dispute, whether by printed sign, by pamphlet, by word of mouth or otherwise, all such activity without exception is within the inclusive prohibition of the statute so long as it occurs in the vicinity of the scene of the dispute.

Fourth. We think that Sec. 3448 is invalid on its face. The freedom of speech and of the press guaranteed by the Constitution embraces at the least the liberty to discuss publicly and truthfully all matters of public concern without previous restraint or fear of subsequent punishment. The exigencies of the colonial period and the efforts to secure freedom from oppressive administration developed a broadened conception of these liberties as adequate to supply the public need for information and education with respect to the significant issues of the times. . . . Freedom of discussion, if it would fulfill its historic function in this nation, must embrace all issues about which information is needed or appropriate to enable the members of society to cope with the exigencies of their period.

In the circumstances of our times the dissemination of information concerning the facts of a labor dispute must be regarded as within that area of free discussion that is guaranteed by the Constitution. Hague v. C.I.O., 307 U.S. 496; Schneider v. State, 308 U.S. 147, 155, 162–163. See Senn v. Tile Layers Union, 301 U.S. 468, 478. It is recognized now that satisfactory hours and wages and working conditions in industry and a bargaining position which makes these possible have an importance which is not less than the interests of those in the business or industry directly concerned. The health of the present generation and of those as yet unborn may depend on these matters, and the practices in a single factory may have economic repercussions upon a whole region and affect widespread systems of marketing. The merest glance at state and federal legislation on the subject demonstrates the force of the argument that labor relations are not matters of mere local or private concern. Free discussion concerning the conditions in industry and the causes of labor disputes appears to us indispensable to the effective and intelligent use of the processes of popular government to shape the destiny of modern industrial society. The issues raised by regulations, such as are challenged here, infringing upon the right of employees effectively to inform the public of the facts of a labor dispute are part of this larger problem. We concur in the observation of Mr. Justice Brandeis, speaking for the Court in Senn's case (301 U.S. at 478):

"Members of a union might, without special statutory authorization by a State, make known the facts of a labor dispute, for freedom of speech is guaranteed by the Federal Constitution."

It is true that the rights of employers and employees to conduct their economic affairs and to compete with others for a share in the products of industry are subject to modification or qualification in the interests of the society in which they exist. This is but an instance of the power of the State to set the limits of permissible contest open to industrial combatants. See Mr. Justice Brandeis in 254 U.S. at 488. It does not follow that the State in dealing with the evils arising from industrial disputes may impair the effective exercise of the right to discuss freely industrial relations which are matters of public concern. A contrary conclusion could be used to support abridgment of freedom of speech and of the press concerning almost every matter of importance to society.

The range of activities proscribed by Sec. 3448, whether characterized as picketing or loitering or otherwise, embraces nearly every practicable, effective means whereby those interestd — including the employees directly affected — may enlighten the public on the nature and causes of a labor dispute. The safeguarding of these means is essential to the securing of an informed and educated public opinion with respect to a matter which is of public concern. It may be that effective exercise of the means of advancing public knowledge may persuade some of those reached to refrain from entering into advantageous relations with the business establishment which is the scene of the dispute. Every expression of opinion on matters that are important has the potentiality of inducing action in the interests of one rather than another group in society. But the group in power at any moment may not impose penal sanctions on peaceful and truthful discussion of matters of public interest merely on a showing that others may thereby be persuaded to take action inconsistent with its interests. Abridgment of the liberty of such discussion can be justified only where the clear danger of substantive evils arises under circumstances affording no opportunity to test the merits of ideas by competition for acceptance in the market of public opinion. We hold that the danger of injury to an industrial concern is neither so serious nor so imminent as to justify the sweeping proscription of freedom of discussion embodied in Sec. 3448.

The State urges that the purpose of the challenged statute is the protection of the community from the violence and breaches of the peace, which, it asserts, are the concomitants of picketing. The power and the duty of the State to take adequate steps to preserve the peace and to protect the privacy, the lives, and the property of its residents cannot be doubted. But no clear and present danger of destruction of life or property, or invasion of the right of privacy, or breach of the peace can be thought to be inherent in the activities of every person who approaches the premises of an employer and publicizes the facts of a labor dispute involving the latter. We are not now concerned with picketing *en masse* or otherwise conducted which might occasion such imminent and aggravated danger to these interests as to justify a statute narrowly drawn to cover the precise situation giving rise to the danger. Compare American Foundries v. Tri-City Council, 257 U.S. 184, 205. Section 3448 in question here does not aim specifically at serious encroachments on these interests and does not evidence any such care in balancing these interests against the interest of the community and that of the individual in freedom of discussion on matters of public concern.

It is not enough to say that Sec. 3448 is limited or restricted in its application to such activity as takes place at the scene of the labor dispute. "[The] streets are natural and proper places for the dissemination of information and opinion; and one is not to have the exercise of his liberty of expression in appropriate places abridged on the plea that it may be exercised in some other place." Schneider v. State, 308 U.S. 147, 161, 163; Hague v. C.I.O., 307 U.S. 496, 515–516. The danger of breach of the peace or serious invasion of rights of property or privacy at the scene of a labor dispute is not sufficiently imminent in all cases to warrant the legislature in determining that such place is not appropriate for the range of activities outlawed by Sec. 3448.

Reversed.

MR. JUSTICE MCREYNOLDS is of the opinion that the judgment below should be affirmed.

NOTES

1. In American Federation of Labor v. Swing, 312 U.S. 321, 61 Sup. Ct. 735, 85 L. Ed. 1145 (1941), the Union engaged in picketing a beauty shop in order to unionize it. An Illinois court enjoined the picketing because it was stranger picketing which was unlawful under state decisions. This injunction was

upheld by the highest Illinois court, but the Supreme Court reversed. Justice Frankfurter, in the majority opinion, said at page 325:

> We are asked to sustain a decree which for purposes of this case asserts as the common law of a state that there can be no "peaceful picketing or peaceful persuasion" in relation to any dispute between an employer and a trade union unless the employer's own employees are in controversy with him.
>
> Such a ban of free communication is inconsistent with the guarantee of freedom of speech. That a state has ample power to regulate the local problems thrown up by modern industry and to preserve the peace is axiomatic. But not even these essential powers are unfettered by the requirements of the Bill of Rights. The scope of the Fourteenth Amendment is not confined by the notion of a particular state regarding the wise limits of an injunction in an industrial dispute, whether those limits be defined by statute or by the judicial organ of the state. A state cannot exclude workingmen from peacefully exercising the right of free communication by drawing the circle of economic competition between employers and workers so small as to contain only an employer and those directly employed by him. The interdependence of economic interest of all engaged in the same industry has become a commonplace. American Foundries v. Tri-City Council, 257 U.S. 184, 209, 42 S. Ct. 72, 78, 66 L. Ed. 189, 27 A.L.R. 360. The right of free communication cannot therefore be mutilated by denying it to workers, in a dispute with an employer, even though they are not in his employ. Communication by such employees of the facts of a dispute, deemed by them to be relevant to their interests, can no more bebarred because of concern for the economic interests against which they are seeking to enlist public opinion than could the utterance protected in Thornhill's case. "Members of a union might, without special statutory authorization by a State, make known the facts of a labor dispute, for freedom of speech is guaranteed by the Federal Constitution." Senn v. Tile Layers Union, 301 U.S. 468, 478, 57 S. Ct. 857, 862, 81 L. Ed. 1229.

2. In Cafeteria Employees v. Angelos, 320 U.S. 293, 64 Sup. Ct. 126, 88 L. Ed. 58 (1943), the Union picketed a restaurant in order to organize it. The management claimed it had no employees because all of the waiters were partners. The New York

Court of Appeals upheld an injunction against the picketing on two grounds: (1) that no labor dispute was involved because there were no employees, and (2) that the statements on the placards were false. 289 N.Y. 498, 507, 46 N.E.2d. 903, 908. The Supreme Court reversed unanimously. Justice Frankfurter, speaking for the court, said at page 295:

> In Senn v. Tile Layers Union, 301 U.S. 468, this Court ruled that members of a union might, "without special statutory authorization by a State, make know the facts of a labor dispute, for freedom of speech is guaranteed by the Federal Constitution." 301 U.S. at 478. Later cases applied the Senn doctrine by enforcing the right of workers to state their case and to appeal for public support in an orderly and peaceful manner regardless of the area of immunity as defined by state policy. A.F. of L. v. Swing, 312 U.S. 321; Bakery Drivers Local v. Wohl, 315 U.S. 769. To be sure the Senn case related to the employment of "peaceful picketing and truthful publicity." 301 U.S. at 482. That the picketing under review was peaceful is not questioned. And to use loose language or undefined slogans that are part of the conventional give-and-take in our economic and political controversies — like "unfair" or "fascist" — is not to falsify facts. In a setting like the present, continuing representations unquestionably false and acts of coercion going beyond the mere influence exerted by the fact of picketing, are of course not constitutional prerogatives. But here we have no attempt by the state through its courts to restrict conduct justifiably found to be an abusive exercise of the right to picket. We have before us a prohibition as unrestricted as that which we found to transgress state power in A.F. of L. v. Swing, supra . . .

3. Milk Wagon Drivers Union v. Meadowmoor Dairies, 312 U.S. 287, 61 Sup. Ct. 552, 85 L. Ed. 836 (1941), decided the same day as the Swing case, placed a distinct limitation on the constitutional protection of picketing. The Union, in attempting to combat the use of the independent peddler system, picketed dairies using the system. Numerous acts of violence occurred including window smashings, bombings, beatings, and shootings. The Illinois court enjoined not only the violence but all picketing no matter how peaceful. The Supreme Court upheld the injunction. Again speaking through Justice Frankfurter, it said at page 292:

The question which thus emerges is whether a state can choose to authorize its courts to enjoin acts of picketing in themselves peaceful when they are enmeshed with contemporaneously violent conduct which is concededly outlawed. . . .

. . . Peaceful picketing is the working man's means of communication. . . .

It must never be forgotten, however, that the Bill of Rights was the child of the Enlightenment. Back of the guarantee of free speech lay faith in the power of an appeal to reason by all the peaceful means for gaining access to the mind. It was in order to avert force and explosions due to restrictions upon rational modes of communication that the guarantee of free speech was given a generous scope. But utterance in a context of violence can lose its significance as an appeal to reason and become part of an instrument of force. Such utterance was not meant to be sheltered by the Constitution.

Still it is of prime importance that no constitutional freedom, least of all the guarantees of the Bill of Rights, be defeated by insubstantial findings of fact screening reality. That is why this Court has the ultimate power to search the records in the state courts where a claim of constitutionality is effectively made. And so the right of free speech cannot be denied by drawing from a trivial rough incident or a moment of animal exuberance the conclusion that otherwise peaceful picketing has the taint of force. . . .

. . . It is not for us to make an independent valuation of the testimony before the master. We have not only his findings but his findings authenticated by the state of Illinois speaking through her Supreme court. We can reject such a determination only if we can say that it is so without warrant as to be a palpable evasion of the constitutional guarantee here invoked. . . . No one will doubt that Illinois can protect its storekeepers from being coerced by fear of window-smashings or burnings or bombings. And acts which in isolation are peaceful may be part of a coercive thrust when entangled with acts of violence. The picketing in this case was set in a background of violence. In such a setting it could justifiably be concluded that the momentum of fear generated by past violence would survive even though future picketing might be wholly peaceful. . . .

. . . We find nothing in the Fourteenth Amendment that prevents a state, if it so chooses, from placing confidence in a chancellor's decree and compels it to rely exclusively on a policeman's club. . . .

. . . The injunction is confined to conduct near stores dealing in respondent's milk, and it deals with this narrow area precisely because the coercive conduct affected it. An injunction so adjusted to a particular situation is in accord with the settled practice of equity, sanctioned by such guardians of civil liberty as Mr. Justice Cardozo. Compare Nann v. Raimist, 255 N.Y. 307, 174 N.E. 690, 73 A.L.R. 669.

Justice Black dissented on the grounds that the Illinois court did not rely upon the presence of violence, and that the record did not show any substantial evidence of violence more recent than four years prior to the injunction. Justice Reed dissented on the grounds that the injunction prohibited peaceful picketing without any showing of a clear and present danger.

c. The Shriveling of the Doctrine

Even before the Angelos case was decided there were intimations that the Supreme Court might not mean all that it seemed to say about picketing and free speech. Two cases decided the same day in 1942 made clear that not all peaceful picketing was shielded by the Constitution. In Bakery & Pastry Drivers Union v. Wohl, 315 U.S. 769, 62 Sup. Ct. 816, 86 L. Ed. 1178 (1942), the Union picketed wholesale bakeries which sold goods to non-union, self-employed peddlers, and retail grocers who bought goods from them. The purpose was to compel the peddlers, who had seriously undermined union standards, to observe union hours and hire union relief drivers. The New York courts enjoined the picketing in spite of the state anti-injunction statute on the ground that there was no "labor dispute." The Supreme Court reversed, saying at page 774:

. . . [O]ne need not be in a "labor dispute" as defined by state law to have a right under the Fourteenth Amendment to express a grievance in a labor matter by publication unattended by violence, coercion, or conduct otherwise unlawful or oppressive. . . .

. . . A state is not required to tolerate in all places and all circumstances even peaceful picketing by an individual. But so far as we can tell, respondents' mobility and their insulation from the public, as middlemen made it practically impossible for petitioners to make known their legitimate grievances to the public whose patronage was sustaining the peddler system except by the means here employed and contemplated; and those means are such as to have slight, if any, repercussions upon the interests of strangers to the issue.

In Carpenters and Joiners Union v. Ritter's Cafe, 315 U.S. 722, 62 Sup. Ct. 807, 86 L. Ed. 1143 (1942), Ritter had made a contract with a nonunion building contractor to erect a building. The Carpenters Union sought to get Ritter to compel the contractor to employ union labor, by peacefully picketing a restaurant which Ritter owned and operated, quite separate from the new building and two miles away from its site. Texas enjoined the picketing as in violation of its antitrust laws. The Supreme Court in a five-to-four decision held that this injunction did not violate the constitutional guarantee of free speech. Justice Frankfurter, for the majority, stated at page 726:

> Texas has undertaken to localize industrial conflict by prohibiting the exertion of concerted pressure directed at the business, wholly outside the economic context of the real dispute, of a person whose relation to the dispute arises from his business dealings with one of the disputants. The state has not attempted to outlaw whatever psychological pressure may be involved in the mere communication by an individual of the facts relating to his differences with another. Nor are we confronted here with a limitation upon speech in circumstances where there exists an "interdependence of economic interest of all engaged in the same industry," . . . The line drawn by Texas in this case, is not the line drawn by New York in the Wohl case. The dispute there related to the conditions under which bakery products were sold and delivered to retailers. The business of the retailers was therefore directly involved in the dispute. In picketing the retail establishments the union members would only be following the subject-matter of their dispute. Here we have a different situation. The dispute concerns the labor conditions surrounding the construction of a building by a contractor. Texas has deemed it desirable to insulate from the dispute an establishment which industrially has no connection with the dispute. . . .

> It is true that by peaceful picketing working men communicate their grievances. As a means of communicating the facts of a labor dispute peaceful picketing may be a phase of the constitutional right of free utterance. But recogni-

tion of peaceful picketing as an exercise of free speech does not imply that the states must be without power to confine the sphere of communication to that directly related to the dispute. Restriction of picketing to the area of the industry within which a labor dispute arises leaves open to the disputants other traditional modes of communication. . . .

Justice Black, in dissenting (Douglas and Murphy concurring), argued at page 730:

> . . . I can see no reason why members of the public should be deprived of any opportunity to get information which might enable them to use their influence to tip the scale in favor of the side they think is right. . . .
> . . . It may be that the petitioners are left free to inform the public at other places or in other ways. Possibly they might, at greater expense, reach the public over radio or through the newspapers, . . . In any event "one is not to have the exercise of his liberty of expression in appropriate places abridged on the plea that it may be exercised in some other place." Schneider v. State, 308 U.S. 147, 163.

[In a concurring opinion in the Wohl case, but apparently referring to both cases, Justice Douglas indicated that although he did not agree with the Ritter decision he did not equate picketing with other forms of expression (315 U.S. 776)]:

> Picketing by an organized group is more than free speech, since it involves patrol of a particular locality and since the very presence of a picket line may induce action of one kind or another, quite irrespective of the nature of the ideas which are being disseminated. Hence those aspects of picketing make it the subject of restrictive regulation.

Were there any hints in Thornhill v. Alabama that the Court might limit the free speech doctrine as they did in the Ritter case?

What does the Court mean by the "economic context of the real dispute" in the Ritter case? If the new building was to be a new restaurant, would the picketing have been protected? If the new building had been Mr. Ritter's residence, adjoining the restaurant, would the picketing have been protected?

What does Justice Douglas mean when he says the picket line may induce action irrespective of the nature of the ideas being disseminated? Is he assuming that every picket line has an actual intimidating effect on those who approach it? Or does he mean that some people will refuse to cross any picket line, on principle, regardless of the merits of the particular dispute? Suppose one defines the idea disseminated as being merely the statement by the union that it desires persons not to deal with the employer?

Can you determine whether the Court in the foregoing decisions is applying the so-called "clear and present danger" test or the "rational basis" test? See Whitaker v. North Carolina, page 486 supra. Could one properly cite any of these cases for the proposition that a state may not prohibit peaceful picketing for a purpose viewed as illegal under the local common law? Compare Colonial Press v. Ellis, 321 Mass. 495, 74 N.E.2d 1 (1947).

GIBONEY v. EMPIRE STORAGE & ICE CO.
Supreme Court of the United States, 1949
336 U.S. 490, 69 Sup. Ct. 684, 93 L. Ed. 834

[Ice and Coal Drivers and Handlers Local Union No. 953 organized 160 out of the 200 ice peddlers in Kansas City, Missouri. The peddlers drove their own trucks in selling ice from door to door. In order to induce the other 40 peddlers to join, the Union obtained agreements from wholesale ice distributors not to sell ice to the nonunion peddlers. All distributors agreed except Empire Storage and Ice Company. The Union then picketed Empire's place of business. About 85 per cent of the truck drivers working for Empire's customers belonged to unions, and they refused to cross the picket line. If they had, they would have been subject to fines or suspension by their unions.

Empire obtained an injunction from a Missouri court restraining peaceful picketing around its place of business. The Missouri Supreme Court affirmed, holding that the purpose of the picketing was to compel Empire to agree to stop selling ice to nonunion peddlers. Such an agreement would have violated the Missouri antitrust laws (Sections 8301–8305, Mo. Rev. Stats. (1939)), and have subjected Empire to criminal prosecution and suits for triple damages.]

JUSTICE BLACK delivered the opinion of the Court:

. . . Attacking the Missouri statute as construed and applied, appellants broadly challenge the power of the state to issue any injunction against their conduct since, they assert, the primary objective of their combination and picketing was to improve wage and working conditions. On this premise they argue that their right to combine, to picket, and to publish must be determined by focusing attention exclusively upon their lawful purpose to improve labor conditions, and that their violation of the state antitrade restraint laws must be dismissed as merely incidental to this lawful purpose.

First.   That states have constitutional power to prohibit competing dealers and their aiders and abettors from combining to restrain freedom of trade is beyond question. . . .

Second.   It is contended that though the Missouri statute can be applied validly to combinations of businessmen who agree not to sell to certain persons, it cannot be applied constitutionally to combinations of union workers who agree in their self-interest to use their joint power to prevent sales to nonunion workers.   This contention appears to be grounded on the guaranties of freedom of speech and press stemming from the Fourteenth and First Amendments.   Aside from the element of disseminating information through peaceful picketers, later discussed, it is difficult to perceive how it could be thought that these constitutional guaranties afford labor union members a peculiar immunity from laws against trade restraint combinations, unless, as appellants contend, labor unions are given special constitutional protection denied all other people.

The objective of unions to improve wages and working conditions has sometimes commended itself to Congress and to state legislatures.   To the extent that the states or Congress, for this or other reasons, have seen fit to exempt unions from antitrust laws, this Court has sustained legislative power to grant the exemptions. . . .   On the other hand, where statutes have not granted exemptions, we have declared that violations of antitrust laws could not be defended on the ground that a particular accused combination would not injure but would actually help manufacturers, laborers, retailers, consumers, or the public in general. . . .

The foregoing holdings rest on the premise that legislative power to regulate trade and commerce includes the power to determine what groups, if any, shall be regulated, and whether certain regulations will help or injure businessmen, workers, and the public in general.   In making this determination Missouri has decided to apply its law without exception *to all* persons who combine to restrain freedom of trade.   We are without constitutional authority to modify or upset Missouri's determination that it is in the public interest to make combinations of workers subject to laws designed to keep the channels of trade wholly free and open.   To exalt all labor union conduct in restraint of trade above all state control would greatly reduce the traditional powers of states over their domestic economy and might conceivably make it impossible for them to enforce their antitrade restraint laws. See Allen-Bradley Co. v. Union, 325 U.S. 797, 810, 65 S. Ct. 1533, 1540, 89 L. Ed. 1939. More than that, if for the reasons here contended states cannot subject union members to such antitrade restraint laws as Missouri's, neither can Congress. The Constituton has not so greatly impaired the states' or nation's power to govern.

Third. It is contended that the injunction against picketing adjacent to Empire's place of business is an unconstitutional abridgment of free speech because the picketers were attempting peacefully to publicize truthful facts about a labor dispute. See Thornhill v. Alabama, 310 U.S. 88, 102, 60 S. Ct. 736, 744, 84 L. Ed. 1093, and Allen-Bradley Co. v. Union, 325 U.S. 797, 807, note 12, 65 S. Ct. 1533, 1539, 89 L. Ed. 1939. But the record here does not permit this publicizing to be treated in isolation. For according to the pleadings, the evidence, the findings, and the argument of the appellants, the sole immediate object of the publicizing adjacent to the premises of Empire, as well as the other activities of the appellants and their allies, was to compel Empire to agree to stop selling ice to nonunion peddlers. Thus all of appellants' activities — their powerful transportation combination, their patrolling, their formation of a picket line warning union men not to cross at peril of their union membership, their publicizing — constituted a single and integrated course of conduct, which was in violation of Missouri's valid law. In this situation, the injunction did no more than enjoin an offense against Missouri law, a felony.

It rarely has been suggested that the constitutional freedom for speech and press extends its immunity to speech or writing used as an integral part of conduct in violation of a valid criminal statute. We reject the contention now. Nothing that was said or decided in any of the cases relied on by appellants calls for a different holding.

Neither Thornhill v. Alabama, supra, nor Carlson v. California, 310 U.S. 106, 60 S. Ct. 746, 84 L. Ed. 1104, both decided the same day, supports the contention that conduct otherwise unlawful is always immune from state regulation because an integral part of that conduct is carried on by display of placards by peaceful picketers. In both these cases this Court struck down statutes which banned all dissemination of information by people adjacent to certain premises, pointing out that the statutes were so broad that they could not only be utilized to punish conduct plainly illegal but could also be applied to ban all truthful publications of the facts of a labor controversy. But in the Thornhill opinion, 310 U.S., at pages 103–104, 60 S. Ct., at page 745, 84 L. Ed. 1993, the Court was careful to point out that it was within the province of states "to set the limits of permissible contest open to industrial combatants." See Lincoln Labor Union v. Northwestern Iron and Metal Co., 335 U. S. 525, 536, 69 S. Ct. 251, 257; Allen-Bradley Local v. Wisconsin Employment Relations Board, 315 U.S. 740, 748–751, 62 S. Ct. 820, 825–826, 86 L. Ed. 1154. Further emphasizing the power of a state "to set the limits of permissible contest open to industrial combatants" the Court cited with approval the opinion of Mr. Justice Brandeis in Duplex Printing Co. v. Deering, 254 U.S. 443, at page 488, 41 S. Ct. 172, at page 184, 65 L. Ed. 349, 16 A.L.R. 196, 216. On that page the opinion stated:

> . . . The conditions developed in industry may be such that those engaged in it cannot continue their struggle without danger to the community. But it is not for judges to determine whether such conditions exist, nor is it their function to set the limits of permissible contest and to declare the duties which the new situation demands. This is the function of the legislature which, while limiting individual and group rights of aggression and defense, may substitute processes of justice for the more primitive method of trial by combat.

After emphasizing state power over industrial conflicts, the Court in the Thornhill opinion, 310 U.S. at page 104, 60 S. Ct. at page 745, 84 L. Ed. 1093, went on to say that states may not "in dealing with the evils arising from industrial disputes . . . impair the effective exercise of the right to discuss freely industrial relations. . . ." This statement must be considered in its context. It was directed toward a sweeping state prohibition which this Court found to embrace "nearly every practicable, effective means whereby those interested — including the employees directly affected — may enlighten the public on the nature and causes of a labor dispute." That the general statement of the limitation of a state's power to impair free speech was not intended to apply to the fact situation presented here is further indicated by the cases cited with approval in note 21 of the Thornhill opinion.

Appellants also rely on Carpenters Union v. Ritter's Cafe, 315 U.S. 722, 62 S. Ct. 807, 86 L. Ed. 1143, and Bakery Drivers Local v. Wohl, 315 U.S. 769, 62 S. Ct. 816, 86 L. Ed. 1178, decided the same day. Neither lends support to the contention that peaceful picketing is beyond legislative control. The Court's opinion in the Ritter case approvingly quoted a part of the Thornhill opinion which recognized broad state powers over industrial conflicts. In the Wohl case, 315 U.S. at page 775, 62 S. Ct. at page 819, 86 L. Ed. 1178, the Court's opinion found no "violence, force or coercion, or conduct otherwise unlawful or oppressive" and said that "A state is not required to tolerate in all places . . . even peaceful picketing by an individual." A concurring opinion in the Wohl case, 315 U.S. at pages 776–777, 62 S. Ct. at pages 819–820, 86 L. Ed. 1178, pointed out that picketing may include conduct other than speech, conduct which can be made the subject of restrictive legislation. No opinions relied on by petitioners assert a constitutional right in picketers to take advantage of speech or press to violate valid laws designed to protect important interests of society.

We think the circumstances here and the reasons advanced by the Missouri courts justify restraint of the picketing which was done in violation of Missouri's valid law for the sole immediate purpose of continuing a violation of law. In holding this, we are mindful of the essential importance to our society of a vigilant protection of freedom of speech and press. Bridges v. California, 314 U.S. 252, 263, 62 S. Ct. 190, 194, 86 L. Ed. 192, 159 A.L.R. 1345. States cannot consistently with our Constitution abridge those freedoms to obviate slight inconveniences or annoyances. Schneider v. State, 308 U.S. 147, 162, 60 S. Ct. 146, 151, 84 L. Ed. 155. But placards used as an essential and inseparable part of a grave offense against an important public law cannot immunize that unlawful conduct from state control. Virginia Electric & Power Co. v. National Labor Relations Board, 319 U.S. 533, 539, 63 S. Ct. 1214, 1218, 87 L. Ed. 1568; Thomas v. Collins, 323 U.S. 516, 536, 537, 538, 539–540, 65 S. Ct. 315, 325, 326, 327, 89 L. Ed. 430. Nor can we say that the publication here should not have been restrained because of the possibility of separating the picketing conduct into illegal and legal parts. Thomas v. Collins, supra, 323 U.S. at page 547, 65 S. Ct. at page 330. For the placards were to effectuate the purposes of an unlawful combination, and their sole, unlawful immediate objective was to induce Empire to violate the Missouri law by acquiescing in unlawful demands to agree not to sell ice to nonunion peddlers. It is true that the agreements and course of conduct here were as in most instances brought about through speaking or writing. But it has never been deemed an abridgment of freedom of speech or press to make a course of conduct illegal merely because the conduct was in part initiated, evidenced, or carried out by means of language, either spoken, written, or printed. See e.g. Fox v. Washington, 236 U.S. 273, 277, 35 S. Ct. 383, 384, 59 L. Ed. 573; Chaplinsky v. New Hampshire, 315 U.S. 568, 62 S. Ct. 766, 86 L. Ed. 1031. Such an expansive interpretation of the constitutional guaranties of speech and press would make it practically impossible ever to enforce laws against agreements in restraint of trade as well as many other agreements and conspiracies deemed injurious to society.

The interest of Missouri in enforcement of its antitrust laws cannot be classified as an effort to outlaw only a slight public inconvenience or annoyance. The Missouri policy against restraints of trade is of long standing and is in most respects the same as that which the Federal Government has followed for more than half a century. It is clearly drawn in an attempt to afford all persons an equal opportunity to buy goods. There was clear danger, imminent and immediate, that unless restrained, appellants would succeed in making that policy a dead letter insofar as purchases by nonunion men were concerned. Appellants' power with that of their allies was irresistible. And it is clear that appellants were doing more than exercising a right of free speech or press. Bakery Drivers Local v. Wohl, 315 U.S. 769, 776–777, 62 S. Ct. 816, 819, 820, 86 L. Ed. 1178. They were exercising their economic power together with that of their allies to compel Empire to abide by union rather than by state regulation of trade.[6] . . .

---

[6] "Picketing by an organized group is more than free speech, since it involves patrol of a particular locality and since the very presence of a picket line may induce action of one kind or another, quite irrespective of the nature of the ideas which are being disseminated. Hence those aspects of picketing make it the subject of restrictive regulation." Bakery Drivers Local v. Wohl, supra, 315 U.S. at pages 776–777, 62 S. Ct. at page 819.

The opinion in Thomas v. Collins, 323 U.S. 516, 537–538, 65 S. Ct. 315, 326, 89 L. Ed. 430, stated: ". . . When to this persuasion other things are added which bring about coercion, or give it that character, the limit of the right has been passed. . . . But short of that limit the employer's freedom cannot be impaired. The Constitution protects no less the employees' converse right. Of course espousal of the cause of labor is entitled to no higher constitutional protection than the espousal of any other lawful cause. It is entitled to the same protection."

A concurring opinion in Thomas v. Collins, 315 U.S. at pages 543–544, 65 S. Ct. at page 329, stated thus: "But once he uses the economic power which he has over other men and their jobs to influence their action, he is doing more than exercising the freedom of speech protected by the First Amendment. That is true whether he be an employer or an employee. But as long as he does no more than speak he has the same unfettered right, no matter what side of an issue he espouses."

. . . While the State of Missouri is not a party in this case it is plain that the basic issue is whether Missouri or a labor union has paramount constitutional power to regulate and govern the manner in which certain trade practices shall be carried on in Kansas City, Missouri. Missouri has by statute regulated trade one way. The appellant union members have adopted a program to regulate it another way. The state has provided for enforcement of its statutory rule by imposing civil and criminal sanctions. The union has provided for enforcement of its rule by sanctions against union members who cross picket lines. . . . We hold that the state's power to govern in this field is paramount, and that nothing in the constitutional guaranties of speech or press compels a state to apply or not to apply its antitrade restraint law to groups of workers, businessmen or others. Of course this Court does not pass on the wisdom of the Missouri statute. We hold only that as here construed and applied it does not violate the Federal Constitution.

Affirmed.

NOTES

1. What weight does the Court give here to the fact that the picket line's effectiveness rested upon the disciplinary power of the Union? What is the significance of the extensive quotation from Thomas v. Collins, set forth in the footnote?

2. How important is the fact that the state's public policy which is being enforced is explicitly stated in a legislative enactment? How important is it that this polcy is almost universally accepted by the states and by the Federal Government? Suppose the state statute prohibited all picketing in the absence of a dispute between the employer and his immediate employees? See Gordon, Giboney v. Empire Storage & Ice Co.: A Footnote to Freech Speech, 36 Va. L. Rev. 25 (1950). The Giboney case is also noted in 62 Harv. L. Rev. 1402 (1949), 44 Ill. L. Rev. 714 (1950).

3. In Building Service Employees Local 262 v. Gazzam, 339 U.S. 532, 70 S. Ct. 784, 94 L. Ed., 1045 (1950), the Union asked a hotel owner in Bremerton, Washington, to sign a contract covering his fifteen employees. He said this was for the employees to decide. The Union solicited for members but had no success, and after a meeting between the Union representative and eleven of the employees, nine voted against joining, one was undecided, and one voted to join. The hotel owner continued to refuse to

recognize the Union, and the Union picketed the premises. The Washington anti-injunction act contained a declaration of policy similar to that in the Norris-LaGuardia Act, stating that although an employee "should be free to decline to associate with his fellows, it is necessary that he have full freedom of labor association . . . and that he shall be free from interferences, restraint, or coercion of employers . . . in the designation of such representatives or in self-organization or in other concerted activities for the purpose of collective bargaining. . . ." The Washington Supreme Court found that the peaceful picketing violated this public policy because it sought to compel the employer to coerce the employees in the exercise of their free choice and that it should be enjoined.

The United States Supreme Court held unanimously that this injunction was not an unconstitutional denial of free speech. Justice Minton, for the Court, said at page 539:

> Respondent does not contend that picketing *per se* has been enjoined but only that picketing which has as its purpose violation of the policy of the state. There is no contention that picketing directed at employees for organization purposes would be violative of that policy. The decree does not have that effect.
>
> We are of the opinion that Giboney v. Empire Storage & Ice Co., 336 U.S. 490, 69 S. Ct. 684, controls the disposition of this case, and that it therefore must be affirmed. In the Giboney case it is true that the state law which made the objective of the picketing unlawful had criminal sanctions. The Washington statute here has no criminal sanctions. Petitioners seek to distinguish Giboney on that ground. . . . It is not the presence of criminal sanctions which makes a state policy "important public law." Much public policy does not readily lend itself to accompanying criminal sanctions. Whether to impose criminal sanctions in connection with a given policy is itself a question of policy.
>
> Here, as in Giboney, the union was using its economic power with that of its allies to compel respondent to abide by union policy rather than by the declared policy of the State. That state policy guarantees workers free choice of representatives for bargaining purposes. If respondent had complied with petitioners' demands and had signed one of the tendered contracts and lived up to its terms, he would have thereby coerced his employees. . . .

. . . The injunction granted was tailored to prevent a specific violation of an important state law. The decree was limited to the wrong being perpetrated, namely, "an abusive exercise of the right to picket." Cafeteria Employees Union, Local 302 v. Angelos, 302 U.S. at page 295, 64 Sup. Ct. at page 127, 88 L. Ed. 58. The judgment is affirmed.

Compare this decision with the dissenting opinion of Justice Butler in Lauf v. E. G. Shinner & Co., page 678 supra.

4. On the same day that the Gazzam case was decided, the Court also upheld a California injunction of peaceful picketing. Hughes v. Superior Court, 339 U.S. 460, 70 S. Ct. 718, 94 L. Ed. 985 (1950).

An organization of Negroes had requested Lucky Stores to hire Negro employees in the same proportion as it had Negro customers, namely, about 50 per cent. When the store refused, the organization picketed the store. The California Supreme Court held that this was picketing to compel an employer to hire on the basis of race. Since it had earlier held in James v. Marinship, 25 Cal. 2d 721, 155 P. 2d 329 (1944), that union action to compel racial discrimination was unlawful, it proceeded to say that this picketing violated the judicially declared public policy and could be enjoined.

Justice Frankfurter for the unanimous Court said at page 464:

First. . . . To deny to California the right to ban picketing in the circumstances of this case would mean that there could be no prohibition of the pressure of picketing to secure proportional employment on ancestral grounds of Hungarians in Cleveland, of Poles in Buffalo, of Germans in Milwaukee, of Portuguese in New Bedford, of Mexicans in San Antonio, of the numerous minority groups in New York, and so on through the whole gamut of racial and religious concentrations in various cities. States may well believe that such constitutional sheltering would inevitably encourage use of picketing to compel employment on the basis of racial discrimination. In disallowing such picketing States may act under the belief that otherwise community tensions and conflicts would be exacerbated. The differences in cultural traditions instead of adding flavor and variety to our common citizenry might well be hardened into hostilities by leave of law. The Constitution does not demand that the element of communication in picketing prevail over the mischief furthered by its use in these situations.

Second. . . . "[T]he domain of liberty, withdrawn by the Fourteenth Amendment from encroachment by the states," Palko v. Connecticut, 302 U.S. 319, 327, no doubt includes liberty of thought and appropriate means for expressing it. But while picketing is a mode of communication it is inseparably something more and different. . . . Publication in a newspaper, or by distribution of circulars, may convey the same information or make the same charge as do those patrolling a picket line. But the very purpose of a picket line is to exert influences, and it produces consequences, different from other modes of communication. The loyalties and responses evoked and exacted by picket lines are unlike those flowing from appeals by printed word. . . .

Third. A State may constitutionally permit picketing despite the ingredients in it that differentiate it from speech in its ordinary context. Senn v. Tile Layers Protective Union, 301 U.S. 468, 57 S. Ct. 857, 81 L. Ed. 1229. And we have found that because of its element of communication picketing under some circumstances finds sanction in the fourteenth Amendment. Thornhill v. Alabama, 310 U.S. 88, 60 S. Ct. 736, 84 L. Ed. 1093; American Federation of Labor v. Swing, 312 U.S. 321, 61 S. Ct. 568, 85 L. Ed. 855; Bakery & Pastry Drivers & Helpers Local v. Wohl, 315 U.S. 769, 62 S. Ct. 816, 86 L. Ed. 1178; Cafeteria Employees Union v. Angelos, 320 U.S. 293, 64 S. Ct. 126, 88 L. Ed. 58. However general or loose the expressions that found their way into opinions, the specific situations have controlled decision. It has been amply recognized that picketing, not being the equivalent of speech as a matter of fact, is not its inevitable legal equivalent. Picketing is not beyond the control of a State if the manner in which picketing is conducted or the purpose which it seeks to effectuate gives grounds for its disallowance. . . .

Fourth. The fact that California's policy is expressed by the judicial organ of the State rather than by the legislature we have repeatedly ruled to be immaterial. . . . For the Fourteenth Amendment leaves the States free to distribute the powers of government as they will between their legislative and judicial branches. . . .

The injunction here was drawn to meet what California deemed the evil of picketing to bring about proportional hiring. We do not go beyond the circumstances of the case.

Generalizations are treacherous in the application of large constitutional concepts.

Affirmed.

How important in the two above cases was the fact that the state policy involved was one which the court looked upon with favor? The Court in both cases emphasizes that the injunction was "tailored to prevent a specific violation." How could the union in each case have engaged in picketing without violating the injunction? The Hughes case is noted in 28 Tex. L. Rev. 106 (1949).

With the Hughes case, compare New Negro Alliance v. Sanitary Grocery Co., page 680 supra.

INTERNATIONAL BROTHERHOOD OF TEAMSTERS v. HANKE

Supreme Court of the United States, 1950
339 U.S. 470, 70 Sup. Ct. 773, 94 L. Ed. 995

[Hanke and his three sons operated a used car lot and auto repair shop. The Hankes joined the Teamsters Union and displayed the union card. The Union negotiated a contract with the Seattle Automobile Dealers Association, to which Hanke did not belong, providing that used car lots be closed at 6 p.m. on weekdays and all day on Saturdays, Sundays, and eight specified holidays. The Union requested that Hanke comply with these rules, and when he refused they removed his union card, omitted his name from the list of recommended dealers published in the Union journal, and picketed the premises. The picket also took the license numbers of all of Hanke's patrons. Drivers from supply houses refused to cross the picket line to deliver parts and other needed material, and Hanke's business fell off heavily. The Trial Court granted a permanent injunction and awarded damages of $250. The Supreme Court of Washington affirmed.]

MR. JUSTICE FRANKFURTER announced the judgment of the Court and an opinion in which the CHIEF JUSTICE, MR. JUSTICE JACKSON and MR. JUSTICE BURTON concurred.

The question is this: Does the Fourteenth Amendment of the Constitution bar a State from use of the injunction to prohibit the picketing of a business conducted by the owner himself without employees in order to secure compliance by him with a demand to become a union shop? . . .

Here, as in Hughes v. Superior Court, 339 U.S. 460, 70 S. Ct. 718, 94 L. Ed. 985 we must start with the fact that while picketing has an ingredient of communication it cannot dogmatically be equated with the constitutionally protected freedom of speech. Our decisions reflect recognition that picketing is "indeed a hybrid." Freund, On Understanding the Supreme Court 18 (1949). See also Jaffe, in Defense of the Supreme Court's Picketing Doctrine, 41 Mich. L. Rev. 1037 (1943). The effort in the cases has been to strike a balance between the constitutional protection of the element of communication in picketing and "the power of the State to set the limits of permissible contest open to industrial combatants." Thornhill v. State of Alabama, 310 U.S. 88, 104, 60 S. Ct. 736, 745, 84 L. Ed. 1093. A State's judgment on striking such a balance is of course subject to the limitations of the Fourteenth Amendment. Embracing as such a judgment does, however, a State's social and economic policies, which in turn depend on knowledge and appraisal of local social and economic factors, such judgment on these matters comes to this Court bearing a weighty title of respect.

These two cases emphasize the nature of a problem that is presented by our duty of sitting in judgment on a State's judgment in striking the balance that has to be struck when a State decides not to keep hands off these industrial contests. Here we have a glaring instance of the interplay of competing social-economic interests and viewpoints. Unions obviously are concerned not to have union standards undermined by nonunion shops. This interest penetrates into self-employer shops. On the other hand, some of our profoundest thinkers from Jefferson to Brandeis have stressed the importance to a democratic society of encouraging self-employer economic units as a counter-movement to what are deemed to be the dangers inherent in excessive concentration of economic power. . . .

Whether to prefer the union or a self-employer in such a situation, or to seek partial recognition of both interests, and, if so, by what means to secure such accommodation, obviously presents to a State serious problems. There are no sure answers, and the best available solution is likely to be experimental and tentative, and always subject to the control of the popular will. That the solution of these perplexities is a challenge to wisdom and not a command of the Constitution is the significance of Senn. v. Tile Layers Protective Union, 301 U.S. 468, 57 S. Ct. 857, 81 L. Ed. 1229. Senn, a self-employer tile layer who occasionally hired other tile layers to assist him, was picketed when he refused to yield to the union demand that he no longer work himself at his trade. The Wisconsin court found the situation to be within the State's anti-injunction statute and denied relief. In rejecting the claim that the restriction upon Senn's freedom was a denial of his liberty under the Fourteenth Amendment, this Court held that it lay in the domain of policy for Wisconsin to permit the picketing: "Whether it was wise for the state to permit the unions to do so is a question of its public policy — not our concern." 301 U.S. at page 481, 57 S. Ct. at page 863.

This conclusion was based on the Court's recognition that it was Wisconsin, not the Fourteenth Amendment, which put such picketing as a "means of publicity on a par with advertisements in the press." 301 U.S. at page 479, 57 S. Ct. at page 862. If Wisconsin could permit such picketing as a matter of policy it must have been equally free as a matter of policy to choose not to permit it and therefore not to "put this means of publicity on a par with advertisements in the press." If Wisconsin could have deemed it wise to withdraw from the union the permission which this Court found outside the ban of the Fourteenth Amendment, such action by Washington cannot be inside that ban.

Washington here concluded that, even though the relief afforded the Hankes and Cline [party in another case] entailed restriction upon communication that the unions sought to convey through picketing, it was more important to safeguard the value which the State placed upon self-employers, leaving all other channels of communication open to the union. The relatively small interest of the unions considerably influenced the balance that was struck. Of 115 used car dealers in Seattle maintaining union standards, all but ten were self-employers with no employees. "From this fact," so we are informed by the Supreme Court of Washington, "the conclusion seems irresistible that the union's interest in the welfare of a mere handful of members (of whose working conditions no complaint at all is made (is far outweighed by the interests of individual proprietors and the people of the community as a whole, to the end that little businessmen and property owners shall be free from dictation as to business policy by an outside group having but a relatively small and indirect interest in such policy." 33 Wash. (2d) at 659, 207 P.2d at page 213.

We are, needless to say, fully aware of the contentious nature of these views. It is not our business even remotely to hint at agreement or disagreement with what has commended itself to the State of Washington, or even to intimate that all the relevant considerations are exposed in the conclusions reached by the Washington court. They seldom are in this field, so deceptive and opaque are the elements of these problems. That is precisely what is meant by recognizing that they are within the domain of a State's public policy. Because there is a lack of agreement as to the relevant factors and divergent interpretations of their meaning, as well as differences in assessing what is the short and what is the long view, the clash of fact and opinion should be resolved by the democratic process and not by the judicial sword. Invalidation here would mean denial of power to the Congress as well as to the forty-eight States.

It is not for us to pass judgment on cases not now before us. But when one considers that issues not unlike those that are here have been similarly viewed by other States and by the Congress of the United States, we cannot conclude that Washington, in holding the picketing in these cases to be for an unlawful object, has struck a balance so inconsistent with rooted traditions of a free people that it must be found an unconstitutional choice. Mindful as we are that a phase of picketing is communication, we cannot find that Washington has offended the Constitution. . . .

What was actually decided in American Federation of Labor v. Swing, 312 U.S. 321, 61 S. Ct. 568, 85 L. Ed. 855; Bakery & Pastry Drivers & Helpers Local 802 v. Wohl, 315 U.S. 769, 62 S. Ct. 816, 86 L. Ed. 1178, and Cafeteria Employees Union, Local 302 v. Angelos, 320 U.S. 293, 64 S. Ct. 126, 88 L. Ed. 58, does not preclude us from upholding Washington's power to make the choice of policy she has here made. In those cases we held only that a State could not proscribe picketing merely by setting artificial bounds, unreal in the light of modern circumstances, to what constitutes an industrial relationship or a labor dispute. See Cox, Some Aspects of the Labor Management Relations Act, 1947, 61 Harv. L. Rev. 1, 30 (1947). The power of a State to declare a policy in favor of self-employers and to make conduct restrictive of self-employment unlawful was not considered in those cases. Indeed in Wohl this Court expressly noted that the State courts had not found that the picketing there condemned was for a defined unlawful object. 315 U.S. 774, 62 S. Ct. 818, 86 L. Ed. 1178.

When an injunction of a State court comes before us it comes not as an independent collocation of words. It is defined and confined by the opinion of the State court. The injunctions in these two cases are to be judged here with all the limitations that are infused into their terms by the opinions of the Washington

Supreme Court on the basis of which the judgments below come before us.   So read, the injunctions are directed solely against picketing for the ends defined by the parties before the Washington court and this Court. . . .   Our affirmance of these injunctions is in conformity with the reading derived from the Washington court's opinions.   If astuteness may discover argumentative excess in the scope of the injunctions beyond what we constitutionally justify by this opinion, it will be open to petitioners to raise the matter, which they have not raised here, when the cases on remand reach the Washington court.

Affirmed.

MR. JUSTICE CLARK concurs in the result.

MR. JUSTICE BLACK dissents for substantially the reasons given in his dissent in Carpenters & Joiners Union of America, Local No. 213 v. Ritter's Cafe, 315 U.S. 722, 729–732, 62 S. Ct. 807, 810–812, 86 L. Ed. 1143.

MR. JUSTICE DOUGLAS took no part in the consideration or decision of these cases.

MR. JUSTICE MINTON, with whom Mr. Justice Reed joins, dissenting.

Petitioners in each of these cases were "permanently restrained and enjoined from in any manner picketing" the places of business of respondents.   The picketing here was peaceful publicity, not enmeshed in a pattern of violence as was true in Milk Wagon Drivers Union of Chicago, Local 753 v. Meadowmoor Dairies, 312 U.S. 287, 61 S. Ct. 552, 85 L. Ed. 836, 132 A.L.R. 1200; nor was there violence in the picketing, as in Hotel & Restaurant Employees' International Alliance, Local No. 122 v. Wisconsin E.R.B., 315 U.S. 437, 62 S. Ct. 706, 86 L. Ed. 946.   The decrees entered in the instant cases were not tailored to meet the evils of threats and intimidation as Cafeteria Employees Union, Local 302 v. Angelos, 320 U.S. 293, 295, 64 S. Ct. 126, 88 L. Ed. 58, indicates they might have been; nor were they limited to restraint of picketing for the purpose of forcing the person picketed to violate the law and public policy of the state, as were the decrees in Giboney v. Empire Storage & Ice Co., 336 U.S. 490, 69 S. Ct. 684, 93 L. Ed. 834, and Building Service Employees Union v. Gazzam, 339 U.S. 532, 70 S. Ct. 784, 94 L. Ed. 1045.   The abuses of picketing involved in the above cases were held by this Court not to be protected by the Fourteenth Amendment from state restraint.

It seems equally clear to me that peaceful picketing which is used properly as an instrument of publicity has been held by this

Court in Thornhill v. State of Alabama, 310 U.S. 88, 60 S. Ct. 736, 84 L. Ed. 1093; Carlson v. People of State of California, 310 U.S. 106, 60 S. Ct. 746, 84 L. Ed. 1104; American Federation of Labor v. Swing, 312 U.S. 321, 61 S. Ct. 568, 85 L. Ed. 855; Bakery & Pastry Drivers & Helpers Local 802 v. Wohl, 315 U.S. 769, 62 S. Ct. 816, 86 L. Ed. 1178; and Cafeteria Employees Union, Local 302 v. Angelos, 320 U.S. 293, 64 S. Ct. 126, 88 L. Ed. 58, to be protected by the Fourteenth Amendment. I do not understand that in the last three mentioned cases this Court, as the majority in its opinion says, "held only that a State could not proscribe picketing merely by setting artificial bounds, unreal in the light of modern circumstances, to what constitutes an industrial relationship or a labor dispute." If the states may set bounds, it is not for this Court to say where they shall be set, unless the setting violates some provision of the Federal Constitution. I understand the above cases to have found violations of the federal constitutional guarantee of freedom of speech, and the picketing could not be restrained because to do so would violate the right of free speech and publicity. . . .

All the recent cases of this Court upholding picketing, from Thornhill to Angelos, have done so on the view that "peaceful picketing and truthful publicity" (see 320 U.S. at page 295, 64 S. Ct. at page 127, 88 L. Ed. 58) is protected by the guaranty of free speech. This view stems from Mr. Justice Brandeis' statement in Senn that "Members of a union might, without special statutory authorization by a State, make known the facts of a labor dispute, for freedom of speech is guaranteed by the Federal Constitution." 301 U.S. 468, 478, 57 S. Ct. 857, 862, 81 L. Ed. 1229. In that case Justice Brandeis was dealing with action of Wisconsin that *permitted* picketing by a labor union of a one-man shop. Of course, as long as Wisconsin allowed picketing, there was no interference with freedom of expression. By permitting picketing the State was allowing the expression found in "peaceful picketing and truthful publicity." There was in that posture of the case no question of conflict with the right of free speech. But because Wisconsin could permit picketing, and not thereby encroach upon freedom of speech, it does not follow that it could forbid like picketing; for that might involve conflict with the Fourteenth Amendment. It seems to me that Justice Brandeis, foreseeing the problem of the converse, made the statement above quoted in order to indicate that picketing could be protected by the free speech guaranty of the Federal Constitution. Whether or not that is what Justice Brandeis meant, I think this Court has accepted that view, from Thornhill to Angelos. It seems to me too late now to deny that those cases were rooted in the free speech doctrine.   I think we should not decide the instant cases in a manner so alien to the basis of prior decisions.

The outlawing of picketing for all purposes is permitted the State of Washington by the upholding of these broad decrees.   No distinction is made between what is legitimate picketing and what is abusive picketing.   "[H]ere we have no attempt by the state through its courts to restrict conduct justifiably found to be an abusive exercise of the right to picket."   Angelos case, 320 U.S. at page 295, 64 S. Ct. at page 127, 88 L. Ed. 58.

Because the decrees here are not directed at any abuse of picketing but at all picketing, I think to sustain them is contrary to our prior holdings, founded as they are in the doctrine that "peaceful picketing and truthful publicity" is protected by the constitutional guaranty of the right of free speech.   I recognize that picketing is more than speech.   That is why I think an abuse of picketing may lead to a forfeiture of the protection of free speech.   Tested by the philosophy of prior decisions, no such forfeiture is justified here.

I would reverse the judgments in these two cases.[87a]

NOTES

1. Could Hanke have complied with the Union's demands without violating any criminal statute or any public policy of the state?   Was there anything improper or unlawful about the Union's demand for fixed closing hours?   Under pre-Thornhill cases would such picketing have been enjoined as for an illegal purpose?   See Fraenkel, Peaceful Picketing — Constitutionally Protected?   99 U. of Pa. L. Rev. 1 (1950).

2. (a) If the Union placed a full-page advertisement in the Seattle newspapers urging Union members not to enter Hanke's premises, could the state court enjoin such an advertisement?

(b) Could the court enjoin the Union from placing Hanke on its ·black list and prohibiting Union members to deal with him?

(c) Could the court constitutionally enjoin the Union from passing handbills to all persons passing or entering Hanke's lot?

3. If Illinois now wishes to issue an injunction like that in the Swing case or New York wishes to issue ones like those in the Wohl and Angelos cases, may they now do so?

[87a] In Local Union No. 10 v. Graham, — U.S. — ,73 Sup. Ct. 585, — L. Ed. — (1953), the United States Supreme Court upheld an injunction by a Virginia court enjoining peaceful picketing when it was carried on for purposes in conflict with the Virginia Right to Work Statute. — ED.

4. Is the right to picket peacefully constitutionally protected in the following situations:

(a) Picketing by a Negro organization, of a restaurant which refuses to serve Negroes?

(b) Picketing by the Catholic War Veterans of a movie theatre showing "The Miracle," a picture personally obnoxious and sacrilegious to them?

(c) Picketing by the National Association for the Advancement of Colored People of a meeting held by Gerald L. K. Smith, an advocate of white supremacy?

(d) Picketing by Zionists of the British Embassy protesting the alleged supplying of arms by the British government to Arab armies fighting Israel?

(e) Picketing by Quakers of a federal court building in which a conscientious objector is being tried for advising other conscientious objectors not to register for the draft?

3. PICKETING UNDER FOREIGN LAW

In contrast to its significance in this country, picketing has not become an important subject of litigation in foreign countries.

German jurisprudence, after having first held conflicting views on the subject, is now agreed on the lawfulness of peaceful picketing during strikes. By peaceful picketing, it is meant that a very few pickets — for mass picketing would not be tolerated — do not go further than to try to convince — by means of fair persuasion — persons willing to work in the struck shop not to do so.[88] Accordingly, the stationing of a picket near the struck factory is allowed.[89] The same result is reached in the other free countries of Europe, particularly France, Austria, Belgium, Sweden,[90] and Norway, where, however, until 1947 even peaceful picketing was included under the prohibition of "boycott," over which a special "boycott court" sat in judgment.[91] However, picketing of customers of the employer is not lawful in any of these countries.

The fact that the plant is under strike and that the union believes that working men should refrain from taking jobs therein, is very frequently publicized in union papers as well as in the political dailies of the labor parties. Also the names of strikebreakers are frequently published in this fashion.

[88] Nipperdey, The Right to Strike, German Reports to the Third International Congress of Comparative Law 744, 765 (1950) (in German).

[89] Compare Sch. v. Schw. 76 R.G.Z. 35, 44 (1911) ; 34 R.G. Str. 12 (1903).

[90] Robbins, The Government of Labor Relations in Sweden 234 (1942).

[91] Galenson, Labor in Norway 128, 131 (1949). The 1947 Law exempted a blockade from the concept of unlawful boycott.

The Continental law on picketing differs from ours in two essential features.   One of these lies in the test applied for determining the illegality of picketing.   The other is found in the denial to the employer of the status of an aggrieved party.   No doubt there is legal logic in the connection between the two characteristics.   European labor law approaches the question of the legality of picketing from the standpoint of penal law rather than private law.   European law condemns picketing only when it constitutes a public offense.

In France, the 1864 amendment to the Penal Code (art. 414) dealing with "threats" and other attacks on freedom to work was at first read to penalize picketing as intimidation which might reasonably be deemed to influence a person to act against his will. Now, however, it provides that demands made upon organized employees not to work during a strike proclaimed by the organization are nôt unlawful in the absence of "displays, demonstrations or physical acts likely to cause a breach of the peace." [92]

Equally, in the view of the highest court of Sweden, a letter written by a union officer to a worker to the effect that the union had declared him a strikebreaker because of his refusal to stop working does not constitute a punishable "threat." [93]   The court did not find an offense in the posting near a struck factory of a public notice declaring everybody who did not quit, a strikebreaker.[94]   One has to realize that in Sweden, with its high percentage of organized workers and close interunion connections, the mere publication of the name of a strikebreaker is very effective.[95]

The highest court of France (Cour de Cassation), deeming jeers and insults by pickets to be "threats," has applied the criminal sanction of Article 414 of the Penal Code.[96]   It is all the more understandable that the French court has affirmed convictions under that article where the strikers had resorted to mass picketing.[97]   In other countries, such as Sweden and Norway, police regulations provide penalties against blocking of communications and other forms of disorderly conduct, and regulate the number of pickets.[98]

More than half a century ago — and forty years prior to the

[92] Cour de Cassation, 1932, quoted in Philip's article, Unionism in France, in Marquand, Organized Labour in Four Continents 35 (1939).

[93] See the decision (1910) in Robbins, op. cit. supra note 90, at 248.

[94] Id. at 248.

[95] Id. at 238.

[96] Cour de Cassation, 1930, Gaz. Pal. 1930. 1. 612.

[97] Rouast and Durand, Précis de législation industrielle, no. 222 (3d ed. 1948).

[98] Galenson, op. cit. supra note 91, at 117.

Thornhill decision of our Supreme Court — the highest court of Germany declared a police regulation of the city of Lübeck, penalizing picketing as such, to be invalid because of its violation of the constitutional guaranty of the "freedom to combine." [99] But German courts have sustained traffic ordinances regulating picketing. The highest German court has pointed out that the validity of a traffic regulation concerning picketing was not affected by the fact that its enforcement impeded pickets.[100]   A prosecution of pickets of course is in order if they have committed acts of coercion, force, and violence against persons or property of persons willing to work.[101]

As has been said, the second difference between our law and the Continental relates to the matter of parties to a proceeding for unlawful picketing.   The idea that the employer should be regarded as the "party" whose rights have been "injured" and that he is, on this ground, entitled to a civil action for damages — an idea deeply engrained in the American law of labor injunctions — is now rejected in Germany.   If there is any action [102] for violation of a legal right, it is a right of the persons willing to work, not that of the employer.[103]

E. Secondary Boycotts

1. INTRODUCTION

In preceding sections it has been indicated that the legality of union action depended upon both the objectives sought and the means used by the union to achieve those ends.   The section on Strikes was devoted primarily to an inquiry concerning the legality of various union objectives.   The section on Picketing emphasized the importance of the means used and its effect on the legality of the concerted action.

In so far as objectives and means can be separated, the secondary boycott also concerns itself primarily with means.   The core of meaning in the elusive term "secondary boycott" is probably the bringing of pressure against a neutral in order to exert pressure, indirectly, against the real adversary.   The immediate objective

[99] Reichsgericht 1900, 34 R.G. Str. 121; see also (1897) 31 R.G. Str. 185.

[100] Reichsgericht 1914, 14 Gewerbe Archiv 169 (1914).

[101] Stier-Somlo, Sicherheits- und Wohlfahrtspolizei, 5 Handwörterbuch der Rechtswissenschaft 452, 458 (1928).   Kaskel, Arbeitsrecht 440 (4th ed. 1932).

[102] For this ground of action in tort by German law, see the note on legality of concerted actions, page 745 supra.

[103] 2 Hueck and Nipperdey, Lehrbuch des Arbeitsrechts 587 (1930).   But see Reichsgericht 1911, 76 R.G.Z. 35, 46.

to induce the neutral to bring pressure against another becomes the means of bringing pressure against the other from whom the economic concessions are sought.

Secondary boycotts thus involve a new factor which affects the legality of concerted action — the point at which the union's economic pressure is applied. An accepted method of union pressure such as a strike, for a lawful objective such as higher wages, may be illegal because the strike is aimed at some employer not directly involved in the wage dispute. It is this factor of the directness or remoteness of the pressure which forms the core of this section.

Secondary boycotts may take a multitude of forms. A strike may be called against an employer who deals with someone with whom the union has a quarrel; or the refusal to work may take the more limited form of refusing to handle "unfair" goods coming from the adversary. Picket lines may be placed around employers who deal with the union's opponent, thereby inducing customers or workmen not to enter; or the picketing may be more restricted, merely urging customers at retail outlets not to purchase the unfair product being sold in the store. The single common factor is the exertion of economic pressure against one person in order to effect a secondary or indirect pressure against the one with whom the underlying dispute exists.

Distinguishing between primary and secondary pressure, however, is often very difficult. If a union includes "Babs Beer" on its "Do Not Patronize" list, this may reduce its sale in local taverns and induce them to cease buying the beer. Is this a secondary boycott? If striking retail employees picket their store it may induce other employees to refuse to work, induce customers not to buy, and induce employers of truckers not to make deliveries. Is the pressure exerted in this manner primary or secondary? Assuming that it is primary, if these persons are kept out not merely by peaceful picketing but by physical violence, by threat of picketing their homes or by threat of expulsion from their own unions, would any of these facts convert the pressure from primary to secondary?

The courts have not clarified the meaning of the term, for the judicial definition has been circular. Secondary boycotts are said to be illegal. Almost any form of pressure except the most direct, when thought to be illegal, may be termed a secondary boycott. Indirect pressure thought to be legal is declared not to be a secondary boycott. The term is a word of opprobrium to label that which the court finds illegal. Obviously, therefore.

the peacefulness of the means and the worthiness of the objective sought, as well as the judges' personal predilections, may vitally influence the label attached.

Secondary boycotts are not peculiar to labor disputes, for they are but an expression of men's tendency to grab and use whatever weapons may be effective. Politicians use the threat of withdrawal of patronage to obtain support for a legislative measure or a candidate; manufacturers give preferences to dealers who do not handle competitors' lines, and threaten to withhold their business if they do. Unions, in using the secondary boycott, are simply attempting to use for collective bargaining the full measure of their economic strength even though it is exerted at a point far removed from the point of actual dispute.

The problem of the secondary boycott involves an extremely difficult question which strikes close to the heart of free collective bargaining. Under free collective bargaining, the terms of employment are determined by the bargaining power of the parties, their relative economic strength. Secondary boycotts are a part of that economic power pattern. To curtail secondary boycotts is to deprive unions of one of their most important economic levers. How, under free collective bargaining, can this be justified? Have any equivalent weapons been taken from the employer?

Restrictions on secondary boycotts are frequently justified on the basis of protecting the innocent third person who is caught in the struggle between the employer and the union. Is this sufficient justification? Are not innocents frequently injured by the repercussions of labor disputes? Is this not one of the costs of free collective bargaining? Furthermore, is the one against whom the pressure is exerted completely innocent or completely neutral? How often does the union in a secondary boycott act from sheer "disinterested malevolence," to take Justice Holmes' phrase from American Bank v. Federal Reserve Bank, 256 U.S. 350, 358, 41 Sup. Ct. 499, 65 L. Ed. 983 (1921).

Although we accept the premise of free collective bargaining, it may not be necessary to accept all of its logical corollaries without qualification. Limits may be placed on the use of economic strength in order to soften the effects of disruption caused by labor disputes. Restrictions placed on secondary boycotts seek to confine the area of the dispute, limit it to the immediate parties. It is a quarantine to prevent the dispute from spreading to parties whose interest is more remote.

Under the color of conspiracy and prima facie tort theories, the courts did limit unions in some respects in their use of indirect pressure. The decisions are hopelessly conflicting. All than can be done here is to suggest some lines of distinction which have been drawn. The Labor Management Relations Act, in Sections 8 (b) (4) and 303, placed explicit limitations on secondary boycotts. Since these restrictions are applicable to all industries "affecting interstate commerce," they are of primary importance today.

2. COMMON LAW BACKGROUND

GOLDFINGER v. FEINTUCH
Court of Appeals, New York, 1937
276 N.Y. 281, 11 N.E.2d 910

FINCH, Judge.

W. & I. Blumenthal manufacture kosher meat products which are sold under the name of "Ukor." The "Ukor" products are the only nonunion-made kosher provisions sold in the city of New York, and the salaries paid by this company range from 50 to 75 cents an hour as compared with the union scale of 95 cents to $1.25 an hour. The defendant Butcher Union Local No. 174 endeavored to obtain a union agreement from the manufacturer of Ukor products. When these efforts were unsuccessful the defendant decided to picket the nonunion-made products at the retail stores. Among the stores picketed was that of the plaintiff, a dealer in kosher meat products. The defendant placed pickets, sometimes one, sometimes two, in front of the plaintiff's store, carrying signs which bore the inscription in English and Yiddish, "This store sells delicatessen that is made in a non-union factory," and "Ukor Provision Company is unfair to Union labor. Please buy Union-made delicatessen only."

The important question in this case is whether, assuming that there has been no violence, force, intimidation, breach of the peace, coercion, fraud, or unlawful threat the act of the defendant in thus picketing the delicatessen store of the plaintiff is legal. . . .

As between an employer and an employee the right of a union to picket peacefully is generally conceded. Its purpose must be to persuade, not to intimidate. So long as the pleas of both employer and employee are lawful the courts have not been constituted arbiters of the fairness, justice or wisdom of the terms demanded by either the employer or employees. J. H. & S. Theatres, Inc. v. Fay, 260 N.Y. 315, 183 N.E. 509. It is only where unlawful acts have been committed that the courts intervene to redress or prevent manifest abuse of the right to picket peacefully with a limited number of pickets. Nann v. Raimist, 255 N.Y. 307, 174 N.E. 690, 73 A.L.R. 669. Picketing is not peaceful where a large crowd gathers in mass formation or there is shouting or the use of loud-speakers in front of a picketed place of business, or the sidewalk or entrance is obstructed by parading around in a circle or lying on the sidewalk. Such actions are illegal, and are merely a form of intimidation. Likewise it is illegal to picket the place of business of one who is not himself a party to an industrial dispute to persuade the public to withdraw its patronage generally from the business for the purpose of coercing the owner to take sides in a controversy in which he has no interest. Nor is it legal to threaten to ruin the custom and trade generally or to accost or interfere with customers at the entrance to the store. Disorderly conduct, force, violence, or intimidation by pickets should be sternly suppressed by the police and administrative authorities.

Within the limits of peaceful picketing, however, picketing may be carried on not only against the manufacturer but against a nonunion product sold by one in unity of interest with the manufacturer who is in the same business for profit. Where a manufacturer pays less than union wages, both it and the retailers who sell its products are in a position to undersell competitors who pay the higher scale, and this may result in unfair reduction of the wages of union members. Concededly the defendant union would be entitled to picket peacefully the plant of the manufacturer. Where the manufacturer disposes of the product through retailers in unity of interest with it, unless the union may follow the product to the place where it is sold and peacefully ask the public to refrain from purchasing it, the union would be deprived of a fair and proper means of bringing its plea to the attention of the public.

An analogous principle has been applied by this court in Bossert v. Dhuy, 221 N.Y. 342, 117 N.E. 582, Ann. Cas. 1918D, 661; Willson & Adams Co. v. Pearce, 264 N.Y. 521, 191 N.E. 545, affirming 240 App. Div. 718, 265 N.Y.S. 624; and in New York Lumber Trade Assn. v. Lacey, 269 N.Y. 595, 199 N.E. 688. The cases of Auburn Draying Co. v. Wardell, 227 N.Y. 1, 124 N.E. 97, 6 A.L.R. 901, and George F. Stuhmer & Co. v. Korman, 241 App. Div. 702, 269 N.Y.S. 788, affirmed, 265 N.Y. 481, 193 N.E. 281, are not in point. . . .

We do not hold more than that where a retailer is in unity of interest with the manufacturer, the union may follow the nonunion goods and seek by peaceful picketing to persuade the consuming public to refrain from purchasing the nonunion product, whether that is at the plant of the manufacturer or at the store of the retailer in the same line of business and in unity of interest with the manufacturer. Such storekeeper may be, as in the case at bar, the sole person required to man his business. If Goldfinger, the delicatessen dealer, had employed any help, legally they could strike or refuse to work for him so long as he sold Ukor products. We have so held in Bossert v. Dhuy, supra. Such employees, having the right to refuse to work for the plaintiff, would likewise have the right to inform the public why they refused to work for the plaintiff. In this respect at least it has been settled that labor may aid its cause. If a union may request its members not to work upon or with materials bought from a nonunion shop or call a strike for such reasons, it is difficult to see why, under the law of this State, it may not peacefully state the grievance by placards similar to those used here. . . .

LEHMAN, Judge (concurring in part).

I agree that peaceful picketing of the plaintiff's place of business by the defendant union for the purpose of inducing the plaintiff's customers to refrain from buying nonunion products of a manufacturer, which are on sale by the plaintiff, is lawful. That is not a "secondary boycott." . . .

RIPPEY, Judge (concurring in part).

I concur in the result reached solely upon the ground that the trial court found upon sufficient evidence that there was complete unity of interest between the plaintiff and the manufacturer. Except for the finding of unity of interest, the facts would establish a secondary boycott and would be illegal. . . .

HUBBS, Judge (dissenting).

I dissent and vote to affirm upon the ground that even if defendant could generally, by publicity, urge people not to purchase the Ukor products, that does not permit the defendant to say to a dealer who does not employ help that they will ruin him and his business and to carry out that threat by picketing his place of business. That is a secondary boycott and I think it is illegal and against public policy. . . .

NOTES

1. In People v. Bellows, 281 N.Y. 67, 22 N.E.2d 238 (1939), the Union picketed a handbag shop which had installed a neon sign made by a company which employed members of a rival

union. The Court of Appeals, in affirming a conviction for disorderly conduct, stated that this was a secondary boycott and illegal because the shop-owner was a mere purchaser of the product and in no sense a party to the dispute. There was no "unity of interest" within the meaning of the Goldfinger case.

However, in People v. Muller, 286 N.Y. 281, 36 N.E.2d 206 (1941), the Union picketed a store which had a burglar alarm serviced by a company which employed nonunion service men. The Union demanded that the store have the alarm serviced by Union workers. The Court of Appeals reversed a conviction for disorderly conduct, holding that the picketing was for the purpose of promoting the lawful interest of the Union and was within the Goldfinger "unity of interest" test. Can these two cases be distinguished on their facts? Was the storekeeper any more neutral in one than the other? To what extent, in each case, was the storekeeper in a position to influence the outcome of the underlying dispute? Is the conduct enjoined though noncriminal?

2. In Back v. Kaufman, 175 Misc. 169, 22 N.Y.S.2d 449 (1940), the Union picketed a dentist's office because he used dental plates made in a nonunion laboratory. The court enjoined the picketing in spite of the state anti-injunction law on the grounds that there was no labor dispute. There was no unity of interest, said the court, because the dentist did not sell a product identified with the laboratory but one made specially for him to be used in his professional services. Accord, on same facts Brennan v. Eisen, 188 Misc. 672, 69 N.Y.S.2d 441 (1947); Tenzer v. Eisen, 104 N.Y.S.2d 561 (1951).

In Feldman v. Weiner, 173 Misc. 461, 17 N.Y.S.2d 730 (1940), the Union picketed a meat wholesaler because he sold his waste material to a nonunion processing plant. The court distinguished Goldfinger v. Feintuck and granted an injunction. Here a different business and only incidental revenue were involved. "To hold otherwise . . . would require a holding that a union-shop furniture manufacturer . . . who sold his products to many customers in different kinds of business, could be subjected to picketing because one of his vendees in an entirely different line of business was not itself unionized. In such cases no one could say that it was a nonunion product which was being picketed, or that identity of interest was present." Id. at 466. Accord, Missouri Cafeteria Inc. v. McVey, 242 S.W.2d 549 (Mo. Sup. Ct., 1951), in which a union was enjoined from threatening to strike a dairy if it continued to deliver milk to a nonunion restaurant.

In Scolaro Marble Co. v. Building Service Employees International Union, 107 N.Y.S.2d 12 (1951), the Union picketed a corporation engaged in marble-setting because one of its stockholders was also a stockholder in a building corporation which employed nonunion help.   The picket signs made clear that the quarrel was with the stockholder.   Held: Picketing is enjoined for lack of unity of interest.   The report does not indicate what percentage of stock this person owned in each corporation.   Would it make any difference?

Is the test applied in these cases one of neutrality?   Is the dentist completely neutral?   Is the meat wholesaler neutral or is he aiding the nonunion supplier?   Is the court placing the emphasis on following the product and allowing only product-picketing?   If so, then can a union ever picket a supplier in order to bring indirect pressure?   See generally, Gromfine, Labor's Use of Secondary Boycotts, 15 Geo. Wash. L. Rev. 327 (1947); 4 Restatement, Torts 799, 801, 808 (1939).

3. Compare the following cases:

The foundry workers of Allis-Chalmers Company struck.   The Company then sent castings to other foundries to have work done on them while its own employees were on strike.   Held: The calling of strikes and picketing at these other foundries would not be enjoined.   Iron Molders' Union v. Allis-Chalmers Co., 166 Fed. 45 (7th Cir. 1908).

Employees of Kingston Trap Rock Company represented by the Hod Carriers, were on strike but operations were continued with the aid of strikebreakers.   The Operating Engineers refused to allow its members to work at laying rock for an employer so long as he purchased rock from the Company.   Held: The strike by the Operating Engineers would not be enjoined.   Kingston Trap Rock Co. v. International Union of Operating Engineers, 129 N.J. Eq. 570, 19 A.2d 661 (1941).

The Typographical Union called a strike of all printing establishments in Seattle in order to obtain a 44-hour week.   The union also ordered its members to cease working for linotype firms which supplied type to the struck printing establishments.   The Union had no dispute over hours or wages with the linotype firms but only sought to cut off the supply of type to the printing companies.   Held: The strike of linotype firms would be enjoined. Pacific Typesetting Co. v. International Typographical Union, 125 Wash. 273, 216 Pac. 358 (1923).

Wright and Yonkers operated a market and employed Owen to handle the meat department.   The Meat Cutters Union demanded that Owen join the Union and abide by Union rules which included closing at 6 P.M.   When Wright and Yonkers refused, the Union picketed the market and solicited wholesalers of meat who were under contract with the Union to refuse to sell to the market.   Some complied with this request, and drivers for others (members of the Teamsters Union) refused to cross the picket line.   Held: Injunction would not issue.   Wright v. Teamsters, 33 Wash. 2d 905, 207 P.2d 662 (1949).

4. Compare also the three following New York cases:

The Carpenters ordered their members, under threat of fine or expulsion, to refuse to handle any material which was made by a nonunion employer or to work on any job where such material was used.   The plaintiff manufactured doors, sash, and other woodwork under an open shop.   He sought to enjoin the Union from enforcing this rule and thereby preventing potential customers from purchasing from him.   Held: Injunction denied.   Bossert v. Dhuy, 221 N.Y. 342, 117 N.E. 582 (1917).

The Teamsters sought to organize the employees of the Auburn Draying Company.   They persuaded the Auburn Central Labor Union, an association of all AFL unions in the city, to declare the Company unfair.   The members of all AFL unions were then ordered to cease working for any employer who continued to use the services of the Drying Company.   Held: Injunction granted.   Auburn Draying Co. v. Wardell, 227 N.Y. 1, 124 N.E. 97 (1919).

The plaintiff bought a house from a nonunion building contractor, built by him as part of a building development.   The Building Trades Council maintained a picket line across the only entrance to the development from the highway.   When the plaintiff tried to have his house connected with gas and electricity, the employees of the Long Island Lighting Company refused to cross the picket line because it would have resulted in their expulsion from their union.   The plaintiff sought to prohibit the unions from interfering with the installation.   Held: In spite of the plaintiff's position outside the labor dispute, and in spite of the Lighting Company's statutory duty to make the installation, this was in its essence a labor dispute and no injunction could issue because of the anti-injunction statute.   Schivera v. Long Island Lighting Co., 296 N.Y. 26, 69 N.E.2d 233 (1946).

5. The use of various boycott techniques might escape the restrictions of state judicial decisions and yet run afoul of the Sherman Act.

In the famous Danbury Hatters' Case (Loewe v. Lawlor) 208 U.S. 274, 28 Sup. Ct. 301, 52 L. Ed. 488 (1908), the Hatters, in support of a strike to unionize a hat manufacturer, called for a nation-wide boycott of the plaintiffs' hats. The AFL cooperated by urging all members not to buy these hats. The Court held that this was an illegal boycott under the Sherman Act and allowed the plaintiff to recover treble damages. Duplex Printing Press v. Deering, 254 U.S. 443, 41 Sup. Ct. 172, 65 L. Ed. 349 (1921), involved not a consumer boycott but a labor boycott. The Machinists, who were on strike against Duplex, ordered their members not to install or repair Duplex presses, and induced members of other unions to refuse to work for any employer handling Duplex presses. This was also held to be an illegal restraint of trade. Bedford Cut Stone Co. v. Journeymen Stone Cutters Assn., 274 U.S. 37, 47 Sup. Ct. 522, 71 L. Ed. 916 (1927), was similar to the Duplex case except that the boycott consisted simply of members of the Stone Cutters themselves refusing to work on stone produced by nonunion employers. This, too, was held unlawful under the Sherman Act.

These cases, however, were overturned by United States v. Hutcheson, 312 U.S. 219, 61 Sup. Ct. 463, 85 L. Ed. 788 (1941), which held that the Norris-LaGuardia Act freed unions from the strictures of the Sherman Act. In that case the Carpenters had a jurisdictional dispute with the Machinists over assignment of certain construction work being done for Anheuser-Busch. To enforce their demands, the Carpenters called a strike at Anheuser-Busch, picketed the plant, picketed an adjoining plant operated by a wholly independent company which rented the property from Anheuser-Busch, and urged all union members not to drink Anheuser-Busch beer. The United States Supreme Court held this was a labor dispute and not a violation of the antitrust laws.

However, if the union boycott is a part of a joint union-employer combination aimed at eliminating competitors, the union may still be subject to the antitrust laws. Local No. 3 of the IBEW combined with manufacturers of electrical equipment and contractors in New York City to control the New York market by refusing to deal with outsiders. The Court held that the Union lost its immunity when it acted in combination with business groups. Allen-Bradley Co. v. Local Union No. 3, IBEW, 325 U.S. 797, 65 Sup. Ct. 1533, 89 L. Ed. 1939 (1945). See also United Brotherhood of Carpenters & Joiners v. United States, 330 U.S. 395, 67 Sup. Ct. 775, 91 L. Ed. 973 (1947).

In Hunt v. Crumboch, 325 U.S. 821, 65 Sup. Ct. 1545, 89 L. Ed. 1954 (1945), the Teamsters had called a strike to compel all truckers hauling for A & P to join the Union. The plaintiff, a trucking partnership, continued hauling for A & P in spite of the strike. Violence occurred, a Union member was killed, and one of the partners was tried for murder but acquitted. The Teamsters finally won the closed-shop agreement with A & P but then refused to allow the partners to join and prevented them from hauling for A & P or any other unionized firm. The Court held that although the Union's conceded object was to drive the plaintiff out of business by means of a secondary boycott, there was no violation of the Sherman Act.

3. SECONDARY BOYCOTTS UNDER THE TAFT-HARTLEY ACT

DOUDS v. METROPOLITAN FEDERATION OF ARCHITECTS, ENGINEERS, CHEMISTS & TECHNICIANS, LOCAL 231
United States District Court, Southern District, New York, 1948
75 F. Supp. 672

[This was a petition brought by Charles T. Douds, Regional Director of the NLRB to enjoin the union from engaging in activities alleged to be in violation of Section 8 (b) (4) (A) of the Taft-Hartley Act.[104] The charge was filed by Project Engineering Company.

Ebasco Services, Inc., is a corporation which furnishes engineering services such as designing installations for public utilities. It had a contract with the Union which represented its workers. This expired on September 1, 1947. A new agreement was not reached and a strike against Ebasco began on September 5.

Project, organized quite independently of Ebasco, does the same kind of work as Ebasco. A year previous to the strike Ebasco began subcontracting some of its work to Project on a cost plus basis. At the time of the strike an appreciable portion of Project's work consisted of work sent to it by Ebasco. After the strike, this increased until Ebasco subcontracting represented 75 per cent of Project's work. Some work which had been begun by Ebasco employees before the strike was sent to Project for completion.

Under the subcontracting arrangement, Ebasco supervisors made regular visits to oversee the work. After the strike these visits to Project of supervisors who were not on strike became much more frequent, and working hours at Project increased. The Union asked Project to refuse to take work which had come

---

[104] The discussion of this provision in the cases that follow will be more readily understood if the student examines the analytical chart on page 802 infra. — ED.

"off the boards" at Ebasco. When this demand was refused, the Union began picketing Project.]

RIFKIN, District Judge. . . . One of the prohibitions of Section 8 (b) (4) (A) of the Act is: "It shall be an unfair labor practice for a labor organization . . . to . . . encourage the employees of any employer to engage in, a strike . . . where an object thereof is . . . requiring . . . any . . . person . . . to cease doing business with any other person."

Is Project "doing business" with Ebasco within the meaning of the Act? The term is not defined in the Act itself. Section 2, 29 U.S.C.A. §152, contains thirteen definitions, but none of doing business. The term itself has, of course, received a vast amount of judicial construction but always in a context so different that it is pointless to explore that field for help in construing the term in the present context. Nor is it possible to attach legal consequences to all the relationships which the dictionary meaning of the term embraces. So to do would destroy the Act by driving it to absurdity. To give such broad scope to the term would, for instance, reach out to and include the business relation between an employee of the primary employer (Ebasco) and the primary employer, or the business relationship between a primary employer and a professional supplier or strikebreakers. Certainly it is an object of very many strikes and picket lines to induce a reduction in the struck employer's business by an appeal to customers — "any person" — to cease dealing with the employer. This is one of the most conspicuous weapons employed in many labor disputes. The effect of a strike would be vastly attenuated if its appeals were limited to the employer's conscience. I shall proceed on the assumption, warranted by the history of the Act, that it was not the intent of Congress to ban such activity, although the words of the statute, given their broadest meaning, may seem to reach it. Moreover, such broad construction would probably run afoul of Section 13 of the Act, 29 U.S.C.A. §163, which reads: "Sec. 13. Nothing in this Act, except as specifically provided for herein, shall be construed so as either to interfere with or impede or diminish in any way the right to strike, or to affect the limitations or qualifications on that right."

To find the limitations to which "doing business" must be confined recourse may be had to the legislative history to discover the mischief which Congress intended to remedy. In describing the "necessity for legislation" the House Committee on Education and Labor reported, Report No. 245, pp. 4–5:

"The employers' plight has likewise not been happy. . . .

"His business on occasions has been virtually brought to a stand-still by disputes to which he himself was not a party and in which he himself had no interest."

The Senate Committee on Labor and Public Welfare reported the bill which it in part described thus, Report No. 105, p. 3: . . .

"Under paragraph (A) strikes or boycotts, or attempts to induce or encourage such action, are made violations of the Act if the purpose is to force an employer or other person to cease using, selling, handling, transporting, or otherwise dealing in the products of another, or to cease doing business with any other person. Thus, it would not be lawful for a union to engage in a strike against employer A for the purpose of forcing that employer to cease doing business with employer B; nor would it be lawful for a union to boycott employer A because employer A uses or otherwise deals in the goods of or does business with employer B (with whom the union has a dispute)." [Id. at 22.]

During the Congressional debates on the Bill, Senator Pepper objected to the provisions relating to the secondary boycott and stated an illustration in which he thought it would be unjust to apply them. Senator Taft, in reply, said: "I do not quite understand the case which the Senator has put. This provision makes it unlawful to resort to a secondary boycott to injure the business of a third person who is wholly unconcerned in the disagreement between an employer and his employees." (April 29, 1947, p. 4323 of the Congressional Record, Vol. 93.)

Examination of these expositions of Congressional purpose indicates that the provision was understood to outlaw what was theretofore known as a secondary boycott. It is to the history of the secondary boycott, therefore, that attention should be directed and it is in the light of that history that the term "doing business" should be evaluated. See Hellerstein, Secondary Boycotts in Labor Disputes, 1938, 47 Yale Law J. 341; Gromfine, Labor's Use of Secondary Boycotts, 1947, 15 Geo. Wash. Law Rev. 327.

When the term is read with the aid of the glossary provided by the law of secondary boycott it becomes quite clear that Project cannot claim to be a victim of that weapon in labor's arsenal. To suggest that Project had no interest in the dispute between Ebasco and its employees is to look at the form and remain blind to substance. In every meaningful sense it had made itself party to the contest. Manifestly it was not an innocent bystander, nor a neutral. It was firmly allied to Ebasco and it was its conduct as ally of Ebasco which directly provoked the union's action.

Significant is the unique character of the contract between

Ebasco and Project. Ebasco did not buy any articles of commerce from Project. Ebasco did not retain the professional services of Project. Ebasco "bought" from Project, in the words of the basic contract, "services of your designers and draftsmen . . . to work under the direction and supervision of the Purchaser." The purchase price consisted of the actual wages paid by Project plus a factor for overhead and profit. . . .

I am unable to hold that corporate ownership or insulation of legal interests between two businesses can be conclusive as to neutrality or disinterestedness in a labor dispute.

The evidence is abundant that Project's employees did work, which, but for the strike of Ebasco's employees, would have been done by Ebasco. The economic effect upon Ebasco's employees was precisely that which would flow from Ebasco's hiring strike-breakers to work on its own premises. The conduct of the union in inducing Project's employees to strike is not different in kind from its conduct in inducing Ebasco's employees to strike. If the latter is not amenable to judicial restraint, neither is the former. In encouraging a strike at Project the union was not extending its activity to a front remote from the immediate dispute but to one intimately and indeed inextricably united to it. See Bakery Drivers Local v. Wohl, 1942, 315 U.S. 769, 62 S. Ct. 816, 86 L. Ed. 1178; cf. Carpenters Union v. Ritter's Cafe, 1942, 315 U.S. 722, 62 S. Ct. 807, 86 L. Ed. 1143.

The nexus between the labor dispute and the firm picketed in the instant case is immeasurably closer than in the Ritter case where the injunction against picketing was upheld, or in the Wohl case where it was condemned. It must be apparent that a construction of the Act which outlaws the kind of union activity here involved would almost certainly cast grave doubts upon its constitutionality. It is preferable to interpret the disputed section so as to restrain only that kind of union activity which does not enjoy constitutional immunity.

The case at bar is not an instance of a secondary boycott.

For these reasons it is clear that there has been no violation of Section 8 (b) (4) (A) and the court is therefore without power to grant the requested relief. . . . Petition denied.

TAFT—HARTLEY ACT

Section 8(b)(4): It shall be an unfair labor practice for a labor organization or its agents:-
Section 303(a): It shall be unlawful..... for any labor organization:-

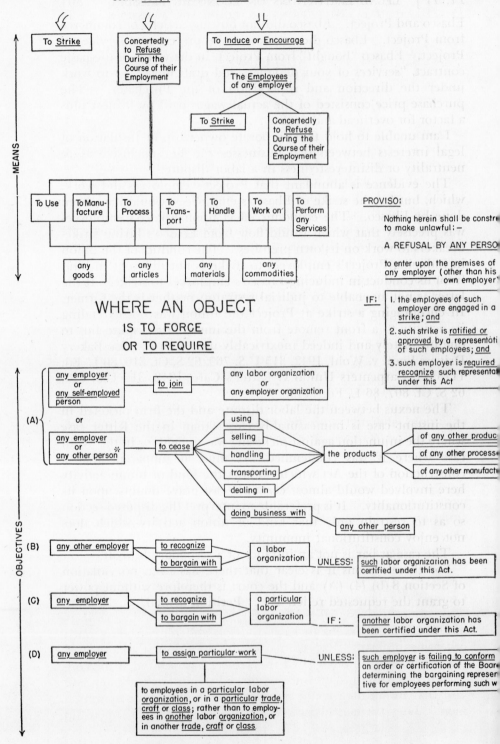

MEANS

To Strike

Concertedly to Refuse During the Course of their Employment

To Induce or Encourage

The Employees of any employer

To Strike

Concertedly to Refuse During the Course of their Employment

To Use | To Manufacture | To Process | To Transport | To Handle | To Work on | To Perform any Services

any goods | any articles | any materials | any commodities

PROVISO:

Nothing herein shall be constru
to make unlawful:—

A REFUSAL BY ANY PERSO

to enter upon the premises of
any employer (other than his
own employer

IF:
1. the employees of such employer are engaged in a strike; and
2. such strike is ratified or approved by a representati of such employees; and
3. such employer is required recognize such representat under this Act

WHERE AN OBJECT
IS TO FORCE
OR TO REQUIRE

OBJECTIVES

(A)

any employer or any self-employed person

to join → any labor organization or any employer organization

any employer or any other person *

to cease → using / selling / handling / transporting / dealing in → the products → of any other produc / of any other process / of any other manufact

doing business with → any other person

(B) any other employer → to recognize / to bargain with → a labor organization

UNLESS: such labor organization has been certified under this Act.

(C) any employer → to recognize / to bargain with → a particular labor organization

IF: another labor organization has been certified under this Act.

(D) any employer → to assign particular work

UNLESS: such employer is failing to conform an order or certification of the Boar determining the bargaining represen tive for employees performing such w

to employees in a particular labor organization, or in a particular trade, craft or class; rather than to employ- ees in another labor organization, or in another trade, craft or class

* second phrase evidently meaning: any other person who is a producer, etc.

NLRB v. DENVER BUILDING & CONSTRUCTION TRADES COUNCIL

Supreme Court of the United States, 1951
341 U.S. 675, 71 Sup. Ct. 943, 95 L. Ed. 1284

MR. JUSTICE BURTON delivered the opinion of the Court.

The principal question here is whether a labor organization committed an unfair labor practice, within the meaning of §8 (b) (4) (A) of the National Labor Relations Act, 49 Stat. 449, 29 U.S.C. §151, as amended by the Labor Management Relations Act, 1947; by engaging in a strike, an object of which was to force the general contractor on a construction project to terminate its contract with a certain subcontractor on that project. For the reasons hereafter stated, we hold that such an unfair labor practice was committed.

In September, 1947, Doose & Lintner was the general contractor for the construction of a commercial building in Denver, Colorado. It awarded a subcontract for electrical work on the building, in an estimated amount of $2,300 to Gould & Preisner, a firm which for 20 years had employed nonunion workmen on construction work in that city. The latter's employees proved to be the only nonunion workmen on the project. Those of the general contractor and of the other subcontractors were members of unions affiliated with the respondent Denver Building and Construction Trades Council (here called the Council). In November a representative of one of those unions told Gould that he did not see how the job could progress with Gould's nonunion men on it. Gould insisted that they would complete the electrical work unless bodily put off. The representative replied that the situation would be difficult for both Gould and Preisner and Doose & Lintner.

January 8, 1948, the Council's Board of Business Agents instructed the Council's representative "to place a picket on the job stating that the job was unfair" to it. In keeping with the Council's practice, each affiliate was notified of that decision. That notice was a signal in the nature of an order to the members of the affiliated unions to leave the job and remain away until otherwise ordered. Representatives of the Council and each of the respondent unions visited the project and reminded the contractor that Gould & Preisner employed nonunion workmen and said that union men could not work on the job with nonunion men. They further advised that if Gould & Preisner's men did work on the job, the Council and its affiliates would put a picket on it to notify their members that nonunion men were working on it and that the job was unfair. All parties stood their ground.

January 9, the Council posted a picket at the project carrying a placard stating "This Job Unfair to Denver Building and Construction Trades Council." He was paid by the Council and his picketing continued from January 9 through January 22. During that time the only persons who reported for work were the nonunion electricians of Gould & Preisner. January 22, before Gould & Preisner had completed its subcontract, the general contractor notified it to get off the job so that Doose and Lintner could continue with the project. January 23, the Council removed its picket and shortly thereafter the union employees resumed work on the project. Gould & Preisner protested this treatment but its workmen were denied entrance to the job.

On charges filed by Gould & Preisner, the Regional Director of the National Labor Relations Board issued the complaint in this case against the Council and the respondent unions. It alleged that they had engaged in a strike or had caused strike action to be taken on the project by employees of the general contractor and of other subcontractors, an object of which was to force the general contractor to cease doing business with Gould & Preisner on that project. . . .

III. The Secondary Boycott. — We now reach the merits. They require a study of the objectives of the strike and a determination whether the strike came within the definition of an unfair labor practice stated in §8 (b) (4) (A).

The language of that section which is here essential is as follows:

" (b) It shall be an unfair labor practice for a labor organization . . .

" (4) to engage in . . . a strike . . . where an object thereof is: (A) forcing or requiring . . . any employer or other person . . . to cease doing business with any other person; . . ." 61 Stat. 141, 29 U.S.C. (Supp. III) §158 (b) (4) (A).

While §8 (b) (4) does not expressly mention "primary" or "secondary" disputes, strikes or boycotts, that section often is referred to in the Act's legislative history as one of the Act's "secondary boycott sections." The other is §303, 61 Stat. 158, 29 U.S.C. (Supp. III) §187, which uses the same language in defining the basis for private actions for damages caused by these proscribed activities.

Senator Taft, who was the sponsor of the bill in the Senate and was the Chairman of the Senate Committee on Labor and Public Welfare in charge of the bill, said, in discussing this section:

". . . [U]nder the provisions of the Norris-LaGuardia Act, it became impossible to stop a secondary boycott or any other kind of a strike, no matter how unlawful it may have been at common law. All this provision of the bill does is to reverse the effect of the law as to secondary boycotts. It has been set forth that there are good secondary boycotts and bad secondary boycotts. Our committee heard evidence for weeks and never succeeded in having anyone tell us any difference between different kinds of secondary boycotts. So we have so broadened the provision dealing with secondary boycotts as to make them an unfair labor practice." 93 Cong. Rec. 4198. . . .

At the same time that §§7 and 13 safeguard collective bargaining, concerted activities and strikes between the primary parties to a labor dispute, §8 (b) (4) restricts a labor organization and its agents in the use of economic pressure where an object of it is to force an employer or other person to boycott someone else. . . .

In the background of the instant case there was a longstanding labor dispute between the Council and Gould & Preisner due to the latter's practice of employing nonunion workmen on construction jobs in Denver. The respondent labor organizations contend that they engaged in a primary dispute with Doose & Lintner alone, and that they sought simply to force Doose & Lintner to make the project an all-union job. If there had been no contract between Doose & Lintner and Gould & Preisner there might be substance in their contention that the dispute involved no boycott. If, for example, Doose & Lintner had been doing all the electrical work on this project through its own nonunion employees, it could have replaced them with union men and thus disposed of the dispute. However, the existence of the Gould & Preisner subcontract presented a materially different situation. The nonunion employees were employees of Gould & Preisner. The only way that respondents could attain their purpose was to force Gould & Preisner itself off the job. This, in turn, could be done only through Doose & Lintner's termination of Gould & Preisner's subcontract. The result is that the Council's strike, in order to attain its ultimate purpose, must have included among its objects that of forcing Doose & Lintner to terminate that subcontract. On that point, the Board adopted the following finding:

"That *an* object, if not the only object, of what transpired with respect to . . . Doose & Lintner was to force or require them to cease doing business with Gould & Preisner seems scarcely open to question, in view of all of the facts. And it is clear at least as to Doose & Lintner, that that purpose was achieved." (Emphasis supplied.)   82 N.L.R.B. at 1212.

We accept this crucial finding. It was an object of the strike to force the contractor to terminate Gould & Preisner's subcontract.

B.   We hold also that a strike with such an object was an unfair labor practice within the meaning of §8 (b) (4) (A).

It is not necessary to find that the sole object of the strike was that of forcing the contractor to terminate the subcontractor's contract. This is emphasized in the legislative history of the section. See also, Labor Board v. Wine, Liquor, & Distillery Workers Union, 178 F.2d 584, 586.

We agree with the Board also in its conclusion that the fact that the contractor and subcontractor were engaged on the same construction project, and that the contractor had some supervision over the subcontractor's work, did not eliminate the status of each as an independent contractor or make the employees of one the employees of the other. The business relationship between independent contractors is too well established in the law to be overridden without clear language doing so. The Board found that the relationship between Doose & Lintner and Gould & Preisner was one of "doing business" and we find no adequate reason for upsetting that conclusion.

Finally, §8 (c) safeguarding freedom of speech has no significant application to the picket's placard in this case. Section 8 (c) does not apply to a mere signal by a labor organization to its members, or to the members of its affiliates, to engage in an unfair labor practice such as a strike proscribed by §8 (b) (4) (A). That the placard was merely such a signal, tantamount to a direction to strike, was found by the Board.

". . . The issues in this case turn upon acts by labor organizations which are tantamount to directions and instructions to their members to engage in strike action. The protection afforded by Section 8 (c) of the Act to the expression of 'any views, argument or opinion' does not pertain where, as here, the issues raised under Section 8 (b) (4) (A) turn on official directions or instructions to a union's own members."   82 N.L.R.B. at 1213.

The further conclusion that §8 (c) does not immunize action against the specific provisions of §8 (b) (4) (A) has been announced in other cases. See No. 108, International Brotherhood of Electrical Workers v. Labor Board, post, p. 694.

Mr. Justice Jackson would affirm the judgment of the Court of Appeals.

Mr. Justice Douglas, with whom Mr. Justice Reed joins, dissenting.

The employment of union and nonunion men on the same job is a basic protest in trade union history. That was the protest here. The union was not out to destroy the contractor because of his antiunion attitude. The union was not pursuing the contractor to other jobs. All the union asked was that union men not be compelled to work alongside nonunion men on the same job. As Judge Rifkind stated in an analogous case, "the union was not extending its activity to a front remote from the immediate dispute but to one intimately and indeed inextricably united to it."

The picketing would undoubtedly have been legal if there had been no subcontractor involved — if the general contractor had put nonunion men on the job. The presence of a subcontractor does not alter one whit the realities of the situation; the protest of the union is precisely the same. In each the union was trying to protect the job on which union men were employed. If that is forbidden, the Taft-Hartley Act makes the right to strike, guaranteed by §13, dependent on fortuitous business arrangements that have no significance so far as the evils of the secondary boycott are concerned. I would give scope to both §8 (b) (4) and §13 by reading the restrictions of §8 (b) (4) to reach the case where an industrial dispute spreads from the job to another front.

NOTES

1. At the same time, the Supreme Court handed down three other decisions in cases involving secondary boycotts. In each, Justices Reed, Douglas, and Jackson dissented. In Local 74, United Brotherhood of Carpenters v. NLRB, 341 U.S. 707, 71 Sup. Ct. 966, 95 L. Ed. 1309 (1951), a property owner engaged in remodeling had contracted with a union contractor to do the carpentry work and with a nonunion contractor to install wall and floor coverings. When this was discovered the business agent of the Carpenters Union ordered all union carpenters off the job. The Union argued that the main object was not to bring pressure on the property owner but merely to enforce the Union's long-established rule of refusing to work on a job with nonunion workers. The Court held this violated Section 8 (b) (4), for it was enough if "one of the objects" of the concerted action is to force the property owner to cease doing business with the nonunion employer.

2. In International Brotherhood of Electrical Workers v. NLRB, 341 U.S. 694, 71 Sup. Ct. 954, 95 L. Ed. 1299 (1951), the effect of Section 8 (c) was more sharply in issue. Giorgi, the general contractor engaged in building a private dwelling, subcontracted the electrical work to Langer, who employed nonunion electricians. The business agent of the Electrical Workers picketed the premises, and the carpenters refused to cross the picket line. There was no evidence that the Carpenters Union ordered a strike, but the workers were merely induced not to work by the picketing. The Court in upholding the Board's finding of a violation of Section 8 (b) (4) said at page 703:

> c. To exempt peaceful picketing from the reach of § (b) (4) would be to open the door to the customary means of enlisting the support of employees to bring economic pressure to bear on their employer. The Board quickly recognized that to do so would be destructive of the purpose of § (b) (4) (A). It said "To find that peaceful picketing was not thereby proscribed would be to impute to Congress an incongruous intent to permit, through indirection, the accomplishment of an objective which it forbade to be accomplished directly." United Brotherhood of Carpenters, 81 N.L.R.B. 802, 811. Also —
>
> "It was the *objective* of the unions' secondary activities . . . and not the *quality of the means* employed to accomplish that objective, which was the dominant factor motivating Congress in enacting that provision. . . . In these circumstances to construe Section 8 (b) (4) (A) as qualified by Section 8 (c) would practically vitiate its underlying purpose and amount to imputing to Congress an unrealistic approach to the problem." (Emphasis in original.) Id., at 812.
>
> The legislative history does not sustain a congressional purpose to outlaw secondary boycotts under § (b) (4) and yet in effect to sanction them under §8 (c).
>
> d. We find no indication that Congress thought that the kind of picketing and related conduct which was used in this case to induce or encourage a strike for an unlawful object was any less objectionable than engaging directly in that strike. The court below, after finding that there was "bare instigation" here rather than an appeal to reason by "the expressing of any views, argument, or opinion," traced the development of the doctrine that he who provokes or instigates a wrong makes himself a party to it. That court then reached

the conclusion that it is "highly unlikely that by §8 (c) Congress meant to abolish a doctrine, so deeply embedded in our civil and criminal law." 181 F.2d at 39.

e. The remedial function of §8 (c) is to protect noncoercive speech by employer and labor organization alike in furtherance of a lawful object. It serves that purpose adequately without extending its protection to speech or picketing in furtherance of unfair labor practices such as are defined in §8 (b) (4). The general terms of §8 (c) appropriately give way to the specific provisions of §8 (b) (4).

5. The prohibition of inducement or encouragement of secondary pressure by §8 (b) (4) (A) carries no unconstitutional abridgement of free speech. The inducement or encouragement in the instant case took the form of picketing followed by a telephone call emphasizing its purpose. The constitutionality of §8 (b) (4) (A) is here questioned only as to its possible relation to the freedom of speech guaranteed by the First Amendment. This provision has been sustained by several Courts of Appeals. The substantive evil condemned by Congress in §8 (b) (4) is the secondary boycott and we recently have recognized the constitutional right of states to proscribe picketing in furtherance of comparably unlawful objectives. There is no reason why Congress may not do likewise.

3. In the third case, NLRB v. International Rice Milling Co., 341 U.S. 665, 71 Sup. Ct. 961, 95 L. Ed. 1277 (1950), the Supreme Court found no violation of Section 8 (b) (4). The Teamsters, in an attempt to organize the Kaplan Rice Mills, established a picket line outside the plant. Two employees of Sales & Service House, a Kaplan customer, came to the mill in a truck to obtain rice. The pickets stopped the truck and told the two men on it the plant was on strike and they would have to go back. They did so, but later proceeded to the mill by a short detour. When the pickets saw this they ran toward the truck and threw stones at it. The Court conceded that the object of the Union's conduct was to force neutral customers to cease doing business with Kaplan for the purpose of exerting pressure on Kaplan. It refused to find a violation, however, saying at page 670:

A sufficient answer to this claimed violation of the section is that the union's picketing and its encouragement of the men on the truck did not amount to such an inducement or encouragement to "concerted" activity as the section proscribes.   While each case must be considered in the light of its surrounding circumstances, yet the applicable proscriptions of §8 (b) (4) are expressly limited to the inducement or encouragement of *concerted* conduct by the employees of the neutral employer. . . .   There were no inducements or encouragements applied elsewhere than on the picket line. The limitation of the complaint to an incident in the geographically restricted area near the mill is significant, although not necessarily conclusive.   The picketing was directed at the Kaplan employees and at their employer in a manner traditional in labor disputes . . .   A union's inducements or encouragements reaching individual employees of neutral employers only as they happen to approach the picketed place of business generally are not aimed at concerted, as distinguished from individual, conduct by such employees.   Generally, therefore, such actions do not come within the proscription of §8 (b) (4) , and they do not here.

On the question of the use of violence, the Court stated at page 672:

In the instant case the violence on the picket line is not material.   The complaint was not based upon that violence, as such.   To reach it, the complaint more properly would have relied upon §8 (b) (1) (A) or would have addressed itself to local authorities.   The substitution of violent coercion in place of peaceful persuasion would not in itself bring the complained-of conduct into conflict with §8 (b) (4) .   It is the object of union encouragement that is proscribed by that section, rather than the means adopted to make it felt.

For a helpful analysis of these cases, see Koretz, Federal Regulation of Secondary Strikes and Boycotts. 37 Cornell L.Q. 235 (1952) .

In re SAILORS' UNION OF THE PACAFIC and MOORE DRY DOCK COMPANY
National Labor Relations Board, 1950
92 N.L.R.B. 547, 27 L.R.R.M. 1108

[Samsoc, a Greek-owned shipping company made a contract with Kaiser Gypsum to carry gypsum from Mexico in the Samsoc ship Phopho. This meant replacement of an American crew for the Greek ship with a Greek crew. To convert the Phopho for this job, it was placed in the Moore Dry Dock Company shipyard. Moore Dry Dock agreed that two weeks before completion Samsoc could put its crew on board for training purposes. In January, 1950, while the boat was in the shipyard, the Union learned of the arrangement. It demanded bargaining rights on the ship, but on February 16, this demand was refused. On the next day it placed pickets at the entrance to the shipyard. The Union also informed the bargaining representatives of Moore's employees that the Phopho was "hot" and requested cooperation. On February 21 all of Moore's employees refused to work on the Phopho, but continued on other work.]

Section 8 (b) (4) (A) is aimed at secondary boycotts and secondary strike activities. It was not intended to proscribe primary action by a union having a legitimate labor dispute with an employer. Picketing at the premises of a primary employer is traditionally recognized as primary action, even though it is "necessarily designed to induce and encourage third persons to cease doing business with the picketed employer . . ."

Hence, if Samsoc, the owner of the S.S. Phopho, had had a dock of its own in California to which the Phopho had been tied up while undergoing conversion by Moore Dry Dock employees, picketing by the Respondent at the dock site would unquestionably have constituted *primary* action even though the Respondent might have expected that the picketing would be more effective in persuading Moore employees not to work on the ship than to persuade the seamen aboard the Phopho to quit that vessel. The difficulty in the present case arises therefore, not because of any difference in picketing objectives, but from the fact that the Phopho was not tied up at its own dock, but at that of Moore, while the picketing was going on in front of the Moore premises.

In the usual case, the *situs* of a labor dispute is the premises of the primary employer. Picketing of the premises is also picketing of the *situs;* the test of legality of picketing is that enunciated by the Board in the Pure Oil and Ryan Construction cases. But in some cases the *situs* of the dispute may not be limited to a fixed location; it may be ambulatory. Thus in the Schultz case, a majority of the Board held that the truck upon which a truck driver worked was the *situs* of a labor dispute between him and the owner of the truck. Similarly, we hold in the present case that, as the Phopho was the place of employment of the seamen, it was the *situs* of the dispute between Samsoc and the Respondent over working conditions aboard that vessel.

When the *situs* is ambulatory, it may come to rest temporarily at the premises of another employer. The perplexing question is: Does the right to picket follow the *situs* while it is stationed at the premises of a secondary employer, when the only way to picket that *situs* is in front of the secondary employer's premises? Admittedly, no easy answer is possible. Essentially the problem is one of balancing the right of a union to picket at the site of its dispute as against the right of a secondary employer to be free from picketing in a controversy in which it is not directly involved.

When a secondary employer is harboring the *situs* of a dispute between a union and a primary employer, the right of neither the union to picket nor of the secondary employer to be free from picketing can be absolute. The enmeshing of premises and *situs* qualifies both rights. In the kind of situation that exists in this case, we believe that picketing of the premises of a secondary employer is primary if it meets the following conditions: (a) The picketing is strictly limited to times when the *situs* of dispute is located on the secondary employer's premises; (b) at the time of the picketing the primary employer is engaged in its normal business at the *situs;* (c) the picketing is limited to places reasonably close to the location of the *situs;* and (d) the picketing discloses clearly that the dispute is with the primary employer. All these conditions were met in the present case.

(a) During the entire period of the picketing the Phopho was tied up at a dock in the Moore shipyard.

(b) Under its contract with Samsoc, Moore agreed to permit the former to put a crew on board the Phopho for training purposes during the last 2 weeks before the vessel's delivery to Samsoc. At the time the picketing started on February 17, 1950, 90 per cent of the conversion job had been completed, practically the entire crew had been hired, the ship's oil bunkers had been filled, and other stores were shortly to be put aboard. The various members of the crew commenced work as soon as they reported aboard the Phopho. Those in the deck compartment did painting and cleaning up; those in the steward's department, cooking and cleaning up; and those in the engine department, oiling and cleaning up. The crew were thus getting the ship ready for sea. They were on board to serve the purposes of Samsoc, the Phopho's owners, and not Moore. The normal business of a ship does not only begin with its departure on a scheduled voyage. The multitudinous steps of preparation, including hiring and training a crew and putting stores aboard, are as much a part of the normal business of a ship as the voyage itself. We find, therefore, that the Phopho was engaged in its normal business.

(c) Before placing its pickets outside the entrance to the Moore shipyard, the Respondent Union asked, but was refused, permission to place its pickets at the dock where the Phopho was tied up. The Respondent, therefore, posted its pickets at the yard entrance which, as the parties stipulated, was as close to the Phopho as they could get under the circumstances.

(d) Finally, by its picketing and other conduct the Respondent was scrupulously careful to indicate that its dispute was solely with the primary employer, the owners of the Phopho. Thus the signs carried by the pickets said only that the Phopho was unfair to the Respondent. The Phopho and not Moore was declared "hot." Similarly, in asking cooperation of other unions, the Respondent clearly revealed that its dispute was with the Phopho. Finally, Moore's own witnesses admitted that no attempt was made to interfere with other work in progress in the Moore yard.

We believe that our dissenting colleagues' expressions of alarm are based on a misunderstanding of our decision. We are not holding, as the dissenters seem to think, that a union which has a dispute with a shipowner over working conditions of seamen aboard a ship may lawfully picket the premises of an independent shipyard to which the shipowner has delivered his vessel for overhaul and repair. We are only holding that, if a shipyard permits the owner of a vessel to use its dock for the purpose of readying and training a crew and putting stores aboard ship, a union representing seamen may then, within the careful limitations laid down in this decision, lawfully picket the front of the shipyard premises to advertise its dispute with the shipowner. . . .

NOTES

1. This case was decided before the Supreme Court decisions were handed down in the four cases previously mentioned. Are

the tests set forth here still valid?   See NLRB v. Service Trade Chauffeurs, Salesmen & Helpers, 191 F.2d 65 (2d Cir. 1951).

2. The Electrical Workers (CIO) called a strike against Bucyrus.   At the time an addition was being built to the Bucyrus plant, the work being done by Ryan Construction Company. When the strike began, a special gate into the plant was made for the Ryan employees.   The Union, however, picketed not only the regular gates where Bucyrus employees entered but also the gate where only Ryan employees entered.   The Ryan employees refused to cross the picket line.   Held: This was merely a picketing of Bucyrus premises and was therefore primary.   It did not "enlarge the economic battleground beyond the premises of the primary employer."   Matter of Ryan Construction Company, 85 N.L.R.B. 417, 24 L.R.R.M. 1424 (1949).

Compare, however, Matter of Richfield Oil Company, 95 N.L.R.B. 1191, 28 L.R.R.M. 1436 (1951).   The Union attempted to organize Superior Tank Company which was installing oil well equipment, at Richfield wells.   The Union placed pickets at the entrance to the Richfield wells with placards saying, "Superior Tank Company Unfair."   The pickets stopped all trucks delivering equipment and urged them not to enter although they were delivering to Richfield and not to Superior.   Held: In spite of the signs the picketing was designed to carry far beyond Superior alone.   This does not fall within the rules of the Moore Drydock case, as no effort was made here to confine the force of picketing to the primary employer.   It was designed to force Richfield to cease doing business with Superior and violates Section 8 (b) (4) (A).

3. The problem of the situs of the dispute becomes particularly difficult where the employer is operating trucks.   In Matter of Schultz Refrigerated Service, Inc., 87 N.L.R.B. 502, 25 L.R.R.M. 1122 (1949), the Board held that where the Union pickets trailed the trucks, and walked around the trucks every time they stopped to load or unload, it was engaged in primary and not secondary activity.   It did not become secondary merely because the employees of another employer then refused to handle the goods being hauled.   On Matter of Sterling Beverages Inc., 90 N.L.R.B. 401, 26 L.R.R.M. 1213 (1950), however, where the pickets marched at the plant gate leading to the platform and started 15 minutes before the primary employer's trucks arrived or remained 15 minutes after they left, the picketing was held to be secondary and illegal.   See also Matter of Howland Dry Goods Co., 97 N.L.R.B. No. 24, 29 L.R.R.M. 1064 (1951).   How much

difference will it make to an employer whether the picketing is at the entrance or around the truck?

If the primary employer were a manufacturer who delivered his product in his own trucks, could the union on strike at the factory trail and picket the trucks? See United Construction Workers, 94 N.L.R.B. 1731, 28 L.R.R.M. 1257 (1951).

4. In the building trades it is a customary union rule that union members must refuse to work on any material or equipment which is produced with nonunion labor or does not carry the union label. If union carpenters working for a union contractor refuse to install doors made by a nonunion mill, do they violate Section 8 (b) (4)? Will it make any difference if the mill is at that time on strike or being picketed to compel recognition? See Douds v. Sheet Metal Workers Union, 101 F. Supp. 273 (E.D.N.Y. 1951).

5. In Matter of Conway's Express, 87 N.L.R.B. 972, 25 L.R.R.M. 1202 (1949), affirmed, Conway's Express v. NLRB, 195 F.2d 906 (2d Cir. 1952), the Teamsters had obtained an area-wide agreement with motor carriers providing that only union drivers should be permitted to drive trucks leased by a carrier to any other employer. The contract further provided that the Union could order its members not to handle for their own employer freight of any other employer engaged in a labor dispute. Conway leased trucks to Middle Atlantic Transportation, Inc., which did not employ union members. The Union called a strike of all Conway employees, and ordered all of its members working for other employers bound by the contract to refuse to handle Conway freight. The Board held that the strike was not secondary because it was not aimed at Atlantic but was in furtherance of a primary dispute with Conway over the violation of a valid collective agreement. Nor was the refusal by Union members working for other employers to handle Conway freight in violation of the Act. These secondary employers had, in effect, consented in advance to the boycott. As they had so consented, the failure to handle Conway freight was not, in a literal sense, a "strike" or "refusal to work." The contracts were not in violation of the Act. The Board said at page 982:

> Section 8 (b) (4) (A) of the Act prohibits *labor organizations* from "forcing or requiring" the participation of neutral employers in secondary boycotts by the use of certain forms of employee pressure, namely, strikes or work stoppages (either actually engaged in, or "induced" or "encouraged" by

the union). This section does not proscribe other means by which unions may induce employers to aid them in effectuating secondary boycotts; much less does it prohibit *employers* from refusing to deal with other persons, whether because they desire to assist a labor organization in the protection of its working standards or for any other reason. . . .

The Union also approached supervisors of other carriers and requested them to refuse Conway freight. This was held not to violate Section 8 (b) (4) because it prohibits inducing or encouraging "employees" to engage in concerted activities. Under Section 2 (3) supervisors are not "employees." Therefore, inducing or encouraging them to act was not within Section 8 (b) (4).

6. Are union "Unfair Lists" outlawed by Section 8 (b) (4)? Compare the following situations. The Building Trades Council lists a general contractor unfair because he employs nonunion workers, or because he deals with nonunion subcontractors? Lists an electrical subcontractor unfair because he employs nonunion workers? Lists a beer company unfair because it had construction done by nonunion workers? The Bar Tenders lists a nonunion tavern unfair? Lists a nonunion beer company unfair? The Bar Tenders Union induces the Building Trades Council to list a tavern unfair because it sells nonunion beer? See Hoover Company v. NLRB, 191 F.2d 380 (6th Cir. 1951); Matter of Grauman Co., 87 N.L.R.B. 755, 25 L.R.R.M. 1168 (1949); Matter of Kimsey Manufacturing Co., 89 N.L.R.B. 1168, 26 L.R.R.M. 1073 (1950).

7. If a textile mill refused to recognize or bargain with a union which had been certified as the majority representative of the Board, could the union call a strike at all clothing factories using any material produced by the mill?

4. BOYCOTTS UNDER FOREIGN LAW

What has been said about the legality of concerted pressure in a previous note (page 744 supra) applies to boycotts. The leniency of European law toward labor boycotts, in contrast to the severity of American law, is more consistent with its attitude toward boycotts practiced by businessmen against their competitors.[105] Our restraint-of-trade concept is part of traditional law; its counterpart, if any, abroad, is of recent vintage. German, French, Swiss,

[105] See, e.g., Swiss Federal Court (1936), B.G.E. 62 II 97 (threat of trade association to boycott nonmember competitor P if P would not comply with anti-price-cut program, held, not unlawful).

and Swedish courts — to mention important examples — have expressed their view that "in business life, the free play of economic forces is an essential ingredient of the present legal and economic system" and that the same rule must control all economic disputes, whether commercial boycotts or labor boycotts; harm done by such boycotts, being inherent in the system, is not actionable.[106]

On this theory, the French highest court has held that strikers, in protecting their own economic interest, are allowed to proclaim a labor boycott against the employer (*mettre un patron à l'index*).[107] Likewise, the court dismissed an employer's action brought against the owner of a restaurant in whose window the teamsters' union had hung a request that teamsters should not ask for employment in plaintiff's shop.[108] As a consequence of their general theory of labor disputes, no essential distinction is made by the German, Swiss, and Swedish courts between consumer boycotts and labor boycotts. Even the emphasis laid in recent legislation of this country upon the distinction between "primary" and "secondary" boycotts is less discernible abroad.

Thus, Germany's highest court has found no legal fault with the customer boycott proclaimed in an economic strike by a bakers' union against certain bakery owners; the boycott was carried out through leaflets and advertisements calling upon workers not to buy the plaintiff's bread.[109] Equally, a boycott advising workers not to patronize a certain restaurant whose owner was a party to a labor dispute has been sustained.[110] But compare Gompers v. Buck's Stove Co., 221 U.S. 418, 31 Sup. Ct. 492, 55 L. Ed. 797 (1911), and Seattle Brewing Co. v. Hansen, 144 Fed. 1011 C.C.N.D. Calif. (1905) in our own country.

A good illustration of the Swiss approach to secondary boycotts is supplied in the following case. An intense competitive fight had been waged by bakery owners organized in a local association against a traveling food store company. The plaintiff, an outsider, supplied that company with all bakery products by under-

---

[106] Swiss Federal Court 1906, B.G.E. 32 II 360. German Supreme Court: V. et al. v. A et al., 1906, 64 R.G.Z. 53. French Court of Cassation, 1905, D. 1905. 1 153; Dame Veuve Boivu v. Syndicate Général, etc., Trib. Civ. de la Seine, 1929, D. H. 1930, 437. For Swedish cases, see Robbins, The Government of Labor Relations in Sweden 238, 264 (1942).

[107] See the decisions in 2 Planiol, Traité élémentaire de droit civil 290 n.3 (9th ed. 1923).

[108] Bloch v. Mallon, Sirey Rec. 1934. 1. 96.

[109] V. et al. v. A. et al., 1906, 64 R.G.Z. 53.

[110] L. et al. v. S., 1907, 66 R.G.Z. 379 (unlawful for other reasons: fraudulent statements). However, French courts have shown some aversion toward a customer boycott. Cour d'Appel, 1933, Gaz. Pal. 1933. 1. 969.

cutting the prices charged by all the association members. As a result, the company sold the products to the public at lower prices than the bakers. The association thereupon resorted to various forms of boycotts against the plaintiff in order to induce him to stop supplying the company. One of the measures consisted in threatening two of the plaintiff's employees with black-listing by the national association of Swiss bakery owners. As one can see, two secondary boycotts were interwoven in the dispute: one was directed against the plaintiff, and the other against two of his employees. The court disapproved the former boycott but did not consider the latter objectionable from the legal standpoint. Concerning the former, the court pointed out that a distinction must be made between competitive devices which aim at winning over a competitor's customer on the one hand, and actions directed at the elimination of such a customer on the other, because this conduct goes beyond competition and is therefore violative of moral standards. However, the other secondary boycott — putting pressure on the plaintiff's employees without inducing a breach of contract — was regarded as being within the allowable area of competition.[111]

The Swedish collective contract statute of 1928 permits "secondary boycotts" declared in aid of others — even during the term of a collective contract — provided that the primary dispute is not unlawful.[112] In the absence of such a statutory provision, foreign courts have held that a boycott is unlawful if called by a union against employers during the term of a collective contract made with the employer's association. This result is derived from the "peace obligation" — discussed at page 420 supra — and is not affected by the fact that the boycott was intended to induce performance of a contractual term.[113]

In the note on legality of concerted actions, found at page 742 supra, there are guides that apply to the law of boycott. But a few aspects of illegality are significant only for boycotts. One is the requisite of exhaustion of all other sanctions of a less severe nature than boycott, before recourse can be had to the latter. (Compare the exhaustion principle established in international law for the resort to pacific blockades.) For legal systems such as those of Sweden, Norway, and Switzerland, which forbid recourse to economic warfare without previous warning, notice,

---

[111] Reich v. B. et al., 1931, B.G.E. 57 II 334.
[112] Collective Contract Act of June 22, 1928, Svensk Fflg. 1928 no. 253, sec. 4 (4); Robbins, op. cit. supra note 106, at 264.
[113] Swiss Federal Court 1943, B.G.E. 69 II 82, 86.

cooling-off period, conciliation, and participation in mediation, the exhaustion of such preliminary measures is required by statute. Germany's highest courts and the French courts arrive at the same result tentatively by what might be termed "judicial experimentation." [114]   Another is the requirement that a boycott must not be out of proportion to the objective of the dispute.   Black-listing of an unorganized worker by a union which virtually controls all jobs in the trade has been regarded as unlawful in Germany, France, Norway, and Switzerland.[115]   Where the loss occasioned by the primary dispute is far less than that imposed by the boycott, then the boycott is unlawful.[116]   It is interesting to note that this principle of balance of equities is familiar to us in labor injunctions and is an express requirement of the Norris-LaGuardia Act (Sec. 7 (c)).

Even prior to the post-war era, marked by the creation of constitutional guaranties for the right to combine, the black-listing of a worker by a whole group of employers — because of his organizational activities — was regarded as proving a shocking lack of a due sense of proportion; the group, therefore, was held liable for damages to the worker.[117]   In many countries, for example in Sweden, Norway, and Denmark, prohibitory laws to this effect have been enacted.[118]   Where the black-listing is for reasons other than organizational activities, it might still be illegal because of the disproportion between its ruinous effect upon his economic existence and the small advantage to the employers from such a boy-

[114] Germany. Supreme Court, Juristische Wochenschrift 1930, p. 410; Supreme Labor Court 1928, 5 Bensh. Slg. 253; 1927, 2 Bensh. Slg. 217. France: Trib. Civ. de la Seine, 1948, Gaz. Pal. 1948. 2. 20; 2 Hueck and Nipperdey, Lehrbuch des Arbeitsrechts 588 (1930). The new French law introducing compulsory conciliation (1950) has been discussed at page 279 supra.

[115] Germany: Supreme Court, Juristische Wochenschrift 1927, p. 2895; id. 104 R.G.Z. 327 (1922); Switzerland: Federal Court 1925, B.G.E. 51 II 532. France: Fédération des Journaux Français v. F. Coty and Société Nationale d'Editions, Cour d'Appel, Paris, 1930, Gaz. Pal. 1930. 1. 928. For previous decisions, see Josserand, De l'Esprit des droits: Théorie dite de l'abus des droits 224 (1927). For Norway, see Boycott Act 1933 in Galenson, Labor in Norway 125 (1949).

[116] Kaskel, Arbeitsrecht, 442 (4th ed. 1932).

[117] Germany: Supreme Court 1904, 57 R.G.Z. 414; Austria: Supreme Court 1905, Gl.U.N.F. 3097; 1915, Gl.U.N.F. 7453.

[118] For Sweden see Robbins, op. cit. supra note 106, at 294 (violation of statutory "right of association"); for Norway see Galenson op. cit. supra note 115, at 126; for Denmark see Act of 1929 (no. 70, sec. 3): "Every kind of economic or personal persecution (including boycott) which aims at unlawfully restricting a person's freedom to engage in business or employment or his or her right to join or to refrain from joining an organization shall be unlawful and punishable by a fine . . ." Where the boycott remains within the limits indicated by the reasonable self-interest of the combination, no action for damages will lie.

cott. The Austrian Supreme Court formerly denied damages to an employee against his former employer,[119] but in a later case it allowed recovery, although the black-listing was done by the defendant employer in compliance with the terms of a cartel agreement — a term which the court held to be invalid — requiring notification to all members of the cartel.[120] By Norwegian law, a boycott is unlawful when it might impair essential public interests or operate unreasonably.[121]

F. *Union Restraint, Coercion, and Discrimination*

NLRB, 15TH ANNUAL REPORT 126–133 (1950)[122]

RESTRAINT OR COERCION OF EMPLOYEES

Section 8 (b) (1) (A) of the act makes it an unfair labor practice for a labor organization or its agents — to restrain or coerce employees in the exercise of the rights guaranteed in section 7 . . .

In determining violations of section 8 (b) (1) (A) during the past year, the Board continued to construe the terms "restraint" and "coercion" by limiting their application to "situations involving actual or threatened economic reprisals and physical violence by unions or their agents against specific individuals or groups of individuals in an effort to compel them to join a union or to cooperate in a union's strike activities."

a. Violence and Threats of Violence

The question whether conduct amounts to unlawful restraint or coercion frequently arises in connection with strike activities. The types of conduct which were found to violate section 8 (b) (1) (A) included: assaults and batteries on nonstriking employees; stoning, threats of physical violence; and erecting barriers to plant entrances during picketing. On the other hand, the Board found that the following strike activities did not come within the statutory proscription: picketing in substantial numbers — up to 100 — in the absence of actual restraint or force; preventing, without violence, supervisory and managerial per-

---

[119] Austrian Supreme Court 1907, Gl.U.N.F. 4040.
[120] Id. 1915, Gl.U.N.F. 7453. But see, contra: State Court, Prague, 1906, Labor Court Reports No. 1240 (employer exonerated from any liability on the grounds of his compliance with bylaws forcing him to denounce name of discharged employee to association).
[121] Galenson, op. cit. supra note 115, at 125.
[122] See also NLRB, 16th Ann. Rep. 206–212 (1951). — Ed.

sonnel from entering the plant where no rank-and-file employees were present; a union practice of following the employer's trucks to delivery points where the trailing union members did not threaten or intimidate the truck drivers; picket-line activities such as calling nonstrikers "finks" and "scabs" and engaging in "horseplay" such as locking the employer's gate but unlocking it when requested to do so.

b. Threats of Economic Reprisal

Union conduct not connected with strikes was held violative of section 8 (b) (1) (A) where it was found to have been reasonably calculated to coerce employees in maintaining or refraining from acquiring union membership. Thus, the Board found coercion where a union agent, in the presence of an employee, told an employer that the employee could not work until he had paid his union dues, and where the union agent then warned the employee, "You know the union is stronger than you. You cannot fight a union and win." The Board similarly held coercive: a speech in front of an employer's store informing the audience that the union intended to organize the store and "that wives and children of employees had better stay out of the way if they didn't want to get hurt"; a union president's warning to rival union supporters not to come to work, accompanied by such threats as that there would be "trouble out there, guns, knives, and blackjacks"; assaults and batteries on nonunion employees during an organizational campaign; and a union official's remark to an employee, in the course of an organizational drive, that "there may be trouble later" if the employees refused to sign a dues checkoff authorization.

In Pinkerton's National Detective Agency, Inc., the Board found that section 8 (b) (1) (A) was violated by a union which, in the absence of a valid union-security agreement, (1) addressed letters to employees calculated to coerce them to retain their union membership; (2) threatened an employee with loss of work unless he joined the union or paid union dues; and (3) engaged in a strike for the primary purpose of compelling the employer to discriminate against employees who failed to maintain membership in good standing in the union.

The Board had occasion during the past year to reaffirm its conclusion in the NMU case that "restraint" and "coercion" within the meaning of section 8 (b) (1) (A) are not automatically present where other subsections of 8 (b) are violated. Thus, the Board held in the ITU cases that union conduct which contravened section 8 sub-sections (b) (2) and (b) (3) was not *per se* violative of 8 (b) (1) (A). In the Di Giorgio case, 8 (b) (4) (A) secondary boycott activities were similarly held not to come within the prohibition of section 8 (b) (1) (A).

However, in several cases, the Board ruled that conduct which violated section 8 (b) (2) also constituted restraint or coercion of employees in violation of 8 (b) (1) (A). Section 8 (b) (2) forbids a labor organization to "cause or attempt to cause" an employer to discriminate against employees because of their union membership or lack of it except under a valid union-shop agreement. . . .

c. Union Rules on Membership

The Board also was called upon to construe the proviso to section 8 (b) (1) (A) which safeguards "the right of a labor organization to prescribe its own rules with respect to the acquisition or retention of membership therein." Thus the proviso in the Board's view, was unmistakably intended to, and did, remove the application of a union's membership rules to its members from the proscriptions of Section 8 (b) (1) (A), irrespective of any ulterior reasons motivating the union's application of such rules or the direct effect thereof on particular employees.

Consequently the Board held in the ITU–ANPA case that the union, whose rules permitted the summary expulsion of members, did not violate section 8 (b) (1) (A) by threatening to expel members who failed to cooperate in enforcing an unlawful "Collective Bargaining Policy." The Board rejected the contention that "coercion" in the statutory sense was present because the threatened expulsion of members would result in their loss of "certain economic perquisites of the union-membership relation." . . .[123]

CAUSING OR ATTEMPTING TO CAUSE AN EMPLOYER
TO DISCRIMINATE AGAINST EMPLOYEES

Section 8 (b) (2) of the act makes it an unfair labor practice for a labor organization or its agents: to cause or attempt to cause an employer to discriminate against an employee in violation of sub-

---

[123] Section 8 (b) (1) (B) prohibits unions from interfering with the free association of employers. Would it be an unfair labor practice for the Teamsters to use their economic pressure to compel one trucking firm to bargain with an association rather than individually? If employers form an association, is it an unfair labor practice for the union to insist on individual bargaining and call a strike against only one of the members of the association to compel it to deal separately? See NLRB, 16th Ann. Rep. 212 (1951). — ED.

section (a) (3) or to discriminate against an employee with respect to whom membership in such organization has been denied or terminated on some ground other than his failure to tender the periodic dues and the initiation fees uniformly required as a condition of acquiring or retaining membership. . . .

In general the Board has held that the insistence by a labor organization upon a closed shop or hiring preference for union members or an illegal union shop violates section 8 (b) (2) . This applies also to a hiring hall arrangement which, although nondiscriminatory on its face, is operated in a discriminatory manner. Insistence upon such illegal union-security devices amounts to an "attempt to cause" discrimination in violation of the statute even though no employee actually suffers discrimination.

Agreeing to an illegal union-security provision also constitutes a violation of section 8 (b) (2) . The insistence upon the discharge, demotion, or discipline of any individual employee in violation of section 8 (a) (3) , of course, is also a violation of this section.

In those cases in which unions were alleged to have violated section 8 (b) (2) by causing unlawful discrimination and the respective employers were charged with the violation of section 8 (a) (3) , the Board was primarily concerned with the question whether or not the actions of the unions and employers involved were justified by validly existing union-security agreements. . . .

The most conspicuous cases in which the Board, during the past year, found that unions *attempted* to cause discrimination against employees in violation of section 8 (b) (2) were the ITU cases. In these cases, the union insisted upon the acceptance by the employers of unilaterally determined "Conditions of Employment" or alternately a "60-day contract," each of which had the effect of compelling the employers to maintain noncontractual closed-shop conditions and, in violation of section 8 (a) (3) , discriminatorily to exclude nonunion men from employment "by the use of a continuing threat to strike."

In one of these cases, the Board reiterated its previous conclusion that a violation of section 8 (b) (2) may be found even though there is no "showing that particular employees were the actual or intended objects of a discriminatory scheme."

G. *Union Responsibility for Acts of Officers and Members*

Section 6 of the Norris-LaGuardia Act provides: "No officer or member of any association or organization, and no association

or organization participating or interested in a labor dispute, shall
be held responsible or liable in any court of the United States for
the unlawful acts of individual officers, members, or agents, except
upon clear proof of actual participation in, or actual authorization
of, such acts, or of ratification of such acts after actual knowledge
thereof."

In United Brotherhood of Carpenters and Joiners v. United
States, 330 U.S. 395, 67 Sup. Ct. 775, 91 L. Ed. 973 (1947), San
Francisco locals of the Carpenters had made agreements with local
manufacturers and dealers in lumber and millwork to exclude
materials coming from outside the area. The international union
and the local unions were convicted of violating the Sherman Act.
The violation, under the rule announced in Allen-Bradley v.
Local 3, page 670 supra, was clear. The issue was whether the instructions to the jury relating to the responsibility of the international union for the contracts made the locals were proper.
The Court, in holding the instructions improper said at page 403:

> We need not determine whether §6 should be called a rule
> of evidence or one that changes the substantive law of agency.
> We hold that its purpose and effect was to relieve organiza-
> tions, whether of labor or capital, and members of those or-
> ganizations from liability for damages or imputation of guilt
> for lawless acts done in labor disputes by some individual
> officers or members of the organization, without clear proof
> that the organization or member charged with responsibility
> for the offense actually participated, gave prior authorization,
> or ratified such acts after actual knowledge of their perpetra-
> tion.
>
> Thus §6 limited responsibility for acts of a co-conspirator
> — a matter of moment to the advocates of the bill. Before
> the enactment of §6, when a conspiracy between labor unions
> and their members, prohibited under the Sherman Act, was
> established, a widely publicized case had held both the unions
> and their members liable for all overt acts of their co-con-
> spirators. This liability resulted whether the members or
> the unions approved of the acts or not or whether or not the
> acts were offenses under the criminal law. While of course
> participants in a conspiracy that is covered by §6 are not
> immunized from responsibility for authorized acts in further-
> ance of such a conspiracy, they now are protected against
> liability for unauthorized illegal acts of other participants in
> the conspiracy. . . . We hold, therefore, that "authoriza-

tion" as used in §6 means something different from corporate criminal responsibility for the acts of officers and agents in the course or scope of employment. We are of the opinion that the requirement of "authorization" restricts the responsibility or liability in labor disputes of employer or employee associations, organizations or their members for unlawful acts of the officers or members of those associations or organizations, although such officers or members are acting within the scope of their general authority as such officers or members, to those associations, organizations or their officers or members who actually participate in the unlawful acts, except upon clear proof that the particular act charged, or acts generally of that type and quality, had been expressly authorized, or necessarily followed from a granted authority, by the association or non-participating member sought to be charged or was subsequently ratified by such association, organization or member after actual knowledge of its occurrence. . . .

The facts in another case, United States v. Brotherhood of Railroad Trainmen, 96 F. Supp. 428 (N.D. Ill. 1951), shows that the Government had seized the railroads on September, 1950, because the Brotherhood of Railroad Trainmen threatened to strike in order to obtain a pay increase. No settlement was reached, and on December 13, the Trainmen in the Chicago yards suffered mass sickness and the Chicago yards were without yardmen. The Government obtained an injunction, but the sickness spread to other cities. The Union claimed the stoppage was unauthorized. President Kennedy sent telegrams to the chairmen of local lodges stating "the unauthorized stoppages must cease forthwith." However, the Union was cited for contempt and fined $25,000. Judge Igoe, in imposing the fine, said at page 431:

As long as the Union is functioning as a Union it must be held responsible for the mass actions of its members. That means this, that when the members go out and act in a concerted fashion and do an illegal act the Union is responsible. They just can't say, "Oh, well, we didn't do that as Union members." . . .

Now, from the way the testimony went on here and from the way this Union functions, these officers — I won't say they were afraid to work or to discharge their duties, but I will be very charitable and I will say that they would be very much embarrassed if they carried out literally all of the provisions of your constitution and filed charges against these members who participated in this illegal work stoppage. That thing, perhaps, would not work out from a human standpoint at all. They didn't do it, and they didn't do it because of — well, just because they were men and they were working alongside of the other men and they simply were not going to file charges against them.

That meant that the Union, in effect, practically approved everything these fellows were doing and they approved it up until the time that action was taken of a definite nature and the men returned to work.

What test of union responsibility is being applied in this case? Why does not the Norris-LaGuardia Act apply?

Section 2 (13) of the Taft-Hartley Act provides: "In determining whether any person is acting as an 'agent' of another person so as to make such other person responsible for his acts, the question of whether the specific acts performed were actually authorized or subsequently ratified shall not be controlling." See also Section 301 (e).

Matter of INTERNATIONAL LONGSHOREMEN'S AND WAREHOUSEMEN'S UNION and SUNSET LINE AND TWINE COMPANY
National Labor Relations Board, 1948
79 N.L.R.B. 1487, 23 L.R.R.M. 1001

. . . We have found that, on various occasions described in the foregoing sections of this opinion, certain acts of restraint and coercion, within the purview of Section 8 (b) (1) (A) of the Act, were committed. The actors were Vail and Lynch, officers of Local 6, assisted on some occasions by striking employees of the Company, other members of the Respondent Unions, regularly detailed pickets, and unidentified persons. None of these individuals is named in the complaint as a respondent. Therefore, the only question before us is whether or not the conduct of these individuals can properly be imputed to one or both of the Respondent Unions, for, unless the record justifies that imputation, there was no violation of the Act in this case. In determining whether or not the evidence does afford a basis for holding the Unions responsible for the episodes in question, the Board has a clear statutory mandate to apply the "ordinary law of agency." The Act, as amended, envisages that the Board shall now hold labor organizations responsible for conduct of their agents which is proscribed by Section 8 (b) of the statute, just as it has always held employers responsible for the acts of their agents which were violative of Section 8 (a). For this purpose we are to treat labor organizations as legal entities, like corporations, which act, and can only act, through their duly appointed agents, as distinguished from their individual members. Hence, our task of determining the responsibility of unions in cases arising under Section 8 (b) of the Act is not essentially new, for the Board has been deciding similar questions in cases involving corporate employers, ever since the statute was enacted in 1935. The fact patterns in Section 8 (b) cases, however, are a novel study in the administration of the Act. We have rarely had occasion to examine the relationships between a labor organization and its officers or other persons allegedly representing it, especially for the purpose of deciding whether or not the officer or other person was acting, in a particular instance, as the agent of the labor organization. Because this is a case of first impression in that sense, we shall set forth, in abstract, those fundamental rules of the law of agency which we believe must control our decision of the issue of responsibility in this and similar cases:

1. The burden of proof is on the party asserting an agency relationship, both as to the existence of the relationship and as to the nature and extent of the agent's authority. In this case, for example, it was incumbent upon the General Counsel to prove, not only that the acts of restraint and coercion alleged in the complaint were committed, but also that those acts were committed by agents of the Respondent Unions, acting in their representative capacity. The Respondents' failure to introduce evidence negating the imputations in the complaint did not relieve the General Counsel of that burden.

2. Agency is a *contractual relationship,* deriving from the mutual consent of principal and agent that the agent shall act for the principal. But the principal's consent, technically called authorization or ratification, may be manifested by conduct, sometimes even passive acquiescence as well as by words. Authority to act as agent in a given manner will be implied whenever the conduct of the principal is such as to show that he actually intended to confer that authority.

3. A principal may be responsible for the act of his agent within the scope of the agent's general authority, or the "scope of his employment" if the agent is a servant, even though the principal has not specifically authorized or indeed may have specifically forbidden the act in question. It is enough if the principal actually

empowered the agent to represent him in the general area within which the agent acted.

In the light of these principles, we shall consider, first, the question of the responsibility of Local 6 and its Petaluma Unit for the several acts of restraint and coercion previously discussed. Vail, an officer of Local 6, figured prominently in most of these episodes, and his role in the conduct of the strike is significant. . . .

Vail has been a business agent of Local 6 for 11 years. . . . The record does not otherwise show how Vail's duties are defined, or what are the limitations of his authority; but neither is there any evidence to rebut the inference, which we might well draw from his title alone, that he was, at the time of the events involved in this case, vested with the powers of a general agent to conduct the Local's business in the Petaluma area. That business consisted, necessarily, of collective bargaining and concerted activities of the membership in furtherance of the Local's objectives in collective bargaining. The strike against the Company in this case was, in that sense, the Local's business. All Vail's actions and conduct reflected in the record indicate that he was the officer of Local 6 who assumed immediate charge of the strike. It was Vail who conducted the bargaining negotiations with the Company both before and after the strike commenced. He conducted the meeting of Local 6 which was held on the eve of the strike; and on August 25, the day the strike began, he addressed a meeting of the strikers and called upon them to serve on the picket line. On that same day, near the plant, he assigned pickets to their posts; thereafter he was frequently seen on the picket line or near the Company's premises apparently directing the activities of the pickets. He was described in the October 31 issue of the Union's official newspaper as the "leader" of the "picket line" and we find that that was his authorized role.

Vail's authority certainly encompassed the planning and direction of lawful activities on the part of the strikers and their sympathizers, such as peaceful picketing, in furtherance of the general purposes of the strike, namely, to hamper or stop the Company's operations at this plant by withdrawal of its labor force, and, of course, to dissuade employees from working so long as the strike was current. It follows that the Local was responsible for the wrongful acts of Vail and individuals under his direction which were performed in furtherance of those same purposes and were of the same general character as, or incidental to, the peaceful picketing, and substantially within the area of this labor dispute in space and time. Of course, the record is barren of evidence showing that Local 6 specifically authorized or ratified Vail's assault on Sousa, for example, but the absence of such proof is immaterial so long as there is evidence that Vail was on that occasion acting within the scope of his general authority to direct this strike and picketing. . . .

. . . On October 10, Vice-President Lynch actively participated in obstructing the ingress of employees. As in the case of Vail, we have no evidence in the record precisely defining Lynch's relationship to Local 6. However, taking cognizance of the customary practices of labor organizations, we can and do infer, in the absence of evidence to the contrary, that, as the first vice president of the Local, Lynch was duly authorized to assist in the conduct of this strike and picketing. We infer that he, like Vail, was authorized to instruct and order the pickets how to conduct themselves. On October 10, Lynch himself was the first man on the picket line to obstruct a car. We find that this act of restraint, designed to further the general purposes of the strike, was the act of Local 6. Under the circumstances, it is immaterial that the pickets who obstructed Simmons' car on October 10, were unidentified. Whoever they were, they were following the pattern set by Lynch a few moments before, and by Vail on the preceding day. We find that Local 6 was responsible for the misconduct of these unidentified pickets on October 10. . . .

We turn, finally, to the question whether or not the International respondent, as well as its Local 6, is responsible for the various acts of restraint and coercion which we have imputed to the Local. We find that it is so responsible.

The record shows the following facts concerning the International's role in the events involved in this case. In the answer to the complaint, the International joined with the Local in alleging affirmatively that it had conducted the strike and picketing against the Company, in the course of which, as we have found, the statutory rights of non-striking employees were infringed. Both Respondents, answering jointly, averred that their strike and picketing at Petaluma was conducted for the lawful purpose of protecting the interests of *their* members, the Company's employees, and compelling the Company to bargain with the respondent Unions — both of them. . . .

. . . The article in the International's official newspaper . . . shows that the episode of October 15 was reported to the International, and that its Regional Director Halling was assigned to "guide" Vail in the conduct of the picketing. Other evidence shows that Halling, like Vail, was present on October 15 when the crowd at the plant gate, among whom were regularly detailed pickets, forcibly blocked the ingress of employees. Like Vail, Halling apparently made no effort on that occasion to stop the violence, which the Local's First Vice-President Lynch was actively inciting.

Thus, it appears from this record that the International was the co-sponsor with its Local of this strike and picketing, conducted for the purpose of gaining a common objective; that the International's Regional Director, who was authorized to render "guidance" in the conduct of the picketing, specifically ratified the most violent episode which occurred on the picket line; and that the International in no way disavowed the misconduct of the Local's officers, Vail and Lynch, on other occasions. We find, therefore, that Vail and Lynch, in directing the picketing activities, were at all times acting on behalf of the International as well as Local 6. . . .

NOTES

1. The union is not responsible per se for the conduct of its members on the picket line although it established the picket line. Membership is not sufficient alone to show agency. Matter of Irwin-Lyons Lumber Company, 87 N.L.R.B. 54 (1949). The illegal conduct must be traced to an officer or some other person who is acting within the scope of his general authority. See Matter of Howland Dry Goods Company, 85 N.L.R.B. 1037, 24 L.R.R.M. 1513 (1949); Matter of Gammino Construction Company, 97 N.L.R.B. No. 52, 29 L.R.R.M. 1103 (1951). Will the union be liable if officers are present when the violence occurs but exercise no leadership and do not themselves engage in violence? See Matter of United Mine Workers, 95 N.L.R.B. 546, 28 L.R.R.M. 1353 (1951). What if the union officials systematically absent themselves from the picket line during change of shift when violence is most likely to occur? See Jaffee v. Newspaper Deliverer's Union, 97 F. Supp. 443 (S.D.N.Y. 1951).

2. To what extent is the international union responsible for the illegal conduct of a local union? Will the international be responsible only through the acts of its officers, who actively participate in the illegal conduct, or will it be liable if it knows of the local's conduct and does not reprimand or discipline it? See Matter of West Kentucky Coal Company, 92 N.L.R.B. 916, 27 L.R.R.M. 1183 (1950). Matter of Chicago Typographical Union

No. 16, 86 N.L.R.B. 1041, 25 L.R.R.M. 1010 (1949); NLRB v. Acme Mattress Company, 192 F.2d 524 (7th Cir. 1951).

3. On responsbility of unions see three excellent student notes, 36 Cornell L.Q. 752 (1951); 63 Harv. L. Rev. 1035 (1950); 16 U. of Chi. L. Rev. 575 (1949).

NOTE ON RESPONSIBILITY OF LABOR ORGANIZATIONS ABROAD FOR CONCERTED ACTION

The French law considers professional organizations (*syndicats professionels*) as corporate entities.[124] The liability of such an organization, e.g., a trade-union, is, therefore, to be distinguished from that of the individual members. The union, like any other corporation, is liable for wrongful acts committed by its officers and employees. Whether or not those acts were expressly authorized, the corporate liability arises when the damage is caused by corporate officers or employees while performing their functions. A strike call given by the secretary of the union in violation of the peace obligation, or his order for a mass picketing, makes the union liable and the fact that the secretary acted without express authority or instructions, or even in complete disregard of them is no defense,[125] provided the giving of such notices is within the scope of his functions. However, the Labor Code of February 11, 1950, released unions from a statutory guaranty of compliance with the collective contract by their members, previously required by a 1946 act. Accordingly, unless the union assumes such a guaranty in the contract, it is not liable for breach of the peace obligation by its members, acting without express or implied advice of the union.[126] But a defamatory attack in a union paper upon an employer or a discharge of an unorganized employee on demand of a union representative, will entitle the employer, and the employee, respectively, to recover from the union.[127] There is no limit set to the amount of damages.

German labor unions would be similarly liable if they were corporate entities. However, one of the principal reasons — there are also others [128] — why German unions have resisted incorporation is that in this way they are able to restrict their lia-

[124] Labor Code, bk. III, tit. I, c. II, art. 10. Rouast and Durand, Précis de législation industrielle, no. 158 (3d ed. 1948).
[125] See the decision in Sirey Rec. 1922. 1. 147. This is derived from art. 1384 of the Civil Code.
[126] Labor Code (as amended by Law of February 11, 1950, J. O. 1688), bk. I, tit. II, c. IV bis, art. 31.
[127] 2 Planiol, Traité élémentaire de droit civil, no. 88 (9th ed. 1923).
[128] Nipperdey, Koalitionsrecht, in 3 Grundrechte 390, n. 16 (1930).

bility for unlawful concerted actions. This is because the laws of Germany, of Switzerland, and of all the countries which succeeded to the erstwhile Habsburg Empire, have not followed the Anglo-American theory of the liability without personal culpability, of a principal for the tortious conduct of his agents and employees while acting in the scope of their employment.[129] In those countries, however, incorporated bodies are subject to general liability for injuries caused by their "corporate organs," that is, the persons who hold representative positions provided for by the corporate constitution and bylaws. But otherwise, principals — corporate and individual alike — are not accountable for wrongful acts of their employees or agents if they used due care in the selection of them or if, though they failed to use such care, the damage would have occurred in any case.[130] Consequently, if a German trade-union is not incorporated, it is not subject to general liability for acts of its representatives appointed or elected according to its constitution and bylaws. This is no different from the non-liability of a principal for wrongful conduct of employees and agents, as discussed above. If, for instance, the union (by majority vote) should pass a strike resolution and appoint a strike committee, no liability for tortious acts committed by the latter or by pickets chosen by the latter would be incurred by the union, provided the committee was chosen with due care.[131] Naturally, the union is liable for acts expressly authorized by the majority of members; the liability, then, is no longer vicarious, for the union is now considered as itself acting rather than acting through its agents.[132] Equally, the individual actors are accountable for their own acts.

The remedies which are available to a complainant vary in the several legal systems:

(a) The remedy of a money recovery for loss caused by the wrongful act is common to all of them. Swedish and Norwegian laws provide, however, for a reduction in the amount of damages by giving the labor courts ample discretion in this regard. The Swedish Act of September 11, 1936, allows such a reduction "if this appears reasonable in view of the slight degree of culpability of the person who has caused the loss, the situation of the person who

[129] Lenhoff, Proceedings, IV Conference on Training of Law Students in Labor Relations 1189, 1196 (1947).

[130] Civil Code, sec. 31, 831 (1); Enneccerus, Lehrbuch des bürgerlichen Rechts 315 (13th ed. 1931).

[131] Hueck and Nipperdey, 2 Lehrbuch des Arbeitsrechts 591 (1930).

[132] Reichsgericht 1926 (April 29), 6 Neue Zeitschrift für Arbeitsrecht 703 (1926).

has suffered loss in respect of the occurrence of the dispute, the extent of the loss in proportion to the means of the person who had caused it, or other circumstances." Complete exemption from liability to pay damages may also be granted.[133] By German law, the employer may, in an action against industrial employees, choose between full damages (including profits prevented by the tortious act) — the burden of proving them is, then, on him — or a claim for liquidated damages, fixed by law at the amount of the usual day's pay for every day of stoppage; if he chooses the latter, he is relieved of proof of any actual damage.[134] Also, French decisions and Swiss statutory law leave it to the discretion of the court — as a general principle not restricted to labor disputes — to reduce damages by taking into consideration the respective economic situation of both parties.[135] The Swedish acts of 1928 and 1936 provide: "If two or more persons are responsible for the loss, the liability to pay damages shall be divided among them in proportion to the degree of culpability established against each."

(b) The German, Austrian, and Swiss law has developed an action to direct the defendant to refrain from certain conduct, for instance, from continuing a boycott where such conduct is unlawful and is likely to continue unless stopped by judgment (*Unterlassungsklage*).[136] Such an action is comparable to our injunction. Even an injunction *pendente lite* can be granted in a particularly dangerous situation.[137] In contrast to this country, courts are very rarely faced with proceedings for permanent injunctive relief and even less with those for provisional injunctions. Once a judicial prohibition is decreed, it is enforceable by fine and arrest.[138]

In Sweden, the labor statute of 1936 (no. 506) enjoins either party to a dispute, even in the absence of a collective contract, from hostile action during a period, fixed in the act for official

---

[133] See Act, 1928 (no. 253), sec. 8; Act, 1936 (no. 506), sec. 23. The Norwegian Act of August 6, 1915, sec. 5, gives the Labor Court similar equitable discretion in reducing damages.

[134] Industrial Code, sec. 124 b.

[135] Swiss Code of Obligations, art. 44 (2) ; Ripert, Réparation du préjudice, no. 95 (1933).

[136] Rabel, Die Grundzüge des Rechts der unerlaubten Handlungen, Deutsche Landesreferate zum Internationalen Kongress für Rechtsvergleichung 11, 24 (1932), referring to decisions of the highest court. 2 Schlesinger-Klang, Commentary [(Austrian) Civil Code] 16 (1934; 1 Egger, Commentary [(Swiss) Civil Code] 267 (1930).

[137] Cf. Oberlandesgericht Frankfurt 1921 (October 20), 2 Neue Zeitschrift für Arbeitrecht 454 (1922).

[138] German Code of Civil Procedure, sec. 888; Austrian Act of 1896 (May 27) on Executions, sec. 355.

negotiations; the act prescribes, also, that notice seven days before hostile action must be given to the other party and to the Department of Social Affairs, and must include a statement of the reasons for the concerted action.   But any action taken during the period when work stoppage is forbidden makes the actors and the organization liable, but exclusively for damages.

In the Romanic laws, damages are the only redress for wrongful acts.   However, French jurisprudence (by an outstanding example of judicial legislation) has evolved the *astreinte:* The court, finding for the plantiff, imposes upon the defendant the payment of an amount larger than merely compensatory damages, but subject to a substantial reduction upon the defendant's discontinuation of his wrongful action, for example, of his boycott against the plantiff, within a certain period of time fixed in the decree.   One may liken this kind of relief to our civil contempt proceedings.[139]

(c) When the wrongful act, for example a strike, constitutes a breach of a collective contract, German, Austrian, and Swiss law gives the other party to the contract — as does our law also — the right of rescission.[140]   At his option the employer may rescind, may sue for damages for breach, or may obtain a judgment enjoining the continuation of the strike.[141]   The discontinuance is in a sense a type of damages (i.e., the restoration of the condition as it existed prior to the breach), a relief provided for by the law of those countries.   By the Romanic laws a rescission requires judicial action.[142]

The Swedish Labor Court Act, 1928 (no. 254) provides for a declaratory judgment to ascertain whether the conduct of the other party is violative of the Collective Contracts Act, 1928 (no. 253), or of the collective contract itself.   By the Collective Contracts Act, Sec. 7, rescission of a collective contract may be decreed upon complaint of a party where the other party "is guilty of an act which substantially violated the contract if the labor court considers such an act to be essential to the contractual relationship in general."   Action for damages also constitutes a very important remedy.   Under the Norwegian Labor Disputes Act, 1927, the Labor Court may render a decree giving the petitioner the right to counter the respondent's breach of the collective contract, by means of concerted action, e.g., a lockout, on his part.

[139] Cf. 2 Planiol, op. cit., supra note 127, at nos. 209, 212; Brodeur, The Injunction in French Jurisprudence, 14 Tulane L. Rev. 210 (1940).

[140] Nipperdey, Das Streikrecht (The Right to Strike), Deutsche Landesreferate zum Internationalen Kongress für Rechtsvergleichung 744, 755 (1950).

[141] Ibid.

[142] France: Civil Code, art. 1184.

III. FEDERAL–STATE JURISDICTION

Federal legislation regulating labor relations is a two-edged sword. While regulating at the national level, it may invalidate controls at the state level. The constitutional doctrine of supremacy of federal power prohibits not only state regulations, which directly conflict with federal regulation but also any controls within areas occupied by the exercise of federal power and intended by Congress to be free from state interference. The increase of federal regulation creates difficult problems concerning the extent to which state controls, both legislative and judicial, have been invalidated.

In a relatively early case, the Supreme Court held that Wisconsin could prohibit union activities such as mass picketing even though the labor dispute involved an interstate industry subject to the National Labor Relations Act. Allen-Bradley Local 1111 v. WERB, 315 U.S. 740, 62 Sup. Ct. 820, 86 L. Ed. 1154 (1942). However, when Florida prescribed that all persons acting as business agents for unions be licensed, and barred aliens or convicted felons from obtaining licenses, the Court held the statute invalid, as applied to unions within the protection of the Wagner Act. Congress provided that employees should have full freedom of choice in selecting their collective bargaining representative. The Florida Act circumscribed this freedom and frustrated the Congressional purpose. Hill v. Florida, 325 U.S. 538, 65 Sup. Ct. 1373, 89 L. Ed. 782 (1945).

This case opened the gates to a series of cases testing the validity of state regulation in industries "affecting interstate commerce" and therefore within the reach of the National Labor Relations Board.

BETHLEHEM STEEL CO. v. NEW YORK STATE LABOR RELATIONS BOARD

Supreme Court of the United States, 1947
330 U.S. 767, 67 Sup. Ct. 1026, 91 L. Ed. 1234

MR. JUSTICE JACKSON delivered the opinion of the Court.

These appeals challenge the validity of the Labor Relations Act of the State of New York as applied to appellants to permit unionization of their foremen. Conflict is asserted between it and the National Labor Relations Act and hence with the Commerce Clause of the Constitution.

After enactment by Congress of the National Labor Relations

Act, July 5, 1935, 49 Stat. 449, 29 U.S.C.S. 151, et seq., New York adopted a State Labor Relations Act following the federal pattern. Laws of New York, 1937, Chap. 443, 30 McKinney's Consolidated Laws of New York, §§700–716.   In the administrative boards they create, the procedures they establish, the unfair labor practices prohibited, the two statutes may be taken for present purposes to be the same.   But in provision for determination of units of representation for bargaining purposes, the two Acts are not identical. Their differences may be made plain by setting forth §9 (b) of the Federal Act, with that part which is omitted from the State Act in brackets and additions made by the State Act as amended, Laws of New York, 1942, Chap. 518, in italics:

> The Board shall decide in each case whether, in order to insure to employees the full benefit of their right to self-organization [and] to collective bargaining, and otherwise to effectuate the policies of this Act, the unit appropriate for the purposes of collective bargaining shall be the employer unit, *multiple employer unit,* craft unit, plant unit, or [subdivision thereof] *any other unit; provided, however, that in any case where the majority of employees of a particular craft shall so decide the board shall designate such craft as a unit appropriate for the purpose of collective bargaining.*

The procedures prescribed for the two boards for investigation, certification, and hearing on representation units and for their election are substantially the same except that the State law adds the following limitation not found in the Federal Act: ". . . provided, however, that the board shall not have authority to investigate any question or controversy between individuals or groups within the same labor organization or between labor organizations affiliated with the same parent labor organization." Laws of New York, 1937, Chap. 443, as amended, Laws 1942, Chap. 518, 30 McKinney's Consolidated Laws of New York, §705.3.

The two boards have at times pursued inconsistent policies in applying their respective Acts to petitions of foremen as a class to organize bargaining units thereunder.   The State Board has in these cases recognized that right; the National Board for a time recognized it.   Union Collieries Coal Co., 41 N.L.R.B. 961; Godchaux Sugars, Inc., 44 N.L.R.B. 874.   Later, there was a period when, for policy reasons but without renouncing jurisdiction, it refused to approve foremen organization units.   Maryland Drydock Co., 49 N.L.R.B. 733; Boeing Aircraft Co., 51

N.L.R.B. 67; General Motors Corp., 51 N.L.R.B. 457. Now, again, it supports their right to unionize. Packard Motor Car Co., 61 N.L.R.B. 4, 64 N.L.R.B. 1212; L. A. Young Spring & Wire Corp., 65 N.L.R.B. 298. The foremen of these appellants, at a time when their desire to organize was frustrated by the policy of the National Board, filed applications with the State Board. It entertained their petitions and its policy permitted them as a class to become a bargaining unit. Both employers, by different methods adequate under State law to raise the question, challenged the constitutionality of the State Act as so applied to them. Their contentions ultimately were considered and rejected by the New York Court of Appeals and its decisions sustaining state power over the matter were brought here by appeals.

Both of these labor controversies arose in manufacturing plants located in New York where the companies employ large staffs of foremen to supervise a much larger force of labor. But both concerns have such a relation to interstate commerce that, for the reasons stated in National Labor Relations Board v. Jones & Laughlin Steel Corp., 301 U.S. 1, federal power reaches their labor relations. On this basis the National Board has exercised power to certify bargaining agents for units of employees other than foremen of both companies. . . . The companies contend that the National Board's jurisdiction over their labor relations is exclusive of state power; the State contends on the contrary that while federal power over the subject is paramount, it is not exclusive and in such a case as we have here, until the federal power is actually exercised as to the particular employees, State power may be exercised.

At the time the courts of the State of New York were considering this issue, the question whether the Federal Act would authorize or permit unionization of foremen was in controversy and was unsettled until our decision in Packard Motor Car Co. v. N.L.R.B., 330 U.S. 485. Whatever constitutional issue may have been presented by earlier phases of the evolution of the federal policy in relation to that of the State, the question now is whether, Congress having undertaken to deal with the relationship between these companies and their foremen, the State is prevented from doing so. Congress has not seen fit to lay down even the most general of guides to construction of the Act, as it sometimes does, by saying that its regulation either shall or shall not exclude state action. Cf. Securities Act of 1933, §18, 48 Stat. 85, 15 U.S.C. §77r; Securities Exchange Act of 1934, §28, 48 Stat. 903, 15 U.S.C. §78bb; United States Warehouse Act, §29, before and after 1931 amendment, 39 Stat. 490, 46 Stat. 1465, 7 U.S.C. §269.   Our question is primarily one of the construction to be put on the Federal Act.   It long has been the rule that exclusion of state action may be implied from the nature of the legislation and the subject matter although express declaration of such result is wanting.   Napier v. Atlantic Coast Line R. Co., 272 U.S. 605. . . .

In the National Labor Relations Act, Congress has sought to reach some aspects of the employer-employee relation out of which such interferences arise.   It has dealt with the subject or relationship but partially, and has left outside of the scope of its delegation other closely related matters.   Where it leaves the employer-employee relation free of regulation in some aspects, it implies that in such matters federal policy is indifferent, and since it is indifferent to what the individual of his own volition may do we can only assume it to be equally indifferent to what he may do under the compulsion of the state.   Such was the situation in Allen-Bradley Local v. Board, 315 U.S. 740, where we held that employee and union conduct over which no direct or delegated federal power was exerted by the National Labor Relations Act is left open to regulation by the state.   However, the power of the state may not so deal with matters left to its control as to stand "as an obstacle to the accomplishment and execution of the full purposes and objectives of Congress."   Hill v. Florida, 325 U.S. 538, 542.   Cf. Maurer v. Hamilton, 309 U.S. 598.   When Congress has outlined its policy in rather general and inclusive terms and delegated determination of their specific application to an administrative tribunal, the mere fact of delegation of power to deal with the general matter, without agency action, might preclude any state action if it is clear that Congress has intended no regulation except its own.   Oregon-Washington Co. v. Washington, 270 U.S. 87.   In other cases, Congress has passed statutes which initiate regulation of certain activities, but where effective regulation must wait upon the issuance of rules by an administrative body.   In the interval before those rules are established, this Court has usually held that the police power of the state may be exercised.   Northwestern Bell Telephone Co. v. Nebraska State Commission, 297 U.S. 471; Welch Co. v. New Hampshire, 306 U.S. 79.   But when federal administration has made comprehensive regulations effectively governing the subject matter of the statute, the Court has said that a state regulation in the field of the statute is invalid even though that particular phase of the subject has not been taken up by the federal agency.   Napier v. Atlantic Coast Line R. Co., 272 U.S. 605.   However, when federal administrative regulation has been slight under a statute which potentially allows minute and multitudinous regulation of its subject, cf. Atlantic Coast Line R. Co. v. Georgia, 234 U.S. 280, or even where extensive regulations have been made, if the measure in question relates to what may be considered a separable or distinct segment of the matter covered by the federal statute and the federal agency has not acted on that segment, the case will be treated in a manner similar to cases in which the effectiveness of federal supervision awaits federal administrative regulation. Northwestern Bell Telephone Co. v. Nebraska State Commission, supra; Welch Co. v. New Hampshire, supra. The states are in those cases permitted to use their police power in the interval. Terminal Railroad Assn. v. Brotherhood of Railroad Trainmen, 318 U.S. 1. However, the conclusion must be otherwise where failure of the federal officials affirmatively to exercise their full authority takes on the character of a ruling that no such regulation is appropriate or approved pursuant to the policy of the statute. Napier v. Atlantic Coast Line, 272 U.S. 605; compare Oregon-Washington Co. v. Washington, 270 U.S. 87, with Parker v. Brown, 317 U.S. 341; cf. Mintz v. Baldwin, 289 U.S. 346.

It is clear that the failure of the National Labor Relations Board to entertain foremen's petitions was of the latter class. There was no administrative concession that the nature of these appellants' business put their employees beyond reach of federal authority. The Board several times entertained similar proceedings by other employees whose right rested on the same words of Congress. Neither did the National Board ever deny its own jurisdiction over petitions because they were by foremen. Soss Manufacturing Co., 56 N.L.R.B. 348. It made clear that its refusal to designate foremen's bargaining units was a determination and an exercise of its discretion to determine that such units were not appropriate for bargaining purposes. Maryland Drydock Co., 49 N.L.R.B. 733. We cannot, therefore, deal with this as a case where federal power has been delegated but lies dormant and unexercised. . . .

. . . The federal board has jurisdiction of the industry in which these particular employers are engaged and has asserted control of their labor relations in general. It asserts, and rightfully so, under our decision in the Packard case, supra, its power to decide whether these foremen may constitute themselves a bargaining unit. We do not believe this leaves room for the operation of the state authority asserted.

The National and State Boards have made a commendable effort to avoid conflict in this overlapping state of the statutes.

We find nothing in their negotiations, however, which affects either the construction of the federal statute or the question of constitutional power insofar as they are involved in this case, since the National Board made no concession or delegation of power to deal with this subject. The election of the National Board to decline jurisdiction in certain types of cases, for budgetary or other reasons presents a different problem which we do not now decide.

We therefore conclude that it is beyond the power of New York State to apply its policy to these appellants as attempted herein. The judgments appealed from are reversed and the causes remanded for further proceedings not inconsistent herewith.

Reversed.

[The separate opinion of Mr. Justice Frankfurter, in which Mr. Justice Murphy and Mr. Justice Rutledge join, is omitted.]

NOTES

1. La Crosse Telephone Corp. v. WERB, 336 U.S. 18, 69 Sup. Ct. 379, 93 L. Ed. 463 (1949), involved a small telephone company which handled interstate calls, and although the NLRB had exercised jurisdiction over similar telephone companies, the Union did not resort to the NLRB, but instituted representation proceedings before the Wisconsin Employment Relations Board. The Wisconsin Board determined the appropriate units, according to the Wisconsin statute which was somewhat different from the Wagner Act and issued a certification. The Court held this certification invalid. Although there was no conflict with any NLRB determination the Court thought (p. 25) "the situation to fraught with potential conflict to permit the intrusion of the State agency." Id. at 25. "The problems of employee representation is a sensitive and delicate one in industrial relations. The uncertainty as to which Board is master and how long it will remain such can be as disruptive of peace between various industrial factions as actual competition between the two boards for supremacy." Id. at 26.

How are the Bethlehem and La Crosse cases affected by the new proviso in Section 10 (a) of the Labor Management Relations Act?

2. The Wisconsin Act, modeled on the Wagner Act, contains a provision similar to Section 8 (3) prohibiting discrimination for union activity except in compliance with a valid union-security provision. However, the Wisconsin Act requires a two-thirds vote of approval by the employees to validate a union-security provi-

sion.   Both Algoma Plywood and Veneer Co. v. WERB, 336 U.S.
301, 69 Sup. Ct. 584, 93 L. Ed. 691 (1949), and Plankinton Packing Co. v. WERB, 338 U.S. 953, 70 Sup. Ct. 491, 94 L. Ed. 588
(1950), involved the power of the Wisconsin board to enforce
this provision in interstate businesses.

In the Algoma case, the War Labor Board had ordered a maintenance-of-membership clause in 1943.   This was adopted and
carried over from year to year, but no vote was taken under the
Wisconsin Act.   When an employee was discharged in January,
1947, because of his failure to maintain his membership, the Wisconsin Board found the union-security provision illegal under
state law and therefore found that the employer was guilty of an
unfair labor practice under the Wisconsin statute.   It then ordered reinstatement and back pay.   The Court held in an opinion
by Justice Frankfurter, with Justices Black and Douglas dissenting,
that this order was within the states' jurisdiction and valid.   Section 8 (3), said the Court, relying on legislative history, did not
affirmatively declare a policy favoring union security, it "merely
disclaims a national policy hostile to the closed shop or other
forms of union security agreement."   The Court found nothing
inconsistent between the provisions of the National Labor Relations Act and the Wisconsin requirement of a two-thirds vote on
a union-security provision.

In the Plankinton case, the War Labor Board had also ordered
a maintenance-of-membership agreement.   It was adopted but not
voted on as Wisconsin law required.   The employee involved
tendered his resignation from the Union in the period allowed by
the maintenance-of-membership provision.   The Union, however, refused to accept his resignation and induced the employer to
discharge him.   The Wisconsin Board found the discharge to be
an unfair labor practice, and ordered reinstatement with back
pay.   Apparently, the discharge would have been illegal under
the National Labor Relations Act as well as under the Wisconsin
Act, because it was in violation of the union-security provision.
The Court in a per curiam opinion held the Wisconsin order invalid, stating only, "The judgment is reversed," and citing the
Bethlehem and La Crosse cases.

How are the above cases affected by Section 14 (b) of the Labor
Management Relations Act?

3. A somewhat different aspect of the problem was involved in
International Union, UAW (AFL) v. WERB, 336 U.S. 245, 69
Sup. Ct. 516, 93 L. Ed. 651 (1949), page 682 supra.   The Union
engaged in intermittent stoppages by using the device of calling

frequent union meetings during working hours. The Wisconsin Board found this to be an unfair labor practice under the state act and ordered the Union to cease and desist. The Court upheld this order as within the states' jurisdiction. This kind of union activity was not "concerted action" within the meaning of the National Labor Relations Act. Therefore, it "was neither forbidden by federal statute nor was it legalized and approved thereby. Such being the case, the state police power was not superseded by congressional Act over a subject normally within its exclusive power . . ."

AMALGAMATED ASSN. OF STREET, ELECTRIC RAILWAY & MOTOR COACH EMPLOYEES, ETC. v. WERB

Supreme Court of the United States, 1951
340 U.S. 383, 71 Sup. Ct. 359, 95 L. Ed. 364

MR. CHIEF JUSTICE VINSON delivered the opinion of the Court.

In these cases, the constitutionality of labor legislation of the State of Wisconsin known as the Public Utility Anti-Strike Law, has been drawn in question.

Petitioners in No. 329 are the union and its officers who represent the employees of the Milwaukee Electric Railway and Transport Company of Milwaukee, Wisconsin, for collective-bargaining purposes. For many years, the transit workers entered into collective-bargaining agreements with the transit company without resorting to strike. In 1948, however, the collective agreement was terminated when the parties were unable to agree on wages, hours and working conditions and the transit workers' union called a strike to enforce union demands. The respondent Wisconsin Employment Relations Board secured immediately an ex parte order from a State Circuit Court restraining the strike and, in compliance with that order, the union postponed its strike. Thereafter, the same Circuit Court entered a judgment under which petitioners are "perpetually restrained and enjoined from calling a strike . . . which would cause an interruption of the passenger service of the (transit company) ." The Wisconsin Supreme Court affirmed the judgment, 257 Wis. 43, 42 N.W.2d 471 (1950), and we granted certiorari, 340 U.S. 874 (1950), to review the important questions decided below. . . .

. . . This provision is part of a statutory pattern designed to become effective whenever collective bargaining results in an "impasse and stalemate" likely to cause interruption of the supply of an "essential public utility service," Wis. Stat., 1949 §111.50, that service including water, heat, gas, electric power, public passenger transportation and communications. . . . In summary, the act substitutes arbitration upon order of the Board for collective bargaining whenever an impasse is reached in the bargaining process. And, to insure conformity with the statutory scheme, Wisconsin denies to utility employees the right to strike.

First. We have recently examined the extent to which Congress has regulated peaceful strikes for higher wages in industries affecting commerce. Automobile Workers v. O'Brien, 339 U.S. 454 (1950). We noted that Congress, in §7 of the National Labor Relations Act of 1935, as amended by the Labor Management Relations Act of 1947, expressly safeguarded for employees in such industries the "right . . . to engage in . . . concerted activities for the purpose of collective bargaining or other mutual aid or protection," "e.g., to strike." We also listed the qualifications and regulations which Congress itself has imposed upon its guarantee of the right to strike, including requirements that notice be given prior to any strike upon termination of a contract, prohibitions on strikes for certain objectives declared unlawful by Congress, and special procedures for certain strikes which might create national emergencies. Upon review of these federal legislative provisions, we held, 339 U.S. at 457: "None of these sections can be read as permitting concurrent state regulation of peaceful strikes for higher wages. Congress occupied this field and closed it to state regulation. Plankinton Packing Co. v. Wisconsin Board, 338 U.S. 953 (1950); La Crosse Telephone Corp. v. Wisconsin Board, 336 U.S. 18 (1949); Bethlehem Steel Co. v. New York Labor Board, 330 U.S. 767 (1947); Hill v. Florida, 325 U.S. 538 (1945)."

Second. The Wisconsin court sought to distinguish Automobile Workers v. O'Brien, supra, on the ground that the industry to which Michigan applied its notice and strike-vote provisions was a national manufacturing organization rather than a local public utility. Congress drew no such distinction but, instead, saw fit to regulate labor relations to the full extent of its constitutional power under the Commerce Clause, Labor Board v. Fainblatt, 306 U.S. 601, 607 (1939). Ever since the question was fully argued and decided in Consolidated Edison Co. v. Labor Board, 305 U.S. 197 (1938), it has been clear that federal labor legislation, encompassing as it does all industries "affecting commerce," applies to a privately owned public utility whose business and activities are carried on wholly within a single state. The courts of appeal have uniformly held enterprises similar to and no more important to interstate commerce than the Milwaukee gas and transit companies before us in these cases subject to the provisions of the federal labor law.   No distinction between public utilities and national manufacturing organizations has been drawn in the administration of the Federal Act, and, when separate treatment for public utilities was urged upon Congress in 1947, the suggested differentiation was expressly rejected.   Creation of a special classification for public utilities is for Congress, not for this Court.

Third.   As we have noted, in 1947 Congress enacted special procedures to deal with strikes which might create national emergencies.   Respondents rely upon that action as showing a congressional intent to carve out a separate field of "emergency" labor disputes and, pointing to the fact that Congress acted only in respect to "national emergencies," respondents ask us to hold that Congress intended by silence, to leave the states free to regulate "local emergency" disputes.   However, the Wisconsin Act before us is not "emergency" legislation but a comprehensive code for the settlement of labor disputes between public-utility employers and employees.   Far from being limited to "local emergencies," the act has been applied to disputes national in scope, and application of the act does not require the existence of an "emergency."   In any event, congressional imposition of certain restrictions on petitioners' right to strike, far from supporting the Wisconsin Act, shows that Congress has closed to state regulation the field of peaceful strikes in industries affecting commerce. Automobile Workers v. O'Brien, supra, at 457.   And where, as here, the state seeks to deny entirely a federally guaranteed right which Congress itself restricted only to a limited extent in case of national emergencies, however serious, it is manifest that the state legislation is in conflict with federal law.

Like the majority strike-vote provision considered in O'Brien, a proposal that the right to strike be denied, together with the substitution of compulsory arbitration in cases of "public emergencies," local or national, was before Congress in 1947.   This proposal, closely resembling the pattern of the Wisconsin Act, was rejected by Congress as being inconsistent with its policy in respect to enterprises covered by the Federal Act, and not because of any desire to leave the states free to adopt it.   Michigan, in O'Brien, sought to impose conditions on the right to strike and now Wisconsin seeks to abrogate that right altogether insofar as petitioners are concerned.   Such state legislation must yield as conflicting with the exercise of federally protected labor rights.

Fourth.   Much of the argument generated by these cases has been considerably broader than the legal questions presented.

The utility companies, the State of Wisconsin and other states as amici stress the importance of gas and transit service to the local community and urge that predominantly local problems are best left to the local governmental authority for solution.   On the other hand, petitioners and the National Labor Board, as amicus, argue that prohibition of strikes with reliance upon compulsory arbitration for ultimate solution of labor disputes destroys the free collective bargaining declared by Congress to be the bulwark of the national labor policy.   This, it is said, leads to more labor unrest and disruption of service than is now experienced under a system of free collective bargainng accompanied by the right to strike.   The very nature of the debatable policy questions raised by these contentions convinces us that they cannot properly be resolved by the Court.   In our view, these questions are for legislative determination and have been resolved by Congress adversely to respondents.

When it amended the Federal Act in 1947, Congress was not only cognizant of the policy questions that have been argued before us in these cases, but it was also well aware of the problems in balancing state-federal relationships which its 1935 legislation had raised.   The legislative history of the 1947 Act refers to the decision of this Court in Bethlehem Steel Co. v. New York Labor Board, 330 U.S. 767 (1947), and, in its handling of the problems presented by that case, Congress demonstrated that it knew how to cede jurisdiction to the states.   Congress knew full well that its labor legislation "preempts the field that the act covers insofar as commerce within the meaning of the act is concerned" and demonstrated its ability to spell out with particularity those areas in which it desired state regulation to be operative.   This Court, in the exercise of its judicial function, must take the comprehensive and valid federal legislation as enacted and declare invalid state regulation which impinges on that legislation.

Fifth.   It would be sufficient to state that the Wisconsin Act, in forbidding peaceful strikes for higher wages in industries covered by the Federal Act, has forbidden the exercise of rights protected by §7 of the Federal Act.   In addition, it is not difficult to visualize situations in which application of the Wisconsin Act would work at cross-purposes with other policies of the National Act.   But we content ourselves with citation of examples of direct conflict found in the records before us.   In the case of the transit workers, the union agreed to continue collective bargaining after the strike became imminent, whereas the company insisted upon invocation of the compulsory arbitration features of the Wisconsin Act. That act requires that collective bargaining continue until an "impasse" is reached, Wis. Stat. 1949, §111.52, whereas the Federal Act requires that both employer and employees continue to bargain collectively even though a strike may actually be in progress. Labor Board v. Mackay Radio & Telegraph Co., 304 U.S. 333, 345 (1938). Further, the transit company was able to avoid entirely any determination of certain union demands when the arbitrators, in accordance with Wis. Stat. 1949, §111.58, ruled that the matter of assigning of workers to certain shifts "infringe (s) upon the right of the employer to manage his business." Yet similar problems of work scheduling and shift assignment have been held to be appropriate subjects for collective bargaining under the Federal Act as administered by the National Labor Relations Board. See Woodside Cotton Mills, Co., 21 N.L.R.B. 42, 54–55 (1940); American National Ins. Co., 89 N.L.R.B. 185 (1950); and cases cited therein.

The National Labor Relations Act of 1935 and the Labor Management Relations Act of 1947, passed by Congress pursuant to its powers under the Commerce Clause, are the supreme law of the land under Art. VI of the Constitution. Having found that the Wisconsin Public Utility Anti-Strike Law conflicts with that federal legislation, the judgments enforcing the Wisconsin Act cannot stand.

Reversed.

Mr. Justice Frankfurter, whom Mr. Justice Burton and Mr. Justice Minton join, dissenting. . . .

A claim of conflict between State and federal labor legislation presents a familiar problem. On eight occasions this Court has considered whether the Taft-Hartley Act, or its predecessor, the Wagner Act, 49 Stat. 49, so collided with State law as to displace it. We have sustained State laws which dealt with mass picketing and intermittent work stoppages. Allen-Bradley Local v. Wisconsin Board, 315 U.S. 740; International Union, United Automobile Workers v. Wisconsin Board, 336 U.S. 245. We have also upheld a State law which required a two-thirds vote for a maintenance-of-membership clause in collective agreements. Algoma Pywood Co. v. Wisconsin Board, 336 U.S. 301.

On the other hand, we have found in five cases that the State law could not consistently stand with the federal law. In Hill v. Florida, 325 U.S. 538, the State was found to have interfered with the freedom in selecting bargaining agents as guaranteed by the federal act.   In Bethlehem Steel Co. v. New York Board, 330 U.S. 767, the State recognized a foreman's union contrary to established policy of the National Board.   In La Crosse Telephone Corp. v. Wisconsin Board, supra, a conflict was found in the bargaining units determined under the State and federal acts.   In Plankinton Packing Co. v. Wisconsin Board, 338 U.S. 953, a State superimposed upon federal outlawry of conduct as an "unfair labor practice" its own finding of unfairness.   In International Union of United Automobile Workers v. O'Brien, 339 U.S. 454, a State act covering all industry permitted strikes at a different time than the federal act and required, unlike federal law, a majority authorization for any strike.   Also, these provisions were applied to only that portion of a bargaining unit, already determined under the federal act, located within the State of Michigan.

"The Principle is thoroughly established that the exercise by the State of its police power, which would be valid if not superseded by federal action, is superseded only where the repugnance or conflict is so 'direct and positive' that the two acts cannot 'be reconciled or consistently stand together.' "   Chief Justice Hughes in Kelly v. Washington, 302 U.S. 1, 10.   It is clear from the decisions just canvassed that the States are not precluded from enacting laws on labor relations merely because Congress has — to use the conventional phrase — entered the field.   It is equally clear that the boundaries within which a State may act are determined by the terrain and not by abstract projection.   Emphasis in the opinions has varied, but the guiding principle is still that set out in the first in the series of immediately relevant cases: whether "the state system of regulation, as construed and applied here, can be reconciled with the federal Act and . . . the two as focused in this case can consistently stand together . . . ."   Allen-Bradley Local v. Wisconsin Board, supra, at 751.   The adjustment thus called for between State and National interests is not attained by reliance on uncritical generalities or rhetorical phrases unnourished by the particularities of specific situations. . . .

An attempt by a State to impose upon industry as a whole a drastic limitation upon the right to strike would conflict with the federal law.   Compare United Automobile Workers v. O'Brien, supra.   And even as to emergency disputes — those involving the obvious public services — it may be urged that the prospect of settlement by arbitration may tend to make one or both parties reluctant to reach an agreement by bargaining.   See Kennedy, The Handling of Emergency Disputes, Proceedings of

Second Annual Meeting of Industrial Relations Research Assn., 14, 21–22 (1949).

But the principle of hands-off collective bargaining is no more absolute than the right to strike. The "national emergency" provisions in the Taft-Hartley Act are an affirmative indication that the force of collective bargaining may be limited in emergency situations. Title II of the Taft-Hartley Act provides for special mediation procedures, a cooling-off period, and ballot by employees on the final offer of the employer, in order to prevent a strike or lockout in "an entire industry or a substantial part thereof" if necessary to avoid peril to "the national health or safety." §206. And Congress apparently expected that additional laws would be enacted if necessary. The "national emergency" provisions were aimed at strikes of nation-wide significance. They have been applied in eight disputes from 1947 to 1950; twice in industry-wide or coast-wide maritime negotiations; three times in industry-wide bituminous-coal negotiations; and in disputes arising in the meat-packing industry, the national telephone industry, and the atomic-energy installation at Oak Ridge. U.S. Dept of Labor, Bureau of Labor Statistics, Federal Fact-Finding Boards and Boards of Inquiry (1950) 2.

Title II would be available for settlement of the disputes involved in the cases before us only if they were a part of a nation-wide utility dispute creating a national emergency. But the careful consideration given to the problem of meeting nation-wide emergencies and the failure to provide for emergencies other than those affecting the Nation as a whole do not imply paralysis of State police power. Rather, they imply that the States retain the power to protect the public interest in emergencies economically and practically confined within a State. It is not reasonable to impute to Congress the desire to leave States helpless in meeting local situations when Congress restricted national intervention to national emergencies. . . .

NOTES

1. The decisions of the Supreme Court have caused considerable confusion in the state courts. Union conduct which has, in the past, been readily enjoined has suddenly achieved an aura of immunity from state action because of the controls over union activity imposed by the Taft-Hartley Act.

In Norris Grain Co. v. Nordass, 232 Minn. 91, 46 N.W.2d 94 (1951), the state court prohibited the enjoining of a secondary boycott because the employer was engaged in interstate commerce. Section 8 (b) (4) gave the NLRB exclusive jurisdiction and barred state control. But in Texas Federation of Labor v. Brown & Root, Inc., 29 L.R.R.M. 2467 (Tex. Cir. App. 1952), the Texas court permitted a suit for injunction and damages against secondary boycott on the grounds that the NLRB could not award damages and therefore could not give adequate relief.

The New York Court of Appeals has formerly enjoined closed unions from enforcing a closed shop against those excluded from the union and thereby barring them from employment. Clark v. Curtis, 297 N.Y. 1014, 90 N.E.8d 536 (1947). Because this is now an unfair labor practice under sections 8 (a) (3) and 8 (b) (2), the state injunction can no longer issue in industries affecting interstate commerce. Costero v. Simons, 302 N.Y. 318, 98 N.E.2d 454 (1951); Ryan v. Simons, 302 N.Y. 742, 98 N.E.2d 707 (1951).

However, where the union has engaged in mass picketing and violence, the state courts have continued to issue injunctions even though the union conduct is an admitted violation of section 8 (b) (1). Williams v. Cedartown Textiles, Inc., 208 Ga. 659, 68 S.E.2d 705, (1952); Erwin Mills v. Textile Workers Union, 234 N.C. 321, 67 S.E.2d 372 (1951); Oil Workers International Union v. Superior Court, 28 L.R.R.M. 2643 (Cal. Dist. Ct. of App. 1951). The states' courts have also enjoined mass picketing where its object was to compel the employer to enforce a closed shop in violation of Section 8 (a) (3). Wortex Mills Inc. v. Textile Workers Union, 369 Pa. 359, 85 A.2d 851 (1952), or to compel the employer to break his contract with a certified union and recognize the picketing union in violation of Section 8 (b) (4) (C). Art Steel Co. v. Velazquez, 109 N.Y.S.2d 788 (1952).

In Goodwins, Inc. v. Hagedorn, 303 N.Y. 300, 101 N.E.2d 697 (1951), the Union picketed the employer with the avowed object of compelling recognition although there was at the time a representation proceeding pending before the NLRB. The New York court held that this could be enjoined by the state because it was not prohibited by any provision of the Taft-Hartley Act. Three judges dissented on the ground that although this conduct was not prohibited by the federal law it was so closely related to activity which was regulated that it was within the area pre-empted by Congress. Since picketing for recognition was prohibited in certain specified instances, Congress must have intended that picketing for recognition in other instances should be free from restrictions.

2. If the NLRB holds that the use of laborsaving devices is

a proper subject for collective bargaining, could New York enjoin a strike against the use of such devices in an industry which
affected interstate commerce?

The NLRB has refused to exercise jurisdiction for purposes of
representation proceedings over certain parts of the construction
industry even though it "affected interstate commerce." Would
this leave a state free to hold representation proceedings under a
state labor relations act? If the Board refused to process unfair
labor practice charges in such a situation, could the state enjoin
a secondary boycott? See Montgomery Building and Construction Trades Council v. Ledbetter Erection Company, 29 L.R.R.M.
2415 (Ala. Sup. Ct. 1952).

What is the significance in these cases of the proviso in Section
10 (a) allowing the Board to cede jurisdiction to states "unless the
provision of the State statute . . . is inconsistent with the corresponding provision of this Act or has received a construction inconsistent herewith"?

PART V

Unions and Their Members

I. INTRA-UNION DEMOCRACY [1]

A. *Introduction*

During recent years there has been a great hue and cry against undemocratic practices within unions. Although undemocratic unions have never constituted more than a small fraction of the labor movement, the tremendous growth of unions in the last fifteen years has increased the number of horrible examples. The extensive use of collective bargaining has focused attention on the structure and functioning of the organizations through which it is done. In this era of upsurge of unions and turbulence of labor relations, dramatized accounts of corruption and oppression by labor "czars" have become one of the main themes of modern muckrakers.

Criticisms of unions usually assume that unions should be democratic in their relationships with their members, without any objective inquiry into the question of why or to what extent they should be democratic. Evaluation of union practices must be made with reference to the society in which they operate and the problems which they face.

First, unions operate in the economic arena as economic organizations, and their governmental structure may reflect the general pattern of economic organizations. How do the rights of a member in his union compare with the rights of an employee in the company for which he works? How do the rights of a

---

[1] American Civil Liberties Union, Democracy in Labor Unions (1952); Aaron and Komaroff, Statutory Regulation of Internal Union Affairs, 44 Ill. L. Rev. 425, 631 (1949); Chafee, The Internal Affairs of Associations Not for Profit, 43 Harv. L. Rev. 993 (1930); Kovner, Legal Protection of Civil Liberties Within Unions, [1948] Wis. L. Rev. 18; Mintz, Trade Union Abuses, 6 St. John's L. Rev. 272 (1932); Pierson, The Government of Trade Unions, 1 Indust. & Lab. Rel. Rev. 593 (1948); Stafford, Disputes Within Trade Unions, 45 Yale L.J. 1248 (1936); Taft, Democracy in Trade Unions, 36 Amer. Econ. Rev., Papers and Proceedings 359 (1946); Witmer, Civil Liberties and the Trade Union, 50 Yale L.J. 621 (1941); Note, Judicial Intervention in Internal Affairs of Labor Unions, 20 Minn. L. Rev. 657 (1936).

member in his union compare with the rights of a stockholder in his corporation? Should a union officer be required to maintain a higher degree of democracy than an employer or a corporation president?

Second, a union is a human organization. Like every other organization it faces the problems of apathetic members, uninformed voters, selfish or disruptive cliques, and struggles for power. It faces these problems and yet is charged with maintaining an elaborate organization, meeting a multitude of needs of its members, and obtaining concessions from a hesitant or hostile management. In the light of these factors, should we expect unions to be more democratic than churches, lodges, or political parties? Should we be surprised if some unions fall into the same state of corruption and control as some of our municipal governments?

This Part is directed principally toward a study of the legal protections which union members have against undemocratic practices by their union leaders. Therefore it consists largely of cases in which the union restricted democratic activities and contains many cases in which the union clearly oppressed individual rights. However, these cases do not indicate that unions are generally undemocratic any more than the cases studied in Contracts indicate that all businessmen are contract breakers, or the cases studied in Domestic Relations indicate that all marriages end in adultery or divorce. These cases do not represent the normal condition within unions but represent the pathology of diseased and disordered unions.

The student should be aware that this law of sick unions has practical significance whether he becomes a specialist in labor law or a general practitioner. The lawyer who customarily represents unions is in a unique position to use his understanding of these cases and the basic problems which they raise in doing valuable preventive work within the union. On the other hand, the general practitioner frequently becomes involved in these cases, for the individual union members who are seeking protection have a natural distrust of any lawyer who is too closely allied with either union or management.

B. *Admission* [2]

1. CONSTITUTIONAL PROVISIONS

(a) "Any white man shall be eligible to membership, who at the time of making application is actually employed in road or yard service on a surface railway where steam and electricity are intermingled or where steam or electricity is the motive power." Constitution of the Order of Railway Conductors of America (1946), Sec. 19.

(b) "All working men and working women, regardless of race, creed, color, or nationality, employed in and around iron and steel manufacturing, processing and fabricating mills and factories, or in any other place now under the jurisdiction of the International Union, in the United States and Canada or officers, staff representatives or employees of the International Union, are eligible to membership.

"No person having the power, in the management of any mill or factory, to hire or fire shall be eligible for membership.

"Persons having supervisory power, excluding the right to hire and fire, shall be eligible to membership subject to the approval of the Local Union and the International Executive Board." Constitution of United Steel Workers (1944), Art. III.

(c) "Sec. 102 (a). Any person to be admitted to membership in this Brotherhood must have followed one of the branches of the trade for three years as enumerated in this Constitution and . . . be competent to command the minimum rate of wages established by the local union or district council of the district in which he applies for membership.

"Sec. 103. Each candidate proposed must be interviewed by a special committee of three who shall examine into the character, experience, competency, health, and other qualifications of the candidate for membership.

"Sec. 104. When a candidate has been reported upon by the committee, the President shall ask whether there are any known reasons why the candidate shall not be admitted to membership. If no objections are stated the local union shall proceed to ballot upon him.

"Sec. 107 (a). No person shall be eligible to become or remain a member in this Brotherhood who holds membership in or

[2] See, generally, Hewitt, The Right to Membership in a Labor Union, 99 U. of Pa. L. Rev. 919 (1951); Summers, The Right to Join a Union, 47 Col. L. Rev. 33 (1947); Summers, Admission Policies of Labor Unions, 61 Q.J. Econ. 66 (1946).

affiliation with any group, club, society or other organization which, in the opinion of the General Executive Board, exercises or claims to exercise duties and functions similar to those exercised by this Brotherhood or its locals, or which claims jurisdiction in whole or in part over matters which are within the jurisdiction of this Brotherhood.

"Sec. 107 (d). Any member who associates himself with any organization or any group that expounds or promotes any doctrine or philosophy inimical to or subversive of the fundamental principles and institutions of the government of the United States or Dominion of Canada, the American Federation of Labor or of this Brotherhood, shall be granted a hearing by the local and, if found guilty, shall be disciplined in the manner provided for in this constitution." Constitution of the Brotherhood of Painters, Decorators and Paperhangers of America (1947).

2. PROBLEM I

The United Framis Makers and Handlers of America is an independent labor organization with exclusive jurisdiction in the framis industry throughout the United States. The total membership is about 150,000 and includes about 95 per cent of all eligible workers in the industry. In most instances, throughout the industry, the UFMHA has secured valid union-shop contracts as provided under the LMRA.

The constitution of the UFMHA contains no membership restrictions based upon race, color, creed, sex, citizenship, or nationality. It originally provided that membership should be denied to persons affiliated with any organization "whose aims, principles, and philosophy are contrary to those of the United Framis Makers and Handlers of America." Following passage of the LMRA, however, this provision was amended as follows:

Otherwise qualified applicants who are affiliated with any organization whose aims, principles, and philosophy are contrary to those of the United Framis Makers and Handlers of America shall be admitted to membership in separate locals, provided that no such local shall be established unless there are at least 10 persons qualifying for membership therein. Where such locals are established, they shall be under the jurisdiction of the officers of the nearest regular local, and shall be represented by those officers in collective bargaining with employers and in all city, district, and national meetings or conventions of the United Framis Makers and Handlers of America.

Of the major companies in the framis industry, only one, Monolith Manufacturing Co., successfully resisted organization by the UFMHA. In 1951, however, Local No. 75, UFMHA was finally certified as exclusive bargaining representative of the Company's 500 employees. In due course, the parties executed a valid union-shop contract. All Monolith employees eligible to join the UFMHA immediately applied for membership and, with some exceptions, all were admitted. However, twelve employees, admittedly affiliated with the White Knights of Christendom, an organization describing itself as opposing "the ruling governmental clique of Communists, Catholics, Jews, and Negroes," were denied membership in Local No. 75. Instead, they were offered membership in a special Local No. 75–A, in accordance with the above-quoted constitutional provision. All twelve refused to join the UFMHA on that basis; and some sixty days after the contract between Monolith and Local No. 75 had been put into effect, they were discharged by the Company at the Union's insistence.

3. LEGAL PROTECTION AGAINST EXCLUSION

FRANK v. NATIONAL ALLIANCE OF BILL POSTERS
Supreme Court, New Jersey, 1916
89 N.J.L. 380, 99 Atl. 134

SWAYZE, J. The defendants are an unincorporated organization, a trade union. They are not shown to have any property, and the plain question is whether the court will interfere by mandamus to compel the other members to receive the relator as a member. The question seems never to have been directly decided in this court. In Zeliff v. Knights of Pythias, 53 N.J. Law, 536, 22 Atl. 63, the local lodge was unincorporated, and the case turned upon the necessity of the relator seeking redress in the tribunals of the order before having recourse to the civil courts. The suggestion of the court that after appealing to the highest tribunal within the order, he might still sue for relief, and that the defendants would still be within reach of the mandatory writ, was not meant to be a decision that such writ would issue. The only authority cited was Sibley v. Carteret Club, 40 N.J. Law, 295, which was a case of a corporation, not a mere unincorporated association. The distinction between incorporated and unincorporated associations was pointed out by Vice Chancellor Emery in O'Brien v. Musical Mutual P & B Union, 64 N.J. Eq. 525, 532, 54 Atl. 150. . . . The reasons are well stated in the opinion by Jessel: [in Rigby v. Connol, L.R., 14 Ch. Div. 482, 49 L.J. Ch. 328]

"The courts as such never dream of enforcing what I may call personal agreements, that is, agreements strictly personal in their nature, whether they are agreements of hiring and service, whether they are agreements of master and servant, or whether they are agreements for the purpose of pleasure or for the purpose of scientific pursuits, or for the purpose of charity or philanthropy. . . ."

He instances the case of a number of gentlemen meeting at each other's houses to play cards, or a number of scientific men meeting from time to time by agreement for scientific purposes. A like view was expressed by V. C. Green in Mayer v. Journeyman Stone-Cutters' Association, 47 N.J. Eq. 519, 20 Atl. 492, although the question there involved was different; two of the complainants who had never been members of the association sought to force an entrance without the aid of the court.

It would be quite impracticable for the courts to undertake to compel men to receive into their social relationships one who was personally disagreeable whether for a good or a bad reason. Property rights the court can deal with; rights in an unincorporated company are of that character, and the right of membership is ordinarily assignable. Voluntary associations are quite different. The courts can deal with property rights of such associations, if there are any, while they cannot, by a mandatory writ, intrude one man's companionship on another. The attempt to do so would be unavailing, as it would lead only to the disintegration of the association. We do not mean to deny the present relator's right to recover damages if his right to labor has been illegally interfered with. Brennan v. United Hatters, 73 N.J. Law, 9 Ann. Cas. 698. All we now decide is that mandamus is not a proper remedy.

The rule is discharged, with costs.

NOTES

1. Exclusionary practices by a professional organization of doctors came before the court in Harris v. Thomas, 217 S.W. 1068 (Tex. Civ. App. 1920). Harris was a licensed osteopath practicing in Amarillo, Texas. The other doctors organized a Medical Association and barred him from practicing at the only hospital

in the city.   Harris sought an injunction against their interfering with his practice.   The court said:

> A voluntary association has the power to enact laws governing the admission of members and to prescribe the necessary qualification for membership.   Mayer v. Stonecutters' Association, 47 N.J. Eq. 519, 20 Atl. 492.   Membership therein is a privilege which the society may accord or withhold at its pleasure, with which a court of equity will not interfere, even though the arbitrary rejection of the candidate may prejudice his material interest . . .   We think such a society as the Potter County Medical Association is legitimate and lawful . . .   If it deemed appellant an osteopath, and that as such he was supporting an exclusive system, the association and its members were within their rights, under its rules, in rejecting him as a member.   To compel appellees to receive appellant into fellowship and accept his view would be to impose his will upon appellees and to force the medical world to accept his theory of the healing art.   Courts have no such power.

2. In what respects is a union a fraternal organization and in what respects does it differ from the typical lodge?   What injury does the plaintiff suffer under the decision in the principal case?   Loss of his job?   Loss of companionship?   Loss of his vote in the union?

JAMES v. MARINSHIP CORPORATION
Supreme Court, California, 1944
25 Cal. 2d 721, 155 P.2d 329

Gibson, Chief Justice.   This is an appeal from an order of the Superior Court in Marin County awarding a preliminary injunction which, among other things, restrained defendants from discharging or causing the discharge of plaintiff and other Negro employees because they are not members of a labor union with which their employer has a closed shop agreement, but which will not grant Negroes full membership privileges.   The basic question presented is whether a closed shop may be enforced by a labor union together with an arbitrarily closed or partially closed union membership.

The defendant International Brotherhood of Boilermakers, Iron Shipbuilders and Helpers of America (hereinafter called the International Brotherhood) is an international labor union and an unincorporated association.   Local Union No. 6 of the International Brotherhood of Boilermakers, Iron Shipbuilders and Helpers of America (hereinafter called Local No. 6) is a local union chartered by and affiliated with the International Brotherhood and does business in California.   Certain officials of both the International Brotherhood and Local No. 6 are also named as defendants.

There is a written contract or "Master Agreement" in effect between Marinship and the International Brotherhood containing a provision for a closed shop.   Under this agreement the International Brotherhood "dispatches" workers for employment at Marinship through the medium and agency of Local No. 6, and workers cannot be employed there in any craft over which the International Brotherhood claims jurisdiction unless they are members in good standing in a local union or auxiliary of the International Brotherhood.

Defendant unions do not admit Negroes to membership.   In 1937, the establishment of separate Negro local lodges was authorized by the International Brotherhood, and by-laws therefor were adopted, effective as of January 1, 1938.   For some time the unions dispatched Negro workers to employment without imposing any condition of union affiliation.   Auxiliary A–41, one of such Negro lodges, was chartered on August 14, 1943, and defendants insisted that plaintiff and other Negro workers must join this local, pay initiation fees and dues, and remain members thereof in good standing in order to obtain work clearances for employment at Marinship.   Upon their refusal to do so, the defendant unions threatened to cause their discharge, and defendant Marinship gave notice that it would discharge them within forty-eight hours unless they complied with the demand and obtained the necessary work clearances.

Plaintiff thereupon brought the present action, setting forth the foregoing facts and further alleging, in substance, that Auxiliary A–41 was not a bona fide union local and did not offer equal privileges and benefits of union membership, but instead was used as a means of discriminating against Negro workers; that they were willing to become members of Local No. 6 on equal terms with the other members; that the threatened action by Marinship would constitute a breach of the anti-discrimination provisions in Marinship's contracts with the Maritime Commission; and that it would be contrary to law and public policy and harmful to the war effort. Plaintiff finally alleges that the Negroes will suffer irreparable damage, that there is no speedy or adequate remedy at law, and that injunctive relief is necessary to prevent a multiplicity of suits.

The fundamental question in this case is whether a closed union coupled with a closed shop is a legitimate objective of organized labor.   The defendants contend in effect that a union may, for any arbitrary reason whatsoever, entirely close its membership to otherwise qualified persons and at the same time may, by enforcing a closed shop contract, demand union membership as a condition to the right to work.   To support this contention they argue, first, that a closed shop is lawful in California, and, second, that private, voluntary associations such as labor unions have always had the right to limit membership to persons mutually acceptable.   The first proposition, the legality of a closed shop agreement in California, is conceded by plaintiff, and this court has held that a union may use economic pressure to enforce a demand therefor even though the employees in the picketed shop do not belong to the union and have no dispute with their employer. . . .   It does not follow, however, that a union may maintain both a closed shop agreement or other form of labor monopoly together with a closed or partially closed membership.   We have found no case in this state that supports such a right and there is no decision of the United States Supreme Court that compels its recognition as a proper labor objective.   The case of Greenwood v. Building Trades Council, 71 Cal. App. 159, 233 P. 823, cited by defendants, involved a dispute between rival local unions, one of which sought to compel its reinstatement as member of a building trades council, an organization composed of a number of local unions.   The court refused to compel reinstatement of the excluded local and, further, refused to restrain the building trades council from calling strikes in shops employing members of such local.   The decision on its facts does not involve the right of any individual to become a member of either the building trades council or its member locals, and there is nothing to indicate that any individual applicants were denied membership by such locals.

In our opinion, an arbitrarily closed or partially closed union is incompatible with a closed shop.   Where a union has, as in this case, attained a monopoly of the supply of labor by means of closed shop agreements and other forms of collective labor action, such a union occupies a quasi public position similar to that of a public service business and it has certain corresponding obligations.   It may no longer claim the same freedom from legal restraint enjoyed by golf clubs or fraternal associations.   Its asserted right to choose its own members does not merely relate to social relations; it affects the fundamental right to work for a living. . . .

Some courts have held that state legislation is necessary in order to announce a public policy restricting a union's right to arbitrarily exclude individuals from membership although as a result thereof excluded persons are unable to find employment in their chosen trade. See, for example, Miller v. Ruehl, 166 Misc. 479, 2 N.Y.S.2d 394; Murphy v. Higgins, 12 N.Y.S.2d 913. As said hereinbefore, however, other authorities have indicated that the courts, without statutory aid, may restrain such conduct by a union on the ground that it is tortious and contrary to public policy. Further, as said in 4 Restatement, Torts, p. 136, comment to section 794; "The expression of public policy is not confined to legislation and criminal law; in passing upon the propriety of an object (of concerted labor action), public policy otherwise defined is an important factor. If the object is an act against which the law has definitely set its face, it is not a proper object of concerted action." . . .

We come now to the question whether the present record discloses such discrimination against Negroes as to bring the case within the scope of the rules discussed above. It is admitted that Negroes are excluded from membership in the union, that is, they cannot become members of Local No. 6. In order to work, however, they must join the Negro auxiliary thereby accepting and consenting to be bound by the "By-Laws Governing Auxiliary Lodges." The defendants argue that this is merely segregation of members and not a denial of membership. But if the union imposes unreasonable and discriminatory restrictions upon Negroes not placed upon members of Local No. 6, and if the auxiliary does not afford its members privileges and protection substantially equal to that afforded to the members of Local No. 6, then to compel the Negroes to join the auxiliary, upon penalty of discharge, is the equivalent of a complete denial of union membership. If a union may not directly exclude certain workers, it may not do so indirectly by prescribing intolerable or unfair conditions of membership for such persons. . . . Upon an examination of the record it becomes readily apparent that the membership offered to Negroes is discriminatory and unequal.

First, as alleged in the complaint, Local No. 6 "controls, manages and supervises all of the affairs and business of Auxiliary A–41." Non-Negro locals are expressly declared in the by-laws to be the "Supervising" lodges. The auxiliary, however, has no voice nor vote in the affairs of Local No. 6. The Negroes are thus deprived of the right to participate in the determination of vital union policies and, as alleged, the auxiliary has no "authority or autonomy with respect to its own affairs."

Second, the auxiliary is not allowed a business agent to act for its members, but must seek representation through the business agents of Local No. 6. It is also without a grievance committee to redress complaints with its employers, although under the by-laws it may have a representative on the committee of the supervising lodge. Thus, although the white workers may choose those whom they wish to represent them, the Negroes are denied the right. Contrary to the ordinary principles of the law of agency, the auxiliary does not have the undivided loyalty of its representatives, and where grievances arise in which whites and Negroes have different interests, it is clear that the Negroes will not be adequately represented and the opportunity for discrimination is obvious. It is asserted by defendants that the business agents or grievance committee chosen by Local No. 6 will act for the Negroes and does act for them without favoritism. This is vigorously denied by plaintiff, but, in any event, is entirely beside the point. The important fact is that the Negroes have no right to compel them to act. Defendant union further seeks to justify the inequality upon the ground that Negroes are a minority group. While it is true that a minority may properly be outvoted, minority members are nevertheless entitled to vote and participate in the affairs of the whole group, and certainly they cannot be forced into a nonparticipating, isolated unit. It is urged by defendants that at the present time Negroes are employed under the same hours, wages and other working conditions as non-Negro employees. But one of the vital purposes of a labor union is to maintain the *continuance* of favorable conditions, — to assure some security as to future employment practices; and, under the union regulations discussed above, the auxiliary is deprived of the customary union machinery essential to watch over and check at the outset future grievances and unequal changes in working conditions fostered by either the employer or the members of the non-Negro local. This is a serious and present discrimination against Negroes, certain to become an even greater handicap when temporary war employment ceases and shipyard jobs become more scarce. Moreover, the important issue between plaintiff and the defendant union is that of discrimination against him as a *union member. . . .*

Third, the members of Auxiliary A–41 are dispatched to employment only through the agency of Local No. 6, and cannot obtain a change of classification of their work, that is, promotions from helper (beginner) to journeyman (skilled craftsman) without the approval of the non-Negro local.   The colored local thus has no right to control the job status of its own members, and the white workers are assured first chance at the better, more highly paid work.

Fourth, the regular union has a permanent status which the Negro local has not.   It appears from the "By-laws Governing Auxiliary Lodges" that auxiliaries may be dissolved, apparently at will, by the International Brotherhood.   In the case of non-Negro locals, however, it is provided that the International Brotherhood may revoke the charter of a lodge "which shall have been proven guilty of violation of this Constitution."   Thus, although no such power is given over non-Negro locals, the International Brotherhood may at any time dissolve the Negro auxiliaries, destroying their right to employment together with any rights attained through past union membership.   As plaintiff points out, this will place Negroes at a great disadvantage with respect to security of employment should shipyard jobs become scarce.   Also, upon dissolution, all funds of the auxiliary (accumulated from fees, dues, and "taxes") must be turned in to the International Brotherhood.

The foregoing illustrations drawn from the complaint and the union rules clearly establish substantial discrimination against Negro workers who accept membership in the auxiliary local.   Since they are denied union membership on terms of equality with other workers, the case is the same as if they were wholly denied the privilege of membership.

The discriminatory practices involved in this case are, moreover, contrary to the public policy of the United States and this state.   The United States Constitution has long prohibited governmental action discriminating against persons because of race or color.   5th, 14th and 15th Amendments.   It has recently been held that these provisions prohibit a political party from denying Negroes the right to vote in primary elections where, under state law, the political party is acting as an agency of the state in conducting the elections.   Smith v. Allwright, 321 U.S. 649, 64 S. Ct. 757, 88 L. Ed. 987, 151 A.L.R. 1110.   And in Steele v. Louisville & Nashville R.R. Co., . . . 323 U.S. 192, 65 S. Ct. 226, 89 L. Ed. —, the court held that the Railway Labor Act clothed the bargaining representative selected by employees with a power which, like that of the Legislature, is subject to limitations, and that, therefore, such representative could not be permitted to discriminate against a minority group of employees because of race.

Where, as here, a labor union has attained a monopoly of the labor supply through closed shop agreements, such a union, like a public service business, may not unreasonably discriminate against Negro workers for the sole reason that they are colored persons. . . .

Defendants urge that Local No. 6 should not have been directly ordered to admit plaintiff as a member.   In accordance with the principles discussed above, the union may not maintain *both* a closed shop and an arbitrarily closed or partially closed union. Negroes must be admitted to membership under the same terms and conditions applicable to non-Negroes unless the union and the employer refrain from enforcing the closed shop agreement against them.   See Wilson v. Newspaper & Mail Deliverers' Union, 123 N.J. Eq. 347, 197 A. 720, . . .   The order of the trial court, when read as a whole, may be interpreted as allowing this alternative.   Under the circumstances of this case, it is unnecessary to determine whether or not the union, in absence of a closed shop agreement, would be required to open its doors to all qualified employees.

The injunction, contrary to defendants' contention, is not so broad as to give Negroes any greater right to membership than that extended to other persons; it was clearly intended to do no more than eliminate discrimination upon the basis of race and color alone. . . .

The judgment is affirmed.

NOTES

1. Although the court in James v. Marinship Corp. placed considerable emphasis on the fact that the Union had a monopoly of the labor market, a year later it held that the existence of a monopoly was not requisite to relief.   Williams v. International Brotherhood of Boilermakers, 27 Cal. 2d 586, 165, P.2d 903 (1946) . For other cases applying the same general rules see Bautista v. Jones, 25 Cal. 2d 746, 155 P.2d 343 (1944) ; Dotson v. International Alliance, 191 P.2d 778 (Cal. Dist. Ct. of App. 1948) ; Riviello v. Journeymen Barbers, 199 P.2d 400 (Cal. Dist. Ct. of App. 1948) ; Walter v. McCarvel, 309 Mass. 260, 34 N.E.2d 677 (1941) ; Carroll v. Local No. 269, 133 N.J. Eq. 144, 31 A.2d 223 (1943) ; Wilson v. Newspaper & Mail Deliverers' Union, 123 N.J. Eq. 347, 197 Atl. 720 (1938) ; Clark v. Curtis, 297 N.Y. 1014, 80 N.E.2d 536 (1948) ; Kelly v. Simons, 87 N.Y.S.2d 767 (1949) ; Colson v. Gelber, 192 Misc. 520, 80 N.Y.S.2d 448 (1948) ; Dorrington v. Manning, 135

Pa. Super. 194, 4 A.2d 886 (1939). See, generally, Summers, The Right to Join a Union, 47 Col. L. Rev. 33 (1947).

2. The California rule against closed unions enforcing a closed shop was greatly expanded in Hughes v. Superior Court, 32 Cal. 2d 850, 198 P.2d 885 (1948). Negro groups demanded that a store, half of whose patrons were Negro, employ Negro clerks in proportion to the number of Negro customers. The store refused, claiming that its hiring policy was based wholly on merit and was nondiscriminatory. When the groups picketed the store, the employer obtained an injunction. The California Supreme Court held that because the picketing was to compel a hiring on the basis of race, it was an attempt to enforce a closed shop and closed union to this extent. Under the principles of James v. Marinship Corp., this arbitrary discrimination was an unlawful purpose and picketing to enforce it could be enjoined. Affirmed, 339 U.S. 460, 70 Sup. Ct. 718, 94 L. Ed. 985 (1950). See page 777 supra for a discussion of the Hughes case.

3. The Brotherhood of Locomotive Firemen & Enginemen, which excludes all Negroes, made a collective agreement with the Louisville & Nashville Railroad providing for seniority and promotion rules which discriminated against Negro firemen and had the effect of eliminating them from their runs. The United States Supreme Court held in Steele v. Louisville & Nashville R.R. Co, 323 U.S. 192, 65 Sup. Ct. 226, 89 L. Ed. 173 (1944), that the enforcement of such discriminatory contracts should be enjoined, and said:

So long as a labor union assumes to act as the statutory representative of a craft, it cannot rightly refuse to perform the duty, which is inseparable from the power of representation conferred upon it, to represent the entire membership of the craft. While the statute does not deny to such a bargaining agent the right to determine the eligibility to its membership, it does require the union, in collective bargaining, and in the making of contracts with the carrier, to represent non-union or minority members of the craft without hostile discrimination, fairly, impartially, and in good faith. Wherever necessary to that end, the union is required to consider the requests of non-union members of the craft and expressions of their views with respect to collective bargaining with the employer, and to give them notice and opportunity for hearing upon its proposed action.

This case is printed at page 236 supra.   See also the companion case, Tunstall v. Brotherhood of Locomotive Firemen & Enginemen, 323 U.S. 210, 65 Sup. Ct. 235, 89 L. Ed. 187 (1944).

These decisions by the Supreme Court have not caused the railroad brotherhoods to abandon their discriminatory policies.   The Negroes have been forced to bring subsequent suits to enjoin enforcement of such contracts, and the unions have vigorously fought these suits on procedural and jurisdictional grounds.   See, e.g., Graham v. Brotherhood of Locomotive Firemen, 338 U.S. 232, 70 Sup. Ct. 14, 94 L. Ed. 22 (1949); Rolax v. Atlantic Coast Line R. Co., 186 F.2d 473 (4th Cir. 1951).   See also Aaron and Komaroff, Statutory Regulation of Internal Union Affairs, 44 Ill. L. Rev. 425, 436 (1949); Creamer, Collective Bargaining and Racial Discrimination, 17 Rocky Mt. L. Rev. 163 (1945); Murray, The Right to Equal Opportunity in Employment, 33 Calif. L. Rev. 388 (1945); cases noted in 58 Harv. L. Rev. 448 (1945), 43 Mich. L. Rev. 982 (1945), 23 Tex. L. Rev. 287 (1945).

4. In a representation hearing under the National Labor Relations Act, In re Larus Brothers, 62 N.L.R.B. 1075, 16 L.R.R.M. 242 (1945), the CIO union charged that the AFL union should not be certified because it maintained segregated locals for its Negro members.   The Board found that the segregated local was given equal rights with the white local, but said at page 1084: "We entertain grave doubts whether a union which discriminately denies membership to employees on the basis of race may nevertheless bargain as the exclusive representative in an appropriate unit composed in part of members of the excluded race."

In spite of this statement of policy by the NLRB which has been repeated a number of times, the Board never acted on this rule.   In all of the cases in which the problem has been raised, the Board has refused to find that such discrimination would bar certification.   See, for example, Carter Manufacturing Company, 59 N.L.R.B. 804, 15 L.R.R.M. 164 (1944); Atlanta Oak Flooring, 62 N.L.R.B. 973, 16 L.R.R.M. 235 (1945); Aaron and Komaroff, Statutory Regulation of Internal Union Affairs, 44 Ill. L. Rev. 425, 438–440 (1949).   Finally, in a recent case the Board repudiated the doctrine of the Larus Brothers case and held that discriminatory admission policies would not be considered in determining the appropriate unit.   In re Balaban and Katz, 87 N.L.R.B. 1071, 25 L.R.R.M. 1197 (1949).

BETTS v. EASLEY
Supreme Court, Kansas, 1946
161 Kan. 459, 169 P.2d 831

HOCH, Justice. . . . The plaintiffs — six in number — are Negro employees of the Santa Fe Railway Company in its Argentine shops in Kansas City, Kansas. They bring the action in their own behalf and — under the authority of Sec. 60–413, G.S. 1935 — in behalf of and for the benefit of the other one hundred or more Negro employees similarly situated. . . .

In November, 1943, in harmony with procedure prescribed in the Railway Labor Act, the Mediation Board, constituted under that Act, conducted in the Argentine shops an election by secret ballot, participated in by all employees involved, for the purpose of determining what labor organization should become the authorized collective bargaining representative of such employees in negotiations with the employer, as contemplated by the Act. As a result of this election, the Grand Lodge Brotherhood Railway Carmen of America was chosen and officially designated as such collective bargaining agent. . . .

Since the organization of Local Lodge No. 850, the defendants have refused to admit the plaintiffs and other Negro employees to full membership in the local lodge although they have paid their membership dues, and "Said defendants have insisted and still insist, and are determined to coerce and to force these plaintiffs and the other Negro employees who are members of said Local Union, to accept membership in a separate, subservient and substandard organization known as a separate or auxiliary lodge for colored employees only."

Plaintiffs assert, in the petition, that the division and classification of employees as above indicated "is not based on experience and skill, but entirely on race and color, and for that reason said division and classification is illegal, unreasonable and arbitrary" and that the alleged acts of exclusion and discrimination were and are being done under a provision of the constitution and by-laws of the defendant union which reads as follows: "On railroads where the employment of colored persons has become a permanent institution they shall be admitted to membership in separate lodges. Where these separate lodges of negroes are organized they shall be *under the jurisdiction of and represented by the delegate of the nearest white local in any meeting of the Joint Protective Board Federation or Convention where delegates may be seated.*" Brotherhood Railway Carmen, Subordinate Lodge

Constitution, Ed. 1941, sec. 6, clause C. (Italics supplied.)

Further allegations particularizing the acts of discrimination may be summarized as follows:

That separate Negro lodge is not permitted to transact its own business, but must be under the absolute jurisdiction of the nearest white local lodge.

Negro workmen, eligible to membership

(a) Are not permitted to attend meetings of Local Lodge No. 850 nor to vote on the election of any officers or on anything pertaining to the business of the Grand or local lodge;

(b) Are not permitted to participate in any determination of policy;

(c) Are not permitted to vote upon the question of the amount of dues to be paid by members of the union;

(d) Are not permitted to vote in the selection of those who are to represent them;

(e) Cannot be delegates in any meeting of the Joint Protective Board Federation or to any meeting or convention where delegates may be seated, but must be represented by a delegate or delegates selected by the white lodge.

The prayer of the petition is that the defendants be restrained "from continuing to enforce the particular provision of the constitution and by-laws, viz.: section 6, clause (c) of the subordinate lodge constitution, which divides and classifies the members of said labor unions on the basis of race and color"; that the defendants be restrained "from being the Bargaining Agent or Agents, or representative or representatives as individuals or as a committee or plan to deal with the defendant the Atchison, Topeka and Santa Fe Railway Company for and on behalf of the employees at the Argentine shops of the aforesaid Railroad Company, concerning grievances, labor disputes, wages, rates of pay, hours of employment, or any other condition of work, unless and until the said defendants, each and all of them, give these plaintiffs and all the other Negro members whom they represent herein, equality of privileges and participation in the affairs of the said defendant Labor Unions, and give them full membership in the same; . . . ."

Before considering the fundamental and controlling questions presented, it is well to make clear at the outset that the pleadings raise no abstract questions as to the power of the union to segregate its white and colored members. To what extent the union may lawfully segregate its membership on the basis of race, color, or any other basis it chooses, in connection solely with local activities which are wholly independent of its functions as the designated bargaining agent, is a question not before us. We are here concerned with a segregation which carries with it alleged inequality of participation in union affairs relating to hours, wages, grievances, working conditions, and other such important matters incident to employment, which are within the scope of negotiation and settlement under the Railway Labor Act.

The questions here may be variously stated as follows:

Is the defendant labor union, in performing its functions as a collective bargaining agent, to be regarded solely as a "private association of individuals" free from the constitutional and statutory restraints which attach to public agencies?

Does the fact that membership is voluntary relieve the union from an obligation, as a collective bargaining agent, to accord to all members equal privileges in connection with its acts and transactions as such agent? . . .

That we are here dealing with acts and transactions affected with a public interest is too clear to require extended comment. The Railway Labor Act was passed by Congress in the exercise of its constitutional power to regulate interstate commerce. . . .

In the light of the history and purpose of the Act, as construed in many decisions, the trial court's view that the acts complained of are solely those of "a private association of individuals" is wholly untenable. The acts complained of are those of an organization acting as an agency created and functioning under provisions of Federal law. This being true, it is unnecessary to consider appellees' contention that the Fifth Amendment is not here applicable because it relates only to action by the Federal government and not to acts of private persons. Nor do we need to inquire whether appellees' statement as to the operation of the Fifth Amendment is too broadly stated. In any event the constitutional guarantees of due process, whether under the Federal or state constitutions, are to be liberally construed to effectuate their purposes, and are a restraint not only upon persons holding positions specifically classed as executive, legislative or judicial, but upon all administrative and ministerial officials who act under governmental authority. 16 C.J.S., Constitutional Law, Sec. 568, pp. 1148, 1149, and cases cited Note 61. While claiming and exercising rights incident to its designation as bargaining agent, the defendant union cannot at the same time avoid the responsibilities that attach to such statutory status.

At this point it should be made clear that when the majority of the craft or class involved have chosen their collective bargaining agent, such agent becomes, under the law, the *sole* bargaining agent for all the workmen.   No minority group is permitted to have its own representative to negotiate for it.   Virginian R. Co. v. System Federation No. 40, [300 U.S. 515]; Steele v. Louisville & Nashville R. Co., 323 U.S. 192, on pages 200, 201, 202, 65 S. Ct. 226, on pages 231, 232, 89 L. Ed. 173, and cases cited.   It is apparent, therefore, that when the Negro workmen, segregated into a separate lodge *under the jurisdiction* of the *nearest white local,* are not permitted to participate in meetings "where delegates may be seated," they are denied rights and privileges accorded to white workmen in vital matters subject to negotiation and adjustment under the Act.

It is urged, however, that since membership in the union is voluntary and not compulsory, the petitioners have no right to complain about limitations placed upon membership under the constitution and by-laws of the union.   The argument is specious and unrealistic.   Note might here be taken of the allegation that in soliciting members, prior to organization of the local lodge, the organizer assured the plaintiffs that all members would have equal rights and privileges.   But passing that, we come to a more fundamental matter.   This court cannot be blind to present-day realities affecting labor in large industrial plants.   The individual workman cannot just "go it alone."   Every person with an understanding of mass production and other features of modern industry long ago recognized the necessity of collective bargaining by labor representatives, freely chosen, if human rights are to be adequately safeguarded.   In the Railway Labor Act, Congress gave clear and firm recognition to this necessity.   This liberal and enlightened view having been written into the statute, it must follow that a union acting as the exclusive bargaining agent under the law, for all employees, cannot act arbitrarily, cannot deny equality of privilege, to individuals or minority groups merely because membership in the organization is voluntary.   To hold otherwise would do violence to basic principles of our American system. . . .

. . . The petition alleges not only that Negro employees are denied the right to take part in such local affairs of the union as the election of officers and the fixing of dues, but are denied the right to participate in determining the position to be taken by the union, as bargaining agent for all employees, as to wages, hours, working conditions, and other such matters vitally affecting their economic welfare.   Such denial is repugnant to every American concept of equality under the law. It is abhorrent both to the letter and the spirit of our fundamental charter. Never was it more important than now to reject such racial discrimination and to resist all erosions of individual liberty. The acts complained of are in violation of the Fifth Amendment. . . .

The rule is firmly imbedded in American law that the guaranty of due process whether under the Fifth Amendment, as a limitation upon the power of the federal government, or under the Fourteenth Amendment, as a limitation upon the power of the states, — is to be liberally construed to effectuate its purpose of protecting the citizen against arbitrary invasion of his rights of life, liberty and property. 12 Am. Jur. 262, 271; 16 C.J.S., Constitutional Law, Sec. 568, p. 1150. Certainly the denial to a workman, because of race, of an equal voice in determining issues so vital to his economic welfare, under the Railway Labor Act, is an infringement of liberty if indeed it may not also be said to be a deprival of property rights. Cameron v. International Alliance T.S.E., 118 N.J. Eq. 11, 176 A. 692, 97 A.L.R. 504, and annotation on page 609. In the opinion in Texas & S.S. Clerks, 281 U.S. 548, 571, 50 S. Ct. 427, 434, 74 L. Ed. 1034, which involved the right of employees to organize and choose their bargaining representative under the Railway Labor Act free from interference by the employing carrier, Mr. Chief Justice Hughes said, for the court: *"If it could be said that it was necessary in the present instance to show a property interest* in the employees in order to justify the court in granting an injunction we are of the opinion that *there was such an interest,* with respect to the selection of representatives to confer with the employer in relation to contracts of service, as satisfied the statutory requirement."   (Italics supplied.)

NOTES

1. In connection with the court's discussion of constitutional issues in Betts v. Easley, Shelley v. Kraemer, 334 U.S. 1, 68 Sup. Ct. 836, 92 L. Ed. 1161 (1948), should be considered. This case held that it constituted state action in violation of the due process clause of the Fourteenth Amendment for a state court to enforce a property owners' "restrictive covenant" which discriminated upon a racial basis.

2. In Courant v. International Photographers of Motion Picture Industry, 176 F.2d 1000 (9th Cir. 1949), cert. denied, 338 U.S. 943 (1950), the court rejected the argument that refusal by a

certified union to admit a qualified worker to membership was a violation of the Fifth Amendment. It further held that even though this exclusion prevented him from obtaining work, it was not a failure to represent fairly, within the doctrine of the Steele case, because the Union owed no duty to those not employed in the unit. It therefore had no jurisdiction to compel the Union to admit him or enjoin it from enforcing its closed-shop contract against him.

3. To what extent would James v. Marinship Corp., Steele v. Louisville & Nashville R.R. Co., and Betts v. Easley be applicable to the twelve men who were excluded from the United Framis Makers in Problem I, page 854 supra? What precise legal relief would each of these decisions provide? What are the points of strength and points of weakness in each rule?

4. What is the comparative effectiveness of the following statutes aimed toward solving the same problem?

(a) "It is hereby declared the public policy of this state that no representative agency of labor . . . shall, in such collective bargaining discriminate against any person because of his race or color." Violations are punishable by fine of $500 to $1000 and imprisonment from 30 to 90 days. Neb. Rev. Stat., Secs. 48–214, 48–216 (1943).

(b) The Pennsylvania Labor Relations Act, modeled after the National Labor Relations Act, in its definitions states: "The term 'labor organization' . . . shall not include any labor organization which . . . denies a person or persons membership in its organization on account of race, creed, color." Pa. Stat. Ann., Tit. 43, Sec. 211.3 (f) (Purdon, 1941).

(c) Labor Management Relations Act, Sections 8 (a) (3) and 8 (b) (2). (See Appendix.)

(d) The New York Anti-Discrimination Act of 1945 established a state commission empowered to make investigations, issue complaints, hold hearings, and issue cease and desist orders against "unfair employment practices." Section 131 provides: "It shall be an unfair labor practice:

"1. For an employer, because of race, creed, color or national origin of any individual, to refuse to hire or employ or to bar or discharge from employment such individual or to discriminate against such individual in compensation or in terms, conditions or privileges of employment.

"2. For a labor organization, because of the race, creed, color or national origin of any individual, to exclude or to expel from its membership such individual or to discriminate in any way against any of its members or against any employer or any individual employed by an employer." [3]

5. The first order against a union ever issued by a state Fair Employment Practices Commission was upheld on court review in Electrical Workers v. Civil Rights Comm., 30 L.R.R.M. 2447 (Conn. Super. Ct. 1952). The court expressed some doubt that racial discrimination had been proved but upheld the Commission's order under a statutory standard which required that the facts found by the Commission be conclusive "if supported by substantial and competent evidence." The court implemented this rule by stating that in cases involving racial discrimination it would allow greater latitude to the Commisson in drawing inferences than would normally be the case because "racial prejudice or discrimination is intangible and elusive and can be established only through inference. . . . One who indulges in discrimination does not shout it from the housetops." Id. at 2448. Discussion of the decision and opinion of the Connecticut Commission in this case will be found in 28 L.R.R.M. 98 (1951).

While the above case is the first involving an order of a Fair Employment Practices Commission directed toward racial discrimination by a union, Railway Mail Assn. v. Corsi, 326 U.S. 88, 65 Sup. Ct. 1483, 89 L. Ed. 2072 (1945), upheld the constitutionality of the New York act prohibiting racial discrimination in union admission policies. It was a declaratory judgment action.

On June 29, 1951, the Seafarers Union of North America (AFL) signed a "No-Racial-Bias" pledge prepared by the New York Commission Against Discrimination. Investigation had showed discriminatory practices against Negroes in the Union hiring halls through the use of separate shipping lists based on racial differences. The agreement pledged the union to act upon applications for membership, work permits, job referrals, and transfers without regard to race, creed, color, or national origin. See 28 L.R.R.M. 97 (1951).

6. To what extent do these cases or statutes (1) prevent discharge, (2) protect getting a job, (3) prevent discrimination in bargaining, and (4) gain admission to the union? Do they protect all persons denied admission to the union or only limited groups?

[3] Fair Employment Practice Acts similar to the New York statute have been passed in Colorado, Connecticut, Massachusetts, New Jersey, New Mexico, Oregon, Rhode Island, and Washington. Five states have established a statutory policy against discrimination without providing any means of enforcing it. These states are Illinois, Indiana, Kansas, Nebraska, and Wisconsin. — ED.

7. In connection with the admission policies of unions, the proviso of Section 8 (b) (1) (A) of the LMRA should be noted. This proviso seems to authorize unlimited restrictive admission policies of unions in so far as federal law is concerned. However, under Section 8 (a) (3) (the union-shop proviso) restrictive union membership policies may not be made the grounds for discharge of an employee not a member of a union under a union-shop contract unless such employee is denied union membership on grounds of nonpayment of dues or initiation fees. See also Section 8 (b) (2) of the Act. Further, Section 8 (b) (5) of the statute provides for NLRB supervision of the reasonableness of union initiation fees when the union is operating under a union-shop contract. These particular statutory provisions are discussed at pages 477–483 supra, and 875 infra.

The proviso of Section 8 (b) (1) (A) has, in operation, served to free unions from any NLRB supervision of admission and expulsion policies other than that required by the specific provisions above mentioned. Thus, the Board has disclaimed any supervision over the grounds of expulsion of union members. See NLRB, 15th Ann. Rep. 129 (1950).

4. EXCLUSIONARY DEVICES

a. Second-class Membership

In James v. Marinship and Betts v. Easley the Negro workers were not excluded from the Union by outright refusal to admit but were relegated to auxiliary locals which were controlled by adjoining white locals. They were not denied admission but were denied most of the rights and privileges of union membership. A number of unions which officially admit Negroes on an equal basis segregate them in autonomous, self-governing locals where they have full membership rights. There is no clear-cut line between an auxiliary local and a segregated local, but there is an imperceptible shading in the degrees of rights recognized. It is fairly clear that in unions, as elsewhere, the process of segregation tends strongly toward second-class citizenship.

A form of second-class membership analogous to that of auxiliary unions was involved in Cameron v. International Alliance, 118 N.J. Eq. 11, 176 Atl. 692 (1935). Local 384 of the Motion Picture Machine Operators voted to accept a number of applicants as "juniors" to fill the need for apprentices which had suddenly arisen with the introduction of sound pictures. However, these new members were compelled to remain in "Junior local" after their apprenticeship terms were served. They had no voice or vote in the Union, were excluded from Union meetings, and were subject to being replaced by "senior" members in their jobs. They could not become senior members except on a two-thirds vote of the seniors and a payment of a $3000 initiation fee. The New Jersey court held that such a classification of union membership was against public policy and ordered the Union to admit the juniors to full membership without payment of the initiation fee.

Another form of second-class membership is effected by use of the work permit. Most unions which restrict admission must make provision for permitting nonunion workers to work with union members during rush periods to meet the peak demands for labor. This is accomplished by issuing permit cards for a fee of $1 or $2 a week. The cards entitle nonmembers to work temporarily but give them no rights within the union. These permit fees have been the subject of considerable legislation, of which the Texas provision is a fairly typical example. The Texas statute was upheld in American Federation of Labor v. Mann, 188 S.W.2d 276 (Tex. Civ. App. 1945). In the course of its opinion in this case, the court stated at pages 281, 284:

> Section 8a prohibits unions or their officers from demanding or collecting work permit fees from any person not a member of the union. . . .
>
> It is the contention of the appellants that unions have for years charged workmen who were not, and did not want to become, union members, pay initiation fees and dues, a work permit fee, as a condition of employment on a closed shop job. It is sought to be justified as a part of the cost to such union in obtaining and maintaining union conditions and servicing the employees on the job. It does not seem to be controverted that the state would have the right to regulate the amount of such work permit fees. But the complaint here is against the prohibition entirely of such charges.
>
> The record shows that the general overall policy of such unions is not to build up a membership in numbers beyond what such unions can normally and reasonably keep adequately employed and properly service, under normal conditions. It was also shown that under the conditions created by war, particularly as to government construction of war plants, camps, training installations, etc., closed-shop contracts were obtained by unions, which, under the emergency condi-

tions could not possibly be fulfilled by employment only of union members. In some such instances the large majority of the employees were non-union, all of whom, before being permitted to work on such job, were required to pay a fee to the union for the privilege of working. Many of them could not qualify for union membership. Thus, in some instances, according to the testimony of one witness, large numbers of non-union employees were required to contribute to the union funds an amount fixed by the unions for the privilege of working on a closed-shop contract, without any voice as to union policy, union activity, or as to what was done by the union with the funds so exacted of them, or how much such permit fee should be. . . . Thus, in the last analysis, the exaction of a work permit fee, under such circumstances, could be deemed by the Legislature, as it evidently was, contrary to the policy expressed in the Preamble to the Act: "The right to work is the right to live." . . .

Are the courts in these cases interested in protecting the right to work, or are they interested in protecting the right of a worker to participate in the formation of union policy? Does the Texas statute deprive a union of a legitimate device in attempting to eliminate abuses? Consider the use of permit fees in the construction industry to provide for temporary workers who do not work long enough to make it worth while for them to join the union.

b. Initiation Fees

In most unions, initiation fees are relatively low, with the great majority charging $50 or less. In many of the large industrial unions the initiation fee is as low as $5. However, unions which seek to restrict their membership frequently resort to setting the initiation fee at a level which will discourage most applicants or effectively exclude them. The New York checkers local of the Longshoremen's Union charges a $500 fee in advance; the Motion Picture Operators locals of New York, Chicago, and other cities have levied fees ranging from $300 to $1000. Local 644, Photographers of the Motion Picture Industry, affiliated with the International Association of Theatrical Stage Employees, has required $500 on application and $500 on admission. Other locals with initiation fees from $200 to $500 have been the Elevator Constructors, the Cement Masons, the Motion Picture Studio Mechanics, the Bill Posters and Billers of America, and the Carpet and Linoleum Layers — all in New York City; the Glaziers in Cincinnati; the Electrical Workers in Perth Amboy and Cleveland; and the Chicago Flat Janitors.   American Civil Liberties Union, Democracy in Trade Unions 22 (1943).   See also Taft, Dues and Initiation Fees in Labor Union, 60 Q.J. Econ. 219 (1946).

A number of states have attempted to regulate this restrictive device by statute.   Consider the wisdom and workability of the following types of provisions:

(a) "Labor unions or labor organizations shall not charge an initiation fee in excess of Fifteen Dollars ($15.00) provided that initiation fees in effect on January 1, 1940 may continue."   Fla. Gen. Laws 1943, c. 21968, Sec. 5.

(b) "It shall be unlawful for any labor union to make any charge or exaction, or to receive any money for initiation fees . . . which will create a fund in excess of the reasonable requirements of such union in carrying out its lawful purpose or activities, if such fees . . . will create an undue hardship on the applicant for admission."   Tex. Rev. Stat. Ann., Tit. 83, Art. 5154a, Sec. 7 (Vernon Supp. 1946).

(c) "Section 8 (b).   It shall be an unfair labor practice for a labor organization or its agents —

    (5)   to require of employees covered by an agreement authorized under subsection (a) (3) the payment, as a condition precedent to becoming a member of such organization, of a fee in an amount which the Board finds excessive or discriminatory under all the circumstances.   In making such a finding, the Board shall consider, among other relevant factors, the practices and customs of labor organizations in the particular industry, and the wages currently paid to the employees affected; . . ."   Labor Management Relations Act, 1947.

c. Other Devices

A number of unions require apprenticeship or competency tests as conditions of membership.   These requirements may be perfectly proper to enable the union to guarantee an employer satisfactory workmanship, maintain the standards of the trade, and protect members from incompetent fellow workers.   However, these requirements can be readily adapted to restrict admission to the union.   By refusing to accept more than a limited number of apprentices or apprentices of a particular race or creed, or by discriminatory and arbitrary administration of competency tests,

unions may effectively exclude unwanted applicants.   See Kotch
v. Pilot Commrs., 330 U.S. 552, 67 Sup. Ct. 910, 91 L. Ed. 1093
(1947).

C. *Union Discipline*

1. INTRODUCTION

If a union is to be effective as a collective bargaining agency,
it must maintain a high degree of discipline among its members.
The very problem of maintaining a functioning organization with
hundreds of local unions and thousands of members scattered
throughout the country and working in thousands of shops makes
necessary a considerable degree of control over the members' activities.   If negotiations with the employer break down, and resort must be had to economic force, the atmosphere within the
union becomes one of a group fighting for self-preservation.
Rigid discipline akin to military regimentation becomes the order
of the day.   When peace returns and a collective agreement is
made, the union then has the difficult and complex job of administering the agreement.   This in turn requires a high degree
of discipline within the union.

The need for union discipline is obvious, and the need to protect the rights of individuals within the union is also obvious.
The difficult problem is one of reconciling group needs with
minority rights.   This is merely a specialized aspect of the broader
problem of democratic government which has received so much
attention with so little definitive conclusions.

Union discipline in its more drastic form may be enforced by
expulsion from the union, but lesser penalties such as suspension, bar from union meetings, or fines may be imposed.   Although the lesser penalties are the ones most frequently imposed,
these cases seldom reach the courts because the disciplined members do not feel the matter worth the costs and uncertainties of
litigation.

Regardless of the penalty imposed, union discipline cases always
raise these principal questions: (1) Was the reason for punishing
a valid one?   (2) Was the procedure within the union adequate?
(3) At what stage of the proceedings will the court intervene to
protect against union action?   (4) To what extent will the court
substitute its judgment for that of the union tribunal?   The material in this section is directed toward raising some of the difficult
problems of union discipline, giving some insight into the methods

by which the discipline power may infringe on individual rights, and indicating the scope of judicial review.

2. PROBLEM II

The United Gismo Workers of America is a national labor organization with about 100,000 members. For some time the membership of the UGWA has been split into left-wing and right-wing factions. The former group opposes "red-baiting" and condemns the Marshall Plan, the Atlantic Pact, and intervention in Korea. It also campaigns militantly for repeal of the Taft-Hartley Act and for improved wages and working conditions in the gismo industry. The latter group opposes "Communist misleaders of labor," and strongly supports the Marshall Plan, the Atlantic Pact, and intervention in Korea. It also campaigns militantly for repeal of the Taft-Hartley Act and for improved wages and working conditions in the gismo industry.

For many years the UGWA has been controlled by the left-wing faction, led by C. P. Rotmann, national president of the Union. Recently, however, the rival group has grown considerably stronger; and there is much talk of its seceding from the UGWA and forming another organization. The focal point of the struggle for power between the two factions is Local 20, whose membership comprises the 30,000 employees of American Gismobile Corporation. This is the largest and richest local in the UGWA.

In the last campaign for election of officers of Local 20, the right-wing minority organized a slate in opposition to the incumbent left-wing candidates. The leader of the right-wing group was A. D. Black. His campaign was characterized by frequent denunciations of the local and national officers. His numerous accusations included the charge that the officers of Local 20 were maintaining "their own little politburo, paid for by Moscow gold." He consistently referred to Rotmann as "one of the Kremlin Kids whose only loyalty is to Uncle Joe."

In a leaflet distributed to all members of Local 20, Black stated: "This is not a fight over unionism and these hypocrites who pretend to tell you that it is a fight over trade union policies are lying — they are lying out of their mouths and from the pits of their dirty bellies — and they know it, they know it, they know it! I wonder ofttimes if they have a conscience."

At the height of the campaign, Black and two of his chief lieutenants were formally charged with engaging in conduct detrimental to the UGWA, libeling and slandering its officers, and bringing the National Union, Local 20, and its officers into disrepute, contempt, and ridicule — all in violation of the National and Local constitutions and bylaws.   At the request of the defendants, their trial was postponed until after the election, which was won by the left-wing group.   Thereafter, the defendants were granted a hearing before a five-man trial board consisting of fellow Union members, appointed by the executive board of Local 20. They were given several months to prepare and present their defense.   In accordance with Union constitutional rule, they were permitted to choose counsel from among the Union membership, but were denied the right to be represented by outside legal counsel.

The trial board found the defendants guilty as charged, and ruled that they be suspended from the Union and prohibited from attending meetings or otherwise participating in Union affairs for periods ranging from two to five years, but that they could continue working in the industry.   This recommendation was approved by a majority vote of the membership of Local 20.

At the request of the defendants, a three-man judiciary committee to reconsider the trial board's decision was appointed by the executive board of Local 20 shortly thereafter.   Its decision, affirming that of the trial board, was also upheld by majority vote of the membership.   The defendants then appealed to the appeals committee of the National Union.   The membership of this five-man committee was drawn from the National Executive Board and was chosen by Rotmann.   The appeals committee granted the defendants a trial *de novo*, but affirmed the original decision of the Local trial board.   Some seventeen months elapsed between the filing of charges against the defendants and the decision of the appeals committee.

According to the constitution of the UGWA, the defendants can appeal the decision of the appeals committee to the next convention, to be held some twenty months hence.   Suppose, instead, that they come to you for advice as to the advisability of instituting a court action to regain their former membership status in the UGWA.   They concede that the actual trial procedures were fair except in two respects: (1) they think they should have been permitted to designate at least a minority of the members on the trial board, the judiciary committee, and the appeals committee, and (2) they think they should have been permitted to employ outside legal counsel to represent them in those proceedings.

3. PUNISHABLE OFFENSES

Constitutional Provisions

CONSTITUTION OF THE INTERNATIONAL BROTHERHOOD OF ELECTRICAL WORKERS, 1947 [4]

Any member may be penalized for committing any one or more of the following offenses:

(1) Urging or advocating that a member, or any L.U., start action in a court of law against the I.B.E.W., or any of its officers, or against a L.U. or any of its officers, without first exhausting all remedies through all the courts of the I.B.E.W.

(2) Violation of any provision of this Constitution and the rules herein, or the by-laws, working agreements, or trade and working rules of a L.U.

(3) Having knowledge of the violation of any provision of this Constitution, or the by-laws or rules of a L.U., yet failing to file charges against the offender or to notify the proper officers of the L.U.

(4) Obtaining membership through fraudulent means or by misrepresentation, either on the part of the member himself or others interested.

(5) Advocating or attempting to bring about a withdrawal from the I.B.E.W. of any L.U. or of any member or group of members.

(6) Publishing or circulating among the membership, or among L.U.'s false reports or misrepresentation.

(7) Sending letters or statements, anonymous or otherwise, or making oral statements, to public officials or others which contain untruths about, or which misrepresent a L.U., its officers or representatives, or officers or representatives of the I.B.E.W.

(8) Creating or attempting to create dissatisfaction or dissension among any of the members or among L.U.'s of the I.B.E.W.

(9) Working in the interest of any organization or cause which is detrimental to, or opposed to, the I.B.E.W.

(10) Slandering or otherwise wronging a member of the I.B.E.W. by any wilful act or acts.

(11) Entering or being present at any meeting of a L.U., or its Executive Board, or any committee meeting, while intoxicated, or drinking intoxicants in or near any such meeting, or carrying intoxicants into such meeting.

(12) Disturbing the peace or harmony of any L.U. meeting or

[4] Article XXVII, Sec. 2 (1–16).

meeting of its Executive Board, using abusive language, creating or participating in any disturbance, drinking intoxicants, or being intoxicated, in or around the office or headquarters of a L.U.

(13) Making known the business of a L.U. to persons not entitled to such knowledge.

(14) Fraudulently receiving any moneys due a L.U. or misappropriating the moneys of any L.U.

(15) Attending or participating in any gathering or meeting whatsoever, held outside meetings of a L.U., at which the affairs of the L.U. are discussed, or at which conclusions are arrived at regarding the business and the affairs of a L.U., or regarding L.U. officers or a candidate or candidates for L.U. office.

(16) Mailing, handing out, or posting cards, handbills, letters, marked ballots or political literature of any kind or displaying streamers, banners, signs or anything else of a political nature, or being a party in any way to such being done in an effort to induce members to vote for or against any candidate or candidates for L.U. office, or candidates to conventions.

4. LEGAL LIMITATIONS ON UNION DISCIPLINE[5]

POLIN v. KAPLAN
Court of Appeals, New York, 1931
257 N.Y. 277, 177 N.E. 833

KELLOGG, J. The plaintiffs were members of an unincorporated association known as the "Moving Picture Machine Operators' Union of Greater New York, Local No. 306." The recording secretary of the union presented charges against the plaintiffs to the association at one of its regular meetings. The charges were three in number. Briefly stated, they were as follows:

Charge No. 1. The plaintiffs had violated section 6, article 10, of the constitution, in that they had brought an action in the Supreme Court of the state in which they had charged the officers of the union with having violated the constitution and by-laws, and had sought redress therefor.

Charge No. 2. The plaintiffs had circulated printed articles of a libelous nature, containing statements charging the

[5] See, generally, Steever, The Control of Labor Through Union Discipline, 16 Cornell L.Q. 212 (1930); Shister, Trade-Union Government; A Formal Analysis, 60 Q.J. Econ. 78 (1945); Notes: 30 Col. L. Rev. 847 (1930), 96 U. of Pa. L. Rev. 537 (1948), 57 Yale L.J. 1302 (1948), 33 Minn. L. Rev. 156 (1949).

officers of the union with violations of the constitution and by-laws, and other illegal practices, and such statements were false and malicious.

Charge No. 3. The plaintiffs had violated their oaths of obligation to the union "by committing the acts charged in specifications 1 and 2, and refusing on numerous occasions to obey the mandates of the union, and also the will of the majority of said union. Also, in failing to keep confidential the work of the body of the union.

The union, at a regular meeting, made the charges cognizable, and referred them to the executive board to try the same and make their report. This was the procedure prescribed by article 10, section 1, of the constitution. The board heard the proof offered in respect to the charges, and made a report sustaining them. Thereupon the union, at a regular meeting, confirmed the report, and imposed these penalties: For the violation specified in charge No. 1, $500; for that specified in charge No. 2, $500; for that specified in charge No. 3, expulsion from the union. Thereafter the plaintiffs instituted these actions to have the proceedings adjudged to be null and void, to procure the plaintiffs' reinstatement, and to recover damages.

The constitution and by-laws of an unincorporated association express the terms of a contract which define the privileges secured and the duties assumed by those who have become members. As the contracts may prescribe the precise terms upon which membership may be gained, so it conclusively defines the conditions which will entail its loss. Thus, if the contract reasonably provides that the performance of certain acts will constitute a sufficient cause for the expulsion of a member, and that charges of their performance, with notice to the member, shall be tried before a tribunal set up by the association, the provision is exclusive, and the judgment of the tribunal, rendered after a fair trial, that the member has committed the offenses charged and must be expelled, will not be reviewed by the regularly constituted courts. Belton v. Hatch, 109 N.Y. 593, 17 N.E. 225, 4 Am. St. Rep. 495; Matter of Haebler v. New York Produce Exchange, 149 N.Y. 414, 44 N.E. 87. A court "cannot review the proceedings or re-examine the merit of the expulsion." Per Miller, J., in Wilcox v. Supreme Council Royal Arcanum, 210 N.Y. 370, 376, 104 N.E. 624, 626, 52 L.R.A. (N.S.) 806. This is not to say, however, that a court will decline to interfere, if an expulsion has been decreed for acts not constituting violations of the constitution and by-laws, and not made expellable offenses thereby, either by terms expressed or implied. In such an instance, the expulsion is not within the power conferred by the contract. Accordingly, the proceedings will be set aside and the associate restored to membership. People ex rel. Bartlett v. Medical Society of Erie County, 32 N.Y. 187; Amalgamated Society of Carpenters v. Braithwaite (1922) 2 App. Cas. 440, 470. . . .

We think also, that in every contract of association there inheres a term binding members to loyal support of the society in the attainment of its proper purposes, and that for a gross breach of this obligation the power of expulsion is impliedly conferred upon the association. It has been said by the Supreme Court of California that an association may expel a member upon one of two grounds, viz.: "First, a violation of such of the established rules of the association as have been subscribed or assented to by the members, and as provide expulsion for such violation; second, for such conduct as clearly violates the fundamental objects of the association, and if persisted in and allowed would thwart those objects or bring the association into disrepute." Otto v. Journeymen Tailors' Protective & Benevolent Union, 75 Cal. 308, 314, 17 P. 217, 219, 7 Am. St. Rep. 156. The Supreme Ct. of Pennsylvania has said that, if the charter of an association contains no express provision for expulsion, it may nevertheless be had if the member "has been guilty of some infamous offense, or has done some act tending to the destruction of the society." Weiss v. Musical Mut. Protective Union, 189 Pa. 446, 451, 42 A. 118, 120, 69 Am. St. Rep. 820. We subscribe to these views.

Charge No. 1. This charge, as we have stated, is that the plaintiffs, in bringing an action against the officers of the corporation, violated section 6 of article 10 of the constitution. That section is entitled "Order of Appeal" and provides in part: "The order of appeal shall be: 1. To the Local Union from its own or its officers' decision." It then provides that subsequent appeals shall be from the decision of the local union to the international president of the alliance in convention assembled. It provides in conclusion: "The penalty for violation of the above order of appeal shall be not less than five hundred ($500.00) dollars or expulsion from this union or both." As the first appeal must be to the local union "from its own or its officers' decision," it is perfectly obvious that the section relates only to appeals from the decisions of a lower tribunal within the association to a higher tribunal within the union. When the plaintiffs brought action against the officers of the union, no decision of the association had then been rendered against them; therefore, they could not take an appeal as provided by the section. Obviously, they violated no express provision of the constitution and by-laws, for which expulsion was provided as a penalty, by bringing the action. Moreover, in so doing, they displayed no disloyalty to the union, and performed no act injurious to the society or tending to its disruption. The purpose of the action was to procure restoration to the treasury of the union of moneys alleged to have been misappropriated by its officers. It was the absolute right of the plaintiffs to bring the suit, whether they could successfully maintain it or not, and they might not be expelled for having so done. Therefore charge No. 1 utterly failed.

Charge No. 2. The plaintiffs were charged with circulating among the members of the union, false and malicious statements setting forth acts of misconduct on the part of its officers, similar to those charged in the action brought. No rule contained in the printed copies of the constitution and by-laws of the union, submitted to us as correctly expressing the same, forbids the circulation among members of statements concerning the union officers, which are libelous, nor does any rule provide, as a penalty for so doing, for the fining or expulsion of the member. Therefore no violation of the express terms of the constitution and by-laws was alleged or shown. Whether such an act might, in any case, constitute a breach of the implied contract term, that a member will remain loyal to his union, and do no act tending to its disruption or disgrace, may be a doubtful question. In People ex rel. Meade v. McDonough, 8 App. Div. 591, 600, 35 N.Y.S. 214, 221, 40 N.Y.S. 1147, Vann, J., wrote: "The charge that the relator slandered the lodge itself was probably sufficient, as that might impair its efficiency, and prove a permanent injury. The willful circulation of false and injurious reports about the organization differs in principle from an attack upon its members, as it involves disloyalty, and a serious violation of corporate duty." In Wilcox v. Supreme Council Royal Arcanum, 210 N.Y. 370, 379, 104 N.W. 624, 627, 52 L.R.A. (N.S.) 806, Miller, J., said: "Undoubtedly it would injure the order; temporarily at least, to accuse its officers of being 'grafters,' but, if the charge were well founded, an impartial judge might conclude that it was made in the discharge of the highest duty to the order, and that the temporary injury resulting from the exposé of wrong-doing was more than offset by the permanent good. It is no longer the law that the greater the truth the greater the libel." If the evidence given before the executive board, which we have not seen, established that the assertions made by the plaintiffs in the circulated statements, concerning the misconduct of the union officers, were unfounded, or were made maliciously without probable cause, and that they tended to the disruption of the union, we are not prepared to say that it would not have justified an expulsion. The difficulty is that the union did not expel the plaintiffs upon this charge.

Charge No. 3. This charges the plaintiffs with a violation of their oaths of obligation to the union, in that they were guilty of misconduct, as set forth in charges 1 and 2. For this charge the penalty decreed was expulsion. We have already shown that charge No. 1 was wholly unfounded, in that the acts charged were not violations of the constitution and by-laws, in respect to any term thereof whether expressed or implied. Thus the plaintiffs stand expelled for two alleged violations in combination, one of which furnished no grounds whatsoever for an expulsion. We cannot assume that the union would have expelled the plaintiffs for the violation asserted in charge No. 2 standing by itself. Especially is this true when it appears that for such violation the plaintiffs were punished by the infliction of no other penalty than a fine of $500. Manifestly, the violation asserted in charge No. 1 entered into the decision, as an essential ground for the expulsion decreed. It follows that the plaintiffs were expelled without power and illegally. They should be reinstated.

It has been found that the plaintiff Polin, as a result of the action of the union in expelling him, has suffered a loss of wages amounting in the aggregate to $1,955. He is entitled to a recovery of this amount. It has also been found that he has incurred expenses for legal services amounting to $5,000. The services involved are those performed in this very action. No recovery may be had therefor.

It has been found that the plaintiff Schneider has suffered a loss of wages amounting to $1,622.40, for which he should have a recovery. His expenses for legal services in this action amounted to $3,500, for which no recovery may be had.

The judgments should be reversed and judgment directed in favor of plaintiff in each action, setting aside the proceedings of the union, restoring plaintiff to membership, and awarding to plaintiff Polin a recovery of $1,955.00, and to plaintiff Schneider, a recovery of $1,622.40, with interest from June 3, 1930, together with costs in all the courts.[6]

[6] This case is discussed in 80 U. of Pa. L. Rev. 452 (1931). — ED.

NOTES

1. Snay v. Lovely, 276 Mass. 159, 176 N.E. 791 (1931), Grace M. Snay was expelled from the Boot and Shoe Workers Union on the charge of engaging in a wildcat strike. Because of this expulsion she was unable to obtain employment in other union shops. The court found that she was clearly not guilty of the offense, but refused to grant relief on the following logic:

> The plaintiff, by becoming a member of the union and agreeing to support it, entered into an obligation in the nature of a contract to become bound by its constitution and governing rules so far as not inconsistent with controlling principles of law. As an incident of membership she consented to be suspended or expelled in accordance with the constitution and rules of the union by its appropriate officers acting in good faith and in conformity to natural justice.
>
> Another obligation impliedly arising from her membership in the union was that the plaintiff must exhaust remedies open to her within the union before seeking relief in the courts for any wrong done her by the organization, unless it appears that resort to those remedies would be illusory or vain. . . . The constitution of the union plainly provides that the plaintiff might have appealed from the adverse decision of the general executive board to the convention. That convention was the body next above the general executive board and had power to reverse and annul its decision. Her failure to avail herself of this remedy for the redress of grievances afforded by the fundamental law of the union prevents her asking the interposition of a court of equity. There is in the record no foundation for a contention that such an appeal would have been fruitless, or that it would not have been treated fairly by the convention. Mulcahy v. Huddell (Mass.) 172 N.E. 796. The factor that the convention did not assemble until a year or more after the suspension of the plaintiff, and then in a city outside of the commonwealth, may be important, in connection with others having an overreaching or crafty aspect, in determining whether a particular contract is so harsh and unreasonable as to be offensive to sound legal principles. See Fritz v. Knaub, 57 Misc. Rep. 405, 103 N.Y.S. 1003, affirmed 124 App. Div. 915, 108 N.Y.S. 1133; Bricklayers', Plasterers' & Stone Masons' Union v. Bowen (Sup.) 183 N.Y.S. 855, affirmed 198 App. Div. 967, 189 N.Y.S.

938; Kunze v. Weber, 197 App. Div. 319, 188 N.Y.S. 644.
But, standing alone, it is not enough in the circumstances here
disclosed to be a basis for relief.   Commonly, contracts voluntarily executed with knowledge of their contents by rational
beings acting on their own judgment ought to be enforced.
The single circumstance that the plaintiff, by reason of her
suspension from membership, was unable to secure work in
union or closed shops, while no doubt resulting in damage to
her, does not create a cause of action in connection with all
the other facts here disclosed.

2. Is it realistic to say that the relationship between the union
and its members is one of contract?   Are the terms of the Electrical Workers Constitution, page 880 supra, sufficiently definite
and fixed to be enforced as a contract?

3. Is it sound to say that a union may punish any offense stated
in its constitution, but only those offenses?   Consider the following cases:

(a) The Plumbers attempt to expel a member who is shown
to be totally lacking in the skills required for the trade.   He
contends that he cannot be expelled because the constitution does
not provide for this offense.   What result?   Cf. Beesley v. Chicago
Journeymen Plumbers Assn., 44 Ill. App. 278 (1892).

(b) The Brotherhood of Railroad Trainmen expels a member
for adultery under a clause specifically providing for this offense.
What result?   Cf. Bonham v. Brotherhood of Railroad Trainmen,
146 Ark. 117, 225 S.W. 335 (1920).

4. Is it sound to say that a member agrees to abide by whatever
procedure the constitution provides?   Consider the following
case: Dame was president of a local of the Telephone Guild.   He
obtained adoption by his local of a resolution stating that the
Executive Board of the National Guild had made an unauthorized
contract and sent copies of this resolution to the Wisconsin Telephone Company.   He was charged with violating the constitutional provision prohibiting revealing Union business in public
and was expelled by the Executive Board without any notice or
hearing.   Held: The expulsion was proper.   The constitution
did not require a hearing in this situation, and Dame was contractually bound by its terms.   Dame v. LeFevre, 251 Wis. 146,
28 N.W.2d 349 (1947).

5. In February, 1948, certain union members filed suit to contest the validity of salary increases recently voted the union officers.
In July of that year the union's national convention adopted a

resolution forbidding resort to court actions until all internal remedies had been exhausted. In June, 1949, the protesting members were summoned to appear at the next convention at a hearing on their alleged violation of the rule of the prior July. They were thereupon tried, convicted, and fined upon this charge. Should they be able to enjoin enforcement of the penalties? Armstrong v. Duffy, 61 Ohio Abs. 187, 103 N.E.2d 760 (1951).

6. Should the court look to the constitution as the final authority on whether a member is entitled to appeal to the court? Under the contract theory, what is the effect of this provision in the constitution of the Switchmens Union (Constitution of Subordinate Lodges, Sec. 71–b), "The bringing of any legal action by a member against this Union, for any cause whatsoever, shall cause such member to be suspended"?

7. Is a suit by a member against his union for wrongful expulsion one in contract or tort? In International Printing Pressmen v. Smith, 145 Tex. 399, 198 S.W.2d 729 (1946), the question arose as to what statute of limitations was applicable. The court held that, based upon the allegations in the complaint, the suit was one in contract. However, the court did not rule out the possibility that a tort action might lie.

CROSSEN v. DUFFY
Court of Appeals, Ohio, 1951
90 Ohio App. 252, 103 N.E.2d 769

THOMPSON, J. This is the third case to come to this Court growing out of various internal controversies of the National Brotherhood of Operative Potters, an Ohio corporation. . . .

In May, 1947, a spirited campaign developed within the Union on the part of the individual members (Finlay, Whippler, et al.) campaigning as a slate opposed to the then officers of the National Brotherhood. These members failed of nomination and the officers who for many years had guided the National Brotherhood policies were reelected at the annual convention in June, 1947. In that National Convention a resolution was introduced and passed by the delegates amending the constitution. The language of the resolution was as follows:

Report of Law Committee Recommendation.

Whereas, The Law Committee has been instructed to offer a solution for unethical tactics and conduct in the past election; and Whereas, the dignity of our organization has been lowered; therefore be it Resolved, That any member contesting for national office shall conduct himself in a proper manner; and be it further Resolved, That any member accused of making false accusations, misrepresentations, untruths or using degrading literature shall be called before the convention following said election, by a majority vote thereof.

The succeeding convention could try accused member or members or elect a body of five members to try said accused, or set up a special court with power to impose a reprimand, fine, suspension or expulsion.

Committee recommends adoption.

Motion by John Thorne that we concur in the report of the committee.   Motion carried unanimously.   [Defendant's Exhibit I, page 21.]

. . . [T]he resolution adopted at the National Convention in June, 1947, . . . in modified form, which modification was made by the National Secretary without the authority of a convention of the Brotherhood, or a referendum of the members, was thereafter embodied in the constitution of the National Union as revised Oct., 1947, and is therein set forth as Sec. 37.   That section provides as follows: "Any member of the N.B. of O.P. who is not a citizen of the United States or Canada shall not be eligible to hold any national office.   Any members contesting for national office shall conduct themselves in a proper manner.   False accusations or misrepresentations, untruths, or use of degrading literature shall be brought to the attention of the delegates in Convention following the National election.   Any candidate convicted by a majority vote of delegates in Convention, of enumerated practices may be reprimanded, fined, suspended or expelled after due and proper hearing.   If the offending member candidate is not a delegate, the Convention shall by a majority vote elect a body of five members as a special court to hear the case, with power to fine, reprimand, suspend or expell." . . .

In addition to Section 37 of the Constitution, it must be noted also that at the 1948 National Convention the following resolution was enacted:

Recommendation of Law Committee:

The Executive Board shall be empowered to summon any member or members before our National Convention for examination of any act or conduct in violation of their obligation, or anything in any manner de*ter*mental to the N.B. of O.P. and its members.

The delegates in the Convention shall have authority to impose suitable and proper penalty in any case where guilt is established.

Failure to present themselves shall not prevent the delegates from disposing of the case in accordance with letter and spirit of this law.

If proven not guilty, the member or members shall be entitled to transportation and hotel expenses to be paid by the national organization.

This law to become effective immediately.

Committee recommends adoption.

Motion by T. J. Desmond that we concur in the report of the committee.   Motion carried unanimously.

Plaintiffs in this case are Crossen, Gilbert, Cranston, Hammond and Snyder. Of these five plaintiffs, the handbill (Plaintiffs' Exhibit 7) bears the names of three, namely, Gilbert, Cranston and Snyder, as members of a committee of six urging a change in national officers and setting forth as worthy of election the names of eight individuals which we refer to in this opinion as the Finlay slate. None of the plaintiffs in this case was a candidate on that slate, the offense charged against the plaintiffs in this case and for which they were tried, being that they either published or circulated improper campaign literature.

Prior to the June, 1949, Convention, each of the plaintiffs in this case had received a letter dated June 20, 1949. Gilbert, Cranston and Snyder received similar letters containing the following notice:

DEAR SIR AND BROTHER:

You are hereby summoned to appear in the National Convention, June 27, 9:30 A.M. Atlantic City Auditorium, Atlantic City, N.J. to defend yourself for the act of publishing malicious misrepresentations regarding present national officials in the last election.

You are being charged with violating the law adopted in the 1947 Convention, prohibiting malicious political activity within the organization.

You are to assume all expense in connection with your getting to Atlantic City. If proven guilty you will not be reimbursed for any expense whatsoever. If adjudged not guilty the N.B.O.P. will pay expenses. We remain,

Fraternally,

JAMES M. DUFFY, *President*

CHARLES F. JORDAN, *Secretary-Treasurer*

The letters to Crossen and Hammond also summoned them to appear at the National Convention on June 27, 1949 at Atlantic City, but these two individuals not having signed the handbill, they were summoned to appear to explain their conduct in distributing handbills to local union memberships during the recent election.   The last paragraph of the letters to Crossen and Hammond contained the identical language contained in the last paragraph of the letters to Cranston, Gilbert and Snyder, informing them that they were to assume the expenses in getting to Atlantic City and advising them that if proven guilty they would not be reimbursed for any expenses incurred.

It becomes important now to examine the handbill, the publication or circulation of which gave rise to the charges in this case. We reproduce the handbill as follows:

Election N.B.O.P.   Officers First Meeting in May

VOTE

We believe the present administration should be changed because of its

1. Reluctance to Accept Laws and Courts of U.S.A.
2. Illegal Salary Increases.
3. Arbitrary Disregard of Wishes and Opinions of Locals and Members.
4. Unfair Election Tactics.
5. Use of Potters Herald for Personal Propaganda Agency and to Impugn Motives and Attack Members.
6. Inefficiency in Office.
7. Denial of Help to W. Va. Federation of Labor in Efforts to Increase Silicosis Benefits.
8. Duffy's Open Shop Attitude.

RESTORE DEMOCRACY IN N.B.O.P.
The following are Honest and Capable —

ELECT

President — Larry Finlay
Sec. Treas. — P. K. Calhoun
First Vice — E. Curry
Second Vice — Harold West
Third Vice — E. C. Armstrong
Fifth Vice — Verne Phillips
Seventh Vice — Charles Boso
Eighth Vice — George Brunt

Committee:
Norman Whippler — No. 124
E. Cranston — No. 9
Frank Applegate — No. 59
Paul Gilbert — No. 33
H. Snyder — No. 133
O. L. Sullivan — No. 201

Plaintiff's Exhibit 7

. . . At the National Convention which commenced on June 27, 1949, the Convention had a number of matters to dispose of and on July 5th, the Convention took up the matter of the alleged misconduct of Crossen, Gilbert, Cranston, Hammond and Snyder pursuant to the summons received by each. . . .

The proceedings of the Convention . . . show that by resolution subsequently adopted, after hearing, a fine of $50.00 was assessed against Gilbert, Cranston and Snyder for putting their names to the green sheet, subject to appeal to the Executive Board. As to the charge of distributing literature on the part of Crossen and Hammond, the fine was originally fixed at $50.00, but the fine as to Crossen was at a later point in the Convention suspended and he was placed on four years probation.

This modification as to Crossen was apparently the result of a statement attributed to Crossen at the Convention and carried in the printed proceedings in which he declared, "I am willing to rub off the war paint and cooperate 100%."

Thereafter, letters were written to each of the five individuals found guilty by the Convention, advising them of the $50.00 fine. As to Crossen, it was declared that his fine was suspended and that he was placed on probation for four years. As to the other four individuals, letters informed them of the fine in the amount of $50.00 each and stated that the fine would be suspended if the individuals appeared before the National Executive Board and gave satisfactory explanation of their recent conduct and assurances of good conduct in the future. The letter closed as follows: "You must however, satisfy the Executive Board in your explanation before the fine is suspended. The fine must be paid to the National Secretary."

Under date of September 2, 1949, Gilbert, Cranston, Snyder, Crossen and Hammond filed their petition in the Common Pleas Court of Columbiana County naming as defendants, the National President and the National Secretary of the Union in their individual capacities and as officers of the Union. . . . Plaintiffs . . .

prayed the Court to restrain the defendants from enforcement of the penalties meted out to the plaintiffs at the Convention of 1949 and for such other and further relief as might be just and proper. . . .

It is apparent from the proceedings of the Convention and the testimony of defendants Duffy and Jordan, that plaintiff's Exhibit 7 was the particular literature to which objection was taken and which furnished the basis for the charges against plaintiff and trial by the Convention.

As to plaintiffs Gilbert, Cranston, Hammond and Snyder, the trial court held that the action of the 1949 Convention in trying these men, and imposing penalties upon them, was void and of no effect and the court therefore enjoined the defendants, Duffy and Jordan, individually, and as president and secretary of the National Brotherhood and also, the National Brotherhood, from collecting or attempting to collect the fines imposed upon plaintiffs. The injunction was denied only as to plaintiff, Crossen.

As a result of the appeal on law and fact to this Court by the defendants, Duffy and Jordan, from the trial court's judgment, this Court has studied carefully the evidence in this case, including the analysis by the trial court of the eight charges published or distributed by plaintiffs in the handbill referred to as plaintiff's Exhibit 7. We do not find that any of these charges fall within the classification of libel. It seems to us rather that the charges complained of fall within the scope of free, if not fair, criticism and the free speech guaranteed by the United States Constitution and the Constitution of Ohio. It is admitted that plaintiff's Exhibit 7 was circulated as part of an election contest in behalf of one of two slates of national officers being presented for election, and to be voted on by the constituent local unions. The slate advocated in plaintiff's Exhibit 7 failed of election. Each slate was warmly espoused by adherents and, in turn, strongly attacked by its opponents. Defendants, as national officers seeking re-election, had available channels of publicity not open to the slate advocated by plaintiffs, since the defendant President was editor of the official newspaper of the Brotherhood sent to all members, and the columns of that paper understandably advocated the defendants' slate and vigorously criticized the opposition, terming these individuals "smear artists," and otherwise belittling them.

In reaching our decision, we recognize that the National Brotherhood of Operative Potters is a strong union, a democratic union. Its record for successful leadership in the industrial field has been outstanding. A strong organization presupposes strong leadership. Such leadership calls forth strong adherents and often strong critics and lively contests, not to be found, because not tolerated, in a totalitarian climate. In our political democracy and in our economic achievements a measure of our strength in this country has been our ability to permit, and benefit by, criticism and the competition which nurtures that strength.

The important and apparently original legal question squarely presented in this case is whether a rule adopted by a mutual benefit association of the character of a labor union may infringe upon and take away fundamental liberties otherwise granted by the Constitution of the United States and the Ohio Constitution. It is quite true that by joining a mutual benefit association an individual consents to be bound as a member by rules and regulations not affecting non-members. How far may a mutual benefit association go in restricting the freedom of members? In this case, the Association involved is an Ohio corporation and it is subject to the Constitution of Ohio and the Constitution and laws of the United States. The Constitution of the United States, Amendment I, declares that Congress shall make no law "abridging the freedom of speech, or of the press." The Constitution of Ohio, Article I, Sec. 11, declares as follows: "Every citizen may freely speak, write, and publish his sentiments on all subjects, being responsible for the abuse of the right; and no law shall be passed to restrain or abridge the liberty of speech, or of the press."

Having in mind the foregoing safe-guards, we may consider the provisions of the regulation or by-law, if any, which the plaintiffs in this case may be said to have violated. Examination of Section 37 of the Constitution of the Union as revised in October, 1947, shows that despite the language of the summons to the Convention, plaintiffs could not have been properly tried for violation of Section 37 because it applies only to candidates. Plaintiffs were likewise not properly able to be tried under the resolution of June, 1947, because, under the procedure there outlined, any member accused of making false accusations, misrepresentations, untruths, or using degrading literature, could be called before the Convention following the election, but could be tried only by the *succeeding* Convention, or by a body of five members or by a special court selected at such succeeding Convention.

We find that despite the letter calling plaintiffs to appear before the June, 1949, Convention to defend themselves for "the act of publishing malicious representations regarding present national officers in the last election," as in the case of Cranston, Gilbert and

Snyder, or to explain their conduct, "in distributing handbills to local union memberships during the recent election for National Officials," as in the case of Crossen and Hammond, the plaintiffs were actually tried or able to be tried by the June, 1949, Convention only for violation of the resolution adopted at the July, 1948, Convention covering "conduct in violation of their obligation or anything in any manner de*ter*mental to the N.B.O.P. and its members." We are loath to say, in view of the provisions of the Constitution of the United States and of the state of Ohio, guaranteeing free speech, that we should construe this indefinite language as intending to deprive members of the union of the right of free and fair criticism, otherwise theirs, although the 1949 Convention appears thus to have construed it and to have punished plaintiffs on that basis. Examination of the facts before us impels us to hold that a member of a mutual benefit association continues to be a citizen of the United States, and the free speech guaranteed by the United States Constitution permits him freedom in criticizing his union officials, as well as his public officials generally, subject always to the limitations imposed by the laws of slander and libel. 64 Harvard Law Review 1071. In so declaring, we recognize that it is not generally the function of courts to control the policies or the internal affairs of labor unions, but the courts may and should protect the democratic processes within unions by which union policies and their leaders are determined. Upon this point, see the illuminating article entitled "Legal Limitations On Union Discipline" by Clyde W. Summers, 64 Harvard Law Review 1049, at page 1073 and also, the article by Joseph Kovner entitled "The Legal Protection Of Civil Liberties Within Unions," (1948) Wisconsin Law Review, at page 18.

Particularly important seems to us the recognition that labor unions constitute a special type of mutual benefit association, standing in special relation to their members and to the state. Membership has become a frequent condition of employment, even as the right of every man to work has become increasingly recognized as one of the most valued rights of a free society. Viewing the important role of labor unions in this era, a court may well determine in a particular case that protection of their democratic processes is essential to the maintenance of our democratic government. . . .

We hold that the action of the 1949 Convention in fining plaintiffs because of publication or distribution of the handbills constituted an infringement of the right of free speech possessed by plaintiffs, calling for exercise, under the peculiar circumstances of this case, of the equity powers of this Court to protect the plaintiffs in their property rights and in their calling. . . .

In the present case, we find that a property right on the part of plaintiffs is clearly involved, since failure within thirty days to pay the fines levied would subject plaintiffs under Section 181 of the Union's Constitution to suspension from the Union. Furthermore, by Section 255 failure to pay a fine expressly deprives any member of all privileges of local membership thus entailing loss of benefits, loss of right to seek office within the Union and possible loss of work opportunities.

Numerous cases hold that where the expulsion or suspension of a member of the Union affects the individual's property rights, a court of equity will award relief to a member wrongfully expelled or suspended from the Union by decreeing his re-instatement, at least where a resort to the internal remedies within the union would be futile, illusory or useless, or would not accord to the members in question substantial or practical justice. See the note in 168 A.L.R. 1462 entitled "Exhaustion of Remedies Within Labor Union As Condition Of Resort To Civil Courts By Expelled Or Suspended Member" and particularly the cases cited at page 1479.

In the court below, the trial judge in his opinion pointed out that the matter of exhaustion of remedies within the Union is not a required prerequisite to court action unless the tribunal is impartial, and in this case it was the Executive Board which brought the charges against plaintiffs and further appeal to that Board would presumably be unavailing. Particularly, was any such gesture to be deemed futile where the objectionable actions of plaintiffs constituted support of an opposition slate and where, in the companion case being decided by this Court today, Armstrong et al. v. Duffy et al., Ohio App., 103 N.E.2d 760, and involving attempted punishment of candidates on the rival slate, the action of the Executive Board had given evidence of intention of silencing further opposition.

Finding that plaintiffs exhausted their remedies within the Union, to the extent feasible, and finding that plaintiffs' property rights were involved, we therefore conclude that the injunction prayed for should issue against the defendants in favor of the five plaintiffs in this case,

Injunction granted.   Exceptions.

NOTES

1. Reilly v. Hogan, 32 N.Y.S.2d 864 (Sup. Ct. 1942), involved expulsion of a Union member on the charge that he had stated that Union officers had "misappropriated" $4500 of Union funds to bring back to the United States members of the Abraham Lincoln Brigade of the Spanish Civil War. There was substantial question raised as to whether "misappropriation" had actually been charged. Also, the alleged statement had been made in the course of a heated election campaign for Union officers. Without actually deciding whether or not the charge had been made, the court ordered reinstatement and awarded damages. The opinion concluded that plaintiff had not been awarded a fair trial, although no details of the unfairness were given, and expressed the determination that the expulsion had been animated by partisan politics rather than by the specific charge made.

2. Elfers, a candidate for secretary-treasurer of a local Union, distributed a pamphlet attacking the present officers and accusing them of misfeasance. As proof he referred to a number of letters, motions and resolutions presented in a Union meeting. He was charged with disclosing Union business to the public and expelled. Held: Expulsion was proper as the pamphlet revealed Union business to outsiders. Elfers v. Marine Engineers Beneficial Assn., 179 La. 383, 154 So. 32 (1934).

3. Statler had an injury and the employer railroad paid his claim but refused to re-employ him. He filed a grievance, but obtained no relief. At the next Union convention he and Love circulated a pamphlet setting out the case and accusing the officers of deceit and tyrannical influence in refusing to prosecute the grievance. Love was charged with violating the constitutional provision prohibiting members from "issuing a circular without the consent of the officers" and was expelled. Held: Expulsion was proper as the offense was clearly within the constitutional prohibition. Love v. Brotherhood of Locomotive Engineers, 139 Ark. 375, 215 S.W. 602 (1919). But cf. Edrington v. Hall, 168 Ga. 484, 148 S.E. 403 (1929).

4. Shapiro brought charges against Gehlman, president of Local No. 1 of the Theatrical and Stage Employees, for mishandling Union funds. The trial committee sustained the charges but recommended exoneration because it had not been willful. Shapiro was then charged with slandering a Union officer and was suspended for one year. He finally obtained a court order of

reinstatement.   Shapiro v. Gehlman, 244 App. Div. 238, 278 N.Y. Supp. 785 (1st Dept. 1935).

5. There has been substantial litigation on the right of a union to expel a member because of that member's opposition to union leadership and union policy manifested through a refusal to obey a union strike call or through the giving of aid and comfort to the "enemy" during a strike.   Burke v. Monumental Division, No. 52, Brotherhood of Locomotive Engineers, 286 Fed. 949 (D. Md. 1922), involved a member of the Union who opposed a strike authorized by Union vote.   The mode of opposition was to negotiate with the struck employer and allow the employer to sue for an injunction in his name.   He was expelled from the Union. The expulsion was upheld in the court.

Similar but less traitorous conduct was involved in Grand International Brotherhood of Locomotive Engineers v. Green, 210 Ala. 496, 98 So. 569 (1923).   Here the Union was discussing a strike vote.   Green stated that he opposed the strike because it was unpatriotic and that he put loyalty to his country above loyalty to his Union.   He was expelled for disloyalty and causing dissension.   The court held the expulsion without just cause and awarded $12,500 damages.

For cases involving punishment of union members for refusing to join wildcat or illegal strikes, see Nissen v. Int. Brotherhood of Teamsters, 229 Iowa 1028, 295 N.W. 858 (1941); Loney v. Wilson Storage & Transfer Co., 14 L.R.R.M. 896 (S.D. Cir. Ct. 1944).

6. To what extent may a union use its disciplinary power as a method of restricting the use of labor-saving devices?   In Harper v. Hoercherl, 153 Fla. 29, 14 So.2d 179 (1943), an employer who had a rush contract with the Army for painting barracks attempted to enjoin the Painters Union from enforcing its rule prohibiting its members from using spray-guns.   Held: The courts will not interfere with the union's power to enforce its duly enacted bylaws unless they are unreasonable, immoral, or contrary to public policy. Injunction denied.   Compare with this Opera on Tour v. Weber, 285 N.Y. 348, 34 N.E.2d 349 (1941), page 692 supra.

7. When a union exercises its disciplinary power to enforce work rules on its members, is this a form of unilateral collective bargaining?   Does the presence of such rules constitute a refusal to bargain collectively on those matters?   Cf. Evans v. International Typographical Union, 81 F. Supp. 675, 22 L.R.R.M. 2576 (S.D. Ind. 1948); In re International Typographical Union, 86 N.L.R.B. 951, 25 L.R.R.M. 1001 (1949).

8. One of the most serious aspects of the expulsion of a union member is that it can cause a forfeiture of valuable insurance and pension rights which have accrued. In most states the courts have strictly construed constitutional provisions to prevent such forfeitures. See Steinert v. United Brotherhood of Carpenters & Joiners, 91 Minn. 189, 97 N.W. 668 (1903) ; Hatch v. Grand Lodge of Railroad Trainmen, 233 Ill. App. 495 (1924) ; Shadley v. Grand Lodge of Railroad Trainmen, 212 Mo. App. 653, 254 S.W. 363 (1923). The New York courts, however, have shown little concern for insurance rights and have upheld strict forfeiture for delinquency of dues. See Hess v. Johnson, 41 App. Div. 465, 58 N.Y. Supp. 983 (2d Dept. 1899) ; Sammel v. Myrup, 12 N.Y.S.2d 217 (1939) ; Simson v. Bugman, 45 N.Y.S.2d 140 (1943).

Because of the harshness of such forfeiture, the Brotherhood of Railroad Trainmen amended their constitution to permit nonmembers to retain their insurance by making payment direct to the General Secretary-Treasurer.

The recent trend toward establishing welfare and pension plans by collective bargaining may increase the potential hardship of expulsion. Almost all of these plans, like that of the United Mine Workers, requires that for a person to be eligible for payments he must be a "union member in good standing." See, in general on this problem, Penello v. International Union, United Mine Workers, 88 F. Supp. 935, 21 L.R.R.M. 2368 (D.D.C. 1950) ; Bureau of National Affairs, Collective Bargaining Negotiations and Contracts 44: 313–323 (1949) ; Gray, Exclusion of Non Union Members from Employee Benefit Plans, 4 Indust. & Lab. Rel. Rev. 265 (1951) ; Rosenthal, Union-Management Welfare Plans, 62 Q.J. Econ. 64 (1947).

9. Did the Gismo Workers Union in Problem II, page 878 supra, have any special needs which justified it in limiting democratic action to prevent dissension and disruption within the Union? Would it make any difference if only half of the gismo industry was organized and the Union was bracing itself for a bitter strike at the American Gismobile Company? See Witmer, Civil Liberties and the Trade Union, 50 Yale L.J. 621 (1941).

10. Is a court adapted to defining the proper limits of union discipline? Do the cases indicate that the present judicial rules are adequate? See Kovner, Legal Protection of Civil Liberties Within Unions, [1948] Wis. L. Rev. 18; Aaron and Komaroff, Statutory Regulation of Internal Union Affairs, 44 Ill. L. Rev. 425, 631 (1949).

11. What protection is given by the Labor Management Rela-

tions Act? To what extent is it adequate to protect internal democracy? What protection would it have given in each of the above cases?

DeMILLE v. AMERICAN FEDERATION OF RADIO ARTISTS [7]
District Court of Appeals, California, 1946
17 A.C.A. 480, 175 P.2d 851

YORK, P.J. As a member of American Federation of Radio Artists, Los Angeles Local (hereinafter referred to as AFRA), which is an affiliate of the national organization bearing the same name, (hereinafter referred to as National), plaintiff by the instant action sought to restrain both organizations and the board of directors of AFRA from suspending him for his refusal to pay a One Dollar assessment which the union levied against its membership for financing its campaign in opposition to the "Right of Employment Act," an initiative measure appearing on the ballot in the State election of November 7, 1944, as "Proposition No. 12."

Proposition No. 12, to which reference has heretofore been made, provided that: "Every person has the right to work and to seek, obtain and hold employment, without interference with or impairment or abridgment of said right because he does or does not belong to or pay money to a labor organization."

Appellant claimed in the trial court, as he does here, that respondents had no authority to levy any assessment for the stated purpose, and that the procedure to suspend him was contrary to and did not conform to the Constitution and By-Laws of AFRA. Appellant also asserts that by respondents' acts his constitutional rights to suffrage, free speech, life, liberty and the pursuit of happiness were invaded; that he was compelled to pay a tax for the exercise of his constitutional right to work, and that section 251 of 2 U.S.C.A., the Corrupt Practices Act of the United States was violated.

As hereinbefore stated, respondent is an open union which admits to membership all persons desiring to work as performers in the radio entertainment industry. Its organic law is set forth in the articles of agreement and constitution of National, and in the articles of agreement, constitution and by-laws of AFRA, by the terms of which each applicant, upon attainment of membership, is bound. Contrary to appellant's contention, the articles of agreement may be consulted for an explanation of the aims and objects sought to be effected by the respective constitutions. The

[7] Affirmed, 31 Cal. 2d 139, 187 P.2d 769 (1947), cert. denied, 333 U.S. 876 (1948).

articles of agreement of AFRA are to the effect that "We, the undersigned, . . . constitute ourselves a voluntary association . . . to advance, protect," etc., all those connected with radio performances, agree that AFRA, its present members, "the undersigned," and persons hereafter becoming members, are to be governed by the constitutions and by-laws and all lawful rules of the National and that "the same shall be binding upon us and all subsequent members of this Local." The articles of agreement of National is substantially in the same form and recites the additional purpose "to secure proper legislation upon matters affecting" the professions of the various members.

Section 1, Article XI of National's constitution provides that initiation fees, dues and assessments shall be fixed by the locals for all members thereof, subject to approval of the National board of directors. This is a direct grant of power to the locals, including AFRA, to levy assessments. Article V provides that no person shall become a member of National or any Local unless he shall sign an application substantially providing that "he agrees to be bound by the respective Constitutions of the Association and Local . . . and by any By-Laws, rules, regulations and orders existing or thereafter lawfully enacted pursuant to such Constitutions and any amendments thereto." Section 5 of Article VIII, provides, among other things: "Subject to the provisions of the Charter and Constitution granted by the Association, and of this Constitution, each Local shall be autonomous and shall manage and govern its own affairs within the territory of its jurisdiction."

Under the power and authority given by the foregoing, the board of directors of AFRA did not exceed its power in levying the assessment herein questioned.

Even though the dangers to AFRA implicit in Proposition No. 12 were debatable, AFRA was convinced of their reality and acted upon that conviction. And to say that AFRA could not legally contribute funds raised by assessment to oppose the proposition and that thereof the assessment was invalid, is to deny to organized labor the right to defend itself from attack.

Appellant argues that he personally favored Propositon No. 12, which would have made union shops illegal, and contends that by paying the assessment to AFRA, he was giving expression to sentiments contrary to those which he holds, in violation of his rights of suffrage, freedom of speech, expression of thought, and the right of assembly.

In clubs, fraternal and civic organizations, business and professional organizations, private corporations and voluntary associations of all kinds, the doctrine of the acceptance by the minority of the decisions of the majority and those whom they have elected to determine the policies of the organization, is the basic principle of their organization and functioning. Also, it is well recognized that the minority in accepting the decisions made by the majority, individually reserve the right to disagree with the decisions so made, because it rarely happens to any action taken by an organization that it represents the unanimous belief of the membership. Therefore, no inference could possibly arise that appellant individually approved either the assessment or AFRA's stand against Proposition No. 12, and furthermore, he was entirely free to work in support of the proposition, regardless of the union's opposition.

From the time appellant became a member of AFRA, he was bound not only by the constitutions and by-laws of the National and Local organizations, but also by the will of the majority of the membership, as lawfully expressed in accordance with such constitutions and by-laws. As a member of AFRA, appellant was contractually bound to submit to disciplinary action for his failure to pay the assessment levied.

The Federal Corrupt Practices Act, 2 U.S.C.A. Sec. 251, denounces contributions by labor organizations "in connection with any election" at which certain designated federal candidates, to-wit, presidential or vice-presidential electors, senators or representatives in Congress "are to be voted for." Proposition No. 12 was on the ballot at which there were candidates for all of these officers, but the funds were used not "in connection with" the election of such officers, but only in opposition to the said proposition. Act of Congress prohibiting expenditures in the election of federal officers cannot interfere with a state election at which electors vote at the same time for state officials, or on proposed amendments to the state constitution, or other matters.

From the foregoing, it appears that the $1 assessment levied by AFRA in connection with its opposition to Proposition No. 12 was for a union purpose, was duly authorized under the constitution and by-laws of said organization and that the suspension of appellant for nonpayment thereof must be sustained.

For the reasons stated, the judgment appealed from is affirmed.

NOTES

1. In a number of cases unions have attempted to control the political activities of their members in order to prevent members from working against union objectives.

(a) A local of the United Electrical Workers (CIO) decided to support the Democratic slate in the 1944 campaign. Morgan, who helped organize the local and who was an officer, objected to its political activities. In order to counteract the Union's effort, he handed out Republican campaign literature. The lower court held that the Union could not expel him. The Union could engage in political activity but could not restrict the freedom of its members. Morgan v. Local 1150, 16 L.R.R.M. 720 (Ill. Super. Ct. of Cook County, 1946). It was reversed on appeal for failure to exhaust internal remedies. 331 Ill. App. 21, 72 N.E.2d 59 (1946).

(b) Spayd, a member of the Railroad Trainmen, signed a petition to the state legislature asking it to reconsider and repeal the Full Crew Law which it had enacted upon the request and pressure of the Union. He was expelled for violating a constitutional provision which specifically prohibited members from interfering with the legislative activities of the Union. In holding that the expulsion was improper, the court said, "Appellant's contention that the application of rule 23 to the plaintiff does not deprive the latter of his right of petition, but merely delegates it to the defendant during his association therewith, cannot be sustained. Any agreement or contract handing over to others such a prerogative to be exercised on the citizens behalf is against public policy and void." Spayd v. Ringing Rock Lodge, 270 Pa. 67, 113 Atl. 70 (1921). Similarly, in Abdon v. Wallace, 95 Ind. App. 604, 165 N.E. 68 (1929), the court held that it was improper for the Locomotive Engineers to expel a member who, in testifying before the Interstate Commerce Commission, opposed the carbon-arc headlights which were advocated by the Union. The charge here was likewise based on a specific clause prohibiting members from interfering with legislative policy.

(c) In connection with organizational control of the political activities of its members, the policy of the American Medical Association in opposition to the proposed National Compulsory Health Insurance program should be considered. To obtain funds to carry on its fight against this program, the AMA requested voluntary $25 contributions from all of its members. About 75 per cent contributed. Finding the funds thus realized insufficient, the AMA, in December, 1949, established dues of $25 annually for membership in the organization. The avowed purpose of the assessment was to obtain funds for this political activity. Any doctor not paying these dues lost his membership in the Association. See 54 Time Mag. 77 (Dec. 19, 1949).

2. Where the union attempts to use its disciplinary power to prevent a member from carrying out his legal responsibilities, the courts have had little difficulty in finding the penalty was improper.

The plaintiffs, union plumbers, were appointed to the Board of Plumbing Examiners in New Orleans. The Union demanded that they vote for McGilravy for inspector. When they refused, they were expelled and black-listed by the Union. The court ordered them reinstated, as the reasons for expulsion were an unwarranted interference with public duty. Schneider v. Local Union No. 60, 116 La. 270, 40 So. 700 (1905).

3. The path has often been rough for those who have participated in legal proceedings against the union, for labor's deep-rooted antipathy for the courts converts such conduct into what is often considered gross disloyalty to the union. The courts have usually given full protection against such discipline.

Thomas Angrisani brought suit against his union to have an assessment declared illegal. He was expelled for "Conducting union business outside of meeting." His brother Arthur was also expelled because he had agreed to testify in Thomas' behalf if subpoenaed. Both were ordered reinstated by the court. Thomas Angrisani v. Stearn, 167 Misc. 728, 3 N.Y.S.2d 698 (1938); Arthur Angrisani v. Stearn, 167 Misc. 731, 3 N.Y.S.2d 701 (1938).

However, there may be a limitation on the protection which the court will give. In Thompson v. Grand International Brotherhood of Locomotive Engineers, 41 Tex. Civ. App. 176, 91 S.W. 834 (1905), a member wrote to the widow of a brother who had been killed in an accident, urging her to sue the railroad, and at the trial he was subpoenaed and testified in her behalf. He was charged with "unbecoming conduct" and expelled. The court stated that if the expulsion had been for writing the letter, it could be proper, but he could not be punished for testifying under subpoena. Since the Union apparently relied on both facts, the expulsion was improper. Likewise, in Strobel v. Irving, 171 Misc. 965, 14 N.Y.S.2d 864 (1939), the court upheld the expulsion of a member who had given financial assistance to another member who was suing the Union. Since he was not compelled to give such support but acted as a mere volunteer, he could be disciplined.

4. Section 304 of the Labor Management Relations Act consists of an amendment to Section 313 of the Federal Corrupt Practices Act directed at circumscribing political expenditures and contributions of labor unions as well as business corporations. The

critical words make it unlawful for a corporation or labor organization "to make a contribution or expenditure in connection with" any election in which federal officers are elected. The validity of this regulation was at issue in United States v. Congress of Industrial Organizations, 335 U.S. 106, 68 Sup. Ct. 1349, 92 L. Ed. 1849 (1948). The question arose through the publication in "The CIO News" of an endorsement of a particular candidate for Congressman. The Court held that the expenditure of funds necessary to print the newspaper containing the political endorsement was not the kind of expenditure Congress intended to prohibit in the statute. The opinion admitted that the Court was interpreting the word "expenditure" narrowly to avoid "grave doubt" as to constitutionality.

5. To what extent does a union's concern over legislation which directly affects it justify the union in disciplining members who oppose its legislative policy? Consider the following case. In 1944, the State, County and Municipal Employees endorsed Representative Homer Ramey for re-election, as he was a member of the Union. When he voted for the Taft-Hartley Act, they brought charges to expel him for violating his obligation as a Union member. What result?

6. The DeMille case, which became a *cause célèbre,* was cited in the majority report of the Senate Committee on Labor and Public Welfare, to show the need for some of the restrictions of the Labor Management Relations Act. To what extent will any provisions in the LMRA give protection in such a case?

Consider also the situation of the union member who supports a rival union in a representation election. Should the union be permitted to expel him? Does the Labor Management Relations Act prevent such an expulsion?

5. DISCIPLINARY PROCEDURE [8]

a. Constitutional Provisions

SUMMERS, DISCIPLINARY PROCEDURES OF UNIONS *

The discipline procedures prescribed in 154 international union constitutions surveyed show a striking similarity in the steps to

[8] See Chamberlain, The Judicial Process in Labor Unions, 10 Brooklyn L. Rev. 145 (1940); Taft, Judicial Procedure in Labor Unions, 59 Q.J. Econ. 370 (1945); Notes: 15 U. of Chi. L. Rev. 232 (1947), 33 Minn. L. Rev. 156 (1949), 96 U. of Pa. L. Rev. 537 (1948), 57 Yale L.J. 1302 (1948).

* The full text of this article by Clyde W. Summers may be found in 4 Indust. & Lab. Rel. Rev. 15 (1950), from which the above selection has been taken with the permission of the editors of that publication. — ED.

be used in any discipline case. At the same time constitutional provisions show a wide divergence in the detail with which those procedures are described.

The typical disciplinary procedure includes the following major steps: making of charges by a fellow member, serving of notice on the accused, naming of a trial committee, holding of a hearing, reporting of recommendations to the local union for vote, and appealing to international officers and the international convention. The number of steps may vary according to the size or structure of the union. In a small union such as the Train Dispatchers, the verdict is rendered by the international officers, while in large unions like the United Auto Workers which have amalgamated locals, the verdict is rendered by the Shop Organization and the first appeal is to the local. There may be many other variations, but the pattern is essentially the same.

A few unions prescribe the procedure which must be followed in great detail. The Musicians provide a virtual maze of procedural rules stated in some 4,000 words and scattered throughout their complex constitution. The Railway Conductors provide extremely complete regulations, and the Rubber Workers provide a model of simple but detailed directions for handling the trial of discipline cases. At the other extreme, 18 unions have no provisions whatever for discipline procedure and others have only very general clauses like the Woodworkers' "every member shall be entitled to be notified in writing of charges preferred against them, an opportunity to be heard in their defense, and a fair trial." Still others, like the Office and Professional Workers, merely provide, "The by-laws of all Local Unions shall provide a fair method for the hearing of charges . . . and shall include an appeal to the General Executive Board." These are the extremes of detail and vagueness, but the other unions are not distributed equally between the extremes. The great majority of unions have wholly incomplete provisions, and less than one-fourth regulate even the bare essentials at each of the major steps.

JOHNSON v. INTERNATIONAL OF THE UNITED BROTHERHOOD OF CARPENTERS AND JOINERS OF AMERICA, LOCAL UNION NO. 971

Supreme Court, Nevada, 1930
52 Nev. 400, 288 Pac. 170

COLEMAN, J. This suit was instituted to enjoin defendants from excluding plaintiff from membership in said organization, for damages, and for general equitable relief.

The complaint pleads section 55 of the constitution and laws of the defendant organization, which provides that charges alleging an offense must be made in writing and must specify the offense or offenses charged and the section violated, and must be signed by the member making the charge; that the charges must be read at the meeting and lay over until the next meeting; that the member charged must be notified and furnished a copy of the charges by registered mail; that all charges must be referred to a trial committee; that the accused shall be allowed until the next regular meeting to appear and reply; that the chairman of the committee shall summon the accused in writing, together with the witnesses for and against him.

The constitution and laws also provide that any member having a grievance may appeal to the general president for redress, subject to a further appeal to the general executive board and a final appeal to the general convention. It also provides that a member must exhaust his resources allowed by the constitution and laws within the organization before taking his case to the civil courts.

The evidence, though conflicting on that point, shows that a written charge was presented against the defendant on September 13, 1926, as follows:

"The following is the statement made by D. E. Johnson in the presence of Charles Varney and Charles Warner.

" 'Why in hell don't they change the name of the S. of a B. of an organization from the United Brotherhood of Carpenters and Joiners of America to the Contractors and Petty Politicians Association.' (Signed) Chas. H. Varney."

After the charge was read, the defendant stated that a part of the matter stated was true and that a part of it was false, and demanded a trial as provided in the laws of the organization. The chairman of the local held that the plaintiff had pleaded guilty and that no trial was necessary.

The minutes of the local, as corrected, read: "Motion by Brother C. H. Varney that Brother D. E. Johnson be expelled for trying to create dissension and working against the harmony of the United Brotherhood."

The motion was adopted, and Johnson was requested to leave the hall. Thereafter, Johnson took an appeal to the General President, who dismissed the appeal on the ground that the local acted for the best interest of the membership; but he took no further appeal.

Section 54, par. B. of the constitution, provides: "Any officer or member who endeavors to create dissension among the members or works against the interest and harmony of the United Brotherhood . . . shall be expelled. . . ."

Paragraph B, Section 55, is as follows: "All charges must be made in writing, and must specify the offense or offenses, and the Section of the Constitution and Laws of the United Brotherhood so violated, and be signed by the member or members making such charges."

The charge fails utterly to comply with this requirement. It does not specify any offense; neither does it specify the section of the constitution and laws alleged to have been violated. To constitute an offense, it must specifically charge that he was guilty of some act or acts prohibited by some law of the organization.

Assuming that it was the intent to charge Johnson with violation of section 54, par. B, an endeavor to create dissension is an essential element of the offense to be embraced in the charge. This element is not embraced in the charge against Johnson; hence he was not charged with the offense of endeavoring to create dissension among the members. While the language Johnson is charged with using is scandalous and reprehensible, it does not necessarily charge him with endeavoring to create dissension. We appreciate that courts should not be anxious to require such charges to be strictly technical, but they should convey to the accused a knowledge of the charge made against him. This was no doubt the purpose of providing that the charge should refer to the section upon which the charge is based.

In Wachtel v. Noah Widows' & Orphans' Soc., 84 N.Y. 28, 38 Am. Rep. 478, it is said: "It is well settled that an association whose members become entitled to privileges or rights or property therein cannot exercise its power of expulsion without notice to the person charged, or without giving him an opportunity to be heard."

While there seem to be some authorities which hold that, whether an expulsion be void or irregular, the aggrieved party must exhaust his remedies within the offending body, the great weight of authority is to the effect that, where the proceedings resulting in suspension, expulsion, or other penalty, are not conducted in compliance with the requirements of the organization itself, or are contrary to law and the fundamental principles of justice, the aggrieved member may apply at once to the civil courts for relief. . . .

b. Fair Procedure

1. In Bricklayers', Plasterers' & Stonemasons' Union v. Bowen, 183 N.Y. Supp. 855 (1920), the court stated at page 861:

> The fact that no such restriction upon the power of the executive board is in terms contained within the book does not relieve it from like obligation of fair play. . . . But both good conscience and law demand, that no member shall be deprived of his rights and privileges until he has had notice of the charges against him and been given opportunity to meet them.   Labor organizations have become an integral part of our business life, and wield a powerful influence upon the everyday affairs of multitudes of our people.   In return for the benefits which, when rightly managed, they insure, their members surrender to them all individual trade freedom, and must rely upon their honest, fair, and efficient management for opportunity to support themselves and their families.   These members constitute a goodly percentage of our citizenship, and the state is vitally interested in their welfare.
>
> The requirements of good government will not permit them to be arbitrarily, or without fair opportunity to defend themselves, deprived by their leaders of their opportunity to work and earn.   Therefore, in the absence of precise stipulation for notice of and hearing of complaints against them, public policy demands that the law intervene to supply such omission.   Kehoe v. Leonard, 176 App. Div. 626, 163 N.Y. Supp. 357 (1917); Williamson v. Randolph, 48 Misc. Rep. 96, 96 N.Y. Supp. 644 (1905).   So necessary is this rule to our public needs that a provision in the constitution of such an organization like that last paragraph of section 4 in article 17, which provides for removal or suspension without notice of a local, or individual member, must be held void as against public policy and utterly unenforceable.

Compare, however, the attitude of the Wisconsin court in State ex rel. Dame v. Le Fevre, Note 4, page 887 supra.

2. Within the general limitations that a union must abide by its constitutional procedure but that it must in any case provide a procedure that insures a fair trial "in accord with principles of natural justice," what procedure will pass the scrutiny of the courts?   See, generally, annotation in 21 A.L.R.2d 1397 (1952).

(a) *Summary procedure.* Blek was suspended from the International Brotherhood of Electrical Workers for taking sound pictures of ex-President Coolidge. He was convicted without notice or opportunity to be heard under a provision of the Constitution which provided for summary procedure. Held: This form of "drum head courts martial" is improper. The constitution will not be interpreted so as to permit a "disregard for natural justice." Blek v. Wilson, 145 Misc. 373, 259 N.Y. Supp. 443 (1932). See also Cotton Jammers & Longshoremen's Assn., No. 2 v. Taylor, 23 Tex. Civ. App. 367, 56 S.W. 553 (1900).

Where the need for immediate action is great, summary procedure provided for in the constitution may be upheld. It has been held that where a member is guilty of dual unionism in fostering secession of the local, he can be summarily expelled, with only a right of appeal to a higher union tribunal. Davis v. International Alliance of Theatrical & Stage Employees, 60 Cal. App. 2d 713, 141 P.2d 486 (1943); Margolis v. Burke, 53 N.Y.S.2d 157 (1945). But see Gilmore v. Palmer, 109 Misc. 552, 179 N.Y. Supp. 1 (1919).

(b) *Notice of charges.* The complete failure to give notice of the charges as required by the constitution will deprive the trial body of jurisdiction and make the proceedings a nullity. Deverell v. Musical Mutual Protective Union, 118 N.Y. 101, 23 N.E. 129 (1889). The notice must be sufficiently specific to enable the member to prepare his defense. Sullivan v. McFetridge, 183 Misc. 106, 50 N.Y.S.2d 385 (1944); Coleman v. O'Leary, 58 N.Y.S.2d 812 (1945).

If the member is not properly served with notice, but he appears and defends, does this constitute a waiver of the defect? The court will not usually require a strict compliance with the constitution and will order a reinstatement where the defect is only technical. If the expelled member has actually had a fair hearing with adequate opportunity to defend, his appearance will constitute a waiver of lack of notice. Clark v. Morgan, 271 Mass. 164, 171 N.E. 278 (1930); McConville v. Milk Wagon Drivers' Union, Local No. 226, 106 Cal. App. 696, 289 Pac. 852 (1930); Kaplan v. Elliot, 145 Misc. 863, 261 N.Y. Supp. 112 (1932); Bachman v. Harrington, 52 Misc. 26, 102 N.Y. Supp. 406 (1906). However, the courts will often scrutinize the proceedings very carefully and if there is any evidence of unfairness or overreaching, the court will use the technical defect as grounds for holding the proceedings void. Spiegel v. Locomotive Engineers, 166 Minn. 366, 207 N.W. 722 (1926); Brennan v. United Hatters of North America, 73

N.J.L. 729, 65 Atl. 165 (1906); Schmidt v. Rosenberg, 49 N.Y. S.2d 364 (1944).

(c) *Right of counsel.* Most unions provide that the member on trial may have the assistance of counsel chosen from the membership. A very few unions permit a member to have the assistance of legal counsel. In Local No. 2 v. Reinlib, 133 N.J. Eq. 572, 33 A.2d 710 (1943), it was held that in the absence of a specific provision in the constitution, a member could not insist on the right of professional counsel. The member was not entitled to all the rights which he might be accorded at common law.

(d) *Double jeopardy.* In Rueb v. Rehder, 24 N.M. 534, 174 Pac. 992 (1918), the plaintiff was charged with interfering with a grievance in the hands of the grievance committee. He was acquitted but then charged and tried for the same offense a second time. Held: Trial for same offense a second time constitutes double jeopardy and is contrary to all sense of justice. The court will not permit such procedure unless the constitution specifically so provides. But in Simpson v. Grand International Brotherhood of Locomotive Engineers, 83 W. Va. 355, 98 S.E. 580 (1919), it was held that double jeopardy was permissible unless specifically prohibited by the constitution.

(e) *Place of trial.* In Gallagher v. Monaghan, 58 N.Y.S.2d 618 (1945), the plaintiff distributed letters in support of one of the candidates during an election in a New York local of the Railway & Steamship Clerks. He was charged with violating a Union rule and ordered to trial in Cincinnati before the Grand President. He refused to appear, was found guilty and expelled. Held: To hold the hearing at such a distance "violated principles of justice to the prejudice of the plaintiff's right to a fair hearing and his right to a proper opportunity to present his defense."

(f) *Presentation of evidence.* "Although formal legal procedure is not required in connection with proceedings for the expulsion of members by such associations as the defendant, those rudimentary rights must be observed which are essential to any fair trial. Among these is the right of the accused member to confront and cross-examine witnesses who appear against him. . . . In the present case the plaintiff was excluded while Louis Steinhauser gave his evidence. Even the identity of the witness was withheld from the plaintiff." Held: Expulsion was improper. Brooks v. Engar. 259 App. Div. 333, 19 N.Y.S.2d 114 (1st Dept. 1940) (two of the five judges dissenting).

In Fales v. Musicians Protective Union, Local 198, 40 R.I. 34, 99 Atl. 823 (1917), the plaintiff asked for continuances because he had to appear in court and consult his attorney. The trial committee proceeded to take evidence in his absence and expelled him. Held: Taking of evidence and closing the case without giving plaintiff an opportunity to defend is grossly unfair. Reinstatement ordered.

(g) *Unbiased tribunal.* A member of the Painters Union wrote a letter for publication in the Newark newspapers, urging unions to clean their own house and remove racketeering leaders. The officers of District 10 of the Union charged him with "creating dissension," tried him, and expelled him. Held: The trial was improper as it was by the same body which had preferred the charges against him. Gaestel v. Brotherhood of Painters, 120 N.J. Eq. 358, 185 Atl. 36 (1936).

Cohen submitted a proposed amendment to the bylaws of Local 802 of the American Federation of Musicians. The proposal recited that it had been "publicly stated" that the election of officers in 1936 was conducted "in such a fraudulent, dishonest and crooked fashion as to cast doubt upon the right of the present officers to hold office." It then recommended that the bylaws be amended to provide for the 1938 elections to be conducted by the Honest Ballot Association. Instead of publishing the proposed amendment as required, the officers charged Cohen with "unfair dealing to the Local and its duly elected officers." A hearing was held by the executive board which consisted of the officers elected in 1936, and Cohen was expelled. Held: Expulsion was invalid. The members of the trial board were disqualified because of bias, prejudice, and interest in the subject matter. Cohen v. Rosenberg, 262 App. Div. 274, 27 N.Y.S.2d 834 (1st Dept. 1941).

In Coleman v. O'Leary, 58 N.Y.S.2d 812 (1945), two shop stewards were charged with refusal to obey instructions given by the officers. They were tried before the executive committee, found guilty and expelled. Held: Expulsion was invalid. Two members on the trial committee were the officers whose orders were disobeyed. They were not only the ones filing the charges but were the chief witnesses against the stewards. Their acting as witness, prosecution, and judge was a violation of the fundamentals of a fair hearing.

As these cases well illustrate, the courts are usually aware of the possibility of bias in the tribunal and strive to give protection against it. However, this is not always true. Hall was elected president of the St. Louis Local of the Bridge and Structural Iron Workers, but International President Morrin declared that the election was invalid. When the local refused to comply, Morrin suspended it and ordered the officers to turn over the books. The local officers then began court action to protect the local. Hall was charged with slandering the international officers, was tried by the General Executive Board and found guilty. The court held that this did not invalidate the trial, as there was no presumption they would violate their obligation to give a fair hearing. The court also held that he must exhaust his internal remedies even though his appeal was to the Geneva Executive Council which included the members of the Board who had convicted him. The "contract between the plaintiff and the association" bound him to appeal. Hall v. Morrin, 293 S.W. 435 (Mo. App. 1927).

3. Queries.

(a) Should the disciplinary procedure within a union be compelled to measure up to the standards of a criminal trial, or should it be governed by the more loose rules of administrative tribunals?

(b) How much leeway should the courts give to union tribunals because they are administered by laymen? Should they be free to prevent so-called technical errors, or should the courts be relatively strict to protect against the layman's tendency to be prejudiced by irrelevant evidence?

(c) Is it possible, as a practical matter, to eliminate bias from the union tribunal in cases where the offense arises out of a deepseated struggle for power within the union?

6. EXHAUSTION OF REMEDIES [9]

It is a well-settled rule that one who is expelled from a fraternal society cannot resort to the courts until he has exhausted his remedies within the society. This rule has been transferred to apply to labor unions and at times has been vigorously enforced. However, its binding effect has been severely weakened by the large number of exceptions which the courts have created to excuse exhaustion of internal remedies. The discussion here will be directed toward describing the various exceptions, which are available if the court does not desire to enforce the rule.

(1) *Action for damages.* It seems well settled that if an expelled member sues for damages rather than reinstatement, he need not exhaust his internal remedies. Grand International

---

[9] See Vorenberg, Exhaustion of Intraunion Remedies, 2 Lab. L.J. 487 (1951); Notes: 35 Col. L. Rev. 951 (1935), 41 Mich. L. Rev. 99 (1942), 168 A.L.R. 1462.

Brotherhood of Locomotive Engineers v. Green, 210 Ala. 496, 98 So. 569 (1923); Mullen v. Seegers, 220 Mo. App. 847, 294 S.W. 745 (1927); Smith v. International Printing Pressmen and Assistants Union, 190 S.W.2d 769 (Tex. Civ. App., 1945). In Bonham v. Brotherhood of Railroad Trainmen, 146 Ark. 117, 225 S.W. 335 (1920), the plaintiff was expelled for commiting adultery with his brother's wife. He sued for damages and reinstatement. The court held that since the suit was primarily for reinstatement and only incidentally for damages, he must exhaust his internal remedies.

(2) *Lack of jurisdiction in trial body.* At a Local meeting, Jose made charges that the officers were guilty of misconduct. The president forbade reading of the charges and then filed charges against Jose for slandering an officer. Instead of being tried before the Local, he was tried by the District Council and suspended. Held: He did not need to exhaust his internal remedies. The District Council did not have jurisdiction. Even if it had had jurisdiction, some of the members on the trial committee were not properly elected. Since there was no legally constituted trial committee, the proceedings were void and there was nothing from which to appeal. Jose v. Savage, 123 Misc. 283, 205 N.Y. Supp. 6 (1924). See also Walsh v. Reardon, 274 Mass. 530, 174 N.E. 912 (1931) (trial by General Executive Board); Gersh v. Ross, 238 App. Div. 552, 265 N.Y. Supp. 459 (1st Dept. 1933).

(3) *Improper grounds for expulsion.* It has been held that where the grounds for expulsion are not within the constitutional power or are against public policy, the expulsion is totally void and there is no need to exhaust the internal remedies. Leo v. Local Union No. 612, 26 Wash. 2d 498, 174 P.2d 523 (1946) (expelled for soliciting membership in another union, which did not violate constitution); Abdon v. Wallace, 95 Ind. App. 604, 165 N.E. 68 (1929) (expelled for testimony given under subpoena before the Interstate Commerce Commission).

(4) *Improper expulsion procedure.* A number of cases have held that where the expulsion procedure either denied a fair trial or failed to follow the constitutional provisions, the proceedings were void and internal remedies need not be exhausted. Rueb v. Rehder, 24 N.M. 534, 174 Pac. 992 (1918); Gilmore v. Palmer, 109 Misc. 552, 179 N.Y. Supp. 1 (1919); Bartone v. Di Pietro, 18 N.Y.S.2d 178 (1939); Coleman v. O'Leary, 58 N.Y.S.2d 812 (1945). But see Dallas Photo-Engravers Union No. 38 v. Lemmon, 148 S.W.2d 954 (Tex. Civ. App. 1941).

(5) *Delay in appeal.* If exhaustion of the internal remedies will cause such delay as to constitute a substantial injustice, then it will be excused and the expelled member can seek legal relief. What constitutes undue delay may vary.   Local Union No. 57 v. Boyd, 245 Ala. 227, 16 So.2d 705 (1944) (2½ months of undue delay); Kaplan v. Elliot, 145 Misc. 863, 261 N.Y. Supp. 112 (1932) (18 months of undue delay); Schultz v. Local 956, 20 Lehigh L.J. 348 (Pa. C.P. 1943) (8 months of delay not unreasonable).   In Mulcahy v. Huddell, 272 Mass. 539, 172 N.E. 796 (1930), appeal was to the convention of the International Union of Operating Engineers.   The convention could be called only upon vote of 55 per cent of membership, and the president effectively controlled the vote.   Although the appeal was against the action of the president, Huddell, the court held the potential delay did not excuse exhaustion of internal appeals.   See also Dallas Photo-Engravers Union No. 38 v. Lemmon, 148 S.W.2d 954 (1941), where it was held that the delay was not unreasonable as it was nothing more than was customary in civil cases.

(6) *Futility of appeal.* Corregan made a speech on the city street stating that the International Typographical Union was rotten to the core; its president, Lynch, was the worst dog in the heap; that he abused his office by working into the hands of management; that Local officers were a lot of labor fakirs.   Corregan was fined $50 and suspended until the fine was paid.   Held: He need not exhaust internal remedies as his appeal would have to be to Lynch whom he had attacked.   Corregan v. Hay, 94 App. Div. 71, 87 N.Y. Supp. 956 (4th Dept. 1904).   See also, Fritz v. Knaub, 57 Misc. 405, 103 N.Y. Supp. 1003 (1907).   Although there are few expulsion cases directly involving this point, a great mass of dictum gives the rule fairly substantial foundation.

A striking example of court insistence that an expelled union member exhaust all his union remedies before attacking the expulsion in court is the British case of Kuzych v. White, 2 W.W.R. (N.S.) 679, 2 All E.R. 435 [1951, Jud. Comm. of the Privy Council].   In this case Kuzych was expelled from the Boilermakers' and Iron Shipbuilders' Union of Canada in Vancouver, British Columbia.   The ground for his expulsion was opposition to the basic union policy of the "closed shop."   Further, because of a closed shop contract, this expulsion meant loss of job.   Without pursuing appeal within the Union, as specifically provided in the Union constitution, Kuyzch brought suit for reinstatement in the Union and damages.   As the result of the enmity Kuzych had incurred in the Union through his outspoken opposition to a basic Union objective and an unsuccessful campaign for Union president in opposition to the then present leadership, it was rather obvious that appeal within the Union would have been futile.

Kuzych won judgment in the trial court, 2 W.W.R. 558 (1949). This judgment was affirmed by the British Columbia Court of Appeal, 2 W.W.R. 193 (1950). The Judicial Committee of the Privy Council reversed on the ground that Kuzych should have exhausted his remedies within the Union. The Privy Council relied heavily upon the oath of obligation to which all members of the Union were required to subscribe which was: "I promise that I will not become a party to any suit at law or in equity against this Union or the Federation, until I have exhausted all remedies allowed to me by said Constitution and By-laws." The opinion of the Privy Council indicated that plaintiff had no right to assume that appeal would be useless, but that even if it was useless the above oath was binding upon him.

After loss of the case, Kuzych did appeal within the Union but this appeal was unsuccessful on the dual grounds that the 60-day limitation upon such appeals had expired (in fact six years had elapsed because of the court fight) and further, that the Union which had expelled him had in the meantime severed its connection with the Federation which constituted the appellate tribunal at the time of the original expulsion.

The entire controversy, which produced nine reported and three unreported decisions and occupied a period of eight years, is discussed in an excellent article by Whitmore in 30 Can. B. Rev. 1 (1952).

(7) *General.* In Nissen v. International Brotherhood of Teamsters, 229 Iowa 1028, 295 N.W. 858 (1941), the court summarized the rule as follows: "Where property rights are involved the member need not first pursue the remedies within the association, if they would be futile, illusory, or vain. . . . Also if the action of the association is wrongful, or without jurisdiction, or is without notice or authority, or not in compliance with the rules or constitutional provisions, or is void for any reason, the obligation to appeal within the order is not imposed but the complaining one may resort directly to the courts. The rule contended for is applicable only when the organization has acted strictly within the scope of its powers."

Although this listing of exceptions to the rule that the aggrieved union member must first exhaust his union remedies tends to indicate that the rule itself is without operative force, this is not the case. In fact, the courts have frequently applied the rule even though it would have been appropriate to have applied one of the exceptions. See, e.g., Dragwa v. Federal Labor Union No. 23070, 136 N.J. Eq. 172, 41 A.2d 32 (1945), 168 A.L.R. 1462 (1947).

Further, the courts will seldom step in before at least *some* kind of action has been taken by the union (i.e., suspension, expulsion, etc.). In Zalnerovich v. Van Ausdal, 65 N.Y.S.2d 650 (1946), the plaintiff sought to enjoin the holding of a trial on the ground that its purpose was to expel him because he refused to join a particular political party. The court refused to issue the injunction. Likewise, in Bernstein v. Robinson, 63 N.Y.S.2d 300 (1946), the plaintiff claimed there was a conspiracy and the trial board had already prejudged his guilt. The court refused to enjoin the trial, saying it would presume the trial board would be fair. But see Sullivan v. McFetridge, 183 Misc. 106, 50 N.Y.S.2d 385 (1944). The court enjoined the Executive Board from trying a Local president on the grounds that under the constitution the Executive Board had no power and so was acting outside its jurisdiction.

Consider the following questions in connection with the exhaustion of remedies rule:

(a) What is the function of the rule? Is it to protect the union from outside interference in its internal affairs? Or is it a rule merely of judicial convenience to protect the court from being burdened by litigation?

(b) To what extent is this rule analogous to the rule that appeals cannot be taken from administrative decisions until all the administrative appeals have been exhausted or a final order has been issued? Do the same principles or rules govern both problems?

(c) Is a court ever bound by the requirement that appeals within the union must be exhausted? In what situation will none of these exceptions apply?

D. *Officers, Elections, and Finances* [10]

1. INTRODUCTION

The preceding sections have dealt with the problem of democracy in government of labor unions with respect to acquisition

[10] See Slichter, The Challenge of Industrial Relations, 114–123 (1947); Shister, The Locus of Union Control in Collective Bargaining, 60 Q.J. Econ. 513 (1946); Taft, The Constitutional Power of the Chief Officer in American Labor Unions, 62 Q.J. Econ. 459 (1948); Dankert, Contemporary Unionism, 206 et seq. (1948).

and retention of membership. While these are of vital importance, they are obviously not enough to establish a well-functioning representative government of the union. Such government requires responsible leadership chosen in free elections and accountable to the rank and file for its conduct of union affairs. If the union is to be effective, large powers must be delegated to officers who can act promptly and forcefully, yet that power must be so checked and controlled as to prevent its being used as an instrument of personal power to the oppression of the members.

Just as in the case of corporations, the power to direct the destinies of a union will sometimes fall into the hands of unscrupulous brigands who use their position for their own advantage, financial and otherwise. Fortunately this is not the usual pattern any more than it is in the business world. However, when it does occur, governmental power is invoked to protect the rank and file of the union and the public from these abuses. The governmental power is applied either through court processes, i.e., judge-made law, or through preventive and protective legislation.

2.   JUDICIAL CONTROL OF OFFICERS, ELECTIONS, AND FINANCES [11]

The following section consists of a series of cases which reveal the struggle of a single local of the Hod Carriers as its members attempted to assert themselves against leaders who governed with a strained sense of democracy. These cases show the attempt of the courts to insure internal democracy, and the maneuvers of those in control to evade judicial action. They pose the serious problem — How effective can the courts be in controlling undemocratic practices within a union?

Prologue

In 1939, President Moreschi of the Hod Carriers, without charges or a hearing, ousted the officers of Sandhogs Local 147 of New York and ordered his henchman, Vice President Bove, to take complete control of the affairs of the Local. The Local secured an injunction to preserve its independence and compelled

[11] See, generally, Ginzberg, American Labor Leaders: Time in Office, 1 Indust. & Lab. Rel. Rev. 283 (1948) ; Perkins, Protection of Labor Union Funds by Members' Representative Suits, 27 B.U. L. Rev. 1 (1947) ; Shister, Trade-Union Government: A Formal Analysis, 60 Q.J. Econ. 78 (1945) ; Summers, Union Powers and Workers' Rights, 49 Mich. L. Rev. 805 (1951) ; Notes: 51 Yale L.J. 1372 (1942), 86 U. of Pa. L. Rev. 885 (1938).

Bove to relinquish control. Moreschi countered this injunction by ordering contractors not to deal with the Local but to hire men from other locals. Local 147 obtained an injunction against this action as beyond the constitutional power of the International. This compelled Moreschi to call the first International Convention in thirty years. The rebels attempted to unseat Moreschi, who had inherited the presidency without the benefit of an election. President Green of the AFL praised Moreschi as a great labor leader and Moreschi then stampeded his way to office. After his victory he stated, "Christ said, 'Forgive them, for they know not what they do.' So do I."

At the convention he succeeded in obtaining an amendment to the constitution which would enable him to forgive his fallen enemies properly. As soon as the convention was over he filed charges against Local 147 under powers granted by the new constitution, held an extended hearing, and revoked the charter. In Moore v. Moreschi, 179 Misc. 475, 39 N.Y.S.2d 208 (1942), Local 147 obtained an injunction restraining the International from all interference with its affairs, and apparently obtained a precarious freedom. (For a more complete account, see Note, 51 Yale L.J. 1372 (1942).)

At an earlier stage of domination over the New York locals, Moreschi had taken jurisdiction for the work on the New York City aqueduct project away from Local 147 and had given it to Local 17. In return for this, the officers of Local 17 turned complete control of the Union over to the International. Nuzzo, former treasurer and one of the sell-outs was given supreme authority, and a process of "milking" the membership was begun. Fred Dusing was the leader of the rebellious faction within Local 17, and he openly challenged Nuzzo's dictatorship by seeking protection from the courts. Here the cases begin.

DUSING v. NUZZO
Supreme Court, New York, Ulster County, 1941
26 N.Y.S.2d 345

MURRAY, J. The motion before the court is for a temporary injunction and also an application by the plaintiffs for discovery and inspection of the books, records, and documents of Local 17. . . .

In support of their accusations, plaintiffs assert that although the constitution of Local 17 specifically provides that there must be held annually by the union a meeting for the election of its officers, that no such election has been held since 1937. There is no dispute as to this fact. Plaintiffs charge that there has been collected from members of the union since 1936, approximately $600,000. That this money was derived from initiation fees, dues and assessments. That after deducting all proper charges and expenses, there should be on hand a balance in the treasury of Local 17 an amount approximating $410,000. Defendants admit collections from 1,900 members in the approximate sum of $200,000. Defendants say that balance of moneys on hand in the general account of Local 17 has been at times less than $2,000.

It is the claim of plaintiffs in support of their charges that defendants are engaged in a conspiracy and act as tools and agents of the International Union. That whenever any member of Local 17 sought any information about the affairs of the union, made any protest about working conditions or the funds of the union, or asked that elections be held or regular monthly meetings take place as provided by the constitution, all such protests and requests were summarily overruled or rejected. That members of Local 17 who made complaints were threatened with violence. That defendants publicly stated on many occasions that any member of the union who spoke adversely would be beaten and properly taken care of in such a manner that he would never be able to open his mouth again.

Furthermore, that in a number of instances, members of the union who dared to make a complaint about the way in which the affairs of Local 17 were being administered were blacklisted and removed from jobs where they were working, at the request of defendant, Nuzzo. Plaintiff, Frederick W. Dusing, deposes by affidavit that on November 29, 1940, while he was working on a construction job in Marlboro, N.Y., for the Pleasantville Construction Company as a brakeman, he was told by the timekeeper that defendant, Samuel Nuzzo, had ordered him to fire Dusing, because he had too much to say about the union. That, consequently, Dusing was discharged and about a week later Nuzzo publicly stated that he ordered Dusing fired and that he would do the same to anybody else who did not like the way in which he was running the union.

Plaintiffs submit further affidavits and proof from various other members of the union to the effect that although it was the duty of the individual defendants to see to it that conditions dangerous to life and limb on the work of the New York City water supply system be corrected, defendants refused to do anything about the matter, despite many accidents and many injuries by reason of such neglect. That members of the union were not paid by the contractors for the class of work they were doing and had moneys due them for overtime and extra work which were not paid. That defendants deliberately ignored their obligations to enforce labor agreements made in behalf of the union members designed for their protection and welfare.

That defendants used a policy of terror and intimidation to stifle all opposition to their rule. That unsuccessful in this method, defendants contrived a new scheme of placing charges against all members who resisted the tyrannical rule of the defendants. These members were accused of "disloyalty to the Local Union and the officers of the Local" and of "endeavoring to create dissension." That spurious charges were made by defendants, a typical example of which is set forth in full in the complaint. That such charges in appearance look genuine, but as a matter of fact the individual defendants herein were not only the complainants, but the judges and jury as well in the matter. That such charges were completely false and unfounded and were and are being used as weapons by defendants to still all opposition to their absolute control of Local 17. That such acts are part of the conspiracy in which the defendants are engaged.

Defendants deny that such accusations are true. They contend such statements are false. One would hardly expect defendants to plead guilty to such atrocious, despotic, savage and wicked deeds, as alleged by plaintiffs.

The fact is undisputed that no election of officers of Local 17 has taken place since 1937. Defendants in their answer allege that by reason of certain complaints of "lack of harmony" in Local 17 that on or about November 3, 1937, the International Union notified the officers of Local 17 to hold no further meetings and until further notice from the International Union, the affairs of Local 17 would be regulated and controlled by the "Executive Board" of Local 17 subject to the veto of a man named James Bove, classified as Vice-President of the International Union. In this connection, it is interesting to note that the International Union directed that the "business representatives" together with the Secretary and Treasurer of Local 17 continue to collect dues, initiation fees and other moneys from the members of Local 17 and make a full report of such collections every two weeks to Mr. Bove.

The charter of Local 17 has not been revoked or suspended, and its constitution is in full force and effect. The Union has not disbanded. The defendants justify their power in conducting the affairs of Local 17 by reason of the so-called order received from the International Union. An affidavit submitted by plaintiff, Dusing, is illuminative as to the kind and type the International Union is as an organization. His affidavit states:

"This International has not held a convention for over a period of 30 years or since 1911. From 1911 down until the present time, there has never been an election of the International, which claims to have 990 local unions affiliated with it and claims to be composed of a membership of 165,000 workers as of September 5, 1938. One Joseph V. Moreschi has held office as President since 1926, when his predecessor, Dominick D'Allesandro, who held office from 1907 to 1926, died. Upon the death of D'Allesandro, Moreschi, who originally came from Chicago, had himself declared President and made himself head of the working destinies of the 165,000 men scattered throughout the 48 states of the Union. Bove was never elected to the office of Vice-President, as provided for in the International constitution, but was appointed a Vice-President and representative for New York State by Moreschi. Not a single one of the 8 people who constitute the officers of the International were ever elected to the office in the manner prescribed by the constitution and the circumstances under which each of them assumed office is shrouded in complete mystery, as far as the membership of the International is concerned."

While it is true that a child should obey its parents, and in this case, if the facts revealed that the parent organization, the International Union, acted upon something more tangible and more substantial than a mere illusory and indefinite "lack of harmony" reason for depriving the members of a local labor union their important and substantial right to elect their own responsible officers, I would be loath to put much faith in complaints made against the teacher.

However, the history and record of the International Union is not impressive. No good reason is shown why it has been so inactive, nor why it has failed to hold meetings for so many years.

It is obviously the duty of defendant, Nuzzo, since he has collected the moneys, to account for same not to some person in Chicago, New York or Boston or elsewhere, but to those working men who gave him part of their hard-earned money. Nuzzo, International Union or no International Union, is nothing more or less than fiduciary, a trustee, and he is personally responsible for his acts and actions. This duty is personal to himself and cannot be transferred to any other person to assume responsibility.

True, it may be, as Mr. Nuzzo says, that the records are open to the inspection of any member, but it is only fair to answer, that if plaintiffs are right in their charges herein that any member of the union who sought such personal inspection would be marked and invite the risk of being fired from his job.

Plaintiffs state that Mr. Nuzzo, as part of his activities, besides being business agent of Local 17, conducts a night club or grill in Newburgh, N.Y. Meetings of Local 17 have been held in this night club. It is charged by plaintiffs that if any attempt is made by a member to state a complaint or a grievance, it is either ignored or met by threats of strong-armed men employed by Mr. Nuzzo as bodyguards. In his affidavit, Mr. Nuzzo states that his night club is sufficiently large to accommodate four or five hundred persons. It may be that a night club is a good place to hold a meeting of a labor union to banish the worry of bothersome problems. That under the stimulus of proper food and drink and the accompaniment of a jazz band with incidentals such as rug cutting, boogie-woogie and other forms of innocent merriment, technical, tedious reports such as financial statements would pass in review without too much critical attention. This court cannot, however, give its assent to such a meeting place for a labor union, however attractive it is to the palate, eye and ear. . . .

The motion for a discovery and inspection of the books, records and documents of the defendant, Local Union No. 17, is likewise granted pursuant to Section 324, Civil Practice Act. All such books, records, documents and papers to be deposited for inspection and discovery by plaintiffs with the County Clerk of the County of Ulster, the place of trial of this action. This court does not desire that this opinion be considered as a determination of this action or any part thereof on the merits. By reason of the kind, type and condition of the persons who compose the body of Local 17, this court believes in the exercise of the equitable power lodged in it that the relief sought by plaintiffs in their motion should be and hereby is granted.

DUSING v. NUZZO

Supreme Court, New York, Ulster County, 1941
177 Misc. 35, 29 N.Y.S.2d 882

BERGAN, J. Plaintiffs are members of the local union. This action is for judgment in the nature of a mandatory injunction requiring that an election be held and for an accounting of the union funds. There is singularly little real dispute of fact in the case. The first question of law presented, and it is crucial, is whether the controversy is justicable, i.e., whether it is a subject requiring any judicial determination of rights. Ordinarily internal disputes in labor unions, as in private associations and fraternal orders, do not present questions for judicial determination.

The concurrence of three elements is necessary for judicial intervention: (a) a property right or its equivalent must be involved; (b) a violation of the constitutional or charter requirements in the act complained of must be shown; (c) resort to the internal processes of the organization for redress must have been exhausted or shown to be futile, which is to say that resort to a court has become an imperative necessity. . . .

In view of these principles and of the fact that the constitution of the local union has been clearly violated, plaintiffs have made out a cause of equitable relief requiring an election and an accounting if they have an interest in the subject of which equity will take cognizance.

It is argued that a court of equity will intervene only to protect property rights, and since it has been held that the elections of officers of fraternal societies are not property rights of members, the argument advances to the point that union members stand in the same position of equitable disability in the right to an election of their officers.

But a labor union is not a social club. It is an economic instrumentality conceived in the necessities of making a living under the expansive influence of modern industrial concepts. The individual workman is impotent to deal with a great industrial organization. Aggregates of capital can only be met on equal terms by labor in the aggregate of union organization. The success of the result is dependent upon the responsiveness and the ability of the leader of the union. He is not the arbiter of social pleasure; he is the dispenser of bread and it is not difficult to hold that the union member has an enforcible interest in union elections of which the court in equity will be cognizant. It is as real and as needful of equitable protection, surely, as money or chattels.

The right to membership in a union is empty if the corresponding right to an election guaranteed with equal solemnity in the fundamental law of the union is denied. If a member has a "property right" in his position on the roster, I think he has an equally enforcible property right in the election of men who will represent him in dealing with his economic security and collective bargaining where that right exists by virtue of express contract in the language of a union constitution. Where an election is required by the law of a union, the member denied the right to participate is denied a substantial right which is neither nebulous nor ephemeral.

Certainly the admitted violations of the fiscal directions of the local constitution, existing over a long period, require that the officers account to the members for their money. The proof indicates that the gross income from dues and fees from 1938 to 1940, inclusive, was about $200,000. The per capita and initiation payments due to the International during the period would be about $40,000. It seems incredible that the local union could have expended $160,000 in the period for administering its own local affairs. Yet, on November 26, 1939, the union's bank balance was $16,153.95, and a little over a year later (December 27, 1940) it was $107.93. Since the accounting directions of the constitution, the observance of which could have checked dissipation, have not been followed, and since the fiscal officers have a fiduciary relationship to the members, I think an accounting is the only complete and adequate remedy. The plaintiffs have "an interest in the general funds of the organization." Blek v. Kirkman, 148 Misc. 522, 266 N.Y.S. 91, 92. See also, by analogy, Insurance Co. of North America v. Whitlock, 216 App. Div. 78, 214 N.Y.S. 697.

Defendants contend they have been acting in respect of supervision of elections and of fiscal matters under the direction of the International Union. In substance, the International vice president directed that meetings be suspended, a direction which was subsequently withdrawn, and further directed that actions of the executive board be ineffective until they receive "my official approval" and that the reports of collections and disbursements be made every two weeks "to me." The specific authority for this action under the International constitution is not apparent, but if there was authority, the prohibition on meetings was withdrawn the following year and acted upon, and the right to the meetings, the elections and the fiscal accounts to members at the meetings was then revived.

I find that the plaintiffs have exhausted whatever remedy exists within the International by application to its officers and that redress has been effectually denied and ignored. Moreover, the International itself has not had an election of officers in thirty years, and defendant Nuzzo, who has been active for years in its affairs, was unable to say by what authority its officers occupy their offices. The futility of applying to an organization thus anti-

pathetic to the elective process for failure of a subordinate union
to comply with the directions of its charter in these respects need
not be labored.

In an elaborate order covering more than ten pages the court
gave detailed orders for the conducting of an election of officers
in Local 17 and for an accounting of funds by Nuzzo. If one has
any illusions about the simplicity of these common equitable
remedies as applied to labor unions, see Dusing v. Nuzzo, 263
App. Div. 59, 31 N.Y.S.2d 849 (3d Dept. 1941).

The election was held in February, 1942, and the insurgents
won a clear-cut victory, electing Canfield, Dusing, and Baxter as
president, business representative, and financial secretary-treasurer.
In the election, one matter was overlooked — the constitution
provided that the length of the term of office, between the limits
of one and five years, should be determined at the time of nominations. The constitution also provided that elections should be
at the first regular meeting in June. Since the court did not
provide for the membership's determining the length of the term,
the International officers ruled that the newly elected officers'
terms expired in June. When the Local refused to hold a new
election, Nuzzo filed a complaint and Moreschi ordered an "investigation." The Local then sought to have the court amend its
order to provide that the officers should serve for a term of one
year. In Dusing v. Nuzzo, 178 Misc. 965, 966, 37 N.Y.S.2d 750,
752 (1942), the court refused to amend its order, stating:

> The boundaries of the judicial power over labor unions
> ought to be plainly stated. Where the management in con-
> trol of a labor union refuses to obey the laws of the union
> requiring that elections be held, or where it arbitrarily expels
> members from the union roster in violation of union law,
> or where it dissipates union funds without accounting, and
> where redress for any of these irregularities cannot be ob-
> tained through constituted local or international officials, the
> court will intervene to grant relief. . . .
> But the courts cannot undertake to run the labor unions
> in detail or to interpret their laws upon every point of inter-
> nal controversy. If the judicial power were exercised in this
> scope it would have an unfortunate consequence upon the
> independence and the vitality of labor unions. Experience
> in responsible self-government is essential to the success of
> union labor in protecting its economic welfare. This in turn

depends upon its independence and the courts should intervene only in cases of grave necessity.

. . . An election has been held under the judgment of the
court. Safeguards were provided to see that the election was
fairly conducted. . . . How long the officers thus elected
should serve and whether there should have been a further
election in June are matters for interpretation and decision
by the union itself and not for the court.

The judgment, based upon gross violations of the union
constitution without adequate redress, cannot be amended to
embrace other controversies subsequently arising from time to
time which may fully be settled within the union itself.

This case gave Moreschi a free hand, and he did not miss his
opportunity to use it fully. Patrick Waldron, whom he had sent
to "investigate," took over the Local and presided at all meetings.
The membership sought to escape this rule by voting for a new
election to be held on November 15, 1942. On November 1,
nominations were made and an election committee was appointed
to investigate the qualifications of the candidates. The two main
contenders for the presidency were Canfield and Nuzzo. When
the election committee refused to disqualify Nuzzo, who had
already been shown to have stolen most of the Union treasury
and who was then under indictment for embezzlement, the local
executive board ordered a postponement of the election until
November 29. Waldron and his dominated election committee
proceeded to hold the election on the 15th, at which Nuzzo was
elected. At a membership meeting on the 22d, a motion was
made to approve the action of the executive board in postponing
the election, but Waldron, who was in the chair, refused to permit a vote. On the 29th another election was held in accordance
with the orders of the executive board, at which Canfield, Dusing,
and Baxter were re-elected. Nuzzo and Waldron appealed to the
International Executive Board, which upheld the election of the
15th and confirmed Nuzzo in office. During this turmoil, the
International attempted to weaken the insurgent officers by taking
away from the Local jurisdiction over all work in Orange County,
thereby depriving them of a large portion of their available
employment.

On January 7, 1943, Nuzzo was convicted of embezzlement and
was sentenced to Sing Sing for a term of ten to twenty years.
Canfield and his fellow rebels again sought the aid of the court
to confirm themselves in office and protect themselves against fur-

ther domination by the International.   In Canfield v. Moreschi, 180 Misc. 153, 40 N.Y.S.2d 757 (1943), they obtained a temporary injunction.

CANFIELD v. MORESCHI
Supreme Court, New York, Ulster County, 1943
182 Misc. 195, 49 N.Y.S.2d 903

[Decision on motion for a permanent injunction.   The facts have been stated above.]

Foster, J.   The foregoing is a rough sketch of the events involved in these lawsuits.   The evidence, both documentary and oral, is extremely voluminous and within the limits of this memorandum it is impossible to fill in all the details.   Despite the ramifications of testimony, the course of events is fairly clear and leads directly to the chief issue of whether plaintiffs have sustained the charge of conspiracy against any or all of the defendants.   To determine this issue the rights and duties under the constitutional set-up of the Local and the International must of course be considered.

The powers of the International and its officers, as defined by its constitution, are very considerable indeed.   The International is defined as sovereign and its powers denoted as legislative, executive and judicial.   The Local is bound by the legitimate exercise of these powers because it owes its charter and very existence to the International itself.   Wherever there is a fairly debatable issue as to the legitimate exercise of any powers given to the International no court has a right to interfere.   The courts cannot undertake to run labor organizations and unless it clearly appears that there has been an abuse of power, above and beyond some internal controversy that merely involves a debatable question, an appeal to the courts is not warranted.   However, great as may be the powers of the International, I think it fundamental that those powers must be exercised by its officials in good faith and for valid purposes.   Due to the dictatorial set-up of the parent organization the welfare of labor is largely in their hands, and they occupy in a very real sense the position of fiduciaries.   Viewed in this light I think the evidence fairly establishes that the acts of Bove, Nuzzo and their associates were clearly beyond the scope of their legitimate powers as responsible labor officials. . . .

To return to the matter of power.   The constitution of the International (Edition of October, 1938, Sec. 18) gave Moreschi as its General President authority to preside, either personally or by deputy, over the meetings of a local in case of disharmony and to depose from office, after trial, officials who were negligent or dishonest. A later edition (adopted September, 1941, Article 6) gave him the power to take over the affairs of a local when its officers were dishonest, negligent or incompetent, or when the local was not being conducted for the purpose it was chartered, or its performance of existing agreements with employers was detrimental to the general welfare and interests of the International Union. Written charges of misconduct were to be preferred in such cases, and pending a trial of such charges local officials might be suspended. The constitution of Local 17, at least the copy before me, recognizes authority thus conferred on the General President of the International (Article XIII, Section 2). When Local 17 was taken over none of the foregoing conditions that might justify such action existed. This action was therefore arbitrary, oppressive and illegal. It resulted in grave injury to the Local, indeed it led directly to the looting of its treasury by Nuzzo. Although arbitrary and illegal control was lifted for a time after the decision in Dusing v. Nuzzo [263 App. Div. 59], attempts were thereafter made in the same familiar pattern to again assume control, and these attempts were at least partially successful. Thus the elements of an illegal conspiracy have been shown.

Of subordinate importance, but nevertheless in my judgment involved in the same pattern, was the action of the General Executive Board in passing on the disputed elections. This board consists of the General President, the Vice-Presidents, and the General Secretary-Treasurer of the International. It cannot be a very large body since there are only six vice-presidents, and two of its members of course were Bove and Moreschi. It had before it the question of whether the Executive Board of the Local, chosen freely by the members, had the right to declare an emergency by reason of the failure of the Election Committee to properly investigate candidates for office, and on the basis of this to postpone for two weeks the election set for November 15, 1942. One of the candidates was Nuzzo, whose unsavory conduct was even then more than a matter of conjecture, and this fact alone was sufficient to cast doubt on any investigation conducted by the Election Committee who passed him. Certainly the membership would have the right to postpone the election under the circumstances, and under the Local's constitution the Executive Board had the power to take any action that the Local Union could take, and which because of an emergency could not be delayed until the next regular meeting. That such a course met with the approval of a majority of the members of the Local is obvious from the record. In spite of all this the General Executive Board held the Local Board to be without power in the matter and declared the election of November 29 illegal and void. In my opinion this action was wrong, both factually and legally, and constituted another step in a program of arbitrary and conspired control.

In view of the foregoing I think that Plaintiffs are entitled to injunctive relief as requested in the complaint against Moreschi as President of the International, Bove individually and as Vice-President of the International, Patrick Waldron, the deputy of Moreschi, Nuzzo and the International itself.

[Affirmed in 268 App. Div. 64, 48 N.Y.S.2d 668 (3d Dept. 1944), and 294 N.Y. 632, 64 N.E.2d 177 (1945).]

Epilogue

In the 1946 International Convention, numerous amendments to the constitution were proposed which would require more frequent conventions and elections of international officers. These were all given unfavorable reports by the Law Committee which was appointed by the International officers and were defeated. Resolutions condemning the action of Moreschi in taking over Local 147 and Local 17 were presented, and though the courts had held his action was illegal, with Moreschi in the chair these resolutions were voted down. In the election for officers, Moreschi was renominated as a "great champion of democracy," and Dusing was nominated in opposition. Although Dusing was solidly supported by Locals 147 and 17, Moreschi won by a landslide.

For an interesting trilogy of Ohio cases involving protested salary increases for national union officers, and union disciplinary action regarding organization elections, see Finley v. Duffy, 88 Ohio App. 159, 94 N.E.2d 466 (1950), Armstrong v. Duffy, 90 Ohio App. 233, 103 N.E.2d 760 (1951) and Crossen v. Duffy, 90 Ohio App. 252, 103 N.E.2d 769 (1951). The Crossen case is reprinted at page 888 supra.

Note on Other Judicial Remedies

(1) *The receivership device.*[12]   An alternative device for court intervention in the affairs of unions has been the appointment of receivers to take control.   President Browne of the Theatrical and Stage Employees took advantage of a minor dispute in the St. Louis Local 143 to send in his agent Nick to take over the Local.   Nick suspended elections, threatened all who opposed him with expulsion, and ordered members not to meet in groups or discuss Union business.   He then proceeded to accept bribes from management for agreeing to lower rates, and misappropriated large amounts of money.   Appeals to Browne by the members were consistently ignored or their names were given to Nick, who then threatened them with expulsion.   In Robinson v. Nick, 235 Mo. App. 461, 136 S.W.2d 374 (1940), the court ousted Nick and ordered appointment of a receiver to preserve the assets pending an election and stated:

> There is ample authority for the proposition that in accordance with general rules, and in a proper case, a receiver may be appointed to conserve the property of an association. . . .
> A labor union, being concededly but a voluntary unincorporated association, falls squarely within such category, and there are cases to be found involving labor unions wherein receivers have been appointed in aid of pending suits in which the matters to be determined were not unlike those in issue in the case at bar.   Collins v. International Alliance of T.S.E., etc., 119 N.J. Eq. 230, 182 A. 37; Mullins v. Merchandise Drivers Local Union No. 641, 120 N.J. Eq. 376, 185 A. 485.
> This is not to say that the receiver in such a case shall be expected to bring pressure to bear upon an employer for a closed shop, or to call a strike, or to take his place in the picket line, for none of such things pertaining to the policies of the union and the personal activities of its members are any part of his function as receiver.   To the contrary, his function as an officer of the court by which he is appointed, and from which he derives whatever power he possesses, is only to receive, manage, protect, and preserve the property committed to his possession, holding it during the pendency of the suit for the benefit of all parties concerned. . . .

[12] Pressman, Appointment of Receivers for Labor Unions, 42 Yale L.J. 1244 (1933).

Appointment of a receiver does not prevent the recalcitrant officers from creating new obstacles. In Local No. 373 v. International Association of Bridge, Structural, and Ornamental Iron Workers, 120 N.J. Eq. 220, 184 Atl. 531 (1936), the insurgents defeated the racketeering business agent in an election. The International officers suspended all meetings and held another election at which their man was elected treasurer. When he failed to account for funds, the insurgents obtained an order from the court appointing a receiver. The treasurer was convicted of embezzling over $21,000 but had no assets. The International refused to make good his loss and refused to issue dues stamps to the receiver. The International was ordered to issue dues stamps but was held not liable to make good the loss of the treasurer.

The receivership may not only come too late to save the assets of the union but may be extremely expensive in itself. In McLane v. Romano, 322 Ill. App. 700, 54 N.E.2d 715 (1944), for an eight-month receivership, the court awarded the receiver $12,750, his attorney $10,000, and the attorney who brought the suit for receivership $2500.

In practice there is no requirement of exhaustion of remedies within the union in these cases. Drastic remedies such as appointing a receiver are never granted except where there is imminent danger to the members. Therefore, the delay in appeal would be, in effect, a denial of any remedy. In addition, most of these cases involve a concerted action by officers in the international and individuals in the locals. Any appeal in such case would be futile. In addition to the cases previously discussed in this section, see Maddock v. Reul, 143 Misc. 914, 256 N.Y. Supp. 915 (1932); Cosentino v. Goldman, 183 Misc. 539, 49 N.Y.S.2d 467 (1944).

(2) *Removal of officers.* Union constitutions usually provide for removal of elected officers either by recall or by trial on charges. Will the court grant as much protection to an officer from being removed from his office as it will to an individual from being expelled from the union? Apparently not. In Balter v. Empire State Motion Picture Operators Union, 167 Misc. 430, 3 N.Y.S.2d 290 (1938), the plaintiff claimed he was removed from the executive board by an unfair trial. The court said: "The petitioner has not been suspended from membership in the union. He has not been deprived of the right to earn a livelihood. It does not appear that membership on the board carried with it any salary, or that it was other than a position of trust and confidence. The court is loath to interfere in the internal affairs of such bodies

unless substantial rights have been wrongfully interfered with. . . . A new member of the board must be elected. It does not appear that the petitioner cannot be a candidate and secure complete vindication and reinstatement at a meeting where all members are present." Accord: Bennett v. Kearns, 88 Atl. 806 (R.I. 1913).

(3) *Judicial control of elections.* Where an election is held in the regular course of events, the courts are very reluctant to inquire into the procedure and void the election. If there is a semblance of complying with the procedure, and no obvious fraud, the court will not intervene. See Rowan v. Possehl, 173 Misc. 898, 18 N.Y.S. 2d 574 (1940); O'Connell v. O'Leary, 167 Misc. 324, 3 N.Y.S.2d 833 (1938); Carey v. International Brotherhood of Paper Makers, 123 Misc. 680, 206 N.Y. Supp. 73 (1924); Maloney v. District No. 1, UMWA, 308 Pa. 251, 162 Atl. 225 (1932).

Court interference in elections does not always obtain as favorable results as in Dusing v. Nuzzo. Very often the union members' antipathy to the courts may serve actually to solidify the position of those whom the court wishes to oust.

In Local No. 11 v. McKee, 114 N.J. Eq. 555, 169 Atl. 351 (1933), the court intervened to end a regime of dictatorship in which meetings had been suspended and local funds misappropriated. It appointed a receiver to preserve the assets and hold an election. In an honest election the old officers were re-elected. In Collins v. International Alliance of Theatrical Stage Employees, 119 N.J. Eq. 230, 182 Atl. 37 (1935), the court found that Kaufman was elected in 1920 and there had been no annual elections in ten years. The officers had perpetuated themselves in office by intimidating the members with loss of their jobs. The court ousted the officers, appointed a receiver and ordered an election. Nine years later the members were still attempting to eliminate the racketeering practices of Kaufman, who apparently had been re-elected business agent. See Gilligan v. Motion Picture Machine Operators Local 244, 135 N.J. Eq. 484, 39 A.2d 129 (1944).

(4) *Judicial control of finances.*[13] Judicial control of union finances may be almost complete when a receiver is appointed. However, this extreme remedy is not resorted to unless there is a history of misappropriation which compels immediate action and strict supervision. Short of this remedy, judicial control seems to be of little consequence. In Russell v. International Alliance of Theatre and Stage Employees, 66 Cal. App. 2d 691,

[13] See Note, 87 U. of Pa. L. Rev. 985 (1939).

152 P.2d 737 (1944), the Court upheld a contract by President Browne and his lieutenant Bioff to pay a tax consultant $10,000 a year.

Where mishandling of finances is involved, the requirement of exhausting internal remedies is much less stringent. In Local No. 104 v. International Brotherhood of Boilermakers, 158 Wash. 480, 291 Pac. 328 (1930), the court said that exhaustion of remedies was required primarily in matters of internal discipline and was not required in disputes over money or tangible assets. In the latter cases, resort to the courts would be barred only on express agreement to submit such controversies to a specified method of arbitration. Frequently the court avoids the requirement by finding that the constitution provides no internal remedies. Therefore, immediate resort to the court is proper. See Bell v. Sullivan, 183 Misc. 543, 49 N.Y.S.2d 388 (1944) ; Warren v. Screen Office Employees Guild, 16 L.R.R.M. 544 (Cal. Super. Ct. 1945).

Early cases held that a member of a union could not be guilty of embezzling union funds. The member was joint-owner, and was therefore taking that which was jointly his. This doctrine has now been repudiated and embezzlement will lie for such a taking. State v. Postal, 215 Minn. 427, 10 N.W.2d 373 (1943) ; People v. Herbert, 162 Misc. 817, 295 N.Y. Supp. 251 (1937).

3. CONTROL BY LEGISLATION

a. The Labor Management Relations Act of 1947

The Labor Management Relations Act contains several provisions intended to promote union democracy by preventing union officers from violating the wishes of individual employees. To the Wagner Act provision for a vote to determine the collective bargaining representative, the Taft-Hartley Act has added a provision which enables individual employees to petition for decertification (Sec. 9 (c) (1) (a)). It has also added the requirement of a vote on the last offer of an employer in a threatened national emergency strike (Sec. 209 (b)), and it originally contained a requirement of an election to authorize a union-shop agreement. This was deleted in 1951 (see present Sec. 8 (a) (3) proviso).

These provisions, however, are the extent to which the Act goes in insuring responsive union leadership. No attempt is made to regulate or supervise union elections or union procedures.

The most important provisions relating to the finances and

officers of the union are those requiring the filing of non-Communist affidavits by union officers and the filing of financial reports by the union, and the limitation on political expenditures by the union.[14]

The constitutionality of the non-Communist affidavit requirement was upheld in American Communications Assn., CIO v. Douds, 339 U.S. 382, 70 Sup. Ct. 674, 94 L. Ed. 925 (1950). The Court laid stress upon the fact that the purpose of the affidavit requirement was to rid the channels of interstate commerce of political strikes inspired by Communists.   In response to the argument that the statute constituted an unconstitutional restriction upon the freedom to speak and to believe, the Court relied upon the fact that there was no actual prohibition of such speech or thought but only certain powers and privileges (union leadership) were taken away and this was done only as part of a detailed federal plan of labor relations control.

Apparently as a means of protesting the enactment of the Taft-Hartley law, the national officers of the AFL and the CIO refused to sign the non-Communist affidavits. The AFL officers finally did comply near the end of 1947; the CIO national officers did not comply until the end of 1949. Meanwhile, the question arose as to whether the various international unions and their locals affiliated with these two national bodies would be deprived of the benefits of the law as the result of this noncompliance. In Matter of Northern Virginia Broadcasters, 75 N.L.R.B. 11, 20 L.R.R.M. 1319 (1947), the Board overruled its General Counsel's earlier interpretation and held that the AFL and the CIO were not "national or international labor organizations" within the provisions of Sec. 9(h) of the law. It was the Board's position that the various national and international labor unions affiliated with the AFL and the CIO were the organizations which Congress meant to be included in the phrase. ' Thus, so long as the national officers of those affiliated unions were in compliance and the officers of the local unions were in compliance, the benefits of the law could be claimed although the officers of the AFL or the CIO were themselves not in compliance.

The Board continued to act upon this interpretation of the law, allowing local unions of internationals affiliated with the AFL and CIO to participate in certifications and union-shop elections, until the decision in NLRB v. Highland Park Mfg., 341 U.S. 322,

[14] See Aaron and Komaroff, Statutory Regulation of Internal Union Affairs, 44 Ill. L. Rev. 425–466, 631–674 (1949). The second part of this article analyzes in detail various legislative proposals then pending before the 81st Congress.

71 Sup. Ct. 758, 95 L. Ed. 969 (1951). In this case, the United States Supreme Court held that the Board's interpretation of the phrase "national or international labor organization" was erroneous and that the officers of the AFL and the CIO had to comply before the various international unions and their locals affiliated with these two organizations could claim the benefits of the Act. Since, at the time of this decision, both the AFL and the CIO officers were in compliance with the non-Communist affidavit requirement, the decision had no prospective effect. However, substantial numbers of certifications as bargaining representatives of local unions affiliated with the AFL and CIO were then operative, and there were many instances of union-shop contracts made by such locals under Board authorization. The impact of the Highland Park decision was to make all of these certifications and union-shop contracts illegal. The Board estimated that a million and a half workers were covered by union-shop contracts now made illegal and 307,000 workers were being represented by unions illegally certified. The Board further estimated that to go through the necessary procedures to re-establish the situation with respect to these workers would cost over one million dollars. In view of these facts, the Congress enacted Section 18 of the amended National Labor Relations Act, in October 1951, to validate retroactively these prior Board determinations which had been made under the erroneous interpretation of the law.

b. State Legislation

"There has been a considerable volume of important state labor legislation since December 7, 1941, most of it relating to the activities of labor unions. Very little of it is legislation for wartime — it is not limited to the duration of the war, but is to remain in effect until amended or repealed. Nevertheless, it is war time legislation not only in the sense that it has been enacted in time of war, but in the more significant sense that it is part of a climate of opinion about labor unions and their activities which, although not entirely the product of war time conditions and war time emotions, has been greatly influenced by them. Some of the new laws contain provisions which are favorable to unions in that they limit the legal right of employers to impede the organization of their employees, but the general trend of the statutes, which are the product of southern and western state legislatures, is in the direction of subjecting the internal affairs of unions to regulation. . . ." Dodd, Some State Legislatures Go to War — On

Labor Unions, 29 Iowa L. Rev. 148 (1944). See also Killings-
worth, State Labor Relations Acts, a Study in Public Policy (1948);
Aaron and Komaroff, Statutory Regulation of Internal Union
Affairs, 44 Ill. L. Rev. 425, 631 (1949) ; Killingsworth, Restrictive
State Labor Relations Acts, [1947] Wis. L. Rev. 546; Millis and
Katz, A Decade of State Labor Legislation, 15 U. of Chi. L. Rev.
282 (1948).

(1) *Licensing and Other Restrictions on Union Officers*

THOMAS v. COLLINS
Supreme Court of the United States, 1945
323 U.S. 516, 65 Sup. Ct. 315, 89 L. Ed. 430

[Section 5 of the Texas Union Regulation Law (Article 5154a,
Vernon's Annotated Civil Statutes, 1943 Supplement, House Bill
No. 100) provides: "All labor union organizers operating in the
State of Texas shall be required to file with the Secretary of State,
before soliciting any members for his organization, a written request by United States mail, or shall apply in person for an organizer's card, stating (a) his name in full; (b) his labor union
affiliations, if any; (c) describing his credentials and attaching
thereto a copy thereof, which application shall be signed by him.
Upon such applications being filed, the Secretary of State shall
issue to the applicant a card on which shall appear the following:
(1) the applicant's name; (2) his union affiliation; (3) a space
for his personal signature; (4) a designation, 'labor organizer'
and, (5) the signature of the Secretary of State, dated and attested
by his seal of office. Such organizer shall at all times, when
soliciting members, carry such card, and shall exhibit the same
when requested to do so by a person being so solicited for membership. The statute is to be enforced by judicial restraining orders
to be issued on the petition of the Attorney General."

In September, 1943, Thomas, president of the United Auto
Workers and vice-president of the CIO, traveled from his home in
Detroit to Houston, Texas, for the sole purpose of addressing a
mass meeting arranged under the auspices of another CIO affiliate
during a campaign to organize the employees of the Humble Oil
and Refining Company. He did not comply with Section 5 of the
Statute. Six hours before he was scheduled to speak he was served
with a restraining order. After consulting his attorneys he decided to go ahead with the meeting as planned because he regarded
the law and the order as an unconstitutional restraint upon free
speech and free assembly. Accordingly, he addressed a meeting

of some 300 persons, in which he discussed, among other things, the State's attempt to interfere with his right to speak, and he concluded by a geneal invitation to join the union to which he added a solicitation of one Pat O'Sullivan a nonunion member in the audience whom he previously had not known. The meeting was orderly and peaceful. Subsequently, Thomas was arrested and the Supreme Court of Texas affirmed a judgment holding him in contempt for violating the restraining order.]

MR. JUSTICE RUTLEDGE delivered the opinion of the Court.

That the State has power to regulate labor unions with a view to protecting the public interest is, as the Texas court said, hardly to be doubted. They cannot claim special immunity from regulation. Such regulation, however, whether aimed at fraud or other abuses, must not trespass upon the domain set apart for free speech and free assembly. This Court has recognized that "in the circumstances of our times the dissemination of information concerning the facts of a labor dispute must be regarded as within that area of free discussion that is guaranteed by the Constitution. . . . Free discussion concerning the conditions in industry and the causes of labor disputes appears to us indispensable to the effective and intelligent use of the processes of popular government to shape the destiny of modern industrial society." Thornhill v. Alabama, 310 U.S. 88, 102, 60 S. Ct. 736, 744, 84 L. Ed. 1093; Senn v. Tile Layers Protective Union, 301 U.S. 468, 478, 57 S. Ct. 857, 862, 81 L. Ed. 1229. The right thus to discuss, and inform people concerning, the advantages and disadvantages of unions and joining them is protected not only as part of free speech, but as part of free assembly. Hague v. Committee for Industrial Organization, 307 U.S. 496, 59 S. Ct. 954, 83 L. Ed. 1423. The Texas court, in its disposition of the cause, did not give sufficient weight to this consideration, more particularly by its failure to take account of the blanketing effect of the prohibition's present application upon public discussion and also of the bearing of the clear and present danger test in these circumstances. . . .

How far the State can require previous identification by one who undertakes to exercise the rights secured by the First Amendment has been largely undetermined. It has arisen here chiefly, though only tangentially, in connection with license requirements involving the solicitation of funds, Cantwell v. Connecticut, [310 U.S. 296]; cf. Schneider v. State, 308 U.S. 147, 60 S. Ct. 146, 84 L. Ed. 155; Largent v. Texas, 318 U.S. 418, 63 S. Ct. 667, 87 L. Ed. 873, and other activities upon the public streets or in public places, cf. Lovell v. Griffin, 303 U.S. 444, 58 S. Ct. 666, 82 L. Ed. 949; Hague v. Committee for Industrial Organization, 307 U.S. 496, 59 S. Ct. 954, 83 L. Ed. 1423, or house-to-house canvassing, cf. Schneider v. State, supra.   In these cases, however, the license requirements were for more than mere identification or previous registration and were held invalid because they vested discretion in the issuing authorities to censor the activity involved.   Nevertheless, it was indicated by dictum in Cantwell v. Connecticut, 310 U.S. 296, 306, 60 S. Ct. 900, 904, 84 L. Ed. 1213, 128 A.L.R. 1352, that a statute going no further than merely to require previous identification would be sustained in respect to the activities mentioned.   Although those activities are not involved in this case, that dictum and the decision in People of State of New York ex rel. Bryant v. Zimmerman, 278 U.S. 63, 49 S. Ct. 61, 73 L. Ed. 184, 62 A.L.R. 785, furnish perhaps the instances of pronouncement or decision here nearest this phase of the question now presented. . . .

If the exercise of the rights of free speech and assembly cannot be made a crime, we do not think this can be accomplished by the device of requiring previous registration as a condition for exercising them and making such a condition the foundation for restraining in advance their exercise and for imposing a penalty for violating such a restraining order.   So long as no more is involved than exercise of the rights of free speech and free assembly, it is immune to such a restriction.   If one who solicits support for the cause of labor may be required to register as a condition to the exercise of his right to make a public speech, so may he who seeks to rally support for any social, business, religious or political cause.   We think a requirement that one must register before he undertakes to make a public speech to enlist support for a lawful movement is quite incompatible with the requirements of the First Amendment.

Once the speaker goes further, however, and engages in conduct which amounts to more than the right of free discussion comprehends, as when he undertakes the collection of funds or securing subscriptions, he enters a realm where a reasonable registration or identification requirement may be imposed.   In that context such solicitation would be quite different from the solicitation involved here.   It would be free speech plus conduct akin to the activities which were present, and which it was said the State might regulate, in Schneider v. State, supra, and Cantwell v. Connecticut, supra.   That, however, must be done, and the restriction applied, in such a manner as not to intrude upon the rights of free speech and free assembly. In this case the separation was not maintained. If what Thomas did, in soliciting Pat O'Sullivan, was subject to such a restriction, as to which we express no opinion, that act was intertwined with the speech and the general invitation in the penalty which was imposed for violating the restraining order. Since the penalty must be taken to have rested as much on the speech and the general invitation as on the specific one, and the former clearly were immune, the judgment cannot stand.

NOTES

1. For comments on Thomas v. Collins see Dodd, The Supreme Court and Organized Labor, 58 Harv. L. Rev. 1018, 1058 (1945); Notes: 25 B.U.L. Rev. 141 (1945), 33 Calif. L. Rev. 317 (1945), 45 Col. L. Rev. 465 (1945), 21 Ind. L.J. 61 (1945), 43 Mich. L. Rev. 1159 (1945), 30 Minn. L. Rev. 204 (1946), 31 Va. L. Rev. 691 (1945).

2. In American Federation of Labor v. Mann, 188 S.W.2d 276, 279 (Tex. Civ. App. 1945), the Texas Court of Civil Appeals, referring to the decision of the United States Supreme Court in Thomas v. Collins, said that Section 5 of the Texas Statute was "a registration statute" applicable to paid labor organizers "who solicit members through other methods than those used by Thomas" and that, if validly applied, it was a proper exercise of the police power.

For decisions in other state courts on similar provisions, see Van Pittman v. Nix, 152 Fla. 378, 11 So. 2d 791 (1943), holding a Florida statute invalid in absence of evidence that the labor organizer created a public nuisance or obstruction to traffic; In re Porterfield, 28 Cal. 2d 91, 168 P.2d 706 (1946), holding a California statute invalid.

3. Section 3 of the Kansas Labor Law of 1943 (Kan. Gen. Stat., Sec. 44–804 (Supp. 1945)) requires every person desiring to operate as a business agent for a labor organization to obtain a license from the Secretary of State. Such licenses are to be granted annually only to citizens of the United States who submit statements by the president and secretary of the union showing their authority to act as agents. The Attorney General of the state, construing the statute as applicable only to salaried union officials who engage in union activities as a livelihood, declared that "it would be absurd to say that the Kansas Legislature intended to inhibit the right of anyone to invite another to join his organization. . . ."

In Stapleton v. Mitchell, 60 F. Supp. 51, 16 L.R.R.M. 560 (D. Kan. 1945), dismissed by stipulation, 326 U.S. 690 (1945), a three-judge court sustained this provision, as construed by the highest enforcement officer of the state, as not inconsistent with the rule of Thomas v. Collins.   Said the court at page 60: "The conclusions of the Supreme Court in Thomas v. Collins are planted squarely upon the fundamental premise that the state may not either by statute or injunctive process, restrain any person from publicly speaking in behalf of unionism at a peaceable assembly, although the speech may have for its purpose the direct solicitation of members in the organization for which he speaks.   But the court did not nullify the Texas Act or any section thereof. . . .   We think it may be fairly implied from what was said in the majority and concurring opinions that the state may, without infringing the constitutional safeguards, condition the right of an individual to personally solicit membership in a union when that solicitation partakes of a commercial transaction in the field of union activities."

4. What criteria, if any, are available to draw the line between advocacy of unionism as an exercise of free speech and as a "commercial transaction"?   In this connection, decisions on the constitutionality of laws and ordinances prohibiting the street distribution of pamphlets and leaflets have relevance.   In Lovell v. City of Griffin, 303 U.S. 444, 58 Sup. Ct. 666, 82 L. Ed 949 (1938), the United States Supreme Court declared unconstitutional an ordinance prohibiting distribution of such leaflets without first obtaining permission of a city official as the ordinance was applied to a religious tract of the Jehovah's Witnesses religious group.   Valentine v. Chrestensen, 316 U.S. 52, 62 Sup. Ct. 920, 86 L. Ed. 1262 (1942), upheld the constitutionality of an ordinance prohibiting the distribution of commercial advertising handbills on the streets.

5. Assuming "commercial transactions" pertaining to labor unions can be clearly identified, are the states entirely free to regulate such transactions?

Note on the Relationship Between State and Federal Controls

The case of Hill v. Florida, 325 U.S. 538, 65 Sup. Ct. 1373, 89 L. Ed. 1782 (1945), involved a challenge of the validity of a Florida statute.   In 1943 the legislature passed a statute establishing various controls over labor unions.   This statute is Chapter 21963 of the Laws of 1943.   The case constituted a challenge of the validity of Sections 4 and 6 of this law.   Section 4 provides that no one shall be licensed as a "business agent" of a labor union who has not been a citizen of the United States for more than ten years, who has been convicted of a felony, or who is not a person of good moral character. Application for a license as a "business agent" must be accompanied by a one-dollar fee and a statement signed by officers of the union setting forth the agent's authority. The statute then provides that the application be held for thirty days to permit the filing of objections to the issuance of a license. A board composed of the Governor, the Secretary of State, and the Superintendent of Education then passes on the application, and if it finds the applicant measures up to the standards of the Act, as it sees them, it authorizes the license to be issued for one year. Section 2 (2) defines "business agent" as any person who for pecuniary or financial consideration acts or attempts to act for a labor union in soliciting or receiving from any employer any right or privilege for employees. Section 6 requires every labor union "operating" in the state to file a written report with the Secretary of State, disclosing its name, the location of its offices, and the names and addresses of its officers. Section 14 makes it a misdemeanor for "any person or labor organization" to violate the statute.

The Attorney General of Florida applied for an injunction against the Union and its business agent, Hill. The courts of Florida upheld the validity of the statutory provisions. The United States Supreme Court reversed.

With respect to Section 4 of the statute, the Supreme Court's opinion written by Justice Black, stated at page 541:

It is apparent that the Florida statute has been so construed and applied that the union and its selected representatives are prohibited from functioning as collective bargaining agents, or in any other capacity, except upon conditions fixed by Florida. The declared purpose of the Wagner Act, as shown in its first section, is to encourage collective bargaining, and to protect the "full freedom" of workers in the selection of bargaining representatives of their own choice. To this end Congress made it illegal for an employer to interfere with, restrain or coerce employees in selecting their representatives. Congress attached no conditions whatsoever to their freedom of choice in this respect. Their own best judgment, not that of someone else, was to be their guide. "Full freedom" to choose an agent means freedom to pass upon that agent's qualifications.

Section 4 of the Florida Act circumscribes the "full free-

dom" of choice which Congress said employees should possess.   It does this by requiring a "business agent" to prove to
the satisfaction of a Florida board that he measures up to the
standards set by the state of Florida as one who, among other
things, performs the exact function of a collective bargaining
representative.   To the extent that Section 4 limits a union's
choice of such an "agent" or bargaining representative, it
substitutes Florida's judgment for the workers' judgment.

Thus, the "full freedom" of employees in collective bargaining which Congress envisioned as essential to protect the
free flow of commerce among the states would be, by the
Florida statute, shrunk to a greatly limited freedom.   No
elaboration seems required to demonstrate that Section 4 as
applied here "stands as an obstacle to the accomplishment
and execution of the full purposes and objectives of Congress.". . .   It is not amiss, however, to call attention to the
fact that operation of this very section has already interfered
with the collective bargaining process.   An employer before
the labor board defended its refusal to bargain with a duly selected representative of workers on the ground that the
representative had not secured a Florida license as a business
agent.   Eppinger and Russell Co., 56 N.L.R.B. 1259.   The
board properly rejected the employer's contention, holding
that Congress did not intend to subject the "full freedom"
of employees to the eroding process of "varied and perhaps
conflicting provisions of state enactments." . . .

Since the Labor Board has held that an employer must
bargain with a properly selected union agent despite his failure to secure a Florida license, it is argued that the state law
does not interfere with the collective bargaining process.   But
here, this agent has been enjoined, and if the Florida law is
valid he could be found guilty of a contempt for doing that
which the act of Congress permits him to do.   Furthermore,
he could, under Section 14 of the state law, be convicted of a
misdemeanor and subjected to fine and imprisonment.   The
collective bargaining which Congress has authorized contemplates two parties free to bargain and cannot thus be frustrated by state legislation.   We hold that Section 4 of the
Florida Act is repugnant to the National Labor Relations
Act.

On the same general grounds as set forth above, the Supreme
Court held Section 6 of the statute invalid.   The court stressed
the fact that under Florida law the Union had been enjoined

from functioning as a labor union and was subject to criminal punishment in case it attempted to bargain or act as a representative of its members. Justices Roberts and Frankfurter dissented.

The history of Hill v. Florida subsequent to the decision of the United States Supreme Court is highly significant. On December 5, 1946, the Attorney General of Florida ruled (Op. 046–502) that "business agents" of labor organizations were required to apply for and procure the license provided for by Section 4 of the Florida statute. The ground of this ruling was that the collective bargaining representative of members of a labor organization, under the National Labor Relations Act, engaged solely in collective bargaining under that act were not "business agents" as defined in Section 2 (2). He further ruled that all labor organizations in Florida had to comply with the provisions of Section 6 of the law.

This opinion was based on the final decree entered on February 1, 1946, by the Circuit Court of Duval County, Florida, in the Hill case, from which the defendant did not appeal. This decree provided that the injunction against Hill, in so far as it prohibited him from functioning as the duly selected representative of the employees in a collective bargaining unit under the National Labor Relations Act, be dissolved. However, the decree provided that the injunction remain in full force and effect until Hill procured a license under the provisions of Section 4 of the Florida law in so far as Hill continued to claim the right to act as a "business agent" for the labor organization. The court enumerated the prohibited activities of "business agent" as consisting of (1) "acting or attempting to act for the defendant labor organization in the issuance of membership or authorization cards, work permits, or any other evidence of rights granted or claimed in, or by, the defendant labor organization," or (2) "acting or attempting to act for the defendant labor organization in soliciting or receiving from any employer any right or privilege for the members, or any number of the members, of the defendant labor organization who are the employees of such employer," provided, that Hill was not enjoined from exercising his functions as representative for collective bargaining purposes of the members of the Union under the National Labor Relations Act.

With respect to Section 6 of the Florida law, the court's decree dissolved the injunction in so far as it restrained the Union from engaging in collective bargaining activities related to work on employment affecting interstate commerce. But the decree also provided that the injunction be continued in full force and effect until the defendant labor union complied with the provisions of Section 6 with respect to registration in so far as the functions of the labor union were not concerned with collective bargaining activities related to work or employment affecting interstate commerce under the National Labor Relations Act.

Is this consistent with the mandate of the Supreme Court of the United States?

Texas provides that aliens and convicted felons shall not serve as union officers or agents. (Act of 1943, c. 104, H.B. 100, Sec. 4a.) This provision was sustained in American Federation of Labor v. Mann, 188 S.W.2d 276 (Tex. Civ. App. 1945).

It should be noted that the question involved in Hill v. Florida and similar cases raises the broad general question of the extent to which a state may regulate in the field of labor relations while Congress is also regulating under the National Labor Relations Act. This question is the subject of detailed consideration at pages 835 et seq. supra.

(2) *Registration and Filing of Financial Reports*

Section 7 of the Alabama Labor Act of 1943 (L. 1943, No. 298, S. 341, Sec. 7; Code of Alabama, Tit. 26, Sec. 382) reads as follows:

Labor organizations to file copies of constitutions and by-laws; reports. — Every labor organization functioning in Alabama shall within sixty days after the effective date of this chapter, and every labor organization hereafter desiring to function in Alabama shall before doing so, file a copy of its constitution and its by-laws and a copy of the constitution and by-laws of the national or international union, if any, to which the labor organization belongs, with the department of labor. Every labor organization functioning in the State of Alabama and having twenty-five or more members in any calendar year shall annually on or before February first in the next succeeding calendar year file with every member of their respective labor organizations and with the director of the department of labor a report in writing showing the facts hereinafter in this section provided as of the close of business on the thirty-first day of December next preceding the date of filing. Such report shall be filed by the secretary or business agent of such labor organization and shall show the following facts: (1) the name of the labor organization; (2) the location of its principal office and its offices in Alabama; (3) the name of the president, secretary, treasurer and other officers, and business agents, together with the salaries, wages, bonuses, and other remuneration paid each, and post office address of each; (4) the date of regular election of officers of such labor organization; (5) the number of its paid up members; (6) a complete financial statement of all fees, dues, fines, or assessments levied and/or received, together with an itemized list of all disbursements, with names of recipients and purpose therefor, covering the preceding twelve (12) months; (7) a complete statement of all property owned by the labor organization. . . .

Section 18 of the same Act (Code of Alabama, Tit. 26, Sec. 393) provides for civil penalties not exceeding $1000 and for criminal punishment not exceeding a fine of $500 or twelve months' imprisonment, or both, for each violation of the statute.

In a suit praying for a judgment declaring the Act unconstitutional, the Supreme Court of Alabama, in Alabama State Federation of Labor v. McAdory, 246 Ala. 1, 18 So.2d 810 (1944), upheld the entire Act, including the reporting requirements and penalties. The Supreme Court of the United States granted a writ of certiorari upon a petition which contended that Section 7 imposes a prior general restraint on petitioners' freedom of speech and assembly, that it is in conflict with the National Labor Relations Act and that it is an arbitrary and unreasonable exercise of the state's police power. The Court, in a unanimous opinion by Chief Justice Stone (Alabama State Federation of Labor v. McAdory, 325 U.S. 450, 65 Sup. Ct. 1384, 89 L. Ed. 1725 (1945)), dismissed the writ for lack of a justiciable case or controversy. With respect to the argument that Section 7 constituted an infringement of freedom of speech and freedom of assembly the Court concluded: "It is not contended that the statute in any way restricts the freedom of assembly and speech of labor organizations after they comply with the filing requirements of the statute, and it nowhere appears that any of the petitioners are so situated that they could not comply with the statute within the period allowed by it for compliance, without incurring any penalty for noncompliance. The attack thus made on section 7 is as to the constitutionality of the section on its face, without reference to its application to any particular defined set of facts, other than those generally catalogued in the section itself. We cannot say that sections 7 and 18 could not be so construed and applied as not to restrain petitioners' functioning in the state in the exercise of their constitutional right of free speech and assembly. The National Labor Relations Act does not extend to all industries and all employees. It is only applicable to those employments in which strikes and labor disputes would affect interstate commerce and are found to be such by the National Labor Relations Board. National Labor Relations Board v. Jones & L. Steel Corp., 301 U.S. 1, 38–40, 81 L. Ed. 893, 912–914, 57 S. Ct. 615, 108 A.L.R. 1352; National Labor Relations Bd. v. Fainblatt, 306 U.S. 601, 604, 83 L. Ed. 1014, 1017, 59 S. Ct. 668; Polish Nat. Alliance v. National Labor Relations Bd., 322 U.S. 643, 647, 88 L. Ed. 1509, 1514, 64 S. Ct. 1196. . . . It nowhere affirmatively appears that any of petitioners act as bargaining representatives of employees in industries within the state which are subject to the National Labor Relations Act."

NOTES

1. The Court's opinion might be taken to approve the imposition of a penalty for failure to file reports required by state law as distinguished from a regulation preventing the union from functioning within the state. Is this analysis persuasive and consistent with Thomas v. Collins, page 937 supra, and Hill v. Florida, page 941 supra?

2. Compare with the McAdory case, American Federation of Labor v. Mann, 188 S.W.2d 276, 282 (Tex. Civ. App. 1945), holding unconstitutional a similar provision requiring unions to file with the Secretary of State of Texas "a complete financial statement of all fees, dues, fines or assessments levied or received, together with an itemized list of all expenditures, with names of recipients and purposes therefor, covering the preceding 12 months." The court said that this imposed "undue burdens upon unions not demanded by the public interest, particularly as to small unions with limited membership. . . ."

(3) *Incorporation of Labor Unions*

American Federation of Labor v. Reilly, 113 Colo. 90, 155 P.2d 145, 160 A.L.R. 873 (1944), noted in 58 Harv. L. Rev. 1256 (1945), was an action for a declaratory judgment by a group of labor organizations, their officers and members, against the members of the Industrial Commission and the Attorney General of Colorado, to test the constitutionality of the Labor Peace Act of Colorado, Chapter 131, Session Laws of 1943. Section 20 of this Act required every local labor union to incorporate, prescribed the manner in which such corporations should be formed, and imposed specific regulations for the internal management of such bodies. Section 21 forbade all labor activities by unincorporated bodies and imposed a fine for failure to incorporate. The court held these provisions unconstitutional on the ground that they denied to unincorporated labor unions and their individual members "any right to assemble and function as such in the promotion of their common welfare by lawful means." The court concluded that compulsory incorporation went beyond the limits of permissible regulation.

For a detailed comment on whether unions should be forced to incorporate, see Seidman: Union Rights and Union Duties 163–179 (1943). The author concludes with the following quotation from a prominent attorney for management:

"All of the regulations which it is desirable to impose on labor unions, can be imposed on them even though they elect to remain unincorporated. The real approach to the problem is to forget the shibboleth of incorporation and to establish proper industrial codes and rules and regulations to govern labor unions whether incorporated or unincorporated. . . . With adequate laws permitting unions to be sued, . . . and requiring democratic administrations of union affairs and strict accounting as to union funds, the public can well leave the question of incorporation where it leaves the same question with employers, to the choice of the unions themselves." (Walter G. Merritt: Regulation of Labor Unions, New York: League for Industrial Rights, 1937, p. 33.)

1. Do we now have "adequate laws" permitting unions to sue and to be sued? See Section 301, Labor Management Relations Act of 1947; New York General Associations Law, Sections 12, 13, and 15.

2. As to the difference between the worker's relation to his union and the stockholder's relation to his corporation, see Dodd, State Legislatures Go to War — On Labor Unions, 29 Iowa L. Rev. 148, 173 (1944).

(4) *Democratic Government of Unions*

A few states — Texas, Tex. Rev. Civ. Stat., Art. 5154 (a) (1948) and Minnesota, Labor Union Democracy Act of 1943, L. 1943, c. 625 — have enacted statutes which prescribe standards for union constitutions, elections, and meetings. But these provisions are incomplete and most of them are not being enforced. The requirements of comprehensive and effective federal legislation are summarized in the following excerpt.

AARON and KOMAROFF, STATUTORY REGULATION OF INTERNAL UNION AFFAIRS *

The power and influence of unions today carry with them the responsibility to maintain a democratic administration of their own internal affairs. Most unions recognize this obligation, but a significant minority do not. Adequate remedies for abuses of union power are not presently available to union members or would-be members, either at common law or under existing state and federal legislation. The enactment of minimal federal legislation regulating internal union affairs is therefore desirable. Such legislation should be designed, not only to afford adequate relief against abuses of union power, but also to encourage and assist unions to improve their own self-government.

It is futile, however, to seek to eradicate undemocratic policies and procedures within unions unless all unjustifiable barriers to membership in those unions and to employment in general are removed. The problem is obviously one of eliminating unfair employment practices by employers and unions alike. Ideally, therefore, this problem should be dealt with in a federal fair employment practices law prohibiting employers, employment agencies, and unions from discriminating against employees because of their race, creed, color, national origin, citizenship, sex or opinion. Since the outlook for such legislation is unfavorable, the question arises whether union admission policies should be regulated even in the absence of similar controls upon the hiring policies of employers. While this type of regulation would probably be less successful than the broader statute mentioned above, it would at least constitute a step in the right direction. If such a restriction were adopted, it might logically be included in the Railway Labor Act and in the National Labor Relations Act. Under these laws a union selected by a majority of employees within an appropriate unit as their bargaining agent becomes the exclusive representative of *all* employees in the unit; and it has a corresponding duty to deal fairly with and on behalf of all those employees.[15] The same statutes which create the right and

---

* The full text of this statement may be found in 44 Ill. L. Rev. 631 (1949), from which the selection, at page 672, has been taken with the permission of the editors of that publication. — Ed.

[15] See Steele v. Louisville & Nashville R.R. Co. and following discussion, page 236 supra. — Ed.

obligation should also include safeguards against their abuse and neglect. No union which denies admission on an equal basis to some employees in the unit can represent them as well as it does its own members; therefore, such a union should be deprived of exclusive bargaining authority.

The rights of union members within the union should be protected by a separate statute. This statute should establish standards governing both substantive rules and procedures. With respect to the former, the standards should be flexible enough to permit reasonable discipline by the union of its members, while at the same time protecting the basic freedoms of speech, press, and assembly. With respect to the latter, the standards should be less flexible and should require in all disciplinary cases that the defendant be presented with written charges, given adequate notice, and accorded a fair hearing before an unbiased tribunal, with opportunity to face his accusers, present evidence in his own behalf, and cross-examine hostile witnesses.

The application of these flexible standards in specific cases can safely be left to the courts. While unions are in many ways quite different from other private associations, such as religious societies and fraternal orders, the relationship between a union and its members is more closely similar to the internal relationships in those groups than to that between a union and an employer. Courts have had long experience in dealing with the internal problems of religious societies and fraternal orders, as well as with those of unions. They have learned to accord the widest latitude possible to the substantive rules of those organizations while at the same time insuring that disciplined members receive procedural due process. Moreover, the courts alone have the power to issue injunctions, which are virtually indispensable in some cases involving abuse by a union of the rights of its members.

Administrative agencies, on the other hand, have had almost no experience in dealing with the internal affairs of private associations. Specifically, the NLRB has steered clear of intraunion controversies. A sudden change in the Board's policy, in obedience to the dictates of a statute, would be likely to produce one of two results, neither of which would be desirable. In its attempt to achieve consistency in its decisions the Board might tend to apply the statutory standards too rigidly; or it might, in order to avoid complicating its relationships with unions in other phases of its work, administer the statute in a purely nominal fashion.

There appears to be no pressing need to regulate such union activities as elections, conventions, or political campaigns, or such union policies as those dealing with seniority, initiation fees, or financial reports.   Members of a union which has non-discriminatory admission policies and democratic disciplinary policies and procedures will be able more successfully to resist attempts by subversive or racketeering elements to destroy their liberties.

E. *Parent-Local Relationships*

1. INTRODUCTION

Almost every union member has a dual relationship — as a member of an international or parent union, and as a member of a local union chartered by that international.   The local exists under the authority of the international and must contribute a certain portion of the member's dues to the international.   Likewise the local is subject to varying degrees of control by the parent in the management of its internal affairs.   The local may be required to obtain parent approval of bargaining agreements, or may even have its negotiations carried on by the international. The local may not be allowed to strike until the international executive board approves, its jurisdiction may be changed by the parent, and its finances may be subject to strict regulation.   The principal problem in this area is determining the extent to which a parent may control a local's internal affairs.   Since means of control is through disciplinary penalties inflicted on the local, the problem is very similar to that of discipline of individual members.   However, the parent-local relationship creates an added problem — that of determining the ownership of assets upon dissolution, suspension, or secession of the local.   The common problem of exhaustion of remedies is still with us, with perhaps a different flavoring because of the nature of disputes which arise.

Underneath these cases runs the all-pervasive struggle between local independence and centralized control which exists in any structure of government.   Many of the fact situations are strikingly analogous to cases involving "home rule" of municipalities or "states rights" within our federal system.

2. PROBLEM III

From 1939 to 1949, Local 999 of the United Farm Equipment Workers, CIO, was the certified exclusive bargaining representative for the production employees of the Mowline Farm Machinery Manufacturing Company in Courtney, Ohio. All of the Local's 2000 members were employed at Mowline, where it maintained a union-shop agreement.

On May 1, 1949, after two months of negotiation, a new two-year agreement was signed with Mowline. This agreement provided for a check-off of union dues without a union shop. Immediately after signing the contract the Union obtained individually signed authorization cards from all but a few of the employees. These cards authorized the employer to "deduct union dues for a period of one year, to be paid over to Local 999 of the United Farm Equipment Workers, CIO."

In October, 1949, the National Convention of the CIO authorized the United Automobile Workers, CIO, to expand its jurisdiction so as to enable the organization of farm machinery and equipment workers and take them into membership in the Automobile Workers. The reason for this authorization was a belief upon the part of the top CIO leadership that the top leadership of United Farm Equipment Workers had become infiltrated with "left-wingers." The effect of the authorization was to allow the Auto Workers to attempt to win farm equipment workers over to the Auto Workers Union without limitation and thus weaken the Farm Equipment Workers Union.

Immediately after the convention, the President of Local 999, Walter Curry, and the Financial Secretary, Milton Goldman, rushed back to Courtney, withdrew all of the Local's funds from the bank ($22,000) and put them in a safe-deposit box in a small bank in Kentucky. It should be added that the local union was not in any way infiltrated with "left-wingers" in its leadership but that Curry and Goldman had bitterly opposed the action of the CIO National Convention on the ground that it would weaken the union of which they were a part.

Next, Curry and Goldman called a meeting of the Local 999 to decide whether it would secede and become an independent union of farm equipment workers. At the meeting, attended by over 1500 members, a resolution was introduced stating that since the independence of farm equipment workers had been compromised by the actions of the CIO National Convention, the International was no longer an independent union and that the Local was no longer affiliated with it in any way. Curry and Goldman made speeches emphasizing the fact that the farm equipment workers had interests independent of automobile workers and stressing that the action of the CIO Convention clearly meant the loss of representation and protection of these independent interests. The resolution passed by a vote of 1326 to 193. A second resolution was then introduced stating that Local 999 was now an independent union, and establishing its name as Independent Farm Equipment Workers, Local No. 999.

The day after this meeting, the dissidents held a meeting and elected new officers, including Joseph Ruby, president. Ruby presented a written notice to the Mowline Company demanding that it bargain with him and his fellow officers concerning pending grievances, and that it pay over to the union which he represented the check-off of union dues. He also served written notice on Curry and Goldman to deliver to him all of the Union funds, and to cease using the name, Local 999. Curry, on the other hand, insisted to the Company that he represented the "true local union" under the agreement and the check-off authorization.

The collective agreement is headed, "An Agreement Between the United Farm Equipment Workers, CIO, and UFEW, Local 999 and the Mowline Farm Machinery Manufacturing Company."

The United Farm Equipment Workers, CIO, Constitution contains the following provisions:

> Sec. 10. Any local union whose good standing members fall below seven may have its charter revoked by the Executive Board. Any disbandment, dissolution, secession or disaffiliation of any local shall be invalid and null and void if seven or more members indicate their desire to retain the local charter.
>
> Sec. 11. If a local disbands, the local secretary shall send all funds and property to the General Secretary-Treasurer who shall hold the property intact for one year. If, within that time, an application is made by 15 former members, a charter will be reissued and the funds and property returned. If not, the funds shall revert to the International Union.
>
> Sec. 12. The General Executive Board shall have the power to revoke the charter of any local when circumstances threaten the existence of the local or threaten to injure the international. If a local's charter is revoked, the local secretary shall send all funds and property belonging to the local to the General Secretary-Treasurer.

3. PARENT CONTROL OF LOCAL AFFAIRS

NILAN v. COLLERAN
Court of Appeals, New York, 1940
283 N.Y. 84, 27 N.E.2d 511

FINCH, Judge. This is an action for an injunction which arises out of an internal dispute in the Operative Plasterers and Cement Finishers International Association. Plaintiff, a local of the International, No. 314, brings this action against the International and another local, No. 852, to compel the cancellation of the charter issued to Local No. 852 and to restore to Local No. 314 as much of its former territory as has been taken from it and transferred to defendant local.

Local No. 314 was chartered in 1904 with jurisdiction over Queens, Nassau and Suffolk counties. Prior to June 7, 1939, it still retained jurisdiction over all but a small part of Queens, Nassau and Suffolk counties as far as Wading River. Within that territory there is the construction of small homes as well as that of multiple dwellings. No satisfactory progress had been made in the unionization of the small homes projects. One means which was proposed to overcome this condition was the establishment of a secondary union scale for the small homes work, allowing longer hours and less wages than are permitted by the regular union standard. Attempts were made to organize the non-union field, but no successful conclusion was reached. Apparently Local No. 314 would not agree to the principle of a secondary scale. On June 7, 1939, by action of the executive committee of the International, Local No. 314 was deprived of about eighty per cent of its territorial jurisdiction which was transferred to a new local simultaneously chartered by the executive board of the International, and which is known as Local No. 852. There is still left to Local No. 314 a substantial field in which to operate, including the populous communities of Long Island City, Corona, Woodside, and other areas. A communication from the executive board of the International to plaintiff local stated that it was the failure of the latter to organize successfully the non-union field which prompted the action of the executive board. This action was taken by the executive board without notice to Local No. 314 or an opportunity for it to be heard on the question of the proposed action. Since its organization there have been admitted to membership in Local No. 852 approximately 483 persons who theretofore were not members of any local of the International and who were working under non-union conditions inferior to those under which they are presently employed. The action of the International executive board was taken without the consent of Local No. 314, which appealed to the convention of the International Association next following the decisions of the executive committee. At that convention a full hearing was accorded to plaintiff local by the convention, which voted to sustain the executive board.

Prior to the 1937 convention of the International, section 34 of the International constitution provided: "No local shall be organized in any city's jurisdiction controlled by another local except with the consent of said local." It has been found by Special Term and affirmed by the Appellate Division upon ample evidence that at the 1937 convention the former section 34 of the constitution was repealed and in its place there was adopted the provisions which provided: "Locals to be organized and charters to be issued at the discretion of the executive board." Thus the action taken by the executive board was not contrary to the constitution of the International for failure to obtain consent of Local No. 314.

Plaintiff contends that the action of the executive board was taken in order to punish plaintiff local, whereas defendants urge that the action was taken as a matter of business judgment in the course of administering the policies of the International. There is a conflict in the record as to the actual motive for the action taken by the executive board.

Clearly the executive board was empowered by the constitution to issue charters in its discretion. Whatever might be the judgment of others, it is the judgment of the executive board which must determine what factors require the issuance of charters and the consequent realignment of jurisdiction of existing locals to accomplish that end. In the case at bar the record reveals that the union was faced with a serious problem in combatting widespread lack of unionization in its field, especially in connection with the small homes problem. The importance of the problem in the territory covered by Local No. 314 was considerable, and clearly a proper subject for some kind of remedial action.

The situation, therefore, is one where the executive board has exercised the power conferred by the constitution, and the power has been exercised for the attainment of a proper object. The question, then, is whether there is any evidence of a reasonable connection between the ends sought to be achieved and the means adopted by the executive board. It cannot be said as a matter of law that the existence of two locals within the territory previously occupied by one may not be a device to solve the problem of unionization in what has been heretofore a predominantly non-union field. Indeed, it has been found that the membership of Local 852 includes at least several hundred workmen who previously belonged to no local of the International and who labored under conditions inferior to those which they have since obtained upon becoming members of Local 852. That is some evidence tending to show a reasonable connection between the action taken by the executive board and the permissible objects of the International. Thus, the action of the executive board may not be assailed on this ground.

Since it has not been shown that the action of the executive board was taken in bad faith and with malice, plaintiff may not succeed. The trial court has not found bad faith or malice and has refused to find that there existed a conspiracy to injure plaintiff. In the absence of any such elements tainting the action of the executive board, the only relevant consideration is whether there is some reasonable basis for the determination of the board to charter a new local within the territory of an existing local. This question has already been considered and no basis discerned which would warrant the courts in setting aside the determination of the executive board.

The judgments should be reversed and the complaint dismissed, with costs in all courts.

HENDREN v. CURTIS
Supreme Court, New York, New York County, 1937
164 Misc. 20, 297 N.Y. Supp. 364

[In February, 1936, various construction companies engaged in the digging of the Sixth Avenue subway in New York City made a collective agreement with the International Hod Carriers', Building and Common Laborer's Union. The agreement provided that the companies would employ only members of Locals 45, 102, 250, 266, and 731 of the Hod Carriers. Subsequently a dispute arose as to the right of carpenters to install certain shoring and underpinning of buildings. Fearing a jurisdictional strike, the Mayor requested that the Building Trades Council call a meeting and settle the dispute. After negotiations, an agreement was reached dividing the work between Hod Carriers and Carpenters, pending an adjudication by the Building Trades Department of the American Federation of Labor.

At the same meeting in February, 1937, representatives of the Hod Carriers locals and the International Hod Carriers Union entered into an agreement with the employers concerning the division of work between the five locals involved. Drill Runners' and Helpers' Union, Local 250 was given jurisdiction over all drill running; Blasters' Union, Local 266 was given all blasting work; Local Union 731 was given all the common labor work outside of the tunnels.

Following the making of this agreement, Locals 45 and 102, the plaintiffs, protested that it deprived them of jurisdiction over drillers, blasters, and laborers in shaft and tunnel work on the Sixth Avenue job. These two locals claimed that they were not adequately represented in the negotiations of the agreement since Local 102 was represented only by the vice president of the International Union with no members of the Local present, and Local 45 had only one member present. The plaintiff unions also claimed that the agreement was entered into in bad faith for the purpose of stripping them of a substantial portion of their jurisdiction on this job and was in violation of an award made in 1934. They appealed to a council of local unions, and at a meeting in April, 1937, this council voted eight to seven to sustain their appeal and to restore the jurisdiction to Locals 45 and 102. The International officers met this act of defiance by exercising a privilege given them by the constitution to "prorogue" the council and vetoed its action. Locals 45 and 102 endeavored to obtain a ruling from the International Executive Board but it refused to take any action whatever. The officers of these two unions then brought this suit to enjoin enforcement of the agreement which deprived them of jurisdiction over the disputed work.]

HARRIS, J. On the claim of conspiracy asserted by the plaintiffs, the court is of the opinion that the agreement of February, 1937, was entered into in good faith by all the parties thereto for the sole purpose of preventing the existing strike from interfering with the progress of the Sixth Avenue subway job. Under the agreement of February, 1936, the corporate defendants had the right and have the right to select from all of the local unions, parties herein, such employees as they desire, providing that such selection was made in good faith and providing the work was divided as much as possible among the different local unions who are parties herein. The court is satisfied by the proof herein that the corporate defendants herein made what appeared to them to be a fair allocation of jobs by means of the agreement of February, 1937. If such corporate defendants herein have not done so, then the plaintiffs herein and the other unions who are parties herein have the right to call for and proceed to arbitration under the provisions of the agreement of February, 1936.

The international has consented to an arrangement by which members may transfer from one local union to the other, and if members of one local union are given employment in preference to the members of another local union, membership is apt to move from the local which is without employment to the local which can provide its members with work. From this it is seen that if the plaintiff unions lose what they claim to be their exclusive right to employment as rock drillers and blasters upon the Sixth Avenue subway work, it may become the loser of its members. Such loss of membership comes from the union law and not from any other source, and it is interesting to note in connection with this that the agreement of February, 1936, makes no allocation of types of jobs to any of the local unions party thereto. The Court is of the opinion that the question of who are to have the jobs is, as has been termed on the trial, a "family matter," and that this question should be disposed of by the International Union or by its executive board and cannot be disposed of in this action. The plaintiffs made claim on trial that the father of the local unions, to-wit, the international, and its officers, had abandoned the family, but even if this is so, such abandonment is a matter for action first within the international to compel the parent to return from such abandonment, and if such abandonment then continues, and if such return is not made, then to compel through the courts the international and its officers to act in this dispute. Until action is taken by the international or its executive board, in view of the fact that there was no allocation of types of work in the February, 1936 agreement, and in view further of the fact that the agreement of February, 1937 was made in good faith, and so long as such agreements of Febuary, 1936 and February, 1937 are carried out in good faith, the court cannot say that the plaintiff unions have the right that they claim for their members for employment as rock drillers and blasters upon the Sixth Avenue subway work.

Based upon the foregoing and from all the proof before it, the court holds that the plaintiffs have not made out a case and that the defendants are entitled to a dismissal of the complaint herein.

NOTES

1. The constitutions of the respective international unions govern the settlement of jurisdictional disputes between locals of the same international unions.

(a) "Sec. 80.   When any dispute or grievance arises between two or more locals of the O.P. & C.F.I.A., or between the O.P. & C.F.I.A., and any subordinate local, such dispute shall be submitted to the General Executive Board for its consideration, final decision and disposition; such decision and disposition shall be appealable to the next Convention in accordance with requirements of Section 20 herein.

"Sec. 84.   Where two or more locals claim jurisdiction over the same territory, said jurisdiction shall be decided by the General President, whose decision shall be final.

"Sec. 85.   Members of the O.P. & C.F.I.A., must abide by the rules of work of the local which has jurisdiction over the locality where they are working.   Subordinate locals shall recognize the right of a member who has been accused of violating their laws to select a representative to properly handle his case, if he so desires.   The representative must be a member of the local where the violation has occurred."   Constitution, Operative Plasterers and Cement Finishers International Association (1946) .

(b) "Sec. 13.   Disputes over Jurisdiction.   Where two or more local unions are in dispute concerning jurisdiction, there shall be no work stoppage of the involved operation, but such controversy shall be submitted for determination to the Joint Council. If any party to such dispute is aggrieved by the decision of the Joint Council, it may appeal to the General President for the appointment of a special committee which in his discretion he may appoint for the purpose of holding a hearing and making a report and recommendations on the issues raised.   The committee shall make its report and recommendations to the General Executive Board for its decision, which shall be final and binding. The parties shall not be entitled to any further hearing or appearances before the General Executive Board."   Constitution, International Brotherhood of Teamsters, Chauffeurs, Warehousemen and Helpers of America (1947) .

2. In these disputes, the executive board of the international union is usually the jurisdictional tribunal and is called upon to settle the dispute.   Sometimes, the contesting unions take their differences to the international convention for consideration.   For an extensive list of such disputes which have been considered

recently and for a discussion of the problems of the "traveling employer," "traveling member," "run-away locals," etc., in regard to jurisdictional problems, see Rottenberg, Intra-Union Disputes over Job Control, 61 Q.J. Econ. 619 (1947).

UNITED BROTHERHOOD v. CARPENTERS LOCAL UNION NO. 14
Court of Civil Appeals, Texas, 1944
178 S.W.2d 558

Suit by the United Brotherhood of Carpenters and Joiners of America against Local Union No. 14 for a mandatory injunction to compel defendant to surrender all its property, books and charter. The defendant by way of cross complaint sought a writ of mandamus directing plaintiff to reinstate defendant in good standing. From a judgment granting the defendant a writ of mandamus and injunctive relief, plaintiff appeals.

PER CURIAM. The United Brotherhood brought this suit contending that Local 14 had been suspended by the parent association and sought to enforce, by way of mandatory injunction, the provisions of Section 30–A of the General Laws of the United Brotherhood, which provide that: "If at any time a Local Union should . . . be suspended . . . all property, books, charter and funds held by, or in the name of, or on behalf of said Local Union must be forwarded immediately by express to the General Secretary, to be held in safekeeping for the United Brotherhood as Trustee for the carpenters in that locality until such time as they shall reorganize."

The controlling questions in the case relate to the powers and authority of the General President, under the constitution and laws of the United Brotherhood, and the extent of the authority of the civil courts to interfere with the internal workings of a voluntary unincorporated association.

. . . The governing laws or rules of the United Brotherhood consist of the Constitution (Sections 1 to 17, inclusive), the General By-Laws (Sections 18 to 24, inclusive) and the General Laws (Sections 25 to 65, inclusive). By Section 25–A of the General Laws, Local Unions are empowered to promulgate trade and working rules, subject to the approval of the First General Vice-President.

. . . Local 14 duly adopted, with the approval of the First General Vice-President, certain trade and working rules, effective as of November 1, 1938, which contained the following provisions:

Article 14, Section 10, Trade Rules. "No carpenter shall at any time work on a job where non-union carpenters are employed, unless they have applications for membership pending; no carpenter shall work for any contractor who employs non-union carpenters."

The United Brotherhood is affiliated as an international organization with the American Federation of Labor. Shortly after the Japanese attack upon Pearl Harbor and the entry of the United States into the war now in progress, the Building Trades Department of the American Federation of Labor agreed with governmental agencies having charge of the constructions on military installations, that there would be no strikes upon such projects by union workmen under its jurisdiction during the war emergency. This agreement is commonly referred to as the "no-strike pledge."

During the early part of 1942, the H. B. Zachry Construction Company, as contractor under an agreement with an agency of the United States Government, began work upon a military installation at Hondo, Texas; which was intended for and is now being used for the purpose of training members of the Army Air Forces of the United States. . . . The Zachry Company maintained what is known as an "open shop," that is, the company did not require as a condition of employment that applicants be members of a labor union, or that they not be members of a labor union. The construction company did agree, however, that it would not interfere with Local 14, or the United Brotherhood in their attempts to recruit members among the carpenters working upon the projects.

During the latter part of 1942, certain members of Local 14 preferred charges against I. G. Paul and some twenty-four other members of Local 14, accusing them of violation of the trade rule of the Local, above set out. As a result of these charges, all twenty-five of the accused were convicted; and the majority of them, including Paul, were find $25.00 and suspended for a period of one year. Paul was fined and suspended on September 28, 1942. . . .

On January 28, 1943, Paul wrote the United Brotherhood protesting the action of Local 14 because only 22 of 226 members on the job were punished. They claimed that they had been organizing the non-union workers on the job and that the expulsion was based on prejudice and was an attempt by their enemies to eliminate them.

A member of the Executive Board was directed to investigate

and report to President Hutcheson. After the report of the investigator, on March 27, 1943, Hutcheson ordered Local 14 to rescind the expulsion and reinstate the members. The Local failed to comply and on April 8 Hutcheson ordered immediate compliance. On April 9 the Local notified President Hutcheson of a vote by the Local to appeal to the Executive Board. On April 15, Hutcheson ordered compliance pending appeal. He sent Roberts, an Executive Board member, to hold a vote in Local 14 as to whether they will comply. The Local was informed that if they voted not to comply, they would be suspended. On April 20, 1943 they voted 97 to 43 not to comply. . . . Roberts then announced that by reason of the vote and under instructions of the General President, Local Union No. 14 was suspended from the parent organization. . . .

Local 14 did attempt an appeal within the organization from both orders of the General President, i.e., the order relieving the accused carpenters of the suspension ordered by the local union, and the order suspending the local union. Copies of the appeals were mailed to the General Secretary and the General President, but they were returned marked "Refused." Thereafter, this suit was filed by the United Brotherhood.

In addition to the provisions of the laws of the United Brotherhood heretofore set out, the following excerpts from the Constitution and Laws of the organization are deemed applicable: . . . "He [the General President] shall decide all points of law, appeals and grievances, except death and disability claims, and have power to suspend any Local Union, District Council, State Council or Provincial Council for violation of the Constitution or International Laws of the United Brotherhood subject to an appeal to the General Executive Board. Any Local or Auxiliary Union, District Council, State Council or Provincial Council which wilfully or directly violates the Constitution, Laws or principles of this United Brotherhood, or acts in antagonism to its welfare, can be suspended by the General President in conjunction with the General Vice-Presidents." Section 10 F Constitution.

It is apparent that under the constitution and laws of the United Brotherhood, the General President is the executive head of the organization. He is clothed with judicial authority and empowered to grant dispensations in extraordinary cases. He has supervision over the entire interests of the United Brotherhood.

The charges contained in the letters which caused the General President to investigate and ultimately to act are these: That Local 14 had permitted its members to work for the Zachry Company, which maintained an open shop; that on the Laredo project some 266 union carpenters were employed, constituting ninety-five per cent of all the carpenters employed. The business agent of Local 14 had ordered these union carpenters to quit the Laredo job under the threat of disciplinary action. To say that the International body, through its General President, has no power to investigate charges of this nature and take action in regard thereto is simply to say that the general organization upon its own initiative is not empowered to enforce the American Federation of Labor "no strike pledge" among its various subordinate bodies.

In our opinion, no such construction of the constitution and laws of the United Brotherhood is compelled by the terms and provisions thereof. The order lifting the suspension of those charged with violation of the Trade Rules of Local 14 may be regarded as the granting of a dispensation which is generally understood in law to mean the relaxation or suspension of a law in a particular case.

Having held that the order of March 27, 1943, was valid, there can be little doubt of the validity of the General President's order suspending Local 14. The refusal of a subordinate body to comply with a mandate of the general organization is a ground for suspension under the laws of the association. This remedy for the suppression of insubordination may be harsh and drastic but it is provided for by the laws of the association to which all members thereof agreed to be bound. District Grand Lodge No. 25, Grand United Order of Odd Fellows v. Jones, 138 Tex. 537, 160 S.W.2d 915.

On Motion for Rehearing

Appellee's motion for rehearing contains an assignment asserting that this Court erred in holding that the manner and method adopted by the General President in suspending the charter of Local 14 did not violate the requirements of "due process law."

Our original view of the question of the validity of the suspension order here involved was that the requisites of due process of law had been complied with, inasmuch as Local 14 had refused to abide by and recognize an order legally promulgated by the General President, and at a meeting of Local 14, the members present were informed that persistence in the adopted course of action would result in a suspension.

The general American rule is that when the constitution or laws of an unincorporated association provide for the suspension or revocation of the charter of a subordinate body (or the suspension or expulsion of a member), but do not provide for charges, notice and hearing relative to such action, the courts will recognize as valid only such actions taken under the association's laws as are taken in pursuance of charges made, notice given and hearing had. Taboada v. Sociedad Espanola De Beneficiencia Mutua, 191 Cal. 187, 215 P. 673, 27 A.L.R. 1508; 10 C.J.S., Beneficial Associations, Sec. 52, p. 295; 63 C.J. 698. This rule may be stated by saying that the law writes into the constitutional or by-law provisions of the association relating to the suspension or revocation of a charter, the requirement that such suspension or revocation must be effected by "due process of law," that is, upon charges, notice and hearing.

The specific question presented here is whether or not a notice given by the general organization to a local subordinate association that if a certain action is taken by the local association a suspension will follow, satisfies the requirements of due process of law as to charges, notice and hearing, or is it necessary to the validity of a suspension order that the general organization, upon the refusal of the local to abide by its order, go further and thereafter prefer charges against the local, give notice thereof and conduct a hearing to determine whether or not the local should be suspended.

Appellee cites Ellis v. American Federation of Labor, 48 Cal. App.2d 440, 120 P.2d 79, decided by one of the District Courts of Appeal of California. In this case it appears that Meyer Lewis, as personal representative of William Green, president of the American Federation of Labor, had informed the Central Labor Council of Santa Clara County, California (a subordinate unincorporated body of the A.F.L.), not to seat a certain disputed delegation until a certain investigation could be completed. Lewis further notified the Central Labor Council that if said delegates were seated by the Council, he, Lewis (presumably acting for and in behalf of William Green, president of the A.F.L.), would "jerk the charter" of the Central Labor Council. The Central Labor Council did seat the delegates and as a result its charter was removed by the president of the American Federation of Labor. The California Court held that the attempted removal or revocation of the charter was void. This holding was not based upon a decision of whether or not the Central Labor Council had "committed any breach of its obligations to the American Federation of Labor, or was guilty of any conduct which would justify the suspension or revocation of its charter," but upon the ground that such action was void as having been accomplished without charges having been filed, notice thereof given, and a hearing had upon the charges preferred. The power of suspension was regarded as a quasi-judicial power. Taboada v. Sociedad Espanola De Beneficiencia Mutua, supra.

We have concluded that the California case should be followed. Consistency in decision of the American authorities upon the point is desirable. . . . We conclude as a matter of law that the suspension order of April 20, 1943, was and is invalid. . . .

NOTES

1. It is generally held that where property rights are involved, a local charter cannot be revoked without a fair trial. Property rights may be found to exist in the assets of the local, members' rights to death benefits, or the members' right to work. See Ellis v. American Federation of Labor, 48 Cal. App. 2d 440, 120 P.2d 79 (1941) ; Gardner v. Newbert, 74 Ind. App. 183, 128 N.E. 704 (1920) ; Local No. 1226 v. Ross, 180 La. 293, 156 So. 357 (1934) ; Swaine v. Miller, 72 Mo. App. 446 (1897) ; Furniture Workers Union, Local 1007 v. United Brotherhood of Carpenters & Joiners, 6 Wash.2d 654, 108 P.2d 651 (1940). The net effect of these cases is obviously to require a fair hearing in practically all charter revocation cases.

However, the problem of giving a fair hearing within the union structure is extremely difficult because of the lack of an unbiased tribunal. Although the two following cases probably involved some objectionable overreaching on the part of the international officers, they may be suggestive of the problem which would exist even though the officers acted in complete good faith.

The New York District Council of the Carpenters & Joiners demanded a general wage increase and voted to strike against those refusing. The General Executive Board prohibited the strike and delegated Hutcheson to settle it. Without consulting the District Council he settled at lower terms than many of the employers had agreed to. The Council refused the settlement and struck. Hutcheson retaliated by suspending the Council and all of the locals. He ordered the members to join new locals set up by him and demanded that all of the locals' books and property be turned over to the new locals. Held: Suspension of locals and interference with their functioning enjoined. The Constitutional provision permitting such summary action is void. Property rights cannot be destroyed without notice and hearing. The right of appeal does not correct this defect as it is not equivalent to a fair trial in the first instance since there would then be a presumption of guilt.   No need to exhaust remedies as appeal is to Hutcheson and Executive Board who have already prejudged the case.   Neal v. Hutcheson, 160 N.Y. Supp. 1007 (1916).

Local No. 7 of the Bricklayers distributed a circular protesting the high salaries of the International officers.   After a hearing the Executive Board ordered the Local suspended.   Appeal was taken to the convention but denied.   Held: Suspension enjoined. The proceedings are void because the Executive Board had no jurisdiction under the constitution to suspend a local for such an offense.   Even if it had jurisdiction, it could not give a fair trial. The very ones who were attacked in the circular attempted to act as judges.   Local No. 7, Bricklayers, Masons & Plasterers International Union v. Bowen, 278 Fed. 271 (S.D. Tex. 1922).   For a similar case, see Riverside Lodge No. 164 v. Amalgamated Assn. of Iron & Steel Workers, 13 F. Supp. 873 (W.D. Pa. 1935).

2.   The revocation of a local charter by the parent automatically expels all members of the local.   Taussig v. Weber, 123 Misc. 180, 205 N.Y. Supp. 605 (1924).   In numerous cases, international officers have attempted to eliminate opposition within rebellious locals by revoking the local charter and refusing readmission of the opposition into other locals.   This device for summary expulsion has almost uniformly been held ineffective to deprive individuals of their membership.   Shadley v. Grand Lodge Brotherhood of Railroad Trainmen, 212 Mo. App. 653, 254 S.W. 363 (1923) ; Kehoe v. Leonard, 176 App. Div. 626, 163 N.Y. Supp. 357 (2d Dept. 1917).

The extent to which this device can be used is well illustrated by a group of cases involving the International Union of Operating Engineers.   In 1930, President Huddell discovered some open opposition within Locals 20 and 184.   He summarily suspended the leaders of the opposition, revoked the locals' charters and created a new Local 125 with his lieutenant, Pat Commerford, as supervisor.   All of the troublemakers were refused admission to the new union and thereby barred from their work.   In Rodier v. Huddell, 232 App. Div. 531, 250 N.Y. Supp. 336 (1st Dept. 1931), the court held that the summary suspension of these members was a denial of a fair hearing and ordered them admitted to Local 125.

This case was only the beginning of a long struggle.   The plaintiffs obtained entry into Local 125 only to find themselves under the dictatorial control of Commerford, who had been appointed as supervisor of Local 125 by Huddell.   He suspended meetings, expelled members without trial, failed to account for funds, admitted members without vote but on payment of exorbitant initiation fees, and prohibited all elections.   In Irwin v. Possehl, 143 Misc. 855, 257 N.Y. Supp. 597 (1932), the court ordered the appointment of a receiver and the holding of an election.   It also held that exhaustion of internal remedies would be excused because an appeal to the general executive board would be futile.

Huddell's successor, Possehl, countered this order by revoking the charter of Local 125 and representing to contractors that the members of Local 125 were not in good standing.   He also established a new local and ordered contractors to deal with it.   In Irwin v. Possehl, 145 Misc. 907, 261 N.Y. Supp. 164 (1932), the court held the revocation of Local 125's charter void and ordered it reinstated.   Possehl then granted the whole jurisdiction of Local 125 to Local 130.   By the time the court got this enjoined, in McGrath v. Dillon, 145 Misc. 912, 262 N.Y. Supp. 90 (1932), Local 130 had been replaced by two new locals.   Possehl then ordered the officers of Local 125 tried for incompetence.   After due trial they were found guilty and suspended from office.   The courts refused to give relief (see Fay v. Robinson, 251 App. Div. 803, 287 N.Y. Supp. 326 (1st Dept. 1936)), and Possehl consolidated Local 125 with the others to form a new local.   Possehl then called a convention in 1938 and obtained modifications in the constitution which would give him greater power over locals who dared challenge his authority.   These provisions were submitted to referendum and were adopted by a vote of 30,975 to 3369.   Most of the voting was not carried out in the regular manner.   In seven locals the vote was unanimous, and in two others it was almost unanimous.   Standing votes in local meetings or votes by mail were used.   In spite of the suspicious circumstances, the court held the members claiming a fraudulent vote had not overcome the "presumption of regularity" and upheld the referendum.   Rowan v. Possehl, 173 Misc. 898, 18 N.Y.S.2d 574 (1940).   See Note, 51 Yale L.J. 1372 (1942), for a more complete account of this controversy.

3. Is it essential to protect autonomy of local unions in order to maintain a democratic union?   To what extent will the remoteness of control affect the vigor of democratic action among the members?

4. To what extent does the structure of the industry affect the structure of the union?   Can a decentralized union deal with a large, highly centralized employer?

5. If local unions are largely autonomous, may they prevent international officers from cleaning out petty racketeers on the local level?   Has the failure of the AFL to clean its own house been due to the autonomy of the internationals within it?

6. Are judicial remedies adequate to effect or maintain any wholesome balance of power between the local and the parent?

4. SECESSION OF LOCALS

CLARK v. FITZGERALD
Supreme Court, New York, New York County, 1949
197 Misc. 355, 93 N.Y.S.2d 768

EDER, Justice.   Motion for injunction is denied.

The organization known as the United Electrical, Radio and Machine Workers of America (hereinafter United Electrical and U.E.) is an unincorporated, voluntary association stated to be an international industrial union in the electrical, radio and machine manufacturing industry.

It is composed of a large number of local unions throughout the United States.   It issues charters to locals and it issued a charter to the organization known as "Local 450 U.E." (hereafter Local 450 or Local).   Local 450 is also an unincorporated, voluntary association, and it has functioned as a chartered local of United Electrical.

United Electrical and Local 450 each have a constitution and bylaws by which they are governed.   The charter issued to Local 450 contains the following provision: "It is hereby agreed in the acceptance of this charter that the aforesaid (local) union shall conform to the constitution, rules and regulations of the United Electrical, Radio and Machine Workers of America."

There is contained in the constitution of United Electrical, in Article 18, Section O, the following provision, so far as here relevant: "Any disbandment, dissolution, secession or disaffiliation of any local shall be invalid and null and void if seven or more members indicate their desire to retain the local charter."

In accepting the charter Local 450 became subject to and bound by the aforementioned provision that it would conform to the constitution of United Electrical.   United Electrical was heretofore affiliated with the organization known as the Congress of Industrial Organizations (hereafter C.I.O.), and the fact of its affiliation with C.I.O. is announced in the heading of its printed booklet which contains the constitution and bylaws of the U.E.

This affiliation of U.E. with the C.I.O. ended on November 2, 1949, when United Electrical was expelled from the C.I.O.

Article I, Section I of the constitution of Local 450 entitled "Name," provides that it shall be known as "Local 450, United Electrical, Radio and Machine Workers of America." Article II, Section I thereof, entitled "Affiliation" reads as follows: "Local 450 shall be affiliated with the United Electrical, Radio and Machine Workers of America, *C.I.O.,* with District 4, United Electrical, Radio and Machine Workers of America *C.I.O.,* and with such other bodies as the membership may determine." (Emphasis, mine.)

Following the expulsion of United Electrical from the C.I.O., meetings of the members of Local 450 were held to discuss the question of continued affiliation with the C.I.O., and as to what course of action should be taken toward accomplishing such continued affiliation, it being asserted that the continued association with the C.I.O. was imperative to secure and assure protection to the members in their field of employment, and that disaffiliation with the C.I.O. could only result in damage to the good and welfare of the membership of Local 450. A motion was proposed and adopted by an overwhelming vote of the members to continue affiliation with the C.I.O.

It is alleged in the moving papers that as a consequence of these meetings and the action taken thereat a recommendation was made by defendant Brady and by other defendants that the title, property, funds and assets of Local 450 be transferred to a committee of seven, consisting of five trustees and two officers, to wit, defendants Fitzgerald and Brady, and that the committee of seven be empowered and authorized to take such steps with respect thereto as they might deem fit, and that the defendants further announced that the Executive Board was seeking affiliation with some other union and that the purpose of establishing a committee of seven was to conceal the property of Local 450 and to make it available for the use and benefit of such other union, and to deprive Local 450 and its membership thereof, and that the defendant Brady and others of the defendants then caused motions to the foregoing effect to be introduced and passed at such meetings over the opposition of more than seven members of Local 450, and that the aforementioned acts on the part of the defendants and members of the Executive Board of Local 450 were in violation of the provisions of the constitution of United Electrical and the bylaws of the Local.

Injunctive relief is sought to restrain the defendants from

committing and continuing the acts complained of and alleged to be illegal. All the alleged illegal acts charged to the defendants are denied by them.

In the opposing papers it is asserted that this action arises from the attempt of the nine plaintiffs herein to harass, by improper action, the entire membership of Local 450 (4200 members) in its fight against Communist control of the union and in its fight to support the policies of the C.I.O. against Communist party interference in the affairs of the union, and that it is also intended by this action to prevent the membership from exercising their right under the Local's constitution to freely choose an affiliation with an organization in the American Labor movement that is not under Communist control. . . .

The principal and fundamental question, then, is whether, in view of the peculiar situation which has arisen by reason of the expulsion of United Electrical from the C.I.O., and resulting in the loss of its affiliation with the latter, the compact between United Electrical and Local 450 has terminated and has rendered nugatory Article 18, Section O of the U.E. constitution, quoted supra.

To resolve this basic question Article 18, Section O, must be viewed in the light of the situation preceding the entry of Local 450 into membership in the U.E.

It appears from the opposing papers that in its organizing campaigns preceding the formation of specific local unions, including Local 450, United Electrical advertised its affiliation with the C.I.O., the strength which it held by virtue of its C.I.O. affiliation, its ability to aid members and prospective members by drawing upon the money, personnel, experience and prestige with the C.I.O.; that at the time Local 450 became affiliated with U.E., the International Union was then an affiliate with C.I.O.; that the organization with which Local 450 became affiliated and from which it accepted a charter, was U.E., *C.I.O.*

The constitution of Local 450 provides in Article II, Section 1 that Local 450 shall be affiliated with United Electrical *C.I.O.*, and with District 4, United Electrical *C.I.O.* and with such other bodies as the membership may determine.

It is thus clear that the membership of Local 450 has considered affiliation with C.I.O. as an essential relationship and prerequisite to protect its welfare and working conditions, and it is alleged that it would never have affiliated with U.E. were it not for U.E.'s affiliation with the C.I.O.

Article 21 of the U.E. constitution requires that the local union's constitution and bylaws must be approved by it. The constitution and bylaws of Local 450 were approved by United Electrical and therefore they are binding upon it. The constitution of Local 450 provides that it shall be affiliated with United Electrical, *C.I.O.* The affiliation with *C.I.O.* cannot be considered as merely a passing reference to a name. Article I, Section 1 of Local 450's constitution provides that it shall be known as "Local 450, United Electrical, Radio and Machine Workers of America." If there was no intention to make *C.I.O.* an important part of its affiliation, the constitution could definitely have rested there. There would have been no need for Article II providing for affiliation with *C.I.O.* It is quite evident, therefore, that it was only because the membership considered affiliation with the C.I.O. as vital that they provided in Article II that the Local should be affiliated with a C.I.O. national union.

In the opposing papers it is pointed out that the Local Union's collective bargaining agreements provide that its contracts with the employer contain C.I.O. as part of the Local Union's name, and also for part of the national union's name, which lends added weight to the conclusion that all of these precautions were taken by the membership because of the determination to be part of C.I.O.

Plaintiffs assert that affiliation with C.I.O. is of no particular significance; that it is unrelated to the contract between the members, the Local and the International, created by the constitution, charter and bylaws, and that United Electrical, like other international unions, was affiliated with C.I.O. for inter-union purposes solely, and that the affiliation can be broken without affecting the international and its locals and its membership.

In support of this premise plaintiffs solicit attention to a statement by the court, Swygart, J., in its findings of fact No. 10 in Seslar v. Union Local 901, Inc., U.S.D.C.N.D.Ind., 87 F. Supp. 447, reading as follows: "The members of the local union have no direct affiliation with the C.I.O. Their only direct affiliation is with their parent body, the United Electrical Radio and Machine Workers of America."

This may be so as a general proposition. However, where, as here, the constitution of the Local definitely requires affiliation by the international union or parent body with the C.I.O., and the constitution with this requirement is approved by U.E., as it was here, it becomes a prerequisite and integral, indispensable element and inducement for the Local Union associating with the parent body, and so long as the required and mandatory affiliation with the C.I.O. exists, the contract of the Local with the parent body exists, and the provisions of the constitution of the respective organizations are binding on the contracting parties. . . .

The affiliation of United Electrical with the C.I.O., as mentioned, was the inducement of Local 450 and its members to enter into the compact with U.E.; indeed such affiliation of the U.E. with the C.I.O. was of the essence of the contract, for the Local and its members were not bound to join with U.E. and would not have joined but for U.E.'s affiliation with C.I.O.

While not so precisely expressed in the contract between U.E. and the Local, both parties must be supposed to have contemplated the continuance of the affiliation of the United Electrical with the C.I.O. as one of the conditions of the compact and such contract is subject to this implied condition.

When performance depends on the continued existence of a given thing and such continued existence is assumed as a basis of the agreement, an implied condition that such existence shall continue is to be read into the contract, and the destruction of the thing puts an end to the contract (Lorillard v. Clyde, 142 N.Y. 456, 37 N.E. 489, 24 L.R.A. 113) ; also where the performance of a contract depends upon the happening of an event over which neither party has control, the implied condition will be read into the contract that it shall be abrogated on the non-happening of such an event (Marks Realty Co. v. Hotel Hermitage Co., 170 App. Div. 484, 156 N.Y.S. 179; Marks Realty Co. v. "Churchills," 90 Misc. 370, 153 N.Y.S. 264) ; the event which renders the contract incapable of performance is the cessation or nonexistence of an express condition or state of things going to the root of the contract. Where an event substantially frustrates the objects contemplated by the parties when they enter into the contract the foundation of the contract is gone. . . .

After due consideration and reflection I have reached the ultimate conclusion that the effectiveness of the U.E. constitution, and particularly the efficacy of Article 18, Section O, thereof, upon which plaintiffs so much rely, are dependent upon the continued affiliation of U.E. with the C.I.O. and that with U.E.'s expulsion from the C.I.O. the compact between U.E. and Local 450 was abrogated, and, hence, the Local and its members were released from any restraint or prohibitions imposed by Article 18, Section O, and that they were at liberty to proceed and act as they did, and that no basis exists for granting the injunctive relief which the plaintiffs seek by this application.

For the reasons set forth the motion is denied.   Settle order.[16]

NOTES

1. Although local disaffiliation problems were not new to the judiciary, the solution arrived at by many of the courts in the UE–IUE actions — the "frustration" doctrine — was a new concept as applied to labor law.   In addition to Clark v. Fitzgerald, many of the cases decided in this controversy followed the doctrine. For example, see Local 1140, United Electrical Workers v. United Electrical Workers, 232 Minn. 217, 45 N.W.2d 408 (1950); Duris v. Iozzi, 6 N.J. Super. 530, 70 A.2d 793 (1949); Bozeman v. Fitzmaurice, 25 L.R.R.M. 2648, 20 CCH Lab. Cas. ¶66,401 (Ohio Ct. App. 1950).

Some courts, however, have held firm to the traditional method for dealing with the assets of a local upon disaffiliation and have refused to allow the seceding local to take the assets with it.   See Seslar v. Union 901, 87 F. Supp. 447 (N.D. Ind. 1949); Kidde & Co. v. United Electrical Workers, 26 L.R.R.M. 2036, 18 CCH Lab. Cas. ¶65,722 (N.J. Super. 1950), reversed in 7 N.J. 528, 82 A.2d 184 (1951); United Electrical Workers, Local 303 v. Kwiecien, 25 L.R.R.M. 2178, 17 CCH Lab. Cas. ¶65,462 (N.Y. Sup. Ct. 1949).   On the problem of United Electrical Workers locals seceding from the International Union see, in general, Petro, The UE–CIO Controversy in the Courts, 2 Labor L.J. 163 (1951); Note, 63 Harv. L. Rev. 1413 (1950).

2. The split of the labor movement and the rise of the CIO resulted in numerous instances in locals breaking away from their old AFL parents and joining a CIO international.   During this period the courts uniformly held that upon secession the assets went either to the deserted parent or the loyal remnant.   Although numerous devices and subterfuges were attempted, the courts refused to permit the secessionists to take the assets with them.   Low v. Harris, 90 F.2d 783 (7th Cir. 1937); Brown v. Hook, 79 Cal. App. 2d 781, 180 P.2d 982 (1947); Liggett v. Koivunen, 227 Minn. 114, 34 N.E.2d 345 (1948); Marvin v. Nanash, 175 Ore. 311, 153 P.2d 251 (1944); Harris v. Backman, 160 Ore. 520, 86 P.2d 456 (1939); Local No. 2508 v. Cairns, 197 Wash. 476, 85 P.2d 1109 (1938).   See also Note, 47 Yale L.J. 483 (1938).

An important recent case following this same traditional ap-

[16] The case is noted in 34 Minn. L. Rev. 357 (1950) and 2 Stanford L. Rev. 588 (1950). — ED.

proach is Harker v. McKissock. Here a local of the Marine and Shipbuilding Workers seceded and formed an independent local. The trial court ruled the disaffiliation was improper because it was not the product of a unanimous vote. The intermediate appellate court held the disaffiliation proper and also held that the withdrawing majority could take the assets. 10 N.J. Super. 26, 76 A.2d 89 (1950). The New Jersey Supreme Court held that while the disaffiliation was proper, the requirement of the contract between the old Local and the International of a forfeiture of the Local's assets upon disaffiliation would be enforced. Harker v. McKissock, 7 N.J. 323, 81 A.2d 480 (1951). This case is discussed with reference to the opinion of the intermediate court in Note, 58 Yale L.J. 1171 (1949). The note contains a useful discussion of the difficulties with the traditional approach and suggests that disposition of funds should be made dependent upon NLRB certification after secession.

3. One authority argues, "Despite the general similarity of international constitutions, the actual relationships of internationals and their locals vary widely and are dependent on factors which have little, if any, connection with the constitutions." He points out that if the "frustration" doctrine had been applied to organizations such as the Amalgamated Clothing Workers, the International Ladies' Garment Workers, and the United Mine Workers, all three of which having at one time or another been affiliated with either the CIO or the AFL, or have been independent, the results would be "absurd." Finally, he warns that the "frustration" doctrine, by giving the courts "wider latitude in giving vent to their economic predilections and prejudices," represents "judicial atavism." Isaacson, The Local Union and the International, Proceedings of New York University Third Annual Conference on Labor 493–529 (1950).

In this connection consider the words of the court in Fitzgerald v. Riverside Labor Hall, 27 L.R.R.M. 2366, 19 CCH Lab. Cas. ¶66,237 (N.Y. Sup. Ct. 1951) : "So UE stands before this Court, in equity, garbed in red as CIO saw it and so accused it, and tries to awaken the court's conscience to claimed wrongs perpetrated against it." In contrast are the words of the court in Fitzgerald v. Abramson, 89 F. Supp. 477, 25 L.R.R.M. 2520 (S.D.N.Y. 1950) : "Behind this dispute may lurk ideological differences of great consequence. The dispute itself, however, relates strictly to property rights and, of course, this Court is not authorized in resolving such a dispute, to apply one ruling of law for Communists and another for anti-Communists."

4. A rather novel disposition of the problem of disposal of the assets of a local union when that union secedes is to be found in Suffridge v. O'Grady, 84 N.Y.S.2d 211 (Sup. Ct. 1948). In this case a local of the Retail Clerks (AFL) voted to secede and join the Distilling Workers (CIO). The Clerks' constitution provided that in cases of secession, the local assets should be held by the International as trustee for the Clerks in that locality for a period of one year, to be turned over to them in case they should reorganize. The court held that the Clerks did reorganize within a year and were entitled to the assets, even though they reorganized in a rival union.

5. Another aspect of the litigation in the UE–IUE controversy was that which involved the struggle over who was entitled to use the name or numerical designation of the local. See Fitzgerald v. Block, 87 F. Supp. 305 (E.D. Pa. 1949); Fitzgerald v. Dillon, 92 F. Supp. 681, 26 L.R.R.M. 2394 (E.D.N.Y. 1950). The NLRB took the position that its exclusive power over representation questions under the Labor Management Relations Act carried with it the exclusive power to decide whether a particular name, used to designate a union on the ballot in an election conducted by the Board, confused the employees in their free choice of a bargaining representative. Thus, in Radio Corporation of America, 89 N.L.R.B. 699, 26 L.R.R.M. 1022 (1950), the Board authorized the IUE local to use the same numerical designation as the UE local on a representation election ballot even though at that time the IUE local had been enjoined from using this numerical designation by a federal court.

6. The same rules do not apply to the secession of the international union from its federation, for the federation is in no sense a parent of its constituent internationals, but merely a voluntary association of them. Textile Workers Union, Local 204 v. Federal Labor Union No. 21,500, 240 Ala. 239, 198 So. 606 (1940), involved the expulsion of the United Textile Workers from the AFL for participating in the CIO. The United Textile Workers then affiliated with the CIO. Local 997B voted to go along and was given a new charter. Dissidents who opposed the CIO formed a local and were chartered by the AFL as Federal Union No. 21,500. They claimed the assets of Local 997B as the true successor. The court held that the obligation of the Local was to its parent international and not to the federation with which the parent was affiliated. When the Local voted to join the CIO it followed its parent. Therefore, the CIO local was the true successor and was entitled to the assets.

BOSTON MACHINE WORKS COMPANY
National Labor Relations Board, 1950
89 N.L.R.B. 59, 25 L.R.R.M. 1508

On August 20, 1948, the UE, as an affiliate of the CIO, together with its then Local 257, executed an agreement with the Employer, covering the employees involved in this case, to be in effect until August 21, 1949. On that date, pursuant to its terms, the contract was automatically renewed for 1 year to August 21, 1950. The UE contends that this contract is a bar to a present determination of representatives. Local 257, IUE–CIO contends, on the other hand, that the facts in this case reveal a schism in the contracting union and that under well-established principles of the Board an immediate election should be directed. The Employer, as the Petitioner, takes a similar position, asserting that it does not know which union represents its employees, and is therefore unwilling to bargain with either until one or the other has been certified by the Board as the exclusive bargaining representative.

The record reveals that on November 8, 1949, at a regular meeting of Local 257, then affiliated with the UE, a motion was proposed that Local 257 disaffiliate from the UE and affiliate with the IUE–CIO. The motion was approved unanimously by the members present. The November 8 meeting was publicized several days in advance by notices on the plant bulletin boards and by oral notification through the shop stewards to individual members. Approximately 118 members out of a total membership of about 198 attended the meeting. After the meeting Local 257 applied for and received a charter from the IUE–CIO. The president and vice president of the former UE Local 257 were elected by the membership of the new local and have continued to serve in their respective capacities as officers of Local 257, IUE–CIO. Uncontroverted testimony indicates that all of the membership of the former UE Local 257 have signed membership cards in Local 257, IUE–CIO, that UE Local 257 in fact has no members, has held no meetings since November 8, 1949, and has processed no grievances. For all practical purposes UE Local 257 is a defunct organization.

On the basis of facts substantially similar, the Board traditionally has held that a current contract between the Employer and a preexisting bargaining representative of its employees cannot operate to bar an immediate election for the purpose of resolving the question concerning representation. As a result of the intra-union split revealed by the record in this case, each of two contending unions challenges with some show of right the other's claim to a representative bargaining status. The Employer reasonably asserts that it does not know with which union to bargain and requests the Board to redetermine the employees' desires with regard to a bargaining representative. It is apparent that the normal bargaining relationship between the Employer and the heretofore exclusive bargaining representative of its employees has become a matter of such confusion, because of the events described above, that the relationship between them no longer can be said to promote stability in industrial relations. Under these circumstances, as we have previously said,[2] to treat the contract as a bar to a present redetermination of representatives would seriously impede rather than encourage the practice of collective bargaining which the Act was designed to foster and protect. We therefore believe that the conflicting claims to representation of the two labor organizations involved can best be resolved by an election.

The unusual circumstances of this and similar cases raise, in addition to the question of representation here considered, other questions relating to the property rights of the parties as well as collective bargaining obligations with reference to the current contract. So far as the property rights of the parties are concerned, that is a matter properly for the courts rather than this Board to decide. With regard to the duty of the Employer and the representative of its employees to bargain now or in the future upon the basis of the current contract or for a new contract, we do not believe it to be this Board's function, in a representation proceeding to pass upon this issue. We find it necessary to determine here only the question of representation as required by Section 9 (c) of the Act. The impact of the resolution of that question upon the collective bargaining duties and rights of the Employer, the employees, and the labor organizations must be determined by the application of other provisions of the Act, in the light of a factual situation not now before us.

Generally, in cases of this nature the Board has not attempted to rule upon the validity or invalidity of the current contract. It has decided only that the employees should be permitted to determine through an election the identity of the labor organization which they desire to have represent them.[3] In several cases,[4] however, it has held that the election would be for the restrictive

---

[2] See Container Corporation of America, 61 N.L.R.B. 823.

[3] See General Motors Corporation, 88 N.L.R.B. 450, where Chairman Herzog . . . relied upon this rationale.

[4] Harbison-Walker Refractories Company, 43 N.L.R.B. 1349; The Register and Tribune Company, 60 N.L.R.B. 360.

purpose of determining the representative to administer the current contract. We need not now decide whether the representative to be certified herein must assume the existing contract. To the extent these cases purport to decide that question and are inconsistent with our decision and direction of election herein, they are hereby overruled.

In his separate opinion Member Reynolds argues that the intervening certification by the Board of another labor organization during the term of a contract otherwise valid between the Employer and the former bargaining representative of its employees can in no manner affect the continued validity of that contract. Under his view the Employer and the union certified as the representative of the employees would be required to engage in collective bargaining on the basis of the preexisting contract. Should the employees vote for no union in the forthcoming election, presumably Member Reynolds would take the position that the contract nevertheless continued in existence between the Employer and the employees. As indicated above, we think it neither necessary nor proper in a representation proceeding to rule upon the collective bargaining duties of the parties or on other issues not before us. The best traditions of Anglo-American law suggest that this Board should neither discuss nor decide matters which are not necessary to resolve the issues presented for specific decision at the time. To the extent we might do so we would be merely stating dictum.

However, to the extent that our colleague's argument goes beyond the expression of a theory that the union is merely the agent of the employees,[5] and may be taken to mean that our certification of any union in this case should be *conditioned* by the requirement that it adhere to the terms of the unexpired contract, it should be noted that this very procedure in representation cases was considered and rejected by the framers of the amended Act.

In reporting to the House, the House conferees explained the deletion of such a provision as follows:

> Under the House bill, in section 9 (f) (8), it was provided that if a new representative were chosen while a collective

---

[5] This theory has not been expressed in Board decisions since the early cases of New England Transportation Company, 1 N.L.R.B. 130, and Swayne & Hoyt, Ltd., 2 N.L.R.B. 282. It has received support in the separate opinions of Member Edwin S. Smith (National Sugar Refining Company of New Jersey, 10 N.L.R.B. 1410) and Member Gerard D. Reilly (J. I. Case Company, 42 N.L.R.B. 85). Cf., however, Member Reilly's dissenting opinion in Container Corporation of America, supra, apparently assuming that an existing contract between the employer and a union would be abrogated by the intervening certification of another labor organization.

bargaining agreement was in effect with another representative, certification of the new representative should not become effective unless such new representative became a party to such contract and agreed to be bound by its terms for the remainder of the contract period. Since the inclusion of such a provision might give rise to an inference that the practice of the Board, with respect to conducting representation elections while collective bargaining contracts are in effect, should not be continued, it is omitted from the conference agreement.[6]

We do not believe that this Board should qualify its certification of the employees' bargaining representative by imposing restrictions not to be found in any provisions of the Act and, indeed, deliberately omitted therefrom. . . .

MEMBER REYNOLDS, dissenting in part: I agree with my colleagues that the collective bargaining contract which is currently in effect is not a bar to the holding of an immediate election. However, wages, hours, and conditions of employment of the employees involved in this proceeding have been stabilized by a currently valid collective bargaining agreement which expires on August 21, 1950, and in view of the fact that the ensuing certification may issue before such expiration date, the Board's action will *doubtlessly* precipitate much uncertainty concerning its effect upon that agreement. The Board should therefore, allay this uncertainty — raised as it is by the Board's own action.

In finding that the unexpired agreement between the Employer and the UE does not bar this proceeding, no implication should be permitted by the Board that the substantive terms of the contract are no longer effective or that the obligations accruing thereunder on the part of either the employees or the Employer are no longer enforceable.[9] In the interest of maintaining stable

[6] House Conference Report No. 510, on H.R. 3020, page 50. We agree with our dissenting colleague that this legislative reference indicates that Congress intended the Board to continue its practice of holding elections albeit during the term of an existing contract. However, as the House conferees pointed out, the requirement that a new union adhere to the terms of a pre-existing contract might have *some effect* upon that practice. It was to leave unimpaired the Board's unqualified right to hold elections whenever a question of representation arose and because that requirement was regarded as a possible impediment to the exercise of this right that Congress decided to eliminate such a provision from the amended Act. Our dissenting colleague would write into the Act the very restriction which Congress, for the reason indicated above, decided to omit.

[9] In The Register and Tribune Company, 60 N.L.R.B. 360, the Board stated: "It is not our intention to invalidate the contract or to disturb it in any respect. The election which we shall hereinafter direct is for the purpose

labor relations, neither the Employer nor the employees should be enabled by virtue of a proceeding before this Board to discard unilaterally any obligations incurred as a result of their collective bargaining agreement. Unilateral termination of such agreements at this time would only frustrate the primary purpose of the Act, i.e., the securing of industrial peace through collective bargaining contracts. The stability attached to these agreements should not depend upon the whim of one of the parties thereto.

My colleagues refer to the failure to include proposed Section 9 (f) (8) of the House bill in the amended Act as indicating a *rejection* by the House conferees of this view. However, as the House Conference Report points out, the only reason for not including the section was because the conferees were concerned about the possibility that an inference might be drawn "that the practice of the Board, with respect to conducting representation elections while collective bargaining contracts are in effect, should not be continued. . . ." This would seem to unequivocally indicate that the deletion was intended merely to eliminate any possible impression that the conferees desired to inhibit the Board's authority to conduct such elections. Therefore, in my opinion, the omission of the section clearly does not support the position that the conferees believed it would be undesirable for the Board to declare explicitly that, although an existing contract is not a bar to the holding of an election, the contract continues in effect for its unexpired term and the obligations thereunder are not vitiated. Furthermore, the framers of the House bill apparently understood that, if a new bargaining representative was chosen while a contract was in effect, it was in accord with Board practice to require such representative to be bound by the substantive provisions of the contract for the remainder of the contract period before a new certification became effective; for in the earlier House Report it was stated that Section 9 (f) (8) "seems to be consistent with present law."

Additional support for continuing in effect the current contract covering the Employer's employees may be found in the language of the Act. Section 8 (a) (5) of the Act compels an employer "to bargain collectively with representatives of his employees, subject to the provisions of Section 9 (a) ." Section 9 (a) states that

---

of determining the identity of the representative which shall administer the contract." See also, Cribben & Sexton Company, 82 N.L.R.B. 1409, wherein the Board stated that, "In directing elections at the present time, we do not thereby intend to abrogate any rights the parties may have under existing contracts." See Joseph Dyson & Sons, Inc., 60 N.L.R.B. 867; Peerless Stages, Inc., 62 N.L.R.B. 1514; and The Ellis Canning Company, 67 N.L.R.B. 384.

these exclusive representatives shall be "designated or selected for the purposes of collective bargaining by the majority of the employees." This language supports the conclusion that in the collective bargaining process the real party in interest, or the principal, is the employees, and that the labor organization is but an agent of such employees, at least for the purposes of negotiating with the Employer. If it can thus be said that a labor organization acts as the agent of the employees in executing a contract, it is clear that the employees cannot repudiate the contract by a change in such agent. The right to change representatives together with the concomitant limitations of the right, was early recognized by the Board when it stated: [15] "The whole process of collective bargaining and unrestricted choice of representatives assumes the freedom of the employees to change their representatives, while at the same time continuing the existing agreements under which the representatives must function."

In accord with the foregoing, I would condition the certification of any new representative chosen in the forthcoming election, by requiring that such representative assume the obligations of the existing contract for the remainder of its term.[16]

NOTES

1. For discussion of the "contract bar rule" see pages 190 et seq. supra.

2. The effect of secession by a local union on the collective bargaining agreement has caused considerable difficulty. The cases are far from consistent in either their approach or conclusions. For considerations of this problem see Lenhoff, The Present Status of Collective Contracts, 39 Mich. L. Rev. 1109, 1126 (1941); Rice, Labor Contracts under the National Labor Relations Act, 37 Mich. L. Rev. 693, 720 (1939); Samoff and Summers, Disaffiliation, 1 Labor L. J. 585 (1950); Willcox, The Triboro Case — Mountain or Molehill? 56 Harv. L. Rev. 576, 603 (1943); Notes: 63 Harv. L. Rev. 1413 (1950), 51 Yale L.J. 465 (1942), 48 Yale L.J. 1059 (1939).

[15] New England Transportation Company, 1 N.L.R.B. 130, 138–9.

[16] My colleagues speculate as to what I would do should the employees vote for no union in the forthcoming election. My answer is simply that I would not permit such a situation to occur because I would not allow a choice for "neither" on the ballot. In my opinion, the purpose of holding an election in a proceeding of this type is to resolve the issue as to which of two contending unions the employees desire to have represent them under the existing contract. To permit them to choose no union under these circumstances is to enable them to achieve by an indirect method a decertification of their bargaining representative. If that is what they desire to accomplish, I would require them to file a proper decertification petition.

3. In the UE–IUE controversy, attempts were made to obtain court determinations with respect to which competing group was entitled to claim "ownership" of the collective bargaining agreement currently in effect. These attempts ended in failure. See Duris v. Phelps Dodge Copper Products Corp., 87 F. Supp. 229, 25 L.R.R.M. 2089 (D.N.J. 1949) ; State ex rel. United Electrical Workers v. Enersen, 230 Minn. 427, 42 N.W.2d 25 (1950) ; Huntsman v. McGovern, 91 N.E.2d 717, 25 L.R.R.M. 2149 (Ohio C.P. 1949) ; Elsner v. Frigidaire Division, General Motors Corp., 25 L.R.R.M. 2514, 17 CCH Lab. Cas. ¶65, 639 (Ohio C.P. 1950) .

4. Perhaps the most critical single problem in determining which competing local union is entitled to claim the existing collective bargaining contract is the problem of who is entitled to claim the dues checked off by the employer pursuant to the collective agreement. Probably the leading case with respect to this aspect of the UE–IUE controversy is General Electric Co. v. Emspak, 94 F. Supp. 601, 26 L.R.R.M. 2439 (S.D.N.Y. 1950) . This case arose out of an interpleader suit brought by the General Electric Co. to determine the disposition of the sums of money which it was collecting under the check-off provisions of the existing collective bargaining agreement. The disposition of the suit was to discharge General Electric and retain the funds thus collected in the court until representative elections were held under the supervision of the National Labor Relations Board to determine the identity of the collective bargaining agent. After such determination, the clerk of the court was to pay over the sums thus impounded to the Union determined to be the bargaining representative. If no union were selected, the sums were to be returned to the employees from whose wages the check-off dues were deducted. For another case using this same technique see Wolchock v. Kovenetsky, 274 App. Div. 282, 83 N.Y.S.2d 431 (1948) .

For cases holding that the union which made the collective bargaining agreement, rather than the new competing local, is entitled to a continuation of the check-off and to receipt of the funds obtained thereby, see Local 60 v. Welin Davit and Boat Corp., 133 N.J. Eq. 551, 33 A.2d 708 (1943) ; United Electrical Workers v. Lawlor, 22 L.R.R.M. 2407, 15 CCH Lab. Cas. ¶ 64, 661 (Conn. Super. Ct. 1948) .

5. A critical problem with respect to job security arises when a seceding local union has a union-shop contract. Under the bare terms of the agreement all employees who are not members of the original local which made the collective bargaining agreement

must be discharged by the employer. There is some indication in the decisions that at least in the situation where the old local continues to function with some members, the employer is free to discharge the employees who went with the seceding local. Colgate-Palmolive Peet Co. v. NLRB, 338 U.S. 355, 70 Sup. Ct. 166, 94 L. Ed. 161 (1949), held that it was not a violation of Section 8 (a) (3) of the Taft-Hartley Act for the employer to dismiss employees who did not maintain membership in the local union having a union-shop agreement even though a question concerning representation had arisen. In M & M Woodworking Co. v. NLRB, 101 F.2d 938 (9th Cir. 1939), the court refused to enforce a cease and desist order of the National Labor Relations Board directing an employer to stop discharging employees because they were members of a seceding local union. On this question, see Note, 63 Harv. L. Rev. 1413, 1423 (1950).

6. In World Trading Corp. v. Kolchin, 166 Misc. 854, 2 N.Y. S.2d 195 (1938), the employer signed a contract with a local union providing for arbitration of disputes. After the contract was made, the local changed its affiliation from AFL to CIO. The employer sought to enjoin it from enforcing the arbitration clause of the contract. The court held that the identity of the local was not changed by a change of affiliation. The contract remained as binding as if a man merely changed his name from Jones to Brown. For other cases dealing with this "substitutionary theory," see Labonite v. Cannery Workers and Farm Laborers, 197 Wash. 543, 86 P.2d 189 (1938); Irwin v. Foley, 259 App. Div. 156, 18 N.Y. S.2d 185 (1st Dept. 1940).

7. In Montaldo v. Hires Bottling Co., 59 Cal. App. 2d 642, 139 P.2d 666 (1943), the employer attempted to justify a violation of the collective bargaining agreement on the ground that the local union had been suspended by the AFL. The court held that the contract was with the local and not with the AFL. Thus suspension in no way affected the operation of the agreement. However, in Klinger v. Krum, 259 App. Div. 309, 19 N.Y.S.2d 193 (1st Dept. 1940), the court held that where the international revoked the local's charter and organized a new local to supplant it, the new local was a new entity and could not enforce the contract against the employer. Neither could the group of secessionists who had affiliated with a rival union enforce the contract.

8. From the standpoint of effective collective bargaining, how practical is it to say that secession leaves the contract intact and with the loyal remnant?

9. What are the rights of the various parties in Problem III, page 951 supra, under the contract which makes the international a party to the contract? What would you advise the employer to do?

10. Does the Labor Management Relations Act contain any provisions which help solve these parent-local problems?

Is the "contract" between the international and the local the kind of contract described in Section 301 of the Labor Management Relations Act? See Snoots v. Vejlupek, 87 F. Supp. 503 (N.D. Ohio 1949) ; Kriss v. White, 87 F. Supp. 734, 25 L.R.R.M. 2130 (N.D.N.Y. 1949).

II. INTER-UNION RELATIONSHIPS (JURISDICTIONAL DISPUTES)

A. *Introduction*

A labor movement composed of two federations, two hundred international unions, and over 50,000 local unions inevitably faces the problem of establishing working relationships among the multitude of diverse units. A degree of tolerance and cooperation is essential — a degree of friction and clash is unavoidable.[17]

Within a single international, local unions ordinarily manifest a high degree of cohesiveness and cooperation. Any disputes between locals are adjudicated by the international, which can use its power of life and death over the local unions to enforce its decisions effectively. Within the AFL or the CIO cohesiveness and cooperation between internationals are the rule, but rivalry, antagonism, or even open warfare is a substantial exception. The tradition that internationals are autonomous strictly limits the power of these loose federations to settle family fights. Between the two federations, and their member internationals, there is little formal cooperation but rather a prevailing attitude of jealousy and distrust. Apart from the two federations, unaffiliated unions may maintain a position of aloofness or belligerent independence.

These divisions within the house of labor, however, seldom break the united front presented to employers. The presence of family fights must not blind one to the underlying sense of unity within the labor movement and the manifold areas of cooperation between unions. Even though engaged in bitter jurisdictional disputes between themselves, construction unions frequently form Building Trades Councils to cooperate in bargain-

---

[17] See Petro, Job-Seeking Aggression, the NLRA, and the Free Market, 50 Mich. L. Rev. 497 (1952).

ing with employers.   Members of CIO unions customarily respect the picket lines established by AFL unions, and contributions to strike funds frequently cross both international and federation lines.

Problems arising from cooperation among unions have been discussed at pages 692, 795, 803, and 815 supra in conjunction with picketing, sympathetic strikes, and secondary boycotts.   The problem arising from competition between unions for the right to represent particular employees in collective bargaining has been discussed at page 140 supra.   This chapter is therefore devoted primarily to a study of the conflict between unions for the right of their members to perform certain jobs.   The material here presented will indicate the causes of these jurisdictional disputes, the effectiveness of attempts to settle them within the union structure, and the outcome of efforts to resolve them by legal processes.

B. *Settlement Within the Union Structure*

Jurisdictional disputes which arise out of union "nationalism" are frequently settled by treaties within the union structure.   Two warring unions may negotiate a treaty allocating the disputed work or territory between them.   (Cf. Hendren v. Curtis at page 956 supra.)   Groups of unions within a particular industry may make a compact to provide methods of adjudicating disputes among them.   Occasionally the federation will attempt to intervene and resolve these bitter quarrels.

Agreement on Jurisdiction

Brotherhood of Painters,
Decorators and Paperhangers of America
and
The Operative Plasterers
and Cement Finishers International Association
New York, N.Y., February 16, 1928

This agreement entered into by and between the Operative Plasterers and Cement Finishers International Association and the Brotherhood of Painters, Decorators and Paperhangers of America, in the matter of Jurisdiction to govern the application of California Stucco "CRAFTEX," "TEXTONE" and other materials of like character shall be as follows:

This agreement shall become effective February 16, 1928, that the applying of all California Stucco shall be the work of the Plasterers Organization. That the finishing of the same it is agreed that the Plasterers shall be permitted to apply one wash and thereafter all washing and the applying of colors, shall be under the Jurisdiction of the Brotherhood of Painters.

It is hereby agreed that all "CRAFTEX," "TEXTONE" or other material of the same character when applied over a scratch or brown coat of plaster shall be the work of the Plasterer, said material to be applied with a trowel, or other usual methods of plastering.

It is hereby agreed that all "CRAFTEX," "TEXTONE" or other material of like character when applied over a sand finish or white coat of plaster shall be the work of the Painter, said material to be applied with a brush, or other usual methods of painting.

It is agreed that when the material in question is applied in show windows for decorative purposes, and does not exceed 150 yards in all, it shall be the work of the Painter, and when the work exceeds 150 yards and applied over a scratch or brown coat of plaster, it shall be the work of the Plasterer.

JAFFE, INTER–UNION DISPUTES IN SEARCH OF A FORUM *

The Federation (A.F. of L.) has occasionally established formal tribunals for settling jurisdictional disputes. Such a tribunal has existed in one or another form in the Building Trades Department, a subsidiary body of the Federation composed of the building unions. Because of the great number of charters in the building trades, the arbitrary craft distinctions which they perpetuate, and the constant change of materials and process, jurisdictional disputes in this field are numerous and costly. Both of the recent indictments under the Sherman Act relate to disputes in the building trades. One of the unions concerned is the Carpenters. This union has been the particular *bête noire* of every attempt to establish an authoritative tribunal in the building trades. In 1909, only one year after affiliation with the department, the Carpenters refused to recognize its decision awarding to the Sheet Metal Workers the jurisdiction to erect metal trim. The department suspended them and asked the Federation to do likewise. This was the occasion for the usual speeches about the value of co-operation. The Federation refused and suggested the inevitable

* The full text of this article by Louis L. Jaffe may be found in 49 Yale L.J. 424 (1940), from which the above selection at page 441 has been taken with the permission of the editors of that publication. — Ed.

conference. The Carpenters then withdrew from the department.
In 1915 they induced the department to reverse its decision and
reaffiliated. They then deigned to confer for some 13 years with
the Sheet Metal Workers; an agreement was reached in 1928. In
1918 the department set up a tribunal composed of representatives
of labor, entrepreneurs and the building professions. This tribunal gave an award against the Carpenters and they promptly
withdrew. In 1927 the department abandoned the board and
its decisions against the Carpenters, who then graciously consented
to reenter. In the meantime the Bricklayers had withdrawn in
1927 because of an adverse decision, and in 1929 the Carpenters
again gained their freedom, this time because of a quarrel over
dues. In 1931 they were joined by the Electricians who were opposed to the participation of employer representatives in settling
jurisdictional disputes. These unions are the big three in the
building trades and their state of mind and consequent defection
substantially lessened the ability of the department to handle
jurisdictional disputes. The department nevertheless gave decisions in cases involving them; it could breathe more easily when
they were not inside the fold and whether they were in or out
seemed to make little difference in their disposition to accept decisions. In 1933 the big three clamored for readmittance because
the department had been given a formal place in the Recovery
Administration's Building Code. The department winced at
the prospect of the return of these ruthless and prodigal sons and
refused to readmit them. They feared particularly a coalition
between them and a dissatisfied group of unions within the department. The officers of the Federation ordered the department
to take them back. Upon refusal, the officers called a purported
convention of the department, superseded the regular department
convention, reinstated the unions and reorganized the department.
The reorganized department then brought a suit in the District
of Columbia for possession of the books and papers. This suit
was lost on the ground that, though the Federation had complete
authority over the department, the officers had exceeded their authority. The clear implication was that the officers might secure
ratification at the next convention. The "regular" department
unions must have seen the futility of their position. In 1935
they agreed upon a form of reorganization.

DUNLOP, JURISDICTIONAL DISPUTES *

The Referee System was established in 1936 as a part of the plan reuniting the Department and was the system in the Constitution of the Department until the present plan became operative on May 1, 1948. For a substantial part of this period no referee was appointed. Under the Referee system the president of the Department, or for a period the vice presidents of the Department resident in Washington, rendered spot decisions to apply to the particular project alone. If an international union objected to such a spot decision it could appeal to the Referee for a decision which would constitute a new national rule. The Referee system was confined to the unions; the contractors had no part in the system.

The National Joint Board for Settlement of Jurisdictional Disputes was created by agreement between the Department and the Associated General Contractors and eight specialty contractors' associations which became effective May 1, 1948. The agreement provided in Article VII that there shall be no stoppages of work in jurisdictional disputes unless work was assigned by contractors contrary to decisions or agreements of record. The plan was made a part of the Constitution of the Building and Construction Trades Department.

The work of this machinery is divided into two phases. First, the Board of Trustees has general responsibility for the administration of the plan. It met thirty times during its first year. The Board of Trustees orders the return of men to work in the event of a strike; it decides whether disputed work is covered by an agreement or decision of work; it has provided procedures for contractors to follow in the assignment of work. In general, the Board of Trustees is concerned with keeping the jobs going.

The second phase of the machinery is concerned with the making of a new decision or agreement of record. If a dispute is determined by the Board of Trustees not to be covered by an existing rule, the President of the Department seeks to secure agreement between the two trades. Failing this mediation, a Joint Board of five members — two general presidents, two contractors' representatives and the chairman of the Board of Trustees — may be established to hear and decide the issue. Any decision is a national

* The full text of this statement by John Dunlop may be found in the Proceedings of the New York University Second Annual Conference on Labor (1949), published by Matthew Bender & Company, Albany 1, N.Y., from which the above selection at page 495 has been reprinted by permission. — ED.

rule and a new decision of record. Each Joint Board is established for a particular case.

JAFFE, INTER–UNION DISPUTES IN SEARCH OF A FORUM *

The constitution of the Federation does not specifically provide
any machinery for settling jurisdictional disputes. But there can
be no doubt now that the Federation is empowered to interpret
the charters it has issued and exclude from its association those
who refuse to abide by its judgment. Nevertheless, the weapon
of revocation or suspension is of limited utility. The Federation,
with an occasional inexplicable exception will rarely invoke it
even in support of its considered and reiterated declarations of
jurisdiction, at least until years of conferences and arbitrations
have worn out even the half-humorous assumption that the dispute
is arbitrable — and then rarely against a powerful union.

A few examples may serve to give meaning to these rather general observations. Let us first consider the dispute between the
Woodworkers (Woodworkers International Union, Amalgamated) and the Carpenters and Joiners Union. It was first
brought before the Convention in 1901. The Convention adopted
a resolution of its committee which found that the Carpenters had
in 1894 conceded to the Woodworkers' jurisdiction over mill
hands, millwrights, and stair builders, roughly persons making
wood objects with factory machines, and that the Carpenters had
consistently violated this so-called agreement by initiating such
persons. The Convention recommended a further effort by the
parties at adjustment. In 1902 the Carpenters, resorting to a
familiar tactic of defense, sought unsuccessfully to secure the revocation of the Woodworkers' charter. Instead, the Convention
ordered the parties to arbitrate. In 1903 the Carpenters claimed
that the arbitral award was procedurally defective and were overruled by the Convention. In 1904 the Executive Council was
authorized to suspend the Carpenters' charter unless the Carpenters
complied. In 1905 the Executive Council reports that it believes
revocation to be a futile step; it suggests instead further conference. The Carpenters give notice that no quarter could be expected except through amalgamation with them. In 1906 the
Executive Council reports no progress, and drops a tear for the
innocent employer: by this time one union was treating, as unfair,

* The full text of this article by Louis L. Jaffe may be found in 49 Yale L.J.
424 (1940), from which the above selection at page 432 has been taken with
the permission of the editors of that publication. — ED.

shops having an agreement with the other. In 1907 the Convention learns that the rank and file of the Woodworkers had, on referendum, rejected amalgamation. At this the Convention begins to lose patience with the persistent little Woodworkers. It refuses to reindorse the award in their favor which only three years before it had approved. It recommends a further conference. The dispute has now entered that stage so familiar in international politics where the stubborn little nation is "inciting" the big one. The Carpenters at the time had approximately 1800 votes in the Convention, the Woodworkers 32. In 1909 the Committee on Adjustments reports a plan of amalgamation. If the Woodworkers refuse, their charter is to be revoked. They are damned if they do and damned if they don't. The secretary of the committee bases this brutal resolve upon the ironic dictates of justice typically appealed to in power politics: "The Committee has come to the concluson that where certain men in this labor movement do not see the benefit of concentration, we believe it is time to compel them to get into line for their own good."

The Convention allowed a decent interval for performing the sacrificial act. In 1912, after further threats, the Woodworkers amalgamated. The Federation in 1917, in a dispute between the Flint Glass Workers and the Machinists, confirmed a voluntary arbitration award giving jurisdiction over glass molder-makers to the former. It was tried often and again to assist the feeble Glass Workers in bringing the powerful Machinists to book. In 1919 Wharton of the Machinists, unabashed, asked why the Machinists should obey decisions when others did not; he said they would obey, if everyone else did. In 1931 the Executive Council was still seeking a solution. If the objective is the settlement of disputes on the best terms possible, it is at least questionable whether this rather Quixotic solution is preferable to the Machiavellism of the other. The case was, however, possibly more difficult to solve: whereas all Woodworkers might find a logical basis of amalgamation with the Carpenters, the Glass Workers as a group, aside from the disputed ones, may have nothing in common with the Machinists; to take away even a small number from a union already small may make administration financially impossible.

The 13th Annual CIO National Convention, meeting in November, 1951, adopted the recommendations of the National Executive Board for an umpire system to settle jurisdictional conflicts between CIO International Unions.   The system provides for a three-step program to settle such disputes.   (1) The responsible representatives of each International concerned shall endeavor to settle the dispute by negotiation.   (2) If step one fails, the CIO National Director of Organization attempts settlement by mediation among the parties.   (3) If step two fails, any International or the CIO National Director of Organization can refer the dispute to the permanent umpire for final settlement.   There is further provision that if the dispute is already in the hands of the NLRB because of a pending representation proceeding, or for any other reason the dispute settlement will not admit of delay, the first two steps in the settlement procedure may be omitted and the dispute may be referred immediately to the permanent umpire for interim or final order.   The plan also provides various guides for the umpire to use in settling disputes as part of an over-all policy that the determination be, "on the basis of what will best serve the interest of the employees involved and will preserve the good names and orderly functioning of the CIO."

C. *Legal Devices for Settling Jurisdictional Disputes*

UNITED UNION BREWING CO. v. BECK
Supreme Court, Washington, 1939
200 Wash. 474, 93 P.2d 772

STEINERT, Justice.

This was an action to recover damages for loss of business sustained by plaintiff through the alleged wrongful and malicious acts of the defendants, and to obtain a permanent injunction restraining defendants from directly or indirectly interfering with the marketing of plaintiff's beer and, specifically, from directly or secondarily boycotting such product.   By stipulation of the parties at the end of the trial, plaintiff's prayer for damages was withdrawn and certain of the defendants were dismissed from the action.

At the conclusion of the hearing by the court, a decree was entered, to which the remaining defendants consented, permanently enjoining them ". . . from employing any threats or intimidations as a means of deterring any merchant from supplying any of plaintiff's customers with the commodities or products used or useful in the conduct of their business," but in all other respects denying the plaintiff's prayer for relief.

Deeming itself aggrieved by the inadequacy of the order, in

that it did not grant the full relief sought, plaintiff has appealed.

The respective contentions of the parties can best be indicated by a resume of the pleadings.

The complaint presents the situation substantially as follows: Appellant is a corporation organized and qualified under the laws of the state of Washington and is engaged in the business of manufacturing beer, known as Old Empire Beer, and wholesaling it throughout the various counties of this state. Its employees are all members of the International Union of United Brewery, Flour, Cereal and Soft Drink Workers of America, which, for brevity, we shall refer to as Brewery Workers Union. There never has been any dispute between appellant and any of its employees over wages, hours, conditions of employment or any other matter.

Respondent Dave Beck is an international organizer for International Brotherhood of Teamsters, Chauffeurs, Stablemen and Helpers, hereinafter referred to as the Teamsters Union. The other respondents are local unions under charter from either the parent Teamsters Union or the Culinary Workers and Bartenders Union, which latter is hereinafter referred to as Culinary Workers Union. As such international organizer, Beck exercises complete domination and control over each of the respondent local unions.

During the year preceding December 1938, respondent Beck, solely for the malicious purpose of destroying appellant's business, directed the respondent local unions in a systematic effort designed to prevent the marketing and distributing of appellant's product. Pursuant to such directions, the respondent locals of the Teamsters Union have refused to deliver products of any kind to any place of business in this state which buys, sells, or possesses appellant's beer, and the respondent locals of the Culinary Workers Union have refused to furnish any bartenders or any employees to any restaurant or tavern that buys, sells, or possesses such beer. Furthermore, the respondent local unions have picketed every retail business in this state which handles appellant's product; the pickets bear signs stating that such picketed premises are unfair to organized labor, although, in fact, no labor dispute exists or has existed at any of such places.

A group of defendants, who by the stipulation were dismissed from the action, are engaged in the business of wholesaling merchandise to restaurants, taverns, and other retail businesses handling beer. Pursuant to respondent Beck's directions these defendants have refused, and still refuse, to sell or deliver any product or furnish any service to such places of business as buy, sell, or possess beer manufactured by appellant. As a consequence, appellant's customers engaged in the retail business are prevented from obtaining desired merchandise and services.

This conduct of respondents has substantially decreased the sale of appellant's beer in this state, and if allowed to continue will cause appellant irreparable damage.

The foregoing constitutes the material allegations of appellant's complaint.

In their answers, respondents deny all the allegations of the complaint except that appellant's employees are members of the Brewery Workers Union. By way of an affirmative defense, respondents present their side of the controversy as follows: Appellant was organized as a corporation by the Brewery Workers Union, and all its stock is closely held by that organization. Both the Brewery Workers Union and the Teamsters Union were organized pursuant to charters issued by the American Federation of Labor, which we will hereinafter refer to as A.F. of L.

In 1933 a controversy arose between the two unions, as to which had jurisdiction over drivers employed on brewery trucks. Pursuant to the constitution and laws of A.F. of L., that controversy was submitted to the General Executive Council of the federation for decision. The council decided that jurisdiction over the drivers belonged to the Teamsters Union and not the Brewery Workers Union. Thereupon the Brewery Workers Union appealed consecutively to the conventions of A.F. of L. held in the years 1934, 1935, and 1936, and at each of those conventions the decision of the general executive council was, after full hearing, sustained. Nevertheless, the Brewery Workers Union and the appellant herein, acting in open defiance of the decisions of A.F. of L., have continued to man all brewery trucks with members of the Brewery Workers Union, and the members of that union have boycotted the products of all breweries in this state which employed members of the Teamsters Union, as a consequence of which the respondent local unions have, in turn, refused, and now refuse, to haul any product of appellant or to patronize or render any service to any retailer of appellant's products.

Appellant, though contending that respondents' affirmative defense is immaterial to the issues here involved, nevertheless comes forward by way of reply and, after admitting that a majority of its stock is owned by members of the Brewery Workers Union, gives its version of the preexisting controversy between the two unions as follows:

Shortly after its organization in 1887, the Brewery Workers Union, which comprised all employees of the brewing industry,

including beer truck drivers, was granted a certificate of affiliation by A.F. of L.   No Teamsters Union or any union of drivers
was granted a certificate of affiliation until twelve years later.   One
of the objects of A.F. of L., as provided by its constitution, is the
establishment of trade unions based upon a strict recognition
of the autonomy of each trade and the promotion and advancement of such bodies.   The constitution further provides that no
charter shall be granted by A.F. of L. to any national, international, trade, or federal labor union without a positive and clear
definition of the trade jurisdiction claimed by the applicant, and
that no charter shall be granted such applicant if the jurisdiction
claimed trespasses on the jurisdiction of any existing affiliated
union, unless such affiliate give its written consent thereto.   The
A.F. of L. has no authority or control over the jurisdiction of the
Brewery Workers Union nor can it transfer such jurisdiction to
another.

The brewing and delivery of beer throughout the United States,
except in the state of Washington and to some extent in the state
of Oregon, are now conducted by the Brewery Workers Union.

In 1934 a proposition that the Teamsters Union be given
jurisdiction over certain drivers was submitted to a referendum
vote of the members of the Brewery Workers Union, and the result of that vote was 170 in favor of such proposal and 14,161
against it.

There are in the United States approximately 12,000 members
of the Brewery Workers Union who are engaged as beer truck
drivers.   For many years the Brewery Workers Union has issued
charters throughout the principal cities of the United States to
local unions composed of members who are either exclusively beer
truck drivers or else handle, in part, deliveries of all brewery products; these locals and their members participate in the sick benefits
and insurance features provided by their parent union.

In spite of these general conditions pertaining to jurisdiction,
respondent Beck and the Teamsters Union have by illegal boycott seized control of all breweries in the state of Washington except that of appellant and are engaged not only in the delivery, but
also in the brewing and bottling, of beer.

The pleadings, as we have summarized them, present the background which gave rise to this controversy and reveal the existence
of a protracted struggle between two powerful international
unions for the right to exercise jurisdiction over a particular type
of employment. . . .

Respondents take the position squarely that the only question involved is whether the Brewery Workers Union or the Teamsters Union has jurisdiction over brewery truck drivers. By "jurisdiction" in this instance is meant the right to accept such drivers as members and to represent them in the negotiation of employment contracts and the settlement of disputes with their employers. Respondents assert that as members of the Teamsters Union, an affiliate of A.F. of L., they have the right to enforce obedience to parental authority by withholding their labor and patronage from all beer taverns that patronize appellant's brewery. Appellant insists that the orders of A.F. of L. through its executive council and in convention, awarding such jurisdiction to the Teamsters Union, are void because in violation of the constitution of the federation.

We will not undertake to decide, in this case, whether such orders were valid or invalid. There are two reasons for the position we take: (1) Neither the A.F. of L., nor the international body of Brewery Workers Union nor any local union of that body, nor the international body of Teamsters Union is a party to this controversy and, so far as this case is concerned, any question regarding the validity of the orders referred to is a collateral matter; and (2) in any event, a decision of that question is unnecessary in the determination of the real issue involved in this case. Whatever may be the background of this controversy and whatever strife between two rival labor organizations may yet lurk therein, the immediate question before us is whether the appellant, a private corporation organized and doing business under the laws of this state, may appeal to the courts for the protection of its property rights.

We clearly recognize the fact that the stockholders of the appellant corporations are members of one of the two rival labor organizations. We are also aware that one of these labor organizations at one time loaned money to the former owner of appellant's brewery for the evident purpose of enabling its members to secure exclusive employment therein adverse to the interests of the other labor organization. Neither of these considerations is material in this case. The mortgage securing the loan was foreclosed, and the brewery was bought at execution sale by the mortgagee. The appellant was organized to take over and operate the brewery which had been subject to the mortgage. Although its stock is owned by members of the Brewery Workers Union, appellant stands exactly in the same position as any other corporation with respect to the right to acquire property and conduct business, so long as it complies with the laws of this state.

In our opinion, this appeal presents, for ultimate determination, two issues, or, more properly perhaps, one issue which may be considered from two approaches.

The first question is whether or not respondents may lawfully use the methods which they have employed, in order to compel appellant to hire, as truck drivers, only those who are members of the Teamsters Union, or to compel appellant's employees to join that union.

The workers employed by appellant have selected their own bargaining agency, as they had the right to do. . . .

It is to be borne in mind that no member of the Teamsters Union has ever been employed by appellant and, further, that there is no dispute whatever upon any subject between appellant and its own employees. . . .

In Blanchard v. Golden Age Brewing Co., 188 Wash. 396, 63 P.2d 397, 407, this same character of controversy was before this court as a result of the concerted action of certain breweries and the members of the Teamsters Union to compel members of the Brewery Workers Union to join the rival union. In upholding the contempt action taken by the trial court following its decree of injunction, we said:

> The action of the owners was contrary to the public policy announced in the very legislative act on which all of the defendants formerly relied and on which the appellant even now relies. But the case goes deeper than that. It is a case where it has been made to appear that one set of employees, through threats of strikes and boycotts, is seeking to compel a group of employers to discharge another set of employees whose relations with their employers have been in all respects harmonious. This is unwarranted. No one has a right to coerce an employer, by threats of violence or of activities which will inevitably lead to great financial loss, in order to compel the discharge of an employee. . . .
>
> The right to earn a livelihood and to continue in employment unmolested by unwarranted activities of third persons is entitled to protection in equity. Truax v. Raich, 239 U.S. 33, 36 S. Ct. 7, 60 L. Ed. 131, L.R.A. 1916D, 545 [Ann. Cas. 1917B, 283]. A correlative principle is that the employer has the right freely to maintain relations of employment with whomsoever he desires, and no one has the right purposely to disrupt or interfere with those relations by the intentional resort to such measures as will obviously, and in the ordinary

course of events, inflict irreparable injury upon the employer. Hitchman Coal & Coke Co. v. Mitchell, 245 U.S. 229, 38 S. Ct. 65, 62 L. Ed. 260, L.R.A. 1918C, 497, Ann. Cas. 1918B, 461. . . .

In the case at bar the purpose of respondents in committing the acts complained of was to compel appellant to substitute for its present employees other employees, or to compel appellant's employees to become members of the Teamsters Union. That purpose was unlawful. To accomplish that purpose, resort was had to acts destructive of appellant's business. Those acts were likewise unlawful and the proper remedy was by injunction.

The second, and principal, question is whether or not, in any event, appellant is entitled to the relief sought, on the theory that the actions of respondents constituted a secondary boycott.

While the term "secondary boycott" is of somewhat vague signification and has no precise and exclusive denotation, the courts, both federal and state, are agreed that any combination will be held to be a secondary boycott if its purpose and effect are to coerce customers or patrons, through fear of loss or bodily harm, to withhold or withdraw their business relations from the employer who is under attack. . . .

While there are some decisions to the contrary, notably in California and Montana, the weight of authority is that a conspiracy, combination or continuance of acts, formed or designed to injure a person's business by coercing his customers, or prospective customers, into withholding or withdrawing their patronage from him by acts or threats of injury to the customer's business if he fails to comply with the demands of the conspirators or combatants, constitutes a secondary boycott and will be restrained by a court of equity. . . .

We have in this case the following elements: (a) Property rights involved; (b) unlawful interference with such rights by acts constituting a secondary boycott and involving (c) intimidations, threats, and violence; and, as a result, (d) the owner of such property rights being threatened with great and irreparable injury.

Appellant is entitled to a decree enjoining respondents from actively interfering with the marketing of appellant's beer; from picketing, or threatening to picket, any of appellant's customers or prospective customers because such customer, present or prospective, handles or attempts to handle beer manufactured by appellant; and from interfering in any way with the delivery of other products or commodities to any of such customers or prospective customers because they handle or attempt to handle such beer.

The cause is remanded to the superior court for modification of the decree as herein indicated. . . .

BLAKE, Chief Justice (dissenting).

Applying the alter ego doctrine, the appellant is in reality the instrumentality of the Brewery Workers' Union. That union and respondent International Brotherhood of Teamsters are both affiliates of the American Federation of Labor. For several years these two unions have been engaged in a dispute over the jurisdiction of drivers of vehicles employed in the brewery business. The instant law suit arises out of that controversy. The controversy has several times been submitted to bodies of the American Federation of Labor having jurisdiction of such matters, and each time there has been a decision confirming the jurisdiction of the Teamsters Union over the drivers. Under such acts as these, it is universally held that the courts will not take jurisdiction of the controversy. In 4 Am. Jur. 466 the applicable rule is stated as follows:

> It is well established that courts will not interfere with the internal affairs of voluntary associations, except in such cases as fraud or lack of jurisdiction. Accordingly, it is held that mandamus will not lie to regulate the affairs of unincorporated societies or associations, at least not in the absence of a permissive statute. Nor will an injunction be granted where the association is proceeding in accordance with its rules and within the scope of its jurisdiction. *The decisions of the tribunals of an association with respect to its internal affairs will, in the absence of mistake, fraud, collusion, or arbitrariness, be accepted by the courts as conclusive.* Moreover, it is held that the courts will not undertake to inquire into the regularity of the procedure adopted and pursued by such tribunals in reaching their conclusions. (Italics supplied.) . . .

Applying this rule, the action should be remanded to the superior court with directions to dismiss.

NOTES

1. The fifty-year feud between the Brewery Workers and the Teamsters involved in United Union Brewing Co. v. Beck has constantly plagued the courts. In addition to this case and

Blanchard v. Golden Age Brewing Co., cited therein, see Yoerg Brewing Co. v. Brennan, 59 F. Supp. 625 (D. Minn. 1945) ; Obergfell v. Green, 29 F. Supp. 589 (D.D.C. 1939) ; International Union of United Brewery Workers v. California State Brewers Institute, 25 F. Supp. 870 (S.D. Cal. 1938) ; California State Brewers Institute v. International Brotherhood of Teamsters, 19 F. Supp. 824 (N.D. Cal. 1937). Settlements of the jurisdictional dispute itself by the courts in the Brewery Workers v. Brewers Institute, and the Obergfell v. Green cases were reversed on appeal on the ground that the jurisdictional dispute was a "labor dispute" within the meaning of the Norris-LaGuardia Act and thus no injunction could issue. Green v. Obergfell, 121 F.2d 46 (D.C. Cir. 1941) ; International Brotherhood of Teamsters v. International Union of United Brewery Workers, 106 F.2d 871 (9th Cir. 1939). For a history of the Brewery-Teamster controversy, see Jaffe, Inter-Union Disputes in Search of a Forum, 49 Yale L.J. 424 (1940).

2. The courts frequently avoid giving even temporary relief in jurisdictional battles. During the construction of a housing project near Baltimore a dispute arose over the right to lay the composition roofs. The Roofers sought an injunction to prevent the Carpenters from depriving them of this particular work which they claimed had been granted them by the AFL. The Carpenters' demurrer was overruled by the lower court and the Carpenters appealed. The Court of Appeals ruled that since the housing project had been completed the case was moot. The Roofers argued that the complaint also asked for an injunction against future projects. The court held that this issue had not been raised in the lower court so the case should be remanded. United Brotherhood of Carpenters and Joiners of America, Local 101 v. United Slate Tile and Composition Roofers, Damp and Waterproof Workers Assn., Local No. 80, 181 Md. 280, 29 A.2d 839 (1943). The Roofers amended their complaint asking for a declaratory judgment that under the jurisdictional awards of the Building and Construction Trades Department of the AFL, they were entitled to lay all roofs except wood, metal, and stone. The Court of Appeals again refused to grant relief, this time on the grounds that the officers of the international unions had not been made parties. In order to discourage further efforts by the persistent Roofers, the Court warned, "We do not mean to intimate that if the necessary parties were here in court . . . we have any right to adjudicate what appears to be a national dispute, or that suit could be otherwise maintained here." 185 Md. 32, 42 A.2d 913 (1945).

3. In International Brotherhood of Teamsters v. International Union of United Brewery Workers, 106 F.2d 871 (9th Cir. 1939), cited in Note 1 above, the court not only relied upon the Norris-LaGuardia Act but also stated that the National Labor Relations Board had the power, under the Wagner Act, to determine the jurisdictional controversy between the Brewers and the Teamsters. What powers and administrative machinery did the Board have available at that time to solve such a dispute?

LOS ANGELES BUILDING AND CONSTRUCTION TRADES COUNCIL
National Labor Relations Board, 1949
83 N.L.R.B. 477, 24 L.R.R.M. 1090

This proceeding arises under Section 10 (k) of the National Labor Relations Act, as amended by Labor Management Relations Act, 1947, which provides that "Whenever it is charged that any person has engaged in an unfair labor practice within the meaning of paragraph 4 (D) of Section 8 (b), the Board is empowered and directed to hear and determine the dispute out of which such unfair labor practice shall have arisen. . . ."

On February 2, 1949, International Association of Machinists, on behalf of its Local Lodge 1235, herein called the Machinists, filed with the Regional Director for the Twenty-first Region a charge alleging that Los Angeles Building and Construction Trades Council, A.F.L. here in called the Trades Council, and Lloyd A. Mashburn, its agent, has engaged in and were engaging in certain activities proscribed by Section 8 (b) (4) (D) of the amended Act. It was alleged, in substance, that they engaged in a strike, with an object of forcing and requiring Westinghouse Electric Corporation, herein called Westinghouse, and/or Stone and Webster Engineering Corporation, herein called Stone, to assign particular work to members of "affiliates" of United Brotherhood of Carpenters and Joiners of America, A.F.L. . . .

Early in 1946 Edison [Southern California Edison Co.] entered into contracts with various contractors for the construction of a new power plant at Redondo Beach, California. Chief among these contractors was Stone, which also acts in an advisory capacity to Edison for the entire project. Before construction of the power plant began, Edison had made arrangements for the purchase and installation of five steam turbine generator units. Two of these generators have already been installed, one each by Westinghouse and General Electric Company; the third was being installed by Westinghouse when the dispute with which we are now concerned began; the fourth is to be supplied and installed by General Electric, and operations on it are scheduled to begin about June 1, 1949; and the fifth is to be supplied and installed at some future date by Westinghouse.

Stone and the other contractors working on the Redondo Beach project, with the exception of Westinghouse and General Electric, have employed only Trades Council members since the construction began. Westinghouse and General Electric had installed the first two generators using two Machinists' members, as well as some Trades Council members. A short time before the installation of the third generator was scheduled to begin, representatives of the Trades Council and the Millwrights approached Stone and attempted to persuade Stone to have Westinghouse replace the Machinists with Millwrights. Stone disclaimed responsibility for the employment of these Machinists, saying that they were Westinghouse employees. On January 31, 1949, installation work on this third generator started. Shortly thereafter, a Trades Council representative, Mashburn, asked William Budge, supervisor of the installation for Westinghouse, to replace the Machinists with Millwrights. Budge refused, whereupon Mashburn said that he had no other recourse "except to take action."

On February 2, 1949, the Trades Council called a general strike of all the building trades employees on the project to enforce its demand on Westinghouse. All of the approximately 650 employees walked out, except the 2 Machinists employed by Westinghouse. The latter worked until February 11, 1949, when Edison requested Westinghouse to cease its installation work until the dispute was resolved. At the time of the hearing, no further installation work had been done on the generator, although work on the rest of the project had been resumed.

Neither Edison nor Stone has advanced any contentions respecting the merits of the dispute, nor has the Millwrights. Westinghouse, although it likewise advanced no contentions, is clearly not a disinterested party; its refusal to accede to the Trades Council's request precipitated the dispute.

The Machinists contends that the work tasks involved in the installation of generators is properly the craft and trade work of its members, and that it has satisfactorily supplied employees for all the generator installation work on the project, including the two completed installations.

The Trades Council contends that the Board is without jurisdiction to determine the dispute for three reasons: (1) this case does not involve a "jurisdictional dispute," but presents a question of representation; (2) the dispute is not one "affecting commerce"; and (3) Section 8 (b) (4) (D) is unconstitutional. The Trades Council also asserts that, in any event, the Millwrights is entitled to the work in question for various reasons: (1) the work falls within the jurisdiction and the trade and craft skills of its members; (2) the Trades Council has a right, under the provisions of its contract with Stone, to demand conformance from Westinghouse with the terms of that contract; (3) A.F. of L. decisions, made while the Machinists was affiliated with the A.F. of L., awarded work of the type in question to the Millwrights; (4) as the Building Trades Department of the A.F. of L. (with which the Machinists was never affiliated) is the only body that can effectively determine a "jurisdictional dispute" between subordinate locals in the construction field, no nonaffiliated union should be permitted to supply workers in this field; (5) the existing assignment of work by Westinghouse to the Machinists is immaterial; otherwise the employer could "oust the Board itself of jurisdiction"; (6) as there are approximately 650 Trades Council members on the project, and the dispute involves only 2 employees not members of the Trades Council, the purposes of the Act will "be better effectuated" by a determination by the Board that will compel Westinghouse to conform its practices to those of the other contractors on the job; and (7) this Section 10 (k) proceeding should be dismissed as "de minimis" because the dispute involves 2 out of 650 employees. . . .

At the time the dispute began, Westinghouse was employing two machinists and two riggers on the project; the former were members of the Machinists, and the latter were members of an affiliate of the Trades Council other than the Millwrights. Westinghouse had assigned the work in dispute to the Machinists. The Respondents insisted that Westinghouse assign the work to the Millwrights. The Board said in Matter of Juneau Spruce Corporation, [82 N.L.R.B. 650 (1949)]: "As we read Section 8 (b) (4) (D) and 10 (k), these Sections do not deprive an employer of the right to assign work to his own employees; nor were they intended to interfere with an employer's freedom to hire, subject only to the requirement against discrimination as contained in Section 8 (a) (3)." And in the Irwin-Lyons case, 82 N.L.R.B. 916 (1949), we held that the question of tradition or custom in the industry is not a governing factor ". . . where a union with no bargaining or representative status makes demands on an employer for the assignment of work to the exclusion of the employer's own employees who are performing the work. . . ." None of the contentions here advanced impels us to reach a different conclusion in this case. Westinghouse had no collective bargaining agreement with any labor organization concerning the employees involved. The fact that Stone, another contractor on the project, was operating under an agreement with the Trades Council, does not subject Westinghouse to any of the obligations of that agreement. It is clear that Westinghouse was not under contract with Stone, and was free to make use of its own employees for the installation, despite the fact that the other employers on the project used Trades Council employees.

We find, accordingly, that neither the Trades Council nor the Millwrights is lawfully entitled to require Westinghouse to assign the work in dispute to members of the Millwrights rather than to employees of Westinghouse who are members of the Machinists.

We are not by this action to be regarded as "assigning" the work in question to the Machinists. Because an affirmative award to either labor organization would be tantamount to allowing that organization to require Westinghouse to employ only its members and therefore to violate Section 8 (a) (3) of the Act, we believe we can make no such award. In reaching this conclusion we are aware that the employer in most cases will have resolved, by his own employment policy, the question as to which organization shall be awarded the work. Under the statute as now drawn, however, we see no way in which we can, by Board reliance upon such factors as tradition or custom in the industry, overrule his determination in a situation of this particular character.

NOTES

1. While Los Angeles Building and Construction Trades Council was pending before the NLRB, the Regional Director filed a petition in the District Court for an injunction under Section 10 (1). Judge Yankwich in a decision handed down after the decision of the Board held there were reasonable grounds for believing that the charge filed with the Board was true and that the dispute had not been adjusted by the parties. He enjoined the AFL Trades Council until "the Board determines the controversy." LeBaron v. Los Angeles Building and Construction Trades Council, 84 F. Supp. 629, 24 L.R.R.M. 2131 (S.D. Cal. 1949).

On June 14, 1949, a hearing was held before a trial examiner. When the Trades Council failed to present evidence of compliance with the Board's determination, the examiner found that the Council had violated the Act by engaging in an illegal jurisdictional strike. His Intermediate Report, made on August 31, 1949, recommended that the unions be ordered to cease and desist from such action. The Board heard the case and on March 14, 1950, remanded it for further hearing. It held (Herzog and Reynolds dissenting) that in proceedings under Sec. 8 (b) (4) (D) the burden of proving noncompliance with the Board's determination was on the General Counsel. 88 N.L.R.B. 1101 (1950). At the time of remanding, the Yankwich injunction was still in force, and presumably the generators had long since been installed and were operating.

This was not all, however. The Yankwich decision granting the injunction was appealed and was affirmed by the Court of Appeals in a brief per curiam decision. Los Angeles Building and Construction Trades Council v. LeBaron, 185 F.2d 405 (9th Cir. 1950). On October 8, 1951, the United States Supreme Court granted petition for certiorari and forthwith vacated the judgment and remanded the case with direction that the petition be dismissed on the ground that the cause was moot. Los Angeles Building and Construction Council v. LeBaron, 342 U.S. 802, 72 Sup. Ct. 25, 96 L. Ed. 23 (1951).

In 94 N.L.R.B. 415, 28 L.R.R.M. 1058 (1951), the Board refused to accept a trial examiner's report finding the Los Angeles Building Trades Council guilty of noncompliance with the order in the principal case. The Board dismissed the complaint. Of significance was the three-to-two split on the Board as to whether the General Counsel had the burden of proof to show noncompliance or whether the defendant had the burden to show compliance. The majority placed the burden on the General Counsel.

2. In International Longshoremen's Union and Juneau Spruce Corp., 82 N.L.R.B. 650, 23 L.R.R.M. 1597 (1949), cited in Los Angeles Building and Construction Trades Council, the Corporation assigned to its own employees, represented by the CIO Woodworkers Union, the job of loading lumber barges. The Longshoremen's Union, CIO, protested this assignment and picketed the Corporation. The Board held that the Corporation was free to assign this work to its own woodworker employees if it so desired. Member Murdock dissented. In the course of his dissenting opinion he said:

. . . By Section 10 (k), as the legislative history demonstrates, and my colleagues of the majority acknowledge, the 80th Congress sought to give the Board the function of *arbitrating* jurisdictional disputes. . . .   But to arbitrate a jurisdictional dispute is to determine which of two or more trade or craft groups of workers, or their respective unions, *ought* to be assigned to perform certain disputed work. . . .

I believe the majority here . . . abdicates the Board's arbitration function. . . .   The foregone conclusion will always be that the work "rightfully" belongs to whatever employee group has already received it under the employer's own award. This result, in my opinion, nullifies the clear purpose of Section 10 (k) of the Act.

At the same time charges were filed before the NLRB in this dispute, the Corporation sued the Union for damages under the provisions of Section 303 of the LMRA.   In International Longshoremen's & Warehousemen's Union v. Juneau Spruce Corp., 342 U.S. 237, 72 Sup. Ct. 235, 96 L. Ed. 201 (1952), the right to recover damages in advance of NLRB determination of the dispute was upheld.

3. The United Telephone Organizations filed a charge under Section 8 (b) (4) (D).   The Board made a preliminary investigation and dismissed the charge.   The complainant then obtained an injunction in the Federal District Court to compel the Board to hold a formal hearing on the charge.   On appeal the Court of Appeals for the District of Columbia reversed, holding that the mandatory language of Section 10 (k) did not compel a hearing unless preliminary investigation showed a prima facie violation of Section 8 (b) (4) (D).   Herzog v. Parsons, 181 F.2d 781. (D.C. Cir. 1950).

4. In 1949, both Administration and anti-Administration forces in the Senate made identical proposals to amend Section 10 (k) of the National Labor Relations Act.   This amendment read:

Whenever it is charged that any person has engaged in an unfair labor practice within the meaning of paragraph (4) (D) of Section 8 (b), the Board is empowered and directed to hear and determine, or appoint an arbitrator to hear and determine, the dispute, and issue an award, first affording the labor organizations involved in the dispute a reasonable opportunity to settle their controversy between or among themselves.   In determining the dispute, the Board or the arbitrator, as the case may be, may consider any prior

Board certification under which any such labor organization claims the right to represent employees who are or may be hired or assigned to perform the work task in dispute, any union charters or inter-union agreements purporting to define areas of jurisdiction between or among the contending labor organizations, the decisions of any agency established by unions to consider such dispute, and the policies of this Act. If an arbitrator is appointed to hear and determine a dispute, he shall proceed in accordance with such rules and regulations as the Board may prescribe; and his award determining the dispute shall have the same effect as an award of the Board. In any proceeding under this section, the employer whose assignment or prospective assignment of a particular work task is in controversy shall have an opportunity to be heard in any hearing conducted by the Board, or an arbitrator, as the case may be. If, at any stage of the proceeding, it shall appear to the Board that the dispute is in fact one concerning representation, it shall treat the case as one instituted under Section 9 (c) of this Act and proceed accordingly.

What deficiencies in the present law was this proposed amendment designed to correct?

5. A good example of a state law providing for the settlement of jurisdictional disputes is that of Minnesota. Minn. Stat. Sec. 179.083 (Mason, 1945). Other states have not attempted to adjudicate jurisdictional disputes but merely outlaw concerted activities in connection with them. The Oregon and California statutes have been held unconstitutional as a denial of free speech through the ban upon picketing. American Federation of Labor v. Bain, 165 Ore. 183, 106 P.2d 544 (1940) ; International Assn. of Machinists v. San Diego County Bldg. and Constr. Trades Council, 14 CCH Lab. Cas. ¶ 64,452 (Cal. Super. Ct. 1948). For discussions of state legislation with respect to jurisdictional disputes, see Killingsworth, State Labor Relations Acts 57–59 (1948) ; Millis and Katz, A Decade of State Labor Legislation, 15 U. of Chi. L. Rev. 282, 304 (1948).

6. Jurisdictional disputes on the railroads are determined by the National Railway Adjustment Board, and such determinations are not reviewable by the courts. Order of Railway Conductors v. Pitney, 326 U.S. 561, 66 Sup. Ct. 322, 90 L. Ed. 318 (1946). Also, a party to such a dispute may not by-pass the Adjustment Board by bringing a declaratory judgment action to determine the dispute through interpretation of the contract or contracts involved.

Slocum v. Delaware, L. & W.R.R. Co., 339 U.S. 239, 70 Sup. Ct. 577, 94 L. Ed. 795 (1950). However, where the Adjustment Board itself, by reason of a conflict between two of its four divisions, is unable to settle a jurisdictional dispute, a declaratory judgment suit will lie to determine which division should decide the dispute.   Order of Railway Conductors of America v. Swan, 329 U.S. 520, 67 Sup. Ct. 405, 91 L. Ed. 471 (1947).

The Adjustment Board consists of representatives of the railroads and representatives of the principal railway brotherhoods. These brotherhoods, which have a long history of racial discrimination, have increasingly encroached on the jobs which were formerly held by Negroes.   Their seizures of jurisdiction can be contested only before the Adjustment Board which they control. Repeated efforts on the part of the Sleeping Car Porters to obtain legal protection have proved futile.   M–K–T R. Co. v. Randolph, 164 F.2d 4 (8th Cir. 1947); Randolph v. M–K–T R. Co., 78 F. Supp. 727, 22 L.R.R.M. 2400 (W.D. Mo. 1948); State ex. rel. St. Louis S.F. Ry. Co. v. Russell, 358 Mo. 1136, 219 S.W.2d 340 (1949).   But cf. Howard v. Thompson, 72 F. Supp. 695, 20 L.R.R.M. 2706 (E.D. Mo. 1947).

7. In general, see on the problem of settlement of jurisdictional disputes, Fisher, The Settlement of Work Jurisdictional Disputes by Governmental Agencies, 2 Indust. & Lab. Rel. Rev. 335 (1949); Hyman and Jaffe, Jurisdictional Disputes, Proceedings of New York University First Annual Conference on Labor 423 (1948).

APPENDIX

APPENDIX

Sherman Anti-Trust Act

26 Stat. 209, 15 U.S.C., Secs. 1 and 2
(approved July 2, 1890)

SEC. 1. Every contract, combination in the form of trust or otherwise, or conspiracy, in restraint of trade or commerce among the several States, or with foreign nations, is hereby declared to be illegal. Every person who shall make any such contract or engage in any such combination or conspiracy shall be deemed guilty of a misdemeanor, and, on conviction thereof, shall be punished by a fine not exceeding five thousand dollars, or by imprisonment not exceeding one year, or by both said punishments, in the discretion of the court.

SEC. 2. Every person who shall monopolize, or attempt to monopolize, or combine or conspire with any other person or persons, to monopolize any part of the trade or commerce among the several States, or with foreign nations, shall be deemed guilty of a misdemeanor, and, on conviction thereof, shall be punished by fine not exceeding five thousand dollars, or by imprisonment not exceeding one year, or by both said punishments, in the discretion of the court.

Clayton Act

38 Stat. 731, 15 U.S.C., Sec. 17; 38 Stat. 738, 29 U.S.C., Sec. 52
(approved Oct. 15, 1914)

SEC. 6. That the labor of a human being is not a commodity or
article of commerce. Nothing contained in the antitrust laws shall
be construed to forbid the existence and operation of labor, agricultural, or horticultural organizations, instituted for the purposes of
mutual help, and not having capital stock or conducted for profit,
or to forbid or restrain individual members of such organizations from
lawfully carrying out the legitimate objects thereof; nor shall such organizations, or the members thereof, be held or construed to be illegal
combinations or conspiracies in restraint of trade, under the antitrust
laws.

SEC. 20. That no restraining order or injunction shall be granted
by any court of the United States, or a judge or the judges thereof,
in any case between an employer and employees, or between employers and employees, or between employees, or between persons employed and persons seeking employment, involving or growing out of,
a dispute concerning terms or conditions of employment, unless necessary to prevent irreparable injury to property, or to a property right,
of the party making the application, for which injury there is no adequate remedy at law, and such property or property right must be
described with particularity in the application, which must be in
writing and sworn to by the applicant or by his agent or attorney.

And no such restraining order or injunction shall prohibit any
person or persons, whether singly or in concert, from terminating any
relation of employment, or from ceasing to perform any work or labor,
or from recommending, advising, or persuading others by peaceful
means so to do; or from attending at any place where any such person or persons may lawfully be, for the purpose of peacefully obtaining or communicating information or from peacefully persuading
any person to work or to abstain from working; or from ceasing to
patronize or to employ any party to such dispute, or from recommending, advising, or persuading others by peaceful and lawful means so
to do; or from paying or giving to, or withholding from, any person
engaged in such dispute, any strike benefits or other moneys or things
of value; or from peaceably assembling in a lawful manner, and for
lawful purposes; or from doing any act or thing which might lawfully
be done in the absence of such dispute by any party thereto; nor shall
any of the acts specified in this paragraph be considered or held to be
violations of any law of the United States.

Norris-LaGuardia Act

47 Stat. 90, 29 U.S.C., Sec. 101
(approved March 23, 1932)

Be it enacted by the Senate and House of Representatives of the United States of America in Congress assembled, That no court of the United States, as herein defined, shall have jurisdiction to issue any restraining order or temporary or permanent injunction in a case involving or growing out of a labor dispute, except in a strict conformity with the provisions of this Act; nor shall any such restraining order or temporary or permanent injunction be issued contrary to the public policy declared in this Act.

SEC. 2. In the interpretation of this Act and in determining the jurisdiction and authority of the courts of the United States, as such jurisdiction and authority are herein defined and limited, the public policy of the United States is hereby declared as follows:

Whereas under prevailing economic conditions, developed with the aid of governmental authority for owners of property to organize in the corporate and other forms of ownership association, the individual unorganized worker is commonly helpless to exercise actual liberty of contract and to protect his freedom of labor, and thereby to obtain acceptable terms and conditions of employment, wherefore, though he should be free to decline to associate with his fellows, it is necessary that he have full freedom of association, self-organization, and designation of representatives of his own choosing, to negotiate the terms and conditions of his employment, and that he shall be free from the interference, restraint, or coercion of employers of labor, or their agents, in the designation of such representatives or in self-organization or in other concerted activities for the purpose of collective bargaining or other mutual aid or protection; therefore, the following definitions of, and limitations upon, the jurisdiction and authority of the courts of the United States are hereby enacted.

SEC. 3. Any undertaking or promise, such as is described in this section, or any other undertaking or promise in conflict with the public policy declared in section 2 of this Act, is hereby declared to be contrary to the public policy of the United States, shall not be enforceable in any court of the United States and shall not afford any basis for the granting of legal or equitable relief by any such court, including specifically the following:

Every undertaking or promise hereafter made, whether written or oral, express or implied, constituting or contained in any contract or agreement of hiring or employment between any individual, firm, company, association, or corporation, and any employee or prospective employee of the same, whereby

(a) Either party to such contract or agreement undertakes or promises not to join, become, or remain a member of any labor organization or of any employer organization; or

(b) Either party to such contract or agreement undertakes or promises that he will withdraw from an employment relation in the event that he joins, becomes, or remains a member of any labor organization or of any employer organization.

SEC. 4. No court of the United States shall have jurisdiction to issue any restraining order or temporary or permanent injunction in any case involving or growing out of any labor dispute to prohibit any person or persons participating or interested in such dispute (as these terms are herein defined) from doing, whether singly or in concert, any of the following acts:

(a) Ceasing or refusing to perform any work or to remain in any relation of employment;

(b) Becoming or remaining a member of any labor organization or of any employer organization, regardless of any such undertaking or promise as is described in section 3 of this Act;

(c) Paying or giving to, or withholding from, any person participating or interested in such labor dispute, any strike or unemployment benefits or insurance, or other moneys or things of value;

(d) By all lawful means aiding any person participating or interested in any labor dispute who is being proceeded against in, or is prosecuting, any action or suit in any court of the United States or of any State;

(e) Giving publicity to the existence of, or the facts involved in, any labor dispute, whether by advertising, speaking, patrolling, or by any other method not involving fraud or violence;

(f) Assembling peaceably to act or to organize to act in promotion of their interests in a labor dispute;

(g) Advising or notifying any person of an intention to do any of the acts heretofore specified;

(h) Agreeing with other persons to do or not to do any of the acts heretofore specified; and

(i) Advising, urging, or otherwise causing or inducing without fraud or violence the acts heretofore specified, regardless of any such undertaking or promise as is described in section 3 of this Act.

SEC. 5. No court of the United States shall have jurisdiction to issue a restraining order or temporary or permanent injunction upon the ground that any of the persons participating or interested in a labor dispute constitute or are engaged in an unlawful combination or conspiracy because of the doing in concert of the acts enumerated in section 4 of this Act.

SEC. 6. No officer or member of any association or organization, and no association or organization participating or interested in a labor dispute, shall be held responsible or liable in any court of the United States for the unlawful acts of individual officers, members, or agents, except upon clear proof of actual participation in, or actual authorization of, such acts, or of ratification of such acts after actual knowledge thereof.

SEC. 7. No court of the United States shall have jurisdiction to issue a temporary or permanent injunction in any case involving or growing out of a labor dispute, as herein defined, except after hearing the testimony of witnesses in open court (with opportunity for cross-examination) in support of the allegations of a complaint made under oath, and testimony in opposition thereto, if offered, and except after findings of fact by the court, to the effect —

(a) That unlawful acts have been threatened and will be committed unless restrained or have been committed and will be continued unless restrained, but no injunction or temporary restraining order shall be issued on account of any threat or unlawful act excepting against the person or persons, association, or organization making the threat or committing the unlawful act or actually authorizing or ratifying the same after actual knowledge thereof;

(b) That substantial and irreparable injury to complainant's property will follow;

(c) That as to each item of relief granted greater injury will be inflicted upon complainant by the denial of relief than will be inflicted upon defendants by the granting of relief;

(d) That complainant has no adequate remedy at law; and

(e) That the public officers charged with the duty to protect complainant's property are unable or unwilling to furnish adequate protection.

Such hearing shall be held after due and personal notice thereof has been given, in such manner as the court shall direct, to all known persons against whom relief is sought, and also to the chief of those public officials of the county and city within which the unlawful acts have been threatened or committed charged with the duty to protect complainant's property: *Provided, however,* That if a complainant shall also allege that, unless a temporary restraining order shall be issued without notice, a substantial and irreparable injury to complainant's property will be unavoidable, such a temporary restraining order may be issued upon testimony under oath, sufficient, if sustained, to justify the court in issuing a temporary injunction upon a hearing after notice. Such a temporary restraining order shall be effective for no longer than five days and shall become void at the expiration of said five days. No temporary restraining order or temporary injunction shall be issued except on condition that complainant shall first file an undertaking with adequate security in an amount to be fixed by the court sufficient to recompense those enjoined for any loss, expense, or damage caused by the improvident or erroneous issuance of such order or injunction, including all reasonable costs (together with a reasonable attorney's fee) and expense of defense against the order or against the granting of any injunctive relief sought in the same proceeding and subsequently denied by the court.

The undertaking herein mentioned shall be understood to signify an agreement entered into by the complainant and the surety upon which a decree may be rendered in the same suit or proceeding against said complainant and surety, upon a hearing to assess damages of which hearing complainant and surety shall have reasonable notice, the said complainant and surety submitting themselves to the jurisdiction of the court for that purpose. But nothing herein contained shall deprive any party having a claim or cause of action under or upon such undertaking from electing to pursue his ordinary remedy by suit at law or in equity.

SEC. 8. No restraining order or injunctive relief shall be granted to any complainant who has failed to comply with any obligation imposed by law which is involved in the labor dispute in question, or who has failed to make every reasonable effort to settle such dispute either by negotiation or with the aid of any available governmental machinery of mediation or voluntary arbitration.

SEC. 9. No restraining order or temporary or permanent injunction shall be granted in a case involving or growing out of a labor dispute, except on the basis of findings of fact made and filed by the court in the record of the case prior to the issuance of such restraining order or injunction; and every restraining order or injunction granted in a case involving or growing out of a labor dispute shall include only a prohibition of such specific act or acts as may be expressly complained of in the bill of complaint or petition filed in such case and as shall be expressly included in said findings of fact made and filed by the court as provided herein.

SEC. 10. Whenever any court of the United States shall issue or deny any temporary injunction in a case involving or growing out of a labor dispute, the court shall, upon the request of any party to the proceedings and on his filing the usual bond for costs, forthwith certify as in ordinary cases the record of the case to the circuit court of appeals for its review. Upon the filing of such record in the circuit court of appeals, the appeal shall be heard and the temporary injunctive order affirmed, modified, or set aside with the greatest possible expedition, giving the proceedings precedence over all other matters except older matters of the same character.

SEC. 11. In all cases arising under this Act in which a person shall be charged with contempt in a court of the United States (as herein defined), the accused shall enjoy the right to a speedy and public trial by an impartial jury of the State and district wherein the contempt shall have been committed: *Provided,* That this right shall not apply to contempts committed in the presence of the court or so near thereto as to interfere directly with the administration of justice or to apply to the misbehavior, misconduct, or disobedience of any officer of the court in respect to the writs, orders, or process of the court.

SEC. 12. The defendant in any proceeding for contempt of court may file with the court a demand for the retirement of the judge sitting in the proceeding, if the contempt arises from an attack upon the character or conduct of such judge and if the attack occurred elsewhere than in the presence of the court or so near thereto as to interfere directly with the administration of justice. Upon the filing of any such demand the judge shall thereupon proceed no further, but another judge shall be designated in the same manner as is provided by law. The demand shall be filed prior to the hearing in the contempt proceeding.

SEC. 13. When used in this Act, and for the purposes of this Act —

(a) A case shall be held to involve or to grow out of a labor dispute when the case involves persons who are engaged in the same industry, trade, craft, or occupation; or have direct or indirect interests therein; or who are employees of the same employer; or who are members of the same or an affiliated organization of employers or employees; whether such dispute is (1) between one or more employers or associations of employers and one or more employees or associations of employees; (2) between one or more employers or associations of employers and one or more employers or associations of employers; or (3) between one or more employees or associations of employees and one or more employees or associations of employees; or when the case involves any conflicting or competing interests in a "labor dispute" (as hereinafter defined) of "persons participating or interested" therein (as hereinafter defined).

(b) A person or association shall be held to be a person participating or interested in a labor dispute if relief is sought against him or it, and if he or it is engaged in the same industry, trade, craft, or occupation in which such dispute occurs, or has a direct or indirect interest therein, or is a member, officer, or agent of any association composed in whole or in part of employers or employees engaged in such industry, trade, craft, or occupation.

(c) The term "labor dispute" includes any controversy concerning terms or conditions of employment, or concerning the association or representation of persons in negotiating, fixing, maintaining, changing, or seeking to arrange terms or conditions of employment, regardless of whether or not the disputants stand in the proximate relation of employer and employee.

(d) The term "court of the United States" means any court of the United States whose jurisdiction has been or may be conferred or defined or limited by Act of Congress, including the courts of the District of Columbia.

SEC. 14. If any provision of this Act or the application thereof to any person or circumstance is held unconstitutional or otherwise invalid, the remaining provisions of the Act and the application of such provisions to other persons or circumstances shall not be affected thereby.

SEC. 15. All Acts and parts of Acts in conflict with the provisions of this Act are hereby repealed.

Railway Labor Act

44 Stat. 577 (approved May 20, 1926) ; amended June 7, 1934
(48 Stat. 926) ; amended June 21, 1934 (48 Stat. 1185) ;
amended June 25, 1936 (49 Stat. 1921) ; amended Aug. 13,
1940 (54 Stat. 785, 45 U.SC., Sec. 151) ; amended Jan. 10,
1951 (64 Stat. 1238, 45 U.S.C., Sec. 152)

TITLE I

DEFINITIONS

SEC. 1. When used in this Act and for the purposes of this Act —
First. The term "carrier" includes any express company, sleeping-car company, carrier by railroad, subject to the Interstate Commerce Act, and any company which is directly or indirectly owned or controlled by or under common control with any carrier by railroad and which operates any equipment or facilities or performs any service (other than trucking service) in connection with the transportation, receipt, delivery, elevation, transfer in transit, refrigeration or icing, storage, and handling of property transported by railroad, and any receiver, trustee, or other individual or body, judicial or otherwise, when in the possession of the business of any such "carrier"; *Provided, however,* That the term "carrier" shall not include any street, interurban, or suburban electric railway, unless such railway is operating as a part of a general steam-railroad system of transportation, but shall not exclude any part of the general steam-railroad system of transportation now or hereafter operated by any other motive power. The Interstate Commerce Commission is hereby authorized and directed upon request of the Mediation Board or upon complaint of any party interested to determine after hearing whether any line operated by electric power falls within the terms of this proviso. The term "carrier" shall not include any company by reason of its being engaged in the mining of coal, the supplying of coal to a carrier where delivery is not beyond the mine tipple, and the operation of equipment or facilities therefor, or any of such activities.

Second. The term "Adjustment Board" means the National Railroad Adjustment Board created by this Act.

Third. The term "Mediation Board" means the National Mediation Board created by this Act.

Fourth. The term "commerce" means commerce among the several States or between any State, Territory, or the District of Columbia and any foreign nation, or between any Territory or the District of Columbia and any State, or between any Territory and any other Territory, or between any Territory and the District of Columbia, or within any Territory or the District of Columbia, or between points in the same State but through any other State or any Territory or the District of Columbia or any foreign nation.

Fifth. The term "employee" as used herein includes every person in the service of a carrier (subject to its continuing authority to supervise and direct the manner of rendition of his service) who performs any work defined as that of an employee or subordinate official in the orders of the Interstate Commerce Commission now in effect, and as the same may be amended or interpreted by orders hereafter entered by the Commission pursuant to the authority which is hereby conferred upon it to enter orders amending or interpreting such existing orders: *Provided, however,* That no occupational classification made by order of the Interstate Commerce Commission shall be construed to define the crafts according to which railway employees may be organized by their voluntary action, nor shall the jurisdiction or powers of such employee organizations be regarded as in any way limited or defined by the provisions of this Act or by the orders of the Commission. The term "employee" shall not include any individual while such individual is engaged in the physical operations consisting of the mining of coal, the preparation of coal, the handling (other than movement by rail with standard locomotives) of coal not beyond the mine tipple, or the loading of coal at the tipple.

Sixth. The term "representative" means any person or persons, labor union, organization, or corporation designated either by a carrier or group of carriers or by its or their employees, to act for it or them.

Seventh. The term "district court" includes the Supreme Court of the District of Columbia; and the term "circuit court of appeals" includes the Court of Appeals of the District of Columbia.

This Act may be cited as the "Railway Labor Act."

GENERAL PURPOSES

SEC. 2. The purposes of the Act are: (1) To avoid any interruption to commerce or to the operation of any carrier engaged therein; (2) to forbid any limitation upon freedom of association among employees or any denial, as a condition of employment or otherwise, of the right of employees to join a labor organization; (3) to provide for the complete independence of carriers and of employees in the matter of self-organization: (4) to provide for the prompt and orderly settlement of all disputes concerning rates of pay, rules, or working conditions; (5) to provide for the prompt and orderly settlement of all disputes growing out of grievances or out of the interpretation or application of agreements covering rates of pay, rules, or working conditions.

GENERAL DUTIES

First. It shall be the duty of all carriers, their officers, agents, and employees to exert every reasonable effort to make and maintain agreements concerning rates of pay, rules, and working conditions, and to settle all disputes, whether arising out of the application of such agreements or otherwise, in order to avoid any interruption to commerce or to the operation of any carrier growing out of any dispute between the carrier and the employees thereof.

Second. All disputes between a carrier or carriers and its or their employees shall be considered, and, if possible, decided, with all expedition, in conference between representatives designated and authorized so to confer, respectively, by the carrier or carriers and by the employees thereof interested in the dispute.

Third. Representatives, for the purposes of this Act, shall be designated by the respective parties without interference, influence, or coercion by either party over the designation of representatives by the other; and neither party shall in any way interfere with, influence, or coerce the other in its choice of representatives. Representatives of employees for the purposes of this Act need not be persons in the employ of the carrier, and no carrier shall, by interference, influence, or coercion seek in any manner to prevent the designation by its employees as their representatives of those who or which are not employees of the carrier.

Fourth. Employees shall have the right to organize and bargain collectively through representatives of their own choosing. The majority of any craft or class of employees shall have the right to determine who shall be the representative of the craft or class for the purposes of this Act. No carrier, its officers or agents, shall deny or in any way question the right of its employees to join, organize, or assist in organizing the labor organization of their choice, and it shall be unlawful for any carrier to interfere in any way with the organization of its employees, or to use the funds of the carrier in maintaining or assisting or contributing to any labor organization, labor representative, or other agency of collective bargaining, or in performing any work therefor, or to influence or coerce employees in an effort to induce them to join or remain or not to join or remain members of any labor organization or to deduct from the wages of employees any dues, fees, assessments, or other contributions payable to labor organizations, or to collect or to assist in the collection of any such dues, fees, assessments, or other contributions payable to labor organizations, or to collect or to assist in the collection of any such dues, fees, assessments, or other contributions: *Provided,* That nothing in this Act shall be construed to prohibit a carrier from permitting an employee, individually, or local representatives of employees from conferring with management during working hours without loss of time or to prohibit a carrier from furnishing free transportation to its employees while engaged in the business of a labor organization.

Fifth. No carrier, its officers, or agents shall require any person seeking employment to sign any contract or agreement promising to join or not to join a labor organization; and if any such contract has been enforced prior to the effective date of this Act, then such carrier shall notify the employees by an appropriate order that such contract has been discarded and is no longer binding on them in any way.

Sixth. In case of a dispute between a carrier or carriers and its or their employees, arising out of grievances or out of the interpretation or application of agreements concerning rates of pay, rules, or working conditions, it shall be the duty of the designated representative or representatives of such carrier or carriers and of such employees, within ten days after the receipt of notice of a desire on the part of either party to confer in respect to such dispute, to specify a time and place at which such conference shall be held: *Provided,* (1) That the place so specified shall be situated upon the line of the carrier involved or as otherwise mutually agreed upon; and (2) that the time so specified shall allow the designated conferees reasonable opportunity to reach such place of conference, but shall not exceed twenty days from the receipt of such notice: *And provided further,* That nothing in this Act shall be construed to supersede the provisions of any agreement (as to conferences) then in effect between the parties.

Seventh. No carrier, its officers, or agents shall change the rates of pay, rules, or working conditions of its employees, as a class as embodied in agreements except in the manner prescribed in such agreements or in section 6 of this Act.

Eighth. Every carrier shall notify its employees by printed notices in such form and posted at such times and places as shall be specified by the Mediation Board that all disputes between the carrier and its employees will be handled in accordance with the requirements of this Act, and in such notices there shall be printed verbatim, in large type, the third, fourth, and fifth paragraphs of this section. The provisions of said paragraphs are hereby made a part of the contract of employment between the carrier and each employee, and shall be held binding upon the parties, regardless of any other express or implied agreements between them.

Ninth. If any dispute shall arise among a carrier's employees as to who are the representatives of such employees designated and authorized in accordance with the requirements of this Act, it shall be the duty of the Mediation Board, upon request of either party to the dispute, to investigate such dispute and to certify to both parties, in writing, within thirty days after the receipt of the invocation of its services, the name or names of the individuals or organizations that have been designated and authorized to represent the employees involved in the dispute, and certify the same to the carrier. Upon receipt of such certification the carrier shall treat with the representative so certified as the representative of the craft or class for the purposes of this Act. In such an investigation, the Mediation Board shall be authorized to take a secret ballot of the employees involved, or to utilize any other appropriate method of ascertaining the names of their duly designated and authorized representatives in such manner as shall insure the choice of representatives by the employees without interference, influence, or coercion exercised by the carrier. In the conduct of any election for the purposes herein indicated the Board shall designate who may participate in the election and establish the rules to govern the election, or may appoint a committee of three neutral persons who after hearing shall within ten days designate the employees who may participate in the election. The Board shall have access to and have power to make copies of the books and records of the carriers to obtain and utilize such information as may be deemed necessary by it to carry out the purposes and provisions of this paragraph.

Tenth. The willful failure or refusal of any carrier, its officers or agents to comply with the terms of the third, fourth, fifth, seventh, or eighth paragraph of this section shall be a misdemeanor, and upon conviction thereof the carrier, officer, or agent offending shall be subject to a fine of not less than $1,000 nor more than $20,000 or imprisonment for not more than six months, or both fine and imprisonment, for each offense, and each day during which such carrier, officer, or agent shall willfully fail or refuse to comply with the terms of the said paragraphs of this section shall constitute a separate offense. It shall be the duty of any district attorney of the United States to whom any duly designated representative of a carrier's employees may apply to institute in the proper court and to prosecute under the direction of the Attorney General of the United States, all necessary proceedings for the enforcement of the provisions of this section, and for the punishment of all violations thereof and the costs and expenses of such prosecution shall be paid out of the appropriation for the expenses of the courts of the United States: *Provided,* That nothing in this Act shall be construed to require an individual employee to render labor or service without his consent, nor shall anything in this Act be construed to make the quitting of his labor by an individual employee an illegal act; nor shall any court issue any process to compel the performance by an individual employee of such labor or service, without his consent.

Eleventh. Notwithstanding any other provisions of this Act, or of any other statute or law of the United States, or Territory thereof, or of any State, any carrier or carriers as defined in this Act and a labor organization or labor organizations duly designated and authorized to represent employees in accordance with the requirements of this Act shall be permitted —

(a) to make agreements, requiring, as a condition of continued employment, that within sixty days following the beginning of such employment, or the effective date of such agreements, whichever is the later, all employees shall become members of the labor organization representing their craft or class: *Provided,* That no such agreement shall require such condition of employment with respect to employees to whom membership is not available upon the same terms and conditions as are generally applicable to any other member or with respect to employees to whom membership was denied or terminated for any reason other than the failure of the employee to tender the periodic dues, initiation fees, and assessments (not including fines and penalties) uniformly required as a condition of acquiring or retaining membership.

(b) to make agreements providing for the deduction by such carrier or carriers from the wages of its or their employees in a craft or class and payment to the labor organization representing the craft or class of such employees, of any periodic dues, initiation fees, and assessments (not including fines and penalties) uniformly required as a condition of acquiring or retaining membership: *Provided,* That no such agreement shall be effective with respect to any individual employee until he shall have furnished the employer with a written assignment to the labor organization of such membership dues, initiation fees, and assessments, which shall be revocable in writing after the expiration of one year or upon the termination date of the applicable collective agreement, whichever occurs sooner.

(c) The requirement of membership in a labor organization in an agreement made pursuant to subparagraph (a) shall be satisfied, as to both a present or future employee in engine, train, yard, or hostling service, that is, an employee engaged in any of the services or capacities covered in section 3, First (h) of this Act defining the jurisdictional scope of the First Division of the National Railroad Adjustment Board, if said employee shall hold or acquire membership in any one of the labor organizations, national in scope, organized in accordance with this Act and admitting to membership employees of a craft or class in any of said services; and no agreement made pursuant to subparagraph (b) shall provide for deductions from his wages for periodic dues, initiation fees, or assessments payable to any labor organization other than that in which he holds membership: *Provided,* however, That as to an employee in any of said services on a particular carrier at the effective date of any such agreement on a carrier, who is not a member of any one of the labor organizations, national in scope, organized in accordance with this Act and admitting to membership employees of a craft or class in any of said services, such employee, as a condition of continuing his employment, may be required to become a member of the organization representing the craft in which he is employed on the effective date of the first agreement applicable to him: Provided, further, That nothing herein or in any such agreement or agreements shall prevent an employee from changing membership from one organization to another organization admitting to membership employees of a craft or class in any of said services.

(d) Any provisions in paragraphs Fourth and Fifth of section 2 of this Act in conflict herewith are to the extent of such conflict amended. [Sec. "Eleventh" was added Jan. 10, 1951; 64 Stat. 1238.]

NATIONAL BOARD OF ADJUSTMENT — GRIEVANCES
— INTERPRETATION OF AGREEMENTS

SEC. 3. First. There is hereby established a Board, to be known as the "National Railroad Adjustment Board," the members of which shall be selected within thirty days after approval of this Act, and it is hereby provided —

(a) That the said Adjustment Board shall consist of thirty-six members, eighteen of whom shall be selected by the carriers and eighteen by such labor organizations of the employees, national in scope, as have been or may be organized in accordance with the provisions of section 2 of this Act.

(b) The carriers, acting each through its board of directors or its receiver or receivers, trustee or trustees, or through an officer or officers designated for that purpose by such board, trustee or trustees, or receiver or receivers, shall prescribe the rules under which its representatives shall be selected and shall select the representatives of the carriers on the Adjustment Board and designate the division on which each such representative shall serve, but no carrier or system of carriers shall have more than one representative on any division of the Board.

(c) The national labor organizations as defined in paragraph (a) of this section, acting each through the chief executive or other medium designated by the organization or association thereof, shall prescribe the rules under which the labor members of the Adjustment Board shall be selected and shall select such members and designate the division on which each member shall serve; but no labor organization shall have more than one representative on any division of the Board.

(d) In case of a permanent or temporary vacancy on the Adjustment Board, the vacancy shall be filled by selection in the same manner as in the original selection.

(e) If either the carriers or the labor organizations of the employees fail to select and designate representatives to the Adjustment Board, as provided in paragraphs (b) and (c) of this section, respectively, within sixty days after the passage of this Act, in case of any original appointment to office of a member of the Adjustment Board, or in a case of a vacancy in any such office within thirty days after such vacancy occurs, the Mediation Board shall thereupon directly make the appointment and shall select an individual associated in interest with the carriers or the group of labor organizations of employees, whichever he is to represent.

(f) In the event a dispute arises as to the right of any national labor organization to participate as per paragraph (c) of this section in the selection and designation of the labor members of the Adjustment Board, the Secretary of Labor shall investigate the claim of such labor organization to participate, and if such claim in the judgment of the Secretary of Labor has merit, the Secretary shall notify the Mediation Board accordingly, and within ten days after receipt of such advice the Mediation Board shall request those national labor organizations duly qualified as per paragraph (c) of this section to participate in the selection and designation of the labor members of the Adjustment Board to select a representative. Such representative, together with a representative likewise designated by the claimant, and a third or neutral party designated by the Mediation Board, constituting a board of three, shall within thirty days after the appointment of the neutral member, investigate the claims of the labor organization desiring participation and decide whether or not it was organized in accordance with section 2 hereof and is otherwise properly qualified to participate in the selection of the labor members of the Adjustment Board, and the findings of such boards of three shall be final and binding.

(g) Each member of the Adjustment Board shall be compensated by the party or parties he is to represent. Each third or neutral party selected under the provisions of (f) of this section shall receive from the Mediation Board such compensation as the Mediation Board may fix, together with his necessary traveling expenses and expenses actually incurred for subsistence, or per diem allowance in lieu thereof, subject to the provisions of law applicable thereto, while serving as such third or neutral party.

(h) The said Adjustment Board shall be composed of four divisions, whose proceedings shall be independent of one another, and the said divisions as well as the number of their members shall be as follows:

First division: To have jurisdiction over disputes involving train- and yard-service employees of carriers; that is, engineers, firemen, hostlers, and outside hostler helpers, conductors, trainmen, and yard-service employees. This division shall consist of ten members, five of whom shall be selected and designated by the carriers and five of whom shall be selected and designated by the national labor organizations of the employees.

Second division: To have jurisdiction over disputes involving machinists, boilermakers, blacksmiths, sheet-metal workers, electrical workers, car men, the helpers and apprentices of all the foregoing, coach cleaners, power-house employees, and railroad-shop laborers. This division shall consist of ten members, five of whom shall be selected by the carriers and five by the national labor organizations of the employees.

Third division: To have jurisdiction over disputes involving station, tower, and telegraph employees, train dispatchers, maintenance-of-way men, clerical employees, freight handlers, express, station, and store employees, signal men, sleeping-car conductors, sleeping-car porters, and maids and dining-car employees. This division shall consist of ten members, five of whom shall be selected by the carriers and five by the national labor organizations of employees.

Fourth division: To have jurisdiction over disputes involving employees of carriers directly or indirectly engaged in transportation of passengers or property by water, and all other employees of carriers over which jurisdiction is not given to the first, second, and third divisions. This division shall consist of six members, three of whom shall be selected by the carriers and three by the national labor organizations of the employees.

(i) The disputes between an employee or group of employees and a carrier or carriers growing out of grievances or out of the interpretation or application of agreements concerning rates of pay, rules, or working conditions, including cases pending and unadjusted on the date of approval of this Act, shall be handled in the usual manner up to and including the chief operating officer of the carrier designated to handle such disputes; but, failing to reach an adjustment in this manner, the disputes may be referred by petition of the parties or by either party to the appropriate division of the Adjustment Board with a full statement of the facts and all supporting data bearing upon the disputes.

(j) Parties may be heard either in person, by counsel, or by other representatives, as they may respectively elect, and the several divisions of the Adjustment Board shall give due notice of all hearings to the employee or employees and the carrier or carriers involved in any disputes submitted to them.

(k) Any division of the Adjustment Board shall have authority to empower two or more of its members to conduct hearings and make findings upon disputes, when properly submitted, at any place designated by the division: *Provided, however,* That final awards as to any such dispute must be made by the entire division as hereinafter provided.

(l) Upon failure of any division to agree upon an award because of a deadlock or inability to secure a majority vote of the division members, as provided in paragraph (n) of this section, then such division shall forthwith agree upon and select a neutral person, to be known as "referee," to sit with the division as a member thereof and make an award. Should the division fail to agree upon and select a referee within ten days of the date of the deadlock or inability to secure a majority vote, then the division, or any member thereof, or the parties or either party to the dispute may certify that fact to the Mediation Board, which Board shall, within ten days from the date of receiving such certificate, select and name the referee to sit with the division as a member thereof and make an award. The Mediation Board shall be bound by the same provisions in the appointment of these neutral referees as are provided elsewhere in this Act for the appointment of arbitrators and shall fix and pay the compensation of such referees.

(m) The awards of the several divisions of the Adjustment Board shall be stated in writing. A copy of the awards shall be furnished to the respective parties to the controversy, and the awards shall be final and binding upon both parties to the dispute, except in so far as they shall contain a money award. In case a dispute arises involving an interpretation of the award the division of the Board upon request of either party shall interpret the award in the light of the dispute.

(n) A majority vote of all members of the division of the Adjustment Board shall be competent to make an award with respect to any dispute submitted to it.

(o) In case of an award by any division of the Adjustment Board in favor of petitioner, the division of the Board shall make an order, directed to the carrier, to make the award effective and, if the award includes a requirement for the payment of money, to pay the employee the sum to which he is entitled under the award on or before a day named.

(p) If a carrier does not comply with an order of a division of the Adjustment Board within the time limit in such order, the petitioner, or any person for whose benefit such order was made, may file in the District Court of the United States for the district in which he resides or in which is located the principal operating office of the carrier, or through which the carrier operates, a petition setting forth briefly the causes for which he claims relief, and the order of the division of the Adjustment Board in the premises. Such suit in the District Court of the United States shall proceed in all respects as other civil suits, except that on the trial of such suit the findings and order of the division of the Adjustment Board shall be prima facie evidence of the facts therein stated, and except that the petitioner shall not be liable for costs in the district court nor for costs at any subsequent stage of the proceedings, unless they accrue upon his appeal, and such costs shall be paid out of the appropriation for the expenses of the courts of the United States. If the petitioner shall finally prevail he shall be allowed a reasonable attorney's fee, to be taxed and collected as a part of the costs of the suit. The district courts are empowered, under the rules of the court governing actions at law, to make such order and enter such judgment, by writ of mandamus or otherwise, as may be appropriate to enforce or set aside the order of the division of the Adjustment Board.

(q) All actions at law based upon the provisions of this section shall be begun within two years from the time the cause of action accrues under the award of the division of the Adjustment Board, and not after.

(r) The several divisions of the Adjustment Board shall maintain headquarters in Chicago, Illinois, meet regularly, and continue in session so long as there is pending before the division any matter within its jurisdiction which has been submitted for its consideration and which has not been disposed of.

NATIONAL MEDIATION BOARD

SEC. 4. First. The Board of Mediation is hereby abolished, effective thirty days from the approval of this Act and the members, secretary, officers, assistants, employees, and agents thereof, in office upon the date of the approval of this Act, shall continue to function and receive their salaries for a period of thirty days from such date in the same manner as though this Act had not been passed. There is hereby Government, a board to be known as the "National Mediation Board," established, as an independent agency in the executive branch of the to be composed of three members appointed by the President, by and with the advice and consent of the Senate, not more than two of whom shall be of the same political party. The terms of office of the members first appointed shall begin as soon as the members shall qualify, but not before thirty days after the approval of this Act, and expire, as designated by the President at the time of nomination, one on February 1, 1935, one on February 1, 1936, and one on February 1, 1937. The terms of office of all successors shall expire three years after the expiration of the terms for which their predecessors were appointed; but any member appointed to fill a vacancy occurring prior to the expiration of the term for which his predecessor was appointed shall be appointed only for the unexpired term of his predecessor. Vacancies in the Board shall not impair the powers nor affect the duties of the Board nor of the remaining members of the Board. Two of the members in office shall constitute a quorum for the transaction of the business of the Board. Each member of the Board shall receive a salary at the rate of $10,000 per annum, together with necessary traveling and subsistence expenses, or per diem allowance in lieu thereof, subject to the provisions of law applicable thereto, while away from the principal office of the Board on business required by this Act. No person in the employment of or who is pecuniarily or otherwise interested in any organization of employees or any carrier shall enter upon the duties of or continue to be a member of the Board.

All cases referred to the Board of Mediation and unsettled on the date of the approval of this Act shall be handled to conclusion by the Mediation Board.

FUNCTIONS OF MEDIATION BOARD

SEC. 5. First. The parties, or either party, to a dispute between an employee or group of employees and a carrier may invoke the services of the Mediation Board in any of the following cases:

(a) A dispute concerning changes in rates of pay, rules, or working conditions not adjusted by the parties in conference.

(b) Any other dispute not referable to the National Railroad Adjustment Board and not adjusted in conference between the parties or where conferences are refused.

The Mediation Board may proffer its services in case any labor emergency is found by it to exist at any time.

In either event the said Board shall promptly put itself in communication with the parties to such controversy, and shall use its best efforts, by mediation, to bring them to agreement. If such efforts to bring about an amicable settlement through mediation shall be unsuccessful, the said Board shall at once endeavor as its final required action (except as provided in paragraph third of this section and in section 10 of this Act) to induce the parties to submit their controversy to arbitration, in accordance with the provisions of this Act.

If arbitration at the request of the Board shall be refused by one or both parties, the Board shall at once notify both parties in writing that its mediatory efforts have failed and for thirty days thereafter, unless in the intervening period the parties agree to arbitration, or an emergency board shall be created under section 10 of this Act, no change shall be made in the rates of pay, rules, or working conditions or established practices in effect prior to the time the dispute arose.

Second.   In any case in which a controversy arises over the meaning or the application of any agreement reached through mediation under the provisions of this Act, either party to the said agreement, or both, may apply to the Mediation Board for an interpretation of the meaning or application of such agreement. The said Board shall upon receipt of such request notify the parties to the controversy, and after a hearing of both sides give its interpretation within thirty days.

Third.   The Mediation Board shall have the following duties with respect to the arbitration of disputes under section 7 of this Act:

(a) On failure of the arbitrators named by the parties to agree on the remaining arbitrator or arbitrators within the time set by section 7 of this Act, it shall be the duty of the Mediation Board to name such remaining arbitrator or arbitrators. It shall be the duty of the Board in naming such arbitrator or arbitrators to appoint only those whom the Board shall deem wholly disinterested in the controversy to be arbitrated and impartial and without bias as between the parties to such arbitration. Should, however, the Board name an arbitrator or arbitrators not so disinterested and impartial, then, upon proper investigation and presentation of the facts, the Board shall promptly remove such arbitrator.

If an arbitrator named by the Mediation Board, in accordance with the provisions of this Act, shall be removed by such Board as provided by this Act, or if such an arbitrator refuses or is unable to serve, it shall be the duty of the Mediation Board, promptly to select another arbitrator in the same manner as provided in this Act for an original appointment by the Mediation Board.

(b) Any member of the Mediation Board is authorized to take the acknowledgment of an agreement to arbitrate under this Act. When so acknowledged, or when acknowledged by the parties before a notary public or the clerk of a district court or a circuit court of appeals of the United States, such agreement to arbitrate shall be delivered to a member of said Board or transmitted to said Board to be filed in its office.

(c) When an agreement to arbitrate has been filed with the Mediation Board, or with one of its members, as provided by this section, and when the said Board has been furnished the names of the arbitrators chosen by the parties to the controversy, it shall be the duty of the Board to cause a notice in writing to be served upon said arbitrators, notifying them of their appointment, requesting them to meet promptly to name the remaining arbitrator or arbitrators necessary to complete the Board of Arbitration, and advising them of the period within which, as provided by the agreement to arbitrate, they are empowered to name such arbitrator or arbitrators.

(d) Either party to an arbitration desiring the reconvening of a board of arbitration to pass upon any controversy arising over the meaning or application of an award may so notify the Mediation Board in writing, stating in such notice the question or questions to be submitted to such reconvened Board. The Mediation Board shall thereupon promptly communicate with the members of the Board of Arbitration, or a subcommittee of such Board appointed for such purpose pursuant to a provision in the agreement to arbitrate, and arrange for the reconvening of said Board of Arbitration or subcommittee, and shall notify the respective parties to the controversy of the time and place at which the Board, or the subcommittee, will meet for hearings upon the matters in controversy to be submitted to it. No evidence other than that contained in the record filed with the original award shall be received or considered by such reconvened Board or subcommittee, except such evidence as may be necessary to illustrate the interpretations suggested by the parties. If any member of the original Board is unable or unwilling to serve on such reconvened Board or subcommittee thereof, another arbitrator shall be named in the same manner and with the same powers and duties as such original arbitrator.

PROCEDURE IN CHANGING RATES OF PAY, RULES, AND WORKING CONDITIONS

SEC. 6. Carriers and representatives of the employees shall give at least thirty days' written notice of an intended change in agreements affecting rates of pay, rules, or working conditions, and the time and place for the beginning of conference between the representatives of the parties interested in such intended changes shall be agreed upon within ten days after the receipt of said notice, and said time shall be within the thirty days provided in the notice. In every case where such notice of intended change has been given, or conferences are being held with reference thereto, or the services of the Mediation Board have been requested by either party, or said Board has proffered its services, rates of pay, rules, or working conditions shall not be altered by the carrier until the controversy has been finally acted upon as required by section 5 of this Act, by the Mediation Board, unless a period of ten days has elapsed after termination of conferences without request for or proffer of the services of the Mediation Board.

ARBITRATION

SEC. 7. First.   Whenever a controversy shall arise between a carrier or carriers and its or their employees which is not settled either in conference between representatives of the parties or by the appropriate adjustment board or through mediation, in the manner provided in the preceding sections, such controversy may, by agreement of the parties to such controversy, be submitted to the arbitration of a board of three (or, if the parties to the controversy so stipulate, of six) persons: Provided, however, That the failure or refusal of either party to submit a controversy to arbitration shall not be construed as a violation of any legal obligation imposed upon such party by the terms of this Act or otherwise.

EMERGENCY BOARD

SEC. 10.   If a dispute between a carrier and its employees be not adjusted under the foregoing provisions of this Act and should, in the judgment of the Mediation Board, threaten substantially to interrupt interstate commerce to a degree such as to deprive any section of the country of essential transportation service, the Mediation Board shall notify the President, who may thereupon, in his discretion, create a board to investigate and report respecting such dispute.   Such board shall be composed of such number of persons as to the President may seem desirable: Provided, however, That no member appointed shall be pecuniarily or otherwise interested in any organization of employees or any carrier.   The compensation of the members of any such board shall be fixed by the President.   Such board shall be created separately in each instance and it shall investigate promptly the facts as to the dispute and make a report thereon to the President within thirty days from the date of its creation. . . .

After the creation of such board, and for thirty days after such board has made its report to the President, no change, except by agreement, shall be made by the parties to the controversy in the conditions out of which the dispute arose.

Labor Management Relations Act, 1947, as Amended by Public Law No.189, 1951

EDITORIAL NOTE. The National Labor Relations Act (popularly known as the "Wagner Act") was approved by the President on July 5, 1935. (49 Stat. 449, 29 U.S.C., Secs. 151–166.) Twelve years later this was amended by Title I of the Labor Management Relations Act of 1947 (popularly known as the "Taft-Hartley Act") passed on June 23, 1947, over the President's veto. (61 Stat. 136, 29 U.S.C., Secs. 141 et seq.) Certain further amendments were added, in 1951.

The opening portion of the LMRA contains its own declaration of policy; then follows Title I amending the earlier act (including an amended policy statement). The remaining four titles of the 1947 act constitute original rather than amendatory legislation. These follow Title I in sequence.

Be it enacted by the Senate and House of Representatives of the United States of America in Congress assembled,

SHORT TITLE AND DECLARATION OF POLICY

SECTION 1. (a) This Act may be cited as the "Labor Management Relations Act, 1947."

(b) Industrial strife which interferes with the normal flow of commerce and with the full production of articles and commodities for commerce, can be avoided or substantially minimized if employers, employees, and labor organizations each recognize under law one another's legitimate rights in their relations with each other, and above all, recognize under law that neither party has any right in its relations with any other to engage in acts or practices which jeopardize the public health, safety, or interest.

It is the purpose and policy of this Act, in order to promote the full flow of commerce, to prescribe the legitimate rights of both employees and employers in their relations affecting commerce, to provide orderly and peaceful procedures for preventing the interference by either with the legitimate rights of the other, to protect the rights of individual employees in their relations with labor organizations whose activities affect commerce, to define and proscribe practices on the part of labor and management which affect commerce and are inimical to the general welfare, and to protect the rights of the public in connection with labor disputes affecting commerce.

Title I

Amendment of National Labor Relations Act[1]

SEC. 101. The National Labor Relations Act is hereby amended to read as follows:

FINDINGS AND POLICIES

SEC. 1. The denial by *some* employers of the right of employees to organize and the refusal by *some* employers to accept the procedure of collective bargaining lead to strikes and other forms of industrial strife or unrest, which have the intent or the necessary effect of burdening or obstructing commerce by (a) impairing the efficiency, safety, or operation of the instrumentalities of commerce; (b) occurring in the current of commerce; (c) materially affecting, restraining, or controlling the flow of raw materials or manufactured or processed goods from or into the channels of commerce, or the prices of such materials or goods in commerce; or (d) causing diminution of employment and wages in such volume as substantially to impair or disrupt the market for goods flowing from or into the channels of commerce.

The inequality of bargaining power between employees who do not possess full freedom of association or actual liberty of contract, and employers who are organized in the corporate or other forms of ownership association substantially burdens and affects the flow of commerce, and tends to aggravate recurrent business depressions, by depressing wage rates and the purchasing power of wage earners in industry and by preventing the stabilization of competitive wage rates and working conditions within and between industries.

Experience has proved that protection by law of the right of employees to organize and bargain collectively safeguards commerce from injury, impairment, or interruption, and promotes the flow of commerce by removing certain recognized sources of industrial strife and unrest, by encouraging practices fundamental to the friendly adjustment of industrial disputes arising out of differences as to wages, hours, or other working conditions, and by restoring equality of bargaining power between employers and employees.

Experience has further demonstrated that certain practices by some labor organizations, their officers and members have the intent or the necessary effect of burdening or obstructing commerce by preventing the free flow of goods in such commerce through strikes and other

[1] In Title I, portions of the National Labor Relations Act which were eliminated by the Labor Management Relations Act are enclosed in brackets, provisions which were added to the National Labor Relations Act are in italics, and unchanged portions of the National Labor Relations Act are shown in roman type. Material added by Public Law No. 189, 82d Cong., 1st Sess. (1951), is set in boldface type.

forms of industrial unrest or through concerted activities which impair the interest of the public in the free flow of such commerce.   The elimination of such practices is a necessary condition to the assurance of the rights herein guaranteed.

It is hereby declared to be the policy of the United States to eliminate the causes of certain substantial obstructions to the free flow of commerce and to mitigate and eliminate these obstructions when they have occurred by encouraging the practice and procedure of collective bargaining and by protecting the exercise by workers of full freedom of association, self-organization, and designation of representatives of their own choosing, for the purpose of negotiating the terms and conditions of their employment or other mutual aid or protection.

DEFINITIONS

Sec. 2.   When used in this Act —

(1) The term "person" includes one or more individuals, *labor organizations,* partnerships, associations, corporations, legal representatives, trustees, trustees in bankruptcy, or receivers.

(2) The term "employer" includes any person acting [in the interest of] *as an agent* of an employer, directly or indirectly, but shall not include the United States *or any wholly owned Government corporation, or any Federal Reserve Bank,* or any State or political subdivision thereof, *or any corporation or association operating a hospital, if no part of the net earnings inures to the benefit of any private shareholder or individual,* or any person subject to the Railway Labor Act, as amended from time to time, or any labor organization (other than when acting as an employer), or anyone acting in the capacity of officer or agent of such labor organization.

(3) The term "employee" shall include any employee, and shall not be limited to the employees of a particular employer, unless the Act explicitly states otherwise, and shall include any individual whose work has ceased as a consequence of, or in connection with, any current labor dispute or because of any unfair labor practice, and who has not obtained any other regular and substantially equivalent employment, but shall not include any individual employed as an agricultural laborer, or in the domestic service of any family or person at his home, or any individual employed by his parent or spouse [.], *or any individual having the status of an independent contractor, or any individual employed as a supervisor, or any individual employed by an employer subject to the Railway Labor Act, as amended from time to time, or by any other person who is not an employer as herein defined.*

(4) The term "representatives" includes any individual or labor organization.

(5) The term "labor organization" means any organization of any kind, or any agency or employee representation committee or plan,

in which employees participate and which exists for the purpose, in whole or in part, of dealing with employers concerning grievances, labor disputes, wages, rates of pay, hours of employment, or conditions of work.

(6) The term "commerce" means trade, traffic, commerce, transportation, or communication among the several States, or between the District of Columbia or any Territory of the United States and any State or other Territory, or between any foreign country and any State, Territory, or the District of Columbia, or within the District of Columbia or any Territory, or between points in the same State but through any other State or any Territory or the District of Columbia or any foreign county.

(7) The term "affecting commerce" means in commerce, or burdening or obstructing commerce or the free flow of commerce, or having led or tending to lead to a labor dispute burdening or obstructing commerce or the free flow of commerce.

(8) The term "unfair labor practice" means any unfair labor practice listed in section 8.

(9) The term "labor dispute" includes any controversy concerning terms, tenure or condition of employment, or concerning the association or representation of persons in negotiating, fixing, maintaining, changing, or seeking to arrange terms or conditions of employment, regardless of whether the disputants stand in the proximate relation of employer and employee.

(10) The term "National Labor Relations Board" means the National Labor Relations Board [created by] *provided for in* section 3 of this Act.

(11) [The term "old Board" means the National Labor Relations Board established by Executive Order Numbered 6763 of the President on June 29, 1934, pursuant to Public Resolution Numbered 44, approved June 19, 1934 (48 Stat. 1183) and reestablished and continued by Executive Order Numbered 7074 of the President of June 15, 1935, pursuant to Title I of the National Industrial Recovery Act (48 Stat. 195) as amended and continued by Senate Joint Resolution 133 [2] approved June 14, 1935.]

The term "supervisor" means any individual having authority, in the interest of the employer, to hire, transfer, suspend, lay off, recall, promote, discharge, assign, reward, or discipline other employees, or responsibly to direct them, or to adjust their grievances, or effectively to recommend such action, if in connection with the foregoing the exercise of such authority is not of a merely routine or clerical nature, but requires the use of independent judgment.

(12) *The term "professional employee" means —*

   (a) *any employee engaged in work (i) predominantly intellectual and varied in character as opposed to routine mental, man-*

---

[2] So in original.

ual, mechanical, or physical work; (ii) involving the consistent exercise of discretion and judgment in its performance; (iii) of such a character that the output produced or the result accomplished cannot be standardized in relation to a given period of time; (iv) requiring knowledge of an advanced type in a field of science or learning customarily acquired by a prolonged course of specialized intellectual instruction and study in an institution of higher learning or a hospital, as distinguished from a general academic education or from an apprenticeship or from training in the performance of routine mental, manual, or physical processes; or

(b) *any employee, who (i) has completed the courses of specialized intellectual instruction and study described in clause (iv) of paragraph (a), and (ii) is performing related work under the supervision of a professional person to qualify himself to become a professional employee as defined in paragraph (a).*

(13) *In determining whether any person is acting as an "agent" of another person so as to make such other person responsible for his acts, the question of whether the specific acts performed were actually authorized or subsequently ratified shall not be controlling.*

NATIONAL LABOR RELATIONS BOARD

SEC. 3 (a) [There is hereby created a board, to be known as the "National Labor Relations Board" (hereinafter referred to as the "Board"), which shall be composed of three members, who shall be appointed by the President, by and with the advice and consent of the Senate. One of the original members shall be appointed for a term of one year, one for a term of three years, and one for a term of five years, but their successors shall be appointed for terms of five years each, except] *The National Labor Relations Board (hereinafter called the "Board") created by this Act prior to its amendment by the Labor Management Relations Act, 1947, is hereby continued as an agency of the United States, except that the Board shall consist of five instead of three members, appointed by the President by and with the advice and consent of the Senate. Of the two additional members so provided for, one shall be appointed for a term of five years and the other for a term of two years. Their successors, and the successors of the other members, shall be appointed for terms of five years each, excepting* that any individual chosen to fill a vacancy shall be appointed only for the unexpired term of the member whom he shall succeed. The President shall designate one member to serve as Chairman of the Board. Any member of the Board may be removed by the President, upon notice and hearing, for neglect of duty or malfeasance in office, but for no other cause.

(b) *The Board is authorized to delegate to any group of three or more members any or all of the powers which it may itself exercise.* A vacancy in the Board shall not impair the right of the remaining members to exercise all of the powers of the Board, and [two] *three* members of the Board shall, at all times, constitute a quorum[.] *of the Board, except that two members shall constitute a quorum of any group designated pursuant to the first sentence hereof.* The Board shall have an official seal which shall be judicially noticed.

(c) The Board shall at the close of each fiscal year make a report in writing to Congress and to the President stating in detail the cases it has heard, the decisions it has rendered, the names, salaries, and duties of all employees and officers in the employ or under the supervision of the Board, and an account of all moneys it has disbursed.

(d) *There shall be a General Counsel of the Board who shall be appointed by the President, by and with the advice and consent of the Senate, for a term of four years. The General Counsel of the Board shall exercise general supervision over all attorneys employed by the Board (other than trial examiners and legal assistants to Board members) and over the officers and employees in the regional offices. He shall have final authority, on behalf of the Board, in respect of the investigation of charges and issuance of complaints under section 10, and in respect of the prosecution of such complaints before the Board, and shall have such other duties as the Board may prescribe or as may be provided by law.*

SEC. 4 (a)   Each member of the Board *and the General Counsel of the Board* shall receive a salary of [$10,000] *$12,000* [3] a year, shall be eligible for reappointment, and shall not engage in any other business, vocation, or employment. The Board shall appoint [without regard for the provisions of the civil-service laws but subject to the Classification Act of 1923, as amended,] an executive secretary, and such attorneys, examiners, and regional directors, and [shall appoint] such other employees [with regard to existing laws applicable to the employment and compensation of officers and employees of the United States,] as it may from time to time find necessary for the proper performance of its duties [and as may be from time to time appropriated for by Congress]. *The Board may not employ any attorneys for the purpose of reviewing transcripts of hearings or preparing drafts of opinions except that any attorney employed for assignment as a legal assistant to any Board member may for such Board member review such transcripts and prepare such drafts. No trial examiner's report shall be reviewed, either before or after its publication, by any person other than a member of the Board or his legal assistant, and no trial examiner shall advise or consult with the Board with respect to exceptions taken to his findings, rulings, or recommendations.* The Board may establish or utilize such regional, local, or other agencies, and utilize such voluntary and uncompensated services, as may from time to time be needed. Attorneys appointed under this section may, at the direction of the Board, appear for and repre-

[3] The salary is now $15,000 (63 Stat. 880).

sent the Board in any case in court. Nothing in this Act shall be construed to authorize the Board to appoint individuals for the purpose of conciliation or mediation, [(or for statistical work, where such service may be obtained from the Department of Labor,] *or for economic analysis.*

(b) [Upon the appointment of the three original members of the Board and the designation of its chairman, the old Board shall cease to exist. All employees of the old Board shall be transferred to and become employees of the Board with salaries under the Classification Act of 1923, as amended, without acquiring by such transfer a permanent or civil service status. All records, papers, and property of the old Board shall become records, papers, and property of the Board and all unexpended funds and appropriations for the use and maintenance of the old Board shall become funds and appropriations available to be expended by the Board in the exercise of the powers, authority, and duties conferred on it by this Act.]

[(c)] All of the expenses of the Board, including all necessary traveling and subsistence expenses outside the District of Columbia incurred by the members or employees of the Board under its orders, shall be allowed and paid on the presentation of itemized vouchers therefor approved by the Board or by any individual it designates for that purpose.

SEC. 5. The principal office of the Board shall be in the District of Columbia, but it may meet and exercise any or all of its powers at any other place. The Board may, by one or more of its members or by such agents or agencies as it may designate, prosecute any inquiry necessary to its functions in any part of the United States. A member who participates in such an inquiry shall not be disqualified from subsequently participating in a decision of the Board in the same case.

SEC. 6[(a)] The Board shall have authority from time to time to make, amend, and rescind, *in the manner prescribed by the Administrative Procedure Act,* such rules and regulations as may be necessary to carry out the provisions of this Act. [Such rules and regulations shall be effective upon publication in the manner which the Board shall prescribe.]

assumes Rule-making power - not exercised by Bd

RIGHTS OF EMPLOYEES

SEC. 7. Employees shall have the right to self-organization, to form, join, or assist labor organizations, to bargain collectively through representatives of their own choosing, and to engage in *other* concerted activities for the purpose of collective bargaining or other mutual aid or protection, *and shall also have the right to refrain from any or all of such activities except to the extent that such right may be affected by an agreement requiring membership in a labor organization as a condition of employment as authorized in section 8 (a) (3).*

Indir right to coll. action

UNFAIR LABOR PRACTICES

Sec. 8. (a) It shall be an unfair labor practice for an employer —

(1) to interfere with, restrain, or coerce employees in the exercise of the rights guaranteed in section 7;

(2) to dominate or interfere with the formation or administration of any labor organization or contribute financial or other support to it: *Provided,* That subject to rules and regulations made and published by the Board pursuant to section 6, [(a)] an employer shall not be prohibited from permitting employees to confer with him during working hours without loss of time or pay;

(3) by discrimination in regard to hire or tenure of employment or any term or condition of employment to encourage or discourage membership in any labor organization: *Provided,* That nothing in this Act, or in [the National Industrial Recovery Act,[4] as amended from time to time, or in any code or agreement approved or prescribed thereunder,] any other statute of the United States, shall preclude an employer from making an agreement with a labor organization (not established, maintained, or assisted by any action defined in *section 8 (a)* of this Act as an unfair labor practice) to require as a condition of employment membership therein *on or after the thirtieth day following the beginning of such employment or the effective date of such agreement, whichever is the later, (i)* if such labor organization is the representative of the employees as provided in section 9 (a), in the appropriate collective bargaining unit covered by such agreement when made; [*and (ii) if, following the most recent election held as provided in section 9 (e) the Board shall have certified that at least a majority of the employees eligible to vote in such election have voted to authorize such labor organization to make such an agreement:*][5] **and has at the time the agreement was made or within the preceding twelve months received from the Board a notice of compliance with sections 9(f), (g), (h), and (ii) unless following an election held as provided in section 9(e) within one year preceding the effective date of such agreement, the Board shall have certified that at least a majority of the employees eligible to vote in such election have voted to rescind th authority of such labor organization to make such an agreement:**[6] *Provided further, That no employer shall justify any discrimination against an employee for non-membership in a labor organization (A) if he has reasonable grounds for believing that such membership was not available to the employee on the same*

[4] U.S.C., Supp. VII, Title 15, Secs. 701–712. The NIRA was declared unconstitutional in the Schecter case (295 U.S. 495 (1935)).

[5] The material in brackets, originally contained in the Labor Management Relations Act, 1947, was repealed by Public Law No. 189, 82d Cong., 1st Sess. (1951).

[6] The boldface material was added by Public Law No. 189 supra.

terms and conditions generally applicable to other members, or (B) *if he has reasonable grounds for believing that membership was denied or terminated for reasons other than the failure of the employee to tender the periodic dues and the initiation fees uniformly required as a condition of acquiring or retaining membership;*

(4) to discharge or otherwise discriminate against an employee because he has filed charges or given testimony under this Act;

(5) to refuse to bargain collectively with the representatives of his employees, subject to the provisions of section 9 (a).

(b) *It shall be an unfair labor practice for a labor organization or its agents —*

(1) *to restrain or coerce* (A) *employees in the exercise of the rights guaranteed in section 7: Provided, That this paragraph shall not impair the right of a labor organization to prescribe its own rules with respect to the acquisition or retention of membership therein; or* (B) *an employer in the selection of his representatives for the purposes of collective bargaining or the adjustment of grievances;*

(2) *to cause or attempt to cause an employer to discriminate against an employee in violation of subsection* (a) (3) *or to discriminate against an employee with respect to whom membership in such organization has been denied or terminated on some ground other than his failure to tender the periodic dues and the initiation fees uniformly required as a condition of acquiring or retaining membership;*

(3) *to refuse to bargain collectively with an employer, provided it is the representative of his employees subject to the provisions of section 9 (a) ;*

(4) *to engage in, or to induce or encourage the employees of any employer to engage in, a strike or a concerted refusal in the course of their employment to use, manufacture, process, transport, or otherwise handle or work on any goods, articles, materials, or commodities or to perform any services, where an object thereof is:* (A) *forcing or requiring any employer or self-employed person to join any labor or employer organization or any employer or other person to cease using, selling, handling, transporting, or otherwise dealing in the products of any other producer, processor, or manufacturer, or to cease doing business with any other person;* (B) *forcing or requiring any other employer to recognize or bargain with a labor organization as the representative of his employees unless such labor organization has been certified as the representative of such employees under the provisions of section 9;* (C) *forcing or requiring any employer to recognize or bargain with a particular labor organization as the representative of his employees if another labor organization has been certified as the representative of such employees under the provisions of section 9;* (D) *forcing or requiring any employer to assign particular work to employees in a particular labor organization or in a particular trade, craft, or class*

rather than to employees in another labor organization or in another trade, craft, or class, unless such employer is failing to conform to an order or certification of the Board determining the bargaining representative for employees performing such work: *Provided*, That nothing contained in this subsection (*b*) shall be construed to make unlawful a refusal by any person to enter upon the premises of any employer (other than his own employer), if the employees of such employer are engaged in a strike ratified or approved by a representative of such employees whom such employer is required to recognize under this Act;

(5) to require of employees covered by an agreement authorized under subsection (*a*) (3) the payment, as a condition precedent to becoming a member of such organization, of a fee in an amount which the Board finds excessive or discriminatory under all the circumstances. In making such a finding, the Board shall consider, among other relevant factors, the practices and customs of labor organizations in the particular industry, and the wages currently paid to the employees affected; and

(6) to cause or attempt to cause an employer to pay or deliver or agree to pay or deliver any money or other thing of value, in the nature of an exaction, for services which are not performed or not to be performed.

(*c*) The expressing of any views, argument, or opinion, or the dissemination thereof, whether in written, printed, graphic, or visual form, shall not constitute or be evidence of an unfair labor practice under any of the provisions of this Act, if such expression contains no threat of reprisal or force or promise of benefit.

(*d*) For the purposes of this section, to bargain collectively is the performance of the mutual obligation of the employer and the representative of the employees to meet at reasonable times and confer in good faith with respect to wages, hours, and other terms and conditions of employment, or the negotiation of an agreement, or any question arising thereunder, and the execution of a written contract incorporating any agreement reached if requested by either party, but such obligation does not compel either party to agree to a proposal or require the making of a concession: *Provided*, That where there is in effect a collective-bargaining contract covering employees in an industry affecting commerce, the duty to bargain collectively shall also mean that no party to such contract shall terminate or modify such contract, unless the party desiring such termination or modification —

(1) serves written notice upon the other party to the contract of the proposed termination or modification sixty days prior to the expiration date thereof, or in the event such contract contains no expiration date, sixty days prior to the time it is proposed to make such termination or modification;

(2) offers to meet and confer with the other party for the pur-

pose of negotiating a new contract or a contract containing the proposed modifications;

(3) notifies the Federal Mediation and Conciliation Service
within thirty days after such notice of the existence of a dispute, and
simultaneously therewith notifies any State or Territorial agency
established to mediate and conciliate disputes within the State or
Territory where the dispute occurred, provided no agreement has
been reached by that time; and

(4) continues·in full force and effect, without resorting to strike
or lockout, all the terms and conditions of the existing contract for
a period of sixty days after such notice is given or until the expiration date of such contract, whichever occurs later.

*limitation -
must give 60
days notice, even
if contr expires -*

The duties imposed upon employers, employees, and labor organizations by paragraphs (2), (3), and (4) shall become inapplicable
upon an intervening certification of the Board, under which the labor
organization or individual, which is a party to the contract, has been
superseded as or ceased to be the representative of the employees subject to the provisions of section 9 (a), and the duties so imposed shall
not be construed as requiring either party to discuss or agree to any
modification of the terms and conditions contained in a contract for
a fixed period, if such modification is to become effective before such
terms and conditions can be reopened under the provisions of the contract...Any employee who engages in a strike within the sixty-period
specified in this subsection shall lose his status as an employee of the
employer engaged in the particular labor dispute, for the purposes
of sections 8, 9, and 10 of this Act, as amended, but such loss of status
for such employee shall terminate if and when he is reemployed by
such employer.

*interpreted in
Jacobs case
32 - 60
what about things
effect out of contr
22615*

By withdrawing rights, Govt power withdrawn if strike within 60 days of notice

REPRESENTATIVES AND ELECTIONS

SEC. 9 (a)   Representatives designated or selected for the purposes
of collective bargaining by the majority of the employees in a unit
appropriate for such purposes, shall be the exclusive representatives
of all the employees in such unit for the purposes of collective bargaining in respect to rates of pay, wages, hours of employment, or
other conditions of employment: *Provided,* That any individual employee or a group of employees shall have the right at any time to
present grievances to their employer [.] *and to have such grievances
adjusted, without the intervention of the bargaining representative,
as long as the adjustment is not inconsistent with the terms of a collective-bargaining contract or agreement then in effect: Provided
further, That the bargaining representative has been given opportunity to be present at such adjustment.*

*Exclusive
Union Rep*

(b)   The Board shall decide in each case whether, in order to [in-
sure] assure to employees the [full benefit of their right to self-

organization and to collective bargaining, and otherwise to effectuate the policies of this Act,] *fullest freedom in exercising the rights guaranteed by this Act,* the unit appropriate for the purposes of collective bargaining shall be the employer unit, craft unit, plant unit, or subdivision thereof: *Provided, That the Board shall not (1) decide that any unit is appropriate for such purposes if such unit includes both professional employees and employees who are not professional employees unless a majority of such professional employees vote for inclusion in such unit; or (2) decide that any craft unit is inappropriate for such purposes on the ground that a different unit has been established by a prior Board determination, unless a majority of the employees in the proposed craft unit vote against separate representation or (3) decide that any unit is appropriate for such purposes if it includes, together with other employees, any individual employed as a guard to enforce against employees and other persons rules to protect property of the employer or to protect the safety of persons on the employer's premises; but no labor organization shall be certified as the representative of employees in a bargaining unit of guards if such organization admits to membership, or is affiliated directly or indirectly with an organization which admits to membership, employees other than guards.*

(c) [Whenever a question affecting commerce arises concerning the representation of employees, the Board may investigate such controversy and certify to the parties, in writing, the name or names of the representatives that have been designated or selected. In any such investigation, the Board shall provide for an appropriate hearing upon due notice, either in conjunction with a proceeding under section 10 or otherwise, and may take a secret ballot of employees, or utilize any other suitable method to ascertain [7] such representatives.]

(1) Whenever a petition shall have been filed, in accordance with such regulations as may be prescribed by the Board —

(A) by an employee or group of employees or any individual or labor organization acting in their behalf alleging that a substantial number of employees (i) wish to be represented for collective bargaining and that their employer declines to recognize their representative as the representative defined in section 9 (a), or (ii) assert that the individual or labor organization, which has been certified or is being currently recognized by their employer as the bargaining representative, is no longer a representative as defined in section 9 (a); or

(B) by an employer, alleging that one or more individuals or labor organizations have presented to him a claim to be recognized as the representative defined in section 9 (a);

the Board shall investigate such petition and if it has reasonable cause to believe that a question of representation affecting com-

[7] So in original.

merce exists shall provide for an appropriate hearing upon due notice. Such hearing may be conducted by an officer or employee of the regional office, who shall not make any recommendations with respect thereto. If the Board finds upon the record of such hearing that such a question of representation exists, it shall direct an election by secret ballot and shall certify the results thereof.

(2) In determining whether or not a question of representation affecting commerce exists, the same regulations and rules of decision shall apply irrespective of the identity of the persons filing the petition or the kind of relief sought and in no case shall the Board deny a labor organization a place on the ballot by reason of an order with respect to such labor organization or its predecessor not issued in conformity with section 10 (c).

(3) No election shall be directed in any bargaining unit or any subdivision within which, in the preceding twelve-month period, a valid election shall have been held. Employees on strike who are not entitled to reinstatement shall not be eligible to vote. In any election where none of the choices on the ballot receives a majority, a run-off shall be conducted, the ballot providing for a selection between the two choices receiving the largest and second largest number of valid votes cast in the election.

(4) Nothing in this section shall be construed to prohibit the waiving of hearings by stipulation for the purpose of a consent election in conformity with regulations and rules of decision of the Board.

(5) In determining whether a unit is appropriate for the purposes specified in subsection (b) the extent to which the employees have organized shall not be controlling.

(d) Whenever an order of the Board made pursuant to section 10 (c) is based in whole or in part upon facts certified following an investigation pursuant to subsection (c) of this section and there is a petition for the enforcement or review of such order, such certification and the record of such investigation shall be included in the transcript of the entire record required to be filed under subsection 10 (e) or 10 (f), and thereupon the decree of the court enforcing, modifying, or setting aside in whole or in part the order of the Board shall be made and entered upon the pleadings, testimony, and proceedings set forth in such transcript.

(e) [(1) *Upon the filing with the Board by a labor organization, which is the representative of employees as provided in section 9 (a), of a petition alleging that 30 per centum or more of the employees within a unit claimed to be appropriate for such purposes desire to authorize such labor organization to make an agreement with the employer of such employees requiring membership in such labor organization as a condition of employment in such unit, upon an appropriate showing thereof the Board shall, if no question of representation ex-*

ists, take a secret ballot of such employees, and shall certify the results thereof to such labor organization and to the employer.

(2) Upon the filing with the Board, by 30 per centum or more of the employees in a bargaining unit covered by an agreement between their employer and a labor organization made pursuant to section 8 (a) (3) (ii), of a petition alleging they desire that such authority be rescinded, the Board shall take a secret ballot of the employees in such unit, and shall certify the results therof to such labor organization and to the employer.] [8]

(1) Upon the filing with the Board, by 30 per centum or more of the employees in a bargaining unit covered by an agreement between their employer and a labor organization made pursuant to section 8(a)(3), of a petition alleging that they desire that such authority be rescinded, the Board shall take a secret ballot of the employees in such unit and certify the result thereof to such labor organization and to the employer. [9]

[3] (2) No election shall be conducted pursuant to this subsection in any bargaining unit or any subdivision within which, in the preceding twelve-month period, a valid election shall have been held.

(f) No investigation shall be made by the Board of any question affecting commerce concerning the representation of employees, raised by a labor organization under subsection (c) of this section, [no petition under section 9 (e) (1) shall be entertained,] [10] and no complaint shall be issued pursuant to a charge made by a labor organization under subsection (b) of section 10, unless such labor organization and any national or international labor organization of which such labor organization is an affiliate or constituent unit (A) shall have prior thereto filed with the Secretary of Labor copies of its constitution and bylaws and a report, in such form as the Secretary may prescribe, showing —

(1) The name of such labor organization and the address of its principal place of business;

(2) the names, titles, and compensation and allowances of its three principal officers and of any of its other officers or agents whose aggregate compensation and allowances for the preceding year exceeded $5,000, and the amount of the compensation and allowances paid to each such officer or agent during such year;

(3) the manner in which the officers and agents referred to in clause (2) were elected, appointed, or otherwise selected;

(4) the initiation fee or fees which new members are required to pay on becoming members of such labor organization;

(5) the regular dues or fees which members are required to pay

[8] The material in brackets, originally contained in the Labor Management Relations Act, 1947, was repealed by Public Law No. 189, 82d Cong., 1st Sess. (1951).

[9] The boldface material was added by Public Law No. 189 supra.

[10] See note 8 supra.

in order to remain members in good standing of such labor organization;

(6) a detailed statement of, or reference to provisions of its constitution and bylaws showing the procedure followed with respect to, (a) qualification for or restrictions on membership, (b) election of officers and stewards, (c) calling of regular and special meetings, (d) levying of assessments, (e) imposition of fines, (f) authorization for bargaining demands, (g) ratification of contract terms, (h) authorization for strikes, (i) authorization for disbursement of union funds, (j) audit of union financial transactions, (k) participation in insurance or other benefit plans, and (l) expulsion of members and the grounds therefor;
and (B) can show that prior thereto it has —

(1) filed with the Secretary of Labor, in such form as the Secretary may prescribe, a report showing all of (a) its receipts of any kind and the sources of such receipts, (b) its total assets and liabilities as of the end of its last fiscal year, (c) the disbursements made by it during such fiscal year, including the purposes for which made; and

(2) furnished to all of the members of such labor organization copies of the financial report required by paragraph (1) hereof to be filed with the Secretary of Labor.

(g) It shall be the obligation of all labor organizations to file annually with the Secretary of Labor, in such form as the Secretary of Labor may prescribe, reports bringing up to date the information required to be supplied in the initial filing by subsection (f) (A) of this section, and to file with the Secretary of Labor and furnish to its members anually financial reports in the form and manner prescribed in subsection (f) (B)... No labor organization shall be eligible for certification under this section as the representative of any employees, [no petition under section 9 (e) (1) shall be entertained,] [11] and no complaint shall issue under section 10 with respect to a charge filed by a labor organization unless it can show that it and any national or international labor organization of which it is an affiliate or constituent union has complied with its obligation under this subsection.

(h) No investigation shall be made by the Board of any question affecting commerce concerning the representation of employees, raised by a labor organization under subsection (c) of this section, [no petition under section 9 (e) (1) shall be entertained,] [12] and no complaint shall be issued pursuant to a charge made by a labor organization under subsection (b) of section 10, unless there is on file with the Board an affidavit executed contemporaneously or within the preced-

[11] The material in brackets, originally contained in the Labor Management Relations Act, 1947, was repealed by Public Law No. 189, 82d Cong., 1st Sess. (1951).

[12] See note 11 supra.

*ing twelve-month period by each officer of such labor organization
and the officers of any national or international labor organization of
which it is an affiliate or constituent unit that he is not a member of
the Communist Party or affiliated with such party, and that he does
not believe in, and is not a member of or supports any organization
that believes in or teaches, the overthrow of the United States Government by force or by any illegal or unconstitutional methods. The
provisions of section 35A of the Criminal Code shall be applicable in
respect to such affidavits.*

PREVENTION OF UNFAIR LABOR PRACTICES

SEC. 10 (a)   The Board is empowered, as hereinafter provided, to
prevent any persons from engaging in any unfair labor practice (listed
in section 8) affecting commerce. This power shall [be exclusive,
and shall] not be affected by any other means of adjustment or prevention that has been or may be established by agreement, law,
or otherwise: *Provided, That the Board is empowered by agreement
with any agency of any State or Territory to cede to such agency jurisdiction over any cases in any industry (other than mining, manufacturing, communications, and transportation except where predominantly local in character) even though such cases may involve
labor disputes affecting commerce, unless the provision of the State
or Territorial statute applicable to the determination of such cases by
such agency is inconsistent with the corresponding provision of this
Act or has received a construction inconsistent therewith.*

(b) Whenever it is charged that any person has engaged in or is
engaging in any such unfair labor practice, the Board, or any agent or
agency designated by the Board for such purposes, shall have power
to issue and cause to be served upon such person a complaint stating
the charges in that respect, and containing a notice of hearing before
the Board or a member thereof, or before a designated agent or
agency, at a place therein fixed, not less than five days after the serving of said complaint: *Provided, That no complaint shall issue based
upon any unfair labor practice occurring more than six months prior
to the filing of the charge with the Board and the service of a copy
thereof upon the person against whom such charge is made, unless the
person aggrieved thereby was prevented from filing such charge by
reason of service in the armed forces, in which event the six-month
period shall be computed from the day of his discharge.* Any such
complaint may be amended by the member, agent, or agency conducting the hearing or the Board in its discretion at any time prior to
the issuance of an order based thereon. The person so complained
of shall have the right to file an answer to the original or amended
complaint and to appear in person or otherwise and give testimony
at the place and time fixed in the complaint. In the discretion of the
member, agent, or agency conducting the hearing or the Board, any

other person may be allowed to intervene in the said proceeding and to present testimony. [In any such proceeding the rules of evidence prevailing in courts of law or equity shall not be controlling.] *Any such proceeding shall, so far as practicable, be conducted in accordance with the rules of evidence applicable in the district courts of the United States under the rules of civil procedure for the district courts of the United States, adopted by the Supreme Court of the United States pursuant to the Act of June 19, 1934 (U.S.C., title 28, secs. 723–B, 723–C).*

(c) The testimony taken by such member, agent, or agency or the Board shall be reduced to writing and filed with the Board. Thereafter, in its discretion, the Board upon notice may take further testimony or hear argument. If upon [all] *the preponderance of* the testimony taken the Board shall be of the opinion that any person named in the complaint has engaged in or is engaging in any such unfair labor practice, then the Board shall state its findings of fact and shall issue and cause to be served on such person an order requiring such person to cease and desist from such unfair labor practice, and to take such affirmative action, including reinstatement of employees with or without back pay, as will effectuate the policies of this Act: *Provided, That where an order directs reinstatement of an employee, back pay may be required of the employer or labor organization, as the case may be, responsible for the discrimination suffered by him: And provided further, That in determining whether a complaint shall issue alleging a violation of section 8 (a) (1) or section 8 (a) (2), and in deciding such cases, the same regulations and rules of decision shall apply irrespective of whether or not the labor organization affected is affiliated with a labor organization national or international in scope.* Such order may further require such person to make reports from time to time showing the extent to which it has complied with the order. If upon [all] *the preponderance of* the testimony taken the Board shall *not* be of the opinion that *the* [no] person named in the complaint has engaged in or is engaging in any such unfair labor practice, then the Board shall state its findings of fact and shall issue an order dismissing the said complaint. *No order of the Board shall require the reinstatement of any individual as an employee who has been suspended or discharged, or the payment to him of any back pay, if such individual was suspended or discharged for cause. In case the evidence is presented before a member of the Board, or before an examiner or examiners thereof, such member, or such examiner or examiners, as the case may be, shall issue and cause to be served on the parties to the proceedings a proposed report, together with a recommended order, which shall be filed with the Board, and if no exceptions are filed within twenty days after service thereof upon such parties, or within such further period as the Board may authorize, such recommended order shall become the order of the Board and become effective as therein prescribed.*

(d) Until a transcript of the record in a case shall have been filed in a court, as hereinafter provided, the Board may at any time, upon reasonable notice and in such manner as it shall deem proper, modify or set aside, in whole or in part, any finding or order made or issued by it.

(e) The Board shall have power to petition any circuit court of appeals of the United States (including the *United States* Court of Appeals [of] *for* the District of Columbia) , or if all the circuit courts of appeals to which application may be made are in vacation, any district court of the United States (including the [Supreme] *District* Court of the *United States for the* District of Columbia) , within any circuit or district, respectively, wherein the unfair labor practice in question occurred or wherein such person resides or transacts business, for the enforcement of such order and for appropriate temporary relief or restraining order, and shall certify and file in the court a transcript of the entire record in the proceedings, including the pleadings and testimony upon which such order was entered and the findings and order of the Board. Upon such filing, the court shall cause notice thereof to be served upon such person, and thereupon shall have jurisdiction of the proceeding and of the question determined therein, and shall have power to grant such temporary relief or restraining order as it deems just and proper, and to make and enter upon the pleadings, testimony, and proceedings set forth in such transcript a decree enforcing, modifying, and enforcing as so modified, or setting aside in whole or in part the order of the Board. No objection that has not been urged before the Board, its member, agent, or agency, shall be considered by the court unless the failure or neglect to urge such objection shall be excused because of extraordinary circumstances. The findings of the Board [as to the facts,] *with respect to questions of fact* if supported by *substantial* evidence [,] *on the record considered as a whole* shall be conclusive. If either party shall apply to the court for leave to adduce additional evidence and shall show to the satisfaction of the court that such additional evidence is material and that there were reasonable grounds for the failure to adduce such evidence in the hearing before the Board, its member, agent, or agency, the court may order such additional evidence to be taken before the Board, its members, agent, or agency, and to be made a part of the transcript. The Board may modify its findings as to the facts, or make new findings, by reason of additional evidence so taken and filed, and it shall file such modified or new findings, which [,] *findings with respect to questions of fact* if supported by *substantial* evidence, *on the record considered as a whole* shall be conclusive, and shall file its recommendations, if any, for the modification or setting aside of its original order. The jurisdiction of the court shall be exclusive and its judgment and decree shall be final, except that the same shall be subject to review by the appropriate circuit court of appeals if application was made to the district court as hereinabove provided, and by the Supreme Court of the United States upon writ of certiorari or certification as provided in sections 239 and 240 of the Judicial Code, as amended (U.S.C., title 28, secs. 346 and 347).

(f) Any person aggrieved by a final order of the Board granting or denying in whole or in part the relief sought may obtain a review of such order in any circuit court of appeals of the United States in the circuit wherein the unfair labor practice in question was alleged to have been engaged in or wherein such person resides or transacts business, or in the *United States* Court of Appeals [of] *for* the District of Columbia, by filing in such court a written petition praying that the order of the Board be modified or set aside. A copy of such petition shall be forthwith served upon the Board, and thereupon the aggrieved party shall file in the court a transcript of the entire record in the proceeding, certified by the Board, including the pleading and testimony upon which the order complained of was entered, and the findings and order of the Board. Upon such filing, the court shall proceed in the same manner as in the case of an application by the Board under subsection (e), and shall have the same exclusive jurisdiction to grant to the Board such temporary relief or restraining order as it deems just and proper, and in like manner to make and enter a decree enforcing, modifying, and enforcing as so modified, or setting aside in whole or in part the order of the Board; [and] the findings of the Board [as to the facts,] *with respect to questions of fact* if supported by *substantial* evidence [,] *on the record considered as a whole* shall in like manner be conclusive.

(g) The commencement of proceedings under subsection (e) or (f) of this section shall not, unless specifically ordered by the court, operate as a stay of the Board's order.

(h) When granting appropriate temporary relief or a restraining order, or making and entering a decree enforcing, modifying, and enforcing as so modified, or setting aside in whole or in part an order of the Board, as provided in this section, the jurisdiction of courts sitting in equity shall not be limited by the Act entitled "An Act to amend the Judicial Code and to define and limit the jurisdiction of courts sitting in equity, and for other purposes," approved March 23, 1932 (U.S.C., Supp. VII, title 29, secs. 101–115).

(i) Petitions filed under this Act shall be heard expeditiously, and if possible within ten days after they have been docketed.

(j) *The Board shall have power, upon issuance of a complaint as provided in subsection (b) charging that any person has engaged in or is engaging in an unfair labor practice, to petition any district court of the United States (including the District Court of the United States for the District of Columbia), within any district wherein the unfair labor practice in question is alleged to have occurred or wherein such person resides or transacts business, for appropriate temporary relief or restraining order. Upon the filing of any such petition the court shall cause notice thereof to be served upon such person, and thereupon shall have jurisdiction to grant to the Board such temporary relief or restraining order as it deems just and proper.*

(k) Whenever it is charged that any person has engaged in an unfair labor practice within the meaning of paragraph (4) (D) of section 8 (b), the Board is empowered and directed to hear and determine the dispute out of which such unfair labor practice shall have arisen, unless, within ten days after notice that such charge has been filed, the parties to such dispute submit to the Board satisfactory evidence that they have adjusted, or agreed upon methods for the voluntary adjustment of the dispute. Upon compliance by the parties to the dispute with the decision of the Board or upon such voluntary adjustment of the dispute, such charge shall be dismissed.

(l) Whenever it is charged that any person has engaged in an unfair labor practice within the meaning of paragraph (4) (A), (B), or (C) of section 8 (b), the preliminary investigation of such charge shall be made forthwith and given priority over all other cases except cases of like character in the office where it is filed or to which it is referred. If, after such investigation, the officer or regional attorney to whom the matter may be referred has reasonable cause to believe such charge is true and that a complaint should issue, he shall, on behalf of the Board, petition any district court of the United States (including the District Court of the United States for the District of Columbia) within any district where the unfair labor practice in question has occurred, is alleged to have occurred, or wherein such person resides or transacts business, for appropriate injunctive relief pending the final adjudication of the Board with respect to such matter. Upon the filing of any such petition the district court shall have jurisdiction to grant such injunctive relief or temporary restraining order as it deems just and proper, notwithstanding any other provision of law: Provided further, That no temporary restraining order shall be issued without notice unless a petition alleges that substantial and irreparable injury to the charging party will be unavoidable and such temporary restraining order shall be effective for no longer than five days and will become void at the expiration of such period. Upon filing of any such petition the courts shall cause notice thereof to be served upon any person involved in the charge and such person, including the charging party, shall be given an opportunity to appear by counsel and present any relevant testimony: Provided further, That for the purposes of this subsection district courts shall be deemed to have jurisdiction of a labor organization (1) in the district in which such organization maintains its principal office, or (2) in any district in which its duly authorized officers or agents are engaged in promoting or protecting the interests of employee members. The service of legal process upon such officer or agent shall constitute service upon the labor organization and make such organization a party to the suit.

In situations where such relief is appropriate the procedure specified herein shall apply to charges with respect to section 8 (b) (4) (D).

Sec. 11.   For the purpose of all hearings and investigations, which, in the opinion of the Board, are necessary and proper for the exercise of the powers vested in it by section 9 and section 10 —

(1) The Board, or its duly authorized agents or agencies, shall at all reasonable times have access to, for the purpose of examination, and the right to copy any evidence of any person being investigated or proceeded against that relates to any matter under investigation or in question.   [Any member of the Board shall have power to issue subpenas.]   *The Board, or any member thereof, shall upon application of any party to such proceedings, forthwith issue to such party subpenas* requiring the attendance and testimony of witnesses [and] *or* the production of any evidence [that relates to any matter under investigation or in question, before the Board, its member, agent, or agency conducting the hearing or investigation.] *in such proceeding or investigation requested in such application.   Within five days after the service of a subpena on any person requiring the production of any evidence in his possession or under his control, such person may petition the Board to revoke, and the Board shall revoke, such subpena if in its opinion the evidence whose production is required does not relate to any matter under investigation, or any matter in question in such proceedings, or if in its opinion such subpena does not describe with sufficient particularity the evidence whose production is required.* Any member of the Board, or any agent or agency designated by the Board for such purposes, may administer oaths and affirmations, examine witnesses, and receive evidence.   Such attendance of witnesses and the production of such evidence may be required from any place in the United States or any Territory or possession thereof, at any designated place of hearing.

(2) In case of contumacy or refusal to obey a subpena issued to any person, any district court of the United States or the United States courts of any Territory or possession, or the [Supreme] *District* Court of the *United States for the* District of Columbia, within the jurisdiction of which the inquiry is carried on or within the jurisdiction of which said person guilty of contumacy or refusal to obey is found or resides or transacts business, upon application by the Board shall have jurisdiction to issue to such person an order requiring such person to appear before the Board, its member, agent, or agency, there to produce evidence if so ordered, or there to give testimony touching the matter under investigation or in question; and any failure to obey such order of the court may be punished by said court as a contempt thereof.

(3) No person shall be excused from attending and testifying or

from producing books, records, correspondence, documents, or other evidence in obedience to the subpena of the Board, on the ground that the testimony or evidence required of him may tend to incriminate him or subject him to a penalty or forfeiture; but no individual shall be prosecuted or subjected to any penalty or forfeiture for or on account of any transaction, matter, or thing concerning which he is compelled, after having claimed his privilege against self-incrimination, to testify or produce evidence, except that such individual so testifying shall not be exempt from prosecution and punishment for perjury committed in so testifying.

(4) Complaints, orders, and other process and papers of the Board, its member, agent, or agency, may be served either personally or by registered mail or by telegraph or by leaving a copy thereof at the principal office or place of business of the person required to be served. The verified return by the individual so serving the same setting forth the manner of such service shall be proof of the same, and the return post office receipt or telegraph receipt therefor when registered and mailed or telegraphed as aforesaid shall be proof of service of the same. Witnesses summoned before the Board, its member, agent, or agency, shall be paid the same fees and mileage that are paid witnesses in the courts of the United States, and witnesses whose depositions are taken and the persons taking the same shall severally be entitled to the same fees as are paid for like services in the courts of the United States.

(5) All process of any court to which application may be made under this Act may be served in the judicial district wherein the defendant or other person required to be served resides or may be found.

(6) The several departments and agencies of the Government, when directed by the President, shall furnish the Board, upon its request, all records, papers, and information in their possession relating to any matter before the Board.

Sec. 12. Any person who shall willfully resist, prevent, impede, or interfere with any member of the Board or any of its agents or agencies in the performance of duties pursuant to this Act shall be punished by a fine of not more than $5,000 or by imprisonment for not more than one year, or both.

LIMITATIONS

Sec. 13. Nothing in this Act, *except as specifically provided for herein,* shall be construed so as *either* to interfere with or impede or diminish in any way the right to strike, *or to affect the limitations or qualifications on that right.*

Sec. 14. [Wherever the application of the provisions of section 7 (a) of the National Industrial Recovery Act (U.S.C., Supp. VII, title 15, sec. 707 (a)), as amended from time to time, or of section 77B, paragraphs (l) and (m) of the Act approved June 7, 1934, entitled

"An Act to amend an Act entitled 'An Act to establish a uniform system of bankruptcy throughout the United States' approved July 1, 1898, and Acts amendatory thereof and supplementary thereto" (48 Stat. 922, pars. (1) and (m)), as amended from time to time, or of Public Resolution Numbered 44, approved June 19, 1934 (48 Stat. 1183), conflicts with the application of the provisions of this Act, this Act shall prevail: Provided, That in any situation where the provisions of this Act cannot be validly enforced, the provisions of such other Acts shall remain in full force and effect.]

(a) *Nothing herein shall prohibit any individual employed as a supervisor from becoming or remaining a member of a labor organization, but no employer subject to this Act shall be compelled to deem individuals defined herein as supervisors as employees for the purpose of any law, either national or local, relating to collective bargaining.*

(b) *Nothing in this Act shall be construed as authorizing the execution or application of agreements requiring membership in a labor organization as a condition of employment in any State or Territory in which such execution or application is prohibited by State or Territorial law.*

SEC. 15. *Wherever the application of the provisions of section 272 of chapter 10 of the Act entitled "An Act to establish a uniform system of bankruptcy throughout the United States," approved July 1, 1898, and Acts amendatory thereof and supplementary thereto (U.S.C., title 11, sec. 672), conflicts with the application of the provisions of this Act, this Act shall prevail: Provided, That in any situation where the provisions of this Act cannot be validly enforced, the provisions of such other Acts shall remain in full force and effect.*

[SEC. 15.] SEC. 16. If any provision of this Act, or the application of such provision to any person or circumstances, shall be held invalid, the remainder of this Act, or the application of such provision to persons or circumstances other than those as to which it is held invalid, shall not be affected thereby.

[SEC. 16.] SEC. 17. This Act may be cited as the "National Labor Relations Act."

Sec. 18. No petition entertained, no investigation made, no election held, and no certification issued by the National Labor Relations Board, under any of the provisions of section 9 of the National Labor Relations Act, as amended, shall be invalid by reason of the failure of the Congress of Industrial Organizations to have complied with the requirements of section 9(f), (g), or (h) of the aforesaid Act prior to December 22, 1949, or by reason of the failure of the American Federation of Labor to have complied with the provisions of section 9(f), (g), or (h) of the aforesaid Act prior to November 7, 1947: *Provided,* That no liability shall be imposed under any provisions of this Act upon any person for failure to honor any election or certificate referred to above, prior to the effective date of this amendment: *Provided, however,* That this proviso shall not have the effect of setting

aside or in any way affecting judgments or decrees heretofore entered under section 10(e) or (f) and which have become final.[13]

EFFECTIVE DATE OF CERTAIN CHANGES

Sec. 102.   No provision of this title shall be deemed to make an unfair labor practice any act which was performed prior to the date of the enactment of this Act which did not constitute an unfair labor practice prior thereto, and the provisions of section 8 (a) (3) and section 8 (b) (2) of the National Labor Relations Act as amended by this title shall not make an unfair labor practice the performance of any obligation under a collective bargaining agreement entered into prior to the date of the enactment of this Act, or (in the case of an agreement for a period of not more than one year) entered into on or after such date of enactment, but prior to the effective date of this title, if the performance of such obligation would not have constituted an unfair labor practice under section 8 (3) of the National Labor Relations Act prior to the effective date of this title, unless such agreement was renewed or extended subsequent thereto.

Sec. 103.   No provisions of this title shall affect any certification of representatives or any determination as to the appropriate collective bargaining unit, which was made under section 9 of the National Labor Relations Act prior to the effective date of this title until one year after the date of such certification or if, in respect of any such certification, a collective bargaining contract was entered into prior to the effective date of this title, until the end of the contract period or until one year after such date, whichever first occurs.

Sec. 104.   The amendments made by this title shall take effect sixty days after the date of the enactment of this Act, except that the authority of the President to appoint certain officers conferred upon him by section 3 of the National Labor Relations Act as amended by this title may be exercised forthwith.

TITLE II

Conciliation of Labor Disputes in Industries Affecting Commerce; National Emergencies

SEC. 201.   That it is the policy of the United States that —

(a) sound and stable industrial peace and the advancement of the general welfare, health, and safety of the Nation and of the best interests of employers and employees can most satisfactorily be secured by the settlement of issues between employers and employees through the processes of conference and collective bargaining between employers and the representatives of their employees;

---

[13] This section was added by Public Law No. 189, 82d Cong., 1st Sess. (1951).

(b) the settlement of issues between employers and employees through collective bargaining may be advanced by making available full and adequate governmental facilities for conciliation, mediation, and voluntary arbitration to aid and encourage employers and the representatives of their employees to reach and maintain agreements concerning rates of pay, hours, and working conditions, and to make all reasonable efforts to settle their differences by mutual agreement reached through conferences and collective bargaining or by such methods as may be provided for in any applicable agreement for the settlement of disputes; and

(c) certain controversies which arise between parties to collective bargaining agreements may be avoided or minimized by making available full and adequate governmental facilities for furnishing assistance to employers and the representatives of their employees in formulating for inclusion within such agreements provision for adequate notice of any proposed changes in the terms of such agreements, for the final adjustment of grievances or questions regarding the application or interpretation of such agreements, and other provisions designed to prevent the subsequent arising of such controversies.

Sec. 202 (a)   There is hereby created an independent agency to be known as the Federal Mediation and Conciliation Service (herein referred to as the "Service," except that for sixty days after the date of the enactment of this Act such term shall refer to the Conciliation Service of the Department of Labor). The Service shall be under the direction of a Federal Mediation and Conciliation Director (hereinafter referred to as the "Director"), who shall be appointed by the President by and with the advice and consent of the Senate. The Director shall receive compensation at the rate of $12,000[14] per annum. The Director shall not engage in any other business, vocation, or employment.

(b) The Director is authorized, subject to the civil-service laws, to appoint such clerical and other personnel as may be necessary for the execution of the functions of the Service, and shall fix their compensation in accordance with the Classification Act of 1923, as amended, and may, without regard to the provisions of the civil-service laws and the Classification Act of 1923, as amended, appoint and fix the compensation of such conciliators and mediators as may be necessary to carry out the functions of the Service. The Director is authorized to make such expenditures for supplies, facilities, and services as he deems necessary. Such expenditures shall be allowed and paid upon presentation of itemized vouchers therefor approved by the Director or by any employee designated by him for that purpose.

(c) The principal office of the Service shall be in the District of Columbia, but the Director may establish regional offices convenient

[14] This rate of compensation has been increased to $16,000 (63 Stat. 880).

to localities in which labor controversies are likely to arise. The Director may by order, subject to revocation at any time, delegate any authority and discretion conferred upon him by this Act to any regional director, or other officer or employee of the Service. The Director may establish suitable procedures for cooperation with State and local mediation agencies. The Director shall make an annual report in writing to Congress at the end of the fiscal year.

(d) All mediation and conciliation functions of the Secretary of Labor or the United States Conciliation Service under section 8 of the Act entitled "An Act to create a Department of Labor," approved March 4, 1913 (U.S.C., title 29, sec. 51), and all functions of the United States Conciliation Service under any other law are hereby transferred to the Federal Mediation and Conciliation Service, together with the personnel and records of the United States Conciliation Service. Such transfer shall take effect upon the sixtieth day after the date of enactment of this Act. Such transfer shall not affect any proceedings pending before the United States Conciliation Service or any certification, order, rule, or regulation theretofore made by it or by the Secretary of Labor. The Director and the Service shall not be subject in any way to the jurisdiction or authority of the Secretary of Labor or any official or division of the Department of Labor.

FUNCTIONS OF THE SERVICE

SEC. 203 (a)   It shall be the duty of the Service, in order to prevent or minimize interruptions of the free flow of commerce growing out of labor disputes, to assist parties to labor disputes in industries affecting commerce to settle such disputes through conciliation and mediation.

(b) The Service may proffer its services in any labor disputes in any industry affecting commerce, either upon its own motion or upon the request of one or more of the parties to the dispute, whenever in its judgment such dispute threatens to cause a substantial interruption of commerce. The Director and the Service are directed to avoid attempting to mediate disputes which would have only a minor effect on interstate commerce if State or other conciliation services are available to the parties. Whenever the Service does proffer its services in any dispute, it shall be the duty of the Service promptly to put itself in communication with the parties and to use its best efforts, by mediation and conciliation, to bring them to agreement.

(c) If the Director is not able to bring the parties to agreement by conciliation within a reasonable time, he shall seek to induce the parties voluntarily to seek other means of settling the dispute without resort to strike, lock-out, or other coercion, including submission to the employees in the bargaining unit of the employer's last offer to settlement for approval or rejection in a secret ballot. The failure or refusal of either party to agree to any procedure suggested by the Director shall not be deemed a violation of any duty or obligation imposed by this Act.

(d) Final adjustment by a method agreed upon by the parties is hereby declared to be the desirable method for settlement of grievance disputes arising over the application or interpretation of an existing collective bargaining agreement. The Service is directed to make its conciliation and mediation services available in the settlement of such grievance disputes only as a last resort and in exceptional cases.

SEC. 204 (a) In order to prevent or minimize interruptions of the free flow of commerce growing out of labor disputes, employers and employees and their representatives, in any industry affecting commerce, shall —

(1) exert every reasonable effort to make and maintain agreements concerning rates of pay, hours, and working conditions, including provision for adequate notice of any proposed change in the terms of such agreements;

(2) whenever a dispute arises over the terms or application of a collective bargaining agreement and a conference is requested by a party or prospective party thereto, arrange promptly for such a conference to be held and endeavor in such conference to settle such dispute expeditiously; and

(3) in case such dispute is not settled by conference, participate fully and promptly in such meetings as may be undertaken by the Service under this Act for the purpose of aiding in a settlement of the dispute.

SEC. 205 (a) There is hereby created a National Labor-Management Panel which shall be composed of twelve members appointed by the President, six of whom shall be selected from among persons outstanding in the field of management and six of whom shall be selected from among persons outstanding in the field of labor. Each member shall hold office for a term of three years, except that any member appointed to fill a vacancy occurring prior to the expiration of the term for which his predecessor was appointed shall be appointed for the remainder of such term, and the terms of office of the members first taking office shall expire, as designated by the President at the time of appointment, four at the end of the first year, four at the end of the second year, and four at the end of the third year after the date of appointment. Members of the panel, when serving on business of the panel, shall be paid compensation at the rate of $25 per day, and shall also be entitled to receive an allowance for actual and necessary travel and subsistence expenses while so serving away from their places of residence.

(b) It shall be the duty of the panel, at the request of the Director, to advise in the avoidance of industrial controversies and the manner in which mediation and voluntary adjustment shall be administered, particularly with reference to controversies affecting the general welfare of the country.

NATIONAL EMERGENCIES

SEC. 206. Whenever in the opinion of the President of the United States, a threatened or actual strike or lock-out affecting an entire industry or a substantial part thereof engaged in trade, commerce, transportation, transmission, or communication among the several States or with foreign nations, or engaged in the production of goods for commerce, will, if permitted to occur or to continue, imperil the national health or safety, he may appoint a board of inquiry to inquire into the issues involved in the dispute and to make a written report to him within such time as he shall prescribe. Such report shall include a statement of the facts with respect to the dispute, including each party's statement of its position but shall not contain any recommendations. The President shall file a copy of such report with the Service and shall make its contents available to the public.

SEC. 207 (a) A board of inquiry shall be composed of a chairman and such other members as the President shall determine, and shall have power to sit and act in any place within the United States and to conduct such hearings either in public or in private, as it may deem necessary or proper, to ascertain the facts with respect to the causes and circumstances of the dispute.

(b) Members of a board of inquiry shall receive compensation at the rate of $50 for each day actually spent by them in the work of the board, together with necessary travel and subsistence expenses.

(c) For the purpose of any hearing or inquiry conducted by any board appointed under this title, the provisions of sections 9 and 10 (relating to the attendance of witnesses and the production of books, papers, and documents) of the Federal Trade Commission Act of September 16, 1914, as amended (U.S.C. 19, title 15, secs. 49 and 50, as amended), are hereby made applicable to the powers and duties of such board.

SEC. 208 (a) Upon receiving a report from a board of inquiry the President may direct the Attorney General to petition any district court of the United States having jurisdiction of the parties to enjoin such strike or lock-out or the continuing thereof, and if the court finds that such threatened or actual strike or lock-out —

(i) affects an entire industry or a substantial part thereof engaged in trade, commerce, transportation, transmission, or communication among the several States or with foreign nations, or engaged in the production of goods for commerce; and

(ii) if permitted to occur or to continue, will imperil the national health or safety, it shall have jurisdiction to enjoin any such strike or lock-out, or the continuing thereof, and to make such other orders as may be appropriate.

(b) In any case, the provisions of the Act of March 23, 1932, entitled "An Act to amend the Judicial Code and to define and limit the jurisdiction of courts sitting in equity, and for other purposes," shall not be applicable.

(c) The order or orders of the court shall be subject to review by the appropriate circuit court of appeals and by the Supreme Court upon writ of certiorari or certification as provided in sections 239 and 240 of the Judicial Code, as amended (U.S.C., title 29, secs. 346 and 347).

SEC. 209 (a). Whenever a district court has issued an order under section 208 enjoining acts or practices which imperil or threaten to imperil the national health or safety, it shall be the duty of the parties to the labor dispute giving rise to such order to make every effort to adjust and settle their differences, with the assistance of the Service created by this Act. Neither party shall be under any duty to accept, in whole or in part, any proposal of settlement made by the Service.

(b) Upon the issuance of such order, the President shall reconvene the board of inquiry which has previously reported with respect to the dispute. At the end of a sixty-day period (unless the dispute has been settled by that time), the board of inquiry shall report to the President the current position of the parties and the efforts which have been made for settlement, and shall include a statement by each party of its position and a statement of the employer's last offer of settlement. The President shall make such report available to the public. The National Labor Relations Board, within the succeeding fifteen days, shall take a secret ballot of the employees of each employer involved in the dispute on the question of whether they wish to accept the final offer of settlement made by their employer as stated by him and shall certify the results thereof to the Attorney General within five days thereafter.

SEC. 210. Upon the certification of the results of such ballot or upon a settlement being reached, whichever happens sooner, the Attorney General shall move the court to discharge the injunction, which motion shall then be granted and the injunction discharged. When such motion is granted, the President shall submit to the Congress a full and comprehensive report of the proceedings, including the findings of the board of inquiry and the ballot taken by the National Labor Relations Board, together with such recommendations as he may see fit to make for consideration and appropriate action.

COMPILATION OF COLLECTIVE BARGAINING AGREEMENTS, ETC.

SEC. 211 (a) For the guidance and information of interested representatives of employers, employees, and the general public, the Bureau of Labor Statistics of the Department of Labor shall maintain a file of copies of all available collective bargaining agreements and other available agreements and actions thereunder settling or adjusting labor disputes.   Such file shall be open to inspection under appropriate conditions prescribed by the Secretary of Labor, except that no specific information submitted in confidence shall be disclosed.

(b) The Bureau of Labor Statistics in the Department of Labor is authorized to furnish upon request of the Service, or employers, employees, or their representatives, all available data and factual information which may aid in the settlement of any labor dispute, except that no specific information submitted in confidence shall be disclosed.

EXEMPTION OF RAILWAY LABOR ACT

SEC. 212.   The provisions of this title shall not be applicable with respect to any matter which is subject to the provisions of the Railway Labor Act, as amended from time to time.

TITLE III

SUITS BY AND AGAINST LABOR ORGANIZATIONS

SEC. 301 (a) Suits for violation of contracts between an employer and a labor organization representing employees in an industry affecting commerce as defined in this Act, or between any such labor organizations, may be brought in any district court of the United States having jurisdiction of the parties, without respect to the amount in controversy or without regard to the citizenship of the parties.

(b) Any labor organization which represents employees in an industry affecting commerce as defined in this Act and any employer whose activities affect commerce as defined in this Act shall be bound by the acts of its agents.   Any such labor organization may sue or be sued as an entity and in behalf of the employees whom it represents in the courts of the United States.   Any money judgment against a labor organization in a district court of the United States shall be enforceable only against the organization as an entity and against its assets, and shall not be enforceable against any individual member or his assets.

(c) For the purposes of actions and proceedings by or against labor organizations in the district courts of the United States, district courts shall be deemed to have jurisdiction of a labor organization (1) in the district in which such organization maintains its principal office, or (2) in any district in which its duly authorized officers or agents are engaged in representing or acting for employee members.

(d) The service of summons, subpoena, or other legal process of any court of the United States upon an officer or agent of a labor organization, in his capacity as such, shall constitute service upon the labor organization.

(e) For the purposes of this section, in determining whether any person is acting as an "agent" of another person so as to make such

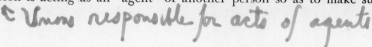
Unions responsible for acts of agents

other person responsible for his acts, the question of whether the specific acts performed were actually authorized or subsequently ratified shall not be controlling.

RESTRICTIONS ON PAYMENTS TO EMPLOYEE
REPRESENTATIVES

SEC. 302 (a) It shall be unlawful for any employer to pay or deliver, or to agree to pay or deliver, any money or other thing of value to any representative of any of his employees who are employed in an industry affecting commerce.

(b) It shall be unlawful for any representative of any employees who are employed in an industry affecting commerce to receive or accept, or to agree to receive or accept, from the employer of such employees any money or other thing of value.

(c) The provisions of this section shall not be applicable (1) with respect to any money or other thing of value payable by an employer to any representative who is an employee or former employee of such employer, as compensation for, or by reason of, his services as an employee of such employer; (2) with respect to the payment or delivery of any money or other thing of value in satisfaction of a judgment of any court or a decision or award of an arbitrator or impartial chairman or in compromise, adjustment, settlement or release of any claim, complaint, grievance, or dispute in the absence of fraud or duress; (3) with respect to the sale or purchase of an article or commodity at the prevailing market price in the regular course of business; (4) with respect to money deducted from the wages of employees in payment of membership dues in a labor organization: *Provided,* That the employer has received from each employee, on whose account such deductions are made, a written assignment which shall not be irrevocable for a period of more than one year, or beyond the termination date of the applicable collective agreement, whichever occurs sooner; or (5) with respect to money or other thing of value paid to a trust fund established by such representative, for the sole and exclusive benefit of the employees of such employer, and their families and dependents (or of such employees, families, and dependents jointly with the employees of other employers making similar payments, and their families and dependents) : *Provided,* That (A) such payments are held in trust for the purpose of paying, either from principal or income or both, for the benefit of employees, their families and dependents, for medical or hospital care, pensions on retirement or death of employees, compensation for injuries or illness resulting from occupational activity or insurance to provide any of the foregoing, or unemployment benefits or life insurance, disability and sickness insurance, or accident insurance; (B) the detailed basis on which such payments are to be made is specified in a written agreement with the employer, and employees and employers are equally represented in the administration of such fund, together with such neutral persons as the representatives of the employers and the representatives of the employees may agree upon and in the event the employer and employee groups deadlock on the administration of such fund and there are no neutral persons empowered to break such deadlock, such agreement provides that the two groups shall agree on an impartial umpire to decide such dispute, or in event of their failure to agree within a reasonable length of time, an impartial umpire to decide such dispute shall, on petition of either group, be appointed by the district court of the United States for the district where the trust fund has its principal office, and shall also contain provisions for an annual audit of the trust fund, a statement of the results of which shall be available for inspection by interested persons at the principal office of the trust fund and at such other places as may be designated in such written agreement; and (C) such payments as are intended to be used for the purpose of providing pensions or annuities for employees are made to a separate trust which provides that the funds held therein cannot be used for any purpose other than paying such pensions or annuities.

(d) Any person who willfully violates any of the provisions of this section shall, upon conviction thereof, be guilty of a misdemeanor and be subject to a fine of not more than $10,000 or to imprisonment for not more than one year, or both.

(e) The district courts of the United States and the United States courts of the Territories and possessions shall have jurisdiction, for cause shown, and subject to the provisions of section 17 (relating to notice to opposite party) of the Act entitled "An Act to supplement existing laws against unlawful restraints and monopolies, and for other purposes," approved October 15, 1914, as amended (U.S.C., title 28, sec. 381), to restrain violations of this section, without regard to the provisions of section 6 and 20 of such Act of October 15, 1914, as amended (U.S.C., title 15, sec. 17, and title 29, sec. 52), and the provisions of the Act entitled "An Act to amend the Judicial Code and to define and limit the jurisdiction of courts sitting in equity, and for other purposes," approved March 23, 1932 (U.S.C., title 29, secs. 101–115).

(f) This section shall not apply to any contract in force on the date of enactment of this Act, until the expiration of such contract, or until July 1, 1948, whichever first occurs.

(g) Compliance with the restrictions contained in subsection (c) (5) (B) upon contributions to trust funds, otherwise lawful, shall not be applicable to contributions to such trust funds established by collective agreement prior to January 1, 1946, nor shall subsection (c) (5) (A) be construed as prohibiting contributions to such trust funds if prior to January 1, 1947, such funds contained provisions for pooled vacation benefits.

BOYCOTTS AND OTHER UNLAWFUL COMBINATIONS

Sec. 303 (a) It shall be unlawful, for the purposes of this section only, in an industry or activity affecting commerce, for any labor organization to engage in, or to induce or encourage the employees of any employer to engage in, a strike or a concerted refusal in the course of their employment to use, manufacture, process, transport, or otherwise handle or work on any goods, articles, materials, or commodities or to perform any services, where an object thereof is —

(1) forcing or requiring any employer or self-employed person to join any labor or employer organization or any employer or other person to cease using, selling, handling, transporting, or otherwise dealing in the products of any other producer, processor, or manufacturer, or to cease doing business with any other person;

(2) forcing or requiring any other employer to recognize or bargain with a labor organization as the representative of his employees unless such labor organization has been certified as the representative of such employees under the provisions of section 9 of the National Labor Relations Act;

(3) forcing or requiring any employer to recognize or bargain with a particular labor organization as the representative of his employees if another labor organization has been certified as the representative of such employees under the provisions of section 9 of the National Labor Relations Act;

(4) forcing or requiring any employer to assign particular work to employees in a particular labor organization or in a particular trade, craft, or class rather than to employees in another labor organization or in another trade, craft, or class unless such employer is failing to conform to an order or certification of the National Labor Relations Board determining the bargaining representative for employees performing such work. Nothing contained in this subsection shall be construed to make unlawful a refusal by any person to enter upon the premises of any employer (other than his own employer), if the employees of such employer are engaged in a strike ratified or approved by a representative of such employees whom such employer is required to recognize under the National Labor Relations Act.

(b) Whoever shall be injured in his business or property by reason or any violation of subsection (a) may sue therefor in any district court of the United States subject to the limitations and provisions of section 301 hereof without respect to the amount in controversy, or in any other court having jurisdiction of the parties, and shall recover the damages by him sustained and the cost of the suit.

RESTRICTION ON POLITICAL CONTRIBUTIONS

SEC. 304. Section 313 of the Federal Corrupt Practices Act, 1925 (U.S.C., 1940 edition, title 2, sec. 251; Supp. V, title 50, App., sec. 1509), as amended, is amended to read as follows:

SEC. 313. It is unlawful for any national bank, or any corporation organized by authority of any law of Congress, to make a contribution or expenditure in connection with any election to any political office, or in connection with any primary election or political convention or caucus held to select candidates for any political office, or for any corporation whatever, or any labor organization to make a contribution or expenditure in connection with any election at which Presidential and Vice Presidential electors or a Senator or Representative in, or a Delegate or Resident Commissioner to Congress are to be voted for, or in connection with any primary election or political convention or caucus held to select candidates for any of the foregoing offices, for any candidate, political committee, or other person to accept or receive any contribution prohibited by this section. Every corporation or labor organization which makes any contribution or expenditure in violation of this section shall be fined not more than $5,000; and every officer or director of any corporation, or officer of any labor organization, who consents to any contribution or expenditure by the corporation or labor organization, as the case may be, in violation of this section shall be fined not more than $1,000 or imprisoned for not more than one year, or both. For the purposes of this section 'labor organization' means any organization of any kind, or any agency or employee representation committee or plan, in which employees participate and which exists for the purpose, in whole or in part, of dealing with employers concerning grievances, labor disputes, wages, rates of pay, hours of employment, or conditions of work."

STRIKES BY GOVERNMENT EMPLOYEES

SEC. 305. It shall be unlawful for any individual employed by the United States or any agency thereof including wholly owned Government corporations to participate in any strike. Any individual employed by the United States or by any such agency who strikes shall be discharged immediately from his employment, and shall forfeit his civil service status, if any, and shall not be eligible for reemployment for three years by the United States or any such agency.

TITLE IV

Creation of Joint Committee to Study and Report on Basic Problems Affecting Friendly Labor Relations and Productivity

SEC. 401. There is hereby established a joint congressional committee to be known as the Joint Committee on Labor-Management Relations (hereafter referred to as the committee), and to be composed of seven Members of the Senate Committee on Labor and Public Welfare, to be appointed by the President pro tempore of the Senate, and seven Members of the House of Representatives Committee on Education and Labor, to be appointed by the Speaker of the House of Representatives. A vacancy in membership of the committee shall not affect the powers of the remaining members to execute the functions of the committee, and shall be filled in the same manner as the original selection. The committee shall select a chairman and a vice chairman from among its members.

SEC. 402. The committee, acting as a whole or by subcommittee, shall conduct a thorough study and investigation of the entire field of labor-management relations, including but not limited to —

(1) the means by which permanent friendly cooperation between employers and employees and stability of labor relations may be secured throughout the United States;

(2) the means by which the individual employee may achieve a greater productivity and higher wages, including plans for guaranteed annual wages, incentive profit-sharing and bonus systems;

(3) the internal organization and administration of labor unions, with special attention to the impact on individuals of collective agreements requiring membership in unions as a condition of employment;

(4) the labor relations policies and practices of employers and associations of employers;

(5) the desirability of welfare funds for the benefit of employees and their relation to the social-security system;

(6) the methods and procedures for best carrying out the collective bargaining processes, with special attention to the effects of industry-wide or regional bargaining upon the national economy;

(7) the administration and operation of existing Federal laws relating to labor relations; and

(8) such other problems and subjects in the field of labor-management relations as the committee deems appropriate.

SEC. 403. The committee shall report to the Senate and the House of Representatives not later than March 15, 1948, the results of its study and investigation, together with such recommendations as to necessary legislation and such other recommendations as it may deem advisable, and shall make its final report not later than January 2, 1949.

Sec. 404. The committee shall have the power, without regard to the civil service laws and the Classification Act of 1923, as amended, to employ and fix the compensation of such officers, experts, and employees as it deems necessary for the performance of its duties, including consultants who shall receive compensation at a rate not to exceed $35 for each day actually spent by them in the work of the committee, together with their necessary travel and subsistence expenses. The committee is further authorized, with the consent of the head of the department or agency concerned, to utilize the services, information, facilities, and personnel of all agencies in the executive branch of the Government and may request the governments of the several States, representatives of business, industry, finance, and labor, and such other persons, agencies, organizations, and instrumentalities as it deems appropriate to attend its hearings and to give and present information, advice, and recommendations.

Sec. 405. The committee, or any subcommittee thereof, is authorized to hold such hearings; to sit and act at such times and places during the sessions, recesses, and adjourned periods of the Eightieth Congress; to require by subpoena or otherwise the attendance of such witnesses and the production of such books, papers, and documents; to administer oaths; to take such testimony; to have such printing and binding done; and to make such expenditures within the amount appropriated therefor; as it deems advisable. The cost of stenographic services in reporting such hearings shall not be in excess of 25 cents per one hundred words. Subpoenas shall be issued under the signature of the chairman or vice chairman of the committee and shall be served by any person designated by them.

Sec. 406. The members of the committee shall be reimbursed for travel, subsistence, and other necessary expenses incurred by them in the performance of the duties vested in the committee, other than expenses in connection with meetings of the committee held in the District of Columbia during such times as the Congress is in session.

Sec. 407. There is hereby authorized to be appropriated the sum of $150,000, or so much thereof as may be necessary, to carry out the provisions of this title, to be disbursed by the Secretary of the Senate on vouchers signed by the chairman.

Title V

DEFINITIONS

Sec. 501. When used in this Act —

(1) The term "industry affecting commerce" means any industry or activity in commerce or in which a labor dispute would burden or ob-

struct commerce or tend to burden or obstruct commerce or the free flow of commerce.

(2) The term "strike" includes any strike or other concerted stoppage of work by employees (including a stoppage by reason of the expiration of a collective bargaining agreement) and any concerted slow-down or other concerted interruption of operations by employees.

(3) The terms "commerce," "labor disputes," "employer," "employee," "labor organization," "representative," "person," and "supervisor" shall have the same meaning as when used in the National Labor Relations Act as amended by this Act.

SAVING PROVISION

SEC. 502. Nothing in this Act shall be construed to require an individual employee to render labor or service without his consent, nor shall anything in this Act be construed to make the quitting of his labor by an individual employee an illegal act; nor shall any court issue any process to compel the performance by an individual employee of such labor or service, without his consent; nor shall the quitting of labor by an employee or employees in good faith because of abnormally dangerous conditions for work at the place of employment of such employee or employees be deemed a strike under this Act.

SEPARABILITY

SEC. 503. If any provision of this Act, or the application of such provision to any person or circumstance, shall be held invalid, the remainder of this Act, or the application of such provision to persons or circumstances other than those as to which it is held invalid, shall not be affected thereby.

INDEX

Index

A

D

I

INDEPENDENT CONTRACTORS
  as employees, 105
  persons included, 106
  union action to protect, 703
INDUSTRIAL REVOLUTION
  bargaining power of individual workers as affected by, 35
  contractual relationship of employer and employee as affected by, 304
  specialization necessitated by, 31
INJUNCTION
  absence of dispute between employer and employees, 652, 676, 688. *See also* secondary boycott *infra*
  Clayton Act, 40, 1012
  exclusion from membership in union as basis for, 856, 857
  generally, 671
  jurisdiction of federal courts in adjudication of subject matter, 717
  "labor dispute," meaning of, 654, 676, 680, 708
  labor-saving devices, enforcement of union bylaw prohibiting use of, 898
  medical practice, interference with, 856
  national emergency, under LMRA, 1060
  Norris-LaGuardia Act, 23, 41, 674, 1013
  notice of application for by NLRB, 1052
  officers, election, and finances of union, 918
  picketing
    collective bargaining, enforcement of demands in, 4
    interference with choice of representatives, 775. *See also* PICKETING
    Norris-LaGuardia Act, 756
    preventing use of equipment not made by members of union, 794
    state jurisdiction, as affected by Taft-Hartley Act, 849
    violence, 764
  secondary boycott. *See also* SECONDARY BOYCOTT
    jurisdictional dispute between unions, 991
    refusal to recognize union, 661
  state jurisdiction, 842, 848
  state legislation, 674
  strikes
    collective bargaining, enforcement of demands in, 4
    government intervention in, 715
    jurisdictional dispute between unions, 1003
    Norris-LaGuardia Act, 682
  union activity by officer failing to comply with licensing requirement, 943
  union discipline, 895, 917
INSUBORDINATION, DISCHARGE BY REASON OF, 528
INSURANCE
  collective bargaining as to, 264
  forfeiture of as result of expulsion from union, 899

J

JOINT COMMITTEE ON LABOR-MANAGEMENT RELATIONS, 1067
JUDGMENT, ENFORCEMENT OF AGAINST LABOR ORGANIZATION, 1062

L

1090 INDEX

RAILROAD LABOR BOARD, 91

RAILROADS

excluded from application of NLRA, 106, 1062

jurisdictional disputes between unions, determination of, 1006

RAILWAY LABOR ACT, 1019

adoption of, 41

arbitration under

agreement for, 1032

suit on award, 1028

check-off, 475

collective bargaining, 1021

commerce, defined, 1019

employees, defined, 1020

grievances and disputes, settlement of, 1022, 1025

discrimination in, 431

union participation in, 446

representation proceedings, 1023

union security, 1023

union shop, 475

unions

dues, 1024

right of employee to join, 1021

REINSTATEMENT. *See also* DISCHARGE

back pay, 531, 628, 730

breach of contract, effect of, 740

burden of proving misconduct, 738

condonation of misconduct of employees, effect of, 741

discharge of Negro employees, strike intended to procure, 739

discrimination in, 725, 729

illegal objective of strike, effect of, 739

Labor Management Relations Act, 1049

mass picketing, employees participating in, 737

mutiny, strike constituting, 739

National Labor Relations Board, authority of, 730, 734, 1049

notice of strike, effect of failure to give, 740

physical disability, effect of, 517

physical violence, employees participating in, 738

probationary period, effect of expiration of, 521

prohibited strike, effect of, 739

sit-down strike, employees participating in, 733

"substantially equivalent employment," 731

union security, employees striking for unlawful contract of, 740

Wagner Act, 42

REPRESENTATION PROCEEDINGS

certification as bar, 190

consent election agreements, 128

contract as bar

generally, 190

secession of local union from parent, effect of, 976

decertification, 199, 934, 1044

decision, 130

discrimination by union, effect of, 243, 865

prevention of, generally, 1048
procedure, 567
  documentary evidence, 569
  filing of charges by union, 567
  hearing, 569
  Labor Management Relations Act, 1048
  orders entered by trial examiner, 569
  report of trial examiner, 569
  subpoena of witnesses, 569
recognition of majority union, refusal of, 692
replacement of striking employees, 725, 729
restraint
  employer, 572
  union, 820
restraint of trade. *See* RESTRAINT OF TRADE
secondary boycott by union. *See* SECONDARY BOYCOTT
solicitation by union, prohibition of by employer, 581
speech and press, employer's use of, 588
surveillance by employer, 580
union security, illegal provision for, 823
union-shop agreements, 253
violence or threats of violence by union, 820
wage increase, granting of during collective bargaining, 231
work stoppage, 841
UNFAIR LISTS, UNION, VALIDITY OF UNDER TAFT-HARTLEY ACT, 816
UNION SECURITY, 446
  advantages and disadvantages, 448
  arbitration compelling acceptance of provision for, 481
  assistance or domination by employer, effect of, 479
  check-off. *See* CHECK-OFF
  closed shop. *See* CLOSED SHOP
  collective bargaining as to, 298
  concerted activity to obtain provision for, 459
  election, 1045
  expulsion of employee from union, 472
  failure of employee to pay dues or initiation fees, discharge for, 481
  illegal provision for
    agreeing to or insisting on, as unfair labor practice, 823
    reinstatement of employees striking for, 740
  Labor Management Relations Act, 478, 1039, 1040, 1041
  maintenance of membership. *See* MAINTENANCE OF MEMBERSHIP
  malicious interference with employment contract, 456
  National Labor Relations Act, 475
  preferential shop, 448
  prior membership in rival union, effect of, 479
  Railway Labor Act, 1023
  restriction of union membership, effect of, 463, 479
  state legislation, generally, 483
  statistics as to coverage in collective contracts, 452
  strike to obtain, legality of, 702
  union shop. *See* UNION SHOP
  United Nations, 495

UNION SECURITY (*Continued*)
validation of provision for, state jurisdiction as to, 840
UNION SHOP. *See also* UNION SECURITY
arbitration as to inclusion of agreement for, 463, 467
collective bargaining as to, 253
defined, 447
expulsion of employee from union, 472
form of agreement for, 447
Railway Labor Act, 475
secession of local union from parent, effect of, 982
union discrimination in connection with, 873
UNION TRUST FUND, COLLECTIVE BARGAINING AS TO PAYMENTS TO, 298
UNION WELFARE FUND, COLLECTIVE BARGAINING AS TO, 253
UNIONS
agents. *See* officers *infra*
agreement not to join, jurisdiction of federal courts as to, 1014
blacklisting by, 658
bylaws of
interference by courts with enforcement of, 898. *See also* discipline *infra*
Secretary of Labor, filing of copy with, 1046
state government, filing of copy with, 945
capacity to sue and be sued, 666, 1062, 1065
certification. *See* REPRESENTATION PROCEEDINGS
closed shop. *See* CLOSED SHOP
coercion of employees by, 820
collective bargaining, duty as to, 217
combination to secure concerted breach of contract, 651
conflicts between. *See* jurisdictional disputes *infra*
constitutions of
disciplinary provisions, 880
membership provisions, 853
relationship of local with parent union, provisions regarding, 953, 959, 962
Secretary of Labor, filing of copy with, 1046
state government, filing of copy with, 945
statutory standards for, 948
suspension provision, validity of, 960
cooperation among, 984
decertification, 199, 934, 1044
discipline, 877. *See also* expulsion *infra*
assessment for contribution to political fund, refusal to pay, 900
bias of tribunal, 912
collective bargaining as affected by provisions for, 898
counsel, right to, 911
criticism of union officers, 888, 895, 897
double jeopardy, 911
evidence, presentation of, 911
injunction against proceeding, 917
limitations on, 880
notice of proceeding, and waiver, 910
place of trial, 911
procedure, 905
provisions for, in union constitutions, 880

V

W